美国管理会计师协会（IMA）

注册管理会计师（CMA）认证考试教材之二

管理会计与报告

（第二版）

（英汉双语）

美国管理会计师协会（IMA）主编

彭韶兵　宋　浩　译

经济科学出版社

图书在版编目（CIP）数据

管理会计与报告：第 2 版：英汉双语／美国管理会计师协会主编；彭韶兵，宋浩译．—北京：经济科学出版社，2007.11
书名原文：Management Accounting and Reporting
注册管理会计师（CMA）认证考试教材
ISBN 978 - 7 - 5058 - 6612 - 6

Ⅰ. 管… Ⅱ. ①美…②彭…③宋… Ⅲ. 管理会计 - 资格
考核 - 教材 Ⅳ. F234.3

中国版本图书馆 CIP 数据核字（2007）第 147105 号

亲爱的读者朋友：

非常高兴你决定参加注册管理会计师（CMA）资格考试并选用这套全新的中文版本教材，我相信这对你来讲是一个明智的决策。这套培训教材的编写以美国管理会计师协会所确认的管理会计知识体系和学习要点为基础，教材在编写中充分利用了一些最为有效的学习技巧，我们相信这套教材能够帮助你顺利通过 CMA 考试。

我很高兴美国管理会计师协会能提供 CMA 考试及这套教材的中文版权。CMA 资格认证只授予全球各行业、各语种中最为优秀的会计人员，它是一个全球性的资格认证。希望读者朋友们能成功通过 CMA 考试并一生好运。

保罗·A·沙曼（Paul A. Sharman），ACMA

IMA 总裁兼首席执行官

2007 年 7 月 12 日

Dear Colleague:

Congratulations on your decision to pursue the Certified Management Accountant (CMA®) certification. You have made a wise choice to pursue this goal and in choosing the new Chinese version of the CMA Learning System to prepare for the exam. The CMA Learning System was developed using IMA's management accounting body of knowledge and subject matter experts. It takes advantage of some of the most effective techniques for learning. We believe that this is a valuable tool to help CMA candidates successfully pass the exam.

I am pleased that IMA can offer a Chinese language version of the CMA exam and the appropriate study materials to help you succeed. I trust you will find that the CMA is a global designation of excellence for accountants working in industry, across all industries and languages. I wish the best of luck to you with your study prep and in your future.

Sincerely,

Paul A. Sharman, ACMA
IMA President and CEO

7/12/07

总目录

The Institute of Management Accountants'
CMA Learning System

Book 2: Management Accounting and Reporting

Contents

About the CMA Learning System

This product is based on the CMA body of knowledge developed by the Institute of Certified Management Accountants (ICMA). Although the text is based on the body of knowledge tested by the CMA exam and the published Learning Outcome Statements covering the four part exams, CMA Learning System program developers do not have access to the current bank exam questions. It is critical that candidates: understand all Learning Outcome Statements published by the ICMA, learn all concepts and calculations related to those statements, and, finally, that they have a solid grasp of how to write the multiple-choice and essay exams in the CMA program.

This material is designed for learning purposes and is distributed with the understanding that the publisher and authors are not offering legal or professional services.

Acknowledgements

IMA would like to acknowledge the subject matter experts who worked on the original English version of this product: Kimberly Frank Charron, Ph.D., CMA; Neal J. Hannon, CMA; Charles R. Hartle, CMA, CPA; Dennis L. Neider, CMA, CPA; and Carl V. Menconi, CMA, CPA.

In addition we would like to acknowledge the following subject matter experts who were instrumental in the 2.0 English version of this product: Jill Bale Ph.D., CMA, CFA; Kent Baker, Ph.D., CMA, CFA; Kenneth Cole, CMA; Saurav Dutta, Ph.D., CMA; Karen L. Jett, CMA; Joe Lanz, CMA, CFA; Paul Miesing, Ph.D.; Lou Petro, Ph.D., CMA; Terri Rittenburg, Ph.D.; Siaw-Peng Wan; Ph.D., CMA

The CMA™ Designation

The Certified Management Accountant (CMA) designation provides corporate management and finance professionals with an objective measure of knowledge and competence in the field of management accounting. The CMA designation is recognized globally as an invaluable credential for professional accountancy advancement inside organizations and for broadening professional skills and perspectives.

The four-part CMA exam is designed to develop and measure critical-thinking and decision-making skills and to meet the following objectives:

- To establish management accounting and financial management as recognized professions by identifying the role of the professional, the underlying body of knowledge, and a course of study by which such knowledge is acquired

- To encourage higher educational standards in the management accounting and financial management fields

- To establish an objective measure of an individual's knowledge and competence in the fields of management accounting and financial management

- To encourage continued professional development

Persons earning the CMA designation benefit by being able to:

- Communicate their broad business competency and strategic financial mastery.

- Obtain contemporary professional knowledge and develop skills and abilities that are valued by successful businesses.

- Convey their commitment to an exemplary standard of excellence that is grounded on a strong ethical foundation and lifelong learning.

- Enhance their career development, salary qualifications and professional promotion opportunities.

The CMA designation is granted exclusively by the Institute of Certified Management Accountants.

Overall Expectations of Candidates

The CMA exam content covers both a depth of technical accountancy and a breadth of organizational topics that are critical for management accountants to be able to assume the 'business partner' role now expected of savvy professionals.

Completing the CMA designation requires a high level of commitment. Dedicating what often amounts to two years of your life to study and complete the four-part exams is a serious investment, one that will provide a solid foundation for your career and that will enhance your career in ways that will pay dividends for a lifetime.

Your success in completing the four-part exams will rest heavily on your ability to create a solid study plan and to execute that plan. The IMA offers many resources, tools and programs to support you during this process. We encourage you to pay the CMA Entrance Fee as soon as you begin the program in order to provide you maximum access to these resources and tools. You are also encouraged to draw on these benefits with rigor and discipline in a way that supports your unique study needs.

For more information about the CMA designation, the CMA exams, or the exam preparation resources offered through IMA visit www.imanet.org.

Introduction

Welcome to Part 2 of the Institute of Management Accountants' CMA Learning System: Management Accounting and Reporting.

Part 2 covers budget preparation methods, cost management tools, information management styles, performance measurement methods, and external financial reporting rules. Each section includes a discussion of relevant terminology, differing methods used, and relevant rules and regulations that a management accountant must know.

The Part 2 CMA Exam

Candidates for the CMA designation are required to take separate exams for Parts 1, 2, 3, and 4. Parts 1, 2, and 3 can be taken in any order; however, Part 4 can be taken only after successful completion of Parts 1, 2, and 3.

The Part 2 CMA exam consists of 140 multiple-choice questions that test all levels of cognitive skills. Candidates have four hours to complete the computer-based exam. This Part 2 book is based upon the Content Specification Outline and the Learning Outcome Statements provided by ICMA for Part 2. That outline is reflected in the table of contents of this book. The ICMA Content Specification Outline and LOS can be obtained from the IMA Web site at www.imanet.org.

It is important when preparing for the Part 2 exam that candidates learn all of the concepts presented and also understand all of the various ways calculations can be performed. It is also important that you learn (or relearn) how to write a comprehensive multiple-choice exam. You are strongly encouraged to create a study plan that details how you will accomplish your Part 2 exam preparation and when you will write the Part 2 exam.

Online Resources

Valuable resources are available to assist candidates to pass the CMA examinations. For information regarding all the resources available please go to www.imanet.org/china/examtools.

Creating a Part 2 Study Plan

The Part 2 certification exam uses a multiple-choice format to test your understanding of Part 2 concepts, terms and calculations. Creating a study plan is a critical ingredient to planning a path to success. Managing your plan is critical to achieving success. The following tips and tactics are included to help you prepare and manage your Part 2 study plan.

1. *Because the Part 2 exam can be written anytime throughout the year, YOU need to bring structure to your exam preparation. This means setting target dates and making them a priority.*

   ▪ *Decide on the date you commit to contacting the ICMA to register for the Part 2 exam. After you register, mark the date you plan to take the exam in pen.*

   ▪ *Based on the dates you commit to register and sit for the exam, decide when you will start and finish studying Part 2. We recommend that you make every effort to write the exam as close as possible to the completion of your studies. A reasonable benchmark for the number of study hours required to prepare for Part 2 is 150. The actual hours you need to invest to prepare will depend on your current level of understanding of the Part 2 content and your familiarity and confidence to write exams of this nature.*

   ▪ *Review each section and topic in Part 2 and rate your familiarity/confidence with each section.*

2. *Create a written plan or chart to track your progress and guide your completion of each component of the self-study books, section by section. We strongly recommend that you create a plan that sees you through to completion of Part 2 within six (6) months or less.*

3. *Use your plan on a regular basis to assess your progress. In addition, be sure to practice the section-specific questions and exercises included in the print material.*

Budget Preparation

Section overview

How do some companies become great successes while others flounder? Successful companies have a strategy that is based on accurate information from both external and internal sources; they match their internal strengths to the best external opportunities available. But a good strategy is not enough. Companies need to convert an overall strategy into action, which is where a budget comes in. A budget is a detailed plan for executing both long-term and short-term goals. A successful budget not only provides cost controls but also makes sure that day-to-day operations take the company where it wants to be in the future. This section covers basic budgeting concepts and various budget systems and explores the master budget in detail.

Learning Outcome Statements

The Certified Management Accountant (CMA) test is based upon a series of Learning Outcome Statements (LOS) developed by the Institute of Certified Management Accountants (ICMA). The LOS describe all the knowledge and skills that make up the CMA body of knowledge, broken down by part, section and topic. The CMA Learning System (CMALS) supports the LOS by addressing all the subjects they cover. Candidates should use the LOS to ensure that they can address the concepts in different ways or through a variety of question scenarios. Candidates should also be prepared to perform calculations referred to in the LOS in total or by providing missing components of a calculation. The LOS should not be used as proxies for exact exam questions; they should be used as a guide for studying and learning the content of the CMA Learning System and ensuring that you can accomplish the objectives set out by the LOS.

The LOS included in the CMALS books are the comprehensive set, current as of the date of publication. Candidates can access the IMA Web site at www.imanet.org and click on the Certification section to locate and download a Portable Document Format (PDF) file of the current LOS.

Learning Outcome Statements

Part 2: Management Accounting and Reporting — Section A. Budget Preparation

Part 2 — Section A1. Budgeting Concepts

- LOS 2.A.1.a—Demonstrate an understanding of the role that budgeting plays in the overall planning and performance evaluation process of an organization.

- LOS 2.A.1.b—Demonstrate an understanding of the interrelationships between economic conditions, industry situation, and a firm's plans and budgets.

- LOS 2.A.1.c—Identify the role that budgeting plays in formulating short-term objectives and planning and controlling operations to meet those objectives.

- LOS 2.A.1.d—Identify the characteristics that define successful budgeting processes.

- LOS 2.A.1.e—Demonstrate an understanding of the role that budgets play in measuring performance against established goals.

- LOS 2.A.1.f—Explain how the budgeting process facilitates communication among organizational units and enhances the coordination of organizational activities.

- LOS 2.A.1.g—Describe the concept of a controllable cost as it relates to both budgeting and performance evaluation.

- LOS 2.A.1.h—Prepare an operational budget.

- LOS 2.A.1.i—Prepare a capital expenditure budget.

- LOS 2.A.1.j—Demonstrate an understanding of the concept of management by objective (MBO) and how it relates to performance evaluation.

- LOS 2.A.1.k—Identify the benefits and limitations of management by objective (MBO).

- LOS 2.A.1.l—Demonstrate an understanding of how the planning process coordinates the efficient allocation of organizational resources.

- LOS 2.A.1.m—Identify the appropriate time frame for various types of budgets.

- LOS 2.A.1.n—Identify who should participate in the budgeting process for optimal success.

- LOS 2.A.1.o—Describe the role of top management in successful budgeting.

- LOS 2.A.1.p—Identify the role of top management or the budget committee in providing appropriate guidelines for the budget and identify items that should be included in these guidelines.

- LOS 2.A.1.q—Demonstrate an understanding of the use of cost standards in budgeting.

- LOS 2.A.1.r—Differentiate between ideal (theoretical) standards and currently attainable (practical) standards.

- LOS 2.A.1.s—Differentiate between authoritative standards and participative standards.

- LOS 2.A.1.t—Identify the steps to be taken in developing standards for both direct material and direct labor.

- LOS 2.A.1.u—Define the role of benchmarking in standard setting.

- LOS 2.A.1.v—Demonstrate an understanding of the techniques that are used to develop standards such as activity analysis and the use of historical data.

- LOS 2.A.1.w—Discuss the importance of a policy that allows budget revisions that accommodate the impact of significant changes in budget assumptions.

- LOS 2.A.1.x—Demonstrate an understanding of the role of budgets in monitoring and controlling expenditures to meet strategic objectives.

Part 2 — Section A2. Budget Systems

- LOS 2.A.2.a—For each of the budget systems identified (annual/master budgets, project budgeting, activity-based budgeting, zero-based budgeting, continuous budgeting, kaizen budgeting, and flexible budgeting), define its purpose, appropriate use, and time frame.

- LOS 2.A.2.b—For each of the budget systems identified (annual/master budgets, project budgeting, activity-based budgeting, zero-based budgeting, continuous budgeting, kaizen budgeting, and flexible budgeting), identify the budget components and explain the interrelationships among the components.

- LOS 2.A.2.c—For each of the budget systems identified (annual/master budgets, project budgeting, activity-based budgeting, zero-based budgeting, continuous budgeting, kaizen budgeting, and flexible budgeting), demonstrate an understanding of how the budget is developed.

- LOS 2.A.2.d—For each of the budget systems identified (annual/master budgets, project budgeting, activity-based budgeting, zero-based budgeting, continuous budgeting, kaizen budgeting, and flexible budgeting), compare and contrast the benefits and limitations of the budget system.

- LOS 2.A.2.e—For each of the budget systems identified (annual/master budgets, project budgeting, activity-based budgeting, zero-based budgeting, continuous budgeting, kaizen budgeting, and flexible budgeting), calculate budget components on the basis of information presented.

- LOS 2.A.2.f—For each of the budget systems identified (annual/master budgets, project budgeting, activity-based budgeting, zero-based budgeting, continuous budgeting, kaizen budgeting, and flexible budgeting), evaluate a business situation and recommend the appropriate budget solution.

Part 2 — Section A3. Annual Profit Plan and Supporting Schedules

- LOS 2.A.3.a—Demonstrate an understanding of the role the sales budget plays in the development of an annual profit plan.

- LOS 2.A.3.b—Identify the factors that should be considered when preparing a sales forecast and evaluate the feasibility of the sales forecast based on business and economic information provided.

- LOS 2.A.3.c—Identify the components of a sales budget and prepare a sales budget based on relevant information provided.

- LOS 2.A.3.d—Demonstrate an understanding of the relationship between the sales budget and the production budget.

- LOS 2.A.3.e—Identify the role that inventory levels play in the preparation of a production budget and define other factors that should be considered when preparing a production budget.

- LOS 2.A.3.f—Prepare a production budget based on relevant information provided and evaluate the feasibility of achieving sales goals on the basis of production plans.

- LOS 2.A.3.g—Demonstrate an understanding of the relationship between the direct materials budget, the direct labor budget, and the production budget.

- LOS 2.A.3.h—Define the use of inventory levels and procurement policies in developing a direct materials budget and the role that labor skills, union contracts, and hiring policies play in the development of a direct labor budget.

- LOS 2.A.3.i—Prepare direct materials and direct labor budgets based on relevant information provided and evaluate the feasibility of achieving production goals on the basis of these budgets.

- LOS 2.A.3.j—Prepare a forecast of employee-related costs and benefits such as employer contributions to Social Security, employment-related taxes, health and life insurance, and pension contributions based on relevant information provided.

- LOS 2.A.3.k—Demonstrate an understanding of alternative ways of allocating employee benefit expense, for example, as a portion of direct labor expense or as overhead, and the effect that allocation has on the financial statements.

- LOS 2.A.3.l—Demonstrate an understanding of the relationship between the overhead budget and the production budget.

- LOS 2.A.3.m—Identify the fixed and variable expenses in an overhead budget.

- LOS 2.A.3.n—Define the components of overhead expense and prepare an overhead budget based on relevant information provided.

- LOS 2.A.3.o—Identify the components of the cost of goods sold budget and demonstrate an understanding of the relationship between the cost of goods sold budget, the pro forma income statement, and the pro forma statement of financial position.

- LOS 2.A.3.p—Demonstrate an understanding of contribution margin per unit and total contribution margin, identify the appropriate use of these concepts, and calculate both unit and total contribution margin.

- LOS 2.A.3.q—Prepare a cost of goods sold budget based on relevant information provided.

- LOS 2.A.3.r—Identify the components of the selling and administrative budget and demonstrate an understanding of the nature of these expenses.

- LOS 2.A.3.s—Describe the relationship between the selling and administrative budget, the pro forma income statement, and the pro forma statement of financial position.

- LOS 2.A.3.t—Demonstrate an understanding of how specific components of the selling and administrative budget may affect the contribution margin.

- LOS 2.A.3.u—Demonstrate an understanding of the relationship between the budget for acquisition of capital assets, the cash budget, and the pro forma financial statements.

- LOS 2.A.3.v—Define the purposes of the cash budget and describe the relationship between the cash budget and all other budgets.

- LOS 2.A.3.w—Identify the elements of a cash budget and demonstrate an understanding of the relationship between credit policies and purchasing (payables) policies and the cash budget.

- LOS 2.A.3.x—Prepare a cash budget from information given and recommend the optimal investment/financing strategy.

- LOS 2.A.3.y—Define the purpose of a pro forma income statement, a pro forma statement of financial position, and a pro forma cash flow statement and understand the relationship among these statements and all other budgets.

- LOS 2.A.3.z—Prepare a pro forma income statement, a pro forma statement of financial position, and a pro forma cash flow statement from relevant information provided.

<table>
<tr><td>Topic 1</td></tr>
</table>

Budgeting Concepts

Topic overview

The future is, by definition, uncertain. Businesses deal continuously with uncertainty and the future. Planning is the process of mapping out the organization's future direction to attain desired goals. Strategy is the organization's plan to match its strengths with the opportunities in the marketplace to accomplish its desired goals over the short and long term. A budget is one of the main methods of planning, and it must be in alignment with the company's strategy or the strategy will have no way of becoming a reality. While a plan or budget may not guarantee success, the lack of a plan can remove opportunities, cause the company to be constantly putting out fires, or cause a complete business failure.

In addition to planning to meet the company's strategy, the second major function of a budget is control. Control is the process of placing checks and balances on the actions of those responsible for aspects of a budget, including the use of performance evaluations tied to the budget. Control is also linked to company strategy; managers must have incentives to make decisions that benefit not only the short-term strategy but also the long-term strategy.

Budget Terminology

The following budget terms are used in this section.

Budget
A **budget** is an operational plan and control tool for an entity that identifies the resources and commitments needed to satisfy the entity's goals over a period. Budgets are primarily quantitative, not qualitative. Financial budgets set specific goals for income, cash flows, and financial position.

Budgeting
Budgeting is undertaking the steps involved in preparing a budget. Along with clear communication of organizational goals, the ideal budget also contains budgetary controls.

Budgetary control
Without a formal system of control, a budget is little more than a forecast. **Budgetary control** is a management process to help ensure that a budget is achieved by instituting a systematic budget approval process, by coordinating the efforts of all involved parties and operations, and by analyzing variances from the plan and providing appropriate feedback to responsible parties. The goals identified in the budget must be considered realistic by employees in order to be motivational in nature.

Pro forma statements
A **pro forma statement** is a budgeted financial statement based on historical documents that is adjusted for events "as if" they had occurred. Budgeted balance sheets, budgeted

statements of cash flows, and budgeted income statements are forecasts of goals for a future period that assist in the allocation of resources.

Note that there are two definitions of pro forma. The definition above relates to the budgeting process for internal users. For external users, pro forma refers to a supplementary disclosure meant to enhance comparability when a company has a change in an accounting principle by retroactively applying the change to prior periods as if the change had been in effect for the whole accounting period. Another external definition of pro forma refers to showing a company's earnings without GAAP-basis amounts for unusual or nonrecurring transactions, but such statements are not regulated, not comparable, and have sometimes misled investors.

Budget cycle

A budget cycle usually involves the following steps:

1. A budget is created that addresses the entity as a whole as well as its subunits, and all managers agree to fulfill their part of the budget.

2. The budget is used to test current performance against expectations.

3. Variations from the plan are examined, and corrective actions are taken when possible.

4. Feedback is collected, and the plan is revisited and revised if needed.

Figure 2-1 shows how these steps revolve back to the beginning to form a cycle.

Figure 2-1: Budget Cycle

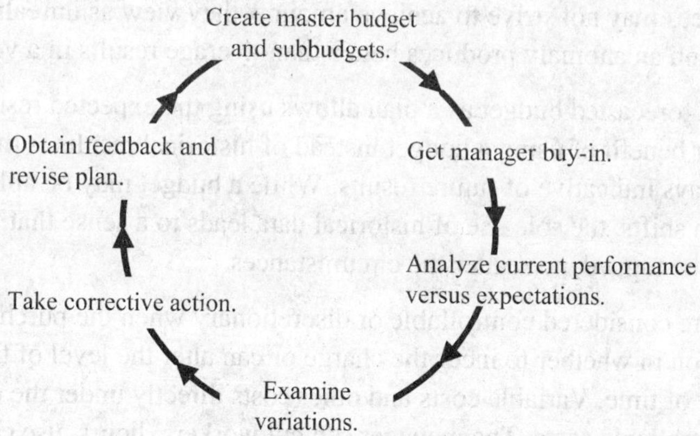

Create master budget and subbudgets.

Get manager buy-in.

Analyze current performance versus expectations.

Examine variations.

Take corrective action.

Obtain feedback and revise plan.

Operations and Performance Goals

As mentioned earlier, a strategic analysis matches an entity's capabilities with available marketplace opportunities. Strategy addresses the objectives of the organization; locates potential markets; considers the impact of events, competitors, and the economy; addresses the structure of the organization; and evaluates the risks of alternative strategies. Strategic analysis is the basis for both long-term and short-term planning. These plans lead, respectively, to long-term and short-term budgets, as summarized in Figure 2-2. These budgets lead in turn to the master budget and its components.

Figure 2-2: Strategy, Planning, and Budgets

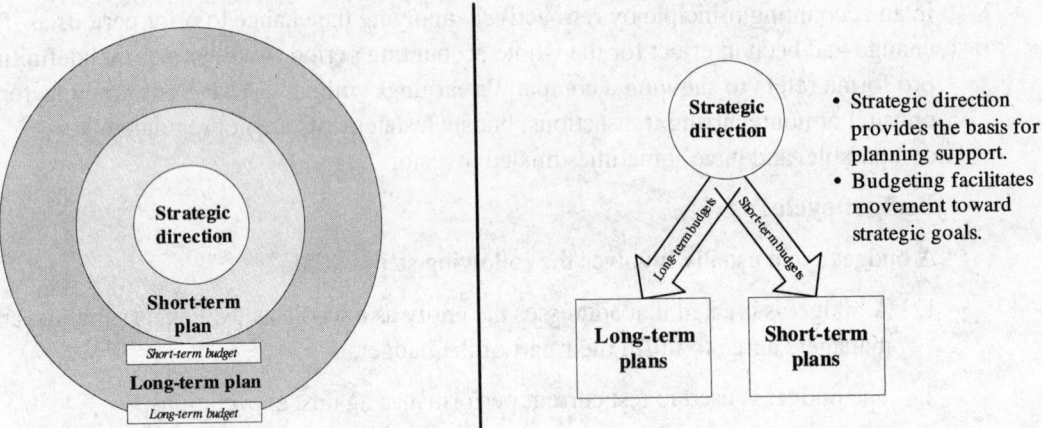

Budgets play a role in measuring performance against established goals. When using past performance solely to evaluate present results, the mistakes and problems that occurred in the past are automatically factored in to the benchmark that is being used. For example, if a company reports poor sales due to a new sales force and that year's data is used as the next year's sales benchmark, the mark would be set lower than necessary and the sales team would not be motivated to work as hard. However, if the benchmark is set too high, employees may not strive to achieve amounts they view as unrealistic. Such can be the case when an anomaly produces better-than-average results in a year.

Using a forecasted budget as a plan allows using the expected results as the benchmark. Another benefit of using a budget instead of historical results is that past performance is not always indicative of future results. While a budget may be able to predict and account for such shifts, the sole use of historical data leads to a sense that the past year must always be topped, no matter the circumstances.

Costs are considered controllable or discretionary when the purchaser or manager has discretion in whether to incur the charge or can alter the level of the charge within a short amount of time. Variable costs and other costs directly under the control of the manager are controllable costs. The manager can cut workers' hours, use cheaper materials, or otherwise restrict such controllable costs. A division manager can control maintenance and advertising costs to a certain degree.

Fixed costs such as administrative salaries or rent are usually not controllable and are therefore called committed costs.

Controllable costs are useful for performance evaluation and budgeting.

- For performance evaluation, using divisional net revenue less controllable costs to rate how a manager or employee is using funds is a more realistic approach that is appreciated by those who are being rated. Holding managers accountable for uncontrollable costs can be unmotivating.

- For budgeting, focusing on controllable costs places the emphasis where the most benefit can be achieved from the effort of budgeting.

Characteristics of Successful Budgeting

Many factors characterize a successful budget, but no single factor can lead to a successful budget.

The common factors in a successful budget include the following:

- The budget must be aligned with the corporate strategy.

- The budget process should be kept separate but flow from the strategic planning and forecasting processes.

  - Strategic plans. Strategic plans are higher-level, longer-term, and structured in company-wide terms such as product lines rather than responsibility centers. However, early budgeting steps can be used to refine the strategic direction of the company because they use more current information.

  - Accountable versus non-accountable forecasts. Many forecasts have lower accountability than a budget, are not usually approved by management, and are not often formally analyzed against variances. For example, a manager may create a forecast for direct materials needed in next week's production to be sure that there is adequate inventory. However, budgets must use the forward-looking information from more comprehensive forecasts. Therefore, the forecasts directly used in the budgeting process, such as the sales forecast, must be kept accountable.

- The budget should be used to alleviate potential bottlenecks and to allocate resources to those areas that will use the funds most efficiently and effectively.

- The budget must contain technically correct and reasonably accurate numbers and facts.

- Management (including top management) must buy in to the budget, meaning that they accept responsibility for reaching the budget goals.

- The budget must be perceived by employees as a planning, communication, and coordinating tool, not as a pressure or blame device.

- The budget must be characterized as a motivating tool to help employees work toward organizational goals.

- The budget must be seen as an internal control device, and internal-use budgets should base evaluations on controllable or discretionary costs.

- Selling and administrative budgets need to be detailed in order that key assumptions can be better understood.

- A higher authority than the team who made the budget must review and approve the budget.

- The final budget should not be easily changed but should include specific provisions for changes to allow budgets to be flexible enough to be useful.

Budgets should compel planning, promote communication and coordination, and provide performance criteria. The budget process must balance input from those who will need to follow the budget against a thorough and fair review of the budget by upper management.

Characteristics of a Successful Budget Process

The budget process can be a very simple affair taking a day or two and involving just one or two people, or it can be a complex process involving a budget committee and many months to complete. Characteristics related to the budget process include the budget period, the participants in the budget process, the basic steps in budgeting, and the use of cost standards.

Budget period

Budgets are most commonly prepared for the company's fiscal year, but three-, five-, and ten-year budgets are planned as well as budgets of shorter duration. A different year basis than the fiscal year is possible, but it is not recommended because fiscal year financial statements can be easily compared to the budget. Budgets are often further broken down into monthly or quarterly subperiods, or a continuous or rolling budget is used. A continuous budget has a month, quarter, or year basis, and as each period ends the upcoming period's budget is revised and another period is added to the end of the budget. Special software makes such budgets simple to implement.

Budget process

Methods of budget preparation differ between companies, but all fall somewhere on a continuum between being entirely authoritative and entirely participative. In an **authoritative budget** (top-down budget), top management sets everything from strategic goals down to the individual items of the budget for each department and expects lower managers and employees affected by the budgets to fulfill these goals. In a **participative budget** (bottom-up or self-imposed budget), managers at all levels and certain key employees cooperate to set budgets for their areas. (Top management usually retains final approval.) The ideal process combines the features of each and falls somewhere between these methods. Figure 2-3 lists benefits and limitations of purely authoritative and participative budgeting and shows how a combined approach provides the greatest number of checks and balances over a budgetary process. Note that the combination approach is sometimes considered to be a form of the participative approach.

Figure 2-3: Comparison of Authoritative, Combined, and Participative Budgeting

Authoritative Approach	Combination Approach	Participative Approach
Top management incorporates strategic goals into their budgets.	**Strategic goals are communicated top-down and implemented bottom-up.**	Strategic goals do not receive priority in the budgetary process.
Better control over decisions.	**Control retained and expertise gained at cost of a slightly longer process.**	Expertise leads to informed budget decisions.
Dictates instead of communicates.	**Two-way communication:** ▪ **Top management understands participants' difficulties/needs.** ▪ **Participants understand management's dilemmas.**	Communicates lower-level perspective (of product/service or market) to management.
Employees: ▪ Resentful ▪ Unmotivated	**Personal control leads to acceptance, which leads to greater, personal commitment.**	Employees ▪ Involved ▪ Empowered
Stringent budgets may not be strictly followed at lower levels.	**Ownership of budget and thorough review leads to tight budgets that get followed.**	Easy or abdicated approval can lead to loose budgets and budget slack.
Not a recommended approach but could work in small or slow-changing environments.	Best for most companies; provides balance between strategic and tactical inputs.	Best for responsibility centers with highly variable situations where area manager has best data.

Steps in a combined budgetary process include the following:

1. Budget participants are identified, involving all levels of management as well as key employees with expertise in a particular area.

2. Top management communicates the strategic direction to budget participants.

3. Budget participants create the first draft of their budget.

4. Lower levels submit budgets to the next higher level for review in an iterative process stressing communication in both directions.

5. Rigorous but fair budget approval sets the final budget.

Budget participants

Three groups make or break a budget: the board of directors, top management, and the budget committee. Middle and lower management also plays a significant role, because they create detailed budgets based on upper management's plan.

Board of directors

The board of directors does not create the budget, but it cannot abdicate its responsibility to review the budget and either approve it or send it back for revision. The board usually appoints the members of the budget committee.

Top management

Top management is ultimately responsible for their budgets, and their primary means of exercising this responsibility is to ensure that all levels of management understand and support the budget and the overall budget control process. If top management is not perceived to be behind a budget, line managers will be less likely to follow the budget precisely. Also, top management should pay close attention to how they are affecting each line manager's budget, because insensitive policies could result in creative budgeting on the part of staff.

Top managers should give their subordinates incentives for making truthful and complete budgets, such as rewarding accuracy. A common problem that needs to be avoided is budget slack. **Budget slack** occurs when budgeted performance differs from actual performance because each manager builds in some extra money for their budget to deal with the unexpected. Budget slack is built-in freedom to fail, and cumulative budget slack at each sublevel can result in a very inaccurate master budget.

Rigid enforcement of budgets will in some situations cost an organization more in the long run than if some flexibility is allowed. For example, a repairs manager at an airline may not approve the temporary transfer of a mechanic because it would use up too much of the repairs budget even though the company overall is losing tens of thousands of dollars per day on a grounded plane.

Budget committee

Large corporations usually need to form a budget committee that is made up of senior management. The chief executive officer or a vice president often leads the budget committee. The size of the committee will vary depending on the organization. The committee directs budget preparation, approves budgets, rules on disagreements, monitors the budget, reviews results, and approves revisions.

Middle and lower management

Once the budget committee sets the tone for the budget process, many others in the organization have some role to play. Middle and lower management will do much of the specific budgeting work. These managers follow budget guidelines, which are general guidelines for responsibility centers preparing individual budgets set by either top management or the budget committee. A responsibility center, cost center, or strategic business unit (SBU) is a segment of a company in which the manager is vested with the authority to make cost, revenue, and/or investment decisions (and therefore also set budgets). The budget guidelines will be formed around the company's strategy and long-term plans. The guidelines govern preparation methods, layout, and new events that have occurred since the publication of the master budget such as new downsizing needs, changes in the economy, and year-to-date operating results.

Budget coordinator

The more people who are involved in a budget process, the greater the need for an individual or team who can identify and resolve discrepancies between various responsibility centers' budgets and between various portions of a master budget.

Process experts

When participative budgeting is used, often certain key nonmanagerial employees are added to the team. Team participants tend to be those that have a detailed understanding of the costs for a particular area, especially for areas that are extremely complex or variable. Such participants will not only bring more focus to a budget but will also take ownership of the budget and increase its likelihood of being followed at the operational level.

Budgeting steps

The steps that responsibility centers take in preparing their budgets include the initial budget proposal, budget negotiation, review and approval, and revision.

Budget proposal

After the CEO decides on the company strategy, a memo or directive is sent to each line manager or responsibility center so they can start aligning their budget process with the strategic plan (that is, a top-down implementation). With this strategy in mind, each responsibility center prepares an initial budget, taking both internal and external factors into account. Internal factors include changes in price, availability, and manufacturing processes; new products or services; changes in related or intertwined responsibility centers; and staff changes. External factors include changes in the economy and the labor market, the price and availability of goods and services, industry trends, and actions of competitors.

Budget negotiation

When the initial budget proposal is submitted to a superior or the budget committee, the budget is reviewed to see if it meets the organization's strategic goals, falls within an acceptable range, and is consistent with similar budgets. Reviewers also determine if the budget is feasible and fits within the goals of units the next level up. Negotiations take up the bulk of time of budget preparations because push-back from a superior will result in renegotiation of priorities for both the superior and the responsibility center.

Budget review and approval

Budgets are reviewed and approved up the chain of command to the level of the budget committee, where the combined budgets become the master budget after review for consistency with the budget guidelines, short- and long-term goals, and strategic plans. Once the committee and the committee leader approve the plan, it is submitted to the board of directors for final approval.

Budget revision

The rigidity of a budget varies from organization to organization. Some budgets must be followed no matter what, others can be revised only under specific circumstances, and others are subject to continuous revision. Rigidly following a budget in the face of differing circumstances is a recipe for disaster. Management should not be required to rely on the budget as the sole operational guideline. Regular revisions may provide better operating guidelines, but managers may anticipate regular changes and not prepare budgets as carefully as they should. Organizations that allow regular revisions should make sure that the threshold for revision is set high enough to keep employees working as efficiently as possible. When regular revisions occur, a copy of the original budget should be kept for comparison with actual results at the end of the period.

Cost standards

Organizations set different types of standards that they strive to achieve. A standard is any carefully determined price, quantity, service level, or cost. Standards in manufacturing are usually set on a per-unit basis. A standard cost is how much an operation or service should cost, or the cost an entity expects to incur assuming that all goes as planned (for example, expected time and capacity). Budget planners use standard costs to prepare budgets, and they update standard costs as circumstances change. In practice, there is not a precise dividing line between a budgeted amount and a standard amount. The shorter the time frame, the thinner the dividing line becomes.

Types of standards

Standards can be either authoritative or participative.

- **Authoritative standards**

    Authoritative standards are determined solely by management. They are more speedily set and can closely match overall company goals but may be a cause for resentment or may not be followed at all.

- **Participative standards**

    Participative standards are set by a dialogue between management and all involved parties. They are more likely to be adopted but take more time and require negotiation to ensure that operating goals are still met.

Specific types of standard costs include ideal standards and currently attainable standards.

- **Ideal standard**

    An ideal standard is a forward-looking goal; it is currently attainable only if all circumstances result in the best possible outcome. Ideal standards work into a continuous improvement strategy and total quality management philosophies. Some firms use progress toward an ideal standard instead of deviations from the ideal to measure and reward success. However, ideal standards are very difficult to attain, and their frequent use can lead to job burnout. If difficult-to-attain ideal standards are constantly required, they can become a disincentive to productivity, because workers will not even attempt to meet such "impossible" goals and may become used to missing goals.

- **Currently attainable standard**

    A currently attainable standard is closer to a historical standard; it sets goals at a level that is attainable by properly trained individuals operating at a normal pace. The standard is expected to be reached most of the time. Setting such a standard too low will encourage employees to work more slowly than needed, so care must be used to allow for expected deviations. Using currently attainable standards discourages continuous improvement strategies.

Standard costs for direct materials and labor

Direct cost items such as direct materials and direct labor are measured by determining the number of units of each type of input required to get one unit of output. This amount is multiplied by the standard cost per input unit. Consider this direct materials example: If three input units are allowed for producing one output unit and an input unit costs $10, then the standard cost would be $30 per output unit. For direct labor, if 0.7 manufacturing labor hours of input are allowed for producing one output unit and labor hours cost $10, then the standard cost would be $7 per output unit. Of course, real standard costs are developed by adding multiple direct materials and labor costs. More specific guidelines for determining the prices for direct materials and labor are as follows.

- **Standard costs for direct materials**
  Standard costs are determined by quality, quantity, and price. Quality must be determined first, as it affects all the other variables. Quality level is determined by the product's targeted market niche. The standard is developed by engineers, production managers, and management accountants, working together, on the basis of the production facilities, the quality of the product, the costs of manufacturing, and the equipment to be used. A price is set as a combination of all prior work done, including quality, quantity, and supply chain costs. Determining supply chain costs includes such things as whether to select the lowest-cost vendor each time (costs will vary) or to establish a relationship with one reliable vendor (costs will be more stable).

- **Standard costs for direct labor**
  Product complexity, personnel skill levels, the type and condition of equipment, and the nature of the manufacturing process will all affect the direct labor costs. Management accountants, engineers, production managers, labor unions, HR, and others affect the direct labor standards. The cost of direct labor is based on gross pay plus benefits, not net pay.

Sources for standards setting

Several sources are often used simultaneously when setting standards: activity analysis, historical data, market expectations, strategic decisions, and benchmarking.

- **Activity analysis**
  An activity analysis, as part of activity-based costing (ABC), identifies, codifies, and analyzes the activities needed to finish a job or operation. (Activity-based costing is discussed in more detail in Section B, Topic 3, of this book.) The most efficient combination of resources and other inputs is calculated by interviewing personnel directly involved with various aspects of the operation. Engineers are involved in calculating the product ingredients and determining the specific steps required in the process. Management accountants help analyze the direct costs of the inputs and allocate a fair amount of the indirect costs (lighting, rent, repairs, and so on) to the operation. Such analyses also evaluate the skill levels required of those who will perform the tasks. Activity analyses in activity-based costing are the most thorough costing method and are also the most expensive to implement.

- **Historical data**

   Relying on historical data for determining costs is relatively inexpensive but is less reliable than activity analysis. When reliable, historical data can be used to find the average or median historical cost for an operation. To implement continuous improvement, the best performance recorded could be used as a standard or at least an ideal standard. Historical data can perpetuate past inefficiencies, however, or fail to take into account the impact of new technologies.

- **Market expectations and strategic decisions**

   Market expectations and strategic decisions can determine a maximum cost level that is allowed for a product, as is the case when using target costing. Target costing is a product design technique in which the product reaches a particular target cost at the end of the production process. However, when a company is a price taker in the market (in other words, it must take the going rate for materials or labor), then target costing must take these actual costs into account when setting standards. Strategic decisions such as a desire for continuous improvement (kaizen costing) or zero defects will be accomplished only if the standards are set high. These concepts are defined later in this section.

- **Benchmarking**

   Benchmarking is the continuous, systematic process of measuring products, services, and practices against the best levels of performance. Many people think of benchmarking as capturing "best-in-class" information, but the practice has a much wider application. Quite often, "best levels" are comparisons to external benchmarks of industry leaders. However, they may also be based on internal benchmarking information or measures from other organizations (outside an industry) that have similar processes. Good benchmarks can lead a company toward continuous improvement. However, a poor benchmark can have significant negative results (for example, an incompatible industry leads to unreachable goals or unchallenging goals). Also, benchmarking typically does not produce breakthroughs that lead to sustainable competitive advantage.

Resource Allocation

All entities have a finite amount of resources and wish to make the most of their capital. The allocation of scarce resources among competing opportunities is accomplished through implementation of a strategy.

Basis for a master budget

A **master budget** is a plan based on a company's strategy for controlling its operations for a specific period of time. A key point is that master budgets are fixed at an expected level of business activity.

Strategy

A company analyzes external factors to identify opportunities and threats; it analyzes internal factors to identify competitive advantages and weaknesses. When a company sees how it can match its strengths with market opportunities, it has a strategy that can be applied to the budget.

When a budget exists without consideration of strategy, it usually begins with the prior year's budget and misses opportunities to change the direction of the company, causing stagnation. Many once-great companies have met their demise because they failed to change in response to market demands. Implementing the strategy requires formulation of long-term plans, and long-term plans are implemented using a budget process.

Long-term planning

While a strategy is the starting point for achieving organizational goals, a long-term plan is needed to ensure that the strategy is implemented. A long-term plan is usually a five- to ten-year plan of actions required to achieve the company's goals. Planning for the long range can involve discontinuing certain operations over time, arranging for equity or debt financing, and allocating resources gradually to new branches of business. Such major reorganizations can be accomplished only over a period of time and usually involve the use of capital budgeting (part of the master budget). Capital budgeting is the process of allocating resources to an entity's proposed long-term projects. Because buildings, equipment, and hiring and training staff are all extremely expensive, such allocations must be made in accordance with strategy.

Short-term objectives

The final aspect that forms the basis for a master budget is short-term objectives. Short-term objectives are the variations in the long-term plan caused as a result of capital budgeting, the operating results of past periods, and expected future results caused by the current economic, social, industrial, and technological environment. These variations are fed into each year's master budget.

Master budget components

The master budget is the overall plan for operations for a company or business unit over a year, an operating period, or a shorter duration. The master budget sets quantitative goals for all operations, including detailed plans for raising the required capital. Figure 2-4 on the next page shows how the factors behind a master budget relate to it.

The master budget is a map showing where the company is heading, and, if it is properly designed, it will show the company heading in the same direction as the strategy and the long-term plan. The budget is more precise and of shorter duration than long-term plans, and it is more focused on responsibility centers than longer-term planning tools.

Figure 2-4: Strategic Goals, Long-Term Objectives, Budgets, and Operations

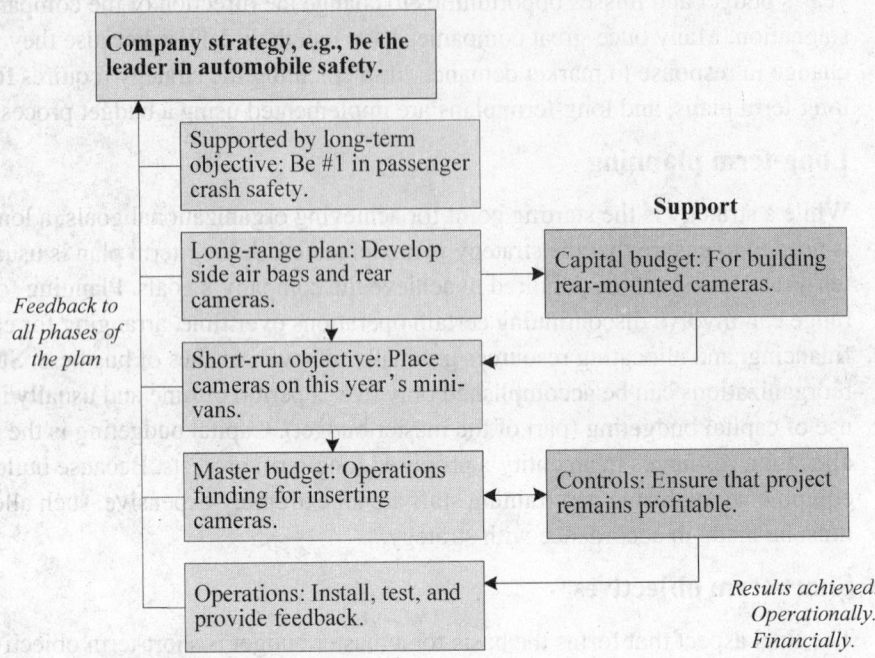

A master budget is broken down into an operating budget, a financial budget, and a capital budget.

- An **operating budget** identifies resources that are needed for operations and is concerned with the acquisition of these resources through purchase or manufacture. Production budgets, purchasing budgets, sales promotion budgets, and staffing budgets are all operating budgets.

- A **financial budget** matches sources of funds with uses of funds in order to achieve the goals of the firm, including budgets for cash inflows, outflows, financial position, and operating incomes.

- A **capital budget** is a budget for evaluating and selecting projects that require huge amounts of funding and provide benefits far into the future. Capital budgets feed into the cash budget and other financial budgets.

Management by Objectives (MBO)

Setting the individual, team, and department goals to reach a master budget is often performed by a system called **management by objectives (MBO)**. MBO is also useful for performance evaluations. MBO is an ongoing process. As Peter Drucker coined the term, MBO is a process in which all levels of management participate to identify the organization's common goals, define areas of responsibility by what is expected of each person, and set these goals as guides for operating the unit and assessing performance over a certain period of time.

The benefits of MBO include that it allows subordinates to participate in the goal-setting procedure, thus getting support for initiatives and feedback from those who will perform the tasks. MBO is more useful for comparing planned nonfinancial goals to actual results than it is for financial budgeting. MBO will help place priorities in nonfinancial terms, such as whether the sales manager opened up a certain number of new accounts. Such actions may reduce current profits but may create more profit for the company in the long run. Asking people to define their own goals also makes people accountable to themselves. The limitations of MBO include that while the goals set for upper levels of management are still clear, the further down in the organization, the more change occurs on a daily basis, and the plans have less relevance after a short period of time. MBO also focuses more on individual manager accountability than on teamwork or accountability to customers.

Part of MBO is responsibility accounting. Responsibility accounting is a method of ensuring that a manager is held accountable for only the items that he or she has under his/her control or discretion. The four elements of responsibility accounting are:

- **Assigning responsibility**
  A manager must understand the distinct items of a budget that he or she is responsible for. Divisional net revenue less controllable costs is an effective means of determining what is under the personal control of each manager.

- **Establishing performance measures**
  The manager must know what items are being measured. Because the manager will seek to maximize (or minimize) only those revenues (or costs) that are measured, care must be taken to ensure that maximizing (or minimizing) these items will result in the overall strategic goals of the firm.

- **Evaluating performance**
  Deviations between actual results and budgeted plans are assessed and separated into their various areas. See Section D for more information on such variances.

- **Assigning rewards**
  Managers should be held responsible for their budgets but should not be penalized if actual results differ negatively due to uncontrollable factors. Managers should be prepared to explain the cause of such differences. They should be rewarded for either meeting their goals or for being able to quickly change course once discrepancies are discovered.

Progress Check

Directions: Read each question and respond in the space provided. Answers and page references appear on the following page.

1. Management interviews a tennis ball line manager and tennis ball machine operators to define a cost standard that each of these parties believes is the best result that could be achieved assuming that nothing went wrong. What sort of standard is being set?

    (   )   a.   Authoritative ideal standard

    (   )   b.   Participative ideal standard

    (   )   c.   Authoritative currently attainable standard

    (   )   d.   Participative currently attainable standard

2. Place the following steps in forming a master budget in the correct order, with 1 being the first step:

    _____   Create master budget.

    _____   Create long-term plans.

    _____   Create short-term plans.

    _____   Analyze the internal and external environment.

    _____   Form strategic goals.

3. Which of the following groups is most likely to introduce slack into a budget?

    (   )   a.   Board of directors

    (   )   b.   Top management

    (   )   c.   Budget committee

    (   )   d.   Middle and lower management

Progress check answers

1. b (p. 2-24)

2. 5, 3, 4, 1, 2 (p. 2-26)

3. d (p. 2-22)

Budget Systems

Topic overview

This topic covers the different types of budget systems, including master budgets, project budgets, activity-based budgets, incremental budgets, zero-based budgets, continuous (rolling) budgets, kaizen budgets, and flexible budgets.

Master Budgets (Annual Business or Profit Plans)

As introduced previously, master budgets (also known as annual business plans or profit plans) are comprehensive budgets for a year or less. Every aspect of the company's cost flows are projected, starting from a sales forecast and sales budget. The benefits of having a master budget are numerous and the drawbacks few; few companies can get away without having some form of master budget. Most of the budgets described in the following pages will also result in a variation on the master budget. Master budgets are described in detail in Topic 3 of this section, "Annual Profit Plan and Supporting Schedules."

Project Budgeting

Project budgets are used when a project is completely separate from other elements of a company or is the only element of the company. A motion picture has a crew and costs that are related solely to that movie. A ship, a road, an aircraft, or other major capital asset is also often budgeted using a project budget. The time frame for a project budget is simply the duration of the project, but a multi-year project could be broken down by year. Successful past project budgets for similar projects should be used as benchmarks when developing project budgets. Project budgets are developed using the same techniques and components as shown for master budgeting in the next topic, except that the focus will be solely on costs related to the project instead of the company as a whole. The overhead budget is simplified because the company will allocate certain portions of the company's fixed and variable overhead to the project, and all remaining overhead for the company is excluded from the project budget.

Project budget advantages include the ability to contain all of a project's costs so that its individual impact can be easily measured. Project budgets work well on both a large and small scale. On a smaller scale, many individuals and firms use programs such as Microsoft Project to budget small projects. A potential limitation of project budgets occurs when these projects use resources and staff that are committed to the entire organization and not just the project. In such situations, the budget will contain links to these resource centers and affected individuals will have two bosses. Care must be taken in dividing costs and lines of authority.

Activity-Based Budgeting

An **activity-based budget** (ABB) focuses on activities instead of departments or products. Each activity is matched with the most appropriate cost driver, which is any volume-based (for example, labor hours, square feet) or activity-based (for example, number of parts to assemble for a machine) unit of measurement of the cost of a job or activity needed to sustain operations. Costs are divided into cost pools such as unit, batch, product, and facility. Cost pools include homogeneous costs that all vary in the same proportion to the rise and fall of production. Fixed costs are in one pool, and different levels of variable costs are in their own pools. The accuracy of these groupings should be evaluated each time a master budget is prepared. See Topic 3 in Section B of this part of the CMA Learning System, "Accumulation Systems," for information on activity-based costing (ABC) and related terms.

Whereas traditional budgeting focuses on input resources and expresses budgeting units in terms of functional areas, ABB focuses on value-added activities and expresses budgeting units in terms of activity costs. Traditional budgeting places emphasis on increasing management performance; ABB places emphasis on teamwork, synchronized activity, and customer satisfaction.

ABB proponents feel that traditional costing obscures the relationships between costs and outputs by oversimplifying the measurements into such categories as labor hours, machine hours, or output units for an entire process or department. Instead of using only volume drivers as a measurement tool, ABB uses activity-based cost drivers such as number of setups to make a clear connection between resource consumption and output. (ABB will also use volume-based drivers if they are the most appropriate measurement unit for a particular activity.) If the relationships are made clear, managers can see how resource demands are affected by changes in products offered, product designs, manufacturing techniques, customer base, and market share. Each planned activity will have its cost implications highlighted. Because of this, companies using ABB will be able to continuously improve their budgeting (and ABB can be linked to kaizen budgeting, discussed later in this topic). Conversely, traditional budgets focus on past (historical) budgets and often continue funding items that would be cut if their cost-effectiveness was better known.

ABB can be used as the foundation of a master budgeting process (detailed in the next topic). The resulting subbudgets would be based on different ways of measuring the costs, so the resulting proportions of costs would be weighted differently. For instance, some portion of the indirect materials or labor that would be part of overhead could be tracked more carefully and be included in direct materials and direct labor amounts.

Robin Manufacturing Company is used as an example in the next topic to show the components of the master budget, and Figure 2-12 in that topic shows that variable indirect labor at the company is applied at $2 per direct labor hour (DLH). For July production of 72,000 units, Robin Manufacturing budgeted 36,000 DLH, for a total of $72,000 in variable indirect labor. It also budgeted $10,000 for salary supervision, which is fixed indirect labor. Assume that the units are produced in two separate departments, subcomponent machining and final assembly, and that each department uses part of this indirect labor for quality control. Under ABB, it is now to be tracked by lots inspected, as shown in Figure 2-5. (Assume that each unit has ten subcomponents.)

Figure 2-5: Sample Cost Determination Using Activity-Based Budgeting

	Subcomponent Machining	Final Assembly
Amount to produce in July	720,000 subcomponents	72,000 units
Subcomponents or units per lot	100 subcomponents/lot	100 units/lot
Number of lots to inspect	720,000/100 = 7,200 lots	72,000/100 = 720 lots
Inspection time per lot	0.2 hours/lot	0.3 hours/lot
Total inspection hours	7,200 × 0.2 = 1,440 hours	720 × 0.3 = 216 hours

If the subcomponent inspection labor costs \$12 per hour and the final assembly inspection costs \$15 per hour, then $1,440 \times \$12 = \$17,280$ and $216 \times \$15 = \$3,240$, for a total of \$20,520. This amount would be included as direct labor and deducted from the indirect labor amounts, which would be recalculated at a new lower hourly rate for the remaining indirect labor. The total of this amount and the new indirect labor charges do not need to result in the same \$72,000 cost, however, as the new, more precise measurements may show that a different amount is expected. Furthermore, the total inspection time of 1,656 hours could be applied to a portion of the fixed overhead costs (supervisory salaries) as well. If ABB determined that one hour of supervisory time is needed for every eight hours of inspection time and supervisory time can be billed at \$30 per hour, then a salary supervision (inspection) fixed cost could be created with the following estimate of the fixed cost:

$$1,656 \text{ hours} \times \left(\frac{1 \text{ hour supervision}}{8 \text{ hours inspection}} \right) \times \$30/\text{hour} = \$6,210$$

Once again, this single fixed overhead cost account is divided into two (or more) cost accounts. The new salary supervision (inspection) account and any other salary accounts will still be fixed overhead accounts, but note that both the fixed and variable amounts are determined using a cost driver. Under ABB (and activity-based costing, on which it is based), both fixed and variable costs are allocated using cost drivers where applicable, meaning that over the short run, both fixed and variable costs are treated the same. This can be important because the new information on how the costs are broken down could be used to allow only one hour of supervisory time per nine hours of inspection, thus lowering a supposedly fixed cost. The more detailed the information, the more precise the planning can be.

As seen from the example, a key advantage of ABB is greater precision in cost determinations, especially where multiple departments or products need to be tracked. These benefits come at a cost, and a potential drawback to ABB can occur if the cost of designing and maintaining the ABB system exceeds the cost savings from better planning. Therefore, ABB is most appropriate in businesses that have complexity in their number of products, number of departments, or other factors such as setups. This is because the more complex a situation becomes, the less useful is the broad brush of traditional costing.

Incremental Budgeting

An **incremental budget** is a general type of budget that starts with the prior year's budget and uses projected changes in sales and the operating environment to adjust individual items in the budget upward or downward. It is the opposite of a zero-based budget. The main drawback to using these types of budgets (and the reason why some companies use zero-based budgets) is that such budgets tend to only increase in size over the years. A sense of entitlement may also arise with the use of an incremental budget.

Zero-Based Budgeting

In order to avoid situations in which ineffective elements of a business continue to exist simply because they were on the prior budget, some companies use **zero-based budgets**, which, as the name implies, start with zero dollars allocated. While the traditional budget focuses on changes to the past budget, the zero-based budget focuses on constant cost justification of each and every item on a budget. Managers must conduct in-depth reviews of each area under their control to provide such justification.

The strength of the zero-based budget is that it forces review of all elements of a business. Zero-based budgets can create efficient, lean organizations and are therefore popular with government and nonprofit organizations. A zero-based budget is a way of taking a new look at an old problem.

The first step in developing a zero-based budget is to have each department manager rank all of its activities from most to least important and assign a cost to each activity. Upper management reviews these lists, called decision packages, and cuts items that lack justification or are less critical. Upper management asks questions such as "Should the activity be performed and if it is not, what will happen?" or "Are there substitute methods of providing this function such as outsourcing or customer self-service?" Managers may also use benchmark figures and cost-benefit analysis to help decide what to cut. Only those items approved appear on the budget. The cost of the accepted items may be arrived at through discussion and negotiation with the department managers. Once the budget figures are determined, the zero-based budget becomes the basis for a master budget and thus uses the same components and steps as shown in the next topic.

Theoretically, zero-based budgets have the advantage of focusing on every line item instead of just the exceptions. They should motivate managers to identify and remove items that are more costly than the benefits provided. These budgets are especially useful when new management is hired. Zero-based budgets have a major drawback in that they encourage managers to exhaust all of their resources during a budget period for fear that they will be allocated less during the next budget cycle. If a manager has incorporated budget slack into the budget, a zero-based budget can encourage a significant amount of waste and unnecessary purchasing. Other drawbacks include the time-consuming and expensive annual review process (so the review is often less thorough than it is intended to be) and the fact that not using prior budgets can lead to ignoring lessons learned from prior years. Zero-based budgets used every year can deteriorate into little more than dressed-up incremental budgets. Managers simply remember their old justifications and figures and use them the next year. The time and expense of a zero-based budget is often mitigated by performing zero-based budgets only on a periodic basis, such as once every five years (and applying a different budget method in the other years), or by performing such a budget for a separate division each year.

Continuous (Rolling) Budgets

A **continuous budget**, or rolling budget, adds a new period on the end of the budget at the end of each period so that there are always several periods planned for the future and the budgets remain up-to-date with the operating environment. As with the other budget types, this budget becomes the master budget for an entity and uses the same components and interrelationships as detailed in the next topic. The difference is that the budget is continually being added to instead of just when the prior budget expires. Therefore, the time frame for this budget always remains the same (for example, one year, no matter if it is viewed in January or July).

For example, if the period is a month, each month (or quarter) a new set of monthly financial statements is issued to each person responsible for preparing the budget. In a monthly budget meeting, managers report on the variances from the past month's budget and make projections for the next month. After review, a budget coordinator updates the master budget. The budget coordinator must perform all of the calculations, such as depreciation or inventory valuation that were not performed by line managers.

Continuous budgets will be more relevant than a budget prepared once a year. The budget can reflect current events and necessities in its estimates. Continuous budgets have the advantage of breaking down a large process into manageable steps. Because managers always have a full period of budgeted data, they tend to view decisions in a longer-term perspective than with a one-year budget, which will cover a shorter and shorter period of time as the year progresses. Potential disadvantages of continuous budgets include the need to have a budget coordinator and/or the opportunity cost of having managers use part of each month working on the next month's budget. Continuous budgets are appropriate for firms that cannot devote a large block of time to a once-a-year budget process. A company that has a seasonal lull may find it easier to budget during this time than one that is continually busy. These types of budgets are also useful for firms that want their managers to have a longer-term view of the firm.

Kaizen Budgeting

A **kaizen budget** is a budgeting method that incorporates continuous improvement ("kaizen" in Japanese). Whereas traditional budgeting continues current practices, a kaizen budgeting process is based on planned future operating practices.

Kaizen budgeting starts by identifying areas of improvement. Because improved practices are usually more efficient, kaizen budgets tend to have lower costs. Such changes are often mandated by company policy (for example, glue costs must fall by 5%). Many firms that use kaizen budgeting also demand that their suppliers show continuous improvement. While traditional budget cuts are reactive and often involve cuts in services or production, kaizen cuts are proactive and try to lower costs without sacrificing productivity.

The master budget using kaizen budgeting would have the same time frame and components as those listed in the following section for master budgets, but within the budget period, each cost driver and/or standard cost may be set at more than one level over time. For example, indirect labor may be allocated at \$2/direct labor hour in the first quarter, \$1.90 in the second quarter, \$1.80 in the third, and \$1.70 in the fourth. Or the direct labor hours per unit could be steadily reduced from 0.5 to 0.4 and so on. Another item may set a standard for units per batch at 200, then 210, and so on. Thus each budget may have a supporting schedule showing how the amounts listed in the final budget are calculated.

The benefits of kaizen are in its proactive setup and its promotion of company ideals. Companies using kaizen usually have fully integrated quality control systems rather than disjointed or sporadic efforts. However, one drawback is that because many budgets are interconnected, for example, if direct labor hour standards are reduced, it may also tighten the amount of variable overhead costs if these are also measured based on direct labor hours. If companies cannot meet the overall goals, the budget will have large variances. Therefore, kaizen is often paired with activity-based budgeting to ensure that all costs are matched to an appropriate cost driver. Another drawback is that managers may lower quality levels or move practices to cheaper labor markets if costs cannot otherwise be lowered. Furthermore, unlike zero-based budgets, the emphasis with Kaizen budgets is on improving existing expenditures, and some projects that should be cut or added might be ignored in place of an incremental improvement.

Flexible Budgeting

Flexible budgeting establishes a base cost budget for a particular level of output (a cost-volume relationship) plus an incremental cost-volume amount that shows the behavior of costs at various volumes. Only the variable costs are adjusted; fixed costs remain unchanged. The most common use of a flexible budget is to show the budget that would have been made if the organization had exactly matched its sales forecast. While flexible budgets from prior periods can be helpful in determining how to modify the next budget, a flexible budget that applies actual production output cannot be used as a type of master budget because the actual production output is not known until the period is complete. Therefore, flexible budgets are used more as an analysis tool for determining variances from plan than for creating the original budget. The time frame for a flexible budget is therefore the same as for the master budget upon which it is based. Because a flexible budget is an adaptation of an existing master budget (or of a month's worth of that budget), components of a flexible budget are the same as those shown for the master budget as detailed in the next topic.

The benefits of using a flexible budget include the ability make better use of historical budget information to improve future planning. Drawbacks to flexible budgeting are few, but one could be that focusing solely on the flexible budget level tends to ignore the fact that the sales target was missed. However, most businesses use flexible budgets because it allows for extremely detailed variance analysis. Flexible budgets are discussed more fully in Section D, "Performance Measurement."

Progress Check

Directions: Read each question and respond in the space provided. Answers and page references appear on the following page.

1. Which of the following budgeting methods might use a cost driver such as number of setups to measure the costs of a batch mixing production job?

   ( ) a. Kaizen budgeting

   ( ) b. Project budgeting

   ( ) c. Continuous budgeting

   ( ) d. Activity-based budgeting

2. Which of the following budgeting methods establishes a base cost budget for a particular level of output plus a marginal cost-volume amount that shows the behavior of costs at various volumes?

   ( ) a. Flexible budgeting

   ( ) b. Continuous budgeting

   ( ) c. Kaizen budgeting

   ( ) d. Activity-based budgeting

3. True or false? A kaizen budget incorporates continuous improvements by creating a new budget for each upcoming month.

   ( ) a. True

   ( ) b. False

4. Bounce Sporting Goods is a currently profitable company that uses an activity-based master budget. Despite their use of activity-based budgeting (ABB), their five-year budget suggests that in a few years their costs will soar above their revenues. Which of the following would be the best choice for Bounce?

   ( ) a. Replace ABB with continuous budgeting.

   ( ) b. Replace ABB with kaizen budgeting.

   ( ) c. Add kaizen budgeting to existing ABB.

   ( ) d. Add continuous budgeting to existing ABB.

Progress check answers

1. d (p. 2-33)

2. a (p. 2-37)

3. b (p. 2-36)

4. c (p. 2-36)

Annual Profit Plan and Supporting Schedules

Topic overview

The master budget, or annual profit plan, has many components and supporting schedules, including operating, financial, and capital budgets and pro forma financial statements. These elements are discussed in this topic.

Master Budget

The master budget provides a comprehensive summation of all of an entity's budgets and its plans for the operating activities of its subunits. It is the place where everything must add up, where strategy and long-term plans meet up with short-term objectives and current realities. Master budgets are usually made yearly, although other short-duration time periods are also used.

The master budget is made up of many different budgets. At the highest level of breakdown, master budgets consist of operating, production, and financial budgets.

The **operating budget** makes up the bulk of the master budget; operating budgets include sales budgets, and sales budgets include production budgets and selling and administrative expense budgets. **Production budgets** determine requirements for the direct materials, direct labor, overhead, and cost of goods sold budgets; these budgets reveal additional product cost data not revealed in the production budget. **Financial budgets** include all pro forma financial statements (budgeted income statement, balance sheet, and statement of cash flows) plus a cash budget. Figure 2-6 shows how the components of the master budget are related.

Figure 2-6: The Master Budget

Master budget

What sales do we predict?

What do we need to produce to meet sales?

What labor, material, and overhead do we need to support production?

What selling and administrative budget do we need to support sales and production?

How much will all of this cost (including capital expenditures)?

What will the financial impact on the company be if we execute this plan?

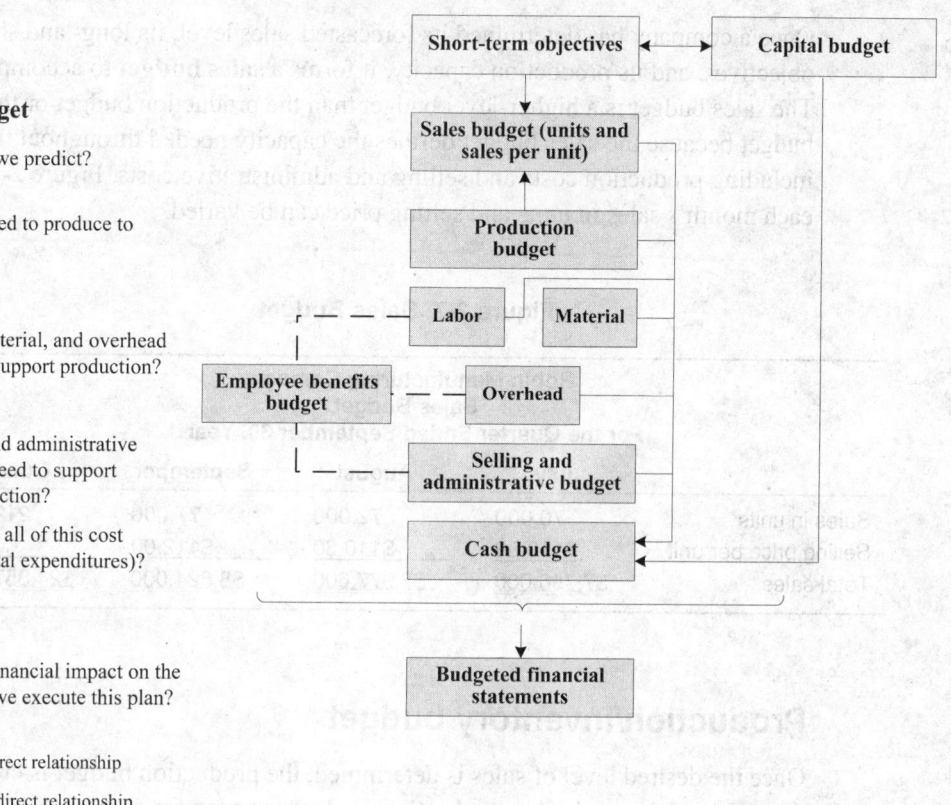

Short-term objectives ↔ Capital budget

Sales budget (units and sales per unit)

Production budget

Labor — Material

Employee benefits budget — Overhead

Selling and administrative budget

Cash budget

Budgeted financial statements

——— Direct relationship

— — — Indirect relationship

Operational Budgets

Sales forecast

Before creating a sales budget, an accurate sales forecast is needed. A **sales forecast** is a subjective estimate of the entity's future sales for the upcoming period. Without an accurate sales forecast, all other budget elements will be inaccurate. Forecasters consider not only historical trends for sales but also economic and industry conditions and indicators, competitors' actions, rising costs, policies on pricing and extending credit, amount of advertising and marketing, numbers of unfilled back orders, and sales in the sales pipeline (unsigned prospects). Sales forecasts should use statistical analysis techniques such as the accounts receivable balance pattern discussed later in this topic. However, sales managers have a great deal of knowledge of their market and their customer needs, and this experience should be leveraged through dialogue between all constituents when deciding on the details of the final sales forecast.

Sales budget

Once a company has determined its forecasted sales level, its long- and short-term objectives, and its production capacity, it forms a **sales budget** to accomplish its goals. The sales budget is a higher-level budget than the production budget or the administrative budget because the sales budget defines the capacity needed throughout the company, including production costs and selling and administrative costs. Figure 2-7 shows how each month's sales in units and selling price can be varied.

Figure 2-7: Sales Budget

Robin Manufacturing Company
Sales Budget
For the Quarter Ended September 30, Year 1

	July	August	September	Quarter
Sales in units	70,000	72,000	77,000	219,000
Selling price per unit	$110.80	$110.80	$112.00	
Total sales	$7,756,000	$7,977,600	$8,624,000	$24,357,600

Production/inventory budget

Once the desired level of sales is determined, the production budget is created to satisfy the expected demand. The **production budget** is a plan for acquiring resources and combining them to meet sales goals and maintain a certain level of inventory. The budgeted production is calculated by adding budgeted sales to desired ending inventory minus the beginning inventory. Inventory levels should be as low as possible without restricting sales. The master budget makes the comparisons between the sales budget and the production budget possible. Figure 2-8 shows a production budget for several months. If presented on a quarterly basis, the total sales would be the total for the three months, but the beginning and ending inventory is the beginning inventory for the first month of the quarter and the ending inventory for the last month of the quarter respectively.

Figure 2-8: Production Budget

Robin Manufacturing Company
Production Budget (in Thousands)
For the Quarter Ended September 30, Year 1

	July	August	September	Quarter
Budgeted sales in units	70	72	77	219
Add: Desired ending inventory of finished goods	10	11	12	12
Total units needed	80	83	89	231
Less: Beginning inventory of finished goods	8	10	11	8
Budgeted production in units	72	73	78	223

Direct materials budget

The **direct materials budget** determines the required materials and the quality level of the materials used to meet production. The direct materials budget is often broken down into a direct usage budget and a direct materials purchase budget. While the production budget specifies only the number of units to be produced, the usage budget specifies the material components and the cost of these materials. The direct materials purchase budget is concerned with direct purchases of material components and finished goods.

Figure 2-9 illustrates the direct materials usage budget; Figure 2-10 illustrates a direct materials purchase budget.

Figure 2-9: Direct Materials Usage Budget

Robin Manufacturing Company
Direct Materials Usage Budget
For the Quarter Ended September 30, Year 1

	July	August	September	Quarter
Production requirement				
Budgeted production	72,000	73,000	78,000	223,000
Pounds of resin per unit of product	5	5	5	5
Total pounds of resin required	360,000	365,000	390,000	1,115,000
Pounds of resin in beginning inventory	35,000	35,000	35,000	35,000
Cost per pound	$13.00	$13.00	$13.25	$13.00
Total cost of beginning inventory	$455,000	$455,000	$463,750	$455,000
Total cost of resin purchases (see Fig. 2-10)	4,680,000	4,836,250	5,253,500	14,769,750
Cost of resin available for production	$5,135,000	$5,291,250	$5,717,250	$15,224,750
Desired ending inventory in pounds	35,000	35,000	40,000	40,000
Cost of desired ending inventory per pound	$13.00	$13.25	$13.30	$13.30
Total cost of desired ending inventory	$455,000	$463,750	$532,000	$532,000
Cost of resin used in production	$4,680,000	$4,827,500	$5,185,250	$14,692,750
(Cost Available for Production – Cost of Desired Ending Inventory)				

Figure 2-10: Direct Materials Purchase Budget

Robin Manufacturing Company
Direct Materials Purchase Budget
For the Quarter Ended September 30, Year 1

	July	August	September	Quarter
Total direct materials needed in production	360,000	365,000	390,000	1,115,000
Add: Desired ending inventory	35,000	35,000	40,000	40,000
Total direct materials required	395,000	400,000	430,000	1,155,000
Less: Direct materials beginning inventory	35,000	35,000	35,000	35,000
Direct materials purchases	360,000	365,000	395,000	1,120,000
Purchase price per pound	$13.00	$13.25	$13.30	
Total cost for direct materials purchases	$4,680,000	$4,836,250	$5,253,500	$14,769,750

Direct labor budget

The **direct labor budget** is prepared by the production manager and human resources. The labor budget can help firms plan production processes to smooth out production over a year and keep a consistent work-force size throughout the year. Firms with unions can begin any required negotiations before a hiring or layoff is needed. Labor budgets are usually broken down into categories such as semiskilled, unskilled, and skilled.

Figure 2-11 illustrates a direct labor budget.

Figure 2-11: Direct Labor Budget

Robin Manufacturing Company
Direct Labor Budget
For the Quarter Ended September 30, Year 1

	July	August	September	Quarter
Budgeted production	72,000	73,000	78,000	223,000
Direct labor hours required per unit	0.5	0.5	0.5	
Direct labor hours needed	36,000	36,500	39,000	111,500
Hourly rate	$15	$15	$15	
Total wages for direct labor	$540,000	$547,500	$585,000	$1,672,500

Overhead budget (factory overhead budget)

All other production costs that are not in the direct materials and direct labor budgets are in the **overhead budget**, sometimes called a fixed costs budget because most of the costs in this category do not vary with the rise and fall of production. For example, rent and insurance remain stable even if production goes up or down.

Variable costs included in this budget are costs that may vary with production, such as batch setup costs or the costs of electricity and other utilities. Fixed costs are easy to budget, but the variable costs require forecasting the number of units to be produced, the production methods used, and other external factors.

Figure 2-12 illustrates an overhead budget.

Figure 2-12: Factory Overhead Budget

	Rate per DLH*	July	August	September	Quarter
Robin Manufacturing Company Factory Overhead Budget For the Quarter Ended September 30, Year 1					
Total direct labor hours		36,000	36,500	39,000	111,500
Variable factory overhead					
Supplies	$0.20	$7,200	$7,300	$7,800	$22,300
Fringe benefits	4.10	147,600	149,650	159,900	457,150
Utilities	1.00	36,000	36,500	39,000	111,500
Maintenance	0.50	18,000	18,250	19,500	55,750
Total variable factory overhead	$5.80	$208,800	$211,700	$226,200	$646,700
Fixed factory overhead					
Depreciation		$20,000	$20,000	$20,000	$60,000
Plant insurance		800	800	800	2,400
Property taxes		1,200	1,200	1,200	3,600
Salary supervision		10,000	10,000	10,000	30,000
Indirect labor		72,000	72,000	72,000	216,000
Utilities		4,000	4,000	4,000	12,000
Maintenance		900	900	900	2,700
Total fixed factory overhead		$108,900	$108,900	$108,900	$326,700
Total factory overhead	$5.80	$317,700	$320,600	$335,100	$973,400

* Direct labor hour (DLH); DLH is assumed to be the cost driver for factory overhead in this example.

Cost of goods sold budget

The **cost of goods sold budget** includes the total and per-unit production cost that is budgeted for a period. This budget is sometimes called the cost of goods manufactured and sold budget, because it often also includes items budgeted to be in inventory. This budget is created only after the production, direct materials, direct labor, and overhead budgets are formed, because it is basically a summary of these budgets.

Figure 2-13 illustrates a cost of goods sold budget.

Figure 2-13: Cost of Goods Sold Budget

Robin Manufacturing Company
Cost of Goods Sold Budget
For the Quarter Ended September 30, Year 1

	July	August	September	Quarter
Beginning finished goods inventory, 7/1/Year 1				$1,575,000
Direct materials used (see Fig. 2-9)	$4,680,000	$4,827,500	$5,185,250	14,692,750
Direct labor used	540,000	547,500	585,000	1,672,500
Manufacturing overhead	317,700	321,600	341,100	980,400
Cost of goods manufactured	$5,537,700	$5,696,600	$6,111,350	$17,345,650
Cost of goods available for sale				18,920,650
Less: Ending finished goods inventory				1,575,000
Cost of goods sold				$17,345,650

Selling and administrative expense budget

Nonmanufacturing expenses are often grouped into a single budget called a **selling and administrative expense budget** or nonmanufacturing costs budget. Sales expenses are included in this category because they are not allowed to be allocated to production processes but must be expensed in the period in which they occur.

The costs in this budget usually satisfy long-term goals, such as customer service, so they are not easy places to make cuts. When using a contribution margin format for selling and administrative expenses, all variable selling and administrative costs as well as variable manufacturing costs are deducted from net sales to find the contribution margin, allowing the budget to be used for internal performance measurement and to help show where costs can be controlled. For more information on contribution margin, see Section D, Topic 2, "Responsibility Centers and Reporting Segments," in this part of the CMA Learning System.

Figure 2-14 illustrates a nonmanufacturing costs budget.

Figure 2-14: Selling and Administrative Expense Budget

Robin Manufacturing Company
Selling and Administrative Expense Budget
For the Quarter Ended September 30, Year 1

	July	August	September	Quarter
Research/design	$95,000	$95,000	$100,000	$290,000
Marketing	240,000	280,000	290,000	810,000
Shipping	135,000	140,000	150,000	425,000
Product support	90,000	90,000	95,000	275,000
Administration	185,000	190,000	192,000	567,000
Total	$745,000	$795,000	$827,000	$2,367,000

Employee benefits budgets

Employee benefits budgets help employers determine the firm's share of payroll costs entailed in budgets. Benefits are becoming ever more important in budgeting: in the U.S. in the 1920s, benefits amounted to about 3% of payroll, while current corporate costs average over 40% of payroll.

Employee benefits tie into the direct labor budget, the overhead budget, and the selling and administrative expense budget, so each of these budgets may have a supporting benefits budget or a schedule to help determine costs to include in each budget. Benefits such as health insurance and retirement benefits are considered to be part of the overhead budget that needs to be allocated usually as part of a tax and benefits charge-out or allocation. Note that in the factory overhead budget previously shown, Robin Manufacturing's benefits are rolled up as "fringe benefits." Benefits such as a schedule of wage and salary increases and budgeted new hires for a period are part of the direct labor budget. Also many of the variable cost benefits are calculated based on budgeted direct labor hours. Benefits such as executive benefits and employee stock options are expensed as part of the selling and administrative expense budget.

Required benefits usually have an employer-paid portion and an employee-paid portion (these amounts are usually equal), but this discussion will focus solely on the employer-paid portions. Optional benefits often also have an employer- and employee-paid portion, such as for health insurance. Figure 2-15 lists some of the common employer-paid employee benefits and indicates which are required by law in the U.S. or are optional for most employers and also which are fixed or variable costs.

Figure 2-15: Common Employer-Paid Benefits

Type	Benefit	Description
Variable, required	Federal Insurance Contributions Act (FICA; Social Security)	Federal law requiring employers to withhold a specific percentage of salary or wages from employee paychecks for deposit in government trust funds for Social Security, disability insurance, and survivor benefits.
	Medicare	Nationwide health insurance program for persons age 65 or older, persons with end-stage renal disease, and persons entitled to Social Security payments for 2+ years.
	Federal unemployment tax (FUTA)	Tax that finances the administrative costs for unemployment insurance.
	State unemployment tax	Tax that finances benefits disbursed from the Unemployment Insurance Fund, required regardless of federal liability.
Fixed, required	Workers' compensation insurance	Insurance that compensates employees for on-the-job injuries. This cost is set annually but can vary year-to-year, depending primarily on the claims history of the firm.
Variable, optional	Payments for time not worked	Payments for holidays, breaks, sick leave, vacations, time off, and family and medical leave; some items may be fixed.
	Bonuses, profit sharing	Defined by employer. Employee stock options must be listed as an expense.
	Retirement benefits, 401(k) matching, and similar programs	Consists of both defined pension plans (a promise to pay a fixed payment at retirement) and defined contribution plans such as a 401(k). Retirement savings accounts: Employers may contribute based on employee's contribution. Employers must recognize defined pension retirement benefits over the course of the employee's career by creating a pension liability. When retired employees receive their benefits, the pension liability account is reduced.
Fixed, optional	Health insurance	Health coverage portion paid by employer.
	Dental insurance	Dental coverage portion paid by employer.
	Short-term disability (STD) insurance	Insurance for accidents or illnesses lasting beyond what is covered by health insurance.
	Long-term disability (LTD) insurance	Insurance for accidents or illnesses lasting beyond what is covered by STD insurance.

Fixed benefits are generally measured at annual cost, but some are measured by cost per employee per year or as a percentage of payroll. Fixed benefits are generally only considered fixed so long as staffing does not change. Variable benefits can be measured by the previous methods or by cents per hour, but the hours may be based on either an arbitrary standard (for example, 2,080 hours per year full time) or on actual hours.

Obviously, required benefits are committed costs that will be difficult to change but must be accounted for. Clearly defining which benefits are optional can help employers determine areas in which they can make cuts or additions.

Financial Budgets

Pro forma financial statements

Pro forma financial statements for internal use are future forecasts of the position the company would like to be in assuming its assumptions prove correct. (Recall that the definition of pro forma statements differs in regard to external statements.) The internal pro forma statements include the income statement, the balance sheet, the schedule of cash receipts and cash disbursements, and the cash budget.

Pro forma income statement

The pro forma income statement, or budget income statement, shows what the profits for the company will be at the end of the year if the company meets its budget and its assumptions prove correct. When budgeted income falls short of the goal, management knows it must take corrective action. The budget is revised to account for these actions. A budgeted income statement is therefore a benchmark to use in evaluating progress.

The pro forma income statement is formed using at a minimum the sales budget, the cost of goods sold budget, and the administrative and selling budget.

Figure 2-16 illustrates a sample pro forma income statement.

Figure 2-16: Pro Forma Income Statement

Robin Manufacturing Company	
Pro Forma Income Statement	
For the Quarter Ended September 30, Year 1	
Sales	$24,357,600
Less: Cost of goods sold	17,345,650
Gross margin	$7,011,950
Less: Operating costs	2,367,000
Operating income	$4,644,950

Pro forma balance sheet

A pro forma balance sheet (also known as budget balance sheet or statement of financial position) shows how operations should affect the company's assets, liabilities, and stockholders' equity. The budget balance sheet is usually the last item prepared in a master budget and is based in part on the budget balance sheet at the end of the current period.

The effects of operations for the budget period are added to the data in the prior balance sheet.

Pro forma schedule of cash receipts and cash disbursements

Prior to creating a cash budget, companies need to determine how much cash will be available in a given period. Due to the use of credit sales, this requires forecasting of cash receipts (inflows) and cash disbursements (outflows). Companies create a pro forma schedule to estimate their cash receipts and another to estimate cash disbursements. The pro forma cash receipts schedule estimates percentages of collections for each period (using the same method as the accounts receivable balance pattern, which is discussed below). The pro forma cash disbursements schedule can also use payment percentage patterns, but these are based on payment history instead of collection history. Often these disbursements are broken down by materials purchases, direct wages (based on current sales), general and administrative expenses, and income taxes. Other schedules separate fixed and variable expenses.

An accounts receivable balance pattern estimates cash inflows, but the same methods can be applied to cash outflows.

An accounts receivable (A/R) balance pattern is a forecasting tool to estimate timing of cash inflows and A/R levels resulting from making sales on credit. Companies use great care in analyzing historical collection trends and use such patterns as assumptions in forecasting cash collections. An A/R balance pattern is derived from a company's collection history and results in a percentage estimate of uncollected credit sales at the end of a specific period, such as a month.

Figure 2-17 shows an A/R sales collection history for Robin Manufacturing Company.

Figure 2-17: Robin Manufacturing Company, A/R Sales Collection History

Interval Since Month Sales	Percentage Collected
Month zero (current month)	40%
Month one (next month)	30%
Month two (month after next)	20%
Month three (three months after)	10%

Using this information, an A/R balance pattern can be applied to monthly sales to predict collections from an upcoming period.

Consider the example in Figure 2-18. Assume that Robin Manufacturing has actual March sales of $9,200,000, April sales of $9,500,000, May sales of $9,032,000, and June through September estimated sales as shown.

Figure 2-18: A/R Balance Pattern for August with Forecast Inflows through September

Month Sales	Sales	Cash Inflows for Month	A/R Remaining from Month Sales at End of August	Remaining A/R as a % of Month Sales
June	$8,520,000	$8,937,600	$852,000	10%
July	$7,756,000	$8,414,800	$2,326,800	30%
August	$7,977,600	$8,125,040	$4,786,560	60%
September	$8,624,000	$8,246,080		

Cash inflows from sales for the month are calculated using the following formula. (The example shows how the final forecast amount was determined for September.)

Cash Inflows for Month

= (Month Zero % Collected × Sales Current Month)

+ (Month One % Collected × Sales Last Month)

+ (Month Two % Collected × Sales Two Months Ago)

+ (Month Three % Collected × Sales Three Months Ago)

For September = (0.4 × $8,624,000) + (0.3 × $7,977,600)

+ (0.2 × $7,756,000) + (0.1 × $8,520,000)

= $3,449,600 + $2,393,280 + $1,551,200 + $852,000 = $8,246,080

A/R remaining from month sales at the end of August and the remaining A/R as a percentage of month sales are calculated as follows:

A/R Remaining from Month Sales at End of Current Month

= Month Sales − [(Month Zero % Collected × Month Sales)

+ (Month One % Collected × Month Sales)

+ (Month Two % Collected × Month Sales)

+ (Month Three % Collected × Month Sales)]

A/R Remaining from June sales at End of August

= $8,520,000 − [(0.4 × $8,520,000)

+ (0.3 × $8,520,000) + (0.2 × $8,520,000) + 0*]

= $8,520,000 − ($3,408,000 + $2,556,000 + $1,704,000)

= $8,520,000 − $7,668,000 = $852,000

A/R Remaining in Current Month as a % of Month Sales

$$= \frac{\text{A/R Remaining From Month Sales at End of Current Month}}{\text{Month Sales}}$$

A/R Remaining in August as a % of June Sales

$$= \frac{\$852,000}{\$8,520,000} = 0.1 = 10\%$$

* Not yet collected

Note that it is possible that the firm would have additional planned cash collections from non-sales sources, such as investment income. In this case, those cash receipts would be added to the cash receipts from sales to find total cash receipts. Using these methods, a pro forma schedule of cash receipts and disbursements can be made, as shown in Figure 2-19. In addition to the assumptions stated previously for Robin Manufacturing, assume that in June, actual direct material purchases were $3,280,000, actual variable factory overhead was $260,500, actual fixed factory overhead (less depreciation) was $16,900, and actual selling and administrative expenses were $705,000. Robin Manufacturing uses data from their other budgets to complete other portions of this schedule. Half of purchases are paid in the same month as the purchase, and the other half are paid one month later. Direct labor is paid in the same month, while overhead is paid the next month. The amounts calculated on this schedule are used in the cash budget. Note that the firm may have additional cash disbursements that can be estimated and added to the cash disbursement schedule.

Figure 2-19: Pro Forma Schedule of Cash Receipts and Cash Disbursements

Robin Manufacturing Company
Pro Forma Schedule of Cash Receipts and Cash Disbursements
For the 3rd Quarter, Year 1

	July expected	August expected	September expected
Sales*	$7,756,000	$7,977,600	$8,624,000
Direct materials (DM) purchases**	$4,680,000	$4,836,250	$5,253,500
Cash receipts			
Sales—40% same month	$3,102,400	$3,191,040	$3,449,600
30%—1-month lag	$2,556,000	$2,326,800	$2,393,280
20%—2-month lag	$1,806,400	$1,704,000	$1,551,200
10%—3-month lag	$ 950,000	$ 903,200	$ 852,000
Total cash receipts	$8,414,800	$8,125,040	$8,246,080
Cash disbursements			
DM purchases**—50% same month	$2,340,000	$2,418,125	$2,626,750
50% following month	$1,640,000	$2,340,000	$2,418,125
Direct labor paid same month***	$ 540,000	$ 547,500	$ 585,000
Variable factory overhead paid following month****	$ 260,500	$ 280,800	$ 284,700
Fixed factory overhead paid following month****	$ 16,900	$ 16,900	$ 16,900
Selling and administrative expenses paid following month*****	$ 705,000	$ 745,000	$ 795,000
Total cash disbursements	$5,502,400	$6,348,325	$6,726,475

*   Sales data taken from sales budget
**   Direct materials purchases data taken from direct materials purchase budget
***   Direct labor data taken from direct labor budget
**** Variable and fixed factory overhead data taken from factory overhead budget; note that depreciation expense of $20,000 was removed each month
***** Selling and administrative expenses data taken from the selling and administrative expense budget

Cash budget

Maintaining adequate liquidity is a requirement for staying in business, and a cash budget is a plan to ensure that liquidity is maintained. Financing can be arranged in an orderly fashion, and investments can be timed to be liquidated at the time the funds are needed. Cash budgets are commonly formulated for monthly periods, but many companies find it useful to have even finer divisions such as by week or even day.

Because cash is needed in all areas of operations, the cash budget gets data from all parts of the master budget and from the pro forma schedule of cash receipts and cash disbursements. A cash budget is divided into cash available, cash disbursements, cash excess or deficiency, and financing.

- **Cash available**

  The first section of a cash budget, cash available, shows the sources of cash for use in operations. These sources include the cash balance at the beginning of the period and cash collections or receipts, which include revenue from accounts and notes receivable, debt capital, equity capital, and gains from disposition of nonoperating assets. Sales levels, collection risk, unusual losses, and credit policy may have an effect on cash available.

  - **Cash balance, beginning**

    This equals the ending cash balance from the prior period.

  - **Cash receipts**

    Cash receipts are all collections in the current period from sales made in the current and prior periods (collections of accounts receivable).

- **Cash disbursements**

  The cash disbursements section includes all outgoing cash payments. These include payments for purchases of materials, wages, operating expenses, taxes, and interest expenses. The ending cash balance before financing is the cash available minus the cash disbursements.

- **Cash excess or deficiency**

  The cash excess or deficiency section is calculated as the beginning cash balance plus receipts and less disbursements and minimum cash balance requirements. The result is either an excess or a deficiency of cash for the period. Deficiencies must be financed, thus the financing section follows.

- **Financing**

  Financing includes finding sources of cash when liquidity levels fall below a point set by management or the board of directors as well as using excess cash for temporary and short-term investments to make use of cash above a certain level. Most firms value capital preservation over returns on investment when choosing investments, so they choose relatively safe investments, for example, money market securities.

The more complex aspects of the financing section involve calculating interest and loan repayments. If financing is needed in one month (see August in Figure 2-20 on the next page), the amount of financing must include enough for the minimum cash balance to be satisfied. Conversely, when calculating the amount of principle and interest that can be repaid, the minimum cash balance must first be deducted (see September in Figure 2-20). Furthermore, it is important to note when the principal and interest are to be repaid (at the beginning or the end of a period) in order to determine what principal the interest charge will be based upon. Calculation of interest must take into account partial periods (for example, 1/12th of 10% per annum for a month's interest).

Figure 2-20 illustrates a cash budget.

Figure 2-20: Cash Budget

Robin Manufacturing Company
Cash Budget
For the Quarter Ended September 30, Year 1

	July	August	September	Quarter
Cash balance, beginning	$1,587,000	$3,499,400	$250,000	$1,587,000
Add receipts				
Collections from customers	8,414,800	8,125,040	8,246,080	24,785,920
Total cash available for needs	$10,001,800	$11,624,440	$8,496,080	$26,372,920
Deduct disbursements*				
Direct materials	3,980,000	4,758,125	5,044,875	13,783,000
Direct labor	540,000	547,500	585,000	1,672,500
Variable factory overhead	260,500	280,800	284,700	826,000
Fixed factory overhead**	16,900	16,900	16,900	50,700
Selling and administrative expense	705,000	745,000	795,000	2,245,000
Capital improvements	1,000,000	7,062,165	50,000	8,112,165
Total disbursements	$6,502,400	$13,410,490	$6,776,475	$26,689,365
Minimum cash needed	250,000	250,000	250,000	250,000
Total cash needed	$6,752,400	$13,660,490	$7,026,475	$26,939,365
Cash excess (deficiency)	3,249,400	(2,036,050)	1,469,605	($566,445)
Financing				
Borrowing (beginning balance)	–	–	2,036,050	0
Borrowing	–	2,036,050	–	2,036,050
Repayment (end of period)	–	–	(1,449,244) ***	(1,449,244)
Interest expense			(20,361) ****	(20,361)
Borrowing (ending balance)		2,036,050	586,806 *****	$586,806
Total financing needs (adjusted for interest payments)	–	$2,036,050	$ (1,469,605)	$586,806
Cash balance, ending	$3,499,400	$250,000	$250,000	$250,000

*   See the pro forma schedule of cash receipts and cash disbursements for information on the timing of cash payments.
**   Depreciation expense removed.
***   Only $1,449,244 could be paid back at this time.
****   Interest on short-term borrowings.
***** Note that interest for the following month will be $5,868.

General notes: Robin Manufacturing Company requires a cash balance of $250,000 at all times. In the month of August, the need to borrow over $2 million was financed with a short-term loan at 12% per annum interest. Note also that the example assumes that excess cash is not being invested (see July).

Capital Budgets

As mentioned earlier, a capital budget is a budget for evaluating and selecting projects that require huge amounts of funding and provide benefits far into the future. Capital investments include purchases of property, plant, or equipment and purchases of new businesses or operating capabilities.

Because all businesses face a scarcity of resources, capital must be rationed. Therefore, capital budgets must first be aligned with the company strategy, and that strategy must be reformed continually to take advantage of internal strengths and external opportunities. Methods of assessing projects are also covered in Section E, Topic 1, Part 3 of the *CMA Learning System*, "Capital Budgeting Process."

Progress Check

Directions: Read each question and respond in the space provided. Answers and page references appear on the following page.

1. Which of the following budgets is the first operating budget prepared because it defines needed capacity for operations?

    ( ) a. Production/inventory budget

    ( ) b. Direct labor budget

    ( ) c. Sales budget

    ( ) d. Overhead budget

2. Which of the following internal pro forma financial statements is usually the last budget prepared at the end of a period?

    ( ) a. Pro forma income statement

    ( ) b. Pro forma balance sheet

    ( ) c. Pro forma statement of stockholders' equity

    ( ) d. Cash budget

3. Which of the following budgets is designed to ensure that the company maintains adequate liquidity?

    ( ) a. Overhead budget

    ( ) b. Sales budget

    ( ) c. Production/inventory budget

    ( ) d. Cash budget

Progress check answers

1. c (p. 2-42)

2. b (p. 2-49)

3. d (p. 2-53)

Cost Management

Section overview

Knowing what costs to include in a budget requires knowledge of how costs are classified. This section starts with an overview of the terminology needed in managing costs. It then covers various methods of measuring and budgeting for costs and various accumulation systems such as job order costing, process costing, and activity-based costing. The final topic of this section covers methods of allocating manufacturing overhead costs.

Learning Outcome Statements

The Certified Management Accountant (CMA) test is based upon a series of Learning Outcome Statements (LOS) developed by the Institute of Certified Management Accountants (ICMA). The LOS describe all the knowledge and skills that make up the CMA body of knowledge, broken down by part, section and topic. The CMA Learning System (CMALS) supports the LOS by addressing all the subjects they cover. Candidates should use the LOS to ensure that they can address the concepts in different ways or through a variety of question scenarios. Candidates should also be prepared to perform calculations referred to in the LOS in total or by providing missing components of a calculation. The LOS should not be used as proxies for exact exam questions; they should be used as a guide for studying and learning the content of the CMA Learning System and ensuring that you can accomplish the objectives set out by the LOS.

The LOS included in the CMALS books are the comprehensive set, current as of the date of publication. Candidates can access the IMA Web site at www.imanet.org and click on the Certification section to locate and download a Portable Document Format (PDF) file of the current LOS.

Learning Outcome Statements

Part 2: Management Accounting and Reporting — Section B. Cost Management

Part 2 — Section B1. Terminology

- LOS 2.B.1.a—Identify and differentiate all cost items reported on the income statement.

- LOS 2.B.1.b—Identify and calculate those costs incurred to complete a product and reported as cost of goods sold.

- LOS 2.B.1.c—Identify and calculate those costs incurred for current operations (period costs) but not included in cost of goods sold.

- LOS 2.B.1.d—Identify and calculate the components of cost concepts such as prime cost, conversion cost, overhead cost, carrying cost, sunk cost, discretionary cost, and opportunity cost.

- LOS 2.B.1.e—Demonstrate an understanding of the characteristics that differentiate fixed costs, variable costs, and mixed costs and evaluate the effect that changes in production volume have on these costs.

- LOS 2.B.1.f—Identify, differentiate, and calculate direct vs. indirect costs.

- LOS 2.B.1.g—Describe the importance of timely and accurate costing information as a tool for strategic planning management decision making.

Part 2 — Section B2. Measurement Concepts

- LOS 2.B.2.a—Demonstrate an understanding of the behavior of fixed and variable costs in the long and short terms and how a change in assumptions regarding cost type or relevant range affects these costs.

- LOS 2.B.2.b—Identify cost objects and cost pools and assign costs to appropriate activities.

- LOS 2.B.2.c—Demonstrate an understanding of the nature and types of cost drivers and the causal relationship that exists between cost drivers and costs incurred.

- LOS 2.B.2.d—Demonstrate a thorough understanding of the various methods for measuring costs and accumulating work-in-process and finished goods inventories and a basic understanding of how inventories are relieved.

- LOS 2.B.2.e—Identify and calculate the components of cost measurement techniques such as actual costing, normal costing, and standard costing; identify the appropriate use of each technique; and describe the benefits and limitations of each technique.

- LOS 2.B.2.f—Demonstrate an understanding of the characteristics of variable costing and absorption costing and the benefits and limitations of these measurement concepts.

- LOS 2.B.2.g—Calculate inventory costs using both variable costing and absorption costing.

- LOS 2.B.2.h—Demonstrate an understanding of how the use of variable costing or absorption costing affects the value of inventory, cost of goods sold, and operating income.

- LOS 2.B.2.i—Determine the appropriate use of joint product and by-product costing and demonstrate an understanding of concepts such as split-off point and separable costs.

- LOS 2.B.2.j—Determine the allocation of joint product and by-product costs using the physical measure method, the sales value at split-off method, the gross profit (gross margin) method, and the net realizable value method; and describe the benefits and limitations of each method.

- LOS 2.B.2.k—Demonstrate an understanding of costing systems used by service sector companies.

Part 2 — Section B3. Accumulation Systems

- LOS 2.B.3.a—For each cost accumulation system identified (job order costing, process costing, activity-based costing, life-cycle costing), define the nature of the system, understand the cost flows of the system, and identify its appropriate use.

- LOS 2.B.3.b—For each cost accumulation system identified (job order costing, process costing, activity-based costing, life-cycle costing), calculate inventory values and cost of goods sold.

- LOS 2.B.3.c—For each cost accumulation system identified (job order costing, process costing, activity-based costing, life-cycle costing), demonstrate an understanding of the proper accounting for normal and abnormal spoilage.

- LOS 2.B.3.d—For each cost accumulation system identified (job order costing, process costing, activity-based costing, life-cycle costing), discuss the strategic value of cost information regarding products and services, pricing, overhead allocations, and other issues.

- LOS 2.B.3.e—For each cost accumulation system identified (job order costing, process costing, activity-based costing, life-cycle costing), identify the benefits and limitations of each cost accumulation system.

- LOS 2.B.3.f—For each cost accumulation system identified (job order costing, process costing, activity-based costing, life-cycle costing), demonstrate an understanding of the concept of equivalent units in process costing and calculate the value of equivalent units.

- LOS 2.B.3.g—For each cost accumulation system identified (job order costing, process costing, activity-based costing, life-cycle costing), define the elements of activity-based costing such as cost pool, cost driver, resource driver, activity driver, and value-added activity.

- LOS 2.B.3.h—For each cost accumulation system identified (job order costing, process costing, activity-based costing, life-cycle costing), calculate product cost using an activity-based system and compare and analyze the results with costs calculated using a traditional system.

- LOS 2.B.3.i—For each cost accumulation system identified (job order costing, process costing, activity-based costing, life-cycle costing), demonstrate an understanding of the concept of life-cycle costing and the strategic value of including upstream costs, manufacturing costs, and downstream costs.

- LOS 2.B.3.j—For each cost accumulation system identified (job order costing, process costing, activity-based costing, life-cycle costing), describe how operation costing is a hybrid cost system utilizing characteristics of both job costing and process costing and identify industry settings where operation costing is appropriate.

- LOS 2.B.3.k—For each cost accumulation system identified (job order costing, process costing, activity-based costing, life-cycle costing), demonstrate an understanding of backflush costing and describe why it is appropriate in a just-in-time setting where manufacturing cells are utilized.

- LOS 2.B.3.l—For each cost accumulation system identified (job order costing, process costing, activity-based costing, life-cycle costing), demonstrate an understanding of how activity-based costing can be utilized in service firms.

Part 2 — Section B4. Overhead Costs

- LOS 2.B.4.a—Demonstrate an understanding of the fixed and variable nature of overhead expenses.

- LOS 2.B.4.b—Determine the appropriate time frame for classifying both variable and fixed overhead expenses.

- LOS 2.B.4.c—Demonstrate an understanding that overhead rates can be determined in a variety of ways, e.g., plant-wide rates, departmental rates, and individual cost driver rates and describe the benefits and limitations of each of these methods.

- LOS 2.B.4.d—Identify the components of variable overhead expense.

- LOS 2.B.4.e—Determine the appropriate allocation base for variable overhead expenses.

- LOS 2.B.4.f—Calculate the per unit variable overhead expense.

- LOS 2.B.4.g—Identify the components of fixed overhead expense.

- LOS 2.B.4.h—Identify the appropriate allocation base for fixed overhead expense and demonstrate an understanding that because the allocation base is generally variable (e.g., direct labor hours), fixed overhead is often overapplied or underapplied.

- LOS 2.B.4.i—Calculate the fixed overhead application rate.

- LOS 2.B.4.j—Demonstrate an understanding of overhead control accounts, overhead allocation accounts, and the expensing of overapplied or underapplied overhead expenses.

- LOS 2.B.4.k—Compare and contrast traditional overhead allocation with activity-based overhead allocation.

- LOS 2.B.4.l—Calculate overhead expense in an activity-based setting and describe the benefits derived from activity-based overhead allocation.

- LOS 2.B.4.m—Demonstrate an understanding of the need to allocate the cost of service departments such as Human Resource or Information Technology to divisions, departments, or activities.

- LOS 2.B.4.n—Understand and use the direct method, the reciprocal method, and the step-down method to allocate service or support department costs.

Terminology

Topic overview

To make the most appropriate decisions, management must have an accurate picture of expected and actual costs. This cost information must be both timely and correct for it to have value in planning for both long-term strategy and daily operations. Understanding cost management terminology helps managers make decisions such as these. They can identify different costs for different purposes, such as direct costs versus indirect costs for a performance evaluation; fixed costs versus variable costs for planning a budget; and opportunity costs, sunk costs, and marginal costs when deciding whether to out-source. This topic defines these and other terms.

Cost Accounting Terms and Concepts

The basic cost terms and concepts are defined below. These terms will be examined in more detail in subsequent content. Note that some differences exist across companies in the way these terms are defined and how costs are classified and measured. For example, one company may differ from another in its definition of what is included and excluded from direct manufacturing costs.

Cost

A **cost** is any resource that must be given up to obtain some objective. Costs can be the monetary amount sacrificed to get a good or service, the creation of a new liability, or the sacrifice of an asset. Costs include actual costs (historical costs) and budgeted costs (forecasted costs).

Cost object

A **cost object** is any object that can have a cost applied to it and is used to determine how much a particular thing or activity costs. Corporate cost objects include products, services, customers, projects, brand categories, departments, responsibility centers, and activities.

Cost pools

A **cost pool** is an aggregation or grouping of cost objects, defined any way that is meaningful to management for assigning accountability. Cost objects such as a wrench and a maintenance worker may be included in the maintenance department cost pool, which is itself a cost object for the operations department.

Cost drivers

A **cost driver** (also called allocation base) is any factor that has a cause-and-effect relationship on costs, such as a level of activity changing the overall cost or the cost of sales commissions rising proportionately with rising sales. Fixed costs have no cost drivers. (However, fixed overhead is allocated to cost pools using an allocation base.)

Cost accumulation

Cost accumulation collects and organizes cost information in an accounting system. Whenever a cost is incurred, such as a purchase or performance of a service, that cost is accumulated over the accounting period. Cost accumulation is directly related to cost assignment.

Cost assignment

Cost assignment both allocates accumulated costs to cost objects and traces accumulated costs to a cost object or cost pool. Costs with an indirect relationship to a cost object are allocated, whereas costs with a direct relationship are traced. Allocation determines the proportional share of a total cost that belongs to a particular cost object. Tracing assigns direct costs to a cost object.

Actual costs

An **actual cost** is the historical cost paid for a good or service.

Direct costs

Direct costs are any costs that can be directly traced to a cost object in a convenient and economical way (usually direct labor and direct materials). Direct costs for a can of tennis balls might include 0.2 labor hours and a quantity of rubber.

Indirect costs

Indirect costs are any costs that are related to a cost object but cannot be traced to the product in a cost-effective manner (e.g., overhead). These costs are allocated through reasonable estimation, taking the cost-benefit constraint into consideration. Indirect costs for producing a can of tennis balls include maintenance costs for the tennis ball machine, the cost of the tennis ball tester, and the sporting goods division supervisor's salary. The supervisor's salary would be allocated to various responsibility centers based on the number of employees in each center. If the supervisor was accountable for 100 employees and the tennis ball responsibility center had 10 employees, then 10% of this supervisor's salary would be allocated to this cost object and 1% could be allocated to an individual employee cost object.

Opportunity costs

Opportunity costs are the potential benefits sacrificed when choosing one alternative over one or more other possibilities. For example, when investing time and funds in a project, the employees cannot work on anything else, and even if there are no other viable projects, the funds could have been invested to earn a return.

Carrying costs

Carrying costs are the costs associated with holding inventory, including inventory itself, warehouse and shipping/receiving labor and overhead for the warehouse space, obsolescence risk, possible markdowns, ongoing financing of inventory, and the opportunity cost from space that could be used for other purposes.

Controllable costs

Controllable costs are those costs that a specific manager or business unit can influence within a year or less. Controllable costs may be fixed or variable.

Noncontrollable costs

Noncontrollable costs are costs that a specific manager or business unit cannot influence within a year or less or may not ever be able to influence. Some costs may be considered controllable by one division or manager but noncontrollable by a different division or manager. Noncontrollable costs may be fixed or variable.

Committed (sunk) costs

Committed or sunk costs are those costs that should be ignored in a decision-making process because the cost was incurred in the past and cannot be changed. Some managers erroneously include committed costs in their analysis in order to justify continued expenditures in a particular area, even if a different investment would earn a higher net return. Instead, managers should focus on noncommitted or differential future costs.

Noncommitted costs

Noncommitted or flexible costs are costs that have yet to be incurred and are therefore likely to be relevant for decision-making purposes. Noncommitted costs are the opposite of a committed or sunk cost.

Differential costs

Differential costs are costs that differ between two or more possible uses of funds and therefore become relevant to a decision maker. For example, if a manager is considering the purchase of a replacement machine and the replacement machine will have depreciation of $100,000 per year whereas the current machine has depreciation of $65,000, the differential cost would be $35,000 of depreciation per year.

Cost management

Cost management is the process of planning and controlling costs in both the short and long term. Managers use accounting information systems to decide how to change processes and setups when managing costs. Cost management is concerned with lowering overall costs but must also consider that to make money an entity needs to spend money, so cost management is linked to profit planning.

Product Versus Period Costs

Product costs

Product costs (also known as inventoriable costs) differ for manufacturers and merchandisers. Manufacturers consider only the costs needed to complete a product to be product costs. These costs include direct materials, direct labor, and overhead. Product costs for a merchandise company are easily determined. Most retailers, wholesalers, and distributors buy goods in a finished state. The costs for product purchased (including associated freight costs) are charged into a single inventory account called merchandise inventory. Product costs are included in the cost of goods sold calculation.

Two ways to categorize product costs include prime costs and conversion costs. Note that direct materials are included in both prime and conversion costs; therefore, prime costs plus conversion costs do not equal product costs.

- **Prime costs**
  Prime costs are the combination of direct labor and direct materials costs, or the total direct cost.

- **Conversion costs**
  When direct labor and overhead are combined, this cost pool is called a conversion cost.

Period costs

Items that cannot be included in product costs must be expensed in the period in which they occur and thus are called **period costs**. Costs that cannot be reasonably allocated to a specific product are expensed because they are not expected to provide measurable future benefits. Selling and administrative costs, advertising costs, data processing costs, and executive costs are all period costs. Period costs are also called operating expenses or selling and administrative expenses. Period costs are not included in cost of goods sold.

Depreciation can be either a product cost or a period cost. Depreciation on fixed assets used directly in operations, such as manufacturing equipment, is a product cost; depreciation on nonoperating fixed assets, such as office equipment, is a period cost.

Manufacturing Versus Nonmanufacturing Costs

Three types of companies exist:

- **Manufacturing companies** purchase or extract materials and combine or convert them into new finished goods. Oil refineries, tennis ball manufacturers, and textile companies are all manufacturing companies.

- **Merchandising companies** such as retailers, distributors, and wholesalers purchase goods for resale at a markup without changing the basic form of the items.

- **Service companies** provide intangible services to customers. They include law firms, hospitals, shipping companies, advertising agencies, and consultants.

Cost flows in manufacturing companies

Manufacturing companies have the most complicated costs of the three types of companies listed above. Manufacturing cost flows begin with purchases of direct and indirect materials for use in production. These materials are initially placed in a materials inventory account (containing only direct materials). The next step is to add the cost elements: direct materials, direct labor, and overhead (which includes indirect materials). In this step, the costs of these three elements are added to work-in-process inventory. When the goods are finished, the costs are transferred as cost of goods manufactured into finished goods inventory. When the goods are sold, the costs are transferred out of finished goods inventory to the cost of goods sold account.

Figure 2-21 shows the cost flows for a manufacturing company.

Figure 2-21: Cost Flows for a Manufacturing Company

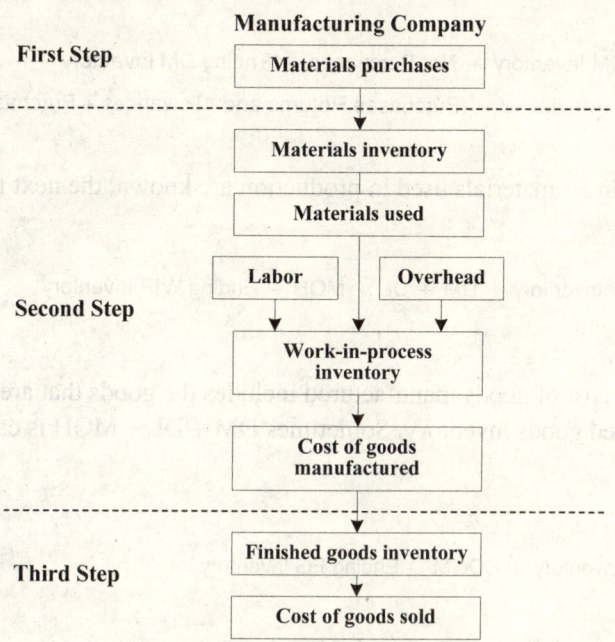

Manufacturing company inventory accounts

The types of inventory are direct materials inventory, work-in-process inventory, and finished goods inventory:

- The **direct materials inventory** contains the cost of all raw materials acquired for the manufacturing process before they are used in production.

- The **work-in-process (WIP) inventory** contains the cost of raw materials, labor, and overhead that have been spent in the production process on any products that are not finished by the end of the reporting period.

- The **finished goods (FG) inventory** contains all product costs for all products that are complete and ready for sale.

Each inventory account has a beginning and ending inventory level for each period.

The amounts held in inventory accounts are calculated using the following formulae, where:

- COGM is cost of goods manufactured.

- COGS is cost of goods sold.

- DM is direct materials.

- DL is direct labor.

- MOH is manufacturing overhead applied.

To calculate cost of goods sold in a manufacturing firm, three steps are required:

1. DM Used = Beginning DM Inventory + Net Purchases − Ending DM Inventory

    where Net Purchases = Purchases − (Purchases Returns and Allowances + Purchase Discounts) + Transportation In

    Once the direct materials used in production are known, the next formula is applied.

2. COGM = Beginning WIP Inventory + DM + DL + MOH − Ending WIP Inventory

    Note: The cost of goods manufactured includes the goods that are completed and moved into finished goods inventory. Sometimes DM + DL + MOH is called manufacturing costs.

3. COGS = Beginning FG Inventory + COGM − Ending FG Inventory

Accounting for cost flows in a manufacturing company

Assume that Robin Manufacturing Company begins a year (e.g., Year 1, but not their first year in business) with $20 (all amounts in thousands) in materials inventory, $20 in WIP inventory, and $15 in finished goods inventory.

As shown in Figure 2-22 on the next page, during the year, Robin Manufacturing purchases $80 in direct materials, spends $55 in wages payable, and applies $120 in overhead. These costs are transferred to WIP inventory.

Of the WIP inventory, Robin Manufacturing completes and transfers out $255 worth of inventory. This amount is the cost of goods manufactured.

The finished goods inventory account receives this $255 of inventory costs. Robin Manufacturing sells $235 worth of inventory during the year, and this amount is the cost of goods sold at the end of the year.

Figure 2-22: Robin Manufacturing Company Accounting Entries, Year 1

	Direct materials (DM) inventory		Labor: Wages payable	Overhead applied
Beginning DM inventory	$20			
During year	$80	$90 →❶	$55 →❷	$120 →❸
Ending DM inventory	$10			

	Work-in-process (WIP) inventory	
Beginning WIP inventory	$20	
During year	❶→ $90 ❷→ $55 ❸→$120	$255 →❹
Ending WIP inventory	$30	

	Finished goods (FG) inventory	
Beginning FG inventory	$15	
During year	❹→$255	$235 →❺
Ending FG inventory	$35	

	Cost of goods sold (COGS)	
	❺→$235	

Key: ❶ Cost of DM used ❷ Cost of labor used ❸ Overhead applied
❹ Cost of goods manufactured (COGM) ❺ Cost of goods sold (COGS)

Note that in each of these accounts, the following relationship is true:

Begining Inventory + Costs Added in Period = Ending Inventory + Costs Transferred Out in Period

For DM: $20 + $80 = $10 + $90

For WIP: $20 + ($90 + $55 + $120) = $30 + $255

For FG: $15 + $255 = $35 + $235

Financial statements for a manufacturing company

The financial statements for a manufacturing company include a statement of cost of goods manufactured and an income statement.

- The cost of goods manufactured statement shows the movement of goods from direct materials inventory to finished goods inventory.

- The income statement starts with sales and subtracts the cost of goods sold to arrive at the gross profit margin and then subtracts all nonoperating expenses to arrive at net income.

Figure 2-23 shows a sample statement for Robin Manufacturing Company.

Figure 2-23: Statement for Robin Manufacturing Company

Robin Manufacturing Company
Statement of Cost of Goods Manufactured
For the Year Ended December 31, Year 1
(in thousands)

Direct materials		
Beginning inventory	$20	
Net purchases	80	
Direct materials available	$100	
Ending direct materials inventory	10	
Direct materials used		$90
Direct labor		55
Factory overhead		120
Total manufacturing cost		$265
Add: Beginning work-in-process inventory		20
Total manufacturing cost to account for		285
Less: Ending work-in-process inventory		30
Cost of goods manufactured		$255
Sales		$335
Cost of goods sold		
Beginning finished goods inventory	$ 15	
Cost of goods manufactured	255	
Cost of goods available for sale	$270	
Ending finished goods inventory	35	235
Gross margin		$100
Selling and administrative expenses		40
Net income		$ 60

* Over- and underapplied overhead would be incorporated: if immaterial, overapplied overhead is subtracted and underapplied overhead is added to the cost of goods manufactured (see "Actual/Normal/Standard Costing" in Topic 2 of this section).

Cost flows in merchandising and service companies

Financial statements in a merchandising company

The income statement for a merchandising company looks similar to that of a manufacturing company. Merchandisers calculate the statement of cost of goods sold using purchases instead of cost of goods manufactured.

Financial statements in a service company

Service companies have little or no inventory, so any inventory they do have would be treated as if the company were a merchandising company if it purchases the goods or as a manufacturing company if it manufactures the goods. Service companies without inventory would prepare a simple income statement starting with revenues, deducting operating expenses such as materials, labor, and other expenses, and arriving at operating income. However, when service companies have services that are not completed within a single period, they may need to include work-in-process inventory.

Direct Versus Indirect Costs

Direct costs

According to the IMA, a direct cost is the quantity of "material (or labor) that can be specifically identified with a cost object in an economically feasible manner." Unanticipated quantities of scrap, waste, or defective units should not be included in direct material cost. Those costs are usually written off to a scrap account, which is included in manufacturing overhead. If the firm adds overhead to direct material (not typical), then the extra material costs would be charged to material overhead. On the other hand, direct material costs should comprise all normal costs of completing the material requirements for the product, including the per-unit costs of scrap, waste, and normally anticipated defective units occurring in the ordinary course of business.

Indirect costs

Indirect materials cost is the cost of materials used in the manufacturing process that cannot be economically traced to the finished product, for example, the amount of ink used to stamp the company name on a tennis ball. **Indirect labor costs** include administrative and supervisory costs as well as the avoidable or unusual nonproductive time spent by production workers because it cannot be specifically identified with a cost object.

Overhead

The indirect labor and indirect materials costs are generally rolled into a cost pool called overhead or factory overhead. Other costs added to overhead include facility costs, operational equipment costs, and support equipment such as a fork lift.

Progress Check

Directions: Read each question and respond in the space provided. Answers and page references appear on the following page.

1. A manufacturing company has a tennis ball manufacturing machine that had maintenance costs, direct labor costs, and depreciation costs during a period. Which of the following is true for this situation?

    (   )   a.   Maintenance and direct labor are period costs, whereas depreciation is a product cost.

    (   )   b.   Maintenance and depreciation are period costs, whereas direct labor is a product cost.

    (   )   c.   Maintenance, direct labor, and depreciation are all product costs.

    (   )   d.   Maintenance and direct labor are product costs, and depreciation is a period cost.

2. What is the cost of goods sold for a manufacturing company that has $100,000 in cost of goods manufactured, $20,000 in beginning finished goods inventory, and $30,000 in ending finished goods inventory?

    (   )   a. $50,000

    (   )   b. $90,000

    (   )   c. $100,000

    (   )   d. $150,000

Progress check answers

1. c (p. 2-65)

2. b (p. 2-67)

Measurement Concepts

Topic overview

Measurement concepts include types of cost drivers, types of costing methods, variable and absorption costing, and joint product and by-product costing.

Fixed Versus Variable Costs

Total cost is made up of variable and fixed costs. A cost can either vary in proportion to activity, volume, or some other cost driver or it can remain fixed over a wide range of cost drivers.

Relevant range

Fixed and variable costs are defined with respect to specific cost drivers for a specific duration of time. Change any quantity by a large enough degree and the fixed costs will no longer remain fixed. Change the quantity to zero and most likely all fixed costs will end along with the demise of the product; change it above a certain level and new plants or other capacity must be added. Therefore, fixed and variable costs are constrained by a **relevant range**. Fixed costs will remain constant over a discrete range of production activity. For example, a professional golf tournament typically schedules six days of activities during the week of the tournament. Even if the weather cancels one or two days of action, the fixed costs will remain constant. A sudden-death playoff on the last day of the tournament typically will not add to the fixed costs of the golf tournament. If the tournament needs to be extended an extra day, however, the extra day would fall beyond the relevant range and require additional fixed costs.

Variable costs

A **variable cost** includes changes in total for a cost object in proportion to each change in the quantity of a cost driver over a relevant range. Variable cost measured on a per-unit basis will remain constant over a relevant range (e.g., $5/unit within a relevant range of 1 to 5,000 units). Direct materials and direct labor are both variable costs because more materials and labor are needed if more units of a cost object are produced. Some indirect costs are also variable costs, such as sealants and adhesives that cannot be measured but must be added to each item.

Using a tennis ball manufacturer as an example, as the quantity of tennis balls increases, the quantity of direct materials such as rubber and the quantity of direct labor will increase across the relevant range defined as the minimum and maximum output of the tennis ball machine (without having to change the size of the work force).

Fixed costs

Fixed costs are the portions of the total cost that do not change when the quantity of a cost driver changes over a relevant range and duration of time. The duration of time is important because fixed costs may be constant one year and be a higher constant level the next. Fixed cost measured on a per-unit basis will decline (become less significant) as quantities increase: At 100 units, a $1,000 fixed cost is $10/unit, but at 1,000 units it is only $1/unit.

Fixed costs can also be discretionary or committed:

- Discretionary costs (also known as managed or budgeted fixed costs) can be included in or cut from the budget, depending on anticipated funds. Examples are advertising, training, or internships, as well as indirect manufacturing labor and selling and administrative labor.

- Committed costs are costs that cannot be omitted due to strategic or operational priorities in the short run. An example is depreciation on equipment previously purchased. Committed fixed costs tend to be facilities-related and result from prior capacity-related decisions.

Fixed costs include many indirect costs such as depreciation, taxes, employees paid on salary, insurance, and lease costs. These costs are usually fixed because no matter the level of output within the relevant range, these costs will remain the same.

Figure 2-24 shows both fixed and variable costs over a relevant range.

Figure 2-24: Fixed and Variable Costs

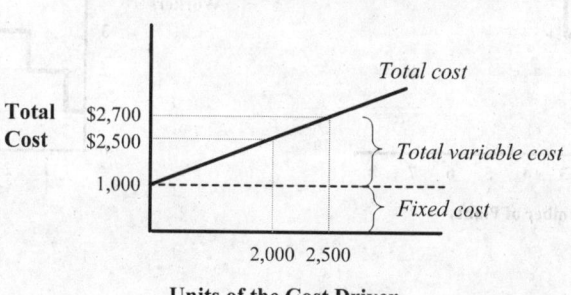

Units of the Cost Driver

For a given output level, the following formula holds true:

Total Cost/Unit at a Given Output Level = Fixed Cost/Unit + Variable Cost/Unit

Total cost per unit will therefore decline as output increases. This occurs because the fixed costs are being allocated over greater quantities.

Step costs

Step costs are fixed costs with very narrow relevant ranges. Step costs tend to be considered fixed costs over the short run but become variable costs over the long run. Consider a company with one plant. In the short run, its plant overhead is a fixed cost. If the plant's capacity is 100 units a day, to produce more than 100 units per day an additional plant must be purchased, which doubles the plant overhead cost and doubles the capacity (assuming that each plant has the same capacity and costs). In the long run, plant overhead becomes a variable cost.

The narrow relevant ranges on step costs can be step-fixed or step-variable. Step-fixed ranges increase in equal-sized chunks over an equal number of cost drivers (e.g., plant overhead increasing by $100,000 for each plant added). Step-variable ranges go up to a higher constant cost in either increasingly larger or increasingly smaller amounts of a cost driver. Step-variable costs can increase or decrease at a predictable rate when they are caused by factors such as increasing learning curve rates for workers, diminishing marginal returns, or economies of scale. (See Part 1 for more information on these subjects.) For example, if one worker (each worker representing an equal-sized step in cost) can produce 0.5 units per day but two workers can produce 1.0 unit, three workers produce 1.5 units, and four workers produce 2.0 units, the resulting step-variable costs would look like those in the right side of Figure 2-25. The left side of this figure shows step-fixed costs using the plant overhead example.

Figure 2-25: Step-Fixed and Step-Variable Costs

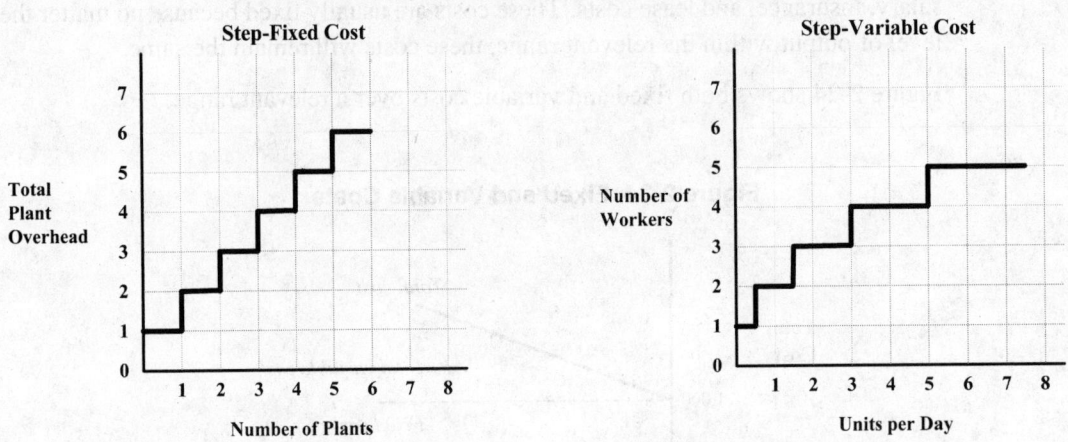

Total cost and mixed cost

Total costs are all fixed and variable costs for a cost object. Total costs are also called mixed costs when they include both fixed and variable components.

Cost type relationships

Direct costs can be fixed or variable, and indirect costs can also be fixed or variable.

Capacity

Capacity measures the constraints or bottlenecks keeping a system from expanding in output or some other measure. Adding plants, employees, or equipment can increase manufacturing capacity; gaining access to new debt or equity financing can increase the financial capacity of the business. Capacity relates to the relevant range, because when the capacity limits are reached, this is often the upper limit of the relevant range. Furthermore, as capacity limits are approached, operations lose efficiency and increase in cost. This leads to the need to define a company's **practical capacity**, which is the highest output level a resource such as a plant can achieve without increasing its costs due to bottlenecks. Output above practical capacity leads to marginal costs exceeding marginal benefits. Practical capacity also takes into account normal operating conditions, such as the average number of errors or breakdowns, holidays and vacation time, and other realistic factors.

When such real-world factors are omitted, capacity is defined as **theoretical capacity**, or the upper limit on output assuming that nothing goes wrong, everything operates at full speed, and no holidays or other scheduling conflicts are included. Theoretical capacity is an ideal.

Capacity decisions in the past determine a company's present fixed costs. Everything from the amount of space and resources devoted to each business unit to the size and cost of plants and the amount of depreciation are fixed costs related to capacity choices. These fixed costs are generally noncontrollable by division managers, who nevertheless feel the effect of these costs. If too much capacity is created, there are opportunity costs and high fixed costs at risk; if too little capacity is created, companies face other costs such as overtime, lost sales, and higher wear and tear on facilities. Separately tracking the cost of excess capacity from the overall cost of an item can help show the cost of underutilized assets. For example, if a plant's budgeted fixed overhead is $500,000, overhead is applied by the units produced, and the plant has a practical capacity level of 5,000 units per period, then overhead would normally by applied at $100/unit. If the plant budgeted only 4,000 units at $100/unit, then $400,000 would be allocated to operations and the remaining $100,000 would be treated as a separate period expense, tracked as the cost of having excess capacity. Then managers are not given incentive to produce to capacity without need, and this cost can be weighed against the costs of increasing output and inventory, etc. Overhead allocation is covered in Topic 4 of this section.

Although the prior definitions of capacity hinged on output, when capacity is defined by the expected demand for output or budgeted demand, it is called capacity utilization. **Normal capacity utilization** is a level of capacity utilization that will meet the average customer demand over a period, including its seasonal and cyclical variations or trends. Normal capacity utilization is a long-term tool that often is used over a several-year period. **Master budget capacity utilization** is normal capacity utilization for the current budget period, such as a year. It is important to use the former for long-term planning and the latter for shorter-term planning, or the end costs can be inaccurate.

Each of these capacity levels can be used to allocate costs, and each will generally show a different amount. For example, in the plant with $500,000 in budgeted fixed overhead, if theoretical capacity is 8,000 units/period, practical capacity is 5,000 units/period, normal capacity utilization is 4,500 units/period, and master budget capacity is 4,000 units/period, the budgeted fixed cost per case would be $62.50, $100, $111, and $125 respectively. Similar results can be found with variable costs. Correct choice of capacity is therefore key to cost analysis, management incentives, and performance evaluation decisions.

Cost Drivers

Firms manage their costs by determining how cost drivers affect a particular cost object. Four types of cost drivers exist.

- **Activity-based cost drivers:** The focus is on operations; they involve manufacturing or service activity such as machine setup, machine use, or packaging.

- **Volume-based cost drivers:** The focus is on output; they involve aggregate measures such as units produced or labor hours.

- **Structural cost drivers:** The focus is on company strategy; they involve long-term plans for scale, complexity, amount of experience in an area, or level of technical expertise.

- **Executional cost drivers:** The focus is on short-term operations; they involve reducing costs through concern with work-force commitment and involvement, production design, and supplier relationships.

Activity-based cost drivers

Firms use an activity analysis to determine a detailed description of each type of activity. These descriptions form the basis for the **activity-based cost drivers**. Each step in the description becomes a different cost driver. The intent is to determine how changing the steps will change the overall cost of the operation. The cost of each step or activity can also be determined, and therefore the overall cost of a cost object can be more reliably determined. This detailed breakdown can help firms determine which activities add value for customers and which do not. Also, when an activity costs more than is expected, activity-based cost drivers will highlight this discrepancy. Figure 2-26 illustrates a few of the activities and cost drivers for a retailer.

Figure 2-26: Retailer Activities and Cost Drivers

Activity	Cost Driver
Accepting cash	Number of cash transactions
Processing of credit card	Number of credit transactions
Payment of credit card fee	Dollar size of transactions
Close-out and supervisor review of clerk	Number of close-outs
Consolidation and deposit of receipts	Number of deposits
Bank account reconciliation	Number of accounts
Updating of customer account balances via computer	Number of accounts updated
Investigation of unusual transactions	Number of transactions investigated
Processing of returns and chargebacks	Number of chargebacks
Maintenance of computer equipment	Number of computer terminals
Training	Number of stores
Mailing of customer statements	Number of accounts

Volume-based cost drivers

Volume-based cost drivers are aggregations of activities based on volume of use. Some cost drivers are inherently volume-based, such as direct materials and direct labor. Direct labor is by definition the level of output for a volume of work at an hourly rate. Volume-based drivers will often have a sloped curve in relation to output levels, as shown in Figure 2-27.

Figure 2-27: Total Cost and the Effect of Capacity Limits

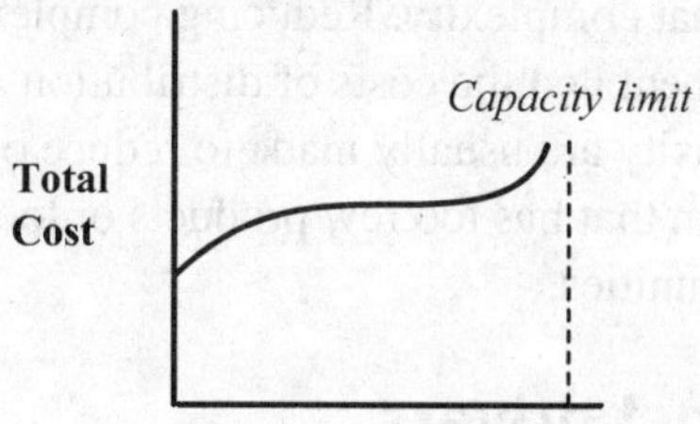

When a volume-based cost driver is very low, factors such as learning curves and efficient use of resources will cause costs to increase more slowly as production increases. (This is called increasing marginal productivity, because the increasing output will use the inputs more efficiently.) At a certain level, the total costs will level off and a rise in volume will have a proportional rise in cost (within the relevant range), until a certain point at which the capacity of the persons or equipment will reach the limit. As the volume increases toward the limit, the costs will rise dramatically because of increased need for repairs, more overtime, and other similar factors. (This is called the law of diminishing marginal capacity.)

Determining costs across the entire range of productivity would be hard to estimate without using higher math, which is why the relevant range is an important element of cost drivers.

Structural cost drivers

Structural cost drivers are long-term cost drivers based on the overall strategy of the company. There are four types of structural cost drivers.

- **Scale**
  The scale of a project or the speed at which a company grows will affect all of the costs of the company overall. Deciding how many stores to open, how many employees to hire, or how much capital to devote to a project will directly affect costs.

- **Experience level**
  The experience level of the company for a particular strategic desire will affect the overall cost of achieving that goal. The areas in which the company has the most expertise will be the cheapest areas to further develop, but if the market no longer

needs such expertise, then developing a new area of expertise could be more cost-effective in the long run.

- **Technology**
  Changing the level of technology for a process can make that process more efficient and therefore less costly. The other benefit of investing in technology is that the products may be of higher quality and therefore the firm may be able to increase market share with a cheaper and better product.

- **Complexity**
  The more complex a firm gets (more products, more levels of hierarchy), the more it costs to sustain that complexity. Reducing complexity will reduce both the costs of product development and the costs of distribution and service. Strategic decisions related to complexity are usually made to reduce overall complexity and cost. Conversely, a firm that has too few products or too small a staff may be missing out on market opportunities.

Executional cost drivers

Executional cost drivers are the short-term decisions that can be made to reduce operational costs. There are three types of executional cost drivers.

- **Work-force involvement**
  The greater the commitment of the work force, the lower the labor costs will be in proportion to the amount of work that gets done. Japanese firms are renowned for developing pride in the workplace through creative team building, emphasis on consensus, and simple activities such as morning group stretches.

- **Production process design**
  Manufacturing costs can be reduced by redesigning inefficient production processes. Many enterprise software packages help remove old bottlenecks in a supply chain, for example, instead of having all customer service orders wait to be checked in by one person before being transferred to the customer service representatives, having the representatives use the new software to check the orders in themselves.

- **Supplier relationships**
  Close relationships with suppliers can reduce overall costs, especially inventory costs. Using electronic data interchange (EDI), many companies now allow suppliers to view the company's inventory levels directly and automatically ship items as they are needed, before the company gets around to creating an invoice and requesting the materials.

Actual/Normal/Standard Costing

Cost allocation is a method of applying costs to products, jobs, or services. Actual, normal, and standard costing are types of cost allocation. The terms "actual" and "normal" refer to the means of overhead application or allocation, which is a method of applying overhead costs to cost objects. Because the actual costs of direct material and labor are usually easy to determine, these actual amounts are used.

Actual costing uses the actual amounts for overhead costs. Normal costing uses the actual costs for labor and direct materials and uses a predetermined overhead rate for overhead. Standard costing differs from the other two types in that it sets standard costs for overhead, direct materials, and direct labor. All three of these methods are types of job order costing. These costing methods are described below.

Actual costing

An **actual costing** system records the actual costs incurred for all costs, including direct labor, direct material, and overhead (actual amounts are allocated). The actual costs are determined by waiting until the end of the accounting period and then calculating the actual costs based on the recorded amounts.

The primary benefit of actual costs is that they are more accurate than other costing systems. However, the reliability comes at the cost of a delay in information. The costs cannot be known until all of the invoices are received, which may not be until the end of the fiscal year or later. Because the number of units produced varies from period to period but fixed costs do not vary with these changes, actual costing makes costs per unit vary for products produced in different periods. Firms that wish to smooth out cost fluctuations in cost per unit turn instead to normal costing.

Normal costing

Similar to actual costing, **normal costing** applies actual costs for direct materials and direct labor to a job, process, or other cost object and then uses a predetermined overhead rate to assign overhead to a cost object.

Normal costing is used for three reasons:

- Actual overhead costs are not readily determinable or cannot be easily allocated within the time frame allowed for period-end statements.

- The company wants to keep product costs current. (Using a standard rate for overhead plus actual labor and actual direct materials cost allows immediate calculation of an item cost.)

- The company wants to smooth out or normalize the fluctuations in factory overhead rates in order to have the same cost per unit per level of production from one period to the next during a year.

The last reason above has made normal costing the most popular method of costing.

The predetermined factory overhead rate is applied to a job or other cost object, as determined in four steps:

1. Create an annual (or other period) budget for overhead costs.

2. Choose cost drivers (usually activity or volume) for charging overhead.

3. Estimate the total annual amount or volume (of the selected cost driver) for the total overhead costs or each cost pool.

4. Calculate the predetermined factory overhead rate as follows:

$$\frac{\text{Budgeted Factory Overhead Costs}}{\text{Estimated Cost Driver Activity Level}}$$

Factory overhead using normal costing will be underapplied in some months and overapplied in others. The net amount overapplied is the amount of applied overhead that exceeds actual costs, and the net amount underapplied is the opposite. The net amount over- or underapplied is disposed of either by adjusting the cost of goods sold account or by prorating the net difference between the current period's applied overhead balances in the work-in-process inventory, finished goods inventory, and cost of goods sold accounts.

- **Adjusting cost of goods sold**
  Suppose that $1,530,000 of actual overhead was incurred and $1,490,000 of overhead was allocated to products under normal costing. This means that overhead was underapplied by $40,000. Assuming that this is immaterial, the cost of goods sold should be increased by $40,000. The adjusting entry to the cost of goods sold account is:

Cost of Goods Sold	$40,000	
Factory Overhead Applied	$1,490,000	
Factory Overhead		$1,530,000

To record the disposition of underapplied overhead

This entry closes the factory overhead applied and factory overhead accounts and debits (increases) the cost of goods sold. If the converse were true—say, if $1,600,000 of overhead was allocated under normal costing and the actual overhead remains the same— if this $70,000 overapplied overhead is immaterial, then the adjusting entry to the cost of goods sold account would be as follows. Note that the entry credits (decreases) cost of goods sold.

Factory Overhead Applied	$1,600,000	
Factory Overhead		$1,530,000
Cost of Goods Sold		$70,000

To record the disposition of overapplied overhead

- **Prorating net difference between inventories and cost of goods sold**
  Factory overhead is accounted for in the work-in-process inventory, finished goods inventory, and cost of goods sold accounts, so when the net variance is material, it should be accounted for in each of these accounts in proportion to their relative size. If all production is complete, all goods are sold by the end of a period, and there is no balance in the WIP and finished goods inventory accounts, then the simple cost-of-goods-sold approach can be used. However, because production usually never ceases, the method described below must be used. The applied overhead in the ending inventories of each of these three accounts at the end of the period is divided by the sum of the applied overhead in the three accounts together to determine the amount to be prorated to each.

Assume that the applied overhead for each account is as follows:

- Ending work-in-process inventory is $200,000.

- Ending finished goods inventory is $300,000.

- Cost of goods sold is $1,000,000.

The ending work-in-process inventory proration is calculated as:

$$\frac{\$200,000}{\$1,500,000} = 0.133 = 13.3\%$$

The finished goods are prorated at 20% and the cost of goods sold at 66.7%. If the variance were an underapplied overhead of $100,000, then the work-in-process account would need to be increased by $13,300. The adjusting entries would be:

Factory Overhead Applied	$1,500,000	
Work-in-Process Inventory	$13,300	
Finished Goods Inventory	$20,000	
Cost of Goods Sold	$66,700	
Factory Overhead		$1,600,000

To record the proration of underapplied overhead

Each inventory account is debited (increased) by the amount shown. If $100,000 of overhead was overapplied (other factors staying the same), the adjusting entries would be:

Factory Overhead Applied	$1,500,000	
Work-in-Process Inventory		$13,300
Finished Goods Inventory		$20,000
Cost of Goods Sold		$66,700
Factory Overhead		$1,400,000

To record the proration of overapplied overhead

Each inventory account is credited (decreased) by the amount shown. If the difference is immaterial, COGS is adjusted; if material, the prorated method is used.

Standard costing

Standard costing applies direct materials, direct labor, and overhead using a predetermined (standard) rate. A standard cost is an expected or target cost for an operation. Standard costing is designed to point out where variances occur so that the company can achieve a better operating result. Each standard cost is usually broken down into:

- A standard number of units of a cost driver adjusted for actual unit production (i.e., set to a flexible budget as discussed in section D of this part), e.g., 40,000 labor hours (assuming 80,000 units produced) = 0.5 labor hours per unit.

- A standard rate per unit of the cost driver, e.g., $20 per labor hour.

Knowing the standard rate and the number of units produced will allow you to derive the standard cost of direct labor or direct materials. Standard costs (e.g., standard number of hours times the standard rate per hour) can then be compared to actual total costs (e.g., total direct labor costs). For example, in a given month with the same 80,000 units produced, actual labor hours may have been 42,000 at an actual rate of $18 per labor hour. These differences between standard costs and actual costs lead to variances from budget, as discussed in section D of this part.

Standards can be ideal or currently attainable, as set by company policy, activity analysis, historical data, market expectations, strategy, and benchmarking. The types of standards are covered in the prior section in this part of the CMA Learning System, "Budget Preparation."

The advantages of standard costs include that they are less likely to incorporate past inefficiencies and they can be adapted as new data indicates expected changes during the budget period. Disadvantages in standard costing can occur when unreasonable standards are set, when they are authoritarian or secretive, or when they are poorly communicated. Inflexible standards or standards that place undue emphasis on profits are also likely to fail.

Absorption (Full) and Variable (Direct) Costing

Absorption costing (or full costing) is an inventory costing system that includes both variable and fixed manufacturing costs. Inventory absorbs all costs of manufacturing. **Variable costing** (or direct costing) is an inventory costing method that includes all variable manufacturing costs as inventoriable costs but excludes fixed manufacturing costs. Variable costing expenses fixed manufacturing costs in the period in which the costs are incurred. Each method expenses all nonmanufacturing costs (both fixed and variable) in the period in which they occur. Therefore, these two methods differ only in how they account for fixed manufacturing costs.

Income statement preparation using absorption and variable costing

Because variable costing and absorption costing have different objectives concerning the importance of what should be presented on the income statement, each is usually presented in its own format. The variable costing method uses a contribution margin format, which highlights the distinction between fixed and variable costs. The absorption method uses the gross margin format, which, in addition to being the format required for external reporting, highlights the differences between manufacturing and nonmanufacturing costs. The variable manufacturing costs are accounted for in the same manner in both income statements.

Examples of each type of costing and each type of format are shown in Figure 2-28 on the next page.

The data used for both sides of the table is the same:

- Units made: 700

- Units sold: 500

- Variable manufacturing costs per unit: $30

- Variable selling (marketing) costs per unit: $20

- Fixed manufacturing costs per unit: $25

- Fixed selling (marketing) costs: $14,000

The primary differences between the two statements in Figure 2-28 are that under variable costing the fixed manufacturing costs are deducted as an expense, whereas the absorption costing method treats each finished unit as having absorbed its share of the fixed manufacturing costs (an inventoriable cost). When production does not equal sales, net income will differ between absorption and variable costing. If more units are produced than sold, absorption costing will have higher net income because costs are all sitting in inventory, whereas variable costing will have lower net income because not as many costs end up in inventory compared to cost of goods sold. Another difference is that when using absorption costing, fixed manufacturing costs in ending inventory are deferred to future periods. On the other hand, variable costing expenses the entire amount in the period in which the inventory is created.

Figure 2-28: Variable Costing vs. Absorption Costing

Variable Costing		Absorption Costing		
Revenues: $200 × 500 units	$100,000	Revenues: $200 × 500 units		$100,000
Variable costs		Costs of goods sold		
Beginning inventory	$0	Beginning inventory	$0	
+ Variable manufacturing costs: $30 × 700	+21,000	+ Variable manufacturing costs: $30 × 700	+21,000	
		+ Fixed manufacturing costs: $25 × 700	+17,500	
= Cost of goods available for sale	21,000	= Cost of goods available for sale	38,500	
− Ending inventory: $30 × 200	− 6,000	− Ending inventory: ($30 variable + $25 fixed) × 200	−11,000	−27,500
= Variable cost of goods sold	15,000	= Cost of goods sold		
+ Variable marketing costs: $20 × 500	+10,000			
= Total variable costs	−25,000			
= Contribution margin	75,000	= Gross margin		72,500
Fixed costs		Operating costs		
Fixed manufacturing costs: $25 × 700	17,500	Variable marketing costs: $20 × 500	10,000	
+ Fixed marketing costs	+14,000	+ Fixed marketing costs	+14,000	
+/− Adjustment for fixed cost variances	0	+/− Adjustment for operating cost variances	0	
= Total fixed costs	− 31,500	= Total operating costs		−24,000
= Operating income	$43,500	= Operating income		$48,500

In summary, when inventory increases, net income under absorption costing will be greater than under variable costing by the amount of the fixed cost of the change in inventory (200 units $\times$ \$25 = \$5,000 in Figure 2-28). When inventory decreases, net income under absorption costing will be less than under variable costing by the amount of the change in inventory fixed cost. However, as methods such as just-in-time production and other inventory reduction methods increase in importance, the differences between variable and absorption costing will grow less material. In fact, if a company has zero inventory at the beginning and end of each accounting period, there is no difference between these two methods of costing.

Benefits and limitations of absorption and variable costing

Absorption costing is the standard method because both the IRS and GAAP require its use. However, absorption costing allows managers to manipulate operating income simply by increasing production. If their bonus or other incentive is tied to operating income, the manager may increase inventory even if no additional demand exists. Also, the manager may produce items that absorb the highest fixed manufacturing costs instead of what is best for the company. To fix this and other improper management incentives, the company could switch to variable costing for internal reporting, allow the manager less latitude in selecting what to produce, or provide a disincentive for accumulating inventory such as a percentage carrying charge for all ending inventory.

Variable costing is used when the emphasis is on what items can be traced to and controlled by a responsibility center. Because fixed costs are generally outside the control of the center's manager, many companies want to focus on areas that can be controlled.

Joint Product and By-Product Costing

Joint products are products that share a portion of the production process and have relatively the same sales value. **By-products** are products that share the same production process with a product or joint product but have relatively minor value in comparison to the main product. By-products from chickens are used in producing dog food. The oil industry uses a joint manufacturing process, where crude oil is refined into joint products such as diesel, gasoline, motor oil, and plastic. Lumber may have finished boards and the scrap could be used in plywood (a joint product), whereas the sawdust is used in other products (by-products). Both joint products and by-products share at least some of the same raw materials and initial processing costs. The split-off point is the point at which products diverge and become separately identifiable. The split-off point is not necessarily the point at which the products become finished goods.

Costing for joint products and by-products includes all manufacturing costs incurred before and after the split-off point. For financial reporting, joint costs incurred before the split-off point are allocated among the joint products. Additional processing costs (separable costs) are any costs that can be specifically identified with a product because the cost occurs after the split-off point where the costs are assigned to the separate products.

Allocation of joint costs to joint products

Two basic approaches can be taken for allocating joint costs to joint products: using data based on the market (such as revenues) or using data based on physical measures (such as weight or volume). The market-based methods include the sales value at split-off method, the gross profit method, and the net realizable value method. These methods are detailed below.

Market-based methods

Sales value at split-off method. The sales value at split-off method (also known as the sales value method) is widely used because of its simplicity. The sales value method can be used only when sales values are available at the split-off point. It allocates joint costs to joint products using their proportional sales value at the split-off point. For example, say that a rabbit farm incurs $8,000 in joint costs when selling rabbit fur for $4 a pound and rabbit meat for $2 a pound. The process produces 1,000 pounds of fur and 3,000 pounds of meat. The steps for allocating this cost to each product are as follows.

1. Calculate the total sales value for each joint product, which is the price per unit multiplied by the number of units. The sales value is not the record of actual sales but a calculation of value.

$$1,000 \text{ Pounds} \times \$4 = \$4,000$$

$$3,000 \text{ Pounds} \times \$2 = \$6,000$$

2. Calculate the proportion of the sales value for each joint product to the total sales value.

$$\frac{\$4,000}{\$10,000} = 0.4 = 40\% \qquad \frac{\$6,000}{\$10,000} = 0.6 = 60\%$$

3. Multiply the joint cost by the proportional amount of the sales value. This becomes the cost of goods sold and is the amount allocated to each product cost.

$$\$8,000 \times 0.4 = \$3,200 \qquad \$8,000 \times 0.6 = \$4,800$$

4. Calculate the cost per unit (pound) by dividing the cost of goods sold (proportional cost) from the previous step by the number of units (pounds). (Note that although the remaining methods do not show this step, the cost per unit can be calculated in the same manner.)

$$\frac{\$3,200}{1,000 \text{ Pounds}} = \$3.20/\text{Pound} \qquad \frac{\$4,800}{3,000 \text{ Pounds}} = \$1.60/\text{Pound}$$

The gross margin for each product can be calculated by subtracting the sales value from the proportional cost:

$$\$4,000 - \$3,200 = \$800 \qquad \$6,000 - \$4,800 = \$1,200$$

Assuming that the sales prices are accurate estimates and if no extra processing is needed on the joint products, then the sales value method has the advantage of providing the same gross margin percentage for both joint products. The gross margin percentage is calculated by dividing the gross margin by the sales value:

$$\frac{\$800}{\$4,000} = 0.2 = 20\% \qquad \frac{\$1,200}{\$6,000} = 0.2 = 20\%$$

The sales value method is widely used because it is both simple to calculate and allocates costs according to the value of the products. Other methods, such as the physical measure method, do not allocate costs according to value and therefore can sometimes allocate so much cost to a product that it has no gross profit margin whereas its counterpart joint product has a huge profit margin. The sales value method has the limitation of not being useful for products that need additional processing after the split-off point before a sales value is established. This method may also be less useful for products that have frequent market price fluctuations.

Gross profit (constant gross margin percentage) method. The gross profit method, also called the constant gross margin percentage method, allocates joint costs so as to provide the same gross margin percentage of profit for each joint product. Assume the same data from the rabbit farm example above, except that in this case the joint products share $5,000 in joint costs, fur has $2,000 in additional processing costs (subsequent to the split-off point), and meat has $1,000 in additional processing costs. The steps for the gross profit method are as follows:

1. Calculate the total gross margin percentage. To do this, first determine the final sales value by multiplying the price per unit by the number of units. (As with the sales value method, the final sales value is the amount produced, not the amount actually sold during the period.)

$$1,000 \text{ Pounds} \times \$4 = \$4,000$$
$$3,000 \text{ Pounds} \times \$2 = \$6,000$$

The total of these amounts ($10,000) less all joint and separable costs is the gross margin:

$$\$10,000 - \$5,000 - \$2,000 - \$1,000 = \$2,000 \text{ Gross Margin}$$

The gross margin percentage is the gross margin divided by the total sales value:

$$\frac{\$2,000}{\$10,000} = 0.2 = 20\%$$

2. To determine the total costs that each product will bear, multiply the gross margin percentage by each individual sales value amount, and then deduct this amount from the sales value to determine the cost:

$$\$4,000 \times 0.2 = \$800 \qquad \$6,000 \times 0.2 = \$1,200$$
$$\$4,000 - \$800 = \$3,200 \qquad \$6,000 - \$1,200 = \$4,800$$

3. Deduct the additional processing costs from the total costs to determine the joint cost that must be allocated to each product:

$3,200 − $2,000 = $1,200 Joint Cost Allocated to Fur

$4,800 − $1,000 = $3,800 Joint Cost Allocated to Meat

$5,000 Total Joint Costs

The final step in this method distinguishes the gross profit method from the other methods because it takes into account the costs incurred before and after the split-off point. Thus this method is not only a joint cost allocation method but also a profit allocation method. Both the joint costs and the total gross margin are allocated to a joint product to maintain a constant gross margin.

One benefit of the gross profit method is that it may be used even when there are additional processing costs. The amount of the joint costs allocated to each product is not always a positive number; a joint product could get a negative allocation of joint costs in order to make the gross margin percentage equal to the overall average for the entity. This is an advantage for companies that wish to keep the same margin for each product, but it could lead to a distortion in the fairness of how costs are allocated.

Net realizable value (NRV) method. The net realizable value (NRV) method, also known as the estimated NRV method, is used when the market price for one or more of the joint products cannot be determined at the split-off point, usually because additional processing is needed. The product's final sales value less additional processing costs is its net realizable value. Assume the same rabbit farm example, except that an additional 1,000 pounds of scrap can now be sold directly to a pet food processor with no additional cost for $1 per pound.

The steps for calculating the net realizable value are as follows:

1. Calculate the net realizable value for each joint product. To do this, start by calculating the sales value for each unit, which is the price per unit multiplied by the number of units.

Fur 1,000 Pounds × $4 = $4,000

Meat 3,000 Pounds × $2 = $6,000

By-Products 1,000 Pounds × $1 = $1,000

The NRV is calculated using this final sales value. (For products with no additional processing cost, the sales value is the NRV.)

NRV = Final Sales Value − Additional Processing Cost

Fur = $4,000 − $2,000 = $2,000

Meat = $6,000 − $1,000 = $5,000

By-Products = $1,000

Total NRV $8,000

2. Calculate the proportion of the NRV for each joint and by-product to the total NRV:

$$\frac{\$2,000}{\$8,000} = 25\% \qquad \frac{\$5,000}{\$8,000} = 62.5\% \qquad \frac{\$1,000}{\$8,000} = 12.5\%$$

3. Multiply the joint cost by the proportional amount of the NRV. This is the amount allocated to each product cost.

$$\$5,000 \times 0.25 = \$1,250$$
$$\$5,000 \times 0.625 = \$3,125$$
$$\$5,000 \times 0.125 = \quad\$625$$

Like the sales value method, this method allocates values in proportion to the value of the product and produces predictable profit margins.

Physical measure (units-of-production) method

The physical measure, or units-of-production, method uses a physical measurement to allocate joint costs to joint products. Physical measures include weight, number, and volume. Measures can be input measures, such as number or pounds of rabbits, or output measures, such as pounds, cans, packages, or crates. The physical measure method is called the average cost method when output is used to allocate joint costs. Assume the first scenario of the rabbit farm: A rabbit farm sells fur for $4 a pound and meat for $2 a pound; the process produces 1,000 pounds of fur, 3,000 pounds of meat, and 1,000 pounds of scrap; and it costs $8,000 for the entire process, with no additional processing costs.

The steps for allocating joint costs using the physical measure method and the input measure of pounds is as follows.

1. Calculate the average cost per unit of the total joint cost by dividing the total joint costs by the total number of pounds (ignoring scrap, waste, and by-products):

$$\text{Average Cost/Unit} = \frac{\$8,000}{4,000 \text{ Pounds}} = \$2/\text{Pound}$$

2. Multiply the average cost per unit by the total number of units to determine the amount of the joint cost to allocate to each product:

$$\$2/\text{Pound} \times 1,000 \text{ Pounds} = \$2,000 \text{ Cost Allocated to Fur}$$

$$\$2/\text{Pound} \times 3,000 \text{ Pounds} = \$6,000 \text{ Cost Allocated to Meat}$$

Thus the gross margin for fur is $2,000 ($4,000 gross profit – $2,000 cost), making the profit margin for fur 50% ($2,000 ÷ $4,000). The gross margin for meat is $0 ($6,000 gross profit – $6,000 cost). Meat has no profit margin.

Although the physical measure method is easy to use and it uses objective criteria for measurement, it has more drawbacks than benefits. As can be seen from the example above, the physical measure method can produce gross profit margins that could frustrate managers and distort actual profits. This is because the value of the joint product is not accounted for at all, unless the relevant physical measure conveys the value of each of the items. For example, gold melted into ounces or bars measured by weight would still be correctly valued (unless the processing added artistic or utilitarian value). Another limitation would be for processes that cannot all be measured using the same units, such as pounds and gallons.

Accounting treatment of joint products and by-products

Joint product costs, once allocated using one of the methods just discussed, become part of inventory costs and are divided among the various finished goods. According to GAAP, all joint costs that can be considered manufacturing costs should be allocated to joint products for purposes of financial reporting and taxation.

By-products can be accounted for in four different ways. If the firm can assign an inventoriable value to by-products at the split-off point (and desires to do so), it uses an asset recognition approach. In this case, in the period in which the by-product is produced, it can record the net realizable value (NRV = Sales Value – Additional Processing Cost) of the by-products as inventory on the balance sheet and as a deduction from the total manufacturing cost on the income statement. Alternately, in the period in which the by-product is produced, the firm can record the NRV of the by-products as other income (or other sales revenue item) on the income statement. These methods follow the matching principle of accrual accounting because the firm matches the value of the by-product with its cost to manufacture. Therefore, recognition at the time of production is considered more appropriate if the amounts are material. When by-product is sold, the inventory cost is recorded as the cost of sales.

If the firm cannot assign an inventoriable value to by-products at the split-off point, it can recognize the by-product at the time of sale using a revenue method. The firm can record the net sales revenue from a by-product as other income (or other sales revenue item) on the income statement. Alternately, at the time of sale, it can record the net sales revenue as a reduction of the total manufacturing cost on the income statement.

The revenue methods are simpler to use and are based on the concepts of revenue realization but should be reserved for immaterial amounts.

Progress Check

Directions: Read each question and respond in the space provided. Answers and page references appear on the following page.

Match the following types of cost drivers with an appropriate example of that cost driver.

1. _____ Activity-based cost driver

2. _____ Volume-based cost driver

3. _____ Structural cost driver

4. _____ Executional cost drivers

a. Redesigning a production process to remove unnecessary steps

b. High technology machine replacing an older unit

c. Labor hours spent driving a truck

d. Number of invoices processed for billing

5. A plant meters electricity usage at the department level. The department contains several product operations, including tennis ball manufacture. For a can of tennis balls, which of the following is electricity considered?

( ) a. A variable indirect cost

( ) b. A variable direct cost

( ) c. A fixed indirect cost

( ) d. A fixed direct cost

6. If a firm is more concerned with reliability of data than with the speed at which the data is available, which of the following costing methods would be the best fit?

( ) a. Variable (direct) costing

( ) b. Standard costing

( ) c. Normal costing

( ) d. Actual costing

7. Assuming that a management accountant wants to maximize reported net income, which of the following costing methods would show the greatest net income when the company increases its ending inventory?

( ) a. Variable costing

( ) b. Normal costing

( ) c. Standard costing

( ) d. Absorption costing

Progress check answers

1. d (p. 2-78)

2. c (p. 2-79)

3. b (p. 2-79)

4. a (p. 2-80)

5. a (p. 2-74)

6. d (p. 2-81)

7. d (p. 2-84)

Accumulation Systems

Topic overview

Accumulation systems accumulate costs and assign them to a particular cost object such as a product or service. Job order costing, process costing, activity-based costing (ABC), life-cycle costing, and other methods of cost accumulation are discussed in this topic. Costing systems have strategic value, and firms use this costing data to manage costs and price their products and services appropriately.

Job Order Versus Process Costing

Companies typically adopt one of two basic types of costing systems when they need to assign costs to products or services.

- **Job order costing (job costing):** assigns costs to a specific job (a distinct unit, batch, or lot of a product or service)

- **Process costing:** accumulates product or service costs by process or department and then assigns them to a large number of nearly identical products by dividing the total costs by the total number of units produced

Thus job order costing is at one end of a spectrum and process order costing is at the other: from specific to general, custom-made to mass-produced. Job costing is to a sit-down restaurant what process costing is to a buffet. Job costing is used for capital asset construction (buildings, ships) in the manufacturing sector; advertising campaigns, R&D, and repair jobs in the service sector; and custom mail-order items and special promotions in the merchandising sector. Process costing is used for multiple nearly identical units that can be organized into a flow such as newspapers, books, and soda pop in the manufacturing sector; check processing and postal delivery in the service sector; and magazine subscription receipts in the merchandising sector.

Both costing systems share the overall purpose of assigning direct materials, direct labor, and overhead to products. Both use the same accounts, including direct materials inventory, work-in-process inventory, finished goods inventory, and cost of goods sold. Job costing differs from process costing in where costs are accumulated: in a job or in a department. Job costing uses a job sheet (or equivalent software) to track specific items; process costing uses a production cost report to track all department costs. Job costing computes unit cost by job at the end of the job; process costing waits until the end of the accounting period to compute the unit cost by department. Although these systems are discussed separately below, most companies use a combination of the two methods, especially when they have some specific and some mass-produced products or services.

Job Order Costing

The procedures outlined previously for actual, normal, and standard costing can be used in job order costing. The basic steps in using job costing to assign costs to a job are as follows:

1. Identify the job. The specific job is usually identified with a unique code or hierarchical reference plus a date. For example, Smith Company may identify the manufacturing of a yacht as job number 123 in 20xx. This example will assume that actual costing is used.

2. Trace the direct costs for the job, for example, $40,000 in direct materials and $60,000 in direct labor.

3. Identify indirect cost pools associated with the job (overhead). For example, the total annual cost for all projects may be $60,000 for the first pool and $120,000 for the second pool.

4. Select the cost allocation base (cost drivers) to be used in allocating indirect cost pools to the job. The first pool is measured in machine hours and the second pool is measured in labor hours. In our example, for all projects for the entire year, the machine hours are 20,000 and the direct labor hours are 30,000.

5. Calculate the rate per unit of each cost allocation base. The actual indirect cost rate is calculated as follows:

$$\text{Actual Indirect Cost Rate} = \frac{\text{Actual Total Cost in Indirect Cost Pool}}{\text{Actual Total Quantity of Cost Driver}}$$

$$= \frac{\$60,000}{20,000 \text{ Machine Hours}} = \$3/\text{Machine Hour}$$

$$= \frac{\$120,000}{30,000 \text{ Labor Hours}} = \$4/\text{Labor Hour}$$

6. Assign cost to the cost object by adding all direct costs and indirect costs. Indirect costs are based on a combination of machine and labor hours, and, in this example, the project took 2,000 machine hours (2,000 × $3 = $6,000) and 3,000 direct labor hours (3,000 × $4 = $12,000), for a total of $18,000 in indirect costs. This amount plus the $40,000 in direct materials and $60,000 in direct labor equals total manufacturing costs of $118,000. If the yacht sells for $140,000, then the gross profit margin is $22,000 and the gross margin percentage ($22,000 ÷ $140,000) is 15.7%.

Spoilage, rework, and scrap in job costing

Companies want to reduce the amount of spoilage, rework, and scrap they produce in order to maximize the value of their raw materials.

Spoilage

Spoilage is any material or good that is considered unacceptable and is discarded or sold for its disposal value. Spoilage can be normal or abnormal. Normal spoilage is any unit of production that is deemed unacceptable during the normal production process, assuming efficient operating conditions. Normal spoilage is considered part of the cost of operations and therefore is part of the cost of good units produced. Normal spoilage can be a direct cost to a particular job or an indirect cost to production in general (allocated to factory overhead). If charged directly to a job, spoilage can be reduced by any estimated salvage value. Abnormal spoilage is any unacceptable product that should not normally exist under efficient and normal operating conditions. Any spoilage over the amount considered normal is allocated to a loss from abnormal spoilage account. Use the following formula to calculate total spoilage:

Total Spoilage =
Beginning Inventory + Units Started – Units Completed and Transferred Out – Ending Inventory

This is a variation of the formula:

Beginning Units + Units Started =
(Units Completed and Transferred Out + Spoilage) + Ending Inventory

Rework

Rework is any finished product that must have additional work performed on it before it can be sold. It is divided into categories as rework needed on the following.

- Normal defective units for a specific job: charged to specific job's work-in-process inventory account (increasing the cost and reducing profits)
- Normal defective units common with all jobs: charged to factory overhead
- Abnormal defective units: charged to loss from abnormal rework account

Scrap

Scrap is a portion of a product or leftover material that has no economic value. It can be categorized by whether it relates to a specific job or is common to all jobs. Specific job scrap is charged to the job's work-in-process inventory account. Scrap that is common to all jobs is charged to factory overhead. Either method increases the cost from the affected account. Scrap costs are not separately accounted for, but if scrap is sold, the accountant will credit (reduce) either work-in-process inventory or overhead accounts by the price received for the scrap.

Job order costing benefits and limitations

Job order costing can provide very detailed results of a specific job or operation, so it is ideal for specific jobs. For large processes, job order costing is less valuable because it is impractical to assign individual costs to mass-produced items on a daily basis. Job order costing can accommodate multiple costing methods, such as actual, normal, and standard costing, so it is flexible enough to be used by a wide variety of companies.

Job order costing can have a strategic value for a business because it gives a detailed breakdown of all of the different types of costs. The gross margin and gross profit margin can be used to compare the company's profitability across different jobs, and, for jobs that did poorly, the company can analyze whether the cost overruns were from direct labor costs, direct materials costs, or one of the indirect cost pools.

Process Costing

As stated previously, process costing is recommended for companies that have mass production processes of identical or nearly identical products. Such companies track their quantities and costs on a departmental production cost report and calculate the unit cost at the end of a period by dividing the total cost of an operation or department by the total units produced.

Process costing is good for any highly automated or repetitive process, such as the U.S. mail. The strategic value of process costing for such companies is that they can be in continuous operations while still receiving timely, accurate, and relatively inexpensive cost information each period, due in part to the use of equivalent units. Process costing also uses production cost reports, which have built-in checks such as balancing units to be accounted for against units accounted for.

Equivalent units in process costing

Unlike job costing, in which partially completed units have a cost already attached to them, process costing cannot easily determine values for partially completed units because the accounting highlights costs for processes or departments, not jobs or items. Therefore, process costing must find the combined cost for all units, including all units partially complete at the beginning and end of the accounting period. Partially complete means that the item is still in work-in-process inventory, so items that are considered complete by one department are not actually complete until they enter finished goods inventory. At the end of the period, either a production manager or an engineer gives an estimate of what percentage of units remains on the production line or in work-in-process inventory.

Because product cost is calculated by determining the cost per unit in each department, partially completed units must be factored into these calculations. At the end of an accounting period, a process costing system accounts for any work-in-process inventory as equivalent units. An **equivalent unit (EU)** is a measure of the amount of work done on partially completed units expressed in terms of how many complete units could have been created with the same amount of work. Equivalent units are necessary because a continuous process is being divided into artificial time periods.

Engineers calculate equivalent units separately for direct labor, direct materials, and overhead because one category may be more complete than another for the same product. Each is calculated in a similar fashion: Multiply the number of units that are partially complete by the estimated percentage that are complete overall. For example, if direct labor on 1,000 cans of tennis balls is 30% complete, they would total 300 equivalent direct labor units. If the same tennis balls were complete but needed to be canned, the material costs could be 90% complete and therefore would total 900 equivalent direct materials units.

Beginning inventory

Beginning inventory items that are a certain percentage complete were accounted for in the last accounting period at that percentage of completion, so the remaining percentage that needs to be completed is used instead. Therefore, if an item in beginning inventory is 30% complete, the remaining 70% incomplete is the basis for the equivalent unit calculation. (1,000 actual units would be 700 equivalent units.) However, not all methods account for beginning inventory in their calculations.

The formula for calculating the total equivalent units of production is as follows:

Equivalent Production Units = [Beginning Inventory Units × (100% − % Complete Beginning Inventory]

+ Units Started and Completed During the Period

+ Equivalent Units in Ending WIP Inventory

Conversion costs

Some firms measure only direct materials separately and combine direct labor and overhead, which are collectively called conversion costs. When the direct labor is not a significant portion of the costs due to a highly automated environment, such firms combine direct labor with overhead when performing calculations such as determining equivalent units.

Conversion cost works well for companies using labor-based cost drivers, but those companies that use nonlabor-based drivers, such as number of setups or machine hours, find it better to calculate labor and overhead separately.

Process costing cost flows

Unlike job costing, which moves costs through jobs directly, the cost flow in process costing is routed through processes and departments. In process costing, each department must have its own work-in-process (WIP) inventory account. Because direct materials, direct labor, and overhead are incurred by each department involved, these charges can be made to each department involved, not just the first department. When departments complete their portion of work on a product, all of the costs are transferred to the next department's WIP inventory account by debiting a transferred-in costs account on the next department's books. When goods are completed, the cost of goods completed is transferred to finished goods inventory.

The accounting entries for two different departments working on the same product are shown in Figure 2-29.

Figure 2-29: T-Account Cost Flow Model Using Process Costing

Materials inventory		Work-in-process inventory—tennis balls		
$100 ▶❶	❶ ▶ Direct materials $100	$800 ▶❹		
$200 ▶❺	❷ ▶ Direct labor $300			
	❸ ▶ Factory overhead $400			

Accrued payroll		Work-in-process inventory—tennis ball cans		
$300 ▶❷	❹ ▶ Transferred-in costs $800	$2,100 ▶❽		
$500 ▶❻	❺ ▶ Direct materials $200			
	❻ ▶ Direct labor $500			
	❼ ▶ Factory overhead $600			

Factory overhead applied		Finished goods inventory		
$400 ▶❸	Beginning inventory $3,500			
$600 ▶❼	❽ ▶ During period $2,100	$1,000 ▶❾		
	Ending inventory $4,600			

Cost of goods sold
❾ ▶ $1,000

Steps in preparing a production cost report

A production cost report is a report for a department that contains all physical units and equivalent units, ending work-in-process inventories, costs incurred during the period, costs assigned to units completed, and costs assigned to units transferred out.

The five steps in preparing a production cost report follow.

1. Determine the flow of physical units. Both input and output units are accounted for when determining the units that are on hand at the beginning of the period, the units that are initiated or received, the units that are finished and transferred out, and the units that are in ending work-in-process inventory. Beginning work-in-process inventory and the units that enter the production department during the period are input units. For a particular department, units that are completed and transferred out and units remaining in WIP inventory at the end of the period are output units.

2. Determine the equivalent units.

(These first two steps analyze production quantities and measure the total work effort for production.)

3. Calculate total manufacturing costs. The costs of any items in the WIP beginning inventory and any current costs are included in the total manufacturing costs that must be accounted for. Material requisition forms, time tickets, and factory overhead allocation sheets collect these costs.

4. Calculate unit costs. To determine product costing and income for a period, the costs per unit are calculated for overall costs as well as for direct materials, direct labor, and factory overhead.

(This step and the prior step are sometimes called unit cost determination.)

5. Assign total manufacturing costs to units (cost assignment). Units completed and transferred out and units remaining in WIP inventory receive the period's manufacturing costs.

Production cost report preparation methods

When using process costing, the production cost report can be prepared according to the first-in, first-out method or the weighted-average method.

First-in, first-out. The **first-in, first-out (FIFO) costing method** is an inventory valuation method that calculates the unit cost using only costs incurred and work performed during the current period.

FIFO keeps the beginning WIP inventory separated from the inventory begun and finished during the current period, and it assumes that the beginning WIP inventory is the first inventory to be completed in the period (and therefore must be complete by the end of the period). The method requires two categories of completed units to correctly cost all inventory: beginning WIP units and units started and completed during the current period.

The costs of work done before the current period on beginning WIP inventory are kept separate from work done in the current period. (But these prior period costs are still included when calculating the costs of units completed from beginning inventory.)

Equivalent units (EU) are determined in a five-step process:

1. Units to be accounted for

2. Units accounted for

3. Equivalent unit costs (using work done in the current period only)

4. Cost to be accounted for (beginning WIP plus current period costs)

5. Costs accounted for

Note that units to be accounted for should equal the units accounted for. Similarly, the costs to be accounted for should equal the costs accounted for.

By definition, the beginning WIP will always be partially complete; otherwise it would have been moved to the next department. Therefore, the objective is to obtain the correct cost of items completed during the month and items left in WIP at the end of the month.

The example in Figure 2-30 on the next page assumes that 100% of the material is added to the product at the beginning of the production process (and is thus 100% complete for beginning inventory) but that beginning WIP conversion costs are only 40% complete. The example also shows how to deal with a partially complete ending inventory (100% complete direct materials and 80% complete conversion costs).

Note that in the costs to be accounted for area, the beginning WIP costs are determined using the prior month's direct material (DM) and conversion (conv.) costs.

Figure 2-30: FIFO Method Production Cost Report

		Physical Quantity	EU DM	EU Conversion	
Units to be accounted for	WIP beginning of month	100			
	Units started in production	700			
	Total units	800			
Units accounted for	Transfers to next department:				
	From beginning WIP, direct material (DM) 100 × (100% − 100%); conv. 100 × (100% − 40%):	100	0	60	
	Started and completed (800 units − 200 ending WIP − 100 beginning WIP completed first)	500	500	500	
	From WIP month-end, DM 200 x 100%, conv. 200 × 80%	200	200	160	
	Accounted for:	800			
	Work done in current period only:		700	720	
		Total Cost			**Whole Unit**
Calculate EU/unit costs and costs to be accounted for	WIP, Beginning of month (cost of work done before current period: (100 DM × $40) + (40 conv. × $30)):	$5,200.00	Not included	Not included	
	Costs added in the current month:	$53,000.00	$30,000.00	$23,000.00	
	Equivalent units of production (see above):		700	720	
	Cost per equivalent unit:		$42.86	$31.94	$74.80
	Total costs to account for:	$58,200.00			
Costs accounted for	Transferred to next department (600 units):				
	WIP, beginning (100 units)	$5,200.00			
	DM	$0	0 x $42.86		
	Conv.	$1,916.40		60 x $31.94	
	WIP, beginning total	$7,116.40			
	Started and completed (500 units):	$37,400.00	500 x $42.86	500 x $31.94	
	Total units completed and transferred:	$44,516.40			
	WIP, month-end (200 units):				
	DM	$8,572.00	200 x $42.86		
	Conv.	$5,110.40		160 x $31.94	
	Total WIP, month-end	$13,682.40			
	Total cost ($1.20 difference due to rounding):	$58,198.80			

Weighted-average method. The weighted-average inventory valuation method calculates the unit cost using all costs, both those for the current period and those for prior periods that are included in the current period's beginning WIP inventory. The weighted-average method finds the average of cost for prior periods and the current period. Whereas the FIFO method is concerned with both input and output measures—

that is, the beginning and ending status of products for the period—the weighted-average method is concerned only with the status of the products at the end of the period. We will look at an example that uses the weighted-average method.

In our example, all costs on the current period's production cost sheet are included in cost calculations, whether or not the cost was actually incurred in the current period. The steps in preparing the production cost report using the weighted-average method follow (along with sample calculations):

1. Determine the flow of physical units.

    Input units:

    - Partially complete beginning WIP inventory—5,000 units

    - Work begun or received during the period—30,000 units

    These 35,000 units are called "units to account for."

    Output units:

    - Units completed—20,000 units

    - Ending WIP inventory—15,000 units

    These 35,000 units are called "number of units accounted for" and should match the units to account for.

2. Determine the equivalent units. Beginning WIP inventory units are not included in equivalent units because they are already included in physical units under this method. Because direct materials are 100% complete and conversion costs are 47% complete, the ending inventory of 15,000 physical units calculates to 15,000 equivalent units (EU) of direct materials and 7,050 EU of conversion costs (direct labor plus factory overhead). This plus the 20,000 units completed equals 35,000 direct materials EU and 27,050 conversion cost EU.

3. Calculate total manufacturing costs. The beginning WIP for direct materials, $10,000, is added to conversion costs, $10,031, for a total of $20,031. The current period's costs for direct materials, $60,000, is added to conversion costs, $40,000, for a total of $100,000. Total manufacturing costs are $120,031.

4. Calculate unit costs as follows.

    $$\text{Direct Materials} = \$10,000 \text{ Beginning WIP Inventory}$$
    $$\underline{\$60,000} \text{ Current Period Costs}$$
    $$\$70,000 \text{ Total Costs}$$

    $$\frac{\$70,000}{35,000 \text{ Units}} = \$2/\text{Unit Direct Materials}$$

    $$\frac{\$50,031}{27,050 \text{ Units}} = \$1.85/\text{Unit Conversion Costs}$$

    $$\$2.00 + \$1.85 = \$3.85/\text{Unit Total Cost}$$

Total manufacturing costs are assigned to units. The unit costs calculated above are multiplied by the number of units in each category, as shown at the bottom of Figure 2-31 (Step 5), a sample production cost report.

Figure 2-31: Production Cost Report—Weighted-Average Method

Production Quantity Information

	Step 1: Determine flow of physical units.		Step 2: Determine equivalent units.	
	Physical Units	**Completion Percentage**	**Direct Materials**	**Conversion Costs**
Input				
Work-in-process, Jan. 1	5,000			
Direct materials				
Conversion costs				
Units started	30,000			
Units to account for	35,000			
Output				
Units completed	20,000	100%	20,000	20,000
Work-in-process, Jan. 31	15,000			
Direct materials		100	15,000	
Conversion costs		47		7,050
Units accounted for	35,000			
Total equivalent units			35,000	27,050

Unit Cost

Step 3: Calculate total manufacturing costs.	Direct Materials	Conversion Costs	Total
Work-in-process, Jan. 1	$10,000	$10,031	$20,031
Costs added during Jan.	60,000	40,000	100,000
Total costs to account for	$70,000	$50,031	$120,031
Step 4: Calculate unit costs.			
Divide by equivalent units	35,000	27,050	
Equivalent unit costs	$2.00	$1.85	$3.85

Step 5: Assign total manufacturing costs.	Completed and Transferred Out	Ending Work-in-Process	Total
Goods completed and transferred out			
(20,000 × $3.85)	$77,000		$77,000
Ending work-in-process:			
Direct materials (15,000 × $2.00)		$30,000	30,000
Conversion costs (7,050 × $1.85)		13,043	13,043
Total costs accounted for	$77,000	$43,043	$120,043 *

* The $12 difference from total manufacturing costs is due to rounding.

Note that the total costs calculated using unit costs should match the total costs calculated in the third step (i.e., $120,031); however, there is a small difference due to rounding.

Production costing in a multidepartment company

Because most processes usually involve more than one department, a more complex example will help show how to deal with costs transferred in from a prior department. This example will also illustrate how to calculate inventory values and the cost of goods sold in process costing using both the FIFO and the weighted-average methods.

Robusto Soup Company has three departments in a continuous process, starting with the mixing department, then the cooking department, and finally the canning department. When each department finishes its work (measured in cans worth of finished product) and transfers the materials to the next department, it also transfers the costs of the batch to that department as transferred-in costs (or prior department costs).

Transferred-in costs are any costs accumulated by prior departments; they are charged to the current department upon assumption of the partially completed units. Thus each department is treated as a separate entity, and the prior department is like a vendor who supplies a semifinished good for a price (cost).

Unlike job order costing, with process costing each production department will have its own work-in-process account. The completed production of a prior department is transferred to the next department's work-in-process account.

Figure 2-32 shows how Robusto's materials and conversion costs are added by department.

Figure 2-32: Percentage of Costs by Department

	Mixing Department	Cooking Department	Canning Department
Direct materials	90%	0%	10%
Conversion costs	60%	20%	20%
Transferred-in costs	N/A	100%	100%

Robusto Soup moves inventory between its accounts as shown in Figure 2-33.

Figure 2-33: Movement of Robusto's Inventory in Units for July

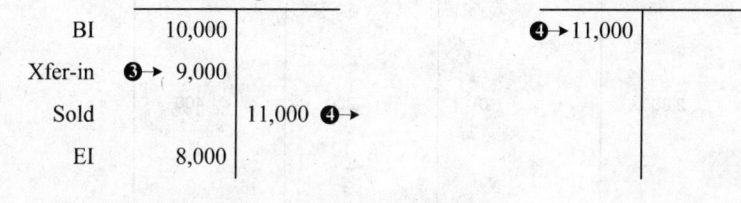

WIP mixing		
BI	1,000	
Started	8,000	
Completed		7,000 ❶→
EI	2,000	

WIP cooking		
BI	3,000	
Xfer-in ❶→	7,000	
Completed		8,000 ❷→
EI	2,000	

WIP canning		
BI	2,000	
Xfer-in ❷→	8,000	
Completed		9,000 ❸→
EI	1,000	

Finished goods		
BI	10,000	
Xfer-in ❸→	9,000	
Sold		11,000 ❹→
EI	8,000	

Units Sold*	
❹→11,000	

Key: Xfer-in = Transferred in   EI = Ending inventory
BI = Beginning inventory

* This account corresponds to cost of goods sold when viewed in dollars instead of in units.

Note that this table shows movements in units and not in costs.

FIFO method for the canning department at Robusto. If the company uses the FIFO method, its canning department has the following costs:

- Work-in-process (WIP) beginning (2,000 units):

  - Cost of work done before current month: (1,800 DM × $1.25/unit) + (1,600 conv. × $2.50/unit) = $6,250

- Costs added in current month:

  - Transferred in from cooking department = $24,000

  - DM = $1,000

  - Conversion = $4,000

Figure 2-34 on the next page shows a completed FIFO method production cost report using this data.

Figure 2-34: Canning Department EU Calculation—FIFO Method

		Physical Quantity	Transferred-in Costs From Cooking Dept.	EU DM	EU Conversion	
Units to be accounted for	WIP beginning of month	2,000				
	Transferred-in	8,000				
	Total units	10,000				
Units accounted for	Transfers to canning department:					
	From beginning WIP, transferred-in 2,000 × (100% − 100%); direct material (DM) 2,000 × (100% − 90%); conv. 2,000 × (100% − 80%):	2,000	0	200	400	
	Started and completed (10,000 units − 1,000 ending WIP − 2,000 beginning WIP completed first)	7,000	7,000	7,000	7,000	
	From WIP month-end, transferred-in 1,000 × 100%; DM 1,000 × 90%, conv. 1,000 × 80%	1,000	1,000	900	800	
	Accounted for:	10,000				
	Work done in current period only:		8,000	8,100	8,200	
		Total Cost				**Whole Unit**
Calculate EU/unit costs and costs to be accounted for	WIP, Beginning of month (cost of work done before current period: (0 transferred in) + (1,800 DM × $1.25) + (1,600 conv. × $2.50)):	$6,250.00	Not included	Not included	Not included	
	Costs added in the current month:	$29,000.00	$24,000.00	$1,000.00	$4,000.00	
	Equivalent units of production (see above):		8,000	8,100	8,200	
	Cost per equivalent unit:		$3.00	$0.1235	$0.4878	$3.6113
	Total costs to account for:	$35,250.00				
Costs accounted for	Transferred to canning department (600 units):					
	WIP, beginning (2,000 units)	$6,250.00				
	Transferred-in	$0	0 × $3.00			
	DM	$24.70		200 × $0.1235		
	Conv.	$195.12			400 × $0.4878	
	WIP, beginning total	$6,469.82				
	Started and completed (7,000 units):	$25,279.10				7,000 × $3.6113
	Total units completed and transferred:	$31,748.92				
	WIP, month-end (1,000 units):					
	Transferred-in	$3,000.00	1,000 × $3.00			
	DM	$111.15		900 × $0.1235		
	Conv.	$ 390.24			800 × $0.4878	
	Total WIP, month-end	$3,501.74				
	Total cost ($0.66 difference due to rounding):	$35,250.66				

Weighted-average method for the canning department at Robusto. If the weighted-average method were used instead, the number of units transferred (Figure 2-35) would remain the same, but the transferred-in costs would differ because each department would include the work done in prior periods (whereas the FIFO method includes only the work done in the current period). Therefore, although all other aspects of the example remain the same, assume that the transferred-in costs to the canning department are now $25,000. Figure 2-35 shows a completed weighted-average method production cost report.

Figure 2-35: Canning Department Production Cost Report—Weighted-Average Method

Production Quantity Information

	Step 1: Determine flow of physical units.		Step 2: Determine equivalent units.		
	Physical Units	Completion Percentage	Transferred-In Costs	Direct Materials	Conversion Costs
Input					
Work-in-process, July 1	2,000				
Transferred-in costs		100%			
Direct materials		90%			
Conversion costs		80%			
Transferred-in	8,000				
Units to account for	10,000				
Output					
Units completed & transferred	9,000	100%	9,000	9,000	9,000
Work-in-process, July 31	1,000				
Transferred-in costs		100%	1,000		
Direct materials		90%		900	
Conversion costs		80%			800
Units accounted for	10,000				
Total equivalent units			10,000	9,900	9,800

Unit Cost

Step 3: Calculate total manufacturing costs.	Transferred-In Costs	Direct Materials	Conversion Costs	Total
Work-in-process, July 1	$6,250	$250	$1,000	$7,500
Costs added during July	$25,000	1,000	4,000	30,000
Total costs to account for	$31,250	$1,250	$5,000	$37,500
Step 4: Calculate unit costs.				
Divide by equivalent units	10,000	9,900	9,800	
Equivalent unit costs	$ 3.125	$ 0.12626	$ 0.5102	$ 3.76146

Step 5: Assign total manufacturing costs.	Completed and Transferred Out	Ending Work-in-Process	Total
Goods completed and transferred out			
(9,000 × $3.76146)	$33,853		$33,853
Ending work-in-process:			
Transferred in (1,000 × $3.125)		$3,125	3,125
Direct materials (900 × $0.12626)		114	114
Conversion costs (800 × $0.5102)		408	408
Total costs accounted for	$33,853	$3,647	$37,500

Figure 2-36 summarizes the data for Robusto Soup, showing the types of T-account transactions and journal entries that would coincide with the data from the weighted-average production cost report.

Figure 2-36: T-Account and Journal Entries for Robusto (Weighted-Average Method)

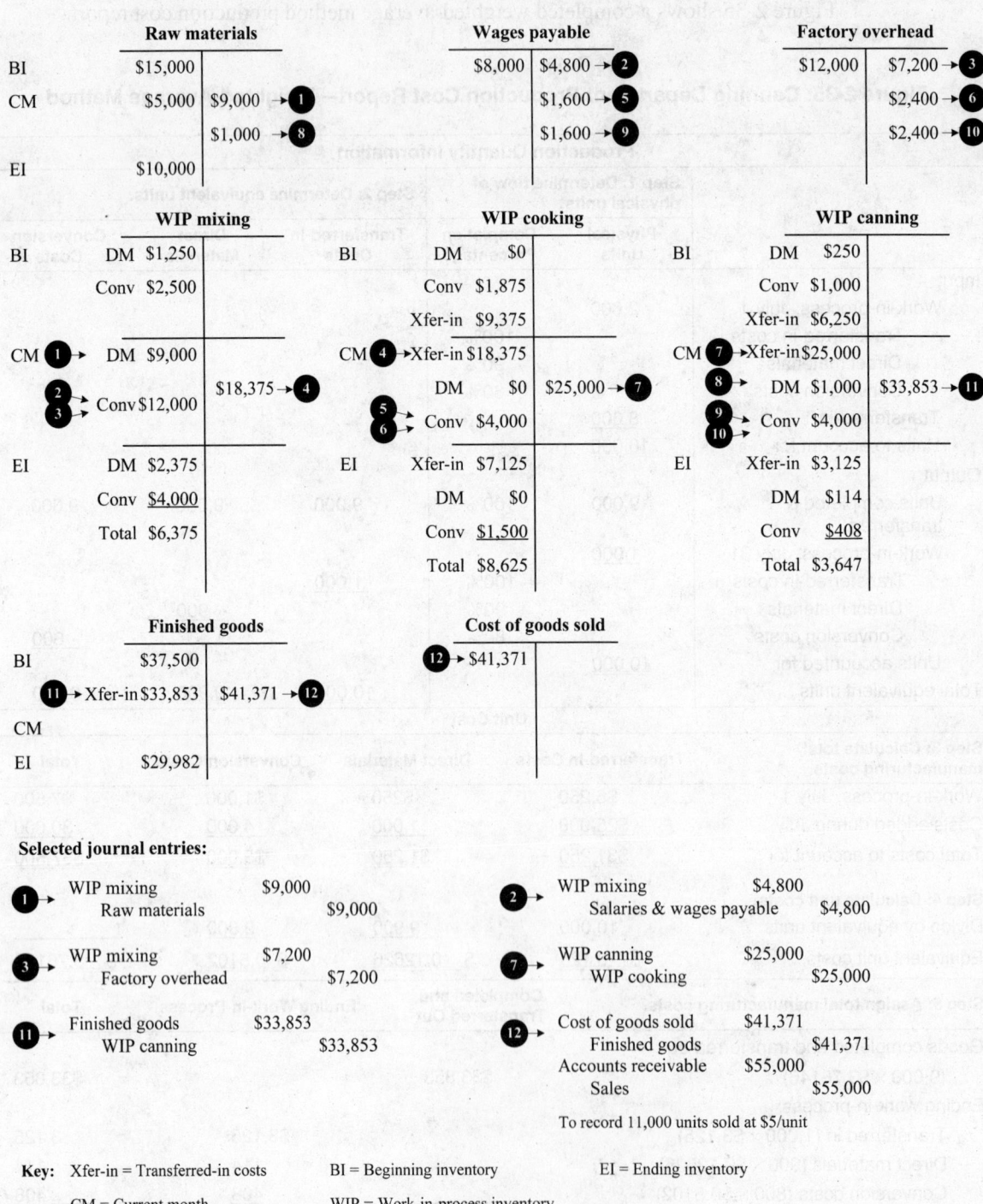

Separate production cost reports for the mixing department and the cooking department would also be needed. (Data for these two accounts is for illustrative purposes only.)

Note that each of the base accounts (raw materials, wages payable, and factory overhead) feeds not only into the first department but into the other departments, as indicated by the percentage of inputs shown in Figure 2-36. The costs transferred out by that department do not directly equal the costs added during the current period; however, beginning inventory plus the costs added in the current month always equal the ending inventory plus the costs transferred out.

Note also that each inventory account's beginning and ending inventory levels are broken down by direct materials, conversion costs, and transferred-in costs.

Determining inventory levels in process costing

The following example will help illustrate the complexities involved in determining inventory levels in process costing. Bounce Sporting Goods buys rubber as a direct material for racquet balls. The molding department processes the racquet balls, and the balls are then transferred to the finishing department, where a coating and a label are applied. The forming department began manufacturing 15,000 "Bouncers" during the month of June. There was no beginning inventory.

Costs for the molding department for the month of June were as follows.

Direct materials:	$60,000
Conversion costs:	46,200
Total	$106,200

A total of 12,000 balls were completed and transferred to the finishing department; the remaining 3,000 balls were still in the molding process at the end of the month. All of the molding department's direct materials were placed in process but, on average, only 40% of the conversion cost was applied to the ending work-in-process inventory.

What is the cost of the units transferred to the finishing department? To find the answer, first determine whether the operation uses the weighted-average or FIFO method. In this example, either method will arrive at the same answer because there is no beginning inventory: beginning work-in-process (WIP) equivalent units (EU) are 0 for direct materials (DM) and 0 for conversion costs.

The answer, $90,000, is calculated as follows:

Determine units started and completed:

DM: 12,000 units × 100% complete = 12,000 EU

Conv: 12,000 units × 100% complete = 12,000 EU

Determine WIP month-end:

DM: 3,000 units × 100% complete = 3,000 EU

Conv: 3,000 units × 40% complete = 1,200 EU

Determine total EU:

DM: 0 + 12,000 + 3,000 = 15,000 EU

Conv: 0 + 12,000 + 1,200 = 13,200 EU

Calculate EU/unit costs:

DM: $\dfrac{\$60,000}{15,000 \text{ EU}} = \$4.00/\text{EU}$

Conv: $\dfrac{\$46,200}{13,200 \text{ EU}} = \$3.50/\text{EU}$

Cost of units started and completed (transferred to finishing department):

(12,000 × $4) + (12,000 × $3.50) = $90,000

To verify, calculate ending WIP:

(3,000 EU DM × $4) + (1,200 EU conv × $3.50) = $16,200

Note that $90,000 + $16,200 = $106,200, the total cost.

Spoilage in process costing

Process costing can have normal and abnormal spoilage, as defined previously under job costing. Spoilage in process costing is handled in one of two ways. The first method counts the number of spoiled units, separately computes the total cost per unit, and then allocates this cost to the good units. The second method omits the spoiled units in the totals so that the cost per unit does not include any spoiled units, making the spoilage cost part of the total manufacturing costs. The first method provides more precise product costs because the individually calculated spoilage cost is spread over only the good units produced. The second method is less precise because the costs are spread to all units including good completed units, units in ending WIP inventory, and abnormal spoiled units.

Benefits and limitations of process costing

Process costing is useful for any highly repetitive flow process such as mass production. Conversely, it is not useful for custom orders or other individual jobs. Process costing allocates costs not only by cost per unit but also to specific departments, allowing individual managers to control their own costs.

Activity-Based Costing (ABC)

Activity-based costing (ABC) is a method of assigning costs to customers, services, and products based on an activity's consumption of resources. An activity is any type of action, work, or movement performed within an entity. An activity center is a logical grouping of activities, actions, movements, or sequences of work. A resource is an element with economic value that is consumed or applied when performing an activity.

Other terms important to ABC include resource cost drivers and activity cost drivers.

A resource cost driver measures the amount of resources consumed by an activity. Resource costs used in an activity are assigned to a cost pool using a resource cost driver. For example, a resource cost driver could be the amount of rubber required to make a batch of tennis balls.

An **activity cost driver** is a measurement of the amount of an activity used by a cost object. Activity cost drivers assign costs in cost pools to cost objects. For example, an activity cost driver is the number of labor hours required for the activity of performing a setup for a particular product.

The basis for ABC is that activities use resources but produce products or services. The resource cost is calculated using a cost driver; the amount of an activity consumed in a period is multiplied by the cost of the activity. The calculated costs are assigned to the product or service.

ABC systems are most necessary for companies that have expanded to multiple products and/or products that use varying amounts of resources, which include not only raw materials and other direct costs but also indirect costs such as customer service, quality control, and supervision. When each product or product line consumes each of these costs at different rates, a broad brush or uniform cost for all items will make some products appear more profitable than they really are and others less profitable than they are. Products can therefore be overcosted or undercosted, where overcosted items consume few actual resources but are charged as if they had consumed more, and undercosted is the opposite. Strategically, ABC should be used when the cost of inaccurate costing data exceeds the added costs of collecting more information and implementing an ABC system. For example, in deciding whether to add or drop a segment, cutting the wrong items could have disastrous consequences. Other strategic choices aided by ABC include product pricing decisions and where to allocate funds to improve processes.

Two-stage allocation is the method used to assign overhead (resource costs) to cost pools and then, based on how a cost object uses resources, from cost pools to cost objects such as products, services, or customers. Cost pools can be either activities or activity centers. ABC has two stages of allocation:

- Stage one: resource cost assignment of overhead costs to activity cost pools or activity centers using pertinent resource cost drivers

- Stage two: activity cost assignment of activity costs to cost objects using pertinent activity cost drivers (measures a cost object's drain on an activity)

Key steps in ABC

The steps for designing an activity-based costing system are identifying activities and resource costs, assigning resource costs to activities, and assigning activity costs to cost objects.

Step 1: Identify activities and resource costs.

An activity analysis identifies the resource costs of performing particular activities by determining the work performed for each activity. The project team makes detailed lists of activities and organizes them into activity centers as well as into the following levels:

- **Unit-level activities** include activities that are performed for each unit produced, such as direct materials or direct labor hours. In other words, these are the same as volume-based or unit-based activities.

- **Batch-level activities** include activities that are performed for each batch of units, such as machine setup, purchase orders, batch inspections, batch mixing, or production scheduling.

- **Product-sustaining activities** include activities that are performed to support the production process, such as product design, expediting, and implementing engineering changes.

- **Facility-sustaining activities** include activities that support production for an entire facility, such as environmental health and safety, security, plant management, depreciation, property taxes, and insurance.

- **Customer-level activities** include activities that are performed to support customer needs, such as customer service, phone banks, or custom orders.

Step 2: Assign resource costs to activities.

Resource costs are assigned to activities using resource cost drivers. A cause-and-effect relationship must be established between the driver and the activity. Resource cost drivers and the related activity that companies often use include the following.

- Number of employees: personnel activities

- Time worked: personnel activities

- Setup hours: setup or machine activities

- Number or distance of movements: materials-handling activities

- Meters: utilities (flow meters, electricity meters, etc.)

- Machine hours: machine-running activities

- Number of orders: production orders

- Square feet: cleaning activities

- Amount of value added: general and administrative

Step 3: Assign activity costs to cost objects.

After determining activity costs, the activity costs per unit are measured using an appropriate cost driver. The activity cost driver should show a cause-and-effect relationship or, in other words, be directly related to the rise and fall of the cost.

The activity cost drivers determine the proportion of a cost to allocate to each product or service using the following formula:

$$\text{Rate} = \frac{\text{Cost Pool}}{\text{Driver}}$$

When to use ABC

ABC helps managers understand their costs, thus highlighting the competitive advantages and weaknesses of their process or product. Computer databases have made tracking individual costs using ABC more feasible. As more firms adopt ABC, using a less accurate costing system is growing relatively more expensive.

Firms that have high product diversity, complexity, or volume have traditionally moved to ABC to help track their costs.

Firms that have a high likelihood of cost distortion, such as firms that have both mass-produced and custom orders, both mature and new products, and both custom delivery and standard delivery channels, should consider ABC. Such mixes make job order costing and process order costing difficult to implement without some form of combination, leaving ABC as an ideal alternative.

Firms that adopt ABC will be able to use it not only in accounting for costs but also for strategic decision making. They can cost products and services, analyze processes, assess management performance, and assess profitability better than firms that use a volume-based (traditional) costing system.

Differences between ABC and traditional costing

The ABC system and traditional costing have many differences. Because the breakdown of costs using ABC is much more specific, these items can be analyzed more carefully. The three primary differences are shown in Figure 2-37.

Figure 2-37: ABC vs. Traditional Costing

ABC	Traditional Costing
Multiple cost drivers: activity and volume-based drivers (whichever fits the cost best)	Up to three cost drivers: only volume-based, chosen for best general fit
Overhead assigned to activities and then from activities to products or services	Overhead assigned to departments and then from departments to products or services
Focus on solving costing and processing issues that cross departmental lines	Focus on assigning responsibility to departmental managers for individual cost and process improvements within their department

Benefits and limitations of ABC

Benefits of using ABC include the following:

- ABC reduces distortions caused by traditional cost allocation methods. In traditional costing, if overhead is high, one product may appear profitable whereas another seems less so; in ABC, the first product may consume more resources and have lower actual profitability than the other product.

- ABC gives managers access to relevant costs so they can compete better in the marketplace.

- ABC measures activity-driving costs, allowing management to alter product designs and activity designs and know how overall cost and value are affected.

- ABC normally results in substantially greater unit costs for low-volume products than is reported by traditional product costing (meaning better decisions can be made to add or drop a product line).

Limitations of ABC include the following:

- Not all overhead costs can be related to a particular cost driver and may need to be arbitrarily allocated, especially when the cost of tracing is greater than the benefit.

- ABC requires numerous development and maintenance hours even with new software and databases. Most projects also take over a year to implement.

- ABC changes the rules for managers, so resistance to change is common. Without top management support, managers could find workarounds.

- ABC viewed only as an accounting initiative will likely fail.

- ABC generates vast amounts of information. Too much information can mislead managers into concentrating on the wrong data.

- ABC reports do not conform to GAAP, so restating financial data adds an expense and causes confusion (unsure whether to rely on the ABC or external data).

Life-Cycle Costing

When a longer-term perspective is needed than other costing methods provide (usually a year), life-cycle costing may be used. Life-cycle costing is a costing process that considers the entire life cycle of a product or service.

For example, the life cycle for a pharmaceutical product starts with research and development, moves through federal testing and product design phases, and then goes on to manufacturing, marketing and distribution, and customer service. In this case, the cycle may be defined as the life span of the patent on the product or the life span of its marketability.

Life-cycle costing is sometimes used on a strategic basis for cost planning and product pricing. It is designed to allow a firm to focus on the overall costs for a product or service. Poor early design could lead to much higher marketing costs, lower sales, and higher service costs. The total costs for a product's life cycle have three phases.

- Upstream costs: costs that are prior to the manufacturing of the product or sale of the service, such as R&D or design (prototypes, tests, and engineering)

- Manufacturing costs: costs involved in producing a product or service, such as purchasing and direct and indirect manufacturing costs

- Downstream costs: costs subsequent to (or coincident with) manufacturing costs, such as marketing, distribution (packaging, shipping and handling, promotions, and advertising), service costs, and warranty costs (defect recalls, returns, and liability)

Life-cycle costing places its strategic focus on improving costs in all three phases. Improving product design is the key to the upstream phase; improving the manufacturing process and relationships with suppliers are highlighted in the manufacturing phase; improving the prior two phases is the key to lowering downstream costs because actions taken in these phases limit the downstream choices that can be made. In other words, life-cycle costing attempts to make managers proactive in the earlier phases so they do not have to be reactive in the downstream phase.

Life-cycle costing is related to life-cycle pricing as detailed in Part 3 of the CMA Learning System.

Other Costing Methods

Two other costing methods are operation costing and backflush costing (in just-in-time production systems).

Operation costing

Operation costing is a costing system that combines job costing with process costing. Similar to job costing, operation costing assigns direct materials to each job or batch, but direct labor and overhead (conversion costs) are assigned similarly to process costing. This hybrid system is most suitable for manufacturers that have similar processes for high-volume activities but who need to use different materials for different jobs. Clothing manufacturers have standard operations: choosing patterns, cutting, and sewing. However, the fabrics used will not only vary by clothing pattern but also by price and choice of color for the same pattern. Other industries that are suitable for operation costing include textiles, metalworking, furniture, shoes, and electronic equipment.

Consider an example. A metalworking company produces handrails that are either unfinished (for painting) or chrome-plated. The company has one department create all of the metal rails and then transfers some to the chrome-plating department. Assume that the company produced 1,000 unfinished rails and 500 chrome rails during a month and that they had no beginning or ending inventory for the month. Operation costing tracks direct materials by job and tracks conversion costs (direct labor and overhead) by department, as shown in Figure 2-38.

Figure 2-38: Total Cost Calculation

Direct Materials

Job 1—Unfinished Rails (1,000)		$30,000
Job 2—Chrome Rails (500)		
Materials for Rails in Metal Department	$15,000	
Chrome Plating Added to Rails in Chrome Department	$10,000	$25,000
Total Direct Materials		$55,000
Conversion Costs		
Metal Department		$45,000
Chrome Department		$10,000
Total Conversion Costs		$55,000
Total Costs		$110,000

The product costs for unfinished rails and chrome rails are calculated in Figure 2-39. Note that the conversion costs for the metal department group all rails together because they are all processed the same in that department.

Figure 2-39: Product Cost Calculation

	Unfinished Rails	Chrome Rails
Direct Materials		
Job 1 $\left(\dfrac{\$30,000}{1,000}\right)$	$30/Rail	
Job 2 $\left(\dfrac{\$25,000}{500}\right)$		$50/Rail
Conversion桜 etal Department $\left(\dfrac{\$45,000}{1,500}\right)$	$30/Rail	$30/Rail
Conversion栈 hrome Department $\left(\dfrac{\$10,000}{500}\right)$		$20/Rail
Total Cost per Rail	60/Rail	$100/Rail

Total product cost

Unfinished Rails $60 × 1,000 = $60,000

Chrome Rails $100 × $500 = $50,000

Total = $110,000

Note that the total costs in figures 2-38 and 2-39 ($110,000) reconcile with each other, proving that the calculations are correct.

Backflush costing in just-in-time production systems

A **just-in-time (JIT) system** produces materials just as they are needed for the next step in production. The trigger for manufacturing at a particular work area is the demand from the next station down the line, thus JIT production systems are a "demand-pull" manufacturing system. Customer demand triggers the initial production need, working backward all the way to raw material purchases at the beginning of the cycle. JIT also reduces manufacturing lead time by organizing manufacturing into cells that are closely coordinated. JIT ensures timely material deliveries and meets customer demands while simultaneously ensuring high-quality products at the lowest possible cost. Therefore, organizations using JIT production have very little inventory, making the choice of inventory valuation methods (e.g., FIFO, weighted-average) and inventory costing methods (e.g., absorption costing, variable costing) irrelevant because the costs flow directly to cost of goods sold during an accounting period. The five most prominent features of a JIT system include the following.

- Manufacturing cells: Each cell groups all of the different types of equipment needed to make a particular product in order to minimize materials-handling costs.

- Multiskilled workers: Workers are cross-trained using job sharing and other means to keep the work force flexible (e.g., workers are trained to maintain machines and make minor repairs).

- Total quality management (TQM): TQM aggressively attempts to eliminate defects because minimal inventories and close links between processing steps make each defect more significant. Therefore, TQM is a required aspect of a JIT production system.

- Reduced manufacturing lead time and setup time: Reducing the time required to set up tools, equipment, and materials for the start of a process (setup) and reducing the time between when a process begins and the product is complete (manufacturing lead time) are strong priorities in JIT systems. Reduced setup allows manufacturers to run smaller batches economically, allowing for reduced inventory. Changes in customer demand can be adopted more quickly when manufacturing lead time is reduced.

- Strong supplier relationships: JIT production requires that suppliers be carefully screened to ensure that they can deliver materials when they are needed. JIT production goes hand in hand with JIT purchasing, which are methods of ensuring that goods arrive just when needed and direct materials inventories are kept low. For example, trusted suppliers could have a direct electronic link to the company so they can send goods when they are required, without waiting for an invoice and a standard purchasing process. Suppliers may also make deliveries directly to a production facility instead of to a warehouse.

Traditional costing systems use sequential tracking, which is any process that records purchases and movements of costs between inventories and accounts in the order in which they occur. Sequential tracking tracks costs through a four-stage cycle:

- Stage A: purchase of direct materials (journal entry in materials inventory)
- Stage B: production (journal entry in WIP inventory)
- Stage C: completion of a good finished unit (journal entry in finished goods inventory)
- Stage D: sale of finished good (journal entry in cost of goods sold)

The journal entries made at each stage are called trigger points.

Backflush costing is a costing system tailored for JIT production systems in which sequential tracking is not used. It omits some or all of the journal entries for the production cycle. The system is called "backflush costing" because when the journal entries are omitted from certain stages of the cycle, normal or standard costs are used to work backward and flush out the costs and make the required journal entries for the missing steps. One of the most common stages skipped is the journal entry for work-in-process inventory, because JIT systems reduce the time that materials remain in this stage.

The use of backflush costing may not be in strict accordance with GAAP, such as the fact that most backflush costing entries ignore WIP inventory even though in reality it does exist and should be recorded as an asset. However, many companies use backflush costing because such items are immaterial. When they are material, these unrecorded costs need to be approximated and adjusting entries made. Backflush costing can save a company money on accounting, but some critics find the lack of a clear audit trail (pinpointing resources at each stage of manufacturing) to be a risk. Many inventories are so low, however, that managers can track operations by simple observation and computer monitoring.

Companies that use JIT production systems are prime candidates for using backflush costing, but any industry that has fast manufacturing lead times and/or very stable inventory levels could use backflush costing.

Progress Check

Directions: Read each question and respond in the space provided. Answers and page references appear on the following page.

1. Which of the following costing systems would work best for a firm that spends a considerable percentage of its overall costs on R&D?

    ( ) a. Job order costing

    ( ) b. Process costing

    ( ) c. Activity-based costing

    ( ) d. Life-cycle costing

2. A post office wants to implement a cost accumulation system for their bulk mail sorting warehouse. Which of the following methods would be best suited to this situation?

    ( ) a. Life-cycle costing

    ( ) b. Activity-based costing

    ( ) c. Process costing

    ( ) d. Job costing

3. Which of the following terms refers to an item with little economic value for the firm?

    ( ) a. Abnormal spoilage

    ( ) b. Normal spoilage

    ( ) c. Rework

    ( ) d. Scrap

4. A company is using process costing (with FIFO). For a period with no beginning WIP inventory and 60% complete ending WIP inventory (10,000 physical units), if there are 20,000 units completed during the period, how many equivalent units are there total?

    ( ) a. 20,000

    ( ) b. 26,000

    ( ) c. 32,000

    ( ) d. 34,000

Progress check answers

1. d (p. 2-114)

2. c (p. 2-94)

3. d (p. 2-96)

4. b (p. 2-100)

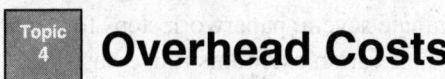

Overhead Costs

Topic overview

Overhead costs can be sizable because they include not only indirect manufacturing costs and administrative and general expenses but also depreciation on plants and factory equipment. Overhead costs can be either product costs or period costs. Product costs can be capitalized into inventory items, whereas period costs must be expensed in the period in which they occur.

This topic covers fixed and variable overhead, plant-wide versus departmental overhead, activity-based costing (ABC) overhead allocation, determining an allocation base (in other words, choosing a cost driver), and the allocation of service department costs.

Fixed and Variable Overhead Expenses

All overhead expenses are either fixed or variable costs. Fixed costs include depreciation on assets, leasing costs, and executive salaries. These costs do not change during an accounting period provided the relevant range is consistent with the level of production. Variable costs include power, water, sewage, engineering support, machine maintenance, and indirect materials. Variable costs change in proportion to the changes in a particular cost driver (volume- or activity-based).

Fixed overhead costs

Most fixed costs are set periodically, so the day-to-day operations of a business have little effect on fixed costs (by definition). The time frame for planning fixed overhead costs has two phases: setting priorities and being efficient in the pursuit of those priorities. Setting priorities means that the firm should determine which fixed overhead costs should or must be undertaken (and which add no value and can be disposed of), plus determining which fixed costs are most important to get right. An auto rental company might set its highest fixed cost priority as the leasing or purchase of the proper number of rental vehicles for a period so that each facility has enough cars to satisfy demand without leaving too much unused capacity.

The second phase is pursuing efficiency in the fixed overhead costs that are on the list of priorities: those costs most likely to be reduced through more careful planning. In the same example, the rental company can decide whether leasing or purchasing is the most cost-effective, choose the most trouble-free brands of cars, or negotiate the best deals with the auto manufacturers.

Variable overhead costs

The time frame for planning variable overhead costs has the same two phases: setting priorities and being efficient in the pursuit of those priorities. Setting priorities for variable costs involves determining which activities add value for customers and which can be eliminated. A car rental company might eliminate several paperwork steps for customers or automate the entire process to reduce their variable administrative costs and improve customer service at the same time. Unlike fixed costs, variable costs can be influenced on a day-to-day basis, so the efficient pursuit of priorities can be an ongoing process, such as scheduling rental car maintenance activities during times of low rentals so that these activities do not hamper business.

Fixed overhead cost allocation rates

Fixed overhead costs are a lump sum that does not change over the course of a period even if wide variations occur in activity. The four steps in determining the budgeted fixed allocation rate are as follows:

1. Determine the proper accounting period. A year basis is usually preferable to a monthly basis because most companies want to smooth over variations due to seasonality or different numbers of days per month. Using an annual period also keeps managers from having to create a new budget each month.

2. Determine the allocation base (cost driver) to use when allocating fixed overhead. Cost drivers have been discussed earlier in the text. A firm could use a volume- or activity-based cost driver. Although fixed costs do not vary, they still must be allocated in proportion to the value they are providing to each cost pool. For example, a tennis ball manufacturer may use machine hours as its fixed cost driver. The company budgets 40,000 machine hours annually to produce 200,000 cans of tennis balls.

3. Determine the fixed overhead costs associated with each cost allocation base (cost driver). Fixed overhead costs could be grouped into any number of pools divided according to which allocation base best measures the value provided by the set of fixed costs. In this example, all fixed manufacturing overhead costs relate to the machine hours allocation base. The fixed overhead costs total $1,000,000 for the year.

4. Calculate the rate per unit of each allocation base used when allocating fixed overhead costs to cost objects:

$$\text{Fixed Overhead Application Rate} = \frac{\text{Total Costs in Fixed Overhead Cost Pool}}{\text{Total Quantity of Allocation Base}}$$

$$= \frac{\$1,000,000}{40,000 \text{ Machine Hours}} = \$25/\text{Machine Hour}$$

Thus more of the fixed cost is assigned to operations that use more of the allocation base than other operations.

Budgeted variable overhead cost allocation rates

The steps and calculations listed for budgeting fixed overhead cost allocation rates are the same for variable rates. Therefore, the steps are not repeated here. Simply substitute "variable" in place of "fixed" above to determine how to develop an applicable rate.

Plant-Wide and Departmental Overhead and ABC Overhead Costing

Firms with two or more production departments can assign factory overhead costs to jobs or products in the following ways:

- Plant-wide overhead rate

- Departmental overhead rate

- ABC overhead costing

Plant-wide overhead rate

A plant-wide overhead rate is a single rate used for all overhead costs incurred at a production facility. The total plant factory overhead is determined using the following calculation:

$$\text{Plant-Wide Overhead} = \frac{\text{Total Plant Overhead}}{\text{Total Units of Cost Driver (Allocation Base) Common to All Jobs}}$$

Because plant-wide allocation is by its nature very general, it can be used only by facilities that have a strong single cost driver that relates to all types of production. If a plant had one portion that was highly automated and another that was labor-intensive, then such a plant should use different cost drivers for each area instead of using a plant-wide overhead rate. Departmental overhead rates are more accurate than plant-wide rates.

Departmental overhead rate

A departmental overhead rate is a single overhead rate calculated for a particular department. Each department could have its own rate calculated based on its own cost drivers. The departmental overhead rate is calculated as follows:

$$\text{Departmental Overhead} = \frac{\text{Total Department Overhead}}{\text{Total Units of Cost Driver Common to All Jobs for the Department}}$$

Accounting for each overhead amount is tracked by keeping separate factory overhead and applied overhead accounts for each department. As with the plant-wide rate, the departmental overhead rate is still a fairly general rate, so misallocations of costs can occur if the cost driver chosen does not truly relate to all activities for a department.

Departmental overhead rates should be used only if the department is homogeneous and if a cause-and-effect relationship can be defined between each job and the selected cost driver. When this is not true, several sets of cost drivers and associated cost pools should be used. The dangers of improperly allocating costs have been elaborated upon earlier: Certain products will appear less profitable than they really are and vice versa, causing mismanagement of the product lines.

ABC overhead costing

When plant-wide and departmental overhead allocation is too inaccurate for allocating costs, an activity-based costing (ABC) method can be used. ABC assigns factory overhead costs to products or services using multiple cost pools and multiple cost drivers. The cost drivers are selected based on a cause-and-effect relationship and can be both activity-based and volume-based.

For more information on ABC, see Topic 3 of this section.

Figure 2-40 shows the cost pools and cost drivers for a sample production facility.

Figure 2-40: Cost Pools, Drivers, and Predetermined Driver Rate

Overhead Cost Pool	Budgeted Overhead Cost	Cost Driver	Units	Predetermined Driver Rate
Utilities	$100,000	Machine hrs.	10,000	$10/machine hr.
Materials Handling	$120,000	Materials weight (lbs.)	40,000	$3/lb.
Setups	$90,000	Number of setups	300	$300/setup
	$310,000			

The predetermined driver rate in the example above is calculated by dividing the budgeted overhead cost by the total number of units of the cost driver. The precision in this system is seen when two or more jobs or products share these costs.

For example, assume that the facility described in Figure 2-40 has two jobs for the current period. Job 1 uses 4,000 machine hours and 30,000 pounds in direct materials weight and has 100 setups. Job 2 uses 6,000 machine hours and 10,000 pounds in direct materials weight and has 200 setups. The costs assigned to each job are calculated as shown in Figure 2-41.

Figure 2-41: ABC vs. Plant-Wide Overhead Allocation

	ABC	Plant-Wide
Job 1 Utilities $10/machine hr. × 4,000 hrs. =	$40,000	
Job 1 Materials handling $3/lb. × 30,000 lbs. =	$90,000	
Job 1 Setups $300/setup × 100 setups =	$30,000	
Total =	$160,000	$124,000
Job 2 Utilities $10/machine hr. × 6,000 hrs. =	$60,000	
Job 2 Materials handling $3/lb. × 10,000 lbs. =	$30,000	
Job 2 Setups $300/setup × 200 setups =	$60,000	
Total =	$150,000	$186,000
	$310,000	$310,000

For comparison, if a plant-wide rate had been used with machine hours as the sole cost driver, the total overhead of $310,000 divided by 10,000 machine hours would be $31/machine hour, multiplied by 4,000 hours for job 1 ($124,000) and 6,000 hours for job 2 ($186,000).

Note that the ABC method produces very different costs for the two products compared to the plant-wide method.

Determination of Allocation Base (Cost Drivers)

Whether plant-wide, departmental, or activity-based cost pools are designated for overhead allocations, the selection of the allocation base(s), or cost driver(s), is of vital importance. The methods and criteria used to determine the allocation base have been covered previously under the discussion of cost drivers.

Allocation of Service Department Costs

There are two basic types of departments in a company: production departments and service departments. Production departments have up to now been the topic of this text. Service departments do not directly perform operating activities but instead assist production departments, customers, and employees. Examples of service departments include maintenance, internal auditing, cafeterias, information technology, human resources, purchasing, company stores, customer service, engineering, and cost accounting.

Allocation of service department costs has three phases:

- Phase 1: Trace all direct costs and allocate overhead costs to all departments (production departments and other service departments).

- Phase 2: Allocate service department costs to production departments or other service departments.

- Phase 3: Allocate production department costs to products.

Service department costs are allocated because most service departments do not generate any revenue: they are cost centers. When a service department does generate revenue, such as the cafeteria or a repairs department, these revenues offset the costs and any net cost is transferred to the production departments, which are revenue-producing departments.

Phase 1: Trace direct costs and allocate overhead costs to departments.

The first activity in Phase 1 is to trace direct costs to production and service departments. This is the same as tracing direct costs to production departments, so it is not covered here. Allocating overhead costs to service departments is also very much the same for service departments as it has been described for production departments. However, the cost drivers (allocation bases) may be slightly different in type. For example, the laundry service might have as a cost driver loads of laundry and the cafeteria might use number of meals served. Other common cost drivers for various service departments are listed below:

- Medical facilities—cases handled

- Data processing—number of personal computers, CPU minutes, disk storage used

- Materials handling—labor hours, volume handled

- Cost accounting—labor hours, customers served

- Shipping and receiving—units handled, number of requisitions, labor hours

- Maintenance—machine hours

- Janitorial services—square feet of building space

Overall, the cost drivers selected should be easily understood by the managers who will have these costs allocated to them. Note that both the cost driver rate selected and the total units of the cost drivers can use actual or standard (budgeted) rates or units (or some combination such as standard cost driver rate times actual units of the cost driver). Use of standard amounts of cost driver rates can motivate service department managers to control costs because the amounts can be calculated during a period. However, variances between standard and actual results will cause amounts to be under- or overapplied. (See "Actual/Normal/Standard Costing" in Topic 2 of this section for more information on over- or underapplied costs.) Using actual cost drivers or actual amounts will allow for precise cost allocation but can only be done after the period is complete, so it cannot be used for control purposes during the period.

There are two basic methods of allocating costs: the single-rate method and the contribution margin method. The single-rate cost allocation method creates a single allocation base for a service department's combined fixed and variable costs, providing a single rate per unit for cost allocation. If a project had $1 million in fixed costs plus variable costs of $50/machine hour and 5,000 machine hours, the total rate per machine hour would be [$1,000,000 + (5,000 × $50)]/5,000 = $250/machine hour. However, when fixed costs are grouped with variable costs, the entire cost seems to be a variable cost and managers could be tempted to out-source to a provider with a lower rate. Because the fixed department costs would be incurred regardless of use (at least in the short term), the department would be adding new external costs while still incurring the fixed portion of the internal costs.

The contribution margin cost allocation method, also called the dual-rate method, creates separate fixed and variable cost pools for allocation of service department costs. Each pool can have its own allocation base, such as labor hours for variable costs but machine hours for fixed costs. Due to the possibility of using different cost drivers, different rates, and use of standard or actual amounts for each variable, the contribution margin method may end up with a different estimate of total costs than if the single-rate method were used. For example, using the same data from the prior paragraph, if the $1,000,000 in fixed costs were allocated based on labor hours and 4,900 labor hours were used, then the fixed allocation rate would be about $204/labor hour and the variable allocation rate would be $50/machine hour. Each type of cost would be separately calculated using one of the allocation methods detailed in Phase 2 below, thus doubling the number of calculations required to find the total costs allocated. If done correctly using the precepts of ABC, this method should lead to more precise allocation of costs and allow better managerial decision making, but it could result in higher administrative costs due to more complex calculations and difficulty in determining proper classification of costs.

Phase 2: Allocate service department costs to production departments or other service departments.

The second phase is to allocate the service department costs to the production departments or to other service departments. Allocating costs to other service departments, such as the costs that custodial services charge to the cafeteria for cleaning, are called interdepartmental or reciprocal services. Three methods can be used to allocate service costs to other departments: the direct method, the step-down method, and the reciprocal method. To keep the focus on the allocation methods, the single-rate method is used in all of the following examples. However, the contribution method can be applied to any of the methods.

Direct method

The direct method, as its name implies, is the most direct and simple method of allocating service department costs. This method cannot be used to allocate costs to other service departments; it can only be used to allocate costs to production departments. Even when one service department does perform a significant amount of service for another department, this method bypasses such considerations and assigns all costs directly to the production departments. The direct method ignores the cost drivers that are related to the service departments and concentrates only on the cost drivers attributable to the production departments. Consider Figure 2-42 showing four of a company's departments.

Figure 2-42: Department Costs and Cost Drivers

	Service		Production	
	HR	Janitorial	Metal Department	Chrome Department
Dept. costs before allocation	$200,000	$80,000	$400,000	$100,000
Labor hours	10,000	5,000	20,000	5,000
Space (sq. ft.)	15,000	500	60,000	20,000

In this example, the HR department's costs use the production departments' labor hours, and the janitorial department uses the production departments' space measurements, as calculated below:

$$\text{Department Allocation} = \frac{\text{Production Department Units}}{\text{Total Units for All Production Departments}} \times \text{Department Costs}$$

$$\text{HR Costs to Metal Dept.} = \frac{20,000}{20,000 + 5,000} \times \$200,000 = 0.8 \times \$200,000 = \$160,000$$

$$\text{HR Costs to Chrome Dept.} = 0.2 \times \$200,000 = \$40,000$$

$$\text{Janitorial Costs to Metal Dept.} = \frac{60,000}{60,000 + 20,000} \times \$80,000 = 0.75 \times \$80,000 = \$60,000$$

$$\text{Janitorial Costs to Chrome Dept.} = 0.25 \times \$80,000 = \$20,000$$

The total cost to the metal department is $620,000 ($400,000 + $160,000 + $60,000), and the total cost to the chrome department is $160,000 ($100,000 + $40,000 + $20,000). These allocations assume that there are only two production departments. Even so, the direct method does not take into account the services performed for other service departments. For example, the janitorial service also cleans the HR department, which means that the two production departments are receiving an inaccurate percentage of these costs.

Step-down method

The step-down method allocates a service department's costs to service departments and to production departments. This method sequentially allocates service department costs, starting with the department that provides the most services to other service departments and finishing with the department that provides the least services to other service departments. Each successive department's allocation is a step down in costs that need to be allocated.

The step-down method takes into account the proportion of work performed for each other service department. As with the direct method, only the departments receiving the allocation are included in the calculation of cost driver proportions to be allocated.

For example, if the same departments are used from the prior metalworking shop example, the HR costs would be allocated first, followed by janitorial services. A real company could have hundreds of service departments.

Figure 2-43 illustrates allocation using the step-down method.

Figure 2-43: Step-Down Method Allocation

	Service		Production	
	HR	Janitorial	Metal Department	Chrome Department
Dept. Costs Before Allocation	$200,000	$80,000	$400,000	$100,000
First Step:	($200,000)	$33,333	$133,334	$33,333
Subtotal	$0	$113,333	$533,334	$133,333
Second Step:		($113,333)	$85,000	$28,333
Total	$0	$0	$618,334	$161,666
Labor Hours	10,000	5,000	20,000	5,000
Space (sq. ft.)	15,000	500	60,000	20,000

The HR department costs are allocated by dividing the department's individual labor hours (5,000) by the total of the labor hours for the janitorial, metal, and chrome departments (30,000 hours). These costs are then added to the departments (first step). (Some rounding was needed to simplify the example.) In the second step, the new total for the janitorial costs is allocated to the two production departments based on square feet. In a realistic situation, these costs would be allocated to many other service departments (the ones with lower costs) than just the production departments. However, all of the costs eventually end up in the revenue-producing production departments.

Comparing these costs to those provided by the direct method, the costs are slightly higher for the metal department and slightly lower for the chrome department. The step-down method provides a more accurate measure of how costs should be allocated. However, as can be seen above, some costs can still be distorted. For example, janitorial costs are still not allocated to the HR department, even though it has many square feet of space that are cleaned.

Reciprocal method

The reciprocal method fully recognizes all interdepartmental service costs using simultaneous equations. In contrast, the step-down method provides only partial recognition because it does not allocate costs backward, only forward.

The first step of the reciprocal method is to set up a system of equations. Referring to the metalworking shop example previously used:

$$HR = \$200,000 + \left(\frac{15,000}{15,000 + 60,000 + 20,000} \times Janitorial \right)$$

$$Janitorial\ (J) = \$80,000 + \left(\frac{5,000}{5,000 + 20,000 + 5,000} \times HR \right)$$

$$HR = \$200,000 + 0.15789(J)$$

$$J = \$80,000 + 0.16667(HR)$$

$$HR = \$200,000 + 0.15789[\$80,000 + 0.16667(HR)]$$

$$HR = \$200,000 + \$12,631.20 + 0.02632(HR)$$

$$1(HR) - 0.02632(HR) = \$212,631.20$$

$$0.97368(HR) = \$212,631.20$$

$$HR = \frac{\$212,631.20}{0.97368} = \$218,378.93$$

$$HR \approx \$218,379$$

Solve for HR's total cost and allocate this to the janitorial, metal, and chrome departments. This amount will be more than the $200,000 department costs. Then allocate the new total in janitorial to HR, metal, and chrome departments. At this point, all costs will be allocated to production departments only.

	HR Department	Janitorial Department	Metal Department	Chrome Department
Costs	$200,000	$80,000	$400,000	$100,000
Step 1	($218,379)	$36,397	$145,586	$36,397
Step 2	* $18,379	($116,397)	*$73,514	*$24,505
	0	0	$619,100	$160,902

* Slightly off due to rounding

Although the reciprocal method is a true recognition method and provides the most accuracy, it is rarely used because of the complexity of its calculations and because the step-down method provides a more cost-effective and reasonable approximation of costs. Computer programs make the reciprocal method easier to calculate, but most companies still do not use it.

Phase 3: Allocate production department costs to products.

This phase has already been covered under the various costing methods described in this section.

Progress Check

Directions: Read each question and respond in the space provided. Answers and page references appear on the following page.

1. Which of the following is often changed on a day-to-day basis?

   ( ) a. Fixed overhead cost priorities

   ( ) b. Variable overhead cost priorities

   ( ) c. Plant-wide overhead rate

   ( ) d. Departmental overhead rate

2. A company has two products—one that is labor-intensive and one that is highly mechanized. Which of the following rates for overhead allocation would be best for this firm?

   ( ) a. Departmental overhead rate

   ( ) b. Activity-based costing overhead rate

   ( ) c. Plant-wide overhead rate

   ( ) d. Departmental rate for the mechanized process and plant-wide rate for the rest of the plant

3. Which of the following allocates service department costs sequentially to both production and other service departments, starting with the department that provides the most services, and finishes in a single pass (does not allocate costs to items higher in the sequence)?

   ( ) a. Direct method

   ( ) b. Step-down method

   ( ) c. Reciprocal method

   ( ) d. Indirect method

Progress check answers

1. b (p. 2-121)

2. a (p. 2-123)

3. b (p. 2-128)

Information Management

Section overview

The advent of computers first allowed individual systems to be automated, such as creating a general ledger database, but the information was still passed on to different departments manually. Such systems were then integrated and the data managed on an enterprise-wide level. This section covers information systems, their types and uses, the design of an information system, basic forms of networking, database basics, forms of artificial intelligence, and forms of electronic commerce.

Learning Outcome Statements

The Certified Management Accountant (CMA) test is based upon a series of Learning Outcome Statements (LOS) developed by the Institute of Certified Management Accountants (ICMA). The LOS describe all the knowledge and skills that make up the CMA body of knowledge, broken down by part, section and topic. The CMA Learning System (CMALS) supports the LOS by addressing all the subjects they cover. Candidates should use the LOS to ensure that they can address the concepts in different ways or through a variety of question scenarios. Candidates should also be prepared to perform calculations referred to in the LOS in total or by providing missing components of a calculation. The LOS should not be used as proxies for exact exam questions; they should be used as a guide for studying and learning the content of the CMA Learning System and ensuring that you can accomplish the objectives set out by the LOS.

The LOS included in the CMALS books are the comprehensive set, current as of the date of publication. Candidates can access the IMA Web site at www.imanet.org and click on the Certification section to locate and download a Portable Document Format (PDF) file of the current LOS.

Learning Outcome Statements

Part 2: Management Accounting and Reporting — Section C. Information Management

Part 2 — Section C1. Nature and Purpose of an Information System

- LOS 2.C.1.a—Identify the different types of business information systems, for example, transaction processing, management information, decision support, and so on.

- LOS 2.C.1.b—Explain the functions of information systems, including business processing and data analysis.

- LOS 2.C.1.c—Differentiate between centralized and decentralized information systems and identify the advantages and disadvantages of each.

- LOS 2.C.1.d—Identify and define the two basic ways that transaction processing systems process data: (i) batch processing and (ii) real-time processing.

- LOS 2.C.1.e—Explain how information systems are used for competitive advantage in organizations by solving temporal and financial problems.

Part 2 — Section C2. Systems Development and Design

- LOS 2.C.2.a—Explain why end users and information technology specialists should design information systems based on an analysis of an organization's business processes and information requirements and that the business process should be well defined and documented.

- LOS 2.C.2.b—Define a systems development life cycle (SDLC).

- LOS 2.C.2.c—Outline the steps of an SDLC and explain how they are related.

- LOS 2.C.2.d—Define prototyping as a systems development tool and demonstrate when prototyping techniques are preferable to traditional SDLC techniques.

- LOS 2.C.2.e—Define rapid application development (RAD) tools.

- LOS 2.C.2.f—Define object-oriented analysis and design (OOAD).

- LOS 2.C.2.g—Demonstrate an understanding of systems feasibility studies—for example, cost/benefit analyses, which include both tangible and intangible benefits.

- LOS 2.C.2.h—Identify the tangible and the intangible benefits of a cost/benefit analysis.

Part 2 — Section C3. Technology of Information Systems

- LOS 2.C.3.a—Identify the advantages of using telecommunications systems, which allow companies to move data from distant points and process information on a global basis at multiple locations, generally at relatively low cost.

- LOS 2.C.3.b—Demonstrate an understanding of the different types of communications networks.

- LOS 2.C.3.c—Describe a wide area network (WAN) and a local area network (LAN).

- LOS 2.C.3.d—Demonstrate an understanding of client/server networks.

- LOS 2.C.3.e—Define "peer to peer" networks.

- LOS 2.C.3.f—Identify where on a client/server network software applications generally reside and where databases generally reside.

- LOS 2.C.3.g—Distinguish between mainframe systems and client/server applications and identify the advantages and disadvantages of each.

- LOS 2.C.3.h—Demonstrate an understanding of a database management system and describe its characteristics.

- LOS 2.C.3.i—Distinguish between a flat database and a relational database.

- LOS 2.C.3.j—Demonstrate an understanding of a relational database system.

- LOS 2.C.3.k—Demonstrate an understanding of Decision Support Systems, how they operate, and the types of decisions that these systems support.

- LOS 2.C.3.l—Define artificial intelligence, including expert systems, fuzzy logic, and neural networks. and explain how they can capture management reasoning in software.

- LOS 2.C.3.m—Demonstrate how to use a spreadsheet for business analysis, planning, and modeling.

- LOS 2.C.3.n—Construct a spreadsheet used for accounting, business reporting, or analysis purposes.

- LOS 2.C.3.o—Analyze the details of a spreadsheet report and determine which formulas are causing errors, and how to correct the formulas.

- LOS 2.C.3.p—Describe the Internet and identify the components of the Internet's backbone.

- LOS 2.C.3.q—Define browser software.

- LOS 2.C.3.r—Define the term intranet and explain its uses.

- LOS 2.C.3.s—Identify how intranets enable companies to share expertise among the organizational units.

- LOS 2.C.3.t—Define a virtual private network and identify how it can be used.

Part 2 — Section C4. Electronic Commerce

- LOS 2.C.4.a—Define and identify the major characteristics of Electronic Data Interchange (EDI).

- LOS 2.C.4.b—Explain how EDI differs from Internet-based electronic commerce applications.

- LOS 2.C.4.c—Define public key cryptography and identify how it is used within networks.

- LOS 2.C.4.d—Define business-to-business (B2B) commerce and its characteristics.

- LOS 2.C.4.e—Summarize the importance of the Internet for business-to-business (B2B) commerce.

- LOS 2.C.4.f—Demonstrate an understanding of how business-to-business (B2B) electronic commerce has affected the supply chain.

- LOS 2.C.4.g—Demonstrate an understanding of other e-commerce technologies, including Online Transaction Processing and Electronic Funds Transfer.

Part 2 — Section C5. Integrated Enterprise-Wide Data Model

- LOS 2.C.5.a—Define enterprise-wide planning (EWP) and its characteristics, including its reliance on an enterprise-wide database.

- LOS 2.C.5.b—Explain why business processes must generally be reengineered and highly integrated to utilize ERP.

- LOS 2.C.5.c—Describe an enterprise-wide database (data warehouse).

- LOS 2.C.5.d—Define data mining.

- LOS 2.C.5.e—Demonstrate an understanding of how data warehousing facilitates data mining.

- LOS 2.C.5.f—Define data marts.

- LOS 2.C.5.g—Define object-oriented databases.

- LOS 2.C.5.h—Demonstrate an understanding of how Structured Query Language (SQL) is used to retrieve, update, and append information to a relational database.

- LOS 2.C.5.i—Define online analytical processing.

Nature and Purpose of an Information System

Topic overview

This section identifies the different types of business information systems and the audiences that primarily use them. These audiences can be types of job roles, such as middle managers or knowledge workers, or they can be departments or business functions. This section also explores how information systems process data.

Business Information Systems

Figure 2-44 on the next page shows the four basic levels of business information, starting with the most refined knowledge at the strategic level (high-level, long-term analysis and decision making) and proceeding to day-to-day record keeping and reporting at the operational end of the spectrum. The numbers of users of the information grows at each level, with very few users at the top of the hierarchy and many users at the bottom. Business information systems are also targeted to the major business functions of an enterprise, such as sales or accounting, and each area usually has software that supports each level, from strategy to operations.

This section covers the basic levels, basic types, and business functions of business information systems (BIS).

Strategic level

Strategic-level systems help executives lead the company over the long term. Such systems provide information on the internal strengths and weaknesses of the firm as well as its external threats and opportunities. Executives can use these tools to help them match their internal strengths with the best available external opportunities, thus forming the strategy of the company.

Strategic-level systems focus on long-term plans (for example, five-year plans) such as product planning, capital budgeting, or staffing.

Figure 2-44: Levels and Types of Business Information Systems

Level	Groups Served	Types	Examples
Strategic	Senior managers	Executive support systems (ESS)	Five-year planning tools (sales trends, operating plans, budget forecasts), profit planning, personnel planning
Management	Middle managers	Management information systems (MIS)	Inventory control, master budgets, capital budgets, sales management, accounting information systems (AIS) summary level
		Decision support systems (DSS)	Production scheduling, product costing, pricing and profitability analysis, sales region analysis
		Expert systems (ES)	Capital budgeting, risk analysis, portfolio management
Knowledge	Knowledge and data workers	Knowledge work systems (KWS)	Workstations (engineering, graphics, managerial)
		Office systems	Word processing, document imaging, date planning and electronic calendars
Operational	Operational managers; department employees	Transaction processing systems (TPS)	Accounting: payroll, A/P, A/R Finance: securities trading, cash management, AIS transaction level Sales and marketing: order tracking and processing Operations: plant scheduling, machine control, and material movement control Human resources: compensation, training, employee record keeping

Executive support systems (ESS)

Executive support systems (ESS) are designed to help executives make strategic, nonroutine decisions by placing the information they need at their disposal. Such systems do not make decisions themselves or solve specific problems but assist the executive in making his or her own decisions. ESS will gather information from decision support systems and management information systems for internal information, plus information from external sources such as new financial reporting requirements or information on competitors. ESS provides relevant information because it filters, aggregates, and tracks critical information, reducing the time required to review all of the data. The information is also presented using advanced graphics, tables, and charts to highlight the significance of the information. ESS provides reliable information because it gets internal real-time information from the other systems in the company and external real-time information from trusted external sources such as Dow Jones, Standard & Poor's, the Gallup Poll, and Internet news feeds.

Unlike decision support systems, ESS does not make much use of analytical models. A model is an abstraction that codifies a process or event into simplified instructions and decision points so that a computer can perform the task. Analytical models attempt to codify decisions requiring higher levels of thinking. Executive-level decisions cannot be defined within a model because executives face varied problems requiring human judgment. Therefore, ESS systems are designed primarily for information synthesis and leave the decision making to the executive.

Management level

Management-level systems help middle managers monitor and control the activities of their employees. These systems also help middle managers make decisions and perform administrative tasks. Most management-level systems provide periodic reports rather than real-time information. These reports help the manager decide whether projects are on budget, such as highlighting exceptions to expected results. Some systems also simulate possible results of various projections—they ask "what-if" questions such as what would be the result of adding a new product line to existing production capacity.

Management information systems (MIS)

Management information systems (MIS) are software designed to provide managers with reports and often online access to real-time business records. Most MIS are internally oriented and provide no access to external information. MIS get information from the company's transaction processing systems and aggregate the information in order to facilitate planning, control, and decision making. Such information could be drawn from multiple departments and databases. For example, an accounting information system (AIS) has MIS features such as forecasts, budget information, and totals per account for management analysis but gets its data from transactional level AIS and other databases, such as a report that integrates actual sales data from the general ledger and master budget data to compare actual to planned results. MIS reports are generally not daily reports but weekly, monthly, and annual reports. Most MIS reports are predefined reports issued on a regular basis, but managers can often define ad hoc reports as needed (and can save these new report types as additional standard reports). MIS can also refer to the information technology (IT) department at an organization, but this is a different type.

Decision support systems (DSS)

Whereas MIS are primarily devoted to historical reporting, decision support systems (DSS) help middle managers make analyses of both internal and external information. Internal information comes from transaction processing systems and from MIS. External information can be information such as stock prices, competitors' prices or discounts, and shipping rates. DSS help solve problems that do not have a predefined procedure and that require fast solutions in a rapidly changing environment. DSS often have preconstructed analytical models that compare various business relationships and generate financial ratios. DSS also aggregate data and present it in a graphical format. Many DSS allow users to generate their own analyses, gather their own sets of data, and ask new questions of the database (ad hoc queries). Decision support systems also include specialized databases, interactive computer-based modeling processes, and the decision maker's own insights and judgments.

DSS are also discussed in Topic 3 of this section, "Technology of Information Systems."

Expert systems (ES)

Expert systems (ES), a variation on artificial intelligence, involve the programming of experts' analytical processes so that these processes can be used to help others make decisions.

Knowledge level

Knowledge-level systems allow knowledge and data workers to collect and integrate new knowledge into the firm. Data workers use these systems to simplify and monitor the flow and amount of paperwork.

Knowledge work systems (KWS)

Knowledge workers are professionals with a degree in their field, such as doctors, lawyers, engineers, scientists, and researchers. A knowledge work system (KWS) is a system specialized in helping each type of professional create new information. For example, an engineering design workstation collects new knowledge from the various engineers and ensures that it is integrated with other engineers' work.

Office systems

Office systems aid knowledge workers and data workers in gathering and processing data. Data workers are employees who primarily process information rather than create it, such as office managers, bookkeepers, and clerks. Office systems are a broad category of software applications covering communications and internal coordination between employees and activities, such as word processing, desktop publishing, document imaging systems (converting paper documents into electronic format), electronic scheduling, Web pages, and e-mail systems.

Operational level

Operational-level systems allow operational managers to record and track the relevant information for their department, such as sales, payroll, credit, invoice receipts, deposits, and all other relevant transactional data. Such systems are often integrated to minimize the redundancy of information. For example, the credit, sales, and customer support databases will all use the same customer information database instead of separately maintaining individual databases that could then differ. Operational-level systems are used in every aspect of the business, from financial reporting to inventory tracking.

Transaction processing systems (TPS)

A transaction processing system (TPS) fulfills a basic business function or functions, such as tracking inventory movements, making journal entries, or scheduling production. Transaction processing systems can be the best-of-breed or enterprise resource planning (ERP) types. Best-of-breed systems, such as Hyperion's suite of accounting information systems, focus on one area of business such as sales and attempt to be the most thorough or industry-specific in their field. ERP systems attempt to be a universal solution for all areas of business in order to achieve close integration and efficiency among business units. A TPS both records data and performs predefined transactions that are structured as the company sees fit. For example, management will decide on whether to use LIFO,

FIFO, or another inventory valuation method, and the system will be set to track inventory in this manner.

A typical TPS is a series of interlaced databases, with the lowest level of information called a data element (for example, customer name or customer address). Data elements are updated as needed and can be combined with other elements to create any type of report or record needed. A payroll database will track payments made, allocate funds to a tax withholding account, and mail paychecks to employees. The five most basic functions of business are all represented by TPS systems: accounting, finance, sales and marketing, operations management, and human resources. In an ERP system, each of these categories is usually called a module. As stated earlier, TPS data is the primary source of information for other database systems. TPS is often so vital a part of a firm that businesses spend vast amounts of money and time setting them up, and if they fail for any length of time, the business itself could fail.

TPS can be a batch processing system or an online input and processing system (also called a real-time processing system).

Batch processing. Batch processing systems accumulate and store transaction input information in groups or batches until a predefined time when the groups or batches are placed into the database and the relevant records are updated. Some batch processing occurs nightly in order to free up daytime processing for other uses. Other batch processing occurs as soon as a certain amount of data is collected. Yet another method is to have the batches update the system according to some business cycle, such as performing a monthly closing of books and preparation of financial statements. Batch processing transactions are accumulated in a transaction file, which is periodically transferred to a master file that contains the permanent information.

Batch processing is common in older systems but is being steadily replaced by online processing because companies need access to more relevant information. For example, in a batch processing system, if two salespersons are selling a product, they both may check the inventory database and see there is only one unit left, and then both may sell it to a different customer, creating a back order issue and a failed promise to deliver. An online system, on the other hand, would record the item as sold and remove it from inventory as soon as the first salesperson entered the sale in the database.

Online (real-time) processing. An online or real-time processing system is the most common type of TPS and continues to gain in usage over batch processing. In online processing, users enter transactional data and the relevant databases are immediately updated as soon as the transaction is saved. Online processing makes use of bar code scanners, magnetic ink character recognition (MICR), and other devices to directly update the database as an activity is performed. Online processing using such devices is more efficient and less prone to user errors.

Business function support

Each of the systems described above is used to support the basic business functions of accounting, finance, sales and marketing, operations, and human resources.

Finance and accounting support

The finance function manages the sources and uses of assets, liabilities, and equity. The finance function arranges for equity (stock issuance) and debt (loans, commercial paper) financing. Financial assets such as cash, stocks, and bonds are managed primarily for preservation of capital and secondarily for return on investment. Capital budgeting and capital investing are also part of the finance function. Financial and accounting software keeps records on all financial transactions such as receipts and disbursements. Financial software is often used for exception reporting (highlighting deviations from planned results). The financial data from other systems or modules is imported into the finance system. For example, payroll information is imported from the human resources system and operational costs are imported from the operations management system.

The finance function determines the opportunity cost of funds, market rates, and market values from external sources and tracks internal information in its general ledger and subsidiary ledger accounts. Finance and accounting software will perform many tasks automatically that used to be very time-consuming physical tasks, such as allocating depreciation or overhead costs.

Accounting functions include accounts receivable and credit, accounts payable, and the general ledger and supporting ledgers. Financial reporting is an output of the finance and accounting functions.

Sales and marketing support

Sales information systems support contacting customers, selling products or services, taking sales orders, and providing sales follow-up. Sales systems track products by product code or possibly a unique identifier such as a bar code. Product descriptions and amounts sold are also tracked. Such systems are usually linked to the inventory system, the finance system (for example, credit function), and the marketing system. Marketing information systems support marketing functions such as identifying and targeting customers, advertising, and collecting both customer information and customer product preferences.

Operations management support

Operations management systems plan, schedule, monitor, and control the production of goods or services. Such systems also include planning new production facilities and setting operational budgets. They include product design and computer-aided design (CAD), materials resources planning (MRP), production planning, and all categories of inventory such as raw materials inventory. Operations management links with finance for recording purchases and assets, with human resources for direct labor costs, and with sales forecasts to determine the amount and type of goods to produce.

Human resources support

The human resources (HR) system supports all personnel functions from recruiting, hiring, training, payroll, and benefits to career development, outplacement, and termination or retirement. The HR system also provides long-term personnel planning. HR tracks prospective employee applications and resumes and often contains a sorting feature and allows HR administrators to advertise for positions. Some firms set up detailed compensation levels and salary grades. The HR function also can be used to set up events and company outings. The payroll portion of HR is usually kept separate from the rest of HR functions for control purposes. HR links to any department that has employees.

Figure 2-45 shows how each function of business contains various types of business information systems.

Figure 2-45: Business Information Systems by Business Function

Business Function	BIS Level	Examples of Use
Finance	Strategic	Executives perform capital budgeting, set long-term investment goals, and generate long-range forecasts.
	Management	Financial MIS tracks and controls the allocation of an entity's resources; financial DSS evaluates specific investment opportunities to help select the best investment at an appropriate risk level. Expert systems (ES) evaluate capital expenditures portfolios and perform risk analyses.
	Knowledge	Analysts use analytical models and workstations to design the right portfolio of investments.
	Operations	Fund flows are controlled using built-in checks and balances.
Sales and marketing	Strategic	Executives follow internal and external evidence (e.g., competitor information) of trends, including sales and new opportunities.
	Management	Managers use MIS to monitor sales, make pricing decisions, and plan advertising; they use DSS to perform market research and analyze individual and overall sales performance.
	Knowledge	Knowledge and data workers generate and publish competitive and other marketing information in marketing analysis workstations.
	Operations	The sales force and the marketing department enter prospective customers, manage customer lists, contact customers, track sales, and process orders. Customer service is a direct user of the data.
Operations	Strategic	Executives use operations management systems to determine long-term plans and set production goals (including capital investment).
	Management	Managers use MIS to monitor and control production tasks and costs; they use DSS to analyze the efficiency of steps and activities to determine which add value to a product or service.
	Knowledge	Knowledge and data workers create and disseminate designs and manufacturing expertise throughout the organization.
	Operations	Line managers use materials resource planning (MRP) to generate lists of needed resources. Data including time, employee number, and inventory status are entered using data entry, bar codes, and fully automated machines.
Human resources	Strategic	Executives analyze staffing needs on a long-term basis, such as long-term plans for costs, number of positions, position types, training, skill, and education level needed.
	Management	Managers use MIS systems to monitor and control costs and payroll; they use DSS systems to analyze recruitment, employee movements, and compensation.
	Knowledge	Knowledge and data workers use HR systems to design jobs, career paths, and training as well as create reporting hierarchies.
	Operations	HR TPS tracks entries for recruitment, new hires, benefits, garnishments, training, placement, terminations, and all other employee transactions.

Progress Check

Directions: Read each question and respond in the space provided. Answers and page references appear on the following page.

1. Which of the following information systems is most likely to automatically generate predefined reports on a periodic basis?

    ( ) a. Knowledge work systems

    ( ) b. Management information systems

    ( ) c. Office systems

    ( ) d. Decision support systems

2. Which of the following system levels would include a human resources job designing workstation?

    ( ) a. Knowledge level

    ( ) b. Strategic level

    ( ) c. Operational level

    ( ) d. Management level

Match the following information system levels to the types of systems included in each level. (Some levels will have more than one type.)

3. _____ Strategic level   a. Office systems

4. _____ Operational level   b. Executive support systems (ESS)

5. _____ Management level   c. Knowledge work systems (KWS)

6. _____ Knowledge level   d. Management information systems (MIS)

                                       e. Transaction processing systems (TPS)

                                       f. Decision support systems (DSS)

Progress check answers

1. b (p. 2-139)

2. a (p. 2-140)

3. b (p. 2-137)

4. e (p. 2-140)

5. d, f (p. 2-139)

6. a, c (p. 2-140)

Systems Development and Design

Topic overview

Information systems are created to solve organizational problems or to take advantage of new opportunities. This topic covers the systems development life cycle and cost-benefit analysis of information systems.

Systems Development Life Cycle (SDLC)

Most computer-based information systems are conceived, designed, and implemented using a systematic development process. Systems development is a structured set of activities designed to create an information systems solution to solve organizational problems or generate opportunities. The process of developing a software package or purchasing the appropriate application software is called the systems development life cycle.

Companies often form an information technology (IT) steering committee not only to perform the first steps of a systems development process but also to monitor ongoing controls in the IT area. An IT steering committee is a group of executives representing the firm's primary functional areas. It is appointed by (and reports to) senior management, and it oversees all normal control functions surrounding the IT function and coordinates strategic and organizational IT processes. Because this committee oversees all IT projects, it helps decide how to allocate resources to various IT projects. It will provide assistance in both setting requirements for user information and providing such information to systems development teams. The committee will hear the recommendations of each individual IT project team and either accept or reject it (or will select between two or more equivalent options presented).

Traditional systems development life cycle (SDLC)

The traditional systems development life cycle (SDLC) divides systems development into sequential portions that must be completed before the next step can begin. This traditional process results in a division of labor that keeps most tasks in the hands of information system specialists and limits end users to providing system requirements and reviewing the system specialists' work.

The traditional process is still used in many large implementation projects that have huge project teams and an even larger user base. The process stresses process control, creating formal specifications and paperwork, and has the advantage of allowing end users to continue their work with little interruption until the conversion process. However, the limitations of the traditional process are that it is costly because it takes a long time to implement and it cannot adapt to newly required changes without great expense. Because the process is sequential, specifications are frozen relatively early in the process and codified into many volumes of documentation. If the specifications must be changed later due to a software upgrade or design flaw, the changes become very expensive because the massive specifications must be redone. Therefore the traditional process often creates a dilemma: Adopt the original plan even though it is not the best solution, or greatly increase the cost and time of implementation.

Alternate SDLC

Several alternate systems development life cycle models exist. For example, some SDLC processes still have most activities occur in sequential order but plan for some repeated steps and some simultaneous steps. Another method, called prototyping, builds a fast experimental system that allows end users to have more interaction with the proposed product so that it can be better tailored to the organization's needs. Simple information systems can be developed by end users, called end-user development. Such projects use a software development tool that simplifies the development process. These projects allow very fast development time, but the firm may have less control over the result and different employees may make conflicting systems. Other firms out-source the entire information system function, where the hardware, software, and staff are all externally operated and controlled.

SDLC steps

The steps in the systems development life cycle are systems analysis, systems design, programming and testing, conversion/implementation, and production and maintenance. Because most firms do not create custom business software but instead purchase it and customize it to their needs, the programming and testing steps are often replaced by a request for proposal (RFP), selection of an application software package, and customization of that package. Figure 2-46 illustrates the SDLC.

Figure 2-46: The Systems Development Life Cycle

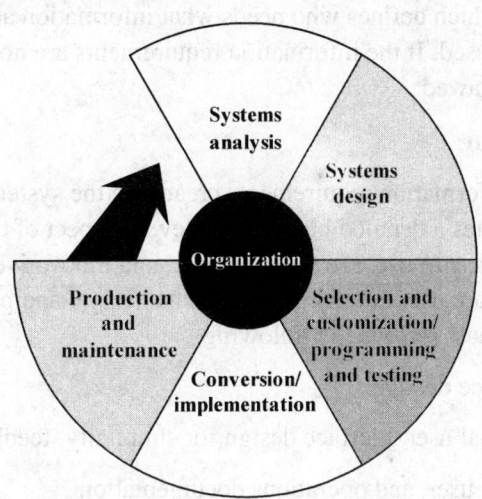

Step 1: Systems analysis/needs assessment/feasibility study

Step 2: Systems design

Step 3: Selection and customization or programming and testing

Step 4: Conversion/implementation

Step 5: Production and maintenance

Systems analysis/needs assessment/feasibility study

Before creating or purchasing a software solution, a firm must take the time to understand its problems (and their causes) or what needs must be met. This process is alternately called a systems analysis, needs assessment, or feasibility study. After analyzing their problems and needs, the company must explore alternate solutions, determine their feasibility, and identify specific data requirements for the system.

A systems analyst or team starts by defining the firm's current practices and business processes, software and hardware, and the parties involved in each process. The IT steering committee may be involved in the strategic phase of this step. The analyst interviews end users and balances their needs with the needs of top management and the IT steering committee. The new process should meet company strategy and remove any steps that do not add value to the final product or service. The systems analysis often reveals that software is only a small part of the solution to a problem and organizational or procedural changes will be needed if the change initiative will be a success.

The systems analysis report includes a feasibility study for each alternative solution presented. The feasibility study incorporates a cost-benefit analysis, looks at the likelihood of technical success, and judges whether the organizational culture can accept the change.

Once a basic solution is chosen, the systems analyst prepares a detailed set of information requirements, which defines who needs what information and how it will be gathered, organized, and used. If the information requirements are not properly chosen, the systems design will be flawed.

Systems design

Based on the information requirements created in the systems analysis step, the systems design step creates a detailed blueprint for every aspect of the proposed system. A good design will be easy to use, efficient, reliable, and innovative. The three major activities of systems design are user interface design, data design, and process design. The design specifications must include the following.

- User interface design:

  - Graphical user interface design for simplicity, feedback, logic, etc.

  - System, user, and operations documentation

  - Input and output methods and timing (for example, bar codes, data entry)

- Data design:

  - Database design (for example, processing requirements, organization, logic data model)

  - Input, output, processing, and storage controls (for example, passwords, character limits, consistency, totals for comparison)

  - Security (for example, audit trails, disaster recovery plans, backups)

- Process design:

  - Manual and electronic procedural steps (for example, who, when, and how; required reports and computations)

  - Required organizational changes

  - Conversion schedule and training methods

End users need to have a major role in defining their business needs because the technical staff may otherwise implement a system that works but does not satisfy the firm's business needs. End-user involvement also boosts acceptance of change, which is a major hurdle to overcome for all change initiatives. Both managers and end users must be convinced to accept change, or unfamiliarity will breed fear, workarounds, and managerial power struggles that can doom a project.

Programming and testing; selection and customization of an application software package

Some companies still develop their own software because they are in an industry that has no ready-made solution to their needs. However, because software programming and testing is extremely time-consuming and expensive, it is usually more cost-effective to purchase an application software package. This is especially the case because custom software often needs to be upgraded, so the costs of bringing in software programmers periodically for an in-house package is never-ending, plus the proprietary program might not be understood by other vendors if the original vendor goes out of business. Therefore, most software is developed by professional software firms.

The programming step of software development involves translating the detailed specifications developed in the systems design step. The testing step involves a great deal of time and many testers. Each transaction must be tested many times under different situations. Furthermore, since the only way to test many business applications is to create test data, the setup and organization of testing can be time-consuming in itself. After each round of testing, the results are reviewed and another round of programming ensues.

Testing has three types: unit testing, system testing, and acceptance testing. Unit testing tests each separable portion of the program by itself. Because it is virtually impossible to remove all bugs from a program, unit testing focuses on finding ways to make a program fail and preventing these events from occurring. System testing tests the program as a whole to see if its various components work together and if they work at the speed that is needed. Acceptance testing is a management and end-user review of the system to see if they will be satisfied with how the program works.

A testing strategy could include an integrated test facility (ITF), which creates a dummy entity in a database to process test transactions simultaneously with live input and can be used to incorporate test transactions into a normal production run of a system. Its advantages are that the testing does not need separate test processes and that it uses the actual system being tested. However, careful planning is needed and test data must be isolated from production data.

An ITF is also considered a useful audit tool (see part 1, section C, "Internal Controls") because it uses the same programs to compare processing using independently calculated data. This involves setting up dummy entities on an application system and processing test or production data against the entity as a means of verifying processing accuracy.

The majority of corporations purchase **application software packages**, which are preprogrammed, pretested software applications that meet business needs. Because most corporations have similar processes such as finance, material requirements planning, or inventory, a general package can be used outright or customized to fit for less than a proprietary system. Software vendors will provide upgrades and support for less than the cost of a proprietary system. Moreover, if a company's vendors and wholesale customers use the same software, they can often integrate shared services electronically and speed up transaction times.

Selection of an application software package starts with the same first steps of the systems development life cycle: systems analysis and systems design. After this step, the company will submit a request for proposal (RFP) to all software vendors that appear to meet their needs. The RFP will contain their detailed information requirements and their proposed system design. The vendors will reply, showing how their software meets each of the business needs. The process is a difficult negotiation.

Customization is a feature in many application software packages that allows the software to be modified to perform different business steps as required by the special needs of the firm. Most customizable software does not actually reprogram the software but changes internal system parameters (i.e., turning on and off selections—a process that still often requires a professional). If a package is customized extensively, the cost of the software will grow exponentially, because when it is time for a software upgrade all of the customizations must be repeated for the new version. Customization can be a hidden cost not seen in the initial price of the product.

Conversion/implementation

Whether a software package is purchased or created internally, the conversion or implementation process must be performed when the software is ready to be used. The conversion process involves change management, planning conversion, preparing documentation, and training end users and technical support staff.

Change management prepares an organization for changes and helps identify resistance to change early so it can be dealt with.

Conversion planning involves determining when and how to adopt the new system. It can be done in one of four ways: direct cutover, parallel strategy, pilot study, or a phased approach.

- **Direct cutover**

  Direct cutover is simply choosing a date to turn off the old system and turn on the new system on the "live date." Such a method is risky because the system may not work properly or users may not be properly prepared. In either case, a loss of productivity for an entire work force costs a great deal of money each day.

- **Parallel strategy**

  A parallel strategy keeps the old system running while the new system is brought up. End users will have more work because they will be required to make the same entry in each system, but at the end of the trial period, the integrity of the system can be seen by comparing output (for example, comparing the general ledger balance in both systems).

- **Pilot study**

  A pilot study introduces the new system to a controlled group who proves that the system works before it is released to the entire end-user base. This method could still have some of the risks of a direct cutover, especially with end-user preparedness.

- **Phased approach**

  A phased approach has multiple "live dates" for different phases of the software implementation. Each area can then receive the benefit of increased individual attention from managers and technical staff. The phases could be determined by functional area, such as human resources, or by geographic area, such as headquarters first. Such staggered implementations increase the overall time and cost of implementation but may result in a smoother transition.

Preparing documentation is necessary because it is the updated blueprint for the software, it contains all the methods used to implement customizations, and it serves as the basis for creating training materials.

Training and involvement of end users and technical support staff is expensive yet necessary for the success of a project. If users do not know how to do their jobs after conversion, the initiative will fail and all prior costs will be a loss. Companies often underbudget for training needs. Training is logistically expensive (for example, lost productivity) and requires extensive lead time for material development, and software changes will require changes in training materials.

Production and maintenance

Production is the "live" stage of a system, when it is actually being used to perform the work it was created for. This stage may involve a series of modifications to improve efficiency and system capability. The system performance will be compared to what was planned or promised, and, if a vendor is involved, the project will not be signed off as complete until the company is satisfied that the vendor has fulfilled its contractual commitments. When this process is formalized, it is called a post-implementation audit. After the audit clears up any remaining contractual requirements, any additional changes will be the responsibility of the corporation.

The maintenance phase of a system involves continuous assessment and improvement of the system to correct errors, add features, or increase efficiency. Maintenance includes changing hardware, software, procedures, or documentation as needed.

Cost-Benefit Analysis

Whether application systems are developed in-house or purchased from a vendor, they are always expensive and many implementations do not live up to their promised results or fail entirely. A system that is both well designed and implemented correctly can lower a firm's costs and increase its profit margin or allow the firm to lower its prices accordingly and increase or maintain its market share. When deciding whether to implement a particular information system, the costs and the benefits must be analyzed to determine if and when the project will pay for itself.

When making a cost-benefit analysis, firms estimate the total costs, tangible benefits, and intangible benefits of each project they are considering. Note that the time frames for benefits and costs must be equal (for example, five years of benefits and five years of costs), though in some of those years the costs or benefits could be zero. After placing a value on the intangible benefits for estimation purposes, analysts will use various financial ratios to determine the overall value of the project to the firm. Ratios used include the payback method, return on investment, the cost-benefit ratio, net present value, the profitability index, and the internal rate of return. These ratios are discussed more fully in Part 1 of the *CMA Learning System*, Section E, "Financial Statement Analysis," and Part 3, Section E, "Investment Decisions." The cost-benefit ratio is provided below as an example:

$$\text{Cost-Benefit Ratio} = \frac{\text{Total Benefits}}{\text{Total Costs}}$$

Costs

The costs for a system project start with the tangible direct costs such as the price for a software package as quoted in an RFP or an internal estimate of software development costs. If not included, firms must also consider hardware, service, telecommunications, customization, training, evaluation, and maintenance costs. Also, the costs for late changes to design can be significant, so the analysis phase should assume a certain amount of modification will be necessary and add a cost for this. As stated earlier, the cost of lost productivity, learning curves, or training must also be accounted for. Also the true costs of a project more often than not overrun the costs that were budgeted, so some allowance for this fact must be made in the analysis phase.

Tangible benefits

The tangible benefits of a system are generally seen only in comparison to the cost of using the current system, in the form of cost savings. Tangible benefits are any benefits that can be assigned a reliable monetary value, including cash savings or increased cash flows. A marketing system that reaches more people at the same cost as the old system will produce a tangible increased cash flow. Tangible benefits include:

- Lower operational costs.
- Lower outside vendor costs.
- Lower administrative and professional costs.
- Lower computer maintenance costs.
- Work-force reduction.
- Reduced rate of expense growth.
- Reduced plant costs.
- Increased productivity.

Intangible benefits

Intangible benefits are any benefits that can be perceived but no monetary value can be easily placed on the benefit. Intangible benefits must be listed and some value or weighting should be applied to them in order to include them in the cost-benefit analysis. Intangible benefits include:

- Fit with strategic plan.
- Faster organizational learning.
- Increased use of assets.
- Better job satisfaction.
- Increased control of resources.
- Improved organizational planning and control.
- More and/or faster information.
- Regulatory compliance.
- Better corporate image.
- Increased customer or client satisfaction.
- Improved decision making.

Cost-benefit example

Assume that a retail store wants to replace its old cash registers with a point-of-sale (POS) system that tracks purchases and saves customer information. The manager begins the analysis by determining specific costs.

New POS system hardware and software (total $40,000):

- 8 network-ready POS terminals with software: $3,000 each
- 1 server: $4,000
- 8 printers: $500 each
- Cables and installation: $3,000
- Sales-tracking database software: $5,000

New POS system training (total $21,500):

- Employee training: 16 employees at $1,000 each
- Database manager training: 1 employee at $4,000
- Manager training: 3 managers at $500 each

Other costs (total ~$24,000):

- Lost sales: ~$5,000
- Lost work hours: 50 person days at $140/day ($7,000)
- Slowed sales due to learning curve for new system: ~$6,000
- New-hire costs for database manager: $6,000

Total costs: $85,500

The manager then estimates all tangible and intangible benefits:

- Reduced cost of marketing mailings due to increased customer knowledge: ~$15,000/year
- Increased ability to manage sales process: $10,000/year
- Increased efficiency for processing one sale: $0.05/sale at ~240,000 sales/year = ~$12,000/year
- More accurate customer information: ~$4,000/year
- Better management and fraud prevention: ~$24,000/year
- Improved customer service and retention: ~$15,000/year
- Better corporate image: ~$16,000/year

Total benefits: $96,000/year.

The cost-benefit ratio for the project is:

$$\frac{\$96,000}{\$85,500} = 1.12$$

For the first year, for every dollar invested in the project, the firm will earn a return of $1.12. Because the estimates used to make the ratio are subjective, the same person or team should make estimates of other prospective projects in order to ensure some consistency to the estimates.

Progress Check

Directions: Read each question and respond in the space provided. Answers and page references appear on the following page.

1. Which stage of the systems development life cycle creates a detailed blueprint for items such as the user interface and the conversion schedule?

   ( ) a. Selection and customization of an application software package

   ( ) b. Conversion/implementation

   ( ) c. Systems analysis

   ( ) d. Systems design

2. Which stage of the systems development life cycle involves submitting an RFP?

   ( ) a. Selection and customization of an application software package

   ( ) b. Conversion/implementation

   ( ) c. Systems analysis

   ( ) d. Systems design

3. Which of the following strategies will generate approximately twice the amount of work for data entry personnel during the conversion process?

   ( ) a. Direct cutover

   ( ) b. Parallel strategy

   ( ) c. Pilot study

   ( ) d. Phased approach

Progress check answers

1. d (p. 2-150)

2. a (p. 2-150)

3. b (p. 2-152)

Technology of Information Systems

Topic overview

This section covers basic information about computer networking, database basics, decision support systems (DSS), business intelligence and other expert systems, spreadsheets, and the Internet.

Data Communications, Networks, Client/Server Systems

Computers are classified as mainframes, midrange computers, personal computers (PCs), workstations, and supercomputers. A **mainframe** is a very large computer that handles all the processing for multiple substations. Mainframes used to be the primary method of business information processing but are now isolated to specific industries needing to process mass data (or are used as servers for some firms).

A midrange computer is either a minicomputer or a server. **Servers** are specialized computers designed to handle requests from multiple PCs linked to them. Servers are specialized for particular tasks such as a file server or a Web server. A company will often have multiple servers or use out-sourced servers that are grouped together and called server farms. A workstation is a PC specialized for a task such as graphics.

A supercomputer is a class of computers where the highest price is paid for the highest performance and capabilities (i.e., applications requiring vast data-processing capabilities such as weather prediction, genome decoding, or military applications).

Computer networks and the client/server model

The combination of computer systems with telecommunications allows companies to move data from distant points, generally at lower costs. This is the basis for computer networks. While mainframe computers use centralized processing, meaning that one large central computer handles all processing tasks, computer networks use distributed processing. **Distributed processing** is when the processing tasks are shared by all computers on the network so that no one computer gets bogged down processing data. The **client/server model** is a distributed processing network that shares processing between clients (PCs) and servers, assigning functions to each machine that best fits its capabilities.

Client/server computing

In client/server computing, the client provides the user interface and some application functions, while the server stores the mass amounts of data, some application functions, and all network resources.

The ratio of how much processing is placed on clients and how much is placed on servers is a continuum. Some client/servers place most of the load on the client, meaning most application functions reside on the client and the PC is responsible for most of its own processing needs. Other client/servers place most of the load on the server(s). The form of distributed processing that places the most processing power in clients is called peer-to-peer computing. Individual PCs linked to each other may not even have a server at all but share data between each other and over the Internet. Peer-to-peer applications called grid computing take over a small amount of unused processing power from each PC to form a large amount of processing power overall.

Applications that reside mostly or entirely on the server are called thin clients (as opposed to client-only applications, which are called fat clients) and are accessed through a Web browser on the client machine. These applications have the advantage of containing all program files in one place for easy maintenance and upgrades (client machines will automatically feel the effect of changes). Server-heavy processing models sometimes replace PCs with network computers, which are scaled-down PCs with minimal memory and processing capabilities. Network computers are becoming less common as PC prices fall, since a network computer is dependent on the server to function but a PC can function without the server.

Local area networks (LANs) and wide area networks (WANs)

Networks that have a set geographic scope are classified as either local area networks (LANs) or wide area networks (WANs). Most LANs and WANs use a client/server model.

LAN. A LAN is a geographically isolated network of PCs and servers confined to one area, such as a building or two that are close together, usually not more than 2,000 feet apart. LANs transmit high amounts of data at high transmission speeds, allow administrators to access PCs on the LAN for maintenance or software upgrades, and are commonly used to share access to peripheral devices such as printers. Servers on the LAN can set access privileges and control external access to the system through a gateway, which is a processor that translates the protocols of dissimilar networks to enable communications. Servers also provide internal and external network security. Servers use network operating systems (NOSs) similar to PC operating systems.

Wireless LANs transmit data over radio waves and can be cheaper than the cost of physical wiring, so these technologies have grown in use. However, transmitting data wirelessly carries the risk that the data could be intercepted by unintended recipients or disrupted by interference.

WAN. A WAN is similar to a LAN except that it is designed to be operated over greater distances, from miles to around the planet. WANs can be made up of switched and dedicated communication lines, microwave, and satellite communications. Switched lines are shared communications lines such as phone lines. Dedicated lines are communication lines that are always available and dedicated to the company's use for a flat fee. WANs exist to keep individual corporations networked together, such as a corporate intranet. Some companies have a WAN that out-sources most of the equipment and software to a telecommunications vendor.

Communications networks. A plethora of communications modes exists to power LANs, WANs, and simple Internet access for others. Methods include the following.

- **Ethernet/Fast Ethernet:** Ethernet is a LAN transmission method that transfers 10 megabits per second (Mbps); Fast Ethernet is a newer standard that carries 100 Mbps.

- **Wireless:** A variety of radio transmission methods that allow computers to send and receive data while physically disconnected from a network.

- **T1:** A dedicated phone connection that transfers data at 1.544 Mbps.

- **Cable:** A broadband Internet connection sent through co-axial TV cables at about 1.5 Mbps.

- **Digital subscriber line (DSL):** A broadband telephone line network that keeps all data digital instead of converting it to analog, thus allowing bandwidths from 128 Kbps to 6 Mbps, depending on the number of users sharing the service.

- **Phone connection:** A narrow-band method of sending and receiving data over phone lines using a modem on each end; becoming obsolete due to faster methods available.

Network topology. Network topology refers to the physical configuration of the computers and servers in a network. Common types include the following.

- **Ring network:** A network that needs no central server because all devices are connected in a ring, meaning that there are two paths any message can travel to get to its destination; can travel long distances because each device repeats the message. A token ring network is a common type.

- **Star network:** A network with a central hub that receives and transmits messages to their proper places. Star networks have no redundancy in message paths but require no other connections between individual end points.

- **Bus network:** All devices are attached to a central network wire or distribution channel, called a bus; the simplest and most common type of LAN topology.

Virtual private network (VPN). A virtual private network (VPN) is a less-expensive alternative to a WAN that uses Internet technology to provide secure intranet communications over the public Web. Many employees who work from home use VPNs. A VPN can be set up through an Internet service provider (ISP) and can also provide low-cost telephone communications because the call is routed to a local ISP, where it travels without long-distance charges. VPNs work using one of several encryption protocols, including Point-to-Point Tunneling Protocol (PPTP), which encrypts data in packets and wraps them in standard Internet Protocol (IP) packets. (IP packets are the standard method of sending data through the Internet.) Because of this security, VPN has become a critical tool for moving data over the Internet. VPN enables many types of business transactions over the Internet that were previously impossible or were too expensive due to the cost of proprietary hookups. VPNs are also called value-added networks (VANs).

Database Management Systems

In the traditional applications approach to data, data was considered a necessary element of each application and data files were designed in a supporting role for that application only. Any place where two applications needed the same data was a source of redundancy. The same record would need to be stored several times (once for each application) and would therefore require multiple updates for a single change, increasing the chance that data errors would occur. Furthermore, data was not shareable among applications due to differences in data layout. These issues led to the separation of data from the applications using the data, which allows the programs to be developed for the user's specific need without having to be concerned with data capture problems. Requiring all applications to use the same source of data also means that applications will communicate in like terminology with each other.

A **database** is a centralized collection of data on a computer that minimizes data redundancy and is organized to provide data as needed by one or more software applications. A centralized database is a database designed to act as a central repository for all applications at a particular entity. There are two basic types of data, source data and reporting data. Source data comes either from a company's legacy systems (applications programmed using the traditional applications approach to data) or data generated by newer applications using a centralized database. Reporting data is data that is generated using the source data and comes from performing transactions and analyzing the source data.

A **database management system** (DBMS) is the software that organizes a database and allows other applications and end users to access the data. Data in a database can be organized by any number of logical views but has only one physical view. A physical view is the actual arrangement of data in the database. A logical view is any way of organizing the data as specified by an application program or an end user. Thus the information can be presented in any order or at any level of aggregation. A data element is any field or single entry in a database, such as First_Name.

A database management system has three components:

- The **data definition language** is a programming language used to create the database's content and structure. It includes a tag uniquely identifying each data element in the database.

- The **data manipulation language** is a simplified language used by end users and software programs to request (or query) information. It manipulates information in the database. Structured Query Language (SQL) is the most common data manipulation language; it can be used by both end users and software applications.

- The **data dictionary** is an automated or manual file recording all of the details of a data element, including who is responsible for maintaining it, who and what programs have access to it, what reports it is included on, and other individual characteristics.

These three components are used to create and manage the database. The data dictionary is useful for both end users and technical staff. For example, if end users are changing a report or technical staff is changing a program, they could use the dictionary to see which other reports or programs will be affected by the change.

Entity-relationship (E-R) diagram. A primary step in creating any type of database is constructing an entity-relationship (E-R) diagram. A database designer such as a systems analyst creates these detailed and logical diagrams to ensure that all of the data works well together. An E-R diagram is a graphical representation of an organization's or business area's entities such as salespersons or inventory, their associations, and their data elements. An entity, represented in the diagram as a square, is anything that data is collected for, such as an agent, an object, or an event. Agents are involved persons such as customers, salespersons, or vendors; objects are items such as inventory, cash, or company trucks; events are transactions such as orders, purchases, or sales. Some objects, agents, and events are not entities for purposes of E-R diagrams because they do not contain any data elements. For example, the company itself is a system consisting of the entities in the diagram and therefore should not be included in the diagram.

The E-R diagram graphically shows the relationships, or associations, as diamonds connecting entities. These relationships can exist between two events (for example, in Figure 2-47, purchase order and receiving), between an object and an event (for example, inventory and purchase order), or between an agent and an event (for example, vendor and receiving). Note that in a real system many more entities and relationships would exist. Ideally, all functions of an enterprise would be integrated to form a comprehensive system such as found in enterprise resources planning (ERP) systems, which are discussed in Topic 5 in this section.

Figure 2-47: Entity-Relationship Diagram for Automated Reordering of Inventory

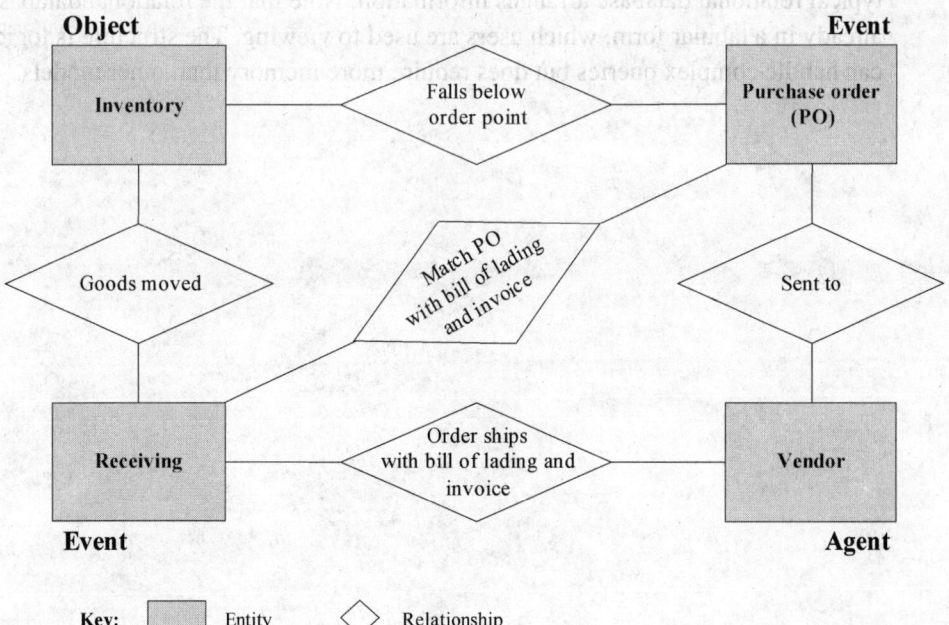

Once a database design team has completed an E-R diagram or the conceptual model of the process flows, the next step is to determine the type of DBMS to use.

DBMS types

Database management systems are divided by how they store and access data, called the logical design for the database. The logical design includes how data items are defined, how items are grouped, and the relationships between the data items. Logical database models include relational, hierarchical, network, and object-oriented.

Relational DBMS

A relational DBMS is the most popular type of DBMS for PCs as well as larger computers and mainframes. Data elements are stored in two-dimensional files called tables. Tables are files set in identically structured rows. (Figure 2-48 on the next page has an order table, a part table, and a supplier table.) When using an entity-relationship diagram, each entity would become a separate table. Each row is a record or individual file. However, unlike a traditional filing system, users can combine information from multiple tables and view a virtual table containing only the pertinent data. The data in one table can be extracted and used in another table whenever each table shares a common data field. Therefore the data in one table can be easily combined with the data in other tables, such as if one table for employees with an employee number field were combined with a table for payroll information that contains the same employee number field. Furthermore, a third table that shares an element with the payroll table, such as a tax table with a common tax withholding field, could also be combined to create a report that combined personnel information, payroll information, and tax information. Common relational databases include Oracle® and Microsoft Access®. Figure 2-48 shows how a typical relational database arranges information. Note that the relational database is already in a tabular form, which users are used to viewing. The structure is logical and can handle complex queries but does require more memory than other models.

Figure 2-48: Relational Data Model

Columns (Fields)

	Order_ Number	Order_ Date	Delivery_ Date	Part_ Number	Part_ Amount	Order_ Total
Order	10034	06/05/06	06/25/06	2245	8	64.80
	10035	06/15/06	07/02/06	1575	9	447.75
	10036	06/16/06	07/03/06	1949	5	276.95

Rows (Records, Tuples)

	Part_ Number	Part_ Description	Unit_ Price	Supplier_ Number
Part	1575	Tennis balls	49.75	48235
	1949	Racquet balls	55.39	25331
	2245	Golf balls	8.10	47432

	Supplier_ Number	Supplier_ Name	Supplier_Address
Supplier	48235	Connor Inc.	101 Jonquil Lane, Lakeville, ND 55044
	25331	OCR Inc.	21035 Howland Avenue, Pine River, TX 33756
	47432	Nicholas Corp.	Route 46, Sandy, UT 89703

Hierarchical and network DBMS

Hierarchical DBMS is an older DBMS structure that resembles a tree. A root is the highest level of the hierarchy, and the levels below it are called segments. At any particular level, the segments are called children and the element above them is called the parent. In such a parent-child relationship, a parent can have many children, but a child can have only one parent, so only a vertical relationship (one-to-many) can be made between elements. Thus a specific customer parent could have an order history child, a credit rating child, and a discounts child. Figure 2-49 shows how a hierarchical DBMS is set up.

Figure 2-49: Hierarchical Database

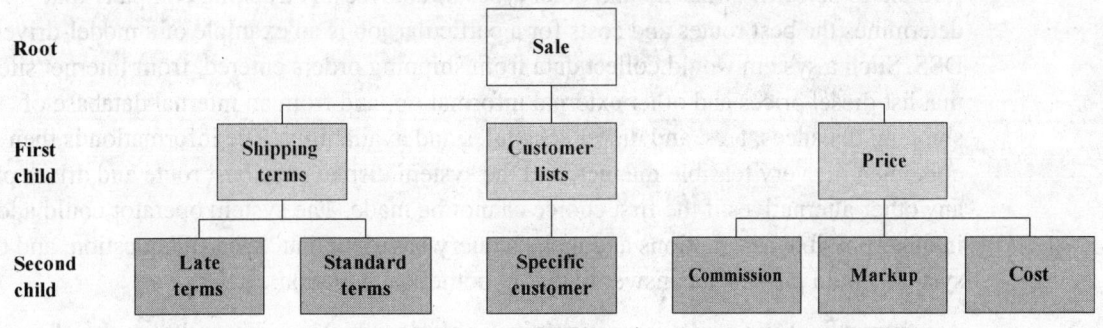

A network DBMS uses a hierarchy and a parent-child relationship similar to a hierarchical DBMS, except that the child can have many parents (a many-to-many relationship). Figure 2-50 shows how a network DBMS can have multiple parents.

Figure 2-50: Network Data Model

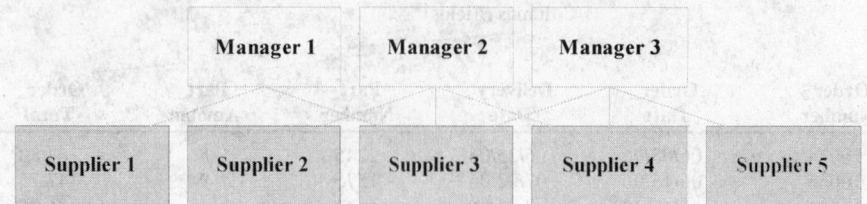

Object-oriented DBMS

Object-oriented DBMS (OODBMS) are designed to process not only alphanumeric data but also java applets, graphics, audio, and video recordings. While relational databases cannot handle such items without extensive programming, every type of data in an OODBMS is considered an object and can be automatically retrieved.

Decision Support Systems (DSS)

A decision support system (DSS) differs from the other type of management tool, a management information system (MIS), in that DSS is designed to provide fast and flexible information for extraordinary situations and analysis for management control choices, while MIS provides standard periodic reports, exception reports, and other structured information flows. DSS is not designed for structured information flows but for unstructured and semistructured problems. An unstructured problem has no predefined solution, and a semistructured problem has some definable elements and some elements that must be defined when the query is made. DSS allows for ad hoc reports, which are queries that are partly or entirely made at the time the report is needed instead of being structured and scheduled in advance. The two basic types of DSS are model-driven and data-driven.

Model-driven DSS

Most model-driven DSS are stand-alone systems that are developed using a data model or formula to perform "what-if" and other types of analyses. A trucking company that determines the best routes and costs for a particular job is an example of a model-driven DSS. Such a system would collect data from shipping orders entered, from Internet sites that list diesel prices and other external information, and from an internal database of shipping distances, fees, and driver schedules and availability. The information is then combined in every feasible manner, and the system displays the best route and driver plus any other alternatives if the first choice cannot be made. The system operator could add in other possible assumptions and make a query based on that "what-if" question, and the system would provide an answer to that hypothetical situation.

A common analysis model is a **sensitivity analysis**, which combines the results of many "what-if" questions, each with a slight variation, to determine the effect of each change. For example, if two parameters are changed, the result would be a table (often presented in an electronic spreadsheet) that listed one variation on the x-axis and the other on the yaxis, with the results listed in the table. The best result can be chosen from each of the many calculations.

Data-driven DSS

Data-driven DSS are used in large corporations that have vast databases. They extract data requested by users and combine it for analysis and decision making. Data from multiple transaction processing systems (TPS) is often first combined in a data warehouse.

The data in the data warehouse is analyzed by data-driven DSS using online analytical processing. **Online analytical processing (OLAP)** is a form of multidimensional data analysis, meaning it allows data to be analyzed from more than two dimensions or perspectives. (See Topic 5 in this section for more information on OLAP.) For example, an OLAP query could compare the actual to budgeted amounts for a particular cost object broken down by department and over a particular duration of time. In other words, OLAP and data-driven DSS allow managers to get just the information they need for a particular question without having to analyze multiple reports. However, the manager must know the question in order for this method to work. Data mining, a technique included in data-driven DSS, allows users to find relationships that are not obvious.

Business Intelligence, Artificial Intelligence, and Expert Systems

Business intelligence and artificial intelligence (AI) are business tools that capture management reasoning in software, including expert systems.

Business intelligence

Business intelligence applications are software applications that help users make decisions by gathering, saving, and analyzing information from multiple internal and external sources. Executive support systems and DSS are forms of business intelligence. Business intelligence stresses fast access to information from multiple sources and is therefore often based on a Web browser, assembling daily information defined by the user. Such Web-based business intelligence software is often called a portal. A portal might assemble the company's and its top competitors' information on the same page with a graph or pie chart.

Artificial intelligence

Artificial intelligence (AI) is any computer-based system that is intended to mimic human choices or behaviors. Speech, robotics, and perceptive systems are all part of AI, but this section confines itself to fuzzy logic, neural networks, and expert systems. These types of business-specific software are designed to capture management reasoning, to create an organizational memory (active memory preserving the expertise of a firm's employees), and to analyze problems that require vast numbers of calculations and vast amounts of data (things a human cannot do in a reasonable amount of time). AI systems used in business are commonly called expert systems (ES).

Fuzzy logic

Fuzzy logic attempts to design software that will make judgment calls, tolerating imprecise data or data from multiple sources. Traditional computers can make only a yes or no or other binary decision, but fuzzy logic is formed with rules that operate over ranges or subjective values.

Traditional computer programs use if-then statements, such as if x equals 1, then open valve A. Fuzzy logic adds nonspecific terms called membership functions to such statements to allow them to solve problems that must have room for error or constant correction. For example, a membership function in an if-then statement for a fuzzy logic clothes dryer could be if the clothes are nearly dry, then reduce the temperature. Such systems often have multiple membership functions, which are called so because they define membership in a category such as nearly dry. Several other factors, such as clothing type, efficiency, or drying speed, could be added, and the fuzzy logic would use programmers' rules to combine these elements and make the correct (most similar to a human) choices about how to best dry the clothes.

Fuzzy logic requires fewer if-then rules to work than traditional programming because programmers do not need to tell the computer what to do in every possible situation that could occur. These systems are cheaper to program, require less memory, and function faster, so they have gained in popularity in the U.S. and especially in Japan. Fuzzy logic has been used in Japan to make subway trains speed up at a rate that keeps passengers from feeling an abrupt jerk. Air conditioners have been programmed with fuzzy logic to reduce energy consumption while providing the same level of service. Fuzzy logic is used to make management decisions on a broad scale, such as checking every medical claim for possible fraud or evaluating stocks for potential investment.

Neural networks

A neural network is a software and hardware system that mimics the learning capacity of the biological brain. Unlike other forms of AI such as expert systems, neural networks are not designed to mimic the behavior of a particular expert or manager but to learn on their own how to solve issues that involve weighing numerous factors. A basic brain cell, or neuron, includes a controlling agent (like an on/off switch) called a soma. The point of contact between two neurons is called a synapse.

Neurons all work in parallel with one another, thus solving a problem much more quickly than if each possibility were tested in sequence. When the brain has a question to answer, each neuron tests possible answers, and the ones that get the answer wrong have their synapses weakened while the ones that get the answer right have their synapses strengthened. Learning is achieved through the strengthening/weakening effect.

To emulate this learning pattern, a neural network uses transistors (on/off switches) or groups of transistors (microchips) as artificial neurons and variable resistors for the synapses. A variable resistor is a device that can vary the level of power being sent through a wire, which is how a neural network mimics the brain's ability to learn (lowering resistance for positive results and increasing resistance for negative results). As with the brain, each artificial neuron works in parallel to test multiple variables simultaneously.

Neural networks are used for business situations that are not clear-cut, such as whether to extend credit or make a particular stock investment. Neural networks are used to detect patterns in large amounts of data, such as detecting credit card fraud or face, voice, and handwriting recognition. Such networks are also being used in medicine and science as well. One medical neural network called Papnet is used to examine Pap smears for cervical cancer. The system rapidly screens Pap smears for possible abnormal cells, providing ten times the accuracy of a manual method. The smears are still checked by humans, but the process is more thorough and less time-consuming.

Expert systems

Expert systems are designed to codify in a software program the knowledge of an expert in a narrowly focused field such as determining a company's credit rating or predicting bankruptcy.

Unlike a neural network, an expert system is given a set of discrete rules to follow when sorting through data. For example, when predicting bankruptcy, the expert system may have rules for each financial ratio, such as the return on investment ratio must be above X. These rules use the if-then programming format discussed earlier, except that the rules are exact: If net income is greater than X, then perform step A. While most programming languages and therefore most software use something akin to the if-then methodology, expert systems are more thorough and have far more such rules, called a rule base. While a standard program might have, say, 100 such rules, an expert system could have up to 10,000 rules, depending on the body of knowledge to be emulated. For this reason, expert systems need to be highly specific. The rules in an expert system are not sequential, but many of the rules are performed simultaneously and many routes can be taken to arrive at the same finite number of results.

Expert systems can be created for almost any narrowly defined business system requiring judgment calls that can be specified by an expert but have shown best results for automating repetitive clerical tasks or providing support such as checklists for service employees. Managers have much greater and more diverse sources of information and diverse problems, and expert systems have so far been unsuccessful in emulating such activities.

Expert systems do not learn. To adapt to changes, they must be reprogrammed with the new factors, and this process can be time-consuming and expensive. Also, expert systems cannot be used for situations that do not result in predefined solutions. Very often, it is less expensive to hire an expert on staff to make complex decisions than it is to spend the effort building and maintaining an expert system.

Spreadsheets

Spreadsheets can be physical or electronic. Electronic spreadsheets duplicate the functions of the accountant's calculator and spreadsheet grid. The most popular spreadsheet software includes Microsoft® Excel and Lotus 1-2-3. Such spreadsheet programs are more powerful than physical spreadsheets because they allow users to automatically apply math functions to columns or rows, such as sums, subtotals, and many other higher math functions. Spreadsheets allow data to be rearranged into different views and compared in different ways. Many of the reports generated in information systems are presented in simple spreadsheet formats so that the report user can manipulate the data as needed.

Internet and Intranet

The Internet is unique compared to other communication technologies in that no one owns the Internet itself. The **Internet** is a network of networks allowing global communications. An **intranet** is a private Internet system run by corporations for internal communications.

Internet

The Internet started in 1969 as a military research project, e-mail was developed in 1972, and in the early 1980s the Internet became a part of the public sector. In 1990, Tim Berners-Lee invented a common way for using hypertext links. Hypertext links instantly transfer a user from one Web site to another. Berners-Lee later led the foundation of the World Wide Web Consortium (W3C), the group that governs many of the standards required to run the Internet.

Other inventions that made the Internet possible include software portability and network and socket programming. Software portability makes Web sites readable by otherwise incompatible operating systems. Network and socket programming makes finding a Web site and using a hypertext link possible and fast. The fast spread of the Internet was caused by the proliferation of inexpensive and powerful PCs and the increase in telecommunications bandwidth.

The physical network that moves the massive amounts of data is called the **Internet backbone**. The Internet backbone consists of several high-capacity communications hookups, such as Internet service providers (ISPs), using fiber-optic cables, linked in a world-wide network. Each major city in America and most major cities through the world are sites for these hubs.

The key to the Internet is information. Information can now be distributed for free or at a very low cost. Vendors can keep their prices and product lists available for customers 24 hours a day and can update these prices at will, instead of being able to change prices only each time they print a new annual catalog. In addition to reducing publication costs, transaction costs and delivery times can also be reduced, especially for products and services that are entirely digital, such as downloading software or accessing a credit report.

The Internet allows information on physical products to be unbundled from the products themselves. Consumers can access a Web site any time and comparison-shop between features and prices (much cheaper than having to travel to each physical showroom). Thus the Internet is changing (and sometimes disrupting) the way traditional companies do business, since if a Web shopper is comparing items and the traditional company has no Web presence, it is likely that they will not get the sale.

The EDGAR database on www.sec.gov is another example of the power of the Internet. This database contains public filings of financial statements for all companies required to file with the SEC. Prior to this service, to obtain such records you would need to write to the SEC and wait for the copies.

The key drawback to the Internet is that it provides access to a company's servers, possibly resulting in malicious attacks, information theft, or other harmful results. Companies therefore encrypt data going over the Internet, set up protections such as firewalls to block unauthorized users and viruses, and set up other security measures. Security is covered in Section C of Part 1 of the CMA Learning System.

Internet assurance services

Real or imagined concerns for the security of Internet-based transactions have historically been a damper on the growth of e-commerce. Many companies have turned to Internet assurance services to test and assure both the security and reliability of the firm's business Internet connections. Assurance is a broad term that includes audits and, according to the American Institute of Certified Public Accountants (AICPA), "Independent professional services that improve information quality or its context." For a fee, an auditor will provide limited assurance that users of a client's Web site will be reasonably secure and e-commerce tools will be reliably accessed. This may entail testing multiple intermediaries, such as network providers and vendors, as well as multiple means of access, such as different browsers. Assurance also commonly requires companies to disclose on their site their business practices for conducting e-commerce.

Additionally, the same or a separate company or association may provide certification of a site's security and reliability. For example, the WebTrust Seal of Assurance is a joint certification offering from the AICPA and the Canadian Institute of Chartered Accountants (CICA). Once an accounting professional gives a site or e-commerce application an unqualified opinion, they are eligible to receive the WebTrust seal to display on their site. The seal has a self-verifying link to prevent unauthorized use. Such certifications must be renewed periodically for continued relevance. Note that Web assurance does not require the use of a CPA or CPA organization.

Intranet

Intranets are identical to the Internet except that they are a network of networks for the sole use of a corporation and its constituents. The primary advantage of an intranet is that it allows a company's many different computing platforms and databases to share data simultaneously without creating a translation program for each different system. Intranets use browsers to allow anyone with security clearance to access company information, post messages on electronic billboards, see prices in a product catalog, search through the company's online database, or use employee self-service technology to fill out a timecard, select benefits, or change personal information.

Intranets feature multimedia displays, such as a video of the CEO giving a speech or a live Web broadcast of a company-wide meeting allowing thousands of end users to view the speakers and ask questions over the Web without ever leaving their desks. Creating a new space for company gatherings, company news, and internal job offers can have an intangible benefit of boosting employee morale and sense of community.

Another cost-saving feature of using an intranet is that directories, phone lists, catalogs, and other information sources can be updated quickly and with little expense compared to publishing the same information on paper. Thus these sources of information are more likely to be up-to-date. Simply moving a corporate newsletter to an intranet saves money in printing and mailing costs. Increased collaboration can also decrease costs by spurring innovation in cost reduction and increased productivity. Many companies have shown a return on investment of their intranet of 23% to 85%, and a few companies have shown exponential returns (Laudon, 2003).

Finance and accounting staff can use an intranet to integrate data from various systems such as the general ledger, annual reports, and the budgeting process when these systems do not otherwise communicate with each other. The intranet helps sales staff out in the field; with access to the Internet and a password, they can view updated prices and sales data, communicate with management, and post orders. Companies have aided the production department using an intranet, such as supplying the profit and loss information on daily operations or giving each production machine a Web site that contains error counts, products produced, and other real-time updates.

Browser software

Browsers read information on the Internet that is posted in languages such as Hypertext Markup Language (HTML), Extensible Markup Language (XML), and Java applets. These languages are designed to be read by any browser on any type of operating system. In business today, browsers are becoming the most-used computing tool to interface with virtual private networks (VPNs), intranets, communication tools, and thin client software applications. A browser and the Internet have also greatly increased the speed of performing research.

Progress Check

Directions: Read each question and respond in the space provided. Answers and page references appear on the following page.

1. Which of the following database management systems (DBMS) can handle and search for a video presentation or a picture as if it were any other type of data?

   ( ) a. Relational DBMS

   ( ) b. Hierarchical DBMS

   ( ) c. Object-oriented DBMS

   ( ) d. Network DBMS

2. Which of the following is true of the various forms of artificial intelligence?

   ( ) a. Expert systems learn.

   ( ) b. Neural networks learn.

   ( ) c. Fuzzy logic requires more coding than traditional software.

   ( ) d. Neural networks use sequential processing.

Progress check answers

1. c (p. 2-166)

2. b (p. 2-168)

Topic 4 — Electronic Commerce

Topic overview

Before the Internet, the only electronic commerce that existed was between proprietary and expensive links. With the Internet, business links are easy to form, stable, and very inexpensive. The transaction costs for traditional versus Internet-enabled transactions are hardly comparable. For example, a phone call to a customer service center costs the company approximately $10 to $45 (in direct labor and overhead), but an e-mail answer costs the company only $1 to $5 and Web self-service costs from 10 to 20 cents (Laudon, 2003).

Using Internet technologies to make payments is also cheaper for both parties, but because the payments arrive sooner than standard mail would take, the sending company misses out on the mail float. Mail float is a delay that entails an opportunity cost of funds, so the payor usually negotiates a discount for early payment when switching to an electronic payment method.

*Electronic commerce (**e-commerce**) is any monetary transaction, sale, or business document transfer traveling over electronic means. One of the oldest but still widely used methods of e-commerce is electronic data interchange (EDI). Business-to-business (B2B) technologies are also discussed in this topic, as well as other e-commerce technologies such as online transaction processing (OLTP) and electronic funds transfer (EFT).*

Electronic Data Interchange (EDI)

Electronic data interchange (EDI) is a highly formalized and structured method of joining two businesses for electronic document transfers. EDI allows two companies to exchange business documents and transaction information in the exact format specified by each party. EDI transmits documents such as invoices, purchase orders, or bills of lading. Originally, EDI was performed solely through proprietary links between two businesses. Both businesses needed to agree on what proprietary software to use. Now EDI usually functions through a third party that handles all of the data translations more efficiently and at less cost. EDI is also frequently performed over the Internet using a virtual private network. The Internet has lowered the cost of EDI so that even small businesses can use it.

EDI differs from e-mail because the forms used to transmit data are formalized and contain standard fields for particular types of data. Because EDI is standardized, companies must make their forms comply with this format. (This comes into account when designing a new information system that will use EDI.) EDI is therefore more secure than e-mail because the fields can be used to verify that the transmission is authentic. When combined with an electronic payment of funds, EDI is used to verify the amount and timing of the funds transfer.

Business-to-Business (B2B)

Business-to-business (B2B) e-commerce is the movement of business transactions between two or more businesses, including sales on the Internet. B2B connects companies with vendors and intermediaries in their industry. Several cooperating entities often band together to form a private industrial network over an extranet. A B2B extranet, private exchange, or private industrial network is a secure network made up of several entities that wish to trade with one another, usually operated through a value-added network (VAN) but owned by the buyer. A VAN is a service company that provides data transmission, extranets, EDI translation, and storage and retrieval of electronic data. A private industrial network provides corporate customers with real-time information on products and prices, allowing the company to reduce its customer representative interactions and costs. Similarly, buyers can also reduce their costs of obtaining information. Private industrial networks focus on continuous coordination and improvement of business processes.

All of the benefits listed for EDI also apply to B2B transactions, since EDI is one of the methods available for conducting B2B. Use of the Internet to facilitate interactions means that small businesses can afford to become B2B partners. Moreover, a private industrial network can be even more advantageous than a pure EDI system because of its emphasis on continuous improvements, its access to multimedia and information databases, and its sharing of product design and development, marketing, inventory management, production scheduling, and secure e-mail.

Another form of B2B is called a net marketplace or an e-hub. A net marketplace is a digital market that links many buyers to many sellers. This concept differs from a private industrial network in that those networks have only one buyer to many sellers. Net marketplaces are either owned by an industry association or are independent entities that act as intermediaries. Some net marketplaces can feature online bidding or auctions, others have fixed prices, and others allow businesses to post requests for quotations (RFQs). Net marketplaces can be classified as those that sell direct goods and those that sell indirect goods. Direct goods are direct materials such as parts and raw materials used directly in the production process. Indirect goods are materials used outside the production process, such as office supplies or tools for repairs. Some net marketplaces support vertical supply chains (for example, the house construction industry), and others support a horizontal market across many industries (for example, shipping). An exchange is a type of net marketplace that connects buyers and sellers for immediate needs (spot purchasing). One example of an online B2B exchange is www.rosettanet.org.

Other E-Commerce Technologies

This section covers online transaction processing (OLTP) and electronic funds transfer (EFT).

Online transaction processing (OLTP)

Online transaction processing (OLTP) is any method of computing that processes transactions as soon as users submit them (as opposed to batch processing). OLTP works effectively because it performs all or a substantial amount of the processing at the client

(PC), the point of entry. This minimizes the traffic sent over the network but requires that transactions be split up into client-side activities and server-side activities. Therefore, OLTP requires that other clients on the network be updated with the changes to the database, a potentially time-consuming event. For example, in the case of an automated teller machine (ATM), when a user withdraws cash, the system updates all other ATMs with the user's new balance. Such data replication functions ensure that current data is available to users.

OLTP is a mainstay of database engineering, allowing users to generate real-time ad hoc reports and update the database with transaction information such as a sales transaction reducing finished goods inventory. OLTP is also a standard part of other common transactions such as processing credit card approvals.

The primary benefit of using OLTP systems is that the transaction database is kept current. The primary drawback of OLTP is that high traffic from multiple transactions can bog down a system or cause it to crash unless it is designed to handle such traffic. Some systems are able to remain stable, but the traffic level still causes the processing time for transactions to be a long wait, especially for complex reports. Other systems are designed to be fault-tolerant (through hardware and software redundancy) so as to avoid system crashes when the system is vital (for example, air traffic control computers).

Systems that do need to be up and running most of the time but do not need to be entirely crash-free can be set up for high-availability computing. High-availability computing involves software and hardware controls designed to back up work continuously and get a system quickly running again after a crash. Such systems use load balancing, mirroring, and clustering as well as a disaster recovery plan to give systems that use OLTP high availability. Load balancing distributes transaction processing among many servers to keep one server from sharing too much of the processing load. Mirroring is establishing a clone of a server that can take over the duties of the primary server when the primary server crashes. Clustering is chaining together two or more computers to act as back-up units or perform parallel processing. A disaster recovery plan is an organizational and technical plan for restoring service quickly in the event of a crash.

Electronic funds transfer (EFT)

Electronic funds transfer (EFT) is a general term for various methods of transmitting payments and payment-related information electronically. EFT and financial EDI are subsets of EDI and are distinguished from EDI in that they involve the actual transfer of value. EFT differs from financial EDI: EFT is performed only between two banks or a Federal Reserve Bank; financial EDI can be between banks and companies or between two or more companies. Companies still use EFT but arrange such transfers through their bank branch. The primary forms of EFT are the automated clearing house (ACH) and wire transfers. Other forms include electronic checks, electronic lockboxes, and electronic cash. The Electronic Funds Transfer Act of 1978 defines the rights and responsibilities of EFT services (the act does not include wire transfers) and limits the liabilities to individuals from unauthorized transactions when using ATMs or point-of-sale (POS) terminals provided that the individual promptly notifies the bank of the problem.

Automated clearing house (ACH) is the electronic exchange of payments, financial documents, and payment information in a standardized format. ACH includes direct deposit of payroll or social security checks. Two banks set up a prearranged trading agreement. ACH is not instantaneous but involves some delay for confirmation. On the other hand, a **wire transfer** is an instantaneous and secure transfer of funds between two banks. Wire transfers cost more than ACH and are therefore used only for larger amounts when the extra transfer speed saves more than the difference in fees (the opportunity cost of funds for the approximate one-day difference). Fedwire is the Federal Reserve's wire transfer system.

An electronic lockbox is similar to a lockbox (a P.O. box that collects checks and deposits the funds directly) except that an electronic lockbox speeds payments by having the lockbox bank enter remittance advice into a database. The remittance data is transferred directly to the collector's accounts receivable transaction processing system.

Electronic checks are similar to paper checks (i.e., both include bank account number, check number, etc.) except that they incorporate a digital signature (for example, the IRS collects a prior year's tax return amount to verify authenticity). Electronic cash is a digital form of cash created by a bank in exchange for real cash. Electronic cash resides in an electronic wallet until the user pays for an online service. Upon receipt, the collector receives actual cash from the bank. Electronic checks and electronic cash are designed to give security to online transactions.

Progress Check

Directions: Read each question and respond in the space provided. Answers and page references appear on the following page.

1. Which of the following technologies allows smaller companies to participate in electronic data interchange (EDI) transactions?

    (   ) a.   The Internet

    (   ) b.   Wide area networks (WANs)

    (   ) c.   Extensible Markup Language (XML)

    (   ) d.   Business-to-business (B2B)

2. Which of the following is the most costly method of sending funds electronically?

    (   ) a.   Electronic check

    (   ) b.   Automated clearing house (ACH)

    (   ) c.   Financial EDI

    (   ) d.   Wire transfer

3. An automated teller machine (ATM) is a form of what technology?

    (   ) a.   Online transaction processing (OLTP)

    (   ) b.   Automated clearing house (ACH)

    (   ) c.   Financial EDI

    (   ) d.   Wire transfer

Progress check answers

1. a (p. 2-175)

2. d (p. 2-177)

3. a (p. 2-176)

Integrated Enterprise-Wide Data Model

Topic overview

The integrated enterprise-wide data model encompasses the ability to store and analyze all data that a company possesses by storing it in a single database. When such a repository is used only for reporting and analysis, it is called a data warehouse. Key tools such as data mining and online analytical processing (OLAP) allow this data to be made into pertinent knowledge. These core elements form the integrated enterprise-wide data model that enables companies to electronically communicate information to multiple departments simultaneously using enterprise resource planning (ERP) systems. Such systems usually include one or more software modules for each department so that the enterprise needs to purchase only certain modules, and each communicates seamlessly with the others. Simultaneous transfers of information allow different departments to begin work on an item simultaneously. For example, a customer order can query accounting and material requirements planning simultaneously.

Data Warehousing and Data Mining

Data warehousing

A **data warehouse** is a database repository of all information from each transaction processing system (TPS). It is used only for queries and analyses, not for transaction processing, so it speeds information retrieval and transaction processing by keeping queries from running on the transactional databases. Thus there are two enterprise-wide databases.

- The primary database includes the transaction processing systems that handle all of the inputs and modifications from daily transactions.

- The secondary database, or data warehouse, is created as a mirror of the primary database.

Such a separation allows complex queries and reports to be run at any time without slowing down the vital operations of the enterprise.

Data warehouses also serve as a collection point for data from transaction processing systems that are all on different and incompatible databases. This grants many of the benefits of having an integrated enterprise-wide database without the cost of creating such a database. Managers can generate complex reports and synthesize large amounts of information for decision-making purposes.

The data in a data warehouse is not real-time information, and the data is read-only. The changes in each transaction processing database that feed into a data warehouse are collected and then sent in a batch update to the data warehouse on a periodic basis, such as overnight. Thus the data may be useful for long-term planning but not as useful for a salesperson checking the inventory levels for an item to be sold. Simple queries such as inventory levels may still be performed in the transaction processing system directly if the information must be relevant.

Data warehouses include reporting and query tools as well as subsets of data called data marts. Query tools include standard reports that automatically run periodically, ad hoc reports that can be created and run anytime, and online analytical processing (OLAP) tools (discussed later in this topic) such as decision support software (DSS). A data mart is a portion of the data in the data warehouse segregated for closer analysis. A marketing data mart would contain all of the data needed for the marketing department so that their queries could be even faster and analytical programs would be able to form connections from a controlled set of data.

Data mining

Data mining is a software application that finds hidden patterns in information and then uses these patterns to create rules to predict future outcomes. It is useful in predicting future results and making organizational decisions. A data mining process creates high-level overviews of trends but allows users to drill down into the data. Many data mining applications are used to target marketing specifically to a customer's likes and dislikes. Some grocery stores use membership cards to give instant coupons and to collect data on the customer's shopping habits so that more targeted promotions can be created.

Data mining can be greatly facilitated when the operation is performed using a data warehouse. The data warehouse aggregates all of the data from all of the transactional databases that a company has, and therefore, the data mining operation can find relatively more associations when it has more information to work with. Because the mining is also occurring outside the transaction processing systems, the data analysis will not bog down these vital systems.

Data mining can be extremely useful to managers because it finds information that the managers did not even consider creating a report for. Data mining creates the following types of information:

- **Associations:** A single event triggers the same occurrences a certain percentage of the time, for example, when it is raining, sales of umbrellas goes up 25%.

- **Sequences:** Links of events over time, for example, when a car is purchased, the new owner uses the dealership oil service for the first three changes 40% of the time.

- **Clustering and classification:** Clustering groups items such as grouping customers by income level. Classification takes groups and finds patterns common to the groups, such as income-level groupings of customers who are most likely to buy a sport coupe.

- **Forecasts:** Forecasting is used for analyzing all related variables for a larger issue, such as forecasting next month's production costs or sales levels.

Online analytical processing (OLAP)

Online analytical processing (OLAP) is a form of multidimensional data analysis, meaning it allows data to be analyzed from more than two dimensions or perspectives. For example, a standard two-dimensional analysis could include sales versus sales region, while a multidimensional analysis could add actual versus budgeted sales data. Thus the spreadsheet becomes more of a cube, as shown in Figure 2-51 on the next page.

Users can rotate such a cube (called "slice and dice") to highlight different comparisons without having to submit a new query to the database. Such tools are commonly used in ERP systems for ad hoc reporting.

Figure 2-51: Multidimensional Data Model

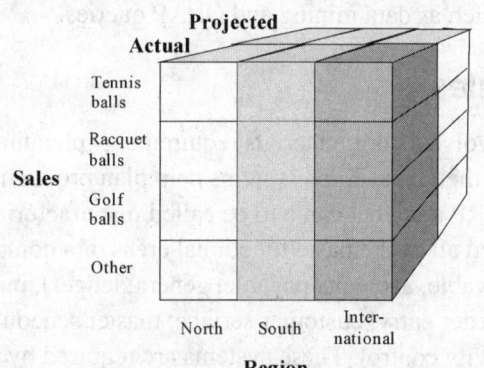

Enterprise Resource Planning (ERP) Systems

An **enterprise resource planning (ERP) system** is a suite of modules such as finance, sales, and human resources; it allows an enterprise to purchase a bundled package of applications that are seamlessly integrated to provide automated interactions and a common data source. ERP systems allow companies to avoid designing interfaces between the modules required in their business. ERP systems can link to outside software or legacy systems through an interface. Industry-specific software and best-of-breed software are also heavily used, often in combination with one of the previously mentioned ERP systems. ERP systems are expensive to purchase, implement (implementations take one to several years), and maintain, but nevertheless the majority of larger firms already have an ERP system and, due to this market saturation, ERP vendors are marketing to smaller companies.

ERP systems are basically transaction processing systems that can be customized to suit each enterprise's needs. There are limits to the amount of customization that is desirable, so most companies instituting an ERP system usually have to change some of the methods they use to do business in order to adapt to the standard processes in an ERP system. Customization has been an issue for many ERP systems, because when implementing an ERP system, many organizations had their functional areas define what each needed in a system by mapping its current and desired functionality. However, each area often added functionality but did not remove non-value-added steps or lower process complexity. Then they selected the closest ERP package and tried to customize it to exactly match each functional area's processes, even if those processes were not more efficient. In so doing, they spent 700% to 800% more than the price of the off-the-shelf software. Companies that redesigned their processes to be both more efficient and more in tune with their ERP system spent only 200% to 300% more than the price of the software and were done implementing the system sooner.

The heart of an ERP system is an enterprise-wide database: a database that stores each type of data in only one place (ideally) so that multiple records do not need to be maintained for the same data. An enterprise-wide database means that if a customer calls to change their address, only one record needs to be updated, not one for the credit department, one for the billing department, and one for the marketing department. Such a database is efficient for data manipulation and also speeds up the processing time for transactions. A duplicate of this database is also commonly kept as a data warehouse (see previous discussion in this topic). It is updated regularly and used for reporting and for analysis tools such as data mining and OLAP queries.

ERP modules

ERP systems evolved from materials requirements planning (MRP) systems and have this functionality at their core. Such systems help plan production and/or purchasing levels. Surrounding MRP are what came to be called manufacturing resource planning (MRP II), and this included all of the basic functional areas of a company: forecasting, accounting (accounts receivable, accounts payable, general ledger), purchasing, inventory management, order entry, customer service, master scheduling, standard costing, and production activity control. These systems are required by any manufacturing firm, and the integration allowed such firms to become more efficient and effective. This core of ERP serves to organize, classify, and standardize data and business processes. Finally, the term ERP came into existence when these MRP/MRPII vendors began to add non-manufacturing-specific modules such as human resources, sales and operations planning, marketing, quality management, manufacturing execution systems, advanced planning and scheduling, decision support systems, demand management, and many others.

Initially, ERP packages had proprietary code that required either using only the modules from that vendor or spending a great deal of time and money on interfaces between different systems. Upgrades in the face of prior customizations and configurations were cost prohibitive. As global and Internet-based commerce expands and firms need to work with many more partners, ERP systems also evolve so that they can connect to external systems more quickly and easily. Most interfaces are now programmed in a universally compatible language such as XML.

Over the years, ERP vendors have added more and more functionality from customer relationship management (CRM), which refines marketing tools to focus on customer needs, to supplier relationship management (SRM), which helps manage a supply chain or network of vendors including semi- or fully automated purchasing functions. While both CRM and SRM are available as stand-alone applications, when integrated fully with an ERP system, the overall CRM and/or SRM system will be more easily automated, such as telling production when to make, purchasing when to buy, and distribution when to ship (for example, after an order is taken) or allowing the customer service representative to know current inventory levels, alternate products available, and customer credit status. Other additions include custom portals and other e-commerce links to the ERP system, easier external application integration (EAI) (linking to other ERP and legacy systems), as well as collaborative planning, forecasting, and replenishment (CPFR) for group collaboration and planning with external partners.

Benefits and limitations of ERP systems

The benefits of ERP systems include that they are primarily event-driven. The system captures both financial and nonfinancial data as an event occurs (such as a sale) and moves the transaction to each affected department simultaneously. ERP systems allow a multinational corporation or a corporation that has grown through multiple acquisitions to standardize its transaction processing at each plant and facility. (ERP systems are available in multiple languages.) ERP enterprise-wide databases allow managers to improve decision making because all company data can be consolidated for reporting. ERP systems can also be expanded to provide new advantages not previously considered feasible. A properly implemented ERP system should make upper management challenge their fundamental assumptions about the business and help them see new opportunities for growth based on the visibility of information provided by the system.

The drawbacks to ERP systems include cost, which must be justified by a similar return on investment (cost savings plus direct benefits). ERP systems force companies to change processes, sometimes for the better, sometimes not. Extensive customization can avoid some of these issues, but overly customized software is expensive to create and even more expensive to upgrade. ERP implementations can fail if buy-in does not occur at all levels of an organization or if end-user training is inadequate to prepare users for the change. Using an enterprise-wide database can create its own traffic jams. Extensive transaction processing coupled with numerous report requests can slow a system down, forcing either batch transaction processing or the use of a data warehouse.

Progress Check

Directions: Read each question and respond in the space provided. Answers and page references appear on the following page.

1. Which of the following is **not** true of enterprise resource planning systems?

    ( ) a. They use bundled modules.

    ( ) b. They are best-of-breed solutions.

    ( ) c. There is no need to create interfaces between modules.

    ( ) d. They use an enterprise-wide database.

2. Which of the following is true of enterprise resource planning systems?

    ( ) a. They keep departmental databases separate.

    ( ) b. They sometimes force different plants to adopt divergent processes.

    ( ) c. Sometimes companies must change their processes to match the ERP system.

    ( ) d. It is easy to achieve a return on investment.

3. Which of the following is **not** true of data warehouses?

    ( ) a. They collect data from multiple databases.

    ( ) b. They display real-time information.

    ( ) c. The data is read-only.

    ( ) d. They keep transactions and reports from interfering with each other.

Progress check answers

1. b (p. 2-183)

2. c (p. 2-183)

3. b (p. 2-181)

Performance Measurement

Section overview

Once an organization has a master budget, it knows where it wants to be, but without feedback on where it is and where it is going, the budgeting process is almost useless. This section shows how to break down variances from the master budget into subcategories that help an organization determine the specific reasons for the variance. It also details how performance feedback from responsibility centers or strategic business units (SBUs) can help manage profitability. The financial measures of profitability used in responsibility centers and in the organization as a whole are also covered.

After covering financial measures, this section shows a balanced approach to performance measurement. The balanced scorecard measures both financial and nonfinancial aspects of an organization and is integrated with strategy so that reading the scorecard will tell anyone in the organization what the strategy is and how to attain it. Finally, this section shows how the principles of total quality management (TQM) can be integrated into all aspects of an organization to improve not only quality but also profitability.

Learning Outcome Statements

The Certified Management Accountant (CMA) test is based upon a series of Learning Outcome Statements (LOS) developed by the Institute of Certified Management Accountants (ICMA). The LOS describe all the knowledge and skills that make up the CMA body of knowledge, broken down by part, section and topic. The CMA Learning System (CMALS) supports the LOS by addressing all the subjects they cover. Candidates should use the LOS to ensure that they can address the concepts in different ways or through a variety of question scenarios. Candidates should also be prepared to perform calculations referred to in the LOS in total or by providing missing components of a calculation. The LOS should not be used as proxies for exact exam questions; they should be used as a guide for studying and learning the content of the CMA Learning System and ensuring that you can accomplish the objectives set out by the LOS.

The LOS included in the CMALS books are the comprehensive set, current as of the date of publication. Candidates can access the IMA Web site at www.imanet.org and click on the Certification section to locate and download a Portable Document Format (PDF) file of the current LOS.

Learning Outcome Statements

Part 2: Management Accounting and Reporting — Section D. Performance Measurement

Part 2 — Section D1. Cost and Variance Measures

- LOS 2.D.1.a—Analyze performance against operational goals using a variety of methods, including measures based on revenue, manufacturing costs, non-manufacturing costs, and profit depending on the type of center or unit being measured.

- LOS 2.D.1.b—Explain why performance evaluation measures should be directly related to strategic and operational goals and objectives and why timeliness of feedback is critical.

- LOS 2.D.1.c—Explain the reasons for variances (as opposed to only generating numerical results) within a performance monitoring system.

- LOS 2.D.1.d—Explain why performance measures should be related to the factors that drive the element being measured, e.g., cost drivers and revenue drivers.

- LOS 2.D.1.e—Recommend performance measures and a periodic reporting methodology given operational goals and actual results.

- LOS 2.D.1.f—Prepare a performance analysis by comparing actual results with the master budget, calculate favorable and unfavorable variances from the budget, and provide explanations for variances based on the situation presented.

- LOS 2.D.1.g—Identify the benefits and limitations of measuring performance by comparing actual results with the master budget.

- LOS 2.D.1.h—Prepare a flexible budget based on actual sales (output) volume.

- LOS 2.D.1.i—Determine the sales-volume variance and the sales-price variance by comparing the flexible budget with the master (static) budget.

- LOS 2.D.1.j—Determine the flexible-budget variance by comparing actual results with the flexible budget.

- LOS 2.D.1.k—Investigate the flexible-budget variance to determine individual differences between actual and budgeted input prices and input quantities.

- LOS 2.D.1.l—Explain management by exception and demonstrate how budget variance reporting is utilized in this environment.

- LOS 2.D.1.m—Define a standard cost system and identify the reasons for adopting a standard cost system.

- LOS 2.D.1.n—Demonstrate an understanding of price (rate) variances and calculate the price variances related to direct material and direct labor inputs.

- LOS 2.D.1.o—Demonstrate an understanding of efficiency (usage) variances and calculate the efficiency variances related to direct material and direct labor inputs.

- LOS 2.D.1.p—Demonstrate an understanding of spending and efficiency variances as they relate to fixed and variable overhead.

- LOS 2.D.1.q—Calculate a sales-mix variance and explain its impact on revenue and contribution margin.

- LOS 2.D.1.r—Demonstrate an understanding that the efficiency (usage) variances can be further analyzed as mix and yield variances.

- LOS 2.D.1.s—Explain how a mix variance results from using direct material and/or labor inputs in a ratio that differs from standard specifications and calculate a mix variance.

- LOS 2.D.1.t—Calculate a yield variance.

- LOS 2.D.1.u—Demonstrate how price, efficiency, spending, and mix variances can be applied in service companies as well as manufacturing companies.

- LOS 2.D.1.v—Analyze variances, identify causes, and recommend corrective actions.

Part 2 — Section D2. Responsibility Centers and Reporting Segments

- LOS 2.D.2.a—Identify and explain the different types of responsibility centers (strategic business units).

- LOS 2.D.2.b—Recommend appropriate responsibility centers given a business scenario.

- LOS 2.D.2.c—Demonstrate an understanding of contribution margin reporting as used for performance evaluation.

- LOS 2.D.2.d—Analyze a contribution margin report and evaluate performance.

- LOS 2.D.2.e—Identify segments that organizations evaluate, including product lines, geographical areas, or other meaningful segments.

- LOS 2.D.2.f—Explain why the allocation of common costs among segments can be an issue in performance evaluation.

- LOS 2.D.2.g—Identify methods for allocating common costs such as stand-alone cost allocation and incremental cost allocation.

- LOS 2.D.2.h—Define transfer pricing and identify the objectives of transfer pricing.

- LOS 2.D.2.i—Identify the methods for determining transfer prices and list the advantages and disadvantages of each method.

- LOS 2.D.2.j—Explain how transfer pricing is affected by business issues such as the presence of outside suppliers and the opportunity costs associated with capacity usage.

- LOS 2.D.2.k—Describe how special issues such as tariffs, exchange rates, and the availability of materials and skills affect performance evaluation in multinational companies.

- LOS 2.D.2.l—Describe how special issues such as taxes, currency restrictions, and expropriation risk affect transfer pricing in multinational companies.

Part 2 — Section D3. Financial Measures

- LOS 2.D.3.a—Demonstrate an understanding of the issues involved in determining product profitability, business unit profitability, and customer profitability, including cost measurement, cost allocation, investment measurement, and valuation.

- LOS 2.D.3.b—Calculate product-line profitability, business unit profitability, and customer profitability given a set of data and assumptions.

- LOS 2.D.3.c—Evaluate customers and products on the basis of profitability and identify ways to improve profitability and/or drop unprofitable customers and products.

- LOS 2.D.3.d—Define and calculate return on investment (ROI).

- LOS 2.D.3.e—Calculate ROI based on the DuPont method and describe how this model enhances the analysis of ROI calculations.

- LOS 2.D.3.f—Analyze and interpret ROI calculations and evaluate performance on the basis of the analysis.

- LOS 2.D.3.g—Define and calculate residual income (RI).

- LOS 2.D.3.h—Analyze and interpret RI calculations and evaluate performance on the basis of the analysis.

- LOS 2.D.3.i—Compare and contrast the benefits and limitations of ROI and RI as measures of performance.

- LOS 2.D.3.j—Define economic value added (EVA®) and calculate it based on a simple (non-complex) scenario.

- LOS 2.D.3.k—Compare and contrast ROI measures using corporation data and external market data.

- LOS 2.D.3.l—Demonstrate an understanding of how EVA® differs from ROI and residual income measures.

- LOS 2.D.3.m—Define market value added.

- LOS 2.D.3.n—Explain how revenue and expense recognition policies may affect the measurement of income and reduce comparability among business units and companies.

- LOS 2.D.3.o—Explain how inventory measurement policies, joint asset sharing, and overall asset measurement may affect the measurement of investment and reduce comparability among business units and companies.

- LOS 2.D.3.p—Define cash flow return on investment.

- LOS 2.D.3.q—Demonstrate an understanding of the effect international operations can have on performance measurement.

Part 2 — Section D4. Balanced Scorecard

- LOS 2.D.4.a—Define the concept of a balanced scorecard and identify its components.

- LOS 2.D.4.b—Define critical success factors and discuss the importance of these factors in evaluating a firm.

- LOS 2.D.4.c—Identify financial measures, such as operating income, revenue growth, revenues from new products, gross margin percentage, cost reductions, EVA®, ROI, RI, and so on, and evaluate their relevance in a specific corporate situation.

- LOS 2.D.4.d—Identify customer satisfaction measures, such as market share, retention, response time, delivery performance, defects, lead time, and so on, and evaluate their relevance in a specific corporate situation.

- LOS 2.D.4.e—Identify internal business process measures, such as new product introductions, technological capability, cycle time, and so on, and evaluate their relevance in a specific corporate situation.

- LOS 2.D.4.f—Identify innovation and learning measures, such as employee skill sets, organizational learning, industry leadership, etc. and evaluate their relevance in a specific corporate situation.

- LOS 2.D.4.g—Describe the characteristics of successful implementation and use of a balanced scorecard.

- LOS 2.D.4.h—Analyze and interpret a balanced scorecard and evaluate performance on the basis of the analysis.

Part 2 — Section D5. Quality Considerations

- LOS 2.D.5.a—Identify the core principles of total quality management (TQM).

- LOS 2.D.5.b—Identify the opportunity costs associated with poor quality management.

- LOS 2.D.5.c—Demonstrate an understanding of the role that communication and training play in successful TQM programs.

- LOS 2.D.5.d—Describe the relationship between quality management and productivity and explain why misconceptions about this relationship can lead to poor decisions.

- LOS 2.D.5.e—Demonstrate an understanding of methods to analyze quality problems such as control charts, Pareto diagrams, and cause-and-effect (fishbone) diagrams.

- LOS 2.D.5.f—Identify how quality considerations factor into the firm's overall performance measurement and evaluation process.

- LOS 2.D.5.g—Identify the purpose of quality audits and gap analyses.

- LOS 2.D.5.h—Define quality as it relates to customer expectations.

- LOS 2.D.5.i—Define conformance as it relates to quality and identify the characteristics of goalpost quality conformance and absolute quality conformance.

- LOS 2.D.5.j—Describe and identify the components of the costs of quality commonly referred to as prevention costs, appraisal costs, internal failure costs, and external failure costs.

Cost and Variance Measures

Topic overview

Feedback is a necessary element of control. Feedback in management is the comparison of planned results, or the budget, to what actually occurred. A variance is the difference between the actual and planned results. This topic covers how flexible budgets and variances can help management control costs and make their business as efficient as possible.

Comparison of Actual to Planned Results

A successful budget cycle has the following characteristics.

- Master budget: planning the performance of the organization as a whole as well as for each subunit

- Standards: establishing a set of specific expectations against which actual results can be compared (See Section A, Topic 1, "Budgeting Concepts," in this part.)

- Investigating variations from plans and taking corrective action if necessary

- Planning again, taking into consideration feedback and changed conditions

When comparing actual to planned results, managers are concerned with the efficiency of the operation and the effectiveness at meeting its goals. **Efficiency** is the budgeted amounts or standards set for a particular cost compared to the actual costs. If a cost is estimated to be $2 per unit, an efficient operation that sells 1,000 units should have a cost of $2,000 or less. An inefficient operation costs more than that amount. **Effectiveness** is measured by how well a firm attains its goals. If the master budget calls for net operating income to be $300 million, an effective operation would have earned that amount or more, and an ineffective operation would have earned less than that amount. An operation can be effective but not efficient or efficient but not effective. An inefficient but effective operation is one that meets its primary goals even though it had cost overruns. An ineffective but efficient operation failed to meet its goals but met its costs. (Note that the ideas of efficiency and effectiveness and the discussion of variance analyses that will follow are directly tied to standard costing and continuous improvement [for example, kaizen] concepts, which are covered in Section A, Topic 1, of this part.)

In order to improve both of these elements, one must know both how the system is acting and how you want it to act. Determining how a system is acting involves standard costing, but such methods won't fix anything by themselves unless combined with variance analysis to determine actual system behavior. Determining how you want the system to act depends on selecting appropriate benchmarks with an appropriate level of stringency (for example, whether to use kaizen with continually increasing goals, target costing with specific types of standards, etc.) in the measure.

A primary means of assessing effectiveness is through the operating income variance, or the difference between budgeted operating income and actual operating income. Such a measure looks at the bottom line of operations. A secondary means of assessing effectiveness is to do a line-by-line comparison of actual to planned results. Figure 2-52 below shows variance from a static budget, which is a budget that is set at the beginning of the year and not changed. (Flexible budgets are covered later in this section.)

Favorable/unfavorable variances

Figure 2-52 shows that some variances are favorable and others are unfavorable. A **favorable variance** exceeds the planned amount of earnings or was less than the planned costs. An **unfavorable variance** is the opposite. A general rule of thumb is that if a variance helps the bottom line, it is favorable; if it hurts the bottom line, it is unfavorable.

Figure 2-52: Analysis of Variance Between Actual and Static Budget

High-Level Analysis—Overview

Actual operating income	$35,760
Budgeted operating income	270,000
Static-budget variance of operating income	$234,240U

Mid-Level Analysis

	Actual Results	Static Budget	Variance (Actual – Static)
Units sold	24,000	30,000	6,000 U*
Revenues	$3,000,000	$3,600,000	$600,000 U
Variable costs			
Direct materials	1,491,840	1,800,000	308,160F**
Direct manufacturing labor	475,200	480,000	4,800 F
Variable manufacturing overhead	313,200	360,000	46,800 F
Total variable costs	2,280,240	2,640,000	359,760 F
Contribution margin	719,760	960,000	240,240 U
Fixed costs	684,000	690,000	6,000 F
Operating income	$35,760	$270,000	$234,240 U

*   U = Unfavorable effect on operating income
** F = Favorable effect on operating income

Note in Figure 2-52 that there is a favorable direct materials variance, $1,491,840 – $1,800,000 = ($308,160), which is a negative but favorable amount. Positive and negative signs are very important to track for variance calculations but do not indicate favorableness/unfavorableness by themselves. Taken together with the fact that this is a cost, a negative number means that the cost is reduced, increasing net income, and therefore the variance is favorable. In contrast, the $600,000 unfavorable revenues variance in Figure 2-52 is unfavorable because it is lower than the revenue that was planned for, adversely affecting net income. Some of the illustrations in this text drop the negative and positive signs to focus more on favorable and unfavorable variances, but if a favorable variance is added to an unfavorable variance, then they have to be netted.

Is the $308,160 favorable direct material variance a good thing for the company? (Even though the operation was ineffective, at least was it efficient?) Not necessarily. Because the operation had an unfavorable number of units sold, the primary reason for the operation being ineffective was that sales were lower than budgeted. Because fewer goods were produced, the direct material costs were lower. The budgeted direct material costs were $1,800,000 for 30,000 units, or $60 per unit. The actual number of units produced was 24,000 units at an actual cost of $1,491,840, so the actual cost was $62.16 per unit. Therefore, favorable and unfavorable are not necessarily indications of a good or bad result per se but show whether the firm is or is not meeting its plan. Budget variances on line items can be misleading and may not indicate either effectiveness or efficiency. Furthermore, variances should be tested against a materiality threshold. If they are individually immaterial, they should be ignored. One must keep in mind, however, that several small variances could point to a much larger problem.

Budget variances can occur because of flawed assumptions when preparing the budget, inefficiencies in execution of the budget, or unforeseen internal or external changes in the environment. Additional analyses that assess the efficiency of operations are needed to determine why targets were missed. Using a flexible budget allows a more detailed level of analysis than using a static budget when determining why a budget has variances.

Use of Flexible Budgets to Analyze Performance

The prior content discussed a static budget and the variances from it compared to actual results. This section defines the flexible budget and discusses using it for performance evaluations.

Static versus flexible budgets

The primary difference between a static budget and a flexible budget is that while both are planned and originally created in the same manner, at the end of the period, a **static budget** is left unchanged and all comparisons are made to the expected output, while a **flexible budget** alters the budget amounts to reflect actual output levels. A manufacturing company would base changes on units of output, while a hospital could use number of patient days and a service company could use billed hours of service.

Extending the prior static budget example, if sales were supposed to be 30,000 units but were actually 24,000 units, the flexible budget would be altered to show 24,000 units and all other corresponding budgeted amounts would be changed to reflect this reality. Creating a flexible budget from a static budget allows managers to compare apples to apples. Using a flexible budget, the favorable variance in direct materials costs changes to an unfavorable variance, because instead of a budgeted amount of $1,800,000 for direct materials, the new budgeted amount of $1,440,000 ($60 per unit × 24,000 units) would be used and the actual amount of $1,491,840 would be $51,840 unfavorable.

When compared to static budgets, flexible budgets yield better managerial control results. The reason for better control lies in the concept of variable and fixed expenses. In theory, management has more control over variable costs because their cost behavior is directly tied to units of production. If a business lowers the number of units produced from the number suggested in the static budget, the variable costs incurred should go down in equal proportion with the drop in units of production.

Flexible budget characteristics

While analyzing a static budget's variances in detail can be misleading, analyzing a flexible budget in its details is possible. A flexible budget alters the output units and corresponding details tied to that unit of output but does not alter unit prices, unit costs, or other items not tied to output. Fixed expenses are also not usually changed because they are by nature fixed over the operating period. A flexible budget that has been altered for an unfavorable and a favorable variance in output units is shown in Figure 2-53 along with changes in other items.

Figure 2-53: Flexible Budgets for Bounce Manufacturing Company

	Flexible Budget at 80%		Flexible Budget at 100%		Flexible Budget at 110%	
Units sold	24,000		30,000		33,000	
Sales	$2,880,000		$3,600,000		$3,960,000	
Variable expenses	2,112,000		2,640,000		2,904,000	
Contribution margin	$768,000	26.67%	$960,000	26.67%	$1,056,000	26.67%
Fixed expenses	690,000		690,000		690,000	
Operating income	$78,000	2.7%	$270,000	7.5%	$366,000	9.2%

Figure 2-53 shows how flexible budgets can be prepared either after the actual results are known or before, as a pro forma flexible budget. Unit changes alter total sales and total variable expenses. Therefore the total contribution margin and operating income change correspondingly, but note that the percentage of the contribution margin stays the same, while the percentage of operating income changes. This is because when the flexible budget has an unfavorable output variance, the fixed costs assume a larger percentage of the costs. In a favorable output variance, the opposite is true.

Flexible budgets can be prepared without any reference to the master budget. While master budgets must be prepared before the accounting period, flexible budgets can be prepared any time and with varying levels of detail (to highlight particular items that need attention). Managers can also use flexible budgets to analyze operating results and determine reasons for changes in operating conditions.

Steps in preparing a flexible budget

Four steps are used when developing a flexible budget.

1. **Prepare a static master budget.**
   This step includes determining a budgeted selling price, budgeted variable costs per unit, and budgeted fixed costs, as these amounts will continue to be used in the flexible budget.

2. **Find the actual quantity of output.**

   The quantity of output is the cost driver for the variable costs.

3. **Calculate the flexible budget amounts for total sales.**

   The following formula is used to calculate total sales in a flexible budget:

   Total Sales = # of Units Sold × Budgeted Selling Price per Unit

   Flexible budget revenues are calculated as follows.

   Flexible Budget Revenues = $120/unit × 24,000 units

   = $2,880,000

4. **Calculate the flexible budget amounts for expenses.**

   The following formula is used to calculate total expenses in a flexible budget:

   Total Expenses = Total Variable Expenses + Total Fixed Expenses

   Total variable expenses equal the number of units sold times budgeted variable costs per unit.

Figure 2-54 shows how the flexible budget is calculated for actual results.

Figure 2-54: Flexible Budget Amounts for Expenses

Flexible budget variable costs	
Direct materials, $60 × 24,000	$1,440,000
Direct manufacturing labor, $16 × 24,000	384,000
Variable manufacturing overhead, $12 × 24,000	288,000
Total variable costs	2,112,000
Flexible budget fixed costs	690,000
Flexible budget total costs	$2,802,000

Flexible budget variance and sales volume variance

A flexible budget can be used to analyze the efficiency of an operation.

The difference between the actual results and the static budget can be split into two different types of variances when a flexible budget is created:

- The **flexible budget variance** is the actual results minus the flexible budget amount (adjusted for actual output).

- The **sales volume variance** is the flexible budget amount adjusted for actual output minus the static budget amount.

Together these two variances form the total of the static budget variance from actual results, as in Figure 2-55.

Figure 2-55: Flexible Budget Variances and Sales Volume Variances

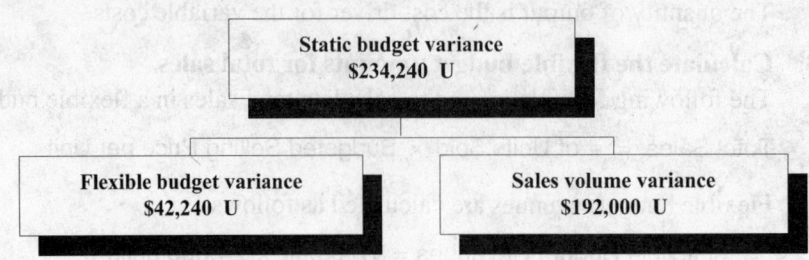

Figure 2-56 shows how the flexible budget variance and the sales volume variance are calculated.

Figure 2-56: Calculating Flexible Budget Variance and Sales Volume Variance

	Actual Results	Flexible Budget	Flexible Budget Variances (Actual – Flexible)	Static Budget	Sales Volume Variances (Flexible – Static)
Units sold	24,000	24,000	0	30,000	6,000 U
Revenues	$3,000,000	$2,880,000	$120,000 F	$3,600,000	$720,000 U
Variable costs					
Direct materials	1,491,840	1,440,000	51,840 U	1,800,000	360,000 F
Direct manufacturing labor	475,200	384,000	91,200 U	480,000	96,000 F
Variable manufacturing overhead	313,200	288,000	25,200 U	360,000	72,000 F
Total variable costs	2,280,240	2,112,000	168,240 U	2,640,000	528,000 F
Contribution margin	719,760	768,000	48,240 U	960,000	192,000 U
Fixed costs	684,000	690,000	6,000 F	690,000	0
Operating income	$35,760	$78,000	$42,240 U	$270,000	$192,000 U

$42,240 U
Total flexible budget variance

$192,000 U
Total sales volume variance

Total static budget variance
$234,240 U

Analysis of the flexible budget variance can show how differences from actual amounts in selling price, variable expenses, and fixed expenses altered operating income from the budgeted amount. Analysis of the sales volume variance shows how differences in output affected the budgeted amounts. Unfavorable amounts indicate that the firm does not have as much market share as was assumed or that the market is smaller than anticipated; favorable amounts indicate that more emphasis should be placed on this product than before. Insignificant sales volume variances mean that the budget predicted accurate sales. Analysis of both variances together will help assess where an operation is efficient and where it is not being efficient.

Activity-Based Management (ABM)

Activity-based management (ABM) is a management style that focuses on cost reduction by drawing on activity analysis, usually activity-based costing (see Section B, Topic 3, "Accumulation Systems"), to continuously improve both operational and management control. While ABC assigns costs, ABM works toward system-wide improvement of costs and enhancement of value to the customer by:

- Eliminating wasteful activities such as an internal reporting requirement.

- Increasing weighting of profitable activities over marginally profitable ones such as increasing production of a profitable subcomponent and decreasing production of a marginally profitable one, buying the latter as needed.

- Simplifying or reducing some activities to bare bones, such as installing automated ticketing booths at a movie theater to reduce staffing.

- Combining activities, such as making the same parts usable in multiple products.

ABM can be divided into strategic ABM and operational ABM. Strategic ABM involves choosing the best activities and creating demand for the most profitable activities. Customer and product mix decisions, supplier relationship management (SRM), process design, strategic pricing (not all pricing decisions), and market segmentation are all components of strategic ABM decisions. Operational ABM includes ways of making activities more efficient through total quality management (see Topic 5, "Quality Considerations," in this section), performance measurement, business process reengineering (see Part 3, Section A, Topic 3, "Business Process Performance"), as well as activity management.

While ABC designates and uses cost drivers for each activity, ABM analyzes these cost drivers for their effectiveness in defining the root causes of activity costs. To explain the effects of cost drivers, ABM uses internal interviews, observation, and quality control tools such as the theory of constraints (see Part 3, Section A, Topic 2, "Manufacturing Paradigms"), benchmarking, Pareto charts, or Ishikawa diagrams (see Topic 5, "Quality Considerations," in this section). The result will be an assessment of how well cost drivers reflect actual costs and actual areas of profitability.

Another main aspect of ABM is performance measurement. ABM helps make performance evaluation measures (discussed in Topics 2 and 4 of this section) relate to the factors that drive the element being measured, that is, cost drivers and revenue drivers. Such measures include revenue, manufacturing cost, nonmanufacturing cost, and profit as well as nonfinancial measures. (See Topic 4, "Balanced Scorecard," in this section.)

Differentiating between value-added and non-value added

Value-added activities must both fulfill an organizational requirement and be perceived as valuable by customers. Non-value-added activities neither fulfill an organizational requirement nor have any impact on customer choices. To determine whether an activity is value-added or not, a manager should begin by determining whether it satisfies the two elements in the definition of value-added. If one of the qualifications is not met or there is some difference of opinion, the following questions can help determine if the activity is value-added:

- Is the activity valuable to one or more customers?
- Do sound business practices require performing the activity?
- Is the activity a waste of time? (If yes, eliminate the activity.)

Examples of value-added activities include product design, product manufacturing, and product delivery. Value-added activities can also be areas for continuous improvement, but the point of determining what is non-value-added is to identify areas where the most improvement can be made the fastest, and the improvements to value-added activities can be delayed until all non-value-added activities have been eliminated. However, such activities can be improved, such as by removing unwanted features during product design, eliminating overproduction, or simplifying manufacturing process steps or distribution methods. Note that broad activities such as product manufacturing could be broken down into smaller steps, and some of these could be deemed non-value-added. Not all non-value-added activities can be removed, but many can be simplified or reduced and so warrant consideration.

Figure 2-57 shows some non-value-added activities and some examples of how they could be eliminated or reduced.

Figure 2-57: Non-Value-Added Activities at a Manufacturing Firm

Non-Value-Added Activity	Example of Improvement
Equipment setups	Schedule production to generate larger batches of each type to reduce setups.
Raw material, work-in-process, and finished goods inventory movements	Redesign the production layout to minimize product movement during production.
Waiting (labor)	Coordinate activities.
Equipment idle time	Coordinate activities.
Rework	Add intermittent inspections to find problems earlier.
Equipment repairs	Schedule routine maintenance for periods of low usage even if repair is a bit early.
Inventory storage	Stop overstocking.
Quality inspections	Select vendors willing to perform and stand by their own quality assurance.
Product exchanges due to failure	Improve quality and final inspection before shipping the product.

Advantages and disadvantages of ABM

ABM has the following advantages over traditional cost management techniques:

- Continuous improvement maintains firm's competitive advantage.

- Allocates more resources to activities, products, and customers that add most value, strategically redirecting management focus.

- Eliminates non-value-added activities.

- Measures process effectiveness and identifies areas to reduce costs or increase customer value.

- Works well with just-in-time (JIT) processes.

- Ties performance measurement to ABC to provide consistent incentives for using ABC.

ABM has the following disadvantages when compared to traditional cost management:

- Changing to ABC/ABM will result in different pricing, process design, manufacturing technology, and product design decisions, and the company must be prepared to support managers who embrace these methods and discourage managers who continue to use the older methods.

- ABC/ABM is not used for external financial reporting, and needing to prepare reports using traditional methods may influence management decision making enough to dilute the impact of ABC/ABM.

- Implementing ABC/ABM is expensive and time-consuming, so a cost-benefit analysis should be done to identify all hidden costs and benefits.

Management by Exception

The breakdown of variances into flexible budget variances and sales budget variances can allow a business to make business decisions based on these variances. Management by exception is a method of focusing management attention on only significant variances from the budget. The significant variances are the exceptions that require more attention than other areas. Some management software will automatically create exception reports. Management by exception flags unfavorable as well as favorable variances. Favorable variances should be tracked to determine if the performance is truly exceptional or perhaps the standard is set too low. Exceptional performance over time should be incorporated into standard practice.

Knowing which exceptions to follow up on requires managerial experience, but the size and frequency of the variances are primary considerations. The relative size of the variance is more important than the absolute size, but managers often have a rule of thumb for both (for example, flag all variances over $30,000 or 5% of the budgeted cost). Small but frequent variances are also worth investigating. Other considerations include following trends, such as a cost that continuously gets larger over time, and the level of control that can be directed to change the cost, such as not paying as much attention to a cost that is rising solely due to market demand.

Management by exception is an efficient way to have managers spend their time because only exceptions are tracked and each exception is tracked or not tracked based on a cost-benefit decision. However, because this method requires management discretion, poor management decisions can cause this benefit to become a drawback. For example, if management believes that a rising raw material cost cannot be controlled and therefore does not flag the cost, it might be overlooking an unorthodox solution such as finding a different vendor or a replacement material. When properly implemented, exception tracking can reduce future costs when causes for unfavorable variances are removed or when causes for favorable variances can be extended.

Use of Standard Cost Systems

Basics of standard costs are discussed in Section A of this part of the CMA Learning System, Topic 1, "Budgeting Concepts." A standard cost is any carefully determined price, quantity, service level, or cost, usually expressed in a per-unit amount. A standard costing system uses standard costs for all elements of a product or service, including standard expenses for manufacturing, administration, and sales. A standard cost is a "should cost." In other words, how much should this activity or cost object cost? Use of a standard costing system will enable the firm to identify variances from the standards they set. Standard cost systems allow for the use of management by exception and a further detailed analysis of price and efficiency variances.

Analysis of Variation From Standard Cost Expectations

While a flexible budget provides a high-level overview of budget variances and flexible budget and sales volume variances provide a more detailed view, a third level of detail is possible by analyzing the cause of these flexible budget variances. Recall that all standards have two components, a standard rate per unit of the cost driver and a standard number of units of a cost driver for a given output level (flexible budget level). Focusing on changes in each of these two components allows flexible budget variances to be broken down into price (rate) variances and efficiency (usage) variances. The total of these two variances equals the flexible budget variance, as shown in Figure 2-58 (where DM is direct materials and DL is direct labor).

Figure 2-58: Variance Breakdown for Direct Costs

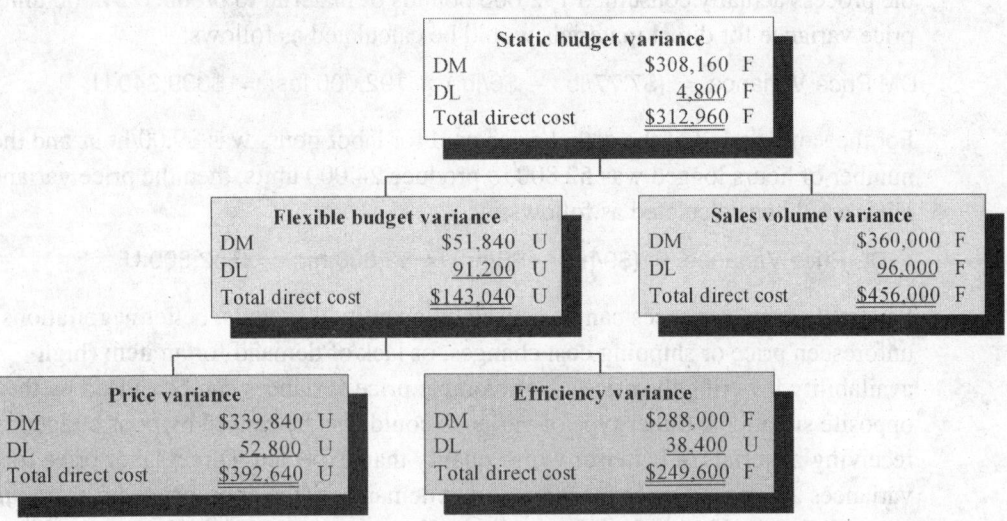

Note that in Figure 2-58, for direct materials, the price variance plus the efficiency variance will equal the flexible budget variance only when the amount of material purchased in the period exactly equals the amount used in production during the period, which means that the inventory balance does not change (that is, a rare event). This problem does not occur in direct labor or overhead because these items cannot be inventoried (amount purchased always equals amount used). Direct costs and fixed and variable overhead require different methods of calculating these variances. This section also covers sales mix variances and their breakdown into mix variances and yield variances.

Price and efficiency variances for direct labor and direct material inputs

Price and efficiency variances result from variances from budgeted input prices or input quantities. A standard input is a predetermined quantity of direct inputs such as labor hours or gallons of a fluid needed to make one output unit.

Price (rate) variances for direct costs

A price variance is the actual input quantity of an item multiplied by the difference between the actual input price and the budgeted (or standard) input price. This formula is:

Price Variance = (Actual Input Price − Budgeted Input Price) × Actual Input Quantity

Suppose the standards for a unit were as follows:

- Direct materials (DM): 10.0 lbs. DM/unit @ $6.00/lb. = $60/unit standard
  (24,000 units × 10.0 lbs./unit = 240,000 lbs. standard)

- Direct labor (DL): 2.0 labor hours/unit @ $8.00/hr. = $16/unit standard
  (24,000 units × 2.0 labor hours/unit = 48,000 labor hours standard)

Assume that for a period, the actual price paid for direct materials was $7.77/pound and the process actually consumed 192,000 pounds of material to produce 24,000 units. The price variance for direct materials would be calculated as follows:

DM Price Variance = ($7.77/lb. − $6/lb.) × 192,000 lbs. = $339,840 U

For the same period, if the actual price paid for labor hours was $9.00/hour and the number of hours logged was 52,800 to produce 24,000 units, then the price variance for labor would be calculated as follows:

DL Price Variance = ($9/hr. − $8/hr.) × 52,800 hrs. = $52,800 U

Favorable price variances can be caused by quantity discounts, better negotiations, unforeseen price or shipping cost changes, or lack of demand for an item (high availability lowering the price). Unfavorable price variances can be caused by the opposite situations. Either type of variance could also be caused by poor budgeting or by receiving materials of better or worse quality than expected. Direct labor price (or rate) variances are caused by changes in market demand for the appropriate labor, requiring either different skill levels to be used or different rates to be paid than set in the standards.

The effect of a variance, whether it is favorable or unfavorable, should be studied. For example, a favorable materials price variance caused by purchasing in bulk could cause a firm to have greater inventory holding costs. Moreover, if the standards reflect the company's strategy, such as differentiation for quality, then variations should be studied for their effect on the company's strategy and corrected when they differ from that strategy.

Efficiency (usage) variances for direct costs

An efficiency variance is the budgeted input price multiplied by the difference between the actual input quantity and the budgeted (or standard) input quantity. This formula is:

Efficiency Variance = (Actual Input Quantity − Budgeted Input Quantity) × Budgeted Input Price

Continuing the prior example, for direct materials the actual input quantity was 192,000 pounds or 8 pounds/unit (192,000/24,000). Because the budgeted input quantity was 240,000 pounds and the budgeted price was $6/pound, the efficiency variance would be calculated as follows:

DM Efficiency Variance = (192,000 lbs. − 240,000 lbs.) × $6/lb. = $288,000 F

For direct labor, the actual input quantity was 52,800 labor hours or 2.2 hours per unit (52,800/24,000). Because the budgeted input quantity was 48,000 labor hours and the budgeted price was $8/labor hour, the efficiency variance would be calculated as follows:

DL Efficiency Variance = (52,800 hrs. − 48,000 hrs.) × $8/hr. = $38,400 U

Because the price variance plus the efficiency variance equals the flexible budget variance, the flexible budget variance can be verified by totaling the price and efficiency variances as follows:

DM Flexible Budget Variance = $339,840 U (price) + $288,000 F (efficiency) = $51,840 U

DL Flexible Budget Variance = $52,800 U (price) + $38,400 U (efficiency) = $91,200 U

Efficiency variances can be caused by poor budgeting or by variances in worker skill level, scheduling, supervision, or setup efficiency. Improperly maintained machines or improper training can also lead to efficiency variances.

Spending and efficiency variances for variable and fixed overhead

As with direct costs, variable and fixed overhead cost variances can be further broken down into price and efficiency variances.

Variances for variable overhead

To break down the variable overhead flexible budget variance requires knowing three calculated amounts:

- Actual cost: actual overhead incurred during the period.

- Applied overhead: actual quantity of cost driver times the standard rate

- Budgeted overhead: standard quantity of cost driver times the standard rate

This variable overhead flexible budget variance can be broken down into a variable overhead spending variance (1 minus 2 in the prior list) and a variable overhead efficiency variance (2 minus 3 in the list).

A variable overhead spending variance is the actual overhead incurred minus the product of the actual quantity of the cost driver times the standard variable overhead rate.

Variable overhead standards are created using a cost driver and a number of units of the cost driver. If machine hours are used as the cost driver for variable overhead and 1.2 machine hours at $10/machine hour are set as the standard for one unit ($12/unit), then 24,000 units should require 28,800 machine hours or $288,000 (see Figure 2-56). Actual variable overhead costs allocated to these 24,000 units are $313,200, and the variable overhead flexible budget variance is $25,200 unfavorable. Therefore, if the actual number of machine hours is 28,000, the variable overhead price variance would be calculated as:

Variable Overhead Spending Variance = Actual Cost − (Actual Units of Cost Driver × Standard Cost Driver Rate)

= $313,200 − (28,000 machine hours × $10/machine hour)

= $313,200 − $280,000 = $33,200 unfavorable

The variable overhead efficiency variance is the product of the actual quantity of the cost driver times the standard variable overhead rate minus the product of the standard quantity of the cost driver times the standard variable overhead rate.

The variable overhead efficiency variance is shown below along with an example. The variable overhead spending plus efficiency variances aggregate to the variable overhead flexible budget variance.

Variable Overhead Efficiency Variance

= (Actual Units of Cost Driver × Standard Cost Driver Rate) − (Standard Units of Cost Driver × Standard Cost Driver Rate)

= (28,000 Machine Hours × $10/Machine Hour) − (28,800 Machine Hours × $10/Machine Hour)

= $280,000 − $288,000 = $8,000 favorable

Variable Overhead Flexible Budget Variance

= Variable Overhead Spending Variance + Variable Overhead Efficiency Variance

= $33,200 U + $8,000 F = $25,200 unfavorable

Variable overhead variance is more likely caused by the imprecision inherent in choosing a single cost driver for overhead that is likely made up of very different costs. In contrast, variance measures for direct materials and direct labor have accurate cost drivers. Activity-based overhead variance measures could perform the variance measures using a variety of cost pools, each with their own cost driver for greater accuracy, but the higher administrative cost is sometimes prohibitive. Variable overhead may also have variances because many types of variable overhead costs are not based on output measures such as units of output but on input measures such as number of setups or batches.

Variable overhead accounting

Recall the discussion of underapplied and overapplied overhead from Section B, Topic 2, of this part. The variable overhead flexible budget variance of $25,200 unfavorable in the prior example is the amount underapplied, because this is the amount by which actual costs exceed applied overhead. If favorable, it would be the amount overapplied.

However, by breaking this variance down into spending and efficiency variances, the accounting for the differences can also become more specific.

Variable Manufacturing Overhead Control	$313,200	
Accounts Payable Control and Other Accounts		$313,200
To record actual variable manufacturing overhead costs incurred		

Work-in-Process Control	$288,000	
Variable Manufacturing Overhead Applied		$288,000
To record variable manufacturing overhead costs applied		
(1.2 machine hours/unit × $10/machine hour × 24,000 units)		

The costs in the work-in-process control account would be transferred to the finished goods control account when production is finished. The costs of items sold are transferred from the finished goods control account to the cost of goods sold account when sales are made.

The following entry would be made to record the variances. (Note that the two variance accounts now replace the single overhead applied account.)

Variable Manufacturing Overhead Applied	$288,000	
Variable Manufacturing Overhead Spending Variance	$33,200	
Variable Manufacturing Overhead Control		$313,200
Variable Manufacturing Overhead Efficiency Variance		$8,000

To record variances for the accounting period

Assuming the amount underapplied (or overapplied) is immaterial, the following accounting entries would write off the difference to the cost of goods sold account at the end of the period.

Cost of Goods Sold	$25,200	
Variable Manufacturing Overhead Efficiency Variance	$8,000	
Variable Manufacturing Overhead Spending Variance		$33,200

To record the disposition of variable overhead variance accounts

Remember, if the amount over- or underapplied is material and unavoidable, the amounts must be prorated among the ending WIP inventory, ending finished goods inventory, and the cost of goods sold based on the relative variable manufacturing overhead allocated to each account.

Variances for fixed overhead

To break down total fixed overhead variance into two subcategories, three amounts must be known:

1. Actual fixed overhead

2. Budgeted fixed overhead: standard quantity times standard fixed overhead rate

3. Applied fixed overhead: actual quantity times standard fixed overhead rate

Actual fixed overhead minus the applied fixed overhead equals the total fixed overhead variance. Therefore, the total fixed overhead variance is also called the underapplied or overapplied fixed overhead.

Actual fixed overhead is the actual amount of overhead incurred in a period. Budgeted fixed overhead uses the standard quantity set in the static budget. The fixed overhead standard rate per unit is the total budgeted fixed overhead cost divided by the budgeted number of units of a cost driver.

The fixed overhead flexible budget variance can be broken down into a fixed overhead spending variance (1 minus 2 in the prior list) and a fixed overhead production volume variance (2 minus 3 in the list). The fixed overhead spending variance is actual fixed overhead minus budgeted fixed overhead. The fixed overhead production volume variance is the budgeted fixed overhead minus applied fixed overhead.

Continuing the prior example (see Figure 2-56), the actual fixed overhead is $684,000. The budgeted fixed overhead is 30,000 units times the standard fixed overhead rate of $23/unit ($690,000/30,000 = $23/unit), or $690,000. The applied fixed overhead is the actual quantity of 24,000 units times the standard rate of $23/unit, or $552,000.

The fixed overhead spending variance and the fixed overhead production volume variance are calculated as follows.

Fixed Overhead Spending Variance

= Actual Fixed Overhead − Budgeted Fixed Overhead

= $684,000 − $690,000 = $6,000 Favorable

Fixed Overhead Production Volume Variance

= Budgeted Fixed Overhead − Applied Fixed Overhead

= $690,000 − $552,000 = $138,000 Unfavorable

Total Fixed Overhead Variance (= Over- or Underapplied Overhead)

= Fixed Overhead Spending Variance + Fixed Overhead Production Volume Variance

= $6,000 + $138,000 = $132,000 Unfavorable

or

Total Fixed Overhead Variance

= Actual Fixed Overhead − Applied Fixed Overhead

= $684,000 − $552,000 = $132,000 Unfavorable

A fixed overhead spending variance shows that the budget procedure missed or failed to predict changes in certain fixed costs. Unfavorable spending variances can also occur if inadequate control is exercised over departmental spending or because of accidents and unexpected repairs. The breakdown of fixed costs into these two categories can highlight when certain variable costs are misclassified as fixed costs, because changes in production volume will be accompanied by changes in some portion of the fixed costs that are actually variable. Also, as with the variable overhead variances, the total fixed overhead variance of $132,000 unfavorable is the total amount of fixed overhead underapplied and would be accounted for using the combination of the fixed overhead spending variance and the fixed overhead production volume variance accounts. The entries would be similar to those shown previously for variable overhead, with the following entry to record the variances.

Fixed Manufacturing Overhead Allocated	$552,000	
Fixed Manufacturing Overhead Production Volume Variance	$138,000	
Fixed Manufacturing Overhead Control		$684,000
Fixed Manufacturing Overhead Spending Variance		$6,000

To record variances for the accounting period

The final entry to adjust the cost of goods sold (if immaterial) is as follows.

Cost of Goods Sold	$132,000	
Fixed Manufacturing Overhead Spending Variance	$6,000	
Fixed Manufacturing Overhead Production Volume Variance		$138,000

To record the disposition of variable overhead variance accounts

Again, if material and unavoidable, such costs would be prorated among the inventory accounts and the cost of goods sold.

The fixed overhead production volume variance can occur when demand for a product changes from what was expected. Often, some measurement of a production variable (labor hours, machine hours) is used as the allocation base for overhead. If the labor usage being measured (actual quantity of allocation base as measured in applied fixed overhead) differs from the budgeted amount used to compute the overhead rate (standard quantity of allocation base as measured in budgeted fixed overhead), this will result in fixed overhead variances being either over- or underapplied.

Other causes of the fixed overhead production volume variance include changes in strategy or unexpected breakdowns. If the company made as many units in the period as they budgeted, there should be no fixed overhead production volume variance. The production volume variance reflects the company's use of its capacity. When volume is low, the price per unit of fixed overhead is higher and capacity is underutilized. The production volume variance does not indicate efficiency but its effectiveness in attaining its cost goals.

Using overhead variance data to solve for other unknowns

Sometimes the variances for a situation are known but some other variables are not known. In such situations, the equation can be solved for the variable in question.

For example, assume that Bounce Sporting Goods is benchmarking a competitor, SportCo. SportCo's actual variable overhead is $432,000, and their actual sales are 28,250 units. SportCo stated in a magazine article that it uses labor hours when allocating variable overhead and it allows a budgeted input of 1.6 labor hours per unit. The article did not mention their variable overhead allocation rates or actual number of labor hours used for the period. SportCo's variable overhead variances are $58,000 unfavorable efficiency variance and $20,000 favorable spending variance. Standard flexible budget units of the cost driver can thus be derived: 28,250 actual units × 1.6 labor hours per unit = 45,200 labor hours.

Based on this information, what is the variable overhead allocation rate per unit? Per labor hour? What was their actual number of labor hours? To find the answers, input the known amounts into the formulae for variances and then solve for the unknown variable. Note that because the actual units of the labor hours cost driver is not known, the first calculation uses units as its cost driver and solves for the answer in units and then uses the answer to solve for the standard labor hours cost driver rate.

Variable Overhead (OH) Spending Variance $=$ Actual Cost $-$ (Actual Units of Cost Driver $\times$ Standard Cost Driver Rate)

$-$ $20,000 F $=$ $432,000 $-$ (28,250 Units $\times$ $X/Unit)

$-$ $20,000 $-$ $432,000 $=$ $-$ (28,250 Units $\times$ $X/Unit)

$452,000 $=$ 28,250 Units $\times$ $X/Unit

$$\frac{\$452,000}{28,250 \text{ Units}} = \$X/Unit = \$16/Unit$$

Budgeted Variable OH Cost Rate/Unit $=$ Budgeted Input/Unit $\times$ Budgeted Variable OH Cost Rate/Input Unit

$16/Unit $=$ 1.6 Labor Hours/Unit $\times$ $X/Labor Hour

$$\frac{\$16/Unit}{1.6 \text{ Labor Hours/Unit}} = \$X/Labor Hour = \$10/Labor Hour$$

Once the budgeted variable overhead cost rate per labor hour is known, the steps below show one way to determine the actual number of labor hours used based on the known variable overhead efficiency variance.

Variable Overhead Efficiency Variance

$=$ (Actual Units of Cost Driver $\times$ Standard Cost Driver Rate)

$-$ (Standard Units of Cost Driver $\times$ Standard Cost Driver Rate)

$=$ (X Labor Hours $\times$ $10/Labor Hour) $-$ (45,200 Labor Hours $\times$ $10/Labor Hour) $=$ $58,000 Unfavorable

$=$ (X Labor Hours $\times$ $10/Labor Hour) $-$ $452,000 $=$ $58,000 Unfavorable

$=$ (X Labor Hours $\times$ $10/Labor Hour) $=$ $58,000 Unfavorable $+$ $452,000

$=$ X Labor Hours $\times$ $10/Labor Hour $=$ $510,000

$$= \text{X Labor Hours} = \frac{\$510,000}{\$10/Labor Hour} = 51,000 \text{ Labor Hours (Actual)}$$

Sales mix variance

Sales mix variance and sales quantity variance can be combined to find the sales volume variance. The sales volume variance is:

Sales Volume Variance $=$ (Units Sold $-$ Units in Static Budget) $\times$ Budgeted Standard Contribution Margin per Unit

The contribution margin is total sales minus variable expenses. The portion of sales volume variance that is not attributable to net changes in sales quantity is caused by variations in the various products a firm offers. For example, if a tennis ball company also makes racquet balls, its sales mix variance would arise from variations in sales of these two products compared to the budgeted amounts for each product. A sales mix is the ratio of any single product or service to the total of all products or services. A sales mix variance is the product of the budgeted contribution margin per unit, the total number of all products sold, and the difference between the actual sales mix ratio and the budgeted sales mix ratio. The sales mix variance is:

$$\text{Sales Mix Variance} = \begin{pmatrix} \text{Actual Sales} & \text{Budget Sales} \\ \text{Mix Ratio for} & - & \text{Mix Ratio for} \\ \text{a Product} & \text{a Product} \end{pmatrix} \times \text{Total All Units} \times \begin{pmatrix} \text{Budget Contribution Margin} \\ \text{per Unit of Product} \end{pmatrix}$$

Consider a situation in which the master budget calls for 10,000 cans of tennis balls to be sold at a unit price of $12 each and for 6,000 cans of racquet balls to be sold at $8 each. The budgeted sales mix ratio for tennis balls is 10,000/16,000 or 0.625 and for racquet balls is 6,000/16,000 or 0.375. To simplify the situation, say that the actual sales for the period were 9,000 cans of tennis balls and 7,000 cans of racquet balls. The total units sold still equals the total units in the master budget, but the sales mix ratios change to 0.5625 for tennis balls and 0.4375 for racquet balls. The sales volume variance equals zero (16,000 units minus 16,000 units times any amount of contribution margin is still zero). However, while the tennis ball department should have had $120,000 in sales and the racquet ball department should have had $48,000 in sales ($168,000 total); they respectively had only $108,000 and $56,000 ($164,000 total) in sales. This $4,000 difference is caused by variances in the sales mix.

Assuming that the budgeted contribution margin per unit of product for tennis balls is $8 and for racquet balls is $4, each product's sales mix variance is calculated as follows.

$$\text{Tennis Ball Sales Mix Variance} = (0.5625 - 0.625) \times 16,000 \text{ Units} \times \$8 \text{ per Unit}$$
$$= -0.0625 \times \$128,000$$
$$= \$8,000 \text{ Unfavorable}$$
$$\text{Racquet Ball Sales Mix Variance} = (0.4375 - 0.375) \times 16,000 \text{ Units} \times \$4 \text{ per Unit}$$
$$= 0.0625 \times \$64,000$$
$$= \$4,000 \text{ Favorable}$$
$$\text{Total Sales Mix Variance} = (\$8,000) + \$4,000 = \$4,000 \text{ Unfavorable}$$

Mix and yield variances

The efficiency (usage) variance for direct costs can be further broken down into two components when a product has two or more ingredients or labor costs that can be substituted for one another. The efficiency variance can be broken down into a direct materials (or labor) mix variance and a direct materials (or labor) yield variance. Three amounts must be known to break an efficiency variance down into its subcomponents:

1. Budgeted Cost/Unit × Actual Total Quantity Used × Actual Mix Ratio for the Item
2. Budgeted Cost/Unit × Actual Total Quantity Used × Budgeted Mix Ratio for the Item
3. Budgeted Cost/Unit × Budgeted Total Quantity Used × Budgeted Mix Ratio for the Item

The mix variance is 1 minus 2 in the prior list and the yield variance is 2 minus 3. The mix ratio is the amount of one substitutable item divided by the total of all substitutable items.

For example, assume that synthetic rubber and natural rubber can be substituted to produce tennis balls and that the standard amounts and prices in the product mix call for 1,000 pounds of synthetic rubber at $2 per pound ($2,000 standard cost) and 600 pounds of natural rubber at $3 per pound ($1,800) to produce 1,000 cans of tennis balls ($3,800 total standard cost). The standard mix ratio for synthetic rubber would be 1,000/1,600 = 0.625 or 62.5%. Similarly the standard mix ratio for natural rubber would be 0.375 or 37.5%. Assume also that the production manager can substitute up to 5% of either product for the other product. In reality, only 988 pounds of synthetic rubber ($1,976 actual cost) and only 532 pounds of natural rubber ($1,596 actual cost) are actually used, for a total of 1,520 pounds (total cost = $3,572, a variance of $228 favorable). This makes the actual mix ratio 65% (988/1,520) for synthetic rubber and 35% for natural rubber. Using this data, the mix variance is calculated as:

1. Budgeted Cost/Unit × Actual Total Quantity Used × Actual Mix Ratio for the Item

   Synthetic Rubber = $2/lb. × 1,520 lbs. × 0.65 = $1,976

   Natural Rubber = $3/lb. × 1,520 lbs. × 0.35   = $1,596

                                                               $3,572

2. Budgeted Cost/Unit × Actual Total Quantity Used × Budgeted Mix Ratio for the Item

   Synthetic Rubber = $2/lb. × 1,520 lbs. × 0.625 = $1,900

   Natural Rubber = $3/lb. × 1,520 lbs. × 0.375   = $1,710

                                                               $3,610

Step 1 − Step 2 = $3,572 − $3,610 = $38 Favorable Mix Variance

The yield variance is calculated as:

2. Budgeted Cost/Unit × Actual Total Quantity Used × Budgeted Mix Ratio for the Item

   Synthetic Rubber = $2/lb. × 1,520 lbs. × 0.625 = $1,900

   Natural Rubber = $3/lb. × 1,520 lbs. × 0.375   = $1,710

                                                               $3,610

3. Budgeted Cost/Unit × Budgeted Total Quantity Used × Budgeted Mix Ratio for the Item

   Synthetic Rubber = $2/lb. × 1,600 lbs. × 0.625 = $2,000

   Natural Rubber = $3/lb. × 1,600 lbs. × 0.375   = $1,800

                                                               $3,800

Step 2 − Step 3 = $3,610 − $3,800 = $190 Favorable Yield Variance

Total Efficiency Variance = ($38) + ($190) = $228 Favorable

The mix variance results from using direct material and/or labor inputs in a ratio that differs from standard specifications. The mix variance is favorable in the example above because a larger percentage of cheaper materials were used to create the product than was budgeted. The yield variance results because the yield (output) obtained differs from the one expected on the basis of input. The larger favorable amount for the yield variance in the example results from the fact that 10% less in materials was used than was expected in order to produce the 1,000 cans of tennis balls. Knowing the breakdown between mix and yield variances can help managers determine how an efficiency variance should be dealt with.

Variations on variance analyses

Each of the prior variances can be broken down into subclasses using the same formulae given. For example, the price (rate) variance can be used to differentiate labor classes to determine more specifically where a favorable or unfavorable variance originated.

Other similar breakdowns or variations include:

- Using mix variance to calculate labor substitution variance (for example, professional versus unskilled labor substitution).

- Labor variance from using substandard materials.

- Price (rate) variance formula to measure the sales price variance or the cost price variance without changing the formula.

Also, some situations occur where some variances are known but other variables must be found, such as in the following example of a highly detailed variance analysis. Bounce Sporting Goods had a very poor month of June according to a flexible budget variance of $76,370 unfavorable. Key data for June follows:

- Budgeted production was for 12,000 units, but a rush order for 8,000 units was added at the last minute and the sales team promised end-of-month delivery.

- Standard costs:

  - Direct material (DM) (from supplier A): 1.5 pounds @ $8/pound = $12/unit

  - Direct labor (DL) (standard Class III [unskilled]): 1.2 direct labor hours (DLH) @ $14/DLH = $16.80/unit

  - Total standard direct costs = $28.80/unit

- Actual costs:

  - After Bounce purchased (and used) 18,200 pounds of DM from supplier A for $144,690, the supplier could not provide more for the rush order, so the purchasing department had to use supplier B, who supplied 18,000 pounds for $142,200 (of which only 15,800 pounds were used, at a cost of $126,400).

  - Actual DM costs charged to production:
    Supplier A DM—18,200 pounds × $8/pound = $145,600
    Supplier B DM—15,800 pounds × $8/pound = $126,400

- To meet the new production quota, Bounce had to transfer some Class II semiskilled employees from a different department, paid on average $16/DLH. (These employees, though more skilled, have a learning curve for the task.)

- Actual DL costs charged to production:
  Class III DL (15,200 hours) = $216,600
  Class II DL (10,300 hours) = $163,770

- Total production costs: $145,600 + $126,400 + $216,600 + $163,770 = $652,370

- Total standard costs at flexible budget level: 20,000 units × $28.80/unit = $576,000

- Flexible budget variance = $652,370 – $576,000 = $76,370 U

Because the DM from supplier B turned out to be very poor, the manager made a breakdown of the time spent by each class of labor in producing units with each set of DM, as shown in Figure 2-59.

Figure 2-59: Units Produced and Labor Used by DM Type

	Supplier A DM		Supplier B DM	
DM used	18,200	pounds	15,800	pounds
Production output				
Class III	7,200	units	4,800	units
Class II	4,800	units	3,200	units
Total output	12,000	units	8,000	units
Actual DLH				
Class III DLH	8,600	hours	6,600	hours
Class II DLH	5,900	hours	4,400	hours
Total DLH	14,500	hours	11,000	hours

What is the DM efficiency (usage) variance for supplier A materials? For supplier B? Figure 2-60 shows how these variances are calculated. Note that in the following calculations, the order of the variance calculations is reversed. While the text earlier presented the following formula,

Efficiency Variance = (Actual Input Quantity – Budgeted Input Quantity) × Budgeted Input Price

the calculations below consistently reverse the order of budgeted versus actual inputs:

Efficiency Variance = (Budgeted Input Quantity – Actual Input Quantity) × Budgeted Input Price

This formula will result in the same number, but it will be positive instead of negative (or vice versa). This complication is presented here because some textbooks present variance formulae in this fashion and it is important to know that there are alternate ways to calculate the same answer. If this reversal is done for one of the variances, it must be consistently done for all of the variances in a set of data. Therefore, in Figure 2-60, the $32,000 unfavorable material usage variance indicates that materials cost $32,000 more than was allocated in the flexible budget.

Figure 2-60: DM Efficiency (Usage) Variance with Multiple Materials

	Supplier A DM		Supplier B DM		Total	
Output—units produced	12,000		8,000		20,000	
Material requirements per unit	× 1.5		× 1.5			
Total standard material requirements	18,000		12,000		30,000	
Actual material consumed	− 18,200		− 15,800		− 34,000	
Usage variance in units (unfavorable)	(200)	U	(3,800)	U	(4,000)	U
Standard cost per unit	× $8		× $8			
Material usage variance	($1,600)	U	($30,400)	U	($32,000)	U
Percent variance from standard	1.1%	U	31.7%	U		

Bounce Sporting Goods also has enough data to break its direct labor variance down into four components: labor rate variance, labor substitution variance, labor variance from substandard materials (supplier B DM), and labor efficiency variance on regular materials (supplier A DM). Figure 2-61 shows the computation of these variances.

Figure 2-61: DL Variance with Multiple Materials and Multiple Types of Labor

	Class III DL	Class II DL	Total DL
Actual DL cost	$216,600	$163,770	$380,370
DL rate variance			
Actual direct labor hours	15,200	10,300	
Standard labor rate	$14.00	$16.00	
Actual labor rate (cost/hours)	− $14.25	− $15.90	
Rate variance per hour	($.25) U	$.10 F	
× Actual direct labor hours	× 15,200	× 10,300	
Labor rate variance	($3,800) U	$1,030 F	($2,770) U
Actual labor hours at standard rate	$212,800	$164,800	$377,600
DL substitution variance			
Class III standard labor rate		$14.00	
Class II standard labor rate		− $16.00	
Substitution rate variance per hour		($2.00) U	
× Actual direct labor hours		× 10,300	
Labor substitution variance		($20,600) U	($20,600) U
Actual labor hours at Class III standard rate	$212,800	$144,200	$357,000
DL variance from substandard materials (Supplier B)			
Units produced—alternative materials	4,800	3,200	
Labor standard per unit	× 1.2	× 1.2	
Standard hours allowed	5,760	3,840	
Actual hours	− 6,600	− 4,400	
Saved/(excess) hours	(840)	(560)	
× Class III standard rate	× $14.00	× $14.00	
Substandard materials labor variance	($11,760) U	($7,840) U	($19,600) U
Subtotal labor costs after substandard materials	$201,040	$136,360	$337,400
DL efficiency variance on regular materials (Supplier A)			
Units produced—regular materials	7,200	4,800	
Labor standard per unit	× 1.2	× 1.2	
Standard hours allowed	8,640	5,760	
Actual hours	− 8,600	− 5,900	
Saved/(excess) hours	40	(140)	
× Class III standard rate	× $14.00	× $14.00	
Labor efficiency variance on regular materials	$560 F	($1,960) U	($1,400) U
Flexible budget labor costs	$201,600	$134,400	$336,000
Total direct labor variances (Flexible – Actual)	($15,000) U	($29,370) U	($44,370) U

Note that the final line of Figure 2-61 is the sum of all variances for each column. What can be learned from this analysis? First, the rush order can be shown to have caused several of the problems. Supplier B's materials accounted for a material usage variance of $30,400 unfavorable (see Figure 2-60), which is much greater than that for supplier A's materials, so the alternate supplies must have had much more scrap or waste. This could have been avoided if the rush order had not been submitted. Second, the labor substitution variance of $20,600 unfavorable is the result of needing to use labor that cost more than the regular workers. Third, the total direct labor variance from use of substandard materials is $19,600 unfavorable, which once again reinforces the conclusion that both types of workers had to waste time working with unsuitable materials.

A detailed analysis such as this can be used for performance evaluation. For example, in keeping with the tenets of responsibility accounting, perhaps the unfavorable variances related to the rush order could be charged to the sales department because they did not provide enough time to produce the rush order, or perhaps purchasing could be charged for the variances related to the substandard materials. Decisions such as these will force the other departments to work more carefully with the production department in the future.

Note that the measures used for the variances discussed in this section make direct use of the most likely cost drivers or revenue drivers that would be used in activity-based costing, such as measuring direct labor hours for a rate variance. This topic also shows that measuring performance against operational goals can take a variety of forms, and in this topic, measuring performance was mostly based on manufacturing costs. However, other performance measures such as those covered in Topic 3 of this section, "Financial Measures"; in Part 1, Section E, "Financial Statement Analysis"; and in Part 3, Section D, "Decision Analysis," are based on revenue, nonmanufacturing costs, and profit, depending on the type of unit being measured. The next topic covers the different types of business units commonly found in the corporate world.

Progress Check

Directions: Read each question and respond in the space provided. Answers and page references appear on the following page.

1. When comparing the variance from a static budget, the budget calls for production of 1,200 units with an overhead cost of $600,000 and a total profit of $120,000. However, only 1,000 units are produced. Total overhead is $550,000 and total profit is $125,000. Actual results are

    ( )   a.   effective and efficient.

    ( )   b.   effective but not efficient.

    ( )   c.   not effective but efficient.

    ( )   d.   not effective and not efficient.

2. Which of the following variances plus the flexible budget variance equals the total static budget variance?

    ( )   a.   Efficiency variance

    ( )   b.   Price variance

    ( )   c.   Sales mix variance

    ( )   d.   Sales volume variance

3. Which of the following results from using direct material and/or labor inputs in a ratio that differs from standard specifications?

    ( )   a.   Yield variance

    ( )   b.   Mix variance

    ( )   c.   Efficiency variance

    ( )   d.   Sales mix variance

Progress check answers

1. b (p. 2-193)

2. d (p. 2-197)

3. b (p. 2-211)

Responsibility Centers and Reporting Segments

Topic overview

A decentralized organization spreads decision making to managers at different responsibility center levels. A responsibility center, also called a strategic business unit (SBU), is any portion of a business that grants the center's manager responsibility over costs, profits, revenues, or investments. Types of responsibility centers include cost centers, profit centers, and investment centers. Reporting segments and contribution reporting are also discussed in this section.

Types of Responsibility Centers

Responsibility accounting is a method of defining segments or subunits in an organization as types of responsibility centers based on their level of autonomy and the responsibilities of their managers and basing performance evaluations on these factors. Responsibility centers are classified by their primary effect on the company as a whole: Revenue or profit centers generate revenues, cost centers generate costs, and investment centers make investments. A cost center such as a service department may generate some revenues, but the department usually has a net cost.

Revenue centers/profit centers

Because profit margin is a function of both revenue and costs, a manager for a **revenue center** or a **profit center** is responsible for generating profits or revenues and for controlling costs. Managers of these departments usually don't have control over investments. A revenue center is used by some companies to designate segments that generate revenues but are not expected to control costs. A sales department could be a revenue center because the primary focus is on revenues and the only costs are salaries and overhead. Other companies do not use the term "revenue center" and call all revenue-generating departments "profit centers" because revenue centers have direct costs and overhead to deduct from gross revenue. A profit center is used to describe an area that generates revenues as well as the major portion of the costs for producing these revenues. Profit centers are often also separate reporting segments. A grocery store that is part of a chain of stores could be a profit center and a separate reporting segment. Managers of such profit centers would be evaluated based on their variance from the master budget profits as compared to their segmented business results.

Cost centers

A manager for a **cost center** is responsible for controlling costs in a department that generates little or no revenue. Therefore, the manager is not responsible for revenue or investments but is rewarded whenever he or she can minimize costs while maintaining an expected level of quality. Finance, administration, human resources, accounting, customer service, and help desks are all examples of cost centers. If the cafeteria isn't expected to make a profit, it is also a cost center. Even plants and manufacturing facilities are sometimes considered a cost center, assuming that the profit center would then be the sales department or a different production department.

Common costs are allocated among all cost centers involved in proportion to the amounts of a selected cost driver. (See the discussion of the allocation of service department costs in Section B, Topic 4, in this part.)

A manager of a cost center would be responsible for following up on variances. The manager's success at removing unfavorable variances and analyzing favorable variances is often part of the basis for their compensation.

Investment centers

A manager for an **investment center** is responsible for investments, costs, and revenues in his or her department. Investment centers can be primarily centered on internal or external investments. An internal investment manager would be responsible for reviewing and approving capital budgeting and other investments, such as in R&D. An external investment manager would be responsible for reviewing and approving temporary and long-term investments for capital maintenance, return on investment, and strategic investments. Managers in such centers would be evaluated based on their function. Strategic investments would be evaluated for their fit with the company strategy, while other investments would be judged on their return on investment and preservation of capital.

Productivity

Increasing productivity is a goal of all businesses. This could be achieved by producing more output with less input, by producing the same amount of output with less input, or by producing more output with the same input amount. Productivity analysis can show, for example, that providing health care coverage for employees results in greater benefits in labor productivity than the health care costs (or it could show the opposite). When firms use fewer resources (for example, labor, property, equipment) than their competitors to produce the same amount (found by benchmarking studies), they enjoy greater long-term success over those competitors.

Productivity is a ratio measuring output against input:

$$\text{Productivity} = \frac{\text{Output}}{\text{Input}}$$

$$= \frac{1{,}000 \text{ Units Produced}}{40 \text{ Hours Total}} = 25 \text{ Units/Hour}$$

Output can be in units produced or in a financial measure such as revenues; input can be in time spent, dollars spent, or quantities of raw materials. The choice of what to use as the numerator and the denominator of this ratio leads to various types of productivity measures.

Financial productivity

The **financial productivity** ratio uses either money or a physical measure for the output value and only money amounts for the input value.

$$\text{Financial Productivity} = \frac{\text{Output in Units or Money}}{\text{Input in Money}}$$

$$= \frac{\$5,000 \text{ Sales Revenue}}{\$1,000 \text{ Raw Rubber}} = \$5 \text{ Revenue}/\$1 \text{ Raw Rubber}$$

Operational productivity

The operational productivity ratio uses physical amounts for the output and input values.

$$\text{Operational Productivity} = \frac{\text{Output in Units}}{\text{Input in Units}}$$

$$= \frac{10,000 \text{ Raquet Balls}}{5,000 \text{ Lbs. Raw Rubber}} = 2 \text{ Raquet Balls/Lb. Raw Rubber}$$

Partial productivity

Partial productivity is a financial or operational productivity ratio that compares total output to a subset of the total inputs, such as just one raw material rather than all ingredients, just one processing machine of several, just one area's labor costs rather than all labor costs, or just fixed overhead rather than total costs. Such ratios highlight the contribution of just one factor to the total output and can help measure change in productivity for specific subsets. All of the prior examples show some type of partial productivity: The first example shows work-force productivity measured by labor hours (but neglects direct material and overhead costs); the second and third examples show revenue produced by one direct material (neglecting other materials, labor, and overhead). Partial productivity is commonly performed for direct materials, called direct materials yield; for a work force, measured as output per labor hour or per employee; and for process productivity, measured in output per machine hour or another cost driver.

Total factor productivity

Total factor productivity (TFP; or **total productivity**) is a financial productivity ratio that compares total output to the cost of total inputs.

$$\text{Total Factor Productivity} = \frac{\text{Total Output in Units}}{\text{Cost of All Inputs Used}}$$

$$= \frac{10,000 \text{ Raquet Balls}}{\$6,000 \text{ DM} + \$15,000 \text{ Conversion}}$$

$$= 0.4762 \text{ Raquet Balls/Dollar of Input Cost}$$

TFP is a useful ratio only when it can be compared to historical and benchmark TFP data from competitors (if it can be acquired). When internal historical data is used, a TFP benchmark ratio can be made by using the units from the current year and flexible budgeting to determine the cost of all inputs that would have been required to produce at the same output level.

$$\text{TFP Benchmark} = \frac{\text{Total Output in Units for Current Year (CY)}}{\text{Cost of Inputs Needed in Prior Year to Make CY Output}}$$

$$= \frac{\text{10,000 Raquet Balls}}{\text{\$7,000 DM} + \text{\$16,000 Conversion}}$$

$$= 0.4348 \text{ Raquet Balls/Dollar of Input Cost}$$

The differential between these two ratios can then be compared without having to adjust for differences in output:

$$\text{TFP Differential} = \frac{\text{Current Year TFP Ratio} - \text{Benchmark TFP Ratio}}{\text{Benchmark TFP Ratio}}$$

$$= \frac{0.4762 - 0.4348}{0.4348} = 0.0952 = 9.52\% \text{ increase in TFP}$$

Contribution and Segment Reporting

Contribution reporting

The contribution approach to reporting on an income statement is useful for internal decision making. It separates fixed from variable expenses, deducting variable expenses first to arrive at the contribution margin and then deducting fixed expenses to arrive at net operating income. The contribution margin is the amount that contributes toward fixed expenses and profits after all variable expenses have been met. The **contribution margin** shows managers how profits are affected by changes in volume, because fixed costs and operating capacity are kept constant.

The primary advantage of such an income statement format is that profit center managers can view the costs by their behavior instead of by departments such as sales, administration, and production (cost of goods sold). Managers can use a contribution income statement when analyzing product lines and when deciding on prices for goods, whether to expand a segment or discontinue it, or whether to make or buy a good. Managers can be more easily evaluated using a contribution income statement, because the items outside their control are separated from the items within their control. However, many fixed costs are controllable, so managers often have their fixed costs further divided into controllable fixed costs and uncontrollable fixed costs. Controllable fixed costs are those that can be changed within a year; uncontrollable costs take over a year to influence. Uncontrollable fixed costs can also come from a nonnegotiable corporate allocation of headquarters expenses. The controllable margin is the contribution margin less the controllable fixed costs.

Figure 2-62 shows two versions of the same income statement, in traditional and contribution formats. If a prior period's statement showed that the uncontrollable fixed production costs were rising and the variable production costs were falling, a traditional statement would not show this fact, but the contribution format could show that the manager had been successful at keeping costs relatively the same even in the face of rising fixed costs outside the manager's control. Note also that the traditional income statement's cost of goods sold, selling, and administrative costs include both fixed and variable expenses, but there is no way to determine how the amounts are broken down.

Figure 2-62: Income Statements in Traditional Versus Contribution Format

Traditional Approach **(Costs Organized by Function)**			**Contribution Approach** **(Costs Organized by Behavior)**		
Sales		$ 31,200	Sales		$ 31,200
Less cost of goods sold		15,600	Less variable expenses:		
Gross margin		15,600	Variable production	$5,200	
Less operating expenses:			Variable selling	1,560	
			Variable administrative	1,040	7,800
Selling	$8,060		Contribution margin		23,400
Administrative	4,940	13,000	Less fixed expenses:		
Net operating income		$ 2,600	Fixed production	10,400	
			Fixed selling	6,500	
			Fixed administrative	3,900	20,800
			Net operating income		$ 2,600

Segment reporting

Reporting segments are portions of a business divided for reporting purposes along product lines, geographical areas, or other meaningful segments to provide individual information about that area. Segmented financial statements are the same as unsegmented statements except that each segment has its own costs traced back to it so that the report shows how profitable each segment is by itself. The **segment margin** is the segment's contribution margin less all traceable fixed costs for the segment. The segment margin is a useful indication of a segment's profitability. If it is not positive, the segment may need to be discontinued unless it adds value to other segments.

Traceable fixed costs that are included in a segment's margin are costs that would not exist were it not for the segment. Administrative salaries for segment managers are an example of a fixed cost that can be traced directly to a segment. Similarly, building maintenance costs or insurance premiums for a specific business segment can be traced to the segment.

Common cost allocation

Unlike traceable fixed costs, common fixed costs cannot be traced to a specific department, such as the CEO's salary, and thus make it more difficult to determine the profitability of an individual segment. A **common cost** is any cost that is shared by two or more segments or entities. When common costs are allocated to segments, it dilutes the value of the segment margin on reporting profitability, so some businesses allocate common costs to segments only when all or most of the cost would disappear if the segment were to be discontinued. Two methods of allocating common costs are the stand-alone method and the incremental method.

- **Stand-alone cost allocation**

  Stand-alone cost allocation is a method that determines the relative proportion of costs for each party that shares a common cost and allocates the costs by those percentages. For example, if a company has a new plant and an older plant, but both plants require some workers to be given on-site training, the traveling trainer's salary of $60,000 plus $10,000 travel and lodging expenses could be allocated based on the number of users that need to be trained at each location (or some other cost driver such as days spent at each location). If the old plant has 40 trainees and the new plant has 60 trainees, then the old plant would receive $28,000 of the cost (40%) and the new plant would receive $42,000 of the cost. This method has the benefit of fairness.

- **Incremental cost allocation**

  Incremental cost allocation is a method that allocates costs by ranking the parties by a primary user and incremental users, or those users that add an additional cost due to the fact that there is now more than one user of the cost. Consider the prior example. If the trainer was hired because the new plant was being opened and therefore has a home base in the new plant's city, the new plant would be the primary user of the trainer cost. If the trainer was at the new plant for three quarters and at the old plant for one quarter, the new plant might be allocated $40,000 of the costs, while the old plant is allocated the remaining $20,000 plus all $10,000 of the travel expenses because these are an incremental cost of having the trainer relocate to serve the incremental user.

  Conversely, if management wanted to give the new plant a head start on costs, it could choose to designate the old plant as the primary user and allocate only a small amount of the costs to the new plant. Because this method allows managers to manipulate how costs are allocated, it is not as balanced as the stand-alone method. Also, when common costs are allocated in this manner, most of the segments want to be incremental users, so this method can cause interdepartmental strife.

Transfer Pricing

Transfer pricing sets prices for internally exchanged goods and services. An **intermediate product** is a good or service that is transferred between two segments of a company. Company strategy is greatly affected by choice of transfer prices. If the company wants the business units to behave independently and keep managers motivated to achieve company goals, transfer prices should be set at arm's length, as if the party were any other external client. When no external suppliers exist for a product or service, the arm's length price is more difficult to determine than simply checking market prices. The amounts set for transfer prices require cooperation between many departments including finance, production, marketing, and tax planning.

Firms that have a high degree of vertical integration will need to carefully set transfer prices. For example, a corporation that owns farms, food warehouses, distributors, and grocery stores will need to set prices for each service that will allow each portion of their business to be financially flexible.

Transfer pricing models

Four models that can be used to set transfer prices include market price, negotiated price, variable cost, and full cost. Firms often combine various methods (dual pricing) to match their needs.

Market price

The market price model is a true arm's length model because it sets the price for a good or service at going market prices. This model can be used only when an item has a market; items such as work-in-process inventory may not have a market price. The market price model keeps business units autonomous, forces the selling unit to be competitive with external suppliers, and is preferred by tax authorities. Businesses that use this model should account for the reduced selling and marketing costs in the price.

Negotiated price

The negotiated price model sets transfer price through negotiation between the buyer and the seller. When different business units experience conflicts, negotiation or even arbitration may be needed to keep the company as a whole functioning efficiently. Negotiated prices can make both buying and selling units less autonomous.

Variable cost

The variable cost model sets transfer prices at the unit's variable cost, or the actual cost to produce the good or service less all fixed costs. This method will lower the selling unit's profits and increase the buying unit's profits due to the low price. This model is advantageous for selling units that have excess capacity or for situations when a buying unit could purchase from external sources but the company wants to encourage internal purchases. The disadvantages of this method include that tax authorities do not prefer that companies use this method and that lowering the profits of a profit center can cause the unit to underreport taxable income.

Full cost (absorption)

The full cost (absorption) model starts with the seller's variable cost for the item and then allocates fixed costs to the price. Some companies allocate standard fixed costs because this allows the buying unit to know the cost in advance and keeps the seller from becoming too inefficient due to a captive buyer that pays for the inefficiencies. Adding fixed costs is relatively straightforward and fair. However, it can alter a business unit's decision making.

Although fixed costs should not be included in the decision to purchase items internally or externally, often managers will purchase the "lower-cost" external item even though the internal fixed costs will still be incurred.

Choosing transfer price models

In general, the market price method is preferred in situations when the market price for a good or service is available. When a market price isn't available, the negotiated price method is preferred. When neither is acceptable, companies may turn to one of the cost models. Cost-based methods are not recommended because they can lead to motivation problems between parties such as the seller not actively controlling costs because they are simply passed on to the buyer.

The logic of choosing a transfer price model and setting transfer prices starts with a make or buy decision. If there are outside suppliers for a product or service, then the market price model should be used. The company should compare the selling unit's variable costs to the market price for the external substitute. If the external market price is lower than the internal variable cost, the buyer should purchase externally to motivate the internal supplier to find ways to lower costs.

When internal variable cost is less than the external market price, then the buying unit should purchase internally so long as the selling unit has excess capacity. The variable cost model is best for low capacity, and the market price model is best for high capacity. If the selling unit is at full capacity, the buying unit should purchase externally if the selling unit can generate more profit from a sale to an external source than will be lost if the buying unit pays the external market price for the item. When the opposite is true, the buying unit should purchase internally and pay market price for the item.

Multinational company transfer pricing considerations

Multinational company transfer pricing issues include the tax liability considerations, risk of expropriation, currency restrictions, consideration of customs charges, and government regulations. In general, if transfer prices are too high, the buyer will not purchase enough units or they will buy externally; if too low, the seller will not produce enough units.

Tax liability

Multinational corporations often use transfer pricing to reduce their overall tax liability. The country with the relatively lower tax rate would recognize the greater share of the profits by charging relatively higher prices. For example, a firm could use market price to sell goods to a country with higher tax rates than the selling unit's country. The buying country's taxable income would be reduced and the selling country's taxable income would be increased, but the net effect would be positive for the company. However, many countries have cracked down on transfer pricing abuses and have assessed additional taxes on companies that perform such activities. The IRS has set up advance pricing agreements (APAs) with firms that set the transfer price in advance so that firms can avoid possible future litigation.

Expropriation

Expropriation occurs when a country takes control of a foreign company's assets and operations in that country. If the risk of expropriation is considered high, transfer pricing can be used to minimize it. The at-risk segment would pay high rates to purchase internal goods from other countries and receive low payments for selling internal goods to other countries, thus transferring the profits away from that segment.

Currency restrictions

Currency restrictions occur when a foreign country limits the amount of a company's profits that can be removed from the country in an attempt to force reinvestment in the country. A multinational firm can set transfer prices to increase the profits distributed to the parent company.

Customs charges

Customs charges and tariffs can be a significant cost for a multinational firm, so minimizing these costs is usually a consideration when setting transfer prices. For example, using the variable cost method would minimize the transfer price and thus the customs charges.

Government regulations

Governments understand that transfer pricing is often used to provide tax and profit advantages for a company, often at the expense of the governments involved. Therefore, many countries have legislated maximum and minimum transfer prices, where the minimum price is cost and the maximum price is the going market rate. Other sets of countries have negotiated treaties agreeing to specific transfer price methods (often at market price).

Reporting of Organizational Segments

The reports created for various organizational segments are of primary internal use for measuring performance. This section includes a brief discussion of external segmented financial reports, followed by a discussion of performance measurement reports and multinational performance measurement issues.

Segmented external financial reports

The FASB requires external financial reports to include segmented data that includes all of the methods and definitions that companies use for internal segmented reports. While segmented financial reports are most useful when they include information such as segment contribution margin, traceable and common costs, and the division of variable and fixed costs, these internally useful methods are not GAAP for external reporting. Therefore companies will need to reconcile their statements at additional cost or prepare them initially according to GAAP, losing out on some of the benefits available for internal reporting.

Performance measurement reports

Performance measurement reports should be tailored to the audience and level of management to which they are directed. Too much information can cloud an issue as easily as not enough information can, so the amount and timing of information delivery is critical to the success of each manager. Timing of performance measurement reports such as variance reports is critical; the information must be relevant for it to be useful. However, reporting can be too frequent if a manager is flooded with information and cannot discern what information is important.

Effective performance measures cause a desired strategic result by causing the manager and other employees to strive for organizational goals. Improper motivation can cause organizations to be counterproductive. To design an effective performance measure, a company should begin by aligning performance measures with company strategy. Each performance measure selected needs to have the following elements:

- A time period for performance measurement (for example, view one year's results or several years simultaneously)

- Common definitions for items (for example, assets are defined as total assets available regardless of function or usage)

- Define specific measurement units used (for example, use historical cost, current cost)

- A target level of performance for each performance measure and each segment

- A feedback timing schedule (for example, feedback supplied daily, weekly, quarterly)

Specific financial performance measurements and the balanced scorecard method of evaluating financial and nonfinancial performance are covered later in this section.

Multinational company performance measurement

Each country has differences in economy, laws, customs, and politics, and these nonfinancial considerations should play a part in evaluating a foreign division's results.

Multinational companies must account for additional concerns such as how tariffs, exchange rates, and the availability and relative cost of materials and skills should affect performance evaluations. Also, as stated previously, multinational companies often use transfer pricing to gain tax and income advantages. This can come into conflict with using transfer pricing to evaluate performance or to create performance incentives. For example, some pharmaceutical companies produce their goods in Puerto Rico and sell the majority of the product in the United States. Because Puerto Rico has a relatively lower tax status than the rest of the U.S., the incentive is for the pharmaceutical company to charge the highest transfer price possible for drugs sold to their U.S. divisions (such as market price), thus retaining the profits in the country that has a lower tax rate. Because the Puerto Rican subsidiary essentially has a captive market, they may not be as efficient as overall corporate management would like.

Conversely, if the producing country has relatively higher taxes than the primary country in which sales occur, the incentive will be to charge the lowest price possible (such as cost) for the goods so that the profits end up in the selling country division. The resulting performance could be that the producing country fails to meet total demand. Also, if the price is actual cost, the producer won't have any incentive to control those costs as they are merely transferred to the other division. One solution to such a dilemma is to use standard costs instead of actual costs. (The standard could be made more stringent over time for continuous improvement.) Another solution is to change the accountability structure of the segments, becoming more centralized if decentralized transfer prices fail to create the desired incentives.

As with any performance evaluation, evaluations in a multinational company should focus on separating controllable from noncontrollable costs, basing assessments only on costs that can be affected by a manager's choices. If a foreign currency becomes devalued, this will affect profits but is outside a manager's control. When foreign governments impose trade restrictions such as tariffs, the performance measurement should take into account reduced profits from such sources. When managers in foreign countries keep their books in a foreign country's currency, their supervisors should consider the effects of currency fluctuations, inflation, and differences in relative purchasing power in the foreign country (for example, a country with lower costs of labor and goods will also have to price goods for sale in that country much lower than in a country where labor and goods are more costly).

However, because performance evaluations should provide incentives for managers to improve overall operations, it is important to determine if any portion of a noncontrollable event could actually have been prevented or deflected. For example, if a manager knows she will not be held accountable for a devalued currency, she may not move as quickly to move funds out of the country than if she was accountable for a portion of such losses. A manager evaluated in such a fashion might employ a market analyst or economist specializing in currency exchange to help forecast such changes.

Another way of enhancing the value of performance measurement is by using benchmark values from other managers or companies in similar local environments. Each distinct area would have its own comparison group. Such a system is analogous to grading on a curve.

Finally, because profits can be so distorted by the various international issues mentioned, performance evaluations could avoid the focus on profit and instead focus on more stable indicators, such as revenues, market share, or operating costs.

Progress Check

Directions: Read each question and respond in the space provided. Answers and page references appear on the following page.

1. Which of the following usually makes a manager responsible for all financial business decisions?

    (   )   a.   Revenue center

    (   )   b.   Cost center

    (   )   c.   Investment center

    (   )   d.   Profit center

2. Which of the following transfer pricing models sets prices at actual cost less all fixed costs?

    (   )   a.   Variable cost

    (   )   b.   Full cost (absorption)

    (   )   c.   Market price

    (   )   d.   Negotiated price

3. Why is including contribution margin on segmented internal income statements an issue for external financial reporting?

    (   )   a.   Including segmented contribution margin on financial statements provides less meaningful information for investors.

    (   )   b.   Including segmented contribution margin on external financial statements is not GAAP, so the statements must be restated.

    (   )   c.   Contribution margin is incompatible with segment reporting.

    (   )   d.   Contribution margin includes all fixed costs for the segment instead of allocating fixed costs to the parent company.

Progress check answers

1. c (p. 2-221)

2. a (p. 2-226)

3. b (p. 2-228)

Financial Measures

Topic overview

Profitability analyses measure the relative success or failure of a company over a period of time. This section covers profitability analyses for products, business units, and customers. It then goes into specific financial analysis ratios.

Profitability Analysis

Product profitability analysis

Product profitability analysis will show which products are the most profitable, which need to have their prices reevaluated, and which should get the greatest marketing and support attention. For product line managers, a product profitability analysis is often used as the basis for compensation or bonuses.

Product lines that are unprofitable in the long run will be discontinued. When determining whether to discontinue a product line, the first step is to remove from the analysis all per-unit fixed costs that would not disappear if the product line were discontinued. The product profitability analysis sums up the benefits of removing all fixed costs that are traceable to the affected unit plus all variable costs for the unit. Then the analysis sums up the opportunity cost of all sales that would be lost if the product line were discontinued. The difference between these amounts is the increase or decrease in profit that would occur from discontinuing the product line.

For example, if a sporting goods company had a profitable tennis ball line and an unprofitable racquet ball line, the racquet ball line could be analyzed to determine what effect removing it would have on company profits. In Figure 2-63, the contribution margin for both product lines shows a positive amount of profit. However, after traceable costs are allocated to each department, the racquet ball department shows a loss. Note that all common costs are deducted only from the total amount for the entire company, so these costs do not play a part in management's decision to discontinue the operation.

Figure 2-63: Profitability Analysis

	Tennis Balls	Racquet Balls	Total
Last year's sales	$780,000	$195,000	$975,000
Relevant costs			
Variable cost	585,000	175,500	760,500
Contribution margin	$195,000	$19,500	$214,500
Other relevant costs (traceable)			
Advertising	19,500	26,000	45,500
Contribution after all relevant costs	$175,500	$(6,500)	$169,000
Nonrelevant costs (not traceable)			
Fixed cost			$100,000
Net income with racquet balls			$69,000

In addition to financial measures, a product line profitability analysis needs to analyze how the line affects overall company strategy. The following questions illustrate types of nonfinancial considerations:

- How will dropping the product line affect company morale?

- If the product line is dropped, how will sales of related product lines be affected?

- Is the product line used as a component of another, more-profitable product?

- Would investing more resources into marketing and sales increase product profitability?

- Could the product become more profitable in the long run?

- Would increasing the price of the product increase profitability or just lower sales even more?

Business unit profitability analysis

Business unit profitability analysis is measured using contribution margin, direct profit, controllable profit, income before taxes, or net income.

Figure 2-64 shows how an income statement could be formed to include these measures for a business unit.

Figure 2-64: Business Unit Income Statement

Revenue	$ 780,000
Cost of sales	500,000
Variable expenses	85,000
Contribution margin	**195,000**
Fixed expenses incurred in the profit center	19,500
Direct profit	**175,500**
Controllable corporate charges	12,500
Controllable profit	**163,000**
Other corporate allocations	40,000
Income before taxes	**123,000**
Taxes	49,200
Net income	**$ 73,800**

Contribution margin

Contribution margin measures the difference between revenue and variable expenses. It is useful for management performance analysis because it eliminates the fixed expenses that are perceived to be beyond the manager's control. However, not all fixed expenses are uncontrollable, so focusing on contribution margin can lead to a manager ignoring possible cost reductions. Furthermore, even fixed costs that cannot be altered must still be managed for efficient use. For example, salaried employees must be kept efficient.

Direct profit

Direct profit is the business unit's contribution margin less its fixed costs. Direct profit does not include fixed costs common to the organization as a whole. Managers evaluated using this measure may be content with a lower level of success than if common costs were also deducted from the measurement.

Controllable profit

If common costs are divided into costs controllable by the business unit and all other costs, then the controllable costs are subtracted from direct profit to arrive at controllable profit. The controllable profit measure includes all costs within the manager's control (and some business unit fixed costs that are not) and therefore is useful in motivating managers to reduce all types of costs where possible. However, this measure is available only on internal financial reports, so if the firm uses this measure, it will be difficult to obtain comparable financial information from competitors.

Income before taxes

Income before taxes deducts all costs for a business unit other than taxes. Using this measure makes the business unit manager seem accountable for costs that are not under the manager's control such as the costs of the human resources department that are allocated to the business unit. One advantage of using this measure is that the manager will have a realistic view of the level of profitability needed to make the business unit successful. The amount can be easily compared to the profitability of competitors. Managers rewarded for maintaining profitability in the face of all overhead may make better long-term decisions such as for product mix and marketing.

Net income

Net income is income after taxes. This method has the same benefits as using income before taxes, but it has other drawbacks. First, tax rates are often the same for each area, so there is often little benefit of examining this amount. Second, when tax rates differ, it is usually a result of corporate manipulation for tax purposes beyond the manager's control. Net income is desirable for foreign business units because each country will have a different tax rate and these will make a difference in overall profitability for a business unit.

Customer profitability analysis

Measuring profitability at the level of the customer involves determining the benefits received from the customer and the costs incurred to service the customer. The benefits will include nonfinancial and financial measures. Nonfinancial measures include customer acquisition, customer retention, customer satisfaction, and overall market share. Nonfinancial measures are discussed more fully in the next topic, "Balanced Scorecard."

Financial measures can usually be collected on a customer level only if the company uses financial software that breaks out costs by customer, a feature typically found in activity-based costing (ABC) software. The financial measures serve as a balance to a company that puts customers first in their strategy, because retaining customers even when the costs outweigh the revenues is a losing strategy. The customer profitability analysis will show when a customer demand should be satisfied, when it should be declined, and when it should include an additional fee for the service.

For strategic reasons, some customer demands will be satisfied even when they are not financially profitable, but an advanced financial management software system such as ABC would at least bring the cost issue to the attention of managers so that a long-term solution can be formed. The emphasis should be on transforming the unprofitable customer into a profitable customer. Lifetime profitability is one reason to retain customers that are initially unprofitable. If the customer can be retained for the long term, the overall profits can be very positive. For example, a real estate agent that spends time on a client trying to purchase a low-cost home may not realize much of a profit on the sale, but the customer's lifetime repeat business could be significant.

Return on Investment (ROI)

Return on investment (ROI) measures profitability by dividing income by the investment made to attain that income. ROI is also called the accounting rate of return or the accrual accounting rate of return.

The formula for ROI follows:

$$\text{Return on Investment (ROI)} = \frac{\text{Return}}{\text{Investment}}$$

Although the time line for the return and the investment are not always equal (for example, investment in a bond in Year 1 with interest returns for the next five years), when comparing two or more investment opportunities, it is important that the time horizons be the same for each project so a fair comparison can be made. When using ROI for a cost-benefit analysis, it is also important to account for any ongoing costs of the investment over the period that the benefits are tracked (that is, net benefit per year).

ROI can be measured for the short term (a single month or year) or the long term (for example, investing in a computer system that will generate six years of benefits and six years of costs). However, when dealing with long-term analyses, use of a discounted cash flow model will be more appropriate because such models take into account the time value of money.

Both return and investment can be defined in different ways to measure different types of profitability, as shown in Figure 2-65 on the next page.

ROI is a broad measure of what you get from what you put in. Often income is used generically to mean contribution margin. Investment is dependent on whose investment one wishes to refer to (to owners' investment, to creditors' debt investment, or to both). Therefore, some companies use total assets, others use assets financed by long-term debt, and others use stockholders' equity plus long-term liabilities.

Figure 2-65: Variations on ROI—Possible Definitions of Return and Investment

Type	Definitions
Return on investment (ROI)	$$\frac{\text{Net Income}}{\text{Investment}}$$ $$\frac{\text{Contribution Margin}}{\text{Investment}}$$ $$\frac{\text{Operating Income}}{\text{Total Assets}}$$ $$\frac{\text{Net Income}}{\text{Total Assets } - \text{ Long-Term Liabilities}}$$
Segment ROI	$$\frac{\text{Divisional Income}}{\text{Investment}}$$
Return on common stockholders' equity or return on equity (ROE)	$$\frac{\text{Net Income } - \text{ Preferred Dividends}}{\text{Average Common Stockholders' Equity}}$$
Return on total assets or return on assets (ROA)	$$\frac{\text{Net Income + Interest Expense}}{\text{Average Total Assets}}$$ $$\frac{\text{Net Profit After Taxes}}{\text{Tangible Total Assets}}$$
Return on operating income	$$\frac{\text{Operating Income}}{\text{Total Shareholders' Equity}}$$
Return on capital investments	$$\frac{\text{Net Income}}{\text{Noncurrent Assets}}$$
Return on invested capital	$$\frac{\text{Net Profit After Taxes + Interest Expense}}{(\text{Total Stockholders' Equity } - \text{ Intangible Stockholders' Equity}) + \text{Long-Term Liabilities}}$$
Return on gross profit	$$\frac{\text{Net Profit After Taxes}}{\text{Gross Profit}}$$
Return on working capital	$$\frac{\text{Net Profit After Taxes}}{\text{Working Capital}}$$
Return on net worth	$$\frac{\text{Net Profit After Taxes}}{\text{Total Stockholders' Equity } - \text{ Intangible Stockholders' Equity}}$$
Profit per employee	$$\frac{\text{Net Profit After Taxes}}{\text{Number of Employees}}$$

When an average is needed, use the sum of this year's beginning (or last year's ending) and this year's ending values divided by two (for example, average total assets are last year's ending total assets plus this year's ending total assets divided by two). How a particular company decides to define both return and investment may depend on industry conventions or internal company conventions. Knowing what figures were used to generate a ratio is the only way to be able to rely on those ratios. If the ratios for a firm are given without any context, it may be more reliable to generate your own ratios from the firm's financial statements. This way you can be sure that each ratio is computed using the same methodology and source data. Be sure to review the disclosures to financial statements, because each company may use different methods to account for inventory, for example, and therefore the results will still not be comparable unless data is converted (for example, companies using LIFO for inventory valuation will report a FIFO equivalent in their disclosures, and this amount can be used when comparing results to another company also using FIFO).

ROI can be expressed as a percentage, and the greater the percentage, the greater the return on investment. ROI is a popular measure of profitability because it combines revenues, investments, and costs all in one figure. However, no financial ratio has meaning by itself; ROI should be used with other financial measures and should be compared to industry averages or to other possible investments.

For internal use, companies use various definitions of income (or profits) and investments; for external use, companies use GAAP definitions of each. However, both internal and external ratios may be hard to compare if the ratios were prepared using different methods of allocating common costs (that is, comparing ROI between business units). When ROI uses average total assets in its investment denominator, it becomes return on assets (ROA), which shows how successful a company is at making a profit using a given level of assets. Firms that are more efficient with their assets are more likely to be profitable. When ROI uses ownership interest for the investment denominator, it is called return on equity (ROE). ROE is calculated only for common equity because preferred stockholders have a set return that is the preferred dividend rate.

There is a relationship between ROE and ROA. In general, a company's ROE should be higher than its ROA, because this implies that the funds borrowed (for example, at 9%) were reinvested to earn a higher rate of return (for example, 15% ROE) than was used in borrowing the funds. A firm uses financial leverage to achieve this difference, which is called trading on the equity. A generic and a specific definition of financial leverage follows:

$$\text{Financial Leverage} = \frac{\text{Assets}}{\text{Equity}} = \frac{\text{Total Assets}}{\text{Average Shareholders' Equity}}$$

Having relatively more assets with relatively less equity increases the financial leverage ratio. From a shareholder's perspective, a higher financial leverage is preferred. For companies making profit above the financing costs, this would yield higher return on invested capital (equity). However, higher financial leverage also exposes the company to greater bankruptcy risk in situations when the company earns less than the interest costs. When revenues are increasing, profits for shareholders are multiplied. (However, when revenues are decreasing, profits shrink at the same accelerated rate because debts must be paid regardless of profits.)

For example, let's say that a sporting goods manufacturer analyzes ROI for two business units using operating income for income and net assets for investment:

- Tennis ball business unit: income of $100,000; net assets of $400,000

$$ROI = \frac{\$100,000}{\$400,000} = 25\%$$

- Racquet ball business unit: income of $60,000; net assets of $300,000

$$ROI = \frac{\$60,000}{\$300,000} = 20\%$$

DuPont method of profitability analysis

The DuPont method of profitability analysis breaks ROI down into investment turnover times return on sales, where investment turnover is revenues (sales) divided by investments and return on sales is income divided by revenues. The formula for the DuPont method follows:

$$DuPont\ Method\ ROI = Investment\ Turnover \times Return\ on\ Sales$$

$$= \frac{Revenues}{Investment} \times \frac{Income}{Revenues}$$

The DuPont method divides profitability into how to produce revenue from assets and how to increase income per dollar of revenue. Investment turnover measures how effectively a manager can increase sales based on a given level of investment. Return on sales measures how effectively a manager can raise profitability by controlling expenses and increasing revenues. Using this version of ROI allows performance evaluations to see whether ROI comes more from how well assets are used or how strong the profit margin is. A firm can set performance goals for both investment turnover and return on sales that encourage each unit to make improvements that fit the company's strategy.

Continuing the prior example, if tennis balls had revenues of $250,000 and racquet balls had revenues of $120,000, the DuPont method ROI would be as follows:

$$Tennis\ balls = \frac{\$250,000}{\$400,000} \times \frac{\$100,000}{\$250,000} = 0.625 \times 0.4 = 25\%$$

$$Racquet\ balls = \frac{\$120,000}{\$300,000} \times \frac{\$60,000}{\$120,000} = 0.4 \times 0.5 = 20\%$$

The calculations above show that the tennis ball business unit owes more of its success to a larger investment base resulting in greater sales but has a lower profit margin. The racquet ball business unit has the opposite: a smaller investment base resulting in lower sales, but a higher profit margin makes up for the difference. Therefore, the tennis ball unit manager might be encouraged to cut costs to increase the profit margin, whereas the racquet ball unit manager might be encouraged to reduce inventory or idle cash to lower the investment base and thus improve their investment turnover (among many other options).

Residual Income (RI)

Residual income (RI) is a dollar amount of income less a chosen required rate of return for an investment. The formula for RI follows:

Residual Income (RI) = Income − (Required Rate of Return × Investment)

The imputed cost of an investment is the required rate of return times the investment, a measure of the opportunity cost of not being able invest the funds elsewhere. Imputed costs attempt to add up the costs of an investment that are not always recognized under accrual accounting, such as the cost of raising capital (for example, a 6% interest rate on long-term debt).

For example, assume that a sporting goods manufacturer decided that the required rate of return for tennis balls was 10% but that the required rate of return for racquet balls was 12% due to greater risks involved in this business unit. The residual income of each business unit is calculated as follows:

Residual Income (RI) = Income − (Required Rate of Return × Investment)

Tennis balls = $100,000 − (0.1 × $400,000) = $60,000

Racquet balls = $60,000 − (0.12 × $300,000) = $24,000

RI implies that so long as the tennis ball unit earns more than $40,000 RI (0.1 × $400,000) and the racquet ball unit earns more than $36,000 RI (0.12 × $300,000), the sporting goods manufacturer should continue to invest in the growth of these operations. Using RI instead of ROI makes managers aim for an actual dollar amount rather than a percentage.

Just as ROI can measure a specific business segment's returns, RI can be used for a business segment, in which case it uses segment income, segment investment, and a segment-specific required rate of return.

RI vs. ROI

Financial ratios must be used in the context of the business and its industry. The nature of a company's business will affect how financial ratios such as ROI are perceived. For example, a particular industry may have lower average ROIs and the market will view a slightly higher ROI favorably even though it is lower than ROIs for most industries. The maturity of the business will also be considered; a firm in its first year of business is not expected to generate as high a return as an established business. Firms entering new markets must set their expectations appropriately (for example, a firm used to a particular ROI for their TV division would have to use a different set of criteria for a new aerospace division). To get past these comparability issues, compute your own ratios for the company and for relevant benchmark companies such as rivals, perhaps narrowing the list to companies at the same maturity level.

Focusing only on ROI is not a good general business policy. Instead, firms should take many factors into account. Perhaps for business development reasons, a firm should take a low ROI project because it promises to add a new long-term client (and therefore a long-term positive ROI). Nonfinancial measures to consider are discussed in the next topic.

Also, when ROI is used as a primary performance evaluation tool, managers of business units with higher profits according to ROI may reject capital investments that do not promise as good or better an ROI than the rate being currently earned even if the investment is strategically beneficial to the organization as a whole. For example, if the tennis ball unit were considering purchasing a new machine for $100,000 that would produce additional revenue of $20,000, the ROI of 20% would lower the business unit's overall ROI of 25%:

$$\text{Tennis Ball Unit with Expansion} = \frac{\$100,000 + \$20,000}{\$400,000 + \$100,000} = 24\%$$

If the manager is compensated on ROI, it is unlikely that he or she will make this investment. Conversely, if the same situation used RI instead, the calculation is as follows:

Tennis Ball Unit with Expansion = $120,000 - (0.1 \times \$500,000) = \$70,000$

Because residual income increases with this investment, a manager compensated based on total RI would have the incentive to make this expansion. Assuming the expansion earned the revenue it promised to earn, the manager will be rewarded for increasing residual income. RI gives managers the incentive to select any project that generates returns above the required rate of return. However, RI is a flat dollar amount, so it is less useful for comparing business units of different sizes (using a percentage value). Also, large business units, even with poor efficiency, will still have a larger RI than a small business unit with good efficiency, so large units tend to be favored by this measure. In contrast, ROI is a more robust measure in some ways because RI is very sensitive to the required rate of return and as the investments become larger, this sensitivity becomes more pronounced.

Economic Value Added (EVA®)

Economic value added (EVA) is a residual income calculation that subtracts after-tax operating income from after-tax weighted average cost of capital (WACC) times total assets less current liabilities.

EVA considers value to be created only if after-tax operating income is greater than the cost of capital. The equation for EVA follows:

EVA = After-Tax Operating Income - [WACC × (Total Assets - Current Liabilities)]

Where:

After-Tax Operating Income = Operating Income × (1 - Marginal Tax Rate)

WACC = (After-Tax Cost of Debt × % of Debt) + (Cost of Equity × % of Equity)

After-Tax Cost of Debt = Average Cost of Debt × (1 - Marginal Tax Rate)

Whereas RI can use a required rate of return that can be set arbitrarily by management, WACC is a precise measurement of the cost of capital. WACC uses the after-tax cost of debt because interest expense is tax-deductible.

For example, assume that a sporting goods manufacturer has a 60% debt ratio and a 40% equity ratio, an average cost of debt of 12%, cost of equity of 15%, and a marginal tax rate of 30%. WACC is calculated as follows:

$$\text{After-Tax Cost of Debt} = 0.12 \times (1 - 0.3) = 0.084 = 8.4\%$$

$$\text{WACC} = (0.084 \times 0.6) + (0.15 \times 0.4) = 0.0504 + 0.06 = 11.04\%$$

Assuming the same income and asset levels as in the prior examples and that the current liabilities are $50,000 for the tennis ball unit and $40,000 for the racquet ball unit, the EVA for each is calculated as follows:

$$\text{After-Tax Operating Income} = \text{Operating Income} \times (1 - \text{Marginal Tax Rate})$$

$$\text{Tennis Ball Unit} = \$100,000 \times (1 - 0.3) = \$70,000$$

$$\text{Racquet Ball Unit} = \$60,000 \times (1 - 0.3) = \$42,000$$

$$\text{EVA} = \text{After-Tax Operating Income} - [\text{WACC} \times (\text{Total Assets} - \text{Current Liabilities})]$$

$$\text{Tennis Ball Unit} = \$70,000 - [0.114 \times (\$400,000 - \$50,000)]$$
$$= \$70,000 - \$39,900 = \$30,100$$

$$\text{Racquet Ball Unit} = \$42,000 - [0.114 \times (\$300,000 - \$40,000)]$$
$$= \$42,000 - \$29,640 = \$12,360$$

To improve their EVAs, businesses often calculate EVA for each proposed change in a business. Each proposed investment, divestment, or change in assumptions is calculated and compared to current EVA to aid in decision making.

EVA vs. RI and ROI

Although RI was intended to minimize the disincentives to investment inherent in ROI, EVA is intended to focus managers' attention on maximizing shareholder value by earning more than the cost of capital. When tax considerations are important, EVA is a better method of judging profitability than RI, but when tax considerations are irrelevant, EVA is simply a more complicated method of arriving at a similar result. Because EVA is tied to the company's actual cost of capital, it is a market-based calculation; as the market-driven cost of equity or debt rises, so does WACC.

Market Value Added

Market value added (MVA) is the market value of a company including debt and equity less the total capital invested. The market value added formula follows:

$$\text{Market Value Added (MVA)} = \text{Market Value} - \text{Invested Capital}$$

Market value is the market value of debt plus the market value of equity that a company holds. When MVA is a positive number, the company is creating value for its investors. MVA is a market-based measure, so it is an objective measure that clearly shows what investors think the organization is worth. MVA as a performance measurement tool emphasizes maximizing shareholder value. Managers using this incentive cannot simply invest more capital to increase MVA because if the extra capital does not increase the market value over the amount that was invested, there will be no net difference in MVA.

One of the drawbacks of MVA over EVA is that MVA ignores the opportunity cost of capital. For example, if a company's market value is $1.7 million after an investment of $1.5 million three years ago, MVA would be $200,000, an apparent value to shareholders. However, if over the course of the three years, the opportunity cost of funds was 10%, the expected return on the investment would be calculated as follows:

$$\$1,500,000 \times (1.1)^3 = \$1,996,500$$

Therefore the investment destroyed some potential wealth that could have been gained from a similar investment over that period. Similarly, MVA does not take into account any dividends that were distributed to shareholders. Such payments would increase value for shareholders but would not be accounted for in the MVA measurement, which measures the company's value only at a moment in time, not over a period of time.

Investment Base Issues

The performance measurement tools discussed above all suffer from the same problems when attempting to compare competing companies or various internal business units. The following differences may make the comparisons less than useful:

- Differing revenue and expense recognition policies

- Differing inventory measurement policies

- Possession of joint or shared assets between business units

- Differing choices on what to consider an asset and how to value those assets

Revenue and expense recognition, inventory measurement, and asset valuation methods are all covered in section E of this part of the CMA Learning System, "External Financial Reporting." Joint or shared assets are similar to other common costs that must be assigned to business units, as covered earlier in this section.

Cash Flow Return on Investment

Cash flow return on investment (CFROI) is a percentage rate of return valuation model that is essentially cash flow divided by market value of capital employed. The actual formula for CFROI is very complicated and is not presented here. For a full explanation of CFROI, see CFROI Valuation—A Total System Approach to Valuing the Firm, by Bartley J. Madden, a partner at HOLT Value Associates LP, the creators of the CFROI analysis. A brief summary of the method is presented here.

CFROI compares the inflation-adjusted after-tax cash flows with the inflation-adjusted gross cash investment amount to determine whether a corporation has earned returns greater than its costs of capital. CFROI includes in its calculations an estimate of the economic life of the company's depreciable assets and a residual value of all other assets.

CFROI assumes stock market prices are based on cash flow instead of on earnings and corporate performance. CFROI is usually calculated on an annual basis.

CFROI and ROI share the fact that they are expressed in percentages, but CFROI is very complex to calculate whereas ROI is very simple. Although CFROI takes into account the present value of money, inflation adjustments, and depreciation charges, ROI does not. Unlike ROI, CFROI removes the influence of accrual accounting because it is based on cash flows. CFROI shares more in common with EVA than with ROI. Both EVA and CFROI motivate management to create value by earning returns on invested capital that are greater than the cost of capital. An advantage of CFROI over the other methods is that CFROI can help compare companies with very different asset compositions, including international companies. Because it is inflation-adjusted, it can also compare companies across time. Another advantage of CFROI is that it bases performance measurement on the ability of a corporation to generate cash flow, a valuable factor to capital markets.

Progress Check

Directions: Read each question and respond in the space provided. Answers and page references appear on the following page.

1. A firm has $100,000 in income, net assets of $500,000, and revenues of $200,000. Its DuPont ROI would be calculated using which of the following numbers?

   ( ) a. 0.1×0.5

   ( ) b. 0.3×0.4

   ( ) c. 0.4×0.5

   ( ) d. 2.5×2

2. Which of the following profitability measures expresses its goals in a dollar amount?

   ( ) a. ROI

   ( ) b. RI

   ( ) c. CFROI

   ( ) d. DuPont ROI

3. Which of the following is a drawback of using market value added (MVA)?

   ( ) a. MVA is a complex calculation requiring many steps.

   ( ) b. MVA gives managers disincentives to invest in projects with MVA less than their current MVA ratio.

   ( ) c. MVA depends on different definitions of income, so comparability is difficult.

   ( ) d. MVA ignores the opportunity cost of capital

Progress check answers

1. c (p. 2-239)

2. b (p. 2-240)

3. d (p. 2-242)

Balanced Scorecard

Topic overview

Until the balanced scorecard and similar holistic techniques evolved, most companies focused solely on financial measures. Although these are objective and quantitative, they are entirely historical in nature. Moreover, they are better at providing short-term forecasts than long-term ones. Although these lagging indicators are important to help in tracking what you have been doing, companies must now focus on the leading indicators, or indicators of future success, too. The balanced scorecard gives companies a simple tool that shows them specific financial and nonfinancial indicators.

The balanced scorecard (BSC) is a strategic measurement and management system that translates a company's strategy into four balanced categories:

- *Financial measures show the past performance of a firm.*

- *Customer, internal business process, and learning and growth measures drive future financial performance.*

Robert Kaplan and David Norton created the BSC to get corporations away from focusing solely on financial data and instead concentrate on this aspect while simultaneously creating the abilities and intangible assets required for long-term growth. This is done by translating a company's strategy into specific measures in each category. Companies use the BSC as a management tool to clarify and communicate strategy, align individual and unit goals to strategy, link strategy to the budgeting process, and get feedback for continuous strategy improvement.

Critical Success Factors

A firm develops its strategies by first performing a SWOT analysis: analyzing internal strengths and weaknesses and then analyzing its external opportunities and threats.

Strengths will include the organization's core competencies, or skills the company performs especially well. Analysis of these factors will help a company determine what its critical success factors are. Critical success factors (CSFs) are specific, measurable goals that must be met in order to achieve a firm's strategy. By codifying CSFs into the SWOT categories, managers will be forced to come to a consensus about how to define each CSF (for example, some managers may classify their product mix as a strength, others as a weakness).

CSFs must be measurable; defining the measurement unit for each CSF is the next step after defining CSFs. According to Kaplan and Norton, "If you can't measure it, you can't manage it." These measurements must encompass more than just financial measures for the BSC to be successful. Examples of CSFs for each of the BSC's four factors are shown in Figure 2-66.

Figure 2-66: CSF Measurement

Factor	Critical Success Factor	Measurement Examples
Financial	Sales	Sales forecast accuracy, return on sales, sales trends
	Liquidity	Asset, inventory, and receivables turnover; cash flow
	Profitability	ROI, residual income, economic value added
	Market value	Market value added, share price
Customer	Market share	Trade association analyses, market definitions
	Customer acquisition	Number of new customers, total sales to new customers
	Customer satisfaction	Customer returns, complaints, surveys
	Customer retention	Customer retention by category, percentage growth with existing customers
	Quality	Warranty expense
	Timeliness	Time from order to door, number of on-time deliveries
Internal business process	Productivity	Cycle time, effectiveness, efficiency, variances, scrap
	Quality	Defects, returns, scrap, rework, surveys, warranty
	Safety	Accidents, insurance claims, result of accidents
	Process time	Setup time, turnaround, lead time
	Brand management	Number of advertisements, surveys, new accounts
Learning and growth	Skill development	Training hours or trainees, skill improvement
	Motivation, empowerment	Suggestions per employee, suggestions implemented
	New products	New patents, number of design changes, R&D skills
	Competence	Employee turnover, experience, customer satisfaction
	Team performance	Surveys, number of gains shared with other teams, number of multiteam projects, percentage of shared incentives

Figure 2-66 is only a sampling of the possible critical success factors that a company could use to form its strategy. However, one measure might be designed to be counterproductive against a different measure. To avoid this possibility, the balanced scorecard uses the process of integration described below.

Effective Use of a Balanced Scorecard

Once the critical success factors and their measurements are defined, they must be linked back to the strategy of the firm. No set of measurement tools will be successful if each manager is motivated to achieve their goals at the expense of the other goals. A successful BSC will create a shared understanding within the organization. The BSC creates an overall view of how the individual contributes to strategic success. The elements of the BSC not only should be created from the strategy, but study of the factors should show what the strategy is. Linking the four categories together with strategy requires understanding three principles:

- Cause-and-effect relationships

- Outcome measures and performance drivers

- Links to financial measures

Cause-and-effect relationships

All of the critical success factors described above should fit within an overall cause-and-effect relationship chain that ends with a relevant financial measure and the achievement of part of the company's strategy. Cause-and-effect situations can be hypothesized using if-then statements: If the firm introduces a new product line, then the firm will attract a new customer base. If the firm attracts a new customer base, then all existing product lines will have new customers . . . and so on. These chains of cause-and-effect relationships should progress through each of the four areas where possible, and the net result of all of the chains should explicitly describe the company's strategy, how to measure each element, and, therefore, how to provide feedback to the process. In the end, all critical success factors should be incorporated into one of these cause-and-effect chains.

Outcome measures and performance drivers

For the cause-and-effect chains of critical success factors to be useful, they must be linked to a definite outcome and a performance driver that says how the outcome can be met. Outcome measures are lagging indicators, or historic indicators of success such as measures of profitability, market share, employee skills, or customer retention. Outcome measures tend to be general measures of what must be achieved at the end of several cause-and-effect chains. Performance drivers are leading indicators, or drivers that are specific to the strategy of a particular business unit such as cycle times, setup times, or new patents. Performance drivers without outcome measures will show how to perform in the short term but will not indicate whether the strategy is successful. Outcome measures without performance drivers will indicate where the department or team needs to be but will not show them how to achieve their goal and will not give relevant information at the time the information is needed.

Links to financial measures

No matter how focused an organization is on an initiative such as total quality management or employee empowerment, without linkage to the bottom line, such programs can become goals in themselves. Furthermore, the lack of a link to a tangible benefit from the program can cause disillusionment because there is no way of measuring its success. Therefore, all cause-and-effect chains need to be linked to financial outcome measures.

Financial measures for the BSC are the same as those that have already been discussed in Topic 3, "Financial Measures," in this section of the CMA Learning System as well as in Part 1, Section E, "Financial Statement Analysis."

Nonfinancial BSC Measures

The following covers the three nonfinancial measures of the BSC in detail; financial measures in the BSC are similar to those described elsewhere in this part of the *CMA Learning System.*

Customer measures

Because customers create all of a company's revenue, customer identification and classification into market segments are of vital importance to all companies. The customer perspective must include specific outcome measures and specific performance drivers. Because a company cannot target everyone without losing its focus on its core customers, a company must shape performance drivers (also known as value propositions) that are specific to market segments and their strategy.

Customer outcome measures

The primary customer outcome measures include:

- Market share.

- Acquisition.

- Satisfaction.

- Retention.

- Profitability.

These outcome measures are discussed below, with the exception of customer profitability, which was discussed in Topic 3 of this section. Figure 2-67 shows how these elements work together in a cause-and-effect relationship chain.

Figure 2-67: Customer Outcome Measures

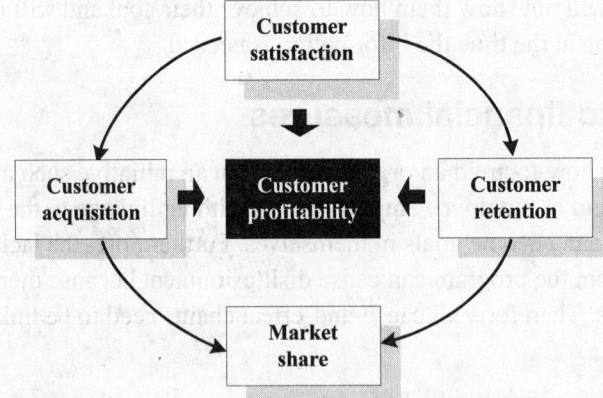

Market share. Market share is the proportion of customers that use a company's product or service out of the total of all users in that particular market segment. A subdivision of market share is account share. Account share is the proportion of a customer's business out of their total spending in the area the company represents, also known as share of the customer's wallet. A food distributor may measure the amount of purchases of their products over all of the targeted customers' food purchases as share of pantry.

Data on the size of the total market segment for a business can be gained from trade associations, industry groups, government studies, and customer surveys. The share of this market controlled by the company can be measured using metrics such as total number of customers, unit volume sold, or dollars spent. Account share is measured using surveys or approximation techniques that estimate the spending of an average user compared to the spending with the company itself. Companies with few customers can track individual customers, whereas companies with many customers must track customer segments.

Customer acquisition. Companies with a growth strategy will focus strongly on the customer acquisition measure, but all companies need to add new customers because customer retention is never 100%. Customer acquisition can be measured in absolute measures (number of new customers) or relative measure (net gain in customers). Customer acquisition could also be measured as total sales to customers. Acquisition can be divided by customer market segment. Customer acquisition is a measure of the success of the funds spent on acquiring the new customers, such as advertising costs and other marketing efforts. Other measures focus on customer conversion rate: the number of new customers divided by the total number of prospect contacts.

Customer satisfaction. Measures of customer satisfaction show how successfully a company has met the needs of consumers. When a company's customers are corporations, getting measurable customer satisfaction feedback is often easily attained from a formal process where the customer will rank each of its vendors on a variety of satisfaction measures. Retail customer satisfaction can similarly be measured using surveys, but when such data is not feasible, some companies use number of customer complaints. Customer surveys can be relatively inexpensive to very expensive, depending on the medium used and the number of desired responses.

Customer retention. Customer retention is an ongoing process that can be directly measured by companies that maintain lists of their customers such as magazines, auto dealerships, distributors, and banks. Similar to account share, customer retention can be further broken down into the percentage change of business with each customer. For retailers, some customer retention data can be gained from credit card receipts, but other data must be approximated.

Performance drivers

Although outcome measures may be broadly defined for most industries, performance drivers are specific to each company's strategy and market. The performance drivers for customer acquisition, retention, and satisfaction are based on meeting the needs of customers. Examples of some common performance drivers include:

- Response time.
- Delivery performance.
- Defects.
- Lead time.

Internal business process measures

After the financial and customer measures are created to meet company strategy, the internal business process measures can be designed to link to these metrics and achieve customer and shareholder value. Instead of creating measures that merely attempt to improve existing business processes, the balanced scorecard suggests that companies start with current and future customer needs, progressing through the cause-and-effect chain via operations, marketing, and other areas all the way to sales and service, keeping only the elements that add value to customers.

Internal business process measures go beyond simple financial variance measures to include output measures such as quality, cycle time, yield, order fulfillment, production planning, throughput, and turnover. However, improving such measures may not be enough to differentiate a company from its competition when they are also working toward these goals. Entirely new internal processes may be needed to make the company a leader in all of these measures simultaneously. A SWOT analysis can help identify weaknesses that require new solutions, not just incremental improvements. For example, a business could radically improve cycle time by eliminating their warehouse and directly shipping goods to retail locations on a just-in-time basis.

The BSC identifies three business process areas that contribute to most companies' business strategies for internal business processes:

- **Innovation**

  The innovation process starts with the SWOT analysis to identify customer needs that the company can satisfy. Because R&D can be extremely expensive and must be written off as a period expense, becoming efficient and effective at producing new products can be just as or more important than concentrating on the efficiency of ongoing production operations. Because the first company to introduce a new product has a distinct edge in market share, time to market is a key metric for evaluating the success of a new product introduction. Other measures employed include percentage of sales from new or proprietary products, new products versus competitors' new products, and variation from project budgets.

  Product development processes can include performance measurements such as yield, cycle time, and cost. For example, research into new computer chips could test numerous materials, and the yield of materials to warrant further study can be judged against the total number tested. The material in each stage can have its time in that phase measured (cycle time), and the overall cost of processing and research can be measured. Thus the progress toward the outcome measurement of time to market and overall cost can be measured.

- **Operations**

  The operations process is the area that has gained the majority of most performance measurements in the past and continues to be important in reducing costs or increasing capabilities. Using only financial measures for operations such as variances and standard costs can lead to line managers making decisions that run counter to the organization's strategy, such as creating too much inventory simply to keep a financial ratio in line with expectations rather than due to customer demand.

Although the financial measurements continue to be important, the BSC recommends supplementing them with measures of quality, technological capabilities, and reducing cycle time to build the company's long-term strategy for differentiation over their competitors.

- **Post-sale service**

  Post-sale service is a method of adding value to a product or service while simultaneously gaining feedback on customer satisfaction. Many companies that sell complex goods or services include post-sale service in their strategic plans. Metrics such as response time for equipment failures and promptness of maintenance calls can be employed to measure the success of post-sale service.

Learning and growth measures

A company develops learning and growth measures after identifying their financial, customer, and internal process strategic needs. If the company created their strategy with ambition and innovation, the company will need to achieve new capabilities through learning and growth. Although it is the last step designed in a BSC strategy, it will be the first step performed. Learning and growth measures are performance drivers for the desired strategic outcomes. Measuring learning and growth using financial measures alone usually tends to show only the short-term results, and short-term training results usually show that the training is unprofitable. However, the long-term consequences of ignoring this element of an organization can be devastating, so new measures must be introduced to guide management's decisions in this area.

The learning and growth perspective can be broken down into three categories.

- **Employee skill sets**

  The automation of repetitive tasks has transformed employee management from an industrial model to one in which employees must think and contribute to ongoing success instead of performing a repetitive task within predefined specifications. Specific outcome measurements of employee results include employee satisfaction, employee retention, and employee productivity. Satisfied employees produce satisfied customers. Employee satisfaction can be measured in the employee's annual review or in surveys. Employee retention is measured by employee turnover and by numbers of years of service. Employees with greater investment in a company tend to be more satisfied. The employee productivity outcome measure is a product of performance drivers such as employee training, autonomy in decision making versus results, and output versus numbers of employees needed to produce the output. Another common and simple productivity measure is revenue per employee, but it should not be the sole measure because overly stressing revenue can lead employees to accept revenue even while the profit level is negative, such as salespersons offering huge price discounts to make sales.

  Employees needing new skill sets can be measured using either the amount of training needed per employee, the proportion of the work force needing training, or the cycle time from an unqualified to a qualified employee. Such measures will indicate the amount of work required to raise the organization's capabilities to the desired strategic level. The strategic job coverage ratio is another metric that tracks the number of employees qualified for a strategic job divided by total organizational needs. This ratio exposes gaps in organizational skill sets.

- **Information system capabilities**

  Measurements of the time needed to access information for customers or of the availability of critical information can assess the capabilities of the current information systems and indicate need for continued investment in such infrastructure. A strategic information coverage ratio can be used to measure current information system capabilities divided by anticipated system needs.

- **Empowerment, motivation, and organizational alignment**

  Empowerment and motivation are measured using metrics such as number of suggestions per employee, number of suggestions implemented, and increases in productivity or cost savings due to employee suggestions. Empowerment and motivation can be enhanced by making such metrics known to employees so that they can see that their efforts are not in vain. Publishing of expectations for improvement, progress toward that improvement, and recognizing individuals who have made good suggestions are motivating factors for all employees.

  Organizational alignment, organizational learning, and teamwork measurements include the goals set versus goals achieved for a department and team-based measures that include team-based rewards. The linking of personal goals and rewards to organizational outcomes is key to achieving the overall company strategy. Performance drivers for organizational alignment include periodic surveys of employees to determine their level of motivation to achieve the critical success factors in the BSC.

Balanced scorecard example

Figure 2-68 shows a completed balanced scorecard for Acme Company. The scorecard gives the company's overall strategic goal and the associated targets. It then covers the specific objectives from each of the four perspectives, numbering them for easy reference by perspective. Each objective has a specific measurable tool and a target for each of the next two years. The "Programs" column is the result of a survey Acme performed that matched planned programs to particular strategic objectives. The targets were set under the assumption that these programs would go forward.

Figure 2-68: Acme Company's Balanced Scorecard (Planned Results)

Acme Company Balanced Scorecard
Overall goal: Grow sales by 20% over the next two years.
Targets

			Current Year (Y0)	Year 1 (Y1)	Year 2 (Y2)
Revenues:			$400,000	$432,000	$484,000

Perspective	Strategic Objectives	Measurements	Y1 Target	Y2 Target	Programs
Financial	F1: Maximize return on equity	Return on equity	9%	13%	
	F2: Positive economic value added (EVA)	EVA	$20,000	$30,000	
	F3: 10% revenue growth	% change in revenues	8%	12%	
	F4: Asset utilization	Utilization rates	85%	88%	
Customer	C1: Price	Competitive comparison	–4%	–5%	
	C2: Customer retention	Retention %	75%	75%	CRM*
	C3: Lowest-cost suppliers	Total cost relative to competition	–6%	–7%	SRM**
	C4: Product innovation	% of sales from new products	10%	15%	
Internal business process	P1: Improve production work flow	Cycle time	0.3 days	0.25 days	ERP***
	P2: New product success	Number of orders	1,000	1,500	
	P3: Sales penetration	Actual vs. plan (variance)	0%	0%	
	P4: Reduce inventory	Inventory as a % of sales	30%	28%	
Learning and growth	L1: Link strategy to reward system	Net income per dollar of variable pay (aggregate)	65%	68%	CRM
	L2: Fill critical competency gaps	% of critical competencies satisfied on tracking matrix	75%	80%	School reimbursement
	L3: Become customer-driven culture	Survey index	77%	79%	CRM
	L4: Quality leadership	Average ranking (on 10-point scale) of executives	8.9	9.2	School reimbursement

* Customer relationship management implementation
** Supplier relationship management implementation
*** Planned upgrade to enterprise resources planning system

At the end of Year 1, the results were as shown in Figure 2-69.

Figure 2-69: Acme Company's Balanced Scorecard (Actual Results)

Acme Company Balanced Scorecard
Overall goal: Grow sales by 20% over the next two years.
Actual

		Y1 Target	Y1 Actual	Variance*	
Revenues:		$432,000	$424,000	$8,000	U
Perspective	**Strategic Objectives**				
Financial	F1: Maximize return on equity	9%	8%	1%	U
	F2: Positive EVA	$20,000	$18,000	$2,000	U
	F3: 10% revenue growth	8%	6%	2%	U
	F4: Asset utilization	85%	87%	2%	F
Customer	C1: Price	–4%	–4%	0	
	C2: Customer retention	75%	70%	5%	U
	C3: Lowest-cost suppliers	–6%	–7%	–1%	F
	C4: Product innovation	10%	8%	2%	U
Internal business process	P1: Improve production work flow	0.3 days	0.25 days	.05 days	F
	P2: New product success	1,000 orders	800 orders	200 orders	U
	P3: Sales penetration	0%	–7%	–7%	U
	P4: Reduce inventory	30%	29%	1%	F
Learning and growth	L1: Link strategy to reward system	65%	63%	2%	U
	L2: Fill critical competency gaps	75%	75%	0	
	L3: Become customer-driven culture	77%	74%	3%	U
	L4: Quality leadership	8.9	8.9	0	

*F = Favorable variance; U = Unfavorable variance

What can Acme learn from the results of Year 1? It may have had trouble implementing its customer relationship management (CRM) program (poorly planned, project cancelled, delayed, etc.), because each of the measures that was linked to that program had an unfavorable variance. A reexamination of that program may find ways to refocus on the customers' needs. On the other hand, Acme's production costs and production efficiencies all have favorable variances, meaning that their SRM and ERP initiatives seem to have been successful. Acme's work force is progressing on pace, and its school reimbursement program is a likely aid to this success. However, although the work force is strong in core competencies and in leadership, they have not become customer-oriented enough, which is the primary reason for their loss of customers and their inability to penetrate new markets and sell new products (which were likely designed with poor information on actual market needs). If Acme wants to turn things around and meet its goals, it must increase its investment in its CRM initiative, including training to change its employees' mindsets toward a customer orientation.

Implementing the balanced scorecard

The information that follows on implementing the BSC was drawn from *The Strategy-Focused Organization* by Kaplan and Norton. Implementing the BSC boils down to executing strategy. Without execution, even the best vision remains a dream. In the past few decades, the average company has gone from about two-thirds of its value being based on tangible assets to about one-third, meaning that companies are moving from being able to describe and measure their success solely in financial terms to needing knowledge-based strategies that rely on more than just slow-reacting tools such as budgets. The BSC lends itself well to strategy execution, because the scorecard itself is a method of describing strategy in a way that can be acted upon. A strategy-focused organization has the following aspects:

- All of the measures used in the BSC (financial and nonfinancial) should be derived from the firm's vision and strategy.

- Processes become participative rather than directive.

- Change is not limited to cost cutting and downsizing but includes repositioning the firm (new or more specialized competitive markets, a customer focus, a performance mindset, etc.).

- The organization must adopt new cultural values and priorities.

Aligning and focusing resources on strategy

According to Kaplan and Norton, like the difference between an energy-glutton light bulb and a miserly but intense laser pointer, the executive team, business units, information technology, human resources, budgets, and capital investments must all be aligned and focused toward narrower and more intense (but not necessarily more capital-intensive) goals than most companies currently work toward. To accomplish this, a firm must implement the following continuous improvement cycle.

- **Describe the strategy in operational terms using strategy maps and the BSC.** A strategy map is a predecessor of the BSC showing the firm what its priorities are so that it can design a scorecard that reflects their strategy. Figure 2-70 shows a strategy map that Mobil North America Marketing and Refining (NAM&R) created to address a new focus on the customer and on those factors that will make customers want to use Mobil stations and products more.

Figure 2-70: Strategy Maps for Mobil NAM&R

Financial Perspective (created first)

Increase ROCE to 12%
- Return on capital employed (ROCE)
- Net margin (vs. industry)

Revenue growth strategy

Productivity strategy

New sources of nongasoline revenue
- Nongasoline revenue and margin

Increase customer profitability through premium brands
- Volume vs. industry
- Premium ratio

Become industry cents leader
- Cash expense (cost per gallon) vs. industry

Maximize use of existing assets
- Cash flow

Customer Perspective

"Delight the consumer"
- Mystery shopper rating
- Share of segment

"Win-win dealer relations"
- Dealer profit growth
- Dealer satisfaction

Basic

Clean	Safe	Quality product	Trusted brand

More consumer products	Help develop business skills

Differentiators

Speedy purchase	Friendly, helpful employees	Recognize loyalty

Internal Perspective

"Build the franchise"

Create nongasoline products and services
- New product ROI
- New product acceptance rate

"Increase customer value"

Understand consumer segments
- Share of target segment

Best-in-class franchise teams
- Dealer quality rating

"Achieve operational excellence"

Improve hardware performance
- Yield gap
- Unplanned downtime

On spec/on time
- Perfect orders

Improve inventory management
- Inventory levels
- Run-out rate

Industry cost leader
- Activity cost vs. competition

"Be a good neighbor"

Improve environmental, health, and safety
- Environmental incidents
- Safety incidents

Learning and Growth Perspective

Motivated and prepared work force

Climate for action
- Aligned
- Personal growth
  - Personal scorecard
  - Employee feedback

Competencies
- Functional excellence
- Leadership skills
- Integrated view
  - Strategic skill coverage ratio

Technology
- Process improvement
- Y2K
  - Systems milestones

Source: *The Strategy-Focused Organization* by Robert S. Kaplan and David P. Norton

- **Align the organization to the firm's strategy using corporate scorecards as well as business unit and support unit synergies.**
  Synergies make the whole worth more than the sum of its parts. Break down functional area silos not by replacing departments or organizational charts but by replacing formal reporting structures with strategic priorities across business units (for example, by having common themes across each unit's different scorecards). Examples of linked scorecards can be found in Kaplan and Norton's The Strategy-Focused Organization.

- **Make strategy everybody's everyday job using personal scorecards, strategic awareness, and balanced paychecks.**
  Replacing top-down direction with top-down communication means that every employee has a clear set of expectations that are already in line with strategy. The BSC becomes the educational tool showing how to measure success, but it may need to be backed up with more formal training (for example, if employees must refine customer segments, they must first be taught about customer segmentation). Also, the lowest or personal level scorecards can be left to the end users to create based on the higher-level priorities communicated. Often this leads to unsought-for synergies when an individual finds ways to help other areas of the company. Such a process helps create a strategic awareness at every level.

  Balanced paychecks link pay to the balanced scorecard measures, usually by business unit performance instead of individual performance. Balanced paychecks apply financial and nonfinancial BSC measures by weighting their importance. Some measures have an individual performance portion and a unit performance portion, and most also tie the compensation to some external factors such as an industry benchmark (to compensate for factors outside of employees' control). Using some form of balanced paycheck raises the interest level of all employees in using the BSC. While the employees may be studying the BSC to see what their compensation will be, they are also simultaneously working to improve corporate goals through their diligence. In the case of Mobil, when truck drivers delivered gasoline to stores, they started reporting poor station conditions because they knew their own compensation was partly based on customer perceptions at the stations.

- **Make strategy a continual process by linking strategy to budgeting, using analytical automation, holding strategy meetings, and implementing strategic learning.**
  Strategy is often neglected in favor of tactical decisions such as setting a budget, so the BSC uses a double-loop process—for example, for budgeting they create two budgets, a strategic budget and an operational budget, thus protecting the long term from suboptimization in the short term. Regular strategy meetings organized around the BSC allows input from a broader group of managers while keeping the meeting focused. Instead of talking about variances or other specifics, managers will use their own balanced scorecard to measure their own performance and then use the meeting to talk about what has gone right and what wrong or what should be continued/discontinued.

  Analytical tool automation found in today's enterprise resource planning (ERP) systems (see section C, topic 5, "Integrated Enterprise-Wide Data Model," in this part) and other sophisticated analytical systems can provide feedback to a broader audience than was traditionally possible, and a BSC can include such analysis. The firm must teach employees how to learn and adapt the strategy such as by providing simple internal brochures explaining how to use a particular type of measure in its specific business context. Other firms may have employees use and then test the cause-and-effect linkages in a scorecard by analyzing actual results.

- **Mobilize change through executive leadership using mobilization, governance processes, and a strategic management system.**
  Active executive involvement is a must, and it involves a focus more on mobilization or getting momentum started than on the metrics in the BSC itself. Governance processes involve how to manage the process once it has begun, using team-based approaches that break up old power structures and focus on executing strategy. In the final phase of implementing the BSC, governance becomes a strategic management system that makes the new methods and values into the new business culture. Governance processes reinforce positive changes such as by determining when and how to link the executive level and other levels of the firm to the BSC, for example, using executive compensation. This last phase is dangerous, as the desire for stability can make future changes more difficult. However, this tendency toward setting standards is universal in organizations and so should be planned for, embraced for a time, and then evaluated and changed to fit evolving strategy.

Progress Check

Directions: Read each question and respond in the space provided. Answers and page references appear on the following page.

1. Which of the following perspectives of the balanced scorecard should every cause-and-effect chain be linked to?

    (   )   a.   Financial

    (   )   b.   Customer

    (   )   c.   Internal business process

    (   )   d.   Learning and growth

2. Which of the following is a customer performance driver?

    (   )   a.   Market share

    (   )   b.   Lead time

    (   )   c.   Retention

    (   )   d.   Profitability

3. Periodic surveys of employee motivation are an example of a

    (   )   a.   learning and growth outcome measure.

    (   )   b.   learning and growth performance driver.

    (   )   c.   customer outcome measure.

    (   )   d.   customer performance driver.

4. The process time critical success factor would be measured best by which of the following?

    (   )   a.   Surveys

    (   )   b.   ROI

    (   )   c.   Customer returns

    (   )   d.   Turnaround

Progress check answers

1. a (p. 2-249)

2. b (p. 2-251)

3. b (p. 2-253)

4. d (p. 2-247)

Quality Considerations

Topic 5

Topic overview

Whereas companies used to be able to ignore quality considerations and still generate sales, global competitors with higher-quality products have now forced all companies to consider how to make quality part of the original design instead of simply inspecting the end result for defects. Japanese manufacturers led the way in integrated quality espoused by management experts such as W. Edwards Deming and J. M. Juran, and the rest of the world was forced to follow if it wished to remain competitive.

Quality

Quality is a product or service that matches or surpasses an expected level of customer expectation at a competitive (expected) price. Customer expectations are the key to understanding quality. A product that seeks to differentiate itself through low prices must still meet customer expectations for quality or the product will not be purchased a second time. Meeting customer needs is not only the objective of quality but of a company's strategy as well. Customer expectations are not absolute but are relative to price and promised level of service.

The Malcolm Baldrige National Quality Award was established by Congress in 1987 to create competition toward quality by rewarding success and communicating successful techniques. Many businesses have found that working toward quality also improves a company's productivity, profitability, and customer and employee satisfaction. Winners of the award have been tracked and compared to the Standard & Poor's 500 index of companies, and the "Baldrige Stock Index" group has outperformed the index three to one.

The International Organization for Standardization (ISO) develops certifications for quality standards such as production inspections, equipment maintenance, worker training, testing, and treatment of customer complaints. The certifications are sought after by businesses around the world.

ISO 9000 (currently implemented by at least 610,000 organizations in 160 countries) is an international reference for quality management requirements in business-to-business interactions. ISO 9000 measures what the organization does to fulfill the customer's quality requirements, applicable regulatory requirements, customer satisfaction, and continual improvement. To become certified, organizations should seek an accredited certification body to perform an audit. (These audits are not performed by the ISO.) Organizations can choose to follow the ISO 9000 guidelines without becoming certified, but the advantages of becoming certified include use in public relations, conformance to applicable standards, and motivation for staff.

The cost of quality and implementing quality initiatives can be up to 20% to 25% of revenue for U.S. firms. However, high-quality products often drive increased sales and greater profits. Sometimes gains in efficiency and effectiveness mean that quality can be achieved with no net increase in costs and can even create cost reductions.

The cost of poor quality also needs to be considered. Losses from scrap, rework, defects, and reinspections are just the tip of the iceberg for the cost of poor quality. Other less visible costs include the following:

- Learning curve losses
- Excess or undercapacity
- Loss of customer satisfaction or trust leading to lost sales
- Expediting back orders and replacements
- Overtime payments to get a plant back on schedule
- Analysis of defective parts
- Excess inventory
- Process and machine redesign
- Downtime

Total Quality Management (TQM) Concepts and Techniques

Quality assurance (QA) used to be related solely to operations. **Total quality management (TQM)** is a management technique that makes the CEO the manager responsible for quality, and all employees and all business processes become a part of quality management. TQM requires full organizational commitment and a cultural change in order to succeed. TQM aligns each manager's, department's, and employee's job role with meeting customer expectations by setting specifications that must be met. TQM is a long-term commitment; organizations that have been using TQM for some time are more successful than newer converts.

TQM can lower product returns, warranty expense, and inventory levels (due to reduced scrap, spoilage, and rework). Furthermore, if customers place a high value on the product due to its quality level, the product's price can be set higher. High-quality goods usually command a large market share. TQM can also reduce cycle times, and faster delivery will reduce costs and increase customer satisfaction and retention.

TQM critical success factors

Figure 2-71 details the factors that are critical to the success of TQM.

Figure 2-71: Critical Success Factors of TQM

Critical Success Factor	Description
Customer satisfaction	• Keep customer needs as a strategy driver. • Identify the needs of both internal and external customers and suppliers. • Customer feedback measures satisfaction.
Continuous improvement (kaizen)	• Keep continuous improvement as a philosophy. • TQM and cost reductions are never-ending, as competitors continue to raise expectations in a global economy. • TQM is a way of life instead of a finite goal.
Top management support and involvement	• Implementing TQM must come from the top. • Using TQM must be a conscious part of every manager's decisions.
Complete work-force involvement	• Satisfying internal customer and vendor requirements for quality keeps all employees active in the pursuit of TQM. • Work-force involvement includes using quality control circles, or groups of employees who meet to discuss problems and implement solutions.
Systematic analysis and objective measures	• Analyze both bad and good processes. • Put resources into prevention. • Minimize variations. • Embrace measurable objectives such as in the balanced scorecard.
Recognizing and rewarding quality achievements	• Without incentives, TQM cannot succeed; however, rewards need not always be financial but could be recognition through publications, awards, or simply seeing suggestions implemented.
Continuous TQM training	• Because TQM requires a culture change, that culture must be continuously reinforced. • Training and education are key to communicating management's commitment to TQM. • Employees need the skills to succeed at TQM.

These elements of TQM are arranged in a hierarchy as shown in Figure 2-72.

Figure 2-72: Total Quality Management Model

Elements	Philosophy	Objective
Systematic analysis		
Total participation	Reducing variation through continuous quality improvements	Customer satisfaction
Internal/external customer		
Internal/external supplier		
Management commitment		

Conformance

The definition of quality used to be conformance to specifications. However, TQM changes the definition of quality to include the many facets of customer needs such as lack of paperwork or speed of service. Conformance in TQM is conformity to quality specifications set by customer expectations. Goalpost or zero-defect conformance sets each specification to fall within a range (for example, 22 mm +/– 0.5 mm). The problem with goalpost conformance is seen in a product with numerous parts. Although all parts may fit within the specified range, when some parts are found acceptable at the high end of the spectrum while other parts are acceptable at the low end, the combination may not be acceptable to the customer overall.

Absolute quality conformance is an approach that sets conformance exactly at a required value (for example, exactly 22 mm). Absolute quality conformance may create a larger number of defective components, but the end product will be far more likely to meet customer satisfaction than when using goalpost conformance.

Compensation systems and TQM

The objectives of a management compensation system are to motivate managers to exert a high level of effort, to reward achievement, and to entice autonomous managers to follow the company strategy as efficiently as possible. When using TQM, rewards and recognition should be revised to place the proper emphasis on TQM. Starting with managers, part of their compensation should be based on meeting the unambiguous and measurable objectives set by TQM. Other employees should get the advantage of either bonus pay for successful quality improvements or a nonfinancial reward such as recognition in a publication or an award. Whenever possible, the ideas should be extended throughout the organization, boosting both quality and employee morale.

Techniques to Analyze Quality Problems

Techniques to analyze quality problems include quality audits, gap analysis, and statistical controls such as control charts, Pareto diagrams, and cause-and-effect (fishbone) diagrams.

Quality audits

A **quality audit** is an in-depth review of a company's processes and strategy from a quality standpoint, including analysis of best and worst practices. Quality audits include systems (or process) audits and product audits. The results of the audit are compared with analyses of other companies with similar processes as part of a benchmarking study. This leads to a long-term plan for strategic quality improvement. The long-term plan will prioritize changes by greatest to least return on investment and will make suggestions for short-term and long-term improvements. Quality audits may be conducted by internal staff or by an external auditor. Internal staff could include production management or designated internal inspectors. External auditors provide quality audits as assurance services for the board of directors or a regulatory body (for example, for a medical or financial product).

Gap analysis

A gap analysis looks at the gap between the company and a benchmark competitor that has the best quality in the industry. A gap analysis frequently follows a quality audit in order to identify specific problems and set distinct targets for improvement. Using the best business in the class sets goals at a high but presumably attainable level. The gap analysis includes the current gap and a projected gap assuming that a certain level of training and other initiatives are pursued.

Statistical controls

TQM can be successful only if it is able to manage the seemingly random variations in a process. Most processes are judged using quantitative or qualitative goals that are set arbitrarily. Such goals often fail to take into account the quantitative maximum output a process is capable of achieving. When the variations in a process are not understood and an arbitrary limit is placed on whether a process is acceptable, managers find themselves reacting to immediate problems instead of being proactive. Reactive fixes are often counterproductive, but even when they work, management does not understand why they worked. Reactive fixes also tend to result in poor quality levels.

Statistical thinking admits that every process or human output has variations and that measuring and managing these variations are the key to effective management and quality control. Expecting variations allows management to plan for and devise methods of measuring these variations. When the variation goes outside of the normal range, then corrective action is applied. This correction should be aimed to raise the entire range to an acceptable level, not just raise an arbitrary minimum level. Normal variation or statistical control is the acceptable range for a process, or what the process is capable of achieving. Abnormal variation is the variation in an element caused by some new factor making the process vary in an unexpected and unacceptable manner.

Methods of gaining statistical control over a process include control charts, Pareto diagrams, and cause-and-effect diagrams.

Control charts

Control charts measure the normal variance of a process by taking periodic measurements of the process and applying them to a chart. This process is performed in a controlled situation to ensure that the process is operating under normal or expected conditions while the measurements occur. For example, if a tennis ball machine produces spheres that are supposed to be 4 cm but vary between 3.97 and 4.03 cm, and the machine is tested to ensure that it is in proper working order, then such variations are what the machine is capable of producing. For a human process, normal conditions for a sales process might be measured using salespersons at known skill levels and given common incentives. Once the normal variation or statistical control is known, variations outside this level can be attributed to a change in the parameters that the statistical control was based upon.

For example, assume that human resources management sets arbitrary goals for employee retention on HR hiring staff, measured using the percentage of new hires still employed after six months. Figure 2-73 shows the performance against the standard for two different departments.

Figure 2-73: Performance Against Arbitrary Goals

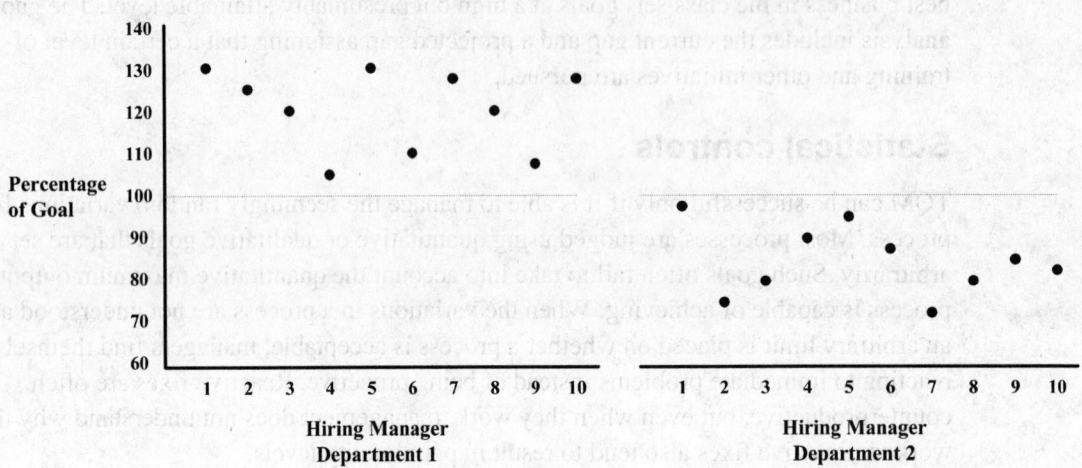

Department 1 appears to have a successful HR manager whereas department 2 does not. However, if statistical control is applied, a study could be performed to set an acceptable range of variation within known parameters, and type of job staffed would be included in the statistical control. Assuming that the same results still occurred, the analysis of the variations from the normal parameters would be accounted for and each process would have its range of normal variations adjusted to account for these factors. Thus if department 1 hired staff for salaried positions that tended to remain on staff longer, the normal range would be set high enough to keep the HR manager challenged. If department 2 hired hourly workers for repetitive jobs, their normal range might be lowered to account for this fact.

Figure 2-74 on the next page shows how these ranges would be set. Now department 1 is not performing as well as it could while department 2 is performing as well as can be expected. These limits can be used for future measurements of each department.

In addition to detecting when a process exceeds its upper and lower control limits, control charts can be used to detect trends that indicate a process may exceed control limits in the future so corrective action can be proactive. When corrective actions are taken, the control chart can show the correction's level of success. The limitations of control charts include that the cause of a variation cannot be determined from the chart alone and that taking samples is a form of estimation that could be erroneous.

Figure 2-74: Performance Using Statistical Control Limits

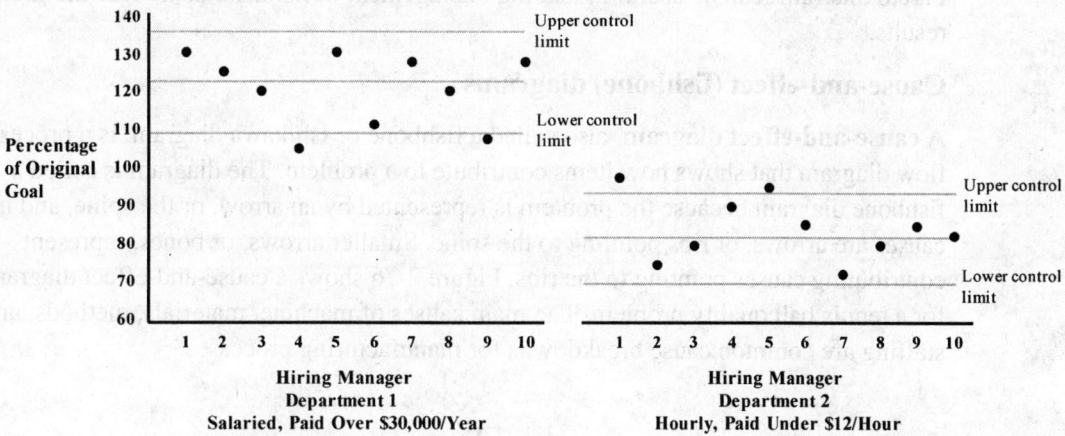

Pareto diagrams

A Pareto diagram is a type of histogram. A **histogram** is a measurement of the frequency of particular elements contributing to an overall set of data. A **Pareto diagram** is a quality histogram that breaks down a quality problem into its various causes and lists them from most to least prevalent. The Pareto diagram operates on Joseph Juran's theory that most quality problems are created by small number of prevalent causes.

Figure 2-75 shows a Pareto diagram for a tennis ball manufacturer expressed as a bar chart. The chart also includes a cumulative total that is calculated by adding the total of the most prevalent amount with the next most prevalent amount. This curve shows the total prevalence of the first two causes together, the first three causes, and so on. The curve of the cumulative amount grows less-sloped as the prevalence of the cause grows less, indicating how correcting the latter causes will have less and less of an effect on resulting quality.

Figure 2-75: Pareto Diagram

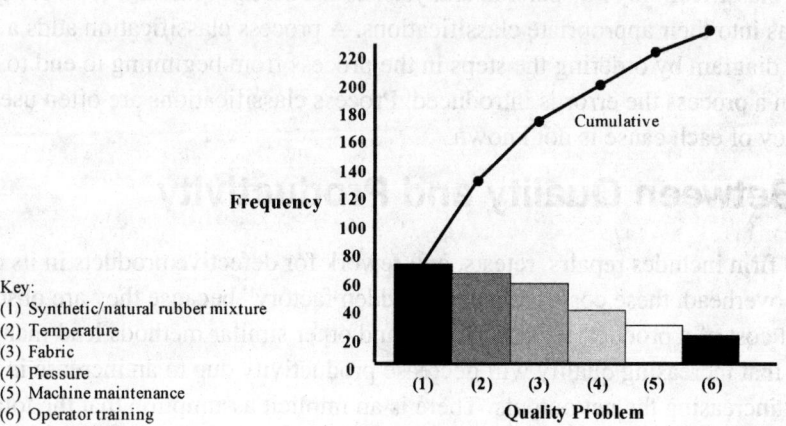

Key:
(1) Synthetic/natural rubber mixture
(2) Temperature
(3) Fabric
(4) Pressure
(5) Machine maintenance
(6) Operator training

A Pareto diagram can often be used as the first analysis of a variation from a control chart. Pareto diagrams can be useful in making management decisions that provide the greatest results.

Cause-and-effect (fishbone) diagrams

A **cause-and-effect diagram**, also called a fishbone or Ishikawa diagram, is a process flow diagram that shows how items contribute to a problem. The diagram is called a fishbone diagram because the problem is represented by an arrow, or the spine, and main causes are arrows, or ribs pointing to the spine. Smaller arrows, or bones, represent contributing causes pointing to the ribs. Figure 2-76 shows a cause-and-effect diagram for a tennis ball quality problem. The main causes of machine, materials, methods, and staffing are common cause breakdowns for manufacturing processes.

Figure 2-76: Tennis Ball Rejection Quality Cause-and-Effect Diagram

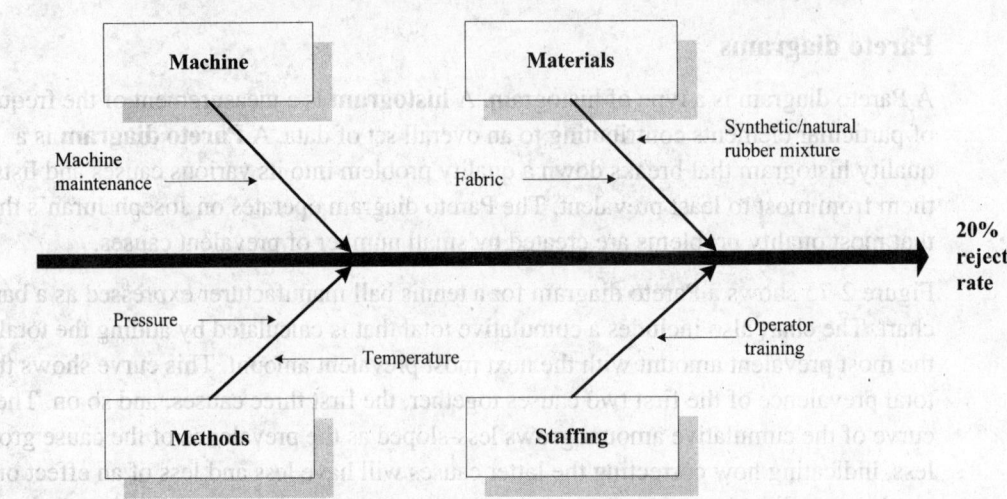

Cause-and-effect diagrams are broken down into two types: dispersion analysis and process classification. A dispersion analysis, as shown in Figure 2-76, places quality problems into their appropriate classifications. A process classification adds a time line into the diagram by ordering the steps in the process from beginning to end to understand where in a process the error is introduced. Process classifications are often used when the frequency of each cause is not known.

Relationship Between Quality and Productivity

When a firm includes repairs, retests, and rework for defective products in its overall factory overhead, these costs are called "hidden factory" because they are obscured from the total cost of a product. Hidden factory and other similar methods lead many firms to believe that increasing quality will decrease productivity due to an increase in net inputs without increasing the net outputs. There is an implicit assumption that the total units produced are good outputs, even though this is not true.

Many firms and studies have shown that increasing quality increases productivity. Not only are the costs of rework, scrap, and defects reduced through a TQM effort, but overall processes often become more efficient. For example, making factory workers responsible for quality levels on the component they manufacture empowers the workers to keep their machines maintained, reducing downtime and removing the need for as many reworked products. Reduced defects could also lower the amount of returns the sales staff needs to process (and also the amount of explaining and apologizing they need to do with customers).

Cost of Quality (COQ) Analysis

Process improvement teams in TQM need to know the specific costs for each part of the production process in order to determine how changes in a quality design affect profitability. For this reason, activity-based costing (ABC) and TQM are frequently used together due to the need for precise data on costs.

Traditional costs

Traditionally, the costs of quality (COQ) were broken down into four categories: prevention costs, appraisal costs, and internal and external failure costs.

- **Prevention costs**
  Prevention costs are the costs of quality system design, implementation, and maintenance, including audits of the quality system itself. Examples include quality planning, review of new products, surveys of supplier capabilities, team meetings for quality, and training for quality.

- **Appraisal costs**
  Appraisal costs are the costs of auditing processes for quality, including formal and informal measurements and evaluations of quality levels and setting quality standards and performance requirements. Examples include inspection and testing of raw materials, work-in-process and finished goods testing, calibration of equipment, and audits of operations or services.

- **Internal failure costs**
  Internal failure costs are the costs involved with defective products and components that are caught before shipping them to the customer. Examples include scrap, rework, spoilage, retesting, and reinspection.

- **External failure costs**
  External failure costs are the costs involved with shipping a defective product to a customer. Examples include customer complaints, returns, product recalls, and warranty claims.

These four categories met with limited success before the implementation of TQM, because most managers felt that quality was the sole responsibility of quality assurance (QA) and because managers defined quality as meeting requirements or keeping within an acceptable range. Therefore most managers felt that the costs of quality were only the costs of inspections and rework, scrap, and testing. The four categories failed to be a method of control for costs, just a method of estimating what those costs were.

Furthermore, once management "fixed" a problem, it was no longer dealt with. Also, the four categories did not fit well with the cost accumulation systems used by many firms and were therefore not well integrated.

On a deeper, more philosophical level, many quality experts disagree on whether the COQ measure should even be used, because it implies that a tradeoff can be made between quality and costs. In other words, it implies that it is acceptable to have less than 100% quality so long as the cost of the poor quality is low. These quality gurus believe that poor quality is unacceptable, however minor. They feel that COQ makes quality into a cost instead of a way to increase overall profits; therefore, some quality experts refer to the cost of poor quality to emphasize that the lack of quality is the reason for the costs.

Figure 2-77 shows a sample cost of quality report. A standardized form provided periodically can be useful in tracking costs and in tracking how successful certain changes have been to the overall product costs. However, some improvement teams can do just as well with a one-time, narrowly focused report and can avoid the expense of a periodic cost of quality report. If the expense of creating and maintaining the report cannot be justified by productivity and quality improvements, then it may not be cost-effective to make such reports regularly. Also note that a balanced scorecard (see Topic 4, "Balanced Scorecard," in this section) could be used to fulfill this and other quality reporting needs.

Figure 2-77: Cost of Quality Report

Quality Cost Summary Report
For the Month Ending _____
(In Thousands of U.S. Dollars)

Description	Current Month			Year to Date		
	Quality Costs	As a Percent of		Quality Costs	As a Percent of	
		Sales	Other		Sales	Other
1.0 Prevention Costs						
1.1 Marketing/Customer/User						
1.2 Product/Service/Design Development						
1.3 Purchasing Prevention Costs						
1.4 Operations Prevention Costs						
1.5 Quality Administration						
1.6 Other Prevention Costs						
Total Prevention Costs						
Prevention Targets						
2.0 Appraisal Costs						
2.1 Purchasing Appraisal Costs						
2.2 Operations Appraisal Costs						
2.3 External Appraisal Costs						
2.4 Review of Test and Inspection Data						
2.5 Miscellaneous Quality Evaluations						
Total Appraisal Costs						
Appraisal Targets						
3.0 Internal Failure Costs						
3.1 Product/Service Design Failure Costs						
3.2 Purchasing Failure Costs						
3.3 Operations Failure Costs						
3.4 Other Internal Failure Costs						
4.0 External Failure Costs						
Total Failure Costs						
Failure Targets						
Total Quality Costs						
Total Quality Targets						

Base Data	Current Month		Year to Date		Full Year	
	Budget	Actual	Budget	Actual	Budget	Actual
Net Sales						
_____						
Other Base (Specify)						

Source: *Principles of Quality Costs* by Jack Campanella

TQM costs

The emphasis of TQM on reducing and eliminating variations, continuous improvement, and other aspects of TQM, plus the failure of traditional quality costs to relate well to cost accumulation systems, have led TQM to abandon the traditional cost categories in favor of measures specific to the cost accumulation system used. When ABC is used, these costs are related to the activities that consume resources. When ABC is used and the quality terminology used matches the accumulation system, the following benefits can be gained:

- Identification of the true source of an abnormal variation

- Proper resource allocation for quality improvement

- Ease of communication of costs between departments

- Immediate feedback to production staff on details such as variation and cycle time

- Integrated financial and quality performance terms

- Monitoring of process and product improvement

Cost of Design Quality

The design of a product affects its overall profitability, quality, marketability, and customer satisfaction. A poor design can create an inefficient production process, inherent defects, and even costly redesign or rework. However, profitability is also greatly affected by time to market, or the time between when the idea is formed and when the product is released for sale. The longer the time to market, the more profits the product must produce. Competitors' products or fads make longer times to market more risky and less profitable. The dilemma between these two conflicting needs forces some products to be released before they are fully tested. These releases commonly end up requiring expensive redesigns to eliminate errors found later.

Old organizational practices worsened the design process. One department ended its responsibility for a design where the next department picked up, so engineers were not held responsible for an inefficient production process. Newer organizations use fewer levels of hierarchy and emphasize interdepartmental communications and teamwork as well as shared responsibility.

Old design processes simply estimated the number of design changes that would be needed based on experience with prior design processes without incorporating any improvement to the process itself. Inspection and sorting was the primary method of quality assurance, and a certain number of defects were expected.

Newer TQM design processes emphasize the satisfaction of customer needs in all parts of the process. One process, called **quality function deployment** (QFD), is a comprehensive planning tool that links customer needs to every part of the design process, and each part is interlinked with design decisions, process controls, and procedures. The result is a plan that shows every aspect of the product development, from production to shipping to customer satisfaction. QFD results in far fewer product redesigns and therefore an overall shorter time to market as well as higher quality. The typical QFD process begins with one element, customer requirements, and then bases each succeeding step on the prior cumulative requirements. Following customer requirements are design requirements, engineering design, product characteristics, manufacturing and purchasing operations, production and quality controls, and customer satisfaction. Thus QFD begins and ends with the customer.

Another common method of speeding up time to market while improving the quality of design is called concurrent engineering. **Concurrent engineering** (CE) involves teamwork to allow various aspects of a design project to be performed simultaneously. CE uses TQM plus modern tools such as computer-aided design to coordinate the efforts of every affected participant such as engineering, marketing, and even vendors for each part of a product's life cycle. Use of CE not only speeds time to market without sacrificing quality in design but also allows each part of the team to begin working on the next product or service sooner than a traditional sequential process would allow.

Progress Check

Directions: Read each question and respond in the space provided. Answers and page references appear on the following page.

1. Critical success factors for total quality management (TQM) include which of the following?

    (   )   a.   Continuous improvement

    (   )   b.   Absolute quality conformance

    (   )   c.   Gap analysis

    (   )   d.   Statistical thinking

2. Which of the following measurement tools usually includes a cumulative total curve that adds the results of the bar chart?

    (   )   a.   Gap analysis

    (   )   b.   Control chart

    (   )   c.   Pareto diagram

    (   )   d.   Quality analysis

3. In the traditional cost of quality analysis, which of the following includes the cost of designing a quality system?

    (   )   a.   Prevention costs

    (   )   b.   Appraisal costs

    (   )   c.   Internal failure costs

    (   )   d.   External failure costs

Progress check answers

1. a (p. 2-264)

2. c (p. 2-269)

3. a (p. 2-271)

External Financial Reporting

Section overview

In 1976 the Financial Accounting Standards Board (FASB) began a conceptual framework project to set out the objectives and fundamentals of financial reporting. The FASB published its first Statement of Financial Accounting Concepts (SFAC) in 1978. This conceptual framework helps the FASB create a coherent set of standards and rules when issuing new Statements of Financial Accounting Standards (SFASs). Although politics plays a role in the development of accounting standards, the FASB was created and is administered by a foundation, the Financial Accounting Foundation (FAF), which should minimize the effect of politics. The FAF is also intended to increase users' understanding of and confidence in financial statements.

The framework helps guide accountant choices when no standards are yet set and helps guide bodies such as the FASB's Emerging Issues Task Force (EITF) in resolving emerging issues more quickly. Although use of the concepts that make up the framework is not mandated by generally accepted accounting principles (GAAP), the concepts have wide acceptance (and the statements based on them are mandated by GAAP). Note that the information in this section on external reporting is solely based on U.S. GAAP and generally accepted auditing standards (GAAS).

This section contains a discussion of the objectives and fundamentals of the conceptual framework as well as the format, elements, and reporting requirements of financial statements. It also contains a discussion of the role of the SEC in shaping external financial reporting and the annual report the SEC requires for public companies.

Learning Outcome Statements

The Certified Management Accountant (CMA) test is based upon a series of Learning Outcome Statements (LOS) developed by the Institute of Certified Management Accountants (ICMA). The LOS describe all the knowledge and skills that make up the CMA body of knowledge, broken down by part, section and topic. The CMA Learning System (CMALS) supports the LOS by addressing all the subjects they cover. Candidates should use the LOS to ensure that they can address the concepts in different ways or through a variety of question scenarios. Candidates should also be prepared to perform calculations referred to in the LOS in total or by providing missing components of a calculation. The LOS should not be used as proxies for exact exam questions; they should be used as a guide for studying and learning the content of the CMA Learning System and ensuring that you can accomplish the objectives set out by the LOS.

The LOS included in the CMALS books are the comprehensive set, current as of the date of publication. Candidates can access the IMA Web site at www.imanet.org and click on the Certification section to locate and download a Portable Document Format (PDF) file of the current LOS.

Learning Outcome Statements

Part 2: Management Accounting and Reporting — Section E. External Financial Reporting

Part 2 — Section E1. Objectives of External Financial Reporting and Section E2. Financial Accounting Fundamentals

- LOS 2.E.1.a—Identify the objectives of external financial reporting, i.e., providing information on resources and obligations, comprehensive income, and cash flow.

- LOS 2.E.2.b—Identify and demonstrate an understanding of basic accounting assumptions and conventions, including going concern, historical cost, accrual accounting, and conservatism.

- LOS 2.E.2.c—Demonstrate an understanding of recognition and measurement concepts as they relate to revenue, expenses, fixed assets, current assets, current liabilities, long-term liabilities, and equity transactions.

- LOS 2.E.2.d—Differentiate between realization and recognition.

- LOS 2.E.2.e—Identify financial statement elements for each of the financial statements.

- LOS 2.E.2.f—Special topics: leases, pensions and other post-retirement benefits, deferred income taxes, stock options, discontinued operations, extraordinary items, accounting changes, early extinguishment of debt, business combinations, consolidated financial statements, and accounting for derivatives and stock options. For each special topic, define and describe its characteristics, demonstrate a basic understanding of the relevant accounting issues, and describe the impact on a firm's financial statements.

Part 2 — Section E3. Financial Statements and Statement Users

- LOS 2.E.3.a—For the Statement of Financial Position (balance sheet), the Statement of Earnings (income statement), the Statement of Cash Flows, and the Statement of Changes in Shareholders' Equity, identify the users of these financial statements and their needs.

- LOS 2.E.3.b—For the Statement of Financial Position (balance sheet), the Statement of Earnings (income statement), Statement of Cash Flows, and the Statement of Changes in Shareholders' Equity, demonstrate an understanding of the purposes and uses of each statement.

- LOS 2.E.3.c—For the Statement of Financial Position (balance sheet), the Statement of Earnings (income statement), Statement of Cash Flows, and the Statement of Changes in Shareholders' Equity, identify the major components and classifications of each statement.

- LOS 2.E.3.d—For the Statement of Financial Position (balance sheet), the Statement of Earnings (income statement), Statement of Cash Flows, and the Statement of Changes in Shareholders' Equity, identify the limitations of each financial statement.

- LOS 2.E.3.e—For the Statement of Financial Position (balance sheet), the Statement of Earnings (income statement), Statement of Cash Flows, and the Statement of Changes in Shareholders' Equity, identify financial statement information that requires supplemental disclosure in the body of the statement or in the footnotes.

- LOS 2.E.3.f—For the Statement of Financial Position (balance sheet), the Statement of Earnings (income statement), Statement of Cash Flows, and the Statement of Changes in Shareholders' Equity, prepare financial statements in the correct format.

- LOS 2.E.3.g—For the Statement of Financial Position (balance sheet), the Statement of Earnings (income statement), Statement of Cash Flows, and the Statement of Changes in Shareholders' Equity, calculate and classify components of each financial statement.

- LOS 2.E.3.h—For the Statement of Cash Flows, demonstrate an understanding of both the "direct" and the "indirect" methods.

- LOS 2.E.3.i—For the Statement of Financial Position (balance sheet), the Statement of Earnings (income statement), Statement of Cash Flows, and the Statement of Changes in Shareholders' Equity, identify how a financial transaction affects the elements of each of the financial statements and determine the proper classification of the transaction.

- LOS 2.E.3.j—For the Statement of Financial Position (balance sheet), the Statement of Earnings (income statement), Statement of Cash Flows, and the Statement of Changes in Shareholders' Equity, identify the basic disclosures related to each of the statements (footnotes, supplementary schedules, and so on).

Part 2 — Section E4. Recognition, Measurement, Valuation, and Disclosure

Required knowledge for each of the subtopics listed

- Define the subtopic and describe the characteristics of its components.

- Demonstrate an understanding of appropriate valuation techniques for the components of each subtopic.

- Demonstrate an understanding of the appropriate accounting conventions for the components of each subtopic.

- Compare and contrast valuation techniques and accounting methods.

- Show the correct financial statement presentation.

- Identify the appropriate disclosure requirements in the body of the financial statements and/or in the footnotes or supplemental schedules.

I. Cash and marketable securities

- LOS 2.E.4.I.a—Subtopic components: cash, cash equivalents, marketable (trading) securities.

- LOS 2.E.4.I.b—Determine when cash is restricted.

II. Accounts receivable

- LOS 2.E.4.II.a—Subtopic components: current, noncurrent, trade, and nontrade receivables; trade discounts, cash (sales) discounts, sales returns and allowances, net realizable value, promissory note, factoring receivables, write-offs and collection of write-offs.

- LOS 2.E.4.II.b—Identify issues related to the valuation of accounts receivable.

- LOS 2.E.4.II.c—Calculate cash discounts using both the gross method and the net method.

- LOS 2.E.4.II.d—Identify two methods of recording uncollectibles and describe why the allowance method is the generally accepted approach.

- LOS 2.E.4.II.e—Calculate the allowance for uncollectibles using both the percentage-of-sales (income statement) approach and the percentage-of-receivables (balance sheet) approach.

- LOS 2.E.4.II.f—Discount a long-term note using the time value of money tables and indicate its correct valuation at time of sale.

- LOS 2.E.4.II.g—Calculate the interest revenue and discount amortized for each time period of the note.

- LOS 2.E.4.II.h—Define and be able to compute an imputed interest rate.

- LOS 2.E.4.II.i—Demonstrate an understanding of receivables when they are used as collateral.

- LOS 2.E.4.II.j—Distinguish between receivables sold on a with-recourse basis and those sold on a without-recourse basis.

III. Inventories

- LOS 2.E.4.III.a—Subtopic components: raw material inventory, work-in-process inventory, finished goods inventory, merchandise inventory; perpetual, modified perpetual, and periodic inventory systems; cost of goods sold, cost of goods available for sale, goods in transit, consigned goods.

- LOS 2.E.4.III.b—Identify issues in inventory valuation, including which goods to include, what costs to include, and which cost assumption to use.

- LOS 2.E.4.III.c—Identify the costs included in inventory.

- LOS 2.E.4.III.d—Differentiate between f.o.b. shipping point and f.o.b. destination.

- LOS 2.E.4.III.e—Demonstrate an understanding of special sale agreements, including sales with a buyback agreement (product financing arrangement), sales with high rates of returns, and sales on installment.

- LOS 2.E.4.III.f—Calculate and indicate the correct entries and financial statement presentation for purchase discounts using the gross method and using the net method.

- LOS 2.E.4.III.g—Identify accounting issues related to purchase commitments.

- LOS 2.E.4.III.h—Identify and compare cost flow assumptions used in accounting for inventories.

- LOS 2.E.4.III.i—Calculate ending inventory and cost of goods sold using the specific identification, average cost, first-in-first-out (FIFO), and last-in-first-out (LIFO) methods.

- LOS 2.E.4.III.j—Calculate the effect on income and on assets of using different inventory methods.

- LOS 2.E.4.III.k—Analyze the effects of inventory errors.

- LOS 2.E.4.III.l—Demonstrate an understanding of the LIFO reserve and LIFO liquidation.

- LOS 2.E.4.III.m—Calculate ending inventory and cost of goods sold using dollar-value LIFO.

- LOS 2.E.4.III.n—Identify advantages and disadvantages of the different inventory methods.

- LOS 2.E.4.III.o—Apply the lower of cost or market rule.

- LOS 2.E.4.III.p—Identify when inventories are valued at net realizable value.

- LOS 2.E.4.III.q—Demonstrate an understanding of the relative sales value method.

- LOS 2.E.4.III.r—Determine ending inventory by using the gross profit method and by using the retail inventory method.

- LOS 2.E.4.III.s—Recommend the inventory method and cost flow assumption that should be used for a firm in a specific industry given a set of facts and management goals.

IV. Investments

- LOS 2.E.4.IV.a—Subtopic components: debt securities: held-to-maturity, trading, and available-for-sale securities; equity securities: less than 20% holdings (available-for-sale and trading), between 20% and 50% holdings, and holdings more than 50%.

- LOS 2.E.4.IV.b—Calculate discounts, premiums, and interest on debt securities using the effective interest method and utilizing time value of money tables.

- LOS 2.E.4.IV.c—Define holding gain or loss.

- LOS 2.E.4.IV.d—Calculate the realized gain/loss on the sale of a debt or equity security.

- LOS 2.E.4.IV.e—Calculate the securities fair value adjustment for available-for-sale and trading debt securities.

- LOS 2.E.4.IV.f—Identify and describe the fair value method, equity method, and consolidated method for equity securities.

- LOS 2.E.4.IV.g—Compare the equity method with the fair value method.

- LOS 2.E.4.IV.h—Demonstrate an understanding of reclassification adjustments.

- LOS 2.E.4.IV.i—Account for impairment of value and indicate the correct cost basis for the impaired security.

- LOS 2.E.4.IV.j—Identify and describe the proper accounting for transfers of investment securities between categories.

V. Property, plant, and equipment

- LOS 2.E.4.V.a—Subtopic components: land, buildings, equipment, and self-constructed assets; additions, improvements, replacements, reinstallations, and repairs; nonmonetary exchanges; depreciation; depletion; impairment.

- LOS 2.E.4.V.b—Calculate depreciation using the activity method, the straight-line method, the sum-of-the-years'-digits method, the declining balance method, the group method, and the composite method.

- LOS 2.E.4.V.c—Calculate and record the gain or loss on the disposition of tangible assets.

- LOS 2.E.4.V.d— Identify the basis on which tangible assets would be valued when payment is in the form of stock.

- LOS 2.E.4.V.e—Demonstrate an understanding of the correct accounting treatment for interest costs incurred for the construction or acquisition of tangible assets.

- LOS 2.E.4.V.f—Determine the effect on the financial statements of using different depreciation methods.

- LOS 2.E.4.V.g—Recommend a depreciation method given a set of data and management goals.

- LOS 2.E.4.V.h—Calculate a depletion base given acquisition, exploration, development, and restoration costs.

VI. Intangibles

- LOS 2.E.4.VI.a—Subtopic components: intangible assets: patents, copyrights, trademarks and trade names, leaseholds, franchises and licensees; purchased intangibles and internally created intangibles; goodwill; internally created goodwill and purchased goodwill; negative goodwill; amortization; research and development; start-up costs, initial operating losses, advertising costs, and computer software costs.

- LOS 2.E.4.VI.b—Demonstrate an understanding of the accounting for impairment of intangible assets.

- LOS 2.E.4.VI.c—Determine the effect on the financial statements of various intangible asset transactions.

VII. Current liabilities

- LOS 2.E.4.VII.a—Subtopic components: current liability: notes payable, accounts payable, current maturities of long-term debt, short-term obligations expected to be refinanced, dividends payable, returnable deposits, unearned (or deferred) revenues, taxes payable, and employee-related liabilities; loss contingencies; warranty costs; premiums and coupons.

- LOS 2.E.4.VII.b—Identify the classification issues of short-term debt expected to be refinanced.

- LOS 2.E.4.VII.c—Identify the different types of employee-related liabilities.

- LOS 2.E.4.VII.d—Apply both the expense warranty approach and the sales warranty approach.

VIII. Long-term liabilities and bonds payable

- LOS 2.E.4.VIII.a—Subtopic components: long-term liabilities/debt: bonds, long-term notes payable, mortgage notes payable, zero-interest-bearing notes, convertible debt.

- LOS 2.E.4.VIII.b—Calculate interest expense, interest payable, bond discount and premium using the straight-line method and the effective interest method (time value of money tables).

- LOS 2.E.4.VIII.c—Identify the proper classification of bond discount and premium as an adjunct account.

- LOS 2.E.4.VIII.d—Identify the proper accounting treatment of debt issuance expenses.

- LOS 2.E.4.VIII.e—Define implicit interest rate and compute imputed interest.

- LOS 2.E.4.VIII.f—Account for notes issued for property, goods, and services.

- LOS 2.E.4.VIII.g—Calculate imputed fair value and note discount where the stated interest rate is unreasonable.

- LOS 2.E.4.VIII.h—Define off-balance sheet financing and identify different forms of this type of borrowing.

- LOS 2.E.4.VIII.i—Indicate the disclosure requirements for off-balance sheet financing.

IX. Equity transactions and earnings per share

- LOS 2.E.4.IX.a—Subtopic components: preferred stock and common stock; capital stock, additional paid-in capital and retained earnings; treasury stock (cost method and par value method); property dividends, scrip dividends; liquidating dividends; stock dividends (large and small); retained earnings.

- LOS 2.E.4.IX.b—Apply the accounting procedures for issuing shares of stock, including par value stock, no-par stock, stock sold on a subscription basis, lump sum sales, and stocks issued in noncash transactions.

- LOS 2.E.4.IX.c—Apply the accounting procedures for the declaration and payment of common stock and preferred stock dividends.

- LOS 2.E.4.IX.d—Define stock options, warrants, and rights and determine the correct presentation in the financial statements for these instruments.

- LOS 2.E.4.IX.e—Identify transactions that affect paid-in capital and those that affect retained earnings.

- LOS 2.E.4.IX.f—Infer the effect on shareholders' equity of large and small stock dividends.

- LOS 2.E.4.IX.g—Define stock split and distinguish from stock dividend.

- LOS 2.E.4.IX.h—Identify reasons for the appropriation of retained earnings.

- LOS 2.E.4.IX.i—Calculate earnings per share (basic and diluted).

X. Revenues and expenses

- LOS 2.E.4.X.a—Apply the revenue recognition principles to various types of transactions.

- LOS 2.E.4.X.b—Identify issues involved with revenue recognition at point of sale, including sales with buyback agreements, sales when right of return exists, and trade loading (or channel stuffing).

- LOS 2.E.4.X.c—Identify instances where revenue is recognized before delivery.

- LOS 2.E.4.X.d—Distinguish between percentage-of-completion and completed-contract methods for recognizing revenue.

- LOS 2.E.4.X.e—Apply the percentage-of-completion and the completed-contract methods.

- LOS 2.E.4.X.f—Compare and contrast the recognition of costs of construction, progress billings, collections, and gross profit recognized under the two long-term contract accounting methods.

- LOS 2.E.4.X.g—Demonstrate an understanding of the proper accounting for losses on long-term contracts.

- LOS 2.E.4.X.h—Identify instances where revenue is recognized after delivery.

- LOS 2.E.4.X.i—Identify the situations in which each of the following revenue recognition methods would be used: installment sales method, cost recovery method, and deposit method.

- LOS 2.E.4.X.j—Demonstrate an understanding of the accounting procedures under the installment method, the cost recovery method, and the deposit method.

- LOS 2.E.4.X.k—Define gains and losses and indicate the proper financial statement presentation.

- LOS 2.E.4.X.l—Discuss the issues and concerns that have been identified with respect to revenue recognition practices.

- LOS 2.E.4.X.m—Demonstrate an understanding of the matching principle with respect to revenues and expenses and be able to apply it to a specific situation.

- LOS 2.E.4.X.n—Demonstrate an understanding of expense recognition practices.

XI. Comprehensive income

- LOS 2.E.4.XI.a—Define comprehensive income and other comprehensive income.

- LOS 2.E.4.XI.b—Identify the three alternative ways that other comprehensive income may be displayed in the financial statements.

- LOS 2.E.4.XI.c—Calculate comprehensive income.

XII. Segment reporting

- LOS 2.E.4.XII.a—Define operating segment.

- LOS 2.E.4.XII.b—Identify the disclosures required for a reportable operating segment.

- LOS 2.E.4.XII.c—Determine if a segment is reportable given a set of data.

XIII. Multinational considerations

- LOS 2.E.4.XIII.a—Identify the challenges inherent in translating foreign entities' financial statements to the parent's reporting currency.

- LOS 2.E.4.XIII.b—Define functional currency.

- LOS 2.E.4.XIII.c—Distinguish between the monetary/nonmonetary method and the current rate method.

- LOS 2.E.4.XIII.d—Translate a foreign entity's financial statements from the entity's functional currency to the reporting currency.

- LOS 2.E.4.XIII.e—Re-measure a foreign entity's financial statement to the functional currency.

- LOS 2.E.4.XIII.f—Describe the significance of a foreign currency transaction gain (loss) on the financial statements.

- LOS 2.E.4.XIII.g—Define "highly inflationary economy" and identify which currency should be used as the reporting currency for a company in this environment.

- LOS 2.E.4.XIII.h—Identify disclosure requirements for translation of foreign currency financial statements.

Part 2 — Section E5. The SEC and Its Reporting Requirements

- LOS 2.E.5.a—Identify the two major acts establishing the SEC and its powers (the Securities Act of 1933 and the Securities Exchange Act of 1934); and demonstrate knowledge of the major provisions of each.

- LOS 2.E.5.b—Describe the general reporting requirements of public companies.

- LOS 2.E.5.c—Define the integrated disclosure system, standardized financial statements, and management discussion and analysis.

- LOS 2.E.5.d—Identify other disclosures regarding business operations.

- LOS 2.E.5.e—Identify and describe the SEC disclosure requirements, including the registration with SEC (initial filing and subsequent filings when issuing securities), the annual report to SEC or Form 10-K, the quarterly report or Form 10-Q, disclosure of material events or Form 8-K, and proxy statements and solicitations.

- LOS 2.E.5.f—Identify and explain the major provisions of the Sarbanes-Oxley Act of 2002.

- LOS 2.E.5.g—Identify the functions and responsibilities of the Public Company Accounting Oversight Board (PCAOB).

Part 2 — Section E6. The Annual Report

- LOS 2.E.6.a—Identify audit services related to the annual report.

- LOS 2.E.6.b—Identify the basic components of the annual report, including management's statement of responsibility for the financial statements and the independent auditor's report.

- LOS 2.E.6.c—Describe the audit committee's level of responsibility for the integrity of the financial information presented in the annual reports.

- LOS 2.E.6.d—Identify the Audit Committee's functions to include (a) nominating the public accounting firm that will conduct the annual external audit, (b) participating in the process of setting the scope of internal and external audits, and (c) inviting direct audit communications on major problems encountered during the course of internal and external audits.

- LOS 2.E.6.e—Discuss how the audit opinion letter published in the annual report can impact the market perception of the firm.

- LOS 2.E.6.f—Identify and describe other sections in the annual report, including the letter to shareholders, management discussion and analysis, and the statement on social responsibility.

Objectives of External Financial Reporting

Topic overview

The FASB began a conceptual framework project with its first Statement of Financial Accounting Concepts (SFAC) to set out the objectives of external financial reporting. Their purpose was to create a basis for all future accounting and reporting standards. Although the concepts are not binding (not GAAP), they serve as the basis for the binding standards (Statements of Financial Accounting Standards, or SFAS). The concept statements are intended to define the reasons for and content and limitations of financial information. The information in this topic is therefore primarily based on SFAC No. 1, "Objectives of Financial Reporting by Business Enterprises."

Financial accounting is external by nature, while managerial accounting is its internal counterpart. While financial accounting is historical and is constrained by GAAP, managerial accounting can be forward-looking and is not constrained by GAAP. However, both types of accounting are constrained by the usefulness of the information and the cost of obtaining the information. These two types of accounting tend to influence each other; financial accounting methods or amounts reported may influence management's decisions or vice versa.

Generally accepted accounting principles (GAAP) are a combination of authoritative pronouncements and an evolution of common practice when authoritative bodies are silent on an issue. GAAP relates to measuring economic activity, the timing of such measurements, and the preparation and presentation of financial information in statements and required disclosures.

Information on Resources and Obligations

Financial reporting is intended to aid investors, creditors, and others in making timely business and economic decisions using relevant and reliable information. The objectives of financial reporting are not restricted to financial statements but apply to any information that would be helpful in decision making. Whatever the format, financial reporting should provide information on the resources and obligations of a company so that external users can allocate their scarce resources to the most efficient business entities. The FASB's Statements of Financial Accounting Concepts (SFACs) set forth general and specific objectives of financial reporting.

General objectives of financial reporting include the following:

- Financial reporting should provide information that is useful to external users in making rational investment, credit, and similar decisions. External users are defined as current and potential investors and creditors (and their advisors) who have a reasonable understanding of business and economics and who are willing to study the information with reasonable diligence.

- Financial reporting should provide information to help external users assess the amounts, timing, and uncertainty of prospective cash flows such as:

  - Cash receipts from dividends or interest.

  - Proceeds from sale, redemption, or maturity of securities and loans.

  - Net cash inflows to the entity (enterprise cash flows).

Specific objectives of financial reporting show the types of information that should be included in specific financial reports:

- Financial reporting should provide information about the economic resources (assets) of an entity, any claims to those resources (liabilities), including obligations to transfer resources to other entities or to owner's equity, and the effects of circumstances, transactions, and events that alter the entity's resources and claims to those resources.

- Financial reporting should provide information about an entity's comprehensive income and its components.

- Financial reporting should provide information about an entity's cash flows.

Economic resources and claims to those resources

Information about an entity's economic resources and claims to those resources is useful to interested parties because it helps them assess liquidity and highlight the entity's financial strengths, limitations, and performance during a period. This information, which is usually found on the balance sheet, can be a direct assessment of the cash flow potential of the entity's resources or of combinations of those resources.

Comprehensive income information

According to SFAC No. 6, comprehensive income is a broad measure of all changes in an entity's equity over a period from transactions and other events and circumstances except those that result from investments by owners and distribution to owners.

Comprehensive income is covered in Topic 4 of this section.

Cash flow information

Information about an entity's cash flow is a specific objective of financial reporting. Without sufficient cash flow, the entity's ability to continue as a going concern may be at risk. Even if the entity is not likely to go out of business, a lack of cash flow, or poor liquidity, may raise the risk of investing in or lending to the entity. Financial reporting gives current and potential investors and creditors an indication of the amount, timing, and uncertainty of an entity's cash flow prospects from business operations or investments.

Cash flows are divided into operating, investing, and financing cash flows. Information on cash flow indicates how an entity borrows and repays cash, how it gets and spends cash, how it invests cash in noncurrent assets, and how it pays dividends and other distributions.

Progress Check

Directions: Read each question and respond in the space provided. Answers and page references appear on the following page.

1. True or false? The SFACs are not part of GAAP and are not binding.

    (   )   a.   True

    (   )   b.   False

2. Which of the following elements of income does comprehensive income exclude?

    (   )   a.   Cumulative effect of a change in accounting principle

    (   )   b.   Investments by and distributions to owners

    (   )   c.   Unrealized gains and losses on available-for-sale securities

    (   )   d.   Income from continuing operations

Progress check answers

1. a (p. 2-287)

2. b (p. 2-288)

Financial Accounting Fundamentals

Topic overview

The fundamentals of financial reporting, as discussed in SFAC No. 5, "Recognition and Measurement in Financial Statements of Business Enterprises," are concepts that guide the selection of accounting methods for recognizing, measuring, and recording transactions, circumstances, and events. The fundamentals also cover the methods used to summarize and report these items to external users and the basic accounting assumptions and conventions.

Accounting Assumptions and Conventions

The financial accounting structure includes the following assumptions and conventions upon which all financial reporting relies.

Monetary unit

The measurement scale used to value entities is nominal units of money. A **nominal unit of money** is money that is not adjusted for changes in purchasing power over time (not adjusted for inflation or deflation).

Economic entity

An **economic entity** is any business enterprise, ranging from a sole proprietorship to a global corporation, that has distinct accountability apart from owners and other entities. The economic entity assumption distinguishes business enterprises from their owners and accounts for each separately.

Going concern

Unless an entity is facing an imminent liquidation, financial accounting assumes that the entity is a going concern that will continue in business for the long term. The going concern assumption does not imply that a business will last indefinitely but that it will continue long enough to fulfill its business objectives and commitments.

Periodicity

Periodicity assumes that economic activities are divided into artificial portions of time such as months, quarters, and years. The portions are artificial because the entity never stops accumulating receivables, payables, and so on until it is out of business. Most financial statements, such as the income statement, encompass results during a period of time (for example, a year). Other financial reports, such as the balance sheet, describe results as of a moment in time (a specific date).

Cost-benefit relationship

The **cost-benefit relationship** assumes that unless the benefits of providing information exceed the costs associated with it, the information should not be prepared.

Materiality

According to FASB's SFAC No. 2, **materiality** refers to the threshold at which the omission or misstatement of an item in a financial report would influence or change the judgment of a reasonable person relying on the report had the item been included or corrected, taking into account the individual circumstances of the situation. In other words, if the item makes a difference, it should be included or corrected.

The FASB has refrained from making a general rule for dealing with materiality, because the majority of the accounting profession believes that materiality judgments can only be made by experienced persons possessing the specific facts of the situation. The SEC also has specific regulations prohibiting materiality thresholds to be used to hide illegal transactions such as bribes, to convert a loss into a profit, to increase the compensation of management, or to preserve a positive earnings trend.

Conservatism

SFAC No. 2 defines **conservatism** as "a prudent reaction to uncertainty to try to ensure that uncertainty and risks inherent in business situations are adequately considered." APB Statement 4 expressed what, for most accountants, conservatism traditionally meant: "that possible errors in measurement be in the direction of understatement rather than overstatement of net income and net assets."

In the past, deliberate and consistent understatement of net assets and profits was considered to give bankers (formerly the primary statement users) a margin of safety. However, such a practice today only makes statements hard to compare and discredits the issuers in the long run. Traditional conservatism has led to undervalued inventories and unreasonable depreciation or income recognition practices. Both conservative and optimistic biases can mislead investors, so the FASB now recommends conservatism be defined by neutrality and honesty in the disclosure of uncertainties, thus allowing users to form their own opinions as to the outcome of uncertain events.

Recognition and Measurement Concepts

Recognition and measurement concepts are the methods of deciding how and when to record business transactions, including historical cost, full disclosure, revenue recognition and realization, and the matching principle.

Historical cost

Historical cost is the amount paid to acquire an asset, or, for noncash exchanges, it is the estimated value of the noncash asset or liability exchanged. Historical cost is the most commonly used valuation method. Depreciation, amortization, or other allocations reduce the historical cost of an asset, if applicable. Other liabilities valued at historical cost include most bonds, notes, and accounts payable. Property, plant, and equipment and intangible assets are generally reported at historical cost less accumulated depreciation or amortization, where appropriate. Many businesses find that historical cost is an effective benchmark that can be used to establish historical trends. It is reliable because it can be verified, but it may lack relevance when it differs from the actual value of an item.

Full disclosure

Full disclosure is a general concept that refers to reporting all known information about a company's finances that would be of sufficient materiality to influence the decisions of a reasonable and informed user. The information should also meet a cost-benefit constraint.

The information may be disclosed in the financial statements, in the notes to the statements, or in supplementary information. Full disclosure and proper accounting must go hand in hand. The financial statements should include only items that fit within the element definitions and that are measurable, reliable, and relevant. Notes should complete an otherwise incomplete or misleading portion of a financial statement. Supplementary information could present information from a different perspective than that in the statements or could be management's explanation of events that cannot be recorded in the financials.

Revenue recognition/realization

Common terminology for revenue recognition and realization includes the following:

- **Realized** means that assets such as goods or services are actually exchanged for cash or claims to cash.

- **Realizable** means that assets held or received are readily convertible into cash or claims to cash through sale on an active market at easily determinable prices.

- **Earned** means that the entity has substantially completed the activity related to the revenue.

Accrual accounting recognizes, or records in the general ledger, revenue when it is realized or realizable and when it is earned; accrual accounting recognizes expenses in the period in which they are incurred rather than when the cash is actually paid.

How do you decide if the conditions of recognition have been met? For most goods, revenue is recognized at the point of sale because the actual sales price can be verified. The period in which the sale is recorded is used in accrual accounting as the point at which the revenue is recognized as earned. However, there are several exceptions to recognizing revenue at the point of sale. The four primary points at which revenue may be recognized are shown in Figure 2-78.

Figure 2-78: Revenue Recognition Timing Exceptions

Recognition	Description
During production	Certain long-term construction projects are allowed to recognize revenues periodically throughout the construction project based on a percentage-of-completion method. Although the transfer of ownership is not completed until the project is finished, at each stage of completion, that portion is considered to be substantially complete. This method may be used only if dependable estimates of progress and costs are available.
End of production	In cases where the selling price and the amount to be sold are certain and verifiable before the sale takes place, revenue can be recognized at the end of production. This holds true only for items sold in a ready market that sets standard prices. For example, a government-set price for an agricultural product could be recognized at harvest time.
Time of sale	Revenue is realized or realizable and earned at the time of sale, in most cases.
Receipt of cash	A cash basis is used when the uncertainty of collection is significant enough to invalidate the assumptions under the time-of-sale method. If a significant portion of sales default, then the actual sales price is undeterminable on average. One method for dealing with uncertainty about cash collections is the installment sales accounting method. In this approach, profits are recognized proportionally as cash installments are collected.

Matching

The concept of **matching** is tied directly to revenue recognition. Entities incur operating expenses such as salaries and production costs far before the usual time of revenue recognition (the point of sale). Matching is associating each expense with the revenue it eventually produces, whenever possible or reasonable. To a degree, however, new accounting rules have deemphasized the matching concept.

Three situations occur in regard to the matching principle: the costs can be associated directly with resulting revenues; the costs cannot be directly associated, but analysis shows a relationship; or the costs are not practical to associate with a revenue. In the first situation, the costs are reported in the same time period as the revenues. In the second situation, most entities use an allocation policy to approximate the matching policy. Long-lived assets need to be amortized over the life of the asset for each period in which they are used productively (that is, depreciation). In the last situation, where expenses are not attributable to a specific revenue, the costs are simply charged as expenses or losses to the period in which they are incurred. This occurs with general expenses such as administrative and executive salaries and other costs.

Financial Statement Elements

FASB's SFAC No. 6, "Elements of Financial Statements," defines the elements of financial statements as the classes of items that comprise all financial statements. Elements are presented in both descriptive words and in numbers (that is, monetary amounts) to express resources, claims to those resources, and the effects of transactions and other events that result in changes to those resources and their claims. Some elements of financial statements are measured at a moment in time (think of a photograph) and others over a period in time (think of a motion picture). "Moment in time" measures are made for permanent accounts; "period in time" measures are made for temporary accounts. The permanent accounts are assets, liabilities, and equity. The temporary accounts show transactions over an interval of time: distributions to owners (dividends), revenues, expenses, gains, and losses.

Assets

Assets are probable future economic benefits obtained or controlled by a particular entity as a result of past transactions or events.

Liabilities

Liabilities are probable future sacrifices of economic benefits arising from present obligations of a particular entity to transfer assets or provide services to other entities in the future as a result of past transactions or events.

Equity

Equity, or **net assets**, is the residual interest in the assets of an entity that remains after deducting its liabilities. Equity of an entity is the difference between the entity's assets and its liabilities, which is the reason that the accounting equation of assets equals liabilities plus equity always balances out. Liabilities have priority over ownership interests, so equity can be a negative amount if the liabilities are greater than the entity's assets. Equity can be directly increased or decreased by the investments by or distributions to owners.

- **Investments by owners** are increases in equity of a particular business enterprise resulting from transfers to it from other entities of something valuable to obtain or increase ownership interests (or equity) in it (for example, purchase of shares). Assets are most commonly received as investments by owners but may also be received as services or satisfaction or conversion of liabilities of the enterprise.

- **Distributions to owners** are decreases in equity of a particular business enterprise resulting from transferring assets, rendering services, or incurring liabilities to owners (for example, for dividends). Distributions to owners decrease ownership interest (or equity) in an enterprise.

(Investments by and distributions to owners are transactions directly between the entity and its owners. By contrast, if a shareholder, or owner, sells part or all of the entity's stock on an exchange market, this transaction does not involve the entity and therefore equity is not affected.)

Comprehensive income

As noted earlier, comprehensive income is the change in equity of a business enterprise during a period from transactions and other events and circumstances from nonowner sources. It includes all changes in equity during a period except those resulting from investments by owners and distributions to owners.

Revenues

Revenues are inflows or other enhancements of assets of an entity or settlements of its liabilities (or a combination of both) from delivering or producing goods, rendering services, or other activities that constitute the entity's ongoing major or central operations.

Expenses

Expenses are outflows or other use of assets or incurrences of liabilities (or a combination of both) as a result of delivering or producing goods, rendering services, or carrying out other activities that constitute the entity's ongoing major or central operations.

Gains

Gains are increases in equity (net assets) from peripheral or incidental transactions of an entity and from all other transactions and other events and circumstances affecting the entity except those that result from revenues or investments by owners.

Losses

Losses are decreases in equity (net assets) from peripheral or incidental transactions of an entity and from all other transactions and other events and circumstances affecting the entity except those that result from expenses or distributions to owners.

Taxes

Taxes are decreases in equity (net assets) from the provision for federal income taxes.

Elements of cash flow

A statement of cash flows shows how the cash receipts and cash payments for a period cause a net increase or decrease in cash for the period as well as dividing how it was used among three major activities: operating, investing, and financing.

- **Net cash flow from operations**
  Net cash flow from operations is net income less increases in accounts receivable or decreases in accounts payable (or plus decreases in A/R and increases in A/P), thus showing the effect of cash transactions on net income.

- **Net cash flow from investing**
  Net cash flow from investing is net cash flow from operations less any investment purchases and plus any investment sales. Investing includes purchase or sale of both debt and equity securities of other entities as well as purchase or sale of property, plant, and equipment.

- **Net cash flow from financing**
  Cash flow from financing activities is net cash flow from investing less any dividends, redemption of debt, or reacquisition of capital stock, plus issuance of debt (for example, notes or bonds) and equity securities. Thus it includes all borrowing and repayment of money from creditors as well as any resources obtained from or paid to owners.

Accounting equation

The accounting equation represents how these elements work together. It represents a balance between the resources of a company on one side of the equation (assets) and all of the claims on those resources on the other side of the equation (liabilities plus equity).

$$\text{Assets} - \text{Liabilities} = \text{Equity}$$

or

$$\text{Assets} = \text{Liabilities} + \text{Equity}$$

Progress Check

Directions: Read each question and respond in the space provided. Answers and page references appear on the following page.

1. True or false? The FASB has promulgated specific guidelines for what amounts are considered material and what amounts are considered immaterial, based on a percentage of the company's net income.

    (   )   a.   True

    (   )   b.   False

2. Property, plant, and equipment and intangible assets are generally valued using which of the following measurements?

    (   )   a.   Historical cost

    (   )   b.   Fair value

    (   )   c.   Net realizable value

    (   )   d.   Lower of cost or market

3. Which of the following is an increase in equity from a peripheral transaction?

    (   )   a.   Revenue

    (   )   b.   Income

    (   )   c.   Gains

    (   )   d.   Comprehensive income

Progress check answers

1. b (p. 2-291)

2. a (p. 2-292)

3. c (p. 2-295)

Financial Statements and Statement Users

Topic overview

The four financial statements discussed in this topic present a basic picture of an entity, are required by the SEC for all publicly traded companies, and are a useful tool for any company. They include:

- *The income statement, which shows the results of business activities.*

- *The statement of shareholders' equity, which shows owner investments, distribution of profits to owners, and profits retained by the company.*

- *The balance sheet, which shows an entity's ending financial position.*

- *The statement of cash flows, which shows an entity's cash receipts, payments, and the cash effects of its operating, investing, and financing activities during the accounting period.*

The financial statements shown in this section are all for a fictitious organization, Robin Manufacturing Company, for a given year, and linkages between the various statements are illustrated with notes and by the amounts themselves. The footnotes to financial statements, which present required disclosures, are also covered.

Most entities provide prior years' financial statement information alongside the current year's information for comparison. For example, both the income and cash flow statements usually show three years of results. This allows analysts to easily compare past performance to present performance and make a determination of future success.

This topic ends with a discussion of the needs of external users and how financial statements satisfy some of those needs.

Statement of Earnings (Income Statement)

The statement of earnings, commonly called an income statement or a profit and loss (P&L) statement, measures the earnings of an entity's operations over a given time period, such as a quarter or fiscal year. The income statement is used to measure profitability, creditworthiness, and investment value of an entity. Along with the other statements, it helps assess the amounts, timing, and uncertainty of future cash flows.

Income and other comprehensive income

The financial statement elements reported on the income statement are revenues, expenses, gains, and losses. These elements were defined earlier in Topic 2 of this section. SFAS No. 130 requires firms to report certain unrealized gains and losses outside of net income as components of other comprehensive income. Comprehensive income is the sum of net income plus (or minus) the items of other comprehensive income.

Firms have the option of presenting the calculation of comprehensive income either as part of an income statement or within the statement of shareholders' equity as an adjustment to the accumulated other comprehensive income account.

Comprehensive income will be covered in detail in Topic 4 of this section.

Format of financial information

The two most common formats are single-step income statements and multiple-step income statements.

Single-step income statement

A single-step income statement subtracts total expenses and losses from total revenues and gains in a single step. No attempt is made to categorize expenses and revenues or arrive at interim subtotals.

Single-step income statements are simple, and some find the lack of priority of one type of revenue or gain (or expense or loss) over another to be a way to avoid classification problems. However, the multiple-step income statement is currently more popular.

Figure 2-79 shows a single-step income statement for Robin Manufacturing Company, Year 1. (Year 1 is used to show a consistent time period; do not assume that this is their first year in business.)

Figure 2-79: Single-Step Income Statement

Robin Manufacturing Company
Income Statement
For the Year Ended December 31, Year 1

Revenues	
Net sales	$2,734,620
Dividend revenue	90,620
Rental revenue	67,077
Total revenues	2,892,317
Expenses	
Cost of goods sold	1,823,938
Selling expenses	416,786
Administrative expenses	322,709
Interest expense	115,975
Income tax expense	61,579
Total expenses	2,740,987
Net income	$151,330
Earnings per common share	$1.89

→ To statement of shareholders' equity (Figure 2-82)

Multiple-step income statement

The multiple-step income statement disaggregates information into operating and nonoperating categories in an attempt to make the information more useful. The sections in the statement that do not relate to operating cash flows are called "other revenues and gains" and "other expenses and losses." These categories could include gains and losses from the sale of equipment, interest revenue and expense, or dividends received.

The multiple-step income statement has subcategories such as cost of goods sold, operating (selling and administrative) expenses, and other revenues, expenses, gains, and losses. These subcategories allow users to compare a company's results over time or with those of a competitor to determine the efficiency with which the entity's scarce resources are used. Such comparisons are especially valuable when several years' income statements are compared.

The multiple-step income statement often reports subtotals for gross profit and income from operations, which are useful for financial statement analysis purposes. For example, gross profit can be used to compare how competitive pressures have affected profit margins.

Figure 2-80 on the next page shows a multiple-step income statement.

Figure 2-80: Multiple-Step Income Statement

Robin Manufacturing Company
Income Statement For the Year Ended December 31, Year 1 (Y1)

Sales Revenue

Sales			$2,808,835
Less: Sales discounts		$22,302	
Less: Sales returns and allowances		51,913	74,215
Net sales revenue			2,734,620

Cost of Goods Sold

Merchandise inventory, Jan. 1, Y1		424,321	
Purchases	$1,830,518		
Less: Purchase discounts	17,728		
Net purchases	1,812,790		
Freight and transportation—in	37,363	1,850,153	
Total merchandise available for sale		2,274,474	
Less: Merchandise inventory, Dec. 31, Y1		450,536	
Cost of goods sold			$1,823,938
Gross profit on sales			910,682

Operating Expenses

Selling expenses

Sales salaries and commissions	186,432		
Sales office salaries	54,464		
Travel and entertainment	45,025		
Advertising expense	35,250		
Freight and transportation—out	37,912		
Shipping supplies and expense	22,735		
Postage and stationery	15,445		
Depreciation of sales equipment	8,285		
Telephone and Internet expense	11,238	416,786	

Administrative expenses

Officers' salaries	171,120		
Office salaries	56,304		
Legal and professional services	21,823		
Utilities expense	21,413		
Insurance expense	15,667		
Building depreciation	16,614		
Office equipment depreciation	14,720		
Stationery, supplies, and postage	2,645		
Miscellaneous office expenses	2,403	322,709	739,495
Income from operations			171,187

Other Revenues and Gains

Dividend revenue		90,620	
Rental revenue		67,077	157,697
			328,884

Other Expenses and Losses

Interest on bonds and notes			115,975
Income before income tax			212,909
Income tax			61,579
Net income for the year			$151,330
Earnings per common share			$1.89

→ To statement of shareholders' equity (Figure 2-82)

Additional income statement presentation items

Occasionally, companies will experience an event that requires separate reporting below income from continuing operations. Additional items that may be located at the end of the income statement include discontinued operations, extraordinary items, and changes in accounting principle.

- **Discontinued operations**
  When a component of an entity that has clearly distinguishable operations and cash flows is disposed of, the item is recorded in a separate section of the income statement after continuing operations and before extraordinary items. Discontinued operations are shown net of tax.

- **Extraordinary items**
  Material items that are both unusual in nature and infrequent in occurrence, such as a government restriction or banning of a product line, require a separate section in the income statement, shown net of tax.

- **Changes in accounting principle**
  The cumulative effect of certain accounting changes between two GAAP methods is shown net of tax after extraordinary items but before net income. (Passage of the FASB Exposure Draft, "Accounting Changes and Error Corrections," as a final statement will require firms to report most discretionary accounting changes using the retroactive method. Under the retroactive approach, the cumulative effect of changing an accounting principle would then be reported as an adjustment to retained earnings rather than on the income statement.)

Figure 2-81 shows how net income is determined when these items are included.

Figure 2-81: Multi-Step Income Statement with Additional Income Statement Items

```
            Net sales
          – Cost of goods sold

            Gross profit on sales
          – Operating expenses

            Operating income
        +/– Other gains and losses

            Earnings before tax
          – Tax expense

            Income from continuing operations
        +/– Discontinued operations
        +/– Extraordinary items
        +/– Changes in accounting principle

            Net income
```

Statement of Shareholders' Equity

When a balance sheet is issued, the FASB requires disclosure of the changes in each separate shareholders' equity account. This requirement satisfies the FASB's suggestion that complete financial statements should include investments by and distributions to owners during the period. The required statement of shareholders' equity is intended to help external users assess how changes in the company's financial structure may affect its financial flexibility.

Major components and classifications

Shareholders' equity includes several components: capital stock (par value of preferred and common shares), additional paid-in capital, retained earnings, and accumulated other comprehensive income. Capital stock is the par value (or face value) for the shares, and additional paid-in capital is the amount paid for the shares in excess of par. Thus, these two categories combine to form contributed capital, also called paid-in capital. Retained earnings can be subdivided into general earnings retained for company use and appropriated earnings set aside for some purpose.

Format of financial information

The statement of shareholders' equity usually lists information in the following order:

- Beginning balance for the period

- Additions

- Deductions

- Ending balance for the period

Figure 2-82 shows a sample statement of shareholders' equity. This example shows the statement listed in a columnar format for a company with only common stock outstanding.

Figure 2-82: Statement of Shareholders' Equity

	Common Stock, $1 Par	Additional Paid-In Capital	Retained Earnings	Total
Robin Manufacturing Company Schedule of Changes in Shareholders' Equity For Year Ended December 31, Year 1 (Y1)				
Balance, Jan. 1, Y1	$24,680	$345,520	$90,251	$460,451
Net income			151,330	151,330
Cash dividends paid			(33,330)	(33,330)
Common stock issued	1,000	14,800		15,800
Balance, Dec. 31, Y1	$25,680	$360,320	$208,251	$594,251

From income statement (figures 2-79 and 2-80) →

→ To balance sheet (Figure 2-84)

Statement of Financial Position (Balance Sheet)

The statement of financial position is an essential tool in assessing the amounts, timing, and uncertainty of prospective cash flows. It is also called a balance sheet because of the balance expressed by the accounting equation:

$$\text{Assets} = \text{Liabilities} + \text{Shareholder's Equity}$$

Alternatively, equity equals assets less liabilities, which is also known as net assets. The balance sheet provides a snapshot of the company's assets and the claims on those assets at a specific point in time.

While the balance sheet does not claim to show the value of the entity, along with the other statements and other information it should allow an external user to make their own estimate of the entity's value.

The balance sheet helps users:

- Evaluate the capital structure of the entity.

- Assess the entity's liquidity, solvency, financial flexibility, and operating capability.

The balance sheet is also essential in understanding the income statement. Revenues and expenses reflect changes in assets and liabilities, so an analyst must evaluate both statements together.

Major components and classifications

The balance sheet is divided into three sections: assets, liabilities, and shareholders' equity. These classifications are designed to group similar items together so they can be analyzed more easily. Assets are listed with the most liquid items first and the least liquid last. Liabilities are listed in the order in which they become due. In the case of equity, the items that have most claim to the equity are listed before items with less claim. Figure 2-83 summarizes the general subdivisions of each category.

Figure 2-83: Balance Sheet Components

Assets	▪ Current assets (cash, A/R, inventory, and so on) ▪ Long-term investments ▪ Property, plant, and equipment (PP&E)	▪ Intangible assets (patents, goodwill, and so on) ▪ Other assets
Liabilities	▪ Current liabilities (A/P, interest payable, current portion of long-term debt, and so on)	▪ Long-term liabilities (bonds, mortgages, and so on) ▪ Other liabilities
Shareholders' equity	▪ Capital stock ▪ Treasury stock (contra equity) ▪ Additional paid-in capital	▪ Accumulated other comprehensive income ▪ Retained earnings

The components of assets, liabilities, and equity are more thoroughly discussed in Topic 4 of this section.

Format of financial information

The two most common formats for the balance sheet are the account form and the report form. All styles of balance sheets break down the assets, liabilities, and shareholders' equity into the categories listed above (current assets, and so on). The account form lists assets on the left side and liabilities and shareholders' equity on the right side. The report form, shown in Figure 2-84, lists assets at the top and liabilities and shareholders' equity at the bottom. These two formats follow the accounting equation; the sum of all assets equals the sum of all liabilities and shareholders' equity. Outside the U.S. other balance sheet formats are used, such as the financial position form, which deducts current liabilities from current assets to show working capital.

In the report form balance sheet in Figure 2-84, the assets and liabilities are also categorized by their levels of financial flexibility. For example, current assets are shown separately from fixed assets.

Figure 2-84: Balance Sheet

Robin Manufacturing Company
Balance Sheet
December 31, Year 1

Assets

Current assets:

Cash and short-term investments	$24,628
Trade receivables, net of $30K allowance	552,249
Other receivables	18,941
Note receivable—related party	80,532
Inventory	252,567
Prepaid insurance	7,500
Total current assets	936,417

Fixed assets:

Property and equipment	209,330
Less: Accumulated depreciation	(75,332)
Net fixed assets	133,998
Total assets	$1,070,415

Liabilities and Equity

Current liabilities

Accounts payable	$175,321
Accrued expenses	2,500
Current portion of long-term debt	36,000
Line of credit	145,000
Total current liabilities	358,821
Long-term debt	117,343
Total current and long-term liabilities	476,164

Shareholders' equity:

Common stock, par	25,680
Additional paid-in capital	360,320
Retained earnings	208,251
Total shareholders' equity	594,251
Total liabilities and shareholders' equity	$1,070,415

From statement of shareholders' equity (Figure 2-82) → → → →

Statement of Cash Flows

Cash is a company's most liquid resource, and therefore it affects liquidity, operating capability, and financial flexibility. SFAS No. 95 says that a statement of cash flows "must report on a company's cash inflows, cash outflows, and net change in cash from its operating, financing, and investing activities during the accounting period, in a manner that reconciles the beginning and ending cash balances." The statement helps interested parties determine if an entity needs external financing or is generating cash flows, meeting obligations, and paying dividends. Keep in mind that a company could have high income but still have negative cash flow.

Components and classifications

Cash receipts and cash payments are classified in the statement of cash flows as related to either operating, investing, or financing activities.

Operating activities

Cash flows from operating activities are those related to the normal course of business. Any transaction that does not qualify as an investing or financing activity is included in the operating activity section. Examples of cash inflows include cash receipts from sales of any kind, collection of accounts receivable, collection of interest on loans, and receipts of dividends. Cash outflows include cash paid to employees, suppliers, and the IRS and to lenders for interest.

GAAP-compliant statements use accrual accounting, so net income includes noncash revenues (for example, uncollected credit sales) and noncash expenses (for example, unpaid expenses). Other items that accrual accounting includes are depreciation, depletion, amortization, and other costs that were incurred in prior periods but are being charged to expense in the current period. These items reduce net income but do not affect cash flows for the current period. Therefore these items are added back when determining net cash flow from operating activities.

Examples of noncash expense and revenue items that must be added back to net income include:

- Depreciation expense and amortization of intangible assets.

- Amortization of deferred costs such as bond issue costs.

- Changes in deferred income taxes.

- Amortization of a premium or discount on bonds payable.

- Income from an equity method investee.

To determine operating cash flows, FASB SFAS No. 95 allows entities to use either the indirect method or the direct method.

Indirect method. The indirect method, or reconciliation method, is the most popular method of converting net income to net cash flow from operating activities. It starts with net income and then adjusts it by adding back noncash expenses and paper losses and subtracting noncash revenues and paper gains that have no effect on current period operating cash flows. Additional adjustments are made for changes in current asset and liability accounts related to operations by adding or subtracting amounts as shown in Figure 2-85. For example, an increase in accounts receivable (a current asset) would be subtracted from net income to arrive at operating cash flows because it means that the amount of cash collected from customers is less than the amount of accrual revenue reported. See Figure 2-85 for an example of the indirect method.

Figure 2-85: Cash Flows from Operating Activities—Indirect Method

Net income

+ Noncash expenses (typically depreciation and amortization expenses)

– Gains from investing and financing activities

+ Losses from investing and financing activities

+ Decreases in current assets

– Increases in current assets

+ Increases in current liabilities

– Decreases in current liabilities

+ Amortization of discounts on bonds

– Amortization of premiums on bonds

Operating cash flow

Direct method. In the direct method, or income statement method, net cash provided by operating activities is calculated by converting revenues and expenses from the accrual basis to the cash basis. Although the FASB encourages the use of the direct method, it is rarely used. Furthermore, if the direct method is used, the FASB requires that the reconciliation of net income to net cash flow from operating activities be disclosed in a separate schedule. Figure 2-86 shows how a direct method statement is arranged (the figure includes sample amounts for illustration).

Figure 2-86: Cash Flows from Operating Activities—Direct Method

Cash received from customers	$100,000
Cash paid to suppliers	(40,000)
Cash paid for interest	(5,000)
Cash paid for taxes	(10,000)
Cash paid for operating expenses	(25,000)
Cash provided by operating activities	$20,000

Investing activities

Most items in the investing activities section come from changes in long-term asset accounts. Investing cash inflows result from sales of property, plant, and equipment (PP&E); sales of investments in another entity's debt or equity securities; or collections of the principal on loans to another entity. (Interest is included in operating cash flows.)

Investing cash outflows result from purchases of PP&E, purchases of other companies' debt or equity securities, and the granting of loans to other entities.

Financing activities

Most items in the financing activities section come from changes in long-term liability or equity accounts. Financing cash inflows come from the sale of the entity's equity securities or issuance of debt such as bonds or notes. Cash outflows consist of payments to stockholders for dividends and payments to reacquire capital stock or redeem a company's outstanding debt. In other words, investing activities involve the purchase or sale of fixed assets and investments in another company's securities, while financing activities involve the issuance and redemption of a company's own equity and debt securities.

Footnotes

The statement of cash flows requires footnote disclosure of any significant non-cash investing and financing activities such as the issuing of stock for fixed assets or the conversion of debt to equity. In addition, when you are using the indirect method for cash flow from operations, both interest paid and income taxes paid need to be disclosed.

Example of a statement of cash flows

The statement of cash flows shown in Figure 2-87 on the next page illustrates the more commonly used indirect approach for calculating operating cash flows. Cash flows from each category (operating, investing, and financing) are separately classified and totaled. The sum of cash inflows (or outflows if negative) from these three categories equals the net increase or decrease in cash for the period. This net cash inflow (outflow) is added to (subtracted from) the cash balance at the beginning of the year to obtain the cash balance at the end of the year (highlighted in gray). Thus the cash flow statement explains the net change in the amount of cash and cash equivalents (short-term, highly liquid investments that are close to maturity) from the beginning to the ending balance sheet.

Figure 2-87: Statement of Cash Flows—Indirect Method

Operating Activities	
Net income	$151,330
Adjustments to convert net income to a cash basis:	
Depreciation and amortization charges*	75,332
Decrease (increase) in accounts receivable	(31,445)
Increase (decrease) in merchandise inventory	(4,165)
Increase (decrease) in accounts payable	6,740
Increase (decrease) in accrued wages and salaries payable	4,543
Increase (decrease) in accrued income taxes payable	3,984
Increase (decrease) in deferred income taxes	(4,950)
Gain on sale of store**	(1,255)
Net cash provided by operating activities	200,114
Investing Activities	
Additions to property, buildings, and equipment	(123,730)
Proceeds from sale of store	3,980
Net cash used in investing activities	(119,750)
Financing Activities	
Increase (decrease) in notes payable	1,100
Increase (decrease) in additional paid-in capital	14,800
Increase (decrease) in long-term debt	(50,500)
Increase (decrease) in common stock	1,000
Cash dividends paid	(33,330)
Net cash used in financing activities	(66,930)
Net increase in cash and cash equivalents	13,434
Cash and cash equivalents at beginning of year	11,194
Cash and cash equivalents at end of year	$24,628

From income statement (figures 2-79 and 2-80) → Net income

From statement of shareholders' equity (Figure 2-82) → Increase (decrease) in additional paid-in capital / Increase (decrease) in common stock / Cash dividends paid

To balance sheet (Figure 2-84) → Cash and cash equivalents at end of year

Note: Changes in various asset and liability accounts (for example, increases/decreases) can be obtained by comparing two consecutive years' balance sheets.

* Depreciation and amortization charges are included in the income statement as part of administrative expenses.
**Gain on sale of store is included in the income statement as part of other revenue.

Limitations of the Financial Statements

The following are limitations of the financial statements.

Historical cost

Most asset accounts of a nonfinancial nature are reported at historical cost. While historical cost measures are considered reliable because the amounts can be verified, they are also considered less relevant than fair value or current market value measures would be for assessing a firm's current financial position.

Different accounting methods

Employing different accounting methods will yield different net incomes. Each choice of two or more accounting methods will further change the results reported, making the task of comparing different entities very difficult, even when these methods are disclosed.

Omit nonobjective items of value

Financial statements exclude valuable assets that are of financial importance but cannot be objectively expressed in numbers. For example, the value of human resources, intangibles such as brand recognition and reputation, or the entity's customer base cannot be exactly or reliably estimated, so they are not included on the balance sheet. Therefore, the balance sheet does not purport to measure the value of the company as a whole.

Use of estimates and judgments

Financial statements incorporate the use of numerous estimates and professional judgments. Differences in estimates mean that the income statements for two or more entities may be difficult to compare. Common estimates include the amount of receivables allocated to an allowance for doubtful accounts and the useful life and salvage value of a piece of equipment.

Off-balance-sheet information

Transactions may be recorded in a way that avoids reporting liabilities and assets on the balance sheet, for example, with an operating lease. The Sarbanes-Oxley Act of 2002 requires publicly traded firms to disclose off-balance-sheet information in their filings with the SEC.

Noncash transactions

The statement of cash flows omits noncash transactions, such as the exchange of stock for a property, exchanges of nonmonetary assets, conversion of preferred stock or debt to common stock, or issuing equity securities to retire a debt. Disclosure of any noncash transactions that affect assets or liabilities would be reported in a note or a supplemental schedule.

Footnotes/Disclosures to Financial Statements

The footnotes or disclosures to financial statements are used when parenthetical explanations would not suffice to describe situations particular to the entity. Typical disclosures include contingencies, contractual situations, accounting policies, and subsequent events.

Contingencies

Contingencies are material events with an uncertain outcome dependent on the occurrence or nonoccurrence of one or more future events. Contingencies can be either gain contingencies or loss contingencies. Accounting recognition is not given to gain contingencies to avoid the premature recognition of income before its realization. However, loss contingencies must be recognized when it is both probable that a loss has been incurred and the amount of the loss is reasonably estimable. Other material loss contingencies should be disclosed in the footnotes to the financial statements; gain contingencies may also be disclosed.

Loss contingencies result from situations such as pending litigation, warranty and premium costs, environmental liabilities, and self-insurance risks. Gain contingencies result from pending litigation (where the outcome is favorable to the company), possible refunds of disputed tax amounts, and tax loss carry-forwards.

Contractual situations

Contractual agreements such as pension obligations, lease contracts, and stock option plans are required to be disclosed in the notes to financial statements. Other significant items should also be included. Contractual situations may require an entity to restrict certain funds, for example, and analysts need to understand how such provisions will affect the entity's financial flexibility.

Accounting policies

Whenever GAAP or industry-specific regulations allow a choice between two or more accounting methods, the method selected should be disclosed. Accounting Principles Board (APB) Opinion No. 22 states that "a description of all significant accounting policies of the reporting entity should be included as an integral part of the financial statements."

APB Opinion No. 22 notes that three types of accounting disclosures related to recognition and asset allocation should be made:

- Selection between acceptable alternatives

- Selection of industry-specific methods

- Unusual or innovative applications of GAAP

Most companies prepare a separate note, "Summary of Significant Accounting Policies," in which they report on the methods used to recognize revenue, calculate depreciation, value inventory, and measure other amounts reported on the financial statements.

Subsequent events

It may take weeks or even months to issue the annual report after the accounting period has closed, and significant business events and transactions may occur during this period. A subsequent event is an event occurring between the balance sheet date and the issuance date of the annual report. If the event provides additional evidence about conditions that existed as of the balance sheet date and alters the estimates used in preparing the financial statements, then the financial statements should be adjusted.

Subsequent events that provide evidence regarding conditions that did not exist on the balance sheet date should be disclosed in a note, supplemental schedule, or pro forma statement.

In addition to the disclosures mentioned above, Figure 2-88 lists other major areas that require some form of disclosure beyond the information presented in the financial statements.

These disclosures are covered in more detail throughout the rest of this book.

Figure 2-88: Summary of Required Footnotes/Disclosures

Category	Footnote/Disclosure
Inventories	• Valuation basis (net realizable value, cost, lower of cost or market) • Cost flow assumption (specific identification, average cost, FIFO, LIFO) • Inventory classifications (purchases, raw materials, work-in-process accounts, finished goods, supplies); classified separately only if significant • Product financing arrangements, if any • FIFO equivalent if the company uses LIFO
Revenue	• Policy on revenue recognition
Accounts receivable	• Collectibility • Collection policy • Determination of bad debt • Allowance for bad debt
Property, plant, and equipment (PP&E)	• Valuation basis • Depreciation expenses for the period • Accumulated depreciation at the balance sheet date • Depreciable asset balances by major class (either by nature or function) • General description of the depreciation methods used by major class of depreciable asset
Intangibles (for example, patents)	• Description of the nature of the intangible • Amount of amortization expense for the period • Method and period of amortization • Remaining useful life of the intangible
Bonds payable	• Par value • Stated and effective interest rate • Call provisions • Maturity date
Preferred stock	• Par or stated value • Changes in the number of shares authorized, issued, and outstanding for the period • Dividend rate • Special features of the preferred stock (convertible, cumulative, participating) • Dividends in arrears
Common stock	• Par or stated value • Changes in the number of shares authorized, issued, and outstanding for the period • Dividends declared (amount and type)
Other	• Amount, nature, duration, and other significant provisions of any restrictions on retained earnings • Prior period adjustments • Employee plans such as an employee stock option plans

Users of Financial Statements

Financial statements are intended to aid in decision making. The most efficient companies will attract investors or will be granted credit first and will also be more likely to produce a higher return on investment. Moreover, a company becomes efficient partly through the proper allocation of its internal resources to those areas most likely to produce a profit. Financial statements are an integral part of the decision-making process for users both internal to the organization and external to it.

Internal and external users

Internal users

Internal users need financial statements for internal decision making (in addition to other sources of information). The information is used to plan and control operations on both a short-term and long-term basis. The quality of these decisions will have an impact on how internal resources are allocated, how profitable the organization is, and, ultimately, whether the organization will survive. Internal users of financial statements include executives, managers, management accountants, and other employees (such as those with stock options or investments in the organization). Unlike external users, internal users may request or generate any type of information that is available in their accounting system. The potential of misuse of such information requires an organization to place internal controls on the use and access to such information but not to the extent that the internal decision makers cannot access the information in a timely manner.

External users

External users are any interested party who must rely on the published financial statements and other publicly available information of an entity when making investment decisions. Some external users, such as lending institutions, may be in a position to demand additional information from an entity that is not publicly available. As mentioned earlier, the FASB defines external users as current and potential investors and creditors (and their advisors) who have a reasonable understanding of business and economics and who are willing to study the information with reasonable diligence. Investors, creditors, unions, analysts, financial advisors, competitors, and government agencies are all external users of information. Investors include individuals and other corporations. Creditors include lending institutions and suppliers of raw materials and other goods.

Needs of external users

Creditors and investors comprise the two main sources of capital for publicly traded entities, so the needs of these two types of users is the primary focus of financial statements. According to the FASB, financial reporting should provide information that is useful to external users in making reasoned choices among alternative investment, credit, and similar decisions. Users cannot absorb infinite amounts of data, and too much information may obscure the most relevant measures of the success of a business. Therefore, the goal of accounting is to summarize the vast amount of information into understandable reports and disclosures. The FASB's statements are intended to require a minimum level of disclosure, but it is still up to each entity to make this information user-friendly.

Needs of investors and creditors

Financial information must be relevant and reliable for it to be useful, and relevance means that it must also be presented in a timely fashion. Investors and lenders are interested in both a return of their investment and a return on their investment. They receive a return of their investment only if the organization can maintain its capital. They receive a return on their investment through dividends and interest.

Investors in the stock market receive a return on their investment if the market perceives that the company is doing well. Actual or potential investors have or are considering a direct ownership stake in an entity, and they need financial information primarily to decide whether to initiate or continue this relationship, that is, buy, hold, or sell the firm's securities.

Actual or potential creditors are interested in the ability of the entity to comply with debt covenants. The four decisions they are concerned with are to extend credit, maintain credit, deny credit, or revoke credit. Creditors are also interested in financial statements to determine the risk level of their loan. Lending institutions expect a higher return on investment for more risky endeavors and will make low-return investments only when the risk is similarly low. Therefore, the entity's credit rating is of particular importance. The credit rating is based primarily on the entity's liquidity, solvency, and financial flexibility, all of which are determined from the entity's financial statements and other disclosures.

Other users of financial statements include stock exchanges (for rule making, listings, and cancellations), unions (for negotiating wages), and analysts (for advising others).

Progress Check

Directions: Read each question and respond in the space provided. Answers and page references appear on the following page.

1. On the statement of cash flows, which of the following is included in the operating activities section?

    ( ) a. Purchase of equipment

    ( ) b. Purchase of treasury stock

    ( ) c. Issuing 1,000 shares of common stock

    ( ) d. Income taxes paid

2. On the balance sheet, which of the following accurately describes the order in which items are listed?

    ( ) a. Assets are listed from most to least liquid; liabilities are listed in the order in which they become due.

    ( ) b. Assets and liabilities are listed in the order in which they become due; equity is listed from least to most liquid.

    ( ) c. Assets are listed from least to most liquid; liabilities are listed in the order in which they become due.

    ( ) d. Assets and liabilities are listed from most to least liquid; equity is listed in the order in which the items are used.

3. True or false? The balance sheet does not show the value of the entity.

    ( ) a. True

    ( ) b. False

4. True or false? The income statement presents the following items net of tax: gains and losses from discontinued operations, extraordinary items, and the cumulative effects of a change in accounting principle.

    ( ) a. True

    ( ) b. False

Progress check answers

1. d (p. 2-308)

2. a (p. 2-304)

3. a (p. 2-304)

4. a (p. 2-303)

Recognition, Measurement, Valuation, and Disclosure

Topic overview

This topic covers the recognition, measurement, valuation, and disclosure requirements for specific accounts of the financial statements presented in Topic 3 of this section.

Cash and Marketable Securities

Cash

Cash is any coin, currency, funds available on deposit, money order, certified check, cashier's check, personal check, bank draft, or savings account. To be reported as cash on the balance sheet, the cash must be readily available for payment of current liabilities and it must not include any contractual restrictions or limits on its use to pay current liabilities.

Cash equivalents

Cash equivalents are marketable securities with maturity of less than three months at the time of acquisition. Short-term commercial paper is a common form of cash equivalent. Cash equivalents are often grouped with cash.

Restricted cash

Restricted cash is cash that is set aside to fulfill the terms of an agreement or for some future use. Restricted cash may include compensating balances, dividend funds, or payroll funds. When the amounts are not material, they can be reported with cash, but if material, they are separately reported as a current or long-term asset. Restricted cash is a current asset if it will be used to pay liabilities within a year or the operating cycle, whichever is longer. Otherwise it is reported as a long-term asset, such as a plant expansion fund or fund for the retirement of a specific long-term debt.

Compensating balances

Many lenders will include a **compensating balance** requirement as part of a loan provision, especially in the case of open or revolving lines of credit. These compensating balances are minimum balance requirements designed to offset part of the risk of lending. Compensating balances may or may not be restricted. They can be used not only for loans but also for the assurance of available future credit and as indirect compensation for services such as check cashing or lockbox management.

The SEC recommends that legally restricted compensating balances be reported as a separate item under cash and cash equivalents if the balance is held against short-term borrowing arrangements and as noncurrent assets (investments or other assets) if the balance is held against long-term borrowing arrangements. Compensating balance arrangements that do not have legal restrictions on their use should be disclosed in the notes to the statements.

Marketable securities

Investments in individual marketable securities that are expected to be converted to cash within one year are classified as current assets. Investments in marketable equity securities are valued at fair value on the balance sheet. The disposition of unrealized gains and losses that arise when these investments are marked to market value depends on whether the securities are classified as part of the trading or available-for-sale investment portfolios. Investments in marketable debt securities are accounted for similarly, except that certain debt investments are classified as held-to-maturity securities and valued at amortized cost rather than at fair value. Accounting for the gains and losses on equity and debt investments under SFAS No. 115 is discussed in more detail later in this topic. Money market funds, money market savings certificates, certificates of deposit (CDs), and short-term commercial paper are classified as temporary investments on the balance sheet because they contain restrictions on their availability or penalties for withdrawal.

Recording and valuation

Marketable securities are initially recorded at their acquisition price plus all incidental costs such as brokerage fees or taxes. If a marketable security is received as a noncash payment or trade, valuation can be based on the more reliable of the fair market value of either the stock or on the item traded. Marketable securities are generally carried at market value because they are by definition generally tradable. However, in a limited number of situations, marketable securities could be reported at historical cost.

Market value

Marketable securities are revalued at the current market price at the time of statement preparation. Rises and falls in the price are reported as gains and losses on the income statement. **Market value** is more relevant than historical cost for reporting liquidity and financial flexibility because it is the current price to acquire or sell the security. Market value is reliable because the price can be definitely determined. SFAS No. 115 prescribes (fair) market value accounting for all securities except held-to-maturity debt instruments.

Accounts Receivable (A/R)

Receivables are claims against a customer for cash, goods, or services. Accounts receivable is a subset of receivables and is detailed below. Receivables result from sellers extending credit to buyers in order to increase sales. Receivables are considered liquid but not as liquid as cash because some accounts will probably not be paid.

Types of receivables

Receivables are classified as current or noncurrent, trade or nontrade. Trade receivables include accounts receivable and notes receivable. Each of these classifications is detailed below. Current receivables are due to be collected within the longer of a year or the current operating cycle. Noncurrent receivables are due after one year or the current operating cycle, whichever is longer.

Trade receivables

Trade receivables are the most common form of receivable because they arise from the normal operations of an entity: credit sales of goods and services.

- **Accounts receivable (A/R)**
  Accounts receivable are promises to pay for a good or service delivered. Most receivables have 30- or 60-day net payment terms and are therefore usually current receivables, but wide variations exist in terms. Accounts receivable are also called open accounts.

- **Notes receivable**
  Notes receivable are more formal trade receivables because they require a written promise to pay on a specified date. They can be either current or noncurrent.

Nontrade receivables

Nontrade receivables contain all types other than those involved in daily operations, including damage deposits and other guarantee deposits, advances to officers or to subsidiaries, dividends and interest receivable, and claims against insurance companies, common carriers, lawsuit defendants, the government, and customers for returned, lost, or damaged goods. Nontrade receivables are usually reported as separate items on the balance sheet.

Impact of sales practices on A/R balances

Accounts receivable are subject to trade discounts and cash discounts.

Trade discounts

Trade discounts (or volume or quantity discounts) allow a business to list a single price in a catalog and then sell the item to various types of customers such as wholesale and retail customers at different percentage discounts from the list price.

Cash discounts

Cash discounts are incentives for early or prompt payment. The buyer can automatically apply this type of discount if they make payment by the specified deadline. Cash discounts are expressed in shorthand such as 2/10, n/30 (two in 10, net 30). This means a 2% discount is available if payment is made within 10 days or the net amount (undiscounted or gross amount) is due within 30 days. A discount of 2/10 net 30 not taken represents an opportunity cost of 37.25%:

$$\text{Effective Cost of Discount} = \frac{\text{Discount \%}}{(100 - \text{Discount \%})} \times \frac{365}{(\text{Net Period} - \text{Discount Period})}$$

$$= \frac{0.02}{0.98} \times \frac{365}{30 - 10} = 0.02041 \times 18.25 = 37.25\%$$

Because the firm can presumably borrow funds for less than this rate, it would be cheaper to borrow funds to pay within the discount period than to use the extended paying period.

Cash discounts can be recorded at either their gross amount or their net amount. Most companies record sales and receivables using the simpler gross method.

- **Gross method**

  The gross method records each receivable and sale at the gross or undiscounted amount. Then sales discounts are recognized in accounting entries if the payment is received within the deadline for the discount. On the income statement, net sales are determined by deducting sales discounts from gross sales.

- **Net method**

  The net method records each receivable and sale at the net amount, assuming all discounts are taken. It more fully embraces the matching principle, because it provides an allowance for expected discounts to be taken and charges these against sales in the period of the sale, thus recording the sale at closer to its realizable value. To account for unused sales discounts, an other revenue item account called sales discounts forfeited is created in which adjusting entries are recorded. Figure 2-89 shows how a receivable of $100,000 with terms of 1/10, n/30, would be recorded under each method, assuming that half of the purchase is paid for within the discount period.

Figure 2-89: Gross and Net Method Accounting for Cash Discounts on A/R

Gross Method		Net Method	
On July 1 sale made:			
A/R	$100,000	A/R	$99,000
Sales	$100,000	Sales	$99,000
On July 10, payment of $50,000 received:			
Cash	$49,500	Cash	$49,500
Sales discounts	$500	A/R	$49,500
A/R	$50,000		
On July 30, payment of $50,000 received:			
Cash	$50,000	A/R	$500
A/R	$50,000	Sales discounts forfeited	$500
		Cash	$50,000
		A/R	$50,000

Sales returns and allowances

When a customer returns goods purchased on credit or receives an allowance (price discount) for imperfect goods, the seller credits accounts receivable and debits sales returns and allowances (a contra account to sales). However, certain companies experience such a high rate of returns that they initially record sales net of an estimate for the expected returns and establish an allowance for sales returns as a contra account to accounts receivable. Sales returns and allowances are covered more later in this topic.

Maturity value vs. present value in trade receivables

APB Opinion No. 21 indicates that long-term receivables should be recorded at their present values but specifically exempts trade receivables due to their short collection times. Trade receivables should instead be recorded at their maturity value, which in the case of a 30- or 60-day receivable is a small enough difference from the present value to make the difference immaterial. GAAP allows for nonrecognition of present value for normal business receivables due in customary trade terms not exceeding one year.

However, trade receivables must be valued and reported at their net realizable value. The **net realizable value (NRV) for trade receivables** is the net amount of cash that the company expects to receive, excluding an estimate of uncollectible amounts (bad debt expense) and of expected returns (if there is a return policy). Note that NRV for trade receivables does not reflect the time value of money and hence present value calculations are not included.

Valuation and uncollectible accounts

Sales made on account raise the possibility that a firm may not be able to collect the full amount of accounts receivable. The two most commonly used methods of recording bad debt expense are the direct write-off method and the allowance method.

Direct write-off method

The direct write-off method recognizes bad debt expense only after an account is deemed uncollectible. The direct write-off method has the advantage of simplicity and reliability, because no estimates are used. However, this method is generally not considered appropriate under GAAP because the costs are not matched against the revenues of the correct period and the receivables are overstated. The direct write-off method is required for federal income tax purposes.

Allowance method

The allowance method makes an estimate of the expected uncollectible accounts from all credit sales or from all outstanding receivables. The allowance for doubtful accounts is netted against accounts receivable to determine net realizable value. This is the amount the company expects to collect. The bad debt expense is also reported as an operating expense. Under the allowance method, bad debt expense is estimated using either a balance sheet approach or an income statement approach.

- **Balance sheet approach (A/R relationship)**

  The balance sheet approach evaluates historical trends between actual bad debts recorded in the past and accounts receivable using one of two methods.

  - **Percentage of outstanding A/R**

    The goal of the percentage of outstanding accounts receivable method is to determine the net realizable value of receivables and report this information on the balance sheet. This method assesses the historical relationship between actual bad debts and accounts receivable over a period without identifying specific accounts (due dates of debts are not accounted for). The resulting percentage of bad debts per average account receivable level is multiplied against the current accounts receivable at the end of a period to determine the required ending balance in the allowance for doubtful accounts. For example, if a company has $100,000 in accounts receivable at the end of a period and they estimate that 4% of receivables result in bad debts, they multiply that sum by the percentage. The net realizable value in this example would be $96,000, and bad debt expense would be $4,000. However, if there is an existing credit balance in the allowance for doubtful accounts, say of $1,000, then bad debt expense would be $3,000, because it is necessary to adjust the balance only to the desired level.

  - **Aging of A/R**

    Accounts receivable become harder to collect as more time passes, a fact that the previous method of estimating bad debts ignores. Aging of accounts receivable using an aging schedule categorizes accounts receivable by the length of time the debts have been outstanding. The older the debts are, the higher the estimated percentage of doubtful accounts.

    Figure 2-90 shows an example of an aging schedule.

Figure 2-90: Accounts Receivable Aging Schedule

Name of Customer	Balance December 31	Under 60 Days	61-90 Days	91-120 Days	Over 120 Days
	Bounce Sporting Goods Company **Aging Schedule**				
East Side Sport Supply	$54,880	$44,800	$10,080		
Rockford Gyms & Courts	179,200	179,200			
Freedom Tennis Supply	30,800				$30,800
Broadway Sporting Goods	41,440	33,600		$7,840	
	$306,320	$257,600	$10,080	$7,840	$30,800

Summary			
Age	Amount	Percentage Estimated to be Uncollectible	Required Balance in Allowance
Under 60 days old	$257,600	5%	$12,880
61-90 days old	10,080	15%	1,512
91-120 days old	7,840	20%	1,568
Over 120 days	30,800	25%	7,700
Year-end balance of allowance for doubtful accounts			$23,660

- **Income statement approach (sales relationship)**

  The income statement approach compares historical bad debts to sales using one of two methods:

  - **Percentage of sales**

    The percentage-of-sales method may be used when there is a stable relationship between cash and credit sales. This approach is based upon the matching principle inherent in the income statement; expenses are matched against revenues in the same period. The historical percentage of bad debts to sales is used to calculate the estimated bad debts for the period. For example, if a company has $100,000 in sales and they estimate that 3% of sales result in bad debts, then bad debt expense is $3,000.

  - **Percentage of net credit sales**

    When the relationship between credit sales and total sales varies widely over time, the percentage of sales method cannot be used as it is. Instead, the method can be applied using net credit sales in place of total sales.

  Both of these income statement methods focus on measuring the expense for the period, which is added to any existing balance in the allowance account.

Write-offs and collection of write-offs in financial statements

When using the allowance method, a specific uncollectible account receivable is written off by debiting the allowance for doubtful accounts and crediting accounts receivable. The write-off confirms the previously estimated loss, so the net carrying value of accounts receivable on the balance sheet is not affected. Bad debt expense is not recorded at the time of write-off. If a written-off receivable is subsequently collected, it is first reinstated by debiting accounts receivable and crediting the allowance for doubtful accounts. Then, the receipt of cash and the reduction of accounts receivable is recorded.

If an account written off using the direct write-off method is subsequently collected, the amount is debited to cash and credited to a revenue account such as uncollectible accounts recovered.

Sales returns and allowances

When a customer returns goods previously sold on credit, accounts receivable is credited and sales returns and allowances is debited, thus reducing net sales. However, in some industries, the return rate is so high that sales are initially recorded net of estimated sales returns, and an offsetting allowance for sales returns is established as a contra account to accounts receivable.

Notes receivable

While accounts receivable are oral promises to pay, notes receivable involve written promises to pay. A **promissory note** documents a note receivable and is signed by a maker (the entity that will owe the money) as an unconditional promise to pay a specific sum of money at a particular date in the future.

Promissory notes are negotiable; they can be bought and sold by the current payee (the one who collects the payment and interest). Because notes are unconditional, they are considered fairly liquid. Notes generally are interest-bearing within a stated rate of interest. Zero-interest-bearing notes include interest as part of their face value.

A note may be accepted from a customer that needs to extend the payment time on an existing receivable or that needs to initiate a lending transaction.

Short-term notes receivable are generally recorded at face value. The interest that is implied in the maturity value for such notes is considered immaterial. Conversely, long-term notes must be reported at the present value of the expected amount to be received.

If a long-term interest-bearing note is issued and the interest stated on the note is equal to the effective (market) rate of interest, the note is issued at face value (future amount owed). When the stated rate differs from the current market rate, the note is issued at a discount or premium, and this amount is amortized over the life of a note to record the effective interest.

These two situations are further illustrated in the sections that follow.

Notes issued at face value

When a note is issued at face value, the stated interest rate of the note would be the same as the going market rate for a new loan of similar risk, so no discount or premium is needed. For example, a lender will lend a borrower $100,000 in exchange for a $100,000 three-year note bearing 8% interest annually when the market rate for an investment of similar risk is also 8%.

The present value tables in figures 2-91 and 2-92 are used to calculate the remaining examples in this section.

Figure 2-91: Present Value of 1 (Present Value of a Single Sum)

$$\text{Present Value } (PV)_{n,i} = \frac{1}{(1 + i)^n} = (1 + i)^{-n}$$

(n) Periods	8%	9%	10%
1	.92593	.91743	.90909
2	.85734	.84168	.82645
3	.79383	.77218	.75132
4	.73503	.70843	.68301
5	.68058	.64993	.62092
6	.63017	.59627	.56447
7	.58349	.54703	.51316
8	.54027	.50187	.46651
9	.50025	.46043	.42410
10	.46319	.42241	.38554

Figure 2-92: Present Value of an Ordinary Annuity of 1

$$\text{Present Value of an Ordinary Annuity (PV-OA)}_{n,i} = \frac{1 - \dfrac{1}{(1 + i)^n}}{i}$$

(n) Periods	8%	9%	10%
1	.92593	.91743	.90909
2	1.78326	1.75911	1.73554
3	2.57710	2.53130	2.48685
4	3.31213	3.23972	3.16986
5	3.99271	3.88965	3.79079
6	4.62288	4.48592	4.35526
7	5.20637	5.03295	4.86842
8	5.74664	5.53482	5.33493
9	6.24689	5.99525	5.75902
10	6.71008	6.41766	6.14457

The exchange price (present value of the funds) of the note is calculated as shown in Figure 2-93, where the interest charge for one period, or $8,000, is used to calculate the overall interest charge using the factor for an ordinary annuity (an annuity that uses compound interest charged at the end of each period).

Figure 2-93: Note Issued at Face Value

Face value of the note		$100,000
Present value of the principal	$79,383	
($100,000 × PV of $1_{3,\,8\%}$) = ($100,000 × 0.79383)		
Present value of the interest	$20,617	
($8,000 × PV-OA of $1_{3,\,8\%}$) = ($8,000 × 2.57710)		
Present value of the note		$100,000
Difference		$0

The present value of the note and the face value are the same, so no discounting is needed.

Notes issued at a discount or premium

A note is issued at a discount when the market rate is higher than the stated rate and at a premium when the market rate is lower than the stated rate.

Zero-interest-bearing notes. Zero-interest-bearing notes have an implicit interest rate based on the difference between the face value (the future value) of the note and the actual amount received by the borrower. The difference between these present and future values is recorded as a discount. The discount must be amortized over the life of the note. For example, the borrower issues a three-year $100,000 zero-interest-bearing note with a present value (based on 8% current market rates) of $79,383. That is, the borrower will receive $79,383 and pay a total of $100,000 after three years. The difference of $20,617 is the total interest that must be paid at the end of the loan, an implicit interest rate of 8%.

Figure 2-94 shows how the issuer of the zero coupon bond records the transaction:

Figure 2-94: Zero-Interest-Bearing Note

Note receivable	$100,000	
Discount on notes receivable		$20,617
Cash		$79,383

The discount on notes receivable is recorded on the balance sheet as a contra asset (valuation) account to notes receivable. The discount is amortized over the term of the note. The effective interest method is used to recognize the annual interest revenue, using an amortization schedule as shown in Figure 2-95.

Figure 2-95: Amortizing a Discount on Notes Receivable

	Cash Received	Interest Revenue	Discount Amortized	Note Carrying Amount
Issue date				$79,383
Year 1 end	$0	$6,351	$6,351	85,734
Year 2 end	0	6,859	6,859	92,593
Year 3 end	0	7,407	7,407	100,000
	$0	$20,617	$20,617	

The interest revenue is calculated by multiplying the carrying amount at the beginning of the period by the 8% interest rate. The note's carrying amount at the end of the period is the sum of the discount amortized and the carrying value at the beginning of the period (for example, $79,383 + $6,351 = $85,734). A small adjustment may be needed in the last period to compensate for rounding.

Interest revenue for the first year is recognized by debiting the discount amortized ($6,351 in the example) to discount on notes receivable and crediting interest revenue for the same amount.

Interest-bearing notes. If a company accepts a three-year $100,000 note bearing interest at 8% but the current market rate for a similar investment is 9%, the note will be exchanged at a discount, as calculated in Figure 2-96.

Figure 2-96: Discount on an Interest-Bearing Note

Face value of the note		$100,000
Present value of the principal	$77,218	
($100,000 × PV of $1_{3, 9\%}$) = ($100,000 × 0.77218)		
Present value of the interest	$20,250	
($8,000 × PV-OA of $1_{3, 9\%}$) = ($8,000 × 2.53130)		
Present value of the note		$97,468
Difference		$2,532

The receipt of the note will be recorded as shown in Figure 2-97:

Figure 2-97: Interest-Bearing Note Journal Entry

Notes receivable	$100,000	
Discount on notes receivable		$2,532
Cash		$97,468

The effective interest method is used to calculate interest revenue and determine the amount of discount amortized, as illustrated in Figure 2-98.

Figure 2-98: Amortized Discount Calculation

	Cash Received	Interest Revenue	Discount Amortized	Note Carrying Amount
Issue date				$97,468
Year 1 end	$8,000	$8,772	$772	98,240
Year 2 end	8,000	8,842	842	99,082
Year 3 end	8,000	8,918	918	100,000
	$24,000	$26,532	$2,532	

At the end of the first year, the buyer recognizes the receipt of $8,000 cash interest at the stated rate and effective interest revenue of $8,772. The difference between these amounts is the discount amortized, which is added to the note carrying amount to determine the year-end note carrying amount. So, in the first year, the buyer recognizes the cash receipt, the discount amortized, and the total interest revenue, as shown in Figure 2-99.

Figure 2-99: Interest-Bearing Note Journal Entry

Cash	$8,000	
Discount on notes receivable	$772	
Interest revenue		$8,772

Premiums are dealt with using the effective yield method as well, except that the premium on a note receivable is recognized as a debit and the amortization is an annual reduction in the amount of recognized interest revenue. (The discount amortized column in Figure 2-99 would read premium amortized and be a negative number.)

Imputed interest rate

When the effective rate cannot be readily determined by means such as valuing the asset or services exchanged for the note, an imputed interest rate is used. An imputed interest rate is an approximation of the market interest rate. The imputed interest rate should be comparable to the prevailing rates based on the same lending risk level and a similar lending instrument. The imputed rate is determined at the time the note is received and is used for the term of the note.

Disposition of accounts and notes receivable

While many companies continue to handle their own receivables until they are collected or written off, companies often dispose of their trade receivables for immediate cash. Most companies need to extend credit, but not all companies can afford the full expense of a credit department. (However, most companies do not transfer their administrative functions when they sell receivables.) The purchasers of trade receivables specialize in account management and collection, so they can do so more efficiently than most companies. Companies may also dispose of receivables to generate cash to satisfy short-term liquidity needs without borrowing more or issuing more stock.

Purchasers of receivables do so mainly because they get a discount on the receivables and can specialize in efficient collection. Banks may purchase receivables to circumvent lending limits. Also, some purchasers desire the greater legal protections given to asset holders than the protections offered to a secured creditor.

Two types of trade receivable dispositions occur: secured borrowing and sales accomplished by factoring or securitization of receivables. Sales can be made with or without recourse.

Secured borrowing

In a secured borrowing, receivables are collateral for a loan. This allows the company to keep its receivables and borrow against them. The individual debtors are often not notified of the transaction, and the borrower will continue to collect the receivables and record discounts, returns and allowances, and bad debts. The lender will charge interest on the note plus a finance charge on the accounts receivable.

Factoring and securitization of receivables

Factoring and securitization are two approaches companies can use to sell receivables. Factoring is generally on a nonrecourse basis, but some sales of receivables may be made with recourse, and these topics are discussed separately following factoring and securitization.

Factoring. In factoring, factors buy receivables and often take on the billing and collection functions. Finance companies and banks are the most common factors. Factoring is common in the textile, furniture, and apparel industries. Credit cards are also a form of factoring. Companies that use factors get immediate cash (not as much as if secured borrowing were used) and can eliminate their credit department, because factors usually take over these tasks. Factors conduct credit reviews for the company and extend or deny credit, take payments directly from customers, and remit cash minus a fee to the company for receivables purchased. The company continues all operational activities directly with the customers such as order placement and fulfillment. Giving the power of credit decisions to the factor mitigates some of the risk for the factor, leading to a lower cost of service than would otherwise be the case, but the company will have to accept the credit decisions of the factor and some sales will not be approved.

Most factors transfer only 80% to 90% of the value of the receivables to allow for sales returns and allowances and bad debts. In addition, factors charge a percentage commission dependent on the gross amount of receivables transferred and on the perceived risk of noncollection. The company records the factor's commission as an expense or a loss.

Securitization. Securitization is a bundling of similar receivables such as mortgages, credit card receivables, or car loans into an investment fund. The principal and interest payments collected on the receivables are available for payment to investors. Unlike factoring, the sellers of the receivables continue to service the receivables. Securitization usually involves a higher quality of receivables and lower fees.

Sale with recourse. In a sale with recourse, the seller must pay the purchaser for any bad debts the purchaser incurs. Because the seller has a continuing involvement with the receivable, the transaction is recorded using the financial components approach. This approach allows the factor and the seller to recognize only the assets and liabilities they control after sale with recourse. All extinguished or sold assets and liabilities are not recognized. For example, using the financial components approach, $100,000 of receivables is sold with recourse to a factor, who assesses a finance charge of 2% of accounts receivable and withholds an additional 3% of accounts receivable as collateral against noncollection. The allowance for doubtful debts (also known as a recourse obligation) carries a fair value of $4,000. First, the net proceeds from sale are calculated, as in Figure 2-100.

Figure 2-100: Calculating Net Proceeds

Cash received ($100,000 less 2% + 3%)	$95,000	
Due from factor	3,000	$98,000
Less: Allowance for doubtful debts		(4,000)
Net proceeds		$94,000

The net proceeds are the assets received in the sale minus the incurred liabilities. A loss on the sale of receivable is recorded as in Figure 2-101:

Figure 2-101: Calculating the Loss on Sale

Carrying (book) value	$100,000
Net proceeds	94,000
Loss on sale of receivables	$6,000

Sale without recourse. Factoring is most commonly a sale without recourse, meaning that the purchaser assumes the risk of bad debts. Because the sale transfers title, it is considered an outright sale in form, and because the sale transfers control of credit granting and collection, it is also an outright sale in substance. Accounting for a sale without recourse was covered above under factoring.

Secured borrowing vs. sale

The FASB has set guidelines in SFAS No. 140 to determine if a sale of receivables has occurred. Generally, a sale exists whenever surrender of control occurs. In addition, three criteria need to be met to recognize a sale of receivables:

- The asset should be outside the reach of the seller and its creditors.
- The buyer should be able to sell the assets or use them as collateral.
- The seller should not have any agreement to repurchase the assets before their maturity.

According to the FASB, if these conditions are not met, the transfer should be recorded as a secured borrowing. Secured borrowings should be recorded as a liability, and the interest should be recorded as an expense. If the FASB criteria allow recognition of a sale and there is continuing involvement (sale with recourse), then the financial component approach detailed above is used. If the sale is final and there is no continuing involvement, the procedure is to record a reduction in receivables and either a loss or an expense.

Accounts receivable disclosure requirements

Material receivables must be kept separate by type on the balance sheet and reported net of any valuation accounts. Receivables in the current assets section are expected to be converted to cash within the longer of a year or the operating cycle. Required disclosures include loss contingencies related to receivables, any pledges of receivables as collateral, any material concentrations of credit risk, and any related party receivables. A partial balance sheet with various types of receivables and disclosures is shown in Figure 2-102.

Figure 2-102: Receivables Disclosures

Bounce Sporting Goods Company (Partial) Balance Sheet For the Year Ended December 31, Year 1		
Current assets		
Cash and cash equivalents		$1,383,985
Accounts receivable*	$6,643,478	
Less: Allowance for doubtful accounts	370,167	
	6,273,311	
Advances to subsidiaries due 9/30/05	1,546,600	
Notes receivable—trade*	1,133,680	
Federal income taxes refundable	108,561	
Dividends and interest receivable	55,870	
Other receivables and claims (including debit balances in accounts payable)	129,219	9,247,241
Total current assets		10,631,226
Noncurrent receivables		
Notes receivable from officers and key employees		278,307
Claims receivable (settlement on litigation to be collected over five years)		432,900

* **Note on accounts and notes receivable**
In July Year 1, the company arranged with a finance company to refinance a part of its indebtedness. The loan is evidenced by a 8% note payable. The note is secured by substantially all the accounts receivable and is payable on demand.

Inventory

Inventory includes assets that are held for sale in the normal course of business, are work in the process of being produced for sale, or are raw materials used to produce salable goods. Items that are not sold in the usual course of business are not inventory. Retail and manufacturing industries often report inventory as their largest asset.

Inventory is classified by its use. Retailers often have only one category: merchandise, which includes retail goods that were purchased ready for sale. Manufacturers will often have three categories: raw materials, work in process, and finished goods. Costs of production, labor, fixed and variable overhead, and storage are divided between these categories as appropriate. Manufacturers often need inventory categories to account for internal use inventory types such as manufacturing supplies, indirect materials, parts inventory, or factory supplies.

Perpetual and periodic inventory systems

Today, companies are trying to reduce their inventories to the minimum levels required for sales to continue unhindered. Businesses need to have the inventory ready when it is ordered but want to avoid accumulating items because they require financing costs until sold and they could become obsolete or otherwise unsalable. Companies have installed enterprise databases, bar code scanning systems, and other technology to track inventory and keep records real-time. Just-in-time (JIT) inventory systems reduce inventory holding times by setting up direct electronic links to suppliers so they know just when a particular raw material or finished good needs to be shipped.

Two approaches to inventory record keeping are in use: perpetual and periodic. The periodic system evolved before computers were used to track inventory and therefore is not widely used today.

Perpetual inventory system

The perpetual inventory system keeps continuous track of the changes in the inventory accounts. All transactions are recorded as they occur. Sophisticated databases are used to update records of sales, purchases, conversions, and transfers in real time. Retail systems record inventory changes directly at the point of sale, updating both inventory and cost of goods sold. Purchases, returns and allowances, discounts taken, and freight-in are also updated.

When a company uses a perpetual inventory system, a journal entry is made with each sale to reduce inventory and increase cost of goods sold (an expense account). However, not all goods necessarily make it to the point of sale. Some goods are stolen, others are accidentally shipped without an invoice (overage in a shipment), and others are damaged and discarded without being recorded. Therefore, inventory recorded on the books will generally be higher than what is actually on hand. (However, overages also can and do occur.) So periodically companies using the perpetual system will count what inventory they do have on hand and write off the difference from what they have on the record, which increases cost of goods sold and decreases inventory. Because the size of the difference between actual and recorded inventory can be measured, management can determine the amount of such losses year to year. A primary drawback of the periodic system is that it cannot make this measurement.

The inventory account is a control account that contains a ledger of individual inventory records. Each individual record maintains the quantities and costs divided among the various categories of inventory. Other perpetual inventory accounting recognition guidelines include:

- Recognize cost of goods sold as a debit to cost of goods sold and a credit to inventory at the time of the sale.

- Recognize resale merchandise or production raw material purchases in inventory (not purchases).

- Recognize purchase discounts, freight-in, and purchase returns and allowances in inventory (not separate accounts).

The basic accounting for the perpetual system is:

Beginning Inventory + Purchases (Net) − Cost of Goods Sold = Ending Inventory

Periodic inventory system

In contrast, the periodic system starts with the same two items but then subtracts ending inventory to arrive at goods sold (an amount already known under the perpetual system). The periodic inventory system is becoming obsolete as more companies in all industries adopt inventory tracking databases. Periodic inventory systems must count inventory on hand once a year to determine inventory levels. Acquisitions of inventory are debited to a purchases account. The balance of the purchases account at the end of the period is added to the beginning cost of inventory to determine cost of goods available for sale during the period. The cost of goods available for sale minus the ending inventory (determined at year-end count) equals cost of goods sold. Because cost of goods sold is determined only once a year, the information is not timely. To deal with this problem, a modified perpetual inventory system is sometimes used. The modified system keeps a detailed record of quantities (but not prices) in a memorandum account off the books.

Inventory valuation

Inventory valuation is the process of determining what items to include in inventory, what costs should be included in inventory, and which cost flow assumptions should be used.

The overall cost of producing goods is allocated among the goods sold and the goods still on hand. The **cost of goods available for sale or use** is the cost of goods on hand at the start of the period plus the cost of goods acquired or produced throughout the period. The **cost of goods sold** is the cost of goods available for sale or use minus the cost of goods on hand at the end of the period. The cost of goods available for sale and the cost of goods sold are calculated as shown in Figure 2-103.

Figure 2-103: Cost of Goods Sold Calculation

Beginning inventory, January 1	$350,000
Cost of goods acquired or produced during the year	670,000
Total cost of goods available for sale	1,020,000
Ending inventory, December 31	400,000
Cost of goods sold during the year	$620,000

Which goods to include in inventory

Purchases of inventory are generally recorded when the goods are received by the buyer, even though ownership legally transfers when the title passes to the buyer. Because the time of this transfer is hard to know, and because the result does not differ materially when the rule is applied consistently, the general practice is to record acquisitions to inventory when the goods are received. Exceptions to this generally accepted practice of recognizing ownership on delivery are detailed below.

- **Consigned goods**

  Consigned goods are a way of mitigating the risk of unsalable inventory by allowing the wholesale seller (the consignor) to retain ownership of the property until a sale is recorded. Only then does the wholesaler receive payment for the goods from the retailer (the consignee). The consignee takes a selling commission for holding, marketing, and exercising due care of the goods. The consignor retains the item on their inventory until the sale to a third party. The consignee never records the item as inventory.

- **Goods in transit**

  Goods in transit are those items that have been shipped but have not yet reached their destination at the end of a fiscal period. Who owns the goods in transit is determined by the shipping terms, which are either FOB (free on board) shipping point or FOB destination. Under FOB shipping point, title is transferred as soon as the seller delivers the item to a common carrier serving as an agent of the buyer. Under FOB destination, title is transferred when the goods arrive. The matter is of considerable importance because damages to the goods are the owner's responsibility. A designation such as FOB Minneapolis would indicate a specific city where title transferred. Before title transfers, the goods are the property of the seller; after transfer, they must be accounted for on the books of the buyer.

- **Sale agreements**

  Some sale agreements involve a transfer of title at a different point than the transfer of the risks of ownership. Three particular situations are sales with high rates of return, sales with buyback agreements, and installment sales. Sales with high rates of return are not unusual in the publishing, sporting goods, music, and other seasonal industries where customers are permitted to return unsold inventory for a full or partial refund. When the number of returns can be reasonably estimated, the goods should be considered sold and a sales return and allowances account established. However, when such an estimate is impossible, the seller should not record a sale until the amount of return is known.

  Sales with buyback agreements are a type of swap where a selling company sells its inventory to a buying company and agrees to repurchase the inventory at a specific price and at a specific time. Such a transaction is called a parking transaction because the seller "parks" their inventory in the buyer's balance sheet for a short duration. Effectively the seller is financing its inventory and retaining the risks of ownership but transfers title to the goods. When a repurchase agreement has a set price that covers all of the buyer's costs plus the cost of the inventory, the inventory and the liability under the repurchase agreement should still be reported on the seller's balance sheet.

What costs to include in inventory

Which costs should be allocated to inventory items when determining the price of the item? The types of costs allowed to be included in the determination of inventory value are discussed below.

- **Manufacturing overhead costs**

  For entities that make their own goods for sale, the direct and indirect costs incurred in production are included in the cost of the inventory produced. Accounting Research Bulletin No. 43 states that acquisition and production costs can be included but general and administrative expenses should not be included except for any portion that is clearly related to production. It also states that selling expenses are not to be included. Both fixed and variable overhead items are included. Fixed overhead is allocated to goods manufactured using a traditional or activity-based approach. For example, a line manager's salary would be part of the fixed overhead pool attributable to a specific product line. However, an executive's salary would not be considered a product cost.

- **Product costs**

  Product costs include all costs recorded as part of inventory, including shipping costs, labor costs, and direct costs of acquisition, production, and processing.

- **Cash discounts**

  Cash discounts, as discussed earlier in this section under accounts receivable, include discounts for early payment. The gross method records all purchases at the gross price, and discounts are recorded only if taken as a deduction from net purchases. The net method records all purchases net of discounts. Purchase discounts lost are then charged to another expense account.

- **Period costs**

  Items not included as part of inventory such as selling, general, and administrative expenses are considered period costs, because such costs are expensed in the period incurred. These costs sometimes are associated with production but in many cases are unrelated to it. Interest costs related to the preparation of inventory are also included in period costs, although some believe that interest should be capitalized as part of inventory. The FASB has decided that only interest costs of internally constructed assets or discrete projects such as ships or real estate for sale or lease can be capitalized. Financing costs associated with inventory that is routinely manufactured are not capitalized.

Cost flow assumptions

During an accounting period, inventory is often purchased at several different prices. Also, inventory from a prior period is included in the beginning inventory for a period and then items are produced and added to the same inventory, each at different costs. Keeping the specific cost for each item separate may be impossible given the permutations and various types of inventory involved. So several methods of accounting for inventory costs have evolved, called cost flow assumptions. The cost flow assumptions are used for accounting and have nothing to do with the actual physical movement of goods. For example, first-in, first-out (FIFO) does not imply that the oldest inventory sold first. Cost flow assumptions simply determine which costs are allocated to inventory and which are allocated to cost of goods sold. Each method will have a different impact on income. However, the primary purpose in choosing a particular cost flow assumption should be to best approximate periodic income. The four cost flow assumptions currently in use are specific identification, average cost, FIFO, and LIFO.

- **Specific identification**
  Specific identification tracks the cost of each individual item and records the item in cost of goods sold or inventory as appropriate. This method is feasible only if all items are uniquely tagged and works best with small numbers of expensive items such as jewelry or automobiles in retail or with special orders and products in manufacturing using a job costing system. Specific identification works best with a perpetual inventory system that uses a real-time database for information storage. It matches costs directly with revenues and may become more popular as new technologies emerge to track individual items. Finally, specific identification can be abused to manipulate profits by selecting units at a particular price for sale to alter the gross profit for a period.

- **Average cost**
  The average cost method aggregates costs for all similar inventory items and produces an average cost for the period. When using the perpetual inventory system, this method is called the moving-average method, because a new average cost must be calculated after each purchase. This amount is used as the cost until another purchase is made. The average cost per unit is calculated as the cost of the units available for sale after each purchase divided by the number of units available for sale. Therefore, as of a particular day, for example, July 7, if the cost of goods available for sale equals $100,000 and the number of units available for sale is 2,000, then the average cost is $50. Whenever a purchase is made, the average cost of the good is recalculated. Figure 2-104 shows the average costs for an entire month.

Figure 2-104: Moving Average Inventory Cost Flow Assumption

	Bounce Sporting Goods Company Moving Average Inventory Cost Flow Assumption (Perpetual Inventory System)	
July 1, beginning inventory	1,000 units @ $40	$ 40,000
July 7, purchases	1,000 units @ $60	60,000
July 7, balance	2,000 units @ $50	$100,000
July 15, sales	(1,000) units @ $50	(50,000)
July 15, balance	1,000 units @ $50	$ 50,000
July 20, purchases	500 units @ $56	28,000
July 20, balance	1,500 units @ $52	$ 78,000
July 28, sales	(300) units @ $52	(15,600)
July 31, balance	1,200 units @ $52	$ 62,400
Cost of goods sold (1,300 units)	$50,000 + $15,600	$ 65,600
Ending inventory (1,200 units @ $52)		$ 62,400

When used with the periodic system, average cost is called the weighted-average method. The total cost of the goods available for sale for a period is divided by the total number of units sold, to arrive at a weighted-average cost per unit. Goods available for sale includes beginning inventory and purchases. Ending inventory is multiplied by the average cost to determine the value of ending inventory. Cost of goods sold can be determined by subtracting ending inventory from the cost of goods available for sale or by multiplying the units sold by the average cost.

The average cost method is objective and simple to use and the results are not as subject to manipulation as other methods, so many businesses use it for practical reasons.

- **First-in, first-out**

The first-in, first-out (FIFO) method (which was discussed earlier in this book) makes the accounting assumption that goods purchased earlier are used or sold before goods purchased later. Therefore, the costs incurred furthest in the past should be included in the cost of goods sold and the costs incurred most recently should be included in ending inventory.

When costs are increasing, FIFO yields a lower cost of goods sold because the oldest costs are used, but ending inventory has a relatively higher cost. If costs are going down, the converse is true; a higher cost of goods sold and lower ending inventory value will result.

Using the data from Figure 2-104, the cost of goods sold and the ending inventory are calculated as shown in Figure 2-105 under the perpetual method. When a quantity sold exceeds the number obtained at the earliest price, the price of the next most recent purchase is used. Cost of goods sold is always based on the earliest costs.

Figure 2-105: Perpetual FIFO

Bounce Sporting Goods Company
First-In, First-Out Inventory Cost Flow Assumption
(Perpetual Inventory System)

Cost of goods sold (1,300 units):
July 15	1,000 units @ $40	$40,000
July 28	300 units @ $60	18,000
Total		$58,000

Ending inventory (1,200 units):
Beginning Inventory + Purchases – Cost of Goods Sold = Ending Inventory
$40,000 + $88,000 – $58,000 = $70,000*

*	700 units @ $60	=	$42,000
	500 units @ $56	=	28,000
			$70,000

If the periodic system is used, the cost of the ending inventory is calculated using the most recent costs. The total cost of goods available for sale minus the ending inventory is equal to the cost of goods sold. The same inventory and cost of goods sold will be computed under FIFO regardless of whether the perpetual or the periodic system is used, because the same costs will always be the first in. Figure 2-106 shows periodic FIFO valuation.

Figure 2-106: Periodic FIFO

Bounce Sporting Goods Company
First-In, First-Out Inventory Cost Flow Assumption
(Periodic Inventory System)

Ending inventory (1,200 units):

700 units @ $60	$42,000
500 units @ $56	28,000
	$70,000

Cost of goods sold (1,300 units):
Beginning Inventory + Purchases – Ending Inventory = Cost of Goods Sold
$40,000 + $88,000 – $70,000 = $58,000

An objective of using FIFO is to approximate the actual flow of inventory. When the oldest goods are sold first, as is the case with all perishables, FIFO approximates the specific identification method. Also, FIFO ending inventory values provide a reasonable estimate of inventory replacement costs, especially when turnover is rapid or prices are stable. However, FIFO does not match current costs with current revenues on the income statement. Because the oldest costs are matched with revenue, FIFO can distort net income. When inventory prices are rising, FIFO produces phantom inventory profits.

- **Last-in, first-out**
  Under the **last-in, first-out (LIFO)** method, the cost of the last goods bought are assigned to cost of goods sold and the ending inventory will include the cost of the earliest purchases. When costs are increasing, LIFO produces the highest cost of goods sold and the lowest ending inventory. LIFO has traditionally been used in department stores and in other industries that carry a constant base stock such as chemical and refining companies.

  When using the perpetual inventory system, which records events in the order they actually occur, the LIFO cost of the most recent purchase is determined as of the date of each sale. Using data from Figure 2-106, Figure 2-107 illustrates the perpetual LIFO method.

Figure 2-107: Perpetual LIFO

Bounce Sporting Goods Company
Last-In, First-Out Inventory Cost Flow Assumption
(Perpetual Inventory System)

Cost of goods sold (1,300 units):

July 15	1,000 units @ $60	$60,000
July 28	300 units @ $56	16,800
		$76,800

Ending inventory (1,200 units):
Beginning Inventory + Purchases – Cost of Goods Sold = Ending Inventory
$40,000 + $88,000 – $76,800 = $51,200*

*	1,000 units @ $40	=	$40,000
	200 units @ $56	=	11,200
			$51,200

Unlike FIFO, the LIFO perpetual inventory system and the LIFO periodic system
will yield different costs of goods sold and ending inventory figures. This is because
the periodic system measures LIFO cost as of the end of the accounting period, while
the perpetual method measures LIFO cost as of the date of each sale.

When using the periodic system, the cost of goods sold is calculated by subtracting
the ending inventory from the cost of goods available for sale. Figure 2-108 shows
how inventory is valued using the periodic LIFO method.

Figure 2-108: Periodic LIFO

Bounce Sporting Goods Company
Last-In, First-Out Inventory Cost Flow Assumption
(Periodic Inventory System)

Ending inventory (1,200 units):

1,000 units @ $40	$40,000
200 units @ $60	12,000
	$52,000

Cost of goods sold (140 units):
Beginning Inventory + Purchases – Ending Inventory = Cost of Goods Sold
$40,000 + $88,000 – $52,000 = $76,000

LIFO has the advantage of providing a better measure of current earnings because it
matches recent costs against current revenues. LIFO also allows income tax deferrals
when costs are rising, and inventory levels remain stable because cost of goods sold
will be higher and net income lower compared with other methods. Lower taxes
means a higher cash flow for a company. LIFO can also be a hedge against price
declines, because it rarely requires the mark-downs to market value as a result of
price decreases, which FIFO inventories may be subject to. However, the lower
reported earnings that reduce taxes are a disadvantage to some companies wishing to
report higher income. LIFO also distorts the balance sheet by understating inventory
values and therefore working capital.

LIFO liquidation. LIFO records inventory in layers separated by different purchase times and costs. The oldest costs are called the base layer. For example, if Bounce Sporting Goods has a three-year history of purchasing raw rubber, they might use their ending inventory and an average unit cost for their LIFO inventory. If usage of raw rubber exceeds purchases during a period, a situation called LIFO liquidation can occur. **LIFO liquidation** is the sale of multiple layers of inventory, resulting in revenues at current prices but costs at a mix of current and old prices. Assuming that prices are rising, LIFO liquidation results in higher income levels being reported and likely higher taxes as well.

Figure 2-109 shows how this could occur when a shortage of raw rubber prevents a firm from purchasing as much of this direct material as is needed. Note that their beginning inventory is made from three layers of costs and that the first two layers are eliminated and the base year layer is reduced permanently. Because these layers are purchased at a lower cost in each of the prior years, using these layers results in higher income levels and thus higher taxes than if the firm purchased the rubber at current market prices (assuming inflation), as illustrated by the footnote in the figure.

Figure 2-109: LIFO Liquidation

Year 3 beginning inventory: 12,000 pounds raw rubber

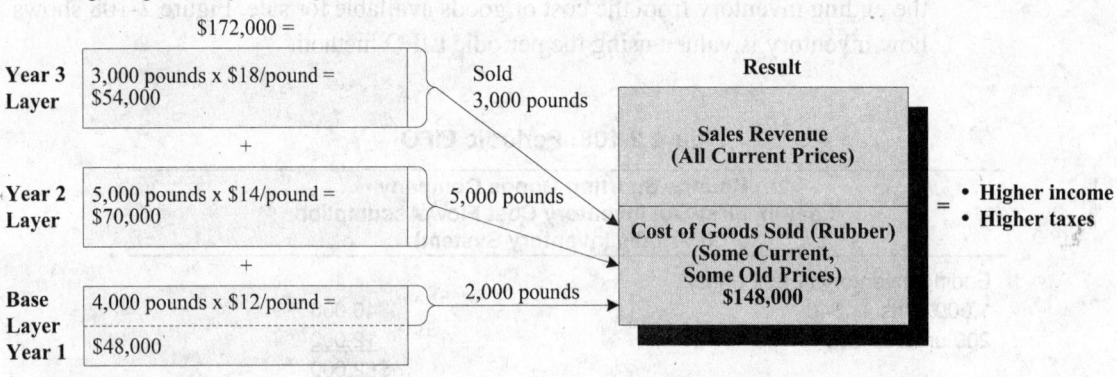

During Year 3, 10,000 pounds raw rubber used;
none available for purchase due to shortage.

* If 7,000 additional pounds of rubber were purchased in year 3 at $18 per pound, then COGS (rubber) would = $180,000, resulting in lower income and lower taxes.

LIFO liquidations can be quite common and can reduce the benefits of using LIFO. Therefore, a common solution is to use the **specific goods pooled LIFO approach**, which groups items into pools of substantially identical items to allow liquidation of one pool to be offset by increases in a different pool. Using pools can reduce fluctuations, but because most companies are continually changing product mixes and therefore inventory items, pools must also be redefined at some expense, and if item mixes change enough, new pools may need to be created, allowing the old pools to be subject to LIFO liquidation.

Dollar-value LIFO. Another solution to LIFO liquidation and to the problems with using pools is to use **dollar-value LIFO**, which measures increases and decreases in a cost pool by their total dollar value instead of using physical quantities. This allows pools to be more vaguely defined to include interchangeable or similar items. The broader the pools, the lower the chances of LIFO liquidation. Dollar-value LIFO calculations are complex; they involve calculating inventory at end-of-year prices and then creating a price index set at 100% for the base year. Each layer above the base has a price index applied that reflects the increases (or decreases) in prices for the period (for example, if prices increased by 16%, then the index would be 116% of the base layer). Using such an index allows each layer to be calculated at base year prices. Figure 2-110 shows how end-of-year inventory at base prices is determined.

Figure 2-110: Dollar-Value LIFO—End-of-Year (EOY) Inventory at Base-Year Prices

December 31	Inventory at End-of-Year (EOY) Prices		Price Index	EOY Inventory at Base-Year Prices
Year 1 (base year)	$450,000	/	100%	$450,000
Year 2	$550,000	/	116%	$474,138

The EOY inventory at base-year prices less the beginning inventory at base-year prices (prior year's data) equals the increase (or decrease) in the quantity of goods. An increase would become a layer of cost. If the difference results in a decrease, then this amount must be subtracted from the most recently added layer. Subtractions are accounted for at the prices that were used to calculate costs for that layer. If a layer is reduced or eliminated, it cannot be rebuilt, and therefore some years might not have a layer. As inventory is used, the most recent layer of costs is used first. Dollar-value LIFO calculations are outside the scope of this text. See an intermediate-level accounting textbook for more information on this subject.

LIFO reserve. An AICPA task force has defined **LIFO reserve** as "the difference between (a) inventory or the lower of LIFO cost or market and (b) inventory at replacement cost or at the lower of cost determined by some acceptable inventory accounting method (such as FIFO or average cost) or market." This definition has been given authoritative status under GAAP. LIFO has advantages for tax preparation and external financial reporting; it is less useful for internal reporting because it does not approximate the physical flow of the product and is cumbersome when applied to interim periods because it relies on estimates of year-end quantities and prices.

Therefore, many companies use a combination of LIFO for taxes and external reporting and an average cost or FIFO method for internal reporting. The internal reporting method is generally followed, and any differences that arise between the two methods are recorded in an allowance to reduce inventory to LIFO account, also called a LIFO reserve. Changes in the balance of the allowance account are called the LIFO effect.

Effect of converting from LIFO to FIFO. When a company decides to switch between inventory accounting methods, what will be the effect on the cost of sales? On income?

Answering such questions will help determine if the change will be an advantage to the company.

For example, when comparing two possible companies to invest in, one reporting with FIFO and the other with LIFO, one will need to be converted to the other method for a true comparison. Because companies that report LIFO are required to disclose their LIFO reserve, it is easier to convert LIFO to FIFO than vice versa. Selected data from a LIFO-basis company is shown in Figure 2-111.

Figure 2-111: Selections from Financial Statements of Company with LIFO Inventory Accounting

	Year 2	Year 1
Excerpts from balance sheet:		
Inventories (approximate FIFO cost)	$338,757	$307,566
– LIFO reserve	– $32,231	–$11,820
LIFO cost	$306,526	$295,746
Excerpts from income statement:		
Cost of goods sold	$2,590,650	
Net income	$108,690	

Because the LIFO reserve increased by $20,411 ($32,231 – $11,820 = $20,411), inventory costs are rising. (Otherwise the LIFO reserve would have fallen.) Also note that in both years the FIFO cost of inventory was greater than the LIFO cost, another indication that costs are rising. (During rising costs, LIFO has the highest cost of goods sold and the lowest net income.) Therefore, the first distinction that can be made is that if the company had used FIFO, its COGS would have been lower and its net income higher, as calculated in Figure 2-112 (the example assumes a 40% tax rate).

Figure 2-112: Converting from LIFO to FIFO

LIFO-basis COGS	$2,590,650
– Increase in LIFO reserve: $32,231 – $11,820 = $20,411	– $20,411
FIFO-basis COGS	$2,570,239
Net income under LIFO	$108,690
Pretax income differential (from COGS change)	+ $20,411
Taxes on differential	– $8,164
Net income under FIFO	$120,937

Using the net income under FIFO, a valid comparison to another FIFO-basis company could now be done. The LIFO reserve is an accumulation of total cost differences between LIFO and FIFO (or another method) since the LIFO method was adopted. Therefore, multiplying the current LIFO reserve by the tax rate will show the amount of income taxes that was saved by using LIFO (disregarding present values). To find this amount, multiply the tax rate by the LIFO reserve (see Figure 2-111): $0.4 \times \$32,231 = \$12,892$. The company therefore has had this much more capital to invest in its operations over the long term.

Effect on income and assets of using different cost flow assumptions. FIFO and LIFO represent extreme ends of a spectrum for their results on income, while average costing falls in the middle. When costs are rising, LIFO will minimize income, which results in lower income tax payments. Because LIFO also matches recent costs with revenues first, some argue that it is the best measure of the cost of goods sold because it approximates replacement costs.

LIFO also excludes inventory holding gains from net income. Holding gains are the difference between the historical cost and the replacement cost of a unit when it is sold. Because LIFO costs approximate replacement costs, the holding gains are minimized and net income is closer to earnings on a current cost basis. In contrast, FIFO includes holding gains in income.

For example, if the most recent unit purchase cost is $90, the oldest cost is $80, and the sale price remains at $200 for a period, then FIFO would record gross profit of $120, which includes a holding gain of $10 (difference between current replacement cost and historical cost). LIFO would record gross profit of $110 and no holding gains. LIFO presents a more realistic picture of the income available for dividends after subtracting the amount needed to replace inventory at the new higher price.

The effects of FIFO, average cost, and LIFO methods are compared in Figure 2-113 using the data from the preceding examples.

Figure 2-113: Comparing Perpetual Inventory Cost Flow Assumptions

Bounce Sporting Goods Company Effects of Inventory Cost Flow Assumptions			
Cost Flow Assumption	**Cost of Goods Available for Sale**	**Cost of Goods Sold**	**Ending Inventory**
FIFO, perpetual	$128,000	$58,000	$70,000
Moving average, perpetual	128,000	65,600	62,400
LIFO, perpetual	128,000	76,800	51,200

Cost flow assumption advantages and disadvantages. All four cost flow assumptions are permitted under GAAP, but there is a wide amount of variance between them. A main disadvantage of allowing so many inventory valuation methods, each resulting in a different net income level, is that it is more difficult to compare various financial statements from different organizations. Because comparison is a primary purpose of financial reporting, this inconsistency complicates matters. However, LIFO companies disclose supplemental information that allows investors to determine what earnings would have been under FIFO.

The International Accounting Standards Board (IASB) considers the LIFO method to be a less acceptable method of inventory accounting. Consequently, as the IASB and the FASB progress in their convergence project, it is likely that inventory valuation methods could be affected.

Effects of inventory errors

Two main types of inventory errors are misstatements in ending inventory and misstatements in purchases and inventory. These misstatements can be in number of units or in valuation methods.

- **Misstated ending inventory**
  When items are not included in ending inventory even though they should have been, the balance sheet will understate inventory, which in turn will understate retained earnings, working capital, and the current ratio. Also, income will be understated because cost of goods sold is overstated. If the error is not corrected in the following period, the opposite effect will result, but the two periods' statements viewed together will result in the same total income as if no error had occurred. However, the net income for each year will have been misstated when viewed individually. When ending inventory is overstated, the converse of this situation occurs; net income, inventory, retained earnings, working capital, and the current ratio are overstated while the cost of goods sold is understated.

- **Misstated purchases and inventory**
  When a purchase is not recorded as a purchase and is not recorded in ending inventory, the balance sheet understates inventory and accounts payable and overstates the current ratio. On the income statement, both purchases and ending inventory are understated, which results in the correct cost of goods sold. Therefore net income will not be affected. The current ratio calculation will be overstated because reducing the size of both current assets and current liabilities will yield a higher ratio. For example, if current assets were $200,000 and current liabilities were $100,000, the ratio would be 2 to 1. However, if both sums were reduced by an error of $50,000, the ratio would be 3 to 1, an overstatement. When both purchases and inventory are overstated, the converse of this situation is true.

Consider a situation in which ending inventory is overstated by $10,000 in Year 0 (the current year). The effects of the error and its correction in Year 1 are shown in Figure 2-114, with the resulting increases and decreases represented by up or down arrows.

Figure 2-114: Correcting an Inventory Misstatement

Cause	Timing	Change
Ending inventory misstated	Year 0	↑ $10,000
Effects (corrected in Year 1)		
Cost of sales	Year 0	↓ $10,000
Operating income	Year 0	↑ $10,000
Tax expense (40% tax rate)	Year 0	↑ $4,000
Net income	Year 0	↑ $6,000
Retained earnings	Year 0	↑ $6,000
Beginning inventory	Year 1	↑ $10,000
Cost of sales	Year 1	↑ $10,000
Operating income	Year 1	↓ $10,000
Tax expense (40% tax rate)	Year 1	↓ $4,000
Net income	Year 1	↓ $6,000
Ending inventory	Year 1	Correct
Retained earnings	Year 1	Correct

This example shows how misstated purchases and inventory can have a material effect on financial statements and how restatements for accounting irregularities can have a large impact on reported numbers.

Lower of cost or market (LCM) rule

While inventory is initially recorded at historical cost, if inventory declines in value due to obsolescence, damage to the goods, or price level changes, then the inventory should be written down to its current value.

The **lower of cost or market (LCM) rule** comes into play when inventory becomes obsolete or declines in value (for example, foreign competition brings prices down). In such situations, inventory is valued at its cost or market value, whichever is lower. Market value is generally considered the cost to replace the item by purchasing or reproducing it (thus it is the value in the purchase market, not the sales market). Inventory is written down in the period in which the value declines rather than in the period the item is sold. This method is based upon the assumption that a decline in the replacement cost of an item normally means the selling price of an item will have to drop to stay competitive.

Net realizable value. Net realizable value (NRV) is the estimate of an item's sale price in an ordinary business situation (not a liquidation) minus all costs to complete the sale and dispose of the asset.

LCM ceiling and floor. When determining what market value should be, two constraints have been placed on the use of replacement cost as a measure of market value:

- Ceiling—Market value should not be greater than the inventory's net realizable value.

- Floor—Market value should not be less than the inventory's net realizable value less an allowance for a normal markup or profit margin.

The ceiling (or upper limit) is designed to make sure that the inventory is not overstated and the loss understated (thus avoiding the need to recognize further losses in future periods). The floor (or lower limit) is designed to make sure that the loss is not overstated and the inventory is not understated (preventing the recognition of excessive future profits).

Applying LCM. According to Accounting Research Bulletin No. 43, the lower of cost or market rule may be applied to individual items, to categories of items, or to the total inventory. When applying LCM to categories or the total inventory, increases in market price in one area tend to offset decreases in a different area, generally leading to a smaller restatement than if LCM is applied to individual items. Item-level LCM is the most common, partly because IRS rules generally require its use. Item-level LCM also produces the most conservative inventory value. Figure 2-115 shows how LCM can be applied in various ways.

Figure 2-115: Applying LCM

Alternative Methods of Applying Lower of Cost or Market Rule					
Inventory	Cost	Market	Individual Items	Category	Total
Rubber products department:					
Tennis balls (box)	$120	$84	$84		
Racquet balls (box)	144	156	144		
	$264	$240		$240	
Racquet department:					
Tennis racquet 1	$192	$230	192		
Tennis racquet 2	240	211	211		
	$432	$441		432	
Total	$696	$681			$681
Inventory valuation			$631	$672	$681
Loss recognition			$65	$24	$15

Recording LCM. When inventory is written down to market, either the direct method or the indirect (allowance) method can be used. The direct method simply substitutes the market value in place of the cost in the inventory, so the loss is not visible on the income statement but is included in cost of goods sold. The allowance method retains the cost in the inventory account and records the write-down in a contra asset account and a loss account.

Relative sales value method

When a group of items is purchased for a lump-sum price and the items differ significantly in type or quality, the purchase price is allocated between the items based upon their relative sales value. Figure 2-116 illustrates the allocation of costs, and Figure 2-117 illustrates the determination of gross profit using the relative sales value method.

Figure 2-116: Allocation of Costs Using Relative Sales Value

Lots	Number of Lots	Sales Price Per Lot	Total Sales Price	Relative Sales Price	Total Cost	Cost Allocated to Lots	Cost Per Lot
A1	50	$6,000	$300,000	3/48	$2,000,000	$125,000	$2,500
A2	200	12,000	2,400,000	24/48	2,000,000	1,000,000	5,000
A3	300	7,000	2,100,000	21/48	2,000,000	875,000	2,917
			$4,800,000			$2,000,000	

Figure 2-117: Calculation of Gross Profit Using Relative Sales Value

Lots	Number of Lots Sold	Sales	Cost of Lots Sold	Gross Profit
A1	25	$150,000	$62,500	$87,500
A2	120	1,440,000	600,000	840,000
A3	230	1,610,000	670,910	939,090
		$3,200,000	$1,333,410	$1,866,590

Accounting issues related to purchase commitments

When customers ask for a product and it is out of stock, it is likely a lost sale. To make sure that their suppliers will have the items they need, some companies engage in purchase commitments, which are agreements to purchase inventory in the future. A purchase commitment does not transfer title to the buyer and no entries are required for commitments that are optional or cancelable.

Noncancellable commitments are not recognized as an asset or a liability, because neither party has exchanged anything yet, but material commitments should be disclosed in the notes to the balance sheet. When the negotiated price is the same or less than the market price, no additional disclosure is required. However, if the contract price is greater than the market price, the amount of the estimated loss should be recorded and reported under other expenses and losses. Assuming the contract price was $300,000 and the market value declined to $200,000, an estimated liability for purchase commitments of $100,000 and an unrealized loss in the corresponding account is recorded. If some or all of the value is recovered, the estimated liability on purchase commitments account and the unrealized holding loss are adjusted.

Estimating inventory

While a physical inventory count is important from an internal control viewpoint, it is usually impractical to take a physical inventory more than once a year. When inventory is not known but needs to be estimated when preparing quarterly statements, either the gross profit method or the retail inventory method can be used.

Estimating inventory using the gross profit method

The gross profit method (or gross margin method) of estimating inventory was developed for situations when it is impossible or impractical to get a precise inventory count. This method is used when preparing quarterly statements because it is not practical to perform physical inventory counts each quarter. The gross profit method is also used by auditors when an estimate of inventory is needed such as when inventory records have been destroyed in a fire.

The gross profit method uses three assumptions:

- Beginning inventory plus purchases equals total goods to be accounted for.

- Goods not sold are in inventory (not stolen, and so on).

- The ending inventory is equal to beginning inventory plus purchases minus sales at cost.

To determine sales at cost, the gross profit percentage is used. This percentage is determined based on records from prior periods. Figure 2-118 shows how to approximate ending inventory using the gross profit method.

Figure 2-118: Gross Profit Inventory Calculation

Beginning inventory (at cost)		$130,000
Purchases (at cost)		410,000
Goods available (at cost)		540,000
Sales (at selling price)	$570,000	
Less: Gross profit (24% of $570,000)	136,800	
Sales (at cost)		433,200
Approximate inventory (at cost)		$106,800

Estimating inventory using the retail inventory method

Retail stores often sell thousands of different items at high volumes, making the inventory tracking method of specific identification impractical. Therefore, the retail inventory method estimates inventory value using retail prices, converting this data to cost using a formula that reflects the firm's average markup. To use the retail inventory method, retail companies must track:

- Period sales.
- Total cost and retail value of purchased goods.
- Total cost and retail value of goods available for sale.

Figure 2-119 shows how this data is applied at Bounce Sporting Goods to estimate the ending inventory value by using the cost to retail ratio for goods available for sale.

Figure 2-119: Retail Inventory Method

	Cost	Retail	Cost to Retail Ratio
Bounce Sporting Goods Year 1			
Beginning inventory	$320,000	$510,000	
Purchases	1,250,000	2,075,000	
Goods available for sale	$1,570,000 /	$2,585,000 =	60.7%
Less sales		– $2,100,000	
Ending inventory (retail prices)		$485,000	
× Cost to retail ratio		× 0.607	
Ending inventory (cost)		$294,395	

Investments

Accounting for investments in debt securities or equity securities of other companies is covered in this section.

Debt securities

A debt security is a form of loan to another entity, including federal and municipal government securities, commercial paper, corporate bonds, securitized debt instruments, and convertible debt. Debt securities are categorized as follows according to SFAS No. 115:

- Held-to-maturity (those that the company has the intent and ability to hold until maturity)—Valued at amortized cost (acquisition cost plus/minus unamortized premium or discount), so no unrealized holding gains or losses are recognized.

- Trading (near-term sale is expected)—Valued at fair value and unrealized holding gains and losses are recognized in net income.

- Available-for-sale (all others)—Valued at fair value and unrealized holding gains and losses are recognized as other comprehensive income (and as a separate component of stockholders' equity).

SFAS No. 115, which superseded SFAS No. 12, requires that on a classified balance sheet companies report individual held-to-maturity, available-for-sale, and trading securities as either current or noncurrent, as appropriate, depending on whether they are expected to be converted to cash within a year or the operating cycle, if longer. [Note that paragraph (17) of SFAS No. 115 dealing with the classification of securities was modified by SFAS No. 135, paragraph 4 t (2).] For securities classified as available-for-sale and held-to-maturity, disclosure is required of the aggregate fair value, gross unrealized holding gains and losses, and amortized cost basis.

In adjusting a portfolio of trading and available-for-sale securities to market value, a valuation allowance (a contra or adjunct account) to the investment account is used. At each balance sheet date, the valuation allowance is adjusted so that the sum of the investment account (at cost) and the valuation allowance are equal to the fair value of the securities. An unrealized gain or unrealized loss is credited or debited as the other side of the adjusting entry. When the securities are sold, the cost is removed from the investment account and a realized gain or loss is recorded.

Held-to-maturity

Because equity securities have no maturity date, only debt securities can be held to maturity. The reporting entity must have both the positive intent and the ability (financial flexibility, risk tolerance) to hold the securities to maturity.

SFAS No. 115 lists several exceptions to this rule, which allow an entity to sell a particular security without calling its intent to hold other securities to maturity into question. Some exceptions include deterioration of issuer's creditworthiness, changes in regulatory requirements altering permissible or maximum investments, or tax law changes that eliminate or reduce tax-exempt status of interest on the debt security.

Debt securities may never be classified as held-to-maturity when the intent is merely to hold them indefinitely or if it is intended that they would be sold in response to changes in market interest rates or the security's prepayment risk, need for liquidity, yield or availability of alternative investments, financing, or foreign currency risk.

Other than such exceptions, sales of held-to-maturity securities should be rare. When they are sold, according to SFAS No. 115, "the amortized cost amount of the sold or transferred security, the related realized or unrealized gain or loss, and the circumstances leading to the decision to sell or transfer the security shall be disclosed in the notes to the financial statements for each period for which the results of operations are presented."

As covered earlier in the discussion of notes receivable, the unamortized discount or premium, if any, is deducted from or added to the acquisition cost to determine the carrying value. Unrealized gains and losses are not accounted for because the assets are not recorded at fair value. As with notes receivable, the effective interest method is used to compute interest income. See the prior section on notes receivable for an example of this method (Figure 2-98).

Trading

Trading securities are intended to be sold in the short term to generate income from the short-term differences in price. Because it is the intention to trade such securities, trading securities are recorded at fair value and any unrealized holding gains or losses must be included in net income. Fair value is determined at the balance sheet date. At the date of acquisition, the security is recorded at its cost including commissions, fees, and taxes. As of the next and all succeeding statement dates, the security is reported at its fair market value. Dividend or interest revenue recognized but not received is accounted for separately as a receivable.

Figure 2-120 shows a sample debt security portfolio including the cost, the fair value, and the unrealized gain or loss (which is the difference between cost and fair value).

Figure 2-120: Computation of Securities Fair Value Adjustment

Trading Debt Security Portfolio **For Year Ended December 31, Year 1**			
Investments	**Cost**	**Fair Value**	**Unrealized Gain (Loss)**
X Corporation 12% bonds	$54,386	$64,860	$10,474
Y Corporation 10% bonds	228,445	216,248	(12,197)
Z Corporation 8% bonds	107,086	114,600	7,514
Total of portfolio	$389,917	$395,708	5,791
Previous securities fair value adjustment balance			(3,201)
Securities fair value adjustment—debit			$2,590

Available-for-sale

Available-for-sale securities include all securities that do not fit in the trading and the held-to-maturity categories, such as securities that have an indeterminate use or indefinite holding time but are not being actively traded to take advantage of temporary differences in market prices. These securities are reported at fair value, and an unrealized gains and losses account is used to record differences between the acquisition cost and the fair value. To reduce the volatility of net income, the unrealized gains and losses on these securities are reported in other comprehensive income and as a separate component of stockholders' equity until realized by a sale.

Figure 2-121 shows how a security would be adjusted to fair value. The example assumes that there was an unrealized loss of $14,257 the prior year. Because the unrealized loss at the end of the current year of $12,000 is $2,257 less than the prior year, an unrealized gain would be recorded.

Figure 2-121: Calculation of Securities Fair Value Adjustment—Available-for-Sale

Available-for-Sale Debt Security Portfolio **For Year Ended December 31, Year 1**			
Investments	**Amortized Cost**	**Fair Value**	**Unrealized Gain (Loss)**
X Corporation 10% bonds (total portfolio)	$300,000	$288,000	$(12,000)
Previous securities fair value adjustment balance—credit			(14,257)
Securities fair value adjustment—debit			$2,257

The balance sheet and the income statement for the available-for-sale security in Figure 2-121 is illustrated in Figure 2-122. (The income statement includes a $6,212 loss on the sale of a security that was sold during the year.)

Figure 2-122: Available-for-Sale Securities on the Balance Sheet and Income Statement

Balance Sheet	
Current assets	
Interest receivable	$xxx
Investments	
Available-for-sale securities, at fair value	$288,000
Stockholders' equity	
Accumulated other comprehensive loss	$12,000
Income Statement	
Other revenues and gains	
Interest revenue	$xxx
Other expenses and losses	
Loss on sale of securities	$6,212

Equity securities

While debt securities are primarily used to preserve capital and generate income, equity securities are those securities that convey an ownership interest in another entity. They include common and preferred stock, other capital stock, and rights to buy or sell ownership interests at set prices (warrants, options, and rights).

Equity securities do not include convertible debt securities or redeemable preferred stocks. They are initially valued at acquisition cost plus brokerage and other fees.

When the investor in a stock acquires an interest in the investee, the percentage of voting stock they acquire determines the method of accounting for the security.

- Holdings of less than 20% (passive interest): Investor uses the fair value method.

- Holdings between 20% and 50% (significant influence): Investor uses the equity method.

- Holdings of greater than 50% (controlling interest): Investor issues consolidated financial statements.

Holdings of less than 20%

Equity securities held at a level of less than 20% ownership interest are accounted for in a similar manner to debt securities and are classified either as available-for-sale or trading. (Having no maturity date, they cannot be classified as held-to-maturity.) The presumption is that investors with less than 20% interest have little or no influence over the investee. If the investor has significant influence over the investee even with less than 20% ownership interest, the equity method is used (see "Holdings between 20% and 50%" in the following pages).

Investments of less than 20% are initially recorded at their acquisition cost including fees and are then revalued at each balance sheet date to fair value. Securities acquired in a noncash exchange (such as for services or land) are recorded at the fair value of the noncash consideration paid or the fair value of the security received, whichever is more reliable. If neither is easy to value, an estimate must be made.

Available-for-sale security portfolio. Cash dividends declared by the investee are reported as income by the investor. Securities are initially recorded at cost. At each balance sheet date, the portfolio is valued at fair value, with any net unrealized gain or loss calculated as shown in Figure 2-123.

Figure 2-123: Calculation of Securities Fair Value Adjustment

Available-for-Sale Equity Security Portfolio For Year Ended December 31, Year 1			
Investments	**Cost**	**Fair Value**	**Unrealized Gain (Loss)**
X Corporation	$228,536	$242,000	$13,464
Y Corporation	279,400	267,520	(11,880)
Z Corporation	124,388	91,520	(32,868)
Total of portfolio	$632,324	$601,040	(31,284)
Previous securities fair value adjustment balance			1,000
Securities fair value adjustment—credit			$(30,284)

The net unrealized gain or loss on the portfolio is reported as part of other comprehensive income and as a component of stockholders' equity (accumulated other comprehensive income). The entry to adjust the portfolio via the valuation allowance (securities fair value adjustment) and record an unrealized loss is illustrated in Figure 2-124.

Figure 2-124: Journal Entries for Securities Fair Value Adjustment

Unrealized holding gain or loss - equity	$30,284	
Securities fair value adjustment (available-for-sale)		$30,284

When a stock in the portfolio is sold, a realized gain or loss is calculated by deducting the acquisition cost from the net proceeds from sale. A realized gain would be accounted for as of the date of the sale as shown in Figure 2-125.

Figure 2-125: Accounting Entries for a Realized Gain on Sale of a Security

Cash	$10,000
Available-for-sale securities	$4,000
Gain on sale of stock	$6,000

Realized gains and losses are recorded when securities are sold. Sales and purchases of securities during the year will change the cost basis of the investments account. Companies often wait until year-end to calculate the net unrealized gain or loss on the portfolio as a whole. When an available-for-sale security is sold during the year, a reclassification adjustment is also required to avoid double-counting the gain or loss. These adjustments are discussed later in this topic.

Trading securities. Accounting for trading securities is the same as the accounting for available-for-sale securities, with the exception that unrealized holding gains or losses are reported in net income instead of other comprehensive income. The account is therefore unrealized holding gain or loss income, and sale of the security requires any remainder of the gain or loss to be recognized in income.

Holdings between 20% and 50%

The equity method of accounting, described in APB Opinion No. 18, is required for any investor who is able to exercise significant influence over an investee's operating and financial policies. The term "significant influence" is not limited to a minimum percentage of ownership of 20% but can also be determined by the amount of representation on the board of directors, material intercompany transactions, and other factors.

However, unless evidence demonstrates otherwise, a 20% or greater investment is presumed to cause significant influence. Those holding greater than 20% interest in an investee can prove that they do not exert significant influence if situations such as those below are true (from FASB Interpretation No. 35):

- Investor signed a contract surrendering significant rights to the investee.

- Investee opposition, such as litigation or other challenges.

- Investee ownership is concentrated among a small group that does not heed the investor's opinions.

- Investor tried and failed to get representation on the board of directors.

- Investor is not allowed access to the required information for using the equity method.

Ownership interest over 50% conveys a controlling interest, so it is not dealt with using the equity method but by requiring the investor to consolidate the investee in its financial statements.

Equity method accounting. Under the equity method, an investment is initially recorded at acquisition cost plus fees. Subsequently, the investment's carrying amount is increased or decreased by the investor's percentage of the earnings or losses of the investee and is decreased by any dividends received from (or declared by) the investee. The investor records its share of the investee's income as an increase or decrease in the carrying value of the investment account obtained by multiplying the percentage of ownership in the investee by its reported income. The equity method presumes a material relationship between the two entities, so in addition to recognizing that the earnings and losses of the investee raise or lower the investor's net assets, several items must be removed from the investor's books to avoid double-counting of assets or liabilities:

- Any intercompany transactions that factor into the investor's net income must be eliminated to the extent of the investor's interest therein.

- The proportionate share of the difference between fair market values and book values of the investee's fixed assets should be depreciated. If investee assets cannot be determined at fair market value, the entire difference between acquisition price and book value is amortized as goodwill.

- The proportionate share of the investee's extraordinary items (discussed later in this topic), results of discontinued operations, and cumulative effects of accounting principles should be treated as the investor's extraordinary items, and so on.

To illustrate the accounting for an equity purchased by an investor company, assume that an investor company purchases a 30% share in an investee company for $20 million. On the date of the investment, the investee's book value is $50 million. The excess of purchase price over the proportionate share of the book value acquired is $5 million ($20 million minus 30% of $50 million). In this example, the difference is allocated among goodwill ($2.5 million), finite-lived intangibles ($1.5 million), and undervalued depreciable assets of the investee's company ($1 million). The intangibles are amortized over five years, and the assets are depreciated over ten years.

At the end of the first year when the investee company releases its end-of-period results, the investor company must account for both ordinary and extraordinary components of income. (Assume that the company reported $4.6 million in net income, which includes a $600,000 extraordinary loss.) A year-end dividend of $1.4 million was also declared. Finally, the amortization and depreciation resulting from the allocation of the excess purchase price must be accounted for. The entries for the end of the year are shown in Figure 2-126.

**Figure 2-126: Year-End Accounting Entries for
Securities Accounted for under the Equity Method**

Investment in X Company stock	$1,380,000	
Loss from investment (extraordinary)	$180,000	
Income from investment (ordinary)		$1,560,000

[To record share of X Company net
income ($4,600,000 × 0.3) and extraordinary loss
($600,000 × 0.3)]

Cash	$420,000	
Investment in X Company stock		$420,000

[To record dividend received
($1,400,000 × 0.3) from X Company]

Income from investment (ordinary)	$400,000	
Investment in X Company stock		$400,000

(To record amortization of investment cost
in excess of book value represented by:

Undervalued depreciable assets $\dfrac{\$1 \text{ million}}{10 \text{ years}}$ = $100,000

Unrecorded intangibles $\dfrac{\$1.5 \text{ million}}{5 \text{ years}}$ = $300,000

Total = $400,000

The carrying amount of the investment is calculated as in Figure 2-127 (assuming that a June dividend of $700,000 was also declared, 30% of which would have been recognized in June, or $210,000).

Figure 2-127: Calculation of Investment Carrying Amount

Investment in Investee Company		
Acquisition cost, 1/1/Year 1	$20,000,000	
Plus: Share of Year 1 income before dividends and amortization	1,380,000	21,380,000
Less:		
Dividends received 6/30 and 12/31	(630,000)	
Amortization of undervalued depreciable assets	(100,000)	
Amortization of unrecorded intangibles	(300,000)	(1,030,000)
Carrying amount, 12/31/Year 1		$20,350,000

Holdings of greater than 50%

When a company achieves a controlling interest in an investee's operations, usually indicated by owning greater than 50% of the investee's stock, each company continues to maintain separate accounting records. Interperiod statements are prepared using the equity accounting method, and the investment is treated as a long-term investment. At the end of the accounting period, the parent company consolidates its results with those of the subsidiary. In the consolidated balance sheet, the investment account is eliminated to avoid double-counting and is replaced with the individual assets and liabilities of the subsidiary. Consolidated statements treat the entities as a single accounting entity. Specifics of consolidated statements are not treated here.

Purchase accounting. When one company acquires more than 50% of another through a merger, acquisition, or statutory consolidation, GAAP requires the use of **purchase accounting** to record the event. Purchase accounting records the value of the acquired firm at the fair market value of the consideration given (stock, cash, debt, or some combination). Also included in the cost of the acquisition are any fees paid to complete the transaction (for example, a pre-acquisition audit or finder's fees paid to an investment banker). Purchase accounting requires that the net assets of the acquired companies be recorded in the consolidated financial statements at their fair market value. Any difference between the amount paid and the fair market value of the acquired company's net assets is recorded as goodwill. Goodwill is an intangible asset that must be tested for impairment annually and written down if impairment occurs. (Goodwill amortization is no longer acceptable under GAAP.)

If the transaction is structured so the acquired firm remains a separate legal entity, that firm is considered a subsidiary of the acquiring (parent) firm and keeps its own set of books. The parent firm carries the subsidiary on its books in an investment in a subsidiary (asset) account. After the date of acquisition, period adjustments are made to the investment in subsidiary account. If the holding company has between 20% and 50% control, the parent company usually tracks its investment in the subsidiary using the equity method. If the parent company has a controlling interest (usually greater than 50% ownership), use of consolidated financial statements and the equity method are required. Under the equity method, the investment account is increased by the subsidiary's net income, decreased for dividends paid, and adjusted for any additional expenses related to the step-up in basis to fair market value. Under the cost method, an adjustment to the investment in subsidiary account is made for a permanent decline in value and additional investments.

Consider an example in which Acme Diversified purchases 60% of Abco Inc.'s stock for $3.84 million. Figure 2-128 compares the differences between the cost and equity methods by showing the accounting entries for the first year of the relationship. The example assumes that the $3.84 million investment exceeded Abco's book value by $480,000. Of this, $240,000 was considered goodwill and $240,000 was considered an excess of market value over book values for depreciable assets. (This amount is amortized over five years, while goodwill is not amortized.) Furthermore, in Year 1, Abco reported:

- Income of $432,000.

- A dividend of $144,000.

Income of $432,000 less the dividend leaves cumulative income after dividends of $288,000.

Figure 2-128: Cost Method versus Equity Method—Parent Company Perspective

Cost Method			Equity Method		
Year 1			**Year 1**		
Investment in Abco	$3,840,000		Investment in Abco	$3,840,000	
Cash		$3,840,000	Cash		$3,840,000
To record the initial investment			To record the initial investment		
Cash	$86,400		Investment in Abco	$259,200	
Dividend income		$86,400	Equity in subsidiary income		$259,200
To record dividends received (0.6 × $144,000)			To record equity in subsidiary income (0.6 × $432,000)		
			Equity in subsidiary income	$48,000	
			Investment in Abco		$48,000
			To adjust equity in subsidiary income for excess depreciation ($240,000/5 years = $48,000)		
			Cash	$86,400	
			Investment in Abco		$86,400
			To record dividends received (0.6 × $144,000)		
			Investment in Abco		$86,400
			To record dividends received (0.6 × $144,000)		

Figure 2-129 shows how the investment account balances are determined in Year 1.

Figure 2-129: Investment Accounts: Cost versus Equity Methods

Investment Account at Year 1 End				
Cost Method		**Equity Method**		
Year 1 cost	$3,840,000	Year 1 cost	$3,840,000	
		Year 1 equity in subsidiary income	$259,200	Year 1 amortization of depreciable assets	$48,000
				Year 1 share of dividend declared	$86,400
Year 1 balance	$3,840,000	Year 1 balance	$3,964,800	

What does the comparison between the two methods tell us?

- Dividends paid or declared are considered income under the cost method but are recorded as a decrease in investment under the equity method.

- Income reported by the subsidiary increases the investment account (asset account) under the equity method but does not get recorded under the cost method.

- Additional depreciation expense of assets marked up during acquisition is included in the equity method but is not in the cost method.

Financial statement presentation issues

Two specific issues in statement presentation have a significant impact on financial statements. These include impairment of value and reclassification adjustments.

Impairment of value

Investments sometimes suffer **impairments** in value, which are losses that are other than temporary. All investments should be evaluated to determine if this is the case. The most common impairments are bankruptcies or other loss of liquidity on the part of an investee. When an impairment is judged to be other than temporary, it is written down to its new cost basis. Impairment losses are considered realized and are included in net income.

Impairment testing is performed in the following manner.

- Debt securities: Determine if it is probable that an investor will be unable to collect all of the amounts due as per the terms of contract.

- Equity securities: If the security's net realizable value is lower than the carrying amount of the investment, consider the duration of time and the extent to which the fair value has been less than cost, the intent and ability of the investor to hold the investment for the period anticipated for the fair value of the investee's stock to regain its value, and the investee's future prospects.

Assume a loss on available-for-sale securities was reported earlier as an unrealized loss in comprehensive income, say, of $100,000 on a $1 million bond. If the loss needs to be recorded as a realized loss because the impairment in value is considered other than temporary, the accounting entry (assuming an available-for-sale debt security) is as shown in Figure 2-130.

Figure 2-130: Realized Loss Due to Impairment

Loss on impairment	$100,000	
Securities fair value adjustment (available-for-sale)	$100,000	
Unrealized holding gain or loss - equity		$100,000
Available-for-sale securities		$100,000

Thus the investment in the debt security has a new cost basis of $900,000.

Reclassification adjustments

Unrealized gains and losses on available-for-sale securities are included in other comprehensive income. When the securities are sold, realized gains and losses are reported as part of net income, so double-counting occurs unless a reclassification adjustment is performed. For example, assume an investor holds the portfolio of stocks in Figure 2-131 for Year 1.

Figure 2-131: Available-for-Sale Security Portfolio

Investments	Cost	Fair Value	Unrealized Holding Gain (Loss)
X Corporation common stocks	$98,400	$129,150	$30,750
Y Corporation common stocks	147,600	166,050	18,450
Total of portfolio	$246,000	$295,200	49,200
Previous securities fair value adjustment balance			0
Securities fair value adjustment—debit			$49,200

The investor's statement of comprehensive income for the period would include the net holding gains for Year 1 as in Figure 2-132.

Figure 2-132: Statement of Comprehensive Income

Bounce Sporting Goods Company	
Statement of Comprehensive Income	
For Year Ended December 31, Year 1	
Net income	$430,500
Other comprehensive income	
Holding gains arising during period	49,200
Comprehensive income	$479,700

The X Corporation stock was sold with a realized gain of $30,750 in Year 2, and the available-for-sale security portfolio at the end of Year 2 is illustrated in Figure 2-133.

Figure 2-133: Available-for-Sale Security Portfolio

Investments	Cost	Fair Value	Unrealized Holding Gain (Loss)
Y Corporation common stocks	$147,600	$190,000	$42,400
Previous securities fair value adjustment balance—debit			(49,200)
Securities fair value adjustment—credit			$(6,800)

The holding gain or loss is computed as in Figure 2-134.

Figure 2-134: Computation of Total Holding Gain (Loss)

Unrealized holding gain (loss)	$(6,800)
Realized holding gain	30,750
Total holding gain recognized	$23,950

The unrealized gain on the X Corporation stock was included in the Year 1 comprehensive income statement, while in Year 2 the realized gain was reported in net income. Because comprehensive income is a component of net income, a reclassification adjustment is required in the Year 2 statement of comprehensive income to eliminate the realized gain from comprehensive income, as shown in Figure 2-135.

Figure 2-135: Statement of Comprehensive Income

Bounce Sporting Goods Company **Statement of Comprehensive Income** **For Year Ended December 31, Year 2**		
Net income (includes $30,750 realized gain on X Corporation shares)		$885,600
Other comprehensive income		
Holding gains arising during period ($190,000 − $166,050)	$23,950	
Less: Reclassification adjustment for gains included in net income	(30,750)	(6,800)
Comprehensive income		$878,800

Property, Plant, and Equipment (PP&E)

Property, plant, and equipment (PP&E) covers all assets of durable nature such as land, office and retail space, factories, warehouses, equipment, machinery, and company vehicles.

Major characteristics of PP&E

To be considered PP&E, an asset must have the following three characteristics:

- **The asset is held for use in operations and not for resale.**
  PP&E includes assets held for use in operations. Assets acquired for investment or resale are not considered PP&E. For example, a vacant building would be classified as an investment.

- **The asset is long-term in nature and if other than land is depreciable.**
  PP&E is expected to provide future benefits over a number of years. Based on the matching principle, the asset's cost is spread over its estimated life and charged to

earnings as depreciation expense. Land, which typically does not decline in value, is not depreciated (but in some cases, its value may become impaired).

- **The asset must be tangible.**
  Assets classified as PP&E have a physical substance, in contrast to intangible assets such as copyrights or patents, which do not.

Cost basis of valuing PP&E at acquisition

The historical cost, or acquisition cost, is the basis used to value PP&E. Issues related to costing land, buildings, equipment, and self-constructed assets is also considered in this section.

Historical cost

Historical cost is measured by the cash or cash equivalent price paid to obtain or construct an asset, including transportation, installation costs, taxes, and related costs. The general rule for determining the cost of an asset, whether PP&E or inventory, is that all the costs necessary to get the asset in place and ready for its intended use are capitalized as part of the cost of the asset.

At the acquisition date, an asset's historical cost and fair value are equivalent. Subsequent to acquisition, changes in fair value are not recognized in the accounts (except when impairment occurs). Some accountants would argue that fair values constitute more relevant measures than historical costs. However, others are concerned that fair values may lack reliability. Consequently, under GAAP, PP&E is valued at amortized historical cost because of its reliability. The costs of additions or improvements are added to the cost of plant assets when an increase in future service potential will result. In contrast, the cost of routine repairs and maintenance would be expensed as incurred.

Cost of land

The cost of land includes:

- The purchase price.

- Closing costs, including title, commissions, legal fees, past-due taxes, and insurance.

- Land preparation costs such as grading, filling, demolition, draining, razing old buildings (net of salvage proceeds), and clear-cutting.

- Cost of surveys.

- Assumption of liens, mortgages, or other possible encumbrances.

Special assessments for municipal improvements such as sewers and street lights are charged to the land account because they are typically permanently maintained by the government. The cost of private improvements of a temporary nature, like driveways and fences, would be recorded in a separate land improvements account and depreciated over the useful life of the improvement. Land held for speculative reasons is considered an investment; land held by a property developer for resale would be considered inventory.

Cost of buildings

The cost of buildings includes all costs to buy or construct a building, including architect's fees, building permits, materials, labor, and overhead. If an old building is razed to make way for a new building, that cost is considered part of the cost of the land, which is being readied for its intended use as a building site, not part of the cost of the new building.

Cost of equipment

All expenditures in purchasing, shipping, preparing a site, and installation of equipment are included in the cost of the equipment. For example, preparing a foundation for equipment is included in the cost. Equipment encompasses office equipment, machinery, delivery equipment, furniture, fixtures, and all other similar fixed assets.

Cost of self-constructed assets

While most companies contract out construction projects to professional firms, some companies, such as those in the telecommunications, rail, and utilities industries, construct their own assets. Lacking an external purchase price, the cost of self-constructed assets is more difficult to determine. An entity must carefully allocate costs and expenses between operating and construction activities to determine the asset's cost.

Allocating direct construction costs, such as materials and direct labor, is straightforward. In theory, indirect costs, such as insurance, property taxes, utilities, depreciation of fixed assets, and supervisory factory labor, might be dealt with in different ways. In practice, a proportional amount of these overhead costs would be allocated to the self-constructed asset. However, some accountants would argue against allocating these overhead costs to construction, because they would be incurred whether or not the construction project was under way. Any costs incurred in excess of the asset's market value should not be capitalized but would be recorded as a loss.

Accounting for interest costs during construction or acquisition of PP&E

In theory, capitalization of interest costs arising during construction of PP&E can be handled in three ways:

- **Capitalize only actual interest costs arising during construction.**
  With a few exceptions, GAAP requires this method because it uses the historical cost principle of recording only actual transactions that are a part of the actual cost of construction. Under GAAP, the amount of interest capitalized is based on the lower of the amount of interest actually incurred during the construction period or the amount of interest that would have been avoidable if expenditures for the asset had not been made.

- **Do not capitalize any interest charges during construction.**
  Those who favor this approach argue that if a firm had used equity rather than debt financing, no interest costs would have been incurred. Therefore interest should be considered a financing cost rather than a construction cost. However, unless the related interest costs are immaterial, such an approach is unacceptable under GAAP.

- **Capitalize all types of finance costs used to construct the asset, whether or not specifically identifiable.**

  Some argue that there is always an opportunity cost to funding construction, whether debt or equity financing is used, and that this should be considered part of the asset's cost. However, because this opportunity cost is a subjective measure that does not fit with the historical cost method, it is not used under GAAP.

Nonmonetary exchanges

Exchanges of nonmonetary assets (such as inventory or PP&E) are recorded based upon fair values, as long as the transaction has commercial substance. A transaction has commercial substance if the exchange will change the timing and amount of the firm's future cash flows. Future cash flows are likely to change when the assets exchanged are dissimilar (inventory for equipment) or when the assets are similar (truck for truck) but have different expected useful lives. In other words, if the two entities will have different economic positions after the exchange, the transaction has commercial substance. If future cash flows are not expected to change significantly, the transaction lacks commercial substance and would be accounted for at book value, with no gain or loss recognized.

Accounting for exchanges with commercial substance—gain recorded

An asset acquired in a nonmonetary exchange is valued based on the fair values of the assets given up. Only in the case when it is more clearly evident would the fair value of the asset received be used instead. Figure 2-136 illustrates the computation of a gain when a warehouse is acquired in exchange for a fleet of cars.

Figure 2-136: Computation of Fair Value of Cars and Gain

Fair value of cars		$147,000
Cost of cars	$192,000	
Less: Accumulated depreciation	66,000	
Book value of car		126,000
Gain on disposal of cars		$21,000

The warehouse would be recorded for $147,000, the fair value of the cars given up. The cars and their related accumulated depreciation account would be written off, and a gain of $21,000 would be recorded as a result of the exchange.

Accounting for exchanges with commercial substance—loss recorded

This situation is illustrated in figures 2-137 and 2-138. The example assumes that a company acquires a new machine (B) with a list price of $25,000 by paying cash and trading in its old machine (A). An analysis of the future cash flow associated with the old and new machines indicates that the exchange has commercial substance. The old machine had an original cost of $18,000, and accumulated depreciation of $8,000 has been recorded on it. The fair value of the old machine is determined to be $7,000, but a trade-in allowance of $12,000 is negotiated for it as part of the purchase agreement.

Figure 2-137: Computation of Cost of New Machine

List price of new machine	$25,000
Less: Trade-in allowance for used machine	12,000
Cash payment due	13,000
Fair value of used machine	7,000
Cost of new machine	$20,000

The accounting entry to record the exchange is shown in Figure 2-138.

Figure 2-138: Accounting Entry for Exchange

Machine B	$20,000
Accumulated depreciation - machines	$8,000
Loss on disposal of machine	$3,000
[Fair value – book value: $7,000 – $10,000]	
Machine A	$18,000
Cash	$13,000

Accounting for exchanges without commercial substance

When the company remains in the same economic position as before the exchange, the asset acquired should be recorded at the book value of the asset disposed of, with no gain or loss recognized. To illustrate this situation, assume that company A exchanges its iron stamping machine for company B's steel stamping machine.

Company A's iron stamping machine has a:

- Fair value of $112,000.

- Book value of $94,500 (cost of $105,000 less accumulated depreciation of $10,500).

Company B's steel stamping machine has a:

- Fair value of $119,000.

- Book value of $95,200 (cost of $140,000 less accumulated depreciation of $44,800).

Company A also pays company B $7,000 in cash. From company A's perspective, the calculation of the unrealized gain on the swap is shown in Figure 2-139.

Figure 2-139: Calculation of Gain (Unrecognized)

Fair value of iron stamper exchanged	$112,000
Book value of iron stamper exchanged	94,500
Total gain (unrecognized)	$17,500

The new machine is expected to produce cash flows similar to those of the old machine, so the exchange is deemed to lack commercial substance. As a result, the total gain on disposal of the old machine is deferred. The cost recorded for the new machine can be calculated based either on the book value of the assets given up or on the fair value of the asset received less the amount of gain deferred, as illustrated in Figure 2-140.

Figure 2-140: Basis of Steel Stamper

Book Value Method			Fair Value Method	
Book value of iron stamper	$94,500		Fair value of steel stamper	$119,000
Cash paid	7,000	or	Less: Gain deferred	(17,500)
Basis of steel stamper	$101,500		Basis of steel stamper	$101,500

The entry to record this exchange on company A's books is shown in Figure 2-141:

Figure 2-141: Company A's Entry for the Exchange

Steel stamper	$101,500	
Accumulated depreciation - machines	$10,500	
Iron stamper		$105,000
Cash		$7,000

If the steel stamping machine is later sold to an outside party, the deferred gain that reduced its basis will be recognized.

Nonmonetary exchanges should be disclosed in the financial statement notes. Disclosure should include the nature of the transaction, the accounting method used, and any gains or losses recognized.

Payment for PP&E in the form of stock

When PP&E assets are acquired through the issuance of stock or other securities, the par value of the stock will be inadequate to measure the true cost of the property. Instead, if the stock is being actively traded, its current market value is used. If the stock value cannot be determined because the stock is not actively traded, an estimate of the market value of the property should be made and used as the basis for recording the value of both the asset and the issuance of the stock.

An example follows of an acquisition when the stock is being actively traded. Acme Company wants to build luxury condominiums and so purchases a warehouse from Robin Manufacturing by issuing them 10,000 shares of $1 par common stock currently trading at $20 per share. Acme's accounting entry would be as shown in Figure 2-142.

Figure 2-142: Acme Company Accounting Entry

Property (10,000 shares × $20/share)	$200,000	
Common stock		$10,000
Additional paid-in capital		$190,000

Accounting for costs subsequent to acquisition

Costs subsequent to the acquisition of PP&E are either capitalized or expensed as operating expenditures. To qualify as a cost to be capitalized (recorded to the asset account), the cost should provide future economic benefits above those that were expected from the existing asset. Future economic benefits can be increased either by:

- Extending the life of the asset.
- Increasing the productivity of the asset by improving either the quantity or quality of the units produced.

Additions, improvements and replacements, reinstallations or rearrangements, and repairs each have special accounting implications.

Additions

Additions should be capitalized because they are effectively a new asset. If the addition results in modifications to the existing structure, the cost of those modifications would be capitalized provided the addition had been planned when the existing structure was constructed; otherwise, the costs would be reported as an expense or loss.

Improvements and replacements

An improvement substitutes a more effective asset for one in place; replacements replace aging assets with newer versions of the same thing. Both should be capitalized. Three approaches are used to account for such capitalizations: the substitution method, capitalizing the new cost, and charging the cost to accumulated depreciation.

- **Substitution method**
  Whenever the book value of the asset to be replaced is known, the substitution method should be used. The book value of the old asset is removed from the asset account and the new item is recorded. Assume that an old boiler needs to be replaced with a new boiler. The old boiler has a scrap value of $300, a current book value of $4,500, and an original book value of $45,000 less accumulated depreciation of

$40,500. The new boiler costs $37,500. The book entry for the substitution is shown in Figure 2-143.

Figure 2-143: Substitution Method Accounting Entries

New boiler	$37,500	
Accumulated depreciation - old boiler	$40,500	
Loss on disposal of old boiler ($4,500 − $300)	$4,200	
Old boiler		$45,000
Cash ($37,500 − $300)		$37,200

- **Capitalizing the new cost**

  Improvements are usually handled by capitalizing the cost of the new item without removing the carrying amount of the old item. This is justified by the assumption that sufficient depreciation was taken on the old item to make the carrying amount close to zero.

- **Charge accumulated depreciation**

  If the quality or quantity of an asset has not been improved but its useful life is extended, the costs are debited to accumulated depreciation because the previous reduction in carrying value has been restored. Such accounting will extend the depreciable life of the asset.

Reinstallations or rearrangements

Movements of assets from one location to another are capitalized and expensed over the period of benefit. If certain of these costs cannot be separated from other operating benefits or if the costs are immaterial, they should be expensed immediately.

Repairs

Repairs that maintain a normal level of asset function are charged to the expense account in the period incurred. An allowance for repairs account is sometimes used when all repairs are performed during particular interim periods but benefit the entire year. For example, assume that a company estimates it will need to spend $1,000,000 on repairs during the year and allocates these costs over the four quarterly periods. Actual repair expenditures were incurred in the second quarter ($520,000), in the third quarter ($256,000) and in the fourth quarter ($235,000). The accounting for each quarter would be as shown in Figure 2-144.

Figure 2-144: Accounting Entries Using a Repair Expense Account

First Quarter End

Repair expense	$250,000	
Allowance for repairs ($\frac{\$1,000,000}{4}$)		$250,000

Second Quarter End

Allowance for repairs	$520,000	
Cash, accrued payroll, inventory, etc.		$520,000
Repair expense	$250,000	
Allowance for repairs ($\frac{\$1,000,000}{4}$)		$250,000

Third Quarter End

Allowance for repairs	$256,000	
Cash, accrued payroll, inventory, etc.		$256,000
Repair expense	$250,000	
Allowance for repairs ($\frac{\$1,000,000}{4}$)		$250,000

Fourth Quarter End

Allowance for repairs	$235,000	
Cash, accrued payroll, inventory, etc.		$235,000
Repair expense	$261,000	
Allowance for repairs		$261,000
[$520,000 + $256,000 + $235,000 − ($250,000 × 3)]		

At the end of the year, the allowance for repairs account must have a zero balance, so any remaining balance should be closed to repairs expense. On interim statements, the allowance for repairs account is reported as a contra account to PP&E.

Depreciation

Depreciation is an accounting method of allocating costs over the useful life of a tangible asset to the periods the asset will benefit. Because depreciation is a method of cost allocation, not a method of asset valuation, the fair market value of an item generally has no relation to its depreciated book value. For natural resources and intangible assets, the terms "depletion" and "amortization" are used instead of depreciation.

In order to calculate depreciation, the following must be determined:

- Depreciable base
- Useful life
- Method of depreciation

An asset's depreciable base is its original cost minus its salvage (or residual) value, which is the estimated value of the asset at the end of its useful economic life. An asset's useful economic life may be shorter than its actual physical life, because, for example, it is expected to become obsolete before it actually wears out. A paper mill may shut down an old but still functioning press because newer machines produce paper more efficiently and cheaply.

When assets are purchased or sold part way through a year, the annual depreciation expense is calculated and then prorated for the partial year (for example, if a full year's depreciation is $120,000 and the asset was purchased on April 1, then $9/12 \times \$120,000 = \$90,000$).

We will consider depreciation methods based upon expected units of use (the activity method) and expected years of use (the straight-line, sum-of-the-years'-digits, and declining balance methods). The sum-of-the-years'-digits and declining balance methods are also considered decreasing charge or accelerated depreciation methods because they result in high depreciation cost in earlier years and decreasing charges in later years.

For comparability, the same asset will be depreciated using each different method: a plastic extruder machine that cost $1,000,000 and has a $150,000 salvage value and an estimated life of 70,000 units produced or seven years of useful life.

Activity method

The activity method (also known as the variable charge approach, units of production method, or units of output method) of depreciation does not depreciate assets by the passage of time but by units of use of the asset, either input units, such as the number of hours used, or output units, such as the number of items produced by the asset. Output measures associate costs with use more closely and should be used if easily determined.

The depreciation charge for a year is calculated in the following manner:

$$\text{Depreciation Charge} = \frac{\text{Depreciable Base} \times \text{Units Produced or Hours Used}}{\text{Total Units of Production or Total Hours Usable Over Life}}$$

If the plastic extruder machine actually produces 9,500 units in the first year and the asset has a depreciable base (cost less salvage) of $850,000, the depreciation charge for the first year is calculated as:

$$\frac{\$850,000 \times 9,500}{70,000} = \$115,357.14$$

The activity method is suitable for equipment and vehicles, but it is not useful for buildings because they depreciate primarily due to time rather than use. The activity method produces lower depreciation during periods of low use and higher depreciation during periods of high use and effectively matches costs with revenues for assets whose utility declines depending on the amount of usage. Therefore, the activity method is considered the best approach under GAAP for items that depreciate through wear or use.

Straight-line method

The straight-line method of depreciation is simple and therefore widely used. When obsolescence is a primary cause of depreciation, this time-based method that allocates equal depreciation to each period is often the most appropriate conceptually. It is also most appropriate for assets that generate revenue consistently over their lives.

Depreciation is calculated as follows:

$$\text{Annual Depreciation Charge} = \frac{\text{Depreciable Base}}{\text{Estimated Service Life}}$$

Referring to our example, this would result in:

$$\text{Annual Depreciation Charge} = \frac{\$850,000}{7} = \$121,428.57$$

One objection to this method is that it makes the unrealistic assumption that the asset's usefulness is the same every year and that repair costs are also the same each year. Also, as the depreciation reduces the asset's book value, if the revenue produced from use of the asset is steady each year, then the rate of return from the asset will continue to increase.

Accelerated depreciation methods

Accelerated depreciation or decreasing charge methods depreciate an asset more in the earlier years and less and less in the later years of the asset's life. The reasoning behind such methods is that assets lose the majority of their value in the first years of use and that repair costs will generally increase over the life of the asset. Repair costs increase as depreciation charges decrease, so that the total asset-related expenses are smoothed out. This method is also conceptually appropriate for assets that generate more revenue in their earlier years than in their later years.

Because depreciation is a noncash expense, it reduces a company's operating income and thereby reduces the company's tax liability. Hence, methods that record higher depreciation expenses early in the lifetime of the asset will reduce their tax liability sooner, which would result in a better cash flow in the earlier periods.

- **Sum-of-the-years'-digits method**
  The sum-of-the-years'-digits method uses the depreciable base (cost less salvage value) and multiplies it by a fraction that decreases each year. The fraction is determined as follows:

$$\text{Depreciation Fraction} = \frac{\text{Years of Useful Life Remaining}}{\text{Sum of All Years of Useful Life}}$$

$$\text{First Year of 7-Year Life} = \frac{7}{7 + 6 + 5 + 4 + 3 + 2 + 1} = \frac{7}{28}$$

or

$$\text{Sum of All Years of Useful Life} = \frac{n(n + 1)}{2} = \frac{7(7 + 1)}{2} = 28$$

(Where n = all years of useful life)

Figure 2-145 shows how this method is applied to the extruder machine. (Note: To avoid rounding issues, the depreciation expense was calculated by multiplying the depreciable base by the numerator of the depreciation fraction and then dividing the total by the denominator. The answers were rounded to the nearest dollar.)

Figure 2-145: Sum-of-the-Years' Digits Method

Year	Depreciable Base	Years of Life Remaining	Depreciation Fraction	Depreciation Expense	End-of-Year Book Value
0					$1,000,000 *
1	$850,000	7	7/28	$212,500	$787,500
2	$850,000	6	6/28	$182,143	$605,357
3	$850,000	5	5/28	$151,786	$453,571
4	$850,000	4	4/28	$121,429	$332,142
5	$850,000	3	3/28	$91,071	$241,071
6	$850,000	2	2/28	$60,714	$180,357
7	$850,000	1	1/28	$30,357	$150,000 **
Totals		28	28/28	$850,000	

* = Book value at date of purchase (that is, cost)

** = Salvage value. Final book value should always equal salvage value.

- **Declining balance method**

  The declining balance method is applied using a percentage of a straight-line depreciation rate. In the straight-line method, an asset with a ten-year life is depreciated at 10% per year (1/10); the declining balance method is usually applied at 150% or 200% of the straight-line rate. (In the latter case, it is called the double-declining balance method.)

  The declining balance method calculates depreciation based on the asset's book value without regard to salvage value (in contrast to the other methods that calculate depreciation based upon the depreciable base, or cost minus salvage value). As the asset's book value declines, applying the constant percentage rate of depreciation results in a lower amount of depreciation each year.

  For example, in the case of the plastic extruder machine with a life of seven years, its straight-line depreciation rate would be 1/7, or 14.29% per year. If 150% declining balance depreciation is used, the rate would be $1/7 \times 1.5 = 1.5/7 = 21.43\%$. The double declining balance would be $1/7 \times 2 = 2/7 = 28.57\%$.

  Depreciation schedules using both 150% declining balance and double-declining balance rates are shown in Figure 2-146. Note that as soon as the asset's residual value is reached, the depreciation ceases. As a result, in the illustration below the normal declining balance computation requires an extra year under the 150%

declining balance rate and the depreciation is settled a year early using the double-declining balance method.

Figure 2-146: Declining Balance Depreciation Methods

Bounce Sporting Goods Company
Declining Balance Depreciation Methods

Year	Book Value of Asset at Beginning of Year	Rate	Depreciation Charge	Book Value at End of Year
150% Declining Balance				
1	$1,000,000	21.43%	$214,300	$785,700
2	785,700	21.43%	168,376	617,324
3	617,324	21.43%	132,293	485,031
4	485,031	21.43%	103,942	381,089
5	381,089	21.43%	81,667	299,422
6	299,422	21.43%	64,166	235,256
7	235,256	21.43%	50,415	184,841
8	184,841	21.43%	34,841 *	150,000 *
			$850,000	

* Depreciation charge of $39,611 in year 8 reduced to arrive at salvage value of $150,000.

Year	Book Value of Asset at Beginning of Year	Rate	Depreciation Charge	Book Value at End of Year
Double Declining Balance				
1	$1,000,000	28.57%	$285,700	$714,300
2	714,300	28.57%	204,076	510,224
3	510,224	28.57%	145,771	364,453
4	364,453	28.57%	104,124	260,329
5	260,329	28.57%	74,376	185,953
6	185,953	28.57%	35,953 *	150,000 *
7	—		—	
			$850,000	

* Depreciation charge of $53,127 in year 6 reduced to arrive at salvage value of $150,000.

To make sure that the asset is not depreciated below its salvage value or to complete the depreciation on the original schedule, some entities switch to a straight-line method near the end of the asset's useful life. For example, if in year 5 of the 150% declining balance example, the book value would be $299,422, and the depreciable base would be $299,422 − $150,000 = $149,422. The asset has two years left from its original estimate, so $149,422/2 = $74,711 is recorded in depreciation for years 6 and 7.

Group and composite methods

The group and composite methods of depreciation are alternate methods that take a group of depreciable assets, average their service lives via a weighted average of the units, and then depreciate the group as if it were a single asset. Because the items are aggregated, gains and losses cannot be recognized when an asset is disposed of. Instead, gains and losses are netted into accumulated depreciation. The group method aggregates similar assets; the composite method aggregates dissimilar assets.

Both methods use the same formula:

$$\text{Depreciation Rate} = \frac{\text{Sum of Straight-Line Depreciation of Each Asset}}{\text{Total Asset Cost}}$$

$$\text{Depreciation Expense} = \text{Depreciation Rate} \times \text{Total Cost for Group or Composite}$$

Selecting a depreciation method

A company can select different depreciation methods for different classes of assets. For example, buildings that provide constant benefits over their useful life might be depreciated using the straight-line method, while equipment that has a greater loss of utility in the initial years might be depreciated using the declining balance method.

Figure 2-147 on the next page compares depreciation methods and notes their effect on depreciation expense, operating income (OI), tax expense and liability, and assets. The straight-line method is used as a base line and the other methods are compared to it.

Note that this comparison is for just one asset, but if the method were consistently applied a similar result would be seen for the entire company. Note also that the activity method is omitted because if units of actual use match their expected values, this will result in the same depreciation as the straight-line method. (When it does not, each company will experience different results.)

Figure 2-147: Comparison of Depreciation Methods to the Straight Line Method

Effect \ Method	Straight-Line Method	Sum-Of-Years'-Digits Method	150% Declining Balance	Double Declining Balance
Depreciation expense				
In Year 1	$121,429	$212,500	$214,300	$285,700
In Year 7	$121,429	$30,357	$50,415	$0
Effect on OI				
In Year 1	—	↓ $91,071	↓ $92,871	↓ $164,271
In Year 7	—	↑ $91,072	↑ $71,014	↑ $121,429
Effect on taxes (40%)				
In Year 1	—	↓ $36,428	↓ $37,148	↓ $65,708
In Year 7	—	↑ $36,429	↑ $28,406	↑ $48,571
Effect on assets				
In Year 1	—	↓ $91,071	↓ $92,871	↓ $164,271
In Year 7	—	↑ $91,072	↑ $71,014	↑ $121,429

For tax purposes, companies usually compute depreciation using the IRS's Modified Accelerated Cost Recovery System (MACRS), which sets different depreciation rates and methods depending on one of eight asset classes determined by asset life. The first four classes cover assets under 15 years of life and use the double declining balance method, the next two classes cover assets between 15 and 27½ years and use the 150% declining balance method, and the last two classes cover assets with lives of 27½ years or longer and use the straight-line method.

Differences in depreciation methods for financial reporting and tax purposes will often lead companies to record deferred tax liabilities. To illustrate the treatment of a tax liability here, assume that a firm used the straight-line method for financial reporting and the sum-of-the-years'-digits method for tax reporting (using the data in Figure 2-145). If the operating income from before this depreciation charge is deducted (with all other depreciation items already deducted) were $1,000,000, then for book purposes, under the straight-line method, income before taxes would be $878,571, with tax owed of $351,428. For tax reporting under the sum-of-years'-digits method, resulting income before taxes would be $787,500, with tax owed of $315,000, for a deferred tax liability of $36,428 (that is, you are paying less taxes now and will therefore owe more later).

Another way of saying this is that the additional $36,428 increases the company's annual depreciation tax shield (the total annual amount saved in taxes from taking depreciation deductions).

If the asset is retained for the seven years, the tax liability would be offset by corresponding increases in taxes owed (for example, $35,429 in year 7), removing this temporary difference. (If sold earlier for a taxable gain, the sale may result in having to pay this deferred tax liability.) However, due to the time value of money, companies prefer to pay lower taxes in earlier years. Companies will also have more money to reinvest in their business in these earlier years.

Deferred taxes are discussed in more detail later in this topic.

Impairment

PP&E is carried at historical cost and is not revalued at each balance sheet date to fair market value. However, when the book value of PP&E cannot be recovered through sale or use, the value of the asset has become impaired and the carrying value must be written down to fair value. Arriving at fair value for PP&E can be difficult and subjective.

SFAS No. 144, "Accounting for the Impairment or Disposal of Long-Lived Assets," indicates that PP&E should be tested for impairment when one of the following circumstances exists:

- Significant decrease in the market value of an asset (asset group)

- Significant adverse change in the extent or manner in which an asset is used or its physical condition

- Significant adverse change in legal factors or in the business climate that could affect the value of a long-lived asset, including an adverse action or assessment by a regulatory body

- Accumulation of costs significantly in excess of the amount originally expected to acquire or construct a long-lived asset

- A current period operating or cash flow loss combined with a history of such losses or a projection or forecast that demonstrates continuing losses associated with an asset

- The expectation that the asset is likely to be sold or retired significantly before the end of its previously estimated useful life

When one of these situations exists, the recoverability test is used to determine whether impairment has occurred. If the sum of the undiscounted future net cash flows expected from the use and disposition of the asset is less than the asset's carrying amount, the asset is impaired. If the undiscounted cash flows are greater than or equal to the carrying value, the asset is not impaired. If impairment exists, the asset is written down to its fair value and the write-down is recorded as an impairment loss. The fair value is the market value of the asset, if determinable; otherwise, the present value of the expected future net cash flows is used.

For example, if an asset has a book value of $1,000,000 and accumulated depreciation of $200,000 (thus a carrying amount of $800,000) and the undiscounted expected future net cash flows from use and disposition of the asset are $700,000, then an impairment has occurred. If the fair value of the asset is estimated to be $650,000, then an impairment loss of $150,000 ($800,000 – $650,000) must be recorded.

The impairment loss is recorded as part of income from continuing operations in a category such as other expenses and losses, not as an extraordinary item. Any recognized impairment loss should be disclosed, including information about the assets impaired, the reason for the impairment, the amount of the loss, and the method of determining fair value.

Disposition of PP&E

PP&E can be sold or exchanged, involuntarily converted, or abandoned. The company should depreciate the asset to the date of the disposal and then remove all related accounts from the books. At the time of disposition, any difference between the depreciated book value and the asset's disposal value must be recognized as a gain or loss. Gains or losses on dispositions of plant assets are reported as part of income from continuing operations unless the disposal is related to discontinued operations.

Sale

When PP&E is sold, depreciation must be recorded from the date of the last depreciation entry until the date of disposal. This brings the book value of the asset up to date in order to correctly measure the gain or loss from the sale of the asset. For example, say a firm has a plastic extrusion machine that originally cost $34,000 and has recorded $3,400 in depreciation for the past seven years. On April 1 of the eighth year (Year 8), the plastic extruder is sold for $10,000. What is the gain/loss on this sale? First, the firm must account for the depreciation for Year 8, which is $3,400 × 3/12 = $850. This amount would normally be added to the total depreciation amount at the end of the year, or it could be separately accounted for by debiting depreciation expense and crediting accumulated depreciation—machinery.

Figure 2-148 shows how to calculate the gain/loss on the disposal of the extruder.

Figure 2-148: Journal Entry on Sale of Machinery

Cash	$10,000	
Accumulated depreciation—machinery	$24,650	
Machinery		$34,000
Gain (loss) on disposal of machinery*		$650

*   ($3,400 × 7) + $850 = $24,650
**   (Selling Price – Net Book Value) = Gain/Loss
      Net Book Value = Cost – Accumulated Depreciation
      $10,000 – ($34,000 – $24,650) = $650 gain

Because a company will often make multiple purchases and sales of equipment or other assets in a single period, a slightly more complex example follows. At the beginning of a year, Bounce Sporting Goods had equipment with a book value of $240,000 and $96,000 in accumulated depreciation. During the year, they sold equipment costing $45,000 with a book value of $1,500 for $10,500. The year-end equipment balance was $330,000, and accumulated depreciation was $120,000. What were the equipment purchases for the year? To find out, first determine the cost from the given book value:

$$\text{Book Value} = \text{Cost} - \text{Depreciation}$$

Beginning Equipment
$$\$240,000 = x - \$96,000$$
$$x = \$336,000$$

Ending Equipment
$$\$330,000 = x - \$120,000$$
$$x = \$450,000$$

The formula below shows how to calculate the equipment purchases (or a different variable in the same equation):

Equipment Purchases
= Ending Equipment Balance Cost – Beginning Equipment Balance Cost + Equipment Sold
= $450,000 – $336,000 + $45,000 = $159,000

Involuntary conversion

Flood, fire, earthquake, theft, or condemnation are types of involuntary conversions of assets. When the event that leads to such a conversion is considered to be both unusual in nature and infrequent in occurrence, the gain or loss on disposition would be reported as an extraordinary item on the income statement.

Even in situations where the asset converted is immediately replaced by another asset, a gain or loss on disposal must be recognized according to FASB Interpretation No. 30.

An example of an involuntary conversion is the loss of a plant by fire. In this example, the asset was bought for $1,600,000 and has accumulated depreciation of $600,000. Figure 2-149 shows the accounting entry that would be used if an insurance settlement paid the firm $1,700,000.

Figure 2-149: Journal Entry on Involuntary Conversion

Cash	$1,700,000	
Accumulated depreciation—Plant assets	$600,000	
Plant assets		$1,600,000
Gain (loss) on disposal of plant assets*		$700,000

* Insurance Payment – Net Book Value = Gain/Loss
Net Book Value = Cost – Accumulated Depreciation
$1,700,000 – ($1,600,000 – $600,00) = $700,000 Gain

Abandonment

Abandoned or scrapped items that do not result in any recovery of cash will produce a loss equal to the book value of the asset. If any scrap value is received, a gain or loss is recognized for the difference between the scrap value and the asset's book value. Fully depreciated assets that are still in use should be disclosed in the notes to financial statements.

Depletion

Natural resources such as petroleum, minerals, and timber can be completely consumed and can be restored only by an act of nature, so they are called wasting assets. Unlike other assets, wasting assets do not maintain their physical characteristics. The cost of natural resources is charged to income as depletion expense.

Depletion accounting requires establishing a depletion base, which includes acquisition costs, exploration costs, development costs, and restoration costs. Acquisition costs include the cost of purchasing property, rights to search for a resource, or rights to use a resource. Exploration costs include all costs of finding a resource. Intangible development costs such as drilling costs are included in the depletion base; tangible development costs for equipment that can be moved from one site to another are not included in the depletion base but are separately depreciated. Restoration costs are the costs of restoring the land to a usable state and are included in the depletion base. The salvage value of a property is deducted from the depletion base.

After establishing the depletion base, this amount is allocated to the appropriate accounting periods, normally using a units-of-production or activity-based approach as discussed previously.

The depletion rate is determined using the following formula:

$$\text{Depletion Cost per Unit} = \frac{\text{Total Cost} - \text{Salvage Value}}{\text{Total Estimated Units Available}}$$

Thus if depletion costs for an oil well are $5 per barrel and 5,000 barrels are extracted in the first year, depletion of $25,000 would be recorded.

Financial statement presentation and disclosure requirements for PP&E

For PP&E and natural resources, the basis of the valuation should be disclosed (for example, historical cost) along with any commitments, pledges, and liens (such as use of the asset as collateral). Liabilities secured by PP&E are reported separately in the liability section of the balance sheet and not netted against the asset.

Also, PP&E used in operations should be segregated from PP&E not currently used in operations. Reporting accumulated depreciation separately informs statement users of the historical cost of the assets and the amount of depreciation recorded to date. Some entities use a similar accumulated depletion account, but others credit depletion directly to the natural resources account. The oil and gas industry has special disclosure requirements, including the accounting method used and the manner of disposing of such costs.

APB Opinion No. 12 (par. 5) indicates that the following information about depreciable assets used should be disclosed:

- Depreciation expense for the period

- Balances of major classes of depreciable assets, classified by function and nature

- Accumulated depreciation, in total or by major classes of depreciable assets

- General descriptions of all methods used in calculating depreciation for each major class of depreciable asset

A sample of the disclosure requirements for PP&E is shown in Figure 2-150.

Figure 2-150: Disclosures for PP&E and Natural Resources for Year 2

Timber and Forest Corporation

Property (Note 1)	Year 2	Year 1
	(expressed in thousands)	
Property and equipment		
Land and land improvements	$46,847	$42,372
Buildings and improvements	425,877	403,087
Machinery and equipment	3,021,216	3,000,748
	3,493,940	3,446,207
Accumulated depreciation	(1,591,285)	(1,507,640)
	1,902,655	1,938,567
Timber, timberlands, and timber deposits	194,810	202,020
	$2,097,465	$2,140,587

Notes to Financial Statements

Note 1 (in part): Summary of Significant Accounting Policies
Property. Property and equipment are recorded at cost. Cost includes expenditures for major improvements and replacements and the net amount of interest cost associated with significant capital additions. Capitalized interest was $992,340 in Year 2, $7,825,500 in Year 1, and $13,155,720 in Year 0. Substantially all of our paper and wood products manufacturing facilities determine depreciation by the units-of-production method, and other operations use the straight-line method. Gains and losses from sales and retirements are included in income as they occur.

Depreciation is computed over the following estimated useful lives:

Buildings and improvements	5 to 40 years
Furniture and fixtures	5 to 10 years
Machinery, equipment, and delivery trucks	3 to 20 years
Leasehold improvements	5 to 10 years

Cost of company timber harvested and amortization of logging roads are determined on the basis of the annual amount of timber cut in relation to the total amount of recoverable timber. Timber and timberlands are stated at cost, less the accumulated cost of timber previously harvested.

Intangibles

The value of intangible assets continues to increase in today's economy. Many intangible assets are difficult to value, such as quality of management or customer loyalty, and so they are not reported on the financial statements. The balance sheet does includes the value of purchased intangible assets, which are measured at amortized cost. This section covers the characteristics of intangibles and then explores valuation, amortization, impairment testing, and accounting for goodwill and research and development.

Characteristics of intangibles

Intangible assets are defined by two main characteristics: They lack physical substance and are not financial instruments. Other factors distinguish intangible assets from tangible assets: Their values may fluctuate due to competitive conditions, they may be valuable only to the company possessing them, their future benefits may not be readily determinable, and they may have indeterminate lives. Intangible assets are typically classified as noncurrent assets.

Types of intangibles

SFAS No. 141, "Business Combinations" (par. A14), defines six categories of intangible assets.

- **Marketing intangibles**

  Marketing intangibles include any assets used to market or promote a business, including trademarks, trade names, company names, Internet domain names, and agreements not to compete. They include words or symbols that identify products, services, or companies. The U.S. Patent and Trademark Office grants indefinite numbers of ten-year renewals for registered marks, but common law protects even unregistered marks. Purchased marketing intangibles are capitalized at their purchase price. Internally developed marketing intangibles are capitalized for the amount of legal fees, registration fees, design and consulting fees, and other costs, excluding research and development. Most marketing intangibles have indefinite lives and therefore their cost cannot be amortized.

- **Customer intangibles**

  Customer lists, order or production backlogs, and other customer contracts and relationships are all customer intangibles because they relate to dealings with third parties. Most customer intangibles have a finite life and are amortized over that period.

- **Artistic intangibles**

  Copyrights on books, movies, plays, poems, music, photos, and audiovisual information are artistic intangibles. Copyrights granted to individuals are good for 70 years past the life of the creator and cannot be renewed. The costs to purchase and defend a copyright would be amortized over the period of expected benefit (which may be shorter than the legal life of the copyright).

- **Contract intangibles**

  Contract intangibles are the rights granted by contract arrangements such as construction permits, broadcast rights, franchises and licensing agreements, and service contracts. The initial costs of securing a franchise (such as legal fees or an advance payment) are recorded in an intangible asset account and amortized over the life of the franchise, if it is limited. However, annual payments required under a franchise agreement are expensed as incurred.

- **Technological intangibles**

  Patented technology, trade secrets, and other innovations are technological intangibles. Patents, which include both product and process patents, have a legal life of 20 years. Purchased patents are capitalized at the purchase price; any legal fees required to secure or defend the patent are also capitalized. However, research and development costs related to the patented product or process must be expensed as incurred. The capitalized cost of a patent is amortized over the shorter of its legal life or its useful life.

- **Goodwill**

  Goodwill is the difference between the price paid to acquire a business and the fair market value of its underlying identifiable assets. The amount paid for a company is first allocated to its identifiable tangible and intangible assets and the remainder is recorded as goodwill, which is discussed more thoroughly later.

Valuation of intangibles

Intangibles are recorded differently depending on whether they were purchased or created internally.

- **Purchased intangibles**

  Purchased intangibles are recorded at cost, plus any additional costs such as legal fees. If intangibles are acquired in exchange for stock or noncash assets, the exchange is recorded at the more reliable of the fair value of consideration given or the intangible asset received. If tangible assets are part of a basket purchase, the lump-sum price is allocated between the assets received based upon relative fair values.

- **Intangibles created internally**

  Research and development costs incurred to develop a patent internally are expensed as incurred. Only direct costs, such as legal fees, related to internally developed patents may be capitalized.

Amortization

Intangibles with an indefinite life are not amortized but are tested for impairment annually. On the other hand, the cost of intangible assets with a limited life would be amortized over the period of expected benefit. An intangible's useful life is estimated using the following factors (described in par. 11 of SFAS No. 142):

- Expected use of the intangible

- Limits placed on an intangible's life through legal, regulatory, or contractual provisions

- Extension rights or other provisions for renewal

- Provisions that allow for renewal or extension of the asset's life without substantial cost

- Effects of technological change, obsolescence, consumer demand, competition, and other economic factors

- Expected useful life of another asset related to the intangible asset

- Levels of maintenance expenditures required to gain the expected future benefits from the asset (If these are material compared to the carrying value of the asset, it suggests a limited life.)

When an intangible asset has a limited life, the capitalized cost minus any residual (salvage) value is amortized over that life. Residual value is usually zero unless the entity believes that the intangible will have some value to another entity at the end of the amortization period (such as a purchase commitment for a mailing list). Intangible assets are amortized using the straight-line method unless another method more clearly reflects the pattern of asset use. Amortization is debited to an expense account and credited either to the intangible asset account or to a separate accumulated amortization account.

Goodwill

According to SFAS No. 141 (par. 43), goodwill is "the excess of the cost of an acquired entity over the net of the amounts assigned to assets acquired and liabilities assumed." This section deals with recording goodwill and testing it for impairment.

Recording goodwill

Only purchased goodwill is capitalized. Internally created goodwill is never reported as an asset. Purchased goodwill is recorded as an asset only when an entire business is purchased; it cannot be separated from the business as a whole but is an integral part of the going concern.

When one company purchases another company, a price is determined based on the fair value of the new subsidiary's assets and liabilities, not on the amounts reported on its balance sheet, because these are listed at historical cost. An audit is usually conducted by the purchasing company or independent agents to arrive at the fair market value of the subsidiary's net assets. The long-term assets and liabilities usually have the greatest variance between book and fair value. The audit also seeks out any unrecorded assets or liabilities and accounts for the method of inventory valuation in its fair value estimate. Once the fair value is determined, the negotiators settle on a purchase price that usually accounts for intangibles that cannot be valued, such as management expertise, reputation, and the like. Therefore, the purchase price will likely be materially higher than the fair value. In very rare instances, negative goodwill occurs, which is a credit on the purchasing company's books in instances where the purchase price was less than the fair value. Also known as bargain purchase, this situation is rare because the seller is more likely to sell off the pieces of the business separately to get the market value.

As an example of goodwill, if a parent company purchases a company as a subsidiary and the net fair market value for the underlying assets and liabilities is $35 million but the purchase price is $40 million, the $5 million difference is accounted for as goodwill.

The calculation in Figure 2-151 demonstrates the allocation of the purchase price.

Figure 2-151: Calculation of Goodwill

Purchase price	$40,000,000
Less:	
Cash	$2,500,000
Receivables	$5,000,000
Inventories	$9,000,000
Property, plant, and equipment	$22,000,000
Patents	$1,500,000
Liabilities	($5,000,000)
Fair value of identifiable net assets	$35,000,000
Goodwill	$5,000,000

Impairment testing of goodwill

Goodwill is not amortized but is tested for impairment and written down when impairment is determined to have occurred. The FASB does not believe that goodwill amortization helps investors analyze financial performance, and goodwill is considered to have an indefinite life.

Goodwill is considered impaired when the fair value of the reporting unit is less than its carrying value, including goodwill. When impairment exists, the loss must be measured. An impairment loss is recognized for the excess of the carrying amount of the reporting unit goodwill over the implied fair value of that goodwill. The implied fair value of goodwill is determined similarly to how goodwill is measured in a business combination. The fair value of the reporting unit is allocated to identifiable net assets (including unrecognized intangibles), and any excess is considered implied goodwill.

For example, if a subsidiary had a fair value of $40 million including goodwill and valued its net identifiable assets (excluding goodwill) at $36 million, then the implied goodwill would be $4 million. If the goodwill recorded on the books was $5 million, it would be written down $1 million, with an impairment loss recorded for that amount. An impairment loss cannot exceed the carrying amount of goodwill, and after a loss is recognized, it cannot subsequently be reversed.

Accounting for impairment of intangible assets

Intangible assets other than goodwill are also tested for impairment. Both limited-life and indefinite-life intangibles are tested.

Impairment testing for limited-life intangibles

Intangible assets that are subject to amortization are reviewed for impairment in the same way as property, plant, and equipment. (See the PP&E section for details on the recoverability test.) An impairment loss is recognized if the carrying amount of an intangible asset is not recoverable and its carrying amount exceeds its fair value. Once an intangible asset has been written down, any recovery in value cannot be recognized.

Impairment testing for indefinite-life intangibles

Intangibles that are not subject to amortization should be tested for impairment annually by comparing the fair value of the intangible asset with its carrying amount. If the carrying amount exceeds the fair value, an impairment loss is recognized for the excess. Once a loss is recognized, it cannot be reversed.

Research and development (R&D)

Research and development costs are charged to expense when incurred. Although R&D expenditures may result in an intangible asset, such as a patent, being created, the difficulty in identifying the costs associated with different projects and the uncertainties inherent in estimating the magnitude of expected benefits led the FASB to require firms to simply expense these costs.

SFAS No. 2 describes research as a planned search to discover new knowledge that may lead to the development of a new product or service. Development involves translating research findings into a plan for a new product or process, including design and testing phases. Routine alterations to existing products are not considered R&D.

Accounting for R&D

The costs of materials, equipment, facilities, and purchased intangibles are expensed as incurred, unless they have alternative future uses. In that case, they are capitalized and charged to expense as used. Personnel and contract services costs are expensed immediately. Other indirect costs are allocated to R&D on a reasonable basis, except that general and administrative costs usually are not included.

Costs similar to R&D

Other costs that are typically expensed as incurred include start-up costs for a new operation or activity, initial operating losses incurred by development stage entities (SFAS No. 7), advertising costs, and costs of developing products or processes (such as computer software) that will be used in a firm's selling and administrative activities.

Financial statement presentation and disclosure requirements for intangibles

On the balance sheet, goodwill should be separately reported and all other intangible assets in the aggregate should, at a minimum, be separately reported. Unlike PP&E, accumulated amortization is normally not separately presented in the balance sheet for intangibles. All amortization charges and impairment losses should be reported as part of income from continuing operations, except for goodwill impairments related to discontinued operations. Disclosure of the following items in the footnotes is required for all intangibles subject to amortization:

- The gross carrying amount and accumulated amortization in total and by major intangible class
- Amortization expense for the periods presented
- Estimated amounts of amortization for each of the five succeeding years

For intangibles not subject to amortization, the total amount and the amounts by major class should be disclosed. Changes in goodwill during the period must also be disclosed, including the amount acquired and the amount of impairment losses recognized.

Current Liabilities

According to SFAC No. 6, **liabilities** are the "probable future sacrifices of economic benefits arising from present obligations of a particular entity to transfer assets or provide services to other entities in the future as a result of past transactions or events." According to the AICPA's Accounting Research Bulletin (ARB) No. 43, **current liabilities** are "obligations whose liquidation is reasonably expected to require use of existing resources properly classified as current assets, or the creation of other current liabilities."

Types of current liabilities

Figure 2-152 shows the types of current liabilities covered in this section.

Figure 2-152: Current Liabilities

Accounts payable	Taxes payable from operations
Notes payable	▪ Sales taxes payable
▪ Interest-bearing	▪ Income taxes payable
▪ Zero-interest-bearing	Employee-related liabilities
Current maturities of long-term debt	▪ Payroll deductions
	▪ Compensated absences
Short-term obligations to be refinanced*	▪ Bonus obligations
Dividends payable	Estimated liabilities
Returnable deposits and advances	▪ Property taxes payable
Unearned or deferred revenues	

* Must show intent and ability to refinance obligation on long-term basis

Accounts payable

Accounts payable are amounts owed to suppliers for goods purchased on credit. A discount may be allowed for early payment, based on the invoice terms. Cash discounts, expressed in terms such as 2/10 net 30, were covered previously under accounts receivable. Accounts payable should be recorded when title to the goods passes or the services have been received, so special attention must be paid to transactions near the end of the accounting period. Accounts payable are easily valued at the amount owed.

Notes payable

Notes payable are more-formal, written agreements to pay a certain sum on a certain date. Notes can be short- or long-term, interest-bearing or zero-interest-bearing.

- **Interest-bearing notes payable**
Interest-bearing notes are recorded as the initial cash received from the lender.

Interest expense and interest payable are recorded ratably over the period during which the note is outstanding. At maturity, the borrower pays back the face value of the note plus interest.

- **Zero-interest-bearing notes payable**

  Zero-interest-bearing notes implicitly carry interest because the lender gives the borrower the present value of the note, which is less than the amount due at maturity. Figure 2-153 shows how the transaction is recorded if a $1,050,000 note payable is signed and the present value of $1,000,000 is received from a lender.

Figure 2-153: Accounting Entry for Zero-Interest-Bearing Notes Payable

Cash	$1,000,000	
Discount on notes payable	$50,000	
Notes payable		$1,050,000
(To record issuance of six-month zero-interest-bearing note to X Bank)		

The discount on notes payable account is used to record the difference between the cash received and the face value of the note. On the balance sheet, notes payable will be reported net of the discount (a contra liability account), as shown in Figure 2-154.

Figure 2-154: Balance Sheet Presentation of Discount

Current liabilities		
Notes payable	$1,050,000	
Less: Discount on notes payable	50,000	1,000,000

Over the term of the note, interest expense will be recorded with an accompanying credit to the discount account. As the contra account is reduced, the net liability is increased and will be equal to the face value by the maturity date.

Current maturities of long-term debt

Current maturities of long-term debts represent the portion of long-term liabilities, such as mortgages, that will become payable within the next year. The balance of these liabilities that is not maturing currently would be reported as a long-term liability. Also included with current liabilities would be debts that are callable on demand within one year. On the other hand, liabilities that are not expected to use current assets are not reported in the current liability section. Examples include debt to be retired using assets accumulated in a long-term asset account, debt to be refinanced on a long-term basis, and debt to be converted into capital stock.

Short-term obligations expected to be refinanced

If a company intends to refinance a short-term obligation and demonstrates the ability to do this by having a refinancing agreement with clear terms, then the debt can be reported in the long-term liability section, according to SFAS No. 6. As the FASB works to converge U.S. GAAP with international standards, firms will be required to have entered into a refinancing agreement by the balance sheet date before reclassification of the debt is permitted.

If the short-term debt is greater than the financing in place or arranged, only the portion of the debt that will be covered by the arrangement may be classified as long-term debt.

Dividends payable

When a cash or property dividend is declared by the board of directors, it is recorded as a current liability and a reduction to retained earnings. When the dividend is paid, the liability is eliminated. Stock dividends do not lead to the creation of liabilities, because a firm's own equity securities, rather than its assets, will be transferred. Preferred stock dividends in arrears are not considered a liability until declared.

Returnable deposits and advances

Returnable cash deposits received from customers or employees are recorded as a liability, which may be classified as either current or noncurrent depending on when it is expected to be repaid. Such deposits might be made to cover performance or property loss or damage, for example.

Unearned or deferred revenues

Unearned or deferred revenues include prepayments for goods or services that the company is obligated to provide in the future. Cash received in advance for magazine subscriptions, airline tickets, or gift certificates would fall in this category. When the cash is received, the unearned revenue account is credited; when the service or product is actually delivered, the unearned revenue is debited and revenue is credited.

Taxes payable from operations

Taxes payable from operations include sales taxes and income taxes. Property taxes payable are discussed later.

- **Sales taxes payable**
  Sales tax is collected from customers and, before the tax is remitted to the government, would be reported as a liability. If the amount owed the government differs from the amount recorded as sales taxes payable, a gain or loss is recognized. If sales taxes are not separately recorded at the time of sale, an adjusting entry must be made later to reduce the sales account for the amount of the tax and credit sales taxes payable.

- **Income taxes payable**
  Corporate income taxes are computed based upon the income reported on state and federal tax returns. The amount due is classified as a current liability until paid. If additional taxes from a prior year are assessed, income taxes payable is credited and

current income is debited. Differences in measuring income for tax reporting and financial reporting lead to recording liabilities or assets for deferred income taxes.

Employee-related liabilities

Employee-related current liabilities include payroll deductions and accruals for compensated absences, retirement benefits, and bonus obligations.

- **Payroll deductions**

  Payroll deductions include taxes, union dues, insurance premiums, employee savings plans, and other amounts that the employee agrees to have (or is legally obligated to have) withheld. If such amounts have not yet been remitted to the entities owed by the end of the accounting period, they are considered current liabilities. In addition to payroll taxes withheld from the employee's paycheck, the employer also has current liabilities for matching Social Security taxes and unemployment taxes.

- **Compensated absences**

  Compensated absences include paid days off for vacations, holidays, or sick days. Such absences are recognized as an expense and a related liability in the year that the benefits are earned, as long as the obligation is attributable to services already rendered, payment is probable, the obligation relates to rights that accumulate or vest, and the amount of the liability can be reasonably estimated. Accumulated rights are those that, if not used, can be carried forward to later periods. Vested rights are those that must be paid even if employment is terminated. Under SFAS No. 43, firms are required to accrue vacation days earned and have the option of recording sick days earned. The FASB has made an exception for sick days because payment is not considered probable (because sickness may not occur).

  The accrual can be made either using the employee's current rate of pay or a projected future rate. If the pay rate used for the accrual differs from the rate in effect when the days are used, the difference is expensed in the period in which the days are used.

- **Bonus obligations**

  Bonuses payable to employees are considered a form of additional wages. When earned, they are recorded as an operating expense and a current liability.

Warranties, premiums, and coupons

Based on the matching principle, costs associated with certain product warranties and with coupon and premium offers are reported as expenses and liabilities in the period in which the related product is sold. Experience serves as a basis for developing estimates of the expected costs of repairing or replacing products covered under warranty. Similarly, the expected cost of fulfilling offers like cash rebates or delivering premiums in exchange for box tops or wrappers is estimated. When the product under warranty is actually repaired, the cash rebate paid, or the premium delivered, the estimated liability is reduced. Warranties are a type of loss contingency (discussed later in this topic).

Accounting for warranty costs. There are two basic ways to account for warranty costs, cash basis and accrual basis, and of the accrual basis, there are two methods, the expense warranty approach and the sales warranty approach.

- **Cash basis**

  When it is improbable that a liability has been incurred or if the liability is not reasonably estimable, the cash basis method is required. This method is optional if warranty costs are immaterial or the warranty period is brief. In this method, no warranty liability is recognized in the period of sale and warranty costs are charged during the period in which the warranty is exercised. The cash basis is the only method allowed for income taxes.

- **Accrual basis**

  Accrual basis is required when it is probable that some amount of warranty claims will be exercised and the firm can make a reasonable estimate of the costs.

  - **Expense warranty approach**

    The expense warranty approach makes an estimate of the warranty expense during the year of the sale. For example, a cash register company sells 1,200 Type A cash registers during a year (Year 1) for $1,000 each with a one-year warranty. They have determined from past warranty claims that approximately $40/unit will go toward warranty expense. During Year 1, they incur $20,000 in actual warranty costs, and, during Year 2, they anticipate incurring an additional $28,000 in actual warranty costs related to Year 1 sales of Type A cash registers. In Year 1, the sale would be recorded as follows:

Figure 2-155: Accounting Entry for Expense Warranty Approach

Cash or accounts receivable	$1,200,000	
Sales		$1,200,000

The warranty expense would also be recognized in Year 1:

Figure 2-156: Accounting Entry for Expense Warranty Approach

Warranty expense	$20,000	
Cash, inventory, accrued payroll		$20,000
To recognize warranty costs incurred		
Warranty expense	$28,000	
Estimated liability under warranties		$28,000
To accrue estimated warranty costs		

The Year 1 balance sheet would include this $28,000 as an estimated liability under warranty under current liabilities, whereas the Year 1 income statement would record warranty expense of $48,000. In Year 2, warranty costs on Type A units sold in Year 1 would be recognized, and after the warranty period expires, any difference between the estimate and the actual expense is netted out of the estimated liabilities under warranties account.

Sales warranty approach

The sales warranty approach is used when the warranty (or extended warranty) is sold separately from the item. In this method, the item and the warranty are recorded separately. Sales revenue from selling the extended warranty is deferred and is usually recognized on a straight-line basis over the life of the warranty. Commissions and other costs that vary directly with the sale of the warranty are also deferred and amortized. Costs that would be incurred regardless of the sale such as salaries are expensed in the period incurred.

If the cash register company mentioned previously also offers an extended warranty on its Type A registers for an additional two years for $100 and it sells 100 of these in Year 1, the sale of the cash registers and the additional warranties are accounted for as follows:

Figure 2-157: Accounting Entry for Sales Warranty Approach

Cash or Accounts Receivable	$1,210,000	
Sales		$1,200,000
Unearned Warranty Revenue		$10,000

At the end of Years 2 and 3 (the period in which the extended warranty begins), warranty revenue is recognized using straight-line amortization ($10,000/2 = $5,000 per year).

Figure 2-158: Accounting Entry for Sales Warranty Approach

Unearned warranty revenue	$5,000	
Warranty revenue		$5,000

The exception to the use of straight-line amortization is if the costs to be recognized fall in a predictable but irregular pattern, in which case the revenue is recognized in proportion to the costs expected to be incurred.

Valuing current liabilities

In theory, liabilities should be valued at the present value of future cash flows. However, current liabilities are typically recorded at their maturity or face amount, because the difference between this amount and the present value is rarely material.

Contingent liabilities and commitments

According to SFAS No. 5 (par. 1), a contingency is "an existing condition, situation, or set of circumstances involving uncertainty as to possible gain (gain contingency) or loss (loss contingency) to an enterprise that will ultimately be resolved when one or more future events occur or fail to occur."

Accounting for gain contingencies

Gain contingencies result if there is a possibility that an entity will receive assets (or reduce its debt) as a result of the receipts of gifts, donations, bonuses; disputed tax amounts; pending court cases (where the company is expected to receive a settlement); or tax loss carry-forwards. Gain contingencies are not recorded in the accounts but may be disclosed in the notes to the financial statements if it is likely that a material gain will occur.

Accounting for loss contingencies

Loss contingencies result when existing situations have the potential to lead to future losses. A **contingent liability** is recorded when it is probable a liability has been incurred as of the financial statement date and the amount of the loss can be reasonably estimated. According to SFAS No. 5, contingent losses are not recorded but are disclosed in the notes to the financial statements when occurrence of the loss is considered only "reasonably possible" rather than "probable" or when the amount of a probable loss cannot be reasonably estimated. Losses with only a "remote" chance of occurring, or those whose amount is immaterial, need not be disclosed.

Types of loss contingencies include the risk of uncollectibility of receivables, warranty obligations, premiums, pending litigation, threatened expropriation of assets, pending claims or assessments, agreements to repurchase sold receivables, and guarantees of the indebtedness of others. Some contingencies, like the risk of uncollectible accounts and the threatened expropriation of assets, result in the reduction of an asset rather than the incurrence of a liability. General business risks and the risks of losses from fires, explosions, and other natural and workplace hazards are not considered contingencies, because an event triggering the possibility of loss has not yet occurred.

Financial statement presentation and disclosure requirements for current liabilities

Financial statement presentation of current liabilities

Current liabilities are usually reported in financial statements at their maturity value. They are presented on the balance sheet in order of liquidation preference or in order of maturity. An example of current liabilities on a balance sheet is presented in Figure 2-159.

Figure 2-159: Current Liabilities on the Balance Sheet

Bounce Sporting Goods Company		
	Current Year	Prior Year
Current liabilities		
Short-term borrowings	$4,214	$18,353
Accounts payable	1,929,825	1,268,743
Accrued payroll-related liabilities	1,331,374	808,778
Accrued liabilities	2,883,832	2,075,038
Deferred service revenues	1,080,614	678,315
Income taxes payable	1,031,201	482,920
Note payable	60,000	102,400
Total current liabilities	$8,321,060	$5,434,547

Supplemental information should be provided to grant full disclosure of current liabilities. Liabilities secured with collateral and the related collateral should be identified. Current liabilities should not be netted against assets intended to be used in their liquidation.

Financial statement presentation of loss contingencies

Disclosure of a loss contingency in the notes to the financial statements is illustrated in Figure 2-160.

Figure 2-160: Disclosure of Loss Contingency

XYZ Corporation

Note 1: Litigation. XYZ is a defendant or codefendant in a substantial number of lawsuits alleging wrongful injury and/or death from rupture of silicone breast implants. The following table summarizes the activity in these lawsuits:

Claims	
Pending at beginning of year	7,411
Received during year	3,775
Settled or otherwise disposed of	(1,213)
Pending at end of year	9,973
Average indemnification cost	$3,826
Average cost per case, including defense costs	$6,459
Trial activity	
Verdicts for the company	32
Total trials	46

The following table presents the cost of defending silicone breast implant litigation, together with related insurance and workers' compensation expenses.

Included in operating profit	$1,572,480
Nonoperating expense	7,624,680
Total	$9,197,160

The company is seeking to reasonably determine its liability. However, it is not possible to predict which theory of insurance will apply, the number of lawsuits still to be filed, the cost of settling and defending the existing and unfiled cases, or the ultimate impact of these lawsuits on the company's consolidated financial statements.

Long-Term Liabilities and Bonds Payable

Long-term liabilities are those that will not be paid with current assets, or, in other words, those that are expected to be paid after one year or the operating cycle, whichever is longer. Bonds payable and notes payable are common types of long-term liabilities.

Valuation of and accounting for long-term notes payable

Like short-term notes payable, long-term notes payable have a set maturity date and either a stated or implicit interest rate. Unlike short-term debt, which may be recorded at maturity amount, long-term liabilities are valued at the present value of their future cash flows, including payments for both interest and principal. Accounting for long-term notes payable mirrors accounting for long-term notes receivable, which was presented earlier. In this section we review the terminology related to notes. We will examine accounting for bonds payable, which is similar to accounting for notes, in a subsequent section.

- **Notes issued at face value**
  When a note is issued at face value, the stated interest rate and the effective interest rate are the same. The note is recorded at its face amount; no discount is recorded. Interest paid on the note (determined by multiplying the face value times the stated rate) is recorded as interest expense, which is recognized as time passes. For example, if a $24,000 8% note payable was issued on August 1, 2005, with the first interest payment due on August 1, 2006, the adjusting entry on December 31, 2005, would record an $800 debit to interest expense and credit to interest payable:

$$\frac{\$24,000 \times 8\%}{\left(\frac{12 \text{ Months}}{5 \text{ Months}}\right)} = \$800$$

- **Notes not issued at face value**
  Notes not issued at face value have a stated rate that is different than the effective rate. One example would be a zero-interest-bearing note, which has a stated rate of zero. The amount of interest paid on these notes is based upon the stated rate, whereas the amount of interest expense recorded is based upon the effective, or imputed, rate. The effective rate is the rate that discounts the maturity amount and/or periodic payments to equal the amount borrowed.

- **Imputed interest**
  Notes payable with rates substantially different than market rates have their rate imputed. See the section on accounts payable for a discussion of imputed interest.

- **Notes issued for property, goods, and services**
  The value of a note issued for cash is readily determinable. However, this is not always the case when a note is issued in exchange for noncash assets or services. The stated rate on such notes is assumed to be fair unless the note has no stated interest rate, the stated rate is unreasonable, or the face amount of the note differs materially from the fair value of the assets or services for which it is exchanged. In that case, the note would be valued based upon the fair value of the noncash consideration for which it is exchanged. If the fair value of that consideration is not readily determinable, the note would be valued by discounting its cash flows at an imputed

interest rate. An imputed rate is determined by estimating what rate the borrower would be expected to pay for a similar type of debt instrument.

Mortgage notes payable

Mortgages are a common type of secured note payable that use property as collateral. Mortgages are either payable in full at maturity or payable in installments. Points paid by the borrower at the inception of the loan reduce the amount of cash borrowed and thus increase the effective rate. Mortgages may be issued with either a fixed rate or a variable (floating) rate. The rate charged on variable rate mortgages fluctuates in tandem with a benchmark interest rate such as the prime rate.

Mortgage notes payable at maturity are reported as long-term liabilities until the year prior to when they become due. If the mortgage is payable in installments, the principal amount of the payments due within the upcoming year would be reported as a current liability and the remainder as a long-term liability.

Off-balance-sheet financing

Over the years, the financial community has developed various types of financing arrangements that enable companies to finance certain types of assets in a manner that permits both the assets and the related liabilities to be omitted from the balance sheet. Such transactions, which include certain operating leases and other transactions, are commonly referred to as off-balance-sheet financing. Changes made to the SEC disclosure requirements after passage of the Sarbanes-Oxley Act require all off-balance-sheet financing to be disclosed by public companies.

Project financing arrangements are a common form of off-balance-sheet financing and are typically accomplished as follows:

- Two or more entities create a new entity for the sole purpose of constructing an operating plant to be used by both entities.

- The new entity borrows funds for the project and pays the debt back using completed project funds.

- The original entities secure the debt with guarantees.

This approach keeps the liability for the funds borrowed on the books of the separate entity rather than on the books of the investing entities. As a result, the companies initiating the project financing arrangement will have balance sheets that look more favorable. They are required to disclose only the loan guarantees.

Enron used a considerable amount of off-balance-sheet financing, which led to one of the largest bankruptcies on record. In response to the Sarbanes-Oxley Act of 2002, the SEC required increased disclosures in the management's discussion and analysis section of the annual report, including tabular disclosure of all contractual obligations and disclosure of contingent liabilities and commitments. (SEC reporting requirements are covered in detail in the next topic of this section of the CMA Learning System.)

Types of bonds

Bonds are long-term debt arrangements usually requiring the approval of the board of directors and involving covenants and restrictions for the protection of both the lender and the borrower. By issuing bonds, a borrower can obtain more cash than a single lender is able to supply. Once issued, bonds can be traded on an active bond market. The fair value of the bonds will fluctuate in this secondary market depending on the current market rate for instruments of similar risk. General economic conditions as well as perceptions about the borrower's level of risk will lead to value changes over time. For accounting purposes, however, the issuer of a bond payable does not recognize fair value changes until the period in which the bond is redeemed.

Some of the different types of bonds are listed below:

- **Secured and unsecured bonds**
  Secured bonds are backed by collateral such as real estate (mortgage bonds) or stocks and bonds of other corporations (collateral trust bonds). Unsecured bonds, or debenture bonds, are backed only by the word of the issuer.

- **Deep-discount bonds**
  Deep-discount bonds are zero-interest debenture bonds that sell at a discount from face value.

- **Callable bonds**
  Callable bonds have an option that allows the issuer to buy back the bonds at a call price set one or two percentage points above the par value (for example, at 101 or 102). A firm issuing a callable bond has three options: wait until maturity to pay off or retire the bonds; buy them on the open market if the market price is less than the call price; or call them at the specified call price. A company may issue such bonds when interest rates are higher in hopes that they can retire the debt early and issue new bonds at a more favorable rate. The gain or loss on early retirement of the debt is recorded as other income (loss) on the income statement. For example, if a firm had issued $400 million in bonds callable at 101 that had an unamortized discount of $20 million at a time when the market price was 103, the gain or loss is calculated as shown in Figure 2-161:

Figure 2-161: Gain or Loss on Retiring a Callable Bond Early

Retire on Open Market	(in millions)	Retire by Calling	(in millions)
Par value of bonds being retired	$400	Par value of bonds being retired	$400
– Unamortized discount	– $20	– Unamortized discount	– $20
Carrying value of the bonds	$380	Carrying value of the bonds	$380
– Market price ($400 × 1.03)	– $412	– Call price ($400 × 1.01)	– $404
Loss on retirement of bonds payable	($32)		($24)

- **Other bond terminology**

  Bonds that all mature on the same date are called term bonds, and those that mature in installments are called serial bonds. Some bonds are convertible into the issuer's stock at the option of the investor (as we will discuss next).

Impact of convertible bonds

Convertible bonds are debt instruments that can be converted into a specific number of shares of common stock (equity). The issuer has the advantage of issuing the debt for lower interest rates than a straight debt issue would require and also limits the potential dilution of stock over a straight equity issuance. For example, to raise $5 million, a company with stock currently selling for $60 per share would need to issue more than 83,333 shares (more than this much because of issuance costs); if the company could sell 2,500 bonds at $2,000 par convertible into 30 shares of common stock apiece, it would only risk diluting equity by up to 75,000 shares. The following accounting for convertible bonds is from the perspective of the issuer.

Issuance of convertible bonds

The bond is recorded as a straight debt issuance with none of the amount being recorded as equity. Discounts and premiums are amortized to their maturity date as shown elsewhere in this section.

Conversion of convertible bonds

Accounting for conversion can be difficult because common stock or other equity securities fluctuate in value. The GAAP practice for recording the conversion is called the **book value method**. This method recognizes no gain or loss upon conversion because at issuance the firm agreed either to pay the value of the bond at maturity or to issue a specific number of shares.

Note that the paid-in capital in excess of par is calculated as the bonds payable plus the premium on bonds payable (or less a discount) less the par value of the common stock. This is done because no gain or loss is recognized on the conversion. The market value of the bond and the market value of the stock are not considered under this method.

Valuation of and accounting for bonds

Prior to issuing bonds, the company establishes a maturity value (also known as par value, face value, or principal amount) and stated interest rate (also known as the coupon or nominal rate). The issuer will pay annual interest on the bond equal to the stated rate multiplied by the face value of the bonds. This interest may be paid semiannually, annually, or quarterly.

However, between the time the bonds are printed and finally come to market, the market interest rate for similar debt may have changed. Alternately, bonds can be planned to be issued at a discount or premium such as if management wanted to set a specific interest rate. In the case of either a timing difference or management choice to issue bonds not at par, investors will pay more (bonds are issued at a premium) or less (bonds are issued at a discount) than face value for the bonds, in order to earn the current market rate (also called effective rate or yield). The issue price of a bond is determined by discounting its cash flows (the interest payments calculated at the stated rate and the maturity value) at the effective interest rate. When the effective rate is higher than the stated rate, the bond sells at a discount. When the effective rate is lower than the stated rate, the bond sells at a premium. If the effective rate is equal to the stated rate, the bond sells at par value.

Bonds issued at par on an interest payment date

If a bond is issued at par on an interest payment date, there is no accrued interest and no premium or discount. The issuer debits cash and credits bonds payable for the face amount of the bonds. In subsequent years, the interest expense equals the amount of cash paid.

Bond discounts or premiums

Bonds issued at a premium or discount on an interest payment date

If a $1 million bond was issued at 95 (95% of par value), then the issuer would debit cash for $950,000, credit bonds payable for $1,000,000, and debit discount on bonds payable for $50,000. The discount account is a contra liability, so the net carrying value of the bond at issuance would be $950,000.

If a $1 million bond was issued at 105 (105% of par value), then the issuer would debit cash for $1,050,000, credit bonds payable for $1,000,000, and credit premium on bonds payable for $50,000. The premium account is a liability, so the net carrying value of the bond at issuance would be $1,050,000.

Interest on the bonds would be recorded using either the effective rate method or the straight-line method (if that produces results that are not materially different from the effective rate method). The effective rate method is discussed later in this section, and an amortization schedule is illustrated in Figure 2-168. Under the effective rate method, interest expense recorded is higher than the interest paid and the difference is amortized to the discount on bonds account (a contra liability account).

Bonds issued between interest dates

For simplicity, bond issuers pay a full period's interest to all bond investors on each interest payment date. However an investor that purchased bonds between interest payment dates would not be entitled to a full period's interest. To compensate for this, the investor prepays interest accrued since the last interest payment date at the time the bonds are purchased. The net result is that the investor is left with the amount they are entitled to for the period the bonds were held. If a ten-year, 8%, $1 million bond, with interest payable semiannually on January 1 and July 1, was issued on April 1, Year 1, at par plus accrued interest, the issuer would record the entry shown in Figure 2-162. (Interest payable could also be credited instead of interest expense.)

Figure 2-162: Issuance of Bonds Between Interest Dates

Cash	$1,020,000	
Bonds payable		$1,000,000
Bond interest expense ($1,000,000 × 0.08 × $\frac{3}{12}$)		$20,000

When the issuer pays interest on July 1, the entry in Figure 2-163 would be recorded:

Figure 2-163: Entry at Interest Payment Date

Bond interest expense	$40,000	
Cash		$40,000

Interest expense would therefore be $20,000 ($40,000 minus $20,000) for the three months the bonds were actually outstanding. If the same bond had been issued at 95 instead of at par, the entry would be as shown in Figure 2-164:

Figure 2-164: Issuance of Bonds at 95, Between Interest Dates

Cash	$970,000	
[($1,000,000 × 0.95) + ($1,000,000 × 0.08 × $\frac{3}{12}$)]		
Discount on bonds payable ($1,000,000 × 0.05)	$50,000	
Bonds payable		$1,000,000
Bond interest expense		$20,000

Effective interest rate method

The effective rate method is the preferred method for computing bond interest expense and amortizing bond discounts and premiums. Under the effective rate method, interest expense is calculated by multiplying the effective rate by the carrying value of the debt at the beginning of the period. (Note that because interest rates are stated in annual terms, they must be adjusted if interest is paid more than once a year. Thus, an 8% annual rate translates to a 4% semiannual rate or a 2% quarterly rate.) The difference between bond interest paid (face value times the stated rate) and bond interest expense (beginning carrying value times effective rate) is the amount of discount or premium amortized. So the amount of discount or premium amortization can be expressed as follows:

Amortization Amount

= (Carrying Value of Bonds at Start of Period × Effective Interest Rate)

– (Face Amount of Bonds × Stated Interest Rate)

In the effective rate method, interest expense is a constant percentage of the bond's carrying value. If the bond was issued at a discount, the carrying value and interest expense will both increase over time. Conversely, if the bond was issued at a premium, the carrying value and interest expense will both decrease over the term of the bond. In contrast, the straight-line method would assign the same amount of interest expense to each period. Regardless of whether the effective rate or straight-line method is used to compute interest expense, over the life of the bond, the same total amount of expense will be reported.

The time value of money tables in figures 2-165 and 2-166 will be used in the examples below.

Figure 2-165: Present Value of 1 (Present Value of a Single Sum)

$$PV_{n,i} = \frac{1}{(1+i)^n} = (1+i)^{-n}$$

(n) Periods	4%	5%	6%
1	.96154	.95238	.94340
2	.92456	.90703	.89000
3	.88900	.86384	.83962
4	.85480	.82270	.79209
5	.82193	.78353	.74726
6	.79031	.74622	.70496
7	.75992	.71068	.66506
8	.73069	.67684	.62741
9	.70259	.64461	.59190
10	.67556	.61391	.55839

Figure 2-166: Present Value of an Ordinary Annuity of 1

$$PV\text{-}OA_{n,i} = \frac{1 - \dfrac{1}{(1+i)^n}}{i}$$

(n) Periods	4%	5%	6%
1	.96154	.95238	.94340
2	1.88609	1.85941	1.83339
3	2.77509	2.72325	2.67301
4	3.62990	3.54595	3.46511
5	4.95182	4.32948	4.21236
6	5.24214	5.07569	4.91732
7	6.00205	5.78637	5.58238
8	6.73274	6.46321	6.20979
9	7.43533	7.10782	6.80169
10	8.11090	7.72173	7.36009

Bonds issued at a discount

If a five-year, $100,000, 9% bond payable with semiannual interest dates is issued at a 12% effective rate, the issue price is calculated as shown in Figure 2-167. Note that the five-year bond that pays semiannual interest includes ten interest payment dates, so the present value is determined using ten periods. The effective rate and stated rate are also adjusted to reflect semiannual interest rates.

Figure 2-167: Computation of Discount on Bonds Payable

Maturity value of bonds payable		$100,000.00
Present value of $100,000 due in 5 years at 12%, interest payable semiannually; FV(PV$_{10,\,6\%}$); ($100,000 × .55839)	$55,839.00	
Present value of $4,500 interest payable semiannually for 5 years at 12% annually; R(PV–OA$_{10,\,6\%}$); ($4,500 × 7.36009)	33,120.41	
Proceeds from sale of bonds		88,959.41
Discount on bonds payable		$11,040.59

The amortization schedule for the bond is shown in Figure 2-168. Based upon the table amounts computed for each interest payment date, the issuer would record a credit to cash, a debit to interest expense, and a credit to discount on bonds payable. (Note: A company with a December 31 year-end would have to accrue interest prior to the scheduled January 1 payment date, and in this adjusting entry would credit interest payable rather than cash for the amount payable.)

Figure 2-168: Bond Discount Amortization Schedule

**Schedule of Bond Discount Amortization, Effective Yield Method—
Semiannual Interest Payments (5-Year 9% Bonds Sold to Yield 12%)**

Date	Cash Paid	Interest Expense	Discount Amortized	Carrying Amount of Bonds
1/1/Y1				$88,959.41
7/1/Y1	$4,500 [a]	$5,337.56 [b]	$837.56 [c]	89,796.97 [d]
1/1/Y2	4,500	5,387.82	887.82	90,684.79
7/1/Y2	4,500	5,441.09	941.09	91,625.88
1/1/Y3	4,500	5,497.55	997.55	92,623.43
7/1/Y3	4,500	5,557.41	1,057.41	93,680.84
1/1/Y4	4,500	5,620.85	1,120.85	94,801.69
7/1/Y4	4,500	5,688.10	1,188.10	95,989.79
1/1/Y5	4,500	5,759.39	1,259.39	97,249.18
7/1/Y5	4,500	5,834.95	1,334.95	98,584.13
1/1/Y6	4,500	5,915.05	1,415.87 *	100,000.00
	$45,000	$56,039.77	$11,039.77	

[a] $4,500 = $100,000 × .09 × 6/12
[b] $5,337.56 = $88,959.41 × .12 × 6/12
[c] $837.56 = $5,337.56 − $4,500
[d] $89,796.97 = $88,959.41 + $837.56

* Note: The final discount amortized was adjusted for rounding errors in order to make the carrying amount of the bond equal to the bond's maturity value.

Bonds issued at a premium

If the five-year, 9%, $100,000 bond is instead issued at an effective rate of 8%, the premium is calculated as in Figure 2-169.

Figure 2-169: Calculation of Premium on Bonds Payable

Maturity value of bonds payable		$100,000.00
Present value of $100,000 due in 5 years at 8%, interest payable semiannually; FV(PV10, 4%); ($100,000 × .67556)	$67,556.00	
Present value of $4,500 interest payable semiannually for 5 years at 8% annually; R(PV–OA10, 4%); ($4,500 × 8.11090)	36,499.05	
Proceeds from sale of bonds		104,055.05
Premium on bonds payable		$4,055.05

The premium amortization schedule for the bond appears in Figure 2-170. Based upon the table amounts computed for each interest payment date, the issuer would record a credit to cash, a debit to interest expense, and a debit to premium on bonds payable. (Note: A company with a December 31 year-end would have to accrue interest prior to the scheduled January 1 payment date, and in this adjusting entry the company would credit interest payable rather than cash for the amount payable.)

Figure 2-170: Bond Premium Amortization Schedule

Schedule of Bond Premium Amortization
Effective Yield Method—Semiannual Interest Payments
5-Year 9% Bonds Sold to Yield 8%

Date	Cash Paid	Interest Expense	Premium Amortized	Carrying Amount of Bonds
1/1/Y1				$104,055.05
7/1/Y1	$4,500 [a]	$4,162.20 [b]	$337.80 [c]	103,717.25 [d]
1/1/Y2	4,500	4,148.69	351.31	103,365.94
7/1/Y2	4,500	4,134.64	365.36	103,000.58
1/1/Y3	4,500	4,120.02	379.98	102,620.60
7/1/Y3	4,500	4,104.82	395.18	102,225.42
1/1/Y4	4,500	4,089.02	410.98	101,814.44
7/1/Y4	4,500	4,072.58	427.42	101,387.02
1/1/Y5	4,500	4,055.48	444.52	100,942.50
7/1/Y5	4,500	4,037.70	462.30	100,480.20
1/1/Y6	4,500	4,019.21	480.20 *	100,000.00
	$45,000	$40,944.36	$4,055.64	

[a] $4,500 = $100,000 × .09 × 6/12
[b] $4,162.20 = $104,055.05 × .08 × 6/12
[c] $337.80 = $4,500 − $4,162.20
[d] $103,717.25 = $104,055.05 − $337.80

* Note: The final discount amortized was adjusted for rounding errors in order to make the carrying amount of the bond equal to the bond's maturity value.

Discount and premium classification

On the balance sheet, the bond is reported at its carrying value, which is the face amount less any discount or plus any premium. The discount and premium accounts are considered contra and adjunct liability accounts respectively.

Financial statement presentation and disclosure requirements for notes and bonds

Long-term debts maturing within a year are classified as current liabilities, whereas all other long-term debts are noncurrent or long-term liabilities. Entities with large numbers of debt securities will often report an aggregate amount on the balance sheet and attach a breakdown in a supporting schedule. Figure 2-171 shows an example of several disclosures for long-term liabilities (current year is Year 2).

**Figure 2-171: Disclosure of Long-Term Obligations for
K-V Pharmaceutical Co. (dates genericized) (continued on next page)**

K-V Pharmaceutical Company—LONG-TERM DEBT
Long-term debt as of March 31, Year 3, consists of:

	Year 3	Year 2
Building mortgages	$43,000	$10,740
Convertible notes	200,000	200,000
	$243,000	$210,740
Less current portion	(1,681)	(973)
	$241,319	$209,767

As of March 31, Year 3, the Company has credit agreements with two banks that provide revolving lines of credit for borrowing up to $140,000. The credit agreements provide for $80,000 in revolving lines of credit along with supplemental credit lines of $60,000 that are available for financing acquisitions. These credit facilities expire in October Year 3 and June Year 3, respectively. The revolving and supplemental credit lines are unsecured and interest is charged at the lower of the prime rate or the one-month LIBOR rate plus 175 basis points. At March 31, Year 3, the Company had $3,900 in an open letter of credit issued under the revolving credit line and no cash borrowings under either credit facility. The credit agreements contain financial covenants that impose minimum levels of earnings before interest, taxes, depreciation and amortization, a maximum funded debt ratio, a limit on capital expenditures and dividend payments, a minimum fixed charge coverage ratio, and a maximum senior leverage ratio.

In March Year 3, the Company entered into a $43,000 mortgage loan agreement with one of its primary lenders, in part, to refinance $9,859 of existing mortgages. The $32,764 of net proceeds the Company received from the new mortgage loan will be used for working capital and general corporate purposes. The new mortgage loan, which is secured by three of the Company's buildings, bears interest at a rate of 5.91% and matures on April 1, Year 16.

On May 16, Year 0, the Company issued $200,000 principal amount of Convertible Subordinated Notes (the "Notes") that are convertible, under certain circumstances, into shares of Class A common stock at an initial conversion price of $23.01 per share. The Notes, which are due May 16, year 31, bear interest that is payable on May 16 and November 16 of each year at a rate of 2.50% per annum. The Company also is obligated to pay contingent interest at a rate equal to 0.5% per annum during any six-month period from May 16 to November 15 and from November 16 to May 15, with the initial six-month period commencing Year 3, if the average trading price of the Notes per $1,000 principal amount for the five trading day period ending on the third trading day immediately preceding the first day of the applicable six-month period equals $1,200 or more. As this contingent interest feature is based on the underlying trading price of the Notes, the contingent interest meets the criteria of and qualifies as an embedded derivative. At the time of issuance and at March 31, Year 3, management determined that the fair value of this contingent interest embedded derivative was de minimis and, accordingly, no value has been assigned to this embedded derivative.

The Company may redeem some or all of the Notes at any time on or after May 21, Year 3, at a redemption price, payable in cash, of 100% of the principal amount of the Notes, plus accrued and unpaid interest, including contingent interest, if any. Holders may require the Company to repurchase all or a portion of their Notes on May 16, Year 5, Year 8, Year 13, Year 18 and Year 23 or upon a change in control, as defined in the indenture governing the Notes, at a purchase price, payable in cash, of 100% of the principal amount of the Notes, plus accrued and unpaid interest, including contingent interest, if any.

**Figure 2-171: Disclosure of Long-Term Obligations for
K-V Pharmaceutical Co. (dates genericized) (concluded)**

The Notes are subordinate to all of our existing and future senior obligations. The net proceeds to the Company were approximately $194,200, after deducting underwriting discounts, commissions and offering expenses. The Notes are convertible, at the holders' option, into shares of the Company's Class A common stock prior to the maturity date under the following circumstances:

- during any quarter commencing after June 30, Year 0, if the closing sale price of the Company's Class A common stock over a specified number of trading days during the previous quarter is more than 120% of the conversion price of the Notes on the last trading day of the previous quarter. The Notes are initially convertible at a conversion price of $23.01 per share, which is equal to a conversion rate of approximately 43.4594 shares per $1,000 principal amount of Notes;
- if the Company has called the Notes for redemption;
- during the five trading day period immediately following any nine consecutive day trading period in which the trading price of the Notes per $1,000 principal amount for each day of such period was less than 95% of the product of the closing sale price of our Class A common stock on that day and the number of shares of our Class A common stock issuable upon conversion of $1,000 principal amount of the Notes; or
- upon the occurrence of specified corporate transactions.

The Company has reserved 8,691,880 shares of Class A common stock for issuance in the event the Notes are converted into the Company's common shares.

The Notes, which are unsecured, do not contain any restrictions on the payment of dividends, the incurrence of additional indebtedness or the repurchase of the Company's securities, and do not contain any financial covenants.

The aggregate maturities of long-term debt as of March 31, Year 3, are as follows:

Due in one year	$ 1,681
Due in two years	1,941
Due in three years	2,058
Due in four years	2,182
Due in five years	2,315
Thereafter	$232,824

Weighted average limited partners' units outstanding—dilutive

The Company paid interest, net of capitalized interest, of $4,692 and $4,156 during the years ended March 31, Year 3 and Year 2, respectively. For the year ended March 31, Year 1, the Company paid interest of $3,215.

The notes to financial statements should include all relevant details of the debt securities, including their nature, maturity dates, interest rates, collateral used, and any other restrictions or rights provided such as call provisions. Companies must also disclose five years' worth of future payment information about principal repayment requirements and maturity closures (see bottom of Figure 2-171). All off-balance-sheet financing arrangements such as project financing arrangements must be disclosed in the notes as well. Companies with callable bonds must disclose any bonds that have become callable due to a violation of a debt agreement, including a description of the violated covenants and disclosure of the long-term debt liabilities and their circumstances on an unclassified balance sheet. Firms must also note if any such bonds are classified as noncurrent because the debt violation is likely to be cured.

Other items of note in Figure 2-171 include the following:

- Disclosure of contractual agreements for the firm's various lines of credit and various covenants
- Disclosure of new long-term debt
- Disclosure of potentially dilutive notes convertible into common stock, including discussion of related contingencies and their likely impact
- Disclosure that notes are redeemable and states the rights of holders; the dates listed can be critical because they show when the company could have cash flow issues due to redemption of notes

Early Extinguishment of Debt

When debt is retired at scheduled maturity, any premium or discount will be fully amortized and the carrying amount will equal the face value. As a result, no gain or loss would be recorded. However, when debt is retired prior to scheduled maturity, a gain or loss may result. The gain or loss would be the difference between the carrying value of the debt (including any unamortized premium or discount and issue costs) and the reacquisition price. If the reacquisition price exceeds the carrying value, a loss results; if the carrying value exceeds the reacquisition price, a gain results.

SFAS No. 145 no longer allows classification of gains or losses on the extinguishment of debt to be treated as extraordinary items, although this treatment had previously been required under SFAS No. 4.

An in-substance defeasance is the creation of an irrevocable trust account that contains funds (principal plus interest earned in the trust) sufficient to service the remainder of a debt. In-substance defeasances do not extinguish the liability on the debtor's balance sheet. (No gain or loss is recorded.)

Equity Transactions and Earnings per Share (EPS)

Although equity is dealt with differently for proprietorships and partnerships, this section deals with equity for the most common form of business, the corporate form. This section also deals with earnings per share.

Corporate capital

Equity in a corporation is called corporate capital, stockholders' equity, or shareholders' equity. Corporate capital is made up of capital stock, additional paid-in capital, and retained earnings. Contributed capital, or paid-in capital, is capital stock plus additional paid-in capital, and it represents the total amount paid by investors for equity securities. Retained earnings represents earned capital, which is the result of profitable operations.

Retained earnings are available (some restrictions apply) for shareholder dividends, which provide investors with a return on their investment.

Legal capital is defined as the par value of the capital stock. Par values are nominal amounts printed on the shares, which are unrelated to fair market values. However, an investor that buys stock for less than par value (an infrequent event) will have a contingent liability to the corporation's creditors in the event of bankruptcy. Par values are typically low to avoid this problem. Shares can also be issued without a par value. In that case, a stated value may be assigned to them, which is accounted for similarly to par value but does not trigger the same contingent liability.

Accounting for the issuance of shares of stock

A corporation can issue stock after it has been granted a charter or certificate by the state of incorporation. The corporation can market its shares directly or through an underwriter. When the shares are sold, the corporation records the receipt of cash and the issuance of the shares. Details of specific types of stock issues follow.

Par value stock. When par value stock is sold, the par value is credited to a separate account. Par value accounts are maintained for different classes of stock, like common and preferred. Any amount paid for the shares in excess of par is credited to additional paid-in capital (also called premium on stock). A discount account would be used for shares that sell for less than par.

For example, the accounting entry for an issuance of 1,000 shares of stock with a par value of $6 per share at a total price of $10,000 would be as shown in Figure 2-172.

Figure 2-172: Stock Issuance at Premium

Cash	$10,000	
Common stock		$6,000
Paid-in capital in excess of par (premium on common stock)		$4,000

No-par stock. No-par stock that has no stated value is recorded in a single account at the selling price, with no additional paid-in capital recorded, as illustrated in Figure 2-173.

Figure 2-173: No-Par Stock Issuance

Cash	$10,000	
Common stock		$10,000

No-par stock to which a stated value has been assigned is accounted for similarly to par value stock. The stated value is recorded in the capital stock account and any excess above stated value is recorded in the additional paid-in capital account.

Stock sold on a subscription basis. In cases where investors buy shares on a subscription basis, the purchase price is paid in installments. The shares are not issued until the price is paid in full. On the balance sheet, the amount of subscriptions receivable is reported as a contra equity account, not as an asset account.

Lump-sum sales. When several classes of stock are sold in a package for a lump-sum price, the total received is allocated between the different securities. If the fair values of each class of stock are known, then the allocation is based on relative fair values (the proportional method). The fair market value of each security divided by the aggregate fair market values of all securities determines the proportion of the purchase price assigned to that security, as shown in Figure 2-174, where 10,000 shares of common stock and 5,000 shares of preferred stock are issued for a lump-sum price of $180,000. On that date the common stock was selling for $14 per share and the preferred stock for $10 per share.

Figure 2-174: Proportional Method for Allocation of a Lump-Sum Price

Fair market value of common (10,000 × $14)	=	$140,000
Fair market value of preferred (5,000 × $10)	=	50,000
Aggregate fair market value		$190,000
Allocated to common: $\dfrac{\$140,000}{\$190,000} \times \$180,000$	=	$132,632
Allocated to preferred: $\dfrac{\$50,000}{\$190,000} \times \$180,000$	=	47,368
Total allocation		$180,000

When the fair value of only one security can be determined, that security is recorded at its fair value and the balance of the lump-sum price is allocated to the remaining security (the incremental method). If none of the fair values can be determined, the allocation may be based on an appraisal or estimate.

Stocks issued in noncash transactions. As with all noncash transactions, the value of the exchange is determined by either the market value of the shares issued or the market value of the noncash items received. If neither of the values can be readily determined, an appraisal or estimate is required.

Stock issuance costs. Direct costs of issuing stock reduce the proceeds received from issuance and so are debited to additional paid-in capital (rather than being treated as expenses). These costs include:

- Printing costs.

- Underwriting fees and marketing costs.

- Legal and accounting fees involved in preparing a registration statement.

- Filing fees and exchange listing fees.

- Clerical, administrative, and mailing costs.

Recurring costs such as maintaining records on investors or registrar or agent fees should be expensed in the period incurred.

Companies sometimes wish to make just one registration of new securities even though they do not plan to issue all of the approved shares to the public immediately. This type of situation is called a shelf registration. Companies can request permission from the SEC to obtain a shelf registration. A shelf registration helps reduce the filing costs when more than one issue of stock is planned. The unissued stock is treated as treasury stock unless it is issued at a subsequent date.

Capital stock

Capital stock is divided into common stock and preferred stock unless the entity has only one type of stock, which is always called common stock. Common stock has already been covered (par stock, no-par stock, and so on). Preferred stock characteristics are explained next.

Preferred stock

Preferred stock gains certain preferences compared to common stock, but preferred shareholders do not have the right to vote. Some preferred stock is convertible into common stock, and other preferred stock is callable at a specified price and date. Preferred stock may be issued instead of debt when an entity's debt to equity ratio is too high. Various features of preferred stock are discussed below.

- **Preference to dividends**

  Preferred shareholders are entitled to receive dividends before common shareholders. Before declaring a dividend, the board of directors should confirm that the company has an adequate balance in retained earnings and sufficient cash available to fund the dividend.

  The dividend rate on preferred stock is stated as a percentage of the par value. For example, 10% preferred stock with a par value of $50 will pay an annual dividend of $5 per share if declared by the board of directors. With cumulative preferred stock, if dividends are not declared during a year, these dividends in arrears accumulate and must be paid before dividends can be declared on common stock. Dividends in arrears are not considered a liability but would be disclosed in the notes to financial statements.

  Another type of preferred stock, participating preferred stock, calls for preferred and common shareholders to share in a total dividend declared based upon a stated allocation.

- **Voting rights**

  Preferred stock usually does not allow any voting rights.

- **Preference in liquidation**

  If the corporation is liquidated, assets will be distributed first to creditors, then to preferred stockholders, and lastly to common shareholders. As a result, in a bankruptcy situation, there may be insufficient assets for shareholder distributions.

- **Debt vs. preferred stock**
  Unlike debt, preferred stock has no maturity date and entails no legal obligation for payment. Therefore it is classified as part of stockholders' equity. However, mandatorily redeemable preferred stock must be redeemed on a specific date and so is, in substance, debt rather than equity. Accordingly, SFAS No. 150 requires that such securities be classified as liabilities.

Treasury stock (reacquisition of shares)

Shares that have been issued by a company and are later reacquired are called treasury stock. Shares may be reacquired for the following reasons:

- To reduce the number of stockholders or prevent takeover attempts

- To have shares available for the exercise of employee stock options

- To increase earnings per share and return on equity

- To make a market in the company's stock and so stabilize or increase the stock price

- To distribute cash to shareholders at favorable capital gains rates

Treasury stock is reported as a reduction of stockholders' equity and is not an asset because an entity cannot own itself. Shares held as treasury stock have no voting or dividend rights. Reacquired shares are accounted for by either the cost method or the par value method. The cost method is more commonly used in practice.

- **Cost method**
  In the cost method, the treasury stock account is debited for the cost of the shares reacquired. When treasury shares are subsequently reissued, treasury stock is credited for the cost of the shares, cash is debited for the selling price, and additional paid-in capital from treasury stock is credited for the excess of the cash received over the cost of the shares. If treasury shares are reissued for less than cost, the difference is debited either to additional paid-in capital from treasury stock or to retained earnings. Under the cost method, the reacquisition of 10,000 shares at $9 per share would be recorded as shown in Figure 2-175.

Figure 2-175: Reacquisition of Shares Under Cost Method

Treasury stock	$90,000	
Cash		$90,000

The reissuance of 4,000 of these shares for $11 per share is recorded as follows.

Figure 2-176: Reissuance of Shares Under Cost Method

Cash	$44,000	
Treasury stock (4,000 shares at $9 per share)		$36,000
Additional paid-in capital from treasury stock		$8,000

- **Par (or stated value) method**

  In the par value method, treasury stock is recorded at par value. When shares are reissued, cash is debited for the selling price, treasury stock is credited for the par value of the stock, and additional paid-in capital is credited for the excess.

Retiring treasury stock

Treasury stock actually is included in three accounts: in the treasury stock account at cost (in the cost method), in the common stock account (for the par value), and in additional paid-in capital on common stock (for the amount at which the stock originally sold in excess of par). When the shares are retired, an appropriate amount must be removed from all three accounts. This entry is illustrated in Figure 2-177, which assumes that 10,000 shares of $5 par common stock are retired from the treasury. The shares had originally sold for $8 per share and had been repurchased as treasury stock at $9 per share.

Figure 2-177: Cost Method of Retiring Treasury Stock

Common stock, $5 par	$50,000	
Additional paid-in capital on common stock*	$30,000	
Retained earnings	$10,000	
Treasury stock (10,000 shares at $9 per share)		$90,000

* ($8 – $5) × 10,000 = $30,000

If the par value method is used, the par value of the retired shares in the treasury stock account offsets the capital stock account. The accounting entry appears as follows.

Figure 2-178: Par Value Method of Retiring Treasury Stock

Common stock, $5 par	$50,000	
Treasury stock (10,000 shares at $5 par)		$50,000

Required disclosures for treasury stock

Disclosures are required for each treasury stock transaction. When treasury stock is purchased or sold, companies should disclose the number of shares issued, the number in the treasury, and the number left outstanding. Additionally, if the treasury stock is accounted for under the cost method, the total cost of the treasury stock should be presented as a deduction of total stockholders' equity. If accounted under the par method, the par value of the treasury stock should be presented as a deduction from par value of issued shares of the same class. Additional paid-in capital from the treasury stock is netted with corresponding additional paid-in capital without needing separate disclosure.

Treasury stock being retired can be either an actual retirement, which means the shares were cancelled through formal application, or a constructive retirement, which is a board-authorized retirement without formal cancellation. Constructive retirement method accounting requires disclosure of the number of shares held in treasury.

Paid-in capital

Paid-in capital, or contributed capital, is recorded when capital stock is issued and can be affected by various other transactions, including:

- Sale of treasury stock at above or below cost.

- Revision of the capital structure to absorb a deficit (as in a quasi-reorganization).

- Conversion of convertible bonds or preferred stock to common stock.

Balance sheet presentation of paid-in capital

Capital stock and additional paid-in capital are reported in the stockholders' equity section of the balance sheet. Disclosure should be provided of the rights and privileges of each type of outstanding stock. After being paid in, the funds become part of a common pool for all shareholders and no individual shareholder has any special claim on the amounts paid in. Changes in these account balances during the year are reported in the statement of stockholders' equity. An example of the stockholders' equity section of the balance sheet is shown in Figure 2-179.

Figure 2-179: Contributed Capital

Bounce Sporting Goods Company Contributed Capital For Year Ended December 31, Year 1	
Stockholders' Equity	
Contributed capital:	
Preferred stock, $70 par (9%, cumulative, convertible, 10,000 shares authorized, 5,500 shares issued and outstanding)	$385,000
Common stock, $4 par (70,000 shares authorized, 46,500 shares issued)	186,000
Treasury stock, at cost (1,000 shares common)	(18,400)
Additional paid-in capital	652,093
Total contributed capital	$1,204,693

Retained earnings

Profitable operations are the primary source of retained earnings. In addition to net income and net losses, the other transactions that can affect retained earnings include prior period adjustments (error corrections and certain changes in accounting principle), dividends of all types, some treasury stock transactions, and quasi-reorganizations.

Stock options, warrants, and rights

Stock options, warrants, and rights are call options that give the holder the right to buy shares of stock at a set exercise price. Because these are equity instruments, accounting for them affects paid-in capital.

Shares issued to employees

Shares may be issued to employees who exercise stock options granted to them as a form of additional compensation. Employees can also purchase shares under an employee share purchase plan.

- **Employee stock ownership plans (noncompensatory plans)**
  Employee stock ownership plans (ESOPs), or employee share purchase plans, are intended to raise capital and provide employees with a sense of ownership rather than provide an additional source of compensation. To be considered noncompensatory, such plans should cover substantially all full-time employees and offer only a small discount from market price (comparable to what might be offered to current shareholders). The plan cannot offer any substantive option feature. Without all of these features, a plan cannot be considered noncompensatory. No compensation expense is recorded; the sale of the shares is recorded as for any other sale of stock.

  Disclosures required for ESOPs include a description of the plan, the basis for making contributions, covered groups, and any notes to help comparability between periods. Significant accounting policies, compensation cost recognized, any repurchase obligations (at aggregate fair value), and the fair value of any unearned compensation must also be disclosed.

- **Equity share options**
  According to SFAS No. 123 (revised), at the date that stock options are granted to employees, the fair value of the options is measured based on market prices of options with similar terms, if available, or estimated using an option pricing model. The fair value of the options is recorded as additional paid-in capital and as compensation expense over the service period. The service period is the period during which the employee renders services in exchange for the compensation and is frequently the period between the date of grant and the date that the options first become exercisable.

  For example, assume that an executive is granted options for the purchase of 1,000 shares of $8 par common stock at $20 per share. There is a four-year service period before the options become exercisable. At the date of grant, the options are determined to have a fair value of $4 each. During each year of the service period, the employee will make the entry as illustrated in Figure 2-180:

Figure 2-180: Annual Entry Recognizing Compensation Expense

Compensation expense	$1,000	
Paid-in capital—stock options		$1,000

When the option is exercised, the entry is as follows.

Figure 2-181: Entry for Option Exercise

Cash ($20 × 1,000 shares)	$20,000	
Paid-in capital stock options	$4,000	
Common stock, $8 par		$8,000
Additional paid-in capital on common stock		$16,000

Firms with stock compensation plans should disclose the nature and terms of the plans, the method of estimating fair value, the effect of the plans on the income statement, and the cash flows associated with the plans.

Warrants and rights

Warrants allow the holder to acquire shares of stock at a certain price within a stated duration of time. Stock options issued to employees are a form of warrant, as are stock rights granted to shareholders. Warrants are sometimes issued in a package with other securities such as bonds or preferred stock. When the stock price rises above the exercise price stated on the option, the potential for profit exists, either by exercising the option and selling the shares or by selling the option itself, which now has an intrinsic value.

Stock rights give current stockholders the right to purchase newly issued shares in proportion to those currently held, thus preventing their ownership stake and voting rights from being diluted without their permission. This right is also called the preemptive right. No entry is recorded when the warrants are issued. When the warrants are exercised, the receipt of cash and the issuance of the shares is recorded, as for any other sale of shares.

Stock warrants issued with other securities

A stock warrant is sometimes issued in a package with bonds or stock as an additional incentive to entice investors. As long as the warrants are detachable and thus can be sold separately from the other security, the issuer must allocate the proceeds of the package between the stock warrant and the other security. The allocation is based upon either the proportional or incremental method. (These methods were previously introduced in the discussion of lump-sum sales of different assets.)

- **Proportional method**
  The proportional method is used when the fair market values of both securities can be determined, often by relying on prices when the securities begin to trade separately

after issuance. The total amount investors paid for the package is allocated between the two securities based on their relative market values. For example, assume that 1,000 shares of preferred stock are issued together with 1,000 warrants, for a total of $20,750. After the sale, the preferred stock is selling for $18.25 per share and the warrants are selling for $3 each. The allocation under the proportional method is shown in Figure 2-182.

Figure 2-182: Proportional Method of Valuing Stock Warrants Grouped with Securities

Fair market value of preferred (1,000 × $18.25)	=	$18,250
Fair market value of warrants (1,000 × $3)	=	3,000
Aggregate fair market value		$21,250
Allocated to preferred: $\dfrac{\$18,250}{\$21,250} \times \$20,750$	=	$17,821
Allocated to warrants: $\dfrac{\$3,000}{\$21,250} \times \$20,750$	=	2,929
Total allocation		$20,750

- **Incremental method**

  When the fair value of one of the securities cannot be determined (for example, the warrants are not being separately traded), the incremental method is used. In this approach, the fair value that is determinable is assigned to that security and the remainder of the price is assigned to the other security. Figure 2-183 illustrates this method, assuming that only the preferred stock in the above example was trading separately.

Figure 2-183: Incremental Method of Valuing Stock Warrants Grouped with Securities

Lump-sum receipt	=	$20,750
Allocated to preferred (1,000 × $18.25)	=	18,250
Balance allocated to warrants		$2,500

Appropriation of retained earnings

An appropriation of retained earnings is a reclassification of these earnings for specific purposes. The board of directors must approve any appropriations of retained earnings. Appropriations reduce unappropriated retained earnings and must be displayed within the stockholders' equity section of the balance sheet. However, according to SFAS No. 5, costs or losses cannot be charged directly to appropriated retained earnings but must be reported on the income statement. Once such costs have been accounted for, the retained earnings appropriation would be reversed. An appropriation of retained earnings is just a means to signal that these earnings are unavailable for dividends. Alternately, a restriction on retained earnings can be disclosed. Among the reasons that a firm might appropriate or restrict retained earnings include:

- Loss contingencies (such as pending lawsuits).
- Legal restrictions related to treasury stock.
- Contractual restrictions related to bond indentures.
- Plant expansion or debt retirement.

Accounting for appropriation of retained earnings

An account such as appropriated retained earnings is set up as a subclassification of retained earnings. When the appropriation is made, the accounting entry is as follows:

Figure 2-184: Accounting for Appropriations of Retained Earnings

Retained earnings	$10,000,000
Retained earnings appropriated for Product X lawsuit loss contingency	$10,000,000

Dividends

Dividend distributions are typically made from retained earnings, but few companies distribute all of their retained earnings as dividends. Retained earnings may be restricted, or firms may wish to retain assets that might be used to pay dividends to fund future growth. Many companies try to maintain a steady record of dividend payments over time, consistent with investors' expectations. On the other hand, some younger companies have never paid a dividend. To the extent that retained earnings are not distributed as dividends, they should contribute to increasing share prices. The types of dividends covered here include cash dividends, property dividends, liquidating dividends, cumulative dividends, scrip dividends, and stock dividends. Stock splits and reverse stock splits are also covered.

Cash dividends

The cash dividend rate on preferred stock is fixed and stated either as a percentage of par or as a per-share amount. Dividends on common stock vary at the discretion of the board of directors. Cash dividends become a current liability on the date they are declared by the board of directors (the date of declaration). Dividends are payable to those stockholders who own shares as of the date of record and are distributed on the date of payment. Assuming that the board of directors declared a dividend of $1 per share on the 200,000 shares outstanding, the entry for the date of declaration is as follows.

Figure 2-185: Accounting for Cash Dividends at Date of Declaration

| Retained earnings | $200,000 | |
| Dividends payable | | $200,000 |

No accounting entry is made of the date of record. On the date of payment, cash is credited and dividends payable debited.

Property dividends

Any nonreciprocal transfer of nonmonetary assets from the entity to its owners is considered a property dividend. Dividends payable in property, merchandise, or investments are called property dividends. Property dividends are accounted for at the fair value of the assets transferred. At the date of declaration, a gain or loss is recognized for the difference between the asset's cost and its carrying value.

Assume that a company declares a property dividend that calls for distribution of securities held as an investment. These securities have a cost and carrying value of $1,000,000 and a fair market value of $1,300,000 to stockholders. The entry at the date of declaration is as follows:

Figure 2-186: Accounting for Property Dividends at Date of Declaration

Investments in securities	$300,000	
Gain on appreciation of securities		$300,000
Retained earnings (property dividends declared)	$1,300,000	
Property dividends payable		$1,300,000

The entry at the date of distribution would be:

Figure 2-187: Accounting for Property Dividends at Date of Distribution

| Property dividends payable | $1,300,000 | |
| Investments in securities | | $1,300,000 |

Liquidating dividends

A dividend that is paid out of paid-in capital rather than retained earnings is a liquidating dividend. A liquidating dividend constitutes a return of the stockholders' investment rather than a return on their investment, as a normal dividend would be.

Liquidating dividends typically occur when a company is ceasing operations. The following entry illustrates the accounting for a dividend that was partly paid from retained earnings (normal dividend) and partly from additional paid-in capital (liquidating dividend).

Figure 2-188: Accounting for Liquidating Dividends at Date of Declaration

Retained earnings	$750,000	
Additional paid-in capital	$250,000	
Dividends payable		$1,000,000

The entry for the date of payment is as follows:

Figure 2-189: Accounting for Liquidating Dividends at Date of Payment

Dividends payable	$1,000,000	
Cash		$1,000,000

Cumulative dividends

A preferred stock can be cumulative, meaning that if a corporation fails to pay a dividend on this stock in a year and owes this dividend in arrears, then the corporation is legally obligated to pay the dividends in arrears plus the current year's dividend before the corporation can pay any dividends to common shareholders. Unless preferred stock is labeled as noncumulative, it is legally considered to be cumulative. Noncumulative stock carries no obligations to pay dividends (like common stock).

Scrip dividends

Scrip is a type of note payable. Therefore a scrip dividend is a promise to pay a specific dividend at a future date. A scrip dividend can be declared when a corporation has sufficient retained earnings for a dividend but is experiencing cash flow problems. A scrip dividend can be used instead of failing to make an expected dividend payment (a negative sign to the market). A shareholder with a scrip dividend can hold it until maturity or sell it on the open market.

Stock dividends

Stock dividends are a nonreciprocal transfer of an entity's own stock to its shareholders on a pro rata basis. Unlike cash or property dividends, stock dividends do not affect total assets or total shareholders' equity. Retained earnings are merely reclassified as paid-in capital. This capitalization of earnings has the effect of retaining them in the corporation on a permanent basis. Small stock dividends involve the distribution of less than 20% to 25% of the number of shares outstanding on the date of declaration and are accounted for by debiting retained earnings for the market value of the shares on the declaration date. In contrast, large stock dividends involve the transfer of more than 20% to 25% of the number of shares outstanding and are accounted for by debiting retained earnings for the par value of the shares.

Stock dividends are often issued when the company wants to give something to the owners while still conserving cash. The company can reinvest its cash by reclassifying it from earned to contributed capital, retaining the funds in the business. The shareholders can sell these extra shares on the open market.

Although shareholders maintain their same proportional ownership in the company after the stock dividend, the fact that there are more shares outstanding will cause the book value per share and market price per share to adjust downward. The impact of this will be more noticeable in the case of large stock dividends, which, like stock splits, are often used to decrease the stock price to a more marketable level. Therefore, the market usually treats large stock dividends as if they were a stock split.

Stock splits and reverse stock splits

A stock split is a tool to reduce the market price per share of a company's stock without changing ownership proportions by issuing a specific number of shares for each share outstanding and reducing the par value per share by the same proportion. For example, a 4-for-1 stock split on 100,000 shares of stock trading at $400 per share would result in 400,000 shares of stock trading at approximately $100. Thus there is no net change to stockholders' equity, unlike with a stock dividend, which increases the number of shares without lowering the par value (increasing the total par value of outstanding shares). The reason for using stock splits is to make the stock more affordable for certain investors, thus increasing the diversification of ownership and theoretically increasing overall trading. No entry is recorded for a stock split; instead, a memorandum notes the changed par value of the shares.

Although rare, a **reverse split** is the opposite of a stock split in that it reduces the number of outstanding shares and proportionally increases the per-share price. For example, a 1-for-20 reverse stock split would transform 200,000 shares at $1 per share into 10,000 shares at approximately $20 per share.

EPS simple capital structure

A company with no potentially dilutive securities outstanding has a simple capital structure, whereas a company with such securities has a complex capital structure. Potentially dilutive securities are those that have the potential to lead to the issuance of additional shares of common stock. These securities include convertible preferred stock, convertible bonds, contingent shares, and stock options, warrants, and rights.

Basic earnings per share (EPS) is reported for a company with a simple capital structure. It is computed as net income available to common stock (net income minus dividends on preferred stock) divided by the weighted average shares of common stock outstanding during the year:

$$\text{Earnings Per Share} = \frac{\text{Net Income} - \text{Preferred Dividends}}{\text{Weighted Average Number of Shares Outstanding}}$$

Preferred dividends and weighted average shares are discussed below.

Preferred stock dividends

Preferred stock dividends declared reduce the amount of earnings available for common stock. They are therefore subtracted from net income (or, if a company reports a net loss, serve to increase the loss). If the preferred stock is cumulative, the annual dividend affects the EPS numerator whether or not it has been declared.

Weighted average number of shares outstanding

Anytime the number of shares outstanding changes during the year, a weighted average number of shares is determined for use in the EPS denominator. The shares outstanding at a given point are weighted by the portion of the year during which they are outstanding:

$$\text{Weighted Average Number of Shares Outstanding} = \text{Shares Outstanding} \times \frac{\text{Months Outstanding}}{\text{12 Months}}$$

The sum of the weighted average number of shares outstanding is totaled to find the weighted average shares for the year. For example, assume that a company had changes to their outstanding shares due to the issuance of additional shares and the purchase of shares for the treasury as shown in Figure 2-190.

Figure 2-190: Shares Outstanding and Ending Balance

Date	Share Changes	Shares Outstanding
January 1	Beginning balance	110,000
March 1	Issued 40,000 shares for cash	40,000
		150,000
June 1	Purchased 46,000 shares	46,000
		104,000
October 1	Issued 35,000 shares for cash	35,000
December 31	Ending balance	139,000

The computations in Figure 2-191 are performed to determine the total weighted average.

Figure 2-191: Weighted Average Number of Shares Outstanding

Dates Outstanding	Shares Outstanding		Fraction of Year		Weighted Shares
January 1–March 1	110,000	×	2/12	=	18,333
March 1–June 1	150,000	×	3/12	=	37,500
June 1–October 1	104,000	×	4/12	=	34,667
October 1–December 31	139,000	×	3/12	=	34,750
Weighted average number of shares outstanding					125,250

Assume that the company has income before extraordinary items of $300,000 and preferred dividends of $100,000. Therefore income before extraordinary items available to common shareholders would be $200,000 and earnings per share would be calculated as in Figure 2-192.

Figure 2-192: Computation of Income Available to Common Stockholders

	Income Information		Weighted Shares		Earnings per Share
Income before extraordinary items available to common stockholders	$200,000	÷	125,250	=	$1.60
Extraordinary gain (net of tax)	50,000	÷	125,250	=	.40
Income available to common stockholders	$250,000	÷	125,250	=	$2.00

Earnings per share related to extraordinary items must be separately disclosed, either on the face of the income statement or in the notes. Income statement disclosure is shown in Figure 2-193.

Figure 2-193: Earnings per Share with Extraordinary Item

Income before extraordinary item	$300,000
Extraordinary gain, net of tax	50,000
Net income	$350,000
Earnings per share:	
Income before extraordinary items	$1.60
Extraordinary item, net of tax	.40
Net income	$2.00

EPS complex capital structure

Companies with potentially dilutive securities outstanding report both basic and diluted EPS. Diluted EPS reflects the hypothetical impact that conversion or exercise of outstanding potentially dilutive securities would have on earnings available to common shareholders.

Diluted EPS = Basic EPS + Impact of Convertibles + Impact of Warrants

The intent of diluted EPS is to show bad news, or a potential decrease in EPS. Sometimes, conversion or exercise of a potentially dilutive security will cause EPS to increase. When that is the case, that security is considered antidilutive and is omitted from the calculation of diluted EPS. As a result, diluted EPS will always be smaller (or a loss per share larger) than basic EPS.

The impact of convertible bonds and convertible preferred stock on diluted EPS is calculated using the if-converted method, whereas the impact of warrants, options, and rights is determined using the treasury stock method.

If-converted method

The if-converted method assumes that convertible securities are converted to common stock at the beginning of the period (or at the date of issuance if issued during a period). The impact of the assumed conversion on the EPS numerator and denominator is then determined. In the case of a convertible bond, conversion to common stock would mean that no bond interest expense would have been incurred, so earnings available for common stock would increase by the after-tax amount of bond interest expense (because interest is deducted before computing tax expense). Conversion would also increase the number of common shares outstanding. Starting with basic EPS, the additional income would be added to the EPS numerator and the additional shares added to the EPS denominator in order to arrive at diluted EPS. Convertible preferred stock is treated similarly, except that dividends on preferred stock do not affect tax expense and so are not subject to the tax adjustment. (Net income is used in the numerator.)

For example, assume a 40% tax rate for a year in which two convertible debenture bonds are issued: a 6% $1,000,000 bond that is convertible into 30,000 common shares is issued at par on January 1 and a 7% $1,000,000 bond that is convertible into 35,000 common shares is issued at par on July 1. The net of tax adjustment for interest for the first bond is calculated as

$$\text{Annual Interest} \times (1 - \text{Tax Rate})$$

$$(\$1,000,000 \times 0.06) \times (1 - 0.40) = \$36,000$$

Because the 7% bond was issued in July, interest expense for only half of a year would have been recorded:

$$\text{Annual Interest} \times (1 - \text{Tax Rate}) \times \frac{\text{Months Outstanding}}{12 \text{ Months}}$$

$$(\$1,000,000 \times 0.07) \times (1 - 0.40) \times \frac{1}{2} = \$21,000$$

If income available for common shareholders from basic EPS was $300,000, the after-tax bond interest expense would be added to that to compute the numerator for diluted EPS: $300,000 + $36,000 + $21,000 = $357,000. The weighted average number of shares in the EPS denominator would be increased by the additional shares issued on conversion, weighted by the portion of the year outstanding (July through December):

$$\text{Convertible Number of Shares} \times \frac{\text{Months Outstanding}}{12 \text{ Months}}$$

$$30,000 \times 1 = 30,000$$

$$35,000 \times \frac{1}{2} = 17,500$$

If 100,000 weighted average shares were used in the calculation of basic EPS, the number of shares used for diluted EPS would be 100,000 + 30,000 + 17,500 = 147,500. As a result, diluted EPS is $357,000 divided by 147,500, or $2.42 per share.

Treasury stock method

The treasury stock method assumes that (1) warrants and options are exercised at the beginning of the year (or on the date of issuance if issued during the year) and (2) the proceeds from exercise are used to repurchase shares (at the average stock price for the year) for the treasury. The second assumption has the effect of mitigating the increase in the number of outstanding shares that would otherwise occur. The excess of the shares assumed to be issued in step 1 less the shares repurchased in step 2 is the number of incremental shares added to the EPS denominator. An incremental amount will exist when the exercise price is less than the stock's market price because the funds won't be enough to buy back all of the shares. Because warrants do not pay interest or dividends, they have no effect on the EPS numerator.

Any time the exercise price of the warrant or option is higher than the market price of the stock, the options will be antidilutive and are ignored for purposes of calculating diluted EPS. Therefore, when the exercise price of the warrant or option is greater than the market price of the stock, exercise is not assumed and no dilution need be accounted for.

For example, assume that a company has 2,000 warrants outstanding, each of which can be exercised for the purchase of one share of common stock at $15 per share, and the average market price of the common stock during the year is $45. The treasury stock method first assumes that all the warrants are exercised, which leads to the issuance of 2,000 shares of common stock, accompanied by a cash inflow of $30,000 (2,000 × $15). Next, the company is assumed to use the cash received to repurchase shares for the treasury. At the average market price, 667 shares can be repurchased ($30,000 ÷ $45). The net result is that 1,333 (2,000 − 667) incremental shares would be outstanding and are added to the EPS denominator in computing diluted EPS.

Alternately, the same result can be arrived at using the formula below.

$$\text{Number of Incremental Shares} = \text{Number of Options} \times \frac{\text{Market Price} - \text{Option Price}}{\text{Market Price}}$$

$$= 2,000 \times \frac{\$45 - \$15}{\$45} = 1,333$$

Assume that basic EPS was $3.00 per share, based on $300,000 in earnings and 100,000 shares outstanding. The incremental shares are added to the denominator, and diluted EPS would be calculated as follows:

$$\text{Diluted EPS} = \frac{\$300,000}{100,000 + 1,333} = \$2.96 \text{ per Share}$$

Diluted EPS with convertible debts and stock warrants

Assuming the examples used for the if-converted method and the treasury stock method were for the same company and period of time, the combined diluted EPS would be calculated as shown below.

$$\text{Diluted EPS} = \text{Basic EPS} + \text{Impact of Convertibles} + \text{Impact of Warrants}$$

$$= \frac{\$300,000 + \$36,000 + \$21,000}{100,000 + 47,500 + 1,333} = \frac{\$357,000}{148,833 \text{ Shares}} = \$2.40/\text{Share}$$

Income statement presentation of the basic and diluted EPS amounts is shown in Figure 2-194.

Figure 2-194: Earnings per Share Disclosure

Net income for the year	$300,000
Earnings per share (Note 1):	
Basic earnings per share ($300,000 ÷ 100,000)	$3.00
Diluted earnings per share ($357,000 ÷ 148,833)	$2.40

Financial statement presentation and disclosure requirements for equity and EPS

Disclosures for simple and complex earnings per share on the income statement were illustrated previously. When irregular items appear on the income statement, per-share amounts should be shown for income from continuing operations, income before extraordinary items, income before accounting changes, and net income. EPS should be shown for each period presented on the statements.

EPS is covered under SFAS No. 128 (February 1997), which superceded APB No. 15. SFAS No. 128 provides guidelines for computation and presentation of EPS for public companies and any nonpublic companies wishing to report EPS. The statement helps integrate EPS practices with international standards and simplifies reporting. Specific requirements of this standard have been covered throughout this section, such as that both basic and dilutive EPS must be listed for any company with potentially dilutive securities. Furthermore, any presentation showing a complex capital structure requires the following disclosures:

- Rights and privileges of outstanding securities

- Reconciliation of the numerator and denominator used for basic and diluted EPS, showing the impact of each individual security

- Effect of conversions that occurred after year-end but before statement issuance

- Weight given to preferred dividends when calculating income available to common stockholders for basic EPS

- Antidilutive securities that were not included in basic or dilutive EPS that could affect EPS in the future

Revenue Recognition

Revenue recognition has been a topic of recent concern to the SEC, because it is often a source of restatements for companies that have prematurely or improperly recognized revenues. This section covers different accounting approaches used in various industries for recognizing revenues.

The revenue recognition principle in FASB Concepts Statement No. 5 states that revenue is recognized when it is realized or realizable and earned. However, this approach is somewhat inconsistent with FASB Concepts Statement No. 6, which defines revenues in terms of inflows of assets or settlement of liabilities as a result of a firm's ongoing or central operations. As a result, the FASB is currently contemplating redefining the revenue recognition concept in terms of changes in assets and liabilities.

The following are some common sources of revenue and the point at which recognition typically occurs:

- Sales of products: recognized as of date of sale or delivery to customers

- Services and fees: recognized after the service is performed and is billable

- Interest, rents, and royalties from permitting others to use an asset: recognized as time passes or the assets are used

- Gains or losses on disposition of noninventory assets: recognized as of the date of sale

The point of sale is the most common point for revenue recognition, but revenue for certain types of transactions can be recognized before delivery (before, during, or on completion of production) or after delivery (as cash is collected or after costs are recovered). These different approaches are discussed below.

Point-of-sale recognition issues

Questions arise about revenue recognition at the point of sale in certain situations, such as when a buyback agreement or right of return exists.

- **Sales with buyback agreements**
  A sale that includes an agreement to buy back the goods later has transferred the title legally, but the seller retains the risks of ownership, so therefore no sale should be recorded. (Note that this was covered earlier in the discussion of inventory.)

- **Sales when a right of return exists**
  Book, magazine, and music publishers, perishable food dealers, and many other industries provide guarantees for return of unsold merchandise in order to increase overall sales. As long as the following conditions are met, firms should report sales less an allowance for estimated returns:

  - The sales price is fixed or determinable.
  - The buyer's obligation to pay the seller is not contingent upon resale of the product.
  - Theft, damage, or destruction of the product will not alter the liability of the buyer to the seller.
  - The buyer has economic substance separate from the seller.
  - The seller has no significant obligations for future performance to directly bring about the buyer's resale of the product.
  - The amount of returns can be reasonably estimated.

- **Trade loading (channel stuffing)**
  Trade loading is the practice of convincing retailers to buy more wholesale product than they can sell in a reasonable amount of time to inflate revenues (and profits) in the near term. The effect is that tomorrow's or next year's revenues are booked today, which will eventually lead to lowered future revenues unless the practice is indefinitely continued. Such window-dressing policies are discouraged.

Recognition after delivery

Three methods are used when revenue recognition is deferred because collectibility of the sales price is not reasonably assured: the installment sales method, the cost recovery method, and the deposit method.

- **Installment sales method**
  The installment sales method recognizes profit as cash is collected rather than at the point of sale. It is used when no reasonable estimate of the amount that can be collected is available. Thus this method is often used when payments for purchases of goods are required in installments (for example, furniture, large, expensive machinery, land development sales). To protect the seller, such agreements may include provisions such as delaying transfer of title until full payment has been made.

  This method recognizes the revenues and costs of goods sold related to installment sales in the period of sale but defers gross profit until the cash is collected. A gross profit rate is computed based on each year's installment sales. As cash is collected, the profit realized is determined by multiplying the cash collections by the gross profit rate applicable to that year's installment sales. Any remaining gross profit not realized is deferred to future years.

  On the balance sheet, deferred gross profit is generally reported as a liability representing unearned revenue, although some accountants argue that it is preferable to treat it as a contra account to installment accounts receivable.

- **Cost recovery method**
  Under the cost recovery method, revenue is recognized only when the cash received by the seller exceeds the cost of goods sold. After this threshold, all cash collections lead to profit recognition. This method is applicable when collectibility cannot be reasonably estimated. In the year of sale, the income statement reports revenue, cost of goods sold, deferred gross profit, and recognized gross profit. For example, if a company had sales on credit of $100,000 and cost of goods sold of $70,000, the closing entry to defer gross profit for Year 1 sales would be as shown as in Figure 2-195:

Figure 2-195: Year 1 Closing Entry Under Cost Recovery Method

Sales	$100,000	
Cost of sales		$70,000
Deferred gross profit		$30,000
(To close sales and cost of sales and to record deferred gross profit on sales accounted for under the cost recovery method)		

If, by the end of Year 2, cash collections on the Year 1 sales totaled $80,000, then $10,000 profit would be recognized as follows:

Figure 2-196: Year 2 Entry Under Cost Recovery Method

Deferred gross profit	$10,000	
Realized gross profit		$10,000
(To recognize gross profit to the extent that cash collections in Year 2 exceed costs)		

The final entries would be made in Year 3 when the remaining profits are recorded:

Figure 2-197: Year 3 Entry Under Cost Recovery Method

Deferred gross profit	$20,000	
Realized gross profit		$20,000
(To recognize gross profit to the extent that cash collections in Year 3 exceed costs)		

- **Deposit method**
  The deposit method is not really a revenue recognition method but rather a procedure applied when advance payment is made for goods or property that have not yet been transferred by the seller. No revenue is recognized until the sale is complete. The cash collected is reported as a liability (customer deposits) and the inventory remains on the books of the seller. When the sale is complete, an appropriate revenue recognition method is applied.

Issues and concerns regarding revenue recognition

In addition to the issues addressed earlier, like channel stuffing, the SEC has become concerned about other issues. For example, some companies acting as intermediaries and earning a fee on the sales they facilitate have recorded the full amount of the sale in their revenues. The SEC has indicated that such companies should report only their own fee as revenues. Another issue concerns revenue on contracts that provide services over the course of several years. Revenue under such contracts should only be recorded as earned and not front-end-loaded at the inception of the contract. Another revenue recognition issue is recognizing all of the revenue as earned on a contract that provides services over the course of several years. Such contracts should record revenue only as it is earned.

Premature or excess revenue recognition has been one of the most common problems that the SEC has discovered in its review of the statements companies file with it. This became an even greater concern during the Internet boom, when the shares of development-stage Internet companies began to trade on revenues multiples instead of the more traditional earnings multiples. In response, the SEC, in Staff Accounting Bulletin (SAB) 101, summarized the four basic criteria under GAAP that must be met for revenue to be recognized:

- Persuasive evidence of an arrangement exists.
- Delivery has occurred or the services have been rendered.
- There is a fixed or determinable price.
- Collectibility is assured.

GAAP for revenue recognition continues to evolve, and issues including accounting for multi-element revenue arrangements covering contracts combining the delivery of goods and services, such as a sale of equipment with ongoing maintenance services, are being addressed on an ongoing basis. In such circumstances, it is necessary to break the transactions into their components and apply the revenue recognition principles to the component parts of the transaction. In the case of the sale of an automobile with lifetime maintenance, it would be necessary to distinguish the portion of the sales price that applies to the sale of the car from the amount that represents a prepayment of the regular maintenance service that is also included in the transaction. The revenue associated with the maintenance services would be deferred and recognized over the period during which the maintenance would be performed.

The FASB currently has a revenue recognition project on its agenda, which seeks to ultimately produce one standard on revenue recognition in place of the numerous standards that address different aspects of this issue under GAAP today.

Accounting for long-term construction projects

Two accounting methods can be applied in recognizing revenue on long-term construction contracts, the percentage-of-completion method and the completed contract method.

Percentage-of-completion method

The percentage-of-completion method is used for recognition of revenues from long-term construction contracts under GAAP, as long as estimates can be made of the extent of job completion and a contract with legally enforceable rights exists. Estimates of completion can be based on input measures, such as costs incurred or labor hours used, or output measures, such as stories completed or miles of road completed. A commonly used input measure (recommended by the Committee on Accounting Procedure in Accounting Research Bulletin No. 45) is based upon the ratio of costs incurred to date to total estimated costs:

$$\text{Cost-to-Cost Percentage Complete} = \frac{\text{To-Date Costs}}{\text{Most Recent Estimate of Total Costs}}$$

This percentage is multiplied by the estimated total gross profit or revenue to determine the amount of revenue and profit to recognize to date. The amount of profit recognized to date less the amount of profit recognized at the end of the prior year determines the profit recognized for the current year.

An inventory account titled contracts in progress is used to collect construction costs plus gross profit earned to date. When the customer is billed, accounts receivable is increased together with billings on contract, which is netted against the construction in progress account on the balance sheet, with the total reported as either an asset or liability.

For example, assume that a company has a construction contract for $11,250,000. During the first year, $2,500,000 of actual costs were incurred, which was 25% of the total estimated contract costs of $10,000,000. The total estimated gross profit on the contract is $1,250,000 ($11,250,000 – $10,000,000) and 25% of this amount, or $312,500, is recognized as gross profit the first year in relationship to the costs incurred to date.

The following journal entries would be made during the year as costs are incurred, billings are made, and collections received.

Figure 2-198: Percentage-of-Completion Entries

Contracts in progress	$2,500,000	
Materials, cash, payables, etc.		$2,500,000
(To record cost of construction)		
Accounts receivable	$2,250,000	
Billing on contracts in progress		$2,250,000
(To record progress billings)		
Cash	$1,875,000	
Accounts receivable		$1,875,000
(To record collections)		

At the end of the year, profit is recognized on the contract, along with expenses, and the total equals the amount of revenue to be recognized the first year.

Figure 2-199: Year-End Percentage-of-Completion Entry

Contracts in progress (gross profit)	$312,500	
Construction expenses	$2,500,000	
Construction revenue		$2,812,500

At completion of the contract, construction in progress is credited and billings on contract is debited to close out the accounts.

Completed-contract method

The completed-contract method is used only when the entity has mostly short-term contracts, when the percentage-of-completion method is inappropriate because estimation of costs isn't practical, or when the contract has hazards that go beyond ordinary business risks.

Under the completed-contract method, revenue and gross profit are recognized only after the contract is complete. A contracts in progress (inventory) account is used to accumulate construction costs. A contra inventory account called progress billings on construction in process is used to accumulate progress billings.

Unlike the percentage-of-completion method, the completed-contract method makes no interim charges or credits for revenues, costs, or gross profit. However, when it is likely that a loss will be incurred on the contract, it should be recorded as discussed below.

In the final year of the contract, the following accounting entries would be made:

Figure 2-200: Contractor's Final Year Accounting Entry Using Completed-Contract Method

Billings on construction in process	$11,250,000	
Revenue from long-term contracts		$11,250,000
Costs of construction	$10,125,000	
Construction in process		$10,125,000

Losses on long-term contracts

Long-term contracts can result in a current period loss on a project that is still going to be profitable or a loss on an unprofitable project.

Loss in a current period

Under the percentage-of-completion method, a change in estimate results if estimated expenses increase but the overall estimate for a project still results in a profit. A loss is recorded in the current period to offset the excess gross profit recognized previously. The current period loss is calculated as shown in Figure 2-201.

Figure 2-201: Computation of Recognizable Loss in Current Period

Cost to date (12/31/Year 2)	$4,315,680
Estimated costs to complete (revised)	3,231,716
Estimated total costs	$7,547,396
Percentage complete ($4,315,680 ÷ $7,547,396)	57.2%
Revenue recognized in Year 2: ($6,660,000* x 57.2%) – $1,665,000**	$2,144,520
Costs incurred in Year 2	2,797,360

Loss recognized in Year 2	$(652,840)

* Revenue recognized in Year 2 on project
** Cumulative revenue recognized up to Year 1 on project

The loss is recorded as follows:

Figure 2-202: Loss In Current Period on Long-Term Contract

Construction expense	$2,797,360	
Construction in process (loss)		$652,840
Revenue from long-term contract		$2,144,520

This loss is the difference between the reported revenue and the actual costs.

Loss on an unprofitable contract

No matter whether the completed-contract method or the percentage-of-completion method is used, if an overall loss on a project is expected, the entire amount of the loss that is estimated must be recognized in the current period.

- **Percentage-of-completion accounting**

  Under the percentage-of-completion method, when a gross profit was recognized in a prior year, that amount has to be recognized as a loss, along with the currently projected loss on the contract. For example, if $100,000 in gross profit was recognized in the prior year and the total loss on the contract is now projected to be $50,000, then the loss recognized in the current year is $150,000. The entry to record the loss is shown below:

Figure 2-203: Loss in Current Period Using Percentage-of-Completion Accounting

Construction expense	$1,000,000	
Construction in process (loss)		$150,000
Revenue from long-term contract		$850,000

- **Completed-contract accounting**

  The completed-contract method simply recognizes the total loss in the year it becomes evident:

Figure 2-204: Accounting Entry for Loss Under Completed-Contract Accounting

Loss from long-term contracts	$50,000	
Construction in process (loss)		$50,000

Neither the balance in construction in process nor the balance in the billings account can exceed the contract price. If the construction in process account exceeds the billings, the loss is deducted from the construction in process account and reported in a current liability account titled estimated liability from long-term contracts.

Comprehensive Income

Comprehensive income information

Comprehensive income is defined in Concepts Statement 6 (par. 70) as "the change in equity [net assets] of a business enterprise during a period from transactions and other events and circumstances from nonowner sources. It includes all changes in equity during a period except those resulting from investments by owners and distributions to owners." These changes result from the effects of exchange transactions, the entity's productive efforts, price changes, and peripheral transactions.

So, comprehensive income includes all revenues, expenses, gains, and losses that affect a business during the period, including both realized gains and losses that are included in net income and unrealized gains and losses that are reported outside of net income as elements of other comprehensive income. The main items of other comprehensive income are:

▪ Unrealized gains and losses on investments in available-for-sale securities.

▪ Unrealized gains and losses on certain derivative financial instruments.

▪ Pension losses that result from the minimum liability adjustment.

▪ Certain foreign currency translation adjustments.

Other comprehensive income

Comprehensive income is the sum of net income and the items of other comprehensive income. Per-share amounts are not reported for comprehensive income.

Net income is closed to retained earnings and other comprehensive income is closed to accumulated other comprehensive income, so each is separately accumulated as a component of shareholders' equity. To avoid double-counting when a gain or loss previously reported in other comprehensive income is later realized and reported in net income, a reclassification adjustment is required. This adjustment removes the effect of the gain or loss, once it has been realized, from accumulated other comprehensive income.

Comprehensive income can be presented either on a combined income statement, on a separate income statement, or on the statement of stockholders' equity. These three presentations are illustrated below.

- **Combined statement of income and comprehensive income**

  A company can choose to present traditional net income as a subtotal, followed by the items of other comprehensive income, with comprehensive income as the total. Although straightforward, this approach gives less prominence to net income, which some companies view as a disadvantage. Figure 2-205 illustrates a combined statement of income and comprehensive income.

Figure 2-205: Combined Income Statement—Comprehensive Income

Bounce Sporting Goods Company Statement of Income and Comprehensive Income For Year Ended December 31, Year 1	
Sales revenue	$1,120,000
Cost of goods sold	840,000
Gross profit	280,000
Operating expenses	126,000
Net income	154,000
Unrealized holding gain, net of tax	42,000
Comprehensive income	$196,000

- **Separate comprehensive income statement**

  The starting point for this separate statement is net income, to which the items of other comprehensive income are added to arrive at the total comprehensive income. This presentation clarifies the relationship between net income and other comprehensive income. Figure 2-206 illustrates separate statements of income and comprehensive income.

Figure 2-206: Separate Income Statement and Comprehensive Income Statement

Bounce Sporting Goods Company Income Statement For Year Ended December 31, Year 1	
Sales revenue	$1,120,000
Cost of goods sold	840,000
Gross profit	280,000
Operating expenses	126,000
Net income	$154,000

Bounce Sporting Goods Company Comprehensive Income Statement For Year Ended December 31, Year 1	
Net income	$154,000
Other comprehensive income	
Unrealized holding gain, net of tax	42,000
Comprehensive income	$196,000

- **Statement of stockholders' equity**

  In practice, the most popular comprehensive income reporting approach has been to show the computation of comprehensive income within the statement of stockholders' equity. When this statement is presented in columnar format, the items of other comprehensive income are shown in a comprehensive income column, with the total for these items closed to the accumulated other comprehensive income account, as illustrated in Figure 2-207.

Figure 2-207: Comprehensive Income in the Statement of Stockholders' Equity

Bounce Sporting Goods Company Statement of Stockholders' Equity
For the Year Ended December 31, Year 1

	Total	Comprehensive Income	Retained Earnings	Accumulated Other Comprehensive Income	Common Stock
Beginning balance	$574,000		$70,000	$84,000	$420,000
Comprehensive income					
Net income	154,000	$154,000	154,000		
Other comprehensive income					
Unrealized holding gain, net of tax	42,000	42,000		42,000	
Comprehensive income		$196,000			
Ending balance	$770,000		$224,000	$126,000	$420,000

Other comprehensive income on the balance sheet

The ending balance in the "accumulated other comprehensive income" account is reported in the equity section of the balance sheet, as illustrated in Figure 2-208.

Figure 2-208: Accumulated Other Comprehensive Income in the Balance Sheet

Bounce Sporting Goods Company
Balance Sheet
For Year Ended December 31, Year 1
(Stockholders' Equity Section)

Stockholders' equity	
Common stock	$420,000
Retained earnings	224,000
Accumulated other comprehensive income	126,000
Total stockholders' equity	$770,000

Leases

A **lease** is a contract between a lessor and a lessee in which the lessor gives the lessee the right to use the lessor's property for a certain period of time in exchange for rent payments that are usually periodic in nature. The lessor retains the title to the property, so the form of a lease agreement is different from a sale. Nevertheless, sometimes the substance of the lease agreement is comparable to a sale, which is the case when the lease transfers substantially all of the risks and benefits of asset ownership to the lessee.

From the perspective of the lessee, there are two types of leases: capital and operating.

Capital leases

SFAS No. 13 lists four criteria used to determine whether the lease transfers substantially all of the risks and benefits of property ownership to the lessee.

A lease is capitalized by the lessee if it meets at least one of the following criteria:

- **Transfer of title.** The lease transfers title in the asset to the lessee at the end of the lease term.

- **Bargain purchase option.** The lease contains a bargain purchase option, which allows the lessee to purchase the property at a price that is significantly lower than its fair market value.

- **75% of useful life.** The lease term is 75% or more of the remaining life of the property.

- **90% of net FV.** The present value of the minimum lease payments is equal to 90% or more of the fair value (FV) of the property at the inception of the lease.

If the lease qualifies as a **capital lease**, the lessee records both a leased asset and a lease liability on its balance sheet. The asset is measured based on the present value of the minimum lease payments (excluding any executory costs, like insurance or maintenance) or the lower fair market value of the leased asset. The leased asset, which is reported with property, plant, and equipment, is depreciated (or amortized) by the lessee. Lease payments reduce the lease liability, or **capital lease obligation**. A capital lease obligation is the present value (PV) of future lease payments. The future cash payment can be divided into an interest expense portion and a reduction in lease obligation portion (analogous to a principal payment for a regular loan). Interest expense is recorded on the liability using the effective rate method. (Therefore, the accounting is similar to that which would be applied if a company had purchased an asset by issuing a note payable.)

For example, say that on January 1, Year 1, Acme Company (the lessee) leases a plastic extrusion machine worth $150,000 (fair value at inception) from Plastcon (the lessor). The noncancellable lease is for four years and includes annual lease payments of $41,933.41 every January 1 starting at inception. The lease cannot be renewed, the equipment reverts back to the lessor at the end of the lease, and the equipment has no residual value due to an estimated economic life of four years. In addition, the equipment is depreciated on a straight-line basis. Acme's incremental borrowing rate is 9% per year, and Plastcon has informed Acme that it has built in an 8% per year rate of return on this asset. If the lessee knows the lessor's actual rate, it should be used in calculations but only if it is lower than the lessee's incremental borrowing rate. Otherwise the lessee's incremental borrowing rate should be used.

First, the four lease capitalization criteria must be tested to determine the proper accounting method:

- **Transfer of title?** No. The lease does not transfer ownership of the asset.

- **Bargain purchase option?** No. The lease does not contain a bargain purchase option.

- **75% of useful life?** Yes. The four years of the lease divided by four years of useful life equals 100%.

- **90% of net FV?** Yes. $41,33.41 × present value of an annuity due of $1 for four periods at 8% = $41,933.41 × 3.57710 (see Figure 2-209, following) = $150,000.00. The fair value at inception is also $150,000. $150,000 PV payments/$150,000 FV = 100% of net FV.

Note that an annuity due presumes that payments are made at the beginning of a period instead of the end (that is, an ordinary annuity) and so uses different PV tables.

Figure 2-209: Present Value of an Annuity Due of 1

$$\text{Present Value of an Annuity Due of 1 (PV-AD)}_{n,i} \ = \ \frac{1 - \dfrac{1}{(1 + i)^{n - 1}}}{i}$$

(n) Periods	8%	9%	10%
1	1.00000	1.00000	1.00000
2	1.92593	1.91743	1.90909
3	2.78326	2.75911	2.73554
4	3.57710	3.53130	3.48685
5	4.31213	4.23972	4.16986
6	4.99271	4.88965	4.79079
7	5.62288	5.48592	5.35526
8	6.20637	6.03295	5.86842
9	6.74664	6.53482	6.33493
10	7.24689	6.99525	6.75902

Because at least one of the criteria was answered by a yes, this lease qualifies as a capital lease. Therefore, the entry on January 1, Year 1, is as shown in Figure 2-210.

Figure 2-210: Entry to Record a Capital Lease (January 1, Year 1)

Leased equipment under capital leases	$150,000.00

Obligations under capital leases	$108,066.59
Cash	$41,933.41

To record a capital lease at inception at the present value of future rental payments (for four periods at 8%: 41,933.41 × [3.57710 − 1]* = $108,066.59) and to record a capital lease payment

* Amount reduced by 1 because the first payment is not being included in the present value calculations.

The $41,933.41 payment has an interest portion and a reduction in lease obligation portion.

Figure 2-211 shows how the annuity due basis and the effective interest methods are used to determine the annual interest on the unpaid obligation and the resulting lease obligation.

Figure 2-211: Lessee Perspective Lease Amortization Schedule on the Annuity Due Basis

	Acme Company Lease Amortization Schedule			
Date	**Annual Lease Payment**	**Interest on Unpaid Obligation***	**Reduction of Lease Obligation****	**Lease Obligation**
Inception				$150,000.00
1/1/Y1	$41,933.41	$0.00	$41,933.41	$108,066.59
1/1/Y2	$41,933.41	$8,645.33	$33,288.08	$74,778.51
1/1/Y3	$41,933.41	$5,982.28	$35,951.13	$38,827.38
1/1/Y4	$41,933.41	$3,106.03 ***	$38,827.38	$0.00
Total	$167,733.64	$17,733.64 ****	$150,000.00	

* 8% interest applied to remaining lease obligation at the end of the year, e.g., (0.08 × $108,066.59 = $8,645.33). Note that the first payment is on the date of inception so no interest has accrued.

** Reduction in lease obligation calculated as annual lease payment less interest on unpaid obligation.

*** Interest reduced by $0.16 to account for rounding errors.

**** Note that $167,733.64 − $17,733.64 = $150,000.00.

At the end of Year 1, Acme records its accrued interest as shown in Figure 2-212.

Figure 2-212: Entry to Record Accrued Interest (December 31, Year 1)

Interest expense	$8,645.33
Interest payable	$8,645.33

To record accrued interest on a leased plastic extrusion machine

Also at the end of Year 1, Acme records its straight-line depreciation as shown in Figure 2-213.

Figure 2-213: Entry to Record Depreciation Expense (December 31, Year 1)

Depreciation expense—Capital leases	$37,500	
Accumulated depreciation—Capital leases		$37,500

To record depreciation expense ($150,000/4 years = $37,500)

Portions of leases due within one year are classified as current liabilities (for example, $33,288.08 in Year 1, which is the amount due within the next year), and longer-term portions are classified as noncurrent or long-term liabilities ($74,778.51 in Year 1, for a total obligation of $108,066.59). On the December 31, Year 1, balance sheet, assets with capital leases are separately identified, and the current liabilities section would list interest payable at $8,645.33 and obligations under capital leases at $33,288.08. Noncurrent liabilities would list obligations under capital leases at $74,778.51. Figure 2-214 shows a lease payment in a year with interest payable (Year 2):

Figure 2-214: Entry to Record Lease Payment (January 1, Year 2)

Interest payable	$8,645.33	
Obligations under capital leases	$33,288.08	
Cash		$41,933.41

To record a lease payment for a plastic extruder machine

When the lease expires, the asset is returned to the lessor and the accumulated depreciation accounts and leased equipment accounts are removed from the books as shown in Figure 2-215.

Figure 2-215: Entry to Remove Leased Asset from Books (January 1, Year 5)

Equipment	$150,000	
Accumulated depreciation—Capital leases	$150,000	
Leased equipment under capital leases		$150,000
Accumulated depreciation—Equipment		$150,000

To remove a leased asset from the books at the end of the lease

Capital lease disclosures include gross amount by major class of assets under capital leases, future minimum payments for each of the next five years, including all of the separate categories of data shown in Figure 2-215, information on noncancellable leases and contingent rentals, and depreciation on capital leases.

Operating leases

Leases that do not meet the criteria for capitalization are recorded as operating leases. Operating leases are similar to ordinary rent. The expense accrues as time passes. Using the operating method, the liability for the rent expense accrues daily and the rent is assigned to each period during which the firm benefited from using the asset. However, recognition of the expense or revenue is generally made on a straight-line basis over the lease term. Commitments to make future payments are not accounted for. If the asset from the prior example met none of the criteria for capitalization, then the payment would be recorded without any reference to the components making up the charge, as shown in Figure 2-216. If there is multi-year agreement of a material amount with an operating lease, then the payment schedule has to be disclosed.

Figure 2-216: Lessee's Entry to Record Rent Payment (January 1, Year 1)

Rent expense	$44,933.41	
Cash		$44,933.41
To record rent payment on a plastic extrusion machine		

Operating leases do not appear on the balance sheet. On the income statement, the lessee will report rental expense and the lessor will report rental revenue. If an operating lease has terms making it noncancellable for a year or more, this must be disclosed.

Lease classifications from the lessor's perspective

- The four possible lease classifications from the perspective of the lessor are:

- Operating (discussed previously for both the lessor and the lessee).

- Sales-type.

- Direct financing.

- Leveraged.

Referring to the four criteria for determining whether or not a lease is a capital lease, from the lessor's perspective, if a lease meets any of these four criteria and both of the criteria to follow, then it is either a sales-type, a direct financing, or a leveraged lease. These leases must have both of the following properties:

- Collectibility of the minimum lease payments is reasonably predictable.

- No important uncertainties exist related to unreimbursable costs the lessor may yet incur.

The three non-operating classifications depend on whether a profit or loss can be recognized due to issuance of the lease. In each of these three capital-type leases, the lessor removes the asset from the balance sheet and replaces it with a lease receivable (or net investment in the lease). The lessor will record interest revenue over the lease term.

Sales-type leases

Sales-type leases are transactions that are used as an alternative to a sale but are otherwise like a sale, such as leasing a new car from a dealership or re-leasing equipment when its prior lease is expiring. When the lessor is a manufacturer or dealer in the leased asset, the lease is usually a sales-type lease, and, in addition to interest revenue, the lessor will also recognize sales and cost of goods sold at the inception of the lease. Technically, a lease is considered a sales-type lease when the fair value (sales price) of the asset differs from the cost of the asset. The difference between the two is the gross profit (or loss). Sales-type lease transactions involving real estate must transfer the title by the end of the lease term.

Direct financing leases

Direct financing leases are transactions that are used as a form of loan, where the cost of the asset is equal to the fair value of the asset (sales price). Therefore, other than interest revenue, the lessor does not realize a profit or loss on the transaction. Lessors are commonly banks who purchase the asset and lease it out. Borrowing funds using the property being purchased as collateral would accomplish the same result, with the exception that with a direct financing lease the lessor keeps title to the assets. Direct financing leases can be used when a borrower cannot otherwise finance 100% of the asset, when there are tax benefits to doing so, or when the residual value on the asset plus the interest earned is more favorable than outright sale for the lessor.

Leveraged leases

Leveraged leases are a type of direct financing lease, but they have separate accounting treatment because they involve three or more parties. In addition to the lessor and the lessee, a long-term creditor serves as an intermediary. Here the lessor is called the equity participant. The long-term creditor must provide financing without recourse to the lessor's general credit but can have recourse to the leased asset. A lease is not a leveraged lease unless the lessor has substantial financial leverage in the transaction. The behavior of a leveraged lease is that the net investment of the lessor will decline in early years and increase in later years.

Pensions and Other Post-Retirement Benefits

A **pension plan** provides benefits to employees after retirement based on services provided during the employees' working years. The matching principle dictates that the costs of these benefits be reported during the periods when employees work to earn the benefits rather than when they are paid. The employer typically makes payments to a separate entity, the pension fund, to accumulate the assets to pay future benefits. Some plans are contributory, with both employees and employers contributing to the pension fund. Other plans are noncontributory, or funded solely by the employer. Accounting for the sponsoring employer, rather than for the pension fund itself, is the topic discussed in this section.

Two major types of pension plans are defined contribution plans and defined benefit plans. In a defined contribution plan, the amount the employer agrees to contribute to the pension fund each period is defined by a formula. The formula may be based on factors such as age, length of service, employer profits, and compensation. No promise is made regarding the amount of future benefits to be paid, so the risk of pension variability rests with the employees. An independent third-party trustee usually collects funds from the employer, safeguards the accumulated income in the trust, and deals with forfeitures of funds from early termination in a manner dictated by the employer. The trustee's beneficiaries are the employees in the plan.

In a defined benefit plan, the employer promises that a specific benefit amount will be paid during the retirement years. This payment is based on a formula that may take into account the number of years worked and the compensation level near retirement. Trustees for defined benefit plans safeguard and invest the employer's contributed assets to build enough funds to pay the employer's obligations. The employer retains ownership of the trust assets. Therefore, the trustee's beneficiary for a defined benefit plan is the employer, not the employees. Employers are at risk with these types of plans because they have to make up any shortfall if the amount accumulated in the pension fund is insufficient to make the defined benefit payments. The present value of the promised payments is a pension liability; the fact that this liability can be measured using several different approaches (projected benefit obligation, accumulated benefit obligation, vested benefit obligation) further complicates the accounting.

Accounting for defined contribution plans

Accounting by the employer sponsoring a defined contribution plan is simple: Pension expense is recorded for the amount of the annual contribution to the plan, cash is credited for the amount paid into the pension fund, and, if necessary, an asset or liability is recorded for any difference. The employer's cost is simply their minimum annual contribution. If they fail to make the full minimum contribution, a liability is created on the employer's balance sheet for the difference. If funds above the minimum are deposited, an asset is created on the balance sheet. Disclosures include a description of the plan with listings of covered employee groups, contribution formulae used, and any other significant matters that could affect comparability between periods.

Accounting for defined benefit plans

Accounting for defined benefit plans is complex because the ultimate cost of the promised benefits can only be estimated during the working years. The employer measures pension expense in accordance with the provisions of SFAS No. 87.

Pension expense is the sum of several components, including service cost (the increase in the pension liability due to one more year of employee service) and interest cost (the increase in the pension liability due to the passage of time). Other components included in pension expense are the return on plan assets, amortization of prior service cost, and certain gains and losses. The employer debits pension expense for this total, credits cash for the amount contributed to the pension fund, and then records the difference as a liability (or asset) account, accrued (or prepaid) pension cost.

Additional adjustments may be required to recognize a minimum pension liability on the balance sheet. This liability is the present value of expected cash flows of one of the following amounts:

- **Vested benefit obligation.** The vested benefit obligation measures the benefit obligation only for vested employees and only at current salary levels. Employees become fully vested after a specific number of years on the job.

- **Accumulated benefit obligation.** The accumulated benefit obligation uses current salary levels to determine the payment that would be required if the employee were to quit today but disregards whether employees are vested or nonvested. The accumulated benefit obligation measures the firm's payment obligation as of the current time without considering additional years of service or anticipated salary increases.

- **Projected benefit obligation.** The projected benefit obligation measures the benefit obligation for vested and nonvested employees and makes a projection for future salary levels (that is, basing the formula on projected final pay). This method results in the highest estimates. The FASB recommends this method because it provides a more realistic measure of the employer's obligation; they also require this method if the plan benefit formula uses it.

As part of the adjustment to recognize this minimum liability, the employer will also record an intangible pension asset and/or a loss reported as a component of accumulated other comprehensive income. The management's choice of discount rates to use in the present value calculations will have a great influence on the projected obligation and so are required to be adjusted each measurement date to reflect current interest rates. Furthermore, actuaries include adjustments for deaths, withdrawals, early retirements, and disabilities in their present value calculations, technically making them actuarial present values.

Pension expense

The annual payments made to a defined benefit plan are broken down into several components because of the need to match costs to the appropriate periods of benefit.

The components are as follows:

- **Service cost.** According to SFAS No. 87, service cost equals the actuarial present value of the benefits attributed by the pension benefit formula to employee service during the period (for example, the projected benefit obligation).

- **Interest expense.** Interest expense, or the interest on the liability, accrues on the projected benefit obligation (because it is a type of discounted debt) outstanding for the period based on the settlement rate, which is an interest rate determined by actuaries that would effectively settle all projected benefit obligations if the plan were to be terminated (includes time value of money calculations).

- **Actual return on plan assets.** The return on plan assets will decrease pension expenses. The return consists of interest earned and dividends received as well as adjustments to the market value of the fund itself.

Actual Return =

(Plan Assets [PA] Ending Balance − PA Beginning Balance) − (Contributions − Benefits Paid)

- **Amortization of unrecognized prior service cost.** Plans are sometimes amended to provide retroactive benefits for completed employee work. These costs are allocated to pension expense to the future remaining service years of the affected employees.

- **Gain or loss.** The difference between the actual and expected return on plan assets form part of any gain or loss, with the remainder made up of amortization of unrecognized net gain or loss from prior periods. Gains or losses can be caused by changes in the benefit obligation estimate or changes in the market value of the pension.

Disclosure of pensions on the balance sheet

On the balance sheet, underfunded pension accounts are listed as a liability. That is, if the amount the employer funds to the pension trust is lower than the amount of the annual expense, the difference is recorded as a long-term liability (or as a current liability if the amount is due within one year) under a term such as accrued pension cost or pension expense not funded.

Any overrfunded amounts would appear as an asset on the balance sheet. The difference would be reported either in the current assets or other assets section (depending on whether or not it is due within a year) under a term such as deferred pension expense or prepaid pension expense.

Another liability can arise when the accumulated benefit obligation is greater than the fair value of the plan assets.

A debit must be made to compensate for the difference:

- **If the debit is greater than the unrecognized prior service cost:**
  Record the liability as a contra account to stockholders' equity called excess of additional pension liability over unrecognized prior service cost. Report the excess debit portion as part of other comprehensive income and the accumulated balance as part of accumulated other comprehensive income.

- **If the debit is lower than the unrecognized prior service cost:**
  Record the liability as an intangible asset called deferred pension cost.

Pension worksheet

Because not all of the aspects of pension expense are tracked through normal journal entries, a pension worksheet tracks the annual pension expense, cash, and prepaid or accrued cost accounts from the general ledger against the unrecognized or noncapitalized pension items: projected benefit obligation and plan assets. Figure 2-217 shows an example of a pension worksheet using sample numbers and a 10% settlement rate. Note that the prepaid accrued cost balance should equal the memo record's net balance. Note also that the debits and credits for both records are used as if they were one journal. (Each transaction has debits equal credits across the two records.) The contributions item refers to the period contributions made to the plan, whereas the benefits refer to actual benefits disbursed to current retirees. The purpose of Figure 2-217 is to show the format of the pension worksheet; it does not illustrate the underlying computations.

Figure 2-217: Pension Worksheet (in thousands)

Items	General Journal Entries			Memo Record	
	Annual Pension Expense	Cash	Prepaid/ Accrued Cost	Projected Benefit Obligation	Plan Assets
Balance, Jan 1, Year 1			$0	$200,000 Cr	$200,000 Dr
Service cost	$16,000 Dr			16,000 Cr	
Interest expense	20,000 Dr			20,000 Cr	
Actual return	20,000 Cr*				20,000 Dr
Contributions		$14,000 Cr			14,000 Dr
Benefits				12,000 Dr	12,000 Cr
Journal entry for Year 1	$16,000 Dr	$14,000 Cr	2,000 Cr**		
Balance, Dec 31, Year 1			$2,000 Cr***	$224,000 Cr	$222,000 Dr

Note: Dr = debit, Cr = credit.

* Actual return = ($222,000 – $200,000) – ($14,000 – $12,000) = $20,000

** Cash less annual pension expense equals the prepaid/accrued cost: $14,000 – $16,000 = ($2,000).

*** Plan assets less projected benefit obligation equals the end-of-year balance in the prepaid/accrued cost: $222,000 – $224,000 = ($2,000).

Financial statement disclosures

Disclosures related to pension plans should be made within the body of the financial statements or in the notes. Figure 2-218 shows an example of a pension disclosure in the notes from a company's 10-Q.

Figure 2-218: Pension Disclosures for New CF&I (dates genericized)

NEW CF&I, INC.
Notes to Consolidated Financial Statements [Pension Disclosures Excerpt] (Unaudited)

Employee Benefit Plans

New CF&I has noncontributory defined benefit pension plans and post-retirement health care and life insurance benefit plans that cover nearly all of its eligible employees. Certain management employees are no longer eligible to participate in the defined benefit plans if they were hired after September 1, Year 1 (Y1). Those employees are instead enrolled in an employer-funded defined contribution plan equal to 3% of annual wages. The new defined contribution plan is funded annually, and participants' benefits vest after five years of service. New CF&I also offers a qualified Thrift 401(k) plan to all of its employees.

Components of net periodic benefit cost related to the defined benefit pension plans are as follows:

	Defined Benefit Pension Plans			
	Three Months Ended June 30		Six Months Ended June 30	
	Year 2 (Y2)	Year 2 (Y2)	Y2	Y1
	(In thousands)		(In thousands)	
Service cost	$ 648	$ 579	$ 1,296	$ 1,158
Interest cost	1,057	1,001	2,114	2,002
Expected return on plan assets	(880)	(586)	(1,760)	(1,200)
Amortization of unrecognized net loss	115	38	230	76
Amortization of unrecognized prior service cost	609	609	1,218	1,218
Total net periodic benefit cost	$ 1,549	$ 1,641	$ 3,098	$ 3,254

Components of net periodic benefit cost related to the post-retirement health care and life insurance benefit plans are as follows:

	Other Benefit Plans			
	Three Months Ended June 30		Six Months Ended June 30	
	Y2	Y1	Y2	Y1
	(In thousands)		(In thousands)	
Service cost	$ 60	$ 55	$ 117	$ 111
Interest cost	309	304	612	607
Amortization of unrecognized net loss	69	54	131	107
Amortization of unrecognized prior service cost	183	180	363	359
Total net periodic benefit cost	$ 621	$ 593	$ 1,223	$ 1,184

New CF&I made contributions of $7.5 million and $11.3 million, respectively, to its pension plans for the three and six months ended June 30, Y2, and contributions of $2.2 million and $5.6 million, respectively, during the three and six months ended June 30, Y1. New CF&I expects to make additional contributions of $8.1 million in Y2.

The first paragraph in Figure 2-218 discloses the types of pension plans the company has and who is eligible. The employer is required to make the following disclosures (see the top half of the figure): projected benefit obligation, pension plan assets, unrecognized prior service costs, and unrecognized net gain or loss. These items are not otherwise recorded on the financial statements. In addition, the following information should be disclosed:

- A schedule showing the components of pension expense

- The funded status of the plan (the difference between the projected benefit obligation measure of the liability and the fair value of the plan assets)

- A schedule showing the changes in the projected benefit obligation and the fair value of the plan assets during the year

- The estimates used for the discount rate, asset return rate, and rate of compensation increases

The final paragraph of the disclosures in Figure 2-218 indicates the firm's actual and planned contributions.

Deferred Income Taxes

Because the IRS tax code has differences from GAAP (and there are many variations within GAAP), the usual result is that pretax financial income will differ from taxable income. **Pretax financial income** (or income before taxes/income for book purposes) is the income derived for financial reporting under GAAP for use by the investment community. **Taxable income** is a term in the Internal Revenue Code (the tax code) denoting the base amount of net income (after all allowed deductions) that is used to calculate income tax payable.

Temporary differences

Many of the differences between the two methods are actually temporary differences. A **temporary difference** is a differential between an asset or liability's reported value (carrying or book) and its tax basis that will reverse itself in a later period, resulting in the same net tax being paid. For example, although GAAP uses full accrual accounting, the tax code allows the use of a modified cash basis for revenue recognition. This means that under GAAP, revenue is generally recognized in earlier periods than under the tax code. Figure 2-219 shows how such a temporary difference in revenues can exist for a time due to differences in the timing of revenue recognition. The figure assumes a 40% tax rate and consistent revenues and expenses for GAAP reporting (for easier comparison).

Figure 2-219: Financial versus Tax Reporting

| | Acme Company | | | |
	Year 1	Year 2	Year 3	Total
GAAP reporting				
Revenues	$100,000	$100,000	$100,000	
Expenses	$60,000	$60,000	$60,000	
Pretax financial income	$40,000	$40,000	$40,000	$120,000
Income tax expense	$16,000	$16,000	$16,000	$48,000
Tax reporting				
Revenues	$70,000	$110,000	$120,000	
Expenses	$60,000	$60,000	$60,000	
Taxable income	$10,000	$50,000	$60,000	$120,000
Income tax payable	$4,000	$20,000	$24,000	$48,000
Difference*	$12,000	($4,000)	($8,000)	

*Difference = Tax Expense – Tax Payable

The temporary difference in Figure 2-219 is a deferred tax liability offset by the two future increases in tax payable. A **deferred tax liability** is a difference that results in paying less taxes now (the $12,000) compensated by paying higher taxes in future periods (the $4,000 and $8,000 differences). A **deferred tax** asset is a difference that results in paying higher taxes now and lower taxes later.

Differences of these sort result in needing to allocate tax between periods, called interperiod tax allocation. Interperiod tax allocation refers to the allocation of total income tax expense or benefit between continuing operations, discontinued operations, extraordinary items, and items charged or credited directly to shareholders' equity between periods. It is needed when items are recorded in different periods for tax accounting and financial reporting (or book) purposes. For example, a company might accrue warranty expense in the period that a product is sold under warranty for financial reporting purposes but deduct the repair costs for tax purposes when warranty service is actually provided. Or, the revenue from an installment sale might be reported in the period of sale for financial reporting purposes but reported as taxable income when cash is received. Under GAAP, the tax effects of these differences lead to the recording of deferred tax assets and liabilities. Stated a different way, deferred tax assets result when book-tax differences result in deductible amounts (like the warranty expense), and deferred tax liabilities result when book-tax differences result in taxable amounts (like the installment sales revenue). A **deductible amount** is an item that decreases taxable income in future periods. A **taxable amount** is an item that increases taxable income in future periods.

Under SFAS No. 109, deferred taxes are measured using the asset and liability method. This method measures the tax effects that arise when the carrying amounts of assets and liabilities differ for financial reporting and tax purposes.

Consider the case of a fixed asset that costs $1,500 and that is being depreciated using the straight-line method for financial accounting purposes and an accelerated method for tax purposes. As illustrated in Figure 2-220, assume that at the end of the year (Year 1), the asset has a carrying value of $1,200 for financial reporting purposes and a tax basis of $1,000. This $200 difference would give rise to a deferred tax liability. Assuming that the tax rate was 40%, a deferred tax liability of $80 ($200 × 40%) would be recorded related to the depreciable asset. The nature of this liability can be understood by assuming that the asset had been sold for $1,200. No gain or loss would be reported on the income statement, but a taxable gain of $200 would result. So, a future sale of the asset may increase taxable income and taxes payable. Of course, any gain on the future asset sale may be more than offset by tax-deductible expenses or losses, so no tax payment may in fact result. Therefore, deferred taxes, although classified as assets and liabilities, are not receivables or payables in the usual sense.

Figure 2-220: Carrying Value Difference

	Book	Tax
Asset cost	$1,500	$1,500
Depreciation to date	(300)	(500)
Basis at balance sheet date	$1,200	$1,000

Assume that the company had a tax rate of 40%, taxable income of $8,000, and no deferred tax assets or liability balances at the beginning of the year. Tax expense would be computed as the difference between the amount of tax payable with the tax return (taxable income times the tax rate) and the adjustment to the deferred tax liability account, as illustrated in Figure 2-221.

Figure 2-221: Entry to Record Tax Expense

Tax expense	$3,280	
Deferred tax liability		$80
Tax payable		$3,200

Tax expense reported on the income statement is the sum of the amount of tax payable with tax returns for the period and the net amount of adjustments made to deferred tax asset and liability balances from the beginning to the end of the year. Because companies that have been operating for more than a year may have interperiod differences over several years, the current year's income tax expense can be calculated as follows:

$$\text{Income Tax Expense} = \left(\begin{array}{l} \text{End-of-Year Deferred Tax Liability (Asset)} \\ - \text{ Beginning-of-Year Tax Liability (Asset)} \end{array} \right)$$
$$+ \text{ Current Period Income Tax Payable}$$

In Year 2, the book depreciation to date is $600 and the tax depreciation is $750, so this $150 difference results in an additional $60 deferred tax liability. The ending deferred tax liability is therefore $140. If taxable income is $7,000, income tax expense = [$140 – $80] + $2,800 = $2,860. A similar accounting entry to Figure 2-221 would be made crediting deferred tax liability by an additional $60. In Year 3, the book depreciation to date is $900 and the tax depreciation is $800, so this $100 difference × 40% = $40 taxable amount and the end-of-year deferred tax liability will be $140 – $40 = $100. If taxable income is $8,000, income tax expense = ($100 – $140) + $3,200 = $3,160. Figure 2-222 shows how the journal entry will partly reverse the amount in the deferred tax liability account.

Figure 2-222: Entry to Record Tax Expense

Tax expense	$3,160	
Deferred tax liability	$40	
Tax payable		$3,200

Because the asset was being depreciated over a five-year life, in the fifth year the difference would be completely reversed. Because the ability to realize the benefit of deferred tax assets is not a certainty, a valuation allowance is provided to reduce deferred tax assets to the extent that it is more likely than not—greater than 50% likelihood—that they will not be realized.

- Examples of temporary differences

- Examples of temporary differences include where different methods are used for:

- Installment sales method for taxes (cannot be used with GAAP).

- Long-term construction contracts.

- Depreciation.

- Goodwill (amortization over 15 years under tax code; not amortized under GAAP).

- Estimated costs such as warranty expense are not recorded until they actually occur under the tax code.

- Prepaid income is part of taxable income when received for taxes but is a liability until earned under GAAP.

- Accounting for investments uses equity method for financial reporting, cost method for taxes.

- Net capital loss recognized currently under GAAP; carried forward to offset future capital gains for taxes.

- Deferred compensation accrues over employee's employment period for GAAP but cannot be deducted until actually paid for taxes.

- Accrued contingent liabilities cannot be deducted for taxes until they are fixed and determinable.

- Excess charitable contributions can be carried over to future years for taxes.

- Cash versus accrual basis: taxes use modified cash; GAAP uses accrual accounting.

Permanent differences

A number of differences between GAAP and tax accounting will never be reversed because some items always affect one method but never another or vice versa.

Examples of permanent differences

The following are some examples of permanent differences.

- Changes in effective tax rate. If the tax rates change, a portion of a temporary difference could become a permanent difference (for example, if a 40% tax rate changes to a 35% tax rate, the 5% change would become a permanent difference because it wouldn't need to be paid when the temporary difference reverses itself).

- Deduction for dividends received. Dependent on ownership interest, some percentage of dividends received by a corporation are nontaxable but must be fully taxed under financial reporting.

- Municipal interest income. 100% exclusion from taxes is allowed for qualified municipal securities (capital gains from the investment are taxable) but is not excluded from financial reporting.

- Percentage depletion. Excess of percentage depletion over cost depletion is allowable as a deduction for taxes but not for financial reporting.

- Government tax exemptions. Governments have passed laws that exempt certain revenues from taxation, permit special deductions above what is allowed by GAAP, or add special taxes on types of businesses to discourage their growth. To spur development in certain geographical areas, some local governments have created tax-free zones. In such situations, a company's effective tax rate will differ from the statutory tax rate (used for financial reporting). The differential will become permanent.

Permanent difference illustration

The best way to illustrate a permanent difference is to show it alongside temporary differences because this will help show how permanent differences are not included in a deferred tax liability or asset account. For example, say that Acme Company reported pretax financial income of $100,000 for Year 1, $110,00 for Year 2, and $120,000 for Year 3, has a 40% tax rate, and received municipal interest income of $20,000 in each of the three years, which is entirely tax deductible for taxes and not deductible for financial reporting. In addition, the company sells a $15,000 asset on an installment account, recognizing the entire sale in Year 1 for financial reporting, but it can recognize only a third of the amount per year for tax purposes. Figure 2-223 shows how to calculate income taxes payable for each of the years.

Figure 2-223: Calculating Income Taxes Payable with Temporary and Permanent Differences

	Year 1	Year 2	Year 3
Pretax financial income	$100,000	$110,000	$120,000
Permanent difference			
Deductible expense	($20,000)	($20,000)	($20,000)
Temporary difference			
Installment sale*	($10,000)	$5,000	$5,000
Taxable income	$70,000	$95,000	$105,000
Income tax payable (40%)	$28,000	$38,000	$42,000

* Installment sale in Year 1: ($15,000) recognized for book + $5,000 recognized for tax = ($10,000)

To determine taxes payable from pretax financial income, deduct those differences making pretax financial income greater than taxable income and add those differences that make pretax financial income less than taxable income. Therefore, the $15,000 asset sold on the books increases Year 1 income by this amount but for taxes only $5,000 can be claimed, so the $10,000 difference is deducted because this is the amount by which pretax financial income exceeds taxable income for the temporary difference. Figure 2-224 shows the journal entries for each of the three years reflects how temporary differences require a deferred tax liability account but permanent differences are simply rolled into income tax payable and income tax expense.

Figure 2-224: Acme Company Journal Entries for Income Taxes in Years 1, 2, and 3

December 31, Year 1		
Income tax expense [$28,000 + ($10,000 × 40%)]	$32,000	
Deferred tax liability ($10,000 × 40%)		$4,000
Income tax payable		$28,000
To record income payment of income taxes		
December 31, Year 2		
Income tax expense [$38,000 − ($5,000 × 40%)]	$36,000	
Deferred tax liability ($5,000 × 40%)	$2,000	
Income tax payable		$38,000
To record income payment of income taxes		
December 31, Year 3		
Income tax expense [$42,000 − ($5,000 × 40%)]	$40,000	
Deferred tax liability ($5,000 × 40%)	$2,000	
Income tax payable		$42,000
To record income payment of income taxes		

Although the statutory tax rate for each of these years remains 40%, the effective tax rate differs. The effective tax rate formula and examples follow.

$$\text{Effective Tax Rate} = \frac{\text{Total Income Tax for Period}}{\text{Pretax Financial Income}}$$

For Year 1 $= \dfrac{\$32,000}{\$100,000} = 32\%$ For Year 2 $= \dfrac{\$36,000}{\$110,000} = 32.73\%$ For Year 3 $= \dfrac{\$40,000}{\$120,000} = 33.33\%$

Financial statement impact

Deferred tax amounts are separated on the balance sheet for financial reporting purposes into current and noncurrent amounts. Deferred tax balances that relate to a current asset or liability are classified as current, and deferred tax balances that relate to a noncurrent asset or liability are classified as noncurrent. For example, the deferred tax balance related to the depreciable asset in the example above would be classified as noncurrent because it relates to a plant asset. The net amount of any current deferred tax assets and liabilities is reported on the balance sheet, as is the net amount of any noncurrent deferred tax assets and liabilities.

The notes to the financial statements should include a reconciliation of the statutory tax rate and the effective tax rate and disclosure of the components of the net deferred tax liability or asset recognized in the balance sheet. Figure 2-225 shows an example of income tax disclosures.

Figure 2-225: Disclosure of Income Taxes

Bounce Sporting Goods Company, International (in Millions)

Note 13: Income Taxes
U.S. and foreign income from continuing operations before income taxes:

		Year 3	Year 2	Year 1
U.S.		$1,401	$1,489	$1,402
Foreign		545	497	(55)
		$1,946	$1,986	$1,347

Provision for income taxes on income from continuing operations:

		Year 3	Year 2	Year 1
Current:	Federal	$(166)	$514	$218
	Foreign	230	95	119
	State	40	51	62
		104	660	399
Deferred:	Federal	117	20	175
	Foreign	3	13	(35)
	State	9	11	(2)
		129	44	138
		$233	$704	$537

Reconciliation of the U.S. federal statutory tax rate to our effective tax rate on continuing operations:

	Year 3	Year 2	Year 1
U.S. federal statutory tax rate	35.0%	35.0%	35.0%
State income tax, net of federal tax benefit	1.7	2.1	3.0
Effect of lower taxes on foreign results	(3.0)	(5.6)	(4.4)
Settlement of prior years' audit issues	(5.6)	(1.9)	(2.8)
Guatemala settlement	(21.4)	—	—
Effect of unusual impairment and other items	3.3	2.3	9.6
Other, net	2.5	3.5	(0.6)
Effective tax rate on continuing operations	12.5%	35.4%	39.8%

Deferred taxes are recorded to give recognition to temporary differences between the tax bases of assets or liabilities and their reported amounts in the financial statements. We record the tax effect of the temporary differences as deferred tax assets or deferred tax liabilities. Deferred tax assets generally represent items that can be used as a tax deduction or credit in future years. Deferred tax liabilities generally represent items that we have taken a tax deduction for but have not yet recorded in the income statement.

Deferred tax liabilities (assets):	Year 3	Year 2
Intangible assets other than nondeductible goodwill	$1,242	$1,172
Property, plant, and equipment	572	430
Safe harbor leases	94	99
Zero coupon notes	68	72
Other	407	288
Gross deferred tax liabilities	2,383	2,061
Net operating loss carry-forwards	(483)	(447)
Post-retirement benefits	(212)	(212)
Various current liabilities	(604)	(439)
Gross deferred tax assets	(1,299)	(1,098)
Deferred tax assets valuation allowance	492	394
Net deferred tax assets	(807)	(704)
Net deferred tax liabilities	$1,576	$1,357
Included in:		
Prepaid expenses, deferred income taxes, and other current assets	$(148)	$(102)
Deferred income taxes	1,724	1,459
	$1,576	$1,357

Deferred tax liabilities are not recognized for temporary differences related to investments in foreign subsidiaries and in unconsolidated foreign affiliates that are essentially permanent in duration. It would not be practical to determine the amount of any such deferred tax liabilities.

Net operating losses of $2.3 billion at year-end Year 3 were carried forward and are available to reduce future taxable income of certain subsidiaries in a number of foreign and state jurisdictions. These net operating losses will expire as follows: $83 million in Year 4, $2.1 billion between Year 5 and Year 17, $173 million may be carried forward indefinitely.

Stock Options

As discussed earlier, a stock option gives selected employees or directors the right to buy common stock at a set exercise price over an specified period of time. The objective of employee stock options is to encourage employees to take an ownership stake in improving the company. Stock options also help retain key employees, provide deferred, long-term compensation that maximizes the employee's after-tax benefits, and help tie employee and company performance to compensation.

Key terms for stock options include the following.

- **Grant date.** A grant date is the date on which the employee receives the options; on the grant date the exercise price and the market price of the stock should be the same (but may not be).

- **Vesting date.** Stock options have a vesting date, which is a date after which the options are allowed to be exercised without any contingent clause of continued employment.

- **Service period.** The service period is the period of time between the grant date and the vesting date during which the employee must continue working for the company (unless otherwise specified).

- **Exercise price.** The exercise price is a price for the stock that is set on the grant date; it is the price the executive will pay for the stock if he or she exercises the options and buys the stock. If the stock price eventually rises above the exercise price, the employee can profit by purchasing shares at the exercise price and selling them at the higher market price.

Stock options can have an effect on the dilution of ownership of a company. Although a stock option is similar to issuing new shares of stock, issuing stock options does not require a company to give current shareholders first right of purchase as is done for normal issuances of new stock. Therefore, current shareholders may experience a drop in their percentage of ownership if large amounts of stock options are issued.

Accounting issues

SFAS No. 123(R) (revised) requires firms to recognize the compensation expense based upon the fair market value of the stock options expected to vest on the grant date. Determining expense using the fair value method is ideally performed by using actual market prices (market-observed) for the stock options. However, this is not usually available because employee stock options lack exchangeability. Therefore, fair value is often based on use of an option pricing model (such as the Black-Scholes-Merton (BSM) model) that determines the fair value of the company (and thus its stock). The BSM model is a closed-form fair value model originally intended to value stocks on the public market (rather than stock options), so some firms have started using an entirely different technique called a "lattice" model, which provides the flexibility to include or exclude variables as fits the situation. The binomial model is the most common example of a lattice model. These models are complex but are becoming easier to apply as sophisticated computer software evolves. SFAS No. 123(R) recommends use of lattice models as being more sensitive to the differences found in stock options.

The fair value method recognizes that there are three aspects to the value of a stock option: the intrinsic value (the difference between the stock price at the grant date and the current market price), the time value of money (investor can invest funds elsewhere while waiting to exercise the options), and the time value of the underlying stock's volatility (employee may profit from appreciation of underlying stock but risks only the option premium, not the full value of the stock). This means that even if the intrinsic value is zero, the total of the other two items will likely show that the option provides some amount of compensation and must be so accounted for. Base data to calculate these three items includes the exercise price of the option, expected dividends, expected volatility of the price of the underlying share, risk-free interest rates for the term of the option, the current price of the underlying share, and the expected term of the option (including contractual term, vesting, and post-vesting employee termination behaviors).

Once the fair value of the company has been determined and applied to the value of the stock options on the grant date, increases or decreases in the stock price do not cause adjustments in the value of the option. The expense is recognized in income over the service period, during which the employee provides services in exchange for the options.

Financial statement impact

Note disclosures related to stock options are illustrated in Figure 2-226. The company in this illustration had been accounting for its stock options using the fair value method, which is now required under SFAS No. 123(R).

Figure 2-226: Disclosure of Stock Option Plans by Inergy Holdings (dates genericized)
(continued next page)

Inergy Holdings, L.P. and Subsidiaries—Accounting for Unit-Based Compensation

The Company and Inergy each have a long-term incentive plan. These plans are accounted for under the recognition and measurement principles of APB Opinion No. 25, "Accounting for Stock Issued to Employees," for all periods presented and presents the **fair value method** pro forma disclosures required under the provisions of SFAS No. 123, "Accounting for Stock-Based Compensation," as amended by SFAS No. 148, "Accounting for Stock-Based Compensation—Transition and Disclosure." No percentage interest or unit-based employee compensation cost is reflected in net income (loss), as all options granted under the plan had an exercise price equal to the market value of the underlying equities on the date of measurement. The following table illustrates the effect on net income (loss) as if the Company had applied the fair value recognition provisions of SFAS No. 123, "Accounting for Stock-Based Compensation," to percentage interest or unit-based employee compensation. For purposes of pro forma disclosures, the estimated fair value of an option is amortized to expense over the option's vesting period. Pro forma information for each of the three years in the period ended September 30, Year 3 is as follows (in thousands, except per unit data).

	Year 3	Year 2	Year 1
Net income as reported	$31,099	$9,533	$7,806
Deduct: Total unit-based employee compensation expense determined under fair value method for all awards	123	37	36
Pro forma net income	$30,976	$9,496	$7,770
Net income per limited partner unit			
Basic—as reported	$ 1.81	$ 0.76	$ 0.63
Diluted—as reported	$ 1.81	$ 0.59	$ 0.49
Pro forma net income per limited partner unit			
Basic	$ 0.63	$ 0.76	$ 0.63
Diluted	$ 1.80	$ 0.59	$ 0.48

Income Per Unit

Basic net income per limited partner unit is computed by dividing net income by the weighted average number of units outstanding. Diluted net income per limited partner unit is computed by dividing net income by the weighted average number of units outstanding and the dilutive effect of unit options granted under the long-term incentive plan. The following table present the calculation of basic and dilutive income per limited partner unit (in thousands, except per unit date).

	Year Ended September 30,		
	Year 3	Year 2	Year 1
Numerator:			
Net income—basic and diluted	$31,099	$ 9,533	$ 7,806
Denominator:			
Weighted average limited partners' outstanding—basic	17,140	12,550	12,373
Effect of dilutive unit options outstanding	46	3,540	3,717
Weighted average limited partners' units outstanding—dilutive	17,186	16,090	16,090
Net income per limited partner unit			
Basic	$ 1.81	$ 0.76	$ 0.63
Diluted	$ 1.81	$ 0.59	$ 0.49

When limited partners' units outstanding are adjusted to give pro forma effect to excess distributions, basic and diluted net income per limited partner unit was $1.68 and $1.67, respectively, for the year ended September 30, Year 3.

Figure 2-226: Disclosure of Stock Option Plans by Inergy Holdings (dates genericized) (concluded)

Segment Information

SFAS No. 131, "Disclosures about Segments of an Enterprise and Related Information" (SFAS No. 131), establishes standards for reporting information about operating segments, as well as related disclosures about products and services, geographic areas, and major customers. Further, SFAS No. 131 defines operating segments as components of an enterprise for which separate financial information is available that is evaluated regularly by the chief operating decision maker in deciding how to allocate resources and assessing performance. In determining reportable segments under the provisions of SFAS No. 131, the Company examined the way it organizes its business internally for making operating decisions and assessing business performance. See Note 13 for disclosures related to the company's propane and midstream segments.

Recently Issued Accounting Pronouncements

On December 16, Year 2, the Financial Accounting Standards Board (FASB) issued Statement of Financial Accounting Standards (SFAS) No. 123 (revised 2004), "Share-Based Payment," which is a revision of SFAS No. 123, "Accounting for Stock-Based Compensation." SFAS 123(R) supersedes APB Opinion No. 25, "Accounting for Stock Issued to Employees," and amends FASB Statement No. 95, "Statement of Cash Flows." Generally, the approach in SFAS No. 123(R) is similar to the approach described in SFAS No. 123. However, SFAS No. 123(R) requires all share-based payments to employees, including grants of employee stock options, to be recognized in the income statement based on their fair values. Pro forma disclosure is no longer an alternative.

SFAS No. 123(R) must be adopted no later than October 1, 2005. Early adoptions will be permitted in periods in which financial statements have not yet been issued. The Company will adopt SFAS No. 123(R) on October 1, Year 3.

SFAS No. 123(R) permits public companies to adopt its requirements using one of two methods:

- A "modified prospective" method in which compensation cost is recognized beginning with the effective date (a) based on the requirements of SFAS No. 123(R) for all share-based payments granted after the effective date and (b) based on the requirements of SFAS No. 123 for all awards granted to employees prior to effective date of SFAS No. 123(R) that remain unvested as of the effective date.

- A "modified retrospective" method that includes the requirements of the modified prospective method described above but also permits entities to restate based on the amounts previously recognized under SFAS No. 123 for purposes of pro forma disclosures either (a) all prior periods presented or (b) prior interim periods of the year of adoption.

The Company will adopt SFAS No. 123(R) using the modified prospective method.

As permitted by SFAS No. 123, during the fiscal year ended September 30, Year 3, the Company accounted for share-based payments to employees using Opinion 25's intrinsic value method and, as such, generally recognized no compensation cost for employee stock options. The impact of adoption of SFAS No. 123(R) will depend on levels of share-based payments granted in the future. However, had we adopted SFAS No. 123(R) in prior periods, the impact of that standard would have approximated the impact of SFAS No. 123 as described in the disclosure of pro forma net income and earnings per share in Note 1. The adoption of SFAS No. 123 (R)'s fair value method is not expected to have a significant impact on our results of operations or on our overall financial position.

SFAS No. 151, "Inventory Costs, an amendment of ARB No. 43, Chapter 4," amends the existing standard that provides guidance on accounting for inventory costs and specifically clarifies that abnormal amounts of costs should be recognized as period costs. This statement is effective for the fiscal year beginning after June 15, Year 3. The adoption of SFAS No. 151 is not expected to have a material effect on the Company's consolidated financial statements.

Backdating is the practice of setting the exercise price on a date when the stock was relatively low. Required disclosures for stock options include any backdating, which while currently legal, must receive the permission of directors and be consistent with company policy, as well as providing full disclosure to investors and reducing earnings by the amount of the added costs. Backdating has been abused by many firms such as by timing the announcement of news that will likely raise their stock price to just after stock options have been issued or by not properly reducing earnings when the backdating occurs. The SEC has forced numerous companies to restate their earnings and is well aware of this issue.

Expiration and adjustment

If stock options expire without being exercised, no adjustment is made to compensation expense. However, if the employee fails to meet the necessary obligations under the agreement, compensation expense must be adjusted as a change in estimate to decrease compensation expense.

Discontinued Operations

A discontinued operation is a common type of irregular item reported on the income statement. When a segment is being disposed of, these operations become discontinued. The results of operations of a component of an entity that has been sold during the year or is being held for sale would be reported under **discontinued operations** net of taxes or benefit, as would losses or gains related to sale or impairment of the asset. Operations that are to be discontinued are transferred from the held and used category to the held-for-sale category on the balance sheet, which may result in gains or losses reported under discontinued operations.

Accounting issues

APB Opinion No. 30 defines the accounting and disclosure provisions for discontinued operations, and SFAS No. 144 modified APB 30 by eliminating the requirement that a discontinued operation had to qualify as a business segment, instead defining a "component of an entity" as any part of a company that can be distinguished by its own cash flows and operations. To qualify as a discontinued operation, according to SFAS No. 144, it is expected that, after disposition, the operations and cash flows of the component will no longer affect ongoing operations and there will be no significant continuing involvement with the component disposed of. The component may be a segment of a business, a reporting unit, or an asset group, but it should have clearly distinguishable operations and cash flows.

If the component is considered impaired, a loss is recognized and the carrying value is written down to fair value less cost to sell. Subsequently, gains may be recognized based on increases in fair value less cost to sell—but not in excess of the total loss previously recognized. At the date of sale, any gain or loss not previously recognized would be recorded.

When a company decides to discontinue an operation, the date of this decision becomes the decision date. On or after the decision date, the operation is officially classified as held-for-sale. When the operation is officially disposed of, this becomes the disposal date.

Calculating the gain or loss on disposal

Two basic amounts must be known to calculate the gain or loss on operations: the loss or gain from operations of the discontinued operation (net of tax) and the loss or gain on disposal of the discontinued operation. The total of these amounts equals the loss or gain on the discontinued operation. The loss from operations is calculated by summing the following.

- The difference between the carrying value of the operations at the beginning of the year and the carrying value after GAAP adjustments are made to bring the operation up to the date it was classified as held-for-sale. Excluding long-lived assets, the carrying value of assets and liabilities must be adjusted according to GAAP. These adjustments are excluded from the gain or loss on disposal because they are included in the gain or loss from operations of the discontinued operation. GAAP adjustments include depreciation, amortization, and adjustment of valuation accounts. For example, the valuation allowance for bad debts on A/R may need to be adjusted to reflect the probabilities of collection when the asset is classified as held-for-sale.

- Losses from operations from the beginning of the year until the date it was reclassified as held-for-sale (includes GAAP adjustments).

- Losses from operations from when it was classified as held-for-sale until sold or until the end of the year if not sold (that is, subsequent to GAAP adjustments).

The gain or loss on disposal is determined by comparing the carrying value of the operation to the fair value less selling costs. The formula for the loss (gain) on disposal is as follows.

Loss (Gain) on Disposal = (Carrying Value – GAAP Adjustments) – (Fair Value – Selling Costs)

GAAP adjustments refer to the adjustments mentioned in the first bullet on the previous page.

The first step in calculating a gain or loss on disposal of an operation is to determine the costs to sell the asset. These costs are deducted from the fair value of the asset. Incremental direct costs of transacting the sale (those costs that arise directly from the decision to sell) include:

- Brokers' commissions and other selling fees.
- Fees for fair value assessment of operation.
- Legal fees.
- Title transfer fees.
- Closing costs.

The next step in calculating the gain or loss on the disposal of an operation is to calculate the carrying value of the operation. This should include capitalization of interest and other costs. With certain exceptions, all material costs that were needed to get the asset ready for its initial use, including any interest costs from financing the asset, should be capitalized to show a more accurate initial investment cost.

Once the carrying value of the operation is determined, the fair value of the operation is assessed by an actuary. If the total carrying amount is greater than the fair value less these costs, then a loss on disposal is recognized in the period in which the asset is classified as held-for-sale. If the opposite is true and there is a gain on disposal, it is not recognized until the period of actual sale.

Financial statement impact

The results of discontinued operations, less applicable income taxes (benefit), are reported as a separate component of income before extraordinary items (if applicable). The gain or loss on disposal may instead be disclosed in the notes to the financial statements. Figure 2-227 illustrates the presentation of discontinued operations on the income statement.

Figure 2-227: Income Statement—Discontinued Operations

Income from continuing operations		$8,000,000
Discontinued operations		
Loss from operation of discontinued X division (net of tax)	$120,000	
Loss from disposal of X division (net of tax)	$200,000	$320,000
Net income		$7,680,000

Future period adjustments

Future losses from the end of the fiscal year until the anticipated date of sale would be dealt with in the periods in which these losses occur in the same way they are accounted for in the prior discussion. In addition, amounts reported in discontinued operations may need to be adjusted in later periods by classifying them separately in discontinued operations for the current period (nature and amount of adjustments should be disclosed).

Extraordinary Items

An extraordinary item is another type of irregular item reported on the income statement. To qualify as an **extraordinary item**, an event or transaction must both have an unusual nature, occur infrequently, and be outside management control, taking into account the environment in which the entity operates. Such events are typically unrelated to the normal activities of the entity and are not expected to reoccur in the foreseeable future. So, for example, damage from a hurricane would be considered extraordinary only if it occurred in a part of the country where such damage was a rare occurrence.

Accounting issues

Because restrictive criteria are applied in determining whether an item is considered extraordinary, there are a number of unusual or infrequent items that are not reported as extraordinary items but are included in income from continuing operations.

Financial statement impact

Extraordinary items are listed net of taxes on a separate line of the income statement below income from continuing operations.

Accounting Changes and Error Corrections

Financial statements must reflect the results of:

- Error corrections.
- Changes in accounting principle.

Changes in accounting principle occur as a result of new rules issued by the FASB or because management has elected to change to another GAAP method where a choice is allowed. When change in accounting principle occurs, GAAS (generally accepted auditing standards) requires a modification of the auditor's report to alert the reader to this fact. For public companies, the SEC requires that the independent auditor provide a letter confirming that the company's chosen method is preferable to the prior method.

Accounting issues

Errors made that affect the income or loss reported in prior years are corrected by adjusting the balance in retained earnings (since prior years' income statement accounts have been closed to retained earnings). When prior years' statements are being reported on a comparative basis, they are restated to corrected amounts. The effect of the error on earlier years than those presented is shown as an adjustment of beginning retained earnings for the earliest year presented.

Under SFAS No. 154, all changes in accounting principle are treated similarly to error corrections, using the retroactive method. Under the retroactive approach, the cumulative effect of changing an accounting principle would then be reported as an adjustment to retained earnings rather than on the income statement.

Assume that a firm decided to change from sum-of-the-years' digits depreciation to straight-line depreciation in Year 3. The effect of the change on prior years' income (before tax) would be $48,000, as illustrated in Figure 2-228.

Figure 2-228: Change in Accounting Principle

Year	Old Method: Sum-of-the-Years'- Digits Depreciation	New Method: Straight-Line Depreciation	Excess of Old Over New Method
Year 2	$96,000	$60,000	$36,000
Year 1	72,000	60,000	12,000
Total			$48,000

Financial statement impact

If prior periods are affected by a change in accounting, the affected prior periods are restated and the required disclosures include the nature of and justification for the accounting change in the period of the change, a report on the effect on income before extraordinary items and net income for all prior presented statements including per-share amounts, and the differences between shareholders' equity accounts opening balances and previously reported balances.

When errors are corrected in prior period statements, the nature of the error and the effect on current period income and per-share amounts should be disclosed.

Disclosure of the cumulative effect of a change in accounting principle, as reported under current GAAP, is illustrated in the income statement section shown in Figure 2-229.

Figure 2-229: Income Statement—Change in Accounting Principle

Income before extraordinary item and cumulative effect of a change in accounting principle	$144,000
Extraordinary item—casualty loss (net of $14,400 tax)	(33,600)
Cumulative effect on prior years of retroactive application of new depreciation method (net of $7,200 tax)	16,800
Net income	$127,200

Business Combinations

SFAS No. 141 states that "a business combination occurs when an entity acquires net assets that constitute a business or acquires equity interests of one or more other entities and obtains control over that entity or entities."

Accounting issues

The purchase method of accounting for business combinations is now required under GAAP; the pooling of interests method is no longer acceptable. In the purchase method, the acquiring company allocates the acquisition purchase price to all tangible and identifiable intangible assets acquired and to liabilities assumed, based on their fair values. Any excess of the purchase price over the fair value of the underlying assets and liabilities is accounted for as goodwill. If the fair value of the net assets acquired exceeds the purchase price, then the values of noncurrent assets, other than financial assets, would be proportionally reduced.

In most cases, the entity to be considered the acquirer in a business combination is evident. The larger entity or the one that issues its equity is normally the acquirer. Business combinations of entities under common control were not affected by SFAS No. 141, so a method similar to the pooling of interests method is used. Common control exists when an individual, a direct family member, or a group of shareholders owns over 50% of the voting interests in each entity in the combination.

Financial statement impact

The notes to the financial statements would include disclosure of the name and a brief discussion of the entity acquired, the percentage interest acquired, the cost of the acquisition, including the number of shares, if any, issued to complete the transaction, the primary reason for the acquisition, and the period for which the results of operations of the acquired entity are included in the consolidated financial statements. Disclosure is also required of a summarized balance sheet of the acquired company, identifying the values allocated to each of the assets and liabilities. Specific disclosure is required of acquired intangible assets, both those that are subject to amortization and those that are not, as well as goodwill arising from the transaction, which should be broken down by the business segments (under SFAS No. 131) to which it relates.

Consolidated Financial Statements

Consolidated financial statements are statements presenting the financial position and results of operations of a parent company and its subsidiaries as if the aggregate were a single entity with divisions. Consolidated financial statements are considered to be the most useful statements of the entity for shareholders and creditors of the entity. A **combined financial statement** is the same as a consolidated financial statement except that it consolidates the statements of legally separate entities related by common ownership. Consolidated and combined financial statements differ in the presentation of the equity section, where the legal status of the entities dictates the information displayed.

Accounting issues

As required by SFAS No. 94, "Consolidation of All Majority-Owned Subsidiaries," all companies with subsidiaries are required to issue consolidated statements including each subsidiary they control (usually meaning 50% or more ownership; however, control can also be exerted in other ways). The limited exceptions that remain allowing the nonconsolidation of majority-owned subsidiaries principally relate to the absence of control over the subsidiary due to legal or other restrictions.

Financial statement impact

To create a consolidated financial statement, first the assets, liabilities, assets, revenue, and expenses of each formerly separate company are combined. Second, any intercompany transactions and balances are eliminated. Finally, the consolidated statements are issued. Intercompany transactions and balances are transactions and balances that appear on both of the company's books, such as the investment account, which contains the investment made to acquire the company (and any previous partial acquisitions) as well as the related stockholders' equity for the subsidiary. An eliminating entry is a workpaper entry (not an accounting entry) used to cancel the effects of intercompany transactions and therefore avoid double-counting of the net assets. The elimination substitutes the subsidiary's net assets for the investment account. In addition to eliminating entries, adjusting entries also occur. An adjusting entry is an entry to correct errors or to account for entries that were made by one party but not the other.

All of the primary financial statements—balance sheet, income statement, statement of cash flows, and statement of stockholders' equity—must be prepared on a consolidated basis, as such information is essential to an understanding of financial position and operating results of the entity by its stakeholders.

To begin the process of consolidating the financial statements, first determine the percentage of stock that has been acquired in the subsidiary if less than 100%. Second, if there is any purchase differential, or a difference between the purchase price and the book value of the acquisition, then this amount is allocated to adjust the underlying assets/liabilities of the acquisition. The percentage acquired times the net assets or of the equity of the acquisition equals the book value. When cost is greater than book value, the net assets will be adjusted upward (or vice versa).

For example, assume that Acme Company acquired 75% of Beta Company's stock for a cash payment of $330,000 (7,500 of 10,000 shares). The initial journal entry by Acme would record a debit of $330,000 to investment in Beta Company with a corresponding credit to cash. The book value of the firm is $400,000. Any difference between the cost and the book value would need to be allocated to specific accounts. When the cost is greater than the book value, some asset accounts would need to be increased in value (or vice versa). The accounts that can be increased are those that have a historical cost that is greater than the market value. Such accounts can be increased but not to the point where they exceed market value (any excess is marked as goodwill). Therefore, in this example, we assume that the property and equipment account and the land account will each be allocated 50% of the excess of cost over book value. Figure 2-230 shows how to determine if there is a difference between the cost and book value.

Figure 2-230: Calculating Difference Between Cost and Book Value and Allocating the Difference

Cost of investment (purchase price)	$330,000
Book value of equity acquired (75% × $400,000)	$300,000
Difference: cost greater than (less than) book value	$ 30,000
Adjust property and equipment upward* (50% × $30,000)	($15,000)
Adjust land upward* (50% × $30,000)	($15,000)
Balance	$ 0
*To mark toward market	

Figure 2-231 shows how a workpaper is used to determine the necessary eliminations.

Figure 2-231: Consolidated Balance Sheet Workpaper

Consolidated Balance Sheet Workpaper
Acme Company and Wholly Owned Subsidiary
January 1, Year 1 (Date of acquisition)

	Acme Co.	Beta Co.	Eliminations (workpaper only, not journal entries)		Non-controlling Interest	Consoli-dated Balances
			Debit	Credit		
Cash	$170,000	$100,000				$270,000
Other current assets	700,000	250,000				950,000
Plant and equipment	600,000	200,000	$15,000**			815,000
Land	200,000	100,000	15,000**			315,000
Investments in Beta Co.	330,000			$330,000*		
Difference between cost & book value			30,000*	$30,000**		
Total assets	$2,000,000	$650,000				$2,350,000
Liabilities	300,000	250,000				550,000
Common stock						
Acme Co.	1,000,000					1,000,000
Beta Co.		250,000	187,500*		$62,500*	
Other contributed capital						
Acme Co.	200,000					200,000
Beta Co.		50,000	37,500*		12,500*	
Retained earnings						
Acme Co.	500,000					500,000
Beta Co.		100,000	75,000*		25,000*	
Noncontrolling interest					$100,000	100,000
Total liabilities and equity	$2,000,000	$650,000	$360,000	$360,000		$2,350,000

*   To eliminate investments in Beta Co: common stock = $250,000 × 0.75 = $187,500 owned, $62,500 not owned; other contributed capital = $50,000 × 0.75 = $37,500 owned, $12,500 not owned; retained earnings = $100,000 × 0.75 = $75,000 owned, $25,000 not owned; difference between cost and book value = $30,000.

** To distribute the difference between cost and book value ($30,000 × 50% to plant and equipment, × 50% to land)

Note also in Figure 2-231 that assets and liabilities are summed to find the consolidated amounts (after factoring in eliminating entries).The fair value markups made to account for the difference between cost and book value would be amortized over the useful lives of the assets selected.

In the subsequent periods, the fair value markups would be amortized over the remaining life of the underlying assets. Similarly, intercompany transactions in the subsequent years will have to be reversed. Discussion of these topics is beyond the scope of the current text.

Derivatives

A **derivative** is a type of financial instrument or contract that generally requires no or minimal initial investment and permits net settlement. A derivatives derives its value from changes in a benchmark known as an underlying, such as mortgage rates, commodity prices, exchange rates, interest rates, or indexes. Changes in the benchmark are measured based upon a notional amount, or unit measure of currency, bushels, shares, and so on.

Derivative contracts include forwards, futures, swaps, and options. The stock options and warrants discussed earlier are a common type of derivative instrument. The market value of a stock option is derived from the value of the underlying stock that can be purchased at an established price. Derivative contracts should have terms that permit net settlement.

Derivatives might be purchased for speculative purposes. But they are often used to hedge, or offset, risks involved in other transactions. For example, the option to purchase a quantity of oil at a set price in the future can offset the risk of oil price variability. Therefore, derivatives are similar to insurance, because the mitigation of risk comes with a price. That price includes not only the cost of the derivative but the reduction of the potential for gain on favorable price changes for the item being hedged.

Accounting issues

SFAS No. 133, as amended by SFAS No. 138 and SFAS No. 149, governs accounting for derivatives and hedging transactions. These FASB statements require that all derivative instruments of any type be recognized at fair value in the balance sheet as assets or liabilities depending on their nature.

How changes in the fair value (that is, gains or losses) of a derivative are accounted for depends on whether it has been designated as and qualifies as part of a hedging relationship and the nature of the hedge.

- **No hedging designation.** When a derivative is held for speculative purposes, the gain or loss is recognized currently in earnings.

- **Fair-value hedge.** A fair-value hedge is used to offset the exposure to changes in the value of an asset, liability, or firm commitment (like a purchase commitment). The gain or loss on the hedging instrument as well as the offsetting loss or gain on the hedged item are recognized currently in earnings in the same accounting period.

- **Cash flow hedge.** A cash flow hedge is used to offset the exposure to variability in future cash flows from an anticipated transaction (such as an anticipated purchase of inventory). Gains and losses on cash flow hedges are reported in other comprehensive income and then reclassified into earnings when the forecasted transaction affects earnings.

- **Foreign currency hedge.** Gains or losses on a derivative instrument or nonderivative financial instrument designated and qualifying as a foreign currency hedging instrument are accounted for as follows:

  - The gain or loss on a hedge of a foreign-currency-denominated firm commitment and the offsetting loss or gain on the firm commitment hedged is recognized currently in earnings.

  - The gain or loss on a hedge of an available-for-sale security and the offsetting loss or gain on the hedged security is recognized currently in earnings.

  - The effective portion of the gain or loss on a hedge of a forecasted foreign-currency-denominated transaction is reported as a component of other comprehensive income and reclassified into earnings in the same period or periods during which the hedged forecasted transaction affects earnings. The remaining gain or loss on the hedging instrument is recognized currently in earnings.

  - The gain or loss on a hedge of a net investment in a foreign operation is reported in other comprehensive income as part of the cumulative translation adjustment to the extent that it is effective as a hedge, and any remaining gain or loss is recorded in earnings currently.

Financial statement impact

Disclosure for derivatives includes the objectives for holding or issuing the instruments (speculative or hedging), the context needed to understand the objectives, and the firm's strategy for achieving those objectives. Fair-value hedges, cash flow hedges, and other types of derivatives should be distinguished. The company's risk management policy should be described, as should the items or transactions for which risks are hedged. Disclosure of the gain or loss recognized in earnings is also required.

The requirements of SFAS No. 133 are complicated, and a clear understanding of hedging strategies is necessary to ensure that the appropriate accounting is made for an entity's transactions in this area.

Segment Reporting

Diversified entities and entities that grow by purchasing other entities are becoming ever more common, and readers of financial statements need more information on the components of such diversified entities in order to get a realistic picture of how each component contributes to the risk, profitability, and growth of the entity.

Some corporations object to releasing segment information, fearing that the information will be misinterpreted or used by competitors and unions. However, the FASB and the SEC feel that not reporting segment information leaves investors with an incomplete picture of a company's operating performance. SFAS No. 131, "Disclosures about Segments of an Enterprise and Related Information," requires that the management approach be used to report financial information. The management approach requires that entities report information on a single basis of segmentation—the basis that is used by management in making capital allocation decisions, such as product line or geographic region.

Operating segment

The operating segment is the basic division that requires disaggregated reporting.

Any component of an entity that meets the following criteria is considered an operating segment:

- The component has separate revenues and expenses earned from business activities.

- A chief decision maker for the entity reviews the component's activities and decides how to allocate funds to the component.

- An internal reporting system tracks individual financial data for the segment.

- The component is materially significant enough to warrant disclosure, as defined by at least one of the following:

    - Revenue is at least 10% of the revenue for the entire entity.

    - The absolute value of its profit or loss is at least 10% of the absolute value of the greater of either the total operating profit of all segments not reporting a loss or the total loss of all segments reporting a loss.

    - Segment assets are at least 10% of the total assets of the entity.

Results of two or more segments may be aggregated provided that they share similar characteristics, in that they:

- Make the same products or services.

- Use the same production process.

- Share the same type of customers.

- Use similar methods of distribution.

- Share the same regulatory environment.

Required segment reporting

A maximum of ten segments would be identified, and the identified segments should account for at least 75% of the total sales to external customers. Allocation of common or corporate costs for financial reporting is not required.

SFAS No. 131 requires disclosure of general information about operating segments, segment assets, and segment income statement information, including sales (both internal and external), interest revenue and expense, tax expense, depreciation and amortization, and unusual and extraordinary items. Other required disclosures relate to operating results for different geographic areas (when segments are not defined on this basis) and information about major customers. Reconciliation of segment revenue, income, and assets to financial statement totals for those amounts is also required.

An example of segment disclosures is shown in Figure 2-232.

Figure 2-232: Disaggregated Information

Segmented Information by Operating Segments

	Tennis Balls	Tennis Racquets	Training Equipment	Clothing	Finance	Totals
Revenues from external customers	$6,900	$6,900	$16,100	$27,600	$11,500	$69,000
Intersegment revenues	—	—	6,900	3,450	—	10,350
Segment profit	460	161	2,070	5,290	1,150	9,131
Interest revenue	—	—	—	—	9,200	9,200
Interest expense	—	—	—	—	6,900	6,900
Depreciation and amortization	460	230	115	3,450	2,530	6,785
Other significant noncash items:						
Cost in excess of billings on long-term contracts	—	460	—	—	—	460
Segment assets	4,600	11,500	6,900	27,600	131,100	181,700
Expenditures for segment assets	690	1,610	1,150	3,910	1,380	8,740

Reconciliation of Revenues and Profit or Loss

Revenues:	
Total segment revenues	$79,350
Revenues of immaterial segments	2,300
Elimination of intersegment revenues	(10,350)
Total revenues	$71,300
Profit or loss:	
Total segment profit or loss	$9,131
Elimination of intersegment profits	(1,150)
Unallocated amounts:	
Interest expense	(1,150)
Litigation settlement received	1,150
Other corporate expenses	(1,725)
Adjustment to pension expense in consolidation	575
Total profit or loss of immaterial segments	230
Income before income taxes and extraordinary items	$7,061

Multinational Considerations

Before preparing consolidated financial statements, a parent must translate the statements of any foreign subsidiaries or branches from its reporting currency to that of the parent. Foreign currency translation issues also arise any time a company enters into a transaction that is denominated in a currency other than its reporting currency.

Functional currency

Choosing the appropriate method for translating subsidiaries' foreign currency financial statements depends upon what an entity's **functional currency** is. SFAS No. 52, "Foreign Currency Translation," defines functional currency as the currency of the primary economic environment in which the subsidiary operates. The subsidiary's local currency would be its functional currency if its operations are relatively self-contained and integrated within a particular country. On the other hand, the parent's currency would be the functional currency if the operations of the branch or subsidiary are essentially an extension of the parent company's operations.

Determining which currency is the functional currency would depend on factors such as where the subsidiary's sales market is, how its sales prices are determined, where its expenses are incurred, its sources of financing, and the extent of intercompany transactions. Self-contained operations would typically have their sales, purchases, and financing denominated in their local currency and would have few intercompany transactions. On the other hand, integral operations would typically have their sales, purchases, and financing denominated in the parent's currency and would have a number of intercompany transactions.

If a subsidiary operates in a hyperinflationary environment (one with inflation of 100% or more over a three-year period), the parent's currency is always the functional currency.

Currency translation methods

When the parent's currency is the functional currency, the statements of the branch or subsidiary are remeasured into the parent's currency using the temporal method. On the other hand, when the subsidiary's local currency is the functional currency, the statements are translated using the current rate method. When the subsidiary uses its local currency but this currency is not the functional currency or the parent's reporting currency, then the statements must first be remeasured to the functional currency and then translated to the parent's reporting currency.

Remeasurement using the temporal method

Under the temporal method, also known as the monetary/nonmonetary method, nonmonetary balances (all balance sheet items other than cash, claims to cash, and cash obligations) are translated by using historical exchange rates, and the expenses associated with them should be translated at the historical exchange rate in effect when the item was originally recorded.

These nonmonetary accounts include:

- Investments carried at cost.

- Inventories carried at cost and cost of goods sold.

- Prepaid expenses such as rent, insurance, and advertising.

- PP&E and depreciation expense.

- Intangible assets and amortization expense.

- Deferred charges and credits.

- Deferred revenue.

- Paid-in capital accounts.

Monetary assets and liabilities (cash, receivables, and payables) and other assets and liabilities measured at current values (market values or discounted cash flows) are translated at the current exchange rate on the balance sheet date. Income statement accounts other than those mentioned above are translated using the average exchange rate for the current year (quarter or month) for simplicity. In the temporal method, translation gains and losses are reported in income.

The example in Figure 2-233 shows a remeasurement from euros to U.S. dollars, the branch's functional currency. As indicated, accounts have been translated using either the current rate on the balance sheet date, the historical exchange rate, or the average rate for the year. The home office account, which represents equity, is not remeasured; rather, the beginning balance in dollars is carried forward.

Figure 2-233: Remeasurement Using the Temporal Method

Bounce Sporting Goods Company
Remeasurement of European Branch Trial Balance to U.S. Dollars
December 31, Year 1

	Balance (euros) debit (credit)	Exchange Rates	Balance (U.S. dollars) debit (credit)
Cash	€19,950	$0.24 *	$4,788
Trade accounts receivable	352,800	0.24 *	84,672
Inventories	157,500	0.21 **	33,075
Home office	(432,250)		(78,400)
Sales	(700,000)	0.225 ***	(157,500)
Cost of goods sold	472,500	0.21 **	99,225
Operating expenses	129,500	0.225 ***	29,138
Subtotals	€0		$14,998
Transaction gain	0		(14,998)
Totals	€0		$0

* Current rate (on December 31, Year 1) = .24
** Applicable historical rate
*** Average exchange rate for the year

Translation using the current rate method

In the current rate method, all assets and liabilities are translated using the current exchange rate on the balance sheet date. Paid-in capital accounts are translated using the historic rate. For simplicity, SFAS No. 52 requires translation of income statement accounts based on the average rate for the current year (although some accountants would argue for using the end-of-year rate on the income statement as well as the balance sheet). Translation gains and losses are not shown in net income but are reported as a component of other comprehensive income.

An example of a translation worksheet from euros to U.S. dollars appears in Figure 2-234. Use of the current, average, or historical exchange rate is indicated. The retained earnings balance is not translated; rather, the dollar amount of beginning retained earnings from the prior year would be carried forward. Ending retained earnings would be the sum of this beginning balance, plus the translated income amount, less any dividends declared during the year.

Figure 2-234: Translation Using the Current Rate Method (Subsidiary Financial Statements) to Reporting Currency from Functional Currency

Bounce International Germany
Translation of Financial Statements to U.S. Dollars
For Year Ended August 31, Year 2

	German Euros	Exchange Rate	U.S. Dollars
Income Statement			
Net sales	€206,400	$0.515 [1]	$106,296
Other revenue	51,600	0.515 [1]	26,574
Total revenue	€258,000		$132,870
Cost of goods sold	€154,800	0.515 [1]	$79,722
Operating expenses and income taxes	82,560	0.515 [1]	42,518
Total costs and expenses	€237,360		$122,240
Net income	€20,640		$10,630
Balance Sheet			
Cash	€8,600	$0.49 [2]	$4,214
Trade accounts receivable (net)	34,400	0.49 [2]	16,856
Inventories	154,800	0.49 [2]	75,852
Short-term prepayments	3,440	0.49 [2]	1,686
Plant assets (net)	275,200	0.49 [2]	134,848
Intangible assets (net)	17,200	0.49 [2]	8,428
Total assets	€493,640		$241,884
Notes payable	€17,200	$0.49 [2]	$8,428
Trade accounts payable	25,800	0.49 [2]	12,642
Common stock	430,000	0.54 [3]	232,200
Retained earnings	20,640		11,146
Cumulative translation adjustments			(22,532)
Total liabilities and stockholders' equity	€493,640		$241,884

[1] Average for year ended December 31, Year 2
[2] Current rate (on December 31, Year 2)
[3] Historical rate (on December 31, Year 1, date of X Corporation's investment)

Financial statement presentation and disclosure requirements for foreign currency

The income statement or notes should list the aggregate gains or losses from foreign entities over the accounting period. Changes in cumulative translation adjustments for the period must also be disclosed in either a separate statement, a note, or the statement of stockholders' equity. Details of translation adjustments include the beginning and ending amounts of cumulative translation adjustments, aggregate adjustments, hedges of net investments, long-term intercompany transactions, income taxes allocated to translation adjustments, and decreases from liquidating a foreign investment.

Progress Check

Directions: Read each question and respond in the space provided. Answers and page references appear on the page following the progress check questions.

Match the following types of receivables with their definitions.

1. _____ Current receivables

2. _____ Noncurrent receivables

3. _____ Accounts receivable

4. _____ Notes receivable

5. _____ Nontrade receivables

a. Receivable evidenced by a written promise to pay on a particular date

b. Interest or dividends receivable

c. Receivables expected to be collected within a year or the operating cycle, whichever is longer

d. Informal customer promises to pay for goods sold on credit in the ordinary course of business

e. Receivables expected to be collected after one year or the operating cycle, whichever is longer

6. If inventory prices have been rising, which cost flow assumption would a firm choose in order to maximize its inventory value and its net income if it sells a high volume of inexpensive items?

( ) a. LIFO

( ) b. FIFO

( ) c. Average cost

( ) d. Specific identification

7. Trading securities should be valued at

( ) a. historical cost.

( ) b. market value.

( ) c. present value.

( ) d. net realizable value.

8. Which of the following costs should not be included in inventory valuation?

( ) a. Manufacturing overhead costs

( ) b. Cash discounts

( ) c. Shipping costs (freight-in)

( ) d. Interest costs related to inventory preparation

9. Which of the following methods of measuring depreciation would be based on units produced?

( ) a. Decreasing charge method

( ) b. Declining balance method

( ) c. Activity method

( ) d. Straight-line method

10. A loss contingency should be recorded if it is

( ) a. probable that a liability has been incurred and the loss can be reasonably estimated.

( ) b. reasonably possible that a liability has been incurred and the loss can be reasonably estimated.

( ) c. probable that a liability has been incurred and the amount of the loss is reliably documented.

( ) d. reasonably possible that a liability has been incurred and the amount of the loss is reliably documented.

Progress check answers

1. c (p. 2-321)

2. e (p. 2-321)

3. d (p. 2-321)

4. a (p. 2-321)

5. b (p. 2-321)

6. b (p. 2-339)

7. b (p. 2-321)

8. d (p. 2-337)

9. c (p. 2-372)

10. a (p. 2-394)

The SEC and Its Reporting Requirements

Topic overview

The Securities and Exchange Commission (SEC) has broad authority over activities of the securities industry, including regulation of securities firms and the stock exchanges. It also has responsibility for monitoring and regulating periodic reporting by companies with publicly issued securities. The principal reason for the SEC's existence is to protect the interests of investors and potential investors and maintain market integrity.

Acts Establishing the SEC and Its Power

SEC legislation

The principal acts establishing the SEC are the 1933 Securities Act and the 1934 Securities Exchange Act. More recently, the Sarbanes-Oxley Act amended the Securities Exchange Act to give the SEC additional responsibilities.

Securities Act of 1933

The **Securities Act of 1933** is principally concerned with the initial sale and distribution of securities rather than the trading in securities subsequent to their initial issuance. The act requires a registration statement to be effective prior to the sale of securities to the general public (initial public offerings as well as subsequent offerings of securities in the primary market) and that a prospectus be delivered to every purchaser of a security prior to the sale.

A registration statement consists of two parts. Part I, which comprises the prospectus, consists of information regarding the securities being offered, the issuer of the securities, the plan of distribution, and the use of proceeds from the offering. It also includes five years of selected financial information together with management discussion and analysis (MD&A) of the results of operation, financial position and liquidity, and capital resources of the issuer as well as audited financial statements for the last three years. (The MD&A is discussed later in this topic.)

Part II of the registration statement is more supplemental and administrative and is generally not provided directly to the general public; however, the entire registration statement is available to the public via the EDGAR system accessible through the SEC's Web site (www.sec.gov), which contains copies of all filings made by registrants with the SEC.

The SEC declares a registration statement effective after it has reviewed and provided comments to the registrant on its content and is satisfied with the registrant's responses to such comments and the amendments made to the registration statement.

Securities Exchange Act of 1934

The **Securities Exchange Act of 1934** regulates the trading of securities on the secondary market and the actions of investors, including:

- Regulation of the securities markets.

- Prevention of market manipulation and fraud.

- Continuous disclosure by Securities Act registrants.

- Control of credit granted for purchase of securities, called margin trading.

- Proxy solicitations and other communications with shareholders.

- Regulation of insider trading.

The Securities Exchange Act requires all U.S.-domiciled companies registered under the Securities Act to file annual reports on Form 10-K, quarterly reports on Form 10-Q, and other reports with the SEC such as current event Form 8-K and proxy statements. (There are comparable reporting forms for foreign companies whose securities are registered with the SEC.) The act also requires the issuer of any over-the-counter securities to register with the SEC if the stock is held by 500 or more stockholders and the company has $10 million or more in total assets. The Securities Exchange Act is concerned not with the specific nature of the securities issued (addressed under Securities Act registration) but with ensuring that the registrant maintains adequate information regarding the financial condition of the company for investors.

Additional legislation

In addition, the SEC has the responsibility for the maintenance of a number of secondary acts, including the Public Utility Act of 1935, the Trust Indenture Act of 1939, the Investment Company Act of 1940, the Investment Advisors Act of 1940, and the Sarbanes-Oxley Act of 2002.

SEC enforcement and regulatory operations

In conducting its enforcement activities under the securities laws, the SEC has the right to commence civil legal action against those who violate the laws; however, it works closely with the Justice Department when criminal enforcement action is required.

As part of its responsibility for periodic reporting by public companies, the SEC has the authority to set accounting principles to be used by public companies in their periodic reports. In this regard, the SEC has determined that at the present time it will support the standards-setting process of the FASB and its accounting standards.

The SEC conducts its regulatory operations through four divisions:

- Corporation Finance

- Market Regulation

- Investment Management

- Enforcement

Of these, the Division of Corporation Finance is the most familiar to accountants. It processes and conducts the reviews of filings under the Securities Act, the Securities Exchange Act, and the Trust Indenture Act of 1939.

The SEC also has a number of staff offices. The Office of the Chief Accountant of the SEC is the one with which accountants have the most contact, as it provides guidance on accounting principles and represents the SEC in its dealings with the FASB and other accounting standards setters.

SEC Reporting Requirements for Public Companies

The SEC's reporting requirements are divided into three categories: regulations S-X, S-K, and S-B. Regulation S-X governs the content required in all financial statements for both registration of companies and periodic reporting. In contrast, regulation S-K governs all nonfinancial information. Regulation S-B was designed to govern all reporting for small businesses and is not covered further here. These reporting requirements apply to the filings under both the Securities Act and the Securities Exchange Act.

Regulation S-X

Regulation S-X requires the issuance of audited financial statements prepared according to U.S. GAAP for Securities Act registrations using Forms S-1, S-2, or S-3 and for Securities Exchange Act compliance with periodic reporting requirements, including the annual report on Form 10-K and quarterly reports on Form 10-Q. Specifically, in Form 10-K, the entity must supply audited balance sheets for the two most recent fiscal years, income statements, cash flow statements, and changes in the components of stockholders' equity for the three most recent fiscal years. Additionally, Regulation S-X requires disclosures of certain information not required by GAAP such as disclosures of compensating bank balances. The regulation also imposes materiality thresholds that must be followed.

Interim financial statements, unlike annual statements, do not need to be audited but must be prepared according to GAAP. Such statements, which are required for the first three quarters of the year, are issued on Form 10-Q. The interim reporting requirements include a condensed balance sheet for both the most recent quarter and the most recent fiscal year (for comparison), a condensed year-to-date income statement, and cash flow statements for the end of the last fiscal quarter and for the same quarter a year prior (for comparison). Regulation S-X also includes the requirements regarding independent auditors and their reports on the financial statements of registrants.

Regulation S-K

Regulation S-K governs all nonfinancial disclosure requirements made in Securities Act and Securities Exchange Act filings. The SEC's requirements in total are called the Basic Information Package (BIP), which includes all of the requirements of Regulations S-X and S-K. Regulation S-K disclosure requirements include, among other things:

- Risk factors relating to the registrant's business and securities.
- A description of the business.
- Cash dividend frequency.
- Summary of the entity's financial trends over five years.

- Eight quarters of sales, gross profit, and earnings data (for larger companies).

- MD&A.

- Any changes in accountants in the past two years and any disagreements with the accountants.

SEC Disclosure Requirements for Public Companies

The concepts of integrated disclosure, standardized financial statements, and MD&A are discussed below. Also discussed in this section are the SEC's disclosure requirements and their public records database, EDGAR.

Integrated disclosure, standard financial statements, and MD&A

Originally, the Securities Act was made to regulate primary market transactions and the Securities Exchange Act to regulate secondary market transactions, so they had different disclosure requirements. To promote full disclosure and comparability between financial statements (and to reduce costs), the requirements for filings with the SEC under the acts have been integrated, financial statements have been standardized, and the inclusion of a section containing an MD&A is now required. These elements are discussed below.

Integrated disclosure

In the past, the requirements for disclosure for filings made under the Securities Act and the Securities Exchange Act differed in their many details. In 1982, the SEC adopted the Integrated Disclosure System (IDS). The IDS continues to be refined, but the primary aspects of the system are as follows:

- Company-specific information for both acts is practically identical, so that Securities Exchange Act filings are essentially updates of the information provided in registration statements under the Securities Act. Not only does this assist the investor, as the information content of the filings is now similar, but it also eases the burden on the registrants who prepare the information.

- When large companies (meeting certain criteria) make additional securities filings, they can incorporate the information from their latest Securities Exchange Act filings into the new issuance by reference. (This saves the company time and money.)

Integrated disclosure gave investors in the secondary market equal standing with primary market investors.

Standardized financial statements

The existence of the IDS and Regulations S-X and S-K and the use of the Basic Information Package ensures that the Securities Act and the Securities Exchange Act have standardized requirements for financial statements. Thus financial statements required by the Securities Act on Forms S-1, S-2, and S-3 are identical to those required in a Form 10-K filed under the Securities Exchange Act.

MD&A

The BIP requires the inclusion of an analysis of the company's operations and financial conditions referred to as an MD&A (**management discussion and analysis**). The intent behind this requirement is to give investors the perspective that management has on a company. Management must analyze their company's liquidity, capital resources, and the results of operations for the past three years. The impact of inflation, when material, must also be disclosed. Financial statements are made up of historical data, so the SEC regulations for the MD&A section of filings require that management focus on all of the events, trends, and uncertainties known to them that could cause past results not to be indicative of future performance. This requirement covers both past events that will no longer influence the future and events that may have had no effect on past events but will begin to have an influence. Only information known to management must be discussed; discussion of hypothetical situations is not required. The format of the MD&A was not specified by the SEC to enable this section to avoid becoming a standard "cookie cutter" form, leaving management free to discuss the qualitative and quantitative factors in their business as they see fit.

SEC disclosure requirements

The most common registration forms required by the SEC are discussed in this section. Note that there are numerous forms listed on the SEC's Web site for the various exceptions and special cases that have arisen over the years.

Forms S-1, S-2, and S-3

Forms S-1, S-2, and S-3 are used for the registration of securities with the SEC. Registration is a complex process involving legal counsel, accountants (both internal and independent) with SEC expertise, and underwriters. Form S-1 is used for IPOs and for companies that do not qualify for streamlined registrations. Form S-2 is available for companies that have not defaulted on any obligation or dividend on preferred stock and that have been filing Securities Exchange Act reports for at least three years in a timely fashion. Form S-3 is similar in its requirements to Form S-2, except that companies are required to have only one year of timely prior filings; it does require, however, that the company have a public float, or market value of its common stock, of at least $75 million. Other exceptions and details apply to each of these forms. Whichever form is used, each will include all information about the offering in the prospectus (part I), and the company-specific sections are all the same. However, when utilizing Forms S-2 and S-3, the company-specific information can be incorporated by reference to previously issued reports (available from the SEC on their EDGAR database online).

Form 10-K

Form 10-K is the annual report most companies with actively traded stock must file with the SEC, providing a comprehensive overview of the registrant's business. As of 2006, the deadline for Form 10-K is 60 days.

Form 10-Q

Form 10-Q is the quarterly report filed for the first three quarters by most publicly traded companies. It includes unaudited financial statements and MD&A. The intent is to provide more relevant information for investors by showing a continuing view of the entity's financial position throughout the year. As of 2006, the deadline for Form 10-Q is 30 days.

Disclosure of Material Events or Form 8-K

Form 8-K is called the current report because it must be used to disclose any material events or corporate alterations of importance to investors that have yet to be reported in a financial statement. The nine categories of items that are included in Form 8-K are as follows:

- Item 1: Changes in control of registrant
- Item 2: Acquisition or disposition of assets
- Item 3: Bankruptcy or receivership
- Item 4: Changes in registrant's certifying accountant
- Item 5: Other materially important events
- Item 6: Resignations of registrant's directors
- Item 7: Financial statements and exhibits
- Item 8: Change in fiscal year
- Item 9: Regulation FD disclosure

Proxy solicitations

Proxy solicitations are used when voting is required by shareholders so that certain shareholders give their rights to specific agents to vote for them in proxy at the appropriate time. The laws of a company's state of incorporation and its bylaws govern when shareholders are entitled to vote. When a vote is required and anyone solicits proxies, that person must provide a proxy statement including information that will help the shareholder vote in an informed manner. The proxy statement includes a proxy card authorizing a specific agent to vote for the shareholder. Most proxy cards involve a specific vote and indicate a specific position that the proxy agent must vote for them, but others are for longer duration and allow the agent to vote as he or she pleases. Proxy filings are publicly available information. The specific items that must be included in a proxy statement are:

- Date, time, and location of the next shareholders' meeting.
- Individual for whom the solicitation is prepared and the estimated cost of the solicitation.
- Amount of shares of issuer's stock held by the directors and executive officers.
- Rights of dissenters, if any, on any voting matter.
- Rights of proxy revocation.

EDGAR

The SEC has created a database called the Electronic Data Gathering, Analysis, and Retrieval, or EDGAR, system. This database, accessible from www.sec.gov, contains the public filings for all companies registered with the SEC. Any member of the public can use this database to access the financial statements of any publicly traded company free of charge by simply entering information in a search engine provided with the database.

Provisions of the Sarbanes-Oxley Legislation

The **Sarbanes-Oxley Act of 2002** (SOX), also called the Public Company Accounting Reform and Investor Protection Act, legislated the relationship between corporate management, boards of directors, and auditors. The act aims to make financial information released by public corporations as accurate and forthcoming as possible by establishing a system of checks and balances between the board of directors, company management, and external auditors.

Provisions of SOX include the creation of a **Public Company Accounting Oversight Board** (PCAOB), with five full-time members, to provide regulatory oversight to the accounting profession. SOX requires firms performing audits for publicly traded companies to register as accounting firms with the PCAOB.

SOX contains nine "titles." Sections of SOX are numbered according to the title in which they appear (for example, Title III contains Sections 301, 302, and so on). A brief summary of these titles is shown in Figure 2-235.

Figure 2-235: Summary of the Sarbanes-Oxley Act of 2002 (continued on next page)

Title	Brief Coverage of Provision
Title I	Establishes the Public Company Accounting Oversight Board (PCAOB). The PCAOB is responsible for overseeing the audits of public companies for the protection of investors and furthering the public interest in the preparation of informative, accurate, and independent audit reports. Unlike the SEC, the PCAOB is not a government agency but rather a private, not-for-profit corporation. The PCAOB is made up of five full-time members who are appointed by the SEC after consultation with the Secretary of the Treasury and the Chairman of the Board of Governors of the Federal Reserve System. PCAOB members serve five-year staggered terms with a two-term limit and must be "appointed from among prominent individuals of integrity and reputation who have demonstrated commitment to the interests of investors and the public and an understanding of the responsibilities for and nature of the financial disclosures required of issuers under the securities laws and the obligations of accountants with respect to the preparation and issuance of audit reports with respect to such disclosures." At least two members must have been CPAs, and the remaining three must not be and cannot have been CPAs. Title I requires firms performing audits for publicly traded companies to register as an accounting firm with the PCAOB. The Sarbanes-Oxley Act also gives the PCAOB broad powers with respect to establishing or adopting auditing standards; however, the act sets certain minimum requirements, including concurring partner reviews and working paper standards. Title I further sets forth ethical standards and provides for inspections, investigations, and discipline of public accounting firms. It further states that foreign accounting firms performing audits for issuers of public securities are subject to the act.
Title II	Title II deals with auditor independence. It provides that any firm auditing the books of an issuer of public securities cannot perform a list of other accounting services for the issuer. The auditor may perform other services (not on the list) if prior approval is received. Title II also allows for some exemptions (approved by PCAOB) if it is in the public interest. The fees for such nonaudit activities must be reported in a company's annual report on Form 10-K or in its annual proxy statement. A public accounting firm may not audit the books of an issuer of public securities if any officer or director of the issuer was employed by the public accounting firm and participated in any audit activity with the issuer within one year. Title II also requires rotation of audit partners for an issuer within a public accounting firm. It provides in section 204 that the auditor shall report to an auditing committee appointed by the board of directors of the issuer.
Title III	Title III addresses management responsibility. It requires that the principal executive officer or officers and the principal financial officer certify the company's periodic filings with the SEC that contain financial statements. Such certifications must verify that the officer has no knowledge of untrue statements or omissions of material fact and that the financial statements are fair representations of financial condition and results of operations. Title III also requires management to design internal controls to ensure that material information is made known to such officers by others within the business and its entities. Section 307 requires the SEC to adopt regulations requiring attorneys to report material breaches of the securities laws.

Figure 2-235: Summary of the Sarbanes-Oxley Act of 2002 (concluded)

Title	Brief Coverage of Provision
Title IV	Title IV requires enhanced financial disclosures in the periodic reports to the SEC. It provides for more disclosure in periodic reports containing financial statements, requiring them to disclose all material off-balance-sheet transactions, arrangements, and obligations (including contingent obligations). Title IV prohibits loans to executives, unless those loans are made as part of the usual business of the company (for example, mortgage company lending to its president for a home purchase). Title IV also requires that management establish and document internal control procedures and certify as to the effectiveness of such controls annually. The company's independent auditor is required to perform an attestation engagement to report upon the assessment of internal controls made by management.
Title V	Title V addresses conflicts of interest regarding financial analysts, placing restrictions on analysts employed by broker-dealers who perform investment banking services (issuing and trading of debt and equity securities) for the issuers.
Title VI	Title VI outlines funding available to the SEC and its authority regarding the Sarbanes-Oxley Act.
Title VII	Title VII charged the General Accounting Office (GAO) with conducting a study to determine the factors that led to the consolidation of public accounting firms since 1989 and the consequent reduction in the number of firms capable of providing audit services to large national and multinational business organizations that are subject to the securities laws.
Title VIII	Title VIII deals with corporate and criminal fraud accountability. It provides for criminal penalties for alteration of documents, disallows discharge of debt if the debt was incurred in violation of securities fraud laws, and requires that auditors maintain all audit and review working papers for five years. **Working papers** are the records kept by the auditor of the procedures applied, tests performed, information obtained, and the pertinent conclusions reached in the audit. Title VIII also provides protection for whistle blowers and provides criminal penalties for defrauding public securities investors.
Title IX	Title IX sets forth enhancements to criminal penalties for white-collar crimes such as mail fraud and ERISA violations.
Title X	Title X requires that corporate tax returns be signed by the chief executive officer of the corporation.
Title XI	Title XI deals with corporate fraud and accountability, providing for criminal penalties of up to 20 years. In addition, the SEC may order escrow for any extraordinary payments going to corporate officers (directors, officers, partners, controlling persons, agents, or employees) during investigation and hearing. Title XI also increased penalties under the Securities Act of 1933 and provides for criminal penalties for anyone who retaliates against an informant.

Insider Trading and Securities Fraud Acts

Section 16 of the Securities Exchange Act of 1934 first addressed insider trading by prohibiting short-swing trading by insiders and by requiring disclosures of insider trading. Despite this only partial prohibition of insider trading, the courts ruled that rule 10b-5 of the act prohibiting fraud could be applied to prohibit insider trading by making it a duty of insiders to disclose material nonpublic information or abstain from trading until such time as this information is disclosed. Two other acts have reinforced the opinions of the courts.

Insider Trading Sanctions Act of 1984

The Insider Trading Sanctions Act of 1984 specifies civil penalties for illegal insider trading to be up to three times the profit gained or three times the loss avoided from the illegal trading.

Insider Trading and Securities Fraud Enforcement Act of 1988

The Insider Trading and Securities Fraud Enforcement Act of 1988 stipulates that brokers, dealers, and investment advisors must enact and enforce policies to prevent insider trading and to prevent the firm, its employers, or any associated persons from misusing material nonpublic information.

Progress Check

Directions: Read each question and respond in the space provided. Answers and page references appear on the following page.

1. Which of the following is **not** governed by the Securities Exchange Act of 1934?

   ( )   a.   Regulation of securities markets

   ( )   b.   Registration of securities to be sold in the primary market

   ( )   c.   Control of margin trading

   ( )   d.   Regulation of insider trading

2. True or false? The SEC's Regulation S-X requires that managers provide a management discussion and analysis (MD&A) statement that includes full disclosure of material events that will affect the company's future earnings.

   ( )   a.   True

   ( )   b.   False

3. The Public Company Accounting Oversight Board was

   ( )   a.   established by the Securities Exchange Act of 1934 to ensure compliance with the act.

   ( )   b.   established by the Securities Exchange Act of 1934 to oversee the audits of public companies.

   ( )   c.   established by the Sarbanes-Oxley Act to ensure compliance with the act.

   ( )   d.   established by the Sarbanes-Oxley Act to oversee the audits of public companies.

Progress check answers

1. b (p. 2-479)

2. b (p. 2-481)

3. d (p. 2-485)

The Annual Report

Topic 6

Topic overview

*The annual report is guided by the **full disclosure principle**, which states that any financial information significant enough to influence the judgment of an informed reader should be included in periodic filings. Because the SEC requires audited financial statements, audit services related to financial reporting are covered first in this topic, followed by a discussion of management's responsibility for financial statements, the role of the audit committee and the board of directors, the independent auditor's report, and other information contained in the annual report.*

*Generally accepted auditing standards **(GAAS)** are a set of ten guidelines developed by the AICPA, divided into general standards, standards of field work, and reporting standards. The general standards require adequate technical training and proficiency, independence in mental attitude, and use of due professional care on the part of the auditor. The standards of field work require proper supervision and planning, a sufficient understanding of internal control (nature, timing, and extent of tests), and gathering sufficient competent evidential matter to form an opinion. The standards of reporting include a requirement to state whether the statements were prepared according to GAAP, identification of situations where GAAP was not consistently followed, an assumption that any disclosures are adequate unless otherwise noted, and a requirement that an expression of an opinion (or a disclaimer) must be made.*

Audit Services Related to Financial Reporting

An audit is defined by the auditor's written expression of opinion on the conformity of financial statements to GAAP in all material respects. Audits are the most prevalent form of business conducted by CPA firms. When an auditor expresses an opinion, he or she becomes liable for defending that opinion, and external financial users look to that opinion when determining the reliability of the entity's assertions. Auditor reports are required for annual financial statements included in every public filing. Public company filings with the SEC can be found on the SEC's EDGAR database. Private companies also will have audits performed, among other reasons, in order to secure credit. The audience for an audit includes management and often the general public and the SEC. Audits provide the highest level of assurance available.

The types of services that auditors offer related to financial reporting are broken down into assurance services and nonassurance services; nonassurance services are not covered in this text. Assurance services include the subcategory of attestation services. An audit is a type of attestation service. Note that many of these services are not allowed to be performed by the same firm or individual who performs other services.

Attestation services

Operational audits

An **operational audit** is a review of an entity's operational procedures to evaluate their efficiency and effectiveness. The auditor usually supplies a recommendation for improving operations at the end of the audit. Operational audits can test the efficiency and effectiveness of any process from supply chain management to the use of software for accounting entries. Because the range of services is broad, the specific actions of or qualifications needed by the auditor cannot be specifically defined. The auditor may be reviewing management's decisions or the effectiveness of sales training. Because this type of audit is subjective, it is closer to management consulting than the other types of audits. Management is the usual recipient of the audit results.

Compliance audits

A **compliance audit** is used to test whether the subject is in compliance with the regulations of a government body or higher authority. Compliance audits can also be performed to see if employees are following internal controls. School districts and other government agencies have numerous audits to ensure compliance with the many regulations. The management of an entity is the recipient of such an audit. Some of the work done on a compliance audit is performed by individuals employed by the affected organizational units, unless the situation requires more independence. For example, when a government agency wants to determine compliance, the auditor is usually employed directly by the agency. IRS tax auditors fall in this category.

Other attestation services

CPAs also provide other attestation services such as independent verification of a debtor's compliance with financial covenants in a loan agreement. Testing a client's internal controls is also a common service. An annual report regarding the effectiveness of internal controls is required for all public companies by the Sarbanes-Oxley Act. Attestation services are also performed on an entity's forward-looking statements when these are used to obtain credit.

Other services include review services, compilation services, and attestation engagements.

- **Review services**

  A review service engagement allows the accountant to express limited assurance that financial statements are in accordance with GAAP or another comprehensive basis of accounting. A nonpublic company that wants to provide assurance on their financial statements without incurring the cost of an audit may find a review adequate for its needs when there is no regulatory requirement for an audit. Less evidence is gathered for a review than for an audit. The accountant should, however, obtain information about the client's business, accounting records, and financial statements and be knowledgeable about accounting principles used in the industry.

- **Compilation services**

  In a compilation service engagement, the accountant prepares a company's financial statements based on information provided by management without any attempt to verify the information's accuracy. Compilation is the minimum service required of CPAs, but the compiler is not required to be independent and does not take any of the liability for material misstatements so long as they are the result of information provided by management. The compiler must, however, possess knowledge about the client, the client's business, the industry, transactions, accounting records, and employees. The auditor should also make simple inquiries to determine if the information provided is satisfactory and should review the statements for compliance with GAAP and for any math errors. If the auditor determines that the statements are not fairly presented, they should either get the problem addressed or withdraw from the engagement.

- **Attestation engagements**
  In an attestation engagement, the accountant issues a written opinion with regard to the reliability of an assertion made by another party. For example, a bank may hire a CPA to state whether a debtor has met all requirements of a loan agreement. Attestation engagements include agreed-upon procedures engagements, in which the procedures to be performed are agreed upon by the accountant, the party making the assertions, and the intended users of the accountant's report.

Other assurance services

Other assurance services are designed to give the client assurance about the reliability and relevance of information in order to improve its quality, for example, assuring that a lottery was conducted fairly. These services do not meet the formal definition of an attestation service, and no written report is required, nor is there a need to attest to the reliability of another party's written assertions. Because non-CPAs can perform these services, the field may have more competitors. Other examples of assurance services include risk assessments, business performance measurements, information systems reliability checks, health care performance measures, electronic commerce assessments, and ElderCare Plus assessments.

Auditor responsibilities

The auditor plans the audit and then performs the audit according to generally accepted auditing standards (GAAS) to obtain reasonable assurance that the financial statements are free of material misstatement, whether caused by error or fraud. However, due to the nature of audit evidence and the characteristics of fraud, the auditor can obtain only reasonable but not absolute assurance that no material misstatement has occurred.

The auditor verifies information in the financial statements by gathering audit evidence or documentation to support the information. For example, invoices, contracts, and bank statements document financial statement amounts. The auditor should evaluate the competence or reliability of documentation, as there have been cases where companies have presented fraudulent documentation. For example, if XYZ Corporation shows that they have a contract with ABC Corporation to provide services, the auditor may need to verify that ABC Corporation exists, that the contract presented to the auditor was indeed signed by the appropriate person at ABC Corporation, and so on.

After the auditor has completed verification of material information found in the financial statements, he or she prepares an audit report that communicates the auditor's findings.

Reasonable assurance

The auditor must obtain reasonable assurance about whether the financial statements are free of material misstatement. Due to the limitations of audit evidence and the nature of fraud, the auditor is not able (or expected) to obtain absolute assurance that material misstatements are detected.

Materiality vs. immateriality

Misstatements are considered material when the combined amount of uncorrected errors and fraud is of a magnitude that is likely to influence the decisions of a reasonable person relying on the financial statements. The auditor is responsible for obtaining reasonable assurance that the financial statements are free from material misstatements but cannot be expected to have responsibility for finding all immaterial misstatements or fraud.

Detecting errors or fraud

The auditor is responsible, through inspection of audit evidence (or lack thereof), for detecting errors and fraud. Information can be misstated or omitted either due to error or due to fraud. An error is unintentional, whereas fraud is intentional misstatement or omission of material facts.

Fraud can take two forms: employee fraud or management fraud. Employee fraud, also called misappropriation of assets, results when funds or other assets are stolen. Assets would be misappropriated if, for example, an employee takes home company supplies or fails to ring up sales and then pockets the cash.

Fraudulent financial reporting is also called management fraud; it occurs when management misstates or omits material information. For example, the overstatement of sales or understatement of bad debt expense to increase income would be fraudulent financial reporting.

Under GAAS, the auditor is required to specifically assess the risk of material misstatement due to fraud. Risk factors for fraud relate to the characteristics of management and the internal control environment (for example, high management turnover, one dominant individual, excessive focus on the earnings trend), industry conditions (for example, declining or rapidly changing industry), and the firm's financial stability and operating characteristics (for example, pressure to obtain additional capital, overly complex transactions or business structure). The existence of risk factors may lead the auditor to modify the types of evidence sought or to take other actions.

Detecting illegal acts

Illegal acts, as defined in AICPA Statement on Auditing Standards (SAS) No. 54, are violations of laws or government regulations other than fraud. An example of an illegal action is hiring foreign workers without work visas or green cards. Direct-effect illegal acts are those that have a direct financial effect on specific account balances in financial statements. An example of a direct-effect illegal act is violation of tax laws, which affects the tax expense and tax payable balances. Indirect-effect illegal acts are those that do not directly have an effect on the financial statements.

The auditor is responsible, regarding direct-effect illegal acts, under SAS No. 54, for evaluating whether or not there is evidence to indicate material violations of federal or state tax laws. This may be done by interviews with employees or findings from reports issued by tax authorities.

Indirect-effect illegal acts affect the financial statements only if the company suffers fines or sanctions. A potential fine or sanction may need to be disclosed as contingent liability. Because auditors are not legal experts, auditing standards do not require the auditor to provide assurance that indirect-effect illegal acts have been detected.

If an auditor does discover an illegal act, the auditor must consider the possible effects on the financial statements and must report knowledge of the illegal activity to the auditing committee. If communication about the illegal act is oral, the discussion should be documented in the working papers.

If the client does not accept the auditor's modified report or fails to take action to correct the illegal activity, the auditor may have to withdraw from the audit. If the client is a publicly traded company, the auditor is required to report the illegal activity to the SEC.

Forensic accounting applies financial, accounting, and investigative skills to research issues in dispute regarding civil and criminal litigation.

Subsequent events

When significant events occur after the balance sheet date (end of the fiscal year) but before the financial statements are actually issued, these events are termed subsequent events or post-balance-sheet events. The difference between the two dates is occupied by preparing the statements, auditing, and printing of the annual report. Subsequent events can be dealt with in two different ways depending on when they occurred:

- Adjustments to the financial statements are required if the events both provide supplementary evidence regarding conditions as of the balance sheet date and affect estimates used to prepare the financial statements (that is, settlement of a contingent liability).

- Adjustments to the financial statements are not required but should be disclosed in the notes to the financial statements if the events did not exist at the balance sheet date but provide a better indication of present conditions in order to prevent the financial statements from being misleading. Events that require disclosure but not adjustments to the statements include:

  - Gains or losses on some marketable securities.

  - Debt incurred, reduced, or refinanced.

  - Discontinued operations.

  - Sale of bonds or capital stock as well as stock splits and stock dividends.

  - Pending or effected business combinations.

  - Litigation.

- Capital stock issued or repurchased.

- Employee benefit plans.

- Fire or flood losses to inventories, plants, or equipment.

- Loss of receivables, for example, due to a major customer's bankruptcy.

Other events such as product changes or union agreements are discussed elsewhere, such as in the management discussion and analysis.

Communications between successor auditors

Policies for when auditors pass the torch to different auditors are covered under Statement on Auditing Standards (SAS) No. 7, "Communications Between Predecessor and Successor Auditors." The obligations of the successor auditor are to explain to the client the process of succession and related standards. Also, the successor auditor must request that the client instruct the predecessor auditor to comply fully with the information requests of the successor. After consent is given, the successor auditor is responsible for initiating contact with the prior auditor and should make the following specific and reasonable inquiries in order to determine if the client should be taken on:

- Integrity of management

- Disagreements with management related to application of GAAP or GAAS

- Predecessor's understanding of why the change in auditors is taking place

The obligations of the predecessor auditor include keeping all information from the audit confidential unless specifically authorized by the client and responding promptly and fully to successor auditor inquiries once the permission has been given. Information supplied can include exchange of working papers used in the audit as well as interviews with the staff from the engagement.

Management's Responsibility for Financial Statements

Management is responsible for the preparation and content of financial statements. The SEC requires that management certify in writing that they are responsible for the contents of their financial statements, that they have an internal control system, and that they have assessed the effectiveness of their internal control systems and report the findings of their assessment.

Types of information used in external decision making

In SFAC No. 5, the FASB distinguished different sources of firm information useful to those making investment, credit, and other decisions, portraying these sources in the exhibit reproduced in Figure 2-236. The information included in the financial reporting area is the responsibility of management. Because management operates the business, they are the most knowledgeable about its operations and assets. Although information outside of the financial reporting system is not under the control of management, savvy managers may try to have a positive influence on this category to the extent possible (for example, plans for dealing with welcome and unwelcome publicity).

Figure 2-236: Responsibility Levels

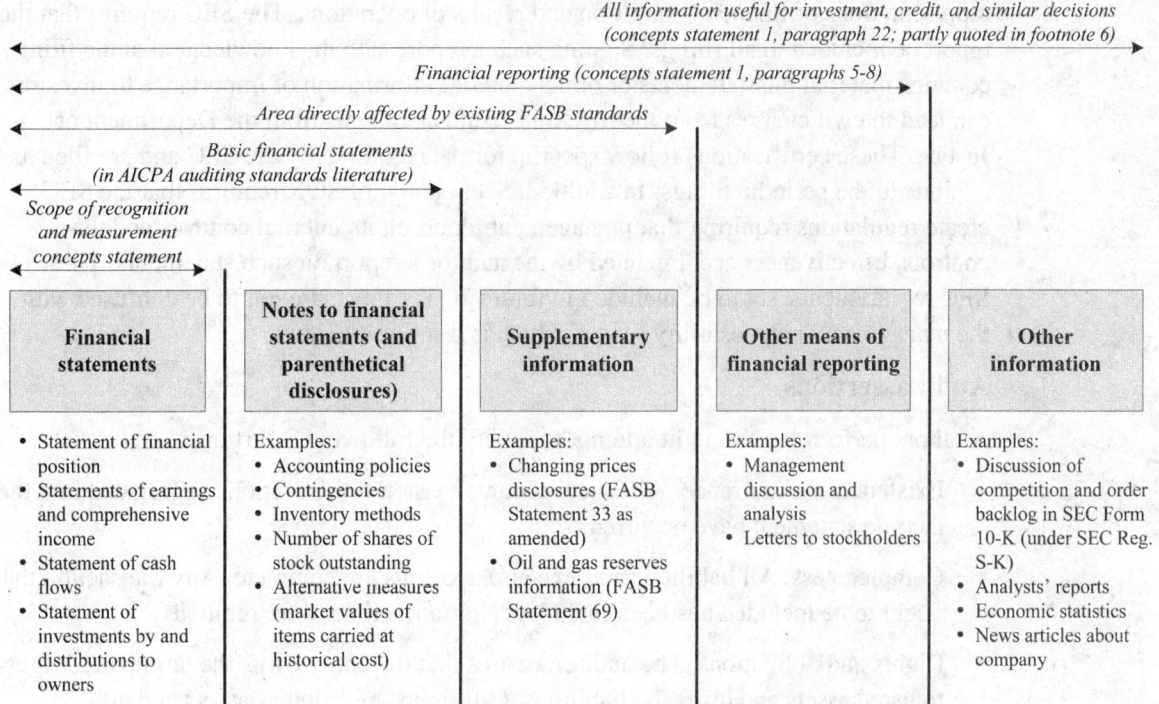

Management responsibilities

Management is responsible for adopting sound accounting policies and developing, documenting, and maintaining internal controls that provide reasonable assurance that management's control objectives will be met. Management must have evaluated the effectiveness of the company's internal controls within 90 days prior to the publication of periodic filings. (Note that internal controls are covered in more depth in Part 1 of the *CMA Learning System*, Section C, "Internal Controls.") Management is responsible for preparation of the financial statements and accompanying footnotes.

Managers signing periodic filings must have disclosed to the auditors and the audit committee of the board of directors (or persons fulfilling the equivalent function):

- All significant deficiencies in internal controls that could adversely affect the issuer's ability to clearly and completely report financial information.

- Any fraud, whether or not material, that involves management or other employees who have a significant role in the issuer's internal controls.

- Whether there were significant changes in internal controls or in other factors affecting financial reporting and internal controls, including any corrective actions with regard to significant deficiencies and material weaknesses.

Sections 302 and 906 of the Sarbanes-Oxley Act created a formal requirement to have management certify the financial statements and other information contained in the entity's periodic reports with the SEC, verify that they have no knowledge of untrue statements or omissions of material fact, and state that the financial statements are fair representations of financial condition and results of operations. The SEC requires that the report be included in all filings. Signing such a report with the knowledge that the filing contains material misstatements or omits material information of importance to investors can lead to civil charges from the SEC and criminal charges from the Department of Justice. These certifications follow specific formats required by the SEC and are filed as exhibits to the periodic filings. In addition, Section 404 of SOX requires that the SEC create regulations requiring that management report on its internal controls and the controls' effectiveness accompanied by the auditor's report on such statements. These SEC requirements, set to be included in future 10-K filings, are not to be confused with the management responsibility report, which is discussed below.

Audit assertions

Auditors performing the audit attempt to satisfy the following assertions:

- Existence or occurrence. All asset accounts exist. All transactions aggregated into the income statement have occurred.

- Completeness. All liabilities and expense accounts are complete. Any transaction that ought to be included has been included. No transactions were omitted.

- Rights and obligations. The auditor assures that the entity owns the unimpaired rights to listed assets and owes the liabilities. (All rights are listed as assets and all obligations are listed as liabilities.)

- Valuation or allocation. All assets, liabilities, equity, revenues, expenses, gains, and losses are all presented in the financial statements according to GAAP, and all allocated items are allocated in a systematic and rational way.

- Presentation and disclosure. All amounts in the financial statement are properly identified, classified, and described. All disclosures are meaningful and conform to GAAP.

Management responsibility report

A management responsibility report has been an elective part of reporting to shareholders for many years. Many companies choose to include such a report to acknowledge their responsibility for the preparation of the financial statements. These reports can take any form desired by management and are usually included in the company's annual report to shareholders, frequently adjacent to the report of the independent auditors. An example of a management's responsibility report is included in Figure 2-237.

Figure 2-237: Management Responsibility Report

XYZ Corporation

Report of Management

The corporation has prepared the consolidated financial statements and related financial information included in this annual report. Management has the primary responsibility for the financial statements and other financial information and for ascertaining that the data fairly reflects the financial position, results of operations, and cash flows of the corporation. The financial statements were prepared in accordance with generally accepted accounting principles appropriate in the circumstances and necessarily include amounts that are based on best estimates and judgments, with appropriate consideration given to materiality. Financial information included elsewhere in this annual report is presented on a basis consistent with the financial statements.

The corporation maintains a system of internal accounting controls, supported by adequate documentation, to provide reasonable assurance that assets are safeguarded and that the books and records reflect the authorized transactions of the corporation. Limitations exist in any system of internal accounting controls based upon the recognition that the cost of the system should not exceed the benefits derived. XYZ Corporation believes its system of internal accounting controls, augmented by its corporate auditing function, appropriately balances the cost-benefit relationship.

The independent accountants provide an objective assessment of the degree to which management meets its responsibility for fair financial reporting. They regularly evaluate internal accounting controls and perform such tests and procedures they deem necessary to express an opinion on the fairness of the financial statements.

The board of directors pursues its responsibility for the corporation's financial statements through its audit review committee composed of directors who are not officers or employees of the corporation. The audit review committee meets regularly with the independent accountants, management, and the corporate auditors. The independent accountants and the corporate auditors have direct access to the audit review committee, with and without the presence of management representatives, to discuss the scope and results of their audit work and their comments on the adequacy of internal accounting controls and the quality of financial reporting.

We believe that the corporation's policies and procedures, including its system of internal accounting controls, provide reasonable assurance that the financial statements are prepared in accordance with the applicable securities laws and with a corresponding standard of business conduct.

Full disclosure principle

The full disclosure principle requires that any financial information significant enough to influence the judgment of an informed reader be disclosed. Full disclosure of financial information helps prevent insiders from using exclusive information to profit abnormally in the secondary markets, and it helps the market itself operate as efficiently as possible, because the most successful concerns will attract the most capital. Full disclosure helps to put competitors on a level playing field; it allows analysts to assess how use of different accounting methods impacts comparisons and to determine whether questionable or deceptive accounting practices are being used. (APB Opinion No. 22 requires disclosure of all accounting policies.)

The cost of full disclosure is significant; Congress, the FASB, and the SEC must weigh the cost of new disclosure requirements against the benefit of receiving such information. The Sarbanes-Oxley Act greatly increases disclosure requirements and therefore has greatly increased the cost of providing such information. However, the loss of investor confidence caused by accounting scandals is costly for the economy as a whole.

Required supplementary disclosures

The Sarbanes-Oxley Act of 2002 has had a significant impact on the disclosures required on the financial statements. Section 401 of the act specifically applies to financial disclosures. This section amends the Securities Exchange Act to include the following requirement:

> The SEC will issue rules requiring quarterly and annual periodic filings filed with the SEC to disclose all material off-balance-sheet transactions, arrangements, obligations (including contingent obligations), and other relationships of the issuer with unconsolidated entities or other persons that may have a material current or future effect on financial condition, changes in financial condition, results of operations, liquidity, capital expenditures, capital resources, or significant components of revenues or expenses. (Section 401, Sarbanes-Oxley Act of 2002)

Role of the Audit Committee/Board of Directors

The board of directors is elected by the shareholders of a corporation to represent their interests. The Sarbanes-Oxley Act requires the board of directors to form an audit committee composed of independent directors with sufficient financial background, including at least one with specific experience in financial reporting. The audit committee is directly responsible for the appointment, compensation, and oversight of the work of the audit firm. Requiring the auditor to report directly to the audit committee, rather than to management, avoids the potential conflict of interest created by having management direct the audit of its own activities.

The audit committee must consist entirely of directors who are independent of the issuer, meaning that they cannot accept any consulting, advisory, or other compensatory fee from the issuer or be a member of the management of the issuer or any of its subsidiaries. The committee:

- Reviews the company's internal control structure.
- Aids in the choice of accounting methods and policies.
- Chooses the auditor.
- Reviews the audit plan.
- Reviews the auditor's suggestions for improved internal control.
- Reviews the audit report and the audited annual report.

Independent Auditor's Report

The independent auditor issues a report on the financial statements at the end of an auditing engagement. The report can be unqualified, qualified, adverse, or a disclaimer of opinion. The report is of great significance to all parties involved. The users of periodic filings depend on the assumption that the auditor has made an unbiased and fair assessment of a company's statements. The auditor will likely be held responsible if an incorrect audit report is signed.

AICPA's Auditing Standards Board

The Statements of Auditing Standards issued by AICPA's Auditing Standards Board require the auditor to sign and date the audit report and include the following statements:

- The auditor is independent.

- An audit was performed on specified financial statements.

- The financial statements are the responsibility of the company's management; the opinion is the responsibility of the auditors.

- The audit was conducted according to GAAS (which in turn require following GAAP).

- The audit was planned and performed to obtain reasonable assurance about whether the financial statements are free of material misstatement.

- The audit included examination, assessment, and evaluation stages.

- The audit provides a reasonable basis for an opinion.

- An expression of an opinion concerning the fair presentation is included.

Report paragraphs

A standard unqualified audit report is shown in the sample report in Figure 2-238.

Figure 2-238: Standard Unqualified Report on Comparative Statements

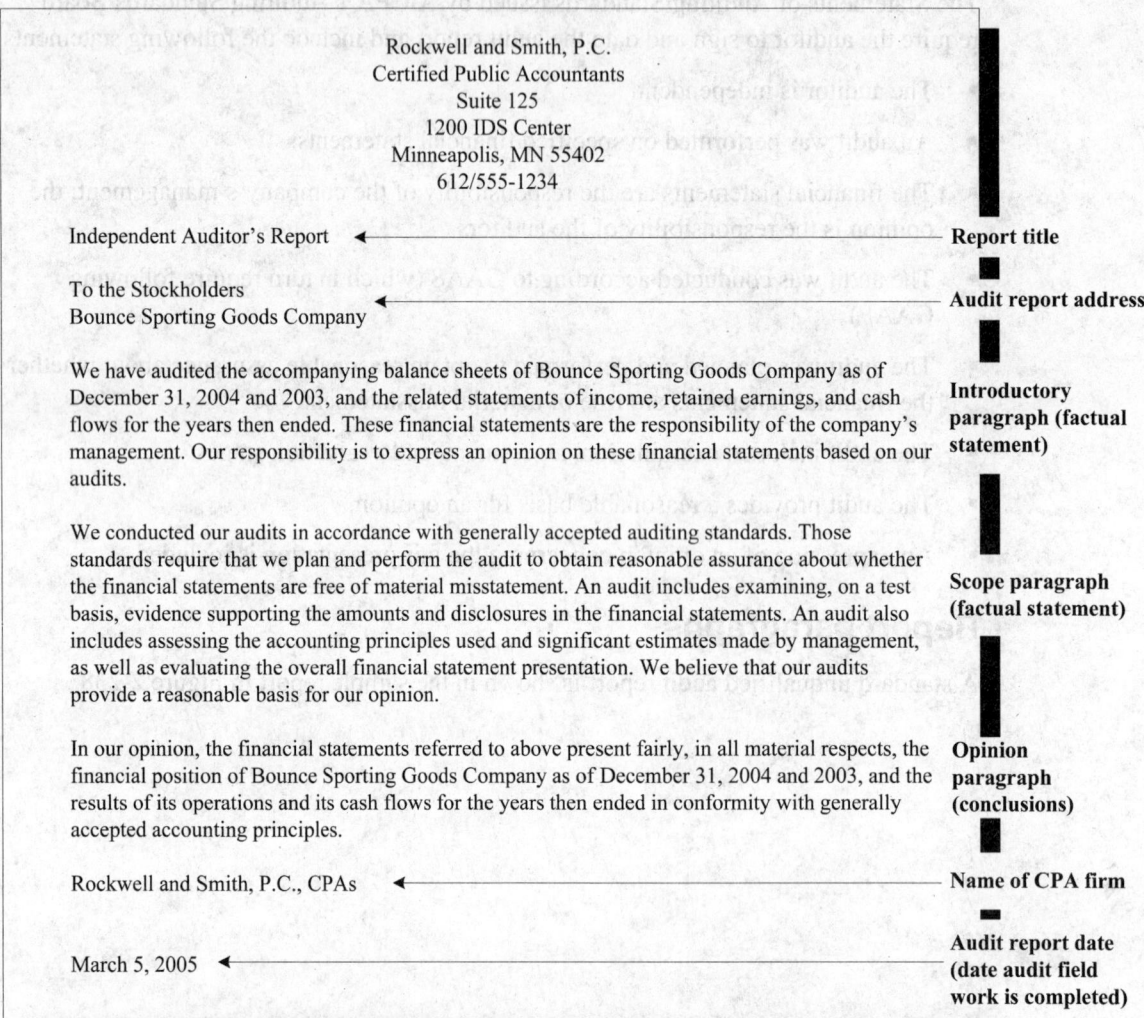

Rockwell and Smith, P.C.
Certified Public Accountants
Suite 125
1200 IDS Center
Minneapolis, MN 55402
612/555-1234

Independent Auditor's Report — **Report title**

To the Stockholders
Bounce Sporting Goods Company — **Audit report address**

We have audited the accompanying balance sheets of Bounce Sporting Goods Company as of December 31, 2004 and 2003, and the related statements of income, retained earnings, and cash flows for the years then ended. These financial statements are the responsibility of the company's management. Our responsibility is to express an opinion on these financial statements based on our audits. — **Introductory paragraph (factual statement)**

We conducted our audits in accordance with generally accepted auditing standards. Those standards require that we plan and perform the audit to obtain reasonable assurance about whether the financial statements are free of material misstatement. An audit includes examining, on a test basis, evidence supporting the amounts and disclosures in the financial statements. An audit also includes assessing the accounting principles used and significant estimates made by management, as well as evaluating the overall financial statement presentation. We believe that our audits provide a reasonable basis for our opinion. — **Scope paragraph (factual statement)**

In our opinion, the financial statements referred to above present fairly, in all material respects, the financial position of Bounce Sporting Goods Company as of December 31, 2004 and 2003, and the results of its operations and its cash flows for the years then ended in conformity with generally accepted accounting principles. — **Opinion paragraph (conclusions)**

Rockwell and Smith, P.C., CPAs — **Name of CPA firm**

March 5, 2005 — **Audit report date (date audit field work is completed)**

The standard unqualified report consists of seven parts.

- Report title: Must include the word independent, such as "Independent Auditor's Report"

- Audit report address: Usually addressed to stockholders

- Introductory paragraph: States that the audit firm has done an audit; lists the financial statements that were audited, including dates and accounting periods; indicates that the statements are the responsibility of management and that the opinion is the responsibility of the auditor

- Scope paragraph: States what the auditor did in the audit; that the audit was designed to provide reasonable assurance that the statements are free from material misstatement; provides a discussion of audit evidence

- Opinion paragraph: The final paragraph; states the auditor's opinion
- Name of the audit firm
- Audit report date: Date of the last day of important auditing procedures in the field

Modified reports may require an additional paragraph describing the reasons for a qualified, adverse, or disclaimer of opinion.

Report opinions

The types of audit reports that can be issued are as follows.

Standard unqualified report

Standard unqualified reports can be issued when each of the following conditions exist:

- All statements (balance sheet, income statement, statement of retained earnings, and statement of cash flows) are included.
- The three general standards of GAAS have been followed in every respect.
- The auditor can conclude that the three standards of field work of GAAS can be met because sufficient evidence was compiled and the auditor conducted the engagement properly.
- Financial statements are presented according to GAAP, including adequate disclosures.
- No explanatory paragraphs or modification of the wording of the report is needed.

Unqualified report with explanatory paragraph

All of the conditions for a standard unqualified report have been met except that the auditor believes an explanatory paragraph is needed to provide additional information. Such explanatory paragraphs are used, for example, when accounting principles are not consistently applied due to a change in accounting method, when there is substantial doubt about the entity's ability to continue as a going concern, or to emphasize a matter.

Qualified report

This type of opinion is issued when the auditor concludes that the financial statements are fairly presented overall but they contain a departure from GAAP or the scope of the audit has been restricted. In either case, the basis for the qualification is explained in the report.

Adverse opinion

The auditor expresses an adverse opinion when he or she concludes that the financial statements are materially misleading due to departures from GAAP or otherwise. The reason for the adverse opinion is included in the report. Adverse opinions are rare.

Disclaimer of opinion

The auditor is either unable to form an opinion concerning whether the financial statements are fairly presented due to severe restrictions on the scope of the audit or the auditor is not independent and cannot express an opinion. The reason for the disclaimer will be included in the report.

An auditor's report does not imply that the company has a clean bill of health. The opinion does not deal with the company's policies, the adequacy of its internal controls, or other management decisions. The report also does not make any claim as to the success or failure of a company. Although the GAAS standards do consider solvency and financial viability of a company, the company's prospects may change rapidly.

Audit reports also do not guarantee that fraud has not been committed by one or more persons at the company, except when such fraud would have caused a detectable material misstatement on the financial statements. Although the independent auditor is trained to be skeptical and the audit is designed to detect instances of fraud, fraud can be concealed by management by collusion and forgery and therefore could escape detection.

Other Components of the Annual Report

The annual report may contain additional information. The management discussion and analysis (MD&A) section is required for SEC submissions, but other items such as a letter to shareholders or a statement on social responsibility are voluntary.

Letter to shareholders

A letter to shareholders can take any form that a company wishes. A portion of a letter to shareholders from Krispy Kreme is shown in Figure 2-239.

Figure 2-239: Abridged Letter to Shareholders from Krispy Kreme (continued on next page)

Dear Shareholder:

As we near the completion of our third year as a public company and our 66th year as a business enterprise, it is gratifying to share the substantial achievements of the past year, especially in the context of a difficult external environment. Consumers, investors, and businesses have had to deal with or sort out challenges including geopolitical issues and unrest, a continuation of stunning disclosures by several respected companies regarding questionable business practices, a domestic economy fighting recession, and extreme weather patterns that yielded record heat and drought, followed by record levels of rain, ice, and snow in many parts of the country. The costs these conditions generated are hard to quantify but are surely significant to most retail businesses. Another challenging dynamic more easily quantified, which Krispy Kreme faced, is the rising cost of our insurance coverages, such as group medical, workers' compensation, and property and casualty.

It has not been our practice to discuss the challenges we've had to face. We tend to focus primarily on results and opportunities. This past year, however, it does not give enough credit to the efforts of our people were it not done in the context of the unusually difficult business environment. With this in mind, we are proud to share the following achievements and milestones:

- System-wide sales of $778.6 million, a 28% increase over last fiscal year (52-week year)
- Net income of $39.1 million, up 51.6% over last fiscal year (52-week year; excludes arbitration ruling)
- Opening a new 187,000-square-foot mix plant and distribution facility in Effingham, Illinois
- Awarding our first two franchise agreements outside of North America for Australia and New Zealand and the United Kingdom and the Republic of Ireland
- Opening 53 factory stores and 10 commissaries
- Acquiring Montana Mills Bread Company, Inc., a Rochester, New York–based bakery concept
- Assisting nonprofit organizations in raising over $43 million through our fund-raising programs
- Celebrating our 65th anniversary on July 13, 2002

The magnitude of several of the year's accomplishments is best illustrated by their impact on our year-over-year improvement in financial results, which also exemplifies our consistent focus on the core strategies that create the greatest leverage on our business model.

Figure 2-239: Abridged Letter to Shareholders from Krispy Kreme (concluded)

(Dollars in thousands except per-share amounts)	FY00	FY01	FY02[1]	FY03[2]	Improvement FY03 vs. FY02[3]
Earnings/share $	.15	.27	.44	.66	48.9%
Net income $	5,956	14,725	25,820	39,146	51.6%
Revenue $	220,243	300,715	386,460	491,549	27.2%
System-wide sales $	318,854	448,129	608,485	778,573	28.0%
Operating margin %	4.9	7.8	10.6	14.0	3.4 ppts.

	Net Income	System-Wide Sales	Total Revenues
Fiscal 2002, as reported	$26,378	$621,665	$394,354
Adjustment for extra week	(558)	(13,180)	(7,894)
Fiscal 2002, pro forma	$25,820	$608,485	$386,460

Notes:

[1] We operate on a 52- or 53-week fiscal year. Fiscal 2002 was a 53-week year. The amounts shown in the table above represent management's estimate of the amounts that would have been reported had fiscal 2002 been a 52-week year. The following table presents a reconciliation of the amounts reported for fiscal 2002 with the above amounts (in thousands).

Diluted earnings per share for fiscal 2002 were $0.45. We estimate that the 53rd week impacted diluted earnings per share by approximately $0.01. Operating margin for fiscal 2002 was 10.6%.

[2] Reported net income for fiscal 2003 was $33.5 million and diluted earnings per share was $0.56. Reported results for fiscal 2003 include a pretax charge of $9.1 million related to an arbitration award against the Company, more fully discussed in Note 18—Legal Contingencies in the notes to our consolidated financial statements. Excluding the effect of the arbitration award, net income for fiscal 2003 would have been $39.1 million and diluted earnings per share would have increased by approximately $0.10. Operating margin, calculated based upon reported amounts for fiscal 2003, was 12.2%.

[3] The percentages reflected in this column are based on the pro forma amounts for fiscal 2002 (adjusted to estimate the results for a 52-week year) and fiscal 2003 (adjusted to exclude the impact of the arbitration award) shown in the table above. Comparing the corresponding reported amounts for fiscal 2002 and fiscal 2003 results in the following comparisons: Diluted earnings per share increased 24.8%; net income increased 26.9%; total revenues increased 24.6%; and system-wide sales increased 25.2%. Operating margin for fiscal 2002 was 10.6%, as compared to 12.2% for fiscal 2003, based upon reported results, representing an increase of 1.6 percentage points.

We realize our accomplishments to date are now history. We believe that a healthy relationship is not based on the past but rather on the potential the future holds. We do hope, however, that the achievements of our people have earned your confidence, and we hope our commitment to the long-term success of Krispy Kreme will encourage your long-term participation as a shareholder.

Warmest personal regards,

Scott A. Livengood
Chairman, President, and CEO

Usually the discussion in the letter to shareholders highlights the entity's successes or gives mitigating or explanatory factors for less-successful operations. The letter usually explains the operating results of the company in layperson's terms. The letter may also provide a forecast for future results and developments. New plants or stores may be discussed as well as other company information that may be of interest to shareholders. The letter may also go into detail on revenues and earnings per share in a simplified format. Finally, the letter may include updates to the company philosophy, mission, or codes of ethics.

Management Discussion and Analysis (MD&A)

The details of the MD&A statement were covered earlier, in the discussion of SEC disclosure requirements for public companies. In general, the MD&A is required under the SEC regulations, including forward-looking information, short- and long-term projections, narrative explanation of financial statements, and the viewpoint of management. Although most private companies are not under the SEC's jurisdiction, the use of the MD&A has spread to these companies as well.

Statement on social responsibility

The optional statement on social responsibility may be included in the annual report. The content of this report is at the discretion of the company. Such reports usually describe company philosophy, values, and goals as well as any active community programs, environmental programs, and other social initiatives. The report may also give shareholders an opportunity to join in these programs. Figure 2-240 shows a portion of a statement on social responsibility from McDonald's.

Figure 2-240: Abridged Statement on Social Responsibility from McDonald's

---

Our Commitment to Social Responsibility—*A Message from the Chairman and Chief Executive Officer*

Thank you for your interest in McDonald's. We welcome your curiosity, and we value your perspectives—whether you are a customer, a neighbor, a supplier, a shareholder, a student, a parent, or a McDonald's employee.

Strong principles are part of our heritage. Our corporation's founder, Ray Kroc, committed McDonald's to being a responsible corporate citizen in 1955 with a very simple idea—that every McDonald's should give back to the community in which it does business. This commitment serves as the foundation for all of our social responsibility efforts.

McDonald's has the honor of serving more customers around the world than anyone else. With this privilege comes a responsibility to be a good neighbor, employer, and steward of the environment and a unique opportunity to be a leader and a catalyst for positive change. We recognize the challenges and the obstacles but believe strongly in the importance of social responsibility.

Since the publication of this report, we have launched several new initiatives that extend our social responsibility commitment to areas that our customers tell us matter to them, including animal welfare, the environment, food safety, and children's charities. We know there is always more work to do, and we are working on our next Social Responsibility Report, which will take a closer look at each of these areas and more.

One of my top priorities is maximizing McDonald's support of healthy, active lifestyles. McDonald's was built upon offering high-quality menu choices. Throughout our history, we have expanded these choices by listening to our consumers. Their input was the impetus for our decision to provide detailed nutritional information about our menu items 30 years ago.

We are now implementing a worldwide, comprehensive approach to active lifestyles, fitness, and nutrition. Important first steps have already been taken. McDonald's is adding more choice to our Happy Meals around the world. Countries are offering various selections, including fruit and vegetable selections, milk, and other healthy choices. We have also established an external global Advisory Council on Healthy Lifestyles composed of leading health and fitness experts to help McDonald's develop superior programs that support our customers' healthy, active lives. You will see an expansion of these efforts in the future.

Acting in the best interests of our customers, the communities we serve, and the environment is an evolving process. Your feedback helps us understand how we're doing. Please let us know what you think.

Jim Cantalupo, Chairman and CEO   May, 2003

Disclaimer: *This McDonald's inaugural Social Responsibility Report, issued in April 2002, provides information about pertinent aspects of our business related to the communities we serve, the environment, our people, and our relationships with suppliers. The report presents our progress through the end of 2001 and a snapshot of our company as it was in early 2002. Forward-looking statements included in the report reflected management's expectations regarding future events and our future performance as of April 2002.*

Progress Check

Directions: Read each question and respond in the space provided. Answers and page references appear on the following page.

1. Which of the following auditor services is sometimes used by private companies as a lower-cost method of providing a moderate level of assurance that their managers are not distorting finances?

   (　)   a.   Audit of historical financial statements

   (　)   b.   Compliance audit

   (　)   c.   Compilation of historical financial statements

   (　)   d.   Review of historical financial statements

2. The audit committee of the board of directors is

   (　)   a.   not allowed to hire external auditors directly.

   (　)   b.   not allowed to direct choices of accounting methods and policies.

   (　)   c.   now required by the Sarbanes-Oxley Act for all public companies.

   (　)   d.   composed of both members of management and independent directors.

3. Which of the following statements is NOT true?

   (　)   a.   Auditors are responsible for creating a system of internal control for the company being audited.

   (　)   b.   Management is responsible for the preparation of the financial statements.

   (　)   c.   Auditors are not responsible for detecting illegal acts that do not affect the financial statements directly.

   (　)   d.   Auditors must report illegal activity discovered during the course of the audit to the audit committee of the board of directors.

Progress check answers

1. d (p. 2-492)

2. c (p. 2-500)

3. a (p. 2-493)

Bibliography

Afterman, Allan B. *SEC Regulation of Public Companies.* Englewood Cliffs, New Jersey: Prentice Hall, 1995.

American Society of Association Executives. *ASAE's Essentials of the Profession Learning System:* Module Five, Membership/Using Technology Effectively, and Module Seven, Finance Administration. Washington, D.C.: American Society of Association Executives and Eagan, Minnesota: Holmes Corporation, 2002.

Arens, Alvin A., and James K. Loebbecke. *Auditing: An Integrated Approach,* 8th edition. Upper Saddle River, New Jersey: Prentice Hall, 1999.

Bernstein, Leopold A. *Financial Statement Analysis: Theory, Application, and Interpretation,* 3rd edition. Homewood, Illinois: Irwin, 1983.

Blocher, Edward J., Kung H. Chen, and Thomas W. Lin. *Cost Management: A Strategic Emphasis,* 2nd edition. New York: McGraw-Hill Irwin, 2002.

Bodnar, George H., and William S. Hopwood. *Accounting Information Systems,* 3rd edition. Boston: Allyn and Bacon, 1987.

Brealey, Richard A., and Stewart C. Meyers. *Principles of Corporate Finance,* 4th edition. New York: McGraw-Hill, 1991.

Campanella, Jack, editor. *Principles of Quality Costs,* 2nd edition. Milwaukee, Wisconsin: ASQ Quality Press, 1990.

Cartin, Thomas J. *Principles and Practices of TQM.* Milwaukee, Wisconsin: ASQ Quality Press, 1993.

"Database Management System," Webopedia Web site, www.webopedia.com/TERM/d/database_management_system_DBMS.html.

Delaney, Patrick R., Ralph Nach, Barry J. Epstein, and Susan Weiss Budak. *GAAP 2003.* Hoboken, New Jersey: Wiley, 2002.

Epstein, Barry J., Ralph Nach, and Steven M. Bragg, *Wiley GAAP 2006.* New York: John Wiley & Sons, 2005.

Evans, Matt H. *Course 11: The Balanced Scorecard,* www.exinfm.com/training/pdfiles/course11r.pdf.

Financial Accounting Standards Board, Statements of Financial Accounting Concepts Nos. 1, 2, 4, 5, 6, 7. Financial Accounting Standards Board: Stamford, Connecticut: 1978-2000.

Frederick, William C., James E. Post, and Keith Davis. *Business and Society: Corporate Strategy, Public Policy, Ethics,* 7th edition. New York: McGraw Hill, 1992.

Garrison, Ray H., and Eric W. Noreen. *Managerial Accounting,* 10th edition. Boston: McGraw-Hill/Irwin, 2003.

Gelinas, Ulric J., Jr., Steve G. Sutton, and Allan E. Oram. *Accounting Information Systems,* 4th edition. Cincinnati, Ohio: South-Western College Publishing, 1999.

Gibson, Charles H. *Financial Statement Analysis: Using Financial Accounting Information,* 7th edition. Cincinnati, Ohio: South-Western College Publishing, 1998.

Greenstein, Marilyn, and Todd M. Feinman. *Electronic Commerce: Security, Risk Management, and Control.* Boston: McGraw Hill Higher Education, 2000.

Hargrave, Lee E. *Plan for Profitability: How to Write a Strategic Business Plan.* Titusville, Florida: Four Seasons Publishers, 1999.

Hilton, Ronald W., Michael W. Maher, and Frank H. Selto. *Cost Management: Strategies for Business Decisions,* 2nd edition. Boston: McGraw-Hill Irwin, 2003.

Horngren, Charles T., George Foster, and Srikant M. Datar. *Cost Accounting,* 10th edition. Upper Saddle River, New Jersey: Prentice-Hall, 2000.

Hoyle, Joe B., Thomas F. Schaefer, and Timothy S. Doupnik. *Advanced Accounting,* 6th edition. Boston: McGraw-Hill Irwin, 2001.

Juran, Joseph M., and Blanton Godfrey, coeditors-in-chief. *Juran's Quality Handbook,* 5th edition. New York: McGraw-Hill, 1999.

Kaplan, Robert S., and David P. Norton. *The Balanced Scorecard: Translating Strategy Into Action.* Boston: Harvard Business School Press, 1996.

Kaplan, Robert S., and David P. Norton. *The Strategy-Focused Organization.* Boston: Harvard Business School Press, 2001.

Kaplan, Robert S., and David P. Norton. "Using the Balanced Scorecard as a Strategic Management System." *Harvard Business Review,* January-February 1996.

Kieso, Donald E., and Jerry J. Weygandt. *Intermediate Accounting,* 9th edition. New York: Wiley, 1998.

Kieso, Donald E., Jerry J. Weygandt, and Terry D. Warfield. *Intermediate Accounting,* 10th edition. New York: Wiley, 2001.

Larsen, E. John. *Modern Advanced Accounting,* 10th edition. New York: McGraw-Hill, 2006.

Laudon, Kenneth C., and Jane P. Laudon. *Management Information Systems*, 8th edition. Upper Saddle River, New Jersey: Pearson Prentice Hall, 2003.

Madden, Bartley J. *CFROI Valuation—A Total System Approach to Valuing the Firm.* Boston: Butterworth-Heinemann, 1999.

McMillan, Edward J. *Budgeting and Financial Management Handbook for Not-for-Profit Organizations.* Washington, D.C.: American Society of Association Executives, 2000.

Moscove, Stephen A., Mark G. Simkin, and Nancy A. Bagrandoff. *Core Concepts of Accounting Information Systems,* 5th edition. New York: Wiley, 1997.

Nicolai, Loren A., and John D. Bazley. *Intermediate Accounting,* 5th edition. Boston: PWS-Kent Publishing Company, 1991.

Olve, Nils-Göran, and Anna Sjöstrand. *The Balanced Scorecard.* Oxford, United Kingdom: Capstone Publishing (a Wiley Company), 2002.

Ratliff, Richard L., Wanda A. Wallace, Glenn E. Sumners, William G. McFarland, and James K. Loebbecke. *Internal Auditing: Principles and Techniques.* Altamonte Springs, Florida: Institute of Internal Auditors, 1996.

Roszkowski, Mark E. *Business Law.* New York: Addison Wesley, 1997.

Tague, Nancy R. *The Quality Toolbox.* Milwaukee, Wisconsin: ASQ Quality Press, 1995.

U.S. Securities and Exchange Commission, www.sec.gov.

Van Horne, James C., and John M. Wachowicz, Jr. *Fundamentals of Financial Management,* 9th edition. Englewood Cliffs, New Jersey: Prentice-Hall, Inc., 1995.

Young, S. David, and Stephen R. O'Byrne. *EVA® and Value-Based Management: A Practical Guide to Implementation.* New York: McGraw Hill, 2001.

Index

目　　录

出版说明

关于 CMA 考试教材

本培训教材的基础是美国管理会计师协会（IMA）所开发的知识体系。虽然本教材的基础是CMA 考试所测试的知识体系以及已经公布的涵盖该考试四个组成部分的学习要点（LOS），但是CMA 考试教材方案的开发者并没有参考当前的题库。而且，阅读本教材并不能保证一定能够通过考试。对考生来说至关重要的是，理解美国管理会计师协会认证部（ICMA）公布的所有学习要点、学习与这些要点有关的概念和计算以及牢牢掌握如何解答 CMA 考试中的单项选择题和问答题。

本教材的目的是为了帮助考生进行学习，但应当认识到出版商和作者并不提供法律或者专业方面的服务。

致谢

IMA 非常感谢对本书的最初英文版本做出贡献的各个专家，他们是注册管理会计师金伯利·弗兰克·沙伦博士（Kimberly Frank Charron），注册管理会计师尼尔·J·汉农（Neal J. Hannon），注册管理会计师和注册会计师查尔斯·R·哈特尔（Charles R. Hartle）、丹尼斯·L·奈德（Dennis L. Neider）以及卡尔·V·孟可尼（Carl V. Menconi）。

此外，我们还非常感谢以下几位专家，这些专家对本书的第二版做出了非常大的贡献，他们是注册管理会计师和特许金融分析师吉尔·贝尔博士（Jill Bale），注册管理会计师和特许金融分析师肯特·贝克博士（Kent Baker），注册管理会计师肯尼思·科尔博士（Kenneth Cole），注册管理会计师索雷弗·杜塔博士（Saurav Dutta），注册管理会计师卡伦·L·杰特（Karen L. Jett），注册管理会计师和特许金融分析师乔·兰兹（Joe Lanz），保罗·迈尔森博士（Paul Miesing），注册管理会计师露·佩特博士（Lou Petro），特里·里坦伯格博士（Terri Rittenburg），注册管理会计师肖彭·万博士（Siaw-Peng Wan）。

最后，我们还要感谢以下几位对本书中文部分的翻译校对工作做出了非常大贡献的专家学者。他们是美国管理会计师协会顾问、香港科技大学会计学教授杨继良，注册管理会计师罗鹏，注册管理会计师韩保庆，以及李若女士。

版权所有

册管理会计师）学习系统资料的行为都属非法，并严重地违背了 IMA（管理会计师协会）的《职业道德规范声明》。

任何 CMA 或 CMA 考生，若未事先获得 IMA 和经济科学出版社的授权，以任何形式复制、翻印或发行 CMA 学习系统资料或内容都会面临法律诉讼，同时还会将这一行为报告给 ICMA（管理会计师协会认证部），并立即取消其 IMA 会员资格和 CMA 考试资格。

读者有责任确保自己所使用的 CMA 考试资料来自有授权的渠道或个人。如果对资料的可信性或资料提供的途径有任何怀疑，请联系 IMA 客户服务处，致电（800）638 - 4427 或（201）573 - 9000，或者 Email：IMA@ imanet. org。

本书所引用的各种 FASB 文件，其版权归财务会计准则委员会（FASB）所有，地址为 401 Merritt 7，P. O. Box 5116，Norwalk，Connecticut 06856，U. S. A，并经允许复印。这些文件的完整版本可从 FASB 处获得。

CMA 资格

注册管理会计师（CMA）资格为公司管理层和财务专业人员提供了衡量管理会计领域知识和能力方面的客观指标。CMA 资格在全球范围内被各种组织内的专业会计人员作为重要的资质证明，它已成为提升专业技能和扩展专业视野的一种重要途径。

CMA 考试包含四个部分，其目的是开发和考核批判性思考能力和决策制定技能，并且可以满足以下目标：

- 通过确定专业人员的作用、知识体系以及获得这些知识的课程，使得管理会计和财务管理成为一种受人认可的专业。
- 鼓励在管理会计和财务管理领域实施较高的教育标准。
- 确定度量个人在管理会计和财务管理领域的知识和技能的客观指标。
- 鼓励持续的职业发展。

获得 CMA 资格的人员可以从以下几个方面受益：

- 可以与其他人员广泛交流业务知识和战略性财务技能。
- 获得最新的专业知识和技能，这些对企业的成功非常重要。
- 致力于卓越，这种卓越建立在强大的职业道德基础与终身学习基础之上。
- 在职业发展、工资水平及升迁机会上获得优势。

CMA 资格由美国管理会计师协会独家授予。

对考生的整体期望

CMA 考试的内容既包括一定深度的会计专业知识，也包括非常广泛的组织问题，这些问题对于管理会计师发挥专业人员的"商业合伙人"角色非常重要。

获得 CMA 资格需要付出很大的努力，完成四个部分的考试可能需要两年的学习时间。但这笔投资将使考生终身受益，能为他们的职业发展奠定坚实的基础，提升其职业发展水平。

如果考生希望通过这四个部分的考试，就必须制定一个严密的学习计划并切实执行该计划。IMA 为考生提供了很多资源、工具和方案，这些都有助于考生的学习和考试。我们鼓励考生在入学开始时就尽快支付入学费，以便充分利用这些有利条件，以最大化自己的学习效果。

如果希望得到关于 CMA 资格、CMA 考试或者 IMA 所提供的考试资源方面的更多信息，请访问网站 www. imanet. org。

前言

欢迎学习 CMA 教材的第二部分：管理会计与报告。

第二部分内容包括预算编制方法、成本管理工具、信息管理方法、业绩评价和外部财务报告规则。每章都会探讨相关术语、不同方法的运用，以及管理会计师必须了解的相关规则和监管条例。

第二部分 CMA 考试

CMA 考生一共需通过四个部分的考试，前三部分的考试可以不按顺序参加，但第四部分的考试只有在成功通过前三部分之后才能参加。

第二部分的 CMA 考试包括 140 道单项选择题，旨在全方位考查应试者的认知能力。应试者有 4 个小时的答题时间，考试在电脑上进行。这部分内容是在参考 ICMA 所制定的考试大纲和学习要点的基础上编写的。ICMA 的考试大纲和学习要点可在美国管理会计师协会（IMA）的网站 www.imanet.org 上找到。

对于准备参加第二部分考试的应试者来说，透彻理解书中的所有概念并掌握各种计算方法非常重要。当然，学会怎样做好选择题也很关键。希望各位考生做好详细的学习计划，以便在第二部分的复习准备和考试中取得成功。

在线资源

这里有许多有用的在线资源可以为参加 CMA 考试的应试者提供帮助，详情请登录网站：www.imanet.org/china/examtools。

制定学习计划

第二部分的考试采用单项选择题的形式考查考生对该部分的概念、术语和计算方法的掌握及了解情况。制定学习计划是迈向成功之路的一个关键因素，认真履行该学习计划同样至关重要。以下是一些帮助你准备和实行第二部分学习计划的窍门及技巧。

1. 因为第二部分的考试可以在全年的任何一天参加，所以考生应做好考试的结构安排。这意味着设定目标考试日期并优先做出考虑和安排。

- 首先决定你的考试日期，并与 ICMA 联系注册第二部分的考试。在注册后，用笔在你计划参加考试的日期上标上记号。
- 在你决定并注册了考试后，就应安排好第二部分学习的起止时间。我们建议你认真协调好考试时间与学习完成时间。第二部分推荐学时为 150 小时。当然，实际学时将取决于你现有的知识水平，你对这部分内容的了解和熟悉程度，以及你的自信心。
- 复习各章以及各节的内容，并为你对每一章的了解/自信程度进行评估打分。

2. 制定一个书面的学习计划，以此指导你的学习，我们强烈建议你制定一个计划，在 6 个月内完成你的自学任务。

3. 定期评估学习计划的履行情况。此外，应认真完成各节后的进度检查练习以及其他资料中的习题。

预算编制

本章内容简介

为什么一些公司取得很大的成就而一些公司却在困境中挣扎？那些卓有成效的公司取得成功的原因在于它们拥有以准确的内外部信息为基础的战略。它们能够将其内部的优点与外部的机会很好地结合在一起。但是，仅拥有好的战略并不够。公司需要将战略转化为行动，这就需要预算。预算是为实现长期和短期目标而制定的详细计划。好的预算不仅能促进成本控制，同时还能确保公司的日常运营与公司的总体目标保持一致。本章探讨预算的基本概念、各种预算系统以及总预算。

学习要点说明

注册管理会计师（CMA）考试包含很多学习要点，这些学习要点由管理会计师协会确定。学习要点描述了注册管理会计师考试要求掌握的所有知识点和技能，并且细分为各个章节。注册管理会计师考试教材解释了学习要点所包含的各个部分，是对学习要点的有力支持。学习要点可以帮助考生以不同的方式或通过不同的问题情景理解这些概念。考生还应该练习学习要点中所提到的全部或者部分计算，或者完成计算过程中的缺失部分。学习要点不能代替对 CMA 考试教材内容的研究和学习，但是可以确保考生达到学习要点所设定的目标。

注册管理会计师教材中所包含的学习要点是一个完整的集合，并且是到目前为止最新的版本。考生可以浏览 IMA 的官方网站 www. imanet. org，点击"认证"部分查看和下载关于学习要点的最新 PDF 文件。

学习要点

1.1 预算概念

- LOS 1.1.1：理解在组织总体计划和绩效评估过程中预算所起的作用。
- LOS 1.1.2：理解经济状况、产业形势及公司计划和预算之间的关系。
- LOS 1.1.3：确认在制定短期目标以及计划和控制经营活动以实现这些目标上预算所起的作用。
- LOS 1.1.4：确定成功的预算编制流程所具备的要素。
- LOS 1.1.5：理解在根据既定目标评估业绩的过程中预算所起的作用。
- LOS 1.1.6：解释预算编制流程如何促进组织各部门的沟通并提升组织活动的协调性。
- LOS 1.1.7：描述与预算编制和绩效评估有关的可控成本的概念。
- LOS 1.1.8：编制一份经营预算。
- LOS 1.1.9：编制一份资本支出预算。
- LOS 1.1.10：理解目标管理（MBO）的概念及其与绩效评估之间的关系。
- LOS 1.1.11：确定目标管理的优点和局限性。
- LOS 1.1.12：理解计划制定流程如何同组织资源的有效配置相协调。
- LOS 1.1.13：确定不同类型预算的合适的时间框架。
- LOS 1.1.14：确定为实现预算流程的最优化应由哪些人员参与该流程。
- LOS 1.1.15：描述成功的预算编制中高层经理所起的作用。
- LOS 1.1.16：确定在制定合适的预算指导方针中高层经理或预算委员会所起的作用，同时确定预算指导方针中应包含哪些项目。
- LOS 1.1.17：理解预算编制对成本标准的作用。
- LOS 1.1.18：区分理想的（理论）标准和当前可实现的（实际）标准。
- LOS 1.1.19：区分权威式标准和参与式标准。
- LOS 1.1.20：确认在制定直接材料标准和直接人工标准中所应采取的步骤。
- LOS 1.1.21：确定在标准设立过程中标杆分析的作用。
- LOS 1.1.22：理解在标准制定中所采用的方法，如作业分析和历史数据的应用。
- LOS 1.1.23：讨论为适应预算假设的重大变化，允许修改预算的政策的重要性。
- LOS 1.1.24：理解在监控和控制支出以达到战略目标的过程中预算所起的作用。

1.2 预算制度

- LOS 1.2.1：对每一个预算制度（年度/总预算、项目预算、作业基础预算法、零基预算、连续性预算、包含改善内容的预算（Kaizen budgeting）、弹性预算），确定其目的、适用的条件和时间框架。
- LOS 1.2.2：对每一个预算制度（年度/总预算、项目预算、作业基础预算法、零基预算、连续性预算、包含改善内容的预算（Kaizen budgeting）、弹性预算），确定预算的组成要素并解释这些组成要素间的内部关系。
- LOS 1.2.3：对每一个预算制度（年度/总预算、项目预算、作业基础预算法、零基预算、连续性预算、包含改善内容的预算（Kaizen budgeting）、弹性预算），理解其编制方法。
- LOS 1.2.4：对每一个预算制度（年度/总预算、项目预算、作业基础预算法、零基预算、连续性预算、包含改善内容的预算（Kaizen budgeting）、弹性预算），比较和对比这些预算制度的优点和局限性。

- LOS 1.2.5：对每一个预算制度（年度/总预算、项目预算、作业基础预算法、零基预算、连续性预算、包含改善内容的预算（Kaizen budgeting）、弹性预算），以当前信息为基础计算预算的组成要素。

- LOS 1.2.6：对每一个预算制度（年度/总预算、项目预算、作业基础预算法、零基预算、连续性预算、包含改善内容的预算（Kaizen budgeting）、弹性预算），评估企业的形势并推荐适当的预算解决方案。

1.3 年度利润计划和附表

- LOS 1.3.1：理解在编制年度利润计划中销售预算所起的作用。

- LOS 1.3.2：确定在编制销售预测并根据所提供的业务信息和经济信息评估该销售预测的可行性时应考虑的因素。

- LOS 1.3.3：确定销售预算的组成要素并根据所提供的相关信息编制销售预算。

- LOS 1.3.4：理解销售预算和生产预算之间的关系。

- LOS 1.3.5：确定在编制生产预算时存货水平所起的作用，并界定在编制生产预算时应考虑的其他要素。

- LOS 1.3.6：根据所提供的相关信息编制生产预算，并根据生产计划评估实现销售目标的可行性。

- LOS 1.3.7：理解直接材料预算、直接人工预算和生产预算之间的关系。

- LOS 1.3.8：确定在编制直接材料预算时对存货水平和采购政策的使用，以及在编制直接人工预算中员工技能、工会合同和雇佣政策的角色。

- LOS 1.3.9：根据所提供的相关信息编制直接材料预算和直接人工预算，并根据这些预算评估实现生产目标的可行性。

- LOS 1.3.10：根据所提供的相关信息预测与员工相关的成本和福利，如雇主对社会保障的贡献份额、与雇佣有关的税收、健康和人寿保险以及养老金贡献等。

- LOS 1.3.11：理解分摊雇员福利费用的不同方法，例如作为直接人工费用的一部分、作为间接费用，理解该分摊对财务报表的影响。

- LOS 1.3.12：理解间接费用（overhead）预算和生产预算之间的关系。

- LOS 1.3.13：确定间接费用（overhead）预算时的固定费用和变动费用。

- LOS 1.3.14：界定间接费用（overhead）的组成要素并根据所提供的相关信息编制间接费用（overhead）预算。

- LOS 1.3.15：确定产品销售成本预算的组成要素，并理解产品销售成本预算、模拟损益表及模拟财务状况报表之间的关系。

- LOS 1.3.16：说明单位边际贡献和总边际贡献，确定对这些概念的恰当应用并计算单位边际贡献和总边际贡献。

- LOS 1.3.17：根据所提供的相关信息编制产品销售成本预算。

- LOS 1.3.18：确定销售和管理费用预算的组成要素并理解这些费用的特点。

- LOS 1.3.19：描述销售和管理费用预算、模拟损益表和模拟财务状况报表之间的关系。

- LOS 1.3.20：理解销售和管理费用预算中具体的组成要素对边际贡献的可能影响。

- LOS 1.3.21：理解资本资产购置预算、现金预算和模拟财务报表之间的关系。
- LOS 1.3.22：界定现金预算的目的并描述现金预算和其他预算之间的关系。
- LOS 1.3.23：确定现金预算的要素并理解信用政策、购买（应付账款）政策和现金预算之间的关系。
- LOS 1.3.24：根据给定的信息编制现金预算并推荐最优投资/融资战略。
- LOS 1.3.25：界定模拟损益表、模拟财务状况报表和模拟现金流量表的目的，理解这些报表和其他预算之间的关系。
- LOS 1.3.26：根据提供的相关信息编制模拟损益表、模拟财务状况报表和模拟现金流量表。

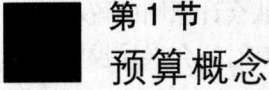

第1节
预算概念

本节内容简介

　　未来是不确定的，企业需要持续应对不确定的未来。计划是制定未来的方向以实现既定目标。战略是将组织优势与市场机会相匹配的计划，以实现既定的长短期目标。预算是计划的主要方法之一，预算必须与公司战略保持一致，否则战略就不可能成为现实。尽管计划或预算并不能保证成功，但缺乏计划会导致错失良机，致使公司频繁应对各种危机，甚至会导致整个运营的失败。

　　除了要与企业的战略相一致之外，预算的第二个主要作用是控制功能。控制对负责预算各个方面的人员的行动施加了制衡机制，包括与预算相联系的绩效评估。控制也与公司战略相关，经理必须有动力为实现长短期战略制定决策。

预算术语

　　这一章应用的有关预算的术语如下所示。

预算

　　预算是一个实体的营运计划和控制工具，它用来确定在一段时间内为实现实体的目标所需要的资源和所需承担的义务。预算主要是定量指标，而不是定性指标。财务预算为损益、现金流量和财务状况设定了具体的目标。

预算编制

　　预算编制是为制定预算所实施的步骤。除了清晰传达组织的目标，理想的预算还包括预算控制。

预算控制

　　如果没有正式的控制系统，预算只不过是预测。预算控制是一个管理过程，目的是通过制定系统性的预算审批流程，协调相关方的努力和相关经营活动，分析实际结果与预算的差异并向负责方提供适当的反馈，以确保预算目标的实现。预算中所设定的目标必须是雇员们认为可实现的，这样目标才具有激励作用。

模拟报表

　　模拟报表是一种以历史信息为基础的预算财务报表，它会假设某些事件已经发生过以对历史信息做出调整。预算资产负债表、预算现金流量表以及预算损益表是对未来一段时间资源配置目标的预测。

　　注意"模拟"有两个定义。上面与预算过程有关的定义针对的是内部使用者。对于外部使用者，当公司会计政策变更时，追溯调整会将这项变更应用于以前期间，就好像这项变化在整个会计期间都起作用一样，在这种情况下，模拟是一个补充的披露，目的是增加可比性。另一个外部定义是说明企业未基于公认会计原则的盈利是非经常性业务产生的，但是这一类报表是不受管制的，不可比，有时还会误导投资者。

预算周期

预算周期通常包括以下步骤：

1. 将一个实体和它的分部门作为一个整体编制预算，所有的经理同意完成预算中应由自己负责的那一部分。

2. 预算被用于比较当前的绩效与期望中的绩效。

3. 检查实际结果与预算的差异，如果可能的话采取纠正措施。

4. 收集反馈信息，重新检查预算，必要时修订预算。

图表 2 – 1 展示了这些步骤如何形成一个周而复始的周期。

图表 2 – 1　预算循环

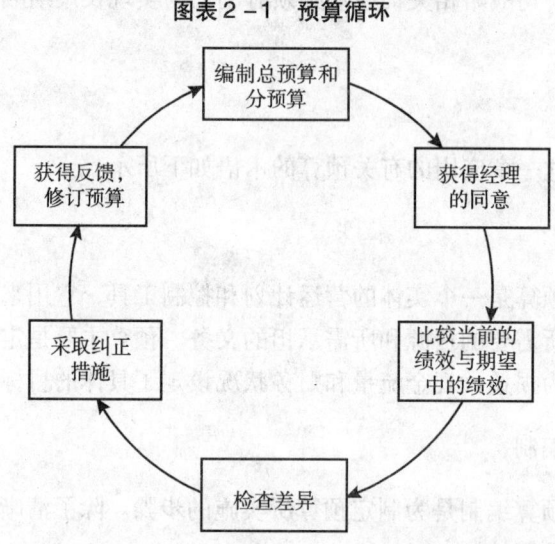

经营及业绩目标

如前所述，战略分析将实体的能力与市场上可利用的机会相结合。战略提出组织的目标，界定潜在市场，并考虑事件、竞争者以及总体经济状况的影响。战略明确了组织结构，同时还会评估替代战略的风险。战略分析是长短期计划的基础，长短期计划分别引导出长短期预算，具体参见图表 2 – 2。长短期预算反过来又引导出了总预算以及构成总预算的各个分预算。

预算可用于根据既定目标进行业绩评估。如果仅仅根据过去的业绩评估当前的表现，过去发生的错误和问题会自动地成为当前的业绩评估基准中的参考因素。例如，某公司由于组建了新的销售团队而导致销售业绩欠佳，如果该公司使用销售业绩欠佳年度的数据作为下一年度的销售业绩评估基准，这一基准明显过低，不利于激励销售团队努力工作。然而，如果评估标准设立得太高，员工也不会努力工作，因为他们认为无论多努力都不可能实现所要求的目标。比如由于某个异常事件的发生使得某一年度的结果好于平均表现，并以该年度的较好结果作为下一年度的评估基准时就会发生这种情况。

图表 2 - 2　战略、计划及预算

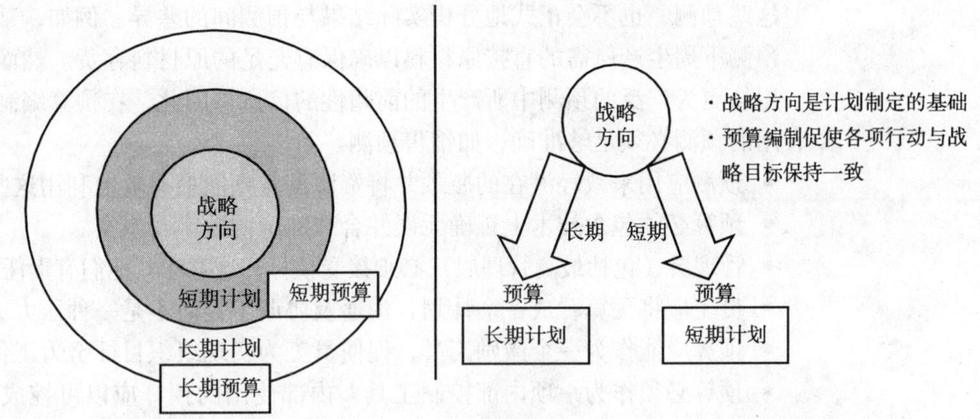

预算的使用允许组织使用期望结果作为评估标准。用预算代替历史结果的另一个好处是过去的业绩并不总能揭示未来的结果。预算能够预见到并考虑到经营环境中所发生的重大变化，而如果仅仅使用历史数据，人们会倾向于认为下一年度必须超越上一年度的表现，而不考虑实际经营环境的变化。

如果采购人员或经理能自主决定是否发生某项成本或在短期内能改变该项成本的水平，这一成本就被认为是可控成本或可自由裁决的任意成本。经理能直接控制的变动成本和其他成本是可控成本。经理可通过削减工人工作时数、使用更为便宜的原料等措施来限制这些可控成本，比如部门经理能够将维修成本和广告成本控制在一定的范围内。

像管理层薪水或租金这样的固定成本通常是不可控的，因此被称作承诺成本。

可控成本这一概念对绩效评估和预算编制十分有用：

● 在绩效评估中，用部门净收入减去可控成本来评估经理或雇员的资金使用效率，这种方法更为现实，并已得到那些被评估者的肯定。让经理负责不可控成本起不到激励作用。

● 在预算编制中，集中关注可控成本可以将重点放在通过预算编制能获得最大效益的地方。

成功的预算编制的特征

成功的预算具备很多特征，但其中任何一个单一的特征都不可能形成一个成功的预算。

成功的预算具备以下共同特征：

● 预算必须与企业的战略相一致。

● 预算过程应保持独立，但应根据战略计划和预测来编制预算。

○ 战略计划。战略计划是高层次、长期、面向整个公司的结构化的规划，比如组建新的生产线就是战略计划，但设立新的责任中心并不是战略计划。然而，早期的预算步骤可用于完善企业的战略方向，因为这些步骤中使用了更多的当前信息。

○ 准确与不准确的预测。很多预测比预算的准确度低，管理层通常不会批准这些预测，也不会正式地分析实际结果与预测间的差异。例如，某个经理可能会预测下周生产所需的直接原材料以确保有充足的原材料存货。然而，预算必须利用从更为广泛的预测中所产生的前瞻性的信息。因此，在预算编制过程中直接运用的预测必须足够准确，如销售预测。

- 预测应用来减轻潜在的瓶颈并将资源配置到能最有效地利用这些资金的领域。
- 预算必须包含技术上正确无误并合理准确的数字及事实。
- 管理层（包括最高管理层）必须接受预算，这意味着他们有责任实现预算目标。
- 员工应将预算看成一个计划、沟通及协调工具而不是一种压力或惩罚措施。
- 预算应能作为一个激励工具，促使员工为实现组织目标努力工作。
- 预算必须作为一项内部控制工具，内部使用的预算应以可控成本或任意成本为基础实施业绩评估。
- 销售及管理费用预算应足够详细以使关键的假设能得到更好的理解。
- 预算编制团队的上级部门必须审查并核准预算。
- 最终的预算不应轻易改变，但应包括为变化所作的具体准备以使预算足够灵活，便于运用。

预算应支配计划，促进沟通与协调，并能提供业绩标准。预算流程必须以高级管理层对预算所作的全面而公正的评估作为依据，以平衡来自丁那些需要遵循预算的相关人员的信息输入。

成功的预算流程的特征

预算流程可以是一个很简单的事件，花费一两天工夫，涉及一两个人即可。预算流程也可以是一个十分复杂的过程，需要一个专门的预算委员会花费几个月的时间才能完成。与预算流程相关的特点包括预算期、预算流程的参与者、基本预算步骤以及成本标准的应用。

预算期

预算主要是为企业的财政年度而编制，但也存在 3 年期、5 年期甚至 10 年期的预算以及期限短于 1 年的预算。不以财政年度为基础的预算也是可行的，但我们不推荐这种预算形式，这是因为财政年度的财务报表可以很容易地与以财政年度为基础的预算作比较。预算通常被进一步分解为月度或季度预算，或者应用连续性预算或滚动预算。连续性预算以月、季度或年为基础，在每一个时期结束时修改下一个时期的预算，添加另一个时期的预算。特定的软件可以非常方便地编制这种连续性预算。

预算流程

不同的公司会有不同的预算编制方法，但是所有的方法都介于完全权威式的预算和完全参与式的预算这两个极端之间。在权威式预算（自上而下的预算）中，高级管理层根据战略目标为每一个部门设定预算的每个具体项目，并期望受预算影响的较低层级的经理及员工能实现这些预算目标。在参与式的预算（自下而上或自愿接受的预算）中，各个层级的经理与某些关键员工一起共同制定本部门的预算（高层经理通常保留最后的批准权）。理想的预算流程是综合采用两种方法的优点。图表 2 – 3 列出了完全的权威式预算以及完全的参与式预算的优点与局限性，并指出了综合预算编制方法如何为预算流程提供最大数量的制衡。注意，综合预算方法有时被看做是参与式预算的一种形式。

图表 2 – 3　权威式预算、综合预算与参与式预算的比较

权威式预算	综合预算	参与式预算
高级管理层将战略目标整合到预算中	自上而下沟通战略目标，并自下而上实施该目标	在预算流程中不优先考虑战略目标
能更好地控制决策	保留了对预算编制的控制权，同时能获得各个组织层级的专业信息，缺点是预算编制流程会比较长	较低层级的专业信息使预算决策更为可靠
用指令代替沟通	双向沟通： • 高级管理层理解参与者的困难与需求 • 参与者理解管理层的两难境地	较低层级与高层经理的全面沟通（产品／服务视角或市场视角）
员工： • 不满 • 不受激励	较低组织层级的参与使他们更好地接受预算，而对预算的普遍接受又使他们能实现预算目标做出更大的承诺	员工： • 参与 • 受激励
较低组织层级可能不会严格地遵循预算	员工对预算拥有责任感加上高级管理层的全面审查，这使得严格的预算能得到遵循	高层经理过松或过严的审批（过严的审批是指压缩较低组织层级的预算申请）会导致预算松弛
不推荐这种方法，但该方法比较适用于小型企业或环境相对稳定的企业	适用于大多数公司；能实现战略与战术间的平衡	适用于高度波动环境中的各个责任中心，在这种情况下，各个领域的经理拥有最为完善的数据

综合预算流程的步骤如下所示：

1. 确定预算参与者，包括各个层级的经理以及在特定领域拥有专长的关键员工。

2. 高层经理与预算参与者沟通战略方向。

3. 预算参与者制定预算初稿。

4. 低层经理将预算提交到下一个较高层级的经理审查，这一过程可能会反复多次，过程中强调双向的沟通。

5. 通过严格而公正的预算审批形成最终的预算。

预算参与者

预算的制定或者废除由三方决定，即董事会、高级管理层以及预算委员会。中低层级的经理也是预算流程的重要参与者，他们根据高级管理层的计划制定详细的预算。

董事会

董事会并不制定预算，但它们拥有审查预算，或予批准或者退回去修改的责任。通常由董事会任命预算委员会的成员。

高级管理层

高级管理层对预算负有最终责任，他们履行这项责任的主要方法是确保每个管理层都能理解并支持预算以及整个预算控制流程。如果高级管理层不明确地支持预算，一线经理也不太可能严格地遵循预算。高级管理层应密切关注自身对一线经理的预算的影响，因为政策的不敏感性会促使部门员工也能制定出富有创造性的预算。

高级管理层应该给予下属以激励如公正的薪酬体系，使他们能制定出真实完整的预算。一个需要避免的常见问题是预算松弛。当预算业绩与实际业绩不同时就会产生预算松弛，这是因为每个经理都会在其预算中预留一笔额外的资金以应对非预期事件。预算松弛使经理对失败无所畏惧，较低组织层级上的预算松弛累积起来会导致总预算极其不准确。

预算的僵化执行在某些情况下会使组织在长期运营中的成本比在预算中增加一些弹性时要高。例如，航空公司的维修经理不会同意一个机械工的临时调职，因为这样做会消耗太多的维修预算，即使公司整体在停飞飞机上每天会损失上万美元。

预算委员会

大型公司通常需要组建一个由高级经理组成的预算委员会，并往往由首席执行官或一名副总裁领导该预算委员会。预算委员会的规模取决于组织的规模。预算委员会指导预算编制工作，核准预算，裁决不同的意见，监控预算，检查结果，并审查修改的预算。

中低层级的经理

一旦预算委员会设定了预算流程的基调，组织中的很多其他人员就需要参与进来。中低层级的经理将会做很多具体的预算工作。这些经理遵循预算指导方针，这些指导方针是高级管理层或预算委员会为各个责任中心制定的预算编制总的指南。责任中心，成本中心或战略性业务部门（SBU）是公司的组成部分，其经理被授权确定成本、收入和/或投资决策（以及制定预算）。预算指导方针围绕公司战略及长期计划制定。预算指导方针中规定了预算编制方法、规划以及自主预算公布后所发生的新的事件，例如新的缩减规模的需要、总体经济状况的变化以及年初至今的运营结果。

预算协调者

参与预算流程的人越多，就越需要某个人或团队能识别并解决不同责任中心在预算上的分歧以及总预算不同部分间的分歧。

流程专家

当实施参与式预算时，一些关键的非管理人员往往会加入到预算团队中。这些人员一般对特定领域的成本有非常细致的了解，尤其是那些很复杂多变的领域。这样的参与者不仅能使预算得到更多的关注，而且亲身参与预算流程使他们对预算拥有一种责任感，从而增加了预算在营运层面得到遵循的可能性。

预算步骤

各责任中心在编制预算时应采取的步骤包括最初的预算提案、预算商议、检查并核准以及修正预算。

预算提案

首席执行官确定了公司的战略之后，一份备忘录或指示就会传达到每个直线经理或责任中心处，这样直线经理或责任中心就可以将其预算流程与战略计划相协调（即一个自上而下的实施过程）。各个责任中心将根据公司战略编制预算的初稿，预算初稿中要兼顾内外部因素。内部因素包括价格变化、可用性的变化以及生产流程的变化，新产品或者新服务，相互关联的责任中心的变化，以及员工的变化。外部因素包括总体经济条件及劳动市场的变化，商品和服务的价格和可用性的变化，产业趋势以及竞争者的行为。

预算商议

一旦预算初稿呈递给高级管理层或预算委员会，后者就会检查预算是否符合组织的战略目标，是否在可接受的范围内，以及是否与类似的预算相一致。检查者还会确定这项预算是否是可行以及是否符合下一个较高组织层级的目标。预算商议会占用很多时间，这是因为从较高管理层处退回来的预算将会引起较高管理层级和责任中心对优先预算项目的重新商议。

预算检查与批准

预算经过一层层的检查和批准直至预算委员会这一层级，预算委员会通过检查预算是否与预算指导方针、长短期目标以及战略计划相一致之后，各个责任中心的单一预算就会合并成总预算。一旦预算委员会和委员会的领导批准了预算，预算就被提交到董事会等待最后的批准。

预算修正

预算的刚性随组织的不同而不同。有些预算不管怎样都要严格执行，有些预算只有在特定环境下才可以被修改，还有一些预算可以频繁地改动。在不同的环境下僵化地执行一项预算将会导致灾难。管理层不应将预算作为其惟一的经营指导方针。定期修改预算可以提供更好的经营指南，但有些经理一旦预期预算会定期修改，他们就不会很认真地编制预算。允许定期修改预算的组织应确保预算修改的门槛设置得足够高，以使员工能尽可能有效地工作。当定期修改预算时，应保留原始预算的副本以便在这一时期结束后同实际结果相比较。

成本标准

组织会设定自己努力想实现的不同类型的标准。标准可以是仔细决定的价格、数量、服务水平或成本。制造业企业的标准通常以单位产品为基础制定。成本标准是一项操作或服务所应耗费的成本，或者是假设所有事项都按计划运行的情况下（如按预期时间和预期产能运行），一个实体预期会发生的成本。预算编制人员利用标准成本制定预算，并随环境的变化而相应更新标准成本指标。实际中，在预算数量和标准数量之间并没有清晰的分界线。时间框架越短，分界线就越模糊。

标准的类型

标准可以是权威式的也可以是参与式的。

● 权威式标准

权威式标准只能由管理层制定。权威式标准可以很快制定出来并能够同整个企业的目标很好地匹配，但权威式标准可能会导致员工不满因此无法得到很好地遵循。

● 参与式标准

参与式标准通过管理层和所涉及各方之间的相互沟通制定。参与式标准更容易被接受但其制定过程需要耗费较多的时间，并需要管理层和所涉及各方之间的协商妥协以确保实现经营目标。

成本标准可分为理想标准和当前可实现的标准这两类。

● 理想标准

理想标准是一个远期目标。它只有当所有情况都产生最佳的可能结果时才能在当下实现。理想标准适用于持续改进战略和全面质量管理理念。一些公司使用在实现理想标准上的进展代替与理想标准的偏离来度量和奖励成功。然而，理想标准很难达到，频繁使用理想标准会导致工作让人不堪重负。如果持续要求达到很难实现的理想标准，这些标准就会丧失激励作用，因为员工没有动力实现这种"不可能"的目标并逐渐习惯于毫无目标。

● 当前可实现的标准

当前可实现的标准与历史标准有些相似；受过恰当培训的人按正常速度操作应能达到当前可实现的标准的要求。绝大多数时候当前可实现的标准都预期可达到。当前可实现的标准也不能设定得太低，否则会导致员工工作过慢，因此标准的设定应适度，应能起到激励作用。当前可实现的标准不符合持续改进战略。

直接材料与直接人工标准成本

类似直接材料和直接人工这样的直接成本项目可以通过确定每一单位的产出所需要的每种类型的投入的数量来度量。然后用投入的单位数量乘以每单位投入的标准成本。考虑一个直接材料的例子：如果 3 单位的投入生产出 1 单位的产出并且单位投入的成本为 \$10，那么每单位产出的标准成本为 \$30。对于直接人工，如果投入 0.7 人工工时得到 1 单位产出并且人工工时成本为 \$10，那么每单位产出的标准成本为 \$7。当然，真实标准成本需要将多个直接材料成本和直接人工成本相加。下面更为具体地讲解在确定直接材料和直接人工成本时应予考虑的因素。

● 直接材料标准成本

标准成本由质量、数量以及价格决定。质量是第一决定要素，因为它对其他所有变量都有影响。质量水平由产品的目标市场决定。该标准由工程师、生产经理以及管理会计人员根据生产设施、产品质量、制造成本以及所利用的设备等进行确定。价格的设定需要参考所有前期数据，包括质量、数量以及供应链成本。供应链成本取决于是否每次都选择价格最低的供应商（成本会变化）或者与一个可信赖的供应商建立合作关系（成本会比较稳定）。

- **直接人工标准成本**

产品复杂性、人工技能水平、设备的类型和条件以及制造工艺都会影响直接人工成本。管理会计人员、工程师、生产经理、工会、人力资源管理以及其他因素也会影响直接人工的标准。直接人工的标准成本以薪金总额加上福利为基础，而不是净薪金。

标准设定中的支持信息

设定标准时要同时应用几种信息来源，包括作业分析、历史数据、市场预期、战略决策以及标杆分析。

- **作业分析**

作业分析是作业成本法（ABC）的一部分，它是指确认、整理以及分析完成一项工作或操作所需要的作业。（本书第 2 章第 3 节对作业成本法有详细的讲解。）可以通过调查直接参与该项操作的人员以确定最有效的资源以及其他投入的组合。工程师参与核算产品的组成部分并确定生产过程中所涉及的具体步骤。管理会计人员帮助分析投入的直接成本以及将一定数量的间接成本（照明、租金、维修费用等）分配到该操作中去。作业分析也用于评估履行任务的人员所应具备的技能水平。作业成本法中的作业分析是最彻底的成本核算法，其实施费用也最大。

- **历史数据**

利用历史数据确定成本相对较容易，但该信息没有作业分析可靠。为提高可靠性，可以利用历史数据确定一项操作的平均成本或历史成本的中值。为实施持续改进，可以将历史上的最佳业绩作为标准或至少是理想标准。然而，使用历史数据无法排除过去的无效率，或者未能考虑到新技术所带来的影响。

- **市场预期与战略决策**

市场预期与战略决策能够决定产品的最大可允许成本水平，这与目标成本法类似。目标成本法是一种产品设计技术，即在生产结束时产品的总成本不能超过特定目标成本。然而，如果一个公司在市场上是价格接受者（换句话说，它必须接受原材料以及人工价格的变化），那么目标成本法在设定标准时就必须考虑到这些市场实际成本。类似于持续改进（改善成本法）或零缺陷这样的战略决策只有在设定高标准时才能实现。本章稍后会给出这些概念的定义。

- **标杆分析**

标杆分析是一个持续、系统化的衡量过程，它与最优业绩相比较来衡量产品、服务以及各项实务的优劣。很多人认为标杆分析是获取"同类最优"信息，但标杆分析在实际中有更广泛的应用。通常，"最好的水平"是针对该行业处于领导地位的公司的外部标杆而言的。然而，"最好的水平"也可以行业外具有类似流程的其他组织的内部标杆信息或指标为依据。好的标杆可以引导公司实现持续改进。相反，不好的标杆会导致显著的负面效应（例如，以一个不相容的行业为标杆会导致制定不现实的目标或缺乏挑战性的目标）。另外，标杆分析一般不会带来能实现可持续竞争优势的重大突破。

资源配置

所有的实体都只拥有有限的资源，它们需要充分利用这有限的资源以获得竞争优势。稀缺资源在竞争性机会中的配置可通过一项战略的实施得以完成。

总预算的基础

总预算是一项计划，它以公司在特定时期内的运营控制战略为基础。关键的一点是，在预期业务活动水平上，总预算保持不变。

战略

公司分析外部因素以确认所面临的机会与威胁；同时分析内部因素以确认自己所具备的竞争优势与劣势。一旦公司知道如何将自己所具备的优势与市场机会相匹配，它就拥有了可据以制定预算的战略。

没有战略的预算通常以前一年的预算为基础，并错过了改变企业战略方向的机会，这不利于企业的发展。许多一度很成功的企业最后销声匿迹就是因为它们未能及时响应市场需求的变化。实施这一战略需要制定明确的长期计划，并利用预算流程实施该长期计划。

长期计划

战略是实现组织目标的起点，为确保战略的顺利实施我们还需要制定一项长期计划。长期计划一般是一项 5～10 年期的计划，计划中会明确为实现公司目标所需采取的行动。长期计划会涉及某些业务的中断，安排权益融资或债务融资，以及将资源逐步配置到新的业务分支上。完成这些大型的重组活动非一朝一夕之事，它是一个时间过程，并且通常需要使用资本预算（总预算的一部分）。资本预算是一个资源配置过程，它将资源配置到实体的长期项目上去。由于厂房、设备以及雇佣和培训员工等项目极耗成本，因此资源的配置应与战略保持一致。

短期目标

构成总预算基础的最后一个要素是短期目标。短期目标是长期计划里的变动，这些变动由资本预算、过去期间的经营业绩以及预期的未来业绩引起，而预期的未来业绩又由当前的经济、社会、产业以及技术环境决定。这些变动应添加到每年的总预算中。

总预算的组成要素

总预算是一个公司或一个业务部门在一年、一个营运期间或短期内的总体经营计划。总预算为所有经营活动设定定量目标，包括筹集必要资本的详细计划。图表 2-4 展示了总预算的各个组成要素。

总预算是展示企业前进方向的地图,设计良好的总预算会指示公司按战略以及长期计划所指定的方向发展。与长期计划相比,预算更精确并且涉及的时间较短,预算更专注于责任中心。

图表2-4 战略目标、长期目标、预算及实施

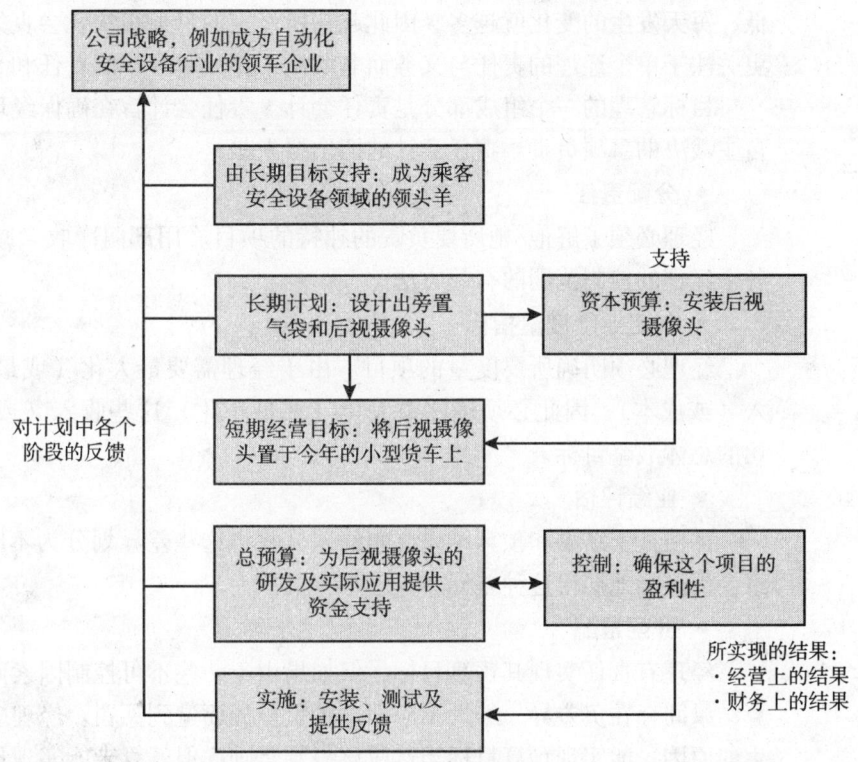

总预算可以分为经营预算、财务预算和资本预算。

● 经营预算确定经营所需要的资源以及如何通过购买或生产获得这些资源。生产预算、采购预算、销售预算以及人员配置预算都属于经营预算。

● 财务预算将资金的来源与资金的使用相匹配以实现公司目标,财务预算包括现金流入预算、现金流出预算、财务状况预算以及经营收入预算。

● 资本预算旨在评估并挑选项目,这些项目需要巨额资金但能在未来提供回报。资本预算应添加到现金预算及其他财务预算中。

目标管理(MBO)

目标管理系统旨在为个人、团队及部门设定目标以达到总预算的要求。目标管理在业绩评估中也很有用。目标管理是一个持续的过程。正像彼德·德鲁克(Peter Drucker)所指出的,目标管理是一个过程,在这个过程中,各个层级的经理参与确定组织的共同目标,界定各人的责任领域,并将这些目标作为组织经营和业绩评估的指南。

目标管理的优点在于它允许下属参与目标设定过程,因此可以获得员工对目标的

支持并能从实际履行任务的人员那里获得反馈。在比较实际结果与计划的非财务目标时，目标管理比财务预算更为有用。目标管理考虑到了非财务指标，例如销售经理是否获得了一定数量的新客户。为获得新客户所付出的努力可能会减少当前的利润但从长远来看能为公司创造更多的利润。明确界定目标可以使人们对其行为负责。目标管理的局限性在于尽管为高层管理部门所设定的目标较容易保持相关性，但组织层级越低，每天发生的变化就越多，因此起初所设定的目标很快就会丧失相关性。目标管理更关注于单个经理的责任与义务而非团队工作或对客户的责任和义务。

目标管理的一个组成部分是责任会计。责任会计旨在确保经理仅对其能控制或能自主裁决的事项负责。责任会计的四个要素是：

- **分配责任**

经理必须了解他/她所要负责的独特的项目。用部门净收入减去可控成本是确定各个经理的控制范围的有效方法。

- **制定业绩度量指标**

经理必须明确所要度量的项目。由于经理需要最大化（或最小化）被度量的收入（或成本），因此必须确保最大化（或最小化）这些收入（或成本）项目符合公司的总体战略目标。

- **业绩评估**

评估真实结果和预算结果之间的差异并将这些差异划分为不同的领域。本书第4章会更详细地探讨这种差异。

- **分配报酬**

经理有责任实现其预算目标，但如果由于一些不可控因素而导致实际结果与预算结果间存在负差异，经理不应因这种负差异而遭到惩罚。经理应能解释这些差异产生的原因。能实现预算目标当然应该得到奖励，但就算未能实现预算目标，只要经理能在发现负差异时迅速采取恰当的应对措施，他们也应受到奖励。

进度检查

提示：完成以下各题。参考答案随后给出。

1. 管理人员与一线经理及网球生产机器的操作员面谈，共同界定在不发生任何意外的情况下所能实现的最优成本标准。则应设定以下哪种类型的标准？

　（　　）a. 权威式理想标准

　（　　）b. 参与式理想标准

　（　　）c. 权威式当前可实现的标准

　（　　）d. 参与式当前可实现的标准

2. 将下面的步骤按正确的顺序形成一个总预算，用1表示第一步：

＿＿＿＿＿＿ 创建总预算

＿＿＿＿＿＿ 制定长期计划

＿＿＿＿＿＿ 制定短期计划

＿＿＿＿＿＿ 分析内外部环境

_____ 形成战略目标

3. 下面哪一项最有可能导致预算松弛？

(　) a. 董事会

(　) b. 高层经理

(　) c. 预算委员会

(　) d. 中低层级的经理

进度检查答案

1. b

2. 5，3，4，1，2

3. d

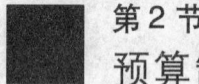

第 2 节
预算制度

本节内容简介

本节探讨不同类型的预算制度,包括总预算、项目预算、作业基础预算法、增量预算、零基预算、连续性(滚动)预算、包含改善内容的预算以及弹性预算。

总预算(年度经营计划或利润计划)

如前所述,总预算(也称为年度经营计划或利润计划)是针对 1 个年度或不到 1 个年度的期间所编制的综合预算。总预算从销售预测和销售预算开始,规划公司成本流的方方面面。编制总预算好处多多,几乎没有坏处;很少有公司能够在没有总预算的情况下应对自如。接下来所要讲述的大多数预算都由总预算变化而来。本章第 3 节"年度利润计划和时间表"会详细地描述总预算。

项目预算

当某个项目完全独立于公司的其他要素或是该公司惟一的要素的时候,我们就会用到项目预算。一部电影有自己的工作人员和仅与这部电影相关的成本。一艘轮船、一条公路、一架飞机或其他主要资本资产经常会用到项目预算。项目预算的时间框架就是项目的期限,但跨年度的项目应按年度分解编制预算。在编制项目预算时,过去相似项目的成功项目预算就可以作为标杆。项目预算的编制同在下一节将要讲到的总预算一样,利用相同的技术并包含相同的组成要素,不同之处仅在于项目预算只关注与项目相关的成本,而总预算关注整个公司的成本。间接费用(overhead)预算被简化了,因为公司将一部分固定和变动间接费用分配到了项目中,剩余的间接费用不再在项目预算中考虑。

项目预算的优点在于它能够包含所有与项目有关的成本,因此能轻易度量单个项目的影响。无论项目规模的大小,项目预算都能很好地发挥作用。在处理比较小的项目时,许多个人及公司利用类似于 Microsoft Project 这样的程序编制预算。当某些项目利用了与整个组织有关而不仅仅是与特定项目有关的资源和人力的时候,项目预算潜在的局限性就会凸现出来。在这种情况下,项目预算将与这些资源中心相关并且受影响的个体将会拥有两个上司。这时就要注意成本的划分与职权结构。

作业基础预算法

作业基础预算法(ABB)关注于作业而不是业务部门或产品。每一项作业都有其相应的成本动因,可以是基于数量的成本动因(如人工工时、平方英尺)或基于作业的成本动因(如组装一台机器所需要的零部件数量)。成本动因是为维持运营所需要的某项工作或作业的成本度量单位。成本可以划分为成本池如单位、批数、产品以及设施等。成本池由同质成本构成，这些成本随生产的上升或下降而同比例变化。固定成本属于同一个成本池，不同层次的变动成本被划分到不同的成本池中。每次编制总预算时，都应对成本池划分的准确性作出评估。本书第 2 章第 3 节"累积系统"中会介绍作业成本法（ABC）及其相关术语。

　　传统预算关注于资源投入并按职能领域编制预算。作业基础预算法关注于增值型作业并按作业成本编制预算。传统预算把重点放在提高管理业绩上，作业基础预算法将重点放在团队合作、同步作业以及客户满意度上。

　　作业基础预算法的支持者认为传统成本会计通过将成本度量过度简化为人工工时、机时、整个流程或部门的产出单位等指标，模糊了成本与产出之间的关系。与传统成本会计仅使用数量动因不同，作业基础预算法使用类似于调整次数这样的作业成本动因，从而能理清资源耗费与产出之间的关系。（如果基于数量的动因对于特定作业来讲是最适合的度量单位，作业基础预算法也会采用数量动因。）理清了资源耗费与产出之间的关系后，经理就可以了解产品供应、产品设计、制造技术、客户基础以及市场占有率的变化对资源需求的影响。由此每一项计划的作业都会有其突出的成本内涵。正因为如此，很多公司应用作业基础预算法以持续改善其预算编制（作业基础预算法与本节稍后将要讨论的包含改善内容的预算之间也具有相关性）。与此相反，传统预算关注于过去（历史）的预算，并且往往由于不了解某些项目的成本效益，因而对那些本应中止的项目仍继续投入资金。

　　作业基础预算法可以作为总预算编制流程（在下一节中详细讨论）的基础。由此编制的分预算会采用不同的成本度量方法，因此成本比例会有不同的权重。例如，作为间接费用的一部分间接原材料或间接人工可以谨慎地归入直接材料和直接人工。

　　下一节将用罗宾制造公司的例子说明总预算的组成，下一节中的图表 2 - 12 表明该公司的变动间接人工按每直接人工工时（DLH）2 美元计算。7 月份产出 72 000 个单位的产品，罗宾制造公司的预算直接人工工时为 36 000 小时，因此总变动间接人工成本为 $72 000。该公司还预算管理人员的薪水为 $10 000，这是一项固定间接人工成本。假设 72 000 个单位的产品由两个独立的部门生产，包括零部件加工和最后的组装，并且每个部门都利用部分间接人工进行质量控制。使用作业基础预算法，我们可以按批次追踪用于质量控制的间接人工，如图 2 - 5 所示。（假设每 1 单位产品有 10 个零部件。）

图表 2 - 5　使用作业基础预算法确定成本的例子

	零部件加工	最后组装
7 月份的产量	720 000 个零部件	72 000 件产品
每批次的零部件数或产品数	每批次 100 个零部件	每批次 100 件产品
要检查的批次数	720 000/100 = 7 200 批次	72 000/100 = 720 批次
每批次的检查时间	每批次 0.2 小时	每批次 0.3 小时
总检查时数	7 200 × 0.2 = 1 440 小时	720 × 0.3 = 216 小时

　　如果零部件检查的人工成本为每小时 $12，最后组装的检查成本为每小时 $15，那么 1 440 × $12 = $17 280，216 × $15 = $3 240，总额为 $20 520。这部分成本将作为直接人工并从间接人工中扣除，余下的间接人工可以按一种新的较低的小时费率来

计算。$20 520 与新的间接人工的和不一定仍等于 $72 000，作为新的、更为准确的度量方法，得出一个不同的结果也在预期之内。此外，1 656 小时的总检查时间会占用部分固定间接成本（管理人员薪水）。如果作业基础预算法规定每 8 个小时的检查时间需要 1 个小时的管理监督时间，并且每 1 小时的管理监督时间的成本为 $30，那么用于检查的管理人员的薪水这一固定成本计算如下：

$$1\ 656\ 小时 \times \left(\frac{1\ 小时管理监督}{8\ 小时检查}\right) \times \$30/小时 = \$6\ 210$$

再次，这个固定间接成本可以分成两个（或更多）的成本项目。用于检查的新的管理人员薪水和其他任何薪水仍为固定间接成本，但注意到这里无论是固定成本还是变动成本都由成本动因决定。在作业基础预算法（基于作业成本法）下，固定成本和变动成本都采用合适的成本动因进行分摊，这意味着在短期内，固定成本和变动成本的处理方式相同。这一点很重要，因为与成本分解有关的新信息可能揭示出每 9 个小时的检查时间只需要 1 小时的管理监督时间，这会降低原先预计的固定成本。信息越具体，预算就越精确。

从本例中可以看出，作业基础预算法的一个主要优点是它可以更准确地确定成本，尤其是在追踪多个部门或多个产品的成本时。但为获得这一优点也需要付出一定的代价，如果设计并维持作业基础预算系统的成本超过了由这一预算系统所带来的成本节约，作业基础预算法的潜在缺陷就会表露无遗。因此，作业基础预算法最适合于在产品数量、部门数量以及诸如设备调整等方面比较复杂的企业。这是因为当经营环境趋于复杂时，宽泛的传统成本法的效用就会大打折扣。

增量预算

增量预算是一种很常用的预算，它以前一年度的预算为起点，根据预计的销售变化和经营环境变化自上而下或自下而上地调整上一年度预算中的各个项目。增量预算与零基预算相反。增量预算的主要缺点（也是零基预算的主要优点）是预算规模会逐年增大。使用增量预算能使人产生一种权利感。

零基预算

为避免前期预算中的无效率因素继续出现，一些企业使用零基预算，顾名思义，"零基预算"是指从零美元开始。传统预算关注于过去预算的变化，而零基预算关注于预算中每一个项目的成本的合理性。经理必须深入地检查受其控制的各个领域才能证明这些领域的成本的合理性。

零基预算的优点在于它促使经理检查所有的业务要素。零基预算有利于创造一个有效、精简的组织，因此在政府机构和非营利组织中很受欢迎。零基预算是从新的视角看待老问题。

制定零基预算的第一步就是要求每个部门的经理按重要性程度的高低列出其部门的所有活动，并为每项活动分配一笔成本。更高层级的经理会检查这些被称为决策包的活动清单，并删除那些不太合理或不是很重要的活动项目。高层经理通常会问这样的问题："这项活动是否必须被施行？如果不施行会发生什么？"或者"能不能利用外包或客户自助服务等替代方法提供该项功能？"经理也可以利用标杆指标及成本效益分析来决定应删掉哪些活动项目。只有那些得到批准的活动项目才会出现在预算中。可以通过与部门经理之间的讨论与协商来确定已被接受的活动项目的成本。一旦确定了预算指标，零基预算就成为总预算的基础，其组成要素和编制步骤与下一节将要探讨的总预算一样。

理论上，零基预算的一个优点是它关注于每个预算项目而不仅仅是例外情况。零基预算帮助经理确认并剔除那些成本大于收益的项目。在雇用新的经理的时候零基预算十分有用。零基预算的一个主要缺陷是，因为担心下一个预算周期中可能会被分配较少的资源，经理倾向于用光当前预算期间的所有已分配资源。如果经理故意在零基预算中加入预算松弛，这一预算编制法就会导致重大浪费和不必要的采购。其他缺陷包括零基预算编制中的年度审查流程极耗时间且极费成本（因此这一审查往往不能像预想的那样全面、彻底），加上零基预算并不使用前期的预算，因此前期的经验教训无法在零基预算中得到反映。每年都使用零基预算会和增量预算一样达不到很好的效果。经理会记住过去的判断和指标，并在下一年继续使用这些判断和指标。为减少零基预算所需要的时间和花费，可以每五年编制一次零基预算（其他年份应用不同的预算法），或者每年只在一个部门中实施零基预算。

连续性（滚动）预算

连续性预算或滚动预算是在每个预算期结束时再添加一个新的预算期，这样预算中的时期数就保持不变，并且还能根据经营环境的变化更新预算。同其他预算类型一样，连续性预算也可以作为总预算，其组成要素和内部关系与下一节将要讨论的总预算一样。区别就在于滚动预算是在前期预算期满时连续添加新一期的预算。因此，连续性预算的时间跨度保持不变（例如，在一年中的任何月份，连续性预算的时间框架都是一年期）。

例如，如果时间段是一个月期，每个月组织都会将一系列新的月度财务报表交予负责预算编制的各个人员。在月度预算会议上，经理会报告实际结果与上月预算间的差异并预计下一个月的预算。审查完下月的预算后，预算协调人员会更新总预算。预算协调人员必须完成直线经理未履行的所有计算，如折旧、存货估价等。

与年度预算相比，连续性预算具有更强的相关性。连续性预算可以反映当前发生的事项并估计未来的需要。连续性预算的优点是将一个很复杂的过程分解为易于管理的步骤。因为经理总有一个完整时段的预算数据，他们更倾向于从一种更长远的视角而不是年度预算视角来审视决策，因为随着时间的推移，年度预算所涵盖的时段会越来越短。连续性预算的潜在缺陷是需要预算协调人员，以及与经理每月都要花费时间编制下月预算相关的机会成本。连续性预算适用于那些不能投入一大块时间编制年度预算的公司。那些有季节性空闲的公司可能会发现在这一空闲时段编制预算比较方便。连续性预算也适合于需要其经理拥有更长远的眼光的公司。

包含改善内容的预算

包含改善内容的预算（Kaizen budget）是一种持续改进的预算方法（"Kaizen"是日语词汇）。与传统的预算基于当前的表现相比，包含改善内容的预算基于计划的未来经营表现。

包含改善内容的预算编制由确认改进领域开始。由于改进后的行为通常更为有效，因此包含改善内容的预算其成本一般较低。这种改变往往由公司的政策（例如，胶水成本必须下降5%）所主导。许多应用包含改善内容的预算的公司也要求其供应商实施持续改进。传统预算中的削减是被动式的，经常涉及服务水平或生产水平的下降；而包含改善内容的预算中的削减是主动式的，它试图在不牺牲生产率的前提下降低成本。

将包含改善内容的预算作为总预算，其时间跨度和组成要素与下一节将要讨论的总预算相同，但在预算期内，每一个成本动因和/或标准成本随着时间的推移可能不只设定一个水平。例如，第一季度的间接人工分摊率可能是 $2/直接人工工时，第二季度为 $1.90，第三季度为 $1.80，第四季度为 $1.70。或者每单位产出的直接人工工时从 0.5 稳步下降到 0.4……，依此类推。另一个预算项目可能将每批次的产出数量设定为 200、210……，依此类推。因此每份预算可能都有一个附表，以说明最终预算中所列出的数额是怎样计算得到的。

包含改善内容的预算的优点在于它的主动性以及它能推动公司目标的实现。应用包含改善内容的预算的公司一般拥有完全整合的质量控制系统，而不是支离破碎或零星的质量控制努力。然而，包含改善内容的预算的一个缺陷就是，由于很多预算是相互联系的，例如，如果直接人工工时标准降低，那么以直接人工工时数为基础计算的变动间接成本也会收紧，如果公司未能实现其总体目标，包含改善内容的预算与实际结果之间就会存在巨大差异。因此，包含改善内容的预算经常与作业基础预算法结合起来应用，以确保所有的成本都有其适当的成本动因。包含改善内容的预算还有一个缺陷，那就是在没有其他选择的情况下，为了降低成本，经理可能会降低质量要求或将业务转移到劳动力更便宜的市场中去。此外，与零基预算不同，包含改善内容的预算将重点放在改进现有的支出上，因此在实现增量改进的同时会忽略一些本应剔除或添加的项目。

弹性预算

弹性预算为特定产出水平确立一个基准成本预算（成本—产量关系），在此基础上加上一个能反映不同产量水平下的成本习性的增量成本—产量关系。弹性预算只调整变动成本，固定成本保持不变。弹性预算最常见的应用是为准确地匹配组织的销售预测。在决定如何修正下期预期的时候，前期的弹性预算会很有用，采用实际产出水平的弹性预算不能作为一种总预算，因为实际产出水平在预算期结束前都是未知的。因此，弹性预算更多地是作为一种分析工具以确定实际结果与预算间的差异，而不是用于制定原始预算。弹性预算的时间框与总预算一样。由于弹性预算是对现有总预算的调整（或对现有总预算中某一个月份的调整），弹性预算的组成要素与下一节将详细讨论的总预算的组成要素相同。

运用弹性预算的优势在于有效利用历史预算信息改进未来的计划。缺陷在于它仅仅关注弹性预算水平，而忽视了未达到销售目标的事实。然而，大多数企业应用弹性预算是因为它可以进行详细的差异分析。本书第 4 章"绩效评估"中会更详细地探讨弹性预算。

进度检查

提示：完成以下各题。参考答案随后给出。

1. 以下哪一种预算方法会运用"调整次数"这样的成本动因度量某一批次混合生产作业的成本？
   （　　）a. 包含改善内容的预算
   （　　）b. 项目预算
   （　　）c. 连续性预算
   （　　）d. 作业基础预算法

2. 以下哪一种预算方法会为特定产出水平确立一个基准成本预算，在此基础上加上一个能反映不同产量水平下的成本习性的边际成本—产量关系。
   （　　）a. 弹性预算
   （　　）b. 连续性预算
   （　　）c. 包含改善内容的预算
   （　　）d. 作业基础预算法

3. 正确或错误？包含改善内容的预算通过为每一个即将到来的月份编制新的预算来实现持续改进。
   （　　）a. 正确
   （　　）b. 错误

4. Bounce Sporting Goods 是一家盈利企业，该企业采用作业基础总预算法。该企业的 5 年期预算表明，在未来几年中企业的成本会明显高于其收入。以下哪项是 Bounce 公司的最好选择？
   （　　）a. 用连续性预算代替作业基础预算法
   （　　）b. 用包含改善内容的预算代替作业基础预算法
   （　　）c. 用包含改善内容的预算辅助作业基础预算法
   （　　）d. 用连续性预算辅助作业基础预算法

进度检查答案

1. d
2. a
3. b
4. c

第3节
年度利润计划和附表

本节内容简介

总预算或年度利润计划有很多组成要素和附表，包括经营预算、财务预算、资本预算以及模拟财务报表。本节将讨论这些要素。

总预算

总预算是实体的所有预算及其各部门的经营活动计划的全面汇总。总预算将所有东西都汇总在一起，包括战略计划与长期计划以及短期目标与当前的现实。总预算通常以年度为基础编制，尽管短于一年的期限也可以应用总预算。

总预算由很多不同的预算所组成。大体上，总预算可以分为经营预算、生产预算与财务预算。

经营预算是总预算的主体部分；经营预算包括销售预算，而销售预算包括产品预算以及销售和管理费用预算。生产预算由直接材料、直接人工，间接费用以及产品销售成本预算组成。生产预算揭示了产品预算中未涉及的额外产品成本数据。财务预算包括所有的模拟财务报表（预算损益表、预算资产负债表以及预算现金流量表）以及现金预算。图表2-6展示了总预算的这些组成要素间的相互关系。

经营预算

销售预测

在编制销售预算之前，需要一份准确的销售预测。销售预测是实体对即将到来的时期的销售额的主观估计。没有准确的销售预测，其他所有预算都不可能正确。销售预测不仅要考虑到销售的历史趋势，还要考虑到经济和产业状况指标、竞争者的行为、不断上升的成本、定价策略和信用政策、广告与市场营销的投入额、未履行的订单的数量以及销售管道（潜在客户前景）中的销售。销售预测使用统计分析技术，比如本节稍后会讨论的应收账款余额模式。销售经理对其所负责的市场以及该市场中的客户需求最为了解，在确定最终的销售预测的细节内容时，应通过充分的交流来利用销售经理的这些经验知识。

销售预算

一旦公司确定了其销售预测、长短期目标以及产能，接下来就可以编制一份销售预算以实现这些目标。销售预算是比产品预算或管理费用预算高一级别的预算，因为销售预算界定了公司整体所要求的产能水平，包括产品成本、销售和管理成本。图表2-7说明了各月销售单位及销售价格的变化。

图表2-6　总预算

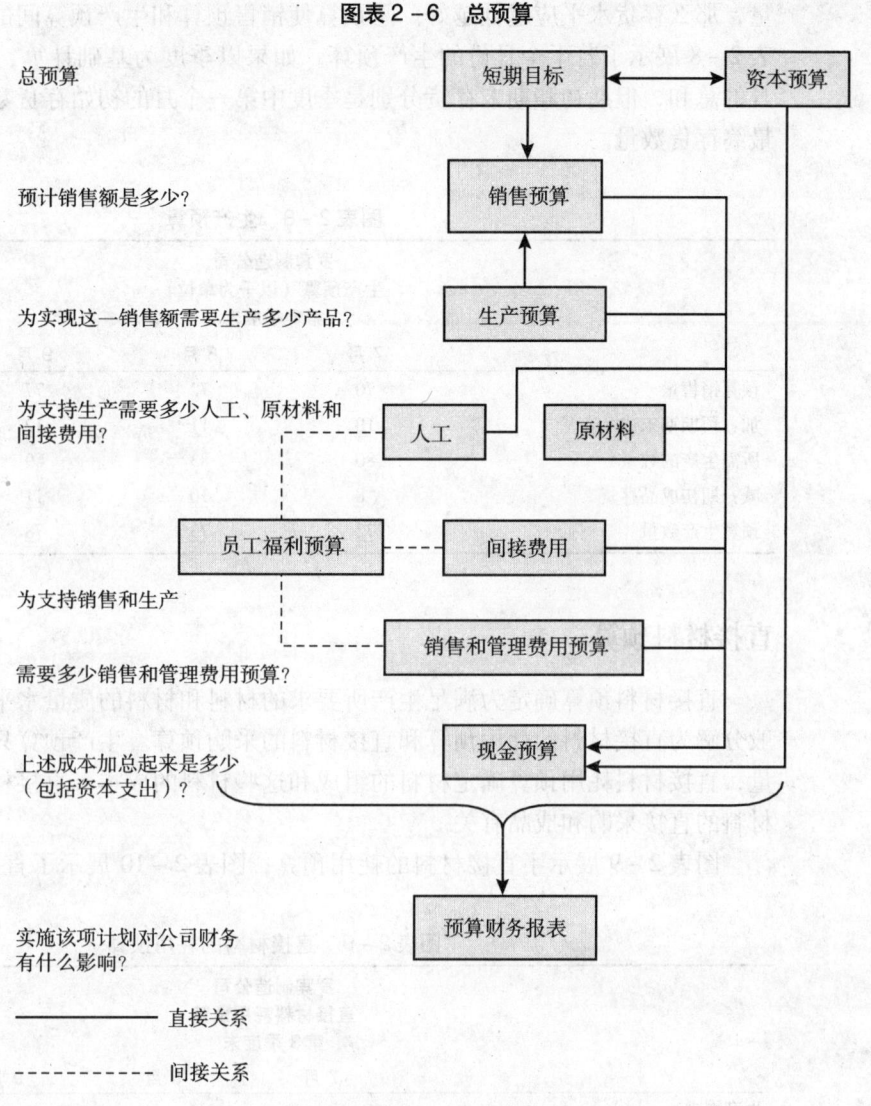

图表2-7　销售预算

罗宾制造公司
销售预算
第3季度末

	7月	8月	9月	季度
销售数量	70 000	72 000	77 000	219 000
单位售价	$110.80	$110.80	$112.00	
总销售额	$7 756 000	$7 977 600	$8 624 000	$24 357 600

生产/存货预算

　　确定了预计的销售水平后，就可以编制生产预算以满足预期需求。生产预算是计划所需购置的资源，并利用这些资源满足销售目标，同时维持一定的存货水平。生产预算通过用预期期末存货加上预算销售量再减去期初存货来计算。如果不限定销售量，那么存货水平应越低越好。总预算使销售预算和生产预算间的比较成为可能。图表2-8展示了若干个月份的生产预算。如果以季度为基础计算，总销售量就是三个月的总和，但期初和期末存货分别是季度中第一个月的初始存货数量和最后一个月的最终存货数量。

图表2-8 生产预算

罗宾制造公司
生产预算（以千为单位）
第3季度末

	7月	8月	9月	季度
预算销售量	70	72	77	219
加：预期期末成品存货	10	11	12	12
所需生产的数量	80	83	89	231
减：期初成品存货	8	10	11	8
预算生产数量	72	73	78	223

直接材料预算

直接材料预算确定为满足生产所要求的材料和材料的质量水平。直接材料预算一般分解为直接材料的耗用预算和直接材料的采购预算。生产预算只确定所要生产的数量，直接材料耗用预算确定材料的组成和这些材料的成本。直接材料采购预算与各种材料的直接采购和成品有关。

图表2-9展示了直接材料的耗用预算；图表2-10展示了直接材料的采购预算。

图表2-9 直接材料的耗用预算

罗宾制造公司
直接材料耗用预算
第3季度末

	7月	8月	9月	季度
生产需求				
预算产量	72 000	73 000	78 000	223 000
每单位产品所需的树脂量（磅）	5	5	5	5
所需树脂总量（磅）	360 000	365 000	390 000	1 115 000
期初树脂存货（磅）	35 000	35 000	35 000	35 000
每磅成本	$13.00	$13.00	$13.25	$13.00
期初存货总成本	$455 000	$455 000	$463 750	$455 000
树脂采购总成本（参见图表2-10）	4 680 000	4 836 250	5 253 500	14 769 750
可用于生产的树脂的总成本	$5 135 000	$5 291 250	$5 717 250	$15 224 750
预期期末存货数量（磅）	35 000	35 000	40 000	40 000
每磅预期期末存货的成本	$13.00	$13.25	$13.30	$13.30
预期期末存货的总成本	$455 000	$463 750	$532 000	$532 000
生产所耗用的树脂的成本	$4 680 000	$4 827 500	$5 185 250	$14 692 750
（可用于生产的树脂的总成本—预期期末存货的总成本）				

图表 2-10 直接材料的采购预算

罗宾制造公司 直接材料采购预算 第3季度末	7月	8月	9月	季度
生产所需直接材料总额	360 000	365 000	390 000	1 115 000
加：预期期末存货	35 000	35 000	40 000	40 000
所需的直接材料总额	395 000	400 000	430 000	1 155 000
减：期初直接材料存货	35 000	35 000	35 000	35 000
直接材料采购数量	360 000	365 000	395 000	1 120 000
每磅采购价格	$13.00	$13.25	$13.30	
直接材料采购总成本	$4 680 000	$4 836 250	$5 253 500	$14 769 750

直接人工预算

直接人工预算由生产经理和人力资源经理共同编制。人工预算帮助公司规划生产流程以使全年的生产平稳运行，并使人力规模与生产要求保持一致。在需要雇用或解聘员工时，公司可以与工会谈判。人工预算可以按照类别划分，如半熟练工人、非熟练工人及熟练工人。

图表 2-11 展示了直接人工预算。

图表 2-11 直接人工预算

罗宾制造公司 直接人工预算 第3季度末	7月	8月	9月	季度
预算产量	72 000	73 000	78 000	223 000
每单位产品所要求的直接人工工时数	0.5	0.5	0.5	
所需直接人工工时数	36 000	365 000	39 000	115 000
小时工资	$15	$15	$15	
直接人工总工资	$540 000	$547 500	$585 000	$1 672 500

间接费用预算（工厂间接费用预算）

除直接材料和直接人工之外的其他所有生产成本的预算都属于间接费用预算有时也称为固定成本预算，因为大部分成本都不随产量的上升和下降而变化。例如，无论产量是上升还是下降，租金和保险费都保持稳定。

间接费用预算中所包含的变动成本会随产量而变化，如批调度成本、电力成本和其他公用设施成本。固定成本很容易预算，但变动成本要求预测所要生产的产品数量、所使用的生产方法以及其他外部因素。

图表 2-12 展示了间接费用预算。

图表 2-12　间接费用预算

罗宾制造公司
间接费用预算
第 3 季度末

	间接费用分摊率 （每 DLH）*	7 月	8 月	9 月	季度
直接人工工时总数		36 000	365 000	39 000	111 500
变动间接费用					
耗用品	$0.20	$7 200	$7 300	$7 800	$22 300
额外福利	4.10	147 600	149 650	159 900	457 150
公用设施	1.00	36 000	365 000	39 000	111 500
维护费	0.50	18 000	18 250	19 500	55 750
变动间接费用总额	$5.80	$208 800	$211 700	$226 200	$646 700
固定间接费用					
折旧		$20 000	$20 000	$20 000	$20 000
工厂保险		800	800	800	2 400
财产税		1 200	1 200	1 200	3 600
管理人员的薪水		10 000	10 000	10 000	30 000
间接人工		72 000	72 000	72 000	216 000
公用设施		4 000	4 000	4 000	12 000
维护费		900	900	900	2 700
固定间接费用总额		$108 900	$108 900	$108 900	$326 700
间接费用总额	$5.80	$317 700	$320 600	$335 100	$973 400

＊本例中假设直接人工工时数是间接费用的成本动因。

产品销售成本预算

　　产品销售成本预算是一个时期内的预算总生产成本和预算单位生产成本。产品销售成本预算有时也称为产品生产和销售成本预算，因为该预算通常包括存货项目。产品销售成本预算在生产预算、直接材料预算、直接人工预算和间接费用预算完成之后才开始编制，因为产品销售成本预算是其他预算基础上的一个总结。

　　图表 2-13 展示了产品销售成本预算。

图表 2-13　产品销售成本预算

罗宾制造公司
产品销售成本预算
第 3 季度末

	7 月	8 月	9 月	季度
期初产成品存货，（某年）7 月 1 日				$1 575 000
耗用的直接材料（参见图表 2-9）	$4 680 000	$4 827 500	$5 185 250	$14 692 750
耗用的直接人工	540 000	547 500	585 000	1 672 500
间接费用	317 700	321 600	341 100	980 400
产品制造成本	$5 537 700	$5 696 600	$6 111 350	$17 345 650
可供出售的产品的成本				18 920 650
减：期末产成品存货				1 575 000
产品销售成本				$17 345 650

销售及管理费用预算

非制造费用通常被归入一个称为销售和管理费用预算或非制造成本预算的预算中。将销售费用划入这一类别是因为销售费用不能分摊给生产流程，并且必须计为销售当期的费用。

销售及管理费用预算中的成本通常是为了满足长期目标，如客户服务，因此这些成本不容易被削减。在使用销售和管理费用的边际贡献模式时，同变动制造成本一样，所有变动销售和管理成本都可以从净销售额中扣除以得到边际贡献，这一特征使得销售和管理费用预算可用于内部业绩评估并可用于揭示哪些成本属可控成本。有关边际贡献的更多信息可参见本书第4章第2节"责任中心和报告部门"。

图表2-14展示了非制造成本预算。

图表2-14 销售和管理费用预算

罗宾制造公司
销售和管理费用预算
第3季度末

	7月	8月	9月	季度
调查/设计	$95 000	$95 000	$100 000	$290 000
市场营销	240 000	280 000	290 000	810 000
运输	135 000	140 000	150 000	425 000
产品支持	90 000	90 000	95 000	275 000
管理	185 000	190 000	192 000	567 000
总额	$745 000	$795 000	$827 000	$2 367 000

雇员福利预算

雇员福利预算帮助雇主确定预算中公司所要承担的薪水成本份额。在预算中，福利变得越来越重要：在20世纪20年代的美国，福利约占薪水的3%，然而现时公司的福利成本平均超过薪水的40%。

雇员福利与直接人工预算、间接费用预算以及销售和管理费用预算有关，所以这些预算中的每一种可能都拥有一个支持性的福利预算，或一个附表以帮助确定每个预算中所应包含的福利成本。比如健康保险和退休福利就被视为是间接费用预算的一部分，并通常作为税收和福利支出的一部分进行分摊。注意到在先前所展示的间接费用预算中，罗宾制造公司的福利由"额外福利"项表示。增加工资和薪水这样的福利以及某一期间新的人员雇佣是直接人工预算的一部分。很多变动成本福利的计算以预算直接人工工时数为依据。管理人员福利和员工股票期权福利视为销售及管理费用预算中的一笔费用。

法定福利通常由雇主和雇员共同支付，但这里只关注雇主支付的部分。可选福利也由雇主和雇员共同支付，如健康保险。图表2-15列出了一些常见的由雇主支付的雇员福利，并指出了哪些是法定福利，哪些是大部分雇员可选择的福利，以及哪些是固定成本福利，哪些是变动成本福利。

图表 2 -15　常见的由雇主支付的福利

类型	福利	描述
变动成本福利，法定福利	美国联邦社会保险捐款法（FICA；社会保险）	联邦法律规定雇主从雇员薪水中保留一定比例，将其存入政府信托基金用于社会保险、伤残保险和遗属津贴。
	医疗保险	针对 65 岁以上公民、患有末期肾脏疾病的公民以及有资格领取社会保障金 2 年以上的公民的全国范围内的健康保险计划。
	美国联邦失业税（FUTA）	为失业保险的管理成本提供融资的税收。
	州失业税	在联邦责任之外的，为失业保险基金所支付的福利提供融资的税收。
固定成本福利，法定福利	员工赔偿保险	赔偿工伤的保险。每年会重新设定额度，各年的额度可能会不一样，额度大小主要由公司的赔偿历史决定。
变动成本福利，可选福利	非工作时间的报酬	假期、休息、病假、事假以及家庭和医疗假期的报酬；一些可能是固定成本福利。
	奖金，分红	由雇主规定。员工股票期权必须计入费用。
	退休福利，401（k），以及类似的计划	包括固定养老金计划（允诺一笔固定的退休支付）和养老金的固定缴款计划如 401（k）。退休储蓄账户：雇主可能以雇员的缴款为基础额外缴款。通过设立养老金负债账户，雇主承认在雇员职业生涯中的固定养老金收益。当退休的雇员获得其收益，养老金负债账户被冲销。
固定成本福利，可选福利	健康保险	由雇主支付的健康保险部分。
	牙医保险	由雇主支付的牙医保险部分。
	短期伤残（STD）保险	健康保险保障期间之外的事故或疾病保险。
	长期伤残（LTD）保险	短期伤残保险保障期间之外的事故或疾病保险。

　　固定成本福利一般计入年度成本，一些固定成本福利也按每年每人的成本或薪水的百分比来计算。只要员工数量不发生变化，固定成本福利通常被认为保持不变。变动成本福利可按前面的方法或按小时成本来计算，工时数可自主决定（如每年全职工作 2 080 小时）或以实际工时数为准。

　　很明显，法定福利是很难改变且必须支付的承诺成本。明确界定哪些福利是可选福利有助于雇主确定可以削减或增加成本的领域。

财务预算

模拟财务报表

　　供内部使用的模拟财务报表是在一系列假设条件下，对公司未来状况的预测。（注意模拟财务报表的定义与外部报表不同）。内部模拟财务报表包括模拟损益表、模拟资产负债表、模拟现金流量表以及现金预算。

模拟损益表

　　模拟损益表或预算损益表展示了在公司满足其预算要求并且各项假设前提正确无误的条件下，公司在年末所能获得的利润。如果预算收益比目标收益小，管理层就应采取修正行动，并根据这些行动修正预算。因此预算损益表是评估业绩进展的基准。

　　模拟损益表的编制至少需要用到销售预算、产品销售成本预算以及销售和管理费用预算。

　　图表 2 -16 展示了模拟损益表。

图表 2 – 16　模拟损益表

罗宾制造公司 模拟损益表 第 3 季度	
销售额	$24 357 600
减：产品销售成本	17 345 650
毛利	$7 011 950
减：经营成本	2 367 000
经营收益	$4 644 950

模拟资产负债表

　　模拟资产负债表（也称为预算资产负债表或预算财务状况报表）展示了公司的经营活动对其资产、负债和所有者权益的影响。预算资产负债表通常是总预算中最后一个需要编制的项目，它部分上以当前期间末的预算资产负债表为基础。

　　在编制预算资产负债表时，应将预算期间经营活动的影响与上期资产负债表中的数据相加。

模拟现金流量表

　　在编制现金预算之前，公司需要确定在给定期间内可使用的现金数量。在采用信用销售的情况下，公司需要预测现金流入与现金流出。公司应编制模拟现金流入表和模拟现金流出表。模拟现金收入表估计每期的回款百分比（使用下面将要讨论的应收账款余额模式法）。模拟现金流出表可以使用支付百分比模式，但这里以支付历史记录而非回款历史记录为依据。现金流出一般包括原材料采购、直接工资（基于当期销售量）、一般管理费用以及所得税，也可分为固定费用和变动费用。

　　应收账款余额模式可用来估计现金流入，也可用于估计现金流出。

　　应收账款（A/R）余额模式是一种预测工具，用于估计现金流入的时间以及由于赊销所产生的应收账款水平。公司应分析历史回款趋势并使用该趋势模式预测未来的现金回收情况。可以利用公司的收款历史记录推导应收账款余额模式，并估计在特定期间末（如每月末）未收回的款项所占的百分比。

　　图表 2 – 17 展示了罗宾制造公司的应收账款回收的历史记录。

图表 2 – 17　罗宾制造公司应收账款回收历史记录

	回收百分比
零月（当月回收）	40%
一个月（下月回收）	30%
两个月后回收	20%
三个月后回收	10%

　　使用该应收账款余额模式信息，我们就可以预计未来期间的现金回收情况。

　　考虑图表 2 – 18 中的例子，假设罗宾制造公司 3 月份的实际销售额为 $9 200 000，4 月份的销售额为 $9 500 000，5 月份的销售额为 $9 032 000，6 月份到

9 月份的估计销售额如图表 2 – 18 所示。

图表 2 – 18　利用应收账款余额模式预测现金流入

月销售额	销售额	当月现金流入	8 月末，月销售额中应收账款余额	月销售额中应收账款余额的百分比
6 月	\$8 520 000	\$8 937 600	\$852 000	10%
7 月	\$7 756 000	\$8 414 800	\$2 326 800	30%
8 月	\$7 977 600	\$8 125 040	\$4 786 560	60%
9 月	\$8 624 000	\$8 246 080		

月销售额中的现金流入使用下面的公式计算（这里以 9 月份为例）。

月现金流入

=（当月回收百分比 × 当月销售额）

+（下月回收百分比 × 上月销售额）

+（两个月后的回收百分比 × 两个月前的月销售额）

+（三个月后的回收百分比 × 三个月前的月销售额）

9 月份

=（0.4 × \$8 624 000）+（0.3 × \$7 977 600）+（0.2 × \$7 756 000）+（0.1 × 8 520 000）

= \$3 449 600 + \$2 393 280 + \$1 551 200 + \$852 000 = \$8 246 080

8 月末，月销售额中的应收账款余额和应收账款余额百分比的计算方法如下所示：

8 月末，月销售额中应收账款余额

=月销售额 –〔（当月回收百分比 × 月销售额）+（下月回收百分比 × 月销售额）

+（两个月后的回收百分比 × 月销售额）+（三个月后的回收百分比 × 月销售额）〕

8 月末，6 月销售额的应收账款余额

= \$8 520 000 –〔（0.4 × \$8 520 000）+（0.3 × \$8 520 000）+（0.2 × \$8 520 000）+0*〕

= \$8 520 000 –（\$3 408 000 + \$2 556 000 + \$1 704 000）

= \$8 520 000 – \$7 668 000 = \$852 000

8 月末的月应收账款余额占月销售额的百分比

$$= \frac{8 \text{ 月末，月销售额中的应收账款余额}}{\text{月销售额}}$$

8 月末，6 月应收账款余额占 6 月销售额的百分比

$$= \frac{\$852\,000}{\$8\,520\,000} = 0.1 = 10\%$$

* 尚未回收

注意到公司可能有额外的非销售现金流入，如投资收入。在这种情况下，应将非销售现金流入与销售现金流入相加以得到总的现金流入。利用这种方法，我们就可以编制如图表 2 – 19 所示的模拟现金流量表。这里继续沿用前面对罗宾制造公司的假设，除此之外，我们还假设在 6 月份，实际直接材料采购成本为 \$3 280 000，实际变动间接费用为 \$260 500，实际固定间接费用（减去折旧）为 \$16 900，实际销售和管理费用为 \$705 000。罗宾制造公司利用其他预算中的数据完成该模拟现金流量表的其他部分。采购成本的一半在采购当月支付，另一半在下月支付。直接人工在当月支

付，间接费用在下月支付。接下来的现金预算要用到该模拟现金流量表中的数据。注意到这个公司或许存在其他现金流出，模拟现金流量表也要考虑到这些额外的现金流出。

图表2-19　模拟现金流量表

罗宾制造公司 模拟现金流量表 第3季度			
	7月 预期	8月 预期	9月 预期
销售额 *	$7 756 000	$7 977 600	$8 624 000
直接材料（DM）采购成本 **	$4 680 000	$4 836 250	$5 253 500
现金流入			
销售额—40%当月回收	$3 102 400	$3 191 040	$3 449 600
30%—下月回收	$2 556 000	$2 326 800	$2 393 280
20%—两个月后回收	$1 806 400	$1 704 000	$1 551 200
10%—三个月后回收	$950 000	$903 200	$852 000
总现金流入	$8 414 800	$8 125 040	$8 246 080
现金流出			
直接材料采购成本 **—50%当月支付	$2 340 000	$2 418 125	$2 626 750
50%下月支付	$1 640 000	$2 340 000	$2 418 125
当月支付的直接人工 ***	$540 000	$547 500	$585 000
下月支付的变动间接费用 ****	$260 500	$280 800	$284 700
下月支付的固定间接费用 ****	$16 900	$16 900	$16 900
下月支付的销售和管理费用 *****	$705 000	$745 000	$795 000
总现金流出	$5 502 400	$6 348 325	$6 726 475

* 从销售预算中得到的销售额数据
** 从直接材料采购预算中得到的直接材料采购成本数据
*** 从直接人工预算中得到的直接人工数据
**** 从间接费用预算中得到的变动和固定间接费用数据；注意每月的数据中都扣除了$20 000的折旧费用
***** 从销售和管理费用预算中得到的销售和管理费用数据

现金预算

组织的经营活动必须保持有足够的流动性，现金预算的目的就是为确保这种流动性。有了现金预算，组织就能有序安排融资，并在需要资金时能及时将投资变现。现金预算通常每月编制一次，但很多公司发现每周甚至每天编制现金预算更为有用。

由于在所有经营领域都需要现金，因此现金预算的数据来自于总预算的所有部分和模拟现金流量表。现金预算分为可用现金、现金流出、超额或短缺现金以及融资这四个部分。

● 可用现金

现金预算的第一部分是可用现金，它展示了经营中所需现金的来源。这些来源包括期初现金余额以及现金流入，现金流入包括销售收入、应收票据、借入资本、权益资本以及非营运资产的处置所得。销售水平、回收风险、非经常性损失以及信用政策等对可用现金都有一定的影响。

　　○ 期初现金余额

　　它等于前一期的期末现金余额。

　　○ 现金流入

　　现金流入是当期收回的当期和前期的销售收入（应收账款的收回）。

● **现金流出**

现金流出部分包括所有的现金支付项目，如原材料采购、工资、经营费用、税收以及利息费用。融资前的期末现金余额等于可用现金减去现金流出。

● **超额或短缺现金**

超额或短缺现金部分等于期初现金余额加上现金流入，然后减去现金流出和最小现金余额要求。所得到的就是当期的现金盈余或短缺。现金短缺就必须借入资金，因此接下来是融资部分。

● **融资**

融资有两层含义，一是在流动性水平低于管理层或董事会所设定的某个值时，着手寻找现金来源；二是将超额现金用于暂时性的投资及短期投资以充分利用高于一定水平的现金。多数公司在进行投资时更看重资本保全而非投资回报，因此它们会选择相对安全的投资，如货币市场证券。

当涉及利息计算和贷款偿付时，融资部分就会比较复杂。如果在某月需要融资（如图表 2－20 中的 8 月），融资额度必须足够大以满足最小现金余额要求。相反，在计算需要偿付的本金和利息的时候，首先要减去最小现金余额要求（如图表 2－20 中的 9 月）。此外，明确何时需要偿还本金和利息（是期初还是期末）十分重要，以便确定用于计算利息的本金基础。计算利息时要注意利率所对应的期间（例如，年利率 10% 的 1/12 是月利率）。

图表 2－20 展示了现金预算。

图表 2－20　现金预算

罗宾制造公司
现金预算
第 3 季度

	7 月	8 月	9 月	季度
期初现金余额	$1 587 000	$3 499 400	$250 000	$1 587 000
加现金流入				
从客户处收回的现金	8 414 800	8 125 040	8 246 080	24 785 920
总可用现金	$10 001 800	$11 624 440	$8 496 080	$26 372 920
减现金流出 *				
直接材料	3 980 000	4 758 125	5 044 875	13 783 000
直接人工	540 000	547 500	585 000	1 672 500
变动间接费用	260 500	280 800	284 700	826 000
固定间接费用 **	16 900	16 900	16 900	50 700
销售和管理费用	705 000	745 000	795 000	2 245 000
资产改进	1 000 000	7 062 165	50 000	8 112 165
总现金流出	$6 502 400	$13 410 490	$6 776 475	$26 689 365

续表

罗宾制造公司
现金预算
第3季度

	7 月	8 月	9 月	季度
最小现金余额要求	250 000	250 000	250 000	250 000
所需现金总额	$6 752 400	$13 660 490	$7 026 475	$26 939 365
超额现金（短缺）	3 249 400	（2 036 050）	1 469 605	（$566 445）
融资				
借入现金（期初余额）	–	–	2 036 050	0
借入现金	–	2 036 050	–	2 036 050
偿还现金（期末）	–	–	（1 449 244）***	（1 449 244）
利息费用			（20 361）***	（20 361）
借入现金（期末余额）		2 036 050	586 806*****	$586 806
所需融资总额（针对利息支付调整后的额度）	–	$2 036 050	$（1 469 605）	$586 806
期末现金余额	$3 499 400	$250 000	$250 000	$250 000

* 有关现金支付时间的信息请参见模拟现金流量表
** 已扣除折旧费用
*** 在当期只偿还 $1 449 244
**** 短期借款利息
****** 注意下个月的利息将是 $5 868
注：罗宾制造公司的最小现金余额要求是 $250 000。在 8 月份，借入年利率为 12% 的 200 万美元的短期贷款。本例中假设超额现金没有对外投资（参见 7 月份）。

资本预算

如前所述，资本预算是为了评估并挑选那些需要巨额资金并且在未来期间才能获利的项目。资本投资包括购买财产、厂房或设备以及购买新业务或新的经营能力。

所有的企业都面临稀缺资源的约束，资本的供给有限。资本预算必须首先与企业战略保持一致，并充分利用内部优势和外部机遇持续改善该战略。项目评估方法在 CMA 教材第三部分第 5 章第 1 节 "资本预算流程" 中有探讨。

进度检查

提示：完成以下各题。参考答案随后给出。

1. 以下哪项预算是应首先编制的经营预算，因为它界定了经营所需的产能？

　（　　）a. 生产/存货预算

　（　　）b. 直接人工预算

　（　　）c. 销售预算

　（　　）d. 间接费用预算

2. 以下哪项内部模拟财务报表通常在期末最后编制？

　（　　）a. 模拟损益表

（　　）b. 模拟资产负债表

（　　）c. 模拟所有者权益变动表

（　　）d. 现金预算

3. 以下哪项预算是为确保公司保持足够的流动性而设计的？

（　　）a. 间接费用预算

（　　）b. 销售预算

（　　）c. 生产/存货预算

（　　）d. 现金预算

进度检查答案

1. c

2. b

3. d

第 2 章
成本管理

本章内容简介

　　为了解预算中包含哪些成本，我们需要知道成本如何分类。本章首先总结了成本管理中需要用到的相关术语，随后探讨了各种成本计量和预算方法，以及各种成本归集制度如分批法、分步法以及作业成本法。本章最后一节讲述了间接制造成本的分摊方法。

学习要点说明

　　注册管理会计师（CMA）考试包含很多学习要点，这些学习要点由管理会计师协会确定。学习要点描述了注册管理会计师考试要求掌握的所有知识点和技能，并且细分为各个章节。注册管理会计师考试教材解释了学习要点所包含的各个部分，是对学习要点的有力支持。学习要点可以帮助考生以不同的方式或通过不同的问题情景理解这些概念。考生还应该练习学习要点中所提到的全部或者部分计算，或者完成计算过程中的缺失部分。学习要点不能代替对 CMA 考试教材内容的研究和学习，但是可以确保考生达到学习要点所设定的目标。

　　注册管理会计师教材中所包含的学习要点是一个完整的集合，并且是到目前为止最新的版本。考生可以浏览 IMA 的官方网站 www.imanet.org，点击"认证"部分查看和下载关于学习要点的最新 PDF 文件。

学习要点

2.1 相关术语

- LOS 2.1.1：确认并区分在损益表中报告的所有成本项目。
- LOS 2.1.2：确认并计算为完成一件产品所发生的并作为产品销售成本列示的成本。
- LOS 2.1.3：确认并计算那些因当期经营发生但不包括在产品销售成本中的成本（期间成本）。
- LOS 2.1.4：确认并计算成本概念中的组成部分，如主要成本、转换成本、间接成本、持有成本、沉没成本、酌定成本和机会成本。
- LOS 2.1.5：理解固定成本、变动成本和混合成本的不同特征，并评价产量的变化对这些成本的影响。
- LOS 2.1.6：确认、区分并计算直接成本和间接成本。
- LOS 2.1.7：描述及时、准确的成本信息作为战略规划管理决策工具的重要性。

2.2 成本计量概念

- LOS 2.2.1：理解固定成本和变动成本在长期及短期内的习性，以及成本类型假设或相关范围假设的变化对这些成本的影响。
- LOS 2.2.2：识别成本对象和成本池以及将成本分配到适当的作业。
- LOS 2.2.3：理解成本动因的属性和类别，以及成本动因和发生的成本之间所存在的因果关系。
- LOS 2.2.4：全面了解各种存货计量方法以及半成品库存和产成品存货的归集法，基本了解存货的补充机制。
- LOS 2.2.5：确认并计算成本计量技术中的组成部分，如实际成本法、正常成本法和标准成本法；确认每种方法的恰当使用；描述每种方法的优点和局限性。
- LOS 2.2.6：了解变动成本法和吸收成本法的特征，以及这两种成本核算法的优点和局限性。
- LOS 2.2.7：计算在变动成本法和吸收成本法下的存货成本。
- LOS 2.2.8：了解变动成本法和吸收成本法的使用如何影响存货价值、产品销售成本以及营运收入。
- LOS 2.2.9：确定联产品成本法和副产品成本法的恰当使用，理解分离点和可分离成本等概念。
- LOS 2.2.10：确定在实体衡量法、分离点销售价值法、毛利法以及可实现净值法下对联合产品成本和副产品成本的分配；描述每种方法的优点和局限性。
- LOS 2.2.11：理解服务部门公司使用的成本核算系统。

2.3 成本归集制度

- LOS 2.3.1：对已确认的每种成本归集制度（分批法、分步法、作业成本法、生命周期法），定义制度属性、理解制度中的成本流、确定其恰当的使用。
- LOS 2.3.2：对已确认的每种成本归集制度（分批法、分步法、作业成本法、生命周期法），计算存货价值以及产品销售成本。
- LOS 2.3.3：对已确认的每种成本归集制度（分批法、分步法、作业成本法、生命周期法），理解正常和异常损耗的恰当会计处理。
- LOS 2.3.4：对已确认的每种成本归集制度（分批法、分步法、作业成本法、生命周期法），讨论与产品、服务、定价、间接费用分摊和其他问题相关的成本信息的战略价值。

- LOS 2.3.5：对已确认的每种成本归集制度（分批法、分步法、作业成本法、生命周期法），确认每种成本累计制的优点和局限性。
- LOS 2.3.6：对已确认的每种成本归集制度（分批法、分步法、作业成本法、生命周期法），理解在分步法下约当产量的概念并计算约当产量的价值。
- LOS 2.3.7：对已确认的每种成本归集制度（分批法、分步法、作业成本法、生命周期法），定义作业成本法的要素如成本池、成本动因、资源动因、作业动因以及增值型作业。
- LOS 2.3.8：对已确认的每种成本归集制度（分批法、分步法、作业成本法、生命周期法），计算在作业制下的产品成本，并同传统方法下计算出的结果作比较。
- LOS 2.3.9：对已确认的每种成本归集制度（分批法、分步法、作业成本法、生命周期法），理解生命周期成本法的概念以及上游成本、制造成本和下游成本的战略价值。
- LOS 2.3.10：对已确认的每种成本归集制度（分批法、分步法、作业成本法、生命周期法），利用分批法和分步法的特征来描述营运成本法如何成为一种混合成本制度，确定适合使用营运成本法的行业领域。
- LOS 2.3.11：对已确认的每种成本归集制度（分批法、分步法、作业成本法、生命周期法），理解及时制造后推成本法，描述为什么采用及时生产制的制造单元适用该成本法。
- LOS 2.3.12：对已确认的每种成本归集制度（分批法、分步法、作业成本法、生命周期法），理解作业成本法在服务性公司中的应用。

2.4　间接成本（overhead costs）

- LOS 2.4.1：理解间接费用的固定和变动属性。
- LOS 2.4.2：为划分变动间接费用和固定间接费用确定恰当的时间框架。
- LOS 2.4.3：理解确定间接费用分摊率的各种方法，如全厂间接费用分摊率、部门间接费用分摊率以及单个成本动因间接费用分摊率，描述每种方法的优点和局限性。
- LOS 2.4.4：确定变动间接费用的组成要素。
- LOS 2.4.5：确定变动间接费用恰当的分摊基础。
- LOS 2.4.6：计算单位变动间接费用。
- LOS 2.4.7：确定固定间接费用的组成要素。
- LOS 2.4.8：确定固定间接费用恰当的分摊基础，理解由于分摊基础的变动性（如直接人工工时），固定间接费用往往会过度分摊或分摊不足。
- LOS 2.4.9：计算固定间接费用分摊率。
- LOS 2.4.10：理解间接费用控制账户、间接费用分摊账户以及过度分摊或分摊不足的间接费用的费用化。
- LOS 2.4.11：对比传统的间接费用分摊法和作业基础间接费用分摊法。
- LOS 2.4.12：计算作业基础下的间接费用，描述作业基础间接费用分摊法的优点。
- LOS 2.4.13：理解将人力资源部门或信息技术部门等服务部门的成本分摊到各分公司、各部门或各作业上的原因。
- LOS 2.4.14：理解并使用直接法、交叉法、按步向下分摊法来分摊服务部门或支持部门的成本。

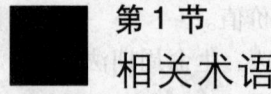

第1节
相关术语

本节内容简介

为了制定最适当的决策，管理层必须有一个准确的期望和实际成本的蓝图。这个成本信息必须及时、准确才能为长期战略和日常经营计划带来价值。理解成本管理术语可以帮助经理制定决策。他们可以为不同的目的确定不同的成本，如绩效评价中的直接成本和间接成本；制定预算时的固定成本和变动成本；以及在决定是否外购时的机会成本、沉没成本和边际成本。本节将详细介绍这些术语。

成本会计术语和概念

下面会介绍基本的成本术语和概念。注意不同的公司在成本定义及成本分类方法和成本计量方法上会存在差异。例如，不同的公司在界定直接制造成本中应包含哪些成本要素时可能会存在差异。

成本

成本是要获得某些对象必须放弃的任何资源。成本可以是获取一件商品或一项服务要付出的货币数额，一项新债务的产生或是一项资产的牺牲。成本包括实际成本（历史成本）和预算成本（预测成本）。

成本对象

成本对象是可以将一项成本分配给其的任何对象并且它可以用来确定某个物品或作业的成本是多少。公司成本对象包括产品、服务、顾客、项目、品牌类别、部门、责任中心和作业。

成本池

成本池是成本对象的集合或分组，成本池可以任何方式进行界定，只要该方式对管理层分配责任有意义。成本对象如一个扳钳和一个修理工也许会被包括在维修部门的成本池中，而这个成本池本身又是营运部门的成本对象。

成本动因

成本动因（也称为分配基础）是任何与成本之间存在因果关系的因素，如影响总成本的作业水平或随销售量增长而成比例增长的销售佣金成本。固定成本没有成本动因（然而固定间接费用会使用某种分摊基础分配到成本池中）。

成本归集

成本归集是指收集和组织会计系统中的成本信息。任何时候成本一旦发生，例如购买或收到一项服务，成本在一个会计期间里归集。成本归集和成本分配直接相关。

成本分配

成本分配即分配归集的成本到成本对象,同时也指将归集的成本追溯到成本对象或成本池中。分配和成本对象有间接关系的成本,追溯和成本对象有直接关系的成本。分配决定在属于某个特定成本对象的总成本中的占有比率。追溯将直接成本分配到成本对象。

实际成本

实际成本是为一件商品或一项服务支付的历史成本。

直接成本

直接成本指以方便、经济的方式,可被直接追溯至成本对象的成本(通常指直接人工和直接材料)。一罐网球的直接成本可能包括 0.2 个工时和一定数量的橡胶。

间接成本(indirect costs)

间接成本(indirect costs)是任何和成本对象相关但无法以成本有效的方式追溯到产品的成本[如间接费用(overhead)]。考虑到成本收益约束,这些成本会在合理估计的基础上进行分配。生产一听网球的间接成本包括网球机器的维修成本、网球检测器的成本和运动产品分厂管理人员的薪水。基于每个责任中心的员工数,管理人员的薪水会被分配到各个责任中心。如果一个经理负责 100 名员工并且这个网球责任中心有 10 名员工,那么 10% 的经理薪水会被分配到这个成本对象,1% 的薪水会被分配到单个员工成本对象。

机会成本

机会成本是当选择一种方法而不是另外一种或其他更多种方法时牺牲的潜在利益。例如:当将时间和资金投资到一个项目时,员工就不能在其他项目上工作;即使没有其他的可行项目,资金亦可以被投资来赚取收益。

持有成本

持有成本是和持有存货相关的成本,包括存货本身、仓库和运输/收货员工以及仓库占地的间接费用、报废风险、可能的减价、正在进行的存货融资和可以用作其他用途的空间的机会成本。

可控成本

可控成本是某个特定的经理或业务单元在一年或一年之内能够施加影响的成本。可控成本可以是固定的也可以是变动的。

不可控成本

不可控成本是某个特定的经理或业务单元在一年或一年之内或者也许任何时候都不能够施加影响的成本。某些成本对于某个分部或某个经理来讲也许是可控的,但对另一个不同的分部或经理来讲则是不可控的。不可控成本可以是固定的也可以是变动的。

沉没成本

沉没成本是那些在决策制定时应忽略的成本，因为这些成本发生在过去并且不能够被改变。一些经理错误地把沉没成本包括在他们的分析中，以证明某个特定的领域的持续支出是合理的，即使另一项投资会赚取更高的回报。经理应忽略沉没成本而关注非沉没成本或未来的差量成本。

弹性成本

弹性成本是那些还没有发生并且也因此和决策制定相关的成本。弹性成本与沉没成本相对应。

差量成本

差异成本是两个或更多可能的资金用途间存在差异的成本并且正是因为这个差异而变得和决策制定有关。例如，如果一个经理正在考虑一台置换机器的购买，该置换机器每年的折旧额是 10 万美元，然而现有机器的折旧额是 6.5 万美元，那么差量成本是每年的折旧额 3.5 万美元。

成本管理

成本管理是在长期和短期内计划及控制成本的过程。经理使用会计信息系统来决定在管理成本时如何改变流程和计划。成本管理关注于降低总成本，但必须考虑到一个经济实体要赚钱就需要花钱，因此成本管理和盈利计划相关联。

产品成本和期间成本

产品成本

产品成本（也称存货成本）对制造商和商业公司是不同的。制造业认为只有在完成一件产品的过程中所需要的成本才为产品成本。这些成本包括直接材料、直接人工和间接成本。商业公司的产品成本很容易确定。大多数零售商、批发商还有分销商购买完工状态下的产品。购买产品的成本（包括相关的运费）被计入一个叫做商品存货的单独存货科目。产品成本包含在产品销售成本的计算中。

给产品成本分类的两种方式包括主要成本和转换成本。注意，直接材料既包含在主要成本中也包含在转换成本中；因此，主要成本加上转换成本不等于产品成本。

- **主要成本**

主要成本是直接人工和直接材料成本或总的直接成本。

- **转换成本**

当直接人工和间接成本结合在一起，这个成本池称作转换成本。

期间成本

不能够包括在产品成本中的项目必须在成本发生期间费用化，并称作期间成本。

不能够合理地分配到某个产品的成本要被费用化，因为不期望它们在将来带来可计量的收益。销售和管理成本、广告成本、数据处理成本和行政成本均为期间成本。期间成本业被称作营运费用或销售和管理费用。期间成本不包括在产品销售成本中。

折旧费用既是产品成本也是期间成本。营运中直接使用的固定资产的折旧是产品成本，如工业设备；非营运固定资产的折旧是期间成本，如办公设备。

制造成本和非制造成本

存在的三种公司：

* 制造企业购买使用原材料并且结合到或转换成新的产成品。炼油厂、网球制造厂还有纺织企业均为制造企业。
* 商业企业诸如零售商、分销商和批发商购买商品再以更高的价格卖出，但并没有改变商品的基本结构。
* 服务企业向顾客提供无形服务，包括法律公司、医院、货运公司、广告代理还有咨询公司。

制造企业的成本流

制造企业的成本是以上列出的三种企业中最复杂的。制造成本流以购买生产中使用的直接和间接原材料为起点。这些原材料最初是被计入原材料存货账户的（只包含直接原材料）。下一步是加上成本要素：直接材料、直接人工和间接成本（包括间接材料）。在这一步，将这三个要素的成本加到半成品库存上。当产品完工后，成本作为制造产品的成本转移到产成品存货上。当产品被卖出时，成本从产成品存货转出到产品销售成本上。

图表 2-21 展示了制造企业的成本流。

图表 2-21　一家制造企业的成本流

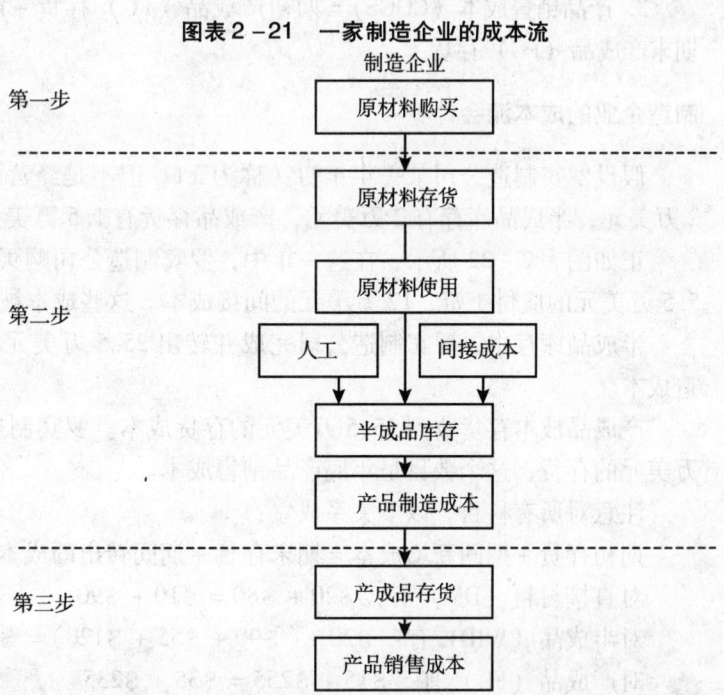

制造企业的存货账户

存货的种类有直接材料存货、半成品库存和产成品存货：

- 直接材料存货包含为制造过程购得并在被使用前购得的所有原材料。
- 半成品库存包含花费在生产过程中的任何产品的原材料成本、人工和间接成本，而这些产品直到报告期末才完工。
- 成品存货包含所有完工准备售出的产品成本。

每个存货账户在每个期间都有期初和期末账户。

存货账户的数额用以下公式计算：

- COGM 是产品制造成本。
- COGS 是产品销售成本。
- DM 是直接材料。
- DL 是直接人工。
- MOH 是应用的间接制造费用。

计算制造企业的产品销售成本，要求有三个步骤：

1. 使用的直接材料（DM）＝期初直接材料（DM）存货＋净采购－期末直接材料（DM）存货

净采购＝采购－（采购退回＋采购折扣）＋运费

一旦知道了生产使用的直接材料，就可以应用下一个公式了。

2. 产品制造成本（COGM）＝期初半成品（WIP）库存＋直接材料（DM）＋直接人工（DL）＋间接制造费用（MOH）－期末半成品（WIP）库存

注意：产品制造成本包括完工的并且转移到产成品存货的产品。DM＋DL＋MOH 有时也称作制造成本。

3. 产品销售成本（COGS）＝期初产成品（FG）存货＋产品制造成本（COGM）－期末产成品（FG）存货

制造企业的成本流会计

假设罗宾制造公司某一年年初（称为 Y1，但不是经营的第一年）原材料存货有 2 万美元，半成品库存有 2 万美元，产成品存货有 1.5 万美元。

正如图表 2－22 所示，在这一年中，罗宾制造公司购买了 8 万美元直接材料，有 5.5 万美元的应付工资，12 万美元的间接成本。这些成本被转移到半成品库存。

半成品库存中，罗宾制造公司完成并转出 25.5 万美元存货。这个数目是产品制造成本。

产成品成本存货收到 25.5 万美元的存货成本。罗宾制造公司在这一年售出 23.5 万美元的存货，这个数目是年底产品销售成本。

注意对所有科目，以下关系成立：

期初存货＋期间新增成本＝期末存货＋期间转出的成本

对直接材料（DM）有：$20 + $80 = $10 + $90

对半成品（WIP）有：$20 + ($90 + $55 + $120) = $30 + $255

对产成品（FG）有：$15 + $255 = $35 + $235

图表2-22 罗宾制造公司会计分录，Y1（单位：千）

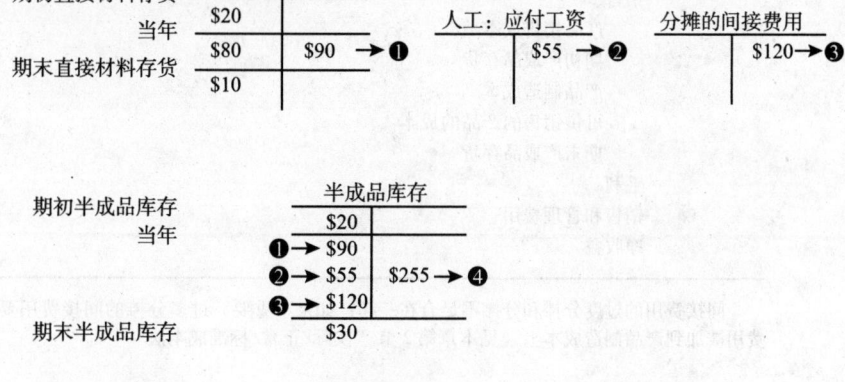

注：❶使用的直接材料（DM）的成本❷使用的人工的成本❸分摊的间接费用❹产品制造成本（COGM）❺产品销售成本（COGS）

制造企业的财务报表

制造企业的财务报表包括产品制造成本表和损益表。

- 产品成本制造表展示了从直接材料存货到产成品存货的运动。
- 损益表始于销售收入，减去产品销售成本得出毛利，然后再减去所有的非营运费用得到净收益。

图表2-23展示了罗宾制造公司的样表。

图表2-23 罗宾制造公司报表

罗宾制造公司 产品制造成本表 Y1年12月31日（单位：千）	
直接材料	
期初存货	$20
净采购	80
可用的直接材料	$100
期末直接材料存货	10
使用的直接材料	$90
直接人工	55
工厂间接成本	120
总制造成本	$265
加：期初半成品库存	20
应考虑的总制造成本	285
减：期末半成品库存	30
产品制造成本	$255

续表

销售		$335
产品销售成本		
期初产成品存货	$15	
产品制造成本	255	
可供销售的产品的成本	$270	
期末产成品存货	35	235
毛利		$100
销售和管理费用		40
净收益		$60

间接费用的过度分摊和分摊不足合在一起：如果不重要，过多分摊的间接费用要被扣除，过少分摊的间接费用被加到产品制造成本上（见本章第 2 节"实际/正常/标准成本法"）

商业和服务企业中的成本流

商业企业的财务报表

商业企业的损益表和制造企业的看起来相似。商人用购买成本而不是产品制造成本来计算产品销售成本。

服务企业的财务报表

服务企业很少或根本就没有存货。如果服务企业有存货，并且是以购买商品的形式持有这些存货，则可以采用类似于商业企业的做法处理这些存货；如果服务企业自己生产商品，则可以采用类似于制造企业的方式处理这些存货。没有存货的服务企业会编制以收入作为起点的简单损益表，扣除诸如原材料、人工和其他费用的经营费用，得出经营收入。然而当服务企业有在一个会计期间内未完工的服务时，它们也需要半成品库存这一科目。

直接成本和间接成本

直接成本

根据美国管理会计师协会的定义，直接成本是"可以经济、可行的方式特别确认为一个成本对象的原材料（或人工）"的数量。预期之外的废品、次品不应包含在直接成本中，废品、次品成本通常核销到一个废品账户，该账户包含在间接制造费用中。如果公司将间接成本加到直接材料上（不是典型做法），那么额外的原材料成本会被计入原材料间接成本。另一方面，直接材料成本应当包括所有正常的完成产品所要求的成本，包含废品、次品的单位成本和正常预计的发生在正常经营过程中的废品成本。

间接成本

间接成本是在生产过程中使用的，不能追踪到产成品的材料成本，如网球上印公司名称使用的墨水。间接成本包括监管成本和工人花费的可避免的或不经常发生的非生产性时间，因为它们不能被追溯到某一个成本对象。

管理费用（overhead）

通常将间接人工和间接材料成本放入一个成本池中称为管理费用或工厂间接制造成本。其他加到间接制造成本中的包括设施成本、经营性设备成本和支持性设备成本如叉车。

进度检查

提示：完成以下各题。参考答案随后给出。

1. 一家制造企业有一个网球生产设备，设备有维修成本、直接人工和一个会计期间的折旧成本。在这种情况下，以下哪项是正确的？
   - ( ) a. 维修费用和直接人工是期间成本，而折旧是产品成本
   - ( ) b. 维修费用和折旧费用是期间成本，而直接人工是产品成本
   - ( ) c. 维修费用、直接人工和折旧费用都是产品成本
   - ( ) d. 维修费用和直接人工是产品成本，折旧是期间成本

2. 一家制造企业有 $100 000 的产品制造成本，期初产成品存货有 $20 000，期末产成品存货有 $30 000，那么这家企业的产品销售成本是多少？
   - ( ) a. $50 000
   - ( ) b. $90 000
   - ( ) c. $100 000
   - ( ) d. $150 000

进度检查答案

1. c
2. b

 ## 第2节
成本计量概念

本节内容简介

成本计量概念包括成本动因的类型、成本核算法的种类、变动成本法、吸收成本法以及联产品成本法和副产品成本法。

固定成本和变动成本

总成本由变动成本和固定成本组成。一项成本既可以随作业、数量或其他成本动因的变化成比例变动，也可以在一个很大的成本动因范围内保持不变。

相关范围

固定成本和变动成本是针对一个特定的成本动因在一个特定的持续期间来定义的。在一个足够大的程度上任意改变生产量，固定成本也将不再保持不变。将生产量减到零，有可能所有的固定成本都会随产品的消失而一同消失；改变生产量超过某个水平，就必须增加新的厂房或其他设备。因此，固定成本和变动成本被限制在一个相关范围内。固定成本在一个离散的作业范围内保持不变。例如，一个职业高尔夫比赛在比赛周中通常安排6天的活动。即使因为天气的原因取消一两天的活动，固定成本也会保持不变。比赛最后一天为打破评分而做的延长比赛一般不会增加比赛的固定成本。如果比赛需要延长一天，这一天不在相关范围之内并且要求额外的固定成本。

变动成本

变动成本包括一个成本对象总体上的变动，这个变动在一个相关范围内同某个成本动因的数量变化成比例。单位变动成本在一个相关范围内保持不变（例如，在1到5 000单位的相关范围内，单位变动成本为 $5）。直接材料和直接人工都是变动成本，因为如果要生产更多单位的成本对象就需要更多的材料和人工。一些间接成本也是变动成本，比如密封剂和粘胶这些不能被计量但必须加到每一件产品上去的间接成本要素。

以网球制造企业为例，网球生产量增加，类似橡胶这样的直接材料的数量以及直接人工量都会在相关范围内增加，这个相关范围定义为网球生产设备的最低和最高产量（不改变劳动力规模）。

固定成本

固定成本是当一个成本动因在一个持续期间以及在相关范围内变动时，总成本中保持不变的那部分成本。持续期间很重要，因为固定成本也许在一年内不变，在下一年会在一个更高的水平上保持不变。当产量增加时，单位固定成本会减少（变的不重要）：在100个单位，固定成本是 $1 000 时，单位固定成本是 $10 每单位，但是

1 000 个单位时，单位固定成本是 $1 每单位。

固定成本可以是酌量的也可以是约束的：

● 酌量性固定成本（也称作管理或预算固定成本）可以包括在预算中也可以从预算中扣除，这取决于预计的资金。例子有广告费、培训费或实习生费用，还有间接制造人工以及销售和管理人工。

● 约束性固定成本是短期内鉴于战略和经营优先权的考虑不能被忽略的成本。一个例子就是之前购买的固定资产折旧。约束性固定成本趋向于同产能相关，源于之前的产能相关决策。

固定成本中包括很多间接成本，比如折旧、税费、员工薪水、保险和租赁成本。这些成本通常是固定的，因为无论产量处于相关范围内的哪个水平，这些成本都保持不变。

图表 2 - 24 展示了相关范围内的固定成本和变动成本。

图表 2 - 24 固定成本和变动成本

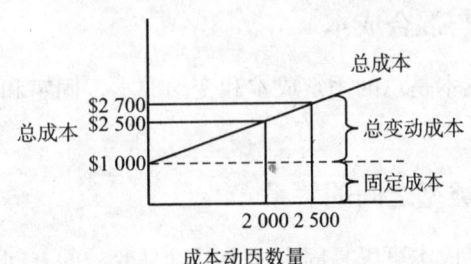

成本动因数量

在给定的产量水平上，下面的公式成立：

在给定产量水平下的单位总成本 = 单位固定成本 + 单位变动成本

产量上升时，单位总成本也会因此而减少。这是因为固定成本被分摊到了更多的产品中。

阶梯式成本

阶梯成本是在一个很狭窄的相关范围内的固定成本。阶梯式成本趋向于被认为是在短期内的固定成本，但是在长期内会变成变动成本。考虑一个只有一个工厂的企业。短期内，工厂间接成本是固定成本。如果工厂的产能是每天 100 单位，那么为每天生产 200 单位，就需要购买额外的工厂，这么做会使工厂间接成本加倍同时也会获得加倍的产能（假设两个工厂有相同的产能和成本）。长期内，工厂间接成本变成变动成本。

严格的阶梯式成本相关范围可以是阶梯式固定的也可以是阶梯式变动的。阶梯式固定的范围在增加相等数量的成本动因时增加相同规模（例如，每增加一个工厂，工厂间接成本增加 $100 000）。阶梯式变动的范围在成本动因越来越大或越来越小时，都变为更高的固定成本。由某些因素导致的阶梯式变动成本能以可预知的比例增加或减少，如递增的工人学习曲线、递减的边际报酬或规模经济（详细内容请参见 CMA 教材第一部分）。例如，如果一个工人（每个工人代表成本中的一个相同规模的梯级）每日可生产 0.5 单位，而两个工人可生产 1 单位，三个工人可生产 1.5 单位，四个工人可生产 2 单位，由此所得的阶梯式变动成本见图表 2-25 右图。左图则显示了以工厂间接成本为例的阶梯式固定成本。

图表 2-25　阶梯式固定成本和阶梯式变动成本

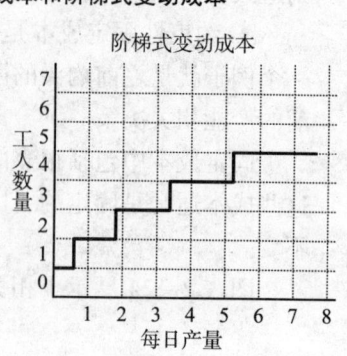

总成本与混合成本

总成本是总的固定成本和变动成本。固定和变动部分都包含在内的总成本也叫混合成本。

各成本类型之间的关系

直接成本可以是固定的也可以是变动的，间接成本也可以是固定或变动的。

产能

产能衡量的是导致一个系统无法扩大其产出或其他衡量指标的约束条件或瓶颈。增加工厂、工人或设备可提高产能；获得新的债务融资或权益融资可提高企业的财务能力。产能与相关范围有关，因为当达到产能极限时，通常也是相关范围的上限。此外，在接近产能极限的同时，经营管理效率也逐渐降低，成本逐渐增加。因此有必要定义企业的实际产能，即企业资源（如工厂）能达到的最高产出水平而并不因为瓶颈增加成本。当产出大于实际产能时，将导致边际成本超过边际收益。实际产能也考虑到了正常经营状况，如平均错误或故障次数、节假日和其他现实因素。

当这些现实因素被忽略时，产能就被定义为理论产能，或者说是假定没有故障，所有事情均全速进行，没有假日或其他安排与之冲突的情况下的产出上限。理论产能是理想的。

过去的产能决策决定了企业现期的固定成本。投入到每个企业单位的场地和资源数量以及折旧数量是与产能选择相关的固定成本。这些固定成本通常不能由部门经理控制，不过部门经理仍然可以感受到这些成本的影响。若产能过剩，就存在机会成本和过高的固定成本风险；若产能太小，企业则面临其他成本如超时、脱销以及设备磨损增加。从一个项目的全部成本中分离、追踪过剩产能成本有助于展示闲置资产的成本。例如，如果一个工厂的预算固定间接成本为 $500 000，间接成本根据产品单位数量分摊，且此工厂拥有每期 5 000 单位的实际产能水平，因此间接成本的分摊率为每单位产品 $100。若工厂预算只生产 4 000 单位，每单位的间接成本为 $100，这样 $400 000 应分配给生产经营过程，剩余的 $100 000 则应看作单独的期间费用，即闲置产能的成本。这样除非需要，经理便没有意愿按产能来进行生产，闲置产能的成本可与增加产出的成本和存货成本相权衡。间接成本的分摊详见本章第 4 节。

虽然前述产能的定义依赖于产出，当产能由产出的期望需求或计划需求来定义时，就是所谓的产能利用率。正常产能利用率是产能利用率的一种水平，它满足一段时间内的平均客户需求，包括需求的季节性和周期性变化。正常产能利用率是一个长期工具，它通常在若干年的期间上使用。总预算产能利用率是用于当前预算期（比如一年）的正常产能利用率。将前者（正常产能利用率）用于长期计划后者（总预算产能利用率）用于短期计划很重要，否则期末成本会不准确。

这些产能水平都可用于分配成本，而每种产能水平通常都会得出不同的金额。例如，一个预算固定间接成本为 $500 000 的工厂，若理论产能是每期 8 000 单位，实际产能是每期 5 000 单位，正常产能利用率是每期 4 500 单位，总预算产能是每期 4 000 单位，则各种情况下的预算固定成本分别为 $62.50、$100、$111 和 $125。变动成本也有类似的结果，因此选择正确的产能对成本分析、管理层激励以及绩效评估决策来说都很关键。

成本动因

企业通过决定成本动因如何影响特定成本对象来管理它们的成本。

成本动因有四种类型。

- 作业成本动因。它关注的焦点在于经营过程，包括生产或服务活动，如设备安装或包装。
- 数量成本动因。它关注的焦点在于产出，包括总量尺度如产品单位量或工时。
- 结构性成本动因。它关注于企业战略，包括规模、综合性、在某一领域经验的多少以及专业技术水平高低的长期性计划。
- 执行性成本动因。它关注于短期经营，包括通过关注劳动力承诺与投入、生产设计以及供应商关系来降低成本。

作业成本动因

企业通过作业分析来确定每种作业的详细描述。这些描述确立了作业成本动因的基本内容。描述中的每个步骤都成为不同的成本动因。这是为了确定这些步骤的变化会导致经营总成本产生怎样的变化。每个步骤或作业的成本也能被确定，因而一个成本对象的总成本就能得到更可靠地确定。这种细节分解可帮助企业确定哪些作业能为客户增加价值而哪些作业不能带来增值。同时，当某项作业比预期花费更多的成本时，作业成本动因会突出这个差异。图表 2－26 举例说明了一个零售企业的一些作业及成本动因。

图表2-26　零售商的作业及成本动因

作　　业	成本动因
收取现金	现金交易数量
信用卡交易处理	信用卡交易数量
支付信用卡费	交易货币规模
收尾工作及主管评价	出清数量
收入合并及账款存入	存款数量
银行账户对账	账户数量
在计算机上更新客户账户余额	更新账户数量
非正常事项调查	调查事项数量
退货及退款处理	退款数量
计算机设备保养	计算机终端数量
培训	商店数量
客户结算表邮寄	账户数量

数量成本动因

数量成本动因是建立在使用数量上的作业总数。一些成本动因注定是数量基础的，如直接材料和直接人工。直接人工由小时工资率和工作量决定。数量基础动因与产出水平间的关系是一条倾斜曲线，如图表2-27所示。

图表2-27　总成本及产能极限的影响

当数量成本动因相当低时，学习曲线和资源的有效利用等因素能使成本的增加速度小于产量的增长（这被称为边际生产率递增，因为递增的产出让投入得到更有效的利用）。在一定水平上，总成本渐趋稳定且数量的增加会带来成本的成比例增加（在相关范围内），直到某一点上人力或设备的产能达到极限。随着产量趋向极限，成本也会因为维修、更多的加班及其他类似因素而显著增加（这被称为边际产能递减律）。

若不使用更高级的数学知识，整个生产范围内成本的确定将会很难估计，这就是为什么相关范围是成本动因的一个重要元素。

结构性成本动因

结构性成本动因是一个长期成本动因，它建立在公司的全面战略上。结构性成本动因有四种类型。

- 规模

一个项目的规模或一个企业的成长速度会影响到整个企业的所有成本。决定开多少商店，雇佣多少职员，或者向一个项目投入多少资金将直接影响到成本。

- 经验水平

公司特定战略需求下的经验水平会影响达成目标所需的总成本。企业拥有最多专业技术的领域将是对于进一步发展来说成本最低的领域，但若市场不再需要这些专业技术，则发展新的专业领域在长期来说更有成本效益。

- 工艺

改变一个流程的工艺能使此流程更有效率，且因此成本更低。投资于工艺的其他好处在于产品质量可能更高，由此企业可用更质优价廉的产品扩大市场份额。

- 综合性

一个企业越综合（更多产品，更多组织层级），维持综合性的成本就越高。减少综合性可同时减少产品开发的成本和分销及服务的成本。关于综合性的战略决策通常用于降低总的综合性和成本。相反，一个产品太少或员工太少的企业将错失市场机会。

执行性成本动因

执行性成本动因属于短期决策，它可用于降低经营成本。执行性成本动因有三种类型。

- **劳动力投入**

劳动力承诺度越高，劳动力成本占完工工作量的比例就越低。日本企业以它们在工作场所培养自豪感而著名，这种自豪感是通过创造性团队的建立、强调多数人的意见和小活动如团体晨练来培养的。

- **生产流程设计**

制造成本可通过重新设计低效率的生产流程来降低。很多企业软件包可帮助企业在供应链中消除旧的瓶颈，例如，不再让所有客户服务订单等待一个职员登记然后传送到客户服务代表手中，而让客户服务代表使用新软件自己登记订单。

- **供应商关系**

与供应商的紧密联系可减少总成本，特别是存货成本。使用电子数据互换（EDI），很多公司现在可让供应商直接查看公司的存货水平，也可在需要时自动传输一些项目，然后公司再去开具发票或索取材料。

实际成本法/正常成本法/标准成本法

成本分配是一种将成本分摊到产品、工作或服务中的方法。实际成本法、正常成本法以及标准成本法是成本分配的不同类型。"实际"和"正常"的含义涉及间接成本的分摊或分配方法，即将间接成本分摊到成本目标上的方法。因为直接材料和人工的实际成本通常很容易确定，因此对直接材料和人工可以直接使用实际成本额度。

实际成本法使用间接成本的实际金额。正常成本法采用人工和直接材料的实际成本，同时对间接成本采用预定的间接成本分摊率。标准成本法与上述两者的不同之处在于它为间接成本、直接材料和直接人工设立标准成本。这三种方法都是分批成本制方法。这些成本方法详述于下。

实际成本法

实际成本制度记录发生的所有实际成本，包括直接人工、直接材料和间接成本（实际金额已分配）。实际成本直到会计期末才能确定，此时就可在所记录的金额基础上计算实际成本。

实际成本的主要优势在于它比其他成本制度都准确。然而，这种可靠性的获得需以信息滞后为代价。在收到所有发票之前，人们无法确定成本，这些发票也许在会计期末或更晚才能得到。因为产品数量每期不同，而固定成本并不因此而变化，实际成本使不同期间生产的单位产品成本各不相同。由于这一原因，想要消除单位成本波动的企业转而使用正常成本法。

正常成本法

与实际成本法类似，正常成本法对工作、流程或其他成本对象的直接材料和直接人工采用实际成本，同时采用预定间接成本分摊率将间接成本分摊到成本对象上。

正常成本法的使用出于三种原因：

- 实际间接成本不能很容易地确定或者不容易在期末报表的时限内分摊。
- 企业想保持生产成本的现时性（对间接成本采用标准分摊率再加上实际人工和实际直接材料成本可迅速计算出科目成本）。
- 企业希望消除或标准化工厂间接成本分摊率的波动，以便在同一年的不同期间得到相同的单位成本。

上面最后一个原因使正常成本成为最受欢迎的成本方法。

预定工厂间接成本分摊率应用于一项工作或其他成本对象中，它由四个步骤确定：

1. 建立年度（或其他期间）的间接成本预算。
2. 为计算间接成本选择成本动因（通常为作业或数量）。
3. 估计总间接成本或每个成本池的总年度金额或数量（按所选成本动因）。
4. 计算预定工厂间接成本分摊率，如下所示：

$$\frac{工厂间接成本预算}{估计的成本动因作业水平}$$

采用正常成本法的工厂间接成本在一些月份会分摊不足，在另一些月份又会过度分摊。过度分摊的净金额是指超出实际成本的间接成本分摊额，分摊不足的净金额与之相反。过度分摊或分摊不足的净额可通过调整产品销售成本账户进行处理，或按比例将净差异分配到半成品、产成品存货以及产品销售成本账户中的当期间接成本分摊余额中。

- **调整产品销售成本**

假定实际间接成本为 $1 530 000，且其中 $1 490 000 已用正常成本法分配到产品中去。这意味着间接成本被少分配了 $40 000。假设这个少分配金额并不重大，则产品销售成本应增加 $40 000。产品销售成本账户的调整分录为：

产品销售成本	$40 000	
工厂间接成本分摊	$1 490 000	
工厂间接成本		$1 530 000

记录间接成本分摊不足的处理

这个分录结算了工厂间接成本分摊账户和工厂间接成本账户且借记（增加）产品销售成本。若情况相反，比如，若正常成本法下分摊了 $1 600 000 的间接成本，而实际间接成本仍保持不变，若这 $70 000 多分摊的间接成本影响不重大，那么产品销售成本账户的调整分录如下。注意这个分录贷记（减少）产品销售成本。

工厂间接成本分摊	$1 600 000	
工厂间接成本		$1 530 000
产品销售成本		$70 000

记录间接成本过度分摊的处理

- **将净差异按比例分配到存货和产品销售成本上**

工厂间接成本是在半成品库存、产成品存货和产品销售成本账户中计量的，所以当净差异重大时，就应根据这些存货和产品销售成本的相对规模按比例分配净差异。若所有生产已完工，所有产品在期末均已销售，且半成品和产成品存货账户中没有余额，那么可以运用简单的产品销售成本法。然而，由于生产是个不会中断的过程，因此必须采用下述方法。用三个账户分配的总间接成本去除其中每一个账户所分配的间接成本，以此可确定每一个账户的分配比例。

假设每个账户分配的间接成本如下：

- 期末半成品库存为 $200 000
- 期末产成品存货为 $300 000
- 产品销售成本为 $1 000 000

期末半成品库存部分的计算为：

$$\frac{\$200\ 000}{\$1\ 500\ 000} = 0.133 = 13.3\%$$

产成品存货分配比例为 20%，产品销售成本分配比例为 66.7%。若差异为分摊不足的间接成本 $100 000，那么半成品账户需要增加分摊 $13 300。调整分录为：

工厂间接成本分摊	$1 500 000	
半成品库存	$13 300	
产成品存货	$20 000	
产品销售成本	$66 700	
工厂间接成本		$1 600 000

按比例分配分摊不足的间接成本

每个存货账户都按所示金额借记（增加）。若有 $100 000 的间接成本被过度分摊（其他因素保持不变），则调整分录为：

工厂间接成本分摊	$1 500 000	
半成品库存		$13 300

产成品存货	$20 000
产品销售成本	$66 700
工厂间接成本	$1 400 000

按比例分配过度分摊的间接成本

每个存货账户都按所示金额贷记（减少）。若差异不重大，调整产品销售成本；若重大，则需使用比例法。

标准成本法

标准成本法采用直接材料、直接人工并使用预定（标准）间接成本分摊率。标准成本是营运的期望或目标成本。标准成本用于展示差异出在哪里，以便企业能够取得更好的营运业绩。每个标准成本通常分解为：

- 实际单位产品的成本动因的标准数量（参见本书第 4 章将要讨论的弹性预算），如，40 000 人工工时（假设生产了 80 000 单位）=0.5 人工工时每单位。
- 每单位成本动因的标准分摊率，如 $20 每人工工时。

已知标准分摊率和产量后就能求出直接人工和直接材料的标准成本。标准成本（如标准工时数乘以每工时的标准分摊率）可与实际总成本（如总直接人工成本）相比。例如，某月生产产品同为 80 000 单位，实际人工工时为 42 000，实际分摊率为每人工工时 $18。标准成本与实际成本之间的差异导致实际结果与预算间的差异，详见第 4 章。

标准可以是理论性的或当前可实现的，标准由企业政策、作业分析、历史数据、市场预期、战略及标杆分析等设定。标准的类型已在第 1 章 "预算编制" 中有讲述。

标准成本的优势包括它们不受过去的无效率的影响，同时在预算期内它们可以作为新数据揭示人们所期望的各种改进。标准成本的缺点在于可能设定不合理的标准，比如标准的设定过于独裁或隐秘，或缺乏沟通。刚性标准或不恰当地强调利润的标准也很可能失败。

吸收成本法（完全成本法）和变动成本法（直接成本法）

吸收成本法（或完全成本法）是一种存货成本法制度，它包括变动和固定制造成本。存货吸收了制造过程中的所有成本。变动成本法（或直接成本法）是一种存货成本方法，它包括所有变动制造成本作为产品成本，但不包括固定制造成本。变动成本法将成本发生期间的固定制造成本作为费用。这两种方法都将成本发生期间的非制造成本（包括固定和变动成本）作为费用。因此，这两种方法只在如何处理固定制造成本上不同。

吸收成本法及变动成本法下的损益表编制

因为在考虑到损益表上应披露的项目的重要性时，变动成本法和吸收成本法目标不同，所以每种方法都以各自的格式进行披露。变动成本法采用边际贡献格式，突出了固定成本和变动成本的区别。吸收成本法采用边际毛利式，突出了制造成本和非制造成本的区别，这也是对外财务报告所要求的形式。变动制造成本在两种损益表下都采用相同的计量方式。

图表2-28展示了这两种成本核算方法及各自的报告格式。

表的两边所用数据相同：

- 生产产品单位量：700
- 产品销售单位量：500
- 每单位变动制造成本：$30
- 每单位变动销售（营销）成本：$20
- 每单位固定制造成本：$25
- 固定销售（营销）成本：$14 000

图表2-28中两份表的主要区别在于在变动成本法下固定制造成本被看做费用来减去，而吸收成本法下每个产成品都被看做已经将相应固定制造成本吸收了（作为产品成本）。当生产与销售数量不等时，吸收成本法和变动成本法下的净利润便不相同。若生产数量大于销售数量，吸收成本法会带来更高的净利润因为成本已全部吸收到存货中，而变动成本法会带来更低的净利润因为相对于销售成本并没有一样多的成本进入到存货中。另一个不同点在于采用吸收成本法时，期末存货中的固定制造成本被递延到未来期间。另一方面，变动成本法在存货生产期间扣除整个固定制造成本。

图表2-28　变动成本法与吸收成本法

变动成本法		吸收成本法	
收入：$200×500 单位	$100 000	收入：$200×500 单位	$100 000
变动成本		产品销售成本	
期初存货	$0	期初存货	$0
+ 变动制造成本：		+ 变动制造成本：	
$30×700	+21 000	$30×700	+21 000
= 可供销售的产品的成本	21 000	+ 固定制造成本：	
− 期末存货：	−6 000	$25×700	+17 501
$30×200		= 可供销售的产品的成本	38 500
= 变动产品销售成本	15 000	− 期末存货：	
+ 变动营销成本：		（$30 变动 + $25 固定）	
$20×500	+10 000	×200	−11 000 −27 500
= 总变动成本	−25 000	= 产品销售成本	
= 边际贡献	75 000	= 边际毛利	72 500
固定成本		营运成本	
固定制造成本：		变动营销成本	10 000
$25×700	17 500	$20×500	
+ 固定营销成本	$14 000	+ 固定营销成本	+14 000
+／− 固定成本差异		+／− 营运成本差异	
调整	0	调整	0
= 总固定成本	−31 500	= 总营运成本	−24 000
= 营运收益	$43 500	= 营运收益	$48 500

总之，当存货增加，净利润在吸收成本法下会比在变动成本下高，高出部分等于存货增加部分中的固定成本金额（200 单位 × $25 = $5 000，见图表2-28）。当存货减少时，吸收成本法下比变动成本法下的净利润低，低的部分等于存货固定成本的变化。然而，随着及时生产和其他存货削减方法变得日益重要，变动成本法和吸收成

本法之间的差异的重要性也会越来越小。事实上，若一个公司每期期初和期末存货均为 0，则两种成本核算方法就没有区别了。

吸收成本法与变动成本法的优势与局限性

吸收成本法是一种标准方法，因为联邦税务局与公认会计原则都要求使用它。然而，吸收成本法让经理仅靠增加存货就能操纵营运收入。若他们的年金或激励计划与营运收入相关，则经理可能会增加存货，即使没有额外需求存在。另外，经理可能会生产一些能吸收最多固定制造成本的产品而不是对企业最有利的产品。为解决这个及其他不适当的管理层激励问题，企业应当对内部报告改用变动成本法，缩小管理层选择生产什么的范围，或抑制存货积累如针对所有期末存货的一定比例的持有费用。

当我们关注那些项目可被追溯至责任中心并可被其控制时，就使用变动成本法。由于固定成本通常不在该中心经理的控制范围之内，所以许多公司希望关注于那些可被控制的领域。

联产品成本法和副产品成本法

联产品是共享一部分生产工序且拥有相对相同的销售价值的产品。副产品是与一种产品或联产品共有相同工序但与主要产品相比拥有相对较小价值的产品。小鸡饲养的副产品就被用于狗粮。石油工业采用联产工序，原油被炼制成联产品，如柴油、汽油、润滑油和塑料。木材可做成板材，同时废料可用来做合板（一种联产品），而锯屑则用于其他产品（副产品）。联产品和副产品均共享至少某些相同的原材料和初始工序成本。分离点在产品分离且分别确认的点上。分离点不必是产品完工的时点。

联产品和副产品的成本核算包括发生在分离点以前及以后的所有制造成本。对于财务报告，发生在分离点前的联合成本就分配到联产品中。附加工序成本（可分离的成本）是可单独确认为某种产品成本的任何成本，因为它发生在分离点之后，可分配给单独的产品。

联合成本在联产品间的分配

将联合成本分配给联产品可采用两种基本方法：使用市场基础数据（如收入）或使用物理指标基础数据（如重量或数量）。市场基础法包括分离法下的销售价值、毛利法及可实现净值法。这些方法详述如下。

市场基础法

分离法下的销售价值。分离法下的销售价值（或叫销售价值法）使用广泛，因为它简单。销售价值法只有当销售价值在分离点上可得时才能使用。它根据分离点上各联产品的销售价值比例对联合成本进行分配。例如，若一个养兔场分别以 $4 每磅和 $2 每磅出售兔皮和兔肉时，发生了 $8 000 的联合成本。生产过程产出 1 000 磅毛皮和 3 000 磅兔肉。对每种产品分配成本的步骤如下。

1. 计算每种联产品的总销售价值，就是用单位价格乘以数量。销售价值不是实际销售额的记录而是价值的计算。

1 000 磅 × \$4 = \$4 000

3 000 磅 × \$2 = \$6 000

2. 计算每种联产品销售价值占总销售价值的比例

$$\frac{\$4\ 000}{\$10\ 000}=0.4=40\% \qquad \frac{\$6\ 000}{\$10\ 000}=0.6=60\%$$

3. 用联合成本乘以销售价值的比例。这成为销售成本同时也是分配给每种联产品的金额。

\$8 000 × 0.4 = \$3 200　　　\$8 000 × 0.6 = \$4 800

4. 计算每单位（磅）成本，用前一步中的产品销售成本（比例成本）除以单位数量（磅）。（注意，虽然其余的方法没有显示这一步，但单位成本可按相同方法计算）。

$$\frac{\$3\ 200}{1\ 000\ 磅}=\$3.20/磅 \qquad \frac{\$4\ 800}{3\ 000\ 磅}=\$1.60/磅$$

每种联产品的边际毛利都能用销售价值减去比例成本来计算：

\$4 000 − \$3 200 = \$800　　　\$6 000 − \$4 800 = \$1 200

假设销售价格估计正确，且联产品不需要额外工序，那么销售价值法的优势在于为联产品提供了相同的边际毛利百分比。边际毛利百分比可用边际毛利除以销售价值计算：

$$\frac{\$800}{\$4\ 000}=0.2=20\% \qquad \frac{\$1\ 200}{\$6\ 000}=0.2=20\%$$

销售价值法使用广泛，因为它不但易于计算而且是根据产品价值来分配成本。其他方法，如物理指标法，并不按照价值来分配成本，因此有时可能对一个产品分配了过多成本使之没有了边际毛利，而它的相对联产品却有很高的边际利润。销售价值法的局限性在于不能用于在分离点后价值形成前需要额外工序的产品。这种方法对于市场价值变化频繁的产品的使用价值也较低。

毛利法（固定边际毛利率法）。毛利法，也叫做固定边际毛利率法，分配联合成本以使各联产品拥有相同的边际毛利率。假设养兔场例子数据同上，除了在这里联产品共享 \$5 000 的联合成本，兔皮有 \$2 000 的额外工序成本（分离点后），兔肉有 \$1 000 额外工序成本。毛利法的步骤如下：

1. 计算总毛利率。为此，首先确定最终销售价值，用单位价格乘以数量。

（与销售价值法一样，最终销售价值是生产出的金额，而不是当期实际销售的金额）

1 000 磅 × \$4 = \$4 000

3 000 磅 × \$2 = \$6 000

总金额（\$10 000）减去联合成本及单独成本就是边际毛利：

\$10 000 − \$5 000 − \$2 000 − \$1 000 = \$2 000　边际毛利

边际毛利率即用边际毛利除以总销售价值：

$$\frac{\$2\ 000}{\$10\ 000}=0.2=20\%$$

2. 为确定每种产品负担的总成本，用边际毛利率乘以单个销售价值金额，然后用销售价值减去这个金额来确定成本：

$4\ 000 \times 0.2 = \$800$　　　$6\ 000 \times 0.2 = \$1\ 200$

$4\ 000 - \$800 = \$3\ 200$　　　$6\ 000 - \$1\ 200 = \$4\ 800$

3. 从总成本中减去额外工序成本来确定分配到每种产品中的联合成本：

$3\ 200 - \$2\ 000 = \$1\ 200$　　　分配给毛皮的联合成本

$\underline{\$4\ 800 - \$1\ 000 = \$3\ 800}$　　　分配给兔肉的联合成本

　　　　$\underline{\$5\ 000}$　　　总联合成本

此方法的最后一步将毛利法与其他方法区别开来，因为它考虑到了分离点前后发生的成本。于是这种方法便不单是联合成本的分配，还是一种利润分配方法。联合成本和总边际毛利都分配给联产品以保持固定边际毛利。

毛利法的一个好处是即使存在额外工序成本时也可使用。分配给每种联产品的联合成本金额并不总是正数；一种联产品可能得到负的联合成本，以让边际毛利率与整个公司的平均水平相同。这对于那些想让不同产品保持相同边际收益的公司来说是个优势，但它可能导致成本分配的扭曲。

可实现净值（NRV）法。可实现净值（NRV）法，也叫做估计可实现净值法，用于当一种或多种联产品市场价格在分离点不能确定的情况，通常是因为需要额外的工序。产品的最终销售价值减去额外工序成本就是它的可实现净值。再次使用养兔场的例子，额外的 1 000 磅废料现在可直接卖给一个宠物食品加工厂而没有了每磅 $1 的额外成本。

可实现净值的计算步骤如下：

1. 计算每种联产品的可实现净值。为此，首先计算每单位的销售价值，即单位价格乘以数量。

毛皮 1 000 磅 × \$4 = \$4 000

兔肉 3 000 磅 × \$2 = \$6 000

副产品 1 000 磅 × \$1 = \$1 000

用此最终销售价值计算 NRV（对于没有额外工序成本的产品，销售价值就是 NRV）。

NRV = 最终销售价值 - 额外工序成本

毛皮 = \$4 000 - \$2 000 = \$2 000

兔肉 = \$6 000 - \$1 000 = \$5 000

副产品　　　　 = $\underline{\$1\ 000}$

总 NRV　　　　　$\underline{\$8\ 000}$

2. 计算每种联产品和副产品的 NRV 占总 NRV 的比例：

$\dfrac{\$2\ 000}{\$8\ 000} = 25\%$　　　$\dfrac{\$5\ 000}{\$8\ 000} = 62.5\%$　　　$\dfrac{\$1\ 000}{\$8\ 000} = 12.5\%$

3. 用联合成本乘以 NRV 百分数。这是分配给每种产品成本的金额。

$5\ 000 \times 0.25 = \$1\ 250$

$5\ 000 \times 0.625 = \$3\ 125$

$5\ 000 \times 0.125 = \$625$

与销售价值法一样，这种方法将价值按比例分配到产品价值中，形成可预知的边际利润。

物理指标（产品单位）法

物理指标法或产品单位法，采用物理指标将联合成本分配给联产品。物理指标包括重量、数量和体积。物理指标可以是对投入的计量如兔子的只数或磅数，或对产出的计量如磅数、罐数、包数或箱数。当产出用于分配联合成本时，物理指标法被叫做平均成本法。假定养兔场情况保持不变，一个养兔场出售 $4 每磅的毛皮和 $2 每磅的兔肉；生产线产出 1 000 磅毛皮、3 000 磅兔肉和 1 000 磅废料；整个生产工序成本为 $8 000，没有额外工序成本。

用物理指标法和投入的磅数来分配联合成本的步骤如下。

1. 计算总联合成本的平均单位成本，用总联合成本除以总磅数（忽略废料、损耗和副产品）：

$$平均成本/单位 = \frac{\$8\ 000}{4\ 000\ 磅} = \$2/磅$$

2. 用单位平均成本乘以总数量来确定分配给每种产品的联合成本金额：

$2 磅 × 1 000 磅 = $2 000 分配给毛皮的成本

$2 磅 × 3 000 磅 = $6 000 分配给兔肉的成本

这样毛皮的边际毛利为 $2 000（$4 000 毛利 – $2 000 成本），使毛皮的边际毛利达到 50%（$2 000 ÷ $4 000）。兔肉的边际毛利是 $0（$6 000 毛利 – $6 000 成本）。兔肉没有边际利润。

虽然物理指标法易于使用且采用客观标准来计量，但它的缺点远超过其优势。从上例中可以看出，物理指标法可能产生让管理层沮丧和让实际利润失真的边际毛利。这是因为联合产品的价值完全没有得到体现，除非相关物理指标表现出了各种产品的价值，例如，熔解的以盎司或条计的黄金按重量计量仍可以得到正确的估值（除非在工序中增加了艺术或实用价值）。另一个局限性在于工序中不可能总是使用相同的计量单位，如磅和加仑。

联产品和副产品的会计处理

联产品成本，一旦用以上某种方法进行分配，便成为存货成本的一部分，同时在各产成品之间进行了划分。根据 GAAP，出于财务报告和计税的目的，所有能看作制造成本的联合成本都应分配给联产品。

副产品可以采用四种不同的方法进行处理。若企业能在分离点前将产品价值归属给副产品（也愿意这样做），就可使用资产辨认法。这种情况下，在副产品产出期间，副产品的可实现净值就可在资产负债表上作为存货计入，同时在损益表上作为总制造成本的抵减项记录。或者，在副产品产出期间，公司可将副产品的 NRV 作为其他收益（或其他销售收入项目）计入损益表。这些方法遵从了权责发生制的配比原则，因为企业将副产品的价值与其制造成本相配比。因此，若金额重大时，在生产时进行确认更合理。当副产品出售时，存货成本就计入销售成本。

如果企业不能在分离点前将产品成本归属给副产品，可以在副产品出售时用收入法确认。企业可将副产品的净销售收入作为其他收益（或其他销售收入项目）计入损益表。或者，在销售时，将净销售收入作为总制造成本的抵减项计入损益表。
收入法更易于使用而且建立在收入确认概念上，但应用于非重大金额。

进度检查

提示：完成以下各题。参考答案随后给出。

将下列成本动因类型与相符的成本动因例子搭配起来。

1. _____ 作业成本动因　　　a. 重新设计生产工序，去掉非必要步骤
2. _____ 数量成本动因　　　b. 高技术设备取代旧设备
3. _____ 结构性成本动因　　c. 驾驶卡车的工时
4. _____ 执行性成本动因　　d. 订单发票的处理数量

5. 一个工厂在部门水平上计量电力的使用。这个部门包含若干产品经营，包括网球生产。对一罐网球来说，电力可以看作以下哪种成本？
   （　　）a. 变动间接成本
   （　　）b. 变动直接成本
   （　　）c. 固定间接成本
   （　　）d. 固定直接成本

6. 若一个企业更看重数据的可靠性而不是获得数据的速度，以下哪种成本核算方法最合适？
   （　　）a. 变动成本法（直接成本法）
   （　　）b. 标准成本法
   （　　）c. 正常成本法
   （　　）d. 实际成本法

7. 假设一个管理会计师想最大化报告净利润，以下哪种成本核算方法能在企业增加期末存货时得到最大的净利润？
   （　　）a. 变动成本法
   （　　）b. 正常成本法
   （　　）c. 标准成本法
   （　　）d. 吸收成本法

进度检查答案

1. d
2. c
3. b
4. a
5. a
6. d
7. d

 **第 3 节**
成本归集制度

本节内容简介

成本归集制度是将各项成本收集起来并将它们分配给特定的成本对象，如一件产品或一项劳务。本节讨论了成本归集的各种方法，包括分批成本法、分步成本法、作业成本法、生命周期成本法和其他方法。成本归集制度具有战略价值，公司运用成本归集数据来管理各项成本并给其产品和劳务合理定价。

分批成本法与分步成本法

公司通常采用成本归集制度中两种基本方法中的一种来将成本分配给产品或劳务。

- 分批成本法。将成本分配到特定的批次。
- 分步成本法。通过加工过程和部门流程来收集产品和劳务的成本，并将其分配到大量同质或近似的产品中，从而用总成本除以总产量来得到单位成本。

因此这两种方法是一个连续体的对立两端：从特殊到一般，从定制到大量生产。分批成本法犹如静坐等候特殊点餐服务的饭店而分步成本法好似提供均一菜食的简便餐车。分批成本法分别用于核算制造业部门的资本资产构建成本（如房屋、船只），核算服务业部门如广告宣传、研发和维修工作的成本，核算商业部门定制的邮政业务和特殊的促销活动。分步成本法用于能够汇成一股成本流的大量近似产品，如制造业部门中的报纸、图书和汽水的生产成本，服务业部门的支票处理和邮递服务以及商业部门的报纸订购收入款。

这两种成本计算系统的相同点是都拥有共同的目的，那就是将直接材料、直接人工和间接成本分配给产品。同时，它们都拥有相同的账户，包括直接材料存货、在产品存货、产成品存货和产品销售成本。分批成本法不同于分步成本法的地方在于成本的归集地：一个批次还是一个部门。分批成本法使用批次表（或软件）来追溯特定的项目；分步成本法使用生产成本报告来追述所有部门的成本。分批成本法通过用最后一个批次来计算单位成本；而分步成本法一直等到本会计年度末期时才按照部门来计算单位成本。虽然我们接下来将分别讨论以上这两种方法，但是大多数公司，尤其是兼有特殊和大额产量的产品或劳务时，都采取了两种方法并用的方式。

分批成本法

之前用于实际、正常和标准成本法计算的步骤可用在分批成本计算之中。使用分批成本法将成本分配到某一批次的基本步骤如下：

1. 确认批次。特定的批次通常用独一无二的代码来识别或用级别索引加日期的方式。例如，史密斯公司会将生产游艇的单号确认为 123 同时加上日期 20××。这一例子假设使用的是实际成本法。

2. 追溯该批次的直接成本，如 $40 000 的直接材料和 $60 000 的直接人工。

3. 确认和批次相关的间接成本池。例如对于所有项目的年间接成本，有 $60 000 在第一个成本池，有 $120 000 在第二个成本池。

4. 选择成本分配基础（成本动因），以便将间接成本分配到该批次中。第一个成本池是以机器小时计量的，第二个成本池以人工工时计量。在我们的例子中，对于全年的所有项目，机器小时数是 20 000，人工工时数是 30 000。

5. 计算每一成本分配基础的单位分摊率。实际间接成本的分摊率计算如下：

$$实际间接成本的分摊率 = \frac{间接成本池中的实际总成本}{总成本动因数量}$$

$$= \frac{\$60\ 000}{20\ 000\ 机器小时} = \$3/机器小时$$

$$= \frac{\$120\ 000}{30\ 000\ 人工工时} = \$4/人工工时$$

6. 加总批次的所有直接成本和间接成本以得到成本对象的总成本。间接成本综合考虑到了机器小时和人工工时，在这个例子中，该项目占用了 2 000 个机器小时（2 000 × $3 = $6 000）和 3 000 个直接人工工时（3 000 × $4 = $12 000），于是得到了间接成本 $18 000。这一数值加上直接材料 $40 000 和直接人工 $60 000 便得到了总的制造成本 $118 000。如果游艇以 $140 000 的价格卖出，则毛利便是 $22 000，毛利率是 15.7%（$22 000 ÷ $140 000）。

分批成本法下的废品、返工品及残料处理

公司应减少生产中的废品、返工品和残料的数量以使其原材料的使用价值达到最大化。

废品

废品指被认为是不可接受的原材料或产品被丢弃或削价处理。废品可以是正常废品和非正常废品。正常废品是指即使在有效经营的条件下，在正常生产流程中产生的废品。正常废品被认为是经营成本的一部分，所以通常被视为完工合格产品成本的一部分。正常废品可以是某一个特定批次的直接成本或生产的间接成本从而分配到工厂的间接成本中去。如果直接让某一批次承担这项成本，废品追加给批次的成本可以由产品估计的残值进行相应的抵减。非正常废品是指在有效生产条件下不应该产生的废品。任何超过正常废品数量的成本都被分配到"非正常废品损失"账户中。计算总废品的公式如下：

总废品数量 = 期初存货数量 + 投入数量 - 完工并结转至合格品的数量 - 期末存货数量

公式的变形为：

期初存货 + 投入量 =（完工并结转至合格品的数量 + 总废品数量）+ 期末存货

返工品

返工品是指已完工产品必须增加工作量返回修理才能作为合格品出售的产品，它们被划分为以下三类：

- 仅与某一特定批次有关的正常返工。将成本分配到该特定批次的在成品存货账户中（增加成本，减少收益）。
- 与所有批次有关的正常返工品。将成本分配到间接成本中。
- 非正常返回。将成本分配到非正常返工损失账户。

残料

残料是产品的一部分或者是生产产品剩下的材料，其并没有经济价值。残料可以划分为与特定批次有关的残料和与所有批次相关的残料。与特定批次有关的残料将其成本追溯到产生该残料批次的半成品库存账中，与所有批次相关的残料成本分摊到间接成本中。这两种方法都增加了受其影响的账户的成本。残料的成本并不单独记录，但是当残料被卖出时，会计人员将按照残料的销售收入金额来贷记（冲减）在产品存货或间接成本。

分批成本法的优点和局限性

分批成本法能够对特定批次和经营情况提供十分详细的结论，所以它是特定批次的理想状态。对于大量的加工处理，分批成本法的使用价值降低了，因为将单个成本分配到每日有大量生产的项目中去是不现实的。分批成本法融合了多种成本计算方法，如实际成本法、正常成本法、标准成本法，这样才可以足够灵活地在更多类型的公司中得到应用。

分批成本法具有商业战略价值因为它对于所有不同种类的成本都给出了详细的分析说明。毛利和毛利率能够用来比较在不同批次情况下公司的盈利情况，并且，对于盈利较差的批次，公司可以分析其过度成本究竟是来自于直接人工、直接材料还是其中的一个间接成本池。

分步成本法

如前所述，分步成本法在有大量同质或近似产品的生产流程中使用。这些公司将它们的产品数量和成本额追溯记录到生产成本报告中并通过总成本除以总产量来得到期末的单位成本。

分步成本法对于具有高度自动化或重复加工流程特点的企业来说很适用，如美国邮政。对于这类公司，分步成本法的战略价值是在持续经营的同时仍然在每一期间可获得及时、准确和相对廉价的成本信息。分步成本法同时使用生产成本报告，报告中具有内置式检查，如要入账的和实际入账的账户余额的对比。

分步成本法下的等价单位

在分批成本法下，部分完工的产品有相匹配的成本，与分批成本法不同，分步成本法下的会计处理高度重视的是加工过程和部门流程产生的成本，并不是各个批次和项目。因此，分步成本法必须找到所有产品单位的联合成本，包括期初和期末部分完工的产品。部分完工意味着这些产品仍处于半成品库存中，因此在一个部门完工的产品并不是真的完工了，直到它们转入产成品存货中才算完工。在期末，生产经理和工程师应对仍处于生产线上的在产品的分比或半成品库存进行估计。

由于生产成本由每一部门单位成本的计算结果决定，部分完成的产品必须纳入其计算之中。在每一个会计年度的期末，分步成本法计算系统将半成品视为约当产量。约当产量是在给定部分完工产品的工作量下本应能够生产的完工品数量。在将持续的加工生产人为地划分为不同的时间区间时，约当产量是不可避免的。

由于相同产品每一部分完成的程度各不相同，工程师们分别以直接人工、直接材料和间接成本来计算约当产量。每一种产品都有相似的计算模式：未完工产品 × 估计完成率，例如，如果 1 000 桶网球有 30% 的直接人工是完成的，那么就有 300 个约当人工工时单位。如果相同的网球已经制作完成，只是需要装箱，那么直接材料中有 90% 已经完成了，所以约当直接材料单位为 900 个。

期初存货

期初存货项目应由用来核算上一年度完成程度的完成率的相反百分比，即剩余完成率来计价。因此，如果一个项目的期初存货有 30% 已经完成了，那么它剩余的 70% 未完成的数额就应作为计算约当产量的基础（1 000 单位未全部完成的实际产量相当于 700 单位约当产量）。当然，并不是所有的方法都要在计算中考虑到期初存货的问题。

产品的约当产量 = [期初存货 × (100% - % 期初存货已完成)] + 当期投入和完工数量 + 期末半成品库存的约当产量

转换成本

一些公司单独计量直接材料，并将直接人工和间接成本合起称做转换成本。当高度自动化生产造成直接人工已不再是成本的重要组成部分时，这些公司就会在计算过程中，例如在确定约当产量的时候，将直接人工和间接成本合并起来一起计算。

转换成本这样的划分在基于人工成本动因下的公司有较好的效果，但是那些采用非人工动因的公司，例如以安装的次数和机器小时为成本分配基础的公司，最好将人工和间接成本分开来计算。

分步成本法的成本流转

分批成本法下是直接通过批次将成本进行结转，与分批成本法不同，分步成本法下的成本流遵循加工过程和部门流程。在分步成本法下，每一个部门都必须有一个半成品库存账户。由于直接材料、直接人工和间接成本在每一个相关部门都会发生，每一个部门都将带来这些成本而不仅仅是第一个部门。当一个部门完成了它所应完成的那部分加工以后，通过借记转入成本账户来将所有的成本转入下一个部门的在产品存货账户中。当产品完工的时候，产品的完工成本被转至完工产品中。

对于两个不同部门先后加工同一产品的会计分录见图表 2 - 29。

图表 2-29　分步成本法下的 T 型账户成本流传模型

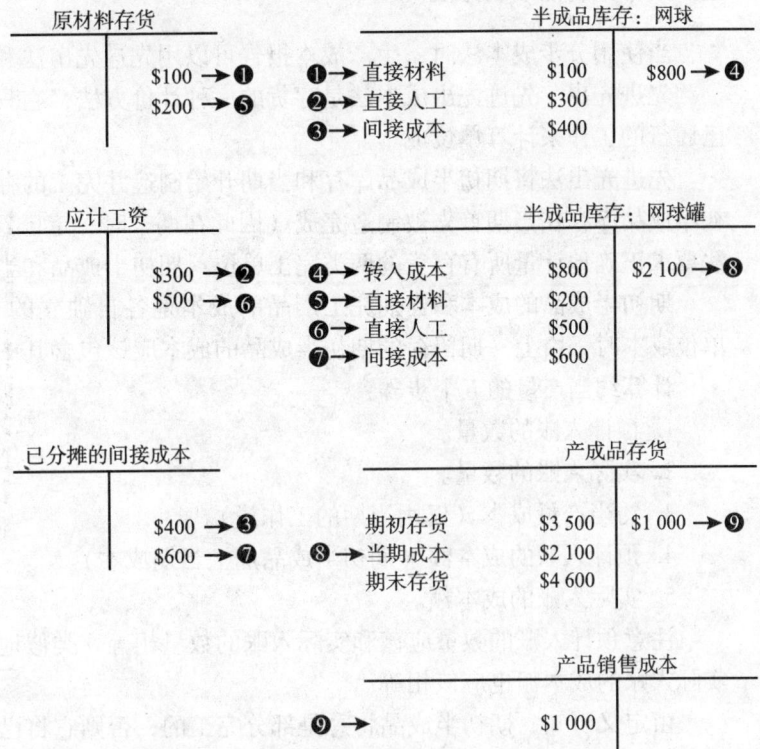

编制生产成本报告的步骤

部门的生产成本报告包含了所有的实物产量、约当产量、期末半成品库存、当期成本、分配给已完工产品的成本以及分配给结转出产品的成本。

编制生产成本报表的五个步骤：

1. 确认实物流。在确认期初拥有多少产品时，投入和产出的产品量都应被考虑，这些产品量包含新加工的或实际收到的数量，完工并结转的产量和期末半成品库存中的数量。期初半成品库存和当期投入生产部门的属于投入产量。对于特殊的部门，完工并结转的产量和期末仍留在存货中的半成品属于产出产量。

2. 确认约当产量。

（以上两个步骤分析了产品数量并计量了生产的总工作量）

3. 计算总制造成本。期初半产品以及当期任何一项需被考虑的成本都应包含在总制造成本当中，领料单、计工单和工厂间接成本分摊表共同集合了这些成本。

4. 计算单位成本。为了确认产品成本和期间收益，应计算总单位成本以及单位直接材料成本、单位直接人工成本和单位间接成本。

（上一步骤和本步骤有时被称为单位成本的确认）

5. 将总制造成本分摊给各个产品单位（成本分配）。产品完成并转出，留存在期末的半成品库存将接受期间制造成本。

生产成本报告的编制方法

当使用分步成本法时，生产成本报告可以用先进先出法和加权平均法来编制。

先进先出。先进先出成本法是存货的一种计价方法，它只用当期已发生的成本和已履行的工作来计算单位成本。

先进先出法将期初半成品库存和当期开始制造并完工的存货分开处理，并假设期初半成品库存在当期首先被制造完成（因此在期末时一定已经是产成品了）。这种方法要求正确地计量所有存货的两类完工单位：期初半成品和当期投入并完工的产品。

期初半成品的成本和当期完工产品的成本是各自独立的（但在计算期初存货的单位成本时，由上一期留存的期初半成品的成本应该包含其中）。

计算约当产量的五个步骤：

1. 预计入账的数量。

2. 实际入账的数量。

3. 约当产量成本（仅用当期的工作量）。

4. 预计入账的成本额（期初半成品加上当期成本）。

5. 实际入账的成本额。

注意预计入账的数量应该和实际入账的数量相等，类似地，预计入账的成本额和实际入账的成本额也应该相等。

由定义可知，期初半成品将总是部分完工的，否则它将已经结转至下一部门。因此，我们的目标是在当月获得正确的已完工产品的成本和月底半成品（WIP）账户下的产品数额。

图表2-30给出了这样一个例子。假设在期初生产加工时，原材料100%都追加到了生产新的产品中去（即期初半成品的原材料汇集已经100%完成了），但是期初半成品的加工只完成了40%。这个例子同时向我们展示如何处理期末半成品（原材料已经100%汇集完毕，但是加工只进行了80%）。

注意在预计入账的成本额这一表格内，期初半成品的成本由上个月的直接材料（DM）和转换（Conv.）成本决定。

图表2-30 生产成本报告：先进先出法

		实物数量	约当产量 直接材料	约当产量 转换成本
预计入账 的数量	期初半成品	100		
	新生产的产量	700		
	总量	800		
实际入账 的数量	结转至下一个部门： 期初半成品，直接材料（DM） $100 \times (100\% - 100\%)$；Conv. $100 \times (100\% - 40\%)$：	100	0	60
	本期新生产的和完工的（800总量－200期末WIP－100期初WIP首先完工） 月底WIP，DM	500	500	50
	$200 \times 100\%$，Conv. $200 \times 80\%$	200	200	160

续表

		实物数量	约当产量 直接材料	约当产量 转换成本
	记录入账：	800		
	只在当期完工的数量：		700	720

		总成本			单位总成本
计算约当产量的成本和预计入账的成本额	月初 WIP（上一期完成的工作的成本：(100DM × $40) + (40Conv. × $30))：	$5 200.00	不被包括	不被包括	
	当月追加成本：	$53 000.00	$30 000.00	$23 000.00	
	约当产量（见上）：		700	720	
	约当产量单位成本：		$42.86	$31.94	$74.80
	预计入账的总成本：	$58 200.00			
实际入账成本额	转入下一个部门（600 件）： 期初 WIP（100 件）：	$5 200.00			
	DM	$0	0 × $42.86		
	Conv.	$1 916.40		60 × $31.94	
	期初 WIP 总额	$7 116.40			
	本期新生产的和完成的（500 件）	$37 400.00	500 × $42.86	500 × $31.94	
	所有完工和结转的产品：	$44 516.40			
	期末 WIP（200 件）：				
	DM	$8 572.00	200 × $42.86		
	Conv.	$5 110.40		160 × $31.94	
	期末 WIP 总额	$13 682.40			
	总成本（由于四舍五入相差 $1.20）	$58 198.80			

加权平均法。加权平均这一存货计价方法是使用当期和上一期已包含在当期期初半成品库存中的成本的总和来计算单位成本。加权平均法旨在求解之前期间和当期的平均成本。先进先出法关心的是投入产出两者的计量，也就是说一定期间内期初和期末的产品状态；加权平均法关心的只是期末时产品的状态。接下来我们将看到一个使用加权平均法的例子。

在我们的例子中，无论成本在当期是否真实发生，列示在生产成本表里的所有成本都被包含在成本计算中。以下是加权平均法下编制生产成本报表的步骤（伴有计算样本）：

1. 确定实物流。

投入量：

- 部分被完成的期初半成品库存：5 000 件。
- 当期开始生产或收到的产品：30 000 件。

这 35 000 件产品称为"预计入账的数量"。

产出量：

- 完成量：20 000 件。
- 期末半成品库存：15 000 件。

这 35 000 件产品称为"实际入账数量"，应该和预计入账的数量相匹配。

2. 确定约当产量。由于在加权平均法下，期初半成品已经包含在实物产量下，所以不应该包含在约当产量中。由于在 15 000 件期末存货实物产品中，直接材料已经 100% 完成，而转换成本只完成了 47%，所以直接材料的约当产量是 15 000，而转换成本（直接人工加工厂间接成本）约当产量是 7 050。这一数值加上已完工的产品数量 20 000 就一共等于 35 000 的直接材料和 27 050 的转换成本约当产量。

3. 计算全部制造成本。期初半成品的直接材料 \$10 000 加上转换成本 \$10 031 总计 \$20 031。当期直接材料成本是 \$60 000，加上转换成本 \$40 000，共计 \$100 000。所以总的制造成本是 \$120 031。

4. 计算单位成本。

直接材料 = \$10 000　期初半成品库存

　　　　　　\$60 000　当期成本

　　　　　　\$70 000　总成本

$$\frac{\$70\ 000}{35\ 000\ 件} = \$2/单位直接材料$$

$$\frac{\$50\ 031}{27\ 050\ 件} = \$1.85/单位转换成本$$

$$\$2.00 + \$1.85 = 3.85/单位总成本$$

总的制造成本就分配到各个产品中去了。以上计算的单位成本再分别乘以每一类的产品数量，参见图表 2-31 生产成本报告样本底部的计算（第 5 步）。

图表 2-31　生产成本报告：加权平均法

	生产数量信息			
	第1步：确定实物流		第2步：确定约当产量	
	实物产量	完成百分比	直接材料	转换成本
投入量				
半成品，1月1号	5 000			
直接材料				
转换成本				
当期新生产的	30 000			
预计入账的数量	35 000			
产出量				
完工产品	20 000	100%	20 000	20 000
半成品，1月31号	15 000			
直接材料		100	15 000	
转换成本		47		7 050
实际入账的数量	35 000			
约当产量总量			35 000	27 050

	单位成本		
第3步：计算总的制造成本	直接材料	转换成本	总　计
半成品，1月1号	\$10 000	\$10 031	\$20 031
1月份的成本追加	60 000	40 000	100 000
预计入账的成本	\$70 000	\$50 031	\$120 031

续表

单位成本			
第 4 步：计算单位成本	直接材料	转换成本	总　计
除以约当产量	35 000	27 050	
约当单位成本	$2.00	$1.85	$3.85
第 5 步：分配总的制造成本	完工并转出的产品	期末半成品	总　计
完工并转出的产品			
（20 000 × $3.85）	$77 000		$77 000
期末半成品：			
直接材料（15 000 × $2.00）		$30 000	$30 000
转换成本（7 050 × $1.85）		13 043	13 043
实际入账的成本总计	$77 000	$43 043	$120 043 *

* 由于近似计算造成了总的制造成本有 $12 的误差。

注意使用单位成本计算出来的总成本应该和第 3 步计算出的总成本（$120 031）相等，其中 $12 的差异是由于计算中的四舍五入造成的。

多部门的生产成本

由于很多加工过程经常牵扯不止一个部门，我们将举出一个更复杂的例子来说明如何处理从上一个部门结转过来的成本。这个例子将同时说明在先进先出和加权平均法下如何计算存货价值和产品销售成本。

Robusto Soup 公司有三个连续加工的部门，产品的加工开始于混合部门，然后是烹饪部门，最后是包装部门，当每一个部门完成其加工并将产品转入到下一个部门时，它同时也将这组产品的成本转入了下一个部门，下一个部门记为转入成本（或上一个部门的成本）。

转入成本是由先前部门积累下来的所有成本；基于该产品是部分完成并在当前部门继续被加工的假设，先前部门的成本需结转至下一个部门。因此，前一个部门就像是向下一个部门提供半成品的卖主，每一个部门都被视为一个独立的实体。

不同于分批成本法，分步成本法下每一个生产部门都有它们自己的半成品账户。上一个部门的完成品将转入下一部门的半成品账户中。

图表 2 – 32 展示了 Robusto 公司的原材料成本和转换成本是如何被追加的。

图表 2 – 32　每个部门的成本百分比

	混合部门	烹饪部门	包装部门
直接材料	90%	0%	10%
转换成本	60%	20%	20%
转入成本	无	100%	100%

图 2 – 33 展示了 Robusto Soup 公司如何在其账户间结转存货。

图表 2-33　Robusto 公司 7 月份的存货结转

混合部门在产品		烹饪部门在产品		包装部门在产品	
期初　1 000		期初　　3 000		期初　　2 000	
新生产 8 000		转入 ❶→7 000		转入 ❷→8 000	
完工	7 000 ❶→完工		8 000 ❷→完工		9 000 ❸→
期末　2 000		期末　2 000		期末　1 000	

产成品		销售产品*	
期初　　10 000			
转入 ❸　9 000		11 000	
卖出	11 000 ❹→		
期末　　8 000			

* 当以货币而不以产量计量时，这个账户和产品销售成本相对应。

注意以上的表显示的是产量而非成本的结转。

先进先出法应用于 Robusto 公司的包装部门。如果公司运用先进先出法，那么包装部门就有下列成本：

- 期初半成品（2 000 件）
- 当月前已经完工的成本：（1 800DM × \$1.25/件）+（1 600Conv. × \$2.50/件）= \$6 250
- 当月追加的成本：
- 从烹饪部门转入的成本 = \$24 000
- 直接材料（DM）= \$1 000
- 转换成本 = \$4 000

图表 2-34 展示了在先进先出法下，以上述数据为基础的一份完整的生产成本报告。

图表 2-34　包装部门约当产量的计算：先进先出法

		实物数量	从烹饪部门转入的成本	约当产量直接材料	约当产量转换成本	
预计入账的数量	月初半成品 转入 总量	2 000 8 000 10 000				
实际入账的数量	转入包装部门：从起初半成品（WIP） 转入成本 2 000 ×（100% - 100%），直接材料（DM）2 000 ×（100% - 90%）； Conv. 2 000 ×（100% - 80%）：	2 000	0	200	400	
	新生产和完成的（10 000 件 - 1 000 期末 WIP - 2 000 最先完成的期初 WIP）	7 000	7 000	7 000	7 000	
	从月末 WIP 转入 1 000 × 100%；DM 1 000 × 90%；Conv. 1 000 × 80%	1 000	1 000	900	800	
	记录入账：	10 000				
	仅当期完工数量：		8 000	8 100	8 200	

		实物数量	从烹饪部门转入的成本	约当产量直接材料	约当产量转换成本	
		总成本				单位总成本
计算约当产量和预计入账的成本额	月初半成品（当期之前完工的成本）：（转入成本为 0）＋（1 800DM × $1.25）＋（1.600conv. × $1.25））：	$6 250.00	不被包括	不被包括	不被包括	
	本月追加成本：	$29 000.00	$24 000.00	$1 000.00	$4 000.00	
	约当产量：		8 000	8 100	8 200	
	约当产量单位成本：		$3.00	$0.1235	$0.4878	$3.6113
	实际入账的成本：	$35 250.00				
实际入账的成本额	转入包装部门（600 件）：期初半成品（2 000 件）	$6 250.00				
	转入	$0	0 × $3.00			
	DM	$24.70		200 × $0.1235		
	Conv.	$195.12			400 × $0.4878	
	期初总的半成品	$6 469.82				
	新生产和完工产品（7 000 件）	$25 279.10				7 000 × $3.6113
	完工结转的总产品：	$31 748.92				
	月末半成品（1 000 件）：					
	转入	$3 000.00	1 000 × $3.00			
	DM	$111.15		900 × $0.1235		
	Conv.	$390.24			800 × $0.4878	
	月末总的半成品	$3 501.74				
	总成本					
	（由于近似计算造成了 $0.66 的误差）：	$35 250.66				

　　加权平均法应用于 Robusto 公司的包装部门。如果使用加权平均法，那么结转的产品数量是一致的（见图表 2 - 35），但是由于每一个部门都包含着前期部分完工的成本，所以转入成本不一样（而先进先出法仅包含在当期完成的成本）。因此，在其他条件保持不变的情况下，假设现在包装部门的转入成本是 $25 000。

　　图表 2 - 35 列出了一个完整的用加权成本法制成的生产成本报告。

图表 2 - 35　包装部门的生产成本报告：加权平均法

生产数量信息				
第 1 步：确定实物流		第 2 步：确定约当产量		
实物产量	完成百分比	转入成本	直接材料	转换成本
投入量				
半成品，7 月 1 号　　2 000				
转入成本	100%			
直接材料	90%			
转换成本	80%			

生产数量信息					
	第 1 步：确定实物流		第 2 步：确定约当产量		
	实物产量	完成百分比	转入成本	直接材料	转换成本
转入产量	8 000				
预计入账的数量	10 000				
产出量					
完工并转出的产品	9 000	100%	9 000	9 000	9 000
半成品，7 月 31 号	1 000				
转入成本		100%	1 000		
直接材料		90%		900	
转换成本		80%			800
实际入账的数量	10 000				
约当产量总量			10 000	9 900	9 800

单位成本				
第 3 步：计算总的制造成本	转入成本	直接材料	转换成本	总　　计
半成品，7 月 1 号	$6 250	$250	$1 000	$7 500
7 月份的成本追加	$25 000	1 000	4 000	30 000
预计入账总成本	$31 250	$1 250	$5 000	$37 500
第 4 步：计算单位成本				
除以约当产量	10 000	9 900	9 800	
约当单位成本	$3.125	$0.12626	$0.5102	$3.76146
第 5 步：分配总的制造成本	完工并转出的产品		期末半成品	总　　计
完工并转出的产品				
（9 000 × $3.76146）	$33 853			$33 853
期末半成品：				
转入（1 000 × $3.125）			$3 125	
直接材料（900 × $0.12626）			114	114
转换成本（800 × $0.5102）			408	408
实际入账的成本	$33 853		$3 647	$37 500

　　图表 2 –36 总结了 Robusto Soup 公司的数据，同时用 T 形账户和分录展示了交易的发生，并同加权成本法下的生产成本报告里的数据相吻合。

　　记录以 $5/件卖出 11 000 件产品的销售混合部门和烹饪部门分别需要一份生产成本报告（这两个账户的数据仅用作解释说明的目的）。

　　注意，正如图表 2 –35 所展示的投入量的百分比，每一个基础账户（原材料、应付工资和工厂间接成本）不仅满足了第一个部门的生产需要同时也为下一个部门提供了准备。部门的转出成本并不直接等于当期追加的成本，但期初存货加上当月的成本追加总是等于转出成本和期末存货。

　　同时也需注意，每一个存货账户的期初和期末存货水平都被分解成直接材料、转换成本和转入成本。

图表2-36 Robusto 公司的 T 形账户和分录（加权平均法）

原材料		应付工资		工厂间接成本	
期初存货 $15 000		$8 000	$4 800 →❷	$12 000	$7 200 →❸
当月 $5 000	$9 000 →❶		$1 600 →❺		$2 400 →❻
期末存货 $10 000	$1 000 →❽		$1 600 →❾		$2 400 →❿

混合部门半成品库存			烹饪部门半成品库存		
期初存货	直接材料 $1 250		期初存货	直接材料 $0	
	转换成本 $2 500			转换成本 $1 875	
当月 ❶→	直接材料 $9 000			转入成本 $9 375	
❷→		$18 375 →❹	当月 ❹→	转入成本 $18 375	
❸→	转换材料 $12 000		❺→	直接材料 $4 000	$25 000 →❼
			❻→	转换成本 $4 000	
期末存货	直接材料 $2 375		期末存货	转入成本 $7 125	
	转换成本 $4 000			直接材料 $0	
	共计 $6 375			转换成本 $1 500	
				共计 $8 625	

包装部门半成品库存		
期初存货	直接材料 $250	
	转换成本 $1 000	
	转入成本 $6 250	
当月 ❼→	转入成本 $18 375	
❽→	直接材料 $1 000	$33 853 →⓫
❾→		
❿→	转换成本 $4 000	
期末存货	转入成本 $3 125	
	直接材料 $114	
	转换成本 $408	
	共计 $3 647	

产成品		产品销售成本	
	$37 500	⓬→ $41 371	
期初存货 ⓫→ 转入成本 $33 853	$41 371 →⓬		
当月			
期末存货	$29 982		

筛选的分录：

❶→	混合部门半成品库存	$9 000	❷→	混合部门半成品库存	$4 800
	原材料	$9 000		应付工资	$4 800
❸→	混合部门半成品库存	$7 200	❼→	包装部门半成品库存	$25 000
	工厂间接成本	$7 200		烹饪部门半成品库存	$25 000
⓫→	产成品	$33 853	⓬→	产品销售成本	$41 371
	包装部门半成品库存	$33 853		产成品	$41 371
				应收账款	$55 000
				销售收入	$55 000

分步成本法下确定存货水平

下一个例子将帮助我们理解在分步成本法下确定存货水平的复杂性。Bounce 体育用品公司为生产壁球购买橡胶作为直接材料。成型部门对壁球进行加工然后转到整理部门进行包装和贴标签。成型部门在 6 月份开始生产壁球 15 000 个，没有期初存货。

6 月份成型部门发生的成本如下：

直接材料：	$60 000
转换成本：	46 200
共计	$106 200

一共 12 000 个球在成型部门完成并转入到整理部门，有 3 000 个球仍然在成型部门的加工中。在成型部门的期末半成品库存当中，所有的原材都已经投放使用，但是应用的转换成本只有 40%。

应向整理部门转移多少成本呢？为了找到答案，我们首先需要明确该公司应用的是先进先出法还是加权法。在这个例子中，由于没有期初存货：期初分摊到直接材料和转换成本的半成品的约当产量都是 0，所以两种方法的结果是一致的。

该问题的答案是 $90 000，具体计算如下：

确定新生产的和完工的产品：

直接材料：12 000 件 × 100% 完工 = 12 000 约当产量

转换成本：12 000 件 × 100% 完工 = 12 000 约当产量

确定月末半成品：

直接材料：3 000 件 × 100% 完工 = 3 000 约当产量

转换成本：3 000 件 × 40% 完工 = 1 200 约当产量

确定总的约当产量：

直接材料：0 + 12 000 + 3 000 = 15 000 约当产量

转换成本：0 + 12 000 + 1 200 = 13 200 约当产量

计算约当单位成本：

直接材料：$\dfrac{\$60\ 000}{15\ 000\ \text{约当产量}} = \$4.00/\text{约当产量}$

转换成本：$\dfrac{\$46\ 200}{13\ 200\ \text{约当产量}} = \$3.50/\text{约当产量}$

新生产和完工产品的单位成本（转入整理部门）

$(12\ 000 \times \$4) + (12\ 000 \times \$3.50) = \$90\ 000$

为了核对正确性，计算期末半成品：

（3 000 约当产量直接材料 × $4）+（1 200 约当产量转换成本 × $3.50）= $16 200

注意总成本为 $90 000 + $16 200 = $106 200

分步成本法下的废品处理

正如前面分批成本法所定义的，分步成本法也有正常废品和非正常废品两种。在分步成本法下，处理废品有两种方法。第一种方法是分别计算废品数量和总的单位成本，并将这些成本分配到好的产品当中。第二种方法是在总的产量中忽略废品数量，每单位的成本中不包含任何废品的成本，将废品的成本待摊到全部的制造成本当中。第一种方法生产成本的计算更为精确，由于个别计算的废品成本只摊销在好的产品当中。第二种方法由于废品成本待摊到所有好的完工产品、期末半成品库存和非正常废品当中，所以欠精确。

分步成本法的优点和局限性

分步成本法对大量生产这种高重复性的流水加工来说十分有用。相反，它对于定制的定购和其他个别订单的生产来说就显得捉襟见肘了。分步成本法不仅按单位来分配成本同时也将成本分配到了各个部门，这样就给各部门的个别管理人员在控制本部门的成本方面提供了机会。

作业成本法

作业成本法基于作业消耗资源这一假设来将成本分派给消费者、各项劳务和产品。一项作业可以是在实体里完成的任何一种经济活动、劳动或运输。作业中心是多种作业、经济活动、运输或一系列劳动的符合逻辑的组合。拥有经济价值的资源在完成这一项作业的同时被消耗了。

其他有助于理解作业成本法的重要术语包括资源成本动因和作业成本动因。

资源成本动因用来衡量一项作业消耗的资源量。在作业中耗用的资源成本利用资源成本动因被分派到成本池中。例如一项资源成本动因可能是做一批网球需要的橡胶数量。

作业成本动因是衡量一个成本对象需要的作业额。作业成本动因将在成本池中的成本分派给成本对象。例如，为一个特定产品的生产进行的机器安装调试的时间便是一个作业成本动因。

作业成本法的基础是作业耗用资源但产出产品和提供劳务。耗用的资源成本应用成本动因来计算；在一定期间内，耗用的作业数量乘以该作业的单位成本。计算出的成本应分配到产品和劳务中去。

作业成本系统对于生产复合型产品同时/或者产品使用多种资源（不仅包括原材料和其他直接成本，同时还有客户服务、质量控制和监管等间接成本的公司十分必要。当各种产品或产品线以不同的消耗率耗用成本的时候，所有产品的成本都一刀切或整齐统一就会使某些产品的实际盈利能力比看似的情况更差或更好。产品的成本因此会被虚增或被低估，成本虚增的产品实际没有消耗那么多资源却要承担更多的成本，成本低估的产品恰好相反。从经营战略这个角度来说，如果不准确的成本信息带来的损失大于搜集更多信息同时执行作业成本系统带来的收益时，作业成本法就应该实施了。比如若在新增或删减某个部门的决策上选择失败的话将会带来灾难性的后果。另一项由作业成本法支撑的战略决策包括产品定价决策以及如何分配资金以改进流程。

两阶段成本分摊制是一种先将间接成本（资源成本）分配到成本池中，再基于一个成本对象耗用的资源量将成本池中的成本分配到如产品、劳务和客户等成本对象中去。成本池既可以是任何一项作业也可以是一个作业中心。作业成本法有两阶段的分配：

- 阶段一：利用适当的资源成本动因将资源成本分配到作业成本池中。
- 阶段二：利用适当的作业成本动因将作业成本分配到成本对象中去。

作业成本法的主要步骤

设计作业成本系统的步骤有：确认作业和资源成本，将资源成本分配到作业中，分配作业成本到成本对象中。

步骤1：确认作业和资源成本

作业分析通过确认每一项作业完成的工作来确定执行特定作业耗用的资源成本。项目小组制定了详细的作业列表并将它们组织成下列不同级别的作业中心：

- 单位级作业是指每一单位产品所涉及的作业，如直接材料或直接人工工时。换句话说，这些作业以产量为基础或以单位为基础。
- 批次级作业是指为了某一批次生产而实行的作业。如生产前的机器调试、采购订单、分批检查、分批混合或生产调度。
- 产品存续作业是指为支持生产流程而实施的作业。如产品设计、产品加速完成和实施工程学变革。
- 设备存续作业是指对所有支持生产的设备实施的作业。如设备运行环境的健康性和安全性、安全检查程序、工厂管理、折旧、财产税和保险。
- 顾客级作业是指为满足顾客需要而发生的作业，如顾客服务、电话银行或客户自定义订单。

步骤2：资源成本分配到作业

资源成本借助资源成本动因以将其分配到各项作业中去。动因和作业之间的因果关系一定要建立起来。企业经常用到的资源成本动因和其相关的作业如下所示：

- 雇员数量：人事作业
- 工作时间：人事作业
- 安装小时：安装和机器作业
- 搬运的次数或距离：材料处理作业
- 仪表测量：公用事业（流量仪表、电表等）
- 机器小时：机器运行作业
- 订单量：生产订单
- 平方英尺：清洁作业
- 价值附加值：一般管理

步骤3：作业成本分配到成本对象

在确定了作业成本之后，单位作业成本就通过合理的成本动因被计算出来。作业成本动因应同成本的上升和下降间具有直接的因果关系。

作业成本动因运用下面这个公式将成本分配到每一件产品和劳务：

$$作业率 = \frac{归集期内作业池里归集的总成本}{动因（归集期内相应的作业量）}$$

什么情况下使用作业成本法

作业成本法帮助管理层获悉本部门的成本情况，因此强调了在产品生产或加工当中的竞争优势和劣势。在作业成本法下，用计算机数据库来追踪单个产品的成本情况变得越发可行了。随着越来越多的公司开始采用作业成本法，使用欠精确的成本计算系统变得越发的昂贵。

那些具有产品多样性、复杂性和高产量的公司传统上已经转向作业成本法以追踪其成本。

那些极容易产生成本扭曲的公司也应考虑作业成本法，比如那些既采用大批量生产也采用客户定制生产的公司，既有成熟产品也有新产品的公司，以及那些既有定制分销渠道也有标准分销渠道的公司。这种生产、产品及分销渠道的复杂性使得公司很难单一实施分批成本法和分步成本法，从而使作业成本法成为了一个理想的替代方案。

公司之所以选择作业成本法已经不仅仅是为了将成本入账同时也是为了战略决策的制定。作业成本法能比数量基础（传统）成本计算系统方法更好地给产品和劳务分配成本、分析加工过程、评价管理业绩和评估盈利能力。

作业成本法和传统成本法的差异

作业成本法和传统的成本计算法之间有着很多差异。由于在作业成本法下，成本的分解更为具体，成本分解的项目将得到更为仔细地分析。图表2-37给出了这两者之间的三项主要区别：

图表2-37　作业成本法和传统成本法

作业成本法	传统成本法
多个成本动因：作业和数量基础动因（无论哪一个都能很好地匹配成本）	仅有三种成本动因：只有数量基础具有普适性
间接成本先分配到各项作业中然后再分配到产品和劳务	间接成本先分配到各部门再分配到各个产品和劳务中
重心放在解决部门间的成本和加工问题	重心放在将单个成本和本部门的流程改进责任分派给各部门经理

作业成本法的优点和局限性

作业成本法的优点如下：

● 作业成本法减少了由传统成本分配造成的失真。在传统成本法下，如果间接成本较高的话，一件产品显得有利可图而另一件则显得逊色；在作业成本法下，第一件产品可能会消耗较多的资源同时其实际盈利能力比其他产品要低。

● 作业成本法给经理提供了一个了解相关产品的途径，从而能使产品在市场上更具竞争力。

● 作业成本法计量作业动因成本，允许管理层在改变产品设计和作业设计的同时了解其对总成本和价值的影响。

● 与传统产品成本法相比，作业成本法一般在较低产量情况下会产生较高的单位成本（这意味着在增加和舍弃某条生产线的问题上可以做出更好的决策）。

作业成本法的局限如下：

● 并不是所有的间接成本都和特定的成本动因相关联，当追踪动因的成本大于收益时，很有可能出现武断的分配。

● 即使有新的软件和数据库，作业成本法仍然需要大量的开发和维护时间。大多数项目的实施都需要一年多的时间。

● 作业成本法让经理改变了规则，所以抵制改变的行为很普遍。在没有高级管理层的支持下，很多经理不得不寻找权宜之计。

● 仅将作业成本法视为一项会计上的创举很可能会导致失败。

● 作业成本法下产生了大量的信息，过多的信息将误导经理将精力集中于不必要的数据上。

● 作业成本法并不遵照公认会计原则，所以重新披露的财务数据将增加费用同时会造成混淆。

生命周期成本法

如果需要提供比其他成本计算方法（通常为一年）更长时间的成本关系，就需要用到生命周期成本法。此种方法是考虑到产品和劳务整个生命周期的成本计算过程。

例如，药产品的生命周期是从研发，经历联邦政府的检验和产品设计期，然后经过生产、市场营销和分销，再到客户服务。在这一例子中，周期将被定义为产品专利权或其市场化的使用期限。

生命周期成本法有时被用作成本计划或产品定价。该方法的实施让公司将重心放在产品和劳务的综合成本上。早期不良设计只能导致更高的市场成本、服务成本和更低的销售额。产品生命周期的总成本一共有三个阶段：

● 上游成本。发生在产品生产和服务出售之前的成本，如研发成本和设计成本（原型、测试和工程）。

● 制造成本。为生产产品和提供劳务消耗的成本，如采购、直接和间接制造成本。

● 下游成本。是生产成本接下来（或同时）发生的成本。如市场营销、分销（包装、运输、装卸、促销和广告宣传）、服务成本和保修成本（残次品的回笼、销售退回和负债）。

生命周期成本法将其战略目标着眼于改善以上这三个阶段上。改善产品设计是上游阶段的关键；改善生产工序和供应商关系是制造阶段所着重强调的；由于在这两个阶段采取的有限措施限制了下游决策的制定，所以改善前两个阶段是降低下游成本的关键。换句话说，生命周期成本法试图让管理层在早期阶段采取积极的应对措施从而不必在下游阶段消极应付。

生命周期成本法与生命周期定价相关，具体参见 CMA 教材第三本书。

其他成本计算法

另外两种成本计算方法是经营成本计算法和（及时生产制中的）后推成本法。

经营成本计算法

经营成本计算法是一种将分批成本法和分步成本法相融合的成本计算方法。经营成本法在分配直接材料的方式上和分批成本法近似，即将直接材料分配到各批次或批量。但直接人工和间接成本（转换成本）则按照近似分步成本法的方式进行分配。这种混合成本系统对高数量作业同时不同批次需要不同的原材料的厂商十分适用。布料工业的成本不仅受衣服样式的影响同时还要受价格和同款不同色的影响。其他适合用经营成本法的产业包括纺织业、金属加工业、家具业、制鞋业和家电业。

考虑一个例子。一个生产扶手的金属加工业公司，其产品是金属和镀铬扶手。该公司有两个生产部门，一个部门生产所有的金属扶手然后将部分扶手转入到镀铬加工部门。假设公司本月生产了 1 000 件未镀铬和 500 件镀铬扶手，并且期初期末存货均为 0。经营成本计算法按批次追溯直接成本，按部门追溯转换成本（直接人工和间接成本），如图表 2-38 所示：

图表 2-38　总成本计算

直接材料		$30 000
批次 1　未镀铬扶手（1 000）		
批次 2　镀铬扶手（500）		
金属加工部门原材料	$15 000	
镀铬加工部门	$10 000	$25 000
总的直接材料		$55 000
转换成本		
金属加工部门		$45 000
镀铬加工部门		$10 000
总的转换成本		$55 000
总成本		$110 000

未镀铬和镀铬扶手的生产成本计算列于图表 2-39。注意，由于所有的扶手都在同一个金属加工部门加工处理，所以金属加工部门的加工成本里包含了所有的扶手。

图表 2-39　生产成本计算

直接材料			未镀铬扶手	镀铬扶手
批次 1	$\left[\dfrac{\$30\,000}{1\,000}\right]$		$30/扶手	
批次 2	$\left[\dfrac{\$25\,000}{500}\right]$			$50/扶手
转换成本　金属加工部门	$\left[\dfrac{\$45\,000}{1\,500}\right]$		$30/扶手	$30/扶手
转换成本　镀铬加工部门	$\left[\dfrac{\$10\,000}{500}\right]$		——	$20/扶手

续表

单位总成本	$60/扶手	$100/扶手

总产品成本
　　未镀铬扶手 $60×1 000 = $60 000
　　镀铬扶手 $100×500 = $50 000
　　总计 = $110 000

注意图表2-38和2-39中的总成本 $110 000 是一致的，这表明计算正确。

及时生产制下的后推成本法

及时制是生产资料仅当下一个生产步骤需要时才进行生产。引发在特定工作区域进行生产的要求来自于生产线的下一个工作站，因此及时生产制也称为"需求拉动"生产系统。顾客需求引发最初的生产，工作一直倒推到生产周期初期的原材料购买。及时制将生产过程划分为十分协调的工作单元，从而减少了生产准备期。及时制同时满足了原材料的及时交付和顾客需求，在保证高品质产品的同时将可能发生的成本降到了最低。因此，使用及时制的企业组织一般都有极少的存货，并且由于在会计期间，成本流直接流入产品销售成本中，所以存货计价方法的选择（如先进先出法和加权平均法）和存货成本计算方法（如吸收成本法和变动成本法）都不再相关。及时制五项最突出的特点为：

- 单元加工。每一个单元都集合了为生产特定产品所需的所有不同种类的仪器设备，目的是将材料处理成本最小化。

- 多技能的员工。员工通过工作分担和其他方式进行交叉训练来维持劳动力的灵活性（例如，那些被训练维持机器正常运转的员工同时要求能进行少量维修工作）。

- 全面质量管理。全面质量管理旨在减少残次品。由于最低的存货储存量和连接紧密的生产加工环节造成每一个残次品的影响都非常严重，因此，全面质量管理是及时生产制的一个必要要求。

- 减少生产准备期和安装调试时间。在及时生产制下，首先要考虑的事情是减少安装工具、仪器和准备初期材料所需的时间，同时减少开始加工和产品完成之间（生产准备期）的时间。考虑到较少的存货，减少的安装调试时间允许厂商可以经济地运行较小批量的生产。一旦生产准备期得到减少，产品的生产就可以迅速响应客户需求的变化。

- 稳固的供应商关系。及时生产制要求严格筛选供应商以确保原材料的及时送达。及时生产的前提是及时采购，以确保原材料按需送达并将原材料存货保持在最低量。例如，值得信任的供应商可以与公司间实现直接电子链接，这样供应商就可以按要求发货，不用等待发票和采用标准的采购程序。供应商也可以直接将货物运至生产车间而不是仓库。

传统的成本计算系统运用的是连续追踪，即按发生顺序记录存货和各账户的采购过程和成本运动过程。连续追踪通过以下四阶段周期来追踪成本：

- 阶段一：购买直接材料（原材料存货分录）。

- 阶段二：生产（半成品库存分录）。
- 阶段三：好的产成品的完成（产成品存货分录）。
- 阶段四：产成品的销售（产品销售成本分录）。

每一阶段的分录被称为触发点。

及时制造后推成本法是为不采用连续追踪的及时生产制量身定做的成本计算系统，它忽略部分或全部生产周期中的会计分录。这一系统之所以被称为及时制造后推成本法是因为当会计分录在生产周期的某些步骤被忽略时，用正常和标准成本逆向追溯发生成本，将成本差异部门冲刷掉，同时对遗失的步骤填写分录。其中一个最常见的被跳过的步骤是半成品库存分录，因为及时生产制减少了材料在这一阶段停留的时间。

及时制造后推成本法并不严格遵守公认会计原则，例如在使用时，即使实际上确实存在半成品并应该将其记为资产，但是通常忽略半成品库存项目。很多企业运用倒溯成本法是因为这些项目并不重要。当这些项目重要时，应估计这些项目的数额并调整入账。及时制造后推成本法可以节省公司的会计成本，但是有人批评说它由于没有清晰的核查记录（给各生产阶段进行资源的精确定位）而造成了风险。有些存货的数量很少，经理可以通过简单的观察或计算机操控便可以进行生产运行的追踪。

运用及时生产制的公司将是以后运用倒溯成本法的主要成员，但具有快速的生产交货周期和/或十分稳定的存货水平的企业都能够使用倒溯成本法。

进度检查

提示：完成以下各题。参考答案随后给出。

1. 下列哪一项成本计算系统最适合于科研成本占总成本相当数量的公司？
   - （　　）a. 分批成本法
   - （　　）b. 分步成本法
   - （　　）c. 作业成本法
   - （　　）d. 生命周期成本法

2. 一个邮局想要为其大量的邮件分类仓库实施一个成本归集系统。下面哪一项方法最适合于这种情况？
   - （　　）a. 生命周期成本法
   - （　　）b. 作业成本法
   - （　　）c. 分步成本法
   - （　　）d. 分批成本法

3. 下列哪一项对公司没有经济价值？
   - （　　）a. 非正常废品
   - （　　）b. 正常废品
   - （　　）c. 返工品
   - （　　）d. 残料

4. 一个公司用分步成本法（先进先出）。在一定的会计期内，没有期初半成品库存，期末半成品完成 60%（10 000 件实物产品），如果当期完成品有 20 000 件，那么总的约当产量是多少？

(　　　) a. 20 000

(　　　) b. 26 000

(　　　) c. 32 000

(　　　) d. 34 000

进度检查答案

1. d

2. c

3. d

4. b

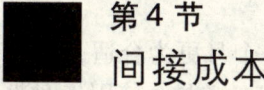

第 4 节
间接成本

本节内容简介

由于间接成本不仅包括间接制造成本、一般管理费用，也包括工厂和机器的折旧，所以间接成本的数额可以相当大。间接成本可以是产品成本也可以是期间成本。产品成本可以资本化到存货项目，而期间成本必须在其发生期间费用化。

本节探讨了固定和变动间接成本、工厂范围和部门间接成本、作业成本法下的间接成本分摊、如何决定分摊基础（换句话说，即选择成本动因）以及服务部门成本的分摊。

固定和变动间接费用

间接费用可以是固定成本或变动成本。固定成本包括资产的折旧、租赁成本和行政工资。这些成本假设在关联范围和产量水平保持一致的条件下，在一定的会计期间内不发生改变。变动成本包括电费、水费、污水处理费、工程支持、机器维修费和间接材料。变动成本随特定的成本动因（数量基础或作业基础）成比例变化。

固定间接成本

根据定义，大多数固定成本都是定期设置的，所以日常经营对固定成本的影响很小。规划固定间接成本的时间框架有两个阶段：设定优先级并有效地履行这些优先级。设定优先级是指公司应决定哪些固定间接成本应该或必须承担（那些是没有附加价值并应处理掉的），同时决定哪些固定成本最为重要。汽车租赁公司应将租用或购买合适数量的汽车作为最高优先级的固定成本，以确保有足够的汽车满足要求，同时不会造成大量待租车辆的闲置。

第二个阶段是有效地履行优先级：哪些成本最有可能通过精心规划而得到降低。在同样的例子下，租赁公司将决定哪一项最具成本效益：是租赁还是购买汽车？同时选择在行驶过程中最不会出现故障的车辆品牌或同车辆生产商协商最优惠的价格。

变动间接成本

规划变动间接成本的时间框架同样也有两个阶段：设定优先级并有效地履行这些优先级。为变动成本设定优先级包括决定哪些经济活动能为客户带来增值以及哪些经济活动应被剔除。汽车租赁公司可能会剔除文书工作步骤或自动化整个流程以降低变动管理成本并改善客户服务。变动成本不同于固定成本，变动成本受日常运营的影响，所以优先级的履行应是一个持续不断的过程，例如在出租业务低迷时，有计划地安排出租车辆的维修将不会影响企业的经营。

固定间接成本分摊率

即使一项经济活动发生大范围的波动，固定间接成本在一定时期内也不会发生改变。固定间接成本分摊率的确定涉及四个步骤：

1. 确定适当的会计期间。以一年作为时间基础通常比用一个月更为合适，原因在于大多数公司想要平滑因为季节性因素和每个月不同天数带来的差异。使用年度期间也能确保经理能够在每个月做出新的预算。

2. 确定固定间接成本的分摊基础（成本动因）。成本动因前面已讨论过。公司可以使用数量基础成本动因和作业基础成本动因。虽然固定成本并不发生变动，但仍需按固定成本所提供的价值比例进行分摊。例如，假如某网球制造商使用机器小时作为固定成本动因，公司预计每年需用 40 000 个机器小时来生产 200 000 箱网球。

3. 确定和每一个成本分摊基础（成本动因）相关的固定间接成本。固定间接成本应被划分到任何一个能够最好地衡量其价值提供的成本池当中。在这个例子中，所有的固定间接成本同机器小时这一成本分摊基础相关。一年中总的固定间接成本是 $1 000 000。

4. 在将固定间接成本分摊到成本对象时，计算每一个分摊基础的单位分摊率：

$$固定间接成本的适用分摊率 = \frac{固定间接成本池中的总成本}{所有分摊基础的数量}$$

$$= \frac{\$1\ 000\ 000}{40\ 000\ 机器小时}$$

$$= \$25/机器小时$$

使用越多分摊基础的业务运营将会分摊到越多的固定成本。

预算的变动间接成本分摊率

预算的变动间接成本分摊率和预算的固定间接成本分摊率的计算过程和步骤相同。因此，其计算步骤就不在这里重复了，只需要在上述适用分摊率的计算过程中，将"固定"简单地替换为"变动"即可。

工厂范围和部门的间接成本以及作业成本法下的间接成本分摊

有两个或更多个生产部门的公司可以将其工厂间接成本按下列方法分摊到批次或产品中去：

- 全厂间接成本分摊率。
- 部门间接成本分摊率。
- 作业成本下的间接成本分摊。

工厂范围间接成本分摊率

工厂范围间接成本分摊率是发生在生产设备上的用来分配所有间接成本的单一分摊率。总的工厂间接成本分摊率由下列公式决定：

$$工厂范围间接成本分摊率 = \frac{总的工厂间接成本}{适合全厂所有作业的总成本动因（分摊基础）}$$

从本质上说，由于工厂范围分摊是非常笼统的，仅适用于该单一成本动因可以和所有类型的生产都相关的时候。如果工厂生产中一部分属高度自动化型，另一部分属劳动密集型，那么在不同的区域应使用不同的成本动因，工厂范围间接成本分摊率就不适用了。部门间接成本分摊率比工厂范围分摊率更为精确些。

部门间接成本分摊率

部门间接成本分摊率是每一个特定的生产部门都使用单一的间接成本分摊率。每一个生产部门都可以基于其成本动因来计算各自的分摊率，部门间接成本分摊率的计算如下：

$$部门间接成本分摊率 = \frac{总的部门间接成本}{适合该部门所有作业的总成本动因}$$

每一个间接成本数额的会计处理都由各个工厂间接成本进行追踪，并将间接成本数额应用到每一个部门中。和工厂范围分摊率一样，部门间接成本分摊率也是一个相当笼统的分摊率。所以，如果成本动因的选择不能和部门内所有的经济业务活动真实相关，那么成本就会被分配不当。

当部门产品是同质同性并且如果每一项工作都和选择的成本动因具有因果关系，那么部门间接成本动因就应采纳使用。当这种情况不存在时，就应设定不同的成本动因和相关的成本池。不当分配成本所带来的危害已经在前面详细阐述过了：一些产品的实际盈利能力大于按错误成本分配所计算的盈利能力（即低估了一些产品的盈利能力），而另一些产品的盈利能力又遭到高估，这都将造成生产线上的错误管理。

作业成本法下的间接成本分摊

当工厂范围和部门间接成本分摊都不够精确时，就应考虑使用作业成本法下的间接成本分摊。作业成本法下的间接成本分摊是使用多种成本池和多种成本动因以将间接成本分摊到产品和劳务中去。成本动因可以基于因果关系选择，同时也能够以作业为基础和以产量为基础。

为更多地了解作业成本法下的间接成本分摊，请参看本章的第 3 节。

图表 2 - 40 展示了一个成本池和成本动因样本。

图表 2 - 40　成本池、动因和预设的动因分摊率

间接成本池	预算的间接成本	成本动因	件　数	预设的动因分摊率
公共事业	$100 000	机器小时	10 000	$10/机器小时
材料处理	$120 000	材料重量（磅）	40 000	$3/磅
安装	$90 000	安装次数	300	$300/安装小时
	$310 000			

上面例子中的预设动因分摊率通过预算的总间接成本除以总的成本动因数量得到。在有两项或更多订单或产品的情况下，这一系统的精确性便展现出来了。

例如，假设如上表所描述的，在当期有两份订单。订单 1 使用了 4 000 个机器小时，30 000 磅的直接材料和 100 次机器安装，订单 2 使用了 6 000 个机器小时，10 000 磅的直接材料和 200 次机器安装。每一份订单所分配的成本其计算过程展示在图表 2 - 41 中。

图表2-41 作业成本和工厂范围间接成本的分摊

			作业成本	工厂范围
订单1	公共事业	$10/机器小时×4 000 小时 = $40 000		
订单1	材料处理	$3/磅×30 000 小时 = $90 000		
订单1	安装	$300/安装次数×100 次 = $30 000		
		总计 = $160 000		$124 000
订单2	公共事业	$10/机器小时×6 000 小时 = $60 000		
订单2	材料处理	$3/磅×10 000 小时 = $30 000		
订单2	安装	$300/安装次数×200 次 = $60 000		
		总计 = $150 000		$186 000
		$310 000		$310 000

为了便于比较，如果全厂分摊率使用机器小时作为惟一的成本动因，则总的间接成本 $310 000 除以 10 000 机器小时得到单位成本为 $31/机器小时，再乘以 4 000 小时，订单1 的成本为 $124 000；6 000 机器小时下计算出来的订单2 的成本是 $186 000。

注意作业成本法下分配得出的两种产品的成本和工厂范围内成本法相比有很大差异。

确定分摊基础（成本动因）

无论是被指定用于间接成本分摊的全厂法、部门法还是作业成本法，分摊基础的选择或成本动因都至关重要。选择分摊基础的方法和标准在前面讨论成本动因问题时已有涉及。

服务部门的成本分摊

公司有两个基本的部门类型，即生产部门和服务部门。到目前为止，我们谈论的都是关于生产部门的问题。服务部门并不直接参与经营活动，而是作为生产部门、客户和员工的辅助部门存在。日常维护、内部审计、企业食堂、信息技术、人力资源、采购、仓储、客户服务、工程服务、成本会计等都属于服务部门的范畴。

服务部门的成本分摊有以下三个阶段：

- 阶段一：追踪所有直接成本并将间接成本分摊到所有部门（生产部门和其他服务部门）。
- 阶段二：将特定服务部门的成本分摊到生产部门或其他服务部门。
- 阶段三：将生产部门的成本分摊到产品中。

将服务部门的成本分摊到其他部门是因为大部分服务部门并不产生利润，服务部门是成本中心。当一个服务部门产生收入时，如食堂或修理部门，我们将这些收入实际冲销成本后的净成本转移到产生直接收入的生产部门。

阶段一：追踪所有直接成本并将间接成本分摊到所有部门

阶段一的第一个作业是追溯直接成本到生产和服务部门。这与追溯直接成本至生产成本的方法一样，因此这里不再赘述。间接成本分摊至服务部门的方法也可参照前面描述的将间接成本分摊至生产部门的方法。然而，成本动因（分摊基础）在类型上有些许不同。例如，洗衣部门可能以要洗的衣服作为成本动因载体；食堂则以可能提供的膳食数量作为成本动因载体。各种服务部门使用的其他常见的成本动因列示如下：

- 医疗部门：处理的就诊次数。
- 数据处理部门：个人电脑的数量、CPU 运行时间、使用的存储空间大小。
- 搬运部门：工作时间、搬运数量。
- 成本会计：工作时间、服务的对象。
- 运输和接收部门：处理的数量、请购数量、工作时间。
- 维护部门：机器工作时间。
- 清洁服务：大厦面积。

总的来说，经理人员是最后分摊这些成本的人，因此我们应选择那些让经理们容易理解的成本动因。成本动因分摊率和成本动因的总单位都可以用实际、标准（预算）分摊率或单位（也可以用一些综合分摊率，如标准成本动因分摊率与实际成本动因单位的乘积）。使用标准成本动因分摊率时，由于某一期间的成本动因分摊率可以计算出来，因此这种方法可以激励服务部门经理控制成本。然而，这样一来，标准成本和实际成本的差异会导致少分配和多分配成本的问题（关于少分配和多分配成本的问题可以参见本章第 2 节的"实际成本法/正常成本法/标准成本法"中的阐述）。运用实际成本动因或实际数量可以准确地分摊成本，但是分摊行为只有在一个期间结束后才能完成，因此这种方法不能达到控制当期成本的目的。

这里介绍两种基本的成本分摊方法：单一比率法和边际贡献法。单一比率成本分摊法为一个部门的固定和变动成本创造一个单一的分摊基础，即为成本分摊提供一个单一的单位比率。如果一个项目固定成本为 100 万美元，变动成本为每机器小时 50 美元、有 5 000 个机器小时，那么总的成本分摊率为 [＄1 000 000 ＋（5 000 × ＄50）]／5 000 ＝ ＄250／机器小时。然而，当我们将固定成本和变动成本集合在一起时，会使整体成本看起来都是变动的，这样一来，可能会诱使经理们寻求外包以获得更低的成本分摊率。由于不管部门是否运行，固定成本都会存在（特别是从短期考虑），因此在这些固定的内部成本发生的同时，部门还会负担新的外部成本。

边际贡献成本分摊法，也叫双重比率法，为服务部门成本的分摊分别创造固定和变动成本池。每个成本池有自己的分摊基础，如变动成本采用人工工时而固定成本采用机器工时。由于采用不同的成本动因和分摊率以及标准或实际成本动因或者标准或实际分摊率的使用，边际贡献法计算出的预计总成本与单一比率法下计算出的预计总成本将存在差异。例如，采用与前例相同的数据，假定 100 万美元的固定成本以人工工时为基础分摊（共耗费了 4 900 个人工工时），那么固定分摊率为 ＄204／人工工时、变动分摊率为 ＄50／机器小时。一种分摊方法下每一类成本都会分别计算（详见阶段二），因而要计算出总成本将需要两倍的计算量。如果正确使用了作业成本法的规则，这种分摊方法更为准确且可产生更佳的管理决策，但是由于复杂的计算和成本分类的难度，它也会带来较高的管理成本。

阶段二：将特定服务部门的成本分摊到生产部门或其他服务部门

阶段二是将特定服务部门的成本分摊到生产部门或其他服务部门。将成本分摊到其他服务部门也称部门间服务或互惠服务，如服务于食堂和清洁部门的保管服务。我们主要使用以下三种方法：直接分摊法、按步向下分摊法以及互相分摊法。从分摊方法上讲，单一比率法被用在以下描述的所有例子中。然而，边际贡献法可以应用在任何一种方法中。

直接分摊法

顾名思义，直接分摊法是最直接和最简单的分摊服务部门成本的方法。这种方法不能用于将成本分摊到其他服务部门，它只能用于将成本分摊至生产部门。即使当一个服务部门为另一服务部门提供了相当可观的服务时，这个方法也绕过此考虑而直接将所有成本分摊至生产部门。直接成本法忽视了与服务部门相关的成本动因而只集中考虑归因于生产部门的成本动因。以图表 2 - 42 为例，它展示了一个公司的四个部门。

图表 2 - 42　部门成本和成本动因

	服　　务		生　　产	
	人力资源	清洁卫生服务	金属加工部门	镀铬部门
分摊前部门成本	$200 000	$80 000	$400 000	$100 000
人工工时	10 000	5 000	20 000	5 000
占用面积（平方英尺）	15 000	500	60 000	20 000

在这个例子中，人力资源部门的成本应使用生产部门的人工工时，清洁卫生部门应使用生产部门的面积指标，计算如下：

$$部门分摊 = \frac{生产部门总产品}{所有生产部门总产品} \times 部门成本$$

$$金属加工部门的人力资源成本 = \frac{20\ 000}{20\ 000 + 5\ 000} \times \$200\ 000 = 0.8 \times \$200\ 000$$
$$= \$160\ 000$$

$$镀铬部门的人力资源成本 = 0.2 \times \$200\ 000 = \$40\ 000$$

$$金属加工部门的清洁卫生成本 = \frac{60\ 000}{60\ 000 + 20\ 000} \times \$80\ 000 = 0.75 \times \$80\ 000$$
$$= \$60\ 000$$

$$镀铬部门的清洁卫生成本 = 0.25 \times \$80\ 000 = \$20\ 000$$

金属加工部门的总成本是 $620 000（$400 000 + $160 000 + $60 000），镀铬部门的总成本是 $160 000（$100 000 + $40 000 + $20 000）。这种分摊是建立在仅有两个生产部门的基础上的。虽然如此，直接分摊法并没有考虑部门间交叉服务的情况。例如，清洁卫生部门同时也为人力资源部门提供清洁服务，这意味着这两个生产部门不精确的成本百分比。

按步向下分摊法

按步向下分摊法将一个部门的服务成本分配到服务部门和生产部门。这一方法循序渐进地分摊服务部门的成本，开始于为其他部门提供服务最多的部门，结束于为其他部门提供服务最少的部门。后续部门需要分摊的成本逐步降低。

按步向下分摊法考虑到了部门之间的相互服务问题。和直接分摊法一样，成本动因分摊率的计算仅涉及那些接收到成本分摊的部门。

例如，继续使用前面的例子，人力资源成本将首先被分摊，然后是清洁卫生部门。一个真实的公司将拥有成百的部门。

图表 2-43 展示了用按步向下分摊法来分摊成本的过程。

图表 2-43 按步向下分摊法

	服 务		生 产	
	人力资源	清洁卫生服务	金属加工部门	镀铬部门
分摊前部门成本	$200 000	$80 000	$400 000	$100 000
第一步：	($200 000)	$33 333	$133 334	$33 333
小计	$0	$113 333	$533 334	$133 333
第二步：		($113 333)	$85 000	$28 333
总计	$0	$0	$618 334	$161 666
人工工时	10 000	5 000	20 000	5 000
占用面积（平方英尺）	15 000	500	60 000	20 000

人力资源部门的成本分摊用该部门的人工工时除以清洁卫生、金属加工和镀铬部门的总人工工时。然后将这些成本追加到各部门中去（第一步；为了简化，例子采用了一些近似计算）。在第二步中，新的总清洁卫生成本按照平方英尺将成本分摊到生产部门。在现实情况下，这些成本不仅分摊到生产部门，同时也分摊到其他各个服务部门（其他具有较低分摊成本的部门）中去。但是，所有成本最后都汇总在创收生产部门。

将计算的成本和直接分摊法相比，金属加工部门的成本略高，镀铬部门的成本略低。按步向下分摊法为成本分摊提供了更为精确的方法。但是，正如以上所看到的，部分成本的分摊仍然是扭曲的。例如，即使人力资源部门有很大平方英尺的地面由清洁部门打扫，但是清洁成本仍没有分摊到人力资源部门。

交叉分摊法

交叉分摊法是使用联立方程对部门间服务成本进行全面确认。相反，按步向下分摊法仅将部分成本进行了分摊，因为其并不向后分摊成本，只向前。

交叉分摊法的第一步是建立一个方程组。使用上述金属加工车间的例子：

$$人力资源部门成本 = \$200\,000 + \left(\frac{15\,000}{15\,000 + 60\,000 + 20\,000} \times 清洁部门成本 \right)$$

$$清洁部门成本 = \$80\,000 + \left(\frac{5\,000}{5\,000 + 20\,000 + 5\,000} \times 人力资源部门成本 \right)$$

$$人力资源部门成本 = \$200\,000 + 0.15789（清洁部门成本）$$

$$清洁部门成本 = \$80\,000 + 0.16667（人力资源部门成本）$$

$$人力资源部门成本 = \$200\,000 + 0.15789[\,\$80\,000 + 0.16667（人力资源部门成本）]$$

人力资源部门成本 = \$200 000 + \$12 631.20 + 0.02632（人力资源部门成本）

（1 − 0.02632）（人力资源部门成本）= \$212 613.20

0.97368（人力资源部门成本）= \$212 613.20

$$人力资源部门成本 = \frac{\$212\ 613.20}{0.97368} = \$218\ 378.93$$

人力资源部门成本 ≈ \$218 379

解出人力资源部门的总成本并将其分摊到清洁、金属加工和镀铬部门。这个数值将大于 \$200 000 部门成本。最后将新的总清洁部门成本分摊给人力资源、金属加工和镀铬部门。最后将所有的成本仅分摊到生产部门。

	人力资源部门	清洁部门	金属加工部门	镀铬部门
成本	\$200 000	\$80 000	\$400 000	\$100 000
步骤一	（\$218 379）	\$36 397	\$145 586	\$36 397
步骤二	* \$18 379	（\$116 397）	* \$73 514	* \$24 505
	0	0	\$619 100	\$160 902

* 由于近似计算造成的差异

尽管交叉分摊法是一种真实确认并且是最精确的方法，但由于其计算的复杂性同时由于按步向下分摊法提供了更具成本效益的合理近似的成本计算方法，所以交叉分摊法很少被使用。虽然计算机程序简化了交叉分摊法的计算，但很多公司仍不愿使用这一方法。

阶段三：将生产部门的成本分摊到产品中

参见本章变动成本法中的讲述。

进度检查

提示：完成以下各题。参考答案随后给出。

1. 下列哪一项往往随日常运营情况而变动？
   （　　）a. 固定间接成本的优先级
   （　　）b. 变动间接成本的优先级
   （　　）c. 工厂范围内间接成本分摊率
   （　　）d. 部门间接成本分配率

2. 一个公司有两种产品，一种是劳动密集型，一种是高度机械化的。该公司应采用下列哪一个间接成本分摊率？
   （　　）a. 部门间接成本分摊率
   （　　）b. 作业成本法下的间接成本分摊率
   （　　）c. 工厂范围内间接成本分摊率
   （　　）d. 机械加工过程采用部门分摊率，在其他领域采用工厂范围分摊率

3. 下列哪一项是将服务部门的成本逐步分摊到生产和其他服务部门，并开始于为其他部门提供服务最多的部门，结束于为其他部门提供服务最少的部门（不将成本分摊给服务成本高于自身的

部门）？

(　　) a. 直接分摊法

(　　) b. 按步向下分摊法

(　　) c. 交叉分摊法

(　　) d. 间接分摊法

进度检查答案

1. b

2. a

3. b

第 3 章
信息管理

本章内容简介

计算机的出现第一次使单个系统自动化，比如创建一个总分类账的数据库，但信息仍然需要通过人工传达到不同部门。这些单个系统此后被整合，数据管理也被置于企业整体层面上运行。本章涵盖了信息系统、信息系统类型和用途、信息系统设计、网络基础、数据库原理、人工智能的形式，以及电子商务的形式。

学习要点说明

注册管理会计师（CMA）考试包含很多学习要点，这些学习要点由管理会计师协会确定。学习要点描述了注册管理会计师考试要求掌握的所有知识点和技能，并且细分为各个章节。注册管理会计师考试教材解释了学习要点所包含的各个部分，是对学习要点的有力支持。学习要点可以帮助考生以不同的方式或通过不同的问题情景理解这些概念。考生还应该练习学习要点中所提到的全部或者部分计算，或者完成计算过程中的缺失部分。学习要点不能代替对 CMA 考试教材内容的研究和学习，但是可以确保考生达到学习要点所设定的目标。

注册管理会计师教材中所包含的学习要点是一个完整的集合，并且是到目前为止最新的版本。考生可以浏览 IMA 的官方网站 www. imanet. org，点击"认证"部分查看和下载关于学习要点的最新 PDF 文件。

管理会计与报告（第二版）

学习要点

3.1　信息系统的性质和用途

- LOS 3.1.1：识别企业信息系统的不同类型，例如，交易处理、管理信息、决策支持等系统。
- LOS 3.1.2：解释信息系统的功能，包括交易处理和数据分析。
- LOS 3.1.3：区分集中式和分散式的信息系统，并识别它们各自的优缺点。
- LOS 3.1.4：识别和定义交易处理系统处理数据的两种基本方式：（1）批处理；（2）即时处理。
- LOS 3.1.5：解释管理信息系统怎样用来解决组织中的暂时性和财务性问题，以提高企业竞争优势。

3.2　系统开发和设计

- LOS 3.2.1：解释为什么最终用户和信息技术专家应根据组织的商务流程分析和信息需求分析来设计信息系统，以及为什么应该对商务流程进行恰当的定义和注释。
- LOS 3.2.2：定义系统开发生命周期（SDLC）。
- LOS 3.2.3：简述 SDLC 的步骤和及其相互关系。
- LOS 3.2.4：定义系统开发工具原型，简述其较传统 SDLC 技术的优越之处。
- LOS 3.2.5：定义快速应用开发（RAD）工具。
- LOS 3.2.6：定义面向对象的分析和设计。
- LOS 3.2.7：阐述系统可行性研究。如成本—收益分析，它包括显性收益的隐性收益。
- LOS 3.2.8：识别成本—收益分析中的显性收益和隐性收益。

3.3　信息系统技术

- LOS 3.3.1：识别使用电信系统的优点，它使企业能以较低的成本进行远程数据传输，在全球范围的多节点进行信息处理。
- LOS 3.3.2：阐述通讯网络的不同类型。
- LOS 3.3.3：描述广域网（WAN）和局域网（LAN）。
- LOS 3.3.4：阐述客户端/服务器网络。
- LOS 3.3.5：定义"对等"网络。
- LOS 3.3.6：识别在客户端/服务器网络上，软件和数据库的应用之处。
- LOS 3.3.7：区分主机系统和客户端/服务器网络的应用，识别各自优缺点。
- LOS 3.3.8：理解数据库管理系统并描述其特征。
- LOS 3.3.9：区分扁平型数据库和关系型数据库。
- LOS 3.3.10：理解关系型数据库系统。
- LOS 3.3.11：理解决策支持系统，理解它们的运作以及系统所支持的决策类型。
- LOS 3.3.12：定义人工智能，包括专家系统、模糊逻辑和类神经网络，以及解释它们怎样用软件得到管理信息。
- LOS 3.3.13：介绍怎样用表格表单来进行商务分析、计划和建模。
- LOS 3.3.14：构造用于会计、商务报告或分析用途的表格表单。
- LOS 3.3.15：分析表格表单的细节，确定引起错误的公式及其改正。

- LOS 3.3.16：描述互联网和识别骨干网的成分。
- LOS 3.3.17：定义浏览器软件。
- LOS 3.3.18：定义企业内部网，解释其用途。
- LOS 3.3.19：理解内部网如何使企业在组织单元中共享专家知识。
- LOS 3.3.20：定义虚拟私有网络，理解如何使用。

3.4　电子商务

- LOS 3.4.1：定义和识别电子数据交换（EDI）的主要特征。
- LOS 3.4.2：解释 EDI 是如何不同于以互联网为基础的电子商务应用。
- LOS 3.4.3：定义公共钥匙密码法，理解如何在网络中使用。
- LOS 3.4.4：定义 B2B（企业对企业）电子商务及其特征。
- LOS 3.4.5：概述互联网对 B2B 电子商务的重要性。
- LOS 3.4.6：理解 B2B 电子商务是如何影响供应链。
- LOS 3.4.7：理解其他的电子商务技术，包括在线交易处理和电子资金转账。

3.5　综合的企业整体数据模型

- LOS 3.5.1：定义企业整体规划（EWP）和它的特征，包括它对于企业整体数据库的依赖。
- LOS 3.5.2：解释为什么运作的流程要重组并与企业资源计划（ERP）高度匹配。
- LOS 3.5.3：描述企业整体数据库（数据仓库）。
- LOS 3.5.4：定义数据挖掘。
- LOS 3.5.5：理解数据仓库是如何帮助数据挖掘。
- LOS 3.5.6：定义数据分库。
- LOS 3.5.7：定义面向对象型数据库。
- LOS 3.5.8：理解结构化查询语言（SQL）是如何用来检索、更新和添加信息到关系型数据库的。
- LOS 3.5.9：定义在线分析处理。

第1节
信息系统的性质和用途

本节内容简介

本节区分了不同类型的企业信息系统及其主要用户，这些用户可以是不同的工作人员，比如可以是中层经理或知识工作者，也可以是企业部门或经营流程。本节还探讨了如何用信息管理系统处理数据。

企业信息系统

图表2-44显示了四种企业信息的基本层次，范围包括最精练的战略层（具有高层次、长期分析和与决策制定紧密相关等特点）直至日常记录和报告的运作层。信息使用者的数量在逐层递增，顶层的使用者很少而底层的使用者很多。企业信息系统还面向企业主要的职能部门，如销售或会计，从战略到运作每个层次都有相关的软件支持。

本节涵盖了企业信息系统（BIS）的基本层次、基本类型和企业职能。

战略层

战略层信息系统帮助高层经理对公司战略的理解和规划。这些系统能够提供有关企业内部的优势和弱势以及企业外部的威胁和机会的信息。高层经理用这些信息帮助他们把企业内部优势和最优的外部机会联系起来，从而制定出企业战略。

战略层信息系统帮助制定长期计划（如五年计划），如产品计划，资金预算，人员编制。

图表2-44 企业信息系统的层次和类型

层次	服务对象	系统类型	举 例
战略	高层经理	高管支持系统（ESS）	五年计划（销售趋势、营业计划、预算预测）、利润计划、人事规划
管理	中层经理	管理信息系统（MIS）	存货控制、总预算、资本预算、销售管理、会计信息系统（AIS）的简略水平
		决策支持系统（DSS）	生产调度、产品成本、价格和盈利分析、销售区域分析
		专家系统（ES）	资本预算、风险分析、投资组合管理
知识	知识和数据员工	知识工作系统（KWS）	工作站（工程的、制图的、管理的）
		办公系统	文字处理、文档成像、日程计划和电子日历
运作	基层经理；部门员工	交易处理系统（TPS）	会计：薪水支付、应付账款、应收账款 财务：安全贸易、现金管理、会计信息系统事项处理 销售和市场营销：订单的跟踪和处理 策划执行：厂房调度、机器控制和材料运转控制 人力资源：薪酬、培训、员工记录

高管支持系统（ESS）

高管支持系统（ESS）向高层经理提供所需信息，帮助他们制定战略，而非日常性决策。这些系统不能直接制定决策或是解决具体问题，而仅仅是帮助高层经理制定决策。ESS 提供的信息来源于决策支持系统和管理信息系统的内部信息，以及诸如新的财务报告要求或竞争对手情况等外部信息，并对其进行汇总。ESS 能提供有效的信息，是因为它过滤、合并和跟踪重要信息，减少了审查所有数据的时间，并通过使用先进的图形、表格和图表来突出重要信息。ESS 能提供可靠的信息，是因为它通过公司的其他系统得到即时的内部信息，通过可信赖的外部渠道如道琼斯、标准普尔、盖洛普民意测验和互联网新闻得到即时的外部信息。

不同于决策支持系统，ESS 只使用少量的分析模型。模型只是一个抽象，它将一个工序或事件进行简化、编码、制成决策点，使电脑能够对其进行处理。分析性模型试图通过更高水平的思考来进行决策。而经理层的决策不能定义为一个模型，因为高管人员面临太多不同的问题而需要人工判断。因此，高管支持系统主要进行信息的综合和分析，而把决策的制定留给高层经理。

管理层

管理层信息系统帮助中层经理监督和控制员工的活动。这些系统还能帮助他们制定决策和完成管理任务。大多数管理层系统只是提供期间报告而不是即时信息。这些报告帮助经理了解项目是否按预算进行，如重点查看与期望结果的偏差。有些系统还能模拟各种项目的可能结果——它们考虑"假如……将会……"问题，例如，如果在现有的生产能力上再增加一条新生产线将会怎样。

管理信息系统（MIS）

管理信息系统（MIS）是为经理提供报告和在线取得即时的商业记录而设计的软件。大多数 MIS 是内部导向的而不提供外部信息。为了方便计划，控制和制定决策，MIS 通过公司的交易处理系统获得信息并对其进行分类归纳。这些信息可以从各个部门和数据库提取。例如，会计信息系统具有某些管理信息系统的特点，如预测、预算和管理分析，不过它是从交易层面的会计信息系统和其他的数据库取得数据的，如为了比较实际与计划的结果，报告需要将来自总分类账的销售数据和来自总预算的数据进行综合比较。MIS 报告不是日常报告而是周、月和年度报告。大多数 MIS 报告是定期发布的，预先规定提交的报告即预定义报告，但是经理也可以在有必要的时候定义特别报告（或把这些新的报告类型另存为标准报告）。MIS 也可使用信息技术（IT）部门的数据，但它属于另外一种类型。

决策支持系统（DSS）

相对于 MIS 主要是历史信息记录报告，决策支持系统（DSS）帮助中层经理用内部和外部信息来做分析。内部信息来自于交易处理系统和 MIS。外部信息是类似于股价，竞争对手的价格或折让和运费等信息。DSS 帮助解决这样的问题，即我们没有预先定义程序和我们需要在快速变化的环境中迅速提出方案，解决问题。DSS 通常会预先构建分析模型，模型能比较各种商务关系和生成财务比率。DSS 也会合并数据并以图形的形式呈现出来。许多 DSS 允许用户进行他们自己的分析，汇总他们自己的各种数据，以及询问数据库新问题（特别问题）。决策支持系统还包括专业数据库，互动的以计算机为基础的建模程序，以及决策制定者个人的看法和判断。

DSS 还在本章的第 3 节中有介绍，"信息系统的技术"。

专家系统（ES）

专家系统（ES）是一种变化了的人工智能，它对专家的分析推理过程进行编程，这些程序能帮助人们制定决策。

知识层

知识层系统允许知识和数据工作者收集和汇总新知识进入企业。数据工作者用系统来简化和监督日常文书工作的流程和工作量。

知识工作系统（KWS）

知识工作者是在其领域内的专业人员，如医生、律师、工程师、科学家和研究员。知识工作系统（KWS）是一个专门帮助各行专业人员创建新信息的系统。例如，一个工程设计工作站从不同的工程师那里收集新的知识，并确保将其他工程师的工作整合起来。

办公系统

办公系统帮助知识工作者和数据工作者收集和处理数据。数据工作者是主要处理信息而非创建信息的工作者，如办公室经理、图书管理员以及秘书。办公系统是软件应用的一个大类，包括员工之间、工作之间的沟通和内部协调，如文字编辑、桌面排版、文档影像系统（把文本文档转化为电子格式）、电子目录、网页、电子邮件系统。

运作层

运作层系统允许基层经理为自己的部门记录和跟踪相关的信息，如销售、薪水支付、赊购、收到发票、存款和所有其他有关的交易数据。这些系统通常被合并以使大量冗长信息最小化。例如，赊购、赊销和客户支持数据库都使用同一客户信息数据库，而不是各自使用自己独立的数据库。从财务报告到存货跟踪，企业的各个方面都使用运作层系统。

交易处理系统（TPS）

交易处理系统（TPS）能执行企业基本的一种职能或多种职能，如跟踪存货、制作日记账或安排生产。交易处理系统可以是 BOB（Best-of-breed）或企业资源规划（ERP）类型。BOB 系统，如会计信息系统的 Hyperion 套件，针对企业的一个领域如销售领域，意图成为该领域最精确或最专业的系统。ERP 系统试图为企业所有领域找到一个普遍的解决方法来提高企业各单位的紧密度和高效度。TPS 不仅记录数据，还模拟企业应该发生的预定义的交易。例如，经理设定是用后进先出法、先进先出法，还是其他的存货价值计量方法，系统将依据此法来追踪记录存货。

一个典型的 TPS 是由各种数据库交织在一起的，它的信息最低层次是数据单元

（如客户姓名或客户地址）。数据单元根据需要而更新，能联合其他数据单元来创建任何类型的报告或需要的记录。一个薪水支付数据库将跟踪发生的支付，分配资金到所得税账户，寄薪水支付单给员工。TPS 系统代表了企业五大最基本的职能：会计、财务、销售和市场、运作管理、人力资源。在一个 ERP 系统中，每一个分类被称作一个基本模块。如前所述，TPS 是其他信息系统的主要信息来源。TPS 是一个企业的重要部分，企业花费大量时间和金钱来建立它们，如果某个时段的系统建立失败将导致企业自身的失败。

TPS 是一个批处理系统，或是一个在线输入和处理的系统（也可叫做即时处理系统）。

批处理。批处理系统是以组或批为单位累积储存交易输入的信息，直到一组组或一批批数据进入数据库并且更新相关记录。为了空出白天时间来处理其他数据，有些批处理在夜间进行。而有些批处理却要在某些数据取得时尽快进行。还有另一方法是根据商业循环成批的更新系统，如每月的转账和准备财务报表。批处理的交易是累积记录在一个交易文件中，而该文件将定期转到储存永久性信息的总文件中。

批处理常用于旧系统，因为公司需要获取更多的相关信息，它正逐步被在线处理所取代。举个例子，在一个批处理系统中，如果两个销售人员正在销售同一项产品，也许他们检查存货数据时都发现还剩一件产品，然后他们把这一件产品销售给不同的客户，收到返回的发货订单，但却实现不了发货的承诺。而另一方面，一个在线处理系统能在销售时记录数据，并在第一个销售人员在数据库中确定销售时马上变更存货记录。

在线（即时）处理。一个在线或即时处理系统是 TPS 最常用的类型，它比批处理更为广泛采用。在线处理系统中，一旦使用者输入交易数据，相关数据库在交易数据存档时就立即更新。当交易发生时，在线处理利用条形码扫描器、磁墨字符识别（MICR）以及其他设备来直接更新数据库。使用了这些设备的在线处理将更加高效，更少出错。

企业职能支持

上述的每一个系统都支持基本的企业职能，即会计、财务、销售和市场营销、运作，以及人力资源职能。

财务和会计支持

财务职能管理资产、负债和所有者权益的来源和用途。财务职能对权益（存货保险）和负债（借款、商业票据）融资进行安排。现金、股票、债券等金融资产的管理主要为了资本保全和投资回报。资本预算和资本投资都是财务职能的一部分。财务和会计软件记录所有的财务交易活动如收入和支出。财务软件经常用来做差异报告（揭露同计划值的差异）。财务数据是从其他系统和模块导入的。例如，薪水支付的信息是从人力资源系统导入的，而运作成本是从运作管理系统导入的。

财务职能利用外部信息，及总账和明细账中的内部信息，决定资金机会成本、市场价格和市场价值。财务和会计软件将自动地进行许多费时的固定工作，如分摊折旧费用或制造费用。

会计职能包括应收账款和信贷、应付账款、总分类账和辅助分类账。财务报告是财务和会计职能的输出。

销售和市场营销支持

销售信息系统支持联系客户，销售产品或服务，下销售订单和提供售后服务。销售系统根据产品号或独特的识别标志如条形码来跟踪产品，还跟踪产品说明和销售数量。这个系统常与存货系统、财务系统（如信贷职能）和市场营销系统联系在一起。市场营销系统支持市场营销职能如识别和面向目标客户、广告，以及收集客户信息和客户的产品偏好。

营运管理支持

营运管理系统计划、安排、监督和控制产品的生产和服务，还包括计划购买新的生产设备和制定经营预算。它们具体包括产品设计和计算机辅助设计（CAD），材料资源规划（MRP），生产计划和所有的存货项目如原材料存货。营运管理由于记录购买和资产而与财务相关，由于记录直接成本而与人力资源相关，由于决定生产产品的数量和类型而与销售预测相关。

人力资源支持

人力资源（HR）系统支持所有的人事职能，从招募、雇用、培训、支付薪水和福利到职业发展规划、新工作的安排、解雇或退休，还提供长期人事计划。HR 跟踪期望雇员的申请和简历，按特点进行分类，让 HR 经理提出招聘职位。有些公司建立了详细的薪酬水平和工资等级。HR 的职能部门也能举办运动竞赛和公司户外活动。为了便于控制，HR 的薪酬支付部分是与其他的人力资源职能相分离的。HR 与任何有员工的部门都相关。

图表 2-45 显示了每一个企业职能是怎样包含了不同类型的企业信息系统。

图表 2-45 企业信息系统的企业职能

企业职能	信息系统层次	应 用 举 例
财务	战略	高层主管制定资本预算，长期投资目标和长期预测
	管理	财务信息系统跟踪和控制企业资源的配置；财务决策支持系统评价投资机会来帮助选择在一定的风险水平内最优的投资方案；专家系统（ES）评价资本性支出的投资组合和进行风险分析
	知识	分析师使用模型和工作站来设计正确的投资组合方案
	运作	通过内部的检查和比较来控制资金流量
销售和市场营销	战略	高层主管根据内部和外部的发展趋势（如竞争对手的信息）作决策，包括销售和新的市场机会
	管理	管理人员用管理信息系统来监控销售，制定价格策略和进行广告策划；他们用决策支持系统做市场研究和分析单独的和总体的销售情况
	知识	知识和数据工人在市场营销分析工作站里生成和显示竞争对手和其他市场营销的信息
	运作	销售部门和市场营销部门分析期望客户，列出客户名单，联系客户，跟踪销售和处理订单。客户服务部门是数据的直接使用者

续表

企业职能	信息系统层次	应用举例
营运	战略	高层主管使用运作管理系统来制定长期计划和生产目标（包括资本投资）
	管理	经理使用管理信息系统来监督和控制生产任务和成本。他们使用决策支持系统来分析经营活动的效率以及看是什么增加了产品或服务的价值
	知识	知识和数据工人在整个企业内进行设计和传播生产技术
	运作	生产线经理使用材料资源计划（MRP）列出需要的资源。通过数据录入、条形码和全自动机器来记录以下数据，包括时间、员工数量和存货状况
人力资源	战略	高层主管分析长期的人员配备需求，比如长期人工成本计划、职位数量、职位类型、培训、技能和需要的教育水平
	管理	经理使用管理信息系统监督和控制成本和薪酬支出。他们使用决策支持系统分析招聘情况、员工活动和员工薪酬
	知识	知识和数据工人使用人力资源系统设计岗位，职业路径，培训和建立报告层次
	运作	人力资源交易处理系统跟踪以下项目，招聘、新雇员、福利、员工发展规划、培训、任命、解雇，以及所有其他的员工状况

进度检查

提示：完成以下各题。参考答案随后给出。

1. 以下哪种信息系统能定期自动产生预定义报告？

　（　　）a. 知识工作系统

　（　　）b. 管理信息系统

　（　　）c. 办公系统

　（　　）d. 决策支持系统

2. 以下哪种系统层次包括了人力资源岗位设计工作站？

　（　　）a. 知识层

　（　　）b. 战略层

　（　　）c. 运作层

　（　　）d. 管理层

把下列信息系统层次同各自层次的系统类型配对。（有些层次不止一种类型）

3. _____ 战略层　　　　　a. 办公系统

4. _____ 运作层　　　　　b. 执行支持系统（ESS）

5. _____ 管理层　　　　　c. 知识工作系统（KWS）

6. _____ 知识层　　　　　d. 管理信息系统（MIS）

　　　　　　　　　　　　　e. 交易处理系统（TPS）

　　　　　　　　　　　　　f. 决策支持系统（DSS）

进度检查答案

1. b

2. a

3. b

4. e

5. d, f

6. a, c

第2节
系统开发和设计

本节内容简介

信息系统的建立是用来解决企业组织的问题或帮助组织利用新的机会。这一节涵盖了系统开发生命周期和信息系统的成本—收益分析。

系统开发生命周期（SDLC）

大多数以计算机为基础的信息系统，通过系统开发过程，进行构想、设计和实施。系统开发是一系列有组织的活动，通过这样活动，建立一个可以帮助组织解决问题、利用机会的信息系统。开发一个软件包或购买适用的应用软件的过程被称为系统开发生命周期。

企业常常成立一个信息技术（IT）指导委员会，它不仅进行系统开发过程的第一步，还在 IT 领域中监督正在进行的控制。IT 指导委员会是由一些代表企业主要职能领域的高层主管人员组成的。委员会是被高层经理任命（和向他们报告），监督所有与 IT 职能相关的常规控制运作，以及协调战略和组织的 IT 过程。因为这个委员会监督所有的 IT 项目，所以它帮助决定怎样向不同的信息技术项目配置资源。委员会将帮助建立使用者信息需求和提供信息给系统开发小组。它还将听取每一个 IT 项目小组的建议，然后接受或拒绝建议（或是在提议的两个或更多等价方案中选择）。

传统的系统开发生命周期（SDLC）

传统的系统开发生命周期（SDLC）把系统开发分成必须一个步骤完成才能进行下一步骤的几个部分。传统的处理导致了劳动的分离，这种分离一方面让大多数的信息掌握在专家手中，一方面又限制了最终用户提出系统需求和检查系统专家工作。

传统的处理仍然用于许多大型实施项目，这些项目有庞大的项目队伍和更大的使用者群体。这种处理重视过程控制，通过建立正规的项目说明书和文档，在程序完成之前，允许终端用户正常工作（仅受较小的影响）。然而，传统处理的局限是成本昂贵，因为它需要长时间来执行，且需要花费大笔费用才能适应新需求的改变。由于处理过程是按顺序进行的，项目说明书在早期处理过程中就会出台并编写许多文档。如果后来由于软件更新或设计有缺陷而必须变更项目说明书，这个变更的费用会很昂贵，因为大量的项目说明书必须重做。因此传统的处理经常陷入两难的境地：采用原计划尽管它不是最优的方案，或花费更多的成本和时间来实施新方案。

交替的系统开发生命周期

存在大量交替的系统开发生命周期模型。举个例来说，有些 SDLC 流程仍然是按顺序处理发生的活动，但也处理一些重复性步骤和同时发生的步骤。另外有种叫做模版的方法，它建立了一个允许终端用户与提供的产品间进行更多互动的快速实验系统，可以更好地满足企业需求。简单信息系统能被最终用户开发，被称为终端用户开发。这个系统使用一种软件开发工具来简化开发过程，只需要很短的开发时间，但是企业可能降低对结果的控制，以及不同类的员工间产生相冲突的系统。另外有些企业将整个信息系统功能外包出去，即硬件、软件和员工都是由外部运作和控制的。

系统开发生命周期的步骤

系统开发生命周期的步骤分别是系统分析、系统设计、编程和测试、转换/实施、生产和维护。因为大多数企业按他们自己的需要购买而不是自建一个企业软件，所以编程和测试的步骤被征求建议书（RFP），应用软件包的选择和该软件包的定制所取代。图表 2-46 说明了 SDLC 的步骤。

图表 2-46　系统开发生命周期

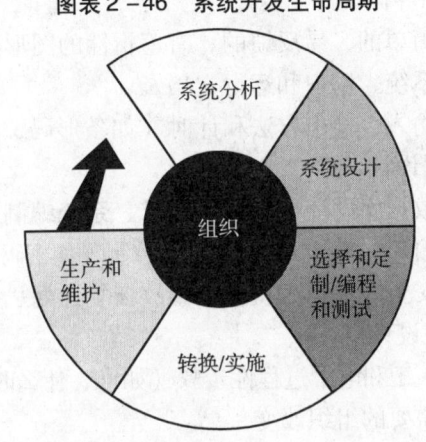

步骤 1：系统分析/需求评估/可行性研究
步骤 2：系统设计
步骤 3：选择和定制或编程和测试
步骤 4：转换/实施
步骤 5：生产和维护

系统分析/需求评估/可行性研究

在建立或购买一个软件方案之前，企业必须花时间了解自身的问题（和产生问题的原因）或必须满足的需求。这个过程可以分别叫做系统分析、需求评估或者是可行性研究。在分析了自身问题和需求后，企业就要为系统设计多个解决方案，研究它们的可行性，以及确定需要的具体数据。

一个系统分析师或分析小组是从定义企业最近的活动和商务进展，软件和硬件，以及每个活动的参与者开始分析的。信息技术指导委员会可能参与了这个步骤的战略框架的设计。分析师采访最终用户并平衡用户与最高管理层和信息技术指导委员会之间的需求。那个新的系统必须符合企业战略，并改变那些不能给最终产品或服务提高价值的步骤。系统分析通常揭示了软件仅仅是解决问题的一个小方面，我们需要组织上或程序上的改变，如果改变初步是成功的话。

系统分析报告包括对每一个选择方案的可行性研究。可行性研究涉及成本—效益分析，查看技术成功的可能性，以及判断企业文化是否能接受这种改变。

一旦确定了基本的解决方案，系统分析师就要准备一系列详细的信息需求，这些需求定义了谁需要什么信息，怎样收集、整理和使用这些信息。如果信息需求没有选恰当，系统设计就会有缺陷。

系统设计

在系统分析步骤建立的信息需求基础上，系统设计是为计划系统的各个方面建立一个详细的蓝图。一个好的设计将是便于使用的、高效率的、可信赖的和创新的。系统设计的三个主要活动是用户界面设计、数据设计和程序设计。设计说明书必须包括以下内容：

- 用户界面设计
  - 简单的、易反馈的、有逻辑性的图形用户界面设计。
  - 系统、用户和运行文档。
  - 输入、输出方法和计时（如条形码，数据加载）。
- 数据设计
  - 数据库设计（如程序需求、系统编制、逻辑数据模型）。
  - 输入、输出、处理和存储控制（如密码、字符限制，一贯性原则和总数比较）。
  - 安全（如审计检查、事故恢复计划、备份）。
- 程序设计
  - 人工和电子过程性步骤（如谁、什么时候、怎么样；需要的报告和计算）。
  - 需要的组织改变。
  - 转换方案和培训方法。

终端用户有必要发挥定义他们企业需求的作用，因为技术员工设计出的系统也许能实施但满足不了企业的需求。终端用户的参与还能提高改变的接受度，接受度是所有改变期初要克服的主要障碍。经理和终端用户应坚定地接受改变，否则对新系统的不熟悉将产生担心，将阻碍变通方案和管理能力，这些将导致项目的失败。

编程和测试；选择和定制应用软件包

一些企业仍在开发自己的软件，因为他们所处的行业没有准备好了的解决方案来满足他们的需要。然而，由于软件开发和测试是非常耗时和昂贵的，它通常比购买应用软件包更耗费成本。特别是这样的情况，由于定制的软件经常需要更新，于是软件开发者定期为内部软件包更新的成本是不会停止的，加上如果原来的卖家不再与企业合作，而另外的卖家可能不能理解原有的程序。因此，许多软件开发是由专门的软件公司来做。

软件开发的开发步骤涉及对系统设计步骤中详细的项目说明书进行翻译。测试步骤涉及大量的时间和测试者，每一个事项必须在不同的状况下测试多次。还有，由于测试许多企业的应用程序的惟一方法是建立测试数据，建立和组织测试就很费时。在每轮测试完后，检察结果并开始另一轮开发。

测试有三种类型：单元测试、系统测试和接受测试。单元测试是自己测试程序的每一个单独的部分。因为从程序中处理掉所有错误是不现实的，单元测试着重找出让程序失败的原因来阻止错误的发生。系统测试是把整个程序作为一个整体来测试，查看不同成分是否能在一起让程序运行，以及它们是否能达到企业要求的运行速度。接受测试是管理层和最终用户查看系统是否能满足程序运行的期望要求。

测试方法包括综合测试设备（ITF），此设备在数据库中建立一个虚拟实体来处理和在线输入测试的事项，并将测试事项合并成一个系统的常规生产运作。它的优点在于测试不需要分开测试过程，只需使用正被测试的实际系统。然而，企业需要精心的计划，测试的数据必须和生产数据分开。

综合测试设备还是一个有用的审计工具（参见第一本书第 3 章"内部控制"），因为它使用相同的程序和独立的计算数据来进行比较处理。它作为一个检验处理准确率的工具，是通过在应用系统上建立一个虚拟企业、处理测试或生产的数据，将其与真实企业的数据进行比较。

大多数企业购买应用软件包，软件包是能满足企业需要的预先编好程和预先测试好的软件应用程序。由于大部分企业有类似的程序，如财务、材料需求规划或存货的程序，因此一个通用的软件包能被完全使用或被定制成适合专业系统的程序。再者，如果一个企业的经销商和整个销售的客户使用同一种软件，那么他们就能电子化地整合共享的服务和加快交易次数。

选择应用软件包是从系统开发生命周期的前两个步骤即系统分析和系统设计就开始了的。在这步骤之后，企业将提交征求建议书（RFP）给所有能满足企业需求软件的卖家。征求建议书将包括企业详细的信息需求和期望的系统设计。卖家将回复企业并说明他们的软件是怎样满足企业每一个需求的。这个过程是一个艰难的协商过程。

定制是许多应用软件包的特点，它把软件改成正如企业特殊需要要求的那样，可以完成不同的企业步骤。许多定制的软件实际上不用重新编制整个软件程序，只需改变内部的系统参数（如变动选项，仍需要一个专业的程序）。如果一个软件包要大部分的定制，软件成本将呈几何倍数地增长，因为当软件到更新的时候，所有的定制部分将更换新版本。定制成本是在首次的产品价格中隐藏的成本。

转换/实施

无论一个软件包是购买还是内部创建，当软件准备使用时必须完成转换或实施程序。转换过程涉及转换管理、转换计划、文档准备、培训终端用户和技术支持工作者。

转换管理为企业转换做好准备，帮助它确定并处理初期转换的阻因。

转换计划涉及决定在什么时候，怎样采用新系统。它可以通过四种方法来完成：直接转换、平行转换、试点转换、分阶段转换。

- 直接转换

直接转换是简单地选一天作为"执行日"，在那天关闭旧系统并开启新系统。因为系统可能会不正常运转或用户没有正确使用，所以此法具有高风险。无论发生哪种情况，每一天整个企业工作部门的生产力损失都会耗费一大笔钱。

- 平行转换

平行转换是当新系统开启时仍保持旧系统的运行。由于要求最终用户在新旧系统中做同样的记录，导致他们将做更多的工作，但在试验的后期，通过比较产出（如在两个系统中比较总分类账的余额）来整合系统。

- 试点转换

试点转换是在将系统发行给整个最终客户群前，把新系统介绍给一群可控制的能验证系统运行的人使用。这种方法仍然有直接转换法的风险，特别要考虑终端用户的使用准备情况。

- 分阶段转换

分阶段转换针对不同的软件实施阶段有多个"执行日"。每个阶段都能从经理和技术人员那里得到更多的关注。阶段可以根据职能来确定，如人力资源，也可以根据地理位置来确定，如总公司优先。这种交错的实施增加了实施的总时间和成本，但是可以让新旧系统更平稳地过渡。

文档准备是有必要的，因为它是软件更新的蓝图，它包括实施定制软件的所有方法，是建立培训材料的基础。

培训终端用户和技术支持人员的花费相当昂贵，但为了系统的成功也是有必要的。如果用户不知道在系统转变后怎样来做他们的工作，前期的结果将会失败，早期的花费也将损失。企业常常低估培训的需要。培训应该会很贵（如损失的生产力），它需要大量引导时间来进行培训资料的开发，而且软件转换将需要改变培训的资料。

生产和维护

生产是一个系统的"现场"阶段，当系统实际进行工作时，生产就发生了。这个阶段可能要一系列的修改才能提高效率和系统能力。系统的表现将与计划或承诺的表现进行比较，如果有卖方，直到企业满意了，即卖方尽到合约上的义务，项目才会结束。当把这个过程形式化，它就叫做事后审计。在审计完所有的合约要求后，任何其他的修改将是企业的责任。

系统维护阶段涉及连续评估，以及对系统进行诸如修改错误、增加作用和提高效率的改进。维护是当需要时对硬件、软件、程序或文档进行改变。

成本—收益分析

无论应用系统是在内部开发还是从卖家购买，它们总是十分昂贵的，而系统实施有时并不能达到他们承诺的结果，有时是彻底失败。一个良好设计和正确实施的系统能降低企业的成本和增加企业的边际收益，或者可以使企业在降低产品价格的同时提高或保持它的市场份额。当决定是否实施某个信息系统时，必须分析成本和收益，以此来决定是否能以及何时能收回成本。

当进行成本—收益分析时，企业要估计所考虑的每个项目的总成本、有形收益和无形收益。要注意成本和收益对应的时间框架要一致（如 5 年的收益对应 5 年的成本），尽管某些年的成本或收益可能为零。在估算出无形收益的价值后，分析师将使用多种财务比率来决定企业项目的总价值。使用的比率包括投资回收期、投资回报率、成本—收益比率、净现值、盈利指数和内部报酬率。这些比率在 CMA 教材第一本书第 5 章"财务报表分析"和第三本书第 5 章"投资决策"中详细讨论过。成本—效益分析的计算公式如下：

$$成本—收益比率 = \frac{总收益}{总成本}$$

成本

系统项目的成本始于有形的直接成本如在征求建议书中的软件包价格或软件开发成本的内部估价。如果不包括上述两项，企业还必须考虑硬件、服务、通信、定制、培训、评估和维护成本。后期改变设计的成本也是很大的，所以分析阶段应当假设一定数量的转换成本并将其加入总成本。正如前面讲到的，损失的生产力、学习曲线或培训成本也须考虑。还须注意到实际成本往往会超过预算成本，因此这些考虑需加在分析阶段中。

有形收益

一个系统的有形收益一般只有在与当前使用系统的成本进行比较才能发现，它是以成本节约的形式出现。有形收益是任何能带来可靠的货币价值的收益，包括现金节约或增加的现金流。一个与旧系统成本相当，但能接触到更多人的市场营销系统将产生更多的有形的现金流。有形收益包括：

- 更低的运行成本。
- 更低的外部购买成本。
- 更低的管理和专业成本。
- 更低的计算机维护成本。
- 劳动力成本降低。
- 降低的费用增长率。
- 降低的厂房成本。
- 增加的生产力。

无形收益

无形收益是任何能轻易增加利润，能估算但没有货币价值形态的收益。为了把它们包括在成本—收益分析中，无形收益必须被列出来并采用适合它们的价值评估或计算。无形收益包括：

- 适合战略计划。
- 更快的组织学习能力。
- 资产的增加使用。
- 更好的工作满意度。
- 增加的资源控制。
- 改善的组织计划和控制。
- 更多和/或更快的信息。
- 调整的适应。
- 更好的企业形象。
- 增加的顾客或用户满意度。
- 改进的决策制定。

成本—收益案例

假如一家零售商店想把自己旧的收银系统更换成销售点（POS）系统来跟踪购买和保存顾客信息。经理从确定具体的成本开始分析。

新的 POS 系统的硬件和软件（总花费 $40 000）

- 8 台联网的 POS 终端和软件：每台 $3 000。
- 一台服务器：$4 000。
- 8 台打印机：每台 $500。
- 电缆和安装：$3 000。
- 销售跟踪数据库软件：$5 000。

新的 POS 系统培训（总花费 $21 500）

- 员工培训：16 个员工每人 $1 000。
- 数据库管理者培训：1 个员工 $4 000。
- 经理培训：3 个经理每人 $500。

其他成本（总花费约 $24 000）

- 损失的销售：约 5 000。
- 损失的工作小时：50 人每天耗费 $140/天（$7 000）。
- 由于学习新系统而降低的销售收入：约 $6 000。
- 新雇的数据库经理成本：$6 000。

总成本：$85 500

然后经理估算所有的有形和无形收益：

- 由于顾客增加了认识而降低的市场营销邮递品成本：约 $15 000/年。
- 管理销售过程的能力增加：$10 000/年。
- 提高了处理一笔销售业务的效率：$0.05/笔×约 240 000 笔/年＝约 $12 000/年。
- 更多准确的客户信息：约 $4 000/年。
- 更好的管理和预防欺骗：约 $24 000/年。
- 改进的顾客服务和顾客保留：约 $15 000/年。
- 更好的企业形象：约 $16 000/年。

总收益：$96 000/年

这个项目的成本—收益比率为：

$$\frac{\$96\ 000}{\$85\ 500} = 1.12$$

在第一年，每投入项目 1 美元企业将获得 1.12 美元的回报。因为估算得到的比率是主观的，因此，为了确保估算的一致性，应当由同一个人或团队估算其他的预期项目。

进度检查

提示：完成以下各题。参考答案随后给出。

1. 系统开发生命周期的哪个阶段为用户沟通和转换方案创建一个详细的蓝图？

（　　）a. 应用软件包的选择和定制

（　　）b. 转换/实施

（　　）c. 系统分析

（　　）d. 系统设计

2. 系统开发生命周期的哪个阶段设计提交征求建议书？

（　　）a. 应用软件包的选择和定制

（　　）b. 转换/实施

（　　）c. 系统分析

（　　）d. 系统设计

3. 下列哪种方法将在转换过程中产生大约两倍的数据录入员工的工作量？

（　　）a. 直接转换

（　　）b. 平行转换

（　　）c. 试点转换

（　　）d. 分阶段转换

进度检查答案

1. d

2. a

3. b

第3节
信息系统技术

本节内容简介

本节内容涵盖计算机网络、数据库基础、决策支持系统、商业智能系统和专家系统、表格表单以及互联网的基本信息。

数据传输、网际网路、客户/服务器系统

计算机被划分为不同的类别，包括：巨型主机、中程计算机、个人计算机、工作站和超级计算机。巨型主机是一个庞大的计算机系统，它常被用来执行各子系统的运算任务。巨型主机是商业信息处理的首选方式，目前根据各个行业的需求用来处理大量的信息（或被当作一些公司的服务器）。

中程计算机可以是一个微型计算机，也可以是一个服务器。服务器是专门处理与其相连接的计算机请求的计算机系统。服务器常用来处理某些特定任务，例如，文件服务器或网络服务器。一个公司经常会使用多个服务器，或使用外包的服务器，这种集中在一起的服务器群被称作服务器工场。工作站是用于特定任务的个人电脑，例如，图形处理。

超级计算机是一个由许多计算机组成的集群系统，在所有的计算机当中，它的性能和处理能力最好，其造价也是最高的（超级计算机常被用在需要处理大量信息的地方，例如，运用于天气预测、基因解析、或军事方面）。

计算机网络和客户端/服务器模型

如果将计算机系统以及电子通信技术联系起来，信息就可以在公司内部不同地点进行低成本传输，这便是计算机网络的基础。巨型主机使用集中式的处理方式，这意味着使用一个大型中央计算机执行所有的运算任务；而计算机网络则是使用分散式的处理方式。分散式处理是指运算任务被分散到网络上的各个计算机上，从而任何单个计算机的错误不会耽误整个运算任务。客户端/服务器模型就是一个分散式处理的网络，它根据各个计算机的运算能力将运算任务分散于客户端（个人计算机）和服务器之间，从而实现优化资源配置。

客户端/服务器运算

在客户端/服务器模型中，客户端提供用户界面和部分应用程序，而服务器则用来储存大量信息，以及部分应用程序和所有网络资源。

运算任务被分配在客户端和服务器之间的比例是一个封闭的连续函数。一些客户端/服务器模型将大部分任务分配给客户端，这意味着大部分的应用程序都将安装在客户端，并且客户端的个人计算机将负责处理大部分运算任务。其他的客户端/服务器模型则将大部分任务分配给服务器，这种将大量的运算能力分配给客户端的分散式处理模式被称作点对点运算，也就是单独的个人计算机与其他计算机相连，可能没有

一个服务器，但它们通过互相的连接或互联网传输信息。这种点对点的运算也被称作计算机网络，它从各个相连的计算机上提取小部分未使用的运算能力，组合在一起提高计算能力。

　　主要或完全依靠服务器的运算模式被称为瘦客户端型（这与只依靠客户端的厚客户端型相对应），客户端计算机通过网络浏览器与之相连。这种运算模式将所有的程序文件储存在一个地方，具有便于维护和升级的优势（客户端计算机会很自然地感觉到这种变化的作用）。这种依靠服务器的运算模式有时会选择网络计算机替代个人计算机，网络计算机是简化的个人计算机，它的储存容量和计算能力都比较小。随着个人计算机价格的不断下降，网络计算机已不再常见，因为网络计算机依靠服务器进行运算而个人计算机可以不需要服务器的帮助单独进行运算。

局域网（LANs）和广域网（WANs）

　　有一定区域跨度的计算机网络常被划分为：局域网（LANs）或广域网（WANs）。大多数的局域网和广域网都使用客户端/服务器模式。

　　局域网。局域网是集中在一定地理区域里，与外界隔绝的计算机和服务器网络，例如，在一栋大楼里或相互离得很近的两台计算机，通常网络中计算机间的距离不会超过 2 000 英尺。通过局域网可以高速传输大量的数据，使得管理员可以对连接在局域网上的计算机进行维护及软件更新，同时也可以连接外围设备，如打印机。局域网上的服务器可以设置链接权限并且通过一个网关控制外部计算机对系统的链接，这种网关通过翻译不同计算机网络的协议使通信成为可能。服务器也可以提供对内部和外部网络安全的保障。服务器使用的是类似于个人计算机操作系统的网络操作系统（NOSs）。

　　无线局域网通过无线电波传输数据，通常比物理连接成本低，因而越来越多地被应用。然而，无线数据传输有被无意接收者拦截和被干扰的风险。

　　广域网。广域网跟局域网相似，不同的只是广域网覆盖区域更广，从几公里直至覆盖全球。广域网可以由交换线、专线、微波和卫星通信组成。交换线是共享的通信线路，例如，电话线。专线是专门针对公司应用并且随时可用的通信线路，通常会收取一定费用。广域网使单个公司能够互相联通，例如，公司内部网络。不少公司使用的广域网的大部分设备和系统都是外包给了电信运营商。

　　通信网络：局域网、广域网和简单的互联网连接是由不同的通信模式支撑的。下面列举了一些手段。

　　● 以太网/高速以太网：以太网是以 10Mbps 传输数据的局域网通信模式；高速的以太网是 100Mbps 的新型网络标准。

　　● 无线网络：多种无线电波传输模式使得计算机可以在不与物理网络连接的时候发送和接收数据。

　　● T1 载体：专门的电话线连接，通常传输速度为 1.544Mbps。

　　● 电缆：通过同轴电视电缆传输数据的宽带互联网连接，传输速度通常为 1.5Mbps。

　　● 数字用户线路：使用数字而非模拟信号传输的宽带电话线网络，带宽通常为 128Kbps – 6Mbps，带宽具体由分享线路的用户数决定。

● 电话线连接：通过窄宽带的电话线进行数据发送和接收，通常在两端都会安装一个调制解调器。随着更快速的传输模式的出现，这种连接方式渐渐退出市场。

网络拓扑。网络拓扑是指网络中的计算机和服务器的物理布局。常见的模式如下：

● 环形网络：在环形网络中没有中央服务器，所有的设备都在环形网络中相连，这意味着任何一条信息都可以通过两条线路到达传输目的地；可以在长距离间传输因为每个设备都可以重复并加强这个信息。令牌环形网络是环形网络中最常见的一种。

● 星形网：星形网通过一个中央服务器接收信息并将其传输至合适的位置。星形网不需要单个网络节点间的连接，因而不会出现信息传输线路中的冗余。

● 总线网络：所有的设备都连接到一个中央网络线路或分解线路上，这被称作总线。这是最简单而且最常见的局域网拓扑结构。

虚拟私有网络（VPN）。虚拟私有网络是通过互联网技术在公共网络上提供安全的内部网络联通网络模式，它是比广域网更加便宜的替代品。许多在家办公的职员都使用虚拟私有网络。虚拟私有网络是由互联网服务提供商构建，因为通信可以被发送至附近的互联网服务提供商，而不用花费长途费用，所以可以提供低成本的电话网络通信联通。虚拟私有网络通过加密协议进行数据传输，包括点对点隧道协议（PPTP），根据这个协议信息被放在加密包中并包裹在标准的互联网协议（IP）包中（互联网协议是在互联网上传输数据的标准模式）。依赖于这种安全性，虚拟私有网络成为在互联网上传输数据的重要手段。虚拟私有网络使得许多以前不可能实现或因专利权转让成本而过于昂贵的网上交易成为可能，因此也被称作增值网络（VANs）。

数据库管理系统

在传统的数据应用方面，数据被认为是每个应用程序的必要构成要素，并且数据文件被设计成该应用程序的重要支撑。任何两个应用程序需要同一份数据时就会出现冗余，而同一份数据记录就被重复储存多次（每次对应其应用程序），从而针对每一次修改都要做多重更新，这无疑增加了出现数据错误的几率，此外，因为数据结构的不同，应用程序间不能实现数据共享，这些因素导致了数据与使用这些数据的应用程序的分离，这样程序可以依照用户的特殊需要去设计，而不用担心数据获取的问题，同时要求所有的应用程序都使用同样的数据源也意味着程序间的交流将使用共通的术语。

数据库是计算机集成化的数据群，它减少了数据冗余同时可以通过一个或多个应用程序提供需要的数据。集成数据库被设计作为一个实体中的所有应用程序的中央数据储存器。数据可以分为两类：源数据和报告数据。源数据来自于公司的遗传系统（使用传统的数据处理方式的应用程序）或使用集成化数据库的更新的应用程序。报告数据来源于对源数据的处理或对交易执行和对源数据的分析。

数据库管理系统（DBMS）作为组织数据库的软件程序可以使其他应用程序和终端用户获取并使用其数据。数据库中的数据可以按照很多种不同的逻辑结构组织，但只能有一种物理结构。物理结构是数据在数据库中的实际布局。逻辑结构是根据不同的应用程序和终端用户的需求而形成的数据布局。因此数据可以按照不同的顺序和不同集合体的层级呈现。一个数据要素可以是任何领域或数据库的一个入口，比如名字。

数据库管理系统由三部分构成：

- 数据定义语言是用于构建数据库内容和结构的程序设计语言。其中包括专门用来识别数据库中每个数据要素的标签。

- 数据操作语言是被终端用户和程序软件用来获取数据的简化语言。它可以在数据库中操作数据。结构化查询语言（SQL）是最常见的数据操作语言，终端用户和程序软件都可以通过它获取数据。

- 数据字典是一个自动或手动的文件程序用于储存关于数据要素的所有细节，包括：谁负责维护数据，谁和什么程序可以有权接触该数据，它包含哪些报告信息和其他有关的信息。

这三个要素都被用作构建和管理数据库。数据字典对于终端用户和技术人员都非常有用。例如，如果终端用户修改了一份报告或技术人员修改了一个程序，它们都可以通过数据字典找出哪些其他报告或程序将会受到影响。

实体—关系图（E-R Diagram）。任何形式的数据库，其创建的第一步就是构建一个实体—关系图。数据库的设计者，例如，系统分析师，通过构建这种详细并且具有逻辑化的图表保证了所有数据相互协调。实体—关系图是用图表的形式，表现一个组织或商业环境的实体情况，例如，销售人员或存货，他们之间的联系以及他们中的各数据要素。实体在图表中用方形表示，是数据收集的目的，如中间人、对象或事件。中间人是指相关的人员，如顾客、销售人员或经销商；对象是指一些项目，如存货、现金或公司卡车等类似的实物；事件是指一些交易，例如，订单、购买行为或销售。一些物品、中间人和事件因为并不包含任何的数据要素，所以并不成为实体—关系图中的实体部件。例如，公司本身作为图表中包含实体的系统，不应该作为实体出现在图表中。

实体—关系图用图表的形式表现了实体之间的关系或联系，这种联系在图中用菱形标志。这种关系可以存在于两个事件之间（例如，在图表 2 - 47 中的购买订单和接收）；或在物品和时间之间（如存货和购买订单）；或中间人和时间之间（如经销商和接收）。需要注意的是，在实际系统中存在更多的实体和关系。理论上，一个组织的所有职能都应该被整合成一个综合的系统，就像企业资源规划管理系统（ERP），这将在本章的第 5 节详细论述。

在数据库设计组完成了实体—关系图和流程理论模型的构建后，下一个步骤就是决定数据库管理系统的类型。

数据库管理系统的类型

数据库管理系统是根据它怎样储存和存取数据进行划分的，这也被称作数据库逻辑设计。数据库的逻辑设计包括：数据要素怎样被定义、要素怎样分组和数据要素之间的关系。数据库逻辑模型包括：关系型、层级型、网络型和事物导向型。

图表 2-47 存货自动登记系统的实体—关系图

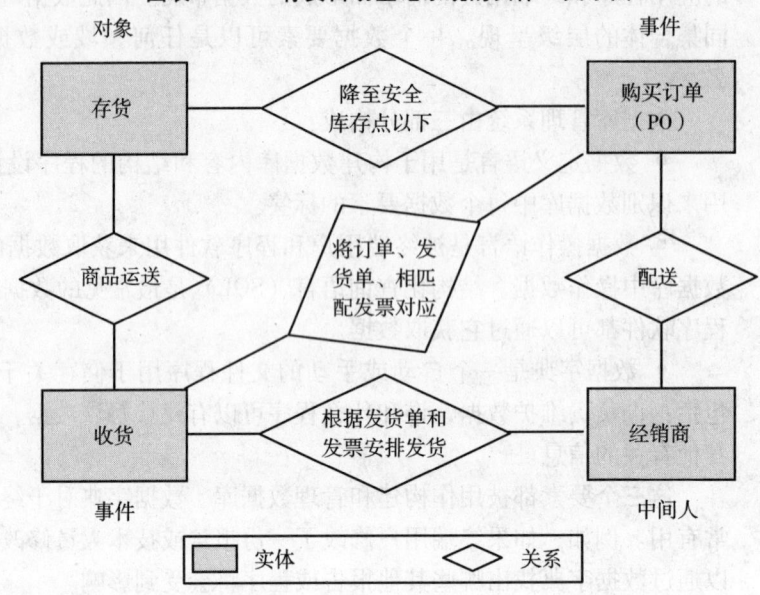

关系型数据库管理系统

关系型数据库管理系统是个人计算机、大型计算机和巨型主机上最常见的数据库管理系统类型。数据要素被储存在二维的表格文件中。表格文件被设计成相同间隔的分栏形式。图表 2-48 展示了订单表格、货单表格和供应商表格。在使用实体—关系图时，每一个实体都应对应一个表格。每一行是一次记录或单个的文件。然而，与传统的文件系统不同，使用者可以通过合并多个表格的数据从而构建只含有相关数据的虚拟表格。在表格有相同的数据项目时，一个表格中的数据可以被提取出来用于另一个表格。因此一个表格中的数据可以很容易地和另一个表格中的数据合并，例如，一个含有雇员编号的雇员表格就可以和一个含有与其雇员编号相同的雇员工资表格合并。此外，与工资表格有相同项目的第三个表格，例如，一个有相同扣缴税款项目的税款表格，也可以合并成为一个报告，其中包含：个人信息、工资表信息和税款信息。常见的关系型数据库包括甲骨文（Oracle）和微软 Access（Microsoft Access）。图表 2-48 展示了典型的关系型数据库是怎样处理数据的。需要注意的是，关系型数据库是以表格形式出现的，这便于使用者的浏览。关系型数据库的逻辑结构使其可以处理复杂的需求，但是同时也比其他的模型需要更多的储存空间。

层级型和网络型数据库管理系统

层级型的数据库管理系统是一个树形的传统数据库管理系统。根部是这个层级的最高级，其下的层级被称作分段。在任何一个特定的层级，这些分段被称作子集，而在其之上的层级被称作母集。在这种母子层级关系中，一个母集可以有很多子集，而一个子集只能有一个母集，所以只有垂直（一对多）的关系才可能存在。所以一个特定的顾客母集可以有一个历史订单子集、一个信用评级子集和一个折扣子集。图表 2-49 展示了一个层级型的数据库管理系统是怎样建立的。

图表 2－48　关系型数据模型

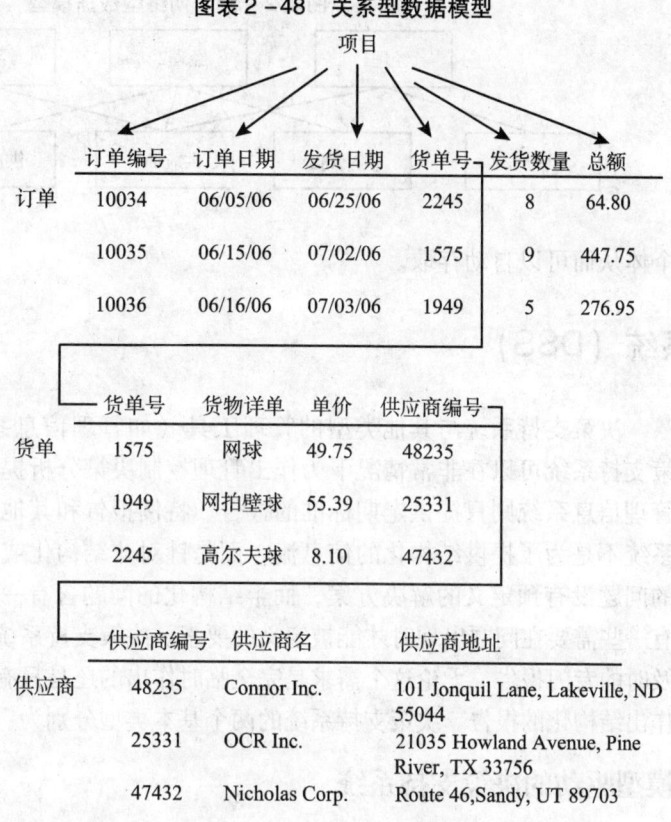

项目

	订单编号	订单日期	发货日期	货单号	发货数量	总额
订单	10034	06/05/06	06/25/06	2245	8	64.80
	10035	06/15/06	07/02/06	1575	9	447.75
	10036	06/16/06	07/03/06	1949	5	276.95

	货单号	货物详单	单价	供应商编号
货单	1575	网球	49.75	48235
	1949	网拍壁球	55.39	25331
	2245	高尔夫球	8.10	47432

	供应商编号	供应商名	供应商地址
供应商	48235	Connor Inc.	101 Jonquil Lane, Lakeville, ND 55044
	25331	OCR Inc.	21035 Howland Avenue, Pine River, TX 33756
	47432	Nicholas Corp.	Route 46,Sandy, UT 89703

图表 2－49　层级型数据库

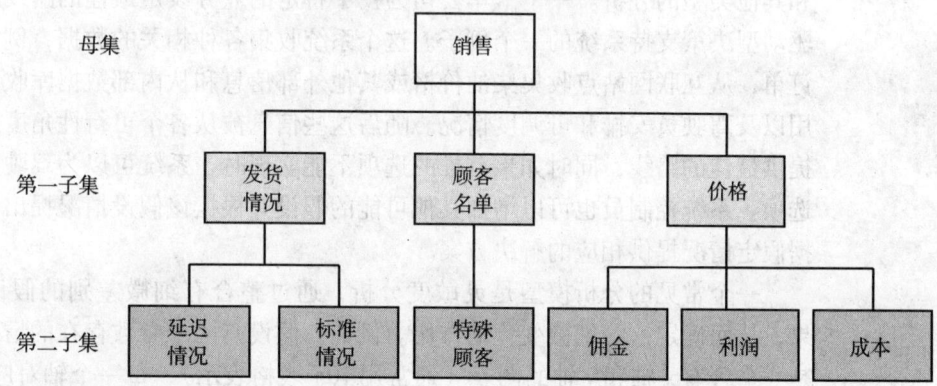

母集　　　　　　销售

第一子集　　发货情况　　顾客名单　　价格

第二子集　　延迟情况　标准情况　特殊顾客　佣金　利润　成本

　　网络型数据库管理系统使用的是类似于层级型数据库管理系统的层级和母子关系形式，所不同的是这里的子集可以有不同的母子（多对多关系）。图表 2－50 展示了网络型数据库管理系统可以有不同的母集。

面向对象型数据库管理系统

　　面向对象型数据库管理系统（OODBMS）不仅仅用来处理文字方面的数据，同时也可以处理 Java 小程序、图形、音频和视频录像。关系型数据库在处理这些数据时并没有加以更多的处理，而在事物导向型数据库管理系统中任何种类的数据都被当作

图表2-50 网络型数据模型

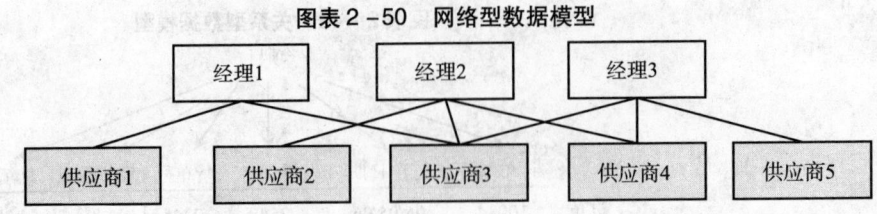

个体从而可以自动存取。

决策支持系统（DSS）

决策支持系统与其他类型的管理工具（如管理信息系统）的区别之处在于，决策支持系统可以在非常情况下为作出管理控制决策分析提供更快捷和灵活的信息，而管理信息系统则只提供定期标准的报告、特例报告和其他结构化的信息流。决策支持系统不是为了提供结构化的信息流，而是针对非结构化或半结构化的情况。非结构化的问题没有预定义的解决方案，而半结构化的问题含有一些预定义的要素，同时也含有一些需要在问题出现时才能被定义的要素。决策支持系统可以在报告需求出现时提供及时的专门报告，无论这个需求是完全临时作出的还是只有部分临时决定，而不用事先作出结构化的报告。决策支持系统的两个基本类型分别为：模型驱动和数据驱动。

模型驱动的决策支持系统

大多数模型驱动型决策支持系统都是独立系统，通过数据模型或方程式进行假设和其他类型的分析。一个卡车公司为一个特定的业务设定最佳的路线和成本就是模型驱动型决策支持系统的一个例子。这个系统收集各种相关的数据，例如，录入的发货订单，从互联网站点收集柴油价格或其他外部信息和从内部数据库收集货运距离、费用以及驾驶员安排和可调度情况。随后这些信息被从各个可行性角度进行整合，从而提供最佳的路线，同时如果首推的选项不能实现时，系统可以为驾驶员提供其他的备选项。系统控制员也可以增加其他可能的假设并根据该假设情况提出请求，系统则根据假定情况提供相应的解决方案。

一个常见的分析模型是灵敏度分析，通过整合有细微差别的假设情况的分析结果，从而确定这些细微变化的作用。例如，假设有两个参数存在的情况，输出的结果是一个含有 x 轴和 y 轴的图表（通常用电子表格表示），每一个轴对应一个参数变量，而表格的中央部分则表示分析的结果。从而最佳的结果可以从这些结算值中选出。

数据驱动的决策支持系统

数据驱动型决策支持系统通常是拥有大型数据库的大公司使用。它根据用户的需求提取数据进行整合，为随后的分析和决策制定做准备。多重交易处理系统（TPS）中的数据通常是首先在数据仓库中被整合的。

数据驱动型决策支持系统将数据仓库的数据采用在线分析处理方式进行分析。在线分析处理（OLAP）是一种多维的数据分析方式，这意味着数据可以从多于二维的角度进行分析处理（有关在线分析处理的更多的信息在本章的第 5 节可以找到）。例如，在线分析处理可以对一个特定的成本项目在不同的部门和一定的时间跨度上进行实际支出和预算额的比较。换言之，在线分析处理和数据驱动型决策支持系统可以使经理们获取有关特定事务的足量信息，而不用去分析研究大量的报告。但是，这个系统的顺利工作必须建立在经理们对自己要了解的问题有清楚认识的基础上。数据挖掘，作为数据导向型决策支持系统中的一种技术，可以使用户发现那些不明显的联系。

商业智能、人工智能和专家系统

商业智能系统和人工智能（AI）是通过软件程序进行管理推理的商业工具，这也包括专家系统。

商业智能系统

作为一种应用程序软件，通过从多种内部和外部来源收集、储存和分析数据，商业智能应用程序可以帮助用户进行决策制定。高管支持系统（ESS）和决策支持系统（DSS）都属于商业智能系统。商业智能系统强调通过多种来源快速地获取信息，因而它依赖网络浏览器聚集用户定义的日常信息。这种以网络为基础的商业智能系统软件常被称作门户。一个门户可以通过图标或饼状图在同一个页面聚集一个公司和其最主要的竞争者的信息。

人工智能

人工智能（AI）是可以模拟人类选择和行为的计算机系统。语言技术、机器人技术和智能感知系统都属于人工智能，但在这个章节中，人工智能专指模糊逻辑、类神经网络和专家系统。这些商业专用软件被用作实现管理推理，构建组织记忆（包含公司职员的专门技术的动态记忆）和作出需要大量数据和计算的情景分析（这种分析在有限的时间内人类是不可能实现的）。在商业中使用的人工智能（AI）常被称作专家系统。

模糊逻辑

模糊逻辑是可以获取来自不同来源的数据，并对不准确的数据进行处理，最终作出逻辑判断的软件程序。传统的计算机系统只能作出是或否或其他二进位的决策，而模糊逻辑却可以依据程序设定在一定范围和主观价值上作出判断。

传统的计算机程序使用"如果……就……"的表达方式，例如，如果 X 等于 1，就开起阀门 A。模糊逻辑通过在这些表达方式中添加被称作从属函数的非特定变量，从而使其可以处理需要容错空间和经常修改的问题情况。例如，一个衣物烘干机的"如果……就……"表达方式的模糊逻辑从属函数可以是：如果衣物快要干了，就降低烘干的温度。这样的系统通常有多重的从属函数，因为这里的从属被定义在了一个类别里，例如，快要干了。其他类似的函数也将被涵盖，例如，衣物的种类、效率或烘干速度，从而模糊逻辑可以根据程序设定整合这些要素最终决定如何烘干衣物的最佳方式（这种方式将和人类的选择十分接近）。

相比传统的计算机程序，模糊逻辑需要更少的"如果……就……"设定，因为程序员不需要告诉电脑在任何一个可能的情况下该怎样做。这些系统构建的成本更低，需要更少的储存器而且运行更快速，所以在美国越来越流行，在日本更是这样。在日本，地铁列车上的模糊逻辑防止乘客在列车加速时有瞬间的急促感觉。空调系统中的模糊逻辑使得人们在享受相同服务的同时降低了能源的消耗。模糊逻辑在商业管理决策领域的应用更加广泛，例如，检查每一份医药索赔以发现可能的舞弊和分析股票的投机前景。

类神经网络

类神经网络是用来模拟生物大脑的学习能力的软件和硬件系统。与专家系统等其他人工智能（AI）所不同，类神经网络不是被设计用于模拟某个特定的专家或经理的行为，而是用于自我学习怎样处理需要权衡多种因素的问题。一个基本大脑细胞或神经元含有一个控制单元（类似开/关控制器），被称作神经细胞本体。两个神经元相接触的点叫做突触。

神经元都是与其他神经元协同工作的，这样在处理问题时就会比将各种可能情况按顺序测试更快捷。当大脑处理问题时，每个神经元都会测试可能的解决方案，那些得到错误答案的神经元突触将会被弱化，而那些得到正确答案的神经元突触将被强化。而正是在这种弱化/强化作用下达到学习的目。

为了模拟这种学习方式，类神经网络用晶体管（开/关控制器）或晶体管群（微芯片）作为人工的神经元，用电位器作为神经突触。电位器可以改变流过线路的电流量，这也是类神经网络模拟大脑学习能力的方式（降低对正确结果的阻碍和提高对错误结果的阻碍）。这就和大脑的工作机理类似，每个人工神经元协同工作同时测试不同的变量。

类神经网络被用于那些非精确定义的商业环境，例如，是否给予更大的信用值或作出特定的股票投资。类神经网络被用于在大量数据中找出规律模式，例如，侦查信用卡欺骗或面部、声音和笔迹鉴定。这样的网络也被用于医药和科学领域。一种被称作电脑抹片系统的医药类神经网络被用于针对子宫癌的子宫颈抹片检查。系统通过对子宫颈抹片快速扫描以发现异常细胞，可以提供比人工检查准确十倍的检验报告。虽然抹片依然由人工检验，但这个过程更加彻底并花费更少的时间。

专家系统

专家系统是将某个专家的知识编码在软件系统中的系统程序，而往往这个专家是关注于某个特定领域的，例如，确定某个公司的信用评级或预测倒闭的可能性。

与类神经网络所不同的是，专家系统为处理信息预制了一系列的离散的程序规则。例如，在预测倒闭可能性时，专家系统也许会对每个财务指标都设定规则，例如，投递回报率必须在 X 以上。这些规则都使用前面介绍的"如果……就……"的程序模式，而在这里这些规则更加精确：如果净收益超过了 X，就实施 A 步骤。事实上大多数的程序语言，因而大多数的软件程序，都是用类似"如果……就……"的方式，而专家系统却更加彻底并且拥有更多的规则，这被称作规则库。一个标准的程序大概有100个这样的规则，而一个专家系统会有10 000个规则，这由需要模拟的知识本身决定。因此，专家系统需要特别高的准确性。这些专家系统中的规则并不是连续的，其中许多规则都是同时起作用的，并且许多的路线可以得到相同数量的有限结果。

专家系统可以应用于基本上任何需要逻辑判断的可详细定义的商业环境，但这些商业环境必须是可以被专家明确定义的，并且通过使重复性的事物工作自动化可以得到最佳结果或为服务雇员提供类似核对表的支持。由于经理们面对更加大量和更多信息来源的数据和多样化的问题，专家系统在这方面至今没能成功地模拟这些活动。

专家系统没有学习程序。如果需要改编或适应新的情况，就需要重新编程添加新的要素，这个过程将会花费很多时间并且成本很高。同时，专家系统不能用于不能得到预设结果的情况。通常，雇用一个专家来制定复杂的决策要比花费精力构建和维护一个专家系统成本要低得多。

表格表单

表格表单可以是物理格式或电子格式的。电子格式的表格表单整合了会计计算器和电子表格扩展表的功能。最常用的电子表格软件包括微软的 Excel 和 Lotus 1 – 2 – 3。这些电子表格软件比物理格式的表格表单功能更加强大，因为他们可以使用户对行或列的数学计算进行自动化处理，例如，加和、小计及其他更高级的数学运算。电子表格可以将数据按照不同的格式整理并进行对比。许多信息系统都是以简单的电子表格方式输出数据结果，从而用户可以根据需要进行数据处理。

互联网和企业内部网络

与其他形式的沟通技术相比，互联网的特殊性在于没有任何一个人拥有互联网。互联网是一系列网络的整合，以促进全球沟通。企业内部网则是由企业构建的私有互联网络，用于企业内部的沟通交流。

互联网

互联网最开始是在 1969 年作为军方的研究项目出现的，1972 年出现了电子邮件，随后在 20 世纪 80 年代初互联网才进入了公众视野。在 1990 年，Tim Berners-Lee 的超文本系统的引进改革了互联网的使用方式。超文本链接可以在瞬间将用户从一个网络站点转到另一个站点。随后 Berners-Lee 率先创建了互联网联盟，该联盟掌握着许多互联网使用需要的标准。

其他促使互联网的推广的发明包括软件可移植性和 Socket 网络编程技术。软件可移植性使得在以往不相匹配的操作系统也可以阅览网页。Socket 网络编程技术使查找网页和运用超文本链接成为可能并且更加快捷。廉价且功能强大的个人计算机的普及和电信带宽的增大都促使了互联网的快速推广。

用以传输大量信息的物理网络被称作骨干网（Internet Backbone）。骨干网由若干高性能的通信链接组成，例如，通过光纤电缆与万维网相连接的互联网服务提供商（ISP）。每个美国主要城市和世界上的主要城市都存在这种枢纽站点。

互联网的关键在于信息。现在信息可以以免费或很低的成本进行传输。厂商可以 24 小时为消费者提供其商品名单和对应价格，并且可以根据需要修改这些价格，而不用只在每年印刷新的商品目录时才能修改价格。除了可以降低发行成本以外，交易成本和送货时间也得到降低，特别是那些完全数字化的产品和服务，例如，下载软件或获取信用报告。

互联网使得关于物理商品的信息可以脱离该商品而存在。消费者可以在任何时间登录互联网站对不同商店的特色和价格进行比较（这将比到每个商店里去要便宜多了）。因此互联网正在改变（有时是在瓦解）传统厂商的经营模式，因为如果一个消费者在网上进行商品比较，而该厂商却没有自己的网站，那么很有可能该厂商将失去这次交易。

美国证监会网站（www. sec. gov）上的 EDGAR 数据库是体现互联网强大作用的另一个例子。这个数据库包含了按规定需要向美国证监会提交报告的所有公司的财务公告。在这个数据库出现前，要获得这些资料需要向美国证监会提出申请并等待接收复印件。

互联网一个重要的不足在于它提供了和公司服务器的链接，这就有可能带来恶意攻击、信息盗窃和其他形式的有害结果。因而公司将在互联网上传输的信息加密，建立例如防火墙的保护措施阻止未授权的用户和病毒，同时还有其他形式的安全措施。安全措施在 CMA 教材第一本书第 3 章中有介绍。

互联网鉴证服务

鉴于以互联网为基础的商业交易的安全性在现实中或想象中的顾虑，电子商务的发展受到了阻碍。许多公司都通过互联网鉴证服务试公司互联网商业链接的安全性和可靠性。鉴证是一个很宽泛的概念，其中包括审计，根据美国注册公共会计师协会（AICPA）的定义就是，"提高环境和信息安全的独立专业服务"。缴纳一定的费用后，审计师可以为用户提供一定的鉴证服务，确保其在浏览客户网站时安全得到保障同时保证电子商务工具使用的可靠性。这使得测试相应的中间媒介成为必要，例如网络提供商和销售商，同时包括多种链接方式，例如不同的浏览器。鉴证服务通常也要求公司在其网站上披露进行电子商务的具体业务流程。

另外，同一个或不同的公司或组织也可以提供站点安全性和可靠性的认证。例如，WebTrust 的鉴证服务就是美国注册公共会计师协会（AICPA）和加拿大特许会计师协会（CICA）颁发的联合认证。一旦专业会计师为一个站点或电子商务应用作出了不合格的鉴定，它们就可以选择在其站点上加盖 WebTrust 的认章。这个认章可以通过一个自我核实的链接阻止未授权的使用。这样的认证需要定期地更新才能保持其有效性。需要注意的是，网络鉴证并不需要注册会计师（CPA）或注册会计师组织的参与。

企业内部网

企业内部网与互联网类似，不同在于它是专为企业及其内部各部门使用的网络。企业内部网的最大的优势在于，它可以使公司内部许多不同的计算机平台和数据库同时分享数据，而不用为不同的系统构建一个转换程序。企业内部网允许任何有安全认证的人员通过浏览器获取公司的信息，在电子布告板上张贴消息，查询产品目录中的价格，查询公司网上数据库中的信息，或通过雇员自助软件填写考勤卡、选择福利计划或更改个人信息。

企业内部网还有多媒体展示功能，例如，可以播出 CEO 的讲话录像，或可以使员工在线观看网上直播的公司范围的会议同时向发言人提问，而这些并不需要大家离开自己的办公桌。同时，为公司聚会、公司新闻和内部职位招聘建立一个新的空间可以带来增强员工士气和团队感的无形利益。

另一个使用公司内部网来节约成本的功能在于，公司指南、电话簿、产品目录和其他的信息可以快速更新，并且要比在纸上打印要便宜得多。这样这些信息更能做到日日更新。将时事通讯发在公司内部网上节约了打印和邮寄的成本。合作的加强同样可以通过激发创新和提高生产效率来降低成本。许多公司都从恭喜内部网的投资中收到了 23% ~ 85% 的收益，少数公司还有指数级的收益（Laudon，2003）。

财务和会计职员可以通过公司内部网将来自不同系统的数据进行整合，例如，基本存款账户、年报和预算流程，而在以前这些系统往往没有相互间的沟通。通过使用密码和公司内部网链接，在卖场的销售人员可以查询最新的价格和销售数据，与经理沟通和录入订货单。公司可以通过公司内部网协助生产部门，例如，为日常生产提供利润和亏损信息，或为每一个生产机械建立相应的网页，其中包括次品数、产品数和其他实时信息。

浏览器软件

浏览器用于阅读互联网上的信息，这些信息由特殊的语言程序书写，例如，超文本标识语言（HTML）、可扩展标识语言（XML）和 Java 语言。这些语言可以被任意操作系统上的任意浏览器解读。在当今的商业环境中，浏览器是最常用的计算机工具，它被用作与虚拟私有网络（VPNs）、公司内部网络、通信工具和少客户端软件应用相链接的接口。互联网和浏览器大大促进了研究发展的速度。

进度检查

提示：完成以下各题。参考答案随后给出。

1. 以下哪一种数据库管理系统，可以像处理其他类型的数据一样处理和查询演示视频或图片？
  （　　）a. 关系型数据库管理系统
  （　　）b. 层级型数据库管理系统
  （　　）c. 面向对象型数据库管理系统
  （　　）d. 网络型数据库管理系统
2. 以下关于人工智能的论述哪一项是正确的？
  （　　）a. 专家系统存在学习能力
  （　　）b. 类神经网络存在学习能力
  （　　）c. 模糊逻辑比传统的软件程序需要更多的编码
  （　　）d. 类神经网络使用顺序处理方式

进度检查答案

1. c
2. b

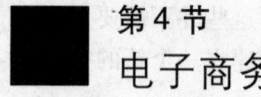

第4节
电子商务

本节内容简介

在互联网出现前，电子商务仅仅是在企业间昂贵的专用网上进行。出现互联网后，企业的连接更加方便，而且稳定、便宜。传统的处理成本比互联网的处理成本高，比如给客户服务中心打一个电话将花费公司大约 $10 ~ $45（在直接人工和制造费用上），但是用电子邮件回复只需花费公司 $1 ~ $5 和大约 10 到 20 美分的网页服务成本（Laudon，2003）。

使用互联网技术来付款对买卖双方都更便宜，但是因为支付的电子货款比传统的邮寄方式更早到达，付款方享受不到用平邮的好处。平邮的延迟能产生资金的机会成本，因此在转换为电子支付以后付款方通常会要求提前付款而给予的折扣。

电子商务（E-commerce）是一种通过电子手段进行的货币交易、销售或企业文档传送。其中一种最旧式但仍广泛使用的电子商务方法是电子数据交换（EDI）。本节还将讨论 B2B 技术，其他的电子商务技术如在线交易处理（OLTP）和电子资金转账（EFT）。

电子数据交换（EDI）

电子数据交换（EDI）是一种通过电子文档的传送联系两个企业的一种方法，它具有高度的形式化和结构化。EDI 允许两个企业用它们各自规定的正确格式来交换企业文档和交易信息。EDI 传送诸如发票、购买订单或船运单之类的文件。最初，EDI 仅在两个企业间的专用网上运行。两企业间需要在使用哪种专用软件上达成一致。现在，EDI 通常是通过第三方来运行的，第三方能更有效地和花费更低成本来完成所有数据的翻译。EDI 还能通过使用虚拟专用网络在互联网上频繁交换数据。互联网大大降低了 EDI 的成本，小企业都能使用。

EDI 不同于电子邮件，因为用于传输数据的形式是形式化的，而且包括特殊数据类型的标准化字段也是形式化的。由于 EDI 是标准化的，企业必须让他们的形式符合这个特定格式（考虑到设计一个信息系统时将用到 EDI）。EDI 用于传输的字段非常可靠，因而 EDI 比电子邮件更加安全。当把 EDI 与电子支付相结合时，EDI 可以确认资金转账的数量和时间。

B2B（企业对企业）

B2B（企业对企业）电子商务是在两个或两个以上企业间的企业交易活动，包括网上销售。B2B 连接了所在行业的企业、卖家以及中间商。在外网上，许多有合作关系的企业常联合在一起建立一个专用商务网络。一个 B2B 的外网，专用交换或专用商务网络是一个由许多期望互相进行贸易的企业所组成的安全网络，它通常通过增值网络（VAN）来运行，但它属于买家。VAN 是一个提供数据传输、外部网络、EDI

翻译、存储和恢复电子数据的网络服务公司。一个专用的企业网络提供给客户有关产品和价格的即时信息，可以降低对客户的代理活动和成本。同样地，买方也可以降低他们取得信息的成本。专用企业网络用于连续的协调和企业交易处理的改进。

因为 EDI 是管理 B2B 的一种方法，所有列出的使用 EDI 的好处也适用于 B2B 的交易。使用互联网来促进企业间的联系意味着小企业也能成为 B2B 的成员。而且，专用企业网络甚至比纯 EDI 系统更为方便，因为它可以不断改进，可以使用多媒体和信息数据库，分享产品设计和开发、市场营销、存货管理、生产计划和安全电子邮件。

另一种 B2B 的形式被称为网络商业中心或电子中心。网络商业中心是一个连接多买方与多卖方的数码市场。这个概念与专用企业网络是相区别的，区别在于专用企业网络是一个买方对应多个卖方。网络商业中心是属于一个企业联盟或是作为中间商的独立的一些企业。有些网络商业中心能进行在线竞标或拍卖，有些提供固定的价格，有些允许企业进行询价（RFQs）。网络商业中心能被划分成销售直接产品的和销售间接产品的。直接产品是再生产过程中直接使用的直接材料如原材料。间接产品是再生产过程之外使用的材料如办公用品或修理工具。有些网络商业中心提供垂直的供应链（如房屋建造业）；另一些提供跨行业的水平的市场（如货运业）。交换是一种网络商业中心的类型，它连接买家和卖家的即时需求（现场购买）。一个在线 B2B 交换的例子是 www.rosettanet.org。

其他的电子商务技术

这部分包括在线交易处理（OLTP）和电子资金转账（EFT）。

在线交易处理（OLTP）

在线交易处理（OLTP）是一个在用户提交交易时进行处理的工具（正与批处理相反）。OLTP 能有效地工作是因为它在客户端上（PC）的进入点处理所有的或大部分的数据。这样做使网络工作的传输拥挤最小化，但需要把交易分成客户方交易和服务方交易。因此，OLTP 需要网络上的其他用户更新数据库，即改变数据库中潜在的耗时交易。以自动提款机（ATM）为例，当用户提取现金时，系统更新所有其他 ATMs 上的用户余额。这种数据复制功能确保了用户对当前数据的可用性。

OLTP 主要支持数据库管理，通过交易信息，如销售交易降低产成品存货这样的信息，它允许用户生成即时特别报告和更新数据库。OLTP 也是一个处理其他交易的标准化过程，如处理信用卡许可。

OLTP 的主要优点在于交易处理的数据库是即时可用的，其主要缺点在于如果不能解决系统拥挤，大量的、多样的交易产生的高度拥挤将降低系统运行速度，或造成系统瘫痪。尽管有些系统能平稳运行，但拥挤度仍将导致交易处理需要长时间等待，特别是处理复杂报告时。另外有些系统增加了故障容忍设计（通过硬件和软件冗余），当系统非常重要时能避免系统故障（如控制空运的计算机）。

我们建立高效率的计算系统，该系统需要不断升级和长时间运行，但并不意味着需要达到没有任何故障的程度。高效率计算涉及支持程序，以及在故障后快速运行的软硬件控制程序。这种系统通过负载均衡、镜像、集群和事故恢复计划技术提高系统使用 OLTP 的效率。负载均衡是在多台服务器间分配交易处理工作以保证一台服务器不会接到过多的工作量。镜像是建立一个与主服务器相同的系统，当主服务器出故障时代替它工作。集群是连接两台或两台以上的计算机像备份单元一样运作或进行平行处理。事故恢复计划是当发生系统故障时，为迅速恢复服务的组织计划和技术计划。

电子资金转账（EFT）

电子资金转账（EFT）是一种电子化支付和传送支付相关信息的通用方法。EFT 和金融 EDI 是属于 EDI，但又区别于 EDI 因它们涉及实际的价值转移。EFT 与金融 EDI 的区别在于：EFT 仅在两个银行间或联邦储备银行内进行；而金融 EDI 能在银行和企业间或两个及两个以上企业间进行。企业仍使用 EFT，不过是通过支行进行转账。EFT 的主要形式有自动清算（ACH）和电汇。其他形式包括电子支票、电子锁箱和电子现金。1987 年的电子资金转账法定义了 EFT 服务的权利和义务（该法案没有包括电汇），限定了个人关于非授权交易的责任（要求个人使用 ATMs 或销售点（POS）终端机时，能即时把问题告知银行）。

自动清算（ACH）采用标准化格式进行有关支付、财务文档和支付信息的电子交换。ACH 包括薪水支付的直接存款或社会安全支票。两个银行建立一个预定的交易协议。ACH 并非马上执行协议，由于认证而要延迟执行。另一方面，电汇是两个银行间迅速而安全的转账。电汇花费比 ACH 高，因此，只有大笔资金转账且当转账速度节约的钱比两者间的费用差（大约相差一天的资金的机会成本）高时才用电汇。联邦电汇是联邦储备的电汇系统。

电子锁箱类似于一个有锁的箱子（一个能收到支票和直接存入资金的专用箱子），只是它是通过锁箱银行把汇款通知记入数据库，而加快了支付速度。汇款数据直接被转移到收款人的应收账款的交易处理系统。

电子支票类似于书面支票（如它们都包括银行账号和支票号等），只是电子支票还包括了数字签名（如 IRS 公司收到上年的税款退回用数字签名来证实可靠性）。电子现金是现金的一种数字形式，它是由银行生成的可与真实现金交换的现金形式。电子现金存在电子钱包里直到用户为在线服务付款。到收款时，收款人从银行收到真实的现金。电子支票和电子现金保证了在线交易的安全。

进度检查

提示：完成以下各题。参考答案随后给出。

1. 以下哪种技术允许小公司参与电子数据交换（EDI）事务？
（　　）a. 互联网
（　　）b. 万维网（WANs）
（　　）c. 可扩展标识语言（XML）
（　　）d. 企对企（B2B）

2. 以下哪一项是电子传送资金费用最高的方法？
（　　）a. 电子支票

　　（　　）b. 自动清算（ACH）

　　（　　）c. 金融 EDI

　　（　　）d. 电汇

3. 自动取款机是什么技术的表现形式？

　　（　　）a. 在线交易处理（OLTP）

　　（　　）b. 自动清算（ACH）

　　（　　）c. 金融 EDI

　　（　　）d. 电汇

进度检查答案

1. a

2. d

3. a

第5节
综合的企业整体数据模型

本节内容简介

综合的企业整体数据模型有储存和分析所有数据的能力，那些数据是储存在一个数据库中，为企业所拥有。当仓库仅仅用于进行报告和分析时，我们称之为数据仓库，例如，数据挖掘和在线分析处理（OLAP）工具，它们允许把数据转化成知识。这些核心成分形成了综合的企业整体数据模型，利用企业资源规划系统，使多个部门通过电子网络进行信息交流。该系统对应的每个部门通常有一个或多个软件模块，企业只需要购买某个模块就能使该部门与其他部门之间的数据传递顺畅。因为信息可以同时转移，企业中的不同部门就可以同时开展同一项工作，如一份客户订单能同时报告给会计和材料需求规划部门。

数据仓储和数据挖掘

数据仓储

数据仓库是一个所有信息来自于交易处理系统（TPS）的数据库仓库。它只被用来查询和分析，但不能进行交易处理，不过由于不需要在交易处理数据库上进行查询，从而加快信息检索和交易处理的速度，所以企业一般都会建立两种内部数据库。

- 主数据库包括交易处理系统，它处理所有日常交易的输入和更新。
- 辅助的数据库，或数据仓库，是作为主数据库的镜像而建立的。

这种划分让复杂的查询和报告能在任何时候运行，而不会降低企业的运行速度。

数据仓库还可当作交易处理系统的数据收集点，它可以在不同的、不兼容的数据库上收集信息，这样相当于有了综合的企业整体数据库的优点，而又节省了建立这种数据库的成本。经理就可以在决策制定时，结合大量信息的分析从而提供综合的报告。

数据仓库的数据是非即时信息，数据是只读的。流入数据仓库的信息，即每个交易处理数据库变动的信息，先被收集再成批地定期（如晚上）送入数据仓库更新。因此，数据对长期计划可能有用，但对一个检查某项售出的存货水平的销售人员来说，数据却不一定有用。如果需要即时的、有用的信息，即便是简单的查询，如存货水平，仍需直接在交易处理系统上处理。

数据仓库包括报告和查询的工具以及被称为数据分库的数据子集。查询工具有定期自动运行的标准报告，能在任何时候建立和运行的特别报告，以及在线分析处理（OLAP）工具（在本节后面讨论），如决策支持软件（DSS）。数据分库是数据仓库中数据的一部分，它被独立化，是进一步分析的需要。一个市场营销数据分库包括市场营销部门所需的所有数据，因此查询会更迅速，并使分析项目可以与相关可控数据组相联系。

数据挖掘

数据挖掘是一个应用软件工具，它能找到信息的隐藏模式，然后用这些模式建立起预测未来结果的规则。它在预测未来结果和制定组织决策上很有用。数据挖掘程序在预测趋势上显示了较高的水平，但有时候仍需用户进一步挖掘数据。数据挖掘大多是为市场营销定位服务，具体到顾客喜欢什么和不喜欢什么。有些杂货店利用会员卡向客户发放优惠券，同时收集有关客户购买习惯的资料，以此制定更多有针对性的促销活动。

数据仓库的运行，为数据挖掘提供了极大的方便。数据仓库从企业的交易处理数据库聚集了所有数据，因此，当数据挖掘需要更多信息要时，数据仓库的运行有利于更好地进行处理。由于挖掘发生在交易处理系统外，数据分析则不会降低系统运行速度。

由于通过数据挖掘可以发现经理没考虑到，但报告需要的信息，因此对经理来说它是非常有用的。数据挖掘产生了下列的信息类型：

- 关联型：一个独立事件的发生能引起另一事件同时发生在某个时间的概率，如当下雨的时候，雨伞的销售额将上升25%。
- 顺序型：有联系的事件按时间顺序发生，如当购买了一辆汽车时，新车主的前三次加油有40%的次数是使用经销商的加油服务。
- 集群和分类：集群项目如果将顾客按收入水平分组。分类是在分好的组中找出每组共同的特点，按收入水平分好组的顾客中谁最有可能购买运动型房车。
- 预测型：预测可以为重大事件分析提供所有变量，如预测下个月的生产成本或销售水平。

在线分析处理（OLAP）

在线分析处理（OLAP）是多维数据分析的一种形式，即它允许从两个以上的维度或角度来分析数据。举例来说，一个标准的二维分析可能包括销售收入对应销售地区，而多维分析可能加入实际的对应预算的销售数据。因此，扩展的表格像个立方体，正如在图表2-51所展示的。

图表2-51　多维数据模型

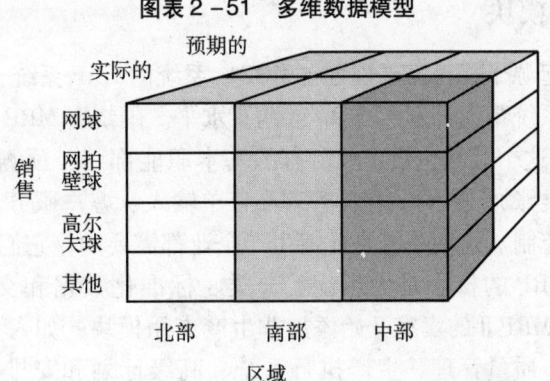

用户可以旋转这个立方体（称之为"切割"）来进行不同的比较，而不用向数据库提交新的查询。这样的工具在ERP系统中被广泛用来进行特别报告。

企业资源规划（ERP）系统

企业资源规划（ERP）系统是一组诸如财务、销售和人力资源的模块；它允许企业购买一套应用软件包，这些软件包能完美地聚集在一起，产生自动的交互作用和提供普通数据来源。ERP系统使企业避免了在企业需要的模块间设计接口，ERP系统可以直接通过接口连接到外部的软件或旧系统。工业专用软件和最优化软件经常被连接到如前所述的一种ERP系统中。ERP系统的购买、实施（实施要一到几年）和维护都非常贵，但是尽管如此，大多数大企业都有ERP系统，而随着这个市场的饱和，ERP的卖家正瞄准了更小的企业。

ERP系统基本上是为企业定制，满足企业需求的交易处理系统。由于期望的定制在数量上有限制，同时为了适应ERP系统的标准程序，多数在建ERP系统的企业不得不改变他们处理事情的某些方式。定制对许多ERP系统来说是个问题，因为当实施ERP系统时，许多组织让他们的职能部门通过构想其现在需要的功能，从而定义各部门需要什么。然而，每个部门通常会加上某些具有功能性的步骤但不删除无法增值的步骤，或降低程序复杂性，然后他们选择最接近的ERP软件包，试图把它定制成完全适合每个职能部门的程序，尽管那些程序效率并不高。事实上，他们这样做，比买成品软件的价格多了700%～800%。为了让程序更有效，与他们的ERP系统更协调，企业需要再设计他们的程序，这就只比软件价格多了200%～300%且能很快实施系统。

ERP系统的心脏是企业整体数据库：数据库把储存的不同类型的数据放在同一地方（理想地），以至于多样的记录不需要为同一数据而保存。企业内部数据库意味着如果某个客户要求更改他的地址，只需要更新一个记录数据，而不用在信贷部门更新一个，在票据结算部门更新一个，在市场营销部门更新一个。这样的数据库对数据处理是高效率的，还能加快事务处理的速度。这种数据库的复制版本一般还被当作数据仓库（见本节前面的讨论）使用。它定期更新，并用作报告和分析的工具，如数据挖掘和OLAP查询。

ERP模块

起源于材料需求规划（MRP）系统的ERP系统，它的核心是材料需求规划功能。这些系统帮助计划生产和/或购买水平。围绕着MRP的是被称为制造资源计划（MRPⅡ），这个计划包括企业所有的基本职能部门：预测、会计（应收账款、应付账款、总分类账）、采购、存货管理、订单输入、客户服务、总调度、标准成本核算和生产活动控制。这些系统是任何生产企业都需要的，它们的整合让企业变得更加高效和有效。ERP的核心是为组织、分类、标准化数据和交易程序而服务。最后，当这些MRP/MRPⅡ的卖家开始添加非生产专用模块，如人力资源、销售和营运计划、市场营销、质量管理、生产执行系统、高级计划和安排、决策支持系统和需求管理等，"ERP"一词就开始存在了。

最初，ERP 有专用的密码，它需要使用来自于卖家的专用模块，或花费大量时间和金钱在不同系统间的接口上。对最初的定制和构造进行更新是非常昂贵的。正当全球和以互联网为基础的商务贸易不断扩大，企业需要与更多的合作者一起工作，ERP 系统也有了改进，使它能更快地、更方便地与外部系统联系。大多数端口现在都是采用通用的可兼容语言如可扩展标识语言（XML）来编程。

近年来，ERP 经销商添加了越来越多的功能，从客户关系管理（CRM）到供应关系管理（SRM），CRM 改进市场营销工具使之能满足顾客需要，SRM 帮助管理经销商的供应链或网络，包括半自动或全自动的购买功能。但是 CRM 和 SRM 都是作为单独的应用程序来使用的，当把它们在 ERP 系统中完全结合时，总体的 CRM 和/或 SRM 系统将更容易自动化，如告诉什么时候开始生产，什么时候开始购买，什么时候分配运货（如在下订单之后）或允许客户服务代表知道目前的存货水平，有哪些替代品和客户信用等级。其他的作用包括把海关和其他的电子商连接进 ERP 系统，易化了外部应用一体化（EAI）（连接到其他 ERP 和旧系统），对于外部合作者的团队合作和计划来说，还易化了合作的计划、预测和补充（CPFR）。

ERP 系统的优点和局限性

ERP 系统的优点是它们主要由事件驱动。当事件发生时（如一笔销售），系统捕捉财务和非财务的数据并把它们同时转移到相关的部门。ERP 系统允许一家跨国企业或一家通过多渠道合并成长的企业，标准化每个厂房和设备的交易处理。（ERP 系统可采用多国语言）ERP 企业整体数据库允许经理改进决策制定，因为所有的企业数据能结合来报告。ERP 系统还能被扩展以提供更多的优点。一个正确实施的 ERP 系统应当让高层管理质疑企业的基础安排，并通过系统提供清晰的信息，帮助企业找到新的增长机会。

ERP 系统的缺点是成本高，成本是通过类似的投资报酬（成本节约加上直接利润）来确定的。ERP 系统让企业改变程序，有时改得更好，有时相反。广泛的定制能避免一些问题，但是过多地采用定制软件则非常昂贵，甚至更新软件也会更贵。如果不能被组织的所有部门认同，或终端用户的培训不足以让他们适应改变，ERP 的实施可能失败，企业整体数据库的使用会造成系统内部的交通堵塞。大量的交易处理和大量的报告需求将降低系统速度，因此，不得不采用批处理或使用数据仓库。

进度检查

提示：完成以下各题。参考答案随后给出。

1. 以下哪一项关于企业资源规划系统的说法不是真的？
   - （　　）a. 它们使用成套的模块
   - （　　）b. 它们是最优的解决方案
   - （　　）c. 没有必要在模块间建立连接口
   - （　　）d. 它们使用企业整体数据库
2. 以下哪一项关于企业资源规划系统的说法是真的？
   - （　　）a. 它们保持各部门的数据库的独立性

（　　）b. 它们有时让不同的工厂采用不同的程序

（　　）c. 有时企业必须改变他们的程序来适应 ERP 系统

（　　）d. 获得投资报酬很容易

3. 以下哪一项关于数据仓库（data warehouses）的说法不是真的？

（　　）a. 它们从多种数据库中收集数据

（　　）b. 它们提供即时信息

（　　）c. 数据是只读的

（　　）d. 它们保存而非处理交易和报告

进度检查答案

1. b

2. c

3. b

业绩评价

本章内容简介

一个组织有了总预算，也就明确了它的目标，但是如果没有及时反馈组织的现状与组织的行进方向，那么这个预算过程是无效的。这一章告诉我们，如何将与全面预算的差异划分为不同类别，以帮助组织判断差异发生的特定原因；如何利用责任中心或企业战略单位的业绩反馈进行利润管理。同时这一章也会涉及到责任中心与组织中用来衡量利润的财务指标。

前一章讲了财务计量，本章将会讨论业绩评价的平衡记分卡法。平衡记分卡同时衡量了企业的财务与非财务状况，并且与企业战略息息相关，所以通过阅读平衡记分卡可以告诉企业的每一个人企业的战略是什么，以及如何实现它。最后，本章还会提到全面质量管理是如何帮助企业提高质量和利润的。

学习要点说明

注册管理会计师（CMA）考试包含很多学习要点，这些学习要点由管理会计师协会确定。学习要点描述了注册管理会计师考试要求掌握的所有知识点和技能，并且细分为各个章节。注册管理会计师考试教材解释了学习要点所包含的各个部分，是对学习要点的有力支持。学习要点可以帮助考生以不同的方式或通过不同的问题情景理解这些概念。考生还应该练习学习要点中所提到的全部或者部分计算，或者完成计算过程中的缺失部分。学习要点不能代替对 CMA 考试教材内容的研究和学习，但是可以确保考生达到学习要点所设定的目标。

注册管理会计师教材中所包含的学习要点是一个完整的集合，并且是到目前为止最新的版本。考生可以浏览 IMA 的官方网站 www.imanet.org，点击"认证"部分查看和下载关于学习要点的最新 PDF 文件。

学习要点

4.1　成本差异计量

- LOS 4.1.1：在收入、制造成本、非制造成本和被衡量的中心或单位种类的利润的基础上，使用多种方式来分析业绩。
- LOS 4.1.2：解释为什么业绩评价方法要直接与公司战略和营业目标相关，以及为什么反馈重要。
- LOS 4.1.3：解释在业绩监督系统中差异产生的原因（不能仅仅关注数字结果）。
- LOS 4.1.4：解释为什么业绩评价与被评价项目的动机因素有关，比如，成本动因和收入动因。
- LOS 4.1.5：推荐业绩评价和比较实际结果和营业目标的定期报告方法。
- LOS 4.1.6：通过比较实际结果与总预算，进行业绩评估，计算有利差异和不利差异，并根据现有情况，解释差异产生的原因。
- LOS 4.1.7：用实际结果与总预算相比进行业绩评价的优点和缺点。
- LOS 4.1.8：以实际销售数量为基础编制弹性预算。
- LOS 4.1.9：通过比较弹性预算与总（静态）预算计算销售数量差异和销售价格差异。
- LOS 4.1.10：通过实际结果与弹性预算的比较计算弹性预算差异。
- LOS 4.1.11：调查弹性预算差异，计算实际投入价格及数量与预算的差异。
- LOS 4.1.12：解释例外管理并讲述在这种情况下如何进行预算差异报告。
- LOS 4.1.13：解释什么是标准成本系统，以及采用这种系统的原因。
- LOS 4.1.14：解释什么是价格差异，以及如何计算与直接材料和直接人工投入相关的价格差异。
- LOS 4.1.15：解释什么是效率差异，以及如何计算与直接材料和直接人工投入相关的效率差异。
- LOS 4.1.16：解释什么与固定和变动间接费用相关的耗费差异和效率差异。
- LOS 4.1.17：计算销售组合差异，阐述对收入和边际贡献的影响。
- LOS 4.1.18：阐述效率差异如何进一步分解成组合差异和产出差异。
- LOS 4.1.19：解释实际直接材料和/或人力的投入比率与标准比率之间的组合差异发生的原因。
- LOS 4.1.20：计算产出差异。
- LOS 4.1.21：解释如何在服务企业和制造企业运用价格、效率差异、耗费差异、组合差异。
- LOS 4.1.22：分析差异，找出原因并找到改进行为。

4.2　责任中心与报告部门

- LOS 4.2.1：阐明和解释各种责任中心（战略业务部门）的区别。
- LOS 4.2.2：公司应如何选择合适的责任中心。
- LOS 4.2.3：业绩评价中边际贡献报告的使用。
- LOS 4.2.4：分析边际贡献报告，进行业绩评价。
- LOS 4.2.5：区分业绩评估的企业分部，包括生产线、地域或其他合理的分部。
- LOS 4.2.6：解释业绩评估中共同成本分配为何会成为一个问题。
- LOS 4.2.7：共同成本的分配方法，如独立成本分配和增量法分配。
- LOS 4.2.8：转移定价的定义及其目标。
- LOS 4.2.9：设定移转产品价格的方法并提出各个方法的优缺点。

- LOS 4.2.10：解释企业存在的各个因素如何影响移转产品价格，比如外部供应商的出现，与资金使用相应的机会成本。
- LOS 4.2.11：阐述关税、汇率、材料和技术的可获取性等特殊因素如何影响跨国公司的业绩评估。
- LOS 4.2.12：讲述税收、货币管制、被没收危险等特殊因素如何影响跨国公司的转移定价。

4.3　财务指标

- LOS 4.3.1：理解产品盈利能力、部门盈利能力、顾客盈利能力，包括成本计量、成本分摊、投资计量和估值等一些盈利指标的决定因素。
- LOS 4.3.2：利用一组数据和假设，计算产品线盈利能力、部门盈利能力和顾客盈利能力。
- LOS 4.3.3：基于盈利能力评估顾客和产品，采取措施提高盈利能力，削减无法获利的顾客和产品。
- LOS 4.3.4：定义和计算投资回报率（ROI）。
- LOS 4.3.5：利用 DuPont 法计算 ROI，并指出这种模型如何改善 ROI 计算分析。
- LOS 4.3.6：分析并解释 ROI 计算，利用分析结果评估绩效。
- LOS 4.3.7：定义和计算剩余利润（RI）。
- LOS 4.3.8：分析并解释 RI 计算，利用分析结果评估绩效。
- LOS 4.3.9：比较 ROI 和 RI 作为绩效指标的优缺点。
- LOS 4.3.10：定义经济增加值（EVA），在简单情形下进行计算。
- LOS 4.3.11：比较分别采用企业数据和外部市场数据计算的 ROI。
- LOS 4.3.12：理解 EVA 与 ROI、RI 指标的差异。
- LOS 4.3.13：定义市场增加值。
- LOS 4.3.14：阐述不同收入和费用会计确认政策将影响收入绩效计量，降低业务部门和企业间数据的可比性。
- LOS 4.3.15：阐述不同存货计价政策、资产的共有和共享、总资产计价政策将影响投资绩效计量，降低业务部门和企业间数据的可比性。
- LOS 4.3.16：定义投资现金流收益。
- LOS 4.3.17：理解跨国经营对绩效计量的影响。

4.4　平衡记分卡

- LOS 4.4.1：引入平衡记分卡的概念并界定其组成部分。
- LOS 4.4.2：定义关键成功因素并讨论这些因素在对公司进行评估时的重要性。
- LOS 4.4.3：界定财务指标，如营业利润、销售额增长、新产品销售额、毛利率、成本削减、EVA、ROI、RI 等等，并且评价它们在特定公司背景下的适用性。
- LOS 4.4.4：界定顾客满意度指标，如市场份额、忠诚度、反应时间、交货表现、缺陷、订货交货时间等等，并且评价它们在特定公司背景下的适用性。
- LOS 4.4.5：界定内部经营过程指标，如新产品的引入、技术能力、周期时间等等，并且评价它们在特定公司背景下的适用性。
- LOS 4.4.6：界定创新和学习指标，如员工技能、组织学习、行业领导者等等，并且评价它们在特定公司背景下的适用性。

- LOS 4.4.7：描述成功实施和使用的平衡记分卡的特征。
- LOS 4.4.8：分析并解释平衡记分卡，并在分析的基础上对业绩进行评价。

4.5 质量因素

- LOS 4.5.1：界定全面质量管理（TQM）的核心原则。
- LOS 4.5.2：界定与低水平质量管理相关的机会成本。
- LOS 4.5.3：证明对交流和培训在成功的 TQM 计划中的作用的理解。
- LOS 4.5.4：描述质量管理和生产率之间的关系，并解释对这种关系的误解会导致不当决策的原因。
- LOS 4.5.5：证明对分析质量问题的方法的理解，如控制图、帕累托图及因果图。
- LOS 4.5.6：界定质量因素如何成为衡量公司整体表现和评估过程的影响因素。
- LOS 4.5.7：界定质量审计和差距分析的目标。
- LOS 4.5.8：界定质量与顾客期望的关联。
- LOS 4.5.9：界定与质量相关的符合性并明确零缺陷质量符合与绝对质量符合。
- LOS 4.5.10：描述并界定质量成本的组成，一般指预防成本、评估成本、内部缺陷成本和外部缺陷成本。

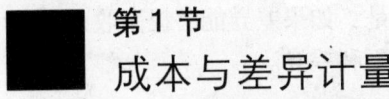

第 1 节
成本与差异计量

本节内容简介

反馈是控制的必要因素。管理中的反馈是指将计划或预算结果与实际结构做比较。差异是指实际结果与计划结果之间的不同。这一节将会介绍弹性预算与差异如何帮助管理人员控制成本，使他们工作效率最大化。

实际结果与计划结果的比较

一个成功的预算应该包括下面的特点。

- 总预算：将组织与其下属部门作为一个整体制定计划。
- 标准：设定一系列具体期望，使实际结果有所参照（参照本书第 1 章的第 1 节"预算概念"）。
- 从计划中调查差异并在必要时采取合适的行动。
- 再次计划：考虑反馈和情况变化。

当实际结果与计划结果相比较的时候，管理人员比较关心经营过程的效率和达到目标的效果。效率是指为与实际成本比较设定的特定成本的计划金额或标准。如果每件产品计划成本是 $2，那么一个有效率的经营过程就是卖了 1 000 件产品的成本是小于或等于 $2 000。一个无效率的经营过程就是大于 $2 000。效果则是衡量一个公司在多大程度上完成了它的目标。如果一个总预算要求营业利润净额达到 $3 亿，那么一个有效的经营过程就是获得大于或等于 $3 亿的净收入，一个无效的经营过程就是获得的净收入小于 $3 亿。一个经营过程可以是有效率但无效的，也可以有效果但无效率的。一个有效果但是无效率的经营过程就是指公司达到了主要目标，但是却费用超标；一个有效率但是无效果的经营过程是指公司没有达到预定目标，但是达到了预定的成本控制（注意：关于效率、效果的想法以及后面提到的差异计算的讨论和本书第 1 章第 1 节讲到的标准成本和持续促进［如：改善］有着直接的联系）。

为了同时达成这两个因素，我们必须知道这个系统是如何运行的以及如何操作。决定系统运行的主要因素包括标准成本，但只有与差异计算相结合才能决定实际系统行为，否则这些方法是不可能单独发挥作用的。而决定操作过程则依赖于在衡量过程中，如何在适当的、严格的水平上去选择恰当的基准（例如，面临不断增长的目标是否使用改善法，用特定类型的标准计算成本等）。

一个衡量效果的方法就是比较营业收入的计划结果与实际结果的差异。这个方法是利用营业利润表中的净利润作比较。第二种方法就是一行一行地比较实际与计划结果的差异。下面的图表 2－52 显示了静态预算中的差异比较，这个预算是在年初时编制且没有发生改变（弹性预算会在后面讲到）。

有利差异与不利差异

图表 2－52 中显示了有利差异与不利差异。有利差异是指超过企业计划收入金额

或低于计划成本，不利差异则相反。判断的惯用方法是：如果差异能够提高收入表最后一行的金额，那么就是有利差异；如果减少，就是不利差异。

图表 2 –52　实际结果与静态预算的差异

总体层次计量			
实际营业收入		$35 760	
计划营业收入		270 000	
静态预算中营业收入差异		$234 240 U	
中间层次计量			

	实际结果	静态预算	差异（实际—静态）
销售数量	24 000	30 000	6 000 U *
总收入	$3 000 000	$3 600 000	$600 000 U
变动成本：			
直接材料	1 491 840	1 800 000	308 160 F **
直接人工	475 200	480 000	4 800 F
变动生产间接费用	313 200	360 000	46 800 F
变动成本总计	2 280 240	2 640 000	359 760 F
边际贡献	719 760	960 000	240 240 U
固定成本	684 000	690 000	6 000 F
营业利润	$35 760	$270 000	$234 240 U

＊U = 对营业利润的不利差异。
＊＊F = 对营业利润的有利差异。

　　注意图表 2 –52 中，直接材料有利差异：$1 491 840 – $1 800 000 =（$308 160）。这是一个负数，但却是我们所偏好的。正负号对于追溯差异计算是十分重要的，但是其本身并不能表示偏好或不偏好。应该结合实际考虑，比如针对成本，负数表示成本减少，增加了净收入，所以是有利差异。相反，表中 $600 000 是非偏好性收入，因为这比计划收入要低，会减少净收入。在文中的很多描述都是强调是有利差异还是不利差异，但是如果把两者相加，那么它们是净得。

　　直接材料中的 $308 160 有利差异是否对公司是好事呢（尽管整个营业过程是无效果的，但至少是比较有效率的）？不一定。因为整个营运过程有在销售数量上的不利差异，这个经营过程之所以无效果就是因为销售低于预算。正因为产品生产减少，所以直接材料成本减少。在预算中，直接材料成本是 $1 800 000，产品数量是 30 000 件，单价是 $60。实际的产品数量只有 24 000 件，其实际成本为 $1 491 840，所以实际的每件成本 $62.16。因此，有利差异与不利差异并不是判断结果好坏的必要手段，只是告诉我们公司是否达到了预定计划。事实上，带横线项目的预算差异容易产生误导，它并不能表明计划的效率与效果。差异应该与材料比较，如果是完全不需要的材料，就应该忽略。但是我们应该切记，一些小小的差异会产生更大的问题。

　　预算差异之所以产生主要是因为我们在编制预算时，假设预算执行效果低下，或内部与外部环境发生不可预见的改变。我们需要多种方式计量经营过程的效率，以便我们可以了解错过目标的原因。而弹性预算的使用能够让我们了解更多的计量细节，从而发现预算差异存在的原因。

使用弹性预算进行业绩评价

前面我们讨论了静态预算以及与实际结果的比较差异。这一章定义了弹性预算并讨论它们在业绩评价中的作用。

弹性预算与静态预算

两者的共同特点在于都是计划性的，最初是以同样方式编制。这两者的主要区别在于，静态预算是不能改变的，而且所有比较都是与预期产量相对比进行的，而弹性预算则改变了预算金额，使它反映现实产出水平。比如制造公司依靠产出数量改变预算，医院依靠每天病人数量改变预算，服务公司依靠服务时间改变预算。

这里我们沿用前面静态预算的例子。如果预计销售为 30 000 件，但是实际销量为 24 000 件，那么弹性预算就会将预计销量改为 24 000 件，那么相应的其他科目也随之发生变化，从静态预算中编制一个弹性预算有利于管理人员进行精细比较。这样，使用弹性预算，直接材料成本中的有利差异就会变成不利差异，使用新的预算金额 $1 440 000（$60 每件 × 24 000 件），实际金额为 $1 491 840，所以就会有 $51 840 的不利差异。

与静态预算相比，弹性预算能提供更好的管理控制结果，因为它可以更好地控制变动成本与固定成本。理论上来说，管理层能更好地控制变动成本是因为他们的成本行为与生产数量紧密联系。如果实际生产数量低于预计生产数量，变动成本就会与销售数量同等比率降低。

弹性预算的特点

虽然静态预算中的差异会产生误导，但是弹性预算的差异却不会。弹性预算改变了产出数量及相应的与产量相关的其他项目，但是没有改变单价、单位成本，以及其他与产量无关的项目。固定成本通常不会改变，因为整个营运期间固定成本没有变动，在图表 2 - 53 中我们能看到在弹性预算中一个不利差异成为一个有利差异。

图表 2 - 53　制造公司的弹性预算

	销售数量达到 80%		销售数量达到 100%		销售数量达到 110%	
销量	24 000		30 000		33 000	
销售收入	$2 880 000		$3 600 000		$3 960 000	
变动成本	2 112 000		2 640 000		2 904 000	
边际贡献	$768 000	26.67%	$960 000	26.67%	$1 056 000	26.67%
固定成本	690 000		690 000		690 000	
营业利润	$78 000	2.7%	$270 000	7.5%	$366 000	9.2%

图表 2 - 53 中显示了弹性预算既可以在知道实际结果之前编制，也可以在知道实际结果以后编制。销量的改变使得收入与变动成本都有所变化，所以边际贡献与营业利润也随之发生相应的改变，但是应该注意：边际贡献率是不变的，变的只是营业利

润率。这是因为当弹性预算产生了不利差异，固定成本就占了成本中较大的比例；如果是有利差异，就正好相反。

弹性预算的编制不会涉及总预算。总预算必须在会计期间开始之前编制，而弹性预算则可以在任何时候编制，任何条件下编制的详细程度也可有所不同（以强调需要引起关注的特殊项目）。管理层可以使用弹性预算去计量营业利润，并找到营业状况发生变化的原因。

编制弹性预算的步骤

编制弹性预算应该包括下面四个步骤：

1. 编制静态总预算

这个步骤中包括决定预算销售单价、预计单位变动成本、预计固定成本，这些金额在后面的弹性预算中都会用到。

2. 找到实际生产数量

产量是变动成本的成本动因。

3. 计算弹性预算中的总收入

在计算总收入时应该用下面的公式：

总收入 = 销售数量 × 预计销售单价

比如，弹性预算中的总收入可以这样计算：

总收入 = \$120/件 × 24 000 件

= \$2 880 000

4. 计算弹性预算的成本金额

下面的公式可用来计算弹性预算中的总成本：

总成本 = 变动成本合计 + 固定成本合计

变动成本合计 = 单位变动成本 × 销售数量

图表 2 - 54 告诉了我们弹性预算的计算过程。

图表 2 - 54　弹性预算的成本金额

弹性预算的变动成本	
直接材料	\$1 440 000（\$60 × 24 000）
直接人工	\$384 000（\$16 × 24 000）
制造费用	\$288 000（\$12 × 24 000）
变动成本合计	2 112 000
弹性预算的固定成本	690 000
弹性预算的成本总额	\$2 802 000

弹性预算差异与销售数量差异

弹性预算可以用来衡量经营过程的效率。

编制了弹性预算以后，实际结果与静态预算结果的差异可以分成两种不同的差异：

- 弹性差异是指实际结果减去调整后弹性预算结果。
- 销售数量差异是指调整后弹性预算金额减去静态预算金额。

在图表2-55中，将静态预算与实际结果的差异分成了两种不同的差异。

图表2-55　弹性差异与销售数量差异

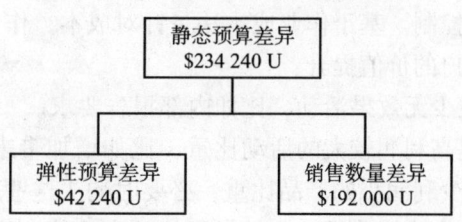

图表2-56告诉我们怎样计算弹性预算差异与销售数量差异。

图表2-56　计算弹性预算与销售数量差异

	实际结果	弹性预算	弹性预算差异	静态预算	销售数量差异
销售数量	24 000	24 000	0	30 000	6 000 U
总收入	$3 000 000	$2 880 000	$120 000 F	$3 600 000	$720 000 U
变动成本：					
直接材料	1 491 840	1 440 000	51 840 U	1 800 000	360 000 F
直接人工	475 200	384 000	91 200 U	480 000	360 000 F
变动制造费用	313 200	288 000	25 200 U	360 000	72 000 F
变动成本总计	2 280 240	2 112 000	168 240 U	2 640 000	528 000 F
边际贡献	719 760	768 000	48 240 U	960 000	192 000 U
固定成本	684 000	690 000	6 000 F	690 000	0
营业利润	$35 760	$78 000	$42 240 U	$270 000	$192 000 U

$42 240 U
弹性预算差异

$192 000 U
销售数量差异

静态预算差异
$234 240 U

　　弹性预算差异能告诉我们由于实际的销售单价、变动成本以及固定成本的差异而带来的预算营业利润的变化。销售数量差异揭示了产出数量对于预算的影响金额。不利差异反映了企业没有最初预计的那么大的市场占有率或市场比预计的要小一些；有利差异则说明应该更比以前注重产生有利差异的这个产品。如果销售数量差异不明显说明企业对于销售数量的预计是比较准确的。同时分析这两种差异能帮助我们评价营业过程是否有效率。

作业管理

作业管理（ABM）是一种管理风格，这个管理风格通过作业分析，通常是作业成本法（见第2章第3节的成本归集制度），关注于减少成本，从而不断促进营业控制与管理控制。基于作业成本法是针对成本，作业管理主要针对系统范围内的成本控制和对客户的价值提升：

- 减少无效果活动，比如内部报告要求。
- 提高利润较大的活动比重，比如增加带来更多利润的产品生产，提高它们的产量，减少利润小的产品比重，必要时购买这些产品。
- 减少或简化活动，仅保留其基本功能，比如在电影院里安装自动售票点以减少雇员数量。
- 结合其他活动，比如在多种产品生产中使用同样有效果的部分。

作业管理可以分成作业战略管理和作业经营管理。作业战略管理包括为能产生较大利润的作业选择最佳策略和创造需求。它包括顾客和产品混合决策、供应商关系管理、过程设计、战略定价（非所有的定价决策）、市场细分等。作业经营管理包括通过全面质量管理（参见本章第5节"质量因素"）、业绩评价、业务重组（参照第三本书第1章第3节"企业流程业绩"），以及作业管理等方法提高经营活动的效率。

作业成本法为企业的每项活动都指定并采用成本动因，作业管理分析这些成本动因在确定作业成本根本原因中的效果性。当解释到成本动因的效果时，作业管理使用了内部访问、观查和质量控制工具，比如约束理论（CMA教材第三本书第1章第2节"生产范式"）、基准榜样、帕累托图、石川图（参见本章第5节"质量因素"）。这些结果将被用来评价成本动因对实际结果和实际利润的影响效果。

另外一个以作业管理的主要方面是业绩评价。它能将业绩评价与被评价对象的驱动因素如成本动因和收入动因联系起来。评价内容包括收入、生产成本、非制造成本、利润以及非财务评价（参见本章第4节"平衡记分卡）。

区分增值与非增值

增值作业必须既达到组织要求，同时也为客户所接受。非增值作业既不能满足组织要求，也不能对客户的选择起到任何作用。决定一个作业是否是增值，管理人员必须以它是否同时满足这两个方面的增值要求为初始条件。如果一项资格不能满足或者存在不同意见，那么下面的问题可以帮助我们决定它是否属于价值增值：

- 这项作业是使一个客户的价值增值还是使多个客户价值增值。
- 好的公司是否是否采用了这项作业。
- 这项作业是否是在浪费时间。

增值作业的例子包括产品设计、产品制造以及产品运输。增值作业也包括一些面向持续改进的领域，但判断什么是非增值作业的关键点在于，识别能够快速取得重大提高的领域。在所有非增值作业削减之前，增值作业的提高会被推迟。但这样的作业是能够得到改进的，比如在产品设计删除不必要部分、减少过度生产、简化制造过程或派送方法。这里我们需要注意，在类似于产品生产这种大范围作业能够被分解成若干个很小的步骤，其中一些步骤是注定不能增值的。不是所有的不能增值作业都能被去掉，它们只能被简化或减少。

图表 2-57 告诉我们一些非增值作业，以及它们如何被去掉或减少。

图表 2-57　制造公司的非增值作业

非增值作业	改进方式举例
设备安装	安排好生产计划，使设备能生产出更大批次的产品，以减少安装次数
原材料、半成品及产成品	重新设计生产布局，以减少产品在生产过程中的移动
闲置劳动力	协作工作
设备闲置期	协作工作
返工	为尽快找出问题进行周期性检查
设备修理	设立降低使用时间的日常计划，甚至可以把修理时间提前
存货储备	防止存货过度积压
质量检查	选择愿意评价和依靠他们自己的质量保证的商贩
由于失败带来的产品更换	提高质量以及在发送产品之前的最后检查

作业管理的优点与缺点

相对于传统的成本控制，作业管理有下面的优点：

- 不断提高公司的竞争优势。
- 为最具有增值性的作业、产品和客户带来更多资源，从而在战略上改变管理重点。
- 消除非增值作业。
- 评价过程效果和指明应该减少成本或提高客户价值的方面。
- 与及时过程有效果配合。
- 与绩效评价相联系，从而为持续使用作业成本提供动力。

相对于传统的成本控制，作业管理有下面的缺点：

- 由于作业管理和作业成本法将导致定价、过程设计、生产技术和产品设计决定等的差异，所以公司必须做好支持管理人员继续执行新的管理方式的准备，而不能鼓励他们用旧方法。
- 作业管理和作业成本法不能用在外部财务报告，需要用传统方式去编制报告。这样才能使管理人员对作业管理和作业成本法的影响考虑充分。
- 执行作业管理和作业成本法是十分昂贵的，也是很费时间的。所以必须做一个成本—利润分析以期发现所有潜在成本和利润。

例外管理

将差异分解成弹性预算差异与销售数量差异能使公司基于这些差异作出决定。例外管理是指引导管理层关注与预算产生重大差异的方法。这些重大差异较其他方面更需要受到关注。一些管理软件可以自动编制例外报告。例外管理既注意不利差异，也注意有利差异。有利差异应该被追溯因为需要评价业绩是否是真的例外还是当初设定的目标过低。长时间的例外业绩应当被归入标准实务中。

知道应该执行哪种例外是需要管理经验的，此时主要考虑例外的大小与频率。差异的相对大小比绝对大小要更重要，但是管理人员一般都同时采用这两种差异（比如，标记差异达 $30 000 以上的总差异或者是预算成本 5% 以上的差异）。数量小但是较频繁的差异也值得调查。其他应该考虑的因素包括跟随趋势，比如长时间经常性的成本超标，与成本改变直接相关的控制水平，如不要对单纯因市场要求而带来的成本提高有过多关注。

例外管理是使管理人员合理安排时间的有效果方法，因为只有例外才会被追溯，每一个例外都是基于成本效益判断是被追溯或不被追溯。但是，由于这种管理方法对经理要求较高，错误的管理决定会使这种优势变成劣势。比如，如果管理人员认为上涨的原材料成本是不可控的，决定不再关注这项成本，很可能忽略了一种非传统的解决方法，比如另外选择供应商或找到一种替代品。如果合理运用例外管理，当产生不利差异的原因被消除或产生有利差异的原因被广泛运用时，例外追溯是能够减少未来成本的。

标准成本系统的使用

在第1章第1节"预算概念"中，我们讨论了标准成本的基础。一项标准成本是经过深思熟虑以后决定的价格、数量、服务水平、成本或经常使用的单位成本费用。一个标准成本制度将标准成本运用到产品或服务的每个方面，包括制造、管理、销售的标准成本。一个标准成本是应该使用的成本。换句话说，这项作业或成本对象应该花费多少成本？使用标准成本系统能使公司从他们设定的标准中找到差异。标准成本系统允许使用例外管理，并允许进一步详细分析价格和效率差异。

分析与标准成本预期间的差异

弹性预算对预算差异进行了高度概述，弹性预算和销售数量差异对其进行了较详细的描绘，而分析这些弹性预算差异产生的原因则可使描述变得更为具体。所有的标准都有两个组成部分，在给定产量水平（弹性预算水平）下，成本动因的单位标准价格及成本动因的标准产量。关注这两方面的变化能使弹性预算差异分解成价格差异和效率差异。这两种差异之和就是弹性预算差异。如图表 2-58 所示。

图表2-58 直接成本的分解

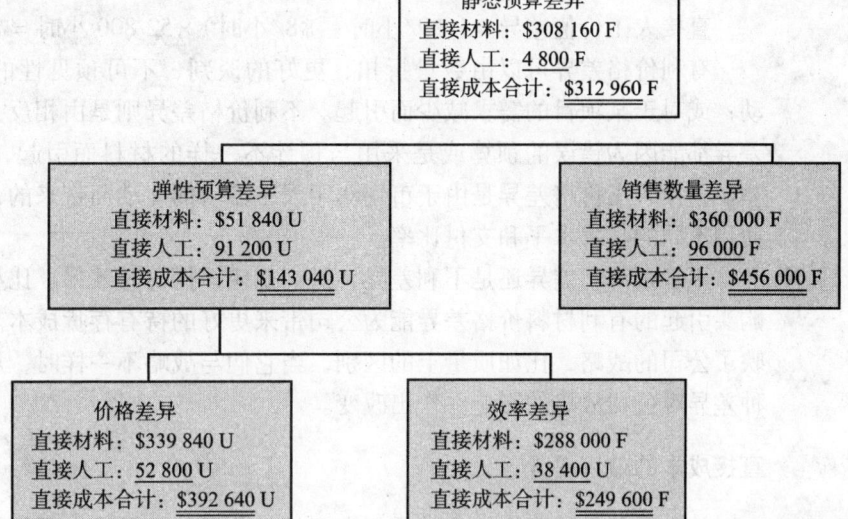

值得注意的是在图表2-58中，对于直接材料，只有某段时间里购买的材料金额与生产使用材料金额正好相等时，价格差异与效率差异的和才等于弹性预算差异，这就意味着存货平衡不变。这种问题在直接人工和制造费用中是不会产生的，因为它们不是存货（采购金额总是等于使用金额）。直接成本、固定成本、变动制造费用差异的计算往往需要不同的方法。本章还会介绍销售组合差异，以及将其分解成组合差异和产出差异。

直接人工与直接材料的价格差异和效率差异

价格差异和效率差异是由与预算中的投入价格或投入数量差异引起的。标准投入是预先决定的直接投入的数量，如工作小时数、或要产出单位数量的产品需要的液体量。

直接成本的价格差异

价格差异等于实际投入数量乘以实际投入价格与预算（或标准投入价格）的差额。公式为：

价格差异 =（实际投入价格 - 预算投入价格）×实际投入数量

假设单位标准如下所示：

- 直接材料：10 磅/件 × $6/磅 = $60/单位标准

  （24 000 件 ×10 磅/件 =240 000 标准磅数）

- 直接人工：2 个工时/件 × $8/小时 = $16/单位标准

  （24 000 件 ×2 小时/件 =48 000 标准工时）

假设在一段时期内，实际花费的直接材料为 $7.77/磅，整个过程花费了 192 000磅生产 24 000 件产品。直接材料的价格差异可以用下面的公式来计算：

直接材料价格差异 =（ $7.77/磅 - $6/磅）×192 000 磅 = $339 840 U

在同样的时间里，如果支付在直接人工上的花费为 $9.00/小时，整个过程里花费了 52 800 个小时生产 24 000 件产品，所以直接人工的价值差异可以用下面的公式计算：

直接人工价值差异 = ($9/小时 – $8/小时) ×52 800 小时 = $52 800 U

有利价格差异可以由数量折扣、更好的谈判、不可预见性的价格或运输成本变动，或对于某项目的需求减少而引起。不利价格差异则是由相反方面引起。任何一种差异都能因为错误的预算或是采用与预计不一样的材料而引起，包括质量更好与更差。直接人工价格差异是由于市场对于人工需求的变动而带来的，它要求有别于标准使用不同的技术水平和支付比率。

不管是有利差异还是不利差异，我们都应该探讨其效果。比如，一个由于大批量购买引起的有利材料价格差异能为公司带来更好的持有存货成本。另外，如果标准反映了公司的战略，比如质量上的区别，当它们与战略不一样时，那么我们应该研究这种差异对公司战略的影响并作出改变。

直接成本的效率差异

效率差异是指预算投入数量与实际投入数量的差异乘上预算投入价格。可以用下面的公式计算：

效率差异 = (实际投入数量 – 计划投入数量) × 预算投入价格

沿用前面的例子，实际人工投入数量为 192 000 磅或 8 磅/件（192 000/24 000）。因为预计投入金额为 240 000 磅，预计价格为 $6/磅，所以效率差异可以这样计算：

直接材料效率差异 = (192 000 磅 – 240 000 磅) × $6/磅 = $288 000 F

对于直接人工，实际投入数量为 52 800 小时或者 2.2 小时/件。因为预算投入为 48 000 小时，预算价格为 $8/小时，效率差异就可以这样计算：

直接人工效率差异 = (528 000 小时 – 48 000 小时) × $8/小时 = $38 400 U

因为价格差异加上效率差异等弹性预算差异，弹性预算差异可以这样计算：

直接材料弹性预算差异 = $339 000 U（价格差异）+ $288 000 F（效率差异）
          = $51 840 U

直接人工弹性预算差异 = $52 800 U（价格差异）+ $38 400 U（效率差异）
          = $91 200 U

效率差异可能是由错误预算或工人技术水平、日程安排、监督、或设置效率差异产生。机器保养不适当或缺少培训也能带来效率差异。

变动制造费用与固定制造费用的耗费差异与效率差异

与直接成本一样，变动制造费用与固定制造费用也能被分解成价格差异与效率差异。

变动制造费用差异

分解变动制造费用的弹性预算差异时要求计算下面的金额：
- 实际成本：一段时期内的实际制造费用。
- 已分配制造费用：成本动因的实际数量乘以标准比率。
- 预算制造费用：成本动因的标准数量乘以标准比率。

变动制造费用的弹性预算差异可被分解成变动制造费用耗费差异（以上列表中的第 1 项减第 2 项）与变动制造费用效率差异（以上列表中的第 2 项减第 3 项）。

变动制造费用耗费差异是指实际发生的制造费用减去成本动因的实际产品数量乘以变动制造费用标准比率。变动制造费用标准是根据成本动因和成本动因下生产数量而确立。如果设备时间被设定为变动制造费用的成本动因，一件产品需要 1.2 的设备时间，每个设备小时的花费为 \$10/设备小时，那么生产 24 000 件产品就需要 28 800 个设备小时或 \$288 000 参见图表 2 – 56。生产 24 000 件产品的实际变动间接成本为 \$313 200，那么变动制造费用就产生了 \$25 200 的不利弹性预算差异。因此，如果实际设备小时为 28 000，那么变动制造费用耗费差异可以这样计算：

$$\begin{array}{l}\text{变动制造费}\\\text{用耗费差异}\end{array} = \text{实际成本} - \left(\begin{array}{l}\text{成本动因的实}\\\text{际生产数量}\end{array} \times \begin{array}{l}\text{成本动因的}\\\text{标准比率}\end{array}\right)$$

$$= \$313\ 200 - (28\ 000\ \text{设备小时} \times \$10/\text{设备小时})$$

$$= \$313\ 200 - \$288\ 000 = \$33\ 200\ \text{不利差异}$$

变动制造费用效率差异是在指成本动因的实际产品数量乘以标准变动制造费用率减去成本动因的标准产品数量乘以标准变动制造费用率。

变动制造费用效率差异的计算在下面的例子中会讲到。变动间接耗费差异加上效率差异的和等于变动制造费用弹性预算差异。

变动制造费用效率差异

$$= \left(\begin{array}{l}\text{成本动因的}\\\text{实际数量}\end{array} \times \begin{array}{l}\text{成本动因}\\\text{标准比率}\end{array}\right) - \left(\begin{array}{l}\text{成本动因的}\\\text{标准数量}\end{array} \times \begin{array}{l}\text{成本动因}\\\text{标准比率}\end{array}\right)$$

$$= (28\ 000\ \text{设备小时} \times \$10/\text{设备小时}) - (28\ 800\ \text{设备小时} \times \$10/\text{设备小时})$$

$$= \$280\ 000 - \$288\ 000 = \$8\ 000\ \text{有利差异}$$

变动制造费用弹性预算差异

$$= \text{变动制造费用耗费差异} + \text{变动制造费用效率差异}$$

$$= \$33\ 200\ \text{不利差异} + \$8\ 000\ \text{有利差异} = \$25\ 200\ \text{不利差异}$$

在多数情况下，变动制造费用的产生是因为多种不同成本组成的制造费用采用单一的成本动因而造成的不准确。相反，直接材料和直接人工的差异衡量却可以有准确的成本动因。以作业为基础的制造费用差异能通过使用多种成本归集方法来衡量差异，每一种成本都有自己的成本动因以达到更大的准确性，但是上升的管理费用有时是不允许的。变动制造费用之所以产生差异是因为多种变动制造费用不是以产出为基础来衡量的，比如产品的产量；而是以投入为基础来衡量的，比如计划数或批次。

变动制造费用会计处理

回顾在第 2 章第 2 节中关于少分配制造费用和多分配制造费用的谈论。在前面的例子中提到的变动制造费用中的 \$25 200 不利差异是少分配制造费用金额，因为这是实际成本超过已分配制造费用的金额。如果是有利差异，那就是多分配制造费用金额。

但是，在将差异分解成耗费差异与效率差异时，这两种差异的会计处理可以更加具体：

变动制造费用控制　　　　　　　　　　　　　　　　　　　　　　\$313 200

应付账款控制与其他账款	$313 200
记录实际发生的变动制造费用	
半成品控制	$288 000
已分配的变动制造费用	$288 000

记录已分配的变动制造费用

（1.2 机器时数/单位 × $10/机器时数 ×24 000 单位）

半成品的成本控制科目在生产结束以后就过渡到产成品的控制科目中。在销售完成以后，销售科目的成本就从产成品的控制科目转到售出货物成本科目。

下面的步骤可以用来记录差异（注意两个差异科目现在取代了单一的已分配制造费用科目）：

变动制造费用	$288 000
变动制造费用耗费差异	$33 200
变动制造费用控制	$313 200
变动制造费用效率差异	$8 000

记录差额核算期

假设少分配或多分配的金额是不重大的，那么，后面的会计记录会在期末冲销与销售产品成本科目中的差异。

销售成本	$25 200
变动制造费用效率差异	$8 000
变动制造费用耗费差异	$33 200

记录变动间接差异科目的处理

记住，如果少分配或多分配的金额是重大的且不可避免的，这部分金额就应该按比例分配到期末的半成品库存、产成品存货和根据分配给各账户的相对变动制造费用，销售成本科目中。

固定制造费用差异

要将固定制造费用差异分解成两个部分，就需要知道下面的三个项目：

1. 实际固定制造费用。

2. 预算固定制造费用：标准数量乘以固定制造费用标准比率。

3. 已分配固定制造费用：实际数量乘以固定制造费用标准比率。

实际固定制造费用减去已分配固定制造费用等于总的固定制造费用差异。所以，总的固定制造费用差异也被称为少分配或多分配固定制造费用。实际固定制造费用是一定时间内的实际制造费用。预算固定制造费用使用静态预算中的标准数量。单位固定制造费用标准比率是用总的预算固定制造费用除以成本动因的预算数量。

固定制造费用的弹性预算差异能分解成固定制造费用耗费差异（以上列表中的第 1 项减第 2 项）和固定制造费用生产数量差异（列表中的第 2 项减第 3 项）。固定制造费用耗费差异是指实际固定制造费用减去预算固定制造费用。固定制造费用生产数量差异是指预算固定制造费用减去已分配固定制造费用。

沿用前面的例子（见图表 2–56），实际固定制造费用为 $684 000，预算固定制造费用为 30 000 件乘以固定制造费用标准比率：$23/件（$690 000/30 000）或

$690 000。已分配固定制造费用为实际生产数量 24 000 件乘以标准比率 $23/件，或 $552 000。

固定制造费用耗费差异与固定制造费用生产数量差异能这样计算：

固定制造费用耗费差异

=实际固定制造费用－预算固定制造费用

= $684 000 － $690 000 = $6 000 有利差异

固定制造费用生产数量差异

=预算固定制造费用－已分配固定制造费用

= $690 000 － $552 000 = $138 000 不利差异

总的固定制造费用差异（ =多分配或少分配间接成本）

=固定制造费用耗费差异＋固定制造费用生产数量差异

= $6 000 ＋ $138 000 = $132 000 不利差异

或

总的固定制造费用差异

=实际固定制造费用－已分配固定制造费用

= $684 000 － $552 000 = $132 000 不利差异

一项固定制造费用耗费差异表示了在预测某种固定成本的变化方面，预算程序出现失误或失败情况。当部门花费没有被控制或由于外部事件或者预计外维修，不利耗费差异就会产生。如果某项变动成本被错误分类成固定成本，将固定成本分解成这两类就能显示这种错误何时发生，因为生产数量的改变总是伴随着固定成本可变部分的变动。同样的，就像变动制造费用差异，$132 000 总的固定制造费用不利差异是少分配的固定制造费用总金额，是固定制造费用耗费差异加上固定制造费用生产数量差异得到的。下面的步骤告诉我们如何去记录差异，这个过程与前面提到了变动制造费用的记录是相似的：

固定制造费用分配	$552 000	
固定制造费用生产数量差异	$138 000	
固定制造费用控制		$684 000
固定制造费用耗费差异		$6 000

记录会计期间的差异

最后调整销售成本（如果不重大）的分录可以这样计算：

销售成本	$132 000	
固定制造费用耗费差异	$6 000	
固定制造费用生产数量差异		$138 000

记录变动制造费用差异的会计处理

再次提出，如果是重大的或不可避免，那么这些成本就应该分配到存货科目和销售成本中。

当产品需求与当初预测有变动时，就会产生固定制造费用生产数量差异。通常情况下，一些产品变动（人工小时、设备小时）的衡量就能在制造费用的分配中使用。如果衡量的人工使用（在计算固定制造费用时使用实际数量分配）与预算中计算间接比率（在预算固定制造费用时使用标准数量分配）的金额不一样，这就会导致固定制造费用差异的少分配或多分配。

其他导致固定制造费用生产数量差异的原因包括战略改变或预料外的分解。如果公司在一段时间内的生产数量与预算一致，那么就不会有固定制造费用生产数量差异。固定制造费用生产数量差异反映了公司生产能力的运用。如果固定制造费用生产数量差异低，那么单位固定制造费用就高，公司生产能力没能达到最大。固定制造费用生产数量差异不能反映效率，但能反映达到成本目标的效果。

使用间接费用差异数据解决其他未知问题

有时，产生的差异是已知的，有时却是未知的。在这种情况下，可以用公式来得到未知的问题。

比如，假设 Bounce Sporting Goods 公司正与其竞争者 Sportco 为基准进行比较。Sportco 公司的实际变动制造费用为 \$432 000，实际销量为 28 250 件。该公司在一篇杂志文章中声称用人工小时分配变动制造费用，每单位产品的人工小时预算投入为 1.6 个人工小时。这篇文章中没有变动制造费用分配率和实际人工小时数量。该公司的变动制造费用差异为 \$58 000 不利效率差异及 \$20 000 有利耗费差异。以成本动因的标准弹性预算单位为：\$28 250 件 × 1.6 人工小时/件 = 45 200 人工小时。

在这些信息基础上，什么是单位变动制造费用分配率？什么是单位人工小时？什么是实际人工小时数？想找到答案，就将已知的金额代入公式中来计算未知的。注意人工小时成本动因的实际数是未知的，第一步应该用数量作为成本动因，得到人工小时的数量，然后使用得到的答案计算人工小时成本动因的标准比例。

变动制造费用耗费差异 = 实际成本 − （成本动因的实际产量 × 成本动因的标准比率）

$$- \$20\ 000\ 有利差异 = \$432\ 000 - (28\ 250\ 件 \times \$X/件)$$

$$- \$20\ 000 - \$432\ 000 = -(28\ 250\ 件 \times \$X/件)$$

$$\$452\ 000 = 28\ 250\ 件 \times \$X/件$$

$$\frac{\$452\ 000}{28\ 250\ 件} = \$X/件 = \$16/件$$

预算变动制造费用成本比率/件 = 预算投入/件 × 预算变动制造费用成本比率/每件投入

$$\$16/件 = 1.6\ 人工小时/件 \times \$X/人工小时$$

$$\frac{\$16/件}{1.6\ 人工小时/件} = \$X/人工小时 = \$10/人工小时$$

一旦知道了预算中单位人工小时的变动制造费用成本比率，下面的步骤就是在变动制造费用效率差异的基础上求出实际人工小时数。

变动制造费用效率差异

= （成本动因的实际产量 × 成本动因的标准比率）− （成本动因的标准产量
  × 成本动因的标准比率）

= （X 人工小时 × \$10/人工小时）−（45 200 人工小时 × \$10/人工小时）

= \$58 000 不利差异

（X 人工小时 × \$10/人工小时）− \$452 000 = \$58 000 不利差异

（X 人工小时 × \$10/人工小时）= \$58 000 不利差异 + \$452 000

（X 人工小时 × $10/人工小时）= $510 000

$$X 人工小时 = \frac{\$510\ 000}{\$10/人工小时} = 51\ 000\ 人工小时（实际）$$

销售组合差异

销售组合差异与销售数量差异可以一起被用于确定销量差异。销量差异可以这样计算：

销量差异 =（销售数量 − 静态预算的数量）× 单位预算标准边际贡献

边际贡献是销售总收入减去变动成本。没有因销售数量的改变而影响边际贡献的那部分销量差异是由于一个公司提供多种产品的变动带来的。比如，一个网球公司同时也制造球拍，在两种产品实际销售金额与预算销售金额的比较后，该公司的销售组合差异就会从比较结果差异中产生。销售组合是指任何一件产品或者服务占总产品或服务的比例。销售组合差异是由单位产品的预算边际贡献、销售产品的总数量，以及实际销售组合比率与预算销售组合比率的差异决定的。销售组合差异是：

销售组合差异 =（一种产品的实际销售组合比率

　　　　　　− 一种产品的预算销售组合比率）× 销售总量

　　　　　　× 单位产品的预算边际贡献

假设总预算计划要求销售 10 000 罐网球，每个售价为 $12，以及 6 000 罐墙网球，每个售价为 $8。预算中销售组合比率为网球 10 000/16 000 或 0.625，墙网球为 6 000/16 000 或 0.375。为了计算简便，实际销售 9 000 罐网球、7 000 罐墙网球。所以销售组合比率变成网球的 0.5625 和墙网球的 0.4375。销量差异为 0（16 000 减去 16 000 乘以任何金额的毛利都是 0）。但是虽然网球部门应该有 $120 000 的销售额，墙网球部门应该有 $48 000 的销售额，但是实际只有 $108 000 和 $56 000 的销售额。这 4 000 差异的产生就是因为销售组合差异。

假设预算中，网球的单位毛利为 $8，墙网球为 $4。那么每种产品的销售组合差异可以这样计算：

网球的销售组合差异 =（0.5625 − 0.625）× 16 000 件 × $8/件

　　　　　　　　　 = − 0.0625 × $128 000 件

　　　　　　　　　 = $8 000 不利差异

墙网球的销售组合差异 =（0.4375 − 0.375）× 16 000 件 × $4/件

　　　　　　　　　　 = − 0.0625 × $64 000 件

　　　　　　　　　　 = $4 000 有利差异

总的销售组合差异 =（$8 000）+ 4 000 = $4 000 不利差异

组合差异与产出差异

当一种产品有两种或两种以上组成成分或人工成本能相互替代，直接成本的效率差异能被进一步分解成两个部分。效率差异能够被分解成直接材料组合差异和直接材料产出差异。这个分解过程需要知道下面三个数据：

1. 单位预算成本 × 实际使用数量总额 × 项目的实际组合比率。

2. 单位预算成本 × 实际使用数量总额 × 项目的预算组合比率。

3. 单位预算成本×预算使用数量总额×项目的预算组合比率。

组合差异是 1 减去 2, 产出差异是 2 减去 3。组合比率是一个替代项目的金额除以总替代项目金额。

比如,假设生产网球需要合成橡胶和天然橡胶,两者相互可以替代生产 1 000 罐(总标准成本为 $3 800)的标准数量和标准金额的组合要求 1 000 磅的合成橡胶,$2/磅($2 000 标准成本),天然橡胶为 600 磅,$3/磅($1 800)。合成橡胶的标准组合比率为 0. 625(1 000/1 600)或 62. 5%。同样天然橡胶的标准组合比率为 0. 375 或 37. 5%。假设管理人员最多可以用其中一种材料替代另一种材料的 5%,实际使用量为合成橡胶 988 磅($1 976 的实际成本),天然橡胶只使用了 532($1 596 的实际成本)磅。总的使用量为 1 520 磅(总成本 = $3 572,有利差异为 $228)。所以实际组合比率为合成橡胶 65%(988/1 520),天然橡胶 35%。使用数据,组合差异可以这样计算:

1. 单位预算成本×实际使用数量总额×项目的实际组合比率

合成橡胶 = $2/磅×1 520 磅×0. 65 = $1 976

天然橡胶 = $3/磅×1 520 磅×0. 35 = $1 596

$3 572

2. 单位预算成本×实际使用数量总额×项目的预算组合比率

合成橡胶 = $2/磅×1 520 磅×0. 625 = $1 900

天然橡胶 = $3/磅×1 520 磅×0. 375 = $1 710

$3 610

第一步 – 第二步 = $3 572 – $3 610 = $38 有利差异

产出差异可以这样计算:

3. 单位预算成本×预算使用数量总额×项目的预算组合比率

合成橡胶 = $2/磅×1 600 磅×0. 625 = $2 000

天然橡胶 = $3/磅×1 600 磅×0. 325 = $1 800

$3 800

第二步 – 第三步 = $3 610 – $3 800 = $190 有利产出差异

效率差异合计 = $38 + $190 = $228 有利差异

组合差异的产生是由于实际直接人工、直接材料的投入比例与预算不相同。上面的例子中,产生有利差异的原因是实际生产时使用的材料比预算便宜很多;而产出差异的产生是由于实际收益与在预算投入基础上计算的预计收益不一样。在上面的例子中,产生有利产出差异主要是因为生产 1 000 罐网球使用的材料比预计少了 10%。了解组合差异和产出差异的分解过程能帮助经理更好地应付效率差异。

差异计量的变动

通过相同的公式,前面的差异都能被分解成更明细的差异。比如,价格差异能用来更细致划分人工等级,这样就能更具体地找到有利差异和不利差异产生的根源。

其他同样的分解有:

- 使用组合差异来计算人工替代差异(比如,职业人工与非技术人工替代)。
- 使用不合格材料带来的人工差异。

- 不改变公式，用价格差异公式来衡量销售价格差异或者成本价格差异。

当然，有时，需要在其他差异已知的情况下才能计算某些差异，比如下面例子中展示的高度分解的差异计算。通过比较六月的预算，Bounec Sporting Goods 公司产生了 $76 370 的不利弹性预算差异。六月的关键数据如下：

- 预计生产数量为 12 000 件，但是在月底突如其来 8 000 件的大宗订单的同时，公司答应一定在月底交货。
- 标准成本：
  - 直接材料（从供应商 A）：1.5 磅 × $8/磅 = $12/件。
  - 直接人工（人工等级为三级，非技术人工）：1.2 直接人工小时 × $14/人工小时 = $16.8/件。
  - 标准成本合计 = $28.8/件。
- 实际成本：
  - 该公司从供应商 A 处花 $144 690 购买（并使用）了 18 200 磅的直接材料，但是供应商 A 不能提供大宗订单所需的材料，所以公司从供应商 B 处花 $142 200 购买了 18 000 磅的直接材料（其中只使用了 15 800 磅，花费了 $126 400）。
  - 实际直接材料花费为：

供应商 A：18 200 磅 × $8/磅 = $145 600。

供应商 B：15 800 磅 × $8/磅 = $126 400。

  - 为达到生产要求，该公司从其他部门调来了二级人工、半熟练人工，平均 $16/人工小时（虽然更为熟练，但是对生产任务需要熟悉过程）。
  - 实际直接人工：

三级人工（15 200 小时）= $216 600。

二级人工（10 300 小时）= $163 770。

- 生产成本合计：$145 600 + $126 400 + $216 600 + $163 770 = $652 370
- 弹性预算的标准成本：20 000 件 × $28.8/件 = $576 000
- 弹性预算差异 = $652 370 - $576 000 = $76 370 不利差异

因为从供应商 B 那购买的直接材料质量不好，管理人员将在生产过程中各个等级的人工的生产时间做了分解，如图表 2 -59 所示。

图表 2 -59　不同的直接材料的生产数量和人工小时

	供应商 A 提供的直接材料	供应商 B 提供的直接材料
使用的直接材料	18 200 磅	15 800 磅
生产数量		
三级人工	7 200 件	4 800 件
二级人工	4 800 件	3 200 件
生产总量	12 000 件	8 000 件
实际人工小时		
三级人工直接人工小时	8 600 小时	6 600 小时
二级人工直接人工小时	5 900 小时	4 400 小时
直接人工小时总量	14 500 小时	11 000 小时

从供应商 A 处得到的直接材料效率差异是多少？供应商 B 呢？图表 2 - 60 告诉我们如何计算这些差异。注意下面的计算，计算差异的顺序与前面提到的刚好相反。前面提到的公式为：

效率差异 =（实际投入数量 - 预算投入数量）×预计投入价格

而下面的公式则调换了实际投入数量与预算投入数量的位置：

效率差异 =（预算投入数量 - 实际投入数量）×预计投入价格

这个公式计算出来的数字是一样的，只是数字前面的符号不一样，我们在这里强调该公式是因为其他教材中有些采用了这个公式，并且我们应该知道要计算同样的数字出来可以选择多种方法。一旦使用这个相反的公式计算差异，那么在后面的计算中，就应该一直使用这个公式。所以在图表 2 - 60 中，$32 000 的不利材料差异表明实际材料比预算中的材料成本多了 $32 000。

图表 2 - 60　多种材料的直接材料效率差异

	供应商 A 的直接材料	供应商 B 的直接材料	合计
生产数量	12 000	8 000	20 000
单位材料需求	×1.5	×1.5	
标准材料需求合计	18 000	12 000	30 000
实际消耗材料	- 18 200	- 15 800	- 34 000
单位效率差异（不利）	(200) U	3 800 U	(4 000) U
单位标准成本	× $8	× $8	
材料效率差异	($1 600) U	($30 400) U	($32 000) U
差异百分比	1.1% U	31.7% U	

Bounec Sporting Goods 公司还拥有足够的数据将直接人工差异分解成四个部分：人工工资率差异、人工替代差异、不合格材料（供应商 B 的直接材料）的人工差异、常规材料（供应商 A 的直接材料）的人工效率差异。图表 2 - 61 中显示了这些差异的计算。

图表 2 - 61　多种材料与多种人工的直接人工差异

	三级直接人工	二级直接人工	合计
实际人工成本	$216 600	$163 770	$380 370
直接人工工资差异			
实际直接人工小时	15 200	10 300	
标准人工工资	$14.00	$16.00	
实际人工工资	- $14.25	$15.90	
单位小时工资差异	($0.25) U	$0.10 F	
×实际直接人工小时	×15 200	×10 300	
人工工资差异	($3 800) U	$1 030 F	($2 770) U
标准工资下的实际人工小时	$212 800	$164 800	$377 600
直接人工替代差异			
三级人工标准工资率		$14.00	

续表

	三级直接人工	二级直接人工	合计
二级人工标准工资率		− $16.00	
单位小时的替代率差异		($2.00) U	
×实际直接人工小时		× 10 300	
人工替代差异		($20 600) U	($20 600) U
三级人工标准率下的实际人工小时	$212 800	$144 200	$357 000
不合格材料的直接材料差异（供应商 B）			
不合格材料的生产数量	4 800	3 200	
单位人工标准	× 1.2	× 1.2	
允许的标准小时	5 760	3 840	
实际小时	− 6 600	− 4 400	
减（超）时	(840)	(560)	
×三级人工标准工资	× $14.00	× $14.00	
不合格材料的人工差异	($11 760) U	($7 840) U	($19 600) U
不合格材料的人工成本合计	$201 040	$136 360	$337 400
常规材料的直接人工效率差异（供应商 A）			
常规材料的生产数量	7 200	4 800	
单位人工标准	× 1.2	× 1.2	
允许的标准小时	8 640	5 760	
实际小时	− 8 600	− 5 900	
减（超）时	40	− 140	
×三级人工标准工资	× $14.00	× $14.00	
常规材料的人工差异	$560 F	($1 960) U	($1 400) U
弹性预算人工成本	$201 600	$134 400	$336 000
直接人工差异合计（弹性 − 实际）	($15 000) U	($29 370) U	($44 370) U

注意图表 2 - 61 的最后一行是每个项目的所有差异合计数。从这个计算中我们能学到什么？首先，这个突如其来的大宗订单导致了几个问题：供应商 B 的材料带来了 $30 400 的较大不利效率差异，这个差异比供应商 A 要高很多，所以供应品替代一定有很多浪费，如果没有这个大宗订单，这是可以避免的；其次，$20 600 的不利人工替代差异是因为需要使用比常规人工成本更高的人工。另外，使用不合格材料的直接人工差异是 $19 600 不利差异，这就印证了一个结论就是，当加工不适当的材料时，两类工人都浪费了时间。

这样的细致计算能够用来进行行业业绩评估。比如，为了与责任会计的宗旨一致，可能与大宗订单有关的不利差异应该归咎于销售部门，因为没有为生产大宗订单提供足够的时间；或将不合格材料而带来的差异归咎于采购部门。这样的决定可以使公司的其他部门在未来更好地与生产部门合作。

注意在这一章差异衡量直接使用了作业成本法中广泛使用的成本动因和收入动因，比如，为工资率差异衡量直接人工小时。这一节也告诉我们针对营业目标的业绩评价可以采取很多形式。本节中，主要是在生产成本的基础上进行业绩评价，但是在本章第3节"财务指标",第一本书第5章"财务报表分析"以及第三本书第4章"决策分析"中,是在收入、非生产性成本和利润的基础上进行业绩评价的。选择哪个作为基础主要是看被评价的单位类型。下节将会讲到企业中经常看到的不同业务单位。

进度检查

提示:完成以下各题。参考答案随后给出。

1. 当与静态预算相比,预算要求生产1 200件产品,制造费用为 $600 000,利润要求为 $120 000。但是,实际生产数量为1 000件,制造费用为 $550 000,利润为 $125 000。则实际结果为:
   (   ) a. 有效率并有效果
   (   ) b. 有效果但无效率
   (   ) c. 无效果但是有效率
   (   ) d. 无效率也无效果

2. 以下哪一项差异加上弹性预算差异等于静态预算差异?
   (   ) a. 效率差异
   (   ) b. 价格差异
   (   ) c. 销售组合差异
   (   ) d. 销售数量差异

3. 与标准预测相比,直接材料与/或直接人工投入的比例差异带来了以下哪一种结果?
   (   ) a. 产出差异
   (   ) b. 组合差异
   (   ) c. 效率差异
   (   ) d. 销售组合差异

进度检查答案

1. b
2. d
3. b

第2节
责任中心与报告部门

本节内容简介

一个分权组织将决策权分散到不同层次责任中心的管理人员。责任中心，也叫战略业务单位，是企业的一个部分，它赋予责任中心管理人员在成本、利润、收入或投资上的权力。责任中心的种类包括成本中心、利润中心和投资中心。本节还会涉及报告部门和贡献报告。

责任中心的种类

责任会计是指根据各个部门的自治权水平以及经理责任，将企业的各个下属部门定义为责任中心，并据此进行业绩评价的方法。责任中心的划分主要是依据他们对企业的主要影响：收入或利润中心产生收入，成本中心产生成本，投资中心进行投资。一个类似于服务部门的成本中心也许会产生收入，但是多数情况下只产生净成本。

收入中心与利润中心

由于利润边际是收入和成本的函数，所以一个收入中心或利润中心的经理既对利润的产生负责，也要控制成本，这些部门的经理一般不会负责投资。有些企业通过收入中心来产生收入，但不需要其控制成本。销售部门可以是一个收入中心，因为它主要关心的是收入，惟一的成本只是工资和制造费用。其他的公司可能不会使用"收入中心"这个名字，而将影响收入的各个部门叫做利润中心，因为收入中心有要从总收入中扣除的直接成本和制造费用。利润中心常用来形容那些产生收入以及为产生收入而发生了主要成本的领域。利润中心通常也是一个独立的报告部门。一家杂货店属于某家连锁店，那么它既可以是利润中心也可以是独立的报告部门。利润中心经理的业绩可以使用该部门的经营结果与总预算利润的差异来评价。

成本中心

成本中心的经理为只产生一点或根本不产生收入的部门负责成本控制。所以，成本中心的负责人不负责收入或者投资，其职责主要是在保持所期望的质量水平的同时，实现成本最少化。财务、行政、人力资源、会计、客户服务都是成本中心的例子。如果自助食堂不以盈利为目的，那么它也是一个成本中心。甚至假定当利润中心是销售部门或一个不同的生产部门时，连车间与生产线有时也可以作为成本中心。

共同成本按照所选取的成本动因比例被分配到所有涉及到的成本中心（参见本书第2章第4节服务部门成本分配的讨论）。

成本中心的经理通常负责差异追溯。如果一个经理成功地驱除了不利差异，并成功分析了有利差异，通常将成为奖励经理的部分基础。

投资中心

一个投资中心的经理为本部门的投资、成本和收入负责。投资中心主要关注内部和外部投资。内部投资经理是负责审批资金预算与其他投资，如研发。外部投资经理负责审批短期和长期投资，关注其资本保全、投资回报和战略投资情况。这些中心的经理是基于他们的职能来得到评价的。战略投资通过它们是否与公司战略保持一致来得到评价的，而其他投资则是通过他们的投资回报与资本保全情况来得到评价的。

生产力

提高生产力是所有企业的目标。它可以通过减少投入、增加产量，或者生产相同的产量所需要的投入减少，或者用相同的投入达到更多的产量等方式实现。例如，生产力分析表明，为员工提供医疗保险金所产过的劳动生产力收益要大于医保成本（否则将出现相反结果）。当一个公司比他们的竞争对手使用更少的资源（比如，人力、财产、设备），却能达到同样的生产数量（基准研究结果揭示出的现象），那么这个公司就能在较长时间内处于优势地位。

生产力是根据投入衡量产出的比率。

$$生产力 = \frac{产出}{投入}$$

$$= \frac{1\,000\ 件}{共\,40\ 小时} = 25\ 件/小时$$

产出可以是数量上的产量，也可以是财务衡量，比如收入；投入可以是花费的时间，消耗的资金，或原材料的数量。我们选择什么样的数字来计算生产力，就会产生多种生产力衡量的方式。

财务生产力

财务生产力对于产出值使用货币指标或实物指标，投入值只使用货币指标。

$$财务生产力 = \frac{生产数量或收入金额}{投入金额}$$

$$= \frac{\$5\,000\ 销售收入}{\$1\,000\ 橡胶原材料} = \$5\ 收入/\$1\ 橡胶原材料$$

营业生产力

营业生产力是使用实物数量作为产出和投入的值来计算的比率。

$$营业生产力 = \frac{生产数量}{投入数量} = \frac{10\,000\ 个墙网球}{5\,000\ 磅橡胶原材料} = 2\ 个墙网球/橡胶原材料（磅）$$

部分生产力

部分生产力是一项财务生产力比率，也可以是一项营业生产力比率。它将总产出与总投入中的一部分相对比，比如，使用一项原材料而不是所有组成成分，几个加工机器中的一个机器，又如所有人工成本中某一个范围的人工成本，或所有成本中的固定间接成本。这样的比率能够突出某一个因素对产出的贡献并能衡量对于特定的投入部分生产力发生的变动。之前的所有例子都是部分生产力的种类：第一个例子解释了用人工小时衡量的劳动力生产力（忽略了直接材料和间接成本）；第二个和第三个例子揭示了一项直接材料带来的收入（忽略了其他材料、人工和间接费用）；部分生产力经常用来衡量直接材料的业绩，也叫做直接材料收益；对于劳动力，通常用单位人工小时或单位员工来衡量产出；又如在流程生产力，是用单位机器小时或其他成本动因来衡量。

总生产力

总生产力是指一项用总产出与投入总成本相比较得到的财务生产力。

$$总生产力 = \frac{总产量}{实际使用总成本}$$

$$= \frac{10\ 000\ 个墙网球}{\$6\ 000\ 直接材料 + \$15\ 000\ 转换成本}$$

$$= 0.4762\ 墙网球/单位投入金额$$

只有将总生产力与历史总生产力，或与竞争对手的公司总生产力基准（如果可以取得）相比较时，才是有用的。当使用了内部历史数据后，利用当年的生产数量和决定总投入成本的弹性预算，就能得到总生产力基准比率。

$$总生产力基准 = \frac{当年总产量}{为达到当年产量上年所需的投入成本}$$

$$= \frac{10\ 000\ 个墙网球}{7\ 000\ 直接材料 + 16\ 000\ 分配成本}$$

$$= 0.4348\ 墙网球/单位投入金额$$

不需要调整产出的差异，我们就能看出这两种比率的区别。

$$总生产力区别 = \frac{当年的总生产力 - 总生产力基准}{总生产率基准}$$

$$= \frac{0.4762 - 0.4348}{0.4348} = 0.0952 = 9.52\%\ 总生产力上升$$

贡献与部门报告

贡献报告

损益表中的贡献法报告对于内部决策是十分有用的。它将固定成本与变动成本分开，首先扣减变动成本后得到边际贡献，然后扣减固定成本后得到营业收益。边际贡献是指当所有变动成本达到标准以后，对于固定成本和利润的贡献金额。边际贡献揭示了产量的变化是如何影响利润的，因为固定成本和营运能力是保持不变的。

采用这种损益表的主要优点就是利润中心的经理可以根据行为来看待成本，而不是根据销售、管理、生产部门。不管是扩大一个部门还是缩减部门，不管是生产一种产品还是购买一种产品，经理可以在分析产品线和决定商品价格时采用边际贡献损益表。边际贡献表也能更轻松地评价经理，因为不应归他们管理的项目可以从归他们管理的项目中分离出来。但是，不是所有的固定成本都是可控制的，所以经理经常将他们的固定成本进一步分解成可控制固定成本和不可控制固定成本。可控制固定成本是指在一年之内可以改变的固定成本；而不可控制成本需要一年以上的时间才能施加影响。不可控制固定成本还有可能产生于总部花费的分配，而这种分配是没有商量余地的。可控边际是指边际贡献减可控固定成本。

图表2-62显示了同一损益表的两种版本，传统损益表和贡献损益表。如果以前年度的报表反映不可控固定成本在上升而变动生产成本在下降，传统损益表是不会显示这个事实的，而贡献损益表则显示虽然固定成本在上升是在经理的控制之外，而经理却能成功地保持总成本与之前相对一致。还值得注意的是传统损益表虽然显示了已经销售产品成本、销售费用、管理费用包括固定成本和变动成本，但却不知道这些金额是如何分解的。

图表2-62 传统损益表和贡献损益表

传　　　统			贡　　　献		
销售		$31 200	销售		$31 200
减已销售产品的成本		15 600	减变动成本：		
毛利		15 600	变动生产成本	$5 201	
减营业			变动销售费用	1 560	
成本：			变动管理费用	1 040	7 800
销售费用	$8 060		边际贡献		23 400
管理费用	4 940	13 000	减固定成本：		
营业收入净额		$2 600	固定生产费用	10 400	
			固定销售费用	6 500	
			固定管理费用	3 900	20 800
			营业收入净额		$2 600

分部报告

分部报告是出于报告目的，企业按照按生产线、地理位置、或其他有意义的方法等划分业务，提供关于这个领域的独立报告。与非分部报表相比，分部财务报表有各自的成本并追溯这些成本使报告能显示这个部门的具体利润。除此之外，分部报告和非分部报告没有任何区别。部门毛利是部门的边际贡献减所有可追溯的该部门的固定成本。部门毛利是一个反映这个部门利润的重要指标。如果这个指标为负数，除非这个部门能为其他部门增加价值，那么这个部门是不能继续存在的。

对于包括在部门毛利里的可追溯固定成本若不是用于该部门，则这些成本将不存在。分部经理的管理工资就是个例子，它能直接追溯于这个分部。同样，一个企业分部的建筑物的维护成本和保险费用也是能直接追溯于这个部门的。

共同成本分配

与可追溯固定成本不同，共同固定成本是不能被归属于某一个部门的，如CEO的工资。这就使判断独立部门的利润出现困难。共同成本可以是被两个或两个以上部门共同占用的成本。当将共同成本分配到各个部门时，会使利润报告的部门毛利贬值，所以有时会出现这样的情况：只有当这个部门丧失继续经营能力，则所有或大部分成本都将消失时，企业才进行共同成本分配。有两种分配共同成本的方法：独立法和增量法。

- **独立成本分配法**

独立成本法是指估计出每个部门分担共同成本的相对比例，然后根据这个比例分配共同成本。比如，一个公司同时拥有一个新工厂和一个老工厂，这两个工厂都要求给职员提供培训，培训人员的工资是 $60 000，加上 $10 000 的往返路费和住宿费。这些费用就应该在需要接受培训的职员人数的基础上分配到两个工厂（或其他成本动因，如在每个地方的停留天数）。如果老工厂接受培训的人数是 40，新工厂接受培训的人数是 60，那么老工厂就该分摊 $28 000（40%），而新工厂就应该分配 $42 000（60%）。这种方法体现了公平性。

- **增量成本分配法**

增量成本分配法是指在分配成本时，将使用者划分为不同等级主要使用者、增量使用者或其他使用者，最后一类使用者增加了额外成本，因为成本使用者人变为不止一个。继续上面的那个例子。如果这个培训师受聘于是由于新工厂刚成立，所以培训师将新工厂所在城市作为主要工作地，因此，可以将这个新工厂当成是主要成本使用者，培训师在新工厂的时间为 3 个季度，在旧工厂为 1 个季度，这个新工厂可能会被分配 $40 000，而老工厂则分配 $20 000 加上 $10 000 的往返路费。因为为了服务于增量使用者，培训师迁移而产生了增量成本。

相反，如果管理层想在新工厂开张时在成本上有好的开始，他们会选择将老工厂作为主要成本使用者，并将很少的一部分成本金额分配到新工厂。因为这种方法使经理能够操纵成本分配方式，所以这个方法相比于独立法不那么具有平衡性。而且如果运用这种方法分配共同成本，那么大部分部门都希望成为增量使用者，这样容易导致内部矛盾。

移转产品价格

移转产品价格是指企业内部进行交换产品和服务时价格的设定。中间产品是指在一个公司内部的两个部门划拨的产品或者服务。移转产品价格的选择对于公司的战略有着很大的影响。如果公司要求各个部门独立运作并激励部门经理达到公司目标，移转产品价格就应该采用市场价格，就像这个部门只是一个外部客户。当不存在外部供应商提供产品或服务时，移转产品价格的设定就比查询市场价格要困难很多。移转产品价格的设定要求企业内部的各个部门包括财务、生产、市场或税收策划的配合。

拥有很多纵向结构层次的公司在设定移转产品价格时要更加小心。比如，拥有自己的农场、食品仓库、经销商和杂货店的公司就需要为相互的服务设定价格，这样就能使企业的每个部门在财务上比较灵活。

移转产品价格模型

在设定移转产品价格时可以使用四种模型，包括市场价格、协商价格、变动成本和完全成本。公司通常结合这几种方法（双重定价）满足它们的需要。

市场价格

市场价格模型是一个真正的公允价值基础模型。因为移转产品价格的设定是以市场上商品或服务的价格为基础的。只有市场上存在这个商品或服务时，才能使用这个模型，如半成品可能就没有市场价格。这个模型赋予了企业各个单位很大的自治权，强迫各个单位与外部供应商竞争，所以这个模型也是为税收部门所喜好的。使用这个模型的企业在价格上要尽力减少销售和市场成本。

协商价格

协商价格模型通过购买方和销售方之间的谈判来商定移转产品价格。当企业各个单位经历冲突时，可能需要谈判甚至是仲裁来使公司在整体上发挥效率。协商价格模型会使购买方和销售方的自治权下降。

变动成本

变动成本模型是通过该单位生产某种产品或提供某种服务的变动成本或实际成本减去固定成本确定的。这种模型会减少销售单位的利润，由于购买方购入价格很低从而会提高购买单位的利润。这种模型对于具有超额生产能力的销售单位来说是有好处的，或者如果企业鼓励那些可从外部渠道采购的单位进行内部采购时，这种模型也是具有优势的。这个模型的缺点就是不为税收监管部门所偏好，因为公司使用这个模型会减少利润中心的利润，从而导致应交税金的减少。

完全成本（吸收法）

完全成本法模型是以销售方的变动成本为起点，在此基础上分配一定的固定成本作为移转产品价格。一些公司甚至会分配标准固定成本，这样就使购买部门能提前知道成本并能避免销售部门的效率低下，原因在于这种效率低下已经转移给了购买者。加上固定成本的做法是相对比较公平的、正直的。但是这能改变公司各单位的决策。

虽然在作出从内部购买还是从外部购买的决定时，是不用考虑固定成本的。但是，有时即使固定成本必会发生，经理还是会从外部购买成本较低的产品。

选择移转产品价格模型

通常情况下，如果在市场中能找到某种产品或服务，那么市场价格模型是应该优先选择的。如果没有某种产品或服务的市场价格，就应该采用谈判价格模型。如果这两者都不能获得，那么就应该采用剩下的两种成本模型。但是尽量不要采用这种成本模型，因为这容易引起企业内部各部门的动机问题，比如，销售方就不会积极地控制成本，因为他们只是将成本转给购买方而已。

选择移转产品价格模型的逻辑和设定移转产品价格是以作出购买还是生产决定为前提的。如果在外部有产品或服务的供应商，那么就应该采用市场价格模型。该公司应该将销售部门的变动成本与外部单位的市场价格比较，如果外部市场价格低于内部变动成本，那么就应该从外部购买，这样就能促使内部供应商尽量降低成本。

但当内部变动成本低于外部市场价格时，购买单位就应该尽可能地从内部购买产品或服务，只要销售单位有超额生产能力。变动成本模型对于低生产能力的企业是最好的选择，而市场结构模型对于高生产能力的企业则是最好的选择。当销售单位有足够的生产能力，且当销售单位向企业外部销售产品得到的利润多于购买单位从企业外购买产品的损失时，购买单位应该尽量从外部购买产品。当与上述情况相反时，购买部门就应该以市场价格从内部购买产品或服务。

跨国公司移转产品定价考虑因素

跨国公司移转产品价格的设定应该要考虑应交税金、被没收的危险、货币限制、海关收费和政府规定。一般情况下，如果移转产品价格太高，就不会购买足够多的产品或者从外部购买；如果移转产品价格太低，销售方就不会生产足够多的产品。

应交税金

跨国公司经常使用移转产品价格来减少应交税金总额。应交税金比率相对较低的国家认可相对提高价格而享受的更大的利润。比如，一个公司使用市场价格模型将产品销售给应交税金比率较高的国家。购买方所在国家的税收就会减少，销售方所在国家的税收就会增加，但是对于公司来说却可以带来净收入。但是，很多国家都在制裁移转产品价格的滥用，并要求有这种行为的公司增加应交税金金额。美国财政局已经与公司达成了提前定价协定。这个协定会提前制定移转产品价格避免公司未来可能出现的不合法行为。

没收

当一个国家控制了外资公司的资产和营业过程时，就出现了没收现象。如果被没收的可能性很大，那么移转产品价格将在一定程度上减少这种危险。处于危险中的部门从其他国家的分部用高比例购买内部产品，并在其他国家的分部用低价销售内部产品，利润就会从这个部门流走。

货币管制

本国政府限制外国公司将从本国获得利润的转移，这样就能使从本国获得的利润再用于本国投资，这种情况下，本国政府就会采用货币限制。一个跨国公司能通过设定移转产品价格来提高分配到母公司的利润。

海关关税

海关收费和税金对一个跨国公司是一笔很大的支出，所以在设定移转产品价格时通常会考虑减少这部分支出。比如，使用变动成本模型就会将移转产品价格缩减到最少，也就使海关收费最少化。

政府规定

政府知道公司经常使用移转产品价格来减少应交税金、提高利润，而这种做法通常是以政府开销为代价的。所以很多国家通过立法来规定移转产品价格的上限和下限，上限是市场价格，下限则是成本。而其他的国家则通过谈判条约，规定用某种特定的移转价格方法（通常是市场价格）。

组织分部报告

组织各部门的报告主要是内部业绩评价工具。本部分会简单地讨论一下企业分部化的对外财务报告、业绩评估报告和跨国公司业绩评估问题。

分部对外财务报告

FASB 要求企业的对外财务报告包含分部数据，数据包括内部分部报告中公司使用的所有数据，包括方法和定义。虽然只有在分部财务报告包括了部门边际贡献、可追溯的及共同成本、固定成本和变动成本分配等信息时，分部财务报告才有用，但是这些对内有效的方法对于对外报告来说并不属于 GAAP。所以公司需要花费额外费用调整报表，或在初始阶段即根据 GAAP 编制报表，这样就牺牲了用于内部报告的一些好处。

业绩评估报告

业绩评估报告应该按照受众和接受报告的经理级别来准备。信息过多会和信息不足一样掩盖一项问题，信息传递的时间设定和数量对于经理的成功十分重要。业绩评估报告中类似于差异报告的时间设定就是一个非常重要的部分。报告中的信息应该具有相关性。但是，如果当经理被大量信息所包围而无法判断哪些属于重要信息时，说明评估报告过于频繁。

一个有效果的业绩评估报告能通过激发经理和员工努力达到企业目标而达到期望的战略结果。不合适的激励会造成相反的结果。要想设计一个有效果的业绩评价，公司必须以业绩评价和公司战略结合为起点。选择的业绩评价必须具备以下各要素：

- 业绩评价的时间段（比如，看一年的结果还是同时看几年的结果）。
- 对项目的普遍定义（比如，资产被定义成所有的资产，不管资产的功效和效率）。
- 定义使用的具体评估单位（比如，使用历史成本还是现时成本）。
- 每一项业绩评估和每个部门的业绩目标水平。
- 反馈时间日程表（比如，反馈时间是每天、每周还是每季度）。

本章稍后还会讲到财务业绩评价以及用于评价财务和非财务业绩平衡记分卡方法。

跨国公司业绩评价

各个国家在经济、法律、习俗、政治等方面都存在很大的不同，所以在评价外国分部的结果时应该考虑到这些非财务因素。

跨国公司必须关注更多的因素比如关税、汇率以及材料和技术的可获得性和相对成本是如何影响业绩评价的。而且，前面提到跨国公司经常使用移转产品价格来减少税金、提高利润。这会与使用移转产品价格来进行行业业绩评估和激发业务动力产生冲突。比如一个药品公司在波多黎各生产产品，主要的产品销售地在美国。由于波多黎各比美国的应交税金比率相对较低，所有药品公司有足够的动机将销售到美国的药品收取最高的移转产品价格（比如市场价格），这样就能将利润留在应交税金较低国家。因为波多黎各的市场是受垄断的，没有公司管理层希望的那么有效果。

相反，如果生产地所在国家的相对主要销售地的税收较高，那么公司就有足够的动力将移转产品价格设定到最低（例如成本），所以销售地部门的利润就降到最低。这样做的绩效结果就是生产地所在国家不能达到要求。同样，如果移转产品价格是实际成本，那么生产部门的经理就没有足够的动力去控制成本，因为他们只是简单地将这些传递到了其他部门。解决这样的困境的一个方法就是使用标准成本而不是实际成本（为实现持续改进，随着时间的推移，标准可以更加严格）。另外一个解决办法就是改变分部的责任结构，如果分散化的移转产品价格不能起到足够的激励作用，就应该更加集中化。

与任何业绩评价一样，跨国公司的业绩评价应该关注于从不可控制成本中分离出可控制成本，只根据受经理选择的影响的成本来进行评价。如果某种货币发生了贬值，这会影响企业的利润但这是不能被经理控制的。当外国政府增加了贸易限制，比如关税，那么公司在业绩评价时应该考虑到由这个因素带来的利润减少。当外国分部的经理采用外币记录会计账簿，他们的上司就应该考虑到汇率波动、通货膨胀及外国相对购买力的不同带来的影响（比如，对于在一个人力资本和产品成本都相对较低的国家生产的产品，在该国的售价应该低于在人力资本和产品成本较高的国家的售价）。

但是，因为业绩评价应该激励经理改善整体运营，所以判断一项不可控制事件的某部分是否实际上本可以加以预防或避免就非常重要。比如，如果经理了解到他不用为货币贬值负责，那么他就不会尽快将货币转移到国外。但如果他需要为货币贬值带来的部分后果负责，情况就完全不一样，他可能会雇用一名市场调查员或货币汇兑的经济学专家来预测未来贬值发生的可能性。

另外一种强化业绩评价作用的方法就是找到在当地相同环境下的其他部门或公司产生的标杆值。每一个领域都有自己可以做比较的公司。这样的一个系统类似于在曲线图上进行等级划分。

最后，由于前面提到的各种国际性因素会扭曲利润，所以业绩评价应该避免只关注利润，取而代之的应该关注更稳定的指标，如收入、市场份额或营业成本。

进度检查

提示：完成以下各题。参考答案随后给出。

1. 以下哪一项在作出企业财务决定时应该让经理负责？
   （　　）a. 收入中心
   （　　）b. 成本中心
   （　　）c. 投资中心
   （　　）d. 利润中心

2. 以下哪一个移转产品价格模型用实际成本减去所有固定成本来设定移转产品价格？
   （　　）a. 变动成本

　　（　　）b. 完全成本

　　（　　）c. 市场价格

　　（　　）d. 谈判价格

3. 为什么将分部内部收益表中的边际贡献增加到对外财务报表会存在争议?

　　（　　）a. 在财务报表中包括部门边际贡献减少了投资者所需的有用信息

　　（　　）b. 对外财务报表中包含部门边际贡献是不符合公认会计原则（GAAP）的，所以报表应
　　　　　　该重新编制

　　（　　）c. 边际贡献与部门报告是不相容的

　　（　　）d. 边际贡献包括分部的所有固定成本，而没有将固定成本分配给母公司

进度检查答案

1. c

2. a

3. b

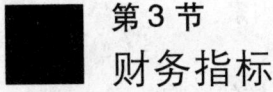

第3节
财务指标

本节内容简介

盈利分析衡量一个公司某段时间内经营的相对成败。这部分内容涵盖了对产品、部门以及顾客的盈利能力分析，然后介绍具体的财务分析比率。

盈利能力分析

产品盈利能力分析

产品盈利能力分析指出哪些产品的盈利性最强，哪些需要重新估价，以及哪些需要引起营销和支持方面足够的重视。对于生产线经理来讲，一种产品的盈利分析常作为薪酬和奖金发放的基础。

长期不能盈利的生产线应当停止。在决定是否停止一条生产线时，首先要去掉与决策无关的单位固定成本。产品盈利能力分析就是将单位变动成本与追溯至单位产品的固定成本加总，即得到如果不发生这些成本的好处。然后计算出机会成本总数，它是指如果停止生产线所带来的销售额的减少。通过比较这两个金额的差异，就可以得到两者对利润或高或低的影响，从而作出是否停止生产线的决策。

例如，一家专门从事运动器材生产的公司同时拥有一条可盈利的网球生产线和一条不能盈利的墙网球生产线。因此，公司就应当分析撤出墙网球生产线后将对公司的盈利产生什么样的影响。从图表2-63可以看出，两条生产线的边际贡献均为正值。然而，当可追溯成本分配至每个部门后，墙网球部门却出现了亏损。我们知道共同成本只从公司整体的利润中减去，因此这些成本并不影响部门经理作出的停止生产线的决策。

图表2-63 盈利分析

	网球	墙网球	合计
上一年销售额	$780 000	$195 000	$975 000
相关成本			
变动成本	585 000	175 500	760 500
边际贡献	$195 000	$19 500	$214 500
其他可追溯相关成本			
广告费	19 500	26 000	45 500
剩余边际贡献	$175 500	$(6 500)	$169 000
非相关成本（不可追溯）			
固定成本			$100 000
网球净利润			$69 000

在产品盈利能力分析过程中，除了对财务指标的考虑外，我们需要分析生产线对

公司整体战略的影响，以下几个问题阐述了需要考虑的非财务因素：

- 放弃本条生产线将在多大程度上影响公司的士气？
- 如果放弃本条生产线，相关生产线的销售额将会受到怎样的影响？
- 本条生产线是另一条更具盈利性生产线的组成部分吗？
- 如果在营销上投入更多资源，产品的盈利性会增大吗？
- 长期来看，本条生产线会变得更具有盈利性吗？
- 提高产品价格将能提高盈利能力还是使销售额变得更低？

部门盈利能力分析

分析部门盈利能力通常用以下指标：边际贡献、直接利润、可控利润、税前利润和净利润。图表 2-64 显示了收入表的组成部分，即它所包括的指标。

图表 2-64 部门收入表

销售收入	$780 000
销售成本	500 000
变动费用	85 000
边际贡献	195 000
利润中心固定费用	19 500
直接利润	175 500
分配的公司可控成本	12 500
可控利润	163 000
分配的其他公司成本	40 000
税前利润	123 000
税金	49 200
净利润	$73 800

边际贡献

边际贡献衡量的是产品销售收入与变动费用之间的差异，由于边际贡献的计算中没有包括部门经理不可控的固定费用，因此这个指标可以用于评价部门经理的业绩。然而并不是所有的固定费用都是不可控的。因此，强调边际贡献会导致部门经理忽视可能削减的成本。此外，即便是无法改变的固定支出也必须有效利用，例如公司应当使领取固定工资的雇员积极工作。

直接利润

直接利润是部门边际贡献减去固定成本后的差额。直接利润不包括公司整体发生的固定共同成本。如果共同成本也要从中减去的话，在使用这种方法对部门经理业绩评价的时候，与共同成本要从中减去相比，部门经理的成功取向会变低。

可控利润

如果共同成本可以分为可被部门控制的成本和所有其他成本，那么将可控成本从部门直接利润中减去即得到可控利润。可控利润的度量要包括部门经理所有可控成本（和一些不可控的部门固定成本）。因此，这个指标可以激发部门经理尽可能降低一切可降低的成本。然而，这种度量只能用于内部财务报告，因此企业从竞争对手那里获得可比较的财务信息有点困难。

税前利润

税前利润是扣除部门除税收外所有成本之后的利润。使用这种度量方式时，部门经理要对其不可控的成本负责，如分配至每个部门的人力资源部门成本。它的一个优点是，部门经理可以从现实的角度考虑本部门需要达到何种盈利水平才可以使部门获得成功。这个数额也可以很容易与竞争企业的盈利能力作出比较。经理因在所有开支都考虑的情况下仍能保持盈利而获得奖赏时，他会作出更好的长期决策，如产品组合和营销决策。

净利润

净利润是税后利润。这种方法有着与使用税前利润一样的优点，但是它有其他缺陷。首先，每个领域内的税率都是相同的，因此考察这个数量几乎没有什么意义。其次，当税率不同时，这往往是公司出于避税的目的而进行操纵的结果，这也不在部门经理的控制范围。净利润是外国企业部门使用的一个理想指标，因为每个国家都有不同的税率，因而这会影响到部门整体的盈利性。

顾客盈利能力分析

从顾客方面衡量盈利性包括明确从顾客那里得到的利益与为顾客服务所发生的成本。所获得的利益包括非财务方面和财务方面。非财务指标包括顾客获得、顾客忠诚度、顾客满意度和整体的市场份额。非财务指标——"平衡记分卡"将在下一节作详细的介绍。

只有当公司使用财务软件按照顾客划分成本时，顾客方面的财务指标才可以获得，这是作业成本法软件的典型特征。财务指标对于将顾客放在战略的第一位的公司来说，是公司的均衡器，因为在成本大于收益的时候保留顾客是战略的失败。顾客盈利能力分析将表明顾客的需求在何时应当被满足，在何时应当被削减，以及在何时需要对服务进行额外的收费。

出于战略的原因，一些在财务上并不能盈利的顾客的需求应当被满足，但是先进的财务管理软件系统如 ABC 至少会使经理人员引起对成本的重视，从而使长期的决策可以完成。应当强调我们要将不能盈利的顾客转化为可盈利的顾客。终生盈利性是保留一开始不能盈利的顾客的原因。如果可以长期保留顾客，那么整体的利润可以显著地为正。例如，一家房地产代理商花费大量时间让顾客购买在销售上可能盈利不大的低成本住宅，但是顾客往后的重复性购买则是比较可观的。

投资回报率（ROI）

投资回报率度量的是每单位投资额所得到的投资回报的大小，它可被称为会计回报率或应计会计回报率。

投资回报率的计算公式如下：

$$投资回报率 = \frac{投资报酬}{投资额}$$

虽然投资和报酬不是常在同一时间点上（例如，在第一年投资的某种债券，在接下来的5年中都可获得利息）。在比较两个或更多投资机会时，应当保证每个项目的时间水平是相同的以便于进行公平比较，这一点是很重要的。当使用投资回报率进行成本—效益分析时，要在收回利润的期间内对投资项目发生的成本予以补偿（即计算出每年的净利润）。

投资回报率可用于短期（1个月或1年）或长期（例如，投资计算机系统将会产生6年的收入和成本）。然而在进行长期分析时，使用折现的现金流量模型将会更加合适，因为它将货币的时间价值也考虑在内。

投资额与报酬均有多种不同的解释，因而可以对应不同类型的报酬率，如图表2-65所示。

投资回报率指标很宽泛地度量了你会从投入中取得多大的回报。收入通常用来代表边际贡献，投资额的选择取决于投资额的主体（所有者的投资、债权人的债务投资，或二者兼有）。因此，有些公司用总资产，其他的使用长期债务支撑的资产，还有的使用股东权益与长期债务之和。

图表2-65　投资回报率的不同表示：投资额和报酬几种可能的定义

类　　　型	定　　　义
投资回报率（ROI）	$\dfrac{净利润}{投资额}$
	$\dfrac{边际贡献}{投资额}$
	$\dfrac{营业利润}{总资产}$
	$\dfrac{净利润}{（总资产 - 长期负债）}$
部门投资回报率	$\dfrac{部门利润}{投资额}$
普通股权益报酬率或权益报酬率	$\dfrac{（净利润 - 优先股股利）}{普通股权益平均数}$
总资产报酬率或资产报酬率（ROA）	$\dfrac{净利润 + 利息支出}{平均总资产}$
	$\dfrac{税后净利润}{有形资产总额}$
营业利润报酬率	$\dfrac{营业利润}{股东权益总额}$
资本投资回报率	$\dfrac{净利润}{非流动资产}$

类　型	定　义
投入资本报酬率	$\dfrac{\text{税后净利}+\text{利息支出}}{(\text{股东权益总额}-\text{股东无形权益})+\text{长期债务}}$
毛利报酬率	$\dfrac{\text{税后净利}}{\text{毛利}}$
营运资金报酬率	$\dfrac{\text{税后净利}}{\text{营运资金}}$
净值报酬率	$\dfrac{\text{税后净利}}{\text{股东权益总额}-\text{股东无形权益}}$
单位雇员报酬率	$\dfrac{\text{税后净利}}{\text{雇员总数}}$

当需要平均数的时候，将本年年初数（或上年年末数）与本年年末数相加后除以 2 即可得到（例如，平均资产就是上年年末总资产与本年年末总资产之和除以 2）。

一个特定公司如何定义投资额和报酬额，取决于行业惯例或公司内部惯例。只有知道比率是用哪些数据计算得到的，我们才可以相信这些比率。如果一家公司的比率是在毫无背景的情况下给出的，我们根据公司的财务报告亲自计算得出的比率或许更加可信。你应当保证每个比率都是在相同的方法和数据来源下计算出来的。同时务必考察一下财务报告的披露部分，因为每家公司都可能采用不同的存货计价方法，因此数据若不经转换是不具可比性的（例如，当公司采用后进先出法为存货计价时，也会在报表披露部分注明采用先进先出法下相对应的结果，这个数据可以与其他采用先进先出法的公司进行比较）。

投资回报率可以用百分比表示，百分比越大就代表单位投资得到的回报越多。投资回报率将收益、投资额与成本结合到一个数据中，因而它是一种比较受欢迎的度量盈利的方法。然而，任何财务比率都没有它自身的含义；投资回报率应当与其他财务度量方式结合运用并与行业平均值或其他可能的投资项目比较。

对于内部使用来讲，公司可以根据需要采用利润和投资额的不同定义；而对于外部使用来讲，公司应当采用公认会计原则中利润与投资额的定义。不管怎样，在计算内部比率和外部比率时如果采用不同的共同成本分摊方法，就可能使比率间的比较有些困难（在这里，比较的是不同部门之间的投资回报率）。

当投资回报率使用平均资产作为它的分母时，它就成为资产报酬率。资产报酬率衡量了给定的资产水平下一个公司的盈利水平。公司利用资产的有效程度越高，其获利的可能性就越大。当投资回报率使用所有者权益作为分母时，它被称为权益报酬率。权益报酬率的计算中只考虑了普通股权益，因为优先股股东有一个固定的投资报酬即优先股股利率。

投资回报率与权益报酬率之间有一定联系。一般来讲，一个公司的权益报酬率应该高于它的投资回报率，因为这表明了公司借入资金（如按 9% 的利率借入）是为了获得一个比借款利率更高的回报率（如 15% 的权益报酬率）而再投资的。公司利用财务杠杆来达到这种目的，这也叫权益交易。通常，财务杠杆按以下方式定义：

$$\text{财务杠杆}=\frac{\text{资产}}{\text{权益}}=\frac{\text{总资产}}{\text{平均股东权益}}$$

拥有较多资产与较少权益会增大财务杠杆。从股东角度看，较高的财务杠杆是可取的。如果公司的利润大于其融资成本，这会使投入资本产生更高的利润额。然而，在公司所获利润低于其利息支出时，高财务杠杆比率使公司面临更大的破产风险。当收入增加时，股东所分得的利润也会成倍增加（不过当收入减少时，由于债务是按固定数额支付的，利润也会以同样的加速度缩水。

例如，我们假设运动器材商用营业利润和净资产两个指标为公司两个部门计算投资回报率如下：

网球部门：利润为 $100 000；净资产为 $400 000

$$投资回报率 = \frac{\$100\ 000}{\$400\ 000} = 25\%$$

墙网球部门：利润为 $60 000；净资产为 $300 000

$$投资回报率 = \frac{\$60\ 000}{\$300\ 000} = 20\%$$

杜邦盈利能力分析法

杜邦盈利分析法打破了以往投资回报率的计算方法，将其表示为投资周转率乘以销售利润率。投资周转率是销售额除以投资额得到，而销售利润率是利润除以销售额。杜邦盈利能力分析法的计算公式如下：

杜邦盈利能力分析法下投资回报率 = 投资周转率 × 销售利润率

$$= \frac{销售额}{投资额} \times \frac{利润}{销售额}$$

杜邦盈利能力分析法将盈利性分解为如何从投入资产中获得更多销售额，以及如何从每美元销售额中赚取获得更多利润。投资周转率度量了管理人员在给定的投资水平下能以多大的效率增加销售额。销售利润率则度量了经理人员通过控制费用和增加销售额来提高盈利性的效率。使用杜邦分析法下的投资回报率使我们通过业绩评价可以看到，投资回报率是更多的来自于资产使用效率还是销售毛利率的高低。公司可以分别为投资回报率和销售利润率设定目标来鼓励各部门作出符合公司整体战略的改进。

继续前面的例子，如果网球的销售额为 $250 000，墙网球的销售为 $120 000，杜邦分析法下的投资回报率计算如下：

网球：$\frac{\$250\ 000}{\$400\ 000} \times \frac{\$100\ 000}{\$250\ 000} = 0.625 \times 0.4 = 25\%$

墙网球：$\frac{\$120\ 000}{\$300\ 000} \times \frac{\$60\ 000}{\$120\ 000} = 0.4 \times 0.5 = 20\%$

以上计算表明网球部门的销售利润率较低，应该把较多的成功归于基于较大的投资额而产生的较高的销售额。而墙网球部门刚好相反：基于较少投资额产生的销售额也偏低，但是一个相对较高的销售利润率使之得到弥补。因此，应当鼓励网球部门经理通过削减成本来增大销售利润率，而墙网球部门经理更可能被鼓励通过降低存货和闲置资金来减少投资额，从而提高部门的投资周转率（这是众多选择之一）。

剩余利润（RI）

剩余利润是一项投资的实际报酬与其要求的报酬之间的差额。剩余利润的计算公式如下：

剩余利润（RI）= 利润 −（投资要求的报酬率 × 投资额）

一项投资的应计成本是指投资额与所要求的报酬率的乘积，度量的是一笔资金不能用于投资其他项目的机会成本。应计成本试图将不在权责发生制下确认的投资成本加总，诸如筹资成本（如一项利率为 6% 的长期负债）。

例如，假设运动器材商为网球部门设定的投资要求的报酬率为 10%，而对风险较大的墙网球部门设定的投资要求的报酬率为 12%。每个部门的剩余利润计算如下：

剩余利润（RI）= 利润 −（投资要求的报酬率 × 投资额）

网球部门：$100\ 000 − (0.1 × $400\ 000) = $60\ 000$

墙网球部门：$60\ 000 − (0.12 × $300\ 000) = $24\ 000$

剩余利润表明，只要网球部门的利润高于剩余利润 $40\ 000$（$0.1 × 400\ 000$），墙网球部门的利润高于剩余利润 $36\ 000$（$0.12 × $300\ 000$），运动器材商就应当继续投资使其业绩增长。用剩余利润替代投资回报率使经理人员可以致力于一个事实的数据而不是一个百分比。

正如投资回报率可以度量具体的部门利润，剩余利润也可以用于部门分析。在这种情况下，就应当使用部门利润、部门投资额以及部门要求的报酬率三个指标。

剩余利润与投资回报率的比较

财务比率要在公司和行业的背景下使用，公司的业务性质会影响到人们对诸如投资回报率等财务比率的理解。例如，某一行业投资回报率的行业平均值可能会偏低，因此市场会对一个相对较高的投资回报率看好，而不论它是否低于多数行业的投资回报率。同时，在分析时也要考虑到公司的成熟度，不能期望刚成立的公司在第一年就产生与其他已成立多年的公司相当的利润。公司在进入新的市场前必须合理地设定其目标（例如，一家公司对其电视机生产部门有一个特定的 ROI 值，但是公司必须为其航天器生产部门设定一个不同的标准）。为了跳过这些比较的话题，亲自计算公司和比率和相关的其他尺度如竞争企业，也许会缩小与处于同一成熟期公司的差距。

仅有对投资回报率的关注是不够的，公司应当将诸多因素考虑在内。也许出于公司发展的原因，公司可以接受一个投资回报率较低的项目，因为它会带来个长期客户（即有长期正的投资回报率）。非财务度量指标将在下节中介绍。

同时，当投资回报率作为业绩评价的主要工具时，部门经理会因为吸收投资后会降低目前的投资回报率而拒绝资本的投入，即使这项投资对公司的整体战略是有益的。例如，如果网球部正在考虑购置一台新机器价值 $100\ 000$，它的投资收益为 $20\ 000$，即投资回报率为 20%，这会降低部门目前的报酬率 25%。

$$投资后网球部门报酬率 = \frac{$20\ 000 + $100\ 000}{$100\ 000 + $400\ 000} = 24\%$$

如果部门经理的 ROI 会因此下降，他将不会作出这项投资。相反，同样情况采用剩余收益时，计算如下：

投资后网球部门的剩余收益 = $120 000 – (0.1 × $500 000) = $70 000

由于剩余利润随这项投资增加，基于剩余利润而补偿的经理就会有投资的动力。假设这项投资可以获得期望的报酬，那么经理就会因剩余利润的增加而获得奖励，剩余利润使经理可以选取任何报酬率高于要求报酬率的项目。然而，剩余利润是一个绝对的数量指标，因此在比较不同规模部门的盈利性时，它的有用性会下降（与百分比指标相比）。同时，对于较大的部门而言，即使其效率很低，也会比高效运行的小部门有一个较大的剩余利润值。因此在使用这种度量方法时，大部门往往更有优势。相比之下，投资回报率是一种更为健全的指标，因为剩余利润对必要投资回报率比较敏感，并随投资额的增加，敏感性会更加明显。

经济附加值（EVA）

经济附加值是剩余利润计算法，它是从税后营业利润中减去税后加权平均成本（WACC）乘以总资产与流动负债的差额。经济附加值只考虑了在税后营业利润大与资本成本时创造的新价值，其计算公式如下：

经济附加值 = 税后营业利润 – [加权平均成本 × (总资产 – 流动负债)]

税后营业利润 = 营业利润 × (1 – 税率)

加权平均成本 = (税后债务成本 × 债务融资比率) + (权益成本 × 权益融资比率)

税后债务成本 = 债务平均成本 × (1 – 税率)

鉴于剩余利润的计算中要用到投资要求的报酬率，它可以出于管理的需要任意确定，而加权平均成本却是对资本成本的精确度量方法。加权平均成本使用税后债务成本，因为债务利息是有一定的避税效应的。

例如，假设运动器材商的负债比率为60%，权益比率为40%，债务平均成本12%，权益资本成本为15%，税率为30%，WACC 的计算如下：

税后债务成本 = 0.12 × (1 – 0.3) = 0.084 = 8.4%

WACC = (0.084 × 0.6) + (0.15 × 0.4) = 0.0504 + 0.06 = 11.04%

假设利润和资产水平与前例相同，网球部门的流动负债为 $50 000，墙网球部门的流动负债为 $40 000，每个部门的 EVA 计算如下：

税后营业利润 = 营业利润 × (1 – 税率)

网球部门：$100 000 × (1 – 0.3) = $70 000

墙网球部门：$60 000 × (1 – 0.3) = $42 000

EVA = 税后营业利润 – [加权平均成本 × (总资产 – 流动负债)]

网球部门：$70 000 – [0.114 × ($400 000 – $50 000)]

= $70 000 – $39 900 = $30 100

墙网球部门：$42 000 – [0.114 × ($300 000 – $40 000)]

= $42 000 – $29 640 = $12 360

为了提高 EVA，公司常为每笔业务计算其可能的 EVA 的变化。每项投资、撤资或假定的改变都要计算 EVA 并与目前的进行比较，从而有助于作出决策。

EVA 与 RI、ROI 的比较

剩余利润旨在降低投资回报率对投资产生的制止因素，而 EVA 旨在使经理人员致力于通过赚取超过资本成本的报酬来最大化股东的价值。当对税金的考虑重要时，在判断盈利性时，EVA 是一种比 RI 更好的办法；但是当对税金的考虑是不相关的时候，EVA 仅仅是一种达到相似结果下更复杂的方法。由于 EVA 与公司实际的资本成本相联系，因而它是一种基于市场的计算方法，当市场上权益与债务的成本上升时，加权平均成本也随之上升。

市场附加值

市场附加值（MVA）是指一个公司包括债务与权益在内的市场价值减去投入资本的总额。市场价值的计算公式如下：

市场附加值 = 市场价值 – 投入资本

市场价值是指一个公司拥有的债务与权益的市场价值，当 MVA 为正时，公司为其股东创造了价值。MVA 是一种基于市场的度量方式，因而它客观地指出投资者认为公司的价值有多大。MVA 作为一种业绩评价工具旨在强调最大化股东价值。当经理人员使用这种激励方式时，不能仅通过投入更多资本来增加 MVA，因为如果额外的投资额没有使其市场价值高于投资成本，MVA 也没有变化。

与 EVA 相比，MVA 的一个缺点是，没有考虑资金的机会成本。例如，一个公司的市场价值是 $1 700 000，三年前投入资本额为 $1 500 000，MVA 为 $200 000，表明股东价值明显地增加了。然而，在这三年中，资金的机会成本率是 10%，投资的期望报酬计算如下：

$$\$1\ 500\ 000 \times (1.1)^3 = \$1\ 996\ 500$$

因此，这项投资使公司丧失了同一时间原本可以从相似投资中获得的潜在价值。企业也并没有考虑到分配给股东的股利。这些支付原本可以增加股东价值的，但是却没有在 MVA 的计算中给予解释。MVA 度量了公司某一时点上的价值，而不是一段时间的价值。

投资基础的争议

以上讨论的业绩评价在试图比较竞争企业间或企业内部不同部门间的业绩时都会遇到相同的问题。下面的几种差异会使比较的有用性下降：

- 收益与费用确认的政策不同。
- 存货计价政策不同。
- 不同部门之间共享或共有资产。
- 在对资产进行评价和估值的时候选择的方法不同。

收益与费用的确认、存货计价方法、资产估价法这些内容均在本书第 5 章"外部财务报告"中讲述。共有资产与其他共同成本是相似的，必须分配给各个部门，这也在本章前面涉及。

投资活动产生的现金流量

投资活动产生的现金流量（CFROI）是对投资回报估价的百分比模型，它实质上是现金流除以资金的市场价值。现实中的 CFROI 的计算公式是十分复杂的，因此不在这里介绍。想了解关于 CFROI 较为全面的解释，可以参考 CFROI 估价———一套对公司估价的系统方法，作者是 Bartley J. Madden，是 HOLT 估价委员会成员、CFROI 分析的开创者。我们这里只对方法的基本概要作简短介绍。

CFROI 通过比较经通货膨胀调整的税后现金流量与经通货膨胀调整的现金投资总额来确定一个公司是否获得了高于其资金成本的回报。CFROI 模型的计算中包括了对公司折旧资产经济寿命以及其他资产残值的估计。CFROI 模型假设存货的市场价格是基于现金流而不是公司的利润或业绩表现制定的。CFROI 常以年度为基础来计算。

CFROI 与 ROI 的共同点是，它们都是用百分比表示的，但是 CFROI 的计算十分复杂，而 ROI 的计算则非常简单。CFROI 将货币的现值、通货膨胀调整，以及折旧费用都予以考虑，而 ROI 则没有。与 ROI 不同的是，CFROI 没有考虑应计会计制的影响，因为它是基于现金流量的。CFROI 与 EVA 比与 ROI 有着更多的共同点。EVA 与 CFROI 均是激励经理人员通过赚取高于资金成本的利润来创造价值。CFROI 相比其他方法的一个优点是，CFROI 可以用于不同资产组成的公司之间的比较，包括跨国公司。由于它是经通货膨胀调整的，CFROI 同样可以比较有时间跨度的公司。CFROI 的另一个优点是它将业绩评价建立在公司产生的现金流量的能力上，这对资本市场来讲是很有价值的一个因素。

进度检查

提示：完成以下各题。参考答案随后给出。

1. 公司的利润为 \$100 000，净资产为 \$500 000，销售额为 \$200 000，则其杜邦 ROI 将通过以下哪些数据计算？
   - (　　) a. 0.1 × 0.5
   - (　　) b. 0.3 × 0.4
   - (　　) c. 0.4 × 0.5
   - (　　) d. 2.5 × 2

2. 以下的盈利指标中哪个是用美元的数量来描述其目标的？
   - (　　) a. ROI
   - (　　) b. RI
   - (　　) c. CFROI
   - (　　) d. 杜邦 ROI

3. 使用市场附加值（MVA）的缺点是以下哪个方面？
   - (　　) a. MVA 是多步骤的较复杂的计算方法
   - (　　) b. MVA 不能激励经理人员投资 MVA 比率比目前低的项目
   - (　　) c. MVA 取决于利润确认的不同口径，因此相互比较是困难的

( ) d. MVA 忽视了资金的机会成本

进度检查答案

1. c
2. b
3. d

第4节
平衡记分卡

本节内容简介

直到平衡记分卡和类似比较全面的方法发展起来之前，大多数公司只关注财务指标。虽然它们是定量指标而且比较客观，但是它们本质上是完全地基于过去的。此外，财务指标更擅长于提供短期预测。虽然这些滞后指标对于帮助我们跟踪过去的行为是很重要的，但是公司现在必须关注一些前置性指标或一些对未来成功的指示。平衡记分卡向公司提供了一种简单的工具，其可以包含财务指标和非财务指标。

平衡记分卡是一种战略性的衡量和管理系统，它将公司的战略转化成平衡的四个方面。

- 财务指标显示的是公司过去的业绩。
- 顾客、内部经营过程、及学习与成长驱动了公司未来的财务业绩。

罗伯特·卡普兰和大卫·诺顿提出了平衡记分卡，旨在使公司摆脱以往仅仅关注财务数据的做法，要对这些方面有所关注。同时创造出公司长期发展所需要的能力与无形资产。这通过将公司的战略转换成每个方面具体的度量方法。公司将平衡记分卡作为一种管理工具用来阐明和传达公司战略，将个人和组织的目标与战略相联系，同时将战略与预算过程相联系，并为持续的战略改进获得反馈。

关键成功因素

公司首先通过 SWOT 分析来规划其战略，分析内部优势和劣势，然后分析外部机会与威胁。优势包括组织的核心能力或公司所擅长的技术。分析这些因素将会帮助一个公司确定其关键的成功因素。关键性因素（CSFS）是具体的、可衡量的目标，并且它是要实现公司战略必须达到的。

通过将关键性因素整理成 SWOT 分析的四个方面，经理人员将会在界定每个关键性因素时达成共识（例如，一些经理也许会将他们的产品组合作为优势，其他的视为劣势）。

关键性因素必须是可度量的，为每个关键性因素定义度量单位是继界定它们之后的下一个任务。根据卡普兰和诺顿"如果你尚不能度量它，你就不能管理它"。若要使平衡记分卡得到认可，不能仅运用财务指标。平衡记分卡的四个维度中的每一项的 CSF 都在图表 2 – 66 中作出了介绍。

图表 2 – 66　CSF 的衡量指标

维　　度	关键性因素	指 标 实 例
财务	销售额	销售预测精确度、销售利润率、销售趋势
	流动性	资产、存货、应收账款周转率、现金流量
	盈利性	投资回报率、剩余利润、经济附加值
	市场价值	市场附加值、股价
	市场份额	贸易联合分析、市场界定
顾客	顾客获得	新顾客数量、新顾客的销售总额
	顾客满意度	顾客退货、投诉、调查

维　度	关键性因素	指标实例
内部经营过程	顾客忠诚度	各类顾客忠诚度、顾客增长百分比
	质量	担保费用
	及时性	订货至交货所需时间、及时送货百分比
	生产力	周期时间、有效性、效率、废品
	质量	缺陷、退货、废品、返工、调查、担保
	安全性	事故、保险索赔、事故后果
	加工时间	准备时间、周转、定货交付时间
学习与成长	商标管理	广告数量、调查、最新报道
	技术发展	员工接受培训时间、技术改进
	积极性、热忱	每个员工的建议、已采纳的建议
	新产品	最新专利、设计变化次数、研发技术
	竞争	员工流动、经验、顾客满意度
	团队合作表现	调查、与其他团队共享利益、多组合作项目次数、共享鼓励百分比

图表 2-66 只是公司用以形成其战略的可能的关键性因素的一个样本，然而，一种指标可能会与其他指标有一定冲突。为了避免这种情况，平衡记分卡利用集成过程，这将在下面介绍。

平衡记分卡的有效利用

关键性因素和它们的衡量指标一旦确定，它们必须联系到公司的战略。如果每个经理人员都被动员以其他目标为代价去达到自身的目标，那么没有一种度量工具是有效的。一种有效的平衡记分卡应当在组织内部营造一种相互理解的氛围。平衡记分卡以一种全局的视角来确定个人对组织战略性的成功作出了多大的贡献。平衡记分卡各因素不仅应当源于战略，而且对这些因素进行研究时应当表明战略是什么。将平衡记分卡的四个维度与战略相联系要求了解以下三个原则：

- 因果关系。
- 业绩衡量指标与业绩动因。
- 与财务指标的联系。

因果关系

以上介绍的所有关键性因素都应当在大体上符合一种因果关系链，它结束于某种相关的财务指标和作为公司战略的业绩表现。因果关系的情形可以用"如果……那么……"表述来假定：如果公司引进一条新的产品线，那么公司将会吸引新的顾客基础；如果公司有了新的顾客基础，那么现在所有的产品线都将有新的顾客，等等。这些因果关系链条应当尽可能地在四个维度的运用中得到改进，所有链条的最终结果应当明确描述公司的战略，如何度量每个因素，怎样为过程提供反馈，最后，所有的关键性因素都应当被合并到这些因果链条中的某一个上来。

业绩衡量指标和业绩动因

由关键性因素构成的因果链条是有用的，它们必须与某种明确的结果及阐述这种结果如何达到的业绩动因相联系。业绩衡量指标是滞后指标，或者说是历史指标，如对盈利、市场份额、员工能力及顾客忠诚度衡量的指标等。业绩衡量指标衡量了在一些因果链条之后会达到什么结果。业绩动因是前置性的指标，是一个特定部门战略的具体化，如周转率、准备时间或新产品。缺乏业绩衡量指标的业绩动因虽然指明了如何在短期内运作，但是不会指明战略是否有效。缺乏业绩驱动的业绩衡量指标会指出部门或团队应当努力的方向，但并没有说明如何达到他们的目标，而且也不会在信息需要的时候提供相关信息。

与财务指标联系

不管一个组织如何明确其目标，如全面质量管理或员工热忱，若没能联系到财务指标，这些规划也仅仅是心中的一个目标而已。不但如此，若不能与计划的可见效果相联系，便会导致理想的破灭，因为并没有可以衡量成功的方法。因此，所有的因果链条都应当与财务结果相联系。

平衡记分卡的财务指标与已经在第 3 节讨论的"财务指标"是相同的，这些内容也在 CMA 教材第一本书第 5 章"财务报表分析"中有所涉及。

BSC 非财务指标

下面具体介绍 BSC 的三种非财务指标；BSC 的财务指标与在 CMA 学习系统其他地方讨论过的类似。

顾客指标

由于顾客创造了公司所有的收益，顾客识别与市场细分对所有的公司都是很重要的。顾客维度包括具体的业绩衡量指标和业绩动因。由于一个公司不能在把每个人都作为目标的同时仍能不失去核心顾客，因此公司必须塑造业绩动因，它们是市场划分与公司战略的具体化。

顾客业绩衡量指标

主要的顾客业绩衡量指标包括：
- 市场份额。
- 顾客获得。
- 顾客满意度。
- 顾客忠诚度。
- 顾客获利能力。

这些业绩衡量指标将在下文予以介绍，除了顾客获利能力已在本章第 3 节中讨论。图表 2 - 67 表明这些因素是如何在因果关系链条中相互作用的。

市场份额。市场份额是指在某一特定市场中，使用一个公司产品或服务的顾客占全部顾客的比例。对市场份额的再分便是会计份额。会计份额是指顾客业务占公司全部开支的比例，也被称为"顾客钱包份额"。一位食品销售商可能将产品的购买量占所有目标顾客的产品购买量的比例作为其市场份额。

图表 2 - 67　顾客业绩衡量指标

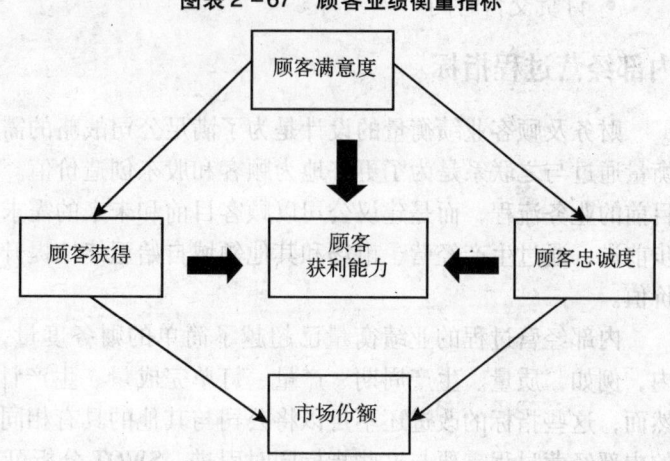

有关企业分割市场的总规模方面的数据可以通过同业公会、行业团体、政府研究以及客户调查而获得。公司掌握的市场份额可以通过客户的数量、出售的货物量或公司的支出来计算。会计份额通过调查或粗略估计来估算出在一个顾客上的支出占公司总支出的比例。拥有较少客户的公司可以追踪客户，然而拥有较多客户的公司必须追踪客户群体。

顾客获得。公司在寻求业务扩大的过程中将十分关注顾客的获得。但由于顾客忠诚度无法达到 100%，因而所有公司需要增加新客户。顾客获得可以用绝对数指标（新顾客数量）或相对数指标（顾客净获得）来表示，同样可以用公司对顾客的销售总额来表示。顾客获得度量了在获得新顾客的过程中所支出资金的效率，如广告费和其他市场费用。其他指标关注客户转化率：即新顾客人数除以潜在的顾客人数。

顾客满意度。对顾客满意度的衡量指出一个公司在满足其消费者需求的过程中成效有多大。当公司的客户更多的是企业时，得到关于顾客满意的反馈是较容易的，顾客会按照一定程序通过满意度指标对其卖主进行评级。零售客户的满意度可以通过调查获得，但当其不可行时，一些公司会采用顾客投诉次数。顾客调查费用高低不等，取决于使用的媒体及顾客回应次数。

顾客忠诚度。顾客忠诚是一种不断发展的过程，对于那些保留客户名单的公司而言，可以直接使用，如杂志社、汽车特许经销处、批发商和银行。与会计份额相似，顾客忠诚度可以转化为对每个顾客业务的百分比变化。对于零售商，一些有关顾客忠诚度的数据可以从信用卡收入中得到，但其他数据必须近似得到。

业绩动因

虽然业绩衡量指标可以广泛地为众多行业所用，但业绩驱动是对每个公司的战略及市场的具体化。顾客获得、忠诚度、满意度的驱动因素是建立在满足顾客需求的基础上的。一些常见的业绩动因如下：

- 反应时间。
- 交货表现。
- 产品缺陷。

- 订货交付时间。

内部经营过程指标

财务及顾客业绩衡量的设计是为了满足公司战略的需要，而内部经营过程的业绩衡量通过与之联系是为了更好地为顾客和股东创造价值。平衡记分卡并没有试图改进目前的业务流程，而是建议公司以顾客目前和未来的需求为出发点，沿着因果链条逐步前进，通过生产经营、市场和其他领域自始至终地提升销售额与服务，为顾客创造价值。

内部经营过程的业绩衡量已超越了简单的财务度量，将衡量产出的指标包括在内，例如，质量、生产周期、产量、订单完成量、生产计划、生产能力以及营业额。然而，这些指标的改进还不足以将公司与其他的具有相同目标的公司加以区分。全新的内部经营过程需要与这些指标同时引进。SWOT 分析可以帮助确定公司的劣势以便寻找新的解决方法，而不仅仅是数量上的改进。例如，公司可以通过一些激进的措施缩短生产周期，在适时供应制度基础上直接将货物送至零售机构从而免去库存。

平衡记分卡定义了内部经营过程的三个方面，为多数公司的内部经营过程的策略提供了一定的帮助。

- **创新**

公司应通过 SWOT 分析来界定其可以满足的客户需求，以此作为创新过程的开始。由于巨额研发费用必须作为期间费用而核销，因此积极有效地研制新产品要比集中于持续的生产经营过程更为重要。由于首先推出新产品的公司在市场份额上占有显著的优势，因此进入市场的时间是评价一种产品的引进是否成功的重要标准。其他衡量指标包括新产品销售额占全部销售额的比重，新产品与竞争对手新产品的比较以及与预算的差异。

产品开发过程包括的业绩衡量指标有产量、周期时间和成本。例如，对一种计算机芯片的研究过程也许需要测试许多材料，因此，用于未来进行研究材料的产量可以通过测试的数量来确定。材料在每个生产阶段都有它可以度量的时间（周期时间），与此同时，研发过程的总成本也是可以衡量的。因此，有关产品投入市场的时间以及全部成本都可以被衡量。

- **经营过程**

经营过程是过去进行业绩衡量的主要对象，而且它在降低成本或增加生产能力方面仍是十分重要的。而仅通过财务指标来评价经营过程，如变动成本和标准成本，会导致生产线经理悖于公司的战略而行动，例如，仅为了保持一个期望的财务比率而储备过多存货，而不是从顾客的角度出发。

虽然财务指标仍是很重要的，但是平衡记分卡建议公司通过实施其他的指标来对其予以补充，如质量、技术能力和缩短周期，从而制定处不同于其他公司的长期战略。

- **售后服务**

售后服务是一种增加产品或服务价值的方法，同时可以得到有关顾客满意度方面的反馈。许多公司在出售复杂产品或服务时，都将售后服务包含在其销售计划中。这一过程使用的指标包括：企业对设备故障的反应时间、接到客户维修电话的响应时间，这些指标都可以衡量售后服务的成效。

学习与成长指标

公司在明确了其财务、顾客及内部经营过程的战略需要后，就引入了学习与成长业绩衡量。如果公司将抱负与创新规划在其战略中，那么公司就需要通过学习与成长获得新的能力。虽然这是平衡记分卡设计中的最后一步，它将是首先被实施的。学习与成长业绩度量是期望战略绩效的绩效动因。用财务指标来衡量学习与成长，往往只能指明短期结果，而短期的培训一般是没有盈利的。然而，如果一个企业长期地将这个因素忽略，那么其后果是很严重的。因此，在这方面必须引进新的衡量方法来引导经理人员作出决策。

学习与成长的衡量包括三方面的内容：

● 员工能力

自动化的重复工作已经将员工管理从一种工业化的模式转化成一种全新的理念。员工必须认真思考，并且对持续的生产经营过程有所贡献，而不是像以往在明确规范下执行重复的任务。具体反映员工能力的指标包括：员工满意度、员工保留度，以及员工生产力。只有满意的员工才能为公司带来满意的顾客。评价员工满意度可以采用年度调查的方法进行，员工保留度可以通过人员流动以及员工服务时间来衡量。为公司投入较多的员工往往会更加满意。员工生产力业绩衡量是绩效驱动的结果，如员工培训、自主决策与结果的比较，产出与应有所产出的员工人数的比较。另一种常用的较为简单的生产力衡量指标是单位员工收益，但它不应成为惟一的度量指标，因为过分强调收益可能会导致员工在盈利水平较低的情况下接受收益。例如，产品推销员为增加销售额而允许大量价格折扣。

衡量员工新技能需要的指标包括：单位员工培训次数，必须经过培训才能完成的工作的比例，或者是将员工培训至合格所需的时间。这些指标也暗含了公司将其能力提升至战略水平所需的工作量。策略性工作涵盖比率是另一个度量方法，它是用有能力担任特定策略性工作的员工人数除以现有员工总数。这个比率揭露了公司在技术上的缺位。

● 信息系统能力

这个指标衡量的是获得客户信息和关键信息所需要的时间，它能评价目前信息系统的能力，并指出对其进行继续投资的必要性，战略信息覆盖率是用目前信息系统能力除以期望的系统需求。

● 热忱、积极性和组织合作

衡量热忱和积极性的指标包括：各位员工提出建议的数量，被采纳的建议的数量及基于员工提议后生产力的提高或成本的削减。员工的热忱和积极性可以通过一些为员工所知的标准来强化，使其相信他们的努力并非徒劳。宣传组织对于进步的期望，基于某项改进而获得的成功，以及将提出建议的员工作为所有员工的动力因素。

组织合作、组织学习，和团队合作的衡量包括某一部门设定的目标与其完成的目标之间的对照，以及包括团队奖励在内的团队度量。将个人目标和奖励与组织绩效相联系对于达到公司的整体战略来讲是十分重要的。组织合作的绩效驱动包括周期性地对员工进行调查，由此确定其积极性水平已达到平衡记分卡中关键性因素的标准。

平衡记分卡实例

图表 2 -68 是 Acme 公司完整的平衡记分卡。它指出了公司全局性的战略目标以及相关目标。它包括了平衡记分卡四个方面具体的目标，为便于指代，分别为它们编号。每一目标都有一个具体的衡量指标和未来两年要达到的目标。"程序"列是针对 Acme 公司特定的战略目标，其调查得到的实际结果与计划结果之间的比较。目标是在这些规划会继续的假设下设定的。

图表 2 -68　Acme 公司平衡记分卡（计划结果）

Acme 公司平衡记分卡
全局目标：在未来两年内增长 20% 销售额
目标

维度	战略目标	指标	今年 （Y0）	第一年 （Y1）	第二年 （Y2）	
销售额			$400 000	$432 000	$484 000	
				第一年目标	第二年目标	程序
财务	F1：权益报酬最大化	权益报酬率		9%	13%	
	F2：正的经济增加值	EVA		$20 000	$30 000	
	F3：销售额增长 10%	销售额变动%		8%	12%	
	F4：资产利用率	利用率		85%	88%	
顾客	C1：价格	与竞争产品相比		-4%	-5%	
	C2：顾客忠诚度	忠诚度%		75%	75%	CRM *
	C3：最低成本供应	总成本与竞争者相比		-6%	-7%	SRM **
	C4：产品创新	新产品销售额%		10%	15%	
内部经营过程	P1：加快生产进度	生产周期		0.3 天	0.25 天	ERP ***
	P2：新产品成功投入	订单数量		1 000	1 500	
	P3：销售额渗透	实际与计划相比（差异）		0%	0%	
	P4：降低存货	存货占销售%		30%	28%	
学习与成长	L1：联系战略与奖励制度	单位变动支付的净利润		65%	68%	CRM
	L2：填补关键能力空白	追踪表中的关键技术满意度		75%	80%	学费报销
	L3：适合顾客文化	调查指数		77%	79%	CRM
	L4：高质量的领导	经理人员平均等级（最大为 10 点）		8.9	9.2	学费报销

*　顾客关系管理实施。
**　供应商关系管理实施。
***　计划提升至企业资源规划系统。

在第一年底，结果如图表 2 -69 所示。

图表 2-69　Acme 公司平衡记分卡（实际结果）

Acme 公司平衡记分卡
全局目标：在未来两年内增长 20% 销售额
实际结果

		第一年目标	第一年实际结果	差异*	
销售额		$432 000	$424 000	$ 8000	U
方面	战略目标				
财务	F1：权益报酬最大化	9%	8%	1%	U
	F2：正的经济附加值	$20 000	$18 000	$2 000	U
	F3：销售额增长 10%	8%	12%	2%	U
	F4：资产利用率	85%	87%	2%	F
顾客	C1：价格	-4%	-4%	0	
	C2：顾客忠诚度	75%	70%	5%	U
	C3：最低成本供应	-6%	-7%	-1%	F
	C4：新产品	10%	8%	2%	U
内部经营过程	P1：加快生产进度	0.3 天	0.25 天	0.05	F
	P2：新产品成功投入	1 000（订单）	800（订单）	200（订单）	U
	P3：销售额渗透	0%	-7%	-7%	U
	P4：降低存货	30%	29%	1%	F
学习与成长	L1：联系战略与奖励制度	65%	63%	2%	U
	L2：填补关键能力空白	75%	75%	0	
	L3：适合顾客文化	77%	74%	3%	U
	L4：高质量的领导	8.9	8.9	0	

* 　F = 有利差异；　* 　U = 不利差异。

　　Acme 公司可以从第一年的结果中得出什么样的结论？公司也许在客户关系管理方案的实施上遇到了问题（计划不周、项目取消或延误等），因为与方案相联系的指标都表现出了不利差异。对方案重新检查后，也许会寻找到将注意力集中于顾客需求的方法。另一方面，Acme 公司的生产成本和生产效率均显示出了有利差异，意味着公司采取的 SRM 和 ERP 行动是有成效的。Acme 公司的劳动力在稳步进展，同时它的短训班补偿方案也与之并驾齐驱。然而，虽然公司在核心竞争力和领导方面的劳动力是充分的，但他们并没有以顾客为导向，这也是公司失去顾客并且不能进入新市场进而卖出新产品的主要原因（这也许基于对实际市场需求的信息不充分的情况下设计）。如果 Acme 公司想扭转这种情况从而实现其目标，它必须增加对 CRM 行动的投资，包括通过培训将员工的心态转变为以顾客为导向。

平衡记分卡的实施

　　有关平衡记分卡实施方面的内容摘自由卡普兰和诺顿编著的《战略集中型组织》，平衡记分卡的实施简化了战略的执行过程。没有实施的战略只是一个"美丽的幻想"。在过去的几十年中，平均来看，有形资产的价值占公司总价值的比例已从2/3 降低到 1/3，这意味着公司已由过去仅从财务术语上衡量其业绩转变为需要知识型战略，不再局限于诸如预算反应较慢的工具。平衡记分卡有助于战略的执行，由于记分卡本身就是用可执行的方式描述战略的一种方法。以战略为核心的组织有以下几方面的特征：

- 平衡记分卡中所使用的所有指标（财务的和非财务的）都应当来自于公司的远景和战略。
- 过程是参与性的，而不是指令性的。
- 改变不局限于成本的削减或降低，还包括公司销售策略的调整（更多专门的竞争市场、顾客聚焦、消费倾向）。
- 公司必须采取新的文化价值观和优先权。

合作并将资源集中于战略

根据卡普兰和诺顿，就如同耗能大的灯泡却没有体积较小的激光指示物的光线强烈一样，执行团队、部门、信息系统、人力资源、预算和资本投资必须结合起来并集中至更具体的目标（没必要提高资本集中度），要比目前大多数公司的目标更加集中和具体。要达到这个目标，公司必须实施以下几方面持续改进的循环：

- 用经营术语来描述战略，使用战略地图和平衡记分卡。

战略地图是在平衡记分卡之前被采用的一种方法，它指出公司优先考虑的重点所在，从而可以设计出反映其战略的记分卡。图表 2－70 是（NAM&R）美孚公司的战略地图，它提出了在顾客方面新的关注点以及一些使顾客使用更多的美孚加油站和产品更多的因素。

- 通过使用公司记分卡以及部门与支撑部门的协同效应，组织与公司战略结合起来。

协同效应使整体价值大于部分价值之和，分解功能性领域不是通过取代部门或组织图表而是用战略优先来取代正式的报告结构（例如，每个部门不同的记分卡都有共同的主题）。与记分卡有关联的实例可参考卡普兰和诺顿的《战略集中型组织》。

- 通过采用个人记分卡、战略意识和平衡薪酬，使战略成为每个人每天的任务。

用自上而下的交流来替代自上而下的指挥，意味着每个员工都有一套清晰且符合战略的期望。平衡记分卡成为一种具有教育意义的工具，它指出如何衡量成功，但是它需要正式的培训来支持（例如，如果员工必须改进，必须首先对他们进行关于顾客分割的讲解）。同时，位于最底层的即个人水平的记分卡，可以由末端使用者基于已被传达的高水平优先权来创建。当个人寻求方法去协助公司的其他领域的时候，协同效应就自然产生了。这种过程可以帮助营造一种在个人水平上的战略意识。

平衡薪酬是将薪金与平衡记分卡相联系，常用于部门业绩而不是个人业绩的衡量。平衡薪酬通过权衡平衡记分卡中财务与非财务指标的重要性来运用它们。一些衡量方法中既有个人业绩部分，也有部门业绩部分，同时必须将薪金与一些外部因素相联系，比如行业基准（为了弥补员工无法掌控的外部因素）。使用平衡薪酬方式使采用平衡记分卡的员工的利益水平得到提高。当员工可能通过学习平衡记分卡来了解他们的报酬时，同时他们也通过勤奋而改进了公司的目标。在美孚案例中，当货车司机将汽油运至仓库时，他们便会通报那里恶劣的环境，因为他们知道自己薪酬的一部分是建立在顾客对加油站的评价之上的。

- 通过将战略与预算相联系，使用自动化分析工具，召开战略会议，开展战略学习，使战略成为一个持续的过程。

图表 2-70 Mobil NAM&R 战略地图

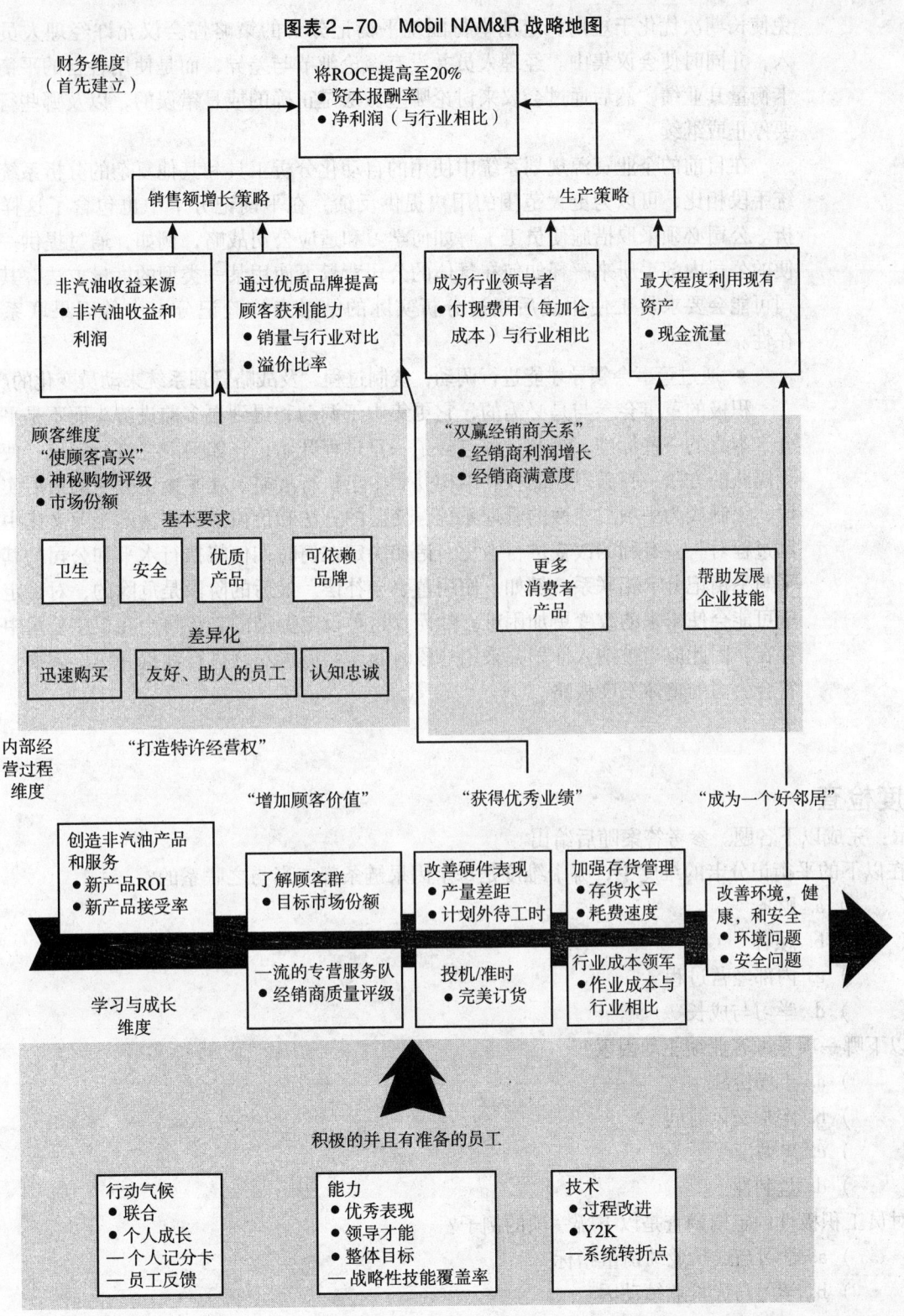

为了有利于一些策略性决策的作出，如设定预算，战略常常被忽视，因此平衡记分卡采用了集成过程。例如，创建两项预算：策略性预算和经营性预算，这样可以避

免使长期次优化于短期。定期举行围绕平衡记分卡的策略性会议允许经理人员的加入，并同时使会议集中。经理人员并没有谈论细节与差异，而是使用各自的平衡记分卡衡量其业绩，然后通过会议来讨论哪些做法是正确的或是错误的，以及哪些行为需要停止或继续。

在目前的企业资源规划系统中使用的自动化分析工具和其他复杂的分析系统与传统手段相比，可以为更大范围的用户提供反馈，在平衡记分卡中也包含了这样的分析。公司必须采取措施使员工了解如何学习和适应公司战略，例如，通过提供一些简便的公司内部手册来解释如何在具体的公司背景下使用某一类型的度量方法。其他公司可能会要求员工使用然后通过分析实际的结果来检验记分卡中的因果联系的存在性。

- 通过董事会领导才能进行调动，统制过程，及战略管理系统来动员变化的产生。

积极的董事会参与是必需的，它更集中于调动和得到更多前进势头而不是平衡记分卡本身的一些标准。统制过程包含了一旦过程开始，将如何对之进行管理，使用基于团队的方法，打破以往的权利结构并集中于执行战略。在平衡记分卡的最后实施阶段，统制成为一项战略性的管理系统，使新的方法和价值融入到新的企业文化中。统制过程对一些有利的改变进行强化，诸如决定在何时如何将执行水平和公司的其他水平与平衡记分卡相联系。例如，使用董事会补偿。最后的阶段是危险的，对稳定的期望可能会使未来的改变更加困难。然而，这种设定标准的趋势将会在很多公司中普遍存在，因此应当被纳入计划并采用一段时间，然后再对之进行评价并作出调整，使其符合公司的整体发展战略。

进度检查

提示：完成以下各题。参考答案随后给出。

1. 在以下的平衡记分卡的维度中，哪个维度是每个因果链条都应当与之联系的？
   - （　　）a. 财务
   - （　　）b. 顾客
   - （　　）c. 内部经营过程
   - （　　）d. 学习与成长

2. 以下哪一项是顾客业绩驱动因素？
   - （　　）a. 市场份额
   - （　　）b. 定货交付时间
   - （　　）c. 忠诚度
   - （　　）d. 盈利性

3. 对员工积极性的定期调查是以下哪一项的例子？
   - （　　）a. 学习与成长业绩衡量指标
   - （　　）b. 学习与成长业绩动因
   - （　　）c. 顾客业绩衡量指标
   - （　　）d. 顾客业绩动因

4. 过程时间的关键成功因素是通过以下哪个指标进行衡量的？

（　　）a. 调查
（　　）b. ROI
（　　）c. 顾客退回
（　　）d. 周转

进度检查答案

1. a
2. b
3. b
4. d

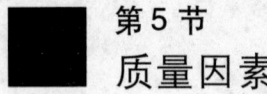

第5节
质量因素

本节内容简介

当公司过去经常在销售产品的时候忽略质量因素，全球生产高质量产品的竞争者目前已经迫使所有的公司考虑如何使质量成为最初设计的一部分，而不是简单地对最终产品质量的检查。日本生产企业继管理学家 W. Edwards Deming 和 J. M. Juran 提出后采纳了全面质量，世界上其他国家若想保持竞争力也要必须执行。

质量

质量是一种产品或服务在竞争（期望的）价格下，等同或超过顾客期望的水平。顾客期望是理解质量的关键。一种产品通过低价策略来进行差异化的前提是满足顾客对质量的期望，否则产品是不会再次被购买的。满足顾客需求不仅是质量的目标，也是公司的战略所在。顾客期望并不是绝对的，而是相对价格和服务的预期水平。

美国国会于 1987 年设立了波多黎各国家质量奖，旨在通过奖励企业成功的沟通技巧来营造产品质量竞争的氛围。许多企业已经发现，向质量方面努力的同时也提升了公司的生产力，盈利性和顾客与员工的满意度。获奖者已经被追踪，并与公司的标准普尔 500 指数（Standard &Poor's 500 index）进行比较，"Baldrige Stock Index"组的指数为 3:1。

国际标准化组织（ISO）为质量标准设立了一些认证，如质量检查、设备维修、员工培训、测试，以及对顾客投诉的处理。这些认证被全世界的公司所推崇。

ISO9000（目前至少在 160 个国家的 610 000 个企业中实施）在公司之间交易的质量管理要求中，是一种国际性参考标准。ISO 衡量了公司如何实现顾客对质量的要求，所适用的管理要求，顾客满意度和持续改进。为了获得认证，公司应当寻求一种已被正式认可的认证机构来完成评估。（这些评估并非由 ISO 完成。）企业可以选择遵循 ISO9000 的准则而不需经过认证，但是经过认证的益处包括：用于公共关系，符合所适用的规范，以及对员工进行激励。

质量和实施质量管理的行为的成本占公司收益 20% ~ 25%。然而，高质量的产品往往能驱动销售额的增长，并带来更多利润。有时在效率和效果方面的改进可以在成本没有净增加甚至降低的时候获得高质量。

由于低质量而带来的成本也应当被考虑。废品、返工、瑕疵、及重新检查只是低质量成本的冰山一角而已。其他相对较不明显的成本包括以下几个方面：

- 学习曲线损失。
- 超产或在生产能力发挥不足。
- 导致销售失败的客户满意度或信任的丧失。
- 出货退回和替换。
- 为赶上生产计划进度而支付加班费。
- 对缺陷部件的分析。

- 过多存货。
- 过程和机器重新设计。
- 停工时间。

全面质量管理（TQM）观念和技术

质量保证（QA）过去常常仅与经营过程相联系。全面质量管理（TQM）是一项管理技术，它使 CEO 等管理人员对质量负责，全体员工及所有经营过程成为质量管理的一部分。TQM 要求全面的组织承诺以及文化的改变以获得成效。TQM 通过设定具体标准来满足顾客的期望，从而将管理人员、部门、员工的工作职责联系起来。TQM 是一项长期的承诺，已使用 TQM 一段时间的企业要比刚采用 TQM 的企业表现好。

TQM 可以降低产品退货、担保费用和存货水平（归因于减少废品、损坏和返工）。不但如此，如果顾客非常看重产品的质量，那么企业就可以为产品制定较高的价格。高质量产品往往拥有较大的市场份额。同时，TQM 也降低了生产周期，加快了供应速度，因而会降低成本，并增加顾客满意度和忠诚度。

TQM 关键成功因素

图表 2-71 具体给出了对 TQM 实施的成效至关重要的几个因素：

图表 2-71

关键性因素	描　述
顾客满意度	<ul><li>将顾客需求作为战略动因</li><li>确定内部和外部的顾客及供应商的需求</li><li>用顾客反馈衡量顾客满意度</li></ul>
持续改进	<ul><li>将持续改进作为宗旨</li><li>全球经济环境下，由于竞争对手不断提高期望，因而 TQM 和降低成本是永无止境的</li><li>TQM 是企业生存的一种方式而不是一个有限的目标</li></ul>
高层经理的支持和参与	<ul><li>TQM 的实施必须从高层开始</li><li>TQM 成为每位经理决策时自觉运用的部分</li></ul>
劳动力的全员参与	<ul><li>满足内部顾客和卖主对质量的要求，来使所有员工积极追随 TQM</li><li>劳动力参与包括使用质量控制周期，或由一组员工来讨论问题及解决的方法</li></ul>
系统化的分析和目标衡量	<ul><li>同时分析正常的和错误的程序</li><li>差异最小化</li><li>采用平衡记分卡中的衡量对象</li></ul>
识别并奖励质量的实现	<ul><li>没有激励，TQM 不能成功；然而，奖励并不能局限于财务方面，可以是来自于公布、奖励、或仅仅是建议被采纳时的认可</li></ul>
持续的 TQM 培训	<ul><li>由于 TQM 的实施需要文化上的转变，必须不断强化那种文化</li><li>培训和教育对于将管理人员的承诺传递给 TQM 是关键的</li><li>员工需要一定技能来使 TQM 获得成效</li></ul>

TQM 的这些要素分级排列如图表 2-72 所示。

图表 2 - 72　全面质量管理模型

要素	宗旨	目标
系统化分析 全员参与 内部/外部 顾客 内部/外部 供应商 管理层承诺	通过持续的质量 改进来降低差异化	顾客满意

符合性质量观

对质量的界定通常是对既定标准的符合。然而，TQM 改变了质量界定的方法，包含了顾客需求的许多方面，如减少文书工作或服务速度。TQM 中的符合是指对顾客期望设定的质量标准的相符程度。球门柱或零缺陷符合将标准设定在一个范围内（如，22mm + / - 0.5mm）。对于有着许多部件的产品来说，零缺陷符合的问题就显现出来了。虽然所有的部件可能都在规定的范围内，当一些部件在范围内较高标准的位置，而其他部件在较低的位置，则就整体而言，它们的结合可能并不在可接受范围内。

绝对质量符合是在要求的水平上精确设定标准（如，恰好为 22mm）。绝对质量符合也许会产生大量的不合格部件，但是最终产品将会有更大的可能性满足顾客。

补偿系统和 TQM

管理层补偿系统的目标是激励管理人员尽可能地去努力，去奖励取得的成就，并且驱使自主的管理人员尽可能有效地遵循公司的战略，当使用 TQM 时，对奖励和认可的设定中应当适度强调 TQM。从管理人员开始，他们的补偿应当基于满足 TQM 设定的明确且可衡量的目标。其他员工可获得由于成功的质量改进而获得的红利支付或诸如公开表彰或奖状等非财务奖励。在一切可能的时候，TQM 观念都应贯穿到整个企业中，使产品质量和员工士气同时得到提高。

分析质量问题的技术

分析质量问题的技术包括质量审计、差距分析和统计控制，如控制表、帕累托图及因果图。

质量审计

质量审计是从质量的角度对公司的流程和战略进行深入地考察，包括对最好的和最差的流程进行分析。质量审计包括系统（或过程）评估和产品评估。评估的结果要与其他有类似流程的公司的分析结果进行比较，从而作为基准研究的一部分。这就为战略性的质量改进提供了长期计划。这项长期计划通过投资回报率的高低来确定各种变化的优先次序。质量审计可能由内部员工或外部审计人员来执行。内部员工可以包括产品经理或指定的内部检查人员。外部审计人员提供质量审计作为对董事会或监管机构提供的保证性服务（例如，对医学的或金融产品的检查）。

差距分析

差距分析立足于公司与同行业质量最高的竞争者之间的差距。差距分析经常伴随质量审计以便明确具体的问题并为改进设定清晰的目标。用行业中最好的企业来设定一个较高的，可以达到的目标。差距分析包括对目前的差距和在采取了培训和其他行动后预计的差距的分析。

统计控制

TQM 成功运用的前提是，它可以对一些看似随机的波动进行管理。大多数过程都是用随意设定的数量或质量目标来进行评价的。这些目标往往缺乏对一个工序所能达到的最大产出量的考虑。当过程的变动不能被理解，并且在过程的可接受性上有随意的限制，管理人员会发现他们是在对即刻出现的文题作出反应而不是前置性的。反应性的举动常会产生相反结果。当他们起作用时，管理人员却不明白为何它们要起作用。反应性的举动也会导致低质量水平。

统计思想容许每个过程或人力输出有一定差异，并且度量和管理这些差异对于有效的管理和质量控制是关键的。当差异在正常范围之外时，就要采取一些校正措施。这种校正应当旨在将整个范围提高至可接受水平，而不仅是提高一个随意的最低水平。正常变动或统计控制是一个过程的可接受范围，或是这个过程所能够达到的。异常波动是由异常因素造成的，它会导致过程以一种未预期的并且不可接受的方式变动。

获得对某一过程统计控制的方法包括控制表、帕累托图和因果图。

控制图

控制图通过对过程进行周期性的测量并运用图表来衡量过程的正常变动。这个过程是处于受控状态的，以保证我们测量的过程是在正常的或预期的情形下进行的。例如，如果网球机器生产高尔夫球的标准是 4cm，并且在 3.97cm 和 4.03cm 之间波动。因此，机器就应当被测试以保证它是处于正常的工作状况，并且这些波动是其能够产生的。对于人力资源过程来讲，销售的正常情况可以通过采用在给定的技术水平和激励水平下的销售人员来衡量。一旦正常的波动或统计控制已知，在这个水平之外的波动就可以归因于参数的改变，统计控制就是基于这些参数之上的。

例如，假设人力资源部门为 HR 所雇用员工的忠诚度设定了随意的目标，使用新雇用人员在 6 个月之后仍被雇用的百分比来衡量。图表 2 - 73 指出了两个部门在不同标准下的业绩表现。

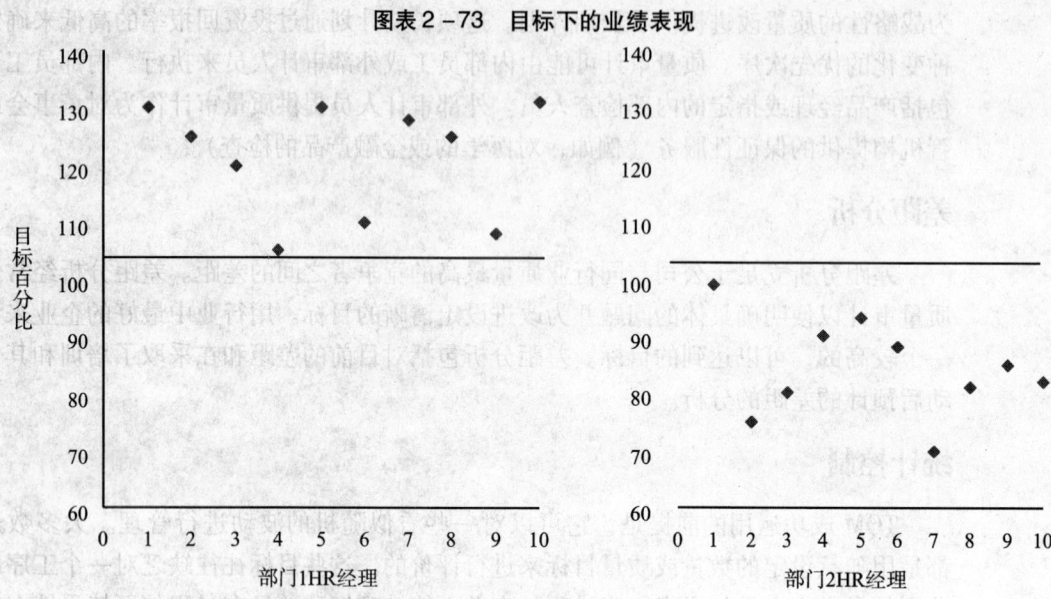

图表2－73　目标下的业绩表现

部门1HR经理

部门2HR经理

部门1似乎有一个成功的HR经理,但是部门2却不是这样。然而,如果采用统计控制,就可以为已知参数的波动设定一个可接受的范围从而进行研究,职位的类型也包括在内。假设相同的结果仍会发生,对正常参数波动的分析将会被解释,每个过程都将有其正常波动的范围来对这些因素作出解释。因此,如果部门1是为领固定薪金的职位招聘员工,那么正常范围将被设置到足够高的位置从而激励HR。如果部门2是雇用小时工人来进行重复性的工作,他们的正常范围就可能会设定得较低。

图表2－74指出了范围将如何设定。现在,部门1并没有表现得如它本来那么好,然而部门2的表现却达到了它的预期。这些范围可以在以后对每个部门进行衡量。

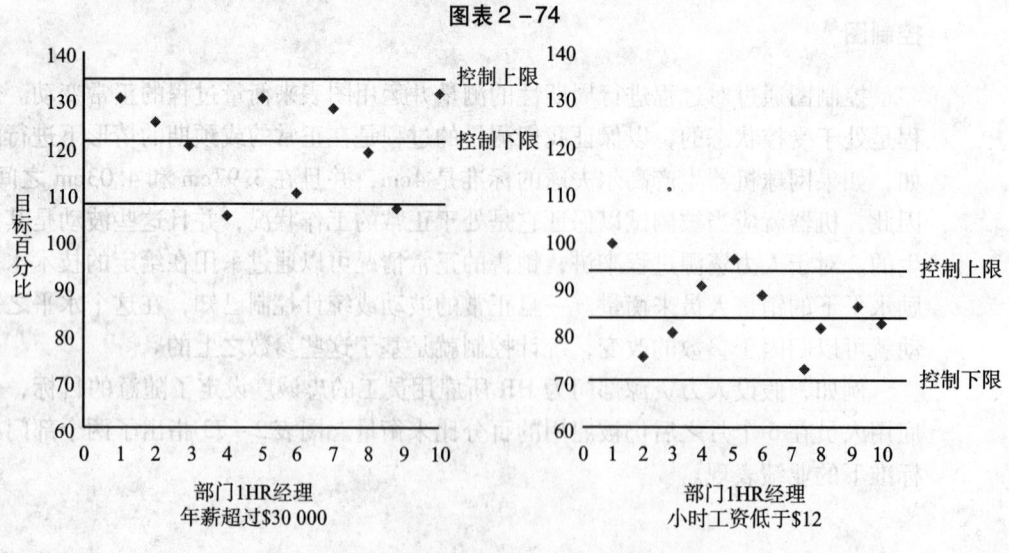

图表2－74

部门1HR经理
年薪超过$30 000

部门1HR经理
小时工资低于$12

除了观察过程超出了它的控制上限和下限,控制图也可以测度从长期来看,过程

管理会计与报告(第二版)

超出控制范围的趋势，因此校正性的措施就能具有前瞻性。当采取了校正措施之后，控制图可以评价改进效果，控制图的局限性在于包括导致波动产生的原因不能从表中得知，同时采用估计方法来取样也可能是错误的。

帕累托图

帕累托图是直方图的一种类型。直方图衡量的是某一特定因素的出现的频率对所有数据的贡献程度。帕累托图是一种质量直方图，它将质量问题按其成因进行分解，并且按其频率的高低进行排列。帕累托图的产生是建立在 Joserph Juran 的理论上的：大多数质量问题是由少数高频率出现的原因所导致的。

图表 2 - 75 是网球部门的帕累托图，它是以直方图的形式来描述的。图表中包括了一个累计的总额，是由最高频率的数量与次高频率数量相加得到的。这条曲线指出前两个因素的总频率、前三个因素等等。累计总额曲线随因素出现频率的下降而逐渐变得平缓，表明了在向后校正了一个因素后将对作为结果的质量产生越来越小的影响。

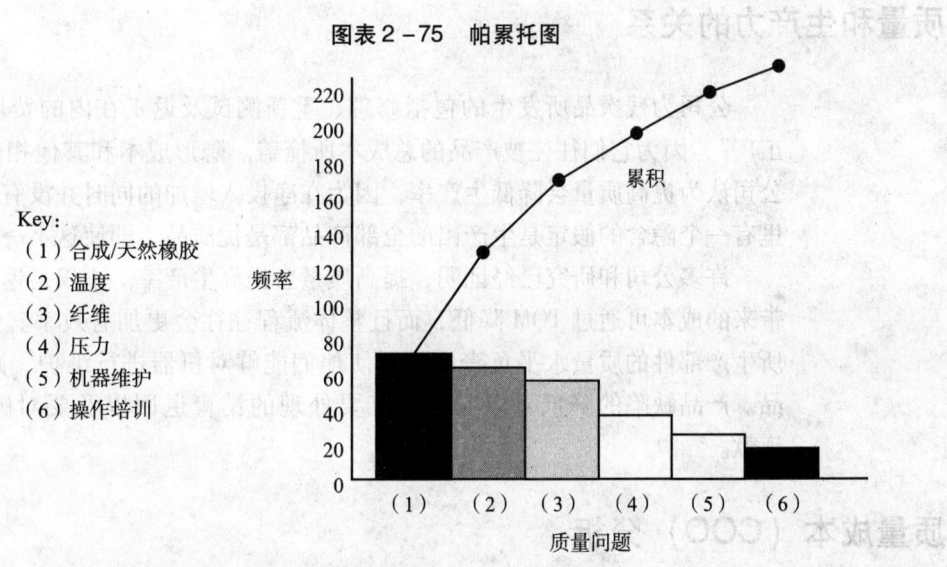

图表 2 - 75　帕累托图

Key:
（1）合成/天然橡胶
（2）温度
（3）纤维
（4）压力
（5）机器维护
（6）操作培训

帕累托图可用于对来自控制图的波动的初步分析。帕累托图在制定管理决策的时候是有用的，如提供最大成果。

因果（鱼骨）图

因果图，又称鱼骨图（Fishbone）或石川图（Ishikawa diagram），是一种流水作业图，它指出了导致问题产生的某些原因。它之所以称为鱼骨图，是因为图中的一个箭头或鱼脊代表出现的问题，其他的箭头或鱼刺代表主要的原因。较小的箭头或鱼骨，代表了对主要原因有影响的一些因素。图表 2 - 76 是一张网球质量问题的因果图。其中机器、原材料、方法和员工是导致生产流程失败的普遍性原因。

图表2-76 网球废品的因果图

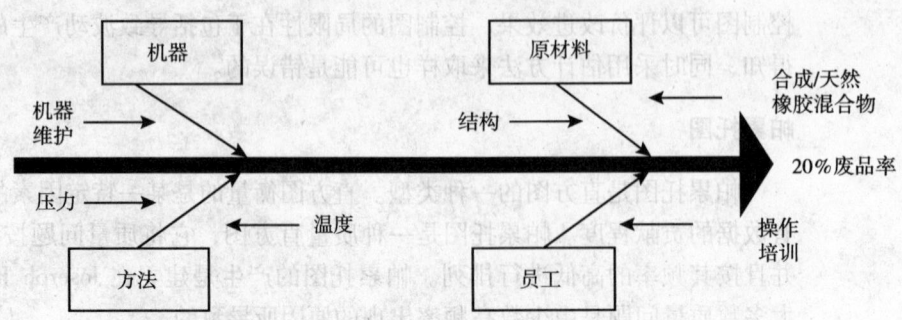

因果图分为两种类型：离差分析和流程分类。离差分析，如图表2-76所示，将质量问题分成恰当的几个方面。流程分类通过加入时线来为流程的步骤进行先后排序，从而指出错误是在哪个环节产生的。流程分类常用于每种原因出现的频率未知的情况。

质量和生产力的关系

公司为残次品所发生的包括修理、重新测试及返工在内的费用被称为"隐藏性工厂"，因为它们往往被产品的总成本所掩盖。隐形成本和其他相似的方法会让很多公司认为提高质量会降低生产率，因为在净投入增加的同时并没有使净产出增加。这里有一个隐含的假定是生产出的全部产品都是优质品，即使这不一定正确。

许多公司和研究已经证明，提高质量会提高生产率。不仅是返工、废品和瑕疵所带来的成本可通过TQM降低，而且整体流程往往会更加有效率。例如，让工人对其所生产部件的质量水平负责，从而使他们能够对机器进行维护，减少故障和返工产品。产品缺陷的降低可以减少员工要处理的销售退回以及要对顾客作出的解释和道歉。

质量成本（COQ）分析

TQM中的流程改进小组需要知道生产流程的每个环节具体发生的成本，从而确定质量设计的改变如何影响盈利性。基于这个原因，作业成本法（ABC）和TQM经常同时运用来获得成本方面精确的数据。

传统成本

传统上质量成本（COQ）分为四类：预防成本、评估成本、外部缺陷成本和内部缺陷成本。

- **预防成本**

预防成本是指质量体系设计、实施和维持的成本，包括对质量体系本身进行审计的成本。具体包括质量计划、新产品检查、供应商能力调查、召开团队质量会议，以及为质量而发生的培训。

- **评估成本**

评估成本是质量的审计过程所发生的成本，包括对质量水平正式和非正式的衡量和评估，以及设定质量标准和业绩要求。例如，对原材料、半成品的检查和测试，对完工产品的检测，校准设备，及流程和服务的评估。

- **内部缺陷成本**

内部缺陷成本是指在产品交付顾客之前由于产品或部件的不合格而发生的成本，包括废品、返工、损坏、重新测试和检查的成本。

- **外部缺陷成本**

外部缺陷成本是指在产品交付顾客之后由于质量问题而发生的费用，包括顾客投诉、退货、产品收回以及担保费用。

在实施 TQM 之前，这四类成本的管理成效是有限的，因为多数经理人员认为质量是质量保证部门（QA）的惟一责任，同时他们认为质量管理的目标在于达到一定标准或将其控制在一个可接受的范围内。因此，大多数经理人员认为质量成本仅仅是检查、返工、废品和测试所带来的。这四类成本的划分并没有成为成本控制的方法，仅是估计成本的一种方法。

除此之外，一旦管理人员明确了一个问题，就可以在近期解决它。同时，这四类成本并不能与多数公司采用的成本归集系统相符合，因此它们不能很好地协调。

从更深层次、更达观的角度上讲，许多质量专家在 COQ 指标是否应当被采用上不能达成共识，因为这表明了在质量和成本之间必然要有一种协调。换句话讲，它意味着低于 100% 的质量是可以接受的，只要低质量所带来的成本足够的低。质量专家认为不论多小的质量缺陷都是不可接受的。他们认为 COQ 将质量视为一种成本，而不是增加整体利润的方法。因此，一些质量专家通过对低质量产生的成本来强调只有低质量才是产生成本的原因。

图表 2-77 是一个质量成本报告的样本。定期提供标准化形式的报告对于成本的追踪是有用的，同时可以衡量一些改进措施对全部产品成本的成效。然而，一些改进小组可以仅做一次集中性的报告从而节约定期的质量报告的费用。如果创建并维持报告的费用不能被证明对生产力和质量的改进是有效的，那么这种定期的质量报告可能并不是具有成本效益的。平衡记分卡（见本章第4节"平衡记分卡"）可以满足此类或其他质量报告的需要。

图表2-77 质量成本报告

质量成本摘要报告 截至_____ （ ）						
描 述	当月			本年迄今		
	质量成本	所占百分比		质量成本	所占百分比	
		销售额	其他		销售额	其他
1.0 预防成本						
1.1 市场/顾客/使用者						
1.2 产品/服务/设计进展						
1.3 购买预防成本						
1.4 营业预防成本						

续表

描　　述	当月			本年迄今		
	质量成本	所占百分比		质量成本	所占百分比	
		销售额	其他		销售额	其他
1.5　质量管理						
1.6　其他预防成本						
预防成本总额						
预防目标						
2.0　评估成本						
2.1　购买评估成本						
2.2　营业评估成本						
2.3　外部评估成本						
2.4　重新检查测试和检查数据						
2.5　各种质量审计						
评估成本总额						
评估目标						
3.0　外部缺陷成本						
3.1　产品/服务设计缺陷成本						
3.2　购买缺陷成本						
3.3　营业缺陷成本						
3.4　其他内部缺陷成本						
4.0　外部缺陷成本						
缺陷成本总额						
目标缺陷						
质量成本总额						
质量总目标						

质量成本摘要报告
截至＿＿＿＿＿＿
（　　　）

基本数据	本月		本年迄今		全年	
	预算	实际	预算	实际	预算	实际
销售净额						
其他基础（具体）						

资料来源：《质量成本原则》，Jack Campanella 著。

TQM 成本

　　TQM 着重强调减少和消除差异、持续的质量改进和 TQM 的其他方面。加之传统的质量成本没能与成本归集系统很好的关联，导致 TQM 抛弃了传统的成本分类，选择了成本归集系统所采用的一些具体的指标。当采用 ABC 时，成本与耗费资源的活动联系起来。使用 ABC 并且用一些质量术语来匹配归集系统的时候，可以得到以下几点好处：

- 明确异常差异的真实来源。
- 为质量改进而合理分配资源。
- 有利于部门之间成本的交流。
- 将差异和生产周期的具体情况迅速反馈给生产线员工。

- 协调财务部门和质量执行团队。
- 监督流程和产品的改进。

设计质量成本

产品的设计会影响到它整体的盈利性、质量、销路及顾客满意度。低水平设计会导致生产流程的低效率、内部缺陷及由重新设计或返工所带来的高昂成本。然而，产品的盈利性同样受其进入市场的时间或是设计思想成熟与产品投入市场所间隔时间的影响。产品进入市场的时间越久，其创造的利润就越多。竞争者的产品停留在市场的时间越长，公司面临的风险增大，盈利性降低。在这种两难选择下，一些产品不得不在充分检测之前就投入市场，这也带来了日后重新设计以消除差异的大量成本。

过去的组织过程使设计流程更加恶化。一个部门完成了其设计责任后，就交付给下一部门，因此设计者对低效率的生产流程是不负责任的。新的组织减少了内部等级水平，同时强调了部门间交流和团队合作，以及共同承担责任。

旧式的设计流程仅是在借鉴之前设计流程的经验后，简单估计需要改动的地方，并没有包含任何对流程本身的改进。检查和挑选是质量保证的主要方法，并且一定数量的缺陷是可以被预计的。

新的 TQM 设计流程在流程中的所有环节都强调了顾客需求满意度。QFD 流程是一种全面计划的工具，它将顾客的需求与设计流程的每个环节都联系起来，每个环节都与设计决策、流程控制及步骤相互关联。结果作为一项计划指出了产品形成的每个方面，从生产到使顾客满意，QFD 使产品重新设计的次数大大降低，因此在保证高质量的同时缩短了产品投入市场的时间。典型的 QFD 流程从一个因素开始，即顾客需求，然后将下一步建立在累积的需求之上。在顾客需求之后的是设计要求、设计策划、产品特性、生产和购买流程、生产和质量控制，以及顾客满意度，因此，QFD 开始于顾客，并结束于顾客。

另外一种在设计质量得到改进的同时加速投入市场的方法叫并行工程（CE）。并行工程包含了团队合作从而使设计项目的不同方面可以同时进行。CE 使用 TQM 和一些现代化工具如计算机辅助设计使相互关联的方面得到协调，如设计、营销和产品生命周期每个阶段的卖主。使用 CE 不仅在不牺牲设计质量的情况下加速产品投入市场，而且允许团队的每个部门可以迅速进入下一产品或服务，这是传统的顺序流程所不能达到的。

进度检查

提示：完成以下各题。参考答案随后给出。

1. 全面质量管理的关键性因素包括以下哪个方面？

(　　) a. 持续改进

(　　) b. 绝对质量符合

(　　) c. 差距分析

(　　) d. 统计思想

2. 以下的衡量工具中，哪一项包含了累积总额曲线作为直方图结果的附加部分？

（　　）a. 差距分析

（　　）b. 控制图

（　　）c. 帕累托图

（　　）d. 质量分析

3. 在传统的质量成本分析中，以下哪类成本包括了质量体系的设计成本？

（　　）a. 预防成本

（　　）b. 评估成本

（　　）c. 内部缺陷成本

（　　）d. 外部缺陷成本

进度检查答案

1. a

2. c

3. a

第5章
外部财务报告

本章内容简介

1976 年美国财务会计准则委员会（FASB）开始构建财务报告目标和基本原则的概念框架。FASB 于 1978 年公布了第一份财务会计概念公告（SFAC）。在发布该概念框架之后，FASB 又在新的财务会计准则公告（SFAS）中建立了一套完整的标准和规则。尽管在会计准则的制定过程中政治也扮演了一定的角色，但 FASB 由财务会计基金会（FAF）建立和管理，因此能最小化政治的影响。财务会计基金会旨在提高用户对财务报告的理解和信心。

在没有相关准则可资参考的情况下，该概念框架可指导会计师作出选择，该概念框架也能为财务会计准则委员会的紧急问题处理小组（EITF）这类机构提供指导，使他们在处理紧急问题时更为快捷。虽然一般公认会计原则（GAAP）并未要求应用该框架中的概念，但这些概念仍被广泛接受（基于这些概念编制的财务报告符合一般公认会计原则）。注意本章有关外部报告的信息仅以美国一般公认会计原则（GAAP）和美国一般公认审计准则（GAAS）为依据。

本章探讨了该概念框架的目标和基本原则，以及财务报表的格式、要素和报告需求。同时也讨论了美国证券交易委员会（SEC）在规范上市公司的对外财务报告和年报时所扮演的角色。

学习要点说明

注册管理会计师（CMA）考试包含很多学习要点，这些学习要点由管理会计师协会确定。学习要点描述了注册管理会计师考试要求掌握的所有知识点和技能，并且细分为各个章节。注册管理会计师考试教材解释了学习要点所包含的各个部分，是对学习要点的有力支持。学习要点可以帮助考生以不同的方式或通过不同的问题情景理解这些概念。考生还应该练习学习要点中所提到的全部或者部分计算，或者完成计算过程中的缺失部分。学习要点不能代替对 CMA 考试教材内容的研究和学习，但是可以确保考生达到学习要点所设定的目标。

注册管理会计师教材中所包含的学习要点是一个完整的集合，并且是到目前为止最新的版本。考生可以浏览 IMA 的官方网站 www. imanet. org，点击"认证"部分查看和下载关于学习要点的最新 PDF 文件。

学习要点

5.1 外部财务报告的目标

- LOS 5.1.1：识别外部财务报告的目标，例如提供资源和债务信息、全面收益信息以及现金流量信息。

5.2 财务会计基础

- LOS 5.2.1：确认和理解会计基本假设和惯例，包括持续性假设、历史成本假设、权责发生制和谨慎性原则。
- LOS 5.2.2：理解收入、费用、固定资产、流动资产、流动负债、长期负债和权益交易的确认和计量。
- LOS 5.2.3："已实现"和"已确认"这两个概念。
- LOS 5.2.4：确认每个财务报表的财务报告要素。
- LOS 5.2.5：专题：租赁、退休金和其他退休福利、递延所得税、股票期权、停止经营、特殊事项、会计变更、提早清偿的债务、企业合并、合并财务报表、衍生工具和股票期权会计。对每个专题，能定义和描述它的特征，基本理解与之相关的会计问题，并描述其对公司财务报表的影响。

5.3 财务报表和报表使用者

- LOS 5.3.1：确认财务状况报表（资产负债表）、收益表（损益表）、现金流量表、股东权益变动表的使用者和他们的信息需求。
- LOS 5.3.2：理解财务状况报表（资产负债表）、收益表（损益表）、现金流量表、股东权益变动表的编制目的和用途。
- LOS 5.3.3：确认财务状况报表（资产负债表）、收益表（损益表）、现金流量表、股东权益变动表的构成要素和分类。
- LOS 5.3.4：确认财务状况报表（资产负债表）、收益表（损益表）、现金流量表、股东权益变动表的局限性。
- LOS 5.3.5：确认财务状况报表（资产负债表）、收益表（损益表）、现金流量表、股东权益变动表需在表内或脚注中披露的补充财务信息。
- LOS 5.3.6：按正确的格式编制财务状况报表（资产负债表）、收益表（损益表）、现金流量表、股东权益变动表。
- LOS 5.3.7：对财务状况报表（资产负债表）、收益表（损益表）、现金流量表、股东权益变动表等财务报表，能正确地计算和准确地分类。
- LOS 5.3.8：理解现金流量表的直接法和间接法。
- LOS 5.3.9：确认金融交易如何影响财务状况报表（资产负债表）、收益表（损益表）、现金流量表、股东权益变动表的要素，确定交易的类别。
- LOS 5.3.10：确认财务状况报表（资产负债表）、收益表（损益表）、现金流量表、股东权益变动表的基本披露形式（包括脚注，附表等）。

5.4 确认、计量、计价和披露

对下列每个子主题的知识要求：。

- 子主题的定义及其构成要素的特征。
- 理解每个子主题的构成要素的合适计价方式。
- 理解每个子主题的构成要素的合适会计惯例。
- 对比其计价方式和会计方法。
- 正确表述财务报表。
- 确认财务报表主体部分和/或脚注或附表的正确披露要求。

Ⅰ. 现金和有价证券

- LOS 5.4.Ⅰ.1：子主题的构成要素：现金、现金等价物、有价（可交易）证券。
- LOS 5.4.Ⅰ.2：确定现金用途何时被限定。

Ⅱ. 应收账款

- LOS 5.4.Ⅱ.1：子主题的构成要素：流动和非流动的应收款，交易性和非交易性的应收款，销售折扣，现金折扣，销售退回和折让，可变现净值，期票，应收账款转让，应收款和代收款注销。
- LOS 5.4.Ⅱ.2：确定应收账款的估值问题。
- LOS 5.4.Ⅱ.3：同时使用总价法和净价法来计算现金折扣。
- LOS 5.4.Ⅱ.4：确认两种坏账的记录方法，解释为什么普遍使用备抵法。
- LOS 5.4.Ⅱ.5：同时使用损益表中的销售百分比和资产负债表中的应收账款的百分比来计算坏账准备。
- LOS 5.4.Ⅱ.6：利用货币时间价值表贴现长期票据，揭示长期票据在销售时刻的真实价值。
- LOS 5.4.Ⅱ.7：计算长期票据每期的利息收入和折价摊销。
- LOS 5.4.Ⅱ.8：定义和计算利率的估计值。
- LOS 5.4.Ⅱ.9：理解应收账款的抵押。
- LOS 5.4.Ⅱ.10：区别有追索权和无追索权的应收账款。

Ⅲ. 存货

- LOS 5.4.Ⅲ.1：子主题的构成要素：原材料存货，半成品库存，产成品存货，商品库存；永续和修正的永续盘存制度，定期清查制度；商品销售成本，可供出售的商品成本，在途产品，代销产品。
- LOS 5.4.Ⅲ.2：确认存货估价方面的问题，包括应给哪些商品估价、估价中应涉及到哪些成本，以及估价中应使用何种成本假设。
- LOS 5.4.Ⅲ.3：确定存货的成本。
- LOS 5.4.Ⅲ.4：区分离岸价的装运点和目的地。
- LOS 5.4.Ⅲ.5：理解特殊的销售协议，包括售后回购（产品融资安排），高回报的销售，以及分期收款销售。
- LOS 5.4.Ⅲ.6：使用总价法和净价法，计算和揭示购买折扣的合适分录和财务报表陈述。
- LOS 5.4.Ⅲ.7：确认与购买约定付款额相关的会计问题。
- LOS 5.4.Ⅲ.8：确认和比较存货会计中所使用的成本流转假设。
- LOS 5.4.Ⅲ.9：使用个别认定法、平均成本法、先进先出法（FIFO）和后进先出法（LIFO），计算期末存货和销售成本。

- LOS 5.4.Ⅲ.10：分析不同的存货计价方法对收入和资产的影响。
- LOS 5.4.Ⅲ.11：分析存货误差的影响。
- LOS 5.4.Ⅲ.12：理解后进先出存货准备，后进先出存货清算。
- LOS 5.4.Ⅲ.13：使用金额数据后进先出法计算期末存货和商品销售成本。
- LOS 5.4.Ⅲ.14：确定不同的存货计价方法的优缺点。
- LOS 5.4.Ⅲ.15：应用成本与市价孰低法。
- LOS 5.4.Ⅲ.16：确定存货何时采用可变现净值计价。
- LOS 5.4.Ⅲ.17：理解相对销售价值法。
- LOS 5.4.Ⅲ.18：使用毛利法和零售盘存价法确定期末存货价值。
- LOS 5.4.Ⅲ.19：在给定经营环境和管理目标的情况下，针对处于特定行业的某家公司推荐合理的存货计价方法和成本流转假设。

Ⅳ. 投资

- LOS 5.4.Ⅳ.1：子主题的构成要素：债务证券：包括持有至到期、交易和可供出售的证券；权益证券：包括持股比例低于20%（可供出售和交易），持股份额在20%~50%之间，以及持股份额大于50%的投资。
- LOS 5.4.Ⅳ.2：用货币时间价值表和有效利率法计算债务证券的折价、溢价及利息。
- LOS 5.4.Ⅳ.3：定义持有损益。
- LOS 5.4.Ⅳ.4：计算与债务证券和权益证券的出售相关的已实现损益。
- LOS 5.4.Ⅳ.5：计算可供出售和交易的债务证券的公平价值调整。
- LOS 5.4.Ⅳ.6：确认和描述权益证券的公平价值法、权益法和合并法。
- LOS 5.4.Ⅳ.7：比较权益法和公平价值法。
- LOS 5.4.Ⅳ.8：理解重新分类调整。
- LOS 5.4.Ⅳ.9：价值损失的会计处理，并指出减值证券的合理成本基础。
- LOS 5.4.Ⅳ.10：确定和描述针对投资证券在不同范畴间的转换（比如从可供出售类别转到交易类别）所适用的恰当会计处理方法。

Ⅴ. 财产、厂房及设备

- LOS 5.4.Ⅴ.1：子主题的构成要素：土地，房屋，设备，自建的资产；扩建，改造，替换，重新装配和维修；非货币性交易；折旧；损耗；减值。
- LOS 5.4.Ⅴ.2：使用工作量法、直线法、年数总和法、余额递减法、分类法及综合法计算折旧。
- LOS 5.4.Ⅴ.3：计算和记录有形资产的处置损益。
- LOS 5.4.Ⅴ.4：确认以股票的形式支付的有形资产的计价基础。
- LOS 5.4.Ⅴ.5：理解与构建或购置有形资产相关的利息成本的合适会计处理方法。
- LOS 5.4.Ⅴ.6：确定不同的折旧方法对财务报表的影响。
- LOS 5.4.Ⅴ.7：在给定配套数据和管理目标的情况下，选择合理的折旧方法。
- LOS 5.4.Ⅴ.8：计算收购、勘探、开发和修复成本的摊销。

Ⅵ. 无形资产

- LOS 5.4.Ⅵ.1：子主题的构成要素：无形资产包括：专利权、版权、商标、租赁权和特许经营权；购买无形资产和自行研发无形资产；商誉；自创商誉和购买商誉；负商誉；摊销；研发；开办成本，初期营运亏损，广告费，电脑软件成本。

- LOS 5.4. Ⅵ.2：理解无形资产减值的会计处理。
- LOS 5.4. Ⅵ.3：确定不同的无形资产交易对财务报表的影响。

Ⅶ. 流动负债

- LOS 5.4. Ⅶ.1：子主题的构成要素：流动负债：应付票据，应付账款，一年内到期的长期负债，短期再融资债务，应付股利，应退回的保证金，递延收益，应付税金，以及与员工相关的负债；或有损失；保证成本；保险及优惠。
- LOS 5.4. Ⅶ.2：确认短期再融资负债的分类问题。
- LOS 5.4. Ⅶ.3：确认各种与员工相关的负债。
- LOS 5.4. Ⅶ.4：应用保证费用计提法和保证收益计提法。

Ⅷ. 长期负债和长期应付债券

- LOS 5.4. Ⅷ.1：子主题的构成要素：长期负债：债券，长期应付票据，应付抵押票据，零息票据，可转债。
- LOS 5.4. Ⅷ.2：使用直线法和有效利率法计算利息费用、应付利息、债券折价和溢价。
- LOS 5.4. Ⅷ.3：确定以附加账户记录债券折价和溢价时的恰当分类。
- LOS 5.4. Ⅷ.4：确定债券发行费用的恰当会计处理方法。
- LOS 5.4. Ⅷ.5：确定隐含利率并计算隐含利息。
- LOS 5.4. Ⅷ.6：解释为财产、商品和服务所发行的票据。
- LOS 5.4. Ⅷ.7：在票面利率不合理时，计算隐含公平价值和票据折扣。
- LOS 5.4. Ⅷ.8：定义表外融资并确认不同形式的表外融资。
- LOS 5.4. Ⅷ.9：说明表外融资的披露要求。

Ⅸ. 权益交易和每股收益

- LOS 5.4. Ⅸ.1：子主题的构成要素：优先股和普通股；股本，资本公积和保留盈余；库藏股（成本法和面值法）；财产股利，票据股利；清算股利；股票股利；保留盈余。
- LOS 5.4. Ⅸ.2：股票发行的会计处理程序的应用，包括有面值股票、无面值股票、股票的认购销售、一次性付款销售和以非现金交易方式发行的股票。
- LOS 5.4. Ⅸ.3：宣告和支付普通股及优先股股利的会计处理程序。
- LOS 5.4. Ⅸ.4：定义股票期权、认股权证和权利，确定其正确的财务报告陈述方式。
- LOS 5.4. Ⅸ.5：确认影响实缴资本和保留盈余的交易事项。
- LOS 5.4. Ⅸ.6：推断股利分配的高低对股东权益的影响。
- LOS 5.4. Ⅸ.7：说明股票分割与股票股利的区别。
- LOS 5.4. Ⅸ.8：说明挪用保留盈余的原因。
- LOS 5.4. Ⅸ.9：计算每股收益（基本每股收益和稀释每股收益）。

Ⅹ. 收入和费用

- LOS 5.4. Ⅹ.1：将收入确认原则应用于不同类型的交易。
- LOS 5.4. Ⅹ.2：销售时点的收入确认问题，包括销售回购协议、销售退回的权利以及存货提前发送（提前确认收入成暗转）。
- LOS 5.4. Ⅹ.3：确认在交付前确认收入的例子。
- LOS 5.4. Ⅹ.4：区别收入确认的完工百分比法和完成合同法。
- LOS 5.4. Ⅹ.5：完工百分比法和合同完工法的应用。
- LOS 5.4. Ⅹ.6：比较和对比两种长期合同会计法下的建设成本的确认、工程进度结算账单、回款以及已确认的毛利。

- LOS 5.4.X.7：理解长期合同损失的恰当会计处理。
- LOS 5.4.X.8：确定交付之后确认收入的例子。
- LOS 5.4.X.9：确认应用下列收入确认方法的情形：分期付款法、成本回收法以及收现营收认前法。
- LOS 5.4.X.10：理解分期付款法、成本回收法和收现营收认前法下的会计程序。
- LOS 5.4.X.11：定义损益并指出对损益的恰当财务报表陈述。
- LOS 5.4.X.12：讨论与收入确认实务相关的问题。
- LOS 5.4.X.13：理解收入和费用的配比原则，并能在具体情形下运用该原则。
- LOS 5.4.X.14：理解费用确认实务。

XI. 全面收益

- LOS 5.4.XI.1：定义全面收益。
- LOS 5.4.XI.2：确定在财务报表上列示全面收益的三种可选方案。
- LOS 5.4.XI.3：计算全面收益。

XII. 分部报告

- LOS 5.4.XII.1：定义经营分部。
- LOS 5.4.XII.2：确定应提供报告的经营分部的披露要求。
- LOS 5.4.XII.3：在给定一系列数据的条件下，确定某分部是否应提供报告。

XIII. 跨国因素

- LOS 5.4.XIII.1：指出将外国子公司报表折算为母公司报告货币时应注意的问题。
- LOS 5.4.XIII.2：定义功能性货币。
- LOS 5.4.XIII.3：区分货币/非货币法和现行汇率法。
- LOS 5.4.XIII.4：将外国子公司报表从功能性货币折算成报告货币。
- LOS 5.4.XIII.5：将子公司财务报表折算功能性货币。
- LOS 5.4.XIII.6：描述外汇交易损益对财务报表的影响。
- LOS 5.4.XIII.7：定义"高通货膨胀经济"并指出处于高通货膨胀经济中的公司应采用哪种货币作为报告货币。
- LOS 5.4.XIII.8：指出外币折算的披露要求。

5.5 证券交易委员会及其报告要求

- LOS 5.5.1：了解与证券交易委员会的成立及其权力相关的两个主要法案（1933 年的《证券法》和 1934 年的《证券交易法》）；了解这两个法案的主要条款。
- LOS 5.5.2：描述上市公司的一般报告要求。
- LOS 5.5.3：定义整合披露制度、标准财务报告和管理层论述及分析。
- LOS 5.5.4：确定与企业经营相关的其他披露要求。
- LOS 5.5.5：确定和描述证券交易委员会的披露要求，包括到证券交易委员会登记、年报或 10 - K 表格、季报或 10 - Q 表格、重大事项的披露或 8 - K 表格以及委托说明书。
- LOS 5.5.6：确定和解释《萨班斯法案》（2002）的主要条款。
- LOS 5.5.7：确定上市公司会计监督委员会（PCAOB）的作用与职责。

5.6 年报

- LOS 5.6.1：了解与年报相关的审计服务。
- LOS 5.6.2：确定年报的基本构成，包括管理层的责任声明和独立的审计报告。
- LOS 5.6.3：说明审计委员会对年报中所展示的财务信息的真实性所应承担的责任。
- LOS 5.6.4：确定审计委员会的作用，包括：（a）任命会计师事务所执行年报的外部审计工作，（b）参与内部和外部审计范围的设定，（c）对内外部审计中所遇到的主要问题展开直接的审计交流。
- LOS 5.6.5：讨论年报审计意见如何影响市场对公司的认知。
- LOS 5.6.6：确定和描述年报的其他部分，包括致股东的公开信、管理层论述及分析以及社会责任声明。

第1节
外部财务报告的目标

本节内容简介

美国财务会计准则委员会的概念框架项目始于该委员会所发布的第一个财务会计概念公告，该公告确立了外部财务报告的目标。财务会计概念的目的是为所有会计准则和报告准则奠定基础。尽管这些概念并不具备约束力（不属于一般公认会计原则），但它们构成了具备约束性的会计准则（财务会计准则公告，SFAS）的基础。此概念公告界定了财务信息的目的、内容和局限性。本节的内容主要基于第1号财务会计概念公告：商业企业财务报告的目标。

财务会计的本质是对外提供信息，而管理会计的本质是为企业内部管理提供信息；财务会计反映历史信息并由一般公认会计原则加以规范，而管理会计则具有前瞻性，不受一般公认会计原则的约束。当然，两种会计都受信息的有用性和信息获得成本的约束。两种会计相互影响：财务会计方法或数据会影响到管理决策，反之亦然。

一般公认会计原则（GAAP）是权威会计声明的综合，并且针对权威声明尚未涉及的问题，一般公认会计原则反映了常见会计实务在该问题上的进展。GAAP涉及到经济活动的度量、实施度量的期间、财务报表的编制和陈述以及财务信息的必要披露。

资源信息和债务信息

财务报告为投资者、债权人以及其他相关方及时制定商业决策和经济决策提供可靠的会计信息。财务报告的目标不仅仅在于提供一份财务报表，而是为决策制定提供相关信息。无论采用何种形式，财务报告的最终目的都是提供与公司资源和债务相关的信息，这样信息的外部使用者就能将其稀缺资源分配给最有效的商业实体。财务会计准则委员会的财务会计概念公告阐明了财务报告的一般目标和具体目标。

财务报告的一般目标是指：

· 财务报告应为信息的外部使用者作出理性投资、信贷及其他相似决策提供有用的信息。信息的外部使用者包括现有和潜在的投资者、债权人（及其顾问）等对经营和经济活动有一定的理解并且愿意付出必要的努力来研究这些信息的人。

· 财务报告应提供必要的信息以使报告的外部使用者能评估预期现金流的数量、时间与不确定性，比如：

· 股利收入或利息收入

· 销售收入、偿付或到期的证券和贷款

· 实体的净现金流（企业现金流）

财务报告的具体目标指明了特定财务报告所包括的信息：

· 财务报告应提供与实体的经济资源（资产）相关的信息、资源的要求权（负债）包括资源转移到其他企业时的责任，以及改变资源和资源要求权的情形、交易和事项的影响。

· 财务报告应提供与实体的全面收益和全面收益的构成相关的信息。

- 财务报告应提供实体的现金流量信息

经济资源与资源的要求权

关于实体的经济资源与资源要求权的信息对相关当事人非常有用，因为它有助于使用者评估实体流动性，突出一定时期的财务优势、局限性与绩效。这些通常基于资产负债表的信息，是评估实体单个资源和综合资源的潜在现金流量的直接信息。

全面收益信息

根据第 6 号财务会计概念公告（SFAC），全面收益能够全面计量企业的权益在一段时期内因交易和其他事件而发生的变动，但不包括所有者的投资和对所有者的分配等情况。

全面收益在本章第 4 节描述。

现金流转信息

实体的现金流量信息是财务报告的具体目标之一。没有足够的现金流量，实体的持续经营将会面临很大的风险。即使不至于破产，但现金短缺或较差的流动性都会提高向实体投资或贷款的风险。财务报告使当前和潜在的投资人及债权人在关注实体运转或投资的同时，也关注实体的预期现金流金额、时间和不确定性。

现金流可以分为经营现金流、投资现金流和融资现金流。现金流信息反映了实体怎样借入和偿还现金，怎样获得和花费现金，怎样将现金投资于非流动资产，以及怎样支付股利和其他分配。

进度检查

提示：完成以下各题。参考答案随后给出。

1. 判断对错。财务会计概念公告不是一般公认会计原则的一部分，且不受一般公认会计原则的约束。

　（　　）a. 对
　（　　）b. 错

2. 下面哪个收入要素包含在全面收益中？

　（　　）a. 会计原则变动的累积影响
　（　　）b. 所有者的投资和对所有者的分配
　（　　）c. 可供出售证券的未实现损益
　（　　）d. 来自持续运营的收入

进度检查答案

1. a
2. b

第2节
财务会计的基础

本节内容简介

根据第5号财务会计概念公告"商业企业财务报表的确认与度量",财务报告的基础是指一些概念,这些概念能够对确认、度量以及记录交易、环境和事件时的会计方法选择给予指导。同时,财务会计基础还包括向外部使用者汇总、报告上述事项的方法,以及基本会计假设和惯例。

会计假设和惯例

财务会计的结构包括下列假设和惯例,所有财务报告都应以这些假设和惯例为依据。

货币单位

评估企业价值所用的计量尺度是名义货币单位。名义货币单位不会因其购买力的变化而进行调整(不受通货膨胀或通货紧缩的影响)。

经济实体

经济实体是指从个人独资经营企业到跨国公司在内的任何一个商业企业,且其责任与所有者和其他实体相独立。经济主体假设是指将企业实体与其所有者分别开来,它们分别进行独立核算。

持续经营

除非企业面临破产清算,那么财务会计应假设企业在未来很长一段时间内都将持续经营下去。持续经营假设并非意味着企业将永远经营下去,而是指有足够长的时间实现其目标和承诺。

会计分期

分期假设是指经济活动的时间被人为地分为不同的期间,如月,季,年。企业总是不间断地获得收入、进行支付直到退出经营,所以只能人为地划分一个期间。大多数财务报表比如损益表就是报告一段时期内的损益情况。而其他财务报告比如资产负债表,则反映某一时刻的信息(某一特定时刻)。

成本与收益关系

成本收益关系假设是指除非提供信息所带来的收益超过它所花费的成本,否则不应收集此信息。

重要性

根据财务会计准则委员会的第2号财务会计概念公告,重要性是对财务报告中某一项目的最低要求。即如果有意省略或对其提供虚假的陈述可能会影响人们的判断，且投资者通过报告已合理信赖此项目的正确性，并将其纳入自己的决策之中，则此项目就具有重要性。换句话说，如果此项目的报告是错误的，它也会被使用者认为是正确的并加以使用。

财务会计准则委员会对此制定了限制性规定，因为大多数会计从业者相信对重要性的判断只能由有经验且了解特定情形下的事实的人来进行。证券交易委员会制定了类似规定，限制利用重要性来掩盖非法交易，如行贿、操纵利润、提高管理人员的薪酬、隐藏合法收入等。

稳健性

第 2 号财务会计概念公告将稳健性定义为："对商业环境中的不确定性和风险因素给予足够谨慎的考虑"。会计原则委员会第 4 号公告对此的解释为：对大多数会计人员来说，谨慎性通常意味着："如净收入和净资产的计量中可能存在错误，则应尽量少披露而不是多披露"。

在过去我们之所以刻意地一致地低估净资产和净利润，是为了保证银行家的安全边际，因为过去银行家是公告的最重要的使用者。然而，这种做法不具有可比性，最终会让公告发行者失去公信力。通常的谨慎性会导致低估存货和不合理的折旧或收入确认等问题。无论是保守还是乐观的偏向都会误导投资者，因此财务会计准则委员会建议披露不确定性时，中性地定义谨慎性，让使用者自己判断不确定事项。

确认与度量概念

确认与度量概念是决定如何、何时记录商业交易的方法，包括历史成本、充分披露、收入的确认与实现以及配比原则。

历史成本

历史成本是指获得资产所支付的金额。如是非现金交易，则是对其非现金资产或债务的估价。历史成本是最常用的计价方式。折旧，摊销或其他分配（如适用）方式可以减少历史成本。其他以历史成本估价的负债包括大部分债券、票据和应付款。财产、厂房和设备以及无形资产一般以历史成本减去累计折旧或摊销进行报告。很多企业发现历史成本是用来建立历史趋势的有效基准。历史成本之所以可信是因为其可核实性，但如果历史成本与资产的实际价值不同，历史成本信息可能会缺乏相关性。

充分披露

充分披露是一个一般概念，它是指应充分披露公司的重要财务信息，这些财务信息足以影响理性使用者的决策。这些信息同时也应满足成本收益的约束。信息可能会被披露在财务报表上，财务报表的附注或补充信息里面。充分披露和合理计量必须同时具备。财务报表只能包含可明确界定的要素，这样才能保证可计量性、可靠性以及相关性。附注应对财务报表中不完整的或可能误导使用者的信息给予说明。补充信息可以对公告中披露的信息给出一些不同的观点或管理层对某一事项的解释等不能以财务信息记录的信息。

收入的确认与实现

与收入的确认和实现相关的术语包括：

● 已实现的　指资产，如商品和服务实际已经通过交易变为现金或现金的要求权。

● 可实现的　指持有或获得的资产很容易通过在活跃市场上以非常确定的价格出售从而变成现金或现金的要求权。

● 获得的　指实体已充分地完成与收入相关的交易程序。

● 根据权责发生制　当收入已实现、可实现或已获得时应确认或记录到总分类账；根据权责发生制，花费的成本应在发生时确认而不是实际支付现金时确认。

如何才能确定满足收入确认的条件已发生？对大多数商品来说，应在实际出售时确认，因为此时的价格才能被准确地核定。记录收入的时间应按照权责发生制在收入已获得时计入。当然，收入确认的时点也有一些例外。图表 2 - 78 列出了四个主要的收入可能被确认的时点。

图表 2 - 78　收入确认时间的例外

确　认	描　述
产品生产期间	特定的长期建设工程项目准予按照建设期间工程完工百分比法来分期确认收入。每完成一部分，此部分都被认为是充分地完成，即使只能到完工时才能完成所有权的转移。完工百分比法只适用于能够可靠计量完工程度和成本时。
产品完工时	在销售行为发生前，只有当销售价格与销售数量能被确定和证实的时候，收入才能在产品完工时确认。这种方式仅适用于有标准价格的商品。例如，在一个政府调节价格的市场上，农产品能在收获时确认收入。
销售时	大多数情况下，收入在销售时都已实现、可实现或已获得。
收取现金时	当销售回款具有高度不确定性，以至于按销售时刻确认收入的方法不成立时，应以现金收付为原则。一旦销售收入中存在严重违约情况，实际售价将不能够按照平均水平来确定。一种处理现金收回的不确定性的方式是分期付款的销售方法。此种方式中，利润按照分期付款收到的现金进行确认。

配比

配比的概念直接与收入确认相关。企业经营中的费用如薪金、产品成本往往早于收入的确认，因为收入只能在销售时确认。配比是指尽可能地将各项费用与其最终带来的收入相匹配。然而，新的会计规则在某种程度上弱化了配比的概念。

与配比原则相关的有三种情形：成本可以直接与收入相配比；成本不能直接与收入配比，但可分析出它们的关系；或成本实际上与收入无关。在上述第一种情形中，成本与收入在相同的时期报告。在第二种情形中大部分实体使用分摊政策近似代替配比政策。长期资产需针对其生命期内每一个实际用于生产的期间进行摊销，这就是所谓的折旧。在最后一种情形中，费用不能归集到特定收入上，则只能作为发生期间的费用或损失，比如一般管理费用。

财务报表的要素

财务会计准则委员会的第 6 号财务会计概念公告，将构成财务报表的所有项目定义为不同类型的"财务报表要素"。财务报表要素由描述性的词语与金额数量共同列示，用来表示资源、资源的要求权，以及交易或其他事项所导致的资源和资源要求权的变化。财务报表中有些要素按某一时点计量，就像电影中的定格；其他要素按某一时段计量。按某一时点计量的财务报表要素记录进永久性账目中，按某一时段计量的财务报表要素记录进临时性账目中。永久性账目包括资产、负债和所有者权益。临时性账目包括具有一定期间的交易：分配给所有者的股利、收入、费用以及损益损失。

资产

资产是由过去的交易或事件形成的，由企业所有的，且可能带来未来的经济收益。

负债

负债是指未来会发生的经济利益的损失。是由过去交易或事件形成的，现在承担的将在未来转移资产或提供劳务给其他企业的义务。

权益

权益或净资产，是企业的资产减去负债以后的剩余权益。企业的权益不同于企业的资产和负债，这就是为什么会计等式中资产永远等于负债加权益。负债有优先权，因此当负债大于资产时，权益就可能为负数。权益随所有者投资的增加而增加，随所有者的分配而减少。

- 所有者的投资会增加企业的权益，它是从其他经济实体转移过来的有价值的投资，目的是获得或增加所有者利益或权益（如购买股份）。所有者投资主要采用资产投资的方式，但有时也表现为负债偿还的形式负债转化的形式。

- 对所有者的分配会减少企业的权益，表现为转移资产、提供劳务、对所有者的经常性负债（如股利分配）。对所有者的分配降低了企业的所有者利益或权益。

（所有者的投资和向所有者的分配是实体与其所有者间的直接交易。相反，如果持股人或所有者在公开市场上出售其持有的全部或部分股票，则这些交易不涉及实体本身，因此对权益不会有影响。）

全面收益

前面已提到过，全面收益是指企业的权益在一段时期内因交易和其他与所有者无关的事件及情况而发生的变动，但不包括所有者的投资和对所有者的分配等导致的权益变动。

收入

收入是指通过交付或生产商品、提供服务或其他企业核心业务所带来的现金流入或资产改善或债务的清偿（或兼有资产的改善和债务的清偿）。

费用

费用是因交付或生产商品、提供服务或进行其他核心业务所导致的现金流出、资产的使用或债务的增加（或兼有资产的使用和债务的增加）。

利得

利得是指由外围交易或附带交易以及对实体有影响的所有其他交易和其他事件与情况所引致的权益（净资产）的增加，但不包括那些由收入或所有者投资所带来的权益增加。

损失

损失是指由外围交易或附带交易以及对实体有影响的所有其他交易和其他事件与情况所引致的权益（净资产）的减少，但不包括那些由费用或向所有者的分配所引起的权益减少。

税金

税金是由缴纳联邦所得税所引起的净资产的减少。

现金流量表要素

现金流量表反映了一定时期内现金的收入与支出如何引起现金的净增加或净减少，该报表将现金的使用划分为三个主要的活动即经营活动、投资活动和筹资活动的现金流。

- **经营净现金流**

经营的净现金流是净收入减去应收账款净增加或应付账款净减少（或加上应收账款应减少或应付账款净增加），反映了现金交易对净收入的影响。

- **投资净现金流**

投资的净现金流是经营活动净现金流减去购买投资的现金支付，加上出售投资的收回现金。投资包括购买其他企业的债券和股票股利以及财产、厂房和设备。

- **筹资净现金流**

筹资活动的净现金流是投资净现金流减去股利、债务清偿或重新取得的股本，再加上发行的债务（如债券或票据）和权益证券。因此，筹资净现金流包括所有来自债权人的借款、所有支付给债权人的债务偿付以及所有来自所有者的融资和向所有者的分配。

会计恒等式

会计恒等式反映了上述要素是如何整合起来的，反映了等式一边（资产项）的公司资源与等式另一边（负债与权益项）对这些资源的要求权间的平衡。

$$资产 - 负债 = 权益$$
或
$$资产 = 负债 + 权益$$

进度检查

提示：完成以下各题。参考答案随后给出。

1. 判断对错。财务会计准则委员会颁布了特别指南，以根据公司净收入的百分比判断多大额度是重要的，多大额度是不重要的。

（　　）a. 对
（　　）b. 错

2. 财产、厂房和设备以及无形资产一般使用下列何种指标计价？

（　　）a. 历史成本
（　　）b. 公平价格
（　　）c. 可变现净值
（　　）d. 成本与市场价格孰低

3. 下列哪项能通过外围交易增加净资产？

（　　）a. 收入
（　　）b. 收益
（　　）c. 利得
（　　）d. 全面收益

进度检查答案

1. b
2. a
3. c

第 3 节
财务报表和报表使用者

本节内容简介

本节讨论了四个财务报表，这四个报表对企业情况提供了基本的描述，对任何公司来讲，这四个报表都是有用的工具。证券交易委员会要求所有上市公司必须编制这四种报表。这四种报表是：

- 损益表，反映了交易活动的结果。
- 股东权益表，反映了所有者的投资、向所有者分配的利润以及公司的未分配利润。
- 资产负债表，反映了企业的最终财务状况。
- 现金流量表，反映了会计期间内企业的现金流入、流出以及经营活动、投资活动、筹资活动对现金的影响。

本章中列举的财务报表都采用虚构的罗宾制造公司在给定年度发布的财务报表。不同的财务报表通过附注和其中的数据相互关联，当然也包括反映披露要求的脚注。

大多数企业提供本年财务报表时也会给出以前年度的信息作为对照。例如，损益表和现金流量表通常同时反映近三年的结果，这便于当前年度与以前年度之间的对比分析，以对未来作出预测。

本节最后讨论了外部使用者对财务报表信息的需求以及财务报表应怎样满足这些需求。

收益表（损益表）

收益表，通常又称为损益表，记录了企业在特定时期如一季度或会计年度内的收益情况。收益表用来衡量企业的盈利能力、商誉和投资价值。在与其他报表一起使用时，收益表还可以用于评估未来现金流量的数量、时机和不确定性。

收益与其他全面收益

收益表中的财务报表要素有收入、费用及损益。本章第 2 节已给出了这些要素的定义。第 130 号财务会计准则公告要求公司将净收益之外的未实现损益作为其他全面收益进行报告。全面收益等于净收益加上（减去）其他全面收益。

公司可以将全面收益的计算作为收益表的一部分或在股东权益报表中展示该计算，以作为对累计其他全面收益账户的调整。

全面收益将在本章第 4 节详细介绍。

财务信息的格式

两个最常用的格式是单步式损益表和多步式损益表。

单步式损益表

单步式损益表是用总收入和利得减去总费用和损失，而没有将收入、费用进行分类或小计。

单步式损益表结构简单，避免了分类问题，但不能反映主要和非主要的收入、利得、费用或损失的区别。因此，多步式损益表当前更为常用。

图表 2-79 反映了罗宾制造公司的单步式损益表，时间为 1 年。

图表 2-79　单步式损益表

罗宾制造公司损益表 截至该年度 12 月 31 日	
收入	
销售收入净额	$2 734 620
股利收入	90 620
租金收入	67 007
总收入	2 892 317
费用	
已销售产品的成本	1 823 938
销售费用	416 786
管理费用	322 709
利息费用	115 975
所得税费用	61 579
总费用	2 740 987
净收益	$151 330 →
每股收益	$1.89

在图表 2-82 股东权益报表中会用到该数据

多步式损益表

为了增强信息的有用性，多步式损益表将信息分为经营性信息与非经营性信息。多步式损益表中将与经营现金流不相关的部分称为"其他收入及利得"和"其他费用及损失"。与经营现金流不相关的部分包括出售设备的损益、利息收入和支出以及收到的股利。

多步式损益表还进一步划分如已销售产品的成本、经营费用（销售和管理费用）、其他收入、费用、利得及损失等范畴。这些进一步的分类让使用者可以将企业一段时间的经营结果与其竞争者相比较，考察本企业对自身稀缺资源的利用效率。

多步式损益表常小计毛利和经营收入，这对财务报告的分析很有用处。例如，毛利可以用来比较竞争压力对边际利润的影响。

图表 2-80 展示了多步式损益表。

图表 2-80　多步式损益表

罗宾制造公司损益表 截至本年度 12 月 31 日		
销售收入		
总收入		$2 808 835
减：销售折扣	$22 302	
减：销售退回和折让	51 913	74 215

续表

	罗宾制造公司损益表 截至本年度 12 月 31 日		
净销售收入			2 734 620
已销售产品的成本			
库存商品，1 月 1 日		424 321	
购入	$1 830 518		
减：采购折扣	17 728		
净购入	1 812 790		
减：采购运费	37 363	1 850 153	
可供销售商品总计		2 274 274	
减：库存商品，12 月 31 日		450 536	
已销售产品的成本			$1 823 938
销售毛利			910 682
经营费用			
销售费用			
销售人员的工资及佣金	186 432		
销售办公室职员的工资	54 464		
差旅和娱乐	45 025		
广告费用	35 250		
销售运费	37 912		
装运材料与费用	22 375		
邮资和办公用品	15 445		
销售设备折旧	8 285		
电话和网费	11 238	416 786	
管理费用			
管理人员工资	171 120		
办公室职员的工资	56 304		
法律和专业服务费	21 823		
公共设施费	21 413		
保险费	15 667		
房屋折旧	16 614		
办公设备折旧	14 720		
办公用品，其他用品，邮资	2 645		
办公杂项费用	2 403	322 709	739 495
经营收入			171 187
其他收入和利得			
股利收入		90 620	
租金收入		67 077	157 697
			328 884
其他费用和损失			
债券和票据利息			115 975
税前收入			212 909
所得税			61 579
本年年净收益			$151 330
普通股每股收益			$1.89

→ 在图表 2 – 82 股东权益报表中会用到该数据

额外损益表报告项目

有时，公司会被要求分开报告不同于持续经营的额外损益。额外项目可能列示在损益表末，且包括非持续性经营、特别事项和会计原则变更。

- **非持续性经营**

如果企业的某一组成部分由明显不同的经营和现金流量构成，该组成部分的事项会被记录在损益表持续经营事项之后，特别事项之前。非持续性经营事项按除税净额列示。

- **特殊事项**

一些重要事项既不同寻常，也很少发生，比如政府的限制或禁止产品的生产。对这些事项要求在损益表上单独以除税净额列示。

- **会计原则变更**

某一会计方法变更后的累积影响以除税净额列示在特别事项之后，净收益之前。（财务会计准则委员会征求意见稿中有一段"会计变更和差错更正"，作为一种决算公告，要求公司对大多数自主性会计变更采用追溯的方法。在追溯的方式下，会计原则变更的累积影响应作为对保留盈余的调整进行报告，而不是调整损益表。

图表2-81展示了在考虑到这些额外项目后的净收益。

图表2-81　多步式损益表与额外损益表事项

```
销售净额
-已销售产品的成本

销售毛利
-经营费用

经营收益
+/-其他损益

税前利润
-所得税费用

持续经营收益
+/-非持续经营损益
+/-特别事项损益
+/-会计原则变更损益

净收益
```

股东权益表

在资产负债表被公布的同时，财务会计准则委员会要求披露每个独立的股东权益账户的变更。此要求符合财务会计准则委员会要求完整的财务报表应包含报告期内的所有者投资和对所有者的分配的建议。对股东权益表的这些要求，目的是利于外部使用者评估公司的财务结构和财务弹性。

主要构成和分类

股东权益包括几个构成部分，即股本（优先股和普通股的面值）、资本公积、保留盈余以及累计其他全面收益。股本是股份的票面价值，资本公积是实缴股本超过票面价值的部分。因此，这两类合称为实缴资本或实收资本。保留盈余可进一步划分为公司使用的一般保留盈余和已拨定用途的保留盈余。

财务信息的格式

股东权益表中的信息按下列顺序排列：

- 本期期初余额。
- 增加项目。
- 扣减项目。
- 本期期末余额。

图表 2 – 82 是一个股东权益表的样本。这里以柱状式表格表示，且只包括发行在外的普通股。

图表 2 – 82　股东权益表

罗宾制造公司
股东权益变动表
截至本年度 12 月 31 日

	普通股	资本公积 面值 $1	保留盈余	总计
余额，1 月 1 日	$24 680	$345 520	$90 251	$460 451
净收益			151 330	151 330
支付的现金股利			(33 330)	(33 330)
已发行的普通股	1 000	14 800		15 800
余额，12 月 31 日	$25 680	$360 320	$208 251	$594 251

来自图表 2 – 79 和图表 2 – 80 中的损益表信息

图表 2 – 84 中的资产负债表会用到该数据

财务状况表（资产负债表）

财务状况表是评估预期现金流量的大小、时间和不确定性的基本工具，它又称为资产负债表，因其是按会计恒等式即资产 = 负债 + 股东权益来陈述的。该恒等式也可以表示为权益等于资产减去负债，后者也称为净资产。资产负债表是公司资产和对这些资产的要求权在特定时间上的静态反映。

尽管资产负债表不要求反映企业价值，但当其与其他报表和其他信息一起使用时，外部使用者应能自行评估企业价值。

资产负债表能帮助使用者：

- 评价企业的资本结构。
- 评估企业的流动性、偿付能力、财务弹性和经营能力。

资产负债表同样是理解损益表的必要工具。收入和费用反映了资产和负债的变化，因此分析时必须将两个报表（资产负债表和损益表）一同评价。

主要构成和分类

　　资产负债表分为三部分，即资产、负债和股东权益。将相同类型的项目归到一起有助于分析的进行。资产按流动性由强到弱列示，负债按偿付时间由短到长列示。对于权益，按每个项目的要求权的大小由强到弱列示。图表2-83概括了每个类别的一般细分。

图表2-83　资产负债表的构成

资产	• 流动资产（现金、应收账款、存货等） • 长期投资 • 财产、厂房及设备（PP&E）	• 无形资产（专利、商誉等） • 其他资产
负债	• 流动负债（应付账款、应付利息、长期负债的当前到期部分等）	• 长期负债（债券、抵押等）
股东权益	• 股本 • 库藏股 • 资本公积	• 累计其他全面收益 • 保留盈余

　　资产、负债及权益的构成在本章第4节有更详细的讨论。

财务信息的格式

　　资产负债表最常用的两种格式是账户式和报告式。这两种格式都将资产负债表如前述一样分为资产、负债和股东权益。账户式将资产列在左边，负债和权益列在右边。报告式，如图表2-84所示，资产列在上面，负债和权益列在下面。这两种格式都符合会计恒等式，即资产之和等于负债加股东权益。在美国之外还有其他的格式，如财务状况式，以流动资产减去流动负债反映营运资本。

　　在图表2-84中，资产和负债进一步按其财务弹性进行分类。比如，分别列示流动资产和固定资产。

图表2-84　资产负债表

罗宾制造公司资产负债表 12月31日	
资产	
流动资产：	
现金和短期投资	$24 628
应收账款，扣除$30 000的坏账准备	552 249
其他应收款	18 941
应收票据—相关方	
存货	252 567
预付保险费	7 500
流动资产总计	936 417
固定资产：	
财产和设备	209 330
减：累计折旧	(75 332)
固定资产净额	133 998

续表

罗宾制造公司资产负债表 12 月 31 日	
资产总计	$ 1 070 415
负债和权益	
流动负债	
应付账款	$175 321
应计费用	2 500
一年内到期的长期负债	36 000
信用额度	145 000
流动负债总计	476 164
长期负债	117 343
流动和长期负债总计	476 164
股东权益：	
普通股（面值）	25 680
资本公积	360 320
保留盈余	208 251
股东权益总计	594 251
负债和股东权益总计	$ 1 070 415

来自图表 2 - 82 中的股东权益表信息 →（对应"普通股（面值）""资本公积""保留盈余""股东权益总计"各行）

现金流量表

现金是一个公司流动性最强的资源，会影响公司的流动性、经营能力和财务弹性。财务会计概念第 95 号公告提出现金流量表"必须报告公司的现金流入、现金流出和会计期间内经营、筹资、投资活动的净现金变化，并应协调期初和期末的现金余额"。现金流量表帮助利益相关者决定企业是否需要外部融资或是否正在产生现金流量、能满足偿债要求并分配股利。公司可能有很高的收益但其现金流可能为负。

构成和分类

现金流量表分为经营、投资、筹资活动的现金收入和支出。

经营活动

经营活动的现金流量是指那些与日常业务过程相关的现金流量。任何不属于投资和筹资的活动都归为经营活动部分。例如，现金流入包括所有销售活动的现金收入、应收账款的收回、贷款利息收入以及收到的股利。现金流出包括支付给员工的工资、供应商的货款、国内税务署的税款和债权人的利息等。

一般公认会计原则（GAAP）要求财务报表使用权责发生制原则，因此净收益应包括非现金收入（如赊销）和非现金费用（如未付费用）。其他权责发生制会计事项包括折旧、损耗、摊销以及一些前期发生，但在当期才计入费用的成本。这些事项减少了净收益，但不影响当期的现金流量。因此，在计算经营活动现金流量时，要针对这些事项进行调整。

应调整到净收益中的非现金费用和收入事项可能包括：

- 折旧费用和无形资产的摊销。
- 递延成本如债券发行成本的摊销。
- 递延所得税的变化。
- 应付债券的溢价和折价的摊销。
- 权益投资收益。

财务会计准则委员会允许企业自行选择直接法或间接法来计算经营现金流量。

间接法：又称调整法，是计算经营活动净现金流时最常用的方法。它是从净收益出发，然后调增非现金费用和账面损失，调减非现金收入和账面利得等对当期现金流量没有任何影响的事项。另外还有与经营活动有关的流动资产和负债变动的调整，通过加上或减去其金额，如图表 2－85 所示。例如，应收账款的增加（流动资产）应从净收益中扣除，因为它意味着从客户那里收到的现金少于所报告的收入的增加。图表 2－85 对间接法进行了说明。

图表 2－85　经营活动现金流量：间接法

净收益
＋非现金费用（代表性的有折旧和摊销费用）
－投资和筹资活动的利得
＋投资和筹资活动的损失
＋流动资产的减少
－流动资产的增加
＋流动负债的增加
－流动负债的减少
＋债券折价摊销
－债券溢价摊销
经营现金流量

直接法：又称损益表法，是将权责发生制下的经营收入和费用转变为收付实现制。

虽然财务会计准则委员会提倡使用直接法，但它很少被采用。并且，如采用直接法，财务会计准则委员会要求在独立的明细表中披露对经营活动净现金流量的净收益调整。图表 2－86 是对直接法的说明（表内配有数据）。

图表 2－86　经营活动现金流量：直接法

从客户处收到的现金	$100 000
支付给供应商的现金	(40 000)
利息费用	(5 000)
税金费	(10 000)
经营费用支付的现金	(25 000)
经营活动提供的现金	$20 000

投资活动

投资活动中的大多数事项都与长期资产账户有关。引起投资现金流入的事项有：出售财产、厂房及设备（PP&E）；出售对其他企业的债券或股权投资；收回对其他企业的贷款本金（利息属于经营现金流量）；投资现金流出有：购买财产、厂房及设备；购买其他公司的债券和股票；以及向其他企业贷款。

筹资活动

筹资活动中的大多数事项与长期负债或权益账户有关。筹资现金流入包括：出售本企业的股权或发行债券与票据。现金流出包括向股东支付股利，回收股份支付的现金或赎回企业的债务。换句话说，投资活动包括购买或销售固定资产和对其他企业的投资，而筹资活动包括发行或赎回本企业的股票和债券。

脚注

现金流量表要求在脚注中披露任何重大的非现金投资和筹资活动，比如为购买或建设固定资产发行的股票、债转股等。另外，如果使用直接法计算经营现金流量，还必须披露支付的利息和所得税。

现金流量表举例

图表2－87的现金流量表对使用间接法计算现金流量给出了更详细的解释。每个类别的现金流量（投资、筹资、经营活动）分门别类地进行了加总。这三类的现金流入（流出）等于本期现金的净增加（减少）。净现金流量加上（减去）期初现金余额就等于期末现金余额。因此，现金流量表反映了现金与现金等价物（短期与即将到期的极具流动性的投资）从本年年初到年末的净变化。

图表2－87 现金流量表：间接法

经营活动	
净收益	$151 330
将权责任发生制转变为收付实现制：	
折旧和摊销费 *	75 332
应收账款减少（增加）	（31 445）
库存商品增加（减少）	（4 165）
应付账款增加（减少）	6 740
应计工资和报酬增加（减少）	4 543
应付税款增加（减少）	3 984
递延所得税增加（减少）	（4 950）
存货销售利得 **	（1 255）
经营活动净现金	200 114
投资活动	
财产、厂房及设备的增加	（123 730）
存货销售收入	3 980
投资活动净现金	（119 750）
筹资活动	
应付票据增加（减少）	1 100
资本公积增加（减少）	14 800
长期负债增加（减少）	（50 500）
普通股增加（减少）	1 000
分配现金股利	（33 330）
筹资活动净现金	（66 930）

数据来自图表2－79和图表2－80中的损益表 →

数据来自图表2－82中的股东权益表 →

续表

现金和现金等价物净增加	13 434
年初现金和现金等价物	11 194
年末现金和现金等价物	$24 628

图表 2 - 84 中的资产负债表会用到该数据

注：不同资产和负债账户的变动（增加或减少）可以通过比较连续两年资产负债表中的账户余额变动取得。

*　折旧和摊销费用属于损益表中的管理费用

**　存货销售利得属于损益表中其他收入

财务报表的局限性

下面是财务报表的局限性。

历史成本

大多数非金融性的资产账户采用历史成本计量。依赖历史成本计量是因该成本不会发生变动，然而在评估公司的当前财务状况时，历史成本的相关性不如公允价值和市场价值。

不同的会计处理方法

采用不同的会计处理方法会产生不同的净收益。采用两种或更多的会计方法会改变报告的结果，即使已披露这些方法，不同公司间的比较仍然非常困难。

省略主观项目

财务报表没有将一些重要的有价值的资产列入报表，因为这些资产不能客观地以数字进行反映。例如，人力资源、无形资产的价值（如品牌和商誉）、企业的客户基础等不能精确可信地估计的事项，因此它们未被列入资产负债表。所以说，资产负债表未能完全地反映、计量企业的全部价值。

会计估计和判断的使用

财务报表包括大量的估计和专业判断。不同的估计方法意味着两个（或更多）公司之间的损益表很难进行比较。常见的会计估计包括与呆账坏账有关的应收款项、设备的使用寿命和和残值。

表外信息

有些交易可能会以避免在表内的资产和负债中反映的方式记录，例如，采用经营租赁方式。萨班斯法案（2002）要求上市公司公开披露它们提交给证券交易委员会的表外信息。

非现金交易

现金流量表省略了非现金交易，比如资产置换股权、非货币性资产交换、优先股或债务置换普通股、发行权益证券偿还债务等。这些影响资产和负债的非现金交易应在注释或补充的附表中披露。

财务报表的脚注/披露

给财务报表作脚注是在母表的解释不足以反映企业的特殊情形时使用。典型的披露包括或有事项、合约情况、会计政策和期后事项。

或有事项

或有事项是指具有不确定性的重要事项，它的结果取决于未来某些事项的发生或不发生。或有事项可能是利得也可能是损失。会计上不确认或有利得是为了避免在收益实现之前对收益的过早确认。然而，当或有损失很可能发生且损失金额能够合理估计时则必须被确认。其他重要的或有损失应在财务报表的脚注中披露；或有利得同样也应披露。

或有损失产生于未决诉讼、担保和保险成本、环境责任、自保风险等。或有收益产生于未决诉讼（结果是对公司有利的）、可能退还争议税金和税务亏损递延。

合约情况

合约协议（如退休金义务、租赁合同与股票期权计划等）按要求应在财务报表注释中披露，同时也包括其他的重要事项。合同情况可能需要企业限制某些资金。例如，分析师需要了解这些规定将如何影响企业的财务灵活性。

会计政策

一般公认会计原则或特定行业法规一直以来都允许在两种或两种以上的会计方法中作出选择，并应披露所选用的方法。会计原则委员会（APB）意见书第 22 号规定："企业实体的财务报告应对所有重大的会计政策给予说明，并作为财务报告整体的一部分。"

会计原则委员会意见书第 22 号提到了应作出的三种涉及确认和资产分配的会计披露：

- 在可接受的备选方案中作出选择。
- 在行业特定的方法中作出选择。
- 对一般公认会计原则的独特或创造性的应用。

大多数公司都会单独编制一项附注：重大会计政策摘要。这项附注是确认收入、计算折旧、评估存货价值以及计量其他事项时的依据。

期后会计事项

在会计期间结束时可能会花数周或数月来发布年度报告，在这段期间可能会发生重要的企业业务和交易事项。期后事项即指在资产负债表日和年报发布日之间发生的事项。如果这些事项提供了截至资产负债表日存在的状况的额外证据，并且修改了编制财务报表的会计估计，那么财务报表就应作相应调整。

如果期后事项未提供关于资产负债表日存在的状况的证据，则应当在脚注、附表或备考报表（Pro forma statement）中披露。

除上述提到的披露事项外，图表 2-88 列出了要求以某种形式披露，且超出了财务报表所能反映的其他重要项目。

图表 2-88 规定脚注/披露汇总

类 别	脚注/披露
存货	• 计价基础（可变现净值、成本、成本与市价孰低） • 成本流转假设（个别鉴别法、平均成本、先进先出、后进先出） • 存货分类（购进的存货、原材料、半成品、产成品、辅料） • 产品融资安排，如果有的话 • 如果公司用后进先出，说明先进先出的结果
收入	• 收入确认政策
应收账款	• 可收回程度 • 收款政策 • 坏账的确定 • 备抵坏账
财产、厂房和设备（PP&E）	• 计价基础 • 本期折旧 • 截至资产负债表日的累计折旧 • 主要财产所使用的折旧方法的通用描述
无形资产（如专利）	• 对无形资产种类的描述 • 本期摊销的费用 • 摊销的方法和时期 • 无形资产的剩余使用寿命
应付债券	• 票面价值 • 市场利率和实际利率 • 赎回条款 • 到期日
优先股	• 票面价值 • 已得到授权和发行的股份数量的变化，以及本期未偿还余额 • 优先股的特点（可转换、可累积、可参与） • 股利分配时间 • 拖欠的股利
普通股	• 票面价值 • 已得到授权和发行的股份数量的变化，以及本期未偿还余额 • 宣告股利（数量和类型）
其他	• 数量、种类、久期和其他重要的对保留盈余有约束的条款 • 前一期间的调整 • 员工计划如员工股权激励

财务报表的使用者

财务报表旨在帮助决策的制定。一家高效率的公司之所以能吸引投资者，是因为投资者认为该公司信誉好，投资该公司能得到较高的回报。此外，这类公司能有效地将内部资源分配到那些最可能产生利润的地方。财务报表是内部和外部使用者在决策制定过程中必不可少的组成部分。

内部和外部使用者

内部使用者

除其他信息外，内部使用者还需要分析财务报表信息以帮助制定内部决策。这些信息用于长期或短期的生产计划和控制决策。这些决策正确与否，会影响企业内部资源的分配、盈利能力，最终决定企业能否生存。财务报表的内部使用者包括公司高管、经理、管理会计人员以及其他员工（如有股票期权或对本公司有投资的）。与外部使用者不同，内部使用者能从会计系统中生成任何所需要的信息。由于这些信息有被误用的可能，企业应内部控制这些信息的使用和查阅，但控制程度不至于影响内部决策者及时地获得信息。

外部使用者

外部使用者是依赖企业的财务报告和其他可用信息来制定投资决策的利益相关者。有些外部使用者（如贷款机构）会要求企业提供一些附加的非公开信息。如前所述，财务会计准则委员会将外部使用者定义为：当前或潜在的投资人或债权人（和他们的顾问）等，对经营和经济活动有一定的理解并且愿意花费必要精力研究信息的人。投资人、债权人、分析师、合作人、财务顾问、竞争对手和政府机构都是信息的外部使用者。投资人包括个人和其他企业。债权人包括贷款机构和原材料与其他商品的供应商。

外部使用者的需求

债权人和投资人构成了上市公司两大主要的资本来源，因此财务报表主要集中满足这两类使用者的需求。根据财务会计准则委员会规定，财务报告应向外部使用者提供在合理制定投资、信贷决策或其他相似决策时所需的有用信息。使用者无法处理无限的数据，太多的信息会使与业务最相关的信息变得不容易识别。因此，会计核算的目标是将大量的信息概括为可理解的报告和披露事项。财务会计准则委员会的声明旨在尽可能地简化披露事项，但企业在提供信息时仍应满足外部使用者的需求。

投资人和债权人的需求

有用的财务信息应具有相关性和可靠性，相关性也即意味着即时性。投资人和债权人不仅对有回报的投资感兴趣，也对投资的回报感兴趣。只有在组织能够保全资本的情况下，投资人才能获得投资回报。投资人通过股利和利息获得投资回报。

如果市场认为企业的经营状况良好，则投资人就能获得投资回报。实际的或潜在的投资者持有或准备持有一个企业的股份时，其主要利用财务信息来决定购买、继续持有或抛售公司股票。

实际或潜在的债权人关注企业履行债务契约的能力。他们主要关注企业的四种决策：扩大债务、维持债务水平、否认贷款以及吊销贷款。同样也关注财务报表信息，以测定贷款的风险水平。贷款机构在风险较高时，会要求更高的投资回报；在低风险时，才接受较低的投资回报。因此，企业的贷款信用等级尤其重要，企业的信用等级主要基于企业的流动性、偿债能力和财务弹性。所有这些信息都来自于财务报表与其他披露事项。

　　财务信息的其他使用者包括股票交易所（用于制定交易规则或取消交易规则）、工会（用于谈判工资）和分析师（向用户提建议）。

进度检查

提示：完成以下各题。参考答案随后给出。

1. 下列哪项活动属于现金流量表中的经营活动？

（　　） a. 购买设备

（　　） b. 购买库藏股份

（　　） c. 发行 1 000 份普通股

（　　） d. 支付所得税税金

2. 下列哪句正确地描述了资产负债表项目的排列顺序？

（　　） a. 资产是按流动性由高到低排列；负债是按到期时间排列

（　　） b. 资产和负债按到期时间排列；权益按流动性由低到高排列

（　　） c. 资产按流动性由低到高排列；负债按到期时间排列

（　　） d. 资产和负债按流动性由高到低排列；权益按用途排列

3. 判断对错。资产负债表不能反映企业的价值。

（　　） a. 对

（　　） b. 错

4. 判断对错。损益表列出了下列除税净额：非持续性经营的损益、特殊事项、会计原则变更的累积影响。

（　　） a. 对

（　　） b. 错

进度检查答案

1. d

2. a

3. a

4. a

第 4 节
确认、计量、计价和披露

本节内容简介

本节探讨前面第 3 节中所提到的财务报表的具体账户的确认、计量、计价和披露。

现金和有价证券

现金

现金是指任何货币、存款中可用的资金、汇票、保付支票、现金支票、个人支票、银行汇票和储蓄账户。资产负债表中的现金必须随时可用来支付流动负债并且在支付时对现金使用没有任何合同限制。

现金等价物

现金等价物是指从取得之日起距到期日不超过三个月的有价证券，通常指短期商业票据。现金等价物常常也被归类为现金。

限制用途的现金

限制用途的现金是指为了满足协议的条款或某些未来需要而留置出来的现金。限制用途的现金往往包括补偿性余额、股利基金和工资基金。当其金额不是很重要时，它可以被归类为现金，但若其金额具有实质性影响，它们就必须单独报告成流动或长期资产。如果它将用来偿还一年或一个经营周期的负债，那它就属于流动资产。否则就属于长期资产，类似于工厂扩充基金或者有明确长期债务的退休基金。

补偿性余额

许多贷款（lenders）人会要求补偿性余额作为其贷款条款的一部分，特别是在开放式或循环信用额度的情况下。补偿性余额是为了降低一部分贷款风险而要求的最低存款余额。补偿性余额可以是受限制的也可以是不受限制的。它不仅仅可以运用于贷款，而且还可以用来为将来的信用提供保证，并且可以作为某些服务项目的间接补偿，如支票结算或保管箱管理。

证券交易委员会规定，受到法律限制的补偿性余额如果由于短期借款计划产生，则应该在现金和现金等价物科目下面列单独科目报告；如果该余额是由于长期借款计划产生的，则应该作为非流动资产（投资或其他资产）。若补偿性余额的用途没有受到法律限制，则应该在报表附注中披露。

有价证券

能够在一年内变现的个别市场证券可以归类为流动资产。有价权益证券投资在资产负债表上以公平价值计价。在以市值计价时，对有价权益证券投资未实现损益的处理取决于这些有价权益证券是交易型投资组合还是可供出售型投资组合的一部分。有价债务证券投资的会计处理与此类似，除了某些债务投资应归类为持有至到期型证券并以摊销成本而非公平价值计价。本节稍后会详细探讨财务会计准则委员会第 115 号公告对权益投资和债务投资损益的会计处理的规定。货币市场基金、货币市场储蓄券、存单以及短期商业票据在资产负债表上都归类为暂时性的投资，因为这些投资项目有可得性限制或提款惩罚。

记录和估价

有价证券的初始记录为购买价格加上所有附带的成本（交易费用），包括经纪人佣金和税金。如果有价证券以非现金支付或非现金交易的方式取得，其价值将基于证券或所交易项目的市场公允价值估计。有价证券一般以市场价值计价，因为它们被定义为可交易的。但是，在少数情况下，有价证券将以历史成本报告。

市场价值

有价证券将在资产负债表日以当前市场价格重新估价。由价格的上升或下降而引起的损益将计入损益表。市场价值在报告流动性和财务灵活性上比历史成本更相关，因为它是买卖证券的现行价格。并且市场价值是可靠的，因为该价格能够明确地确定。SFAS 第 115 号公告规定了除持有至到期日的债务工具之外的所有证券的市场公允价值估计。

应收账款

应收款项是指因销售产品或提供劳务而向客户形成的债券。应收账款是应收款项的一部分。应收款项是由于销售方为了增加销售额而向购货方扩大信用而产生，应收款项被认为是可流动的，但其流动性没有现金强，因为某些应收款项将不被支付。

应收款项的类型

应收款项被分为本期的和非本期的，交易性的和非交易性的。交易性应收款项包括应收账款和应收票据。本期的应收款项是指在一年期内或本经营周期内的应收款项；非本期的应收款项是指长于一年或本经营周期或者时间更长的应收款项。

交易性应收款项

交易性应收账款是应收账款最常见的形式，因为它是由于企业正常经营引起的：销售商品或提供劳务产生的赊销。

- **应收账款**

应收账款是对已交付的货物和提供的劳务的付款承诺。大多数应收款项有 30 天或 60 天的净付款期限，因此通常是本期应收款项，但也存在一些变化。应收账款也称作未结算账目。

- **应收票据**

应收票据是更正式的交易性应收款项，因为它要求一个确定日期付款的书面承诺，它可能是本期的也可能是非本期的。

非交易性应收款项

非交易性应收款项包括日常经营中未涉及的其他所有应收款项类型，包括损害存款和其他担保存款、向职工和管理人员的预付款项、应收股利、应收利息，针对保险公司，向承运商、诉讼被告和政府的索赔款项，以及向退回、遗失、损坏货物的客户应收的款项。非交易性应收款项通常在资产负债表内用单独项目列报。

销售实务对应收账款余额的影响

应收账款计价应考虑商业折扣和现金折扣。

商业折扣

商业折扣（或数量或质量折扣）是指企业列出一个商品标价目录，针对不同的顾客如批发商和零售商，在商品标价上给予不同比例的扣除。

现金折扣

现金折扣是为了鼓励客户提前或立即偿付货款。若购货商在某一期限内付款，他就会得到这种折扣。现金折扣可以简化表示为 2/10、n/30。这表示在 10 天内付款按售价给予 2% 的折扣或者在 30 天内付款不给予折扣。未利用的 2/10、n/30 的折扣表示机会成本为 37.25%：

$$折扣的有效成本 = \frac{折扣百分比}{(1 - 折扣百分比)} \times \frac{365}{(信用期 - 折扣期)}$$

$$= \frac{0.02}{0.98} \times \frac{365}{30 - 10} = 0.02041 \times 18.25 = 37.25\%$$

如果企业能以低于 37.25% 的利率借入资金，那么在折扣期内用借入的现金支付货款比展期付款更便宜。

存在现金折扣的情况下，应收账款入账金额的确认有两种方法，一种是总价法，另一种是净价法。大多数企业在记录销售应收款项时采用较为简单的总价法。

- **总价法**

总价法是将未减去现金折扣前的金额作为实际售价，记作应收账款的入账价值。如果在折扣期限内收到货款，现金折扣就予以确认。在损益表中，净销售额就是扣除现金折扣的总销售额。

- **净价法**

净价法是假设客户会取得所有折扣，将扣除现金折扣后的金额作为实际售价，据以确认应收账款的入账价值。它更符合配比原则，因为它提供了一个享受预期折扣的许可，并在销售期对其进行冲销，这样对销售额的记录就更接近它的可变现价值。而没有享受的折扣金额就在"销售折扣失效"账户中通过调整分录进行反映。图表 2 - 89 反映了一笔额度为 $100 000 的应收账款在不同方法下的确认，规定的现金折扣为

1/10、n/30，假设有一半的货款在折扣期内付款。

图表 2-89　现金折扣的总价法和净价法

总价法			净价法		
7月1日销售确认					
借：应收账款	$100 000		借：应收账款	$99 000	
贷：主营业务收入		$100 000	贷：主营业务收入		$99 000
7月10日 收到货款 $50 000					
借：银行存款	$49 500		借：银行存款	$49 500	
财务费用	$500		贷：应收账款		$49 500
贷：应收账款		$50 000			
7月30日 收到货款 $50 000					
借：银行存款	$50 000		借：应收账款	$500	
贷：应收账款		$50 000	贷：财务费用		$500
			借：银行存款	$50 000	
			贷：应收账款		$50 000

销售退回和销售折让

当客户退回赊销的商品或因货物质量不合格而取得销售折让时，销售方就借记"销售退回和折让"（与销售收入相反的账户），贷记"应收账款"。可是，如果某些企业销售退回率较高，那么它们在初始确认销售额时就应扣除预计的销售退回，并建立"销售退回折让"作为应收账款的相反账户。本节稍后会更为详细地探讨销售退回和折让。

交易性应收款项的现值和到期值

APB 第 21 号意见书指出长期应收款项应以其现值记录，但收回时间很短的交易性应收账款除外。交易性应收账款应以其到期值确认记录，在 30 或 60 天以内的应收款项其现值和到期值并没有实质性不同。GAAP 允许对由那些不超过一年的正常交易而形成的常规交易应收款项不采用现值确认。

可是，交易性应收款项必须以其可变现净值估计和报告。交易性应收款项的可变现净值是指企业可能收到的净现金总额，包括估计的不可收回金额（坏账损失）和预期收入（若存在销售退回政策）。请注意，交易性应收款项的可变现净值（NRV）并不反映货币的时间价值，因此并没有现值的计算。

坏账准备的估计

赊销提高了企业无法收回全部应收账款的可能性。坏账最通常的核算方法有两种：直接转销法和备抵法。

直接转销法

直接转销法是在坏账实际发生时才确认为坏账损失。直接转销法的优点是账务处理简单直接，因为不需要做任何估计。但是，这种方法一般与 GAAP 不符，因为其成本和当期收入不配比，导致应收账款被高估。直接转销法主要用于联邦所得税核算。

备抵法

备抵法是对所有的赊销和所有未偿付的应收款项可能发生的不能收回的金额进行估计。这个备抵账户使应收账款反映可变现净值。它是企业期望可收回货款的总额。坏账损失记入经营费用。在备抵法下，坏账损失的估计可以用资产负债表法，也可以用损益表法。

- **资产负债表法（基于应收账款）**

资产负债表法是通过以前真实发生的坏账记录和应收账款金额之间的历史趋势来估计坏账损失的一种方法。

- **余额百分比法**

余额百分比法的目的是确定应收款项的可变现净值，并将这一信息反映在资产负债表中。这种方法是根据历史资料评估真实发生的坏账损失与一段时期的应收账款之间的关系，用所得出的坏账占应收账款的比率乘以会计期末应收账款余额，据此来确定"坏账准备"账户的期末余额。例如，如果企业在期末有 $100 000 的应收账款，提取坏账准备的比例为 4%，然后将它们相乘。在本例中，应收账款的可变现净值为 $96 000，计提的坏账损失为 $4 000。但是，如果在坏账准备中存在 $1 000 的贷方余额，那么计提的坏账准备为 $3 000，因为只需要将余额调整到期望的水平。

- **账龄分析法**

随着时间的推移，应收账款更难回收，因为以前估计坏账的方法不再有效。账龄分析法根据应收账款入账时间的长短来估计坏账损失。账款的拖欠时间越长，坏账估计比率就越高。图表 2 - 90 是采用账龄分析法的一个例子。

图表 2 - 90　应收账款账龄分析

\multicolumn{5}{c}{Bounce 体育用品公司账龄分析}				
客户名称	12 月 31 日余额	不超过 60 天	61~90 天	91~120 天	超过 120 天
East side	$54 880	$44 800	$10 080		
rockford	179 200	179 200			
freedom	30 800				$30 800
broadway	41 440	33 600		$7 840	
合计	$306 320	$254 600	$10 080	$7 840	$30 800

\multicolumn{4}{c}{一览表}			
应收账款账龄	应收账款余额	估计坏账损失	估计损失金额
不超过 60 天	$257 600	5%	$12 880
61~90 天	10 080	15%	1 512
91~120 天	7 840	20%	1 568
超过 120 天	30 800	25%	7 700
合计			$23 660

- **损益表法（基于赊销金额）**

损益表法是将过去的坏账与赊销金额进行比较的一种方法。

- **销售百分比法**

当企业的销售金额与收到的现金存在稳定的关系时，就可以采用销售百分比法。

这种方法基于损益表中内在的配比原则，认为当期的收入和费用应相配比。历史的销售坏账百分比用来估计当期的坏账。例如，如果企业的销售金额为 $100 000，并估计基于销售额的坏账损失率为 3%，那么计提的坏账准备为 $3 000。

- **净赊销百分比法**

当赊销金额与总销售额之间的关系随时间呈较大幅度的变化时，就不能采用销售百分比法而应采用净赊销额代替总销售额，即采用净赊销百分比法。

上述两种损益表法都注重当期费用的计量，将它们记入准备账户的现有余额中去。

转销坏账和转销坏账的收回

采用备抵法时，当转销坏账准备时，借记"坏账准备"，贷记"应收账款"。坏账转销是确认以前估计的损失，所以应收账款在资产负债表中的净现值并不受影响。在转销时并没有坏账损失的记录。如果转销的应收账款最后收回，就应借记"应收账款"，贷记"坏账准备"，将其账面价值恢复。当收到现金时就冲减应收账款。

在直接转销法下，已转销的坏账收回时，就借记"银行存款"，贷记收入账户如"坏账收回"。

销售退回和折让

当客户退回以前赊销的商品时，就借记"销售退回和折让"，贷记"应收账款"，冲减销售额。但是，在某些销售退回率很高的企业，应将扣除预计销售退回的销售额作为初始记录，并将销售退回折扣的冲销作为应收账款的一个相反账户。

应收票据

应收账款是付款的口头承诺，而应收票据是付款的书面承诺。本票就是应收票据的一种，它由开票人（付款的企业）签发，承诺在将来某一特定时间无条件支付确定的金额给持票人。

本票是可以流通的，收款人（收到本金和利息的人）能够将其进行买卖。因为它是无条件支付，因此可以认为它们的流动性很强。大多数票据是带息票据，具有一定的利息。零息票据（不带息票据）的利息包含在它的账面价值之内。

当客户需要将目前的应收款项延期支付或需要贷款时，就可以将票据进行承兑。

短期应收票据通常按票面价值确认，其隐含在到期值中的利息不具有实质性。相反，长期应收票据必须以预期可收到金额的现值确认。如果流通的长期带息票据上标明了利率，且票面利率和市场利率相等，那么该应收票据的价值就等于票面价值。如果票面利率不等于市场利率，那么该票据的价值就高于或低于票面价值，其差额将按市场利率在票据的整个有效期进行分摊。

稍后会进一步探讨这两种情况。

以面值发行票据

当票据以面值发行时，其票面利率应等于具有相同风险的贷款的市场利率，没有折价和溢价。例如，一个贷款人将贷给借款人 $100 000，以一张 $100 000，期限为 3

年，票面年利率为8%的票据作抵押，具有类似风险的投资的市场利率也为8%。

图表2-91和图表2-92是现值系数表，用来计算这里的例题。

图表2-91 现值系数表

现值系数 $(PV)_{n,i} = \dfrac{1}{(1+i)^n} = (1+i)^{-n}$

(n) 期数	8%	9%	10%
1	0.92593	0.91743	0.90909
2	0.85734	0.84168	0.82645
3	0.79383	0.77218	0.75132
4	0.73503	0.70843	0.68301
5	0.68058	0.64993	0.62092
6	0.63017	0.59627	0.56447
7	0.58349	0.54730	0.51316
8	0.54027	0.50187	0.46651
9	0.50025	0.46043	0.42410
10	0.46319	0.42241	0.38554

图表2-92 普通年金现值系数

普通年金现值系数 $(PV-OA)_{n,i} = \dfrac{1 - \dfrac{1}{(1+i)^n}}{i}$

(n) 期数	8%	9%	10%
1	0.92593	0.91743	0.90909
2	1.78326	1.75911	1.73554
3	2.57710	2.53130	2.48685
4	3.31213	3.23972	3.16986
5	3.99271	3.88965	3.79079
6	4.62288	4.48592	4.35526
7	5.20637	5.03295	4.86842
8	5.74664	5.53482	5.33493
9	6.24689	5.99525	5.75902
10	6.71008	6.41766	6.14457

票据交易价格（资金的现值）的计算如图表2-93所示，在该表中，每期的利息费用为 \$8 000，可当作普通年金（指在每期期末采用复利得出的年金）。

图表2-93 以面值发行的票据

票据面值	\$100 000
票据本金的现值	\$79 383
$\$100\ 000 \times (PV)_{3,8\%} = (\$100\ 000 \times 0.79383)$	
票据利息的现值	\$20 617
$\$8\ 000 \times (PV-OA)_{3,8\%} = (\$8\ 000 \times 2.57710)$	
票据的现值	\$100 000
差异	\$0

票据的现值与其面值相等，没有折价。

折价或溢价发行的票据

当市场利率高于票面利率时，票据价值就低于面值；当市场利率低于票面利率时，票据价值就高于面值。

零息票据。零息票据具有内含利息，因为在票据面值和实际收到的借款者的金额之间具有差额。在现实价值和未来价值之间的差额就作为贴现折价，并将其在整个票据有效期内摊销。例如，借款人（borrower）将票面金额为 $100 000 的 3 年期零息票据贴现，其现值为 $79 383（目前市场利率为 8%）。这样，借款人得到 $79 383 并在 3 年后支付 $100 000。而 $20 617 的差额就作为总的利息在贷款期结束时支付，其内含利率为 8%。

图表 2 - 94 展示了零息票据的持有人如何确认这笔交易：

图表 2 - 94　零息票据

借：应收票据	$100 000	
贷：财务费用（应收票据折价）		$20 617
现金		$79 383

应收票据折价额作为应收票据的相反资产账户在资产负债表中确认，并将折价在票据的有效期内进行摊销。每年利息收入的确认采用实际利率法，其摊销过程见图表 2 - 95。

图表 2 - 95　应收票据折价额的摊销

	收到的现金	每年的利息	折价摊销金额	票据价值
贴现期				$79 383
第 1 年末	$0	$6 351	$6 351	85 734
第 2 年末	0	6 859	6 859	92 593
第 3 年末	0	7 407	7 407	100 000
合计	$0	$20 617	$20 617	

利息收入的计算是将每期初的票据价值乘上 8% 的利率。每期末的票据价值就等于当期的摊销金额加上期的票据价值（例如，$79 383 + $6 351 = $85 734）。可能在最后一期需要调整一下余额的误差。

确认第 1 年利息收入就借记"折价摊销"（如 $6 351），减少应收账款金额，并以相同的金额记入贷方"利息收入"。

带息票据。如果企业收到一张 3 年期的面值为 $100 000，票面利率为 8% 的带息票据，但相同投资的市场利率为 9%，该票据就会折价交易，其计算过程见图表 2 - 96。

图表 2 - 96　带息票据的折价

票据票面价值		$100 000
票据本金的现值	$77 218	
$100 000 × (PV)$_{3, 9\%}$ = ($100 000 × 0.77218)		
票据利息的现值	$20 250	
$8 000 × (PV - OA)$_{3, 9\%}$ = ($8 000 × 2.53130)		
票据的现值		$97 468
差异		$2 532

收到的票据额度的确认如图表 2 - 97 所示：

图表 2 - 97　带息票据分录

借：应收票据	$100 000	
贷：应收票据折价		$2 532
现金		$97 468

其利息收入采用有效利率法，以确定所摊销的折价金额，计算过程如图表 2 - 98 所示。

图表 2 - 98　折价摊销的计算

	收到的现金	每年的利息	折价摊销金额	票据价值
贴现期				$97 468
第 1 年末	$8 000	$8 772	$772	98 240
第 2 年末	8 000	8 842	842	99 082
第 3 年末	8 000	8 918	918	100 000
合计	$24 000	$26 532	$2 532	

在第 1 年年末，买方确认以票面利率计算出的 $8 000 现金作为利息收入，但实际利率计算出的利息收入为 $8 772。两者之间的差额计入折价摊销，将其加上当期的票据价值就是期末的票据价值。因此，在第 1 年，买方确认现金收入、折价摊销和总的利息收入，其过程见图表 2 - 99。

图表 2 - 99　带息票据分录

借：现金	$8 000	
应收票据折价	$772	
贷：利息收入		$8 772

溢价时通常也采用实际利率法，但是应收票据的溢价应确认在借方，而其每年的摊销额作为利息收入的减项。（图表 2 - 99 中的折价摊销额若换成溢价摊销其金额就应为负数。）

估计利率

当不能通过对票据交换的资产或劳务的估价等方式来确定实际利率时，就采用估计利率。估计利率是市场利率的近似值，估计利率应与具有相同贷款风险水平或相同贷款项目的现行利率具有可比性。估计利率在收到票据时确定，并运用于整个票据有效期。

应收账款和应收票据的处置

在企业持有其应收款项至收到款项或转销之日期间，企业通常会将其交易性应收款项进行处理换成现金。大多数企业需要提供信用贷款，但并不是所有企业都能支付信贷部门的全部费用。（但是，大多数企业在出售应收款项时，并没有转移它们的行政职能。）交易性应收款项的买方擅长于应收账款的管理和回收，因此，它们比大多数企业在这方面更有效率。企业也可能为了保持较好的短期流动比率而处置应收款项来换取现金，而不需要借款或发行新股。

应收款项的买方也乐意如此，因为它们以折价得到应收款项，并善于高效率将其收回。银行可能为规避贷款限制而买入应收款项。一些应收款项购买人希望该交易给资产持有人提供的法律保障高于担保债权人。

应收款项处置的两条主要途径。是担保借款和通过保理或证券化出售应收款项。应收款项的出售可以有追索权也可以无追索权。

担保借款

在担保借款形式下，将应收账款作为贷款的抵押。这使公司可以保留应收账款并以这些款项为担保获得借款。单个债权人一般并不会被告知这一担保借款交易，而借款人们继续回收应收账款并记录折扣、退回和折让以及坏账。贷款人将收取利息和融资费用。

代理和证券化

代理和证券化是公司出售应收款项的两种方式。代理一般没有追索权，但有些应收款项的出售可能具有追索权。

保理。在代理这种方式下，保理人购买应收款项并且往往会承担起应收款项的回收职能。财务公司和银行是最常见的代理人。应收款项保理常应用于纺织业、家具业和服装产业。信用卡也是应收款项代理的一种方式。利用应收款项代理的公司可以立即得到现金（但所获得的现金没有担保借款形式下多），同时可以取消自己的信用部门，因为应收款项的风险随即也将转移给保理人。保理人将代替公司进行信用审查，根据信用审查结果决定授信或不予授信，并直接从客户手中获得应收款项的支付，用现金减去相关收费即为购买应收账款应支付的款项。公司继续与客户直接开展各种业务，如下单和履行订单。将信用决策权转移给保理人有利于降低保理人的风险，并降低服务成本，但是公司必须接受保理人的信用决策，因此一些销售可能不被批准。

大多数保理人因为考虑到销售退回和折让以及坏账的可能性，因此一般只对80%～90%的应收款项价值提供融资。另外，保理人还会根据应收款项转让净额和所感知到的呆坏账风险提取一定比例的佣金。公司将保理人提取的这部分佣金计入费用或损失。

证券化。证券化是指将一系列相似的应收款项如抵押、应收信用卡款、汽车贷款打包成一个投资基金。应收款项本金和利息的支付对于投资者来说是可实现的。与应收款项保理不通，应收款项的出售者对售出的应收款项仍附有义务。证券化对应收款项的质量要求较高但收费较低。

附有追索权的应收款项出售。在附有追索权的应收款项出售中，应收款项的出售者必须承担任何可能发生的坏账。因为应收款项出售者仍附有对应收款项的义务，该项交易适用财务组成分析法。该方法规定，购买者和出售者在进行附有追索权的购买后只确认具有控制权的资产和负债，已经出售的资产和负债不在确认范围内。例如，采用财务组成分析法，将 $100 000 的应收款项以具有追索权的形式出售给保理人，保理人按应收款项额度的 2% 收取融资费用，并按应收款项额度的 3% 收取坏账担保。坏账准备（也称不追索权义务）的公平价值为 $4 000。首先，出售应收款项的净收益的计算如图表 2 - 100 所示。

图表 2 - 100　净收益的计算

收到现金（ $100 000 减去 2% +3%）		$95 000
从保理人处获得的款项	3 000	$98 000
减：坏账准备		(4 000)
净收益		94 000

净收入 = 销售得到的资产 - 发生的负债，图表 2 - 101 展示了应收款项的出售损失。

图表 2 - 101　出售损失的计算

账面价值	$100 000
净收益	94 000
应收款项出售损失	$6 000

不附有追索权的应收款项出售。应收款项保理是最常见的不附有追索权的应收款项出售，这意味着购买者要承担可能的坏账风险，因为应收款项的所有权随着销售的实现，已经完全转移给购买者，因此它被认为是一种形式上完全的销售，另外随着销售的实现，信用决策权与收款义务也随之转移，因此它实质上也是一种完全的销售。

担保借款与销售的区别

FASB 在 SFAS 第 140 号中规定了应收款项出售的确认指南。一般来说，当控制权发生转移时，就可以确认销售的实现。另外，应收款项销售的实现必须满足以下三个条件：

- 该项资产必须独立于它的出售者和债权人。
- 该项资产的购买者有使用资产作抵押或出售资产的权力。
- 在条件不符合的条件下，出售者没有权力进行回购。

根据 FASB 的有关条款，如果不满足上述条件，该项交易将确定为有担保借款。有担保借款应确认为一项负债，其利率被确认为一项费用。如果 FASB 的规定允许销售的确认以及存在继续参与（附有回购条件的销售），则适用财务组成分析法，相反，则不适用财务组成分析法，业务的发生将被确认为应收款项的减少或费用、损失。

应收账款的披露要求

重要的应收账款应在资产负债表上单独列示并报告其净值。流动资产部分的应收账款应披露为一年以内或一个会计年度内的现金，规范的应收账款披露包括与应收账款相关的可能发生的损失、与应收账款相关的担保、重要的信贷风险以及关联企业应收账款。

资产负债表中展示应收账款的部分如图表 2 - 102 所示。

图表 2-102　Bounce 体育用品公司部分资产负债表

财年结束于第 1 年的 12 月 31 日

流动资产		
现金以及现金等价物		$1 383 985
应收账款*	$6 643 478	
减：资产减值准备	370 167	
	6 273 311	
预付补贴款	1 546 600	
应收票据－交易	1 133 680	
返还联邦所得税	180 561	
应收股利和应收利息	55 870	
其他应收款项和要求权（包括应付账款的借方余额）	129 219	9 247 241
流动资产总额		10 631 226
非流动应收项目		
来自管理人员和关键员工的应收票据		278 307
应收索赔（过去五年内的诉讼款项）		432 900

*关于应收账款和应收票据的附注

在第 1 年的 7 月，Bounce 体育用品公司同一家金融公司达成了一项安排，对 Bounce 公司的部分债务进行再融资。贷款凭证是利率为 8% 的应付票据。该票据为即期应付票据，并由全部应收账款提供担保。

存货

存货是指企业在正常经营生产过程中以备出售的资产，包括产成品、商品、半成品，或者将被加工成出售商品的原材料等。那些不是由于正常生产经营过程而出售的资产不属于存货。在零售和制造业中，存货是资产最重要的组成部分。

存货通常按照其用途分类。零售业往往只有一种即商品，它包括购买进来用于出售的所有零售商品。制造业通常有三种类别：原材料、半成品和产成品。生产成本、人工费用、固定和变动间接费用、仓储费用将在这些类别之间进行合理分配。制造企业通常根据存货内部的不同用途来对存货进行分类，分为制造供给品、辅助材料、工厂供给品、半存货。

永续盘存制和定期盘存制

目前，企业都在极力减少存货储备，使其控制在正常销售的最低水平。当企业接到订单时需要准备一定的存货，但要极力避免存货累积，因为这些累积的存货在它们销售出去之前是需要财务成本的，并且它们可能发生霉烂或滞销。企业需要建立相关数据库、条形码扫描系统或其他数据系统来对存货进行管理，使存货记录实时更新。JIT（Just-in-time）存货管理系统通过与供应商建立直接电子数据连接减少了存货的储存时间，当某种特定原材料或产成品需要装船时，企业就会知道。

两种确定存货最佳持有量的方法是永续盘存制和定期盘存制（实地盘存制）。永续盘存制是利用电脑信息来管理存货，目前被广泛运用于存货管理。

永续盘存制

永续盘存制持续记录存货账户的变化轨迹。所有的交易都在其交易时确认。复杂的数据库每天都进行更新，记录着存货第一时间的销售、购买、转移、交易情况。零售系统则在存货销售时记录其变化情况，使存货和销售成本同时发生变化。购买量、销售商品退回、可能的折扣以及进货运费也同时更新。

当企业采用永续盘存制时，每一次销售的分录就是减少存货同时增加销售成本（一个费用账户）。可是，并不是所有商品在销售时都照此确认。因为有些商品可能失窃，有些没有开票的商品可能误发（多于开票单要求发送的数量或种类），有些可能由于毁损或报废等原因而没有被确认。因此，在账面上确认的存货数量通常要高于实际持有量。（但是，有时也可能低于实际持有量。）所以，采用永续盘存制的企业将对其持有的存货进行定期盘点，并注销实际数量与其账面价值的差异，增加销售成本，减少存货。由于能够计量实际数量和账面数量之间的差异，每年的累计损失就可以确定。以前采用的定期盘存制的缺点就在于不能对此加以计量。

存货账户是一个统驭账户，其包括一系列存货的单独分类账户。每个单独账户包含存货的数量和在多个存货类别之间分配的成本。其他永久性存货账户确认原则包括：

- 在销售时，按确认的商品成本借记"商品成本"，贷记"存货"。
- 将转售商品、产品和购买的原材料确认为存货。
- 将采购时取得的折扣，采购运费和采购商品退回计入存货成本（不记入单独账户）。

永续盘存制的基本等式为：

期初存货成本 + 本期购货成本（净） - 本期销货成本 = 期末存货成本

定期盘存制

相反，定期盘存制虽然也是从这两个相同项目开始，但是通过减去存货期末余额倒轧出本期销售成本（其在永续盘存制下是已经知道的）。当许多企业采用相关数据库对存货进行记录时，定期盘存制在大多数企业里已经不再适用。定期盘存制必须每年对存货进行一次实地盘点以确定存货数量。所有取得的存货将记在采购账户的借方。在期末，采购账户的余额与期初存货成本相加，确定整个期间内供销售存货的总成本。供销售存货的总成本减去期末存货成本（由年末盘点决定）就得到本期销售成本。由于销售成本一年只确认一次，其信息并不及时。为了解决这个问题，有时采用调整定期盘存制。调整定期盘存制在备用账簿中记录存货的数量（没有价格）。

存货的估价

存货的估价是决定何种项目将计入存货成本的过程，即何种成本将被计入存货以及采用何种存货流转假设。

所有生产产品的成本会在出售的产品和期末存货之间进行分配。待出售或使用的产品的成本是期初存货成本加上本期采购或生产的存货成本。已销售产品的成本是待出售或使用的产品的成本减去期末持有的存货成本。待出售产品的成本和已出售产品的成本的计算见图表 2 - 103。

图表2-103 已出售产品成本的计算

期初存货1月1日	$350 000
本期采购或生产的产品的成本	670 000
待出售产品的总成本	$1 020 000
期末存货	400 000
本期已出售产品的成本	$620 000

何种货物应计入存货

当买方收到货物时，才应确认存货采购，即使买方已收到发票拥有法律上的所有权。由于存货转移时间很难确定，并且与采用上述原则的结果并没有实质性差异，因此在实务中普遍采用收到货物时确认存货采购。但对于该原则的利用，下列情况例外。

● 代销商品

代销商品是为了减少存货滞销的风险而允许批发商（委托人）在商品销售出去之前保留所有权的一种销售方式。然后零售商（受托人）将销售的货款支付给批发商，受托人得到由于代批发商保管、销售存货的销售佣金。代销商品在出售给第三方之前应作为委托方的存货处理，受托方不能将其作为存货。

● 在途商品

在途商品是那些已经发送但在会计期末没有到达目的地的商品。在途商品归谁所有取决于装货项目，是采用FOB（Free on board）装货地还是FOB目的地。在装货地离岸价格下，卖方将货物发给作为买方代理人的一般承运商时，所有权就发生转移。在目的地离岸价格下，当货物到达时所有权才发生转移。需要考虑的是，货物的毁损应由所有者负责。例如明尼阿波利斯离岸价格可能就指出了所有权转移的地点。在所有权转移之前，该货物的所有权由卖方所有；在所有权转移之后，就由买方对货物负责。

● 销售协议

在某些销售协议中包含了所有权转移的内容，它与所有权风险转移的时点不相一致。有三种销售的特殊情况分别是：高退回率销售、售后回购、分期付款销售。高退回率在出版业、体育用品、音乐制品和其他一些季节性行业中很常见，在这种情况下，企业允许客户将滞销的存货予以退回，并退还全部或部分货款。当退回的数量能够合理估计时，企业就应设立销售商品退回账户，并在销售时加以考虑。但是，当其数量不能估计时，企业就应在商品退回时再进行确认。

售后回购协议指销售方将货物销售给购买方后，同意在日后某一确切的时间以确切的价格重新买回这批商品的一种交易。这种交易被称作暂放交易，因为销售方短时期将其存货暂放在购货方的资产负债表中。由此，销售方可以有效地为其存货融资，在保留风险的情况下将所有权转移给购买方。当协议中商议的重新购买价包含了购买方所有成本加上存货成本，对于售后回购协议中所包含的存货和负债应在销售方的资产负债表中进行确认。

哪些成本应归集于存货

在确定存货的价格时，哪些成本应归集于存货项目呢？计入存货价值的成本包括下面几个项目：

- **间接制造费用**

当企业生产产品用于销售时，在生产过程中发生的直接或间接成本均要计入存货成本。会计研究第43号公告指出，外购或自制发生的成本均要计入存货成本，但一般管理费用除外，除非有明确证据表明一般管理费用的某一部分与生产制造明显相关。同时，公告指出销售费用也不得计入存货成本。固定和变动间接费用均应计入存货成本。固定间接费用按传统方法或作业成本法分配给已生产的产品。例如，车间管理人员的工资就是固定间接费用的一部分，并归属于确定的生产车间。但是，执行人员的薪水就不能作为产品成本。

- **产品成本**

所有的产品成本都要计入存货成本，包括运输费用、生产工人工资、外购成本、生产制造成本、加工成本等。

- **现金折扣**

现金折扣指在提前付款时享受的折扣。正如本章前面在应收账款部分中讨论的一样，在总价法下，将购买的商品以全部价格计入。只有当折扣发生时才将折扣减除。在净价法下，商品以扣减折扣的价格计价。折扣损失作为另一个费用账户。

- **期间费用**

期间费用不能计入存货成本，比如销售和一般管理费用，因为这些费用是包含在整个期间内的。这些费用有时会在生产过程中产生，但大多数情况下并不和生产直接相关。与存货相关的利息成本也属于期间费用，虽然有人认为这部分利息应该资本化并将其计入存货。FASB指出只有那些像船舶制造、房产销售和租赁等行业，为内部建造的资产而发生的利息才能资本化。那些与存货有关的日常生产发生的利息费用则不能资本化。

存货成本流转假设

在整个会计期间，存货通常在许多不同的时期购入。上一期的存货也包含在本期存货的期初，并且在本期又会生产出相同的存货，但是它们的成本各不相同。由于存货的流转和类型纷繁复杂，对每一项存货项目明确地计价似乎不太可能。所以，就产生采用某种存货成本流转假设，来对存货成本进行计量。存货成本流转假设仅适用于对存货成本的计量，与其实物流动无关。例如，先进先出法（FIFO）并不表示在实际中先进来的存货先卖出。存货成本流转假设仅仅用于将成本在期末存货和发出存货之间进行分配。每种方法对利润有不同的影响。但是，选择某种存货流转假设的最终目的是使其与每期的真实利润最接近。目前采用个别计价法、平均成本法、先进先出法和后进先出法这四种存货流转假设。

- **个别计价法**

个别计价法是按照各种存货，逐一辨认每个项目，将成本计入发出存货和期末存货。个别计价法适用于一般不能替代使用的存货或少数贵重物品项目如珠宝、汽车或为特定项目专门购入或制造的存货。个别计价法通常采用永续盘存法，利用实时数据库反映存货信息。它符合收入配比原则，并随着存货技术的发展变得流行起来。最后，企业可能滥用个别计价法，通过对某些存货采用特殊价格来调节当期利润。

- **平均成本法**

平均成本法将同类存货进行合计，然后确定本期存货的平均成本。在永续盘存制下，新的平均成本在每次采购之后要重新计算，因此这种方法也叫做移动平均法。单位平均成本等于可供销售的总存货成本除以可供销售的存货数量。因此，在某个时期如7月7日，如果可供销售的总存货成本为 $100 000，可供销售的存货数量为2 000，则存货的平均单位成本为 $50。不论是何时购买，存货的平均单位成本都要重新计算。图表2-104反映了某月的平均成本变化。

图表2-104 移动平均法的存货流转假设

Bounce 体育用品公司移动平均法（永续盘存制下）		
7月1日 期初余额	数量1 000 × 单价 $40	$40 000
7月7日 购入	数量1 000 × 单价 $60	60 000
7月7日 结存	数量2 000 × 单价 $50	$100 000
7月15日 发出	数量（1 000）× 单价 $50	(50 000)
7月15日 结存	数量1 000 × 单价 $50	$50 000
7月20日 购入	数量500 × 单价 $56	28 000
7月20日 结存	数量1 500 × 单价 $52	$78 000
7月28日 购入	数量（300）× 单价 $52	(15 600)
7月31日 结存	数量1 200 × 单价 $52	$62 400
发出存货成本（1 300件）	$50 000 + $15 600	$65 600
期末存货成本（1 200件 × $52）		$62 400

在实地盘存制下，平均成本法也叫做加权平均成本法。本期可供销售的总成本除以总的存货数量，就得到加权平均法下的单位成本。其中可供销售的成本包括期初存货成本和本期购入成本之和。存货期末成本就用期末结存存货数量乘以单位成本。本期发出成本就用可供销售的存货总成本减去期末存货成本或用平均成本乘以销售数量。

平均存货法比较客观，简单易行，并且不像其他几种方法那样容易受人为操纵的影响，因此在实务中得到了广泛应用。

● 先进先出法

先进先出法（FIFO）（在本书的前面部分已经讨论过）是以先购入的存货先发出这样一种存货实物流转假设为前提。因此较早以前购入存货的成本应该包括在发出存货成本中，而近期购入的存货成本应包括在期末存货成本之中。

当存货成本上涨时，先进先出法会高估期末存货成本，低估发出存货成本价值。当物价下降时，情况正好相反，会高估发出存货成本，低估期末存货成本。

利用图表2-104的数据，在永续盘存制下，发出存货成本和期末存货成本的计算过程如图表2-105所示。当发出存货的数量超过最早购入存货数量时，就需采用下一个最早时期的价格。发出存货成本总是基于最早的成本。

图表2-105 永续盘存制下的先进先出法

Bounce 体育用品公司 先进先出法的存货成本流转假设（永续盘存制下）	
发出存货成本（1 300 单位）	
7月15日 数量1 000 × 单价 $40	$40 000
7月28日 数量 300 × 单价 $60	18 000

续表

Bounce 体育用品公司 先进先出法的存货成本流转假设（永续盘存制下）	
合计	$58 000

期末存货成本（1 200 单位）

期初存货成本 + 本期购买成本 − 本期发出成本 = 期末存货成本

$40 000 + $88 000 − $58 000 = $70 000 *

* 数量 700 × 单价 $60 =	$42 000
数量 500 × 单价 $56 =	$28 000
合计	$70 000

在实地盘存制下，期末存货成本采用最近时期的价格计算。可供销售的存货总成本减去期末存货成本就得出发出存货成本。不管是在实地盘存制还是在永续盘存制下，利用先进先出法可以得到相同的本期发出成本，因为最先购进的成本总是相同的。图表 2 – 106 反映了实地盘存制下的先进先出法。

图表 2 – 106　实地盘存制下的先进先出法

Bounce 体育用品公司 先进先出法的存货成本流转假设（实地盘存制下）	
期末存货成本（1 200 单位）	
数量 700 × 单价 $60	$42 000
数量 500 × 单价 $56	28 000
	$70 000
发出存货成本（1 300 单位）	
期初存货成本 + 本期购买成本 − 期末存货成本 = 本期发出成本	
$4 000 + $88 000 − $70 000 = $58 000	

先进先出法的目的是为了与真实的存货实物流转相一致。使先购入的存货先发出时，先进先出法与个别计价法相似。并且，在先进先出法下，对期末存货的价值计入成本的部分提供了一个合理的估计，特别是当存货周转较快且价格相对稳定时。但是，先进先出法并不能使利润表中当期成本与当期收入配比，因此扭曲了净利润，因为当期收入是与最早时期的成本相配比。当存货价格上涨时，先进先出法会虚增企业利润。

- **后进先出法**

在后进先出法（LIFO）下，最近购入存货的成本将计入发出存货成本中，而期末存货成本将包括最早期购入的存货成本。当成本价格上涨时，后进先出法会高估发出存货成本而低估期末存货成本。后进先出法通常用于大型超市或一些具有持续基本存量的企业，如化工、冶炼企业。

在永续盘存制下，在销售商品的当天，就采用后进先出法确定最近购入存货的成本。利用图表 2 – 106 的数据，图表 2 – 107 反映了永续盘存制下的后进先出法。

图表 2 – 107　永续盘存制下的后进先出法

Bounce 体育用品公司
后进先出法的存货成本流转假设（永续盘存制下）

发出存货成本（1 300 单位）		
7 月 15 日	数量 1 000 × 单价 $60	$60 000
7 月 28 日	数量　300 × 单价 $56	16 800
		$76 800
期末存货成本（1 200 单位）		
期初存货成本 + 本期购货成本 − 本期发出成本 = 期末存货成本		
$40 000 + $88 000 − $76 800 = $51 200*		
* 数量 1 000 × 单价 $40 = $40 000		
数量　200 × 单价 $56 =　11 200		
$51 200		

与先进先出法不同，采用永续盘存制下的后进先出法和采用实地盘存制下的后进先出法会得到不同的发出存货成本和期末存货成本。其原因是在实地盘存制下，后进先出法是在会计期末来记录存货成本，而在永续盘存制下是在每一个销售日记录存货成本。

在实地盘存制下，发出存货成本是用可供销售的存货总成本减去期末存货成本而计算出的。图表 2 – 108 反映了在实地盘存制下如何运用后进先出法来计量存货成本。

图表 2 – 108　实地盘存制下的后进先出法

Bounce 体育用品公司
后进先出法的存货成本流转假设（在实地盘存制下）

期末存货成本（1 200 单位）	
数量 1 000 × 单价 $40	$40 000
数量　200 × 单价 $60	12 000
	$52 000
发出存货成本（140 单位）	
期初存货成本 + 本期购制成本 − 期末存货成本 = 发出存货成本	
$40 000 + $88 000 − $52 000 = $76 000	

后进先出法能够很好地反映本期收益，因为它是本期的成本与当期收入相配比。当成本价格上涨时，发出存货成本会上升而净利润会下降，与其他方法相比，采用后进先出法能使存货成本水平较稳定，且可以达到延迟交税的目的。延迟交税就意味着能为企业节约更多的现金。当价格下降时，后进先出法也可以成为套期保值工具，因为它并不需要由于市场价格降低而降低存货标价来计量存货价值，而先进先出法就会受其影响。但是，可以产生减税作用的报告期低盈利对于那些要求高盈利的公司来讲就是一项不利影响。采用后进先出法同时会导致存货的价值估计过于保守以及低估营运资本，从而扭曲了资产负债表。

后进先出法下的存货清算。后进先出法对不同批次的存货根据不同的时间和成本加以计量。最早批次的存货叫做基本层。例如，如果 Bounce 体育用品公司有三年前购买的橡胶原料,它们可能使用期末存货,并得出采用后进先出法下的单位成本。如果本期使用的原材料超过了本期购买量,就会发生后进先出法下的存货清算。后进先出法下的存货清算是指由于销售多种不同批次的存货而导致采用现行价格计量收入而采用现行价格和历史价格共同计量成本的状况。假设价格上涨的情况下,后进先出法下的存货清算会导致报告期间较高的收入和相应较高的所得税。

图表2-109反映了当橡胶原料短缺,企业无法购买到所需要的这些直接材料时产生的结果。注意,它们的期初存货由三个批次的存货成本组成,并且最近两个批次的存货被清除,最初批次的存货永久地减少。因为这些批次的存货在先前以较低成本购入,当使用这些存货时就会比以目前的市价购入存货产生较高的当期收入和随之产生的较高所得税,详见下图的脚注。

图表2-109 后进先出法下的存货清算

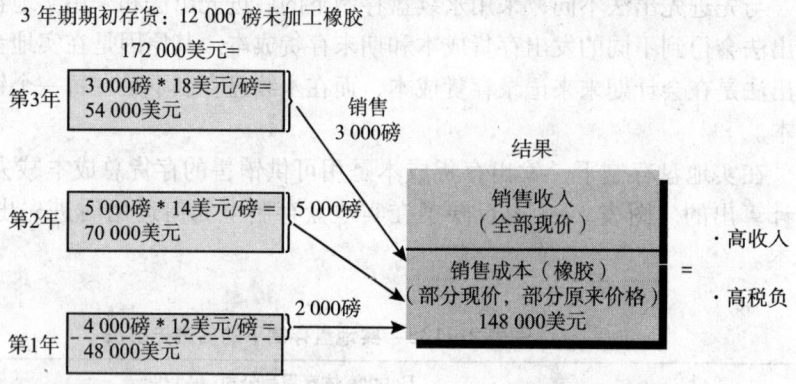

3年期初存货:12 000磅未加工橡胶

3年期间,所用未加工橡胶为10 000磅;
由于原料短缺导致没有新的原料采购。
  *如果第3年多购进18美元/磅的橡胶7 000磅的话,那么销售成本(橡胶)=180 000美元,从而带来低收入与低税负。

广泛运用的后进先出法下的存货清算会降低采用后进先出法的效益。因此,通常的解决方法是采用指定货物的后进先出法,这种方法将各项存货进行不同归类,而对该类进行清算,通过不同种类的增加数来进行冲销。采用这种方法会减少波动,但是由于某些企业会频繁改变归类的成本,因此存货类别必须重新定义,如有某些项目变化较大,就需要进行新的归类,而以前的存货归类项目就要进行后进先出法下的存货清算。

余额后进先出法。解决后进先出法下存货清算和存货归类问题的另一种方法是余额后进先出法,这种方法采用总的货币价值来计量成本项目的上升和下降,而不是采用实物数量。这种方法允许称模糊地确认归类项目,可以包括相互交叉的类似项目。项目的范围越广,后进先出法下的存货清算可能性就越小。余额后进先出法的计算方法比较复杂;它包括计算年末存货价格和并据此创建一个价格指数(基期年份的指数值设为100%)。基期年份以后的各年都采用一个价格指数来反映该价格的上升(或下降,例如,如果价格上涨16%,价格指数就是基期年份的116%)。采用价格指数就可以在基期年份的基础上进行计算。图表2-110展示了这一方法的使用。

图表2-110 金额后进先出法

12月31日	年末存货价值		价格指数	年末存货
第1年（基期年份）	$450 000	/	100%	$450 000
第2年	$550 000	/	116%	$474 138

年末存货价值减去期初存货价值（先前年份的数据）等于货物数量的增加（或减少）。增加的数量可能成为一个成本层。如果年末存货小于期初存货，那么应从最近增加的成本层中减去该数量（即减去年末存货小于期初存货的数量），计算中所使用的价格等于最近增加的成本层中所采用的价格。如果某成本层被减少或清除，且不能恢复，因此在某些年份就没有成本层。当使用存货时，最近成本层的存货先采用。金额后进先出法的计算方法已超出本书范围。关于该主题的详细信息可以参看中级财务会计相关书籍。

后进先出法计提准备。AICPA对后进先出法计提准备的定义如下"指以下两项的区别（a）在后进先出法下，采用成本与市价孰低法的存货成本，（b）存货的重置成本或在其他可接受的存货成本计量方法下（如先进先出法或平均成本法），采用成本与市价孰低法的存货成本"。

该定义得到了GAAP的权威认可。后进先出法在税收准备和对外财务报告时具有优势；但它很少用于对内财务报告，因为它并不与产品的实物流转相符，并且当其用于期中时就变得十分麻烦，因为它是基于年末数量和价格的估计。

因此，许多企业将两种方法结合运用，利用后进先出法进行税收和对外财务报告，而利用先进先出法进行对内报告。两种方法之间产生的任何差异记录为后进先出法账户下的存货减少，也叫做后进先出法计提准备。减免账户的余额变动叫做后进先出法效应。

后进先出法转化为先进先出法的影响。当决定转换存货成本计量方法时，会对销售成本产生何种影响呢？对收入呢？答案取决于这种转换是否能给企业带来好处。

例如，当比较两个可能的投资对象（两家公司）时，一家公司采用先进先出法，另一家采用后进先出法。为使比较切实可行，需要把一家公司的方法变成另一种。因为采用后进先出法的公司需要披露其后进先出法计提准备，因此将后进先出法转换成先进先出法就更容易些。基于后进先出法的公司的某些数据见图表2-111。

图表2-111 采用后进先出法公司的财务报表部分摘要

	期末	期初
资产负债表摘录：		
存货（采用先进先出法）	$338 757	$307 566
－后进先出法计提准备	－ $32 231	－ $11 820
后进先出法成本	$306 526	$295 746
损益表摘录		
发出存货成本	$2 590 650	
净利润	$108 690	

因为后进先出法计提准备增加了$20 411（$32 231 － $11 820 = $20 411），存货的成本增加（否则后进先出法计提准备将会降低）。注意，在这两年中，采用先进先

出法的存货成本大于采用后进先出法的存货成本，表明存货成本在增加。（在成本增加期间，后进先出法产生较高的发出存货成本和较低的净利润。）因此，产生的第一个区别是，如果企业先采用先进先出法，其发出存货成本就较低而净利润较高，计算过程见图表2－112（税率为40%）。

图表2－112 从后进先出法到先进先出法的转化

基于后进先出法的发出存货成本	$2 590 650
－增加的后进先出法计提准备：$32 231 － $11 820 = $20 411	－ 20 411
基于先进先出法的发出存货成本	$2 570 239
后进先出法下的净利润	$108 690
税前利润差异（由于发出存货成本变化）	+ 20 411
所得税差异	－ 8 164
先进先出法下的净利润	$120 937

采用先进先出法下的净利润，就可以与另一个采用先进先出法的企业进行有效的比较。后进先出法计提准备是在采用后进先出法时，后进先出法和先进先出法（或其他方法）之间总成本差异的累计。因此，用税率乘后进先出法计提准备得到采用后进先出法时节约的所得税总额（忽略现值）。将税率与后进先出法计提准备相乘（见图表2－111）：0.4 × $32 231 = $12 892。因此，公司需要额外的 $12 892 的资本投资于长期经营。

采用不同的存货流转假设对资产和利润的影响。先进先出法和后进先出法代表利润结果的两个极端，而平均存货成本法处于中间。当成本上涨时，后进先出法使利润最小化，从而产生较低的所得税费用。由于后进先出法也使最近成本和最初收入配比，所以有人认为它是计量发出存货成本的最好方法，因为它和重置成本最接近。

后进先出法也排除了来自净利润的存货持有利得。持有利得指在销售存货时其历史成本和重置成本之间的差异。由于采用后进先出法计量的成本最接近重置成本，因此其持有利得最小，且利润最接近基于现行成本得到的利润。相反，在先进先出法下，持有利得包含在利润中。

例如，如果最近一批购货成本是 $90，最早批次的存货成本为 $80，本期销售价格为 $200，在先进先出法下，总利润为 $120，其包含 $10 的持有利得（现行重置成本和历史成本的差额），在后进先出法下，总利润为 $110，且没有持有利得。后进先出法反映了在减去需要用新的较高的价格计算存货成本的金额后，更现实的可供分配利润。

采用先进先出法、平均成本法和后进先出法产生的结果比较见图表2－113，其数据来自于前面各表。

图表2－113 永续盘存制下存货成本流转假设的比较

Bounce 体育用品公司 存货成本流转假设的结果			
存货成本流转假设	可供销售的存货成本	发出存货成本	期末存货成本
先进先出法，永续盘存制下	$128 000	$58 000	$70 000
移动平均法，永续盘存制下	128 000	65 600	62 400
后进先出法，永续盘存制下	128 000	76 800	51 200

存货成本流转假设的优点和缺点。GAAP 允许采用所有四种成本流转假设，但是它们之间具有显著的差异。由于每种方法会导致不同的净利润水平，因此允许采用多种存货成本流转假设的主要不利影响就是使不同公司的不同财务报表缺乏可比性。由于可比性是财务报表的主要目的，这种矛盾使问题变得更复杂。但是，采用后进先出法的企业会披露相关补充信息，这就使得投资者可以确定若采用先进先出法会产生的利润。

国际会计准则委员会（IASB）认为后进先出法不太适合存货成本的计量。因此，随着 IASB 和 FASB 的日益趋同，存货价值的计量方法可能会产生一些变化。

存货计量差错的影响

两种主要类型的存货计量差错分别是，期末存货成本的差错和采购存货成本的差错。这些差错可能是在数量上也可能是在计量方法上的问题。

- **期末存货成本的差错**

当项目没有包含在期末存货中时，即使它们本应包含在内，资产负债表就会较少反映存货，随之而来就会低估保留盈余、营运资本和流动比率。并且由于发出存货成本会多计，就会使利润少计。如果该差错没有在以后年度纠正，就会产生不好的影响，但将两个时期的财务报表比较阅读时会产生相同的总利润，仿佛没有产生差错。但是，当单独看一期的报表时，每年的净利润都会有差错。当期末存货成本多计时，情况正好相反；净利润、存货、保留盈余、营运资本和流动比率就会多计，而发出存货成本会少计。

- **采购成本的差错**

当采购没有计入采购成本，并且没有计入期末存货时，资产负债表就会少计存货和应付账款，且多计流动比率。在损益表中就会同时少计采购和期末存货成本，而发出存货成本计量正确。因此，不会对净利润产生影响。由于同时减少了流动资产和流动负债的规模，因此流动比率会被高估。例如，如果流动资产是 $200 000，流动负债是 $100 000，流动比率为 2:1。但是，如果两个金额同时由于差错少计 $50 000，则比率变为 3:1，该比率上升了。当采购成本和期末存货成本均多计时，情况正好相反。

考虑期末存货成本在第 0 年多计 $10 000 的情况。差错的影响和在第 1 年的更正如图表 2 – 114 所示，表中上升或下降的箭头表示结果的增加与减少。

图表 2 – 114　存货计量差错更正

事件	时间	变化
期末存货差错	第 0 年	↑ $10 000
影响（第 1 年更正）		
销售成本	第 0 年	↓ $10 000
营业利润	第 0 年	↑ $10 000
所得税（税率 40%）	第 0 年	↑ $4 000
净利润	第 0 年	↑ $6 000
保留盈余	第 0 年	↑ $6 000
期初存货成本	第 1 年	↑ $10 000
销售成本	第 1 年	↑ $10 000

续表

事件	时间	变化
营业利润	第 1 年	↓ $10 000
所得税（税率 40%）	第 1 年	↓ $4 000
净利润	第 1 年	↓ $6 000
期末存货成本	第 1 年	更正
保留盈余	第 1 年	更正

该案例反映了采购成本和存货差错对财务报表会产生何种实质影响，以及更正会计差错对报告数据的巨大影响。

成本与市价孰低法

存货在最初是以历史成本计量，但如果由于报废、货物损坏、价格水平变化而引起存货价值下降时，就应采用现行价值对存货计价。

当存货报废或价值下降时（例如，国外的竞争导致价格下降），就应采用成本与市价孰低法（LCM）计量。在这种情况下，存货按其成本或市场价值中的较低者计量。市场价值是指通过购买或重新制造（该价值是指购买市场的价值而不是销售市场的价值）该项目而产生的重置成本。存货应在其价值下降的期间按该方法记录而不是在存货出售期间。该方法是基于这样的假设：存货重置成本的下降通常意味着为保持竞争力存货的销售价格必须下降。

可变现净值。可变现净值（NRV）是存货在通常买卖情况下（不是清算状况）销售价格的估计值减去所有完成销售和处理资产的成本。

LCM 上限和下限。在确定市场价值时，采用重置成本来计量市场价值有两个约束：
- 上限。市场价值不应大于存货的可变现净值。
- 下限。市场价值不应小于存货的可变现净值减去正常利润限额或边际利润。

设置该上限的目的是使存货不会被高估，而损失不会被低估（避免在以后期间内确认过多的损失）。设置该下限的目的是使损失不会被高估，而存货不会被低估（避免在以后期间确认过多收益）。

存货成本与市价孰低法的运用。根据会计研究公告第 43 号，成本与市价孰低法可以按单个存货项目、按存货类别或按存货总体来运用。当按存货类别或存货总体运用成本与市价孰低法时，某一地区存货市场价格的上涨会弥补不同地区价格下降的部分。单个存货项目的成本与市价孰低法最常见，部分原因是 IRS 要求采用该方法。单个存货项目的成本与市价孰低法也会得到最保守的存货价值。图表 2–115 反映了成本与市价孰低法不同方式的运用。

成本与市价孰低法的记录。当存货以市价记录时，可以采用直接法或间接（抵扣）法。直接法就是用市场价值替代存货成本，所以其损失包含在发出存货成本中但在损益表中并不反映。抵扣法就是保留存货账面成本，将差额通过另外的资产账户和损失账户反映。

图表 2-115　成本与市价孰低法的运用

成本与市价孰低法的各种运用					
存货	成本	市价	单个项目	存货类别	存货总体
橡胶产品部门:					
网球（盒）	$120	$84	$84		
墙球（盒）	114	156	114		
	$264	$240		$240	
球拍生产部门:					
网球拍1	$192	$230	192		
网球拍2	240	211	211		
	$432	$411		432	
总计	$696	$681			$681
存货价值			$631	$672	$681
确认损失			$65	$24	$15

相对销售价值法

当采用一次性支付购买一批存货，且该批存货在种类和质量上都有显著不同，采购价格就应该基于各自的相对销售价值在该批存货中分配。图表 2-116 反映了成本的分配，图表 2-117 反映采用相对销售价值法如何确定毛利润。

图表 2-116　采用相对销售价值法分配成本

批次	批次数量	销售价格	总售价	相对售价	总成本	分配成本	单位成本
A1	50	$6 000	$300 000	3/48	$2 000 000	$125 000	$2 500
A2	200	12 000	2 400 000	24/48	2 000 000	1 000 000	5 000
A3	300	7 000	2 100 000	21/48	2 000 000	875 000	2 917
			$4 800 000			2 000 000	

图表 2-117　采用相对销售价值法计算毛利润

批次	批次数量	销售额	销售成本	毛利润
A1	25	$150 000	$62 500	$87 500
A2	120	1 440 000	600 000	840 000
A3	230	1 610 000	670 910	939 090
		$3 200 000	$1 333 410	$1 866 590

与采购承诺有关的会计事项

当顾客要购买产品但该产品已脱销，就可能发生失销。为了确保供应商备有其需要的存货，某些企业会签订采购承诺，达成在未来某一时间购买存货的协定。采购承诺并没有将所有权转移给购买方，因此并不需要对其可选择或可能取消的承诺做分录。

不可撤销承诺不能确认为资产或负债，因为任意一方都没有进行交换，但是实质性承诺应该在资产负债表附注中进行披露。当协定价格等于或低于市价时，就不需进行额外披露。但是，如果合同价格大于市场价格，就应该确认估计的损失金额并在费用和损失栏目的下面披露。假设合同价格为 $300 000，而市场价格下降到 $200 000，采购承诺的预计负债为 $100 000 且未实现的损失要在相关账户确认。如果某些或全部价值得到恢复，就要调整采购承诺的预计负债账户和未实现持有损失。

存货的估价

存货的实地盘点对企业内部管理非常重要，但一年内多次进行存货实地盘点是不现实的。在编制季报而存货金额不知道时就要进行估算。这时可以采用毛利润法和零售价法。

采用毛利润法估算存货

当精确计量存货成本不可能或不现实时，就采用毛利润法（或边际利润法）估算存货成本。由于每季都进行存货实地盘点不太现实，所以编制季报时主要采用这种方法。当存货记录被毁而需要估算存货时，一些审计人员也采用毛利润法。

毛利润法的三个假设：

- 期初存货成本加上采购存货成本等于存货总成本。
- 未销售的产品都计入存货（没有被偷盗等情况）。
- 期末存货成本等于期初存货成本加上采购成本减去销售存货成本。

为了确定销售成本，就要采用毛利率。毛利率根据前几期的记录确定。图表2-118反映了如何采用毛利润法计算期末近似存货成本。

图表2-118 采用毛利润法估算存货

期初存货成本		$130 000
采购成本		410 000
可供销售存货成本		540 000
销售金额	$570 000	
减：毛利润（$57 000 的 24%）	136 800	
销售成本		433 200
近似存货成本		$106 800

采用零售价法估算存货成本

零售企业通常销售大量不同种类的存货，这使得分别确认存货的方法不可行。因此就采用零售价法来估算存货价值，运用反映企业平均利润的公式将数据转化为成本。零售价法所需的信息如下所示：

- 本期的销售额。
- 零售商品购货总成本。
- 可供销售的零售商品的总成本。

图表2-119反映了 Bounce 体育用品公司采用可供销售零售商品的成本零售率来估算期末存货成本的过程。

图表 2－119　零售价法

Bounce 体育用品公司			
	成本	零售额	成本零售率
期初存货成本	$320 000	$510 000	
采购存货成本	1 250 000	2 075 000	
可供销售存货成本	$1 570 000　／	$2 585 000	＝60.7%
减：销售		－ $2 100 000	
期末存货金额（零售价）		$485 000	
×成本零售率		×0.607	
期末存货成本		$294 395	

投资

本节将探讨对其他企业的债务证券和权益证券投资的会计处理。

债务证券

债务证券是向其他实体提供贷款的一种形式，包括联邦或市政证券、商业票据、公司债券、负债证券化和可转换债券。根据 SFAS 115 号公告，债务证券的分类如下：

- 持有至到期（是指企业有能力和意图持有至到期）。采用摊销成本计价（取得成本加上／减去来摊销的溢价或折价），因此不需要确认未实现的持有损益。
- 交易性的（可望近期出售的）。采用公允价值计量，未实现的持有损益在净利润中确认。
- 可供出售的（除前两项以外的其他情况）。采用公允价值计量，未实现的持有损益作为其他全面收益（作为所有者权益的一个独立组成部分）确认。

SFAS 第 115 号公告要求在分类资产负债表中，企业要单独报告持有至到期、可供出售的和交易性的证券，根据它们是否可望在一年内或一个经营周期内转换成现金来判断其属于流动资产还是非流动资产。（注意，SFAS 第 115 号公告的第 17 段关于证券的分类在 SFAS 的 135 号公告的第 4 段 t（2）中进行了修改。）对于可供出售的和持有至到期的证券，需要披露公允价值总额、未实现持有损益和摊销成本。

将交易性的和可供出售的证券投资组合根据市值进行调整时，需要对该投资账户的进行估价备抵（相反或附属账户）。在资产负债表日，调整估价备抵使投资账户（成本）和估价备抵之和等于其公允价值。作为调整分录的另一方，未实现损益可以记入借方或贷方。当出售证券时，将成本转出投资账户，确认实现的损益。

持有至到期的证券

由于权益证券没有到期日，故只有债务证券才能持有至到期。报告企业必须具有明显意图和能力（财务灵活性和风险容忍度）将投资持有至到期。

SFAS 第 115 号公告列出了该规则的几条例外情况，在证据表明企业没有意图将证券持有至到期的情况下，允许企业出售特定证券。相关证据包括被投资方信用等级降低、税法规定债务证券的利息收入必须交税。

当证券持有人的意图仅仅是无限期地持有该证券或其意图是为了应对市场利率的

波动或证券提前偿付风险而出售该证券，或是为了流动性、收益率、其他投资、融资或外币风险而出售该证券时，该债务证券就不应归类为持有至到期的投资。

除了上述例外，通常不会出售持有至到期的证券投资。根据 SFAS 第 115 号公告，在出售该债务证券投资时，"应在经营期内各期财务报告附注中披露出售或转让证券的摊销成本、已实现或未实现的损益和导致决定出售或转让证券的原因。"

和前面所讨论的应收票据一样，如果有未摊销的折价或溢价，那么应从证券取得成本中减去未摊销折价或加上未摊销溢价以得到当前的证券价值。并不确认未实现的损益，因为资产并不是以公允价值计量。与应收票据相似，同样采用有效利率法来计算利息。可以参见之前应收票据中的案例（图表 2－98）。

交易性的证券

交易性的证券指在通过短期价格变动产生收益而在短期内将其出售的证券。由于这些证券将在短期内被出售，交易性证券以公允价值确认而未实现的持有损益将包含在净利润中。公允价值在资产负债表日确定。在证券取得日，该证券以其成本计量，包括佣金、收费和税金。在以后持有期间的每个财务报告日，该证券都要以公允价值计量。股利或利息收入也要确认，但是未收到的将单独确认为应收款项。

图表 2－120 反映了包含成本、公允价值和未实现损益（反映成本和公允价值的差异）的某种债务证券投资组合。

图表 2－120　证券公允价值计算调整

交易性债务证券投资组合 12 月 31 日			
投资	成本	公允价值	未实现的损益
持有 X 公司 12% 的债券	$54 386	$64 860	$10 474
持有 Y 公司 10% 的债券	228 445	216 248	(12 197)
持有 Z 公司 8% 的债券	107 086	114 600	7 514
投资组合总额	$389 917	$395 708	5 791
调整前证券的公允价值			(3 201)
调整证券公允价值—借方			$2 590

可供出售的证券

可供出售的证券包括不属于交易性和持有至到期这两个类别的其他所有证券，例如没有明确目的或没有确定到期日的证券并且没有活跃的交易以利用暂时的市场价格差异。这些证券以公允价值计量，且取得时的成本与公允价值之间的差异计入未实现损益。为了减少净利润的不稳定性，在出售实现的那天之前，未实现的损益将作为所有者权益的一个独立组成部分记录在其他全面收益中。

图表 2－121 反映了如何根据公允价值调整证券价值。该例假设以前年度未实现损失为 $14 257。由于本年年末未实现损失为 $12 000，比前年减少 $2 257，因此要确认未实现利得。

图表 2 - 121　可供出售证券公允价值调整计算

可供出售的债务证券投资组合 12 月 31 日			
投资	摊销成本	公允价值	未实现的损益
持有 X 公司 10% 债券	$300 000	$288 000	$(12 000)
以前公允价值调整余额—贷方			(14 257)
调整证券公允价值—借方			$2 257

图表 2 - 121 中可供出售的证券可在资产负债表和损益表中进行反映，如图表 2 - 122 所示（损益表中包含本年出售证券的损失 $6 212）。

图表 2 - 122　资产负债表和损益表对可供出售证券的反映情况

资产负债表	
流动资产	
应收利息	$ xxx
投资	
可供出售的证券，公允价值计量	$288 000
所有者权益	
累计其他全面损失	$12 000
损益表	
其他收入和利得	
利息收入	$ xxx
其他费用和损失	
出售证券损失	$6 212

权益证券

如果说债务证券主要用于保全资本、增加收益的话，那么权益证券就主要是为了获得另一个实体的所有权利益。权益证券包括普通股、优先股、其他股本和以约定的价格买进或卖出所有者权益的权利（认股权证股票期权和权利）。

权益证券不包括可转换债券或可赎回优先股。在初始取得时，以取得成本加上支付的经纪费和其他费用作为初始确认金额。

当股票投资者获得投资收益时，其所拥有的持股比例决定了投资方应采用何种会计方法来确认投资。

- 持股比例小于20%（被动收益）：投资者采用公允价值法。
- 持股比例大于20%，小于50%（重大影响）：投资方采用权益法。
- 持股比例大于50%（完全控制）：投资方应合并财务报表。

持股比例小于20%

当权益投资持股比例小于被投资方所有者权益的20%时，与债务证券相同，应将其分类为可供出售的权益证券和交易性权益证券（由于权益证券没有到期日，因此没有持有至到期日这种类型）。当投资方持股比例小于20%时，其对被投资方的影响就很小或几乎没有。若投资方持股比例小于20%，但对被投资方有重大影响，就应采用权益法（参见后面的持股比例在20%与50%之间的情形）。

如果持股比例小于20%，在初始取得时，将取得成本包括交易费用计入初始成本，并在每个资产负债表日以公允价值报告。通过非现金交易取得的证券（如通过提供劳务或土地等形式）以非现金资产的公允价值或所收到的证券的公允价值计量。如果两种公允价值都无法取得，就需要采用估计。

可供出售的证券投资组合。被投资者公布的现金股利作为投资者的收入。证券按成本进行初始记录。在每个资产负债表日，投资组合按公允价值计价，其中未实现净损益的计算见图表 2 – 123。

图表 2 – 123　证券公允价值调整计算

投资	成本	公允价值	未实现损益
	可供销售的权益证券投资组合 12 月 31 日		
X 公司	$228 536	$242 000	$13 464
Y 公司	279 400	267 520	(11 880)
Z 公司	124 388	91 520	(32 868)
投资组合合计	$632 324	$601 040	(31 284)
调整前证券公允价值			1 000
调整证券公允价值——贷方			$(30 284)

投资组合中包含的未实现净损益计入其他全面收益，并作为股东权益的组成部分（累计其他全面收益）。通过估价备抵（证券公允价值调整）调整该投资组合并记录未实现损失的具体分录，如图表 2 – 124 所示。

图表 2 – 124　证券公允价值调整日记账分录

未实现持有损益—权益	$30 284	
证券公允价值调整（可供出售）		$30 284

当投资组合中有股票售出时，已实现损益通过从销售净额中扣除购置成本来计算。出售日已实现利得的会计分录见图表 2 – 125。

图表 2 – 125　证券销售已实现利得的会计分录

现金	$10 000	
可供出售证券		$4 000
股票出售利得		$6 000

当证券售出时，已实现损益要作记录。年中销售或购买证券将改变投资账户的成本基础。企业通常在年终将投资组合的未实现净损益作为整体计算。若该年度内有可供出售的证券出售，为避免重复计算损益应进行重分类调整。这些调整将在稍后讨论。

交易性证券。交易性证券的计算与可供销售证券的计算基本相同，但交易性证券中未实现持有损益计入净收入而不是其他全面收益。未实现损益以及转让时发生的损益一并在损益表中确认。

持股比例大于 20% 小于 50%

根据 APB 第 18 号意见，当投资方可以对被投资方的日常经营和财务政策产生重大影响时，就应采用权益法。"重大影响"并不局限于至少要持股 20%，还要关注董事会成员中投资方拥有的席位，以及公司间重要的关联方交易情况等因素。

但是，除非有其他证据表明情况相反，否则当投资方持股比例大于 20% 时就应当被认为有重大影响。如果出现下列情况，即使拥有被投资方 20% 以上的股份，也不能认为具有重大影响（根据 FASB 第 35 号公告）：

- 投资双方签订协议，投资方放弃行使某些重大权利。
- 被投资方反对，如诉讼或其他情况。
- 被投资方股权集中于某一集团中，而投资方的意见不被留意。
- 投资方在董事会中没有表决权。
- 投资方不能获得采用权益法的相关数据。

当持股比例大于 50% 时就意味着完全控制。因此就要求投资方不仅采用权益法，还要合并被投资方的财务报表。

权益法。在权益法下，应将取得成本加上相关收费作为投资初始成本。在持有期间，应当按照应享有或应分担被投资单位实现净利润或发生净亏损的份额，调整投资账面价值。当被投资方发放或宣告发放股利时再调减其账户金额。将持股比例乘以被投资方报告净损益就得出投资方应享有被投资方实现净损益的份额，并调增或调减以市场价值确认的投资账户。权益法假设这两个实体之间具有实质性关联，因此投资方不仅要随着被投资方的盈利或亏损确认相应的收益或损失，而且还要将某些科目剔出投资方账户，以避免资产和负债的重复计量。

- 任何引起投资企业净利润变动的关联方交易都要剔出，调整投资企业的利润。
- 对被投资企业固定资产的公允价值和账面价值之间的差异部分所享有的份额应进行摊销。如果被投资企业资产不能由公允价值确认，则企业账面成本和取得价格之间的差异应作为商誉摊销。
- 对被投资方由于清算或会计政策累积影响而产生的非常项目（将在本节稍后讨论）所享有的份额应被当作投资方非常项目。

下面是一个投资企业权益投资的例子。假设某一投资企业投资 $20 000 000 占被投资企业 30% 的持股比例。在投资日，被投资企业的账面价值为 $50 000 000。购买价与按账面价值分享份额之间的差异是 $5 000 000（$20 000 000 减去 30% 乘以 $50 000 000 之积）。在该例中，其差异分别是商誉（$2 500 000）、有限期无形资产（$1 500 000）、被投资方资产被低估的价值（$1 000 000）。无形资产应该在五年内摊销，资产在十年内计提折旧。

被投资企业公告财务报告的年末，投资方必须对正常和超常收益进行确认。（假设被投资企业年净利润为 $4 600 000，包括 $600 000 的非常损失。）宣告发放股利 $1 400 000。最后，购买价超出部分的折旧与摊销也应该确认。企业在年末时的情况见图表 2 – 216。

图表 2 – 126　会计年末企业采用权益法下的投资确认

借：投资于 X 公司股票	$1 380 000	
投资损失（非常损失）	$180 000	
贷：投资收益（正常收益）		$1 560 000

［确认对 X 公司净利润的享有份额（$4 600 000×0.3）和非常损失（$600 000×0.3）］

借：现金	$420 000	
贷：投资于 X 公司股票		$420 000

［确认从 X 公司分得的股利（$1 400 000×0.3）］

借：投资收益（正常收益）	$400 000	
贷：投资于 X 公司股票		$400 000

确认超出以下账面价值的投资成本的摊销

被低估可折旧资产$\dfrac{\$1\,000\,000}{10}=\$100\,000$

未确认无形资产$\dfrac{\$1\,500\,000}{5}=\$300\,000$

总额 = $400 000

投资的账面金额计算如图表 2 – 127 所示（假设 6 月宣告发放股利 $700 000，公司将确认 30% 的份额即 $210 000）。

图表 2 – 127　投资的账面金额计算

取得成本，1 月 1 日	$20 000 000	
加：在分红或摊销前享有的利润份额	1 380 000	21 380 000
减：		
应收股利（6 月 30 日和 12 月 31 日）	(630 000)	
被低估的可折旧资产的摊销	(100 000)	
未确认无形资产的摊销	(300 000)	(1 030 000)
到期值，12 月 31 日		$20 350 000

持股比例大于50%

一旦企业拥有被投资方大于 50% 的股权，就能完全控制被投资企业的经营状况，但每个企业都要进行独立的会计核算。期间报告采用权益法，并将投资作为长期投资。在会计年末，母公司就要合并各子公司的会计报表。在合并报表中，为避免重复计量，投资账户要进行抵销，变成相应资产和子公司的负债。合并会计报表将整个企业集团视为一个会计主体。在此不对合并财务报表进行详细说明。

购买法。当某一企业通过并购、收购、法定合并等形式获得另一方大于 50% 的股权时，根据 GAAP 的要求应当采用购买法确认。在购买法下，从被合并方取得的资产（股票、现金、负债、其他财产）都应以公允价值确认。取得成本中应包括交易收费（如审计费或佣金）。购买法要求被并购企业的净资产在合并报表中以公允价值确认，而购买价格与被并购企业净资产公允价值的差异确认为商誉。商誉是一种无形资产，企业需要在每年末对商誉进行资产减值测试，并对测试结果进行记录（GAAG 规定不再对商誉进行摊销）。

当并购以后被并购方仍然保留独立法人地位时，虽然该公司是并购方的子公司，但仍然保留其会计账簿。母公司将子公司的情况记录在其账簿的子公司投资账户里。

在持有期间，每一会计年度都要对其子公司投资账户进行调整。当其持股比例在
20%到50%之间时，母公司按权益法确认对子公司的投资。当母公司对子公司完全
控制时（通常持股比例大于50%）不仅要采用权益法还要编制合并财务报表。在权
益法下，投资账户应随着从子公司分回的收益而增加账面价值，随着子公司支付股利
而减少，并调整任何与公允价值变动有关而增加的费用。在成本法下，当相关投资价
值持续下降且预计不可恢复时，就应调整子公司投资账户。

例题：Acme Diversified 公司支付 $3 840 000 获得 Abco Inc. 公司 60% 的股权。图表
2-128 对比反映了企业在第一年采用成本法和权益法的差异。假设投资成本 $3 840 000
高于 Abco Inc. 公司账面价值 $480 000。其中 $240 000 确认为商誉，另外的 $240 000
确认为可折旧资产的公允价值高出账面价值的部分。（另外的 $240 000 在五年内摊
销，而商誉不能摊销。）并且，第一年，Abco 公司报告如下：

- 利润 $432 000
- 股利 $144 000

利润 $432 000 减去股利 $144 000 的差额 $288 000 是股利分配后的累计收益。

图表 2-128　成本法和权益法：母公司视角

成本法		权益法	
第 1 年		第 1 年	
投资于 Abco 公司　$3 840 000		投资于 Abco 公司　　$3 840 000	
现金	$3 840 000	现金	$3 840 000
记录初始投资		记录初始投资	
现金　　$86 400		对 Abco 的投资　　$259 200	
股利收益	$86 400	在子公司收益中的权益	$259 200
记录收到的股利（0.6 × $144 000）		记录在子公司收益中的权益（0.6 × $432 000）	
		在子公司收益中的权益　　$48 000	
		对 Abco 的投资	$48 000
		由于超额折旧而调整在子公司收益中的权益	
		（$240 000/5 年 = $48 000）	
		现金　　$86 400	
		对 Abco 的投资	$86 400
		记录收到的股利（0.6 × $144 000）	
		对 Abco 的投资	$86 400
		记录收到的股利（0.6 × $144 000）	

图表 2-129 显示在第 1 年里投资账户余额的确定。

图表 2-129　投资账户：成本法与权益法

第一年末的投资账户					
成本法		权益法			
第一年成本	$3 840 000	第一年成本	$3 840 000	第一年可折旧资产的摊销	$48 000
		第一年在子公司收益中的权益	$259 200	第一年宣布发放的股利	$86 400
第一年余额	$3 840 000	第一年余额	$3 964 800		

对上述两种方法的比较告诉我们什么？

• 应付的或宣告的股利在成本法下被确认为收入，但在权益法下则是作为投资的减少。

• 在权益法下被投资企业报告盈利会增加投资账户（资产账户），但是在成本法下不作任何记录。

• 在权益法下，收购过程中额外的资产的折旧费用会得到考虑，而在成本法下不会考虑这项费用。

财务报表陈述事项

在财务报表的陈述事项中，价值减值和重分类调整两个具体的事项对财务报表具有深远影响。

价值减值

投资者的投资常常会因为价值减值的出现而蒙受损失，并且这些损失是永久损失。所有的投资都必须通过价值重估来确定其是否出现价值减值。最为常见的价值减值事项包括破产以及投资对象的资产流动性减弱等。一旦价值损失被确认为永久性的，那么必须以此调整账面价值，重新确定资产价值，其价值减值就被认定为实现了的并且记入净利润。

价值减值的测试方式：

• 债务证券：确认投资者是否有可能无法按合同规定收回到期所有款项。

• 权益证券：如果股票的可变现净值低于账面价值，这时就需要考虑其公允价值低于投资成本的持续时间段、投资者为了投资公司的股票重新获利而拥有持有至到期投资的期限以及投资对象的未来前景。

例如可供出售证券中有一项损失在之前的报告中被确认为全面收益中的未实现损失，假设 $1 000 000 的债券中有 $100 000 的价值损失，如果这些损失由于属于永久性的损失需要被确认为已实现损失，那么所作分录如图表 2－130 所示（以可供出售债券为例）。

图表 2－130　由减值而确认的已实现损失

减值价值	$100 000	
可供出售证券—公允价值调整	$100 000	
未实现持有损益—权益		$100 000
可供出售证券		$100 000

所以，此债券投资新的账面价值为 $900 000。

重分类调整

可供出售证券的未实现损益包含在其他全面收益中。当债券被出售，已实现的收益在报告中属于净利润的一部分，如果不进行重分类调整则会出现重复确认。例如，一个投资者持有一年期的如图表 2－131 所示的股票投资组合。

图表 2 - 131　可供出售证券投资组合

投资项目	投资成本	公允价值	未实现持有损益
X 公司普通股	$98 400	$129 150	$30 750
Y 公司普通股	147 600	166 050	18 450
合计	$246 000	$295 200	49 200
过去公允价值调整余额			0
公允价值调整—借项			$49 200

　　投资者在这个时期的全面收益表中就会包括一年内的净持有利得，如图表 2 - 132 所示。

图表 2 - 132　全面收益表

Bounce 体育用品公司
全面收益表
第一年，截至 12 月 31 日

净利润	$430 500
其他全面收益	
期间持有利得	$49 200
全面收益	$479 700

　　X 公司的普通股票在第二年出售以后得到已实现利得 $30 750，并且在第二年末可供出售的证券投资组合如图表 2 - 133 所示。

图表 2 - 133　可供出售证券投资组合

投资项目	投资成本	公允价值	未实现持有损益
Y 公司普通股	$147 600	$190 000	$42 400
过去公允价值调整余额—借项			(49 200)
公允价值调整—贷项			$(6 800)

　　持有损益计算结果如图表 2 - 134 所示。

图表 2 - 134　总持有损益计算结果

未实现持有损益	$(6 800)
已实现持有收益	$30 750
总已确认持有收益	$23 950

　　全面收益表中包括 X 公司股票的未实现利得，已实现利得包括在第二年的净利润中。由于全面收益是净利润的组成部分，所以，第二年的全面收益表就需要进行重分类调整来消除已实现利得，如图表 2 - 135 所示。

图表 2–135 全面收益表

Bounce 体育用品公司
全面收益表
第二年，截至 12 月 31 日

净利润（包括 X 公司股票 $30 750 的已实现利得）		$885 600
其他全面收益		
期间持有利得（$190 000 – $166 050）	$23 950	
减：净利润中的利得重分类调整	(30 750)	(6 800)
全面收益		$878 800

财产、厂房及设备（PP&E）

财产、厂房及设备（PP&E）包括所有的长期保持原有的实物形态的资产，如土地、办公室、零售场所、工厂、仓库、设备、机器以及交通工具。

财产、厂房及设备（PP&E）的主要特征

资产必须符合以下三个特征才能被确认为财产、厂房及设备（PP&E）：

• 持有该项资产是为了供本公司所用，而不是用于再出售。

持有财产、厂房及设备（PP&E）的目的是供本公司所用，那些因投资或者再出售而被持有的资产不能被确认为财产、厂房及设备（PP&E）。例如，空置建筑就被归类为其他投资，而不属于财产、厂房及设备（PP&E）。

• 该资产长期保持原有的实物形态，除土地之外，该资产需要计提折旧。

财产、厂房及设备（PP&E）能够在未来很长一段时间为企业带来相关的经济利益流入。根据配比原则，在财产、厂房及设备（PP&E）的使用寿命内，按照确定的方法对应计折旧额进行系统分摊。土地一般不会出现减值，不需计提折旧（但在某些特殊情况下，会出现价值减值）。

• 该资产必须是实物形态的。

属于财产、厂房及设备（PP&E）的资产必须具有实物形态，与之相比，无形资产如著作权和专利权就不具备实物形态。

财产、厂房及设备（PP&E）的计价基础

历史成本或购置成本是财产、厂房及设备（PP&E）的计价基础。本部分将讨论与土地、建筑、设备和自行建造的固定资产的成本计量相关的事项。

历史成本

历史成本是通过购置或建造资产所支付的现金或现金等价物来计量的，它包括运输费、安装费、税金和相关成本。不管是财产、厂房及设备（PP&E）还是存货，确认其成本的通用方法是购置以及让其达到预定可使用状态的相关成本都应该计入成本。

在资产购置当天，资产的历史成本和其公允价值相等。购置完成以后，资产的公允价值变化在账目中不用确认（出现价值减值时才予以确认）。一些会计人员认为，

公允价值的计量比历史成本的计量更具相关性。但是，也有人担心公允价值的可靠性。因此，在一般公认会计原则（GAAP）中规定，考虑到可靠性原则，财产、厂房及设备（PP&E）的价值都是通过摊销历史成本来计量的。如工厂未来潜在的由增加或者改善资产而产生的成本就必须计入其成本，与此不同的是，这些资产的例行维修费用和维护费用直接计入当期损益。

土地成本

土地成本包括：

- 购买价款。
- 成交价，包括物权转让价格、佣金、律师费、应交税金和保险费。
- 整地费用，包括土地评价、灌压、爆破、下水道、拆迁（扣除施救收益后的净值）、皆伐等。
- 调查成本。
- 留置权、抵押等或有支出项。

在城市改良中，由政府长期出资进行维护的下水道和路灯的公共项目的特别估价费用都计入土地成本。而暂时的针对私人设施的改良，例如车道和栅栏的改良支出往往记入几个分开的土地账户，在改良以后的有效期内进行摊销。因为投机目的而持有土地一般被认为是投资，而开发商用于再出售而持有的土地被划分为存货。

建筑成本

建筑成本包括购买或者建造的所有成本，其中含设计费、建房许可证、材料、人工以及间接费用等。如果拆除旧有的建筑用于建造新的建筑，那么旧有建筑的成本会被作为土地成本（建筑用地）的一部分，而不是作为新建筑成本的一部分。

设备成本

设备成本包括所有的购买价款、装运费用、准备设备安置地点以及安装费用等。例如，为设备选择安装地而产生的费用属于设备成本的一部分。设备包括办公设备、机器、运输器材、家具、装置器具以及其他类似的固定资产。

自建资产成本

与许多将建筑工程外包的企业不同，电信、铁路、电力工业等行业的企业更倾向于自建资产。在这种缺乏外部购买价格的情况下，自建资产的成本很难确定。实体必将成本和费用仔细地分配到经营活动和建造活动中去，以此来确定资产的成本。

分配直接建造成本很简单，如材料费和直接人工费用的分配。理论上，间接成本的处理方法截然不同，如保险费、财产税、电费、固定资产折旧以及工厂管理人员薪水等的处理，而在实际工作中，这些管理费用一般都分配在自建资产里面。然而，有些会计人员对此有不同见解，他们认为不管自建工程处于何种状态（施工中、停工状态），这些管理费用都会发生。任何成本的发生导致资产的价值高于市场价值的话，就要资本化；反之就被确认为损失。

建造或购置财产、厂房及设备（PP&E）时对利息成本的会计处理

理论上，财产、厂房及设备（PP&E）建造期间所涉及的利息成本的资本化可以用以下三种方法处理：

- 只将实际发生于自建时期的利息成本资本化。

这是一般公认会计原则（GAAP）提出的要求，对此很少有例外。原因是，它使用历史成本原则，这一原则只记录那些属于建造过程中的实际成本组成部分的实质性交易。在公认会计原则（GAAP）下，资本化利息总量的计量是建立在资产建造期间实际发生的较低的利息总量基础上的，或者是那些资产建造费用未发生时，可以避免的利息支出的总额基础上的。

- 建造期利息费用不资本化。

这一观点的支持者提出，公司一旦全部使用其权益资产，而不是负债来进行资产建造，那么就不会发生利息成本。因此，利息成本与其被确认为建造成本还不如确认为财务费用。但是，除非这些相关利息成本都是非实质性的，否则这一观点并不会在GAAP下被接受。

- 资产建造中产生的所有利息成本都应资本化，不管它是否能够被特别确认。

有人指出，不管是使用债务融资还是权益融资，资产建造的机会成本一直都存在，应当确认为资产建造的成本。但是，机会成本只是一个主观尺度，并不适用于历史成本计量方法，也不适用于GAAP。

非货币交换

非货币性资产交换（如存货或财产、厂房及设备（PP&E）的交换）只要存在商业实质，都是在公允价值基础上进行记录。商业实质是指交换会改变企业未来现金流量的时间、金额。未来现金流量变化很可能是由于交换资产不同（存货与设备交换）或者交换资产类似（卡车与卡车交换）但预期使用寿命不同两方面原因造成的。换句话说，如果两个交换实体在交换后具有不同的商业价值，那么这个交易就具有商业实质。如果未来现金流量并不存在明显变化，那么这个交易就不具有商业实质，应以账面价值入账，不确认损益。

具有商业实质交换的会计处理：确认利得

在非货币性资产交换中获得的资产的计量基础是换出资产的公允价值。如果有确凿证据表明换得资产的公允价值更加可靠，应以换入资产公允价值作为基础确认。图表2-136计算了用车队换仓库时所确认的利得。

图表2-136　轿车的公允价值以及交换利得

轿车的公允价值		$147 000
轿车成本	$192 000	
减：累计折旧	66 000	
账面价值		126 000
处置汽车的利得		$21 000

仓库的价值应以 $147 000 入账，这是换出资产轿车的公允价值。汽车以及相关累计折旧可以注销，$21 000 作为交换利得记录入账。

具有商业实质交换的会计处理：确认损失

这种情况在图表 2 - 137 和图表 2 - 138 中进行说明。例子中假设一公司通过支付现金和旧机器 A 获得了报价为 $25 000 的新机器 B。与新旧机器相关的未来现金流量表明此项交易具有商业实质。旧设备的初始价格为 $18 000，其中包括 $8 000 的累计折旧。经确认，旧设备的公允价值为 $7 000，但合同中的旧货换新折让为 $12 000。

图表 2 - 137　新机器成本

新机器报价	$25 000
减：旧货换新折让	12 000
支付现金	13 000
旧机器公允价值	7 000
新机器成本	$20 000

相关会计分录如图表 2 - 138 所示：

图表 2 - 138　交换的会计分录

机器 B	$20 000	
累计折旧—机器 B	$8 000	
处置损失	$3 000	
[公允价值—账面价值：$7 000—$10 000]		
机器 A		$18 000
现金		$13 000

不具有商业实质的非货币性资产交换的会计处理

当公司在交换以后的经济状况同交换以前无异，换入资产的成本应以换出资产的账面价值入账，并且不确认损益。为了说明这种情况，假设 A 公司用铁冲压机器交换 B 公司的钢冲压机器。

A 公司的铁冲压机器：
- 公允价值 $112 000
- 账面价值 $94 500（成本 $105 000 减去累计折旧 $10 500）

B 公司的钢冲压机器：
- 公允价值 $119 000
- 账面价值 $95 200（成本 $140 000 减去累计折旧 $44 800）

A 公司还向 B 公司支付了 $7 000 的现金。对 A 公司来讲，在交换中未实现的利得如图表 2 - 139 所示。

图表2 – 139　计算利得（未确认）

铁冲压机器的公允价值	$112 000
铁冲压机器的账面价值	94 500
总利得（未确认）	$17 500

由于预计新机器带来的未来现金流量与旧机器相似，所以这个交易被认为不具有商业实质。这就导致旧机器的处置总利得被递延。新机器入账基础可以基于换出资产的账面价值或者是换入资产的公允价值减去延期的处置利得，如图表2 – 140 所示。

图表2 – 140　钢冲压机器的成本基础

账面价值法		公允价值法	
铁冲压机器的账面价值	$94 500	钢冲压机器的公允价值	$119 000
支付现金	7 000	减：递延利得	(17 500)
钢冲压机器的成本基础	$101 500	钢冲压机器的成本基础	$101 500

公司 A 的这笔资产交换分录如图表2 – 141 所示：

图表2 – 141　公司 A 的资产交换会计分录

钢冲压机器	$101 500	
累计折旧—机器	$10 500	
铁冲压机器		$105 000
现金		$7 000

如果钢冲压机器随后被出售给另一方，则递延利得将被确认。

非货币交换应在财务报表的附注中予以披露。披露内容包括该交易的性质、所使用的会计方法以及任何已确认的损益。

利用证券发行购置的 PP&E

如果利用发行股票或其他证券的形式购置财产、厂房及设备等资产，证券的面值将不足以度量这些资产的真实成本。相反如果证券在市场中交易活跃，则可以采用证券的当前市值来度量财产、厂房及设备的真实成本。相反，如果因为证券不存在活跃的交易市场而无法确定证券的价值，则应估计证券的市场价值，并以此价值为基础记录财产、厂房及设备的价值和证券发行。

下面举例说明证券存在活跃交易时的利用证券发行购置财产、厂房及设备。Acme 公司希望建造一栋高级公寓，并从 Robin 制造公司手中购买了一个仓库，仓库购买用发行 10 000 股面值为 1 美元的普通股融资，该普通股当前的交易价格为每股 20 美元。则 Acme 公司的会计分录如图表2 – 142 所示。

图表2 – 142　Acme 公司的会计分录

股票的市场价值（10 000 股 × $20/股）	$200 000	
普通股		$10 000
资本公积		$190 000

购置后成本的会计处理

财产、厂房及设备购置后的成本可以被资本化，也可以计为经营支出中的费用。将成本资本化（记入资产账户）的前提条件是，该项成本所提供的未来经济收益高于现有资产预期提供的经济收益。未来的经济收益包括：

- 延长资产的寿命。
- 提高资产的生产率，比如改善产品质量或增大产品数量。

资产扩建、改进及重置现有资产、重新安装或重新安排现有资产以及资产的修理等都具有特别的会计含义。

资产扩建

资产扩建应被资本化，因为资产扩建实际上带来了新的资产。如果资产扩建导致对现有资产结构的修正，修正成本也应被资本化，但前提条件是在设计现有结构时就计划好了资产的扩建，否则修正成本应计入费用或损失。

改进及重置现有资产

改进是用更有效的资产替代现有资产，重置是用更新的相同资产取代老化的资产。改进及重置都应被资本化。这一资本化可以采用三种会计处理方法，即替代法、资本化新成本以及将成本计为累计折旧。

- **替代法**

如果被取代资产的账面价值已知，这时就可以采用替代法，即从资产账户中剔除旧资产的账面价值并记入新资产的价值。假设用新锅炉取代旧锅炉。旧锅炉的残值为 $300，当前账面价值为 $4 500 即用初始账面价值 $45 000 减去累计折旧 $40 500。新锅炉的成本为 $37 500。则替代法下的会计分录如图表 2-143 所示。

图表 2-143　替代法下的会计分录

新锅炉	$37 500	
累计折旧—旧锅炉	$40 500	
旧锅炉的处置损失（$4 500 - $300）	$4 200	
旧锅炉		$45 000
现金（$37 500 - $300）		$37 200

- **资本化新成本**

改进经常通过资本化新项目的成本而不冲销原有项目的账面价值来处理，前提条件是旧项目有足够多的折旧以至于其账面价值接近于零。

- **将成本计为累计折旧**

如果某种资产的质量或数量没有被改进但其使用寿命被延长了，则相关成本通过累计折旧记入借方，因为先前账面价值的减值被恢复了。这样的会计处理将延长资产可进行折旧的期间。

重新安装或重新安排现有资产

资产从一个地方移到另一个地方，这个过程需要在受益期内资本化和费用化。如果某些相关成本不能与其他运营收益分开或者没有实质内容，这些成本应立即被费用化。

修理

修理的目的是为了保持资产的正常运行水平，它应该在发生期间归集到成本账户上。如果所有的修理都发生在某个特定期间而受益期是整个年度，在这种情况下有时会运用一个修理预提账户。例如，假设某公司估计它在本年将需要花费 $1 000 000 用于修理，并把这些成本平均分摊到四个季度里。确切的修理支出发生在第二季度（$52 000），第三季度（$256 000），第四季度（$235 000）。每个季度的会计处理如图表2-144所示。

图表2-144 修理费用账户的会计分录

第1季度末

修理费用		$250 000
预提修理费用 $\left(\dfrac{\$1\,000\,000}{4}\right)$		$250 000

第2季度末

预提修理费用		$520 000
现金、应付职工薪酬、存货等		$520 000
修理费用		$250 000
预提修理费用 $\left(\dfrac{\$1\,000\,000}{4}\right)$		$250 000

第3季度末

预提修理费用		$256 000
现金、应付职工薪酬、存货等		$256 000
修理费用		$250 000
预提修理费用 $\left(\dfrac{\$1\,000\,000}{4}\right)$		$250 000

第4季度末

预提修理费用		$235 000
现金、应付职工薪酬、存货等		$235 000
修理费用		$261 000
预提修理费用		$261 000
$[\$520\,000 + \$256\,000 + \$235\,000 - (\$250\,000 \times 3)]$		

在年末，预提修理费用账户必须结平，因此任何账户余额应转入修理费用账户。在期中时，预提修理费用账户应作为 PP&E 账户的抵减账户列报。

折旧

折旧是一种会计处理方法，它是在资产受益期内分摊有形资产的成本。因为折旧是一种成本分摊方法，而不是资产估价方法，所以某个项目的公允价值一般和折旧后的账面价值无关。对于自然资源和无形资产，用"损耗"和"摊销"代替折旧。

为了计量折旧，必须确认以下内容

- 可折旧基础。
- 使用寿命。
- 折旧方法。

一项资产的可折旧基础是指它的初始成本减去它的残留（或剩余）价值，残值是资产经济寿命末的估计价值。资产的经济使用寿命可能短于它的实际物理寿命，因为，比如，它可能被预计在它真正报废之前变得过时。一个造纸厂可能会停止使用一件老的但是还能正常运转的造纸机是因为最新的机器生产纸显得更有效率也更便宜。

当资产在年中被购买或售出，应先算出一年的折旧费用然后按比例分摊到这种发生在年中的情况（比如，一项资产的全年折旧额是 \$120 000，该资产在 4 月 1 日购买，则当年的折旧额为 $9/12 \times \$120\,000 = \$90\,000$）。

考虑两种折旧方法，一是基于预期使用量（作业法），二是基于预期使用年限（直线法、年限总和法、双倍余额递减法）。年限总和法和双倍余额递减法也称为加速折旧法，因为使用这两种方法的结果将导致资产使用前期折旧额高而在资产使用后期折旧额低。

作为比较，选取同一种资产但使用不同的折旧法：一台塑料压制机的成本是 \$1 000 000，它的残值是 \$150 000，它预计的工作量为生产 70 000 单位产品或者预计的使用寿命是 7 年。

作业法

作业法（也称为变动成本法、产量法、产出法），它不是根据经过的时间来对资产折旧而是通过资产的使用量或产出单位来折旧。比如使用的小时数或者生产出的产品数，或者资产生产所要耗费的资源数。产出量指标能更紧密地联系成本和使用，该指标如果能很容易地确定，就应使用这种方法。

一年的折旧费用的计算方法如下：

$$\text{年折旧额} = \frac{\text{折旧基础} \times \text{产量单位或使用工时}}{\text{资产生命期内的总产量或总的使用工时}}$$

如果这台塑料压制机在第一年的实际产量是 9 500 单位，它的可折旧基础是（扣除残值）是 \$850 000，则第一年的折旧费用的计算如下：

$$\frac{\$850\,000 \times 9\,500}{70\,000} = \$115\,357.14$$

工作量法适合用于机器设备和运输工具，但它不用于建筑物，因为建筑物的折旧主要与时间有关而一般与使用无关。工作量法使资产在使用强度低的时候折旧费用低而在使用强度高的时候折旧费用高，因此能有效地匹配资产的成本和它带来的收入，使得资产的效用下降依赖于使用量。因此，工作量法被一般公认会计原则（GAAP）认为是在资产因耗用或使用而折旧的情况下最好的方法。

直线法

直线法折旧比较简单，所以被广泛使用。当过时成为折旧的主要原因时，这种在每个时期平均分摊折旧额的基于时间的方法在理论上最为适当。它也最适合于在整个使用寿命期都能一贯地产生收益的资产。

折旧的计算方法如下：

$$年折旧额 = \frac{折旧基础}{估计使用年限}$$

结合上面的例子，这种方法的计算结果是：

$$年折旧额 = \frac{\$850\ 000}{7} = \$121\ 428.57$$

这种方法的一个缺陷是它基于一个不真实的假设：资产的使用效用在每一年都是一样的并且每年的维修成本也是一样的。随着折旧不断减少资产的账面价值，如果在资产的使用过程中产生的收入在每年都是稳定的话，则资产的回报率将持续上升。

加速折旧法

加速折旧法或递减折旧费用法是指对一项资产的折旧在前期多些并且越到资产使用的后期越少。这种方法的依据是：资产在它使用的最初几年里消耗掉了它的大部分价值而维修费用会在整个寿命期间逐渐提高。当维修费用提高的同时而折旧费用减少，因此整个资产的相关费用会得到平滑。这种方法也通常在这种情况下被广泛接受：一类资产，它在前期产生的收益多于后期。

因为折旧是一种非付现成本，它减少一个公司的营业收入相应地减少了公司的税收负担。因此，采用在资产使用期的前期确认较多的折旧费用将减少较早的税收负担，这样就会在早期产生一个比较好的现金流量。

- **年限总和法**

年限总和法使用折旧基础（扣除残值）然后乘以一个逐年减少的因子。这个因子的确定如下所示：

$$折旧因子 = \frac{剩余使用年限}{所有使用年限之和}$$

$$7 年中的第一年 = \frac{7}{7+6+5+4+3+2+1} = \frac{7}{28}$$

$$所有的使用寿命加总 = \frac{n(n+1)}{2} = \frac{7(7+1)}{2} = 28$$

（n = 总使用年限）

图表 2 - 145 展示了年限总和法的应用（说明：为了避免小数问题，折旧费用的计算是用折旧基础去乘以折旧因子的分子，然后除以折旧因子的分母。结果用美元列示）。

图表2-145 年限总和法

年数	折旧基础	剩余年数	折旧因子	折旧费用	年终账面余额
					$1 000 000 *
1	$850 000	7	7/28	$212 500	$787 500
2	$850 000	6	6/28	$182 143	$605 357
3	$850 000	5	5/28	$151 786	$453 571
4	$850 000	4	4/28	$121 429	$332 142
5	$850 000	3	3/28	$91 071	$241 071
6	$850 000	2	2/28	$60 714	$180 357
7	$850 000	1	1/28	$30 357	$150 000 **
合计		28	28/28	$850 000	

* =购买日的账面价值（即成本）

** =残值，最后的账面价值总是等于残值

- **余额递减法**

双倍余额递减法需要运用到直线法折旧率的一定百分比。在直线法下，一项使用寿命为10年的资产的折旧率为每年10%（1/10）；而双倍余额递减法通常是用150%或者200%的直线法下的折旧率。（在后面的这种情况下，又称之为双倍余额递减法）

双倍余额递减法下的折旧计算基础是资产的账面价值且不考虑残值（形成对比的是其他方法的折旧计算基础是可折旧基础或者扣除了残值后的成本）。随着资产的账面价值不断减小，持续使用不变的折旧率将导致越来越低的折旧额。

例如，一台使用寿命为7年的塑料压制机，它的直线法折旧率应该是1/7，或者是每年14.29%。如果使用150%的余额递减法，折旧率将是 $1/7 \times 1.5 = 1.5/7 = 21.4\%$。双倍余额递减法应该是 $1/7 \times 2 = 2/7 = 28.57\%$。

图表2-146展示了150%余额递减法和双倍余额递减法。注意到一旦达到资产的残值点，折旧即停止。结果，在150%的余额递减法下将多一年折旧期，而在双倍余额递减法下会提前一年结束折旧。

图表2-146 余额递减法

年数	资产的期初账面价值	折旧率	折旧费用	资产的期末价值
Bounce 体育用品公司 余额递减法				
150%余额递减法				
1	$1 000 000	21.43%	$214 300	$785 700
2	785 700	21.43%	168 376	617 324
3	617 324	21.43%	132 293	485 031
4	485 031	21.43%	103 942	381 089
5	381 089	21.43%	81 667	299 422
6	299 422	21.43%	64 166	235 256
7	235 256	21.43%	50 415	184 841
8	184 841	21.43%	34 841 *	150 000 **
			$850 000	

* 折旧费用在第8年应该是 $39 611，但被减少到使其能得到残值 $150 000

续表

Bounce 体育用品公司 余额递减法				
年数	资产的期初账面价值	折旧率	折旧费用	资产的期末价值
双倍余额递减法				
1	$1 000 000	28.57%	$285 000	$714 300
2	714 300	28.57%	204 076	510 224
3	510 224	28.57%	145 771	364 453
4	364 453	28.57%	104 124	260 329
5	260 329	28.57%	74 376	185 953
6	185 953	28.57%	35 953 *	150 000 *
7	—		—	
			$850 000	

* 折旧费用在第 6 年应该是 $53 127，但被减少到使其能得到残值 $150 000

为了保证资产不被折旧到其残值以下，以及能够在最初的折旧表上完成折旧，一些公司在资产使用寿命的末期将折旧法改成直线法。比如，以 150% 余额递减法的第 5 年为例，此时账面价值是 $299 422，折旧基础是 $299 422 - $150 000 = $149 422。此时资产还剩两年的使用寿命，因此 $149 422/2 = $74 711 被记为第 6 年和第 7 年的折旧额。

分类和综合法

分类和综合折旧法是一种替代方法，它将一组需要折旧的资产通过加权平均分配它们的服务，并视同一项资产对这组资产进行折旧。因为这是一个合计数，当其中的一项资产被处置掉，它自身的损益将不会被确认，而是将其净损益计入到累积的折旧中。分类法适用于相同的资产，综合法适用于不同的资产。

两种方法都使用同一个公式：

$$折旧率 = \frac{所有资产按直接法折旧额之和}{所有资产成本}$$

折旧费用 = 折旧率 × 资产组的总成本或综合成本

选择折旧方法

公司可以为不同类别的资产选择不同的折旧方法。比如，建筑物在它的使用期提供持续的经济利益，因此应选用直线法；而一些设备在最初几年的效用更大则应使用余额递减法。

图表 2 - 147 比较了不同的折旧方法，并注明了它们对折旧费用、营运收入、所得税以及负债、资产的影响。直线法作为一种基础方法，其他方法和直线法进行比较。

注意这个比较是针对一项资产，但如果这个方法应用于所有资产的话，对于整个公司而言，会得到类似的结果。同样需要注意的是工作量法没被使用，原因是如果产量或耗用量与其预期价值相匹配，这样会和直线法产生的折旧额相同。（当它们不能匹配时，每个公司将出现不同的结果）

图表 2 -147　不同折旧方法与直线法作比较

影响 \ 方法	直线法	年数总和法	150% 余额递减法	双倍余额递减法
折旧费用				
在第 1 年	$121 429	$212 500	$214 300	$285 700
在第 7 年	$121 429	$30 357	$50 415	$0
对营运收入的影响				
在第 1 年	—	↓ $91 071	↓ $92 871	↓ $164 271
在第 7 年	—	↑ $91 072	↑ $71 014	↑ $121 429
对所得税的影响 40%				
在第 1 年	—	↓ $36 428	↓ $37 148	↓ $65 708
在第 7 年	—	↑ $36 429	↑ $28 406	↑ $48 571
对资产的影响				
在第 1 年	—	↓ $91 071	↓ $92 871	↓ $164 271
在第 7 年	—	↑ $91 072	↑ $71 014	↑ $121 429

考虑到税收政策，公司在计算折旧时通常参照美国国内税务署（IRS）的修正加速成本回收体系（MACRS），它依据资产寿命长短确定了 8 类资产进而根据不同资产制定不同的折旧率和折旧方法。前四类资产的使用寿命在 15 年以下，使用双倍余额递减法；接下来的两类资产使用寿命在 15 年到 $27\frac{1}{2}$ 年之间，使用 150% 余额递减法；最后两类资产的使用寿命在 271/2 年或以上，使用直线法。

由于财务报告与税收政策存在差异，这会导致公司记录递延所得税负债。为了说明纳税义务的处理，假设一个公司使用直线法来编制财务报告，但用年限总和法来进行纳税申报（使用图表 2 - 145 的数据）。如果营业利润在扣除折旧费用以前（其他费用已经扣除）是 $1 000 000，那么在直线法下，税前利润是 $878 571，应交所得税为 $351 428。在纳税申报时使用年限总和法，结果导致税前利润为 $787 500，应交所得税为 $315 000，因此递延所得税负债为 $36 428（即是现在缴纳的税金少而以后缴纳的税金相应多）。

换句话说，这额外的 $36 428 提高了公司的年度折旧税盾（通过折旧扣除使得年纳税总额被节约了）。

如果这项资产保持使用 7 年，则纳税负债将会消失，因为通过相应增加应纳税额（比如，在第 7 年纳税 $35 429），会弥补临时差异。（如果资产在应纳税期内出售了，将不得不补交递延的所得税负债。）尽管如此，考虑到货币时间价值，公司情愿在前期负担较少的税负。公司可以把前期节约下的资金用来投资。

本节稍后会详细探讨递延所得税问题。

减值

财产、厂房及设备以历史成本取得，并且不会在每个资产负债表日以公允价值进行重估。尽管如此，在财产、厂房及设备的账面价值不能通过出售或使用而收回的情况下，资产的价值就会发生减值，并且必须用公允价值记录其账面价值。但是要确定财产、厂房及设备的公允价值比较困难并且比较依赖主观判断。

美国财务会计准则公告 144 号（SFAS NO. 144），"长期资产减值和处置的会计处理"规定当财产、厂房及设备存在以下某种情况时，应进行减值测试：

- 一项资产（或资产组）的市场价值明显下降。
- 一项资产的使用环境或物理环境出现在范围上和方式上的明显不利变化。
- 出现影响长期资产的明显不利法律或社会环境的变化，包括由监管机构采取的反向行动或重估。
- 累计成本明显超过原计划用于购买或构建长期资产的数额。
- 过去期间及当前期间都面临经营损失或现金流损失，并且预计与某种资产相关的损失还会继续存在。
- 预计资产将很可能在它先前估计的使用寿命的基础上明显提前出售或报废。

当其中任意一种情况出现时，可恢复性测试被用来确定是否减值已经发生。当预期从资产使用或处置中产生的未贴现的未来现金流量之和小于资产的账面净值时，则资产发生了减值。如果这个未贴现的现金流量大于或等于资产的账面价值，则资产没有减值。如果发生了减值，则资产将减记到其公允价值并且减记要作为减值损失记录。公允价值是该资产的市场价格，前提是价格能够确定。否则，以未来现金流量的现值作为其公允价值。

比如，如果一项资产的取得成本是 $1 000 000，累计折旧是 $200 000（即账面净值是 $800 000）。未贴现的从使用或处置资产得到的未来现金流量净值是 $700 000。则减值发生了。如果这项资产的公允价值被评估为 $650 000，则一笔 $150 000（$800 000 – $650 000）的减值损失将被记录。

减值损失作为持续经营收益的一部分记录，就像其他的费用和损失一样，而不是作为一个额外的内容。任何已经确认了的减值损失都应被披露，包括减值资产的信息、发生减值的原因、减值额以及公允价值的确定方法。

财产、厂房及设备的处置

财产、厂房及设备能够出售、交换、转化或者废弃。公司应折旧到资产的处置日，然后冲销掉所有资产相关的账面金额。在处置的时候，折旧过后的账面价值与处置价值的差异必须确认为损益。资产处置的损益应作为持续经营收益的一部分。除非处置涉及清算。

出售

当财产、厂房及设备被出售时，从最后一笔折旧入账到处置日期间的折旧必须被记录。这样会提供最新的资产账面净值以便于计算资产出售的损益。比如，一家公司有台塑料压制机历史成本是 $34 000，过去的 7 年里每年的折旧额是 $3 400。在第 8 年的 3 月 1 日，这台塑料压制机以 $10 000 卖出。求其出售的损益。首先，公司必须把第 8 年的折旧入账，金额是 $3 400 × 3/12 = $850。这笔金额通常应加到年底的折旧总额中，或者应单独进行会计处理，借方记入折旧费用，贷方记入累计折旧—机器设备。

图表 2 – 148 展示了怎样计算这个压制机的处置损益。

图表 2 – 148　销售机器的日记账分录

现金	$10 000	
累计折旧—机器设备	$24 650	
机器		$34 000
资产处置的损益*		$650

* ($3 400 × 7) + $850 = $24 650

（出售价格 – 账面净值）= 损益

账面净值 = 成本 – 累计折旧

$10 000 – ($34 000 – $24 650) = $650 利得

因为公司在一个时期内会多次购买或出售设备或其他资产，一个比较复杂的例子如下。在年初，Bounce 体育用品公司的设备账面价值为 $24 000，累计折旧为 $96 000。在这年中，它们出售设备的成本为 $45 000 其账面净值为 $1 500，出售价为 $10 500。年末，设备余额为 $330 000，累计折旧为 $120 000。求，今年购买的设备是多少？为了求出该答案，首先应根据给定的账面净值求出成本：

账面净值 = 成本 – 折旧

期初设备

$240 000 = x – $96 000

x = $336 000

期末设备

$330 000 = x – $120 000

x = $450 000

下面的公式展示了怎样计算设备的购置（也可利用该公式计算其他变量）：

设备购置 = 期末设备成本余额 – 期初设备成本余额 + 设备出售

= $450 000 – $336 000 + $45 000 = $159 000

不可抗力改变

洪水、火灾、地震、盗窃或罚没是资产不可抗力改变的几种类型。当那些导致这种改变的事件被认为是既非正常情况，并且发生又非常罕见，则处置的损益应作为损益表的营业外项目列报。

甚至在这种情况下，当已经改变了的资产突然被其他资产替换时，处置损益还必须根据 FASB 的第 30 号解释进行记录。

这里有一个例子，一家公司由于火灾引起不可抗力改变损失。在这个例子中，这项资产的买价是 $1 600 000，累计折旧是 $600 000。图表 2 – 149 显示当保险赔款为 $1 700 000 时的会计处理。

废弃

废弃或丢弃不会产生任何现金回收，这将导致产生与账面价值相同的损失。如果任何废弃价值被回收，则账面价值与回收价值之间的差异应作为损益被记录。折旧完毕的资产如果仍然使用应在资产负债表中披露。

图表 2 –149　不可抗力改变的日记账分录

现金	$1 700 000	
累计折旧—企业资产	$600 000	
企业资产		$1 600 000
企业资产处置损益*		$700 000

* 保险赔款 – 账面净值 = 损益
账面净值 = 成本 – 累计折旧
$1 700 000 –（$1 600 000 – $60 000）= $700 000 利得

折耗

自然资源比如石油、煤、木材能够被完全地消耗，并且只能通过自然的方式恢复，因此它们被称为耗用资产。不像其他资产，耗用资产不会保持它们的物理特性。自然资源的折耗应作为成本与其收入匹配。

折耗的计量需要确定一个折耗范围，这包括取得成本、勘探成本、开采成本及恢复成本。取得成本包括购买的资源开发权或使用权。勘探成本包括所有与探明资源相关的成本。无形的开采成本比如钻井费用应包括在折耗范围内。有形的开采成本主要针对设备，这种设备能够从一个地点移动到另一个地点，这种成本不包括在折耗的范围内，但是应单独折旧。恢复成本是指使土地恢复到可使用状态，这应包括在折耗范围内。财产的残值应从折耗中扣除。

在确定了折耗的范围后，金额将会被分配到适当的会计期，通常使用先前讨论过的产量法或作业法。

折耗率用下面的公式进行确定：

$$每单位折耗成本 = \frac{总成本 – 残值}{总的估计产量}$$

这样，如果一口油井的折耗成本是每桶 $5，第一年开采出 5 000 桶石油，则 $25 000 的折耗应该被记录。

PP&E 的财务报表陈述和披露要求

对于财产、厂房、设备及自然资源，其计价基础（比如历史成本）连同其任何委托、抵押及留置情况应被披露。以财产、厂房及设备作担保的债务应在资产负责表负债部分单独报告，不应冲减资产的成本。

当然，正在使用的财产、厂房及设备应与目前没有使用的财产、厂房及设备区分开。报出的累计折旧应分别告知报表使用者资产的历史成本和报表日的折旧额。一些公司使用一个类似的累计折耗账户，但是其他公司把折耗直接记入自然资源账户的贷方。石油、天然气工业有其特殊的披露要求，包括会计处理方法和成本处置方式。

美国会计原则委员会第 12 号意见第 5 段（APB Opinion No. 12（par. 5））指出关于应折旧资产的下列信息应该披露：

- 本期折旧费用。
- 主要类别应折旧资产的余额，类别是按功能和性质划分。
- 累计折旧总额或者主要类别应折旧资产的累计折旧总额。
- 大概描述各主要类别应折旧资产的折旧计算方法。

一个关于对财产、厂房及设备的披露要求的例子如图表2-150所示。

图表2-150 财产、厂房及设备和自然资源的披露

木材和林业公司		
	第2年	第1年
		（以千为单位进行列示）
财产（附注1）		
财产和设备		
土地和土地改良	$46 847	$42 372
建筑物和建筑物改良	425 877	403 087
机器和设备	3 021 216	3 000 748
	3 493 940	3 446 207
累计折旧	(1 591 285)	(1 507 640)
	1 902 655	1 938 567
木材、林地和木材存储	194 810	202 020
	$2 097 465	$2 140 587

报表附注

附注1（部分内容）：主要会计政策概要

财产。财产及设备以成本入账。成本包括的支出有：主要的改良、替换以及与重大资产扩建相关的净利息成本。

资本化的利息在第2年为$992 340，第1年为$7 825，500，第0年为$13 155 720。所有的纸张和木材生产设备的折旧用的是产量法，其他营运资产用的是直线法。出售或报废资产的损益在当其发生时计入利润。

在折旧所适用的使用年限如下所示：

建筑物及其改良	5～40年
家具和固定资产	5～10年
机器、设备和卡车	3～20年
租赁物改良	5～10年

公司木材的砍伐成本和伐木道路的摊销的确定是基于在总可重获木材量下的本期伐木量。木材和林地以成本计价，减去目前砍伐木材的累计成本。

无形资产

在当今的经济中，无形资产的价值在持续上升。许多无形资产很难估价，比如管理层的能力和顾客的忠诚，因此它们不在财务报告中划出。资产负债表确实包括无形资产的购买价格，它是用来摊销的成本。本部分的内容包括无形资产的特征和其开发价值、摊销、减值测试以及商誉和研发的会计处理。

无形资产的特征

无形资产的定义是基于两个主要特征：它们没有物理实体，不是金融工具。其他的区别于有形资产的因素有：它们的价值随竞争环境而波动，它们仅仅在公司持有时才能表现出价值，它们带来的未来收益不容易被确定，它们的使用寿命也不容易确定。无形资产是典型的非流动资产。

无形资产的种类

SFAS NO. 141，"商业合并"（A14段）定义了6类无形资产。

● **市场无形资产**

市场无形资产包含任何用于市场的资产和促进经营的资产，包括商标、商品名

称、公司名称、公司域名以及非竞争性协议。它们包含定义产品、服务和公司的文字及符号。美国专利和商标局对注册商标授予数目不限的 10 年续注期。但普通法甚至会保护非注册商标。购进的市场无形资产应以购买价格进行资本化。内部开发的市场无形资产可以资本化的范围是：法律费用、注册费用、设计和咨询费用，以及其他成本但不包括研发费用。大部分的市场无形资产没有确定的使用年限，因此它们的成本不能进行摊销。

- **客户无形资产**

客户名单和订单以及其他的客户合同和关系都是客户无形资产，因为它们与第三方的交易有关。大部分客户无形资产都有一个确定的寿命，可以在期限内摊销。

- **艺术无形资产**

书籍、电影、戏剧、诗歌、音乐、美术图片，以及视听信息的版权是艺术无形资产。版权授予创作者在他终生及死后 70 年对作品的权利，版权不能延长期限。购买和保护版权的成本应在可预见的收益期内摊销（通常短于版权的法律保护期）。

- **合同无形资产**

合同无形资产指的是合同规定的权利，比如建设许可、播放权利、特许权和执照以及服务合同。取得一项特许权的初始成本（比如法律费或预付款）应计入无形资产，然后在特许权的使用期内摊销，前提是使用期是有限的。但是，每年根据特许合同规定的付款在发生时作为费用。

- **技术无形资产**

专利技术、产品秘密以及其他革新都是技术无形资产。专利包括产品和工艺专利，有 20 年的法律期限。购买专利的支出应资本化；任何关于取得和保护专利的法律收费也应资本化。尽管如此，与产品和工艺专利相关的研发成本必须在发生时计入费用。专利的资本化成本应在法律期限与使用寿命两者孰短确定的期限内摊销。

- **商誉**

商誉是指购买一个企业的买价与这个企业的可确认资产的公允价值之间的差额。购买一个公司的金额首先应分摊到该公司的可确认有形资产和无形资产上，然后其剩余值被确认为商誉。商誉将在后面进行更详细地讨论。

无形资产的计价

无形资产的计价比较困难，它主要取决于这些无形资产是购买的还是内部创造的。

- **购买无形资产**

购买的无形资产以其成本入账，再加上一切额外成本比如法律费。如果无形资产需要用股票或非货币资产来交换，则交换成本应以支出的资产与收到的无形资产之间谁的公允价值更可靠来确认。如果有形资产是一篮子交易的一部分，则总的价格应该在接收到的资产之间以相关公允价值分配。

- **内部创造无形资产**

为开发专利而发生的内部研发成本在发生时作为费用入账。只有一些直接成本比如与内部开发专利相关的法律费，才能资本化。

摊销

没有确定的使用寿命的无形资产不能摊销，但是每年要进行减值测试。另一方面，使用寿命有限的无形资产的成本应在可预计的受益期内摊销。一项无形资产的使用寿命可以按以下方法估计（见 SFAS NO. 142 的第 11 段）：

- 无形资产的预期使用。
- 限制无形资产使用寿命的有关法律、监管及合同规定。
- 延长权或其他关于无形资产可以重新获得的规定。
- 允许无形资产可以重新获得或延长寿命期限而又不发生真实成本的规定。
- 技术进步、过时、顾客要求、竞争以及其他经济因素的影响。
- 与无形资产使用相关的其他资产的使用寿命。
- 为获得资产的预期未来收益而发生的维护支出的水平（如果这些支出与资产的账面价值相比是重要的，则暗示使用寿命有限）。

当一项无形资产的使用寿命有限，则其资本化的成本减去任何剩余（残留）价值后的值在使用寿命期进行摊销。剩余价值通常是零，除非公司相信无形资产在其摊销期末将带来一些价值给其他公司。无形资产使用直线法摊销，除非其他方法更能清晰地反映出资产使用模式。摊销是借方计费用账户，贷方计该无形资产账户或单独的累计摊销账户。

商誉

根据 SFAS NO. 141（见第 43 段），商誉的定义是"收购成本超过被收购实体的资产净值的部分"。这部分被确认为商誉，并需进行减值测试。

商誉的记录

仅仅购买的商誉可以资本化。内部创造的商誉不能作为资产来报告。购买的商誉作为资产来记录的前提是仅当整个实体被购买时；它不能脱离整个实体，并需作为持续经营的内在组成部分。

当一家公司购买另一家公司，购买价格的确定是基于新的附属公司的资产和负债的公允价值而不是资产负债表上的数字，因为资产负债表上的数字是按历史成本列示。通常买方或独立机构要对被购买公司进行审计，以期能够确定净资产的公允价值。长期资产和负债的账面价值与其公允价值相比通常有最大的差异。审计也用于发现任何没有记录的资产和负债，并说明存货用估计的公允价值计价的方法。当公允价值被确定后，谈判代表会提出一个购买价格，这个价格通常包括没有被估价的无形资产如经理的能力、名誉等。因此，购买价格很可能实际上会高于公允价值。在很少的情况下会出现负商誉，在这种情况下，负商誉将被贷记入买方公司的账上，这时买价将低于公允价值。当然就所知道的谈判而言，这种情况的发生比较少见，因为卖方更有可能出售企业的一部分，从而得到市场价格。

这里有一个关于商誉的例子，如果一家家族企业购买了一家公司作为其附属公司，被收购公司拥有的资产与负债的净公允价值是 $35 000 000，但买价是 $40 000 000，则 $5 000 000 的差额被列为商誉。图表 2－151 中的计算过程展示了购买价格的分配。

图表 2 - 151　商誉的计算

购买价格		$40 000 000
减去：		
现金	$2 500 000	
应收账款	$5 000 000	
存货	$9 000 000	
财产、厂房和设备	$22 000 000	
专利	$1 500 000	
负债	$5 000 000	
确定了的净资产的公允价值		$35 000 000
商誉		$5 000 000

商誉的减值测试

商誉不进行摊销但是要进行减值测试，当减值被确认发生时，应记录下来。FASB 认为商誉的摊销不会帮助投资者分析财务状况，且商誉被认为其使用寿命不确定。

当报告企业的公允价值低于账面持有价值并包括商誉，这时商誉被认为发生了减值。当减值存在时，损失必须被计量。减值损失被认为是报告公司的商誉的账面价值比隐含的商誉公允价值多出的那一部分。隐含的商誉公允价值的确定类似于企业合并时商誉价值的确定。报告公司的公允价值被分摊到确定的净资产（包括不能识别的无形资产），任何一项的增加额会被认为是隐含的商誉。

比如，如果一家附属公司的包括商誉在内的公允价值是 $40 000 000，对其可辨认的净资产（不包括商誉）估价为 $36 000 000，则隐含的商誉为 $4 000 000。如果账上记录的商誉是 $5 000 000，则应记录下 $1 000 000，作为该账户的减值损失。减值损失不能超过商誉的账面价值，当减值损失被确认后，不能以后转回。

无形资产减值的会计处理

除商誉之外的其他无形资产也应进行减值测试。使用寿命有限和使用寿命不确定的无形资产都需要进行测试。

使用寿命有限的无形资产的减值测试

要摊销的无形资产的减值方法与财产、厂房和设备减值的方法相同（参见财产、厂房和设备部分的可恢复测试）。当一项无形资产的账面价值不能恢复且它的账面价值超过其公允价值时，减值损失应被确认。一旦无形资产被减值，任何价值上的恢复都不能确认。

使用寿命不确定的无形资产的减值测试

不进行摊销的无形资产应每年进行减值测试，比较无形资产的公允价值与其账面价值。如果账面价值超过了公允价值，则超出部分被确认为减值损失。一旦减值损失被确认了，则不允许转回。

研发

研发成本在其发生时作为费用。尽管研发支出可能会产生无形资产，比如专利，但是由于很难确认与不同项目相关的成本以及估计预期收益时的内在不确定性，这使得 FASB 只是简单地要求公司将这些成本费用化。

SFAS NO.2 定义的研究是指为了发现可以促成开发出新的产品和服务的知识而进行的有计划的探索。开发是指把研究中的发现转化为新产品或流程的计划，包括设计和测试阶段。对现有产品的常规更新不包括在研发中。

研发的会计处理

材料、设备、工具的成本以及购买无形资产的成本应在发生时计入费用。除非它们存在可选择的未来使用，在这种情况下，这些成本应资本化而在使用时费用化。人力资源成本与合同服务成本应在发生时立即费用化。其他的间接成本应在合理的基础上分摊到研发费用中。而一般管理成本通常不包括在其中。

研发的类似成本

其他的成本一般在发生时费用化，包括新操作或新作业的开办成本、开发阶段产生的前期运营损失（SFAS NO.7）、广告成本以及开发产品或程序（比如电脑软件）的成本。这些成本将在公司的销售与日常管理活动中运用。

无形资产的财务报表陈述与披露要求

对于资产负债表，商誉应单独列报，而所有其他的无形资产至少应作为总体单独列报。与财产、厂房和设备不同，累计摊销一般不会在资产负债表上的无形资产项目里单独列示。所有的摊销费用与减值损失应作为持续经营下的损益列报，而商誉的减值是在非持续经营下。所有可摊销的无形资产应在脚注中披露以下项目：

- 主要类别无形资产的账面总额与累计摊销总额。
- 报告期的摊销费用。
- 接下的五年每年估计的摊销额。

对于不能摊销的无形资产，其总额和主要类别无形资产的金额应该披露。本期发生的商誉的变动必须披露，包括获得的金额和确认的减值损失。

流动负债

根据 SFAS NO.6，负债的定义为"基于过去的交易和事项引起的一家公司未来将转移资产或提供劳务给另一家公司的现实义务，履行该义务将可能导致未来经济利益的流出"。根据 AICPA 的会计研究公告（ARP）第43号关于流动负债的定义为"一种义务，它的履行将预期要求使用存在的被分类为流动资产的资源或者是产生其他流动负债"。

流动负债的种类

图表 2 - 152 列示了这部分包含的流动负债的种类。

图表 2 - 152　流动负债

应付账款	经营应交税金
应付票据	• 应交销售税金
• 带息票据	• 应交所得税
• 无息票据	与员工相关的负债
将要到期的长期负债	• 薪酬扣项
预期再融资的短期债务 *	• 离职补偿
应付股利	• 分红
需要归还的押金和预收款	预计负债
不应得的或递延的收入	• 应交财产税

* 必须显示基于长期的再融资的意图和能力

应付账款

应付账款是购买商品时对卖方的负债，记入贷方。相对于发票金额，较早付款将获得折扣。现金折扣，比如列示 2/10，n/30，将提前确认为应收账款。应付账款应在当约定的货物已经收到或劳务已经提供完毕时确认。因此应特别关注发生在会计期末的交易。应付账款很容易估计。

应付票据

应付票据非常正式，会注明确定的付款额和确定的到期日。票据可以按期限长短来分类，也可以按是否带息分类。

• 带息应付票据

带息应付票据作为先前从出借人处借入现金来记录。利息费用和应付利息在票据没有到期的期间进行记录。到期时，出票人偿付票面价值和利息。

• 无息应付票据

无息票据也带有利息，因为出借人给借人人的期初价值小于票据到期日的数额。图表 2 - 153 列示了记录的一笔交易，该应付票据的面值是 $ 1 050 000，而从出借人处得到的初始金额是 $ 1 000 000。

图表 2 - 153　无息应付票据的会计处理

现金	$1 000 000
应付票据折价	$50 000
应付票据	$1 050 000

（该分录记录了 6 个月期的无息应付票据）

应付票据折价账户是用来记录收到的现金与票据的票面价值之间的差异。在资产负债表里，应付票据应报告其折价（负债账户的备抵账户），如图表 2 - 154 所示。

图表 2 – 154 折价在资产负债表上的列示

流动负债		
应付票据	$1 050 000	
减：应付票据折价	<u>50 000</u>	1 000 000

在票据持有期，利息费用将被记录，作为一个调整账户，贷方记入折价账户。随着这个备抵账户的减少，负债的净值将上升，最终将在到期日等于面值。

将要到期的长期负债

将要到期的长期负债代表了长期负债中的一部分，比如将要在下一年内偿付的抵押。这些负债的余额如果没有将要到期时，作为长期负债列报。当然也包括在本期随时都可以要求偿付的流动负债。另一方面，不能预期使用流动资产的债务不能列报为流动负债。比如基于长期资产账户里的累积资产的负债，基于长期再融资的负债，以及可以转化为股本的负债。

预期再融资的短期债务

如果一个公司签订了有明确期限的再融资合同，说明其有意图进行再融资短期债务并且显示有能力进行。因此根据 SFAS NO.6 的规定，这笔负债将在长期负债部分列示。随着 FASB 的工作目标是使美国的 GAAP 与国际会计准则趋同，公司被要求在负债的重分类被允许之前，在资产负债表日记录一项再融资合同。

如果短期债务的金额比适当的或安排的融资额大，则仅仅能够由安排的金额覆盖的那一部分债务能够被分类为长期负债。

应付股利

当现金或财产股利被董事会宣布时，它将被作为流动负债记录，作为保留盈余的减少额。当股利被发放时，这项债务消失了。股票股利不会导致产生负债，因为它是公司的权益证券而不是它的资产，并且将被转移。优先股股利在未付时不能作为一项负债，直到宣告时再确认。

需要归还的押金和预收款

从顾客和员工中收取的需要归还的押金应作为一项负债，而它应归于流动负债还是非流动负债主要取决于它预期什么时候偿付。这些押金主要是用来保障交易或财产的损失或损坏。

不应得的或递延的收入

不应得的或递延的收入包括为购买货物或劳务而支付的定金，这使得公司有义务在未来提供货物或劳务。因杂志征订、机票或礼券等收取的现金都归在这类。当现金收到时，则贷方记入不应得收入账户；当劳务或产品实际上已经转移时，则不应得账户记入借方，贷方记入收入。

经营应付税金

经营应付税金包括销售税和所得税。财产税在接下来进行讨论。

• 应交销售税

销售税是从顾客处收取，在没有缴入政府之前，应作为负债列报。如果实际应交的金额与应交销售税账户上的金额不同，其差异应确认为损益。如果销售税没有在销售时单独记录，则需要一个调整分录来减少计税销售额，同时贷方记入应交销售税。

• 应交所得税

企业所得税的计税基础是基于向州和联邦税收部门报送的收入。其金额应作为流动负债，一直到缴纳为止。如果额外的税负在先前一年被估计出，则贷方记入应交所得税，借方记入经常收入。为了报税而计算的收入与财务报告报出的收入之间的差异导致产生计入资产或负债的递延所得税。

与员工相关的负债

与员工相关的流动负债包括薪酬扣项、应付缺席补偿、应付退休金以及应付红利。

• 薪酬扣项

薪酬扣项包括税收、工会经费、保险费、员工储蓄计划以及其他员工同意的（或法律强制的）扣除金额。如果这些金额在会计期末前没有交入相关部门，则应作为流动负债。除了工资税在员工的工资中扣除外，雇主也要把相应的社会保障税和失业税计入流动负债。

• 缺勤补偿

缺勤补偿包括为假期、节日或病假而需要付出的金额。这些缺勤在相关收益获得年度被确认为费用和相关的负债，只要这项义务被归因于已经发生的服务，付款是很可能的，这项义务与积累权或归属权相联系，因此，负债金额能够合理地估计。积累权是指，如果不使用，能结转到下期的权利。归属权是指，这些金额必须给付，而不管雇佣关系是否已经解除。SFAS NO. 43 规定，公司需要累计带薪假期和有选择地记录带薪病假。FASB 对病假排除在外，因为付款被认为不一定发生（因为生病不一定会发生）。

这些应付项目的计算可以使用目前员工的工资率或预计的未来工资率。如果用工资率计算的应付款与实际发生的金额不同，则差异在发生期间费用化。

• 红利义务

应付红利作为员工工资额外的一部分。当盈利时，红利将作为营业费用和流动负债记录。

保证、保险及优惠

根据配比原则，与提供产品保证及保险和优惠相关的成本应在相关产品售出时计入费用和负债。在保证情况下，过去的经验应作为估计预计发生的维修或更换成本的基础。同样，现金折扣或保险的预期成本应被估计。当一件处于保修期的商品实际发生了修理或已提供了现金折扣或赠品时，预计的负债将会减少。保修费用是一种或然损失（本节稍后会探讨或有损失）。

保修成本的会计处理。修成本的会计处理有两种基本方法，即现金制和应计制。而在应计制下又有两种方法，即保修费用化法和出售保修法。

- **现金制**

当一项负债极不可能发生，或者其金额不能合理地估计，则适用现金制。如果保修成本是很小或保修期间很短，这种方法是可选择的。在这种方法下，保修负债不会在销售期确认，在修理情况发生时，把保修成本费用化。现金制是所得税法规中惟一允许的方法。

- **应计制**

应计制适用于，当预计一定的保修费用很可能会发生，并且公司能够合理地估计保修成本。

○ 保修费用化法

保修费用化法指估计销售期的保修费用。比如，一家生产收银机的企业在本期销售出 1 200 台 A 类收银机，每台售价 $1 000，保修期为一年。企业根据以往的修理情况认定应该会发生大约每单位 $40 的保修费用。本期实际发生的保修成本是 $20 000；而在下期，企业预计会发生关于本期出售的 A 类收银机的额外保修费用 $28 000。在本期，销售的会计处理如图表 2－155 所示：

图表 2－155　保修费用的会计分录

现金或应收账款	$1 200 000
销售	$1 200 000

本期应该确认的保修费用见图表 2－156：

图表 2－156　保修费用化的会计分录

保修费用	$20 000
现金、存货、应付工资	$20 000
确认实际发生的保修成本	
保修费用	$28 000
预计保修负债	$28 000
应计估计的保修成本	

本期资产负债表上应包括关于保修的 $28 000 的预计负债，作为流动负债，而本期损益表将记录 $48 000 的保修费用。在下期，本期出售 A 类产品的保修成本将被确认，当保修期满之后，预计费用与实际费用之间的差异抵销后，从保修费用的预计负债账户中转出。

○ 出售保修法

出售保修法的适用条件是当保修（或者延长的保修）从这个项目中单独出售。在这种方法下，收入和保修要分开记录。来自出售延长的保修的收入应该进行递延，通常用直线法在整个保修期内确认。佣金和其他直接影响保修费用的成本也要递延和摊销。那些与销售无关的成本比如工资在发生期费用化。

如果前面提到的收银机制造公司也对 A 类收银机提供一种延长的保修，额外延长两年，需要每台额外收取 $100，在本期共出售 100 份延长保修，则出售收银机和保修的会计处理如图表 2 – 157 所示：

图表 2 – 157 出售保修法的会计分录

现金或应收账款	$1 210 000	
销售		$1 200 000
未实现保修收入		$10 000

在下期和再下期（即延长保修时期）用直线法确认的保修收入（每年：$10 000/2 = $5 000）见图表 2 – 158：

图表 2 – 158 出售保修法的会计分录

| 未实现保修收入 | $5 000 | |
| 保修收入 | | $5 000 |

用直线法摊销的例外情况是，如果确认的成本是可以预测的，但是没有一定的模式，在这种情况下，收入应按实际发生的成本的比例确认。

流动负债的计量

在理论上，流动负债应按未来现金流量的现值计量。尽管如此，流动负债通常还是以它们到期时的面值计量，因为账面价值与现值的差异并不重要。

或有负债和承诺

根据 SFAS NO. 5（第 1 段），或有事项是指"目前存在的情况、条件或环境引起的不确定性，它将给公司带来可能的收入（或有收入）或损失（或有损失）。当未来一件或几件事项发生或不发生时，这些不确定性就得到解决了"。

或有收入的会计处理

或有收入的结果是，会出现这样一种可能性，那就是企业将会收到资产（或减少负债）作为接受礼物、捐赠或分红的结果；作为未定税额、未决诉讼的结果；或者是作为税收损失延后的结果。或有收入不在账户中反映，但当实际收益在未来很可能发生时，可以在财务报表附注中披露。

或有损失的会计处理

或有损失结果是目前存在的情形将导致未来的潜在损失。一项或有负债应在这种情况下确认：这项负债在资产负债表日起很可能发生，并且损失的金额能够合理地估计。根据 SFAS NO. 5 的规定，当发生损失的可能性被认为是"有可能"而不是"很可能"或者很可能发生的损失不能合理估计时，或有损失不应确认但应在财务报表附注中披露。损失发生的可能性"极小"或损失额度不大时，则不应披露。

或有损失的种类包括应收项目无法收现的风险、保修责任、保险、未决诉讼、资产被征用的风险、未决的要求权或估价、回购条款以及为第三方提供的担保。一些或有损失，像不能收现的风险和资产被征用的风险，将产生资产的减少而不是产生新的负债。一般的营业损失和火灾、爆炸以及其他自然灾害和操作失误引起的损失的风险不能确认为或有损失，因为一项能引起出现损失的可能性的事项并没有发生。

流动负债的财务报表陈述和披露要求

流动负债在财务报表上的列示

流动负债通常在财务报表上以其到期价值报告。它们在资产负债表上按流动性强弱顺序或到期日长短顺序列示。关于流动负债在资产负债表上列示的例子如图表2-159所示。

图表2-159　流动负债在资产负债表上的列示

Bounce 体育用品公司	本期	上期
流动负债		
短期借款	$4 214	$18 353
应付账款	1 929 825	1 268 743
应付与员工相关的负债	1 331 374	808 778
应计负债	2 883 832	2 075 038
递延劳务收入	1 080 614	678 315
应交所得税	1 031 201	482 920
应付票据	60 000	102 400
流动负债合计	$8 321 060	$5 434 547

补充信息也应提供以对流动负债进行全面披露。有担保保证的负债和相关担保保证应予以确认。

财务报表对或有损失的列示

在财务报表附注中对或有损失进行的披露如图表2-160所示。

图表2-160　或有损失的披露

XYZ 集团

附注1：诉讼。XYZ 在关于由于硅胶假体植入胸部后破裂而致人受伤或死亡的大量诉讼中充当被告或共同被告。下面的图表中列出了这些诉讼的大概情况。

要求	
年初未决诉讼数	7 411
本年新增数	3 755
已判决或者以其他方式解决数	(1 213)
年末未决诉讼数	9 973

续表

XYZ 集团	
平均赔偿额	$3 826
平均每个案件的成本，包括律师费	$6 459
判决情况	
对公司有利的判决数	32
总判决数	46

以下给出了与硅胶假体胸部植入案相关的辩护成本，以及相关的保险费用和工人补偿费用。

包含于营业利润中的费用	$1 572 480
营业外费用	7 624 680
合计	$9 197 160

公司正在为合理确定其负债而努力。尽管如此，但是不可能预测到：哪种保险将会申请，进入诉讼程序的案子数量，以及为解决或辩护目前存在和没有提起诉讼的案子的成本，或者是这些案子对公司合并财务报表的最终影响。

长期负债与应付债券

长期负债指不用流动资产偿还的负债，或者换句话说，是指预期在一年以后或者一个营业周期以后甚至更长时间以后偿还的负债。应付债券和应付票据是两种典型的长期负债。

长期应付票据的计量和会计处理

与短期应付票据一样，长期应付票据也有到期日和固定利率或内含利率。与短期应付票据不同，短期应付票据可以用到期日的金额入账，而长期应付票据的价值应用未来现金流量的现值计量，其中包括偿付利息和本金。长期应付票据的处理与长期应收票据的处理相反，长期应收票据的处理前面已经讨论过。本部分先回顾一下与票据相关的术语，随后将考察应付债券的会计处理，这和应付票据的会计处理相似。

- **票据以面值发行**

当一张票据以票面金额发行时，则票面利率与有效利率相同。票据以其面值入账；没有折价需要计入。应付利息（取决于面值乘以票面利率）作为利息费用入账，随着时间的推移进行确认。例如，一张面值为 $24 000，年利率为 8% 的应付票据，发行日为 2005 年 8 月 1 日，第一次付息日是 2006 年 8 月 1 日，在 2005 年 12 月 31 日，应确认一笔 $800 的利息费用，同时贷方记入应付利息：

$$\frac{\$24\,000 \times 8\%}{\left(\dfrac{12\ 个月}{5\ 个月}\right)} = \$800$$

- **票据不以面值发行**

不以面值发行的票据的票面利率与有效利率不同。无息票据的票面利率是零。应付利息的确定基于有效利率，而利息费用的金额则要基于有效利率或应计利率。有效利率是指以该利率贴现到期金额和/或定期支付后所得到的现值等于实际借入金额。

- 应计利息

应付票据的利率明显与市场利率不同，则会出现应计利率。参看应付账款部分讨论的应计利息。

- 为取得财产、商品和劳务而发行的票据

为获取现金而发行的票据的价值很容易确定。但情况并不总是如此，有时票据发行会用于交换非现金资产和劳务。这些票据的票面利率被认为是公平的，除非该票据没有票面利率，或者是票据的面值与所交换的资产或劳务的公允价值之间有明显差异。在这种情况下，票据的价值应基于所交换的非货币资产的公允价值。如果非货币资产的公允价值不容易取得，则票据的价值应该用应计利率下的贴现现金流量来确定。应计利率应用估计的借款人为获得类似的负债项目而预期付出的利率来确定。

抵押应付票据

抵押应付票据是一种常见的有担保的应付票据，它通常用财产作担保。抵押要么在到期时担保应付项目的全部金额，要么是应付项目的一部分金额。借款开始时借款人支付的相关费用会减少实际借到的金额，因此会增加实际利率。抵押应付票据的发行会采用固定利率或变动（浮动）利率。使用变动利率的抵押应付票据的利率围绕基准利率比如最优惠利率波动。

抵押应付票据作为长期负债列报直到到期日的前一年。如果抵押是分期支付，则在下一年到期的支付本金应作为流动负债列报，而剩余部分作为长期负债。

表外融资

多年来，金融界已经开发出几种融资安排，它使得公司能够以某种方式给几种资产融资，并且能够使得该资产和与之相关的负债不在资产负债表上反映。比如某些交易，其包含了确定的经营租赁和其他交易，这些交易通常称为表外融资。《萨班斯－奥克斯利法案》通过后，该法案要求上市公司披露所有的表外融资，这使得联邦证券交易委员会（SEC）改变了披露要求。

项目融资安排是表外融资的常见形式，其典型的实现方式如下：

- 两家或更多的公司创办一家新公司，创办这家新公司的目的只是为了建造能被两家母公司使用的厂房。

- 新的公司为该项目借入资金并使用完成的项目的资金来偿付债务。

- 母公司为这笔债务提供担保。

这种方法使得借入款项负债在独立实体的账上反映，而不是在投资实体的账上反映。结果，使用项目融资安排的公司将会使得资产负债表看上去更好一些。它们仅仅需要披露贷款的担保情况。

安然公司使用大量表外融资，导致了历史上最大的破产案之一。作为对《2002萨班斯－奥克斯利法案》的反应，联邦证券交易委员会（SEC）要求新增披露管理层对年报的讨论和分析部分，这部分包括披露全部合同义务以及披露或有负债和承诺（下一节将详细探讨联邦证券交易委员会的报告要求）。

债券种类

债券是长期债务安排，通常需要董事会的批准，债券包含有以保护债权人和债务人利益为目的的保护性条款以及限制条件。通过发行债券，债务人可以得到多于向单个债权人融资的资金。一旦发行，债券可以在活跃的债券市场上流通。债券的公允价值会在这个二级市场上随着反映相似风险的市场利率而波动。同宏观经济环境一样，对债务人的风险水平的判断随着时间的推移也会导致债券价值的变化。尽管如此，从会计的角度来讲，债券发行者在债券赎回之前是不会确认其公允价值的变化的。

一些债券种类例示如下：

● 担保债券和无担保债券

担保债券有担保支持，比如房地产（不动产抵押债券）、其他公司的股票或债券（抵押信托债券）。无担保债券只有发行者的口头承诺。

● 深度折扣债券

深度折扣债券是指折价销售的零息无担保债券。

● 可赎回债券

可赎回债券含有期权，它使发行者可以高于票面价值 1~2 个百分点的价格赎回债券（比如 101、102 个百分点的价格）。可赎回债券的发行者有三个选择：在到期日清偿债券；当债券市值小于可赎回价格时回购债权；或者在一定的赎回价格上将其赎回。当利率较高时，公司会发行可赎回债券，它们希望能早日回收旧债券并在未来更好的利率出现时发行新的债券。在回收债券时产生的利得和损失计入损益表中的其他收益（损失）。比如，如果一个公司发行了价值 4 亿美元的债券，在 101 处可赎回，在市场价格为 103 时，未摊销折价为 2 000 万美元，利得或损失的计算如图表 2 - 161 所示：

图表 2 - 161　提早回收可赎回债券产生的利得或损失

在公开市场上回收	（单位：百万美元）	通过赎回回收	（单位：百万美元）
被收回债券的面值	$400	被收回债券的面值	$400
一未摊销折价	- $20	一未摊销折价	- $20
债券账面价值	$380	债券账面价值	$380
一市场价值（$400 ×1.03）	- $412	一赎回价格（$400 ×1.01）	- $404
回收应付债券的损失	（$32）		（$24）

● 其他债券术语

在同一时间到期偿付的债券叫做定期债券，通过分期分批偿还的债券叫做分期债券。一些债券可转换为发行者的股票，而这一权利的行使在于投资者的决定（接下来将会讨论这一问题）。

可转换债券的影响

可转换债券是债务工具，可以转换为特定数量的普通股（股权融资）。与直接债务融资不同，其发行者可以获利于一个更低的债券利率，同时减少了全部用股权融资所带来的对股权的稀释作用。举个例子：需要融资 500 万美元，一个即时股价为 $60

的公司需要发行至少 83 333 份股票（多于这一数目是考虑到发行成本）；如果该公司可以 $2 000 的价格发行 2 500 份可转换债券，每份债券可转换为 30 份股票，则最终权益只会被 75 000 份股票稀释。以下的可转换债券会计处理是从发行者的角度出发。

可转换债券的发行

债券发行的记录完全依照一般的债券进行，在所有者权益下不计入任何数目。折价和溢价的摊销处理与本章其他地方相同。

可转换债券的转换

普通股或其他权益证券价值的波动会给债券转换的会计处理带来困难。GAAP 用账面价值法来记录。这种方法不确认任何转换带来的任何利得或损失，因为在发行时，公司同意在债券到期时按债券价值清偿或发行一定数量的股票清偿。

注意高于面值的实缴资本等于应付债券加上溢价（或减去折价）减去普通股面值。这样计算是因为不能确认任何转换带来的任何利得或损失。债券和股票的市场价值在这一方法下不予考虑。

债券的价值及会计处理

在发行债券之前，公司会确定一个到期价值（又称面值、本金）和票面利率（又称名义利率）。发行者在一份债券上付出的利息等于债券的面值乘以票面利率。利息可以是半年付息一次、一年付息一次或每季付息一次。

但是，在债券被印刷出来到其最后上市有一段时间，此间，类似债券的市场利率可能会发生变化。同样，如果管理层想要保持既定的利率，也可以计划债券溢价或折价发行。由于时间差异或管理层选择，投资者为了获得当前市场收益率（又称有效利率），其支付会高于（溢价发行）或低于（折价发行）票面价值。债券的发行价格是由其现金流（由票面利率决定的利息支付和到期价值）按照有效利率贴现确定。当有效利率高于票面利率时，债券折价发行，当有效利率低于票面利率时，债券溢价发行，当二者相等时，债券平价发行。

付息日平价发行债券

如果债券在付息日平价发行，此时没有应计利息也没有溢价或折价。发行者以票面价格借记现金，贷记应付债券。在接下来的年度里，利息费用等于支付的现金。

债券折价或溢价

债券在付息日折价或溢价发行

如果价值 100 万美元的债券以 95 的折价发行（面值的 95%），那么发行者应借记现金 $950 000，贷记应付债券 $1 000 000，并且借记应付债券折价 $50 000。折价账户属于反向负债账户，所以发行时债券的净值为 $950 000。

如果价值 100 万美元的债券以 105 的溢价发行（面值的 105%），那么发行者应借记现金 $1 050 000，贷记应付债券 $1 000 000，并且贷记应付债券溢价 $50 000。

溢价账户属于负债，所以发行时债券的净值为 $1 050 000。

债券的利息可以用有效利率法或直线法（如果其结果与有效利率法没有实质上的差异）记录。有效利率法将会在本章稍后讨论，其摊销将会在图表2-168中进行说明。在有效利率法下，记录的利息费用高于实际支付的利息，差异会摊销到应付债券折价账户上（反向负债账户）。

债券在付息日之间发行

为了简化起见，证券发行者会在每一个付息日支付此期间的利息。但是，在付息日之间购入债券的投资者不能获得整个期间的利息。为了弥补这一点，投资者预付直到买入债券那一天的应计利息。其结果便是，投资者能够获得其在持有债券期间的利息。如果一个债券于4月1日以票面价格加应计利息发行，价值100万美元，10年到期，票面利率为8%，半年付息一次，分别在1月1日和7月1日。发行者会按照图表2-162所示作分录（应付利息应取代利息费用记在贷方）。

图表2-162 债券在付息日之间发行

现金	$1 020 000
应付债券	$1 000 000
债券利息费用 $\left(\ \$1\ 000\ 000 \times 0.08 \times \dfrac{3}{12}\right)$	$20 000

当发行者在7月1日支付利息时，应作如图表2-163所示的分录：

图表2-163 付息日的分录

债券利息费用	$40 000
现金	$40 000

实际在外流通3个月的债券利息费用应为 $20 000（$40 000 - $20 000）。如果相同的债券以95的折价而非票面价值发行，分录应按照图表2-164所示来做：

图表2-164 以95折价在付息日间发行债券

现金$\left[(\ \$1\ 000\ 000 \times 0.95) + \left(\ \$1\ 000\ 000 \times 0.08 \times \dfrac{3}{12}\right)\right]$	$970 000
应付债券折价（$1 000 000 \times 0.05$）	$50 000
应付债券	$1 000 000
债券利息费用	$20 000

有效利率法

有效利率法是计算债券利息费用和债券折价溢价摊销中更为可取的方法。在有效利率法下，利息费用通过有效利率乘以期初债券账面价值计算得到（注意利率以年利率的形式出现，当一年多次付息时利率必须进行调整。所以，8%的年利率即是4%的半年利率也是2%的季利率）。实际支付利息（票面价值乘以票面利率）和债券利息费用（有效利率乘以期初债券账面价值）之间的差额为债券折价溢价的摊销额。所以，债券折价溢价摊销额可以表示如下：

摊销额 = （期初债券账面价值 × 有效利率）- （票面价值 × 票面利率）

在有效利率法下，利息费用占债券账面价值的恒定比例。如果债券以折价发行，债券的账面价值和利息费用会随着时间的推移而上升。相反，如果债券以溢价发行，债券的账面价值和利息费用会随着时间的推移而下降。不管债券是折价还是溢价发行，在债券的整个存续期，利息费用的总额是相同的。

图表 2 - 165 和图表 2 - 166 的货币时间价值会在接下来的例子中用到。

图表 2 - 165 1 的现值（单位量的现值）

$$PV_{n,i} = \frac{1}{(1+i)^n} = (1+i)^{-n}$$

(n) 期	4%	5%	6%
1	0.96154	0.95238	0.94340
2	0.92456	0.90703	0.89000
3	0.88900	0.86384	0.83962
4	0.85480	0.82270	0.79209
5	0.82193	0.78353	0.74726
6	0.79031	0.74622	0.70496
7	0.75992	0.71068	0.66506
8	0.73069	0.67684	0.62741
9	0.70259	0.64461	0.59190
10	0.67556	0.61391	0.55839

图表 2 - 166 1 的普通年金现值

$$PV - OA_{n,i} = \frac{1 - \dfrac{1}{(1+i)^n}}{i}$$

(n) 期	4%	5%	6%
1	0.96154	0.95238	0.94340
2	1.88609	1.85941	1.83339
3	2.77509	2.72325	2.67301
4	3.62990	3.54595	3.46511
5	4.95182	4.32948	4.21236
6	5.24214	5.07569	4.91732
7	6.00205	5.78637	5.58238
8	6.73274	6.46321	6.20979
9	7.43533	7.10782	6.80169
10	8.11090	7.72173	7.36009

折价发行的债券

以 12% 的有效利率发行价值 $100 000 的债券。此债券 5 年到期，票面利率为

9%，半年付息一次。发行价格计算如图表 2 – 167 所示。注意 5 年期、半年付息一次的债券有 10 个付息日，所以现值的计算使用的是 10 期。有效利率和票面利率都调整为半年利率。

图表 2 – 167 应付债券折价的计算

应付债券到期价值		$100 000.00
以 12% 贴现 5 年后价值为 $100 000，半年付息的现值；FV（PV$_{10,6\%}$）；（$100 000 ×0.55839）	$55 839.00	
以 12% 贴现 5 年期、半年付息 $4 500 的现值；R（PV – OA$_{10,6\%}$）；（$4 500 ×7.36009）	33 120.41	
债券发行收入		88 959.41
应付债券折价		$11 040.59

债券摊销安排如图表 2 – 168 所示。根据表中数值计算出每个付息日的数额，在此基础上发行者应贷记现金，借记利息费用，贷记应付债券折价（注意：以 12 月 31 日为会计年度末的公司应当计提在 1 月 1 日应计的利息，调整分录是贷记应付利息而非现金）。

图表 2 – 168 债券折价摊销安排表

债券折价摊销安排表，有效利率法
半年付息一次（5 年期票面利率为 9% 有效利率为 12% 的债券）

日期	付现	利息费用	折价摊销	债券账面价值
Y1, 1, 1				$88 959.41
Y1, 7, 1	$4 500[a]	$5 337.56[b]	$837.56[c]	89 796.97[d]
Y2, 1, 1	4 500	5 387.82	887.82	90 684.79
Y2, 7, 1	4 500	5 441.09	941.09	91 625.88
Y3, 1, 1	4 500	5 497.55	997.55	92 623.43
Y3, 7, 1	4 500	5 557.41	1 057.41	93 680.84
Y4, 1, 1	4 500	5 620.85	1 120.85	94 801.69
Y4, 7, 1	4 500	5 688.10	1 188.10	95 989.79
Y5, 1, 1	4 500	5 759.39	1 259.39	97 249.18
Y5, 7, 1	4 500	5 834.95	1 334.95	98 584.13
Y6, 1, 1	4 500	5 915.05	1 415.87*	100 000.00
	$45 000	$56 039.77	$11 039.77	

a $4 500　　= $100 000 ×0.09 ×6/12
b $5 337.56 = $88 959.41 ×0.12 ×6/12
c $837.56　= $5 337.56 – $4 500
d $89 796.97 = $8 895 941 + $837.56

* 注：为了使最后的账面价值等于票面价值，最后一次折价摊销是调整过的。

溢价发行的债券

如果一个 5 年期、价值 $100 000、票面利率为 9% 的债券以 8% 的有效利率发行，其溢价计算如图表 2-169 所示：

图表 2-169 应付债券溢价的计算

应付债券到期价值	$100 000.00
以 8% 贴现 5 年后价值为 $100 000，半年付息的现值； FV（$PV_{10,4\%}$）；（$100 000 ×0.67556）	$67 556.00
以 8% 贴现 5 年期、半年付息 $4 500 的现值；R（PV- $OA_{10,4\%}$）；（$4 500 ×8.11090）	36 499.05
债券发行收入	104 055.05
应付债券溢价	$4 055.05

  债券摊销安排如图表 2-170 所示。根据表中数值计算出每个付息日的数额，在此基础上发行者应贷记现金，借记利息费用，借记应付债券溢价（注意：以 12 月 31 日为会计年度末的公司应当计提在 1 月 1 日应计的利息，调整分录是贷应付利息而非现金）。

图表 2-170 债券溢价摊销安排表

债券溢价摊销安排表，有效利率法
半年付息一次（5 年期票面利率为 9% 有效利率为 12% 的债券）

日期	付现	利息费用	溢价摊销	债券账面价值
Y1, 1, 1				$104 055.05
Y1, 7, 1	$4 500[a]	$4 162.20[b]	$337.80[c]	103 717.25[d]
Y2, 1, 1	4 500	$4 148.69	$351.31	103 365.94
Y2, 7, 1	4 500	$4 134.64	$365.36	103 000.58
Y3, 1, 1	4 500	$4 120.02	$379.98	102 620.60
Y3, 7, 1	4 500	$4 104.82	$395.18	102 225.42
Y4, 1, 1	4 500	$4 089.02	$410.98	101 814.44
Y4, 7, 1	4 500	$4 072.58	$427.42	101 387.02
Y5, 1, 1	4 500	$4 055.48	$444.52	100 942.50
Y5, 7, 1	4 500	$4 037.70	$462.30	100 480.20
Y6, 1, 1	4 500	$4 019.21	$480.20 *	100 000.00
	$45 000	$40 944.36	$4 055.64	

  a $4 500 = $100 000 ×0.09 ×6/12
  b $4 162.20 = $104 055.05 ×0.08 ×6/12
  c $337.80 = $4 500 - $4 162.20
  d $103 717.25 = $104 055.05 - $337.80

* 注意：为了使最后的账面价值等于票面价值，最后一次折价摊销是调整过的。

折价和溢价的分类

  在资产负债表上，债券以其账面价值报告。账面价值等于票面价值减去所有折价或加上所有溢价。折价和溢价账户分别是反向负债账户或是附加负债账户。

票据与债券的财务报表陈述和披露要求

在一年内到期的长期债务划入流动负债，而不会在一年内到期的长期债务仍旧作为非流动或长期负债。有大量债务证券的实体会在资产负债表上报告其金额并附上数字细目。长期负债的一些披露要点如图表2-171所示（当前年度是第二年）。

图表2-171　K-V制药公司长期负债披露（概括性数据）

K-V制药公司长期债务
第3年3月31日的长期债务

	第三年	第二年
房产抵押贷款	$43 000	$10 740
可转换票据	200 000	200 000
	$243 000	$210 740
减去：短期部分	(1 681)	(973)
	$241 319	$209 767

在第3年的3月31日，本公司与两个银行达成了信用协议，该协议提供了最高可借款$140 000的循环信用额度，其中包括$80 000的循环信用额度和$60 000的补充信用额度。这些信用额度分别在第3年10月和6月到期。循环信用额度和补充信用额度没有担保，利率取基准利率和LIBOR月利率上浮175个基点的较低者。在第3年3月31日，公司在循环信用额度下发行了价值$3 900的开放式信用证，而此时公司并未借入任何现金。信用协议含有保护性条款，要求了息、税、折旧和摊销前的最低利润水平以及最高负债率、资本性支出和股利支付限制、固定费用最小覆盖率、最大杠杆率。

在第3年3月，公司与其主要的债权人签署了本金为$43 000的抵押贷款协议，其中$9 859用于现有抵押贷款的再融资。公司从新的抵押贷款中所收到的净收入的$32 764将用于营运资本和公司主要目标。新的抵押贷款使用了公司的3处房产作为抵押，其利息为5.91%于第16年4月1日到期。

在第0年5月16日，公司发行了本金为$200 000的可转换次级票据（简称"票据"），这些票据在一定条件下可以$23.01的转换价格转换为A类普通股。票据于第31年5月16日到期，年利率为2.50%，每年5月16日和11月15日付息。在第3年的前6个月，如果每$1 000本金在第三个交易日的5日交易平均价大于或等于$1 200，此时公司在任何6个月期（从5月16日到11月15日以及从11月16日到5月15日）都存在或有利息支出，其利率为年利率的0.5%。因为这项或有利息是建立在票据的基本价值之上，所以它符合内嵌衍生金融工具的性质。在第3年3月31日，管理层认为这项或有利息内嵌衍生金融工具的公允价值不存在，所以，这个内嵌衍生金融工具未分到任何利润。

在第3年5月21日当天或之后，公司可以回购价格用现金的方式回购一些或所有票据。总支出为100%的本金加上所有应计未付的利息（含或有利息，如果存在）。根据票据管理契约，持有者有权在第5、8、13、18、23年的5月16号或是控制权变化时要求公司用现金回购全部或部分票据。回购包括100%的本金加上所有应计未付的利息（含或有利息，如果存在）。

该票据对于已有的和将有的高级负债而言是次级债务。公司在减去承销折扣、佣金和上市费用后的净收入大约是$194 000。票据可在到期前根据持有者的选择转换为公司A类普通股，前提如下：

- 在第0年6月30日后的任何一季度，如果公司A类普通股日收盘价中超过上期最后一个交易日的票据转换价格120%的个数超过规定数目，票据可以每股$23.01的价格转换。这个价格等于每$1 000本金的票据大约转换为43.4594股。
- 如果公司要求回购票据。
- 连续9天每天每$1 000本金票据交易价格小于公司A类普通股收盘价的95%以及每$1 000本金票据可转换的普通股数接下来的5个交易日。
- 视具体公司业务的发生而定。

公司已经保留了8 691 880股A类普通股以为票据转换为公司普通股做准备。

无担保票据没有股利分配、更多借款和公司证券回购的限制，也没有任何财务保护性条款。

在第3年3月31日，长期负债的到期值如下所示：

1年到期	$1 687
2年到期	1 941
3年到期	2 058
4年到期	2 182

续表

5 年到期	2 315
5 年以后	$232 824
加权平均有限合伙人的流通单位票据—稀释后	

公司在第 2 年和第 3 年的 3 月 31 日在扣除资本化利息后，分别支付了 $4 692 和 $4 156 利息。在第 1 年 3 月 31 日，公司支付了 $3 215 的利息。

　　在财务报表附注中应披露债务证券的所有详细资料，包括性质、到期时间、利率、所使用的担保和其他限制条件或提供的权利比如赎回条款等。公司还必须披露未来 5 年的利息支付信息和本金偿还要求及到期时间（见图表 2 – 171 的底部）。所有表外融资安排，比如项目融资安排，也必须在附注中披露。有可赎回债券的公司必须披露因违反债务安排而可赎回的债券，包括描述被违背的保护性条款以及对长期负债及其所处状态的披露。公司还必须说明，是否由于违背情况可能得到纠正，因此有些债券会被归类为非流动负债。

　　其他未包含于图表 2 – 171 中的附注内容如下所示：

- 公司各种信用额度和保护性条款的合约披露。
- 新的长期负债的披露。
- 披露潜在的稀释性可转换为普通股的票据，包括相关或有事项及其可能影响的讨论。
- 可回购票据及其持有者权利的披露。

债务的提前偿付

　　当债务按照日程表偿还，则所有的折价或溢价将会被完全摊销，债务的账面价值将等于面值。因此，不会记录任何利得或损失。但是，当债务在到期日前提前清偿时，便可能产生利得或损失。利得或损失是债务账面价值（包括任何未摊销的溢价和折价以及发行成本）与回购价格的差异。当回购价格大于账面价值时，产生损失；当账面价值大于回购价格时，产生利得。

　　SFAS 第 No. 145 不再允许债务提前偿付的利得或损失划入非经常项目，虽然在第 4 号公告里有这样的要求。

　　视同清偿产生于不可撤销信托账户，此账户有足够基金（本金加信托中获得的利息）能够偿还剩余债务。视同清偿并不代表负债清偿反映在债务人的资产负债表上（不确认任何利得或损失）。

权益交易及每股收益

　　虽然独资企业和合伙制企业对权益的处理不同，但这里所探讨的权益针对的是最常见的所有者权益形式，即公司制。这里同时也会介绍每股收益。

公司资本

　　在公司中的所有者权益又称为公司资本、股东权益。公司资本由股本、资本公积和保留盈余组成。已投入股本或实缴资本等于股本加上资本公积，它代表了投资者对权益证券的总投入。保留盈余代表已赚资本，是盈利性业务带来的经营成果。保留盈余可用于股利分配（有一些限制条件），股利代表投资者的投资回报。

法定资本定义为股本的面值。面值是印在股票上的名义数额，与公允价值无关。但是，当投资者以低于面值的价格购入股票（不常发生的情况），在公司破产时，会给公司的债权人带来或有负债。为了避免这一问题，面值通常很小。股票也可以在没有面值的情况下发行。在这种情况下，每股设定价值可能出现，其作用类似面值但不会带来债权人或有负债的问题。

股票发行的会计处理

公司可以在获得了批准后发行股票。公司可以直接发行股票或由承销商经手发行。当股票卖出时，公司记录下收到的现金和发行的股票。具体情况讨论如下。

有面值的股票。当有面值的股票售出时，面值贷记入一个单独账户。对不同类的股票，比如普通股和优先股，有不同的面值账户。超过面值的部分贷记资本公积（又称股票溢价）。折价账户用来记录低于面值发行的部分。

举个例子，发行 1 000 股面值为 \$6 的股票，收入 \$10 000。会计分录如图表 2 – 172 所示：

图表 2 – 172　溢价发行股票

现金	\$10 000	
普通股股本		\$6 000
超过面值的实缴资本（普通股溢价）		\$4 000

没有面值的股票。没有面值的股票记录在一个单一账户中，不确认资本公积。如图表 2 – 173 所示。

图表 2 – 173　没有面值股票的发行

现金	\$10 000	
普通股股本		\$10 000

没有面值但有设定价值的股票发行与有面值的股票发行会计处理类似。设定价值记在股本账户，任何超过设定价值的部分记在资本公积账户上。

以认购方式发行的股票。在以认购方式发行股票时，投资者以分期付款的方式出资，直到价格完全付清后股票才会发行。在资产负债表上，应收认购款作为所有者权益的反向账户列示而非资产类账户。

一次付款发行。当各类股票采用一揽子交易时，总的收入将在不同的股票间进行分配。如果已知各类股票的公允价值，则分配的基础建立在相对公允价值上（比例法）。用每类股票的公允价值除以总的公允价值作为比率，再乘以购买价格，所得价值分配到该类股票上，如图表 2 – 174 所示。10 000 股普通股和 5 000 股优先股以 \$180 000 的一次性付款价格发行。当日普通股股价为 \$14，优先股股价为 \$10。

图表 2 – 174　分配一次性付款发行价格的比例法

普通股公允价值（10 000 × \$14）	=	\$140 000
优先股公允价值（5 000 × \$10）	=	50 000
总公允价值		\$190 000
分配到普通股： $\dfrac{\$140\ 000}{\$190\ 000} \times \$180\ 000$	=	\$132 632
分配到优先股 $\dfrac{\$50\ 000}{\$190\ 000} \times \$180\ 000$	=	\$47 368
总额		\$180 000

当只能确定其中一个证券的公允价值时，则该证券以其公允价值入账，剩下的金额计入另外一个证券的账户中（增量法）。如果不能取得任何公允价值，价值的分配将取决于评价或估计。

以非货币性交易方式发行的股票。对于所有非货币性交易，交易的价值由发行股票的市场价值决定或由收到的非货币性资产的市场价值来确定。如果二者都不能取得任何公允价值，价值的分配将取决于评价或估计。

股票发行成本。直接股票发行成本冲减发行收入，借计入资本公积（而不是作为费用）。这些成本包括：

- 打印成本。
- 承销费用和市场营销成本。
- 在准备注册时发生的法律和会计成本。
- 上市费。
- 文员、管理以及邮寄费用。

循环发生的费用，比如对投资者的备案记录、注册或代理成本应计入当期费用。

即使公司没有打算立即将所有获得许可的股票公开发行，公司会希望对于新的股票只注册一次。这种情况叫做储架注册。通过向 SEC 申请获得许可，公司可以储架注册。储架注册可以帮助公司减少上市费用。未发行的股票作为库藏股票直到在未来的某一天发行。

股本

股本分为普通股和优先股除非实体只有其中一种股票，这一种通常是普通股。普通股的性质已经在前面介绍过了（有面值的股票、没有面值的股票等）。接下来介绍优先股的性质。

优先股

与普通股相比，优先股具有一些优先权利，但不具备投票权。一些优先股可转化为普通股，一些优先股可以在一定的时间、以一定价格赎回。当公司的负债权益比过高时，优先股可以替代债券发行。优先股的一些性质讨论如下。

- **股利优先权**

优先股股东有权比普通股股东优先获得股利。在宣告分配股利之前，董事会必须确定公司有足够的保留盈余和现金支付股利。

优先股股利率设定为票面价值的百分比。比如，发行面值为 $50 的优先股，优先股年股利率为 10%。对于累积优先股，如果当年没有宣告股利的，拖欠股利将会积累下来，到下次股利发放时必须优先于普通股股利发放。拖欠股利并不认为是负债但会在财务报表附注上披露。

另一种优先股即参与分红优先股，是将优先股和普通股股东将获得的总股利放在一起按照一定的方式分配。

- **投票权**

优先股通常没有投票权。

- **清偿优先权**

在公司清偿时，资产将首先分配给债权人，其次是优先股股东，最后才是普通股股东。所以，在破产的情况下，偿付给股东的资产可能不够。

- **债务 VS. 优先股**

与债务不同，优先股没有到期日也没有必须偿还的法律责任，所以它归类为所有者权益。但是，强制赎回优先股必须在某一天赎回，实质上，它更像是债务而非所有者权益。于是，SFAS 第 150 号文件要求将其归类为负债。

库藏股（股票回购）

公司已发行而后又重新买回的股票叫做库藏股。股票可能因为以下几个原因而重新买回：

- 减少股东防止收购。
- 为员工股票期权做准备。
- 增加每股收益及权益回报。
- 为公司股票建立市场使价格能较为稳定或上涨。
- 在资本利得率较好的情况下发放股利。

库藏股作为股东权益的减项报告，不作为资产因为一个实体不能拥有自己。作为库藏股的股票没有投票权也没有股利。库藏股可以用成本法或面值法进行会计处理。在实务上，成本法用得更多。

- **成本法**

在成本法下，股票再次购买的成本借计入库藏股账户。当库藏股再次发行时，成本再贷计入库藏股账户，售出价格借计入现金账户，现金收入超过库藏股成本的部分贷计入库藏股资本公积。如果库藏股以低于成本的价格再次发行，二者差异可以借计入库藏股资本公积或保留盈余。在成本法下，以 $9 的价格回购 10 000 股应如图表 2 – 175 所示的会计处理。

图表 2 – 175　在成本法下记录股票回购

库藏股	$90 000	
现金		$90 000

以 $11 的价格再次发行 4 000 股记录如下：

图表 2 –176　在成本法下记录股票再发行

现金	$44 000	
库藏股（4 000 股每股 $9）		$36 000
库藏股资本公积		$8 000

- **面值法**

在面值法中，库藏股以面值记录。当再次发行时，已售出价格借记现金，面值贷记库藏股，超过部分贷计入资本公积。

库藏股的退出

库藏股实际上包含于三个账户中：其回购成本在库藏股账户中（在成本法下），在普通股账户中（面值）和在资本公积中（售价超过面值的部分）。当库藏股退出时，这三个账户中的相关余额将会被冲减掉。具体分录如图表 2 – 177 所示。假设有面值为 $5 的 10 000 股库藏股退出。最初发行价为每股 $8，回购价为每股 $9。

图表 2 –177　库藏股退出成本法

普通股，面值 $5	$50 000	
普通股资本公积 *	$30 000	
保留盈余	$10 000	
库藏股（10 000 股，每股 $9）		$90 000
*（$8 – $5）× 10 000 = $30 000		

如果使用的是面值法，则用在库藏股账户中的面值冲减其在股本中的面值。会计分录如图表 2 – 178 所示：

图表 2 –178　库藏股退出面值法

普通股，面值 $5	$50 000	
库藏股（10 000 股，每股 $5）		$50 000

库藏股的披露要求

库藏股的每个交易都要求披露。当库藏股购入或出售，公司应当披露发行的股票数额、库藏股数额以及在外流通的股票数。此外，如果库藏股以成本法计量，库藏股的总成本作为总股东权益的减项。如果使用面值法，库藏股的面值应作为同类股票面值的减项。库藏股的资本公积直接列示到了同类资本公积下，因此不再需要单独披露。

股票的退出可以采取实际退出即通过正式的申请将其取消；或通过建设性退出即只有董事会的授权而没有正式的取消。对于后者要求披露库藏股股数。

实缴资本

实缴资本或已投入股本在股票发行时记录且会受到其他一些业务的影响，包括：

- 以高于或低于成本的价格售出库藏股。
- 为消化赤字而对资本结构的修订（账面重组）。
- 将可转换债券或优先股转化为普通股。

实缴资本在资产负债表上的陈述

股本和资本公积都列示在资产负债表的股东权益下。各类流通股的权利及特权都必须披露。在资本注入后，这个基金变成了所有股东的投资池，单个股东对一定的价格并不具有特殊要求权。在这些账户中的变化将会反映到股东权益表上。资产负债表中股东权益部分如图表 2–179 所示。

图表 2–179　已投入股本

Bounce 运动商品公司	
已投入股本	
12 月 31 日	
已投入股本：	
优先股，面值 $70（9%，累计可转换，10 000 股票中有 5 500 股流通在外）	$385 000
普通股，面值 $4（70 000 股票中有 46 500 股流通在外）	186 000
库藏股，成本法（1 000 普通股）	(18 400)
资本公积	652 093
总已投入股本	$1 204 693

保留盈余

保留盈余主要来源于盈利性经营活动。除了净利润（损失），其他能影响到保留盈余的还有：以前年度调整（修正差错或会计政策变更）、各种股利、库藏股票相关业务及账面重组。

股票期权、认股权证和权利

股票期权、认股权证和权利都是看涨期权，它给了持有者在规定行权价上购买一个公司股票的权利。因为它们是权益融资工具，它们的会计处理会涉及实缴资本。

发行给员工的股票

当股票期权行权时，向员工发行股票可以作为员工的额外薪酬。员工也可以按照员工股票认购计划购买股票。

- **职工持股计划（非酬劳性计划）**

职工持股计划（ESOP）或员工股票认购计划的目的是在融资的同时让员工感受到所有者的感觉而非作为额外薪酬。考虑到是非酬劳性计划，这个计划基本上会包含所有全职职工且其折价也会很小（与现有股东获得的折价相比）。这个计划不具有任何期权性质。没有这些性质，一个计划不能被认为是具有酬劳性的。记录上不会有任何酬劳性支出，这类股票的出售与其他一般股票的处理相同。

职工持股计划的披露要求包括：关于计划的描述、投资基础、包括的人群及有助于比较各期情况的附注。同时，确认的重大会计政策、薪酬成本，任何回购责任

（公允价值总额）和任何未实现的报酬都要披露。

- **权益分享计划**

根据 SFAS No. 123（修订版），在员工收到股票期权当日，期权的公允价值由类似期权的市场价值确定，如果存在这样的类似期权；或者通过期权定价模型估计。期权的公允价值计入资本公积，作为员工服务期的薪酬费用。员工服务期是指员工用自己的劳动换取薪酬的时期，通常指在期权收到日和期权第一次可执行日之间的时间段。

举个例子，假设一个执行官得到了一个期权，以 \$20 购买面值为 \$8 的 1 000 股普通股。此期权可执行日在四年后。在收到日，期权的公允价值被认为是 \$4 每单位。在员工服务期的每年，分录记录如图表 2 – 180 所示：

图表 2 – 180　每年记录薪酬费用的分录

薪酬费用	\$1 000	
实缴资本—股票期权		\$1 000

当行权时，分录记录如下：

图表 2 – 181　记录期权行权的分录

现金（\$20 1 000 股）	\$20 000	
实缴资本—股票期权	\$4 000	
普通股，面值 \$8		\$8 000
资本公积，普通股		\$16 000

有股票薪酬计划的公司必须披露这些计划的性质、估算公允价值的方法、对损益表的影响和带来的现金流变化。

认股权证和权利

认股权证允许持有者在一定的时期内以某一价格购买股票。针对员工的股票期权也是一种权证，正如股东的股票权利。权证有时会和其他证券如债券或优先股一起打包销售。当股票价格高于权证上的价格，则会有潜在的盈利存在，不管是行权卖掉股票还是直接卖掉此时已有内在价值的权证本身。

股票权利给了当前股东购买其手中持有股份百分比部分的权利，以此来防止他们的所有权的转换和未经他们允许的投票权稀释。这一权利也被称为先买权。此项权证发行时不用作任何分录。当行权时，和其他股票销售一样，必须记录收到的现金和发行的股票。

与其他证券一起发行的股票权证

权证有时会和其他证券比如债券或普通股一起打包销售，作为诱惑投资者的激励机制。只要权证能够从中分离出来单独销售，发行者就必须在权证和其他债券之间分配发行收入。分配采用比例法或增量法（这两种方法在前面讨论一揽子交易时介绍过）。

- **比例法**

当可以确定二者的市场价值时，通常采用比例法。一般使用二者在发行后单独上市交易的价格。总的发行收入以二者的相对市价进行分配。比如，假设有 1 000 股优先股和 1 000 份权证同时发行，获得收入 $20 750。在发行后，优先股市场价值为 $18.25，权证为 $3。在比例法下的具体分配如图表 2 - 182 所示：

图表 2 - 182   比例法下计量打包销售中股票权证的价值

优先股公允价值（1 000 × $18.25）	=	$18 250
权证公允价值（1 000 × $3）	=	3 000
总公允价值		$21 250
分配到优先股：$\dfrac{\$18\ 250}{\$21\ 250} \times \$20\ 750$	=	$17 821
分配到权证：$\dfrac{\$3\ 000}{\$21\ 250} \times \$20\ 750$	=	2 929
总额		$20 750

- **增量法**

如果其一公允价值无法获得（比如权证可能无法单独交易），此时将使用增量法。在这个方法下，可确定的公允价值会直接进入该项证券，剩下的部分进入另一个证券。图表 2 - 183 展示了这一方法，假设在上面那个例子中只有优先股可以确定公允价值。

图表 2 - 183   增量法下计量打包销售中股票权证的价值

总收入	=	$20 750
分配到优先股	=	18 250
剩下的分配到权证	=	$2 500

保留盈余的分配

保留盈余的分配是指将收益以一定目的重新分类。保留盈余分配必须得到董事会的同意。分配会减少不适量的保留盈余并且必须在所有者权益内部进行。但是，根据 SFAS No.5，成本或损失不能直接由保留盈余的分配来抵减且必须报告到损益表上。一旦这些成本计算在内，那么保留盈余的分配便应做反向记录。保留盈余的分配只是传递这样一个信号，那就是这些收益不再能作为股利分配出去。作为另一个选择，保留盈余限制要被披露。导致保留盈余的分配或限制的原因有以下几点：

- 或有负债（比如未决诉讼）。
- 对库藏股的法律限制。
- 与债券保护性条款有关的合同限制。
- 工厂扩张或债务清偿。

保留盈余分配的会计处理

保留盈余分配账户设立为保留盈余的子账户。当分配时，会计分录如图表2－184 所示：

图表2－184　保留盈余分配的会计处理

保留盈余	$10 000 000	
保留盈余分配—X 产品诉讼的或有损失		$10 000 000

股利

股利分配总是从保留盈余里支付的，但是很少有公司发放它们所有的保留盈余。保留盈余可能被限制使用了，或公司可能希望保留一些资产以备未来发展需要。很多公司都努力保持平稳的与投资者期望相一致的股利发放政策。另一方面，一些年轻公司从来没有发放过股利。只要保留盈余没有被发放为股利，它们应该对股价有贡献作用。我们讲解的股利类型包括：现金股利、财产股利、清算股利、可累积股利、代价券股利以及股票股利。同样，我们也会介绍股票拆分和反向股票拆分。

现金股利

在优先股上的现金股利是固定的，它是面值或设定价值的一个百分比。普通股的股利由董事会酌情决定。现金股利在董事会宣布发放时便成为了负债（宣告日）。在除权日当天持有公司股票的股东将会在付息日得到股利。假设董事会为 200 000 股在外流通股发放每股 $1 的股利，宣告日的会计处理如图表2－185 所示：

图表2－185　宣告日现金股利的会计处理

保留盈余	$200 000	
应付股利		$200 000

在除权日当日不需要作任何分录。在付息日，贷记现金，借记应付股利。

财产股利

任何一个不可逆将非货币资产从公司转向其所有者都认为是财产股利。以财产、商品或投资为应付股利形式的都叫做财产股利。财产股利以被转换资产的公允价值为计量基础。在宣告日，资产的成本和账面价值之间的差额被确认为利得或损失。

假设公司宣告发放财产股利，股利内容是作为投资持有的证券。证券成本和账面价值为 $1 000 000，公允价值为 $1 300 000。在宣告日的分录如图表2－186 所示：

图表2－186　宣告日财产股利的会计处理

证券投资	$300 000	
证券利得		$300 000
保留盈余（发放财产股利）	$1 300 000	
应付财产股利		$1 300 000

股利发放日的分录如图表 2 – 187 所示：

图表 2 – 187　发放日财产股利的会计处理

应付财产股利	$1 300 000	
证券投资		$1 300 000

清算股利

通过投资资本发放而非保留盈余发放的股利叫做清算股利。清算股利是对股东投资的回收而非像正常股利一样回报股东投资。

清算股利通常会发生在当公司停止营业时。图表 2 – 168 所示的分录描述了分别从保留盈余（正常股利）和资本公积（清算股利）中发放股利的会计处理：

图表 2 – 188　在宣告日发放清算股利的会计处理

保留盈余	$750 000	
资本公积	$250 000	
应付股利		$1 000 000

支付日的会计分录如图表 2 – 169 所示：

图表 2 – 189　在支付日发放清算股利的会计处理

应付股利	$1 000 000	
现金		$1 000 000

可累积股利

优先股股利是可累积的，意思是说如果一个公司在某一年没能发放股利那就存在股利拖欠，则公司有法律责任在发放普通股股利前，如果有任何拖欠股利，则必须先支付拖欠股利。除非优先股表明了是非累积的，否则，从法律上来讲它们就是累积的。非累积股没有支付以前年度拖欠股利的法律责任（如普通股）。

代价券股利

代价券是应付票据的一种，因此，代价券股利是未来支付一定股利的承诺。代价券股利主要是在公司有足够保留盈余但没有足够现金流时支付。在公司无法发放满足市场预期的股利（一个不利的信号）时，也可以使用。股东持有代价券股利至到期日时可以将在公开市场上出售。

股票股利

股票股利是指企业不可逆地将自己的股票按比例分派给股东。与现金股利和财产股利不同，股票股利不会影响总资产或所有者权益，只是将保留盈余重新划分为实缴资本。非盈余资本化可以将该部分盈余永远保留在公司里。股票股利发放额小于宣告日在外流通股数 20% 或 25% 的，属于小额股票股利发放，在宣告日以市场价值借记保留盈余。相对地，股票股利发放额大于宣告日在外流通股数 20% 或 25% 的，属于大额股票股利发放，在宣告日以面值借记保留盈余。

在公司想要分红利给股东同时又想要节省点现金时，公司会考虑发放股票股利。通过将现金从盈利转化为实缴资本，公司将现金进行了再投资。股东可以在公开市场上交易这些多余的证券。

尽管在股票股利发放后股东仍旧保持其在公司中的持股比例不变，但更多股票在外流通会导致每股账面价值和每股市场价格下降。在大规模股票股利发放中，其产生的影响尤为明显。所以，通常市场把大额股票股利发放当成股票拆分。

股票拆分和反向股票拆分

股票拆分是一种在不改变各股东持股比例的情况下，降低每股市价的工具。它通过对每一在外流通股发行一定数量的股票并将面值按相应比例调整，达到这一效用。举个例子，100 000 份流通股，$400 市价，4:1 的股票拆分比例，结果为 400 000 份流通股，$100 市价。与股票股利不同，股票拆分不会导致所有者权益的变化；股票股利的发放只会带来在外流通股的增加而不会带来面值的减少（流通股的总面值会增加）。使更多的投资者能够买该公司股票是股票拆分的原因之一，这样可以稀释公司所有权还可以增加总交易量。在股票拆分中不用做会计分录，但应该留有股票面值变动的备案。

反向股票拆分与股票拆分方向相反，尽管反向股票拆分很少发生，反向股票拆分减少了在外流通股并按比例增加了股票面值。比如，200 000 份流通股，$1 市价，1:20 的反向股票拆分，结果为 10 000 份流通股，$20 每股市价。

每股收益（EPS）：简单资本结构

没有在外流通的潜在稀释性证券的公司有简单资本结构，反之则拥有复杂资本结构。潜在稀释性证券是指可能导致潜在的更多普通股发行的证券，包括可转换优先股、可转换债券、或有股及股票期权、认股权证或权力。

基本每股收益由具有简单资本结构的公司报告。计算时用普通股享有的净利润（净利润减去优先股股利）除以该年加权平均在外流通股数。

$$每股收益 = \frac{净利润 - 优先股股利}{年加权平均在外流通股股数}$$

优先股股利和加权平均股数讨论如下。

优先股股利

优先股股利代表着普通股享有净利润的减少。所以，优先股股利总是从净利润中减去（或者当公司有净损失时，它会增大公司的损失）。当优先股是可累积的，那么各年股利是否会影响每股收益数字也应被披露。

年加权平均在外流通股数

只要在外流通股的股数发生变化，加权平均在外流通股数就被用来计算每股收益。在某一时刻的流通股数以其在外时间占总年度时间的比例为权重计量：

$$加权平均在外流通股股数 = 在外流通股 \times \frac{在外流通月数}{12\ 月}$$

将一年的加权平均在外流通股数加起来构成年加权流通股股数。比如，假设公司因为发行新股和回购股票作为库藏股而改变了公司的在外流通股股数，如图表2－190所示：

图表2－190　在外流通股

日期	股票变化	在外流通股股数
1.1	期初余额	110 000
3.1	发行40 000收回现金	40 000
		150 000
6.1	买回46 000股	46 000
		104 000
10.1	发行35 000股收回现金	35 000
12.31	期末余额	139 000

计算总加权平均在外流通股股数的过程如图表2－191所示：

图表2－191　加权平均在外流通股股数

在外流通时间	在外流通股数		占本年度比例		加权平均值
1.1 ~ 3.1	110 000	×	2/12	=	18 333
3.1 ~ 6.1	150 000	×	3/12	=	37 500
6.1 ~ 10.1	104 000	×	4/12	=	34 667
10.1 ~ 12.31	139 000	×	3/12	=	34 750
加权在外流通股股数					125 250

假设在非正常项目前收益为 \$300 000，优先股股利 \$100 000。则在非正常项目前普通股享有的收益为 \$200 000，则每股收益计算如下：

图表2－192　普通股享有收益的计算

	收益		加权平均股数		每股收益
非正常项目前普通股享有的收益	\$200 000	÷	125 250	=	\$1.60
税后非正常利得	50 000	÷	125 250	=	0.40
普通股享有的收益	\$250 000	÷	125 250	=	\$2.00

与非正常项目相关的每股收益必须单独披露，可以在损益表中披露或在附注中披露。损益表披露如图表2－193所示：

图表2－193　与非正常项目相关的每股收益

非正常项目前的收益	\$300 000
税后非正常利得	50 000
净收益	\$350 000

续表

每股收益：	
非正常项目前的收益	$1.60
税后非正常项目	0.40
净收益	$2.00

每股收益（EPS）：复杂资本结构

有在外流通潜在稀释性证券的公司具有复杂资本结构，既要报告基本每股收益，也要报告稀释每股收益。稀释每股收益反映了这样的假设影响，即潜在稀释性证券的行权或转换会稀释普通股享有的收益。

稀释每股收益＝基础每股收益＋可转换证券的影响＋认股权证的影响

披露稀释每股收益的目的是显示不良信息或每股收益潜在的降低。有时，潜在稀释性证券的行权或转换会带来每股收益的增加。当这种情况发生时，这种证券认定为反稀释证券且在计算稀释每股收益时不考虑在内。所以，稀释每股收益（损失）总是会比基础每股收益小。

可转换债券和可转换优先股对稀释每股收益的影响使用如果转换法计算，而认股权证、股票期权和权利对稀释每股收益的影响使用库藏股法计算。

如果转换法

如果转换法假设可转换证券可在期初转换为普通股（在当期发行的，则在发行日可转换），之后，这个假设对每股收益分子和分母的影响就确定了。在可转换债券的情况下，如果债券转换了，那么就不再存在相应债券利息费用的减项，所以在计算时要先把税后利息费用（因为利息费用先于所得税抵减）加回。转换同时会增加在外流通股股数。从基本每股收益开始，要得到稀释每股收益，分子和分母都必须加上相应调整数。可转换优先股的调整类似，只是可转换优先股股利不会影响到税收（分子中使用的是净收益）。

举个例子，假设税率为40%，发行了两组可转换债券：6%面值为$1 000 000的可转换债券可在1月1日转换为30 000股普通股；7%面值为$1 000 000的可转换债券可在7月1日转换为35 000股普通股。对第一组债券的净税收调整计算如下：

每年利息费用×（1－税率）

（$1 000 000×6%）×（1－0.40）＝$36 000

因为第二组债券在7月发行，在计算时只能计算半年的利息：

$$每年利息费用×（1－税率）×\frac{在外流通月数}{12\ 月}$$

$$（\$1\ 000\ 000×7\%）×（1－0.40）×\frac{1}{2}＝\$21\ 000$$

如果根据基础每股收益，普通股享有的净收益为$300 000，则要得到稀释每股收益，税后债券利息费用应加到分子上：$300 000＋$36 000＋$21 000＝$357 000。加权平均在外流通股股数，每股收益的分母，应该加上假设转换后的股数乘以占该年的比例（从7月到12月）。

$$可转换得到的股票票数 \times \frac{在外流通月数}{12\,月}$$

$$30\,000 \times 1 = 30\,000$$

$$35\,000 \times \frac{1}{2} = 17\,500$$

如果在计算基础每股收益时使用的是 100 000 的股数，那么在计算稀释每股收益时，其分母应该为：100 000 + 30 000 + 17 500 = 147 500。则稀释每股收益等于 $357 000 除以 147 500，即 $2.42。

库藏股法

库藏股法假设（1）认股权证和股票期权在年初行使（如果在当期发行的，则在发行日行使），（2）行权的收入全部用来以该年的平均价格回购股票作为库藏股。第二个假设有利于缓和行权之后可能带来的股票增加。在第（1）步发行的股票数和第（2）步回购的股票数之间的差额，作为每股收益分母的净增加。当行权价低于市场价时，这会是一个增量，因为要买回所有发行的股票，收入不够。因为权证不用付利息或股利，所以其不会对每股收益的分子产生影响。

当权证或期权的行权价高于市场价时，期权便具有反稀释性质，在计算稀释每股收益时便不再考虑。所以，当行权价低于市场价时，认为没有发生行权，也没有稀释发生。

举个例子，假设一个公司有 2 000 个权证在外流通，每个权证行权后可以用来以每股 $15 的价格购买普通股，当年公司普通股平均市场价值为 $45。库藏股法的第一个假设：假设所有权证和期权在年初行使，会带来 2 000 股普通股的发行，获得现金流入 $30 000（2 000 × $15）。接下来，假设公司以平均市价回购了 667 股（$30 000 ÷ $45）。这样的净结果为 1 333（2 000 − 667）净增股数加到计算稀释每股收益的分母上。

$$股票增量 = 期权数 \times \frac{市价 - 期权行权价}{市价}$$

$$= 2\,000 \times \frac{\$45 - \$15}{\$45} = 1\,333$$

假设基础每股收益为每股 $3.00，因为收益为 $300 000 而流通股股数为 100 000。增加的股数将加到分母上，稀释每股收益的计算如下：

$$稀释每股收益 = \frac{\$300\,000}{100\,000 + 1\,333} = \$2.96 \,（每股）$$

在有可转换债务和认股权证的情况下计算稀释每股收益

假设上面的用如果转换法和库藏股法的例子发生在同一公司的同一时间，则联合稀释每股收益的计算如下所示：

稀释每股收益 = 基础每股收益 + 可转换证券的影响 + 权证的影响

$$= \frac{\$300\,000 + \$36\,000 + \$21\,000}{100\,000 + 47\,500 + 1\,333} = \frac{\$357\,000}{148\,833\,股} = \$2.40 \,（每股）$$

基础每股收益和稀释每股收益的损益表陈述如图表 2 − 194 所示：

图表2-194 每股收益披露

当年净收益	$300 000
每股收益（附注1）	
基础每股收益（$300 000 ÷ 100 000）	$3.00
稀释每股收益（$357 000 ÷ 148 833）	$2.40

所有者权益及每股收益的财务报表陈述和披露

有关简单和复杂的每股收益在损益表中的披露前面已经介绍过了。当损益表中出现非经常项目时，应披露持续经营的每股收益、非经常项目之前的每股收益、会计政策变化前的每股收益及每股净收益。在报表上的每一期都必须计算每股收益。

在 SFAS No. 128（1997 年 2 月）取代了 APB No. 15，提供了公共公司计算和列示每股收益的指南。第 128 号公告整合了国际准则每股收益实务处理并简化了报告。本章已讲到了该准则的具体要求，比如对于具有潜在稀释性证券的公司要求既要披露基本每股收益又要披露稀释每股收益。进一步讲，对复杂资本结构公司有以下披露要求：

- 在外流通证券的权利及特权。
- 计算基础和稀释每股收益所用的分子和分母，说明每种证券的影响。
- 年终之后、报表发布之前的转换事件的影响。
- 在计算基础每股收益时优先股所占的权重。
- 在基础或稀释每股收益中没有包含但会对未来每股收益产生影响的反稀释证券。

收入确认

收入确认成为 SEC 最近非常关注的问题，因为很多被要求重新出具报告的公司就是因为提前确认了或不当确认了一项收益。下面重点介绍在不同行业里收入确认的方法。

FASB 第 5 号概念公告中所指出的收入确认原则要求在收入已实现或可实现或已收到的情况下确认收入。但是，这一原则与第 6 号概念公告并不完全一致，第 6 号概念公告中将收入定义为资产的流入或是在公司持续经营或主营业务活动中负债的降低。所以，FASB 正在从资产和负债改变的角度重新定义收入确认原则。

以下是收入的常见来源，也是典型的收入确认点：
- 产品销售：在销售当日或产品发出日确认。
- 提供服务：在服务提供后或账单寄出时确认。
- 允许对方使用自己的资产而收到的利息、租金及允许权使用费按照时间的推移或随资产被使用而确认。
- 对非存货资产处置的利得或损失：在售出日确认。

收入的确认通常是在售出时，但有些收入确认可在产品发出前（在产品生产之前、生产过程中或生产之后）或产品发出后（当收到现金或成本得到补偿时）。下面探讨不同的收入确认方法。

销售点确认的一些问题

有时在销售日确认收入存在一些问题，比如有售后购回协议或退回权时。

- **有售后回购协议的销售**

含有购回协议的销售从法律意义上讲已转移了商品的相关权利，但卖方仍保留了所有权风险，所以不能确认任何销售收入（注意在对存货的讨论中已涉及这类问题）。

- **有退回权的销售**

书籍、杂志和音乐发行商，易腐食品的交易商和其他许多产品行业为提高销售而提供退回权。只要以下条件满足，公司应用销售收入减去估计退回备抵：

- 售价固定或可确定。
- 买方付款给卖方的责任不是以产品的转售来衡量的。
- 偷盗、损失或产品的毁坏不会改变买方对卖方的责任。
- 经济实质上，买方与卖方是分开的。
- 买方没有在未来帮助卖方重新售出产品的明显责任。
- 退回量可合理估计。
- **提前确认收入（暗转）**

提前确认收入是指与分销商签订协议，让分销商超出市场需求地大量吃进他们的货物，以造成公司销售额（或利润）很高的样子。其效果是提前确认明年或明天的收入，最终将导致未来收入降低，除非这种暗转操作能一直进行下去。这种报表粉饰行为不受鼓励。

产品发出后确认

当销售价格的收回不能确定时，可以采用三种方法确认收入：分期付款销售法、成本回收法和收现营收认列法。

- **分期付款销售法**

分期付款销售法随着现金的收回确认收入，而不是在销售发生点就确认。当可收回价值无法合理估计时，通常采用这一方法。所以，在需要分期付款时，通常采用这一方法（比如家具、大型贵重商品、土地开发等）。为了保护卖方，这些协议通常都有保护性条款，比如在完全付清后才能转移资产所有权。

这种方法在销售期间确认收入和销售成本，但在现金收回时才确认毛利润。毛利润根据每年收回的分期付款来计算。随着现金的收回，应确认的利润等于当年收回现金乘以毛利润率。未确认的毛利润递延到以后年度。

在资产负债表日，虽然一些会计师认为毛利润应该作为应收分期付款账户的反向账户列示，但递延毛利润通常作为未实现收入反映在负债方。

- **成本回收法**

在成本回收法下，只有当收到现金大于销售成本时才确认收入。因此，现金的收回意味着利润的确认。当回收能力无法确认时，可使用这种方法。在销售当年，损益表报告收入、销售成本、递延毛利润和已确认的毛利润。比如，如果一个公司赊销 $100 000，销售成本为 $70 000，确认第一年递延毛利润的结账分录如图表 2 - 195

所示：

图表 2 - 195　成本回收法下第一年结账分录

销售收入	$100 000	
销售成本		$70 000
递延毛利润		$30 000
（结转销售收入和成本，同时确认递延毛利润）		

如果在第二年，第一年销售收回现金为 $80 000，则 $10 000 的毛利润的确认如图表 2 - 196 所示：

图表 2 - 196　成本回收法下第二年结账分录

递延毛利润	$10 000	
实现的毛利润		$10 000
（在第二年的现金收回超过了成本，确认毛利润）		

在第 3 年确认实现利润的最终会计分录如下：

图表 2 - 197　成本回收法下第三年结账分录

递延毛利润	$20 000	
实现的毛利润		$20 000
（在第三年的现金收回超过了成本，确认毛利润）		

- **保证金法**

这种方法不是真正的收入确认方法，而是在商品或财产已支付预付款但卖方尚未转移该商品或财产时所应用的一种程序。在销售完成之前不能确认任何收入。收到的现金作为负债（买方的保证金），存货仍留在卖方的账簿上。当销售完成时，再使用合适的销售收入确认方法。

收入确认的问题和关注要点

除了前面提到的问题，如提前确认收入等，SEC 还在考虑一些其他的问题。比如，一些公司以交易双方中介人的身份收取费用，但将销售总额确认为销售收入。SEC 已经要求这些公司只能确认自己收到的收入为销售收入。另一个关注要点是跨年度的服务提供。这种情况下服务收入的确认只能按照合同分年度来确认，不能提前确认。另一个要点是在合同有效期内逐年确认所有收益，这样的收益只能在实现时才确认。

在 SEC 的报告中，过早或过度的收入确认已经成为了普遍性的问题。这在信息经济泡沫时代成了更大的关注点，当时，在成长期的高科技企业已经开始采用营收倍数代替更为传统的盈余倍数。作为回应，在 SAB 101 号公告中，SEC 总结了在 GAAP 下确认收入的四个基本条件：

- 有足够说服力的证据表明其存在性。

- 已发出或服务已提供。
- 价格一定或可确定。
- 回收可保障。

与收入确认相关的一般公认会计原则仍在不断发展，与商品和服务联合交割合同有关的多要素收入确认问题正逐步得到解决，如附带终生维修服务的设备销售。在这种情况下，应把该项业务分解成各个组成部分，再根据各个组成部分的性质使用不同的收入确认方式。在附带终生维修服务的汽车销售中，将销售价格和预付维修费分开确认很有必要。预付的维修费应递延直到在维修确实发生的年度确认。

FASB 已经将收入确认提上日程，希望能够以一个收入确认原则替代现有的从不同方面对收入确认的描述。

长期在建工程会计处理

长期在建工程的会计处理主要有两个方法：完工百分比法和合同完工法。

完工百分比法

只要完工程度可合理估计且合同具有法律强制权利，则根据 GAAP 可以采用完工百分比法。完工百分比的估计可以采用投入作为标准，比如发生的成本或使用的人工工时数，或者以产出作为标准，比如完成的进度或公路已建完工英里数。常用的投入标准（会计程序委员会第 45 号会计研究公告推荐）是用已发生的成本占完工总成本的比例：

$$完工成本比例 = \frac{目前为止已发生成本}{总成本的最近估计}$$

用这个比例乘以预计总毛利润或收入得到目前应该确认的毛利润或收入。目前为止应确认的毛利润减去以前年度已确认的毛利润得到当年应确认的毛利润。

一个名为在建工程的存货账户用来汇总在建工程和目前为止应确认的毛利润的总合。当客户付款时，应收账款与工程款项同时增加。工程款项用来在资产负债表上抵减在建工程，其结果可作为资产或负债。

举个例子，假设公司有在建合同，价值 \$11 250 000，在第一年，实际发生成本 \$2 500 000，占总估计成本 \$10 000 000 的 25%。合同估计总毛利润为 \$1 250 000（\$11 250 000 - \$10 000 000），总毛利润的 25% 即 \$312 500 应随着第一年发生的成本确认为毛利润。

随着成本的发生、费用的付清或应收账款的收回，应编制以下分录，如图表 2 - 198 所示：

图表 2 - 198 完工百分比法会计分录

在建工程	\$2 500 000	
材料、现金、应付账款等		\$2 500 000
（记录在建成本发生额）		
应收账款	\$2 250 000	
在建工程款		\$2 250 000

（记录在建工程款）

| 现金 | $1 875 000 | |
| 应收账款 | | $1 875 000 |

（记录应收账款收回）

在年末，确认第一年的收益、费用和收入，如图表2－199所示。

图表2－199　完工百分比法年末会计分录

在建工程（毛利润）	$312 500	
在建工程费用	$2 500 000	
在建工程收入		$2 812 500

在合同完工后，贷记在建工程和借记在建工程款二者将结账。

合同完工法

企业只有在以下情况下才使用合同完工法：企业大部分合约都为短期合约；由于估计成本缺乏实践意义使完工百分比法不恰当时；当合约超越了常规的营业风险时。

在合同完工法下，只有当合约完全履行后，才确认收入和总利润。在建工程账户（存货）用来累计建设成本。在建工程账户下可以建立一个相反的存货账户（工程进度收款账户）以累计工程进度账款。

与完工百分比法不同，合同完工法在履行合约过程中并不确认收入、成本或毛利润。然而，当一项合约将发生损失时，应做下述处理参见下文"长期合约损失"。

在合约履行的最后一年，应做以下会计分录，如图表2－200所示。

图表2－200　合同完工法下最后年度的会计分录

在建工程款	$11 250 000	
长期合约收入		$11 250 000
建设成本	$10 125 000	
在建工程		$10 125 000

长期合约损失

长期合约可能导致未来可盈利项目的当期损失或非盈利项目的损失。

当期损失

在完工百分比法下，如果预计费用增加而整体项目预计仍能产生利润，那么各项目估计将会发生变化。此时，当期应确认相应的损失以抵销前期确认的额外利润。当期确认的损失计算方法如图表2－201所示：

图表 2-201　长期合约当期损失的计算

已耗费的成本（第 2 年的 12 月 31 日）	$4 315 680
预计完工成本（修正后）	3 231 716
预计总成本	$7 547 396
完工比率（$4 315 680/ $7 547 396）	57. 2%
第 2 年确认的收入（$6 660 000 * ×57. 2%）– $1 665 000 **	$2 144 520
第 2 年确认的成本	2 797 360
第 2 年确认的损失	$（652 840）

* 项目第 2 年确认的收入

** 第 1 年已确认的累计收入

损失的记录如图表 2-202 所示：

图表 2-202　长期合约当期损失

建设费用	$2 797 360	
在建工程（损失）		$652 840
长期合约收入		$2 144 520

报告收入和实际成本的差额即为损失。

非盈利合约的损失

不管前一年使用的是合同完工法还是完工百分比法，如果整体项目预计会产生损失，那么预计的总损失都应在当期确认。

- **完工百分比法下的会计处理**

在完工百分比法下，当毛利润在前期已确认，已确认的利润金额应连同当前预计的损失一同确认为当期损失。例如，如果前一年确认了 $100 000 的利润，而当前预计的损失为 $50 000，那么当年应确认的损失为 $150 000。记录损失的分录如图表 2-203 所示：

图表 2-203　完工百分比法下的当期损失

建设费用	$1 000 000	
在建工程（损失）		$150 000
长期合约收入		$850 000

- **合同完工法下的会计处理**

合同完工法下只确认当期确定的损失，如图表 2-204 所示：

图表 2-204　合同完工法下损失的会计分录

长期合同损失	$50 000	
在建工程（损失）		$50 000

不论在建工程的余额还是在建工程款的余额都不能超过合同价。若在建工程账户超过在建工程款，损失从在建工程账户抵减且作为长期合同的估计负债计入流动负债账户。

全面收益

全面收益信息

全面收益在第 6 号概念公告（第 70 段）中定义为"一个时期内由来自非所有者的交易或其他事项和事件导致的商业企业所有者权益（净资产）变动。它包括一个时期内所有者权益的所有变动，除了所有者的投资和分红"。这些变动来自于交易事项、企业的生产性工作、价格变动和外部事项。

因此，全面收益包括期间内所有影响经营的收入、费用、利得和损失，包括计入净收益的已实现损益以及净收益之外的未实现损益（作为其他全面收益）。其他全面收益的主要项目有：

- 投资于可供出售证券的未实现损益。
- 特定衍生金融工具的未实现损益。
- 最低负债调整带来的退休金损失。
- 特定外币业务调整。

其他全面收益

全面收益是净收益和其他全面收益项目的总和。每股额度不作为全面收益列示。

净收益结算转入保留盈余，而其他全面收益结算转入累计其他全面收益，因此两者均独立累计作为所有者权益的组成部分。为避免前期已在其他全面收益中列报的利得和损失在后期实现且计入净收益时被重复计算，重分类调整是必要的。这种调整消除了利得和损失的影响（一旦它从累计其他全面收益中实现）。

全面收益可披露在合并损益表、独立损益表或股东权益变动表中。这三种披露举例说明如下。

- **全面收益与合并损益表**

企业可选择将传统净收益列示为小计，列在其他全面收益项目后，全面收益列为总和。虽然简明，但这种方法较少突出净收益，一些企业认为这是一个缺点。图表 2–205 举例说明了全面收益的合并损益表。

图表 2–205　合并损益表：全面收益

Bounce 运动用品公司
全面收益合并损益表
第 1 年 12 月 31 日

销售收入	$1 120 000
销售成本	840 000
毛利	280 000
经营费用	126 000
净利润	154 000
未实现持有利得，税后	42 000
全面收益	$196 000

- **独立全面收益表**

独立全面收益表起始于净利润，将其他全面收益项目加之于上以得到总全面收益。这种方式表明了净利润和其他全面收益间的相互关系。图表 2-206 举例说明了全面收益的独立损益表。

图表 2-206　独立损益表和全面收益表

Bounce 运动用品公司 损益表 第 1 年 12 月 31 日		Bounce 运动用品公司 全面收益表 第 1 年 12 月 31 日	
销售收入	$1 120 000	净利润	$154 000
销售成本	840 000	其他全面收益	
毛利	280 000	未实现持有利得，税后	42 000
经营费用	126 000	全面收益	$196 000
净利润	$154 000		

- **股东权益变动表**

实际上，使用最广泛的全面收益披露方法是在股东权益变动表中列示出全面收益的计算过程。当此表用纵栏式编制时，其他全面收益项目列示于全面收益栏，这些项目结算转入累计其他全面收益账户，如图表 2-207 所示。

图表 2-207　股东权益变动表中的全面收益

Bounce 运动用品公司股东权益变动表 第 1 年 12 月 31 日					
	总金额	全面收益	保留盈余	累计其他全面收益	普通股
期初余额	$574 000		$70 000	$84 000	$420 000
全面收益					
净利润	154 000	154 000	154 000		
其他全面收益					
未实现持有利得，税后	42 000	42 000		42 000	
全面收益					
		$196 000			
期末余额	$770 000		$224 000	$126 000	$420 000

资产负债表中的其他全面收益

累计其他全面收益账户中的期末余额在资产负债表的权益部分列示，如图表 2-208 所示。

图表 2-208　资产负债表中的累计其他全面收益

Bounce 运动用品公司资产负债表 第 1 年 12 月 31 日 （股东权益部分）	
股东权益	
普通股	$420 000

续表

<table>
<tr><td colspan="2" align="center">Bounce 运动用品公司资产负债表
第 1 年 12 月 31 日
（股东权益部分）</td></tr>
<tr><td>保留盈余</td><td align="right">224 000</td></tr>
<tr><td>累他全面综合收益</td><td align="right">126 000</td></tr>
<tr><td>总股东权益</td><td align="right">$770 000</td></tr>
</table>

租赁

　　租赁是出租人与承租人之间的一种合同，其中出租人给承租人在一定期限内使用出租人财产的权利，以交换租金，租金通常情况下均为定期性的。出租人保留财产的所有权，因此租赁合同与销售合同具有不同格式。然而，有时租赁合同的实质与销售相当，这种情况出现在租赁实质上将所有资产所有权风险和收益都转移给了承租人。

　　从承租人的角度来看，租赁有两种类型：资本租赁和经营租赁。

资本租赁

　　SFAS NO.13 列出了四个条件，用于确定租赁是否实质上向承租人转移了财产所有权的所有风险和收益。

　　以下条件如果满足至少一项则承租人可确认为资本租赁：

- 所有权转移。租赁期满时资产的所有权转移给承租人。
- 廉价购买任择权。租赁包含廉价购买任择权，它允许承租人以明显低于资产公允价值的价格购买资产。
- 使用寿命的 75%。租赁期占财产剩余寿命的 75% 或以上。
- 公允价值的 90%。最低租赁付款的现值等于租赁开始时财产公允价值的 90% 或以上。

　　若一项租赁属于资本租赁，承租人应在资产负债表中同时记录一项租赁资产和一项租赁负债。这项资产根据最低租赁付款（不包括任何执行成本，如保险费或维修费）的现值与租赁资产公允价值中的孰低者计量。与财产、厂房和设备一起列报的租赁资产也由承租人进行折旧。租金支付减少租赁负债或融资租赁负债。资本租赁负债是未来租金付款的现值。未来现金支付可分为利息费用部分和租赁负债部分的抵减（与普通贷款的本金支付类似）。利息费用用实际利率法计入负债（因此，会计处理类似于企业通过开具应付票据购买资产的情况）。

　　例如，若第 1 年 1 月 1 日时，Acme 公司（承租人）从 Plastcon 公司（出租人）处租赁了一台价值 $150 000（租赁时的公允价值）的塑料压制机。这项不可撤销租赁为期 4 年，包括自租赁开始日起每年 1 月 1 日的年租金支付额 $41 933.41。这项租赁是不可续租的，设备在租赁期满时将归还给出租人，设备没有残值，因为估计经济寿命为 4 年。另外，设备采用直线折旧法折旧。Acme 的边际借款利率为每年 9%，且 Plastcon 已告知 Acme，此资产已形成每年 8% 的回报率。若承租人知道出租人的实际利率，就应用于计算中，但前提条件是它应低于承租人的边际借款利率。否则就应使用承租人的边际借款利率。

首先，为确定合理的会计处理方法必须考查四个融资租赁条件：

- 所有权转移？没有。并没有将资产的所有权转移。
- 廉价购买任择权？没有。租赁合同并未包含廉价购买任择权。
- 使用寿命的75%？有。4年租赁期除以4年使用寿命等于100%。
- 公允价值的90%？有。$41 933.41 利率为8%，4期的期初年金现值周 r = $41 933.41 ×3.57710（见图表2－209）= $150 000。初始时的公允价值也为 $150 000，则 $150 000 现值支付/ $150 000 公允价值 =1

注意期初年金假设在期初支付款项，而不是在期末付款（普通年金），所以使用了不同的现值表。

图表2－209 $1 期初年金现值表

$$PV - AD_{n, i} = \frac{1 - \frac{1}{(1+i)^{n-1}}}{i}$$

(n) 期	8%	9%	10%
1	1.00000	1.00000	1.00000
2	1.92593	1.91743	1.90909
3	2.78326	2.75911	2.73554
4	3.57710	3.53130	3.48685
5	4.31213	4.23972	4.16986
6	4.99271	4.88965	4.79079
7	5.62288	5.48592	5.35526
8	6.20637	6.03295	5.86842
9	6.74664	6.53482	6.33493
10	7.24689	6.99525	6.75902

因为至少满足一个条件，因此这项租赁划分为融资租赁。所以在第1年1月1日的分录如图表2－210所示：

图表2－210 记录融资租赁的分录（第1年1月1日）

融资租赁租人设备	$150 000.00	
融资租赁负债		$108 066.59
现金		$41 933.41

以现值记录融资租赁（8%，4期：$41 933.41 ×［3.57710－1］* = $108 066.59）

* 减1是因为首次支付款项不参与贴现。

$41 933.41 既包含利息部分，又包含租赁负债部分的抵减。

图表2－211 显示了在期初年金基础上，用有效利率法计算的年金利息及租赁负债款项。

图表2－211 承租人角度，期初年金基础，租赁摊销表

	ACME 公司租赁负债摊销表		
日期	每年租赁支付额	未决负债利息*	租赁负债抵减**	租赁负债
期初				$150 000.00

续表

ACME 公司租赁负债摊销表			
日期	每年租赁支付额	未决负债利息*	租赁负债抵减**	租赁负债
Y1，1，1	$41 933.41	$0.00	$41 933.41	$108 066.59
Y2，1，1	$41 933.41	$8 645.33	$33 288.08	$74 778.51
Y3，1，1	$41 933.41	$5 982.28	$35 951.13	$38 827.38
Y4，1，1	$41 933.41	$3 106.03 ***	$38 827.38	$0.00
总额	$167 733.64	$17 733.80 ****	$150 000.00	

* 利息以 8% 计，比如（0.08）× $108 066.59 = $8 645.33。第一个付款日与期初重合，所以没有利息。

** 租赁负债抵减等于每年租赁付款额减去未决负债利息。

*** 利息减少了 0.16 以调整保留小数误差。

**** 注意：$167 733.64 – $17 733.80 = $150 000.00

在第 1 年年末，Acme 记录应计利息的分录如图表 2 – 212 所示：

图表 2 – 212　记录应计利息的分录（第 1 年，12 月 31 日）

利息费用	$8 645.33	
应付利息		$8 645.33
记录融资租赁租入设备应计利息		

同时也在第 1 年年末，Acme 记录租赁资产的折旧，采用直线折旧法，如图表 2 – 213 所示。

图表 2 – 213　记录折旧费用的分录（第 1 年 12 月 31 日）

折旧费用—融资租赁	$37 500	
累计折旧—融资租赁		$37 500
计提折旧费用（$150 000/4 年 = $37 500）		

一年以内到期的租赁部分被划分为流动负债（如第 1 年的 $33 288.08 将会在第 2 年到期），一年以上的被划分为非流动或长期负债（第 1 年的 $74 778.51，总负债金额为 $105 066.59）。在第 1 年 12 月 31 日，即资产负债表日，资产和融资性租赁分别列示，流动负债部分应列示应付利息 $8 645.33 以及融资性租赁的短期部分 $33 288.08。非流动负债下应列示的融资性租赁额为 $74 778.51。图表 2 – 214 是第 2 年租赁付款额的分录。

图表 2 – 214　计提租赁付款额（第 2 年 1 月 1 日）

应付利息	$8 645.330	
融资性租赁负债	$33 288.080	
现金		$41 933.410
计提塑料挤压机的租赁付款		

租赁期末，资产归还给出租人，累计折旧额和租赁资产账户从承租人账簿上清除，如图表 2 – 215 所示。

图表2-215 租赁资产从账簿上移除的分录（第5年1月1日）

设备	150 000	
累计折旧——融资性租赁	150 000	
融资性租赁——设备		150 000
累计折旧——设备		150 000
租赁期末租赁资产从账簿上移除		

　　资本租赁的披露包括融资性租赁下主要资产类别的总额，未来5年中每年最小租赁付款额，包括所有图表在2-215中列示的范畴，不可取消合同的租赁和或有租赁，以及资本租赁资产的折旧额。

经营租赁

　　不符合资本租赁标准的租赁称为经营性租赁。经营性租赁类似于一般的租借，费用随时间增加。使用运营法，租赁费用在资产的受益期间内摊销。收入和费用在租赁期内直线摊销。未来付款的承诺不能进行确认。如果上一例中的资产不符合任何一项确认为资本租赁的条件，那么租赁付款将如图表2-216所示。如果关于经营性租赁有大于一年的支付协议，支付的进度应予以披露。

图表2-216 承租人支付租赁费用的分录（第1年，1月1日）

租赁费	$44 933.41	
现金		$44 933.41
计提塑料挤压机租赁费用		

　　经营性租赁不在资产负债表中列示。在损益表中，承租人报告租赁费用，出租人报告租赁收入。如果有一年或以上期间内不能取消经营性租赁合同的条款，必须进行披露。

从出租人角度对租赁进行分类

　　从出租人角度可以把租赁分为四类：

- 经营性租赁（前面已从出租人和承租人的角度进行了阐述）。
- 销售性租赁。
- 直接融资租赁。
- 杠杆租赁。

　　按照确认资本租赁的四个原则，从出租人的角度来看，如果一项租赁满足四个原则中的一个，或者同时满足以下两个条件，它就可能是销售性租赁、直接融资租赁或杠杆租赁这三种中的一种。

　　这样的租赁必须同时满足以下两个特征：

- 最小租赁付款额能够可靠计量。
- 出租人将会发生的或有费用不存在重大的不确定性。

　　这三种非经营性租赁的分类取决于租赁的利润或者损失是否能通过保险进行确认。在这三种资本租赁中，出租人资产负债表中的出租资产由应收租赁费（或租赁投资净额）取代，并在租赁期间内确认利息收入。

销售性租赁

销售性租赁是出售的一种替代方式，比如从代理商处租借一辆新车或者在设备租借期满后续租。如果出租人是制造商或租赁资产的代理商，这种租赁往往就是销售性租赁。除了利息收入以外，出租人还会在租赁期一开始就确认收入和产品成本。一般来讲，如果租赁资产的市场价格（售价）与成本价格不一致，这样的租赁就有可能是销售性租赁。市场价格和成本价格的差额确认为毛利润（或损失）。销售性租赁如果涉及房地产，在租赁期末需转移房地产所有权。

直接融资租赁

直接融资租赁是以借款的形式发生的，租赁资产的市场价格（售价）与成本价格相同。因此，除了利息收入以外，出租人不能确认利润（或损失）。出租人往往是购买资产并将资产出租的银行。这和使用购买资产进行抵押借款的作用相同，惟一不同的是在直接融资租赁中，出租人保留资产所有权。当借款人不能完全为资产融资，又存在税收优惠或者资产残值与利息收入之和大于直接出售资产所得收入时，可以考虑使用直接融资租赁。

杠杆租赁

杠杆租赁是直接融资租赁的一种，但由于涉及3个或3个以上的交易方，所以会计处理不同。除了有出租人和承租人外，还有一个长期债权人充当中介角色。出租人被称为权益人。长期债权人须为出租人提供无追索权的融资，但对出租的资产享有追索权。只有在出租人通过贷款融资的时候租赁才能成为杠杆租赁。杠杆租赁的特点是出租人的净投入在前面几年会减少，后面的年份会增加。

退休金和其他退休后福利

退休金计划根据雇员工作时提供的服务来为员工提供退休后福利。配比原则规定这些福利的成本在雇员工作期间而不是福利发生时予以确认。雇主把钱交给退休金基金管理公司，用这些基金及其收益来支付日后的福利支出。一部分退休金基金需要雇主与雇员共同出资。而另一些则只需要雇主单方面出资。这里主要探讨雇主的会计处理方法。

退休金计划主要有两种：固定缴款计划和固定收益计划。固定缴款计划中，每个期间雇主向退休金基金交纳的份额由一定的公式计算得出。公式可能由年龄、工作时间长度、雇主利润和平时福利等因素组成。退休金计划并没有规定未来福利支出，所以雇员的收益存在风险。独立的第三方托管人往往从雇主处收集退休基金，保管其收益，并根据雇主的需要处理退休金提前支付的事务。受托关系中的受益人为退休金计划中的雇员。

在固定收益计划中，雇主保证在退休后每年给予固定的福利。福利的大小由工作的年限和退休时的待遇水平决定。托管人对退休金账户进行管理和投资，确保有足够多的资金来履行雇主的责任。雇主对所委托的资产拥有所有权。雇主承受该账户中资金不足以支付固定收益的风险。退休后每年固定福利的现值为退休金负债，可以通过多种方法计量（预计给付义务、累计给付义务、既定给付义务）。这些计量方法使得退休金会计更加复杂。

固定缴款计划的会计处理

对雇主而言固定缴款计划的会计处理很简单：退休金费用以每年投入退休金计划的金额计量，贷记投入到退休金基金的现金，差额作为资产或负债记录。雇主的费用则是每年最低交纳数。如果实际交纳数大于每年最低缴纳额，差额作为资产列示在资产负债表上。退休金计划所包括的人群、每年应投入金额的计算方法和其他对期间比较有重大影响的事件都应进行披露。

固定收益计划的会计处理

固定收益计划的会计处理比较复杂，因为在工作年限内对未来的福利金额只能估算。雇主根据第 87 号财务会计准则公告计量退休金费用。

退休金费用由很多部分组成，包括服务成本（每多工作一年退休金负债的增加）和利息成本（时间的延长导致退休金负债的增加）。退休金费用还包括资产收益、前期服务成本的摊销和特定的损益。雇主借记以上全部金额作为退休金费用，贷记实际交纳的现金，差额记为负债（或资产），作为应计或预付退休金费用。

最低退休金缴纳额作为负债列示在资产负债表上。该项负债是以下金额之一的现金流量现值：

- 既定给付义务。既定给付义务用来计量在现在工资水平上给予既定的雇员福利的义务。既定的雇员是指工作了一定年限后的雇员。

- 累计给付义务。累计给付义务以现有工资水平计算如果雇员今天辞职应该给付的金额，不管雇员是否属于既定范围。累计给付义务计量的是公司现有的给付义务，不包括未来工作年限和工资的增长。

- 预计给付义务。预计给付义务计量对既定和非既定雇员的给付义务，并对未来工资水平进行预测（基于预测公式）。这种方法使用了更多的估算。财务会计准则委员会推荐这种方法，因为它更现实地计量了雇主的义务。财务会计准则委员会同时规定，如果使用了退休金计划的受益公式，则必须使用这种方法。

作为对最低债务额的调整，雇主同时也应将无形退休金资产和/或损失作为累计其他全面收益的一部分进行确认。管理层在计算现值时对贴现率的选择对预计给付义务有重大影响，所以必须在每个计量日根据现行利率对贴现率进行调整。另外，调整还应包括死亡、提款、提前退休和残疾对现值的影响，让其更能反映真实的现值。

退休金费用

为了满足成本与相应期间配比，每年支付给固定收益计划的数额应分成以下几个部分：

- 服务成本。第 87 号财务会计准则公告规定，服务成本等于在该时期内根据退休金计划的受益公式计算出的受益数额现值（比如预计给付义务）。

- 利息费用。利息费用或称为债务利息，按该时期预计给付义务（因为这是一种贴现债务）和结算日利率计提。结算日利率指所有预计给付义务被支付时的利率（包括货币时间价值）。

- 资产实际收益。资产的实际收益将会使退休金费用降低。收益包括利息收入、股利收入和根据市场价格对退休基金进行的调整。

实际收益＝（资产期末余额－资产期初余额）－（投入数－支付数）

- 未确认前期服务成本的摊销。计划有时会根据雇员已完成的工作进行追溯调整。这些成本被分配到相关雇员未来剩余服务期间的退休金费用上。

- 损益。包括实际和预期资产回报的差额以及以前年度未实现的净损益的摊销。损益可能由预计给付义务的变化或退休金的市场价格变化所引起。

资产负债表上退休金的披露

在资产负债表上，不足额的退休金账户作为负债列示。即，如果雇主交给管理人的金额低于本年规定的退休金费用，差额作为长期负债（如果一年之内到期则作为短期负债）列示。

如果超过本年规定的退休金费用，则差额以流动资产或其他资产列示（根据是否在一年内到期）。

此外，如果累计给付义务超过资产现行价值，也可能产生负债。

差额计入借方账户：

- **如果借方账户大于前期未实现服务成本**

把负债作为股东权益的对冲账户，叫做退休金负债超过未实现前期服务成本的剩余部分。剩余部分在其他全面收益中列示，累计数作为累计其他全面收益的一部分。

- **如果借方账户小于前期未实现服务成本**

负债作为无形资产在递延退休金成本中确认。

退休金工作表

并不是所有的退休金费用都是通过一般日记账结算，退休金工作表把总账中的年度退休金费用、现金、预付或应计费用账户结转到未实现或非资本化退休金项目：预计给付义务和计划资产项目。图表 2 - 217 是一个使用样本数据和 10% 结算日利率的退休金工作表例子。应注意的是，预付的应计成本余额应等于备忘录记录的净余额。并且同时使用了借方和贷方，就像一个会计分录（每项交易在两个记录中分别有借方和贷方，且借方、贷方金额相等）。贡献项目指的是每个期间存入退休金计划的数额，福利则指退休人员实际得到的好处。图表 2 - 217 说明了退休金结算表的形式，而没有说明具体的计算过程。

图表 2 - 217　退休金工作表（单位：千美元）

项目	总账			备忘录记录	
	年度退休金费用	现金	预付/应计成本	预计给付义务	计划资产
年初余额				贷 $200 000	借 $200 000
服务成本	借 $16 000			贷 16 000	

续表

项目	总账			备忘录记录	
	年度退休金费用	现金	预付/应计成本	预计给付义务	计划资产
利息费用	借 20 000			贷 20 000	
实际回报	贷 20 000 *				借 20 000
贡献		贷 $14 000			借 14 000
受益额				借 12 000	贷 12 000
年度分录	借 $16 000	贷 $14 000	贷 2 000 **		
年末余额			贷 $2 000 ***	贷 $224 000	借 $222 000

注：

* 实际回报 =（$222 000 – $200 000）–（$14 000 – $12 000）= $20 000

** 现金减去年度退休金费用等于预付/应计成本：$14 000 – $16 000 =（$2 000）

*** 计划资产减去预计给付义务等于年末预付/应计成本余额：$222 000 – $224 000 =（$2 000）

财务报表披露

退休金计划应在财务报表中或附注中进行披露。图表 2 – 218 是一个退休金计划在报表附注中披露的例子。

图表 2 – 218　NEW CF&I 公司退休金披露

合并报表附注【退休金披露摘录】（未审计）

员工福利计划

NEW CH&I 公司为所有员工提供固定收益退休金计划、退休后健康保健以及人寿保险计划。一些在第 1 年 9 月 1 日后被聘用的雇员不再参加固定收益计划，而是加入了雇主出资的固定缴款计划，每年缴款额是年薪的 3%。新的固定缴款计划需要每年注资，参加计划的员工在工作 5 年以后就能得到福利。NEW CH&I 公司同时也向所有员工提供相应的储蓄计划。

与固定收益计划相关的净期间福利费用由以下部分组成：

	固定收益退休金计划（单位：千）			
	3 个月 6 月 30 日		6 个月 6 月 30 日	
	第 2 年	第 2 年	第 2 年	第 1 年
服务成本	$648	$579	$1 296	$1 158
利息成本	1 057	1 001	2 114	2 002
预期计划资产的回报率	(880)	(586)	(1 760)	(1 200)
未确认净损失的摊销	115	38	230	76
未确认前期服务成本的摊销	609	609	1 218	1 218
净期间福利成本总计	$1 549	$1 641	$3 098	$3 254

与退休后健康保健以及人寿保险计划相关的净期间福利成本由以下部分组成：

| | 其他福利计划（单位：千） | | | |
| | 3 个月 6 月 30 日 | | 6 个月 6 月 30 日 | |
	第 2 年	第 2 年	第 2 年	第 1 年
服务成本	$60	$55	$117	$111
利息成本	309	304	612	607
未确认净损失的摊销	69	54	131	107
未确认前期服务成本的摊销	183	180	363	359
净期间福利成本总计	$621	$593	$1 223	$1 184

NEW CH&I 公司对结束于第 2 年 6 月 30 日的 3 个月和 6 个月期的退休金计划分别投入了 $750 万和 $1 130 万，对结束于第 1 年 6 月 30 日的 3 个月和 6 个月期的退休金计划分别投入了 $220 万和 $560 万。NEW CH&I 公司计划在第 2 年继续投入 $810 万。

图表 2－218 的第一段披露了公司所拥有的退休金计划的种类和符合条件的员工。雇主必须披露以下内容（见图表上半部分）：预计给付义务、计划资产、未确认前期服务成本以及未确认的净损益。这些项目都没有记录在报表上。另外，还需要披露下列信息：

- 退休金费用组成部分的表格。
- 退休金账户的状况（预计给付义务和计划资产公允价值之差）。
- 该年中预计给付义务和计划资产公允价值变化的表格。
- 贴现率、资产回报率和补偿率增加的估计。

图表 2－218 的最后一段披露了公司实际和计划的投入。

递延所得税

国家税法和一般公认会计原则有很多不一致的地方（在公认会计原则内部就有很多不一致的地方），通常会导致税前会计利润和应税利润的不一致。税前会计利润（或报表上的税前收入）是一个经济实体用公认会计原则计算出的供财务报告使用的收入。应税利润是根据税法在净收入的基础上（扣除可抵扣项）计算出的应纳税所得额。

暂时性差异

两种计算方法的不同所导致的差异往往是暂时性差异。暂时性差异是指资产、负债的账面价值与其计税基础不同产生的差额。比如，尽管公认会计原则也采用权责发生制，但税法在收入确认上采用修正过的收付实现制。这意味着采用公认会计原则通常比税法提前确认收入。图表 2－219 是一个收入确认时间不同而导致的暂时性差异的例子。我们假设税率为 40% 并在报表期间保持不变。

图表 2 -219　会计上和税法上的处理差异报告

	Acme 公司			
	第 1 年	第 2 年	第 3 年	总计
公认会计准则下				
收入	$100 000	$100 000	$100 000	
费用	$60 000	$60 000	$60 000	
税前利润	$40 000	$40 000	$40 000	$120 000
所得税费用	$16 000	$16 000	$16 000	$48 000
税法下				
收入	$70 000	$110 000	$120 000	
费用	$60 000	$60 000	$60 000	
应税利润	$10 000	$50 000	$60 000	$120 000
应付所得税	$4 000	$20 000	$24 000	$48 000
差异*	$12 000	($4 000)	($8 000)	

差异* = 所得税费用 - 应交税金

　　图表 2 -219 中的暂时性差异是一个递延所得税负债，它由后两期的应交税金增加来抵销。递延所得税负债是指现在少交的所得税（ $12 000），该少交部分由以后期间多交所得税（ $4 000 和 $8 000 的差异）弥补。递延所得税资产是指现在多交税而以后期间少交税的额度。

　　因为这些差异的存在，税款必须在各期间分配，叫做期间税收分配。期间税收分配指在持续期间、非持续经营、非正常损益和一些直接贷记到所有者权益项下的项目之间分配总的所得税费用或收益，这种方法在会计和税法上对项目归属期间划分不同时使用。比如，一个公司在财务报告中在货物售出的时候就计提保修费用，而在税法上修理成本只有在保修服务真正发生的时候才能予以抵扣。或者，分期付款的收入在出售时会在财务报表上确认收入，而根据税法，只有当现金收到时才能确认应税收入。在公认会计原则中，与税法不同产生的差异导致了递延所得税资产和负债的出现。换种方式说，当出现可抵扣差异时（如保修费用）会产生递延所得税资产，而应纳税差异（如分期付款收入）会产生递延所得税负债。可抵扣项目是指未来可以减少应税所得的项目，应纳税项目是指未来会增加应税所得的项目。

　　在 SFAS No. 109 中，用资产负债法来计量递延所得税。这种方法计量资产和负债在会计和税法下计算价值不一致时的差异。

　　考虑以下例子：固定资产原值为 $1 500，会计上使用直线法折旧而税法上使用加速折旧。如图表 2 - 220 所示，假设在第一年末该资产会计上的账面价值为 $1 200,税法上为 $1 000, $200 的差异会使递延所得税负债增加。假设税率为40%，递延所得税负债为 $80（ $200 ×40%），这也可以理解为资产以 $1 200 的价格现在售出。所以，未来售出资产会使应税收入和应交税金增加。当然，未来资产出售产生的任何利得可能会大于可抵扣所得税费用或损失，而不会有实际的税费产生。因此，递延税费虽然归结为资产或负债，但不会导致通常意义上的应收或应付。

图表 2 –220　账面价值的差异

	会计上	税法上
资产原值	$1 500	$1 500
累计折旧	($300)	($500)
资产负债表日账面价值	$1 200	$1 000

假定公司税率为 40%，应税收入为 $8 000，期初没有递延所得税资产或负债。所得税费用通过应交税金（应纳税所得乘以税率）和递延所得税负债账户的调整的差异计算得出，如图表 2 – 221 所示。

图表 2 –221　计提所得税费用的分录

所得税费用	$3 280	
递延所得税负债		$80
应交税金		$3 200

损益表上的所得税费用是当期应交税金和从期初到期末递延所得税资产或负债调整净额的总和。对于在不同年度经营的公司，会产生跨年的差异分配，当期的所得税费用可以用以下公式计算：

所得税费用 = [期末递延所得税负债(资产) – 期初递延所得税负债(资产)] + 当期应交税金

第 2 年，会计上累计折旧为 $600，税法上为 $750，$150 的差异使递延所得税负债增加 $60。递延所得税负债期末余额为 $140。如果应税收入为 $7 000，所得税费用 = [$140 – $80] + 2 800 = $2 860。与图表 2 – 221 相似的会计分录用来贷记增加的递延所得税负债 $60。在第 3 年，会计上累计折旧为 $900，税法上为 $800，$100 的差额 × 40% = $40 的应纳税额，年末的递延所得税负债为 $140 – $40 = $100。如果应税收入为 $8 000，所得税费用 = [$100 – $140] + 3 200 = $3 160。图表 2 –222 是一个部分冲销递延所得税负债账户的分录。

图表 2 –222　计提所得税费用的分录

所得税费用	$3 160	
递延所得税负债	$40	
应交税金		$3 200

因为资产的折旧期为 5 年，在第 5 年暂时性差异会完全消除。而递延所得税资产是否能实现不能确定，所以我们用一个估价备抵账户来反映不太可能实现（小于 50% 的可能性）的递延所得税资产。

- 暂时性差异的例子。
- 暂时性差异的例子中包括不同的计算方法：
- 税收中使用分期付款方法（公认会计原则中不允许）。
- 长期建造合同。
- 折旧。

- 商誉（根据税法在 15 年内折旧，在公认会计原则中不折旧）。
- 根据税法估计的费用如保修费用在实际发生时确认。
- 预收收入根据税法在收到时确认，而在公认会计原则中在获取收入的行为发生前只能确认为负债。
- 会计上用权益法确认投资，而税法上用成本法计量。
- 净资本损失在公认会计原则下在发生时确认，在税法下可以留到以后年度抵销资本利得。
- 公认会计原则下员工福利可以在员工服务年限中摊销，而根据税法只有实际发生时才能抵扣。
- 根据税法或有负债只有在实际发生时才能抵扣。
- 根据税法超额的慈善捐款可以留到以后年度计算税收优惠。
- 收付实现制还是权责发生制：税法上使用修正过的收付实现制；公认会计原则使用权责发生制。

永久性差异

由于公认会计原则和税法之间的不同导致的一些不能转回的差异，因为一些项目只影响其中一种方法。

永久性差异的例子

以下是一些永久性差异的例子。

- 实际税率的变化。由于税率改变，一部分暂时性差异可能会变成永久性差异（比如，如果税率从 40% 降到 35%，5% 的变化会变成永久性差异因为这部分不用再交税）。
- 收到股利的抵扣。根据持股比例的不同，一部分公司收到的股利可以免税，但根据公认会计原则必须全额计算在应税所得中。
- 政府证券的利息收入。从一些符合规定的政府证券中取得的收入（投资的资本利得要缴税）可以 100% 不纳税，但在会计上要确认收益。
- 按比例扣除。扣除比例以外的费用根据税法可以抵免，但根据公认会计原则则不行。
- 政府税收豁免。政府立法豁免了一些应税收入，并允许一些超出公认会计原则的抵扣项，或对一些特定行业增加税收以限制其发展。为了促进某些地区的发展，一些地方政府设立了免税区。在这些时候，公司的实际税率会与官方税率（财务报表中使用的税率）不同。这些差异是永久性差异。

永久性差异说明

解释永久性差异最好的方法就是把它同暂时性差异作比较。比如，Acme 公司在第 1 年报告了 $10 000 的税前会计利润，第 2 年报告了 $110 000，第 3 年报告了 $120 000，税率为 40%，且每一年中都会得到 $20 000 的市政利息收入，其根据税法可以完全抵扣而根据公认会计原则不能抵扣。另外，公司通过分期收款的方式出售了 $15 000 的资产，在第 1 年的财务报告中全部确认为收入，但根据税法第 1 年只有

1/3 可以确认为收入。图表 2 – 223 显示了计算每年应交所得税的过程。

图表 2 – 223 在有暂时和永久性差异下应交所得税的计算

	第 1 年	第 2 年	第 3 年
税前会计利润	$100 000	$110 000	$120 000
永久性差异			
可抵扣费用	($20 000)	($20 000)	($20 000)
暂时性差异			
分期收款销售*	$10 000	$5 000	$5 000
应税收入	$70 000	$95 000	$105 000
应交税金（40%）	$28 000	$38 000	$42 000

* 第 1 年分期收款销售：会计上确认($15 000) + 税法上确认 $5 000 = ($10 000)

用税前会计利润来计算应交税金时，减去差异会使税前会计利润大于应税所得，加上差异会使税前会计利润大于应税所得。因此，$15 000 账面价值的资产的售出使第 1 年会计利润增加 $15 000，在应税所得只增加 $5 000，$10 000 的暂时性差异被扣除因为这是税前会计利润大于应税所得的部分。图表 2 – 224 是近 3 年的会计分录，暂时性差异产生递延所得税负债账户，而永久性差异只在应交税金和所得税费用中表现出来。

图表 2 – 224 Acme 公司在第 1、2、3 年的所得税分录

第 1 年 12 月 31 日		
所得税费用 [$28 000 + ($10 000 × 40%)]	$32 000	
递延所得税负债 ($10 000 × 40%)		$4 000
应交税金		$28 000
计提所得税费用		
第 2 年 12 月 31 日		
所得税费用 [$38 000 – ($5 000 × 40%)]	$36 000	
递延所得税负债 ($5 000 × 40%)	$2 000	
应交税金		$38 000
计提所得税费用		
第 3 年 12 月 31 日		
所得税费用 [$42 000 – ($5 000 × 40%)]	$40 000	
递延所得税负债 ($5 000 × 40%)	$2 000	
应交税金		$42 000
计提所得税费用		

虽然法定税率每年都是 40%，但实际税率发生了改变。实际税率公式如下：

$$实际税率 = \frac{该期间所得税总和}{税前会计利润}$$

第 1 年 = $32 000/ $100 000 = 32%，第 2 年 = $36 000/ $110 000 = 32.73%，第 3 年 = $40 000/ $120 000 = 33.33%。

对财务报表的影响

递延税款在资产负债表上以当期和非当期项目分别列示。与短期资产或负债有关

的递延税款划分为当期项目，与长期资产或负债有关的递延税款划分为非当期项目。比如，上例中的与资产折旧有关的递延税款余额被划分为非当期项目，因为其与固定资产相关。任何当期或非当期递延所得税资产和负债的净额都在资产负债表上列示。

　　财务报表附注应包括法定税率和实际税率的调整项并披露递延所得税资产或负债净额的组成部分。如图表 2 – 225 所示。

图表 2 – 225　所得税的披露

Bounce 体育用品公司（单位：百万美元）			
注13：所得税			
美国和外国的税前持续经营收入			
	第 3 年	第 2 年	第 1 年
美国	$1 401	$1 489	$1 402
外国	545	497	(55)
	$1 946	$1 986	$1 347
所得税			
当期　　联邦	($166)	$514	$218
外国	230	95	119
州	40	51	62
	104	660	399
递延　　联邦	117	23	175
外国	3	13	(35)
州	9	11	(2)
	129	44	138
	$233	$704	$537
美国联邦法定税率和我公司实际税率差异调整：			
美国联邦法定税率	35%	35%	35%
州税率，扣除所得税优惠	1.7	2.1	3.0
国外低税率影响额	(3.0)	(5.6)	(4.4)
前一年度审计因素影响	(5.6)	(1.9)	(2.8)
危地马拉事务解决	(21.4)	–	–
非正常损失的影响	3.3	2.3	9.6
其他影响净额	2.5	3.5	(0.6)
实际税率	12.5%	35.4%	39.8%

　　递延税费是用来计量资产和负债在税法上的数额和会计报表中数额的暂时性差异。我们把暂时性差异对税收的影响计为递延所得税资产或负债。递延所得税资产一般代表未来可抵扣税额，递延所得税负债一般代表在税法已经扣除但在损益表中尚未扣除的项目。

递延所得税负债（资产）：		
除掉不能抵扣商誉部分后的无形资产	$1 242	$1 172
财产、厂房和设备	$572	$430
避风港租赁	$94	$99
零息票据	$68	$72
其他	$407	$288
总递延所得税负债	$2 383	$2 061
以前年度经营损失	(483)	(447)
退休人员福利	(212)	(212)
流动负债	(604)	(439)
总递延所得税资产	(1 299)	(1 098)
递延所得税资产估价备抵项	$492	$394
净递延所得税资产	(807)	(704)
净递延所得税负债	$1 576	$1 357

续表

Bounce 体育用品公司（单位：百万美元）		
包括在：		
预付费用、递延所得税和其他流动资产	$(148)	$(102)
递延所得税	$1 724	$1 459
	$1 576	$1 357

外国子公司的投资和未合并外国子公司的暂时性差异产生的递延所得税负债没有确认，因为这样的确认并不可行。第3年末的净经营损失$2.3亿留到以后年度作为某些外国和本国子公司应税所得的扣减项。这些净经营损失的到期时间分别是：$83亿在第4年到期，$2.1亿在第5年到第17年到期，$173亿没有到期日。

股票期权

股票期权授予特定的员工或管理层在一定期间以一定价格买入公司股票的权利。授予员工股票期权的目的是鼓励员工以所有者的身份来更好地管理公司。另外，股票期权还能起到留住重要员工，为员工提供递延的、能使税后收益最大化的长期利益，并使员工利益和公司业绩联系起来的作用。

股票期权中的一些关键词：

● 授权日。授权日指员工被授予期权的日期。在授权日行权价和股票的市场价格应一致（也可能不一致）。

● 得权日。在这个日期以后股票期权就可以在不附带任何继续聘用条款的条件下执行。

● 服务期间。服务期间是指从授权日到得权日的这段期间，在这段期间内员工必须继续为该公司工作（除非其他例外情况）。

● 行权价格。行权价格是在授权日所设定的股票价格；它是员工行使期权购买公司股票时所支付的价格。如果股票市场价格高于行权价格，员工可以通过以行权价格购买再以市场价格卖出而获益。

股票期权会分散公司所有权。尽管股票期权同发行新股类似，但发行股票期权与发行新股的不同之处在于公司不用当期给予股东购买股票的权利。因此，如果发行了大量的股票期权，现有股东的所有权比例将会下降。

会计处理

修正后的 SFAS No. 123（R）要求公司在授权日根据预计股票期权行权时的市场价格来确认员工福利费用。公允价值法估算费用常使用期权的实际市场价格。但市场价格不太容易取得，因为员工股票期权缺乏流动性。所以公允价值常用一些期权定价模型通过计算公司公允价值来计算得出（如布莱克—斯科尔斯—默顿模型）。布莱克—斯科尔斯—默顿模型（BSM模型）是一个封闭式的公允价值模型，最初用来计算公开市场上公司股票（而非股票期权）的价值。所以一些公司使用另外一种可以根据实际情况加减变量的完全不同的模型，叫做"格子"（Lattice）模型。二项式期权定价模型是最常用的格子模型。这些模型虽然复杂，但随着智能计算机软件的使用变得越来越方便。SFAS No. 123（R）要求公司使用对变化更加敏感的格子模型。

公允价值模型中关于股票期权价值有 3 个参数：内在价值（授权日股票价格和现在市场价格的差额）、货币的时间价值（在等待行权之前投资者可以投资其他项目）以及标的股票波动率的时间价值（投资者可以从股票价格上升中获利，而最大损失额是期权费而非整个股票的价格）。因此，即使内在价值为零，另外两项价值也会为员工带来一定收益。用来计算这三项价值的数据有：行权价格、预计股利、预计股票价格波动和期权同期的无风险利率、股票现时价格以及期权预计期间。

对财务报表的影响

图表 2 - 226 是一个附注披露股票期权的例子。案例中的公司采用 SFAS No. 123（R）要求的公允价值法计量股票期权。

图表 2 - 226　Inergy 控股公司股票期权计划的披露

Inergy 控股公司和其子公司对股票期权计划的会计处理

长期激励计划根据 APB 第 25 号意见进行会计处理，并在相应会计期间根据 SFAS No. 123 "股权激励的会计处理"，使用公允价值法计量，SFAS No. 148 "股权激励的会计处理：转移和披露" 对 SFAS No. 123 进行了修正。净利润（损失）中未反映期权计划成本，因为该计划中所有股票期权的行权价都和计量时的市场价格相同。下表说明了如果公司采用 SFAS No. 123 "股权激励的会计处理" 中的公允价值条款来计量员工期权福利对净利润（损失）的影响。为了满足备考披露的要求，期权的估计公允价值将在权利期内摊销。第 3 年 9 月 30 日前的 3 年备考信息如下所示（除每单位数据之外，其他数据的单位都是千）：

	第 3 年	第 2 年	第 1 年
报告净利润	$31 099	$9 533	$7 806
扣除：公允价值法计算的员工期权福利费用总和	123	37	36
备考净利润	30 976	9 496	7 770
每有限责任股东单位的净利润			
基本的	$1. 81	$0. 76	$0. 63
稀释后的	$1. 81	$0. 59	$0. 49
每有限责任股东单位的备考净利润			
基本的	$0. 63	$0. 76	$0. 63
稀释后的	$1. 80	$0. 59	$0. 49

单位利润

每有限责任股东单位的基本净利润是用净利润除以加权平均股票期权数得到的。稀释后的净利润则是用净利润除以加权平均期权数和长期激励计划下期权对所有者权益的稀释影响合计数。下表具体列示了上述两个数值是如何计算的（以千计，单位数值除外）。

	9 月 30 日结束的会计年度		
	第 3 年	第 2 年	第 1 年
分子			
净利润—基本的和稀释后的	$31 099	$9 533	$7 806
分母			
加权平均有限责任股东单位—基本的	17 140	12 550	12 373
稀释效应	46	3 540	37 717
加权平均有限责任股东单位—稀释后的	17 186	16 090	16 090
每有限责任股东单位的净利润			
基本的	$1. 81	$0. 76	$0. 63
稀释后的	$1. 81	$0. 59	$0. 49

在 9 月 30 日结束的第三个会计年度，如果调整有限责任股东单位数，以反映超额分配对备考数据的影响，基本的和稀释后的每有限责任股东单位的净利润分别为 $1. 68 和 $1. 67。

Inergy 控股公司和其子公司对股票期权计划的会计处理
分部信息 SFAS No. 131 "公司分部报告和相关信息披露" 为报告业务分部信息以及相关的产品或服务、地理位置、主要顾客等的披露设立了标准。SFAS No. 131 还进一步定义了业务分部，即公司主要决策者在分配资源和评估项目时所参照的可以单独获得的财务信息的各组成部分。根据 SFAS No. 131 对分部的划分标准，本公司根据内部营运决策和业绩评估的组织形式来划分分部。参见附注 13。 **最近公布的会计公告** 第 2 个会计年度的 12 月 16 日，财务会计准则委员会（FASB）公布了第 123 号财务会计准则公告（2004年修订）"基于股权的支付"，它是对 SFAS No. 123 "基于股权的福利的会计处理" 的修订。SFAS No. 123（R）取代了 APB 第 25 号意见 "向员工出售股票的会计处理"，并修正了 FASB 第 95 号公告 "现金流量表"。SFAS No. 123（R）所使用的方法与 SFAS No. 123 相似。SFAS No. 123（R）要求披露所有基于股权的支付，包括在损益表中确认员工股票期权的公允价值，而不是用备考披露代替。 SFAS No. 123（R）必须在 2005 年 10 月 1 日以前执行。如果需要提前执行，应在财务报告公布前获得批准。本公司在第 3 年 10 月 1 日开始执行该标准。 SFAS No. 123（R）允许上市公司从以下两种方法中任选一种： •　"修正的预期" 法。员工股票期权计划的成本从该有效日（第 3 年的 10 月 1 日）开始确认（a）根据 SFAS No. 123（R）的要求对所有在有效日以后基于股权的支付适用，和（b）根据 SFAS No. 123（R）的要求对所有在 SFAS No. 123（R）实施之前支付并在 SFAS No. 123（R）实施日（有效日）仍有行权效力的支付适用。 •　"修正的追溯" 法。包括了上述 "修正的预期" 法，但同时也允许经济实体在根据 SFAS No. 123 的要求而先前确认的额度的基础上（为备考披露的目的），将 SFAS No. 123（R）的要求应用于（a）所有先前已得到陈述的时期或（b）在第 3 年采用 SFAS No. 123（R）前的过渡时期。 本公司执行 SFAS No. 123（R）时使用 "修正的预期" 法。 SFAS No. 123（R）允许，在 9 月 30 日结束的第 3 个会计年度中，本公司用第 25 号意见的内涵价值法确认了给员工的基于股权的支付，因此并没有确认员工股票期权的成本。采用 SFAS No. 123（R）的影响取决于未来的基于股权支付的水平。但是，如果我们对之前的期间也采用 SFAS No. 123（R），该准则的影响将同 SFAS No. 123 一样，具体可参见附注 1 中的备考净利润披露和每股收益披露。采用 SFAS No. 123（R）中的公允价值法不会对我们的经营结果和总体财务状况产生重要影响。 •　SFAS No. 151 "存货成本，对 ARB No. 43，第 4 章的修订"，在存货计价方面对现有准则进行了修正，并特别指出非经常性损益应计入期间费用。本公司从第 3 年 6 月 15 日后开始的会计年度里实施此项准则。我们预计 SFAS No. 151 的采用不会对本公司合并财务报表产生重大影响。

当股价相对较低时，决定行权价格往往采用回溯法。股票期权的披露包括任何推延（必须得到董事会批准并和公司政策相符），对投资者进行充分披露，并针对增加的成本相应降低盈余。很多公司都会滥用回溯，比如特意安排某些消息的公布时间，以使股票期权发行后，公司股价会因这些消息的发布而上升，或不恰当地降低公司的盈余。证券交易委员会已经让一些公司重新调整了它们的盈余数字，并高度重视这种情况。

到期和调整

如果股票期权到期未被执行，福利费用不必调整。但是，如果是员工没有履行合约中应尽的义务，福利费用必须根据预计减少的金额进行调整。

非持续性经营

非持续经营是损益表上的非正常项目。当一个分部将被出售，其经营就是非持续的。该会计年度的出售或者为了出售而持有的分经营项目的税后业绩在非持续性经营下反映，与出售该资产相关的损益或资产永损也在此项目反映。非持续性经营的资产需从资产负债表上的持有并使用类转移到为了出售而持有类，这将会导致非持续性经营项目下的损益。

会计处理

APB 第 30 号意见中规定了非持续经营的会计处理和披露。SFAS No. 144 修订了 APB 第 30 号意见，降低了非持续经营必须满足商业分部的要求，指出"经济实体的一个部分"可以是能区分出现金流和经营的任何部分。根据 SFAS No. 144，非持续性经营必须满足在处置以后，该分部的经营和现金流不会影响到其他分布的持续经营，并不会产生持续的影响。一个部分可以是一个商业分部，一个报告单元或资产组，但它必须有明确的可区分的经营和现金流。

如果认定一个分部贬值，应确认损失，账面价值应降低到公允价值减去销售成本的净额。当公允价值上升，也该确认利得，但不高于没有计提减值时的账面价值。在出售时，前期未确认的损益都应确认。

当一家公司决定处置一项经营时，做决定的日期就是决策日。决策日或以后，该项经营应划分到持有并出售类。真正出售的日期为处置日。

计算处置损益

要计算处置损益必须知道两个数据：非持续性经营的经营税后损益以及处置的损益。两者之和就是非持续性经营的损益。经营损失是以下数值的总和：

- 期初经营的账面价值和划分为持有并出售类别时根据公认会计原则对经营的账面价值的调整间的差额。除了长期资产，资产和负债的账面价值都应按照公认会计原则进行调整。调整额被包括在非持续性经营的经营损益中，而非处置损益。根据公认会计原则的调整包括折旧、摊销和对估值账户的调整。比如，当资产划分为持有并出售时，对应收账款计提的坏账准备应根据其收回的可能性进行调整。

- 年初到重分类日的经营损失（包括根据公认会计原则进行的调整）。

- 重分类日到年末（如果年末未被售出）的经营损失（即根据公认会计原则进行调整以后）。

通过比较资产的账面价值与公允价值减销售成本后的结果，可以确定处置损益。计算处置损益的公式如下：

处置损失（利得）=（账面价值 – 根据公认会计原则进行的调整）–（公允价值 – 销售成本）

据公认会计原则进行的调整指上述第一个项目符号（•）后所讲到的调整。

计算处置损益的第一步是确认销售成本。销售成本应从资产公允价值中扣除。

销售的直接增量成本（直接由销售决策导致的成本）包括：

- 经纪人的佣金和其他销售收费。
- 公允价值评估收费。
- 律师费。
- 所有权转移费。
- 结算成本。

计算处置损益的第二步是确认经营的账面价值，包括利息和其他费用的资本化。除了个别例外情况，所有使资产达到最初可用状态的重大成本，包括为购买资产而借款的利息，都应资本化以更准确地反映初始投资成本。

经营的账面价值一旦确定，其公允价值就由精算师来估算。如果总的账面价值大于公允价值，在资产划分为持有并处置期间内应确认处置损失。相反，则等到真正处置时再确认处置利得。

对财务报表的影响

除去所得税（或税收优惠）后非持续性经营的结果在非经常损益项后作为单独损益项列示。处置损益也可以在附注中披露。图表 2 – 227 是一个损益表中对非持续性经营报告的例子。

图表 2 –227 损益表：非持续性经营

持续经营收益		$8 000 000
非持续性经营		
×分部的非持续性经营损失（税后）	120 000	
×分部的处置损失（税后）	$200 000	$320 000
净利润		$7 680 000

日后调整

从本年末到正式处置期间的未来损失与前面所述处理相同。另外，已确认的非持续性经营数额在以后期间应分别分类调整（调整金额和原因应披露）。

非经常性项目

非经常性项目是损益表上的另一种非正常项目。要满足非经常性项目的条件，一项交易必须具有不经常发生的特征，而且是管理层不能控制的（把事件发生时公司的环境考虑在内）。这样的交易通常与正常的交易无关，并在可预见的将来不会再发生。比如，飓风带来的损失就是非经常性项目，如果灾害只在一部分地区出现而且损害很少发生。

会计处理

判断一个项目是否是非经常性项目使用的是限制性标准，有很多不正常或者不经常发生的项目包括在持续经营损益中，而不是作为非经常性项目。

对财务报表的影响

损益表中，非经常性项目在持续经营收益下单独以税后金额列示。

会计变更和差错更正

财务报表必须反映以下结果：
- 差错更正。

- 会计原则变更。

会计原则变更是由财务会计准则委员会（FASB）颁布的新准则或者是管理层根据公认会计原则对会计方法进行重新选择引起的。一旦发生会计原则变更，一般公认审计准则（GAAS）要求审计师修正审计意见以让使用者了解这一情况。对于上市公司，证券交易委员会要求有独立的审计师出具书面证明说明公司选择的新方法比以前的方法更适用。

会计处理

对以前年度损益有影响的会计差错应通过调整保留盈余余额加以更正（因为以前年度的损益表项目已经结转到保留盈余中）。如果是为了提供比较报表，以前年度报表的数据应重新调整。以前年度的差错更正应调整保留盈余而不是损益表。

SFAS No. 154 号指出，任何会计政策的变更都和差错更正一样采用追溯调整法。在追溯调整法下，会计政策的变更带来的累计影响也通过调整保留盈余而不是损益表来完成。

假定一个公司决定在第 3 个会计年度把折旧政策从年数总和法变更为直线折旧法。这对以前年度税前收益的累计影响为 $48 000，如图表 2 - 228 所示。

图表 2 - 228 会计原则变更

年份	旧方法：年数总和法	新方法：直线折旧法	旧方法超过新方法的金额
第 2 年	$96 000	$60 000	$36 000
第 1 年	$72 000	$60 000	12 000
总计			$48 000

对财务报表的影响

如果会计政策变更影响到了以前年度，应根据影响重新调整，并披露会计政策变更的性质和理由，并报告会计政策变更对不考虑非经常性项目前的利润的影响，以及对所有之前编制的报表的净利润（包括每股收益等数据）的影响，同时披露股东权益账户期初余额与先前报告的余额间的差异。

如果差错更正涉及以前年度报表，差错产生的原因以及差错对本年度利润和每股收益的影响都应该披露。

公认会计原则要求对会计政策变更产生的累计影响进行披露，如图表 2 - 229 所示。

图表 2 - 229 损益表—会计政策变更

会计政策变更对不考虑非经常性项目前的利润的累计影响	$144 000
非经常性项目 - 偶然损失（扣除 $14 400 税费）	(33 600)
对新折旧方法追溯调整得到的对以前年度的累计影响额	
（扣除 $7 200 税费）	16 800
净利润	$127 200

商业合并

SFAS No. 141 指出"商业合并是指一个实体通过收购一个或多个实体的净资产或股权继而获得那个或那些实体的控制权的行为"。

会计处理

公认会计原则要求使用购买法来计量商业合并。权益结合法不再适用。使用购买法时，购买方将购买价款根据公允价值分配给所有的有形和可确认的无形资产以及负债。购买价款超过资产和负债公允价值的部分被确认为商誉。如果所购买的净资产的公允价值高于购买价格，长期资产而不是所有资产的价值应按比例减少。

多数情况下，商业合并中的购买方可以确认。规模大的一方或发行股权的一方往往是收购方。共同控制下的商业合并可以不遵循 SFAS No. 141，所以可以使用与权益结合法类似的方法。当个人、直接家庭成员或同一组股东拥有商业合并中各个实体 50% 以上的控制权，就称为共同控制下的合并。

对财务报表的影响

财务报表附注必须披露被收购公司的名称和简介、拥有的股权百分比、收购成本，如果为了完成收购发行了股票，还应包括发行股票数、收购意图，以及被并购实体经营结果显示在合并报表中的时期。披露还应包括被并购公司总结性的资产负债表，指明分配到各项资产和负债上的价值。另外，收购的无形资产（无论是否需要摊销）和交易中产生的商誉都需要额外披露，交易中产生的商誉需要分配到各个相关商业分部中（SFAS No. 131）。

合并财务报表

合并财务报表是指反映母公司和其全部子公司形成的企业集团的整体财务状况和经营成果的财务报表。合并财务报表被认为是对企业集团股东和债权人用处最大的报表。联合财务报表与合并财务报表相似，但前者合并的范围是共同控制下的独立的法律实体。合并财务报表和联合财务报表在权益部分表述不同，因为各个实体的法律地位不同。

会计处理

SFAS No. 94"合并所有拥有控制权的子公司"要求所有拥有子公司的企业提供包括所有控股子公司（通常指拥有 50% 以上的控制权，但不排除其他实际控制的情况）的合并报表。如果因为法律或其他限制不能实质控制拥有控制权的子公司，可以不纳入合并报表范围。

对财务报表的影响

编制合并报表，首先要合并各个公司的资产、负债、收入和费用账户。其次，抵销内部交易及余额。最后，公布合并报表。内部交易及余额是指在两个公司报表上同时反映的金额，如投资账户既包括了母公司的投资额，也包括了子公司的股东权益。抵销分录是一个工作表分录（而非会计分录），用来消除内部交易所导致的被重复计量的净资产。除了抵销分录，还有调整分录。调整分录用来更正差错并对某个公司确认而另一个公司尚未确认的报表数进行调整。

所有基本财务报表，包括资产负债表、损益表、现金流量表以及所有者权益变动表，都需要编制合并报表，因为这样的信息对利益相关者了解公司的财务状况和经营业绩至关重要。

编制合并报表首先要确认拥有非全额控股子公司股权的百分比。其次如果存在购买差价，或购买价款和账面价值不同，差额应分配给所购买的资产和负债。购买百分比乘以净资产或收购股权应等于账面价值。当收购价款大于账面价值，净资产价值应升高（反之同理）。

例如，Acme 公司用 $330 000 现金收购了 Beta 公司 75% 的股票（10 000 股中的7 500 股）。Acme 公司的原始分录应借记 $330 000 的投资，贷记等额现金。Beta 公司的账面价值为 $400 000。收购价款和账面价值间的差额应分摊到各个账户。当收购价款大于账面价值，应增加历史成本大于市场价值的资产账户的价值（反之同理）。但增加后的金额不能超过市场价格（超过部分应确认为商誉）。因此，在该例中，我们假定财产和设备账户及土地账户各分摊收购价款大于账面价值的 50%。如图表2－230所示。

图表 2－230　收购价款与账面价值间的差额的计算和分摊

投资成本（收购价格）	$330 000
所收购权益的账面价值（75% × $400 000）	$300 000
差额：收购价格大于（或小于）账面价值的部分	$30 000
分摊到财产及设备＊（50% × $30 000）	（$15 000）
分摊到土地＊（50% × $30 000）	（$15 000）
余额	$0

＊根据市场价格

图表 2－231 是关于如何进行抵销的工作表。

图表 2－231　合并资产负债工作表

合并资产负债工作表
Acme 公司和其全资子公司
第 1 年 1 月 1 日（收购日）

	Acme 公司	Beta 公司	抵消（仅限于工作表，而非会计分录）		少数股东权益	合并后余额
			借方	贷方		
现金	$170 000	$100 000				$270 000
其他流动资产	700 000	250 000				950 000
设备和厂房	600 000	200 000	$15 000＊＊			815 000
土地	200 000	100 000	15 000＊＊			315 000

续表

合并资产负债工作表
Acme 公司和其全资子公司
第 1 年 1 月 1 日（收购日）

	Acme 公司	Beta 公司	抵销（仅限于工作表，而非会计分录）		少数股东权益	合并后余额
			借方	贷方		
对 Beta 公司的投资	$330 000			$330 000 *		
投资成本与账面价值间的差额			$30 000 *	$30 000 **		
总资产	$20 000 000	$650 000				$2 350 000
负债	$300 000	$250 000				$550 000
普通股						
Acme 公司	$1 000 000					$1 000 000
Beta 公司		$250 000	$187 500 *		$62 500 *	
其他已投入股本						
Acme 公司	$200 000					$200 000
Beta 公司		$50 000	$37 500 *		$12 500 *	
保留盈余						
Acme 公司	$500 000					$500 000
Beta 公司		$100 000	$75 000 *		$25 000 *	
少数股东权益					$100 000	$100 000
负债和权益总额	$2 000 000	$650 000	$360 000	$360 000		$2 350 000

　　* 抵销对 Beta 公司的投资：普通股 = $250 000 × 0.75 = $187 500（持有数），$62 500 非持有数；其他已投入股本 = $50 000 × 0.75 = $37 500（持有数），$12 500 非持有数；保留盈余 = $100 000 × 0.75 = $75 000（持有数），$25 000 非持有数；收购价格和账面价值间的差额 = $30 000

　　** 分摊收购价格和账面价值间的差额（$30 000 × 50% 给厂房和设备，$30 000 × 50% 给土地）

　　图表 2−231 中展示了资产和负债合并后的金额（抵销分录后）。因为收购价格和账面价值间的差额而提高的资产价值应在资产剩余年限内摊销。同样，以后年度的内部交易应转销。这些内容超出了本书的范围。

衍生工具

　　衍生工具是一种几乎不需要前期投入并允许相互抵销的金融工具或合约。衍生工具的价值随标的物价格的变化而变化，标的物可以是抵押贷款利率、商品价格、汇率、利率或指数。标的物价格的变化用名义数值或单位货币、现货商品、股价等来衡量。

　　衍生工具合约包括期货、远期合约、互换和期权合约。前面所提到的股票期权和认股权证是常见的衍生工具。股票期权的市场价格是从可以固定价格购买的标的股票的价值衍生而来的。衍生工具合约应包括允许抵销支付的条款。

　　衍生工具可以是为了特定目的而购买，但它们常用于套期保值或抵销其他交易带来的风险。比如，在未来以一定价格购买一定质量的石油的期权可以消除石油价格变动的影响。因此，衍生工具和保险一样都能通过支付一定的代价来减少风险。代价不仅包括购买衍生工具的成本，还包括未来潜在收益的减少。

会计处理

SFAS No. 133 以及由 SFAS No. 138 和 SFAS No. 149 提供的修正，规定了对衍生工具和套期交易的会计处理。这些准则要求任何形式的衍生工具都应在资产负债表中按公允价值确认为资产或负债。

衍生工具公允价值变化的计量方法取决于其是否是套期关系的一部分或者套期的性质。

- 无套期。为了特定目的持有的衍生工具所产生的损益计入当期损益。
- 公允价值套期。公允价值套期用来抵销资产、负债或承诺（如购货承诺）的价值变化风险。套期工具的损益以及被套期部分的损益计入当期损益。
- 现金流量套期。现金流量套期用来抵销未来将要发生交易带来的现金流量变动风险（如预计购买存货）。现金流量套期的损益计入其他全面收益中，当交易实际发生时重新计入当期损益。
- 外币套期。衍生或非衍生金融工具产生的损益符合外币套期保值工具的按如下原则进行会计处理：
  - 以外币交易为主的公司承诺的套期产生的损益以及被套期部分的损益计入当期损益。
  - 对持有并出售证券的套期产生的损益以及被套期部分的损益计入当期损益。
  - 以外币交易为主的公司对预期交易的套期部分产生的损益计入其他全面收益。在交易实际发生时重新计入当期损益。
  - 对国外净投资的套期部分产生的损益作为累计折算调整计入其他全面收益，其余部分计入当期损益。

对财务报表的影响

对衍生工具的披露包括持有或发行衍生工具（投机或套期保值）的目的，为了理解这些目的应该知道的内容，为了达到该目的的公司的政策。公允价值套期、现金流量套期和其他类型的衍生工具应区分开来。公司的风险管理政策、已对冲风险的项目或交易以及已确认的损益也应该披露。

SFAS No. 133 的要求很复杂，为确保恰当处理公司的衍生交易，有必要明确理解公司的套期保值战略。

分部报告

由于出现了很多通过并购经营而变得多元化的企业，财务报表的使用者需要获取企业各个分部的信息以对该企业面临的风险、盈利状况及成长情况有全面的了解。

一些必须提供分部报告的企业担心分部报告所披露的信息不能被正确理解或被竞争对手利用，但财务会计准则委员会和证券交易委员会认为如果不提供分部报告会使信息使用者不能全面了解企业的经营业绩。SFAS No. 131 "企业分部信息和相关信息的披露"，规定了提供财务信息时使用的管理方法。管理方法要求企业按管理层做资本分配决策相同的原则来提供分部信息，比如按生产线或地理位置。

业务分部

业务分部是需要分开报告的一个基本部分。

任何满足以下标准的部分应考虑单独作为一个业务分部：

- 这一部分有可区分的收入和费用。
- 公司的主要决策者考虑该部分的活动来做资金分配决策。
- 内部报告系统对该分部的财务信息单独报告。
- 该分部对披露有重大影响，至少满足以下一个条件：
  - 收入占整个企业收入 10% 以上。
  - 利润或损失占这个企业所有分部经营损益的 10% 以上。
  - 该分部的资产占整个企业资产的 10% 以上。

两个或两个以上的业务分部或地区分部同时满足下列条件的，可以予以合并：

- 生产同样的产品或提供同样的服务。
- 使用相同的生产过程。
- 相同的客户群。
- 使用相同的产品销售方法。
- 拥有相同的政策环境。

分部报告要求

分部不能大于 10 个，包括在分部中的收入应占对外销售收入的 75% 以上。对共同成本或总公司成本的分配不做要求。

SFAS No. 131 要求披露关于业务分部的一些基础信息，分部的资产，分部的损益表信息包括对内和对外销售、利息收入和费用、折旧和摊销以及非经常性项目。其他披露要求还包括不同地理位置的经营业绩（如果不是按地区来划分分部）以及主要客户信息。还需要根据各个分部的收入、利润及资产调整财务报表总额。

图表 2－232 是一个分部披露的例子。

图表 2－232　分部信息

	网球	球拍	训练器材	服装	金融	总计
	\multicolumn{6}{业务分部的分部信息}					
对外交易收入	$6 900	$6 900	$16 100	$27 600	$11 500	$69 000
内部交易收入	—	—	$6 900	$3 450	—	$10 350
分部利润	$460	$161	$2 070	$5 290	$1 150	$9 131
利息收入	—	—	—	—	$9 200	$9 200
利息费用	—	—	—	—	$6 900	$6 900
折旧和摊销	$460	$230	$115	$2 450	$2 530	$6 785
其他重要的非现金项目：						
长期合同成本	—	$460	—	—		$460
分部资产	$4 600	$11 500	$6 900	$27 600	$131 100	$181 700
分部资产支出	$690	$1 610	$1 150	$3 910	$1 380	$8 740

续表

业务分部的分部信息					
网球	球拍	训练器材	服装	金融	总计
收入以及利润或损失的调整					

收入：

总的分部收入	$79 350
非重大分部收入	2 300
内部交易收入抵销	(10 350)
总收入	$71 300

利润或损失：

总分部损益	$9 131
内部交易利润抵销	(1 150)
未分配金额：	
利息费用	(1 150)
诉讼了结后收入	$1 150
其他总公司费用	(1 725)
合并中对退休金费用的调整	$575
非重大分部损益总和	$230
税前扣除非经常性损益后的利润	$7 061

跨国因素

在编制合并报表之前，母公司须把外国子公司报表折算成本国货币。当一个公司进行以非本国货币结算的交易时，同样会涉及到外币折算。

功能性货币

合理的外币折算方法的选择取决于该公司的功能性货币。SFAS No. 52 "外币折算"将功能性货币定义为子公司经营所处主要经济环境中的货币。如果子公司的经营具有很大的自主性，则子公司的当地货币就是功能性货币。另一方面，如果子公司的业务都是母公司业务的延伸，则母公司的货币是子公司的功能性货币。

决定功能性货币的因素有很多，比如子公司的销售市场在哪里，销售价格如何决定，费用在哪里发生，如何融资，以及内部交易的多少等。自主型子公司拥有独立的用当地货币进行的销售、购货和融资，且具有较少的内部交易。另一方面，非自主型的子公司往往以母公司货币进行销售、购货和融资，内部交易也较多。

如果子公司在高通货膨胀率（通货膨胀率超过3年高于100%）下运营，母公司货币就是功能性货币。

外币折算方法

当母公司货币作为功能性货币时，子公司的报表金额应使用时态法折算成母公司货币。而当子公司货币就是功能性货币时，使用现行汇率法核算。如果子公司使用当地货币，而当地货币非功能性货币或非母公司报告所用货币时，报表应首先折算成功能性货币，然后再折算成母公司报告所使用货币。

使用时态法折算

时态法也称做货币/非货币法，非货币性资产（除了现金、对现金的要求权、现金债务以外的资产负债表项目）都用历史汇率折算，与它们相关的费用必须用发生时的历史汇率折算。

非货币性项目包括：

- 以成本计价的投资。
- 以成本计价的存货和销货成本。
- 预付费用，如租金、保险和广告费。
- 财产、厂房及设备折旧费用。
- 无形资产及摊销费用。
- 递延费用和赊购。
- 递算收入。
- 实缴资本账户。

货币性资产和负债（现金、应收项目和应付项目）以及其他用现时价值计量的资产和负债（市场价格或现金流量贴现值）使用资产负债表日的现行汇率折算。损益表中除以上账户外的其他账户为了方便都用当年（当季度或当月）的平均汇率折算。如果使用时态法，折算损益都要计入当期损益。

图表 2 - 233 是一个从子公司功能性货币欧元折算到美元的例子。折算中使用了资产负债表日的汇率、历史汇率以及当年的平均汇率。家庭办公室账户是权益性账户，所以没有进行折算，而直接使用期初美元余额。

图表 2 - 233　使用时态法折算

Bounce 体育用品公司
欧洲子公司试算表折算为美元
第 1 年 12 月 31 日

	余额（欧元）借方（贷方）	折算汇率	余额（美元）借方（贷方）
现金	€19 950	$0. 24 *	$4 788
应收账款	352 800	0. 24 *	84 672
存货	157 500	0. 21 **	33 075
家庭办公室	(432 250)		(78 400)
销售收入	(700 000)	0. 225 ***	(157 500)
销售成本	472 500	0. 21 **	$99 225
营业费用	129 500	0. 225 ***	$29 138
小计	€0		$14 998
交易利得	0		(14 998)
总计	€0		$0

* 第 1 年 12 月 31 日的现行汇率 = 0. 24
** 使用的历史汇率
*** 当年平均汇率

使用现行汇率法折算

在现行汇率法下，所有的资产和负债都以资产负债表日的现行汇率折算。实缴资本账户使用历史汇率折算。为简便起见，SFAS No. 52 规定损益表科目都以当年平均汇率折算（尽管一部分科目在资产负债表和损益表中应该使用年末的现行汇率）。折算损益不计入当期净利润，而是作为其他全面收益的一部分。

图表 2 - 234 是一个从欧元折算到美元的例子。折算中使用了现行、平均和历史汇率。保留盈余余额没有进行折算，而直接使用的年初余额。年末的保留盈余余额则是由年初余额加上折算后的当年利润，并减去当年派发的股利计算所得。

图表 2 - 234　使用现行汇率法折算
（子公司的财务报表）从功能性货币到报告货币

德国 Bounce 国际公司
财务报表折算为美元
第 2 年 8 月 31 日

	欧元	折算汇率	美元
损益表			
净销售收入	206 400	$0.515[1]	$106 296
其他收入	51 600	$0.515[1]	26 574
总收入	258 000		$132 870
销售成本	154 800	$0.515[1]	$79 722
营业费用和所得税	82 560	$0.515[1]	42 518
总成本和费用	237 360		$122 240
净利润	20 640		$10 630
资产负债表			
现金	8 600	$0.49[2]	$4 214
净应收账款	34 400	0.49[2]	16 856
存货	154 800	0.49[2]	75 852
短期预付款	3 440	0.49[2]	1 686
厂房（净值）	275 200	0.49[2]	134 848
无形资产（净值）	17 200	0.49[2]	8 428
资产总计	493 640		$241 884
应付票据	17 200	$0.49[2]	$8 428
应付账款	25 800	0.49[2]	12 642
普通股	430 000	0.54[3]	232 200
保留盈余	20 640		11 146
累计折算调整数			(22 532)
负债和股东权益总计	493 640		$241 884

[1] 8 月 31 日结束的第 2 个会计年度的平均汇率
[2] 现行汇率（第 2 年 8 月 31 日）
[3] 3 历史汇率（第 1 年 12 月 31 日）

外币的财务报表陈述和披露要求

损益表或附注中应列示外国子公司在该会计期间的所有损益。累计折算调整额的变化应计入单独的报表或在附注中披露，或者计入所有者权益表中。折算调整应包括期初和期末累计折算调整余额、累计调整额、净投资的套期保值、长期内部交易项、折算调整分摊的所得税以及国外投资额的减少。

进度检查

提示：完成以下各题。参考答案随后给出。

把下列应收款项和它们的定义配对

1. _____短期应收款
2. _____长期应收款
3. _____应收账款
4. _____应收票据
5. _____非交易性应收款项

    A. 有书面协议在固定日期收回的款项

    B. 应收的利息或股利

    C. 在一年或一个经营周期（孰长）内应收的款项

    D. 为了商业目的允许顾客推迟支付货款

    E. 在一年或一个经营周期（孰长）之后应收的款项

6. 如果存货价格一直在上涨，公司现在销售的是低成本的商品，为了提高存货价值和净利润公司应使用何种存货计价方法？

    (　) a. 后进先出法

    (　) b. 先进先出法

    (　) c. 平均成本法

    (　) d. 个别计价法

7. 交易证券应以哪种价值计量

    (　) a. 历史价格

    (　) b. 市场价格

    (　) c. 现值

    (　) d. 可变现净值

8. 下列哪项成本不能包括在存货计价中？

    (　) a. 间接制造成本

    (　) b. 现金折扣

    (　) c. 运输成本

    (　) d. 与存货相关的利息成本

9. 下面哪项计算折旧的方法以生产数量为基础？

    (　) a. 递减折旧法

    (　) b. 余额递减法

    (　) c. 工作量法

    (　) d. 直线法

10. 如果满足以下条件，应确认或有损失

    (　) a. 负债可能发生，损失能可靠估计

    (　) b. 负债很有可能发生，损失能可靠估计

    (　) c. 负债可能发生，损失有可靠的记录

    (　) d. 负债很有可能发生，损失有可靠的记录

进度检查答案

1. c
2. e
3. d
4. a
5. b
6. b
7. b
8. d
9. c
10. a

第 5 节
证券交易委员会及其报告要求

本节内容简介

美国证券交易委员会（SEC）对证券行业各种行为有广泛的监督权，包括对证券公司与股票交易所的规范，它还负责对那些公开发行证券公司的定期报告进行监督与规范。美国证券委员会存在的主要理由是保护投资者与潜在投资者的利益，并维护市场的诚信。

成立 SEC 的法案与 SEC 的权力

SEC 立法

成立证券交易委员会的主要法案是依据 1933 年的《证券法》（1933 Securities Act）与 1934 年的《证券交易法》（1934 Securities Exchange Act）而来。而在最近，《萨班斯－奥克斯利法案》（Sabanes-Oxley Act）对《证券交易法》进行了一些修正，赋予了证券委员会更多的责任。

1933 年《证券法》

1933 年《证券法》主要关注证券的首次销售与分配，而不是证券在首次发行后的交易过程。根据该法律要求，在证券公开销售之前（包括在一级股票市场的首次公开发行与再发行），申请上市的注册登记表必须生效，同时招股章程要递送到每一个证券购买者手上。

申请上市的注册登记表包括两个部分。第一部分是招股章程，它包括证券及证券发行公司、分配计划以及发行后的资金使用计划等方面的信息。招股章程还包含 5 年的经过选择的财务信息和管理层对发行公司经营情况、财务状况、流动性与资本资源的论述与分析，以及最近 3 年的经过审计的财务报表。（本节稍后会探讨管理层论述与分析）

申请上市的注册登记表的第二部分更具补充性与管理性，它通常不直接向社会公开；然而社会公众可以通过证券交易委员会网站（www. sec. gov）上的 EDGAR 系统了解到整个注册登记表的信息，它包含各种登记者的所有文件备案。

1934 年《证券交易法》

1934 年的《证券交易法》管制着二级市场的证券交易与投资者的行为，包括：

- 证券市场的规章。
- 防止出现市场操纵与舞弊。
- 根据《证券法》登记的公司的连续披露。
- 对证券购买者的信用的控制，即保证金交易。
- 委托说明书及其他与股东间的沟通。

- 内部人交易的监管。

《证券交易法》要求所有的美国本土公司根据《证券法》进行注册登记，并提供 10-k 年报文件、10-Q 季报文件以及其他证券交易委员会的报告要求比如提供近期事项的 8-k 报告和委托说明书。（对在美国证券交易委员会注册的国外公司也有相应的报告要求）1934 年《证券交易法》还要求，对证券进行场外交易的发行公司，如果它的投票持有者不低于 500 人并且其总资产不低于 1 000 万美元，也需要在证券交易委员会登记注册。《证券交易法》不仅关注具体的证券发行，同时还会保证注册登记公司向投资者公布足够的财务状况信息。

其他立法

另外，证券交易委员会有责任维护一些二级法律，包括 1935 年《公共事业法》、1939 年《信托契约法》、1940 年《投资公司法》、1940 年《投资顾问法》和 2002 年《萨班斯-奥克斯利法》。

SEC 的执法与监管活动

在根据证券相关法律进行执法的过程中，证券交易委员会有权对违反法律的人员采取民事法律行为，在涉及刑事行为的时候，证券交易委员会也会与司法部门紧密合作。

由于其部分责任是管制上市公司的定期报告，证券交易委员会有权制定用于上市公司定期报告的会计原则。在这方面，证券交易委员会已经决定它将支持 FASB 的会计准则制定过程和其制定的会计准则。

证券交易委员会通过以下四个部门来执行其监管业务：

- 公司融资监管部。
- 证券市场管理部。
- 投资活动管理部。
- 执行部。

其中，公司融资监管部对于会计工作者来说最为熟悉不过。它是根据《证券法》、《证券交易法》和 1939《信托契约法》来对备案进行处理和管理。

证券交易委员会还有许多职能办公室。证券交易委员会的总会计师办公室是会计工作者最常联系的办公室，因为它提供对会计原则的指导，并代表证券交易委员会同 FASB 和其他会计准则制定者交涉。

SEC 对上市公司的报告要求

证券交易委员会的报告要求分为三个种类：S-X 管理条例、S-K 管理条例和 S-B 管理条例。S-X 管理条例对公司登记注册和定期报告所用到的财务报表的内容进行规范。相反，S-K 管理条例规范所有非财务信息。S-B 管理条例用来规范所有小型企业的报告，这里不准备进一步讲解。这三个报告要求也同时应用于《证券法》和《证券交易法》下的归档过程。

S-X 管理条例

S-X 管理条例要求按照 GAAP 公开审计过的财务报表时，根据《证券法》的登记注册要求必须使用 S-1、S-2 或 S-3 表格，还要根据《证券交易法》的要求呈示定期报告，包括 10-K 年报和 10-Q 季报。具体来说，10-K 表格要求公司实体必须提供最近两个会计年度经审计过的资产负债表以及最近三个会计年度的损益表、现金流量表和所有者权益变动表。另外，S-X 管理条例还要求披露一些 GAAP 并不要求披露的信息，比如补偿银行存款余额。该条例还规定了一些必须遵循的重要性门槛。

中期财务报表与年度报表不同，它不需要经过审计，但是必须按照 GAAP 编制。这些在一年中的前三个季度均需要提供的报表，按照 10-Q 表格编制。中期财务报表包括最近一季度和最近一个会计年度的简明资产负债表（以便对比）和今年年初到现在的简明损益表，以及到上一个会计季度末和上年度同一季度（以便对比）的现金流量表。S-X 管理条例还包括对独立审计师与其对登记上市公司所出具的报告的一些要求。

S-K 管理条例

S-K 管理条例要求所有非财务性质的披露要按照《证券法》与《证券交易法》备案进行。整个证券委员会的要求被称为基本信息包（Basic Information Package，BIP），它包括所有 S-X 管理条例与 S-K 管理条例的要求。S-K 管理条例要求披露除其他事项以外的以下内容：

- 与登记上市公司的业务和证券相关的风险因素。
- 业务的描述。
- 现金股利发放频率。
- 5 年公司实体的财务趋势总结。
- 8 个季度的销售额、毛利润和收益数据（大型公司）。
- 管理层论述与分析（MD&A）。
- 最近两年会计人员的任何变动情况和会计人员的任何不同意见。

SEC 对上市公司的披露要求

下面论述整合披露、标准化的财务报表和管理层论述与分析这些概念。本部分还将探讨证券交易委员会的披露要求与公共记录数据库 EDGAR。

整合披露、标准化的财务报表和管理层论述与分析

最初，《证券法》是用来规范一级市场事务，《证券交易法》是规范二级市场事务，因此它们对披露有不同的要求。为了促进全面披露和财务报表之间的可比性（还为了降低成本），证券交易委员会对文件的要求被整合，财务报表被标准化，同时还要求加入管理层论述与分析。下面将逐一探讨这些要素。

整合披露

过去，按照《证券法》和《证券交易法》的要求进行的文件披露在细节上存在很多不同。1982 年，证券交易委员会采用了整合披露制度（IDS）。这个制度一直都在改进之中，该制度的主要内容如下：

- 公司的具体信息对于两个法案来说，实际上是相同的，因此《证券交易法》文件是《证券法》下所提供的登记上市信息的必要补充资料。这样由于信息内容很相似，不仅可以帮助投资者，还消除了登记注册公司提供信息的累赘。
- 当大型公司（要满足一定的条件）在提供额外的证券文件时，它们可以合并根据《证券交易法》而提供的文件，为公司新的发行提供参考。

整合披露使处于二级市场的投资者与一级市场的投资者具有同等的地位。

标准化财务报表

IDS、S-X 管理条例、S-K 管理条例的存在和基本信息包的使用，确保了《证券法》和《证券交易法》对财务报表具有标准化的要求。因而按《证券法》的 S-1、S-2 和 S-3 表格与按《证券交易法》的 10-K 表格编制财务报表具有一致性。

管理层论述与分析

BIP 要求一份与公司的经营成果和财务状况相关的分析，指的就是管理层论述与分析（MD&A）。该要求的潜在意义是给予投资者管理当局对公司的观点。管理层必须分析公司的流动性、资本资源和过去三年的经营成果。当通货膨胀的影响达到重要性程度时，也必须被披露。财务报表是根据历史数据编制的，因此证券交易委员会在制定管理层论述与分析部分要求的文件规范时，强调管理层必须关注他们知道的所有事件、趋势与不确定性，以表明过去的结果并没有对未来的表现起到预示作用。这个要求包括了过去事件不再影响未来的情况和事件可能在过去没有影响但现在会产生影响的情况。只有管理层了解的信息才能被分析讨论，而假设情况是不需要讨论的。证券交易委员会并没有规定管理层论述与分析的格式，目的是为了避免这部分变成一种千篇一律的形式，以让管理层自由地讨论他们认为适当的定性和定量业务因素。

SEC 的披露要求

本部分将讨论证券交易委员会要求的最常见的登记表格。要注意的是，证券交易委员会的网站上有许许多多的表格，这些表格是用于最近几年才出现的例外情况与特殊事例。

S-1、S-2 和 S-3 表格

S-1、S-2 和 S-3 表格用于与证券交易委员会进行证券登记注册。登记注册是一个复杂的过程，涉及法律顾问、拥有 SEC 专业技能的会计师（内部会计师或独立会计师）和包销商。S-1 表格适用于 IPO 和那些没有资格进行简化注册的公司。S-2 表格适用于那些没有拖欠任何义务或优先股股利，并且至少三年及时地提交

《证券交易法》要求的报告。S-3 表格同 S-2 表格在要求方面基本相同，除了公司只需有一年的及时报告历史，然而它要求公司有公众持股量或者普通股的市场价值至少达到 7 500 万美元。其他例外事项及细节均适用于这三个表格。无论要用到哪一个表格，每个表格都应包括招股说明书提供的信息（Part I）以及公司具体的信息。在用到 S-2 表格和 S-3 表格时，公司的具体信息可以通过参考之前发布的报告而整合（通过 SEC 的在线 EDGAR 数据库）。

10-K 表格

10-K 表格是大多数股票可以自由交易的公司按照证券交易委员会的要求提供年度报告的文件，它提供了注册公司业务的结合性概述。截至 2006 年，10-K 表格的期限是 60 天。

10-Q 表格

10-Q 表格是最近公开交易的公司前三个季度的季度报告文件。它包括未经审计的财务报表和管理层论述与分析。它旨在通过连续展现公司的财务状况，给投资者提供更相关的信息。截至 2006 年，10-Q 表格的期限是 30 天。

重大事件披露或 8-K 表格

8-K 表格又称作即时报告，因为它必须对投资者披露任何重大事件，或者公司重大变动，这些在财务报表中未能报告。8-K 表格包含的 9 类条款如下所示：
- 条款 1：公司控制的变动
- 条款 2：资产的取得与处置
- 条款 3：破产或破产管理
- 条款 4：公司的注册会计师变动
- 条款 5：其他重大事项
- 条款 6：注册公司董事辞职
- 条款 7：财务报表和展示
- 条款 8：会计年度的变动
- 条款 9：公开披露规则

委托说明书

当股东要求投票时，一些股东将其权力给予特定的机构并委托其在适当的时候为自己投票。委托说明书便用于这一过程。公司章程及其附则决定了何时需要股东投票。当需要投票并且要求委托代理时，股东必须提供一个代理声明，包括授权给特定代理机构为股东投票的代理卡。大多数代理卡包括具体的投票与指定的投票立场，代理机构必须为它们投票，但是有一些代理卡有长期性，允许代理机构任意投票。代理文件是公开的信息。代理声明包括的具体项目有：
- 日期、时间和下一次股东大会的地点。
- 为谁代理投票、估计代理成本。
- 董事会和执行官持有的发行商股票的股份数。

- 在投票事件中的异议权（如果有的话）。
- 代理撤销权。

EDGAR

美国证券交易委员会已经创建了一个数据库，名为 EDGAR 系统。该数据库可以从 www. sec. gov 登录进入，它包括所有在证券交易委员会注册的公司的公开数据，任何成员都能通过该数据库免费获得任何公开交易的公司的财务报表，用户只需使用由该数据库提供的搜索引擎便可很容易地获得所需信息。

萨班斯法案的条款

《萨班斯法案》（2002）也叫做上市公司会计改革与投资者保护法案，确定了公司管理层、董事会和审计人员之间的法律关系。该法案的目的在于通过建立一个检测系统使得上市公司的财务信息得以准确披露，并平衡董事会、公司管理层和外部审计人员之间的关系。

《萨班斯法案》的条款包括上市公司会计监察委员会的创立，该委员会由五个全职成员组成，为会计专业人员提供监管监督。《萨班斯法案》要求对为发行证券的公司出具审计报告的注册会计师事务所进行注册。

《萨班斯法案》包括 9 章，《萨班斯法案》的所有条款都根据章节所在位置进行了编号（例如，第 3 章包括 301 节、302 节等）。图表 2 - 235 简要概述了这些条款。

图表 2 - 235　《萨班斯法案》（2002）的简要概述

章	条款的简要概述
第 1 章	上市公司会计监察委员会的组建。为了保护投资者以及公众的利益，兹组建上市公司会计监察委员会。委员会的目的是监督上市公司的审计以及相关事项，以便为购买及持有其证券的公司或公众投资者编制准确、独立的审计报告。不同于证券交易委员会，该委员会应当是一个法人，作为非营利公司持续经营，直至被国会出台的法案解散。 上市公司会计监察委员会由五位全职人员组成，该五位委员首先由财政部秘书处和美联储理事会主席共同协商再由证券交易委员会最后任命。委员会的五名委员任职为五年，任期不超过两届而且必须是"从具有诚信和名誉的著名人士中任命，他们应当证明自己对投资者和公众的利益负责，并且理解发行证券的公司根据证券法规定披露财务信息的义务及性质，理解为这种信息披露编制、出具审计报告的会计师的义务及性质"。至少有两名委员是注册会计师而其余三名不能为注册会计师。第 1 章还要求对为发行证券的公司出具审计报告的注册会计师事务所进行注册。 《萨班斯法案》同时还赋予了委员会建立或修改审计准则的权力；尽管如此，法案制定了某些最低要求，包括共同合伙人复查以及工作底稿的标准。 第 1 章进一步制定了道德标准，对公众会计师事务所进行检查、调查以及处罚。它还进一步阐明外国会计师事务所对公开发行债券的发行者实施审计的也适用于此法案。
第 2 章	审计师的独立性。该章指出任何事务所在对公开发行债券的发行方的账簿进行审计时不得再为其提供某些特定的会计服务。如果之前获得允许，审计师也可为其提供不在特别规定之内的其他会计服务。该章也允许某些豁免，如果涉及公众利益的话。此类非审计业务的收费必须在该公司的年报（10 - K 表格）或年度委托声明中披露。会计师事务所可以不对公开发行债券的发行方的账簿进行审计，如果该发行方的任何一位董事受聘于该会计师事务所以及在一年内参与了该发行方的审计业务。 第 2 章同时还要求审计合伙人的轮换。该章中的第 204 条指出审计师应向发行方董事会所委派的审计委员会提供报告。

章	条款的简要概述
第 3 章	公司管理层的责任。它要求公司的首要执行官员（们）及首要财务官（们）（或担任同等职务的人员）在每一年度报告或季度报告中保证其披露的内容符合证券交易委员会的规定。这些声明还必须证明该官员认为报告中不存在重大的错报、漏报以及报告中的会计报表及其他财务信息在所有重大方面，公允地反映了公司在该报告期末的财务状况及该报告期内的经营成果。 该章还要求管理层设计所需的内部控制，以保证这些官员能知道该公司及其并表子公司的所有重大信息，尤其是报告期内的重大信息。 第 307 条要求证券交易委员会制定立法以使作为发行证券公司代理人的律师报告其违反证券法律的行为。
第 4 章	第 4 章要求在向证券交易委员会提供的定期报告中强化财务信息披露。它要求在公司申报的年度报告和季度报告中披露所有重大的资产负债表外业务、合同、义务（包括或有义务）。 该章禁止向管理人员提供个人贷款，除非这些贷款属于公司的经营性业务（例如，抵押公司贷款给总裁用于住房购买）。 该章还强调公司管理层应建立和维护内部控制系统及保证相应控制程序充分有效；公司的独立董事应对管理层制定的内部控制进行测试和评价，并出具评价报告。
第 5 章	第 5 章强调了财务分析师的利益冲突问题。对于公开发布由经纪人和交易商雇佣的从事投资银行业务的人员提供的研究报告有严格限制。
第 6 章	第 6 章概述了分配给 SEC 的资金以保证 SEC 能够正常履行其职能以及财政拨款方面的权利。
第 7 章	第 7 章要求审计总署研究自 1989 年以来导致会计师事务所不断合并的原因，合并导致会计师事务所数量减少，但可以执行证券法律规定的大型国内及跨国公司审计业务。
第 8 章	第 8 章主要解决公司会计欺诈的犯罪行为。包括篡改文件的刑事责任、违反证券欺诈法的债务以及要求审计师保存五年之内的所有审计与复查的工作底稿。工作底稿是指审计师保留的申请程序记录、业绩考核、所获信息以及在审计中的相关结论。第 8 章同时也保护提供欺诈证据的上市公司的雇员以及对欺诈公开证券投资者的行为处以罚金。
第 9 章	第 9 章进一步强化白领犯罪（例如利用邮件和电传进行犯罪）的刑事责任。
第 10 章	第 10 章要求公司首席执行官签署联邦所得税的退税证明。
第 11 章	第 11 章解决公司的会计欺诈行为。规定了高达 20 年的处罚。此外，证券交易委员会可以对公众证券的发行人和它的董事、管理人员、合伙人、主管、代理人或雇员涉嫌违反联邦证券法的行为签发临时命令。第 11 章同时也按照 1934 年《证券交易法》加重刑事责任以及对举报人进行打击报复的行为处以罚款。

内部人交易和证券欺诈法案

　　1934 年《证券交易法案》第 16 节在禁止内部人短线操纵交易以及要求对内部人交易进行披露时首次提出内部人交易这一概念。除了这仅有的对内部交易的部分禁令，法院规定 1934 年《证券交易法案》的 10b–5 关于禁止舞弊的法规可以运用于禁止内部交易，把内部人员对符合重要性原则的非公开信息的披露作为一种义务或者不进行交易直到这些信息被披露为止。另外两部法案已经加强了法院的这些意见。

1984 年的《内部人交易制裁法》

　　1984 年的《内部人交易制裁法》特别规定对于非法内部交易的罚金将高达所获利润的三倍或者避免非法交易所造成损失的三倍。

1988 的《内部人交易与证券欺诈执行法案》

1988 的《内部人交易与证券欺诈执行法案》规定，经纪人、交易商和投资顾问必须加强相关政策以防止内部交易和公司、雇主或者任何相关人员滥用重要的非公开信息。

进度检查

提示：完成以下各题。参考答案随后给出。

1. 以下哪一项不属于1934年《证券交易法案》的规定？
   （　　）a. 证券市场的规范
   （　　）b. 登记在初级市场上销售的证券
   （　　）c. 控制保证金交易
   （　　）d. 内部交易的规范

2. 判断对错。
   证券交易委员会的 S－X 管理条例要求管理层所提供的管理层论述及分析报告中包括对重大事件的完全披露，重大事件是指会影响公司未来收益的事件。
   （　　）a. 对
   （　　）b. 错

3. 上市公司会计监察委员会是
   （　　）a. 由1934年《证券交易法案》组建用以保证其遵从该法案
   （　　）b. 由1934年《证券交易法案》组建用以监督上市公司的审计师
   （　　）c. 由《萨班斯法案》组建用以保证其遵从该法案
   （　　）d. 由《萨班斯法案》组建用以监督上市公司的审计师

进度检查答案

1. b
2. b
3. d

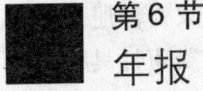

第 6 节
年报

本节内容简介

　　年报的指导原则是充分披露原则，这一原则要求任何能够在很大程度上影响年报使用者进行财务决策的财务信息都应包括在定期报告文件中。因为，美国证券交易委员会（SEC）要求在年报中应首要包括被审计的财务报表和与财务报告有关的审计内容，其次是关于管理层责任的讨论、审计委员会和董事会的作用说明、独立审计报告和其他年报相关内容。

　　公认审计准则（GAAS）是由美国注册公共会计师协会（AICPA）提出的，包括10个对审计以及财务报告的制定具有指导性作用的方针。这些通用标准要求足够的专业技术培训和专业熟练程度，独立态度以及对审计工作合理的职业判断。审计工作的标准要求适当的监督和计划，对内部控制的充分理解（本质、时间以及控制测试的范围）以及从意见中提取具有足够说服力证据的能力。财务报告的标准包括财务报告必须说明报表是否符合一般公认会计原则（GAAP）的要求、确认有违反公认会计原则的内容、假设报表满足充分披露的要求（如果不满足应指出）以及出具审计意见（或者拒绝表达审计意见）。

财务报告的审计工作

　　审计的定义就是注册会计师在所有相关资料基础上确认报表是否满足公认会计原则的要求而表达书面审计意见。大多数审计工作都由注册会计师事务所从事。当注册会计师表达某个审计意见时，他/她就要对审计意见负法律责任，外部使用者以此作为对投资对象可靠性的判断依据。审计报告必须包含在所有的对外年度审计报告中。上市公司的报告必须能够在美国证券交易委员会（SEC）官方网站上的 EDGAR 数据库中得到。私人公司同样需要进行审计，因为它们需要以此来保障其信用水平。审计的受众包括公司管理层、公众以及证券交易委员会，审计工作为他们提供最高水平的可靠性保证。

　　注册会计师提供的审计服务根据不同的财务报告类别分为保证性服务和非保证性服务。本文不探讨非保证性服务。保证性服务包括鉴证服务的子项目，而审计就是鉴证服务的一种。需要注意的是很多服务不允许由同一家事务所或个人提供（这些公司和个人同时提供其他业务）。

鉴证服务

经营审计

　　经营审计是对公司实体经营过程的复核，以此来评价其经营效率和效用。在审计结束之时，注册会计师会向公司提出如何提高经营绩效的建议。经营审计可以测试从供应链管理到用于会计分录的软件使用的效率和效用。由于它的服务范围很广，注册会计师的具体工作活动或者作为注册会计师需要的资格都很难具体定义。注册会计师可能对管理层的决策进行评价或者对销售培训效果进行评价。由于这类审计具有主观性，比起其他的审计类型这更像是管理咨询。

合规审计

合规审计是用来检验审计对象是否符合政府相关部门的规定，合规审计还能够用于检验员工是否遵守内控制度，校区和其他政府机构也会进行大量的审计工作以保证相关法规制度的执行，公司实体的管理层对合规审计很是青睐。在条件允许的情况下（如对独立性要求不高），有些合规审计工作由被审计组织单位聘用的个人来进行，例如：一个政府机构需要进行合规审计工作，那么这个机构可以由自己出资直接聘请审计师（如美国国税局的税务审计师）。

其他鉴证服务

注册会计师也可以提供如对贷款协议中债务人对财务契约的履行情况进行独立验证的服务，为客户进行内控检验也是其业务之一，《萨班斯法案》要求所有公司的年报中必须包含关于公司内部控制效率的信息。鉴证服务也用于对公司实体前瞻性报告的审计，以提高公司的信用度。

其他的服务包括复核业务、报表编制业务和核证业务。

- **复核业务**

复核业务允许注册会计师作出有限的保证，来确保财务报告是符合公认会计原则（GAAP）或其他综合会计准则的标准。由于相关法规没有对非上市公司的审计作出具体要求，那些想要提供财务报告保证而又不想为此支付审计费用的非上市公司或许可以通过复核来满足它们的需要。复核需要的证据收集数量要比审计的证据收集少得多。可是，进行复核的注册会计师应获取客户的业务资料、会计记录、财务报告以及熟悉相关行业的会计准则。

- **报表编制业务**

在报表编制业务中，注册会计师应为客户公司编制财务报告，这些报告是建立在由本公司管理层所提供的信息的基础上的，同时对这些信息的准确性不作确认。虽然报表编制是注册会计师最低的服务要求，但是由于所提供的信息来源于被审计公司的管理层，所以此业务对注册会计师的独立性要求并不高并且不需要为报表中的错报负法律责任。但是报表编制人员必须掌握客户、客户业务、行业、交易、会计记录以及公司员工的资料。注册会计师也应该作出简单的询证来确定提供的信息是否合理，复核财务报告是否符合公认会计原则并且无数据错误。在注册会计师认为报告内容不公允时，应选择披露问题或者放弃编制业务。

- **核证业务**

在核证业务中，注册会计师要对其他方所作出的判断结论的可靠性发表书面意见。例如，一个银行可能要聘请一名注册会计师来审查它的债务人是否满足贷款合同所规定的所有要求，而合同所规定的所有程序已经被第三方注册会计师以及报表使用者所认可。

其他保证服务

其他保证服务是为客户提供关于信息的可靠性以及相关性的保证服务，用以提高信息质量。例如保证彩票行业的公正性。这些服务并不满足鉴证服务的一般定义，不要求书面报告，并且也不需要对第三方的书面建议的可靠性作出判断。由于非注册会计师都可以从事类似工作，这就导致了激烈的行业竞争。其他保证服务还包括风险评估、业绩评估、信息系统可靠性检测、卫生保健情况测试、电子商务评估以及老年保健附加项目评估。

注册会计师的责任

注册会计师规划审计工作并且在公认审计准则（GAAS）下实施审计，合理地保证财务报告不存在错报或舞弊。但是，所收集审计材料的本质以及舞弊行为的特征决定了注册会计师只能作出合理保证，而不是绝对程度上的保证。

注册会计师是通过对审计证据或审计相关文件材料的收集来验证财务报告信息的相关性的，如发票、合同、银行对账单财务报表数据。由于过去曾出现过公司提供虚假的文件资料作为审计材料，所以注册会计师应就文件材料的使用价值以及可靠性进行评估。例如，被审计的 XYZ 公司与 ABC 公司签订了一项合同，向 ABC 公司提供相关服务，注册会计师就需要确认是否存在 ABC 公司，ABC 公司所派的签署合同的人员身份是否符合规定等。

在注册会计师检验完财务报表中发现的材料信息的时候，就应编制一份审计报告说明这些审计材料信息的情况。

合理保证

注册会计师必须对财务报告中不会出现错报作出合理的保证。只作出合理保证的原因是审计证据的局限性、错误的不可避免以及注册会计师不能够获得绝对可靠的证据来作出绝对保证。

重要性 VS. 非重要性

财务报告的错报是财务报告中所有的非人为错误的组合，具有重要性；而舞弊是那些可能影响到报表使用者作出正确决策的人为虚报财务信息。注册会计师有责任作出合理保证来确保财务报告中没有具有重要性的错报内容，但没有责任甄别所有的非重要性的错报和舞弊内容。

检测错误或舞弊

注册会计师有责任通过对所有的审计证据进行检测，来发现错误和舞弊。由于错误或舞弊的存在会使信息被错误陈述或遗漏。错误是非人为的，而舞弊不是。

舞弊有两种形式：非管理舞弊和管理舞弊。非管理舞弊也叫做资产私占，是通过窃取资金或资产实现的。例如，公司资产被员工私自占有或者私自动用公司销售现金等。

舞弊性财务报告也叫管理舞弊，主要表现是信息的错报和漏报。例如，通过夸大销售量或低估坏账费用来提高利润。

在公认审计准则（GAAS）下，由于舞弊的存在，使得注册会计师被要求对符合重要性的错报进行风险评估。舞弊的风险因素主要与公司的管理以及内控环境有关（如较高的经理流动率、关键管理人、过度关注收入目标），行业环境（如不断恶化或迅速改变的行业状况）、公司的财务稳定性和经营特点（如筹资压力、过度复杂的交易和经营结构）。风险因素的存在可能会使注册会计师更改其所寻找的审计证据的类型并采取其他行动。

检测违法行为

美国注册公共会计师协会（AICPA）第 54 号审计准则公告（SAS No. 54）中将违法行为定义为：比舞弊更为严重的违反法律或政府规定的行为。公司雇佣没有取得工作签证或绿卡的外籍员工就是其中一例。有直接影响的违法行为是指对财务报告中的具体账户余额有直接的财务影响。例如，违反税法，这就直接影响到税收费用以及应税余额。间接影响违法行为对财务报告并不存在直接的影响。

SAS No. 54 规定，针对有直接影响的违法行为问题，注册会计师有责任评估是否有证据表明公司有违反联邦法律和州税法的重大违法行为，而这些可以通过对员工的采访和由税务相关部门提供的报告推断出来。

间接影响的违法行为只有在公司接受罚款或制裁时才对公司的财务报告产生影响。公司的潜在罚款或制裁一般由或有负债造成。由于注册会计师不属于法定鉴定专家，审计准则不要求注册会计师对检测到间接影响的违法行为作出保证。

如果注册会计师发现发现了一项违法行为，他/她就需要考虑这个行为是否会对财务报告产生影响并且向审计协会提交违法行为的相关报告。如果违法行为是通过口头传达的，则应将相关讨论内容记录在工作底稿中。

如果客户不接受注册会计师修改报告或者没有作出任何措施来纠正违法行为，注册会计师可以撤回审计服务。如果这个客户是上市公司，注册会计师有义务向证券交易委员会提供相关报告。

法务会计将财务知识、会计知识和侦察技术运用于民法和刑法中有争议的问题。

后期事项

如果一项重要事项发生在资产负债表日之后、财务报告公布之前，它就被称为后期事项或结账后会计事项。资产负债表日到财务报告公布之日，其间的主要工作内容包括报告编制、审计工作和打印年报。后期事项根据其发生的时间可以通过以下两个不同的方法处理：

• 如果后期事项不仅为财务报告提供了补充的审计证据，而且影响到财务报告的编制预期（通常是或有债务的发生），则需要对财务报告进行调整。

• 如果后期事项没有发生在资产负债表日，但它的披露能够防止对财务报告产生误解，这时就不需要将其在财务报告中进行调整，而应在会计报表附注中进行披露。这些事项包括：

• 部分有价证券的资本利得或损失。

• 债务的发生、减少或再融资。

- 停止经营。
- 出售债券、出售股本、分股和分配股票股利。
- 即将或已经发生的公司合并。
- 诉讼事项。
- 发放新股或回购股票。
- 采取福利措施。
- 火灾、洪水造成的存货、厂房或设备的损失。
- 应收账款的损失，如债务人破产。

其他事项诸如产品转换或工会协议将在其他部分讨论，如管理层论述及分析。

后任审计师间的沟通

第 7 号审计准则公告（SAS No. 7）"前任与后任审计师之间的沟通"对后任审计师的工作作出了相关规定。后任审计师有义务向客户解释工作交接流程和相关标准。后任审计师还应要求客户通知前任审计师满足其全面的信息要求。一旦同意，后任审计师有责任就相关事项起草合同并同前任审计师进行签署，并且根据以下具体的和合理的调查来确定是否向客户提供服务：

- 管理的完整性。
- 在与 GAAP 与 GAAS 应用相关的管理问题上持有异议。
- 前任审计师对替换审计师的事项表示理解。
- 前任审计师的义务包括：在未经客户具体授权的情况下，应对审计信息保密；对相关要求要作出迅速的答复；当客户批准后，应满足后任审计师的相关要求。提供的信息包括：审计中使用的会计底稿的交换、业务中采访员工的相关资料。

管理层的财务报告责任

管理层对财务报告的编制和财务报告的内容都负有责任。证券交易委员会要求管理层作出书面保证，以对财务报告的内容负责。保证的内容包括：公司具有内控系统、公司已经对内控系统的效用进行评估以及对评估发现进行报告。

外部决策中的信息种类

财务会计准则委员会（FASB）在第 5 号财务会计概念公告（SFAC No. 5）中将对投资、贷款以及其他决策有用的公司信息来源进行了分类，如图表 2 - 236 所示。管理层对图表中包括在财务报告范围内的信息负责。由于管理层对公司进行管理经营，所以他们对公司的经营状况和资产情况都很清楚。虽然没有包括在财务报告系统内的信息不在管理层的控制之下，但资深的经理会试着对这些信息在一定程度上施加积极的影响（例如，制订方案应对受欢迎公众和不受欢迎的公开报道）。

图表 2-236 责任分层

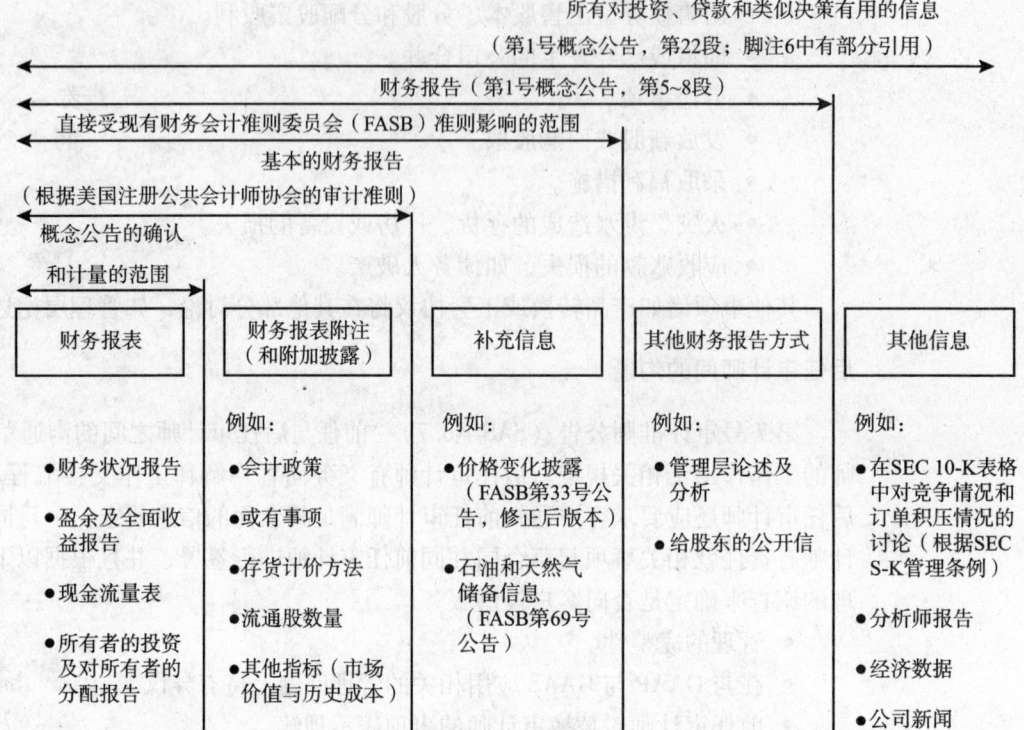

所有对投资、贷款和类似决策有用的信息
（第1号概念公告，第22段；脚注6中有部分引用）

财务报告（第1号概念公告，第5~8段）

直接受现有财务会计准则委员会（FASB）准则影响的范围

基本的财务报告
（根据美国注册公共会计师协会的审计准则）

概念公告的确认
和计量的范围

财务报表	财务报表附注（和附加披露）	补充信息	其他财务报告方式	其他信息
	例如：	例如：	例如：	例如：
●财务状况报告	●会计政策	●价格变化披露（FASB第33号公告，修正后版本）	●管理层论述及分析	●在SEC 10-K表格中对竞争情况和订单积压情况的讨论（根据SEC S-K管理条例）
●盈余及全面收益报告	●或有事项		●给股东的公开信	
●现金流量表	●存货计价方法	●石油和天然气储备信息（FASB第69号公告）		●分析师报告
●所有者的投资及对所有者的分配报告	●流通股数量			●经济数据
	●其他指标（市场价值与历史成本）			●公司新闻

管理层责任

管理层不仅应对会计政策的合理选择负责，而且还应对内部控制的发展、记录以及维护负责，这些内部控制系统为管理目标的实现提供了合理的保证。在公布定期报告的前90天内，管理层必须对公司内部控制系统的效用进行评估（注意：内部控制在 CMA 教材第一部分第3章"内部控制"中有深入讨论）。管理层也要对财务报告的编制和附注负责。

签署定期文件的经理必须将以下信息向审计师和董事会的审计委员会（或履行同等职能的个人）披露：

● 内部控制中的重要缺陷。这些缺陷会对信息公布者准确、完整地报告财务信息的能力产生负面影响。

● 任何舞弊行为，不管是否具有重要性，只要涉及那些在内部控制信息公布中起重要作用的管理层或员工。

● 内部控制本身的显著变化或对财务报告和内部控制有影响的其他因素的显著变化，包括对显著不足或者重大缺陷进行的改进。

《萨班斯法案》在第302和906节对管理层就财务报告以及其他包括在定期报告中的相关信息向证券交易委员会提供保证作出了正式要求，保证他们对不真实的报告和漏报重要事实不知情，保证财务报告是对公司财务状况和经营成果的公允表述。证券交易委员会要求所有的文件中都包括此报告。如果签订事先知道文件中包括重要性错报和漏报信息的财务报告，会导致来自证券交易委员会提起的民事诉讼和来自司法部门的刑事诉讼。证券交易委员会对此要求具体的格式并在定期文件中记录在案。另外，《萨班斯法案》在第404节中提到：证券交易委员会应制定相关规定要求公司的管理层就内部控制作出报告并附上对内部控制有效性情况的报告。这些证券交易委员会的要求都被设置在10-K文件中，这样就不容易与管理层责任混淆，下文将讨论这个问题。

审计认定

审计师进行审计就是试图实现以下认定：

- 存在与发生。所有的资产账户都存在。所有在损益表中进行合计的交易事项都发生了。

- 完整性。所有的负债和费用账户都是完整的。任何应被包括在其中的交易都在，不存在遗漏的情况。

- 权利和义务。审计师要保证公司实体在资产和负债上享有不可侵犯的权利。（所有的权利由资产列示，所有的义务由负债列示）

- 估价和分配。根据公认会计原则（GAAP），所有的资产、负债、所有者权益、收入、费用、利得和损失都应在财务报告中表述，所有的分配项目都应按照系统、合理的方式进行分配。

- 表述和披露。财务报表中所有的数据都需要合理地确认、分类和描述。所有的披露事项要有意义并且符合公认会计原则（GAAP）的规定。

管理层责任报告

多年来，管理层责任报告对股东来讲一直是财务报告中可选择的部分。很多公司选择在财务报告中附带管理层责任报告来承认他们在报告编制工作中的责任。管理层责任报告可以根据管理层的需要选择任意格式，一般包括在公司向股东公布的年度报告中，往往与独立审计师出具的报告相邻。关于管理层责任报告的例子如图表2-237所示。

图表2-237 管理层责任报告

XYZ公司

管理报告

在年度报告中，本公司编制了合并财务报表和相关的财务信息。管理层对此财务报告、其他财务信息承担主要责任，并且保证数据都公允地反映了公司的财务状况、经营成果和现金流量。财务报告的编制都是在遵循公认会计原则的标准并结合实际环境进行的，并且在适当考虑重要性原则的情况下对其中的数据进行了必要的估计和判断。在年度报告中对财务信息的陈述是建立在与财务报告保持一致性的基础上的。

公司在足够的文件证据的支持下，拥有一个内部会计控制系统，用于提供资产被保护、账户记录反映真实交易的保证。内部会计控制系统也有局限性，这是由"系统成本不得高于系统收益"的认识造成的。XYZ公司的公司审计职能使得它相信其内部会计控制系统合理地平衡了成本—收益关系。

独立会计师对管理层履行其对公允财务报告的责任的程度进行客观评价，他们定期对内部会计控制作出评估，当他们认为有必要在符合财务报告公允性的基础上表达审计意见时，他们就会采取相应的测试和程序。

董事会通过由董事组成的审计意见委员会对公司的财务报告负责，这些董事不是本公司的经理或员工。审计意见委员会定期与独立会计师、管理层以及审计师开会。独立会计师和审计师可以不通过公司管理层代表表述而直接联系审计意见委员会，讨论公司审计工作的范围和结果，对公司内部会计控制系统的作用、公司财务报告是否合格作出评价。

我们相信本公司包括内部会计控制系统在内的政策和程序能够保证公司的财务报告遵循了适用的证券法律和相关业务操守标准。

全面披露原则

全面披露原则要求任何足够影响非正式读者判断的财务信息应被披露。财务信息的全面披露有利于预防内部人员使用专有信息在二级市场获取非正当盈利，并促使市场尽量有效运作，这样才能吸引更多的资本进入。全面信息披露有利于各个竞争者处于公平竞争的平台；允许分析家研究不同会计方法产生的不同影响，以此来判断公司是否采用了有问题和带欺骗的会计行为。（APB 第 22 号意见要求对所有会计政策进行全面披露）

全面披露的成本很高。美国国会、美国财务会计准则委员会（FASB）和美国证券交易委员会必须对新披露要求的成本和采用新披露要求所产生的效益作出权衡。《萨班斯法案》很大程度上增加了披露要求，所以也同样增加了实施成本。然而，因会计丑闻而丧失的投资者信心对整个经济来讲是更为严重的损失。

补充披露要求

2002 年的《萨班斯法案》对财务报表的披露已经产生了重要影响。该法案的第 401 条就是专门针对财务信息披露所制定的，该条款修改了《证券交易法案》的相关要求，包括：

证券交易委员会将出台相应的规定，要求在公司申报的年度报告和季度报告中披露所有重大的资产负债表外业务、合同、义务（包括或有义务），如果发行人同非并表实体和其他个人之间存在可能对公司财务状况及其变动、经营成果、流动性、资本性支出、资本来源以及收入或费用构成产生重大影响的其他关系，也应当同时披露。(2002 年的《萨班斯法案》，401 条款)

审计委员会/董事会的角色

由公司股东选举出来的董事会代表股东的利益。《萨班斯法案》要求董事会成立一个由独立董事构成的审计委员会，这些独立董事都应具备较强的财务背景，其中至少一位独立董事具有财务报告方面的专业经验。该审计委员会直接负责对审计师事务所的委派、补偿以及监督。要求审计师向审计委员会直接报告而不是向管理层报告，以避免由于管理层审计自己的活动而造成的潜在利益冲突。

审计委员会必须完全由与发行方相独立的董事组成，这就意味着这些董事不能接受发行方给予的任何咨询费或报酬，同时，他们也不能是发行方或其子公司管理层的成员。

审计委员会的职责：
- 审查公司的内控结构。
- 协助公司关于会计方法与会计政策的选择。
- 选择审计师。
- 审查审计计划。
- 审查审计师为加强公司内控所提出的建议。
- 审查审计报告和经审计的公司年报。

独立审计师的报告

独立审计师在审计期末出具关于财务报告的审计报告。该审计报告可以是无保留意见的审计报告、有保留意见的审计报告、否定意见或拒绝发表意见。这份报告对于所有利益相关者都非常重要。定期报告的使用者基于审计师已经对公司的财务报告作出公正评价的假设，如果审计师在虚假审计报告上签字那么他将很可能需要为此负责。

AICPA 的审计准则委员会

美国注册公共会计师协会出台的审计准则条例要求审计师在审计报告上签明名字和日期，审计准则条例包括：

- 审计师是独立的。
- 该审计是对指定的财务报表进行审计。
- 财务报表是公司管理层的责任；而发表的审计意见是审计师的责任。
- 该审计的实施必须遵从公认审计准则（GAAS）。（遵从公认审计准则意味着需要遵守一般公认会计原则）
- 该审计的计划和实施都是为财务报表免于实质性的错漏报而获得合理保证。
- 审计包括检查、评估与估价阶段。
- 审计为发表意见提供合理的基准。
- 审计应包括与公允表述有关的意见表达。

审计报告段

标准的无保留意见的审计报告样本见图表 2 - 238。

图表 2 - 238　关于比较财务报表的标准无保留意见书

Rockwell &Smith，P. C.
注册会计师事务所
125 号
1200 IDS Center
Minneapolis，MN 55402
612/555 - 1234
独立审计意见书——————————————————————————————意见书标题
Bounce 体育用品公司的股东们：——————————————————审计意见书的称呼

我们已经对所附的 Bounce 体育用品公司 2003 年和 2004 年 12 月 31 日的资产负债表以及相关的损益表、股东权益变动表和现金流量表进行了审计。这些财务报表之编制系管理阶层之责任，本会计师之责任则为根据查核结果对这些财务报表表示意见。————————————————————介绍段（实际陈述）

我们依照会计师查核鉴证财务报表规则暨一般公认审计准则规划并执行查核工作，以合理确信财务报表有无重大不实表达。此项查核工作包括以抽查方式获取财务报表所列金额及所揭露事项之查核证据、评估管理阶层编制财务报表所采用之会计原则及所作之重大会计估计，暨评估财务报表整体之表达。本会计师相信此项查核工作可对所表示之意见提供合理之依据。————————————展开段（实际陈述）

依我们的意见，所述之财务报表在所有重大方面系依照一般公认会计原则编制，足以允当表达 Bounce 体育用品公司 2003 及 2004 年 12 月 31 日之财务状况以及经营成果与现金流量。————————观点段（总结）

Rockwell &Smith，P. C. CPAs——————————————注册会计师事务所的名字
2005 年 3 月 5 日——————————————————————审计报告的日期

标准的无保留意见报告书包括7部分

- 报告书的标题。必须包括"独立的"字样，如"独立的审计报告"。
- 审计报告书的称谓。通常是称呼股东们。
- 介绍段。陈述审计公司已经完成一项审计；列出所审计的财务报表，包括日期和计算阶段；指出这些财务报表之编制系管理阶层之责任，本会计师之责任则为根据查核结果对这些财务报表表示意见。
- 展开段。陈述审计者在审计中所做的工作；审计是为了对财务报表不是严重失实报告提供合理的证据；并提供审计证明讨论。
- 观点段。也是最后一段，陈述审计者的意见。
- 审计公司的名称。
- 审计报告的日期。在这个阶段中重要审计程序的最后日期。

修改报告书需要一个附加段来陈述有保留意见、否定意见或拒绝发表意见的原因。

报告书的观点

审计报告书的分类如下：

标准无保留意见书

无保留意见书在满足下列情况时开出：

- 包含所有报表（资产负债表、损益表、股东权益变动表以及现金流量表）。
- 在任何方面都遵守了 GAAS 的三个一般原则。
- 有充足的证据且审计者恰当地进行了审计时，审计者就可以得出符合 GAAS 三原则的结论。
- 财务报表根据 GAAP 提交，包括充分的披露。
- 没有解释性段落或者对报告文字的修改。

有解释性段落的无保留意见书

除审计者认为需要有一个解释性段落来补充信息外，所有条件都和标准的无保留意见书的条件一致。由于会计方法的改变而使得会计原则不能完全一致地实施，对于企业的持续经营能力有实质性怀疑，或者是为了强调某个事情时使用这些解释性段落。

保留意见书

在审计者的结论中认为财务报表全部提交但是包含着 GAAP 不符点或是审计的范围受到限制时，给出这种类型的观点。在任何一种情形下，保留意见的理由需要在报告中指出。

否定意见

审计者认为由于与 GAAP 不符或其他原因，以致财务报表存在实质性误导时给出相反意见。给出否定意见的原因也要在报告中指出，给出否定意见的情况极少。

拒绝发表意见

审计者考虑到由于审计范围严重受限，财务报表不能被公正表示而不能形成意见，或者是审计者不是独立的不能表达意见时，采用拒绝发表意见。拒绝发表意见的理由要在报告中指出。

审计报告并不能揭示公司的财务健康状况。审议意见并不处理公司的制度，内部控制的充足性，或者其他管理决策。报告也不涉及公司的成败与否。尽管 GAAS 准则要考虑公司的偿付能力以及财务可行性，但公司的前景总是在快速变化。

审计报告不保证公司的一个或多个人的欺诈行为，除非这些欺诈行为已经产生了可以觉察出的实质性的对财务报表的虚假陈述。尽管独立的审计员被训练或具有质疑精神，审计也被设计为检查欺诈，但是欺诈还是会被管理部门的共谋和虚报来隐藏，从而逃脱了检查。

年报的其他组成部分

年报可能包含附加信息。管理层论述及分析部分（MD&A）需要提示给 SEC，但其他文件如给股东的公开信或关于社会责任的陈述报告的提交都是自愿的。

给股东的公开信

给股东的公开信可以采取公司需要的任何形式。图表 2 – 239 中是 Krispy Kreme 公司的一封股东信摘录。

图表 2 – 239　Krispy Kreme 公司致股东的公开信节选

尊敬的股东们：

在我们迎来上市公司 3 年以及企业的 66 年庆时，我们很高兴和大家一起分享去年经营的巨大成果，特别是正处于一个困难的外部环境中。消费者、投资者和企业都必须面对和处理挑战，这些挑战包括地缘政治问题和不稳定性，一些有问题的公司不断被一些有声誉的公司揭露，国内经济不景气，极端的气候结构引起的高温以及旱灾，在国家的部分地区紧接着又是大量的降雨、冰雹、降雪天气。这些情况所产生的代价很难量化，但可以肯定的是对于大多数零售企业来说具有很大影响。另一个 Krispy Kreme 所面临的动态、更容易量化的挑战是我们的保险费成本的增加，如企业的医疗、工伤保险以及贫困和事故。

我们的关注点不是讨论我们曾经不得不面对的挑战。我们倾向于最初就把注意力放在结果和机遇上。过去的一年并没有给员工的付出给予足够的回报，但是，我们并没有陷入异常的经济环境之中。有着这样的想法，我们很自豪地共享下列成果和里程碑：
- 77 860 万美元销售总额，比上一个会计年度（52 周）增长了 28%。
- 净收入 3 910 万美元，比上一个会计年度（52 周，不包括仲裁裁定）增长了 51.6%。
- 建立了一个新的 187 000 平方英尺的混合工厂以及在伊利诺伊州埃芬加姆市开设了分销系统。
- 奖励我们在北美洲之外的面向澳大利亚、新西兰、爱尔兰共和国以及英国的两个特许经营店。
- 建立了 53 个工厂仓库以及指派了 10 名委托人。
- 并购了 Montana Mills Bread Company, Inc，一家位于纽约州、罗彻斯特市的面包店。
- 通过我们的基金项目帮助非营利组织募集了 4 300 多万美元。
- 于 2002 年 7 月 13 日庆祝了企业 65 周年庆。

过去数年的成果的价值在年复一年的财务成果的增长中得到了最好的体现，同时也为我们树立了继续致力于核心战略以创造最大效益的经济模式。

（除每股数量外，其他数据的单位都是千美元）	FY00	FY01	FY02①	FY03②	FY03 与 FY02 对比增量③
每股收益 $	0.15	0.27	0.44	0.66	48.9%
净收入 $	5 956	14 725	25 820	39 146	51.6%
收入 $	220 243	300 715	386 460	491 549	27.2%
总销售 $	318 854	448 129	608 485	778 573	28.0%
营业毛利%	4.9	7.8	10.6	14.0	3. 4ppts

续表

	净收入	总销售	总收入
2002 财年报告数据	$26 378	$621 665	$394 354
额外星期调整	(558)	(13 180)	(7 894)
2002 财年预计数据	$25 820	$608 485	$386 460

注释：

①一个会计年度有 52 或 53 个星期。2002 会计年度有 53 个星期。上部分表中所示的数字代表管理部门估计的数量，把 2002 会计年度作为 52 个星期来看。下部分表代表的是 2002 会计年度所报告的数字与上部分表中的数字相比较后所作的调整。

2002 会计年度的稀释每股收益是 0. 45 美元。我们估计第 53 个星期对稀释每股收益的影响大概是 0. 01 美元，2002 会计年度的营业毛利是 10. 6%。

②报告的 2003 会计年度的净收入是 3 350 万美元，稀释每股收益是 0. 56 美元。所报告的 2003 会计年度的经营成果包括对公司的仲裁裁定，税前是 910 万美元，将在注释即合并财务报表的法律成本费用中具体讨论。不包括仲裁裁定的影响，2003 会计年度的净收入是 3 910 万美元，稀释每股收益应增加大约 0. 10 美元。基于 2003 会计年度所报告的数字计算的营业毛利是 12. 2%。

③反映于表中的百分比是基于对上表中所示的 2002 会计年度的预计（调整至作为一个 52 个星期的会计年度的经营成果的估计）以及对 2003 会计年度的预期（调整至除去仲裁裁定的影响）。比较 2002 会计年度与 2003 会计年度的相应报告数字，结果如下：稀释每股收益增加了 24. 8%；净收入增加 26. 9%；总收益增加 24. 6%；总销售增加 25. 2%。2002 会计年度的营业毛利是 10. 6%，相较于 2003 会计年度的 12. 2%，基于这些数据，显示了 1. 6% 的增长。

我们知道今天所记载的成果已是历史。我们相信一个健康的关系不是建立在过去而是建立在潜在未来的基础上的。我们希望我们企业所取得的成就能够增强你们的信心，希望我们 Krispy Kreme 公司长期成功的承诺将会鼓励你长期作为我们的股东，参与我们企业的成长。

最诚挚的敬意

Scott A. Livengood
董事会主席、总裁和 CEO

通常，股东公开信中的讨论能突出企业的成功或者缓解或解释经营不是很成功的因素。股东公开信通常是以一个外行人的角色来解释公司的经营成果。股东公开信也能够提供一些将来的经营结果和发展的预测。信中可能会讨论新的工厂或仓库，以及股东可能感兴趣的其他公司信息。股东公开信也会用一个简单的表格给出利润和每股收益的具体信息。最后，股东公开信可能会更新公司的理念、使命或商业道德标准。

管理层论述及分析（MD&A）

前面在讨论 SEC 对上市公司的披露要求时已提到过 MD&A 报告的细节。通常，管理层论述及分析是 SEC 规定要提高的信息，包括前瞻信息、短期和长期项目、财务报表的文字解释以及管理部门的观点。尽管大多数私人公司并不属于 SEC 的控制范围，但管理层论述及分析在这些公司中也得到了应用。

社会责任报告

社会责任报告可以被有选择地包含于年报中。报表的内容由公司决定。这样的报表经常是描述公司的理念、价值观、目标以及所参加的社区项目、环境项目以及其他社会活动。报表也给股东们提供了加入这些项目的机会。图表 2 - 240 是麦当劳社会责任报表的节选。

图表2-240 麦当劳的社会责任报告

我们对社会责任的承诺：来自董事会主席兼首席执行官的一份声明

感谢您关注于我们麦当劳。我们欢迎您的好奇并欣赏您的眼力，不论您是一位顾客、邻居、供应商、股东、学生、父亲/母亲还是麦当劳的雇员。

坚持道义是我们的一份企业文化遗产。我们公司的创始人，雷·克拉克（Ray Kroc）先生在1955年就承诺麦当劳将成为一位负责任的企业公民，并秉承一个非常简单的理念，那就是每一家麦当劳店都应回报于它经营地所在的社区。该承诺是我们所有社会责任努力的基石。

能够为世界上更多的消费者服务是我们麦当劳的荣幸，伴随这份荣幸的还有成为一位好邻居、好雇主和好的环境维护者的责任，成为行业领导者的难得的机遇以及向积极的方向发展的催化剂。虽然我们意识到我们所面临的挑战与困难，但我们坚信社会责任对于我们的重要性。

自从这份社会责任报告公布以后，我们已经开创了几点创新之见，把我们的社会责任承诺扩展到其他更广的领域，这些领域都是我们的顾客所关注的领域，包括动物保护、环境问题、食品安全以及儿童慈善基金。我们知道还有更多的工作需要我们去做，这将在我们的下一份年度社会责任报告中列出，它将使我们更加紧密与广泛地关注这些领域。

我们的最高目标之一是要使得麦当劳所倡导的健康积极的生活方式得到最大程度的推广，麦当劳是建立在为顾客提供高质量菜单选择基础之上的。随着我们的发展，通过采纳消费者的意见，我们已经大大丰富了我们的菜单选项。消费者提出的意见是我们决策的巨大推动力，它为我们30年前的菜单项目的设置提供了详尽的营养信息。

我们目前正在世界范围内推广积极的生活方式、健康以及营养理念。我们已经迈出了关键的第一步。麦当劳正在整个世界范围内为"快乐儿童套餐"提供更多的选择。在各个国家提供各式各样的选择，包括水果蔬菜的选择，牛奶以及其他健康食品的选择。我们已经为"健康的生活方式"建立了一个全球化的咨询委员会，这个委员会由顶级的健康专家组成，为麦当劳顾客健康积极的生活提供服务。您将在以后看到我们的更大努力。

为了我们的顾客、所在社区以及周围环境的利益最大化所采取的行动是一个不断发展的过程。您的反馈将有助于我们理解应该如何做。请让我们知道您的想法。

Jim Cantalupo，董事会主席兼首席执行官   2003年5月

免责条款：这份麦当劳的最初的社会责任报告发布于2002年4月，为我们业务相关的社区、环境、消费者以及供应商提供了有用信息。这份报告向外界展现了我们自2001年底以来所取得的成绩以及我们公司在2002年初经营情况的剪影。这份报告中所包括的前瞻性预测反映了截至2002年4月公司管理层对未来发展的预期以及未来将采取的行动。

进度检查

提示：完成以下各题。参考答案随后给出。

1. 以下哪种审计师的服务业务是经常被私营企业所采用以作为较低成本的方法，该方法旨在保证该企业的经理不滥用企业资金？
   ( ) a. 对历史财务报告进行审计
   ( ) b. 合规审计
   ( ) c. 对历史财务报告进行汇总
   ( ) d. 对历史财务报告进行复查

2. 董事会的审计委员会是
   ( ) a. 不允许直接雇用外部审计师
   ( ) b. 不允许指导会计方法和政策的选择
   ( ) c. 目前《萨班斯法案》要求所有上市公司都必须设立
   ( ) d. 由管理层的成员和独立董事共同组成

3. 以下哪种表述不正确？
   ( ) a. 审计师有责任为被审计的公司设计一套内部控制体系

（　　）b. 管理层需负责公司财务报告的编制工作

（　　）c. 审计师没有责任查明对财务报告不产生直接影响的非法行为

（　　）d. 审计师必须向审计委员会报告在审计过程中发现的非法行为

进度检查答案

1. d
2. c
3. a

参考文献

Afterman, Allan B. *SEC Regulation of Public Companies*. Englewood Cliffs, New Jersey: Prentice Hall, 1995.

American Society of Association Executives. *ASAE's Essentials of the Profession Learning System*: Module Five, Membership/Using Technology Effectively, and Module Seven, Finance Administration. Washington, D. C.: American Society of Association Executives and Eagan, Minnesota: Holmes Corporation, 2002.

Arens, Alvin A., and James K. Loebbecke. *Auditing: An Integrated Approach*, 8th edition. Upper Saddle River, New Jersey: Prentice Hall, 1999.

Bernstein, Leopold A. *Financial Statement Analysis: Theory, Application, and Interpretation*, 3rd edition. Homewood, Illinois: Irwin, 1983.

Blocher, Edward J., Kung H. Chen, and Thomas W. Lin. *Cost Management: A Strategic Emphasis*, 2nd edition. New York: McGraw-Hill Irwin, 2002.

Bodnar, George H., and William S. Hopwood. *Accounting Information Systems*, 3rd edition. Boston: Allyn and Bacon, 1987.

Brealey, Richard A., and Stewart C. Meyers. *Principles of Corporate Finance*, 4th edition. New York: McGraw-Hill, 1991.

Campanella, Jack, editor. *Principles of Quality Costs*, 2nd edition. Milwaukee, Wisconsin: ASQ Quality Press, 1990.

Cartin, Thomas J. *Principles and Practices of TQM*. Milwaukee, Wisconsin: ASQ Quality Press, 1993.

"Database Management System," Webopedia Web site, www. webopedia. com/TERM/d/database_management_system_DBMS. html.

Delaney, Patrick R., Ralph Nach, Barry J. Epstein, and Susan Weiss Budak. *GAAP 2003*. Hoboken, New Jersey: Wiley, 2002.

Epstein, Barry J., Ralph Nach, and Steven M. Bragg, *Wiley GAAP 2006*. New York: John Wiley & Sons, 2005.

Evans, Matt H. *Course 11: The Balanced Scorecard*, www. exinfm. com/training/pdfiles/course11r. pdf.

Financial Accounting Standards Board, Statements of Financial Accounting Concepts Nos. 1, 2, 4, 5, 6, 7. Financial Accounting Standards Board: Stamford, Connecticut: 1978 – 2000.

Frederick, William C., James E. Post, and Keith Davis. *Business and Society: Corporate Strategy, Public Policy, Ethics*, 7th edition. New York: McGraw Hill, 1992.

Garrison, Ray H., and Eric W. Noreen. *Managerial Accounting*, 10th edition. Boston: McGraw-Hill/Irwin, 2003.

Gelinas, Ulric J., Jr., Steve G. Sutton, and Allan E. Oram. *Accounting Information Systems*, 4th edition. Cincinnati, Ohio: South-Western College Publishing, 1999.

Gibson, Charles H. *Financial Statement Analysis: Using Financial Accounting Information*, 7th edition. Cincinnati, Ohio: South-Western College Publishing, 1998.

Greenstein, Marilyn, and Todd M. Feinman. *Electronic Commerce: Security, Risk Management, and Control.* Boston: McGraw Hill Higher Education, 2000.

Hargrave, Lee E. *Plan for Profitability: How to Write a Strategic Business Plan.* Titusville, Florida: Four Seasons Publishers, 1999.

Hilton, Ronald W., Michael W. Maher, and Frank H. Selto. *Cost Management: Strategies for Business Decisions*, 2nd edition. Boston: McGraw-Hill Irwin, 2003.

Horngren, Charles T., George Foster, and Srikant M. Datar. *Cost Accounting*, 10th edition. Upper Saddle River, New Jersey: Prentice-Hall, 2000.

Hoyle, Joe B., Thomas F. Schaefer, and Timothy S. Doupnik. *Advanced Accounting*, 6th edition. Boston: McGraw-Hill Irwin, 2001.

Juran, Joseph M., and Blanton Godfrey, coeditors-in-chief. *Juran's Quality Handbook*, 5th edition. New York: McGraw-Hill, 1999.

Kaplan, Robert S., and David P. Norton. *The Balanced Scorecard: Translating Strategy Into Action.* Boston: Harvard Business School Press, 1996.

Kaplan, Robert S., and David P. Norton. *The Strategy-Focused Organization.* Boston: Harvard Business School Press, 2001.

Kaplan, Robert S., and David P. Norton. "Using the Balanced Scorecard as a Strategic Management System." *Harvard Business Review*, January-February 1996.

Kieso, Donald E., and Jerry J. Weygandt. *Intermediate Accounting*, 9th edition. New York: Wiley, 1998.

Kieso, Donald E., Jerry J. Weygandt, and Terry D. Warfield. *Intermediate Accounting*, 10th edition. New York: Wiley, 2001.

Larsen, E. John. *Modern Advanced Accounting*, 10th edition. New York: McGraw-Hill, 2006.

Laudon, Kenneth C., and Jane P. Laudon. *Management Information Systems*, 8th edition. Upper Saddle River, New Jersey: Pearson Prentice Hall, 2003.

Madden, Bartley J. *CFROI Valuation – A Total System Approach to Valuing the Firm.* Boston: Butterworth-Heinemann, 1999.

McMillan, Edward J. *Budgeting and Financial Management Handbook for Not-for-Profit Organizations.* Washington, D. C.: American Society of Association Executives, 2000.

Moscove, Stephen A., Mark G. Simkin, and Nancy A. Bagrandoff. *Core Concepts of Accounting Information Systems*, 5th edition. New York: Wiley, 1997.

Nicolai, Loren A., and John D. Bazley. *Intermediate Accounting*, 5th edition. Boston: PWS-Kent Publishing Company, 1991.

Olve, Nils-Göran, and Anna Sjöstrand. *The Balanced Scorecard.* Oxford, United Kingdom: Capstone Publishing (a Wiley Company), 2002.

Ratliff, Richard L., Wanda A. Wallace, Glenn E. Sumners, William G. McFarland, and James K. Loebbecke. *Internal Auditing: Principles and Techniques.* Altamonte Springs, Florida: Institute of Internal Auditors, 1996.

Roszkowski, Mark E. *Business Law.* New York: Addison Wesley, 1997.

Tague, Nancy R. *The Quality Toolbox.* Milwaukee, Wisconsin: ASQ Quality Press, 1995.

U. S. Securities and Exchange Commission, www. sec. gov.

Van Horne, James C. , and John M. Wachowicz, Jr. *Fundamentals of Financial Management*, 9th edition. Englewood Cliffs, New Jersey: Prentice-Hall, Inc. , 1995.

Young, S. David, and Stephen R. O'Byrne. *EVA® and Value-Based Management*: *A Practical Guide to Implementation*. New York: McGraw Hill, 2001.

管理会计与报告（第二版）

B

C

D

E

F

G

H

I

N

O

Q

R

S

责任编辑：周国强
责任校对：徐领柱
版式设计：代小卫
技术编辑：邱 天

管理会计与报告（第二版）（英汉双语）

美国管理会计师协会（IMA） 主编

彭韶兵 宋 浩 译

经济科学出版社出版、发行 新华书店经销

社址：北京市海淀区阜成路甲 28 号 邮编：100142

编辑部电话：88191350 发行部电话：88191540

网址：www. esp. com. cn

电子邮件：zgq@esp. com. cn

北京密兴印刷有限公司印装

880×1230 16 开 58 印张 1600000 字

2007 年 11 月第 1 版 2011 年 7 月第 4 次印刷

印数：5501—8000 册

ISBN 978 - 7 - 5058 - 6612 - 6/F · 5873 定价：155.00 元

（图书出现印装问题，本社负责调换）

（版权所有 翻印必究）